Eleventh Edition
Antique Trader Books
ANTIQUES & COLLECTIBLES
PRICE GUIDE

1995 ANNUAL EDITION

ANTIQUE TRADER BOOKS

Antiques & Collectibles Price Guide

Edited by
Kyle Husfloen

An illustrated comprehensive price guide to the entire field of antiques and collectibles for the 1995 market

Antique Trader Books
P.O. Box 1050
Dubuque, IA 52004

STAFF

Assistant Editor ....Marilyn Dragowick

Production Coordinator/Editorial Assistant . . . .Louise Paradis

Production Assistant/Editorial Assistant ....Ruth Willis

Production Assistant ....Kristen Bushman

Cover Design ....Jaro Sebek

Subscription Manager ....Bonnie Rojemann

ISBN: 0-930625-10-2
Library of Congress Catalog Card No. 85-648650

Other books and magazines published by Antique Trader Publications:

Ceramics Price Guide
Toy Trader
Discoveries
Postcard Collector
The Antique Trader Weekly
Collector Magazine & Price Guide
Big Reel
Baby Boomer Collectibles
Military Trader

To order additional copies of this book or other publications listed above, contact:

Antique Trader Publications
P.O. Box 1050
Dubuque, Iowa 52004
1-800-334-7165

A WORD TO THE READER

The Antique Trader has been publishing a Price Guide for twenty-four years. *The Antique Trader Price Guide to Antiques and Collectors' Items* was available by subscription and on newsstands across the country, first as a semi-annual and then as a quarterly publication and from 1984 until February 1994 it was published on a bi-monthly basis. It has now been incorporated, to a certain extent, in the monthly publication entitled *Antique Trader's Collector Magazine & Price Guide.*

In 1985, in response to numerous requests to combine the material of the bi-monthly issues and provide a large, complete price guide, the first edition of *The Antique Trader Antiques & Collectibles Price Guide* was issued. The book you now hold in your hands is the 1995 guide, our Eleventh Annual Edition.

This book is the most current price listing available. We think it is also the most reliable book for dealers and collectors to turn to for realistic values of antiques and collectibles. Prices listed in this guide have not been unrealistically set at the whim of an editor who has no material at hand to substantiate the listed values. The Antique Trader Price Guide staff has always used a very methodical compilation system that is supported by experts from across the country as we select listings for the various categories. Prices are derived from antiques shops, advertisements, auctions, and antiques shows, and on-going records are maintained. Items are fully described and listings are carefully examined by experts who discard unreasonable exceptions to bring you the most reliable, well-illustrated and authoritative Price Guide available.

Our format enables us to maintain a wide range of both antique and collectible items in a running tabulation to which we are continually adding information and prices. Items are diligently researched and clearly described. As new areas of collecting interest develop, new categories are added and if a definite market is established, this material becomes a part of the Price Guide. In this issue we have added several new categories in the Ceramics Section. For a more in-depth coverage of ceramics see the recently released book entitled *Pottery & Porcelain Ceramics Price Guide* from Antique Trader Books. Another reference which will be useful to collectors is our forthcoming price guide on glassware, also from Antique Trader Books.

Six popular areas of collecting are highlighted in well-illustrated "Special Focus" features which provide background material and tips on collecting. Our 1995 edition includes focuses on Classic Disney Collectibles, Furniture of the 1890s, Collectible Table Top Radios, 1930 to 1960, Vintage Phonographs, Patents for Kitchen Collectibles and Cookie Jars by Metlox and Twin Winton.

This book should be used only as a *guide* to prices and is not intended to set prices. Prices do vary from one section of the country to another and auction prices, which are incorporated into this guide, often have an even wider variation. Though prices have been double-checked and every effort has been made to assure accuracy, neither the compilers, editor nor publisher can assume responsibility for any losses that might be incurred as a result of consulting this guide, or of errors, typographical or otherwise.

This guide follows an alphabetical format. All categories are listed in alphabetical order. Under the category of Ceramics, you will find all types of pottery, porcelain, earthenware, parian and stoneware listed in alphabetical order. All types of glass, including Carnival, Custard, Depression, Pattern and so on, will be found listed alphabetically under the category of Glass. A complete Index and cross-references in the text have also been provided.

We wish to express sincere appreciation to the following authorities who help in selecting material to be used in this guide: Sandra Andacht, Little Neck, New York; Lillian Baker, Gardena, California; Susan N. Cox, El Cajon, California; Marilyn Dipboye, Warren, Michigan; Robert T. Matthews, West Friendship, Maryland; Cecil Munsey, Poway, California; Ruth Schinestuhl, Marmora, New Jersey; and Tim Timmerman, Beaverton, Oregon.

The authors of the "Special Focus" segments deserve special recognition: "Classic Disney Collectibles," by David Longest, New Albany, Indiana; "Furniture of the 1890s," by Connie Morningstar, Salt Lake City, Utah; "Collectible Table Top Radios, 1930 to 1960," by Harry Poster, South Hackensack, New Jersey; "Patents for Kitchen Collectibles," by Linda Campbell Franklin, Charlottesville, Virginia; "Metlox and Twin Winton Cookie Jars," by Joyce Roerig, Waltersboro, South Carolina; and "Vintage Phonographs," by Louise Paradis, Galena, Illinois.

Photographers who have contributed to

this issue include: Adele Armbruster, Dearborn, Michigan; E.A. Babka, East Dubuque, Illinois; Al Bagdade, Northbrook, Illinois; Stanley L. Baker, Minneapolis, Minnesota; Dorothy Beckwith, Platteville, Wisconsin; Donna Bruun, Galena, Illinois; Marie Bush, Amsterdam, New York; Herman C. Carter, Tulsa, Oklahoma; Susan N. Cox, El Cajon, California; J.D. Dalessandro, Cincinnati, Ohio; Jeff Grunewald, Chicago, Illinois; Jim Martin, Monmouth, Illinois; Kevin McConnell, Pilot Point, Texas; the late Don Moore, Alameda, California; Gale Morningstar, Salt Lake City, Utah; Louise Paradis, Galena, Illinois; Joyce Roerig, Waltersboro, South Carolina; Ruth Schinestuhl, Marmora, New Jersey; Molly Schroeder, Danville, Illinois; and Paul Sherman, Chicago, Illinois.

For other photographs, artwork, data or permission to photograph in their shops, we sincerely express appreciation to the following auctioneers, galleries, museums, individuals and shops: Donna Bauerly, Dubuque, Iowa; Bell Tower Antique Mall, Covington, Kentucky; Bertoia/Brady Auctions, Vineland, New Jersey; Block's Box, Trumball, Connecticut; Burmese Cruet, Montgomeryville, Pennsylvania; Busby Land & Auction Company, Ridge Farm, Illinois; Butterfield & Butterfield, San Francisco, California; Norm & Diana Charles, Hagerstown, Indiana; Christie's, New York, New York; Collector's Auction Services, Oil City, Pennsylvania; Collector's Sales & Services, Middletown, Rhode Island; DeFina Auctions, Austenburg, Ohio; William Doyle Galleries, New York, New York; Marilyn Dragowick, Dubuque, Iowa; DuMouchelle's, Detroit, Michigan; Dunnings Auction Service, Elgin, Illinois; T. Ermert, Cincinnati, Ohio; Frasher's Auctions, Oak Grove, Missouri; The Galena Shoppe, Galena, Illinois; Garth's Auctions, Inc., Delaware, Ohio; Glass-Works Auctions, East Greenville, Pennsylvania; Glick's Antiques, Galena, Illinois; Morton M. Goldberg Auction Galleries, New Orleans, Louisiana; Grunewald Antiques, Hillsborough, North Carolina; and Guarisco Gallery, Ltd., Washington, D.C.

Also to Hake's Americana & Collectibles, York, Pennsylvania; Vicki Harmon, San Marcos, California; the Gene Harris Antique Auction Center, Marshalltown, Iowa; the late William Heacock, Marietta, Ohio; The House in the Woods Auction Gallery, Eagle, Wisconsin; International Carnival Glass Assoc., Mentone, Indiana; Doris Johnson, Rockford, Illinois; James Julia; Fairfield, Maine; Just Kids Nostalgia, Huntington, New York; Kirsner Antiques, Minneapolis, Minnesota; Sherry Klabo, Seattle, Washington; Agnes Koehn Antiques, Cedar Rapids, Iowa; Peter Kroll, Sun Prairie, Wisconsin; Beverly Kubesheski, Dubuque, Iowa; Bobby Lowell and Company, El Paso, Texas; Jim Ludescher, Dubuque, Iowa; Joy Luke Gallery, Bloomington, Illinois; J. Martin, Mt. Orab, Ohio; McMasters Doll Auctions, Cambridge, Ohio; Dr. James Measell, Berkley, Michigan; Merritt's Antiques, Inc., Douglassville, Pennsylvania; William Miller, Rockford, Illinois; Virginia Mills, Peabody, Massachusetts; Kurt & Cindy Moe, Springfield, Minnesota; Neal Auction Company, New Orleans, Louisiana; The Nippon Room, Rexford, New York; Nostalgia Galleries, Elmont, New York; Nostalgia Publications, Inc., Hackensack, New Jersey; Dave Rago Arts & Crafts, Trenton, New Jersey; R.A.M. Quality Auctions, Joliet, Illinois; Rare and Esoteric Books, Three Bridges, New Jersey; Jane Rosenow, Galva, Illinois; Running Rabbit, Nashville, Tennessee; Carlton & Rosa Schleede, Spencerport, New York; Shirley's Glasstiques, Brunswick, Ohio; Robert W. Skinner, Inc., Bolton, Massachusetts; Slawinski Auction Company, Felton, California; Sotheby's, New York, New York; Stanton's Auctioneers & Realtors, Vermontville, Michigan; Michael Strawser, Wolcottville, Indiana; Sweet Water Ranch, Cody, Wyoming; Temples Antiques, Minneapolis, Minnesota; Theriault's, Annapolis, Maryland; Town Crier Auction Service, Burlington, Wisconsin; Trader Luke's, Wilmington, California; Trailer House Antiques, Grand Junction, Iowa; Don Treadway Auction Service, Cincinnati, Ohio; Victorian Images, Marlton, New Jersey; Lee Vines, Hewlett, New York; Doris Virtue, Galena, Illinois; Mrs. William Wade, Glendale, Arizona; Wolf's Auctioneers and Appraisers, Cleveland, Ohio; Woody Auctions, Douglass, Kansas; Yankee Peddler Antiques, Denton, Texas; and Yesterday's Treasures, Galena, Illinois.

The staff of *The Antique Trader Antiques & Collectibles Price Guide* welcomes all letters from readers, especially those of constructive critique, and we make every effort to respond personally.

Kyle Husfloen, Editor

Booklet, "Smith Premier Typewriter," die-cut cover, 1890s 50.00

Bowl, "Schweppes Indian Tonic," ceramic, Blue Willow design, 4¾" d... 65.00

Bowl, cereal, "Wheaties," sports personalities pictured & "Breakfast of Champions" 19.00

Brush, "Consumers Builders Supply," celluloid, w/logo, dated 1924, in box 65.00

Cake carrier, "Pepsi Cola," tin, 1960s... 95.00

Cake pan, "Mother's Oats," aluminum, ring-type, 6" d............................... 32.50

Calendar, 1895, "Phoenix Mutual Life Insurance Co.," little girls pictured, matted 145.00

Calendar, 1898, "Youth's Companion," three-paneled, pictures Victorian scenes, full pad 45.00

Calendar, 1905, "Youth's Companion," w/colorful lithograph of a Victorian girl in the center panel 45.00

Calendar, 1906, "John Hancock Insurance," pictures Colonial shipboard scene, full pad 20.00

Calendar, 1908, "Excelsior Stove Co., Quincy, Illinois," pictures a little girl in a red dress holding a kitten & illustrates the National Stoves' gold medal award that was presented at the 1904 World's Fair 37.50

Calendar, 1909, "Collins Baking Company," lithographed cardboard, diamond shaped, a wood-grained ground centered by a round vignette of a Victorian girl in a winter outfit w/a cluster of holly, small pointed calendar pad at the bottom, printed at the top "Compliments of Collins Baking Co....," printed on the vignette "Collins Celebrated Bread," minor soiling & corner wear, 8" w., 8" h. (ILLUS.) 27.50

Calendar, 1909, "McCormick Harvesters," pictures a battleship, 14 x 20" 135.00

1922 Texaco Calendar

Calendar, 1922, "The Texaco Company," die-cut cardboard, a round disc at the top w/a red circle printed in white "The Texas Company-Petroleum and Its Products," framing a red star overprinted "Texaco," large complete calendar pad below w/further advertising, taped tear at top center, yellow paper, 13" w., 25" h. (ILLUS.) 203.50

Calendar, 1923, "Schofield's Garage, Morning Sun, Iowa," pictures little boy w/dog & entitled "Good Friends," mint w/original mailing envelope 100.00

Calendar, 1927, "First National Bank of Lowell, Indiana," pictures a young girl dressed in her mother's clothing, entitled "Just Like Mother" 95.00

Calendar, 1928, "Round Oak Stove," scene titled "Civilization Advances" 150.00

Calendar, 1937, "McCord Groceries," picture of sailing ship 22.50

Calendar, 1937, "DeLaval Cream Separators," w/picture of pretty girl, full pad 35.00

Calendar, 1944, "John Morrell," w/twelve N.C. Wyeth illustrations, 8¼ x 17¾" 50.00

Calendar, 1949, "Hochgreve Brewing Co., Green Bay, Wisconsin," scenes entitled "The Four Seasons," by Norman Rockwell 25.00

Calendar, 1955, "John Deere," pictures a wildlife scene, full pad 35.00

Cane, "M.C. Mathews Co., Crystal Lake, Ill.," wooden yardstick markings on side, 37" l. 27.50

Can opener, "Pet Milk," metal 12.50

Cards, "Arm & Hammer," second series, "Useful Birds of America," full set of 15 cards in original envelope ... 75.00

Cartoon book, "Volkswagen," includes work by Charles Addams & many others, 1967 .... 45.00

Cereal box, sample size, "Clapp's," pictures baby & a caption w/"Sample - With Compliments of Your Doctor!" 15.00

Cigarette carton, "Lucky Strike," cardboard, colorful Christmas graphics, ca. 1940 .... 38.00

Cigarette lighter, "Kool Cigarettes," metal, model of a penguin, hinged head opens to reveal lighter, ca. 1930s, 4¼" h. 195.00

Cigarette paper dispenser, "Zig Zag," tin 30.00

Clock, "Clapperton Spool Cotton," wall-mounted regulator, large round top lettered "Clapperton Spool

Cotton is the Best" around the dial above a smaller round drop, Baird, ca. 1880 ....950.00
Clock, "Pepsi-Cola," wall-mounted electric, square glass front in metal frame, face lettered "Time For Pepsi-Cola," ca. 1940, 15" sq. 250.00
Clock, "St. Joseph Aspirin," electric light-up wall type, round, white dial w/blue Arabic numerals & blue center w/white lettering, marked "St. Joseph- 2 - Telechron Inc., Ashland, Mass., U.S.A. C.A.P.," w/original box, 15" d. (very minor rust)....132.00
Clock, "S. & H. Green Stamps," electric wall-type, framed metal, rectangular w/a round white dial at the top above "We Give S. & H. Green Stamps" in green & white against a dark green ground, black and gold wood frame, 15¼" w., 22¾" h. (very minor scratches) 82.50
Coaster, "Moxie," w/baseball scorecard reverse 24.00
Coffee cup, "The Nut Tree," china, tree logo....20.00
Coffee cup, "Stewart & Ashby," china, 1933....55.00
Comb, "Ramon's," pocket-type w/leather case, pictures little boy doctor....20.00
Comic book, "Planters Peanuts," entitled "The Personal Story of Mr. Peanut," fiftieth anniversary publication, 1956....20.00
Comic book, "Poll Parrot Shoes," entitled "Bandit Buster," 1959 ....22.50
Cookbook, "Bisquick," pictures several movie stars including Betty Grable & Joan Crawford, 1935 ....24.00
Counter dispenser, "Becker's Improved Stomach Bitters - Patented Sept. 7th, 1869" in gold, black, green & red lettering & scrolling decoration, white porcelain ground w/two upper & two lower gold ring bands, modified barrel-form w/spigot, 10" d., 10" h. 1,320.00
Counter display, "Bausch & Lomb Sports Glasses," cardboard, decorated w/colorful die-cut elves, ca. 1920, 2 pcs. 48.00
Counter display, "Dr. West's Tooth-brush," a model of a large wooden toothbrush in dark red w/white bristles, printed w/beige lettering reading "Dr. West's Germ Fighter," early 20th c., 17½" l. (letter fading & overall scratches)....33.00
Counter display, "Heinz," plastic, model of a pickle, 19" l....135.00
Counter display, "Willard's Tablets," cardboard, three-tiered, four colors, 17" h....22.50
Counter display bottle, "Hoyt's German Cologne," clear glass, oversized bottle w/paper label 225.00
Counter display box, "Clark Coconut Bars," pictures candy bar inside coconut shell, ca. 1940 ....130.00
Counter display box, "Parisian Washing Blue," wooden, stenciled lid w/red, white & blue paper label inside 50.00
Counter display box, "Wrigley's Juicy Fruit," cardboard, colorful illustrations, ca. 1920....40.00
Counter display case, "Ferris Woolens," fold-out cardboard, a rectangular box w/a fold-down flap front w/advertising & a fold-up lid w/the interior decorated w/a colorful scene of people at an early airport & printed "Ferris Woolens - for - Autumn and Winter - 1929-30," case in green, 19" l. (some edge wear & exterior fading) 220.00
Counter display case, "G. Washington's Coffee," painted tin rectangular case w/a glass front, interior shelves, red w/white lettering, printed across the top "Better Coffee Made An Easier Way," across the bottom "The New G. Washington's Coffee - The Coffee Part of the Coffee Bean," early 20th c., 11½" w., 13" h. (scratches, some overall paint loss & top chipping)....55.00
Counter display case, "Ide Collars," a tall, slender glass-sided case w/a wooden frame, top & bottom, w/original collars inside, wooden back opens, early 20th c., 6¾ x 7½", 4' h. (minor soiling)....209.00
Counter display case, "Gruen Watches," hardwood, an arched crest w/a metal nameplate above an upright rectangular case w/two rows of nine slots for displaying watches, flat base, early 20th c., 8¾" w., 15" h. (scratches, minor chipping) ...104.50
Counter display case, "Rice's Seeds," lithographed tin, tiered shelves, lower front embossed w/"Try Rice's Seeds" & picture of two seed packets, 22 x 24", 32" h. 1,250.00
Counter display case, "Ruff-Stuff," painted metal, divided sections for various types of sandpaper, red, cream & green lettering w/green & cream background, pictures Indian on mountain overlooking industry below in valley at sunrise, minor paint chipping & scratches, some rust, 12 x 14", 23" h. (ILLUS.) 110.00

Ruff-Stuff Sandpaper Display

Counter display figure, "Allen's Red Tame Cherry," chalkware, a standing figure of a young Victorian girl holding her apron, barefoot on a rockwork base embossed "Drink Allen's Red Tame Cherry," green dress w/gold apron, lettering in brown, late 19th - early 20th c., 26" h. (overall paint chipping & wear) 495.00

Beefeater Gin Display Figure

Counter display figure, "Beefeater Gin," wood & composition, standing figure of a Beefeater on a rectangular base in black w/yellow lettering reading "Beefeater Gin - The Imported One," man in red w/gold trim, very minor chipping, 17" h. (ILLUS.) 82.50

Counter display figure, "The Clinic Shoe," papier-maché figure of a nurse, 23" h. 225.00

Counter display figure, "Lamb Knit," papier-maché model of a lamb in white w/wording in black on the side, 15" h. (black repainted, some wear) 357.50

Counter display figure, "RCA," papier-maché model of mascot dog Nipper, 12" h. 185.00

Counter display figure, "RCA," jointed wood & composition, 'Radiotron,' figure of a man wearing short pants, knee-high boots, wrist bands & a radio tube on his head, designed by Maxfield Parrish, 1926, 15½" h. 950.00

Counter display jar, cov., "Carnation Malted Milk," clear glass barrel-shaped jar w/embossed tin lid 22.00

Counter display jar, cov., "LaPalina Cigars," clear glass, twelve-sided w/embossed lettering 65.00

Counter display jar, cov., "Seyfert's Original Butter Pretzels," clear glass jar, 10½" h. 60.00

Crock, cov., "Heinz Apple Butter," wide semi-ovoid pottery body w/inset cover & wire bail handle w/wooden handgrip, cream-colored glaze, original multicolored paper label reading "Heinz Apple Butter, Pittsburgh, Pa.," ca. 1885-95, 5¾" h. 302.50

Cup, "Armour's Vigoral," china w/floral decoration, 4" h. 45.00

Cup, demitasse, "Dobbs," black glass w/embossed picture of top hat 15.00

Cup & saucer, demitasse, "Kelly," ceramic, nylon tire pictured 50.00

Cup & saucer, demitasse, "Van Houten's Rona Dutch Cocoa," china, decorated w/blue sailing ship scene & gold lettering 60.00

Cuspidor, "Havana Cigars - 5c," brass 65.00

Die-cut display piece, "Alliance Coffee," die-cut cardboard, the half-length portrait of a smiling chef holding a cup, printed in color, the cup w/"Alliance Coffee," the lower half w/white lettering on a dark ground reading "For Coffee Contentment Serve Alliance," early 20th c., 12½" l., 16⅛" h. (wear to top of hat, stand torn on fold, wrinkled) 247.50

Die-cut display piece, "Billings-Chapin Paint," lithographed cardboard w/clockwork mechanism, half-length profile portraits of a painter holding a can of paint & facing an older gentleman, advertising across the bottom, painter's arm & gentleman's head move when activated, early 20th c.,soiling, water marks, tear in man's head, 32" l., 29" h. (ILLUS. top next column) 330.00

Billings-Chapin Paint Mechanical Display

Die-cut display piece, "Great Atlantic and Pacific Tea Company," lithographed cardboard, an older gent pushing a wheelbarrow holding a late Victorian girl w/flowers & a boy in a sailor suit holding a flag, a small dog running along side, printed in red, blue, brown, white & black, advertising on the front & back, ca. 1884, 5½" w., 8½" h. (very minor edge wear) 27.50

Doll, "C & H Sugar," cloth, dressed in Hawaiian costume 12.00

Doll, "Kellogg's Rice Krispies," Crackle, vinyl 16.00

Doll, "Kellogg's Rice Krispies," Pop, uncut cloth, by Arnold Printworks, 1948 ....42.50

Door push plate, "Colonial Bread," embossed "Colonial Is Good Bread," blue & black paint, w/adjustable extensions, 3 x 22" 35.00

Door push plate, "Grapette Soda," metal, embossed "Grapette - Thirsty or Not" 110.00

Door push plate, "Mrs. Cotton's Bread & Cakes," red & white paint, 3 x 26" 35.00

Door push plate, "Royal Crown Cola," metal, embossed "Best By Taste Test" 125.00

Door push plate, "Town Talk Bread," brass, embossed "Town Talk is Better Bread," ca. 1920, 3 x 18" 225.00

Egg separator, "Jamo Coffee," metal ...20.00

Egg separator, "Puritan Meats," tin.......12.00

Fan, "Hotel Knickerbocker Restaurant," paper, folding-type..............23.00

Fan, "Kools," scene of penguin carrying cigarettes, promoting Tommy Dorsey & NBC radio show 65.00

Fan, "Moxie," cardboard, color picture of a boy on the Moxiemobile, 1922, 7 x 8"..75.00

Fan, "Pepsi-Cola," cardboard w/wood-en handle, lithographed picture of pretty girl drinking a bottle of Pepsi & "Drink Pepsi-Cola," 1912-13..100.00

Fan, "The Singer - 20th Century Sewing Machine," paper, folding-type 23.00

Sleepy Eye Die-Cut Fan

Fan, "Sleepy Eye Milling Co.," die-cut cardboard bust portrait of Sleepy Eye, w/tassels of wheat in headband, advertising on back (ILLUS.) 200.00

Fan, "Ross W. Weir & Sons - Coffee & Tea Importers, New York," paper, folding-type 23.00

Figure, nodding-type, "Kentucky Fried Chicken," composition, "Colonel Sanders" 100.00

Flask, whiskey, "Celebrated Montezuma Rye Whiskey - James Maguire, 470 & 472 N. 3rd St., Phila., Pa.," metal & copper, flask-shaped, w/original cork stopper on a chain, 4½" d. 110.00

Game, "Cracker Jack" prize, entitled "Mind Reading Game" 20.00

Game, card-type, "Post Cereal," entitled "Doctor Dolittle," 1967, sealed in original box 32.50

Goblet, "Pepsi-Cola Bottling Company," glass, 50th Anniversary logo of Seattle, Washington bottling Company (ILLUS. top next column) 41.00

Gum stand, "Clark's Teaberry," vaseline pressed glass ......75.00 to 100.00

Hat, "Robin Hood Flour," Sherwood Forest-style 20.00

Pepsi-Cola Goblet

Ice pick, "Pevely Dairy," metal..............12.00

Ice pick, "Piggly Wiggly," metal.............15.00

Insignia guide, "Wonder Bread," cardboard, rectangular w/turning disc, compares ranks of Army & Navy by turning disc, 4 x 5½"..12.00

Jigsaw puzzle, "Campbell's," depicts tomato soup can, in original can........20.00

Jigsaw puzzle, "Dr. S. A. Richmond's Epileptine - the only cure for Epilepsy," ca. 1890..............................5.00

Jigsaw puzzle, "Quaker Oats," scene w/Cap'n Crunch, mint in unopened package..25.00

Jug, whiskey, "The Kintor Scotch Whiskey," pottery, tan glaze w/brown lettering..................................49.00

Jug, whiskey, "Spring Lake, Handmade Sour Mash Bourbon," china, white glaze w/maroon lettering, marked "KTK China" on base...89.00

Jug, whiskey, "White Lily - Pure Rye, S.B. Co.," ceramic, maroon glaze w/white lettering...............................79.00

Ketchup bottle topper, "Heinz," model of a dinosaur.....................................10.00

Key, "Use Eclipse Soap," cast iron, 10" l..45.00

Key chain, "Milwaukee Harvester," metal, w/four mower bar section.........27.50

Knife, pocket-type, "Kinney Shoes," multicolored marbleized case............15.00

Letter opener, "Cash Clothes," bronze, figural nude man in barrel.....20.00

Letter opener, "Lincoln Telephone & Telegraph Co., Lincoln, NE," metal model of a candlestick telephone, "Silver Ann. 1904-1929"...................125.00

Letter opener, "Marshall Best Flour," brass, ornate handle w/girl..................45.00

Letter opener, "Nabisco," figural "Uneeda Biscuit Boy," w/sticker on handle...75.00

Letter opener, "The Prudential Life Insurance Both Sexes," metal, early 20th c. 18.00

Letter opener/cigar cutter, "Home Insurance Company," brass, 1903.....65.00

Measuring cup, "Eastman-Kodak," clear glass..27.00

Measuring cup, "Rozien Metal Co., Woodward, OK," brass......................12.00

Milk bottle opener, "Diamond Crystal Salt," metal w/celluloid emblem attached, 4" l.......................................15.00

Mirror, pocket-type, "Angelus Marshmallows," two cherubs w/product.......82.00

Mirror, pocket-type, "Beeman's Pepsin Gum," pictures Mr. Beeman.......200.00

Bell Coffee Pocket Mirror

Mirror, pocket-type, "Bell Roasted Coffee," celluloid, shows bell, 2" d. (ILLUS.)..65.00

Mirror, pocket-type, "Boat & Shoe Worker's Union," oval 30.00

Mirror, pocket-type, "Brundage's Maple Ridge Butter," product illustrated 115.00

Mirror, pocket-type, "Campbell's Soup," pictures soup can, embossed "10¢ a can," mint condition 150.00

Mirror, pocket-type, "J.I. Case," oval, w/picture of an eagle.......................135.00

Mirror, hand-type, "Consolidated Ice Company," celluloid back illustrated w/an arctic scene w/a ship in the ice, a hunter & a polar bear, scroll-embossed gilt-metal handle, tarnished, crazing & loss to mirror face, early 20th c. (ILLUS. top next column) 88.00

Mirror, pocket-type, "Kleinert's Dress Shields," celluloid, pictures a woman & reads "I Use Kleinert's Dress Shields"..55.00

Consolidated Ice Hand Mirror

Mirror, pocket-type, "Kleinert's Dress Shields," celluloid, pictures a woman & reads "I Use Kleinert's Dress Shields" 55.00

Mirror, pocket-type, "Mennen's Flesh-Tint Talcum," illustration of a can.......45.00

Mirror, pocket-type, "Pilgrim Specialty Company," pictures a Pilgrim............30.00

Mirror, pocket-type, "Regal Shoes," pictures a pretty girl 75.00

Mirror, pocket-type, "Stacey Chocolates," illustration of the sun over water 35.00

Travelers Insurance Mirror

Mirror, pocket-type, "Travelers Insurance Co., Hartford, Conn.," oval, shows train (ILLUS.).................60.00

Mirror, pocket-type, "Warren Tanner Dry Goods," pictures a building 32.50

Model of a telephone, "Swedish-American Telephone Co., Chicago," nickel-plated brass & black finish, candlestick-type phone, marked on bottom, 1⅛" h...................225.00 to 275.00

Money clip, "Philip Morris," celluloid 25.00

Mug w/pedestal base, "City Squire Motor Inn," ceramic, marked "Hall China" on base 25.00

Mug, shaving-type, "Maryland Casualty Insurance," ca. 1905.........125.00

Mug, "Planters Peanuts," green plastic, embossed figure of Mr. Peanut, ca. 1960, 4" h. 35.00

Mug, electric company, china, illustration of "Reddy Kilowatt," Syracuse China 38.00

Mug, "Richardson's Root Beer," clear glass, paneled, 7" h. 49.00

Mug, "Round Oak Stoves - Doe-Wah-Jack (Dowagiac, Michigan)," ceramic, illustrated w/a full-figure portrait of Chief Doe-Wah-Jack, in green on a shaded ochre ground, ca. 1907 ....175.00

Needle case, "R.H. Macy," leather case w/gold embossing, holds over 200 gold-eyed needles 40.00

Notepad holder, "Fortune Fisheries," brown metal w/an adjustable day-month calendar at the top & a metal tag in red outlined in gold & printed w/"Fortune Fisheries - San Francisco, Calif." & a fish, 4¼ x 6½" (very minor scratches) 66.00

Nut serving spoon, "Planters Peanuts," gold-washed metal, pierced bowl, figural Mr. Peanut handle, 5" l. 18.00

Nut serving spoon, "Planters Peanuts," silver plate, pierced bowl, figural Mr. Peanut handle, 5" l............25.00

Oil bottle, "Thomas Edison Battery Oil," w/embossed signature 26.50

Badger Insurance Co. Paperweight

Paperweight, "The Badger Mutual Fire Insurance Co.," "1887-1937," cast iron, lettering has wear (ILLUS.) 49.50

Paperweight, "Crawford Shoe Store - 612 Olive Street, St. Louis - 1892," glass 45.00

Paperweight, "Crescent Hotel, Eureka Springs," ruby & clear glass, 3" sq.....45.00

Paperweight, "Missouri-Kansas Telephone Company," bell-shaped, blue glass..78.00

Party horn, "Weatherbird Shoes," cardboard, 1950s..............................12.00

Pencil, mechanical, "Harley-Davidson" 110.00

Pencil, mechanical, "Indian Motorcycle," silvered metal w/shirt clip, round disc top w/inset picture of an Indian head & "Indian Motorcycle" in black on white, ca. 1920s, 4¾" l. (minor wear) 302.50

Pencil, mechanical, "Oxydol," celluloid, pictures a mammy & "Sho Makes Clothes White," 1920s 45.00

Photographic slide, "Castoria," glass, very early view of New York City skyline & the Brooklyn Bridge, w/billboard for "Castoria," 7 x 10" 45.00

Pinback button, "Sunoco Winter Oil & Grease," celluloid, pictures old man winter blowing snow 35.00

Plate, "Jones, McDuffee & Stratton Co., NYC," china, four photos w/names & buildings on front & history of the company on the back, blue transfer on white, ca. 1910, Wedgwood 150.00

Plate, "Walgreen," china, drugstore fountain, three-section 35.00

Platter, oval, "Steak 'n Shake," china, marked "Buffalo China" 10.00

Playing cards, "Omar Wonder Flour," mint in box 30.00

Playing cards, "Remington Arms Co.," "First in The Field," scene of ducks in marsh 27.50

Pepsi-Cola Pop Machine

Pop machine, "Pepsi-Cola," blue w/white lettering, Pepsi caps are red, white & blue w/cream & red lettering, overall scratches w/some touch-up, some letter fading, 18 x 24", 52" h. (ILLUS.) 935.00

Postcard, "Alka-Seltzer," w/illustration of Speedy...............................10.00

Potato sack, "Winchester 50 lb," illustrates rifle & covered wagon 10.00

Radio, "Planters Peanuts," figural peanut 70.00

Planters Peanuts Figural Scale

Scale, "Planters Peanuts," figural, floor-model, drop penny into slot in hat for weight, 20 x 22", 45" h. (ILLUS.) 18,150.00

Sheet music, "Bromo Seltzer," entitled "Starlight Polka" 5.00

Shot glass, "RCA," aluminum, colorful enameled raised logo 45.00

Sign, "Dauntless Coffee," cardboard, pictures young Roman soldier 50.00

Sign, "Pepsi-Cola," embossed tin, rectangular, "Drink Pepsi-Cola," spaced on three lines, ca. 1930, 10 x 30" 325.00

Soda fountain tap knob, "Pepsi-Cola," celluloid & metal, musical-type, 1940s, 4" h. 250.00

Soda pop cooler, "Nehi," metal cabinet-type, a rectangular compartment w/two lift lids raised on metal legs w/corner brackets above a lower shelf, on wheels, army green w/red & black lettering on yellow, Nehi bottle in red, yellow & blue & a woman's leg shown behind the bottle (overall paint wear) 533.50

Stickpin, "Victor Talking Machine Company," celluloid, model of Nipper 85.00

Tape measure, "Boon's Knoll Bourbon," celluloid, pictures woman w/flowing hair 95.00

Tape measure, "Buckeye Disc Drill," aluminum 50.00

Thermometer, "Abbott's Bitters," painted wood, a tall narrow shape w/rounded top, yellow ground decorated w/a waiter serving in black at the top above the thermometer & printed in black at the bottom "Abbott's Bitters - Best For Cocktails," narrow blue border, late 19th early - 20th c., 5⅛" w., 21" h. (paint cracked & chipped, scratches, soiling) 203.50

Thermometer, "Doan's Pills," w/wooden cut-out figure of a man stooped in pain & "Is Your Back Day Today?" 185.00

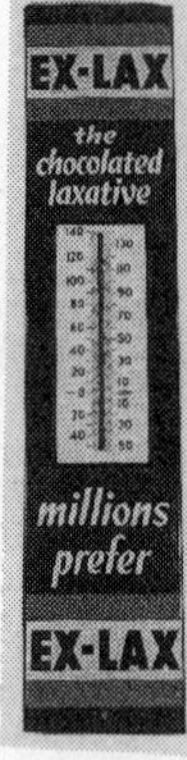

Ex-Lax Thermometer

Thermometer, "Ex-Lax," porcelain, rectangular, dark blue w/black & white lettering above & below the thermometer, chipping around mounting holes. scratches & paint spotting to left side, very minor fading, 8⅛" w., 36⅛" h. (ILLUS.) 99.00

Thermometer, "Frostie Root Beer," painted tin, oblong, smiling bearded elf in tall cap at top w/"Drink Frostie Root Beer" above the thermometer & "A Real Taste Treat" w/a bottle of the product, brown & blue w/black & brown lettering, 8" w., 36" h. (minor scratches & overall paint chipping) 99.00

Thermometer, "Genuine Scotch Anthracite Coal," porcelain, rectangular, red & white lettering on a black ground in a box at the top reading "When You Buy Coal - Buy Genuine Scotch Anthracite," another box at the base w/a trash can & "Don't buy Ash or Clinker," all on a red & green plaid ground, 8" w., 30¼" h (very minor chipping) 357.50

Thermometer, "Occident Flour," painted wood, oblong w/round Occident logo at the top, thermometer in the center & "Occident Flour Makes Better Bread" at the bottom, cream ground w/black & red lettering, early 20th c., 4" w., 15" h. (minor paint cracking & soiling) 220.00

Thermometer, "Red Goose Shoes," porcelain, long rectangular w/rounded ends, red goose w/white lettering reading "Red Goose School Shoes" flanked by black lettering "Finest & Best," goose above "For Boys - For Girls" above the thermometer, emblem of International Shoe Co. at the bottom, 7" w., 27" h. 286.00

Toy fortune teller, "Cracker Jack" prize, lithographed tin 40.00

Toy jump rope, "Kool-Aid," w/figural Mr. Kool-Aid handles 25.00

Toy milk wagon w/horse, "Borden's Milk," wood, 1930s 425.00

Toy play set, "Boston Sunday Globe," lithographed cardbroad, "Iron Horse Railroad train," w/stand up Victorian figures, produced by the Forbes Co., uncut 85.00

Toy play set, "Kellogg's," The Singing Lady punch-out circus, premium created by artist Vernon Grant, near mint 75.00

Toy stuffed animal, "Post Wheat Puffs," Sugar Bear, mint in box 30.00

Toy truck, "Burger King," refrigeration truck, Matchbox w/original box, 12" l. 100.00

Trivet, "Westinghouse," tin, w/eight pictures of stoves, 1942 .... 25.00

Tumblers, "Borden's," clear glass, Bicentennial theme depicting Elsie & others playing fife & drum, boxed set of 6 .... 75.00

Tumblers, "Nestle's World," glass, set of 4 .... 120.00

Watch fob, "Kellogg's Corn Flakes," die-cut brass w/red & black enamel detailing, box-shaped, ca. 1920 .... 95.00

Whiskey jug, "Happy Days - Famous - Old Rye Whiskey," stoneware, w/pictures of graduates, 1 qt. 89.00

Whiskey jug, "O'Keefe's," stoneware, 1 qt. 39.00

ALMANACS

Almanacs have been published for decades. Commonplace ones are available at $4 to $12; those representing early printings or scarce ones are higher.

An Almanac for the Year of Our

Lord God - by John Goldsmith, 1747, printed in London by Charles Ackers $100.00
Ayer's American Almanac, 1910 ....12.00
Ayer's American Almanac, 1917 ....6.00
Boston Almanac, 1847, w/map....75.00
Confederate States Almanac & Repository of Useful Knowledge, by H.C. Clarke, Vicksburg, Mississippi, 176 pp. (some foxing) 85.00
Dr. Miles' Almanac, 1935....10.00
Dr. Morse's Almanac & Weather Forecaster, 1937....5.00
Herbalist Almanac, 1943 ....4.00
Home Almanac, Columbia Exposition article, 1893 ....35.00
Hostetter's Almanac, 1878 ....25.00
Hostetter's Almanac, 1893 ....15.00
Rumford Almanac & Cook Book, 1888, illustrated by Palmer Cox, 6 pp....25.00
Watkins' Almanac, 1911 ....9.00

ARCHITECTURAL ITEMS

Arts & Crafts Fireplace Mantel

In recent years the growing interest in and support for historic preservation has spawned a greater appreciation of the fine architectural elements which were an integral part of early buildings, both public and private. Where, in decades past, fine structures might be razed and doors, fireplace mantels, windows, etc., hauled to the dump, today all interior and exterior details from unrestorable buildings are salvaged to be offered to home restorers, museums and even builders who want to include a bit of history in a new construction project.

Baluster, cast iron, the central shield within an ellipse bordered by ornate scrollwork & surmounted by stylized foliage, designed by Adler & Sullivan, executed by the Yale & Towne Manufacturing Co. for the Guaranty Building, Buffalo, New York, 1894-95, 34¾" h. $3,335.00

Building ornaments, molded copper, each fashioned w/a grimacing head of a man surrounded by a stylized shell form & mounted on a paneled rectangular section, weathered to an overall green verdigris, American-made, late 19th c., 15 x 42", 33" h. 1,725.00

Doors, four-panel style w/two long raised panels above two short raised panels, dark brown framing & original yellow & brown graining in the panels, 19th c., 32" w., 6' 7¼" h., set of 5 (one w/applied moldings & weathered white paint on reverse, one w/old grey paint on reverse) 275.00

Doors, grained-painted wood, six raised panels grained to simulate bird's-eye & tiger maple, New England, 19th c., 35¼" & 35½" w., 7' 5½" & 7' 6" h., pr. 495.00

Doors, wood & leaded glass, in the manner of Frank Lloyd Wright, the upper half w/a long rectangular leaded glass panel composed of small colored & clear squares & rectangles, the lower half w/a raised panel, early 20th c., 28¾" w., 6' 10½" h., pr....6,900.00

Downspout, molded tin, in the form of an elaborate cornice & central socle, the upper portion decorated w/applied sunburst motifs having applied tin stars at sides & applied ridged sea horse tail motifs continuing to the tubular spout, America, mid-19th c., 33" h....1,725.00

Fireplace mantel, oak, Arts & Crafts style, the molded cornice above a paneled section, the panels incised w/poppies & leafage, stained green, above a fire surround, losses to moldings, America, ca. 1900, 6½" w., overall 60" l., 6' 3" h. (ILLUS.) 2,530.00

Fireplace mantel, carved oak, Louis XV Provincial style, a serpentine-fronted rectangular top above the curved apron, the centrally carved scallop shell flanked by foliate sprays, raised on rectangular supports w/carved foliate panels, France, mid-18th c., 77½" l., 4' h. 3,450.00

Fireplace mantel, painted & carved pine, Federal style, a projecting molded shelf above recessed end pilasters w/incised fans & a raised center panel w/a pinwheel, designs picked-out in white on a light slate blue ground, probably New York state, ca. 1830, 9 x 82", 5' 2½" h. 5,463.00

Fireplace mantel & surround, carved mahogany, Art Nouveau style, the arched cornice w/shaped corners & foliate-molded whiplash sides enclosing a large ovoid beveled mirror surrounded by four smaller mirrors & single centered shelf, supported by an arched fireplace surround w/conformingly molded foliage centered by a firebox lined in pink silk fabric & mounted on a molded base, ca. 1900, 64" w., 9' 8" h. (firebox electrified) 4,025.00

Gates, painted wrought iron, each centered w/a basket issuing flowers beneath a scrolling floral top rail, 5' 3" h., pr.....................................6,900.00

Hinges, wrought iron, scrolling ram's horn form, w/pins, 7½" l., pr. 126.50

Hinges, wrought iron, strap-type w/bird's head ends, 16½" l., pr.........104.50

Hinges, wrought iron, strap-type w/scroll detail, complete w/scroll ends, 31" l., pr.................................187.00

Ornament Designed by Sullivan

Ornament, cast iron, open oval form incorporating Celtic interlace & organic forms, designed by Louis Sullivan for the Guaranty Building, Chicago, Illinois, 1894, ends cut, 9¾" l. (ILLUS.) 12,650.00

Ornaments, painted stone, the rectangular block w/high-relief design of flamboyant acanthus above a scroll border, painted black, designed by Louis Sullivan for the Schiller Building, Chicago, Illinois, 1891, 7 x 13 x 20½", pr................2,070.00

Railing, wrought iron & bronze, Art Deco style, the rectangular section w/a panel wrought w/fan-like sections of geometric & stylized scrolling floral designs, set w/hammered bronze spheres at various intervals, in the manner of Edgar Brandt, France, ca. 1925, 7' l., 29½" h. 7,763.00

Skylight panel, leaded glass, rectangular w/deep burgundy Celtic interlace design against a pale amber ground, designed by Adler & Sullivan for the theater of the Auditorium Building, Chicago, Illinois, ca. 1890, framed, 38 x 62" 6,900.00

ART DECO

Art Deco Magazine Rack

Interest in Art Deco, a name given an art movement stemming from the Paris International Exhibition of 1925, is at an all-time high and continues to grow. This style flowered in the 1930s and actually continued into the 1940s. A mood of flippancy is found in its varied characteristics—zigzag lines resembling the lightning bolt, sometimes steps, often the use of sharply contrasting colors such as black and white and others. Look for Art Deco prices to continue to rise. Also see JEWELRY (MODERN).

Bowl, aluminum & brass, plain elliptical form w/gently out-curved sides, fluted silver-gilt footring, impressed marks of Hagenauer, Austria, ca. 1925, 13½" l., 3" h. $220.00

Cocktail shaker, blue glass & chrome, w/original box 65.00

Compotes, open, hand-hammered aluminum, wide rounded elliptical bowl w/curved fluted applied tab handles at the rim, raised on a slender tapering stem w/a flat disc foot, impressed marks of WHW Hagenauer, Austria, ca. 1925,

6¼" h., pr. 467.50

Dresser set: three cylindrical covered containers on a rectangular tray; butterscotch Catalin w/beige trim & covers, the matching pair of containers & a larger container in ribbed cylindrical form w/a flat cover w/bar finial, the tray w/low curved end handles, unsigned, ca. 1930, tray 10⅜" l., 4 pcs. 165.00

Lamp, table-type, patinated metal & glass, in the form of a seated monkey holding a glass umbrella, 16" h. 1,045.00

Lamp, table-type, figure of a seated female nude facing a ball-shaped end-of-day glass shade, Nuart 255.00

Magazine rack, cast iron, each side cast w/a racing hound within a double circle conjoined w/stylized leafage above, America, ca. 1925, 12¼" l., 14" h. (ILLUS.) 1,725.00

Rouge pot., cover w/figural nude lady finial, silver-tone metal, marked Marinello 25.00

Rug, wool, irregular areas of olive, salmon, light brown, ivory, light blue & teal w/stylized floral designs in brown, rust, light blue & mauve, bordered by interlocking linear segments in the above-mentioned colors, France, ca.1925, 6' 3½" w., 9' 9" l. 2,750.00

Tureen, cov., silver plate, circular w/symmetrical stepped handles, the cover w/a cylindrical finial, 7¼" h...460.00

Wine cooler, silver plate, flaring cylindrical body w/symmetrical angular handles, stamped "Wiskemann," 9⅜" h. 920.00

ART NOUVEAU

Art Nouveau Mantel Clock

Art Nouveau's primary thrust was between 1890 and 1905 but commercial Art Nouveau productions continued until about World War I. This style was a rebellion against historic tradition in art. Using natural forms as inspiration, it is primarily characterized by undulating or wave-like lines. Many objects were made in materials ranging from glass to metals. Interest in Art Nouveau still remains high, especially for jewelry in the Nouveau taste. Also see JEWELRY (Antique) and MUCHA (Alphonse) ARTWORK.

Card tray, silver plate, figural, the irregular tray cast w/a maiden in flowing gown opposite a spray of iris blossoms & leafage, Wurttembergische Metallwarenfabrik (WMF), Model No. 290., ca. 1906, 12¼" l...$805.00

Charger, pottery, bust of a long-haired woman flanked by orchids in slip & enamel against a blue ground, incised "Julius Dressler," Austria, ca. 1900, 13" d. 495.00

Clock, mantel-type, enamel & gilt-bronze, arched rectangular form, the main body enameled in mottled seafoam green & blue streaked against a deep green ground, the gilt-bronze mount cast w/sprigs of clover, stamped "PARIS LOUCHET CISELEUR," 9¼" h............1,035.00

Clock, mantel-type, gilt-bronze, the shaped rectangular dial housed within a floral-cast case, signed "M. Miagnon and E. Colin & Cie, Paris," ca. 1900, 15½" h. (ILLUS.) 2,875.00

Easel, floor-type, mahogany, the arch-topped framework w/curved cross-bars at the top above the adjustable rack, on arched & molded trestle base, in the manner of Eugene Gallaird, France, ca. 1900, 28 x 33½", 6' 9" h.......................12,650.00

Art Nouveau Figural Mirror

Mirror, wall-type, bronze, the frame cast w/leafage at the top, the lower section w/a nude maiden standing ankle-deep in a lily pond w/a little frog seated on a lily pad, greenish-brown patina, signed "EG," France, ca. 1900, 10⅞" w., 21¾" h. (ILLUS.) 2,013.00

Mirror, silver-colored metal & brass, the arch-topped rectangular beveled mirror plate within conforming wooden surround, decorated w/applied hammered silver-colored metal w/stylized blossoms & leafage about a textured brass ground, first quarter 20th c., 43 x 72¾" 2,300.00

Parasol handle, tortoiseshell & enamel, the fancy carved & molded tortoiseshell handle elaborately decorated w/stylized foliage, multi-colored enameling & amethysts, signed "Tiffany & Co.," together w/gold rib terminals, all in the original fitted box..........................8,050.00

Shoe horn, sterling silver, hollow handle, woman's head on front & back 25.00

Umbrella stand, ceramic, the bulbous tripod base beneath fluted columns, molded w/stylized floral pattern, glazed in celadon & hunter green alternating w/slate & pale blue, impressed "21146," 21¾" h.............230.00

Vase, ceramic & bronze, the flattened flaring ovoid body glazed in salmon streaking to black, within a whiplash foliate two-handled bronze mount, unsigned, Continental, ca. 1900, 14¾" h...288.00

Vase, pewter overlay, pine cones & branches in pewter over an amethyst satin glass cylinder w/flaring base, France, 16" h. 595.00

AUDUBON PRINTS

John James Audubon, American ornithologist and artist, is considered the finest nature artist in history. About 1820 he conceived the idea of having a full color book published portraying every known species of American bird in its natural habitat. He spent years in the wilderness capturing the beauty in vivid color only to have great difficulty finding a publisher. In 1826 he visited England, received immediate acclaim, and selected Robert Havell as his engraver. "Birds of America," when completed, consisted of four volumes of 435 individual plates, double-elephant folio size, which are a combination of aquatint, etching and line engraving. W.H. Lizars of Edinburgh engraved the first ten plates of this four volume series. These were later retouched by Havell who produced the complete set between 1827 and early 1839. In the early 1840s, another definitive work, "Viviparous Quadrupeds of North America," containing 150 plates, was published in America. Prices for Audubon's original double-elephant folio size prints are very high and beyond the means of the average collector. Subsequent editions of "Birds of America." especially the chromolithographs done by Julius Bien in New York (1859-60) and the smaller octavo (7 x 10½") edition of prints done by J.T. Bowen of Philadelphia in the 1840s are those that are most frequently offered for sale.

American Magpie

American Beaver - Plate XLVI, hand-colored lithograph by J.T. Bowen, Philadelphia, ca. 1845, framed, 21½ x 27" (pale mat stain & foxing, a few creases in margins) $1,725.00

American Elk - Wapiti Deer - Plate LXII, hand-colored lithograph by J.T. Bowen, Philadelphia, ca. 1845, unframed (pale foxing & soiling, few handling creases, small tear, stitch holes & losses along disbound edge) 2,530.00

American Magpie - Plate CCCLVII, hand-colored engraving by Robert Havell, Jr., London, 1827-38, framed, faint mat stain & slight fox marks in margins, 26½ x 39⅝" (ILLUS.) 3,450.00

Arkansaw Flycatcher, Swallow-Tailed Flycatcher, Says Flycatcher - Plate CCCLIX, hand-colored engraving by Robert Havell, Jr., London, 1827-38, unframed (traces of soiling & foxing in margins, repaired tears, a few creases, stitch holes along disbound edge) 2,185.00

Barnacle Goose - Plate CCXCVI, hand-colored engraving by Robert Havell, Jr., London, 1827-38, unframed (foxing, discoloration in edges, remnants of old hinges & offprint) 3,450.00

Black-bellied Plover - Plate CCCXXXIV, hand-colored engraving by Robert Havell, Jr., London, 1827-38, 15⅛ x 21" (pale staining & a few fox marks, several backed tears at margin edges) 495.00

Brown Pelican

Brown Pelican - Plate CCLI, hand-colored engraving by Robert Havell, Jr., London, 1827-38, framed, colors slightly faded, mat stain, minor foxing & soiling, several tears & losses in margins, 25⅛ x 37⅞" (ILLUS.) 19,550.00

Common Cormorant - Plate CCLXVI, hand-colored engraving by Robert Havell, Jr., London, 1827-38, framed, 25¼ x 38" (foxing, mat stain, few small edge tears & two repaired tears) 1,150.00

Green Black-Capt Flycatcher - Plate CXXIV, hand-colored engraving by Robert Havell, Jr., London, 1827-38, unframed, 26½ x 39⅜" (some spots of foxing in margins, some soiling in edges, stitch holes along disbound edge, offprint on verso) 1,150.00

Horned Grebe - Plate CCLIX, hand-colored engraving by Robert Havel, Jr., London, 1827-38, 17⅞ x 20⅝" (cut margins, pale staining, colors slightly attenuated, rubbed patch at bottom, small tear in right margin edge)..1,320.00

The Jaguar - Plate CI, hand-colored lithograph by J.T. Bowen, Philadelphia, ca. 1845, 21½ x 27⅜" (a few tiny spots of foxing, bit of light soiling in the margins, minor discoloration in the extreme sheet edges) 4,025.00

Labrador Falcon - Plate CXCVI, hand-colored engraving by Robert Havel, Jr., London, 1827-38, 26⅛ x 39" (few fox marks, soiling & creases in the sheet edges, few tiny losses in extreme sheet edges, stitch holes along disbound edge) 2,875.00

Long-tailed or Dusky Grouse - Plate CCCLXI, hand-colored engraving by Robert Havell, Jr., London, 1827-38, framed, 25¾ x 38¼" (trimmed margins, pale staining & soiling, laid down on board).......1,430.00

Maria's Woodpecker, Three-toed Woodpecker, Phillips' Woodpecker, Canadian Woodpecker, Harris's Woodpecker, Audubon's Woodpecker, Plate CCCCXVII, hand-colored engraving by Robert Havel, Jr., London, 1827-38, 25⅜ x 38⅜" (very pale staining & scattered foxing, mat stain in margins, backed splits & creases in margins) 3,500.00

Maryland Yellow Throat - Plate 23, hand-colored engraving by Robert Havell, Jr., London, 1827-38, 26 x 39¾" (minor soiling in margins, tears & associated paper losses along sheet edges, some repaired, & soiling on verso) 1,610.00

Passenger Pigeon - Plate LXII, hand-colored engraving by Robert Havel, Jr., London, 1827-38, 25⅜ x 38" (faint light stain, a few small tears in sheet edges, bottom left sheet corner repaired, stains from old tape)...13,225.00

Polar Bear

Polar Bear - Plate XCI, hand-colored lithograph by J.T Bowen, Philadelphia, ca. 1845, framed, very pale mat stain, soiling in margins, few creases, two small losses to edge, 21½ x 27⅛" (ILLUS.) ....3,000.00 to 3,900.00

Rocky Mountain Sheep - plate LXXIII, hand-colored lithograph by J.T. Bowen, Philadelphia, ca. 1845, 21⅜ x 26¾" (some discoloration & soiling in the margins, 8" repaired tear in right margin, linen-backed) 1,725.00

Snowy Owl - Plate CXXI, hand-colored engraving by Robert Havel, Jr., London, 1827-38, 26 x 38¾" (light foxing, minor soiling in margins, traces of glue in the edges verso) 47,150.00

Texan Lynx - Plate XCII, hand-colored lithograph by J.T. Bowen, Philadelphia, ca. 1845, 21⅝ x 27½" (faint mat stain, small tear & a few creases in the right sheet edge, stitch holes along the disbound edge) 805.00

Three-Toed Woodpecker - Plate CXXXII, hand-colored engraving by Robert Havell, Jr., London, 1827-38, 26⅛ x 38⅞" (some soiling & small tears in the sheet edges, stitched holes along disbound edge) 3,220.00

Virginian Partridge - Plate 76, hand-colored engraving by Robert Havell, Jr., London, 1827-38, 25⅜ x 38¾" (few spots of foxing, repaired tear running through the title space into the image, repaired tear in the top left sheet edge, bottom left sheet corner repaired, pinhole in upper right margin) 12,650.00

White-headed Eagle - Plate CXXVI, hand-colored engraving by Robert Havell, Jr., London, 1827-38, 26 x 39⅛" (faint mat stain, spot of foxing to the right of bird's chest, few soft creases in upper left margin, edges of paper hinged to back mat w/linen tape) 3,450.00

Yellow-Billed Cuckoo - Plate II, hand-colored lithograph by W. H. Lizars, London, ca. 1834, 24¾ x 36⅞" (few tears in bottom sheet edge, edges of paper glued to the back mat by linen tape, two printer's creases in image just above the bird at left) 2,300.00

AUTOGRAPHS

Value of autographs and autograph letters depend on such factors as content, scarcity and the fame of the writer. Values of good autograph material continue to rise. A.L.S. stands for "autographed letter signed," L.S. for "letter signed," D.S. for "document signed" and S.P. for "signed photograph."

Signed Photo of Charlie Chaplin

Baker, Josephine, (1906-75) American-born dancer & entertainer, S.P., gelatin silver print of Baker in a feather & silver stage costume, dated "June 20, 1927" & inscribed in French, left hand corner signed "Walery-Paris," 8¾ x 11" $1,380.00

Begin, Menacheim, (1914-92) Prime Minister of Israel, S.P., 3½ x 5", w/envelope 60.00

Burr, Raymond, (1917-93) American actor, S.P., 8 x 10" 8.00

Chaplin, Charlie, (1889-1978) British-born actor, producer & director, S.P., gelatin silver print of Chaplin in bow tie & jacket, signed in lower right corner "Yours Truly Charlie Chaplin," 7¼ x 9" (ILLUS.) 575.00

Crawford, Joan, (1908-77) American actress, L.S., w/envelope 75.00

Dean, James, (1931-55) American actor, white paper napkin signed in blue ink "Love ya Jim Dean" 805.00

Dietrich, Marlene, (1901-92) actress, S.P., 8 x 10" 50.00

Fields, W.C., (1879-1946) American actor-comedian, S.P., black & white glossy photo of the comic shooting pool, still from the 1944 film "Follow the Boys," inscribed in green ink "To Mr. Cary from W.C. Fields," 8 x 10" 605.00

Garland, Judy, (1922-69) American actress, S.P., black & white glossy half-length shot inscribed "To George: Many More Rainbows Judy Garland," 8 x 10" 880.00

Grant, Ulysses S., (1822-85) 18th President of the United States & Civil War general, D.S., land deed for Sioux Indian Trust Lands, dated August 5, 1869, w/papered seal 165.00

Hitchcock, Alfred, (1899-1981) movie director, black marker portrait sketch of Hitchcock's famous profile, done by Hitchcock & signed "Alfred Hitchcock," 8 x 10" 2,185.00

Howe, Julia Ward, (1819-1910), Battle Hymn of the Republic author, A.L.S., 2 pp. (mounting traces on back, otherwise very good) 235.00

Lincoln, Abraham, (1809-65) 16th President of the United States, D.S. nominating George H. French as First Lieutenant in the Veterans Reserve Corps, co-signed by Edward Stanton, Secretary of War, dated August 1, 1864, on vellum,unframed 10,000.00

Nixon, Richard M., (1913-94) 37th President of the Unites States, L.S., typed letter to actor Pat O'Brien, contents include entertainment, World Campaign Suport, election victory, nation's upcoming 200th birthday, 1972 ....195.00

O'Brien, Pat, (1899-1983) American actor, S.P. 35.00

Power, Tyrone, (1913-58) American actor, S.P., inscribed "Don't Let The Power Fool You," 8 x 10" 325.00

Presley, Elvis, (1935-77) American singer & actor, A.L.S., dated 3-11-61, to an Army friend asking that he come & stay w/ Elvis as he feels he can't trust many people................1,725.00

Shatner, William, (1931-) American actor, S.P. 35.00

Turner, Tina, (1941-) female American rock singer, autographed self-portrait sketch in purple felt tip pen on board, matted & framed w/a plaque, 18 x 24" 2,070.00

Autograph & Photo of Richie Valens

Valens, Richie, (1941-59) American musician, signed autograph album page, black ink on blue paper, matted & framed w/a color photo of Valens, ca. 1958, 9 x 12" (ILLUS.) 575.00

AUTOMOBILE LITERATURE

Book, "AAA Service Station Directory," 1942 ....$22.00

Book, "A Complete Reference on the Universal Car, Truck & Tractor," Ford Motor Company, 1924 ....35.00

Book, "Audel's Automobile Guide," 1915..55.00

Book, "Official Automobile Blue Book," 1917, Vol. 2...35.00

Book, "Official Automobile Blue Book," 1925, Vol. 1 ....38.00

Book, "Treasury of the Automobile," by Stein, 1961, hard cover, w/dust jacket 18.50

Book, "Treasury of Foreign Cars," by Clymer, 1957 ....12.50

Books, "Handbook of Gasoline Automobiles," statistics, prices, good picture of each car of every licensed manufacturer, 1904-18, Vols. 4 - 18.......................................795.00

Buick "D-Six" owner's manual, 1944 ....80.00

Chevrolet dealer's brochure, 1949 ....24.00

Chevrolet trucks brochure, 1936, colorful illustrations, 9½ x 10½", 24 pp..25.00

Chrysler Imperial dealer data book, 1970..18.00

DeSoto "Sketch Book," 1941, show-room booklet, in color 24.00

Dodge owner's manual, 1917..............80.00

Ford Model A owner's manual, 1928....25.00

Ford operator's manual, 1926 ....35.00

Hudson auto parts & price list, 1918.....50.00

Hudson booklet, "The New 1950 Hudson" 26.00

Hudson owner's manual, 1940, "Your New Hudson," 31 pp. 22.00

Hudson promotional booklet, 1949, 24 pp..30.00

Hudson "Super Six" instruction booklet, 1926 ....15.00

Kaiser salesman's fact book, 1947, pictures, facts about 1947 Kaiser automobile, paint chips & charts, 135 pp. (slight cover damage) 87.50

Magazine, Motor Age, 1905, March 16, features new cars & four pages of European auto body designs, etc. 18.00

Magazine, Motor Age, 1908, November 12, new Cadillac shown, entries for Chicago Show, advertisements, etc. 15.00

Magazine, Motor Age, 1910, January 6, Madison Square Garden Show Number, color & black & white, over 420 pp. 40.00

Magazine, Motor Age, 1920, June 3, w/Indy 500 race results 12.50

Magazine, Motor Age, 1925, May 7, Indy 500 entries, new Packard, etc. 13.50

Magazine, Motor Magazine, 1932, November, color cover, nice ads, etc. 8.50

Mercury owner's manual, 1976 ....10.00

Oldsmobile showroom booklet, 1952, "Rockets to New Highs," full-color 21.00

Plymouth "Deluxe" showroom booklet, 1939, full-color, 20 pp. 22.00

Pontiac owner's manual, 1961 ....10.00

Willys-Overland equipment & parts list, 1930 ....40.00

Willys-Overland owner's manual, 1946 ....35.00

AUTOMOBILES

1949 Ford Sedan

Chevrolet, 1967 Impala Super Sport, 327/275 h.p., all power operation including Comfortron air, automatic on floor, blue & white interior, bucket seats, original spare tire in trunk, no rust, 21,200 actual miles $12,000.00

Dodge, 1930 four-door sedan, V-8 engine, two-tone, 12,448 original miles, restored 15,000.00

Edsel, 1959 Ranger, new paint, tires & exhaust system.................2,900.00

Ford, 1929 Model A Tudor, restored to original condition....................23,500.00

Ford, 1949 "Custom" four-door sedan, V-8 flathead engine, standard transmission, royal blue body, restored interior (ILLUS.) 6,000.00

Ford, 1972 Ranchero, rebuilt 302 engine, five original Frog mag wheels, new tires, white body, blue upholstery, tilt wheel, split bench seat, Voyager gem top canopy, front Ford stock bumper guards, completely restored 7,650.00

AUTOMOTIVE COLLECTIBLES

Pontiac Hood Ornament

Also see CANS & CONTAINERS.

Banner, "Chevrolet," canvas, picture of convertible parked at the beach, 1950s, 6' l. $135.00

Badge, "Ford Twin City Plant," raised scenes, early 50.00

Battery tester, "Beede No. 209," in box 15.00

Chauffeur's badge, 1916, Michigan....115.00

Chauffeur's badge, 1918, New York.....40.00

Chauffeur's badge, 1919, Minnesota....85.00

Chauffeur's badge, 1920, Colorado (no eagle) 35.00

Chauffeur's badge, 1927, Michigan......30.00

Chauffeur's badge, 1931, California.....65.00

Chauffeur's badge, 1937, Illinois 40.00

Chauffeur's badge, 1938, Indiana 17.50

Chauffeur's badge, 1941, Iowa............12.00

Chauffeur's badge, 1951, Arizona........40.00

Coin, commemorative, "Ford V8 - 1903 - 1933" 15.00

Display cabinet, "Schrader Tire Gauges," shaped like a tire gauge, 20" h..............................185.00

Drink mixer, battery-operated, a 4" l. model of a Jaguar car spins on top of a 6" h. red Lucite & chrome mixer 75.00

Driving goggles, "Willson," patented August 28, 1916, w/original case.......20.00

Gasoline pump globe, "Martin - Purple Martin - Ethyl," wide milk white glass frame...350.00

Gasoline pump globe, "Socony Motor Gasoline," milk white glass insert in metal frame 1,395.00

Gasoline pump globe, "Standard Red Crown Ethyl," crown-shaped, milk white glass etched in red, 1914-31 ....1,800.00

Gasoline pump globe, "Texaco Sky Chief," milk white glass, 1940s 400.00

Gas tank measuring stick, "Ford," wood, w/advertisement for "Ladd & Peffer, Havana, ND," 1908 ....65.00
Gearshift knob, glass, orange & blue streaks 20.00
Gearshift knob, glass, red & cream swirl...45.00
Hood ornament, chrome, figure of a nude woman, signed "Tetty" 75.00
Hood ornament, "Pontiac," depicts bust of Indian in feathered headdress (ILLUS.)...................................45.00
Hubcap, "LaSalle," 1920s....................45.00
Hubcap, "Mercury Monterey," 1956......30.00
License plate, 1915, Pennsylvania, blue porcelain..........................85.00
License plates, 1920, Missouri, pr.........39.00
License plates, 1927, Texas, pr..........100.00
License plates, 1933, Nevada, mint in original Highway Department mailer, pr...50.00
License plates, 1933, Texas, pr...........70.00
Match pack, 1936 NBC Radio "Broadcast by Buick," cover depicts Joe Louis fighting Max Schmeling, 1936 Buick pictured inside, oversized 50.00
Motometer, "Buick" in script across square 45.00
Padlock, "Ford Motor Company," brass 75.00
Paperweight, "Oldsmobile," glass, illustrates a 1926 touring car convertible on a white ground, signed "M," colored pebbled base 65.00
Pin, "Corvette - 1958-1978 - Anniversary," enameled metal 60.00
Radiator cap, brass, figural woman's head & wings 50.00
Radiator cap, "Ford," screw-on type.....14.00
Spark plug, "Rentz," visible-type...........55.00
Tire chain repair kit, "Monkey Links," for broken cross chains, depicts monkey fixing a tire, 1948, mint in box 10.00
Tire pressure gauge, brass, w/leather carrying case......................16.00
Tire pump, brass, "Ford" in script on base 55.00
Tire repair kit, "Goodyear No Rim-Cut," w/flying shoe logo 16.00
Vases, marigold carnival glass, for a Model T Ford, w/original brackets, pr...125.00
Wrench, "Ford," three way-type............15.00

AVIATION COLLECTIBLES

Recently much interest has been shown in collecting items associated with the early days of the "flying machine." In addition to relics, flying adjuncts and literature relating to the early days of flight, collectors also seek out items that picture the more renowned early pilots, some of whom became folk-heroes in their own lifetimes, as well as the early planes themselves.

Side Table with Airplane Model

Airplane propeller, wide wood blades w/rounded green-painted tips, dark stain, 61" l. (minor wear to edges).......................................$176.00
Ashtray, "TWA," metal, a model of a red, white & silver TWA jet raised on an upright bar above a dished square ashtray base, 10" w., 6" h. (metal spotted, some paint wear & decal loss).......................................137.50
Badge, "National Air Races," 1928.....100.00
Book, "The Big Aviation Book," by Joseph Lewis French, 1929, for children, introduction by Admiral Byrd, w/photographs..........................45.00
Book, "National Air Races Official Directory," 1930 ....35.00
Book, "United States Air Force Pictorial Yearbook," 1960 ....20.00
Cigarette cards, "Royal Air Force Badges," British, 1937, set of 50........65.00
Coloring book, "Pan American - Flying Clippers," 1951 ....25.00
Goggles, "American Optical Co.," in original aluminum case 35.00
Model, "Lockheed Sirus," pressed steel, two seater, painted to resemble Lindbergh's Lockheed that he flew around the world, ca. 1930, 22" l...550.00
Pencil box, "Lucky Lindy - Spirit of St. Louis," tin, by Wallace, w/original contents, ca. 1920s...........................60.00
Perfume bottle, clear glass w/ red glass insert, "Lucky Lindy Perfumes," decorated w/a black & gold airplane sticker, Nipola Co., St.

Paul, Minnesota, 2½" h....................45.00

Photograph, formal portrait of Charles Lindbergh, Paris, France, 1927 ....85.00

Pin, "American Airlines - Lead Mechanic," wing-shaped................125.00

Plate, china, illustrated w/Lindbergh, a plane, the Statue of Liberty & the Eiffel Tower, Limoges China, sold by Dispatch in 1927, clipping of advertisement taped on back, 7½" sq...35.00

Postcard, sepia-tone, pictures Charles Lindbergh at microphones, cameraman, official & stadium in background, late 1920s 45.00

Poster, "Dare Devil Stunts," Flying Knights Air Circus, 1933 ....55.00

Sheet music, "Lindy, Lindy," 1927 ....15.00

Side table, chrome & milk white glass, Art Deco style, the reeded standard w/a circular top surmounted by an illuminated airplane finial, the base fitted w/a vasiform support & a molded glass plinth, w/maker's label, ca. 1930, 15¾" d., 36" h. (ILLUS.) 1,150.00

Ticket, "International Aviation Meet, Long Island," 1911, unused 22.00

BABY MEMENTOES

Victorian Baby Carriage

Everyone dotes on the new baby and through many generations some exquisite and unique gifts have been carefully selected with a special infant in mind. Collectors now seek items from a varied assortment of baby mementoes, once tokens of affection to the newborn babe. Also see CHILDREN'S BOOKS and CHILDREN'S MUGS.

Carriage, cast iron & painted wood, shallow sleigh-form body w/raised panels, cast iron frame raised on two large back wheels & two smaller front wheels, ornate supports holding a fringed sun shade, Victorian, late 19th c. (ILLUS.) $495.00

Carriage, wicker w/wire wheels, original upholstery & lace umbrella, Heywood Brothers, Victorian, 53" l., 61" h...800.00

Cup, aluminum, "Baby" embossed on front..8.00

Cup, sterling silver w/applied roses, textured surface, engraved "Rudolph Otto - Greenwood Lake, August 10, 1884," by Wood & Hughes, 5 oz., 3⅛" h...300.00

Feeding dish, china, depicts little girl w/two puppies, back w/"Royal Baby Plate, patd 2 - 1905"........................75.00

Feeding spoon, silver plate, Vintage Grape patt...35.00

Nursery scale, green enamel finish, w/wicker basket, Hanson 150.00

Rattle, sterling silver, dumbbell shape..50.00

Rattle, sterling silver, w/coral handle, marked "GU" & Birmingham, England date mark for 1871-72, 4¾" l. (one piece missing).........................357.50

Rattle, sterling silver, model of an elephant, marked .925 ....85.00

Rattle, sterling silver, model of Peter Rabbit forms handle, England, 1910...75.00

Rattle, twisted wire w/six bells, blue glass beads & wooden handle, 7½" l...137.50

Record book, "A Record of Our Baby," illustrated by M.M. Grimball, 1921, unused 25.00

BAKELITE

Bakelite is the trade-mark for a group of thermoplastics invented by Leo Hendrik Baekeland, an American chemist who invented this early form of plastic in 1909, only twenty years after immigrating to New York City from his native Belgium where he had taught at the University of Ghent. Bakelite opened the door to modern plastics and was widely used as an electrical insulating material replacing the flammable celluloid. Jewelry designers of the 1920s considered Bakelite the perfect medium to create pieces in the Art Deco style and today Bakelite bracelets, earrings and pins of this period are finding favor with another generation of modish women. Also see JEWELRY, MODERN.

Box, cov., Art Deco-style, diamond-shaped, tortoiseshell coloration, 6" w. $30.00
Bracelet, bangle-type, geometric rectangular design, yellow 50.00
Knives & forks, marbleized green handles, set of 6 each, 12 pcs. 45.00
Napkin ring w/ rhinestone polka dot decoration, black...............................35.00
Napkin rings, carved figural rabbit, four different colors, 4 pcs. 125.00
Pencil sharpener, model of a Scottie dog, green.......................................30.00
Pin, cluster of carved red cherries on carved wood 55.00
Pin, carved heart-shaped leaf w/nine dangling cherries, red 165.00
Pin, model of an anchor, black w/red & white braided rope.........................35.00
Pins, model of a Scottie dog w/movable head, red, pr. 60.00

BANKS

Original early mechanical and cast-iron still banks are in great demand with collectors and their scarcity has caused numerous reproductions of both types and the novice collector is urged to exercise caution. The early mechanical banks are especially scarce and some versions are seldom offered for sale but, rather, are traded with fellow collectors attempting to upgrade an existing collection. Numbers before mechanical banks refer to those in John Meyer's Handbook of Old Mechanical Banks. *However, a recently published book,* Penny Lane - A History of Antique Mechanical Toy Banks, *by Al Davidson, provides updated information and the number from this new volume is indicated in parenthesis at the end of each mechanical bank listing. In past years, our standard reference for cast-iron still banks was Hubert B. Whiting's book* Old Iron Still Banks, *but because this work is out of print and a beautiful new book,* The Penny Bank Book - Collecting Still Banks *by Andy and Susan Moore pictures and describes numerous additional banks, we will use the Moore numbers as a reference preceding each listing and indicate the Whiting reference in parenthesis at the end. The still banks listed are old and in good original condition with good paint and no repair unless otherwise noted. An asterisk (*) indicates this bank has been reproduced at some time.*

MECHANICAL

Always Did `Spise A Mule Bank

5 Always Did 'Spise a Mule, riding mule, PL 251 (ILLUS.).........$1,200.00 to 1,450.00
Artillery - Round Trap, PL 12 ....1,450.00
56 Darktown Battery (PL 146) ....3,400.00 to 3,800.00
61 Dog - Barking (Watch Dog Safe), PL 560 ....900.00
62 Dog - Bull Savings Bank (PL 65) 7,000.00
64 Dog - Charges Boy (PL 49) 1,093.00

Speaking Dog Bank

69 Dog - Speaking, PL 447 (ILLUS.) 1,550.00
71 Dog - Trick (PL 481) 1,425.00
75 Eagle & Eaglets (PL 165) ....1,550.00 to 2,200.00
88 Elephant & Three Clowns onTub (PL 170) 2,025.00
118 Hall's Excelsior (PL 228) ....350.00 to 450.00
121 Hen - Setting, PL 236 (ILLUS. top next column) ..4,250.00
126 Horse Race, w/original label (PL 247)................. 28,600.00
127 Humpty Dumpty (PL 248) 4,300.00

Setting Hen Bank

137 Jolly Nigger - moves ears, Starkie Patent, red coat, white collar, blue tie, aluminum (PL 271) 450.00

135 Jolly Nigger with High Hat (PL 277) 600.00

146 Lilliput - Hall's (PL 230) ....700.00 to 900.00

150 Little Joe (PL 304) 300.00

Mammy and Child Bank

155 Mammy and Child, PL 318 (ILLUS.) 6,200.00

156 Mason and Hod Carrier (PL 321) 9,500.00

Monkey and Coconut

163 Monkey and Coconut, PL 332 (ILLUS.) ...2,400.00 to 2,800.00

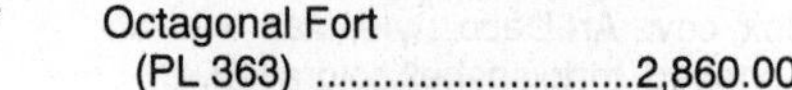

7 Octagonal Fort (PL 363) 2,860.00

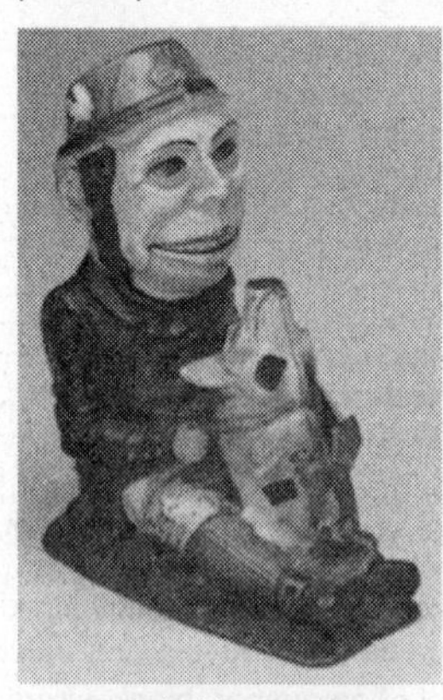

Paddy & His Pig Bank

185 Paddy & His Pig, PL 376 (ILLUS.) ....3,500.00 to 4,000.00

194 Pig in High Chair (PL 390) ....650.00 to 750.00

201 Professor Pug Frog's Great Bicycle Feat (PL 400) 14,500.00

205 Rabbit - large (PL 406) 475.00

212 Rooster (PL 419) 600.00 to700.00

STILL

"Teddy" Bear Bank

909 Barrel - Barrel, cast iron, Judd, ca. 1873, 2" top d., 2¾" h. (W. 283) 95.00

917 Basket - Basket Bank (woven), cast iron, Charles A. Braun, designer, American-made, ca. 1902, 3¾" d., 2⅞" h. 68.00

1440 Battleship - "Maine" (small), cast iron, Grey Iron Casting Co., 1897-1903, 4½" l., 4⅝" h. (W. 142) 275.00

698 Bear - "Teddy" Bear

(embossing), cast iron, Arcade, 1910-25, 4" l., 2½" h.,W. 331 * (ILLUS.) 165.00

80 "Billiken,'" on base, embossed "Billiken Shoes Bring Luck" across chest, cast iron, A.C. Williams, ca. 1909, 4¼" h. (W. 50) ....55.00 to 65.00

73 "Biliken" on Throne, cast iron, A.C. Williams Co., 1909 3 ⅛" w., 6½" h. 145.00

174 Black Man - Darkey (Sharecropper), toes visible both feet, cast iron, American-made, early 1900s, 5¼" h. ....275.00 to 300.00

173 Black Man - Darkey (Sharecropper), toes visible on one foot, cast iron, A.C. Williams, ca. 1901, 5½" h. (W. 18) 145.00

175 Black Woman - Mammy with Basket, clothes basket under right arm, white metal, key locked trap, American-made, 5¼" h. 87.50

1069 Building - Columbia, Administration Building at Columbian Exposition, cast iron, Kenton, 1893-1913,3½" sq., 4½" h. (W. 431) 210.00

1081 Building - Deposit Bank (large print), cast iron, Columbia Grey Casting Co., ca. 1897, 3" w., 4¼" h............................ 85.00

1180 Building - "Domed Bank," building w/cast iron mesh sides & solid cast iron domed roof, A.C. Williams, 1899-1934, 1¾ x 2", 3" h., (W. 424) 50.00

1181 Building - Domed "Bank," building w/cast iron mesh sides & solid cast iron domed roof, A.C. Williams, ca. 1899, 1¾ x 2¼",3⅝" h. (W. 423) 55.00

1183 Building - Domed "Bank," building w/cast iron mesh sides & solid cast iron domed roof, A.C. Williams, 1899-1934, 2⅜ x 4",4¾" h. (W. 421) 78.00

Flat Iron Building Bank

1161 Building - Flat Iron Building (no trap), cast iron, Kenton, 1912-26, 3 x 3½, 5½" h., W. 409 (ILLUS.) 115.00

1126 Building - Home Savings Bank, cast iron, Shimer Toy Co. 1899 & J.& E. Stevens, 1896, 3⅜ x 4½", 5⅞" h. (W. 369) ...105.00

1167 Building - Presto, cast iron, Kenton(?), 1911-13,$3\frac{9}{16}$" w., $4\frac{1}{16}$" h.(W. 425) 150.00

1239 Building - Skyscraper, w/four turrets, cast iron, A.C. Williams, 1900-31, 2 ⅛" sq. base, 4⅜" h. (W. 413) 55.00

1083 Building - State Bank, cast iron, Arcade, 1913-25, Grey Iron, 1889, 2⅜ x $3\frac{1}{16}$", 4⅛" h. 95.00

1080 Building - State Bank, cast iron, Kenton, ca. 1900, 3½ x 4⅝", 5⅞" h. (W. 455) ...190.00

767 Camel - Camel, Large, cast iron, A.C. Williams,1920s, 6¼" l., 7¼" h. (W. 201) .... 300.00 to 350.00

163 "Campbell Kids," cast iron, A.C. Williams Co., 1910-20, 3¼ h., (W. 45) * 275.00

365 Cat - Cat seated with Bow, cast iron, John Wright, 2 ⅞ x 4 ⅜" 60.50

1537 Clock - Clock w/movable hands which tally coin deposit, cast iron, Judd(?), 1890s, 4½" h. (W. 223) 450.00

1541 Clock - "Grandfather's Clock," cast iron, England(?), late 1800s, 5⅜" h. (W. 222) 365.00

1316 Coronation Crown (Edward VII), cast iron crown on mahogany base, John Harper, Ltd., England, 1901,3⅛" w., $3\frac{9}{16}$" h.(W. 321) 165.00

357 Dog - Boxer (Bulldog), seated animal, cast iron, A.C. Williams, 1912-28 & Hubley (no date), 4½" h. (W. 105) * 75.00 to100.00

403 Dog - Bulldog, Standing, cast iron (converted paperweight), Arcade, 1910-13, 2¼" h. 160.00

407 Dog - "Lost Dog," cast iron, possibly by Judd Mfg. Co., possibly 1890s, 5⅜" h. (W. 115) 625.00

435 Dog - Scottie, Standing, cast iron, American-made, $3\frac{5}{16}$" h. (W. 108) 150.00

180 Dutch Boy on Barrel, cast iron, Hubley, 1930s, 5⅝" h. (W. 36) 150.00

446 Elephant - Elephant on

Wheels, cast iron, A.C. Williams, 1920s, 4⅜" l.,4⅛" h. (W. 75) 225.00

Elephant with Howdah Bank

457 Elephant - Elephant w/Howdah (tiny), cast iron, A.C. Williams, 1934, 3" l., 2½" h., W. 69 (ILLUS.) 65.00

453 Elephant - ``McKinley/Roosevelt," cast iron, American-made, ca. 1900, 2½" h. (W. 71) 1,500.00

791 Globe - Globe on Wood Base, metal w/lithographed paper-covered globe, Miller Bank Service Co., 1930s, 4¼" h. 95.00

1381 Hat - Derby ("Pass 'Round the Hat"), cast iron, American-made, 3⅛" d., 1⅝" h. (W. 260) ....165.00 to 200.00

Decker's Pig & Horse "Beauty"

532 Horse - "Beauty," cast iron, Arcade, 1910-32, 4¾" l., 4⅛" h., W. 82 (ILLUS. right) 83.00

510 Horse - Horse on Tub, undecorated, cast iron, A.C. Williams, 1920s, 5 5/16" h. .225.00

509 Horse - Horse on Tub, Decorated, cast iron, A.C. Williams Co., 1920-34, 5 5/16" h. (W. 56)* 180.00

531 Horse - "My Pet" (slot in belly), cast iron, Arcade, 1920s, 4 15/16" l., 4¼" h. (W. 85)..........135.00

517 Horse - Prancing Horse, cast iron, Arcade, 1910-32, A.C. Williams Co., 1910-20s, & Dent Hardware Co. (no date), 4⅞" l., 4¼" h. (W. 77) 67.50

533 Horse - Work Horse, cast iron, Arcade, ca. 1910, 4¾" l., 4⅛" h. (W. 81)*.......................70.00

763 Lion - Lion, Tail Left, cast iron, Hubley, 1910-29, 5⅜" l., 3¾" h. (W. 93) 65.00

164 Mary & Little Lamb, cast iron, American-made, 1902, 4⅜" h. (W. 1)*...............................485.00

Mutt & Jeff Bank

157 Mutt & Jeff, cast iron, A.C. Williams, 1912-31, 4¼" h., W. 13 (ILLUS.) 190.00

603 Pig - "Decker's Iowana," gold-painted cast iron, American-made, 4⅜" l., 2 5/16" h., W. 182 (ILLUS. left) 130.00

330 Pig - Republic Pig, pig standing on hind legs & dressed in suit & tie, "Bank on Republic Pig Iron," cast iron, Wilton Products, 1970, 7" h. 95.00

565 Rabbit - Rabbit Lying Down, cast iron, American-made, 5⅛" l., 2⅛" h. (W. 101) 350.00

569 Rabbit - Rabbit on Base, embossed "Bank" one side, "1884" other, cast iron, American-made, 2¼" h. (W. 97) ....900.00 to 1,000.00

568 Rabbit - Seated Rabbit (small), cast iron, Arcade, 1910-20, 3⅝" h. (W. 96)*.....................110.00

827 Radio - "Majestic" Radio, cabinet-style on legs, cast iron w/steel back, Arcade, 1932-34, 4½" h..........75.00 to 95.00

1335 Refrigerator - "Electrolux," white metal, American-made, 2" l., 4" h...................................75.00

548 Rooster, silver w/red comb & wattles, cast iron, Hubley Mfg. Co. (no date) & A.C. Williams Co., 1910-34, 4¾" h. W. 187* (ILLUS.) 140.00

Rooster Bank

883 Safe - "Japanese Safe," embossed dragon guarding keyhole, cast iron, key locked trap, Kyser & Rex, ca. 1882, 4⅝" sq., 5⅜" h. (W. 349) 80.00

897 Safe - "Junior Safe Deposit," w/combination lock, cast iron, American-made, 2⅛ x 3⅜", 4⅝" h. 49.50

889 Safe - "Security Safe," cast iron, American-made, ca. 1894, 2¼ x 3¼", 4½" h. 169.00

59 Santa Claus, standing figure in old-fashioned red suit, cast iron, Wing, ca. 1900, Hubley ca. 1906, 5⅞" h. (W. 30)* 300.00

1457 Ship - Fortune Ship, embossed "When My Fortune Ship Comes In" on deck, cast iron, England (?), 5⅜" l., 4⅛" h. (W. 249) 1,050.00

1357 Stove - Parlor Stove, cast iron, American-made, 2¾" sq., 6⅞" h. (W. 138) 275.00

1468 Trolley Car - Street Car, cast iron, Columbia Grey Iron Casting Co., 1891, 4½" l., 2⅞" h. (W. 265) 170.00

854 U.S. Mail - "U.S. Mail"(slot in rear), cast iron, A.C. Williams, 1920s, 1¼ x 3¼", 4¼" h. 93.50

GLASS

Cat, clear figure w/metal cap, container for "Grapette" drink ....40.00 to 50.00

Elephant, clear figure w/metal cap, container for "Grapette" drink 17.50

Fishbowl, embossed "Bower Mfg. Co.," 3½" d., 5" h. 20.00

Glass block, advertising "Corning Glass," clear, 1¾ x 3 x 3" 35.00

Abe Lincoln, "Lincoln Foods, Inc., Lawrence,Mass.," 9" h. 20.00

Lucky Joe Glass Bank

Lucky Joe, clear figure, container for "Nash's Mustard" (ILLUS.) 28.00

Owl, "Wise Old Owl" on base, 7" h. 17.50

Pig, clear figure, container for "New England Syrup" marked "Piggy Bank Bottle" 20.00

Pig, clear figure embossed "Brother Can You Spare A Dime" 15.00

Uncle Sam's top hat, milk white glass, painted in red & blue stripes & stars, 2½" h. (paint worn) 66.00

POTTERY

Stoneware Log Cabin Bank

Bust of a man w/large grin, slightly protruding ears, white clay w/green glaze, bottom impressed "W.W.," 3" h. 115.50

Chest of drawers w/yellow slip knobs & name "Albert Stewart," molded label "Savings Bank," redware, 7½" h. (minor edge chips) 137.50

Domed shape w/a pair of loop

handles at the top flanking the pointed finial & coin slot, overall black Albany slip glaze, 10¼" h. 214.50

Log cabin, stoneware, the small house model w/molded logs, windows & door, the roof w/two chimneys centered by a reclining opossum, cobalt blue brushed trim, coin slot on underside, probably Philadelphia, 19th c., one chimney repaired, 4" h. (ILLUS.) 3,450.00

Fort Edward Pottery Stoneware Bank

Ovoid body, stoneware, tapering at the top to a pagoda-form finial, cobalt blue neck band & tooled shoulder bands, one side w/coin slot, the sides incised w/birds & a basket of flowers centering the inscription "Causton Earnest Soper's Bank, Fort Edward, Feb. 27th, 1883," Fort Edward Pottery, Fort Edward, New York, 7" h. (ILLUS.) 8,625.00

Ovoid body tapering up to a small knob finial, coin slot on shoulder, greyish amber salt glaze w/black blob of glaze on back, 4¼" h. 71.50

Ovoid body tapering to a small pointed finial, redware w/worn brown finish, incised inscriptions "Save all you can is a very good plan -John Albert Willars, March 14th 1883 - Economy is the true source of wealth," 7½" h. (hole in bottom damaged inscription there, top broken & glued) 137.50

Pig, large seated animal in sewer pipe pottery w/molded & simple tooled detail, overall greenish brown salt glaze, 9¼" h. (no bottom) 423.50

Pig, running tan & brown glaze, 6¼" l. (small chips) 60.50

Pig standing, cream-colored ground w/blue & brown sponging, 6" l. 302.50

Pig standing, two-tone marbleized olive brown, tan & green glaze, 6⅜" l. 55.00

Policeman, bust of Keystone-type cop, blue glaze, 3¼" h. .. 235.00

Rabbit, large crouching animal in sewer pipe pottery, incised "AL," overall dark glaze, 10½" l. 412.50

TIN

Advertising, "Atlas Battery," replica of 6-volt car battery...... 30.00

Advertising, "Gulf Oil," oil tanker replica 22.00

Queen's Doll House, Chubb Safe Co., England, early 1920s, 2¹¹⁄₁₆ x 3⁵⁄₁₆ x 4⁵⁄₁₆" 65.00

BARBERIANA

A wide variety of antiques related to the tonsorial arts have been highly collectible for many years, especially 19th and early 20th century shaving mugs and barber bottles and, more recently, razors. We are now combining these closely related categories under one heading here for easier reference. A selection of other varied pieces relating to barbering will also be found below.

BARBER BOTTLES

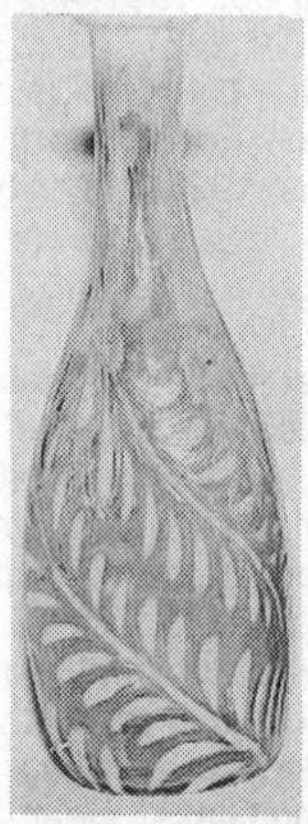

Fern Pattern Barber Bottle

Amber blown glass, decorated w/pewter floral engraved w/gadroon border applied on shoulder & pewter applied cover around rim $165.00

Amethyst blown glass, bulbous base tapering to a tall lady's leg neck, decorated w/dotted bands forming diamonds w/a daisy blossom within each diamond, rolled rim, open pontil, ca. 1900, 8⅜" h., pr..............165.00

Amethyst blown glass w/interior ribbing, bulbous base tapering to a thick bulbous lady's leg neck, white dot diamond chain decoration flanked by white & orange enameled flowerheads, ca. 1880-1920, 8½" h. 71.50

Blue opalescent glass, Seaweed patt. 375.00

Blue opalescent glass, Stripe patt. 295.00

Bristol satin glass w/h.p. florals & gold trim, w/fancy neck, 7⅞" h. 110.00

Cobalt blue blown glass w/interior ribbing, ovoid form tapering to a tall 'stick' neck, enameled w/orange & white flowerheads decoration, ca. 1880-1920, 7⅞" h. 154.00

Cobalt blue blown glass w/enameled dot flower design..............................175.00

Cranberry opalescent glass, Daisy & Fern patt. 295.00

Cranberry opalescent glass, Fern patt. (ILLUS.) 295.00

Cranberry opalescent glass, triangular-shaped, Seaweed patt........395.00

Cranberry opalescent glass, Stars & Stripes patt......................................450.00

Cranberry opalescent glass, Swirl patt., bulbous body w/angled shoulder to the tall slender neck w/rolled rim, ca. 1900, 9" h. (light inside stain)....................................231.00

Milk white glass, cylindrical body tapering to a lady's leg neck & tooled rim, h.p. w/large colorful daisies & leaves w/a central band inscribed "HAIR TONIC" or "WITCH HAZEL," ca. 1900, 8⅝" h., pr. 209.00

Milk white glass, slightly tapering cylindrical body w/a thin ring above & below the center band decorated w/landscape scene of a house framed by trees, thin rings on the cylindrical neck, personalized below the scene w/the owner's name & "Lavender," ca. 1900, 8¾" h. 440.00

Robin's egg blue opalescent glass, Hobnail patt., body w/opalescent raised swirl neck, sheared top, pontil base 125.00

Rubina blown glass, Inverted Thumbprint patt..............................395.00

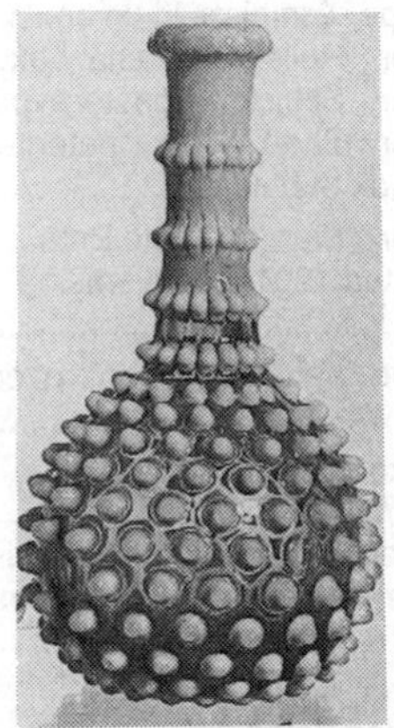

Hobnail Barber Bottle

Sapphire blue opalescent glass, Hobnail patt., bulbous base w/tall stick neck & rolled lip, ca. 1880-1920, three hobnails have chips, 7¼" h. (ILLUS.) 209.00

Turquoise blue opalescent glass, Spanish Lace patt., deeply waisted body below a tall slender neck w/rolled rim, ca. 1900, 7¾" h. (light interior stain) 385.00

Vaseline opalescent glass, Spanish Lace patt. 185.00

White opalescent glass, Daisy & Fern patt., bulbous melon-lobed body tapering to a tall slender neck w/rolled rim, ca. 1900, 7⅜" h. 88.00

White opalescent glass, Swirl patt., tall cylindrical body tapering to a cylindrical neck w/rolled rim, ca. 1880-1920, 8" h. 93.50

Yellowish amber blown glass, Hobnail patt., bulbous base tapering to a cylindrical neck w/tooled rim, ca. 1880-1920, 6⅞" h. 60.50

Yellowish green blown glass, bulbous base w/tall swelled neck & rolled lip, h.p. white enamel Mary Gregory-style decoration of a young girl surrounded by flowers, ca. 1880-1920, 7¾" h......................264.00

RAZORS

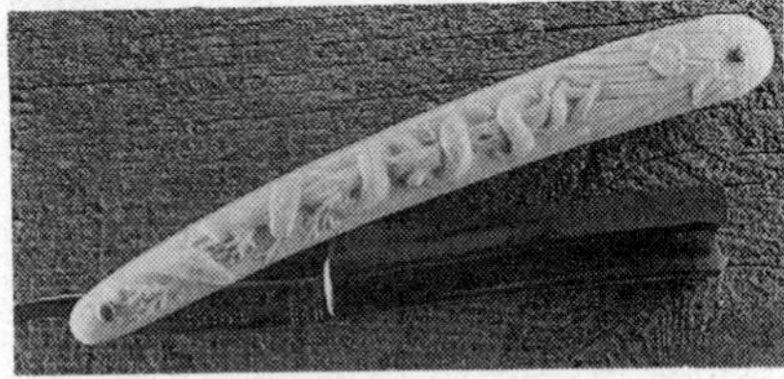

Straight Razor with Celluloid Handle

Corn razor, "Liliput," in original box.......20.00

Safety razor, "The Laurel," vest

pocket-type, complete in tin box 20.00
Safety razor, "Rolls," w/original box......12.50
Safety razor, "Schick," repeater-type....20.00
Safety razor, "Sha-Ve-Zee," patented 1918, w/box of blades........................15.00
Safety razor, "Star," Kampfe Bros., patent-dated 1901, in advertising tin...85.00
Safety razor, "Valet Autostrop" razor kit, brass w/metal box 20.00
Straight razor, celluloid handle molded w/a design of a snake wrapped around a tree facing a bird, cattails below, blade marked "Jamre Garantie" (ILLUS.) 466.00
Straight razor, celluloid handle w/embossed horse.............................35.00
Straight razor, "Colonial - Improved Eagle," embossed blade, Germania Cutlery, in case 15.00
Straight razor, "Gold Nugget" 25.00
Straight razor, "Pathfinder," Big Chief, Indian pictured on blade, in box.........34.00

Razor with Pressed Horn Handle

Straight razor, pressed horn handle w/a panel embossed w/"New York" between an American eagle & shield & crossed cannons, by Joseph Elliot (ILLUS.) 50.00
Straight razor, "Temperite," bone handle, in case..................................20.00

SHAVING MUGS

(Porcelain unless otherwise noted)

Fraternal

Knights of Columbus 85.00
Knights of Pythias...............................160.00
Knights Templar, decoration & name in gold 110.00

Occupational

Bartender, bartender w/five people 450.00
Furniture maker, a scene of a man assembling a piece of furniture & finished pieces of furniture in the background 475.00
Mortician, decorated w/purple drape & flowers...85.00
Railroad engineer, depicts wood burning locomotive, excellent colors, name in gold, left-handed 295.00
Railroad engineer, scene includes steam train engine & passenger car..300.00

General

China, flowers, lilies & name in gold, K.P.M. Germany blank.........................75.00
China, pink flowers on a shaded blue ground, unmarked R.S. Prussia.........75.00
Glass, milk white, President Garfield memorial, footed rounded body w/brush holder well & ring handle beside base, ca. 1881 ....295.00
Ironstone china, scuttle-type, brown transfer-printed picture w/barber, soap & brush, Burleigh 50.00
R.S. Prussia china, green & ivory ground w/pink roses decoration, marked...175.00

GENERAL ITEMS

Early Faience Barber Bowl

Barber bowl, faience, oval w/wide flanged rim w/chin notch, painted in iron-red & blue in the center w/a basket of flowers on a foliate-scroll support encircled above the well w/six stylized flowering branches, the rim w/an iron-red hatchwork border interrupted w/four blue-ground panels of demi-flowerheads, Rouen, France, 1740-50, minor imperfections, 12 3/16" l. (ILLUS.).......460.00
Barber chair, oak, round seat & back, hydraulic mechanism, "Koken".....1,450.00

Figural Barber Pole

Barber pole, figural, carved wood, a standing figure of a black man wearing a tan shirt & sea green pants & holding a tapering pointed red & white pole in one hand, cigars in the other, on a rectangular base marked "Elijah Cook - Barber," ca. 1930s, paint scratches & minor letter fading, base 15½ x 20½", 5' 1" h. (ILLUS.) 2,310.00

Barber pole, carved & painted pine, a tapering column surmounted w/a gold-painted ball finial above heavy ring- and baluster-turnings, on a square block foot, painted w/decorative paint w/red, white & blue stripes, late 19th c., 7' 1" h. 2,070.00

Hair clippers, "Keen Kutter No. 4," w/cover 30.00

Herpicide sterilizer, Bakelite frame & covers & two glass containers, the set 125.00

Razor blade bank, celluloid, advertising "Bobolink Eveready"................25.00

Razor blade bank, ceramic, model of a pig w/floral decoration, marked "Occupied Japan," 3¼" l. 35.00

Razor blade bank, china, model of a frog, "Listerine Shaving Cream".........25.00

Razor blades, "St. Regis," double-edged, one box of five blades 5.00

Razor blades, "Segal," double-edged, one box of five blades 5.00

Razor blade sharpener, "Warner Jones," boxed 27.00

Razor hone, "Keen Kutter No. K20," in original tin box.................................28.00

Shaving mirror, country-style, table model, walnut, rectangular mirror plate in plain frame pivoting between block- and ring-turned supports on a low turned base, refinished, 16½" h...110.00

Mission Style Shaving Mirror

Shaving mirror, Mission-style (Arts & Crafts movement), table model, oak frame w/inverted "V" top enclosing a rectangular mirror plate swiveling between square posts w/stretcher, raised on beveled shoe feet, cast-iron swivel pulls, red decal mark of Gustav Stickley, 7 x 21½" x 24" (ILLUS.) 1,540.00

Shaving mirror, table model, painted cast iron, an oval mirror within a wide pierced oval frame supported between two Victorian ladies in crinoline dresses atop curved willow tree branches above a monument w/shield, arrows & American flag raised on a scrolled palm leaf base, polychrome trim, ca. 1860-80, 13¾" w., 21" h. (some surface rust)...522.50

Sterilizer jar, cov., clear glass base w/chrome cover 55.00

Towel steamer, copper, a large spherical globe w/a slide opening raised on a pedestal base, a small raised sign at the top reads "The Sun Sterilizer," on a new black metal stand, 4' 10" h. 176.00

BASEBALL MEMORABILIA

Andy Pafko Baseball Card

Baseball was named by Abner Doubleday as he laid out a diamond-shaped field with four bases at Cooperstown, New York. A popular game from its inception, by 1869 it was able to support its first all-professional team, the Cincinnati Red Stockings. The National League was organized in 1876 and though the American League was first formed in 1900, it was not officially recognized until 1903. Today, the "national pastime" has millions of fans and collecting baseball memorabilia has become a major hobby with enthusiastic collectors seeking out items associated with players such as Babe Ruth, Lou Gehrig, and others, who became legends in their own lifetimes. Though baseball cards, issued as advertising premiums for bubble gum and other products, seem to dominate the field there are numerous other items available.

Baseball, autographed by Christy Mathewson, Official National League model, signed in black ink $5,500.00

Baseball, autographed by Honus Wagner in blue ink & dated "4-13-54," Official National League model 2,200.00

Baseball, autographed by Roberto Clemente, Official National League model, signed in black ink....2,640.00

Baseball, 1907 Detroit Tigers game-used pennant game ball, used in the decisive game, inscribed "Detroit Tigers - Pennant Ball - Compliments of Hugh Jennings - Baltimore," shellacked & dark 2,350.00

Baseball, 1925 Detroit Tigers team-signed, official American League model signed by twenty-one team members including player-manager Ty Cobb, also Heilmann, Blue, Wingo & Haney, dated "June 1925," excellent condition in original box 1,495.00

Baseball, 1928 Philadelphia Athletics, signed by 26 members of the team including Ty Cobb, Al Simmons, Eddie Collins & Jimmie Foxx, Official National League model....1,045.00

Baseball, 1929 New York Yankees team-signed, official American League model w/twenty-three signatures including Babe Ruth on the sweet spot & Lou Gehrig on the side panel, also Lazzari, Hoyt, Durocher & others, excellent condition 2,185.00

Baseball, 1948 World Series game ball, inscribed "This ball used in 1948 World Series game at Cleveland, largest crowd in World Series history, 86,277," & autographed by homeplate umpire George Barr 440.00

Baseball, 1950 Brooklyn Dodgers, signed by 25 members of the team including Campanella, Hodges, Reese, Snider, Robinson & Furillo, Official National League model....1,210.00

Baseball, 1962 New York Yankees World Championship baseball, signed by 24 members of the team on a Yankee promotional ball, includes Mantle, Maris, Berra & Ford 880.00

Baseball cap, game-worn Minnesota Twins model used by Harmon Killebrew in the game where he broke Mantle's home run record of 536, signed by Killebrew inside the band & w/a letter of authenticity from Killebrew, 1972 ....550.00

Baseball card, 1886, Lone Jack Cigarettes, sepia photograph of Chris Von Der Ahe, owner of the St. Louis Browns, 1½ x 2½" 825.00

Baseball card, 1890, Old Judge Cigarettes, photograph of Mike "King" Kelly, shown standing & holding a bat....770.00

Baseball card, 1909, Piedmont Cigarettes, Sherwood Magee "Magie" error card, colored lithograph bust portrait, advertising on reverse....26,400.00

Baseball card, 1911, Piedmont Cigarettes, Roger Bresnahan, colored lithograph bust portrait w/facsimile signature, gold edge border band, advertising on reverse....418.00

Baseball card, 1914, Cracker Jack, Ty Cobb, half-length color portrait of Cobb holding a bat, player biography & advertising on reverse ...9,350.00

Baseball card, 1933, DeLong Gum Company, Vernon "Lefty" Gomez, black & white outlined photograph of Gomez in a pitching pose against a color background of a stadium, a pitching tip from Austen Lake on reverse....660.00

Baseball card, 1933, Goudey Gum, Lou Gehrig, No. 92 (centered slightly askew) 863.00

Baseball card, 1933, Goudey Gum Co. - Big League Chewing Gum, Babe Ruth, full-length color portrait of Ruth in a batting stance, No. 144, brief player biography on reverse....9,900.00

Baseball card, 1949, Bowman Gum, Leroy "Satchell" Paige, colored overlay black & white bust photograph against a light green ground, information on reverse 1,540.00

Baseball card, 1952, Topps Gum, Willie Mays, color photograph of the player, name & facsimile signature under the photo....2,420.00

Baseball card, 1952, Topps Gum, Andy Pafko, No. 1 (ILLUS.) 1,150.00

Baseball card, 1953, Bowman Gum, Roy Campanella, No. 46, autographed....552.00

Baseball card, 1963, Topps Gum, Yogi Berra, No. 340 ....40.00

Baseball card, 1963, Topps Gum, Pete Rose rookie card, No. 537.......529.00

Baseball card, 1981, Topps Gum, Rickey Henderson, No. 261...............15.00

Baseball card, E-103 Honus Wagner card, produced by Williams Caramel Co., color photo front & blank back, early 20th c., excellent to mint condition 978.00

Baseball card set, 1965, Topps Gum "Push-Pull" set, each card contains two player images viewed by sliding slats, mint set of 36.......................1,035.00

Baseball schedule, 1956 New York Giants, cardboard, tri-fold, depicts Russ Hodges & Polo Grounds seating, opens to 4½ x 9" 15.00

Bat, rosewood, 1883 John Ward game-used model, manufactured by S.D. Kehoe, New York City, offered w/letter authenticating the piece & the newspaper box score of the game it was used in, 1½ x 2¼" d., 39 ¾" l...4,600.00

Bat, game-used by Lou Gehrig, a Hillerich & Bradsby Model 125 Louisville Slugger, weighing 37½ oz., stamped "Powerized - Bone Rubbed," engraved facsimile signature of Gehrig, w/letter of authenticity documenting that this bat was used in Gehrig's four homer game against the Athletics in June 1932, 35" l.................................28,600.00

Bat, game-used by Mickey Mantle, a Louisville Slugger 125 powerized model, stamped on the barrel "All-Star Game - Mickey Mantle - Baltimore 1858" 19,800.00

Bat, wood, All-Star Game-used, made by Hillerich & Bradsby, Model 125, also marked "All-Star Game, Roberto Clemente, Atlanta, 1972," number 21 on end of shaved knob, used by Clemente in his final All-Star Game, near mint 5,980.00

Book, "Athletic Sports in America, England and Australia," by Palmer, Fynes, Richter & Harris, 1889, illustrated in black & white & color, 460 pp. concerning baseball, hard cover, excellent condition, 711 pp...518.00

Book, "Baseball Techniques," by Ethan Allen, illustrated, 1951 ....10.00

Book, "Pride of the Yankees - Lou Gehrig," by Gallico, 1942..................35.00

Book, "Jackie Robinson, My Own Story," by Jackie Robinson, 1948, signed by Robinson on the flyleaf, hard cover.......................................552.00

Book, "Signals, Secret Language of Baseball in Finger Tip Moves," Gillette promotional item, featuring Paul Richards, 1957 ....45.00

Joe DiMaggio Pinback

Button, pinback, Tip-Top Bread advertising-type, photograph of Joe DiMaggio with advertising "Winners Eat - Joe DiMaggio Eats - Tip-Top Bread," ca. 1941, l½" d. (ILLUS.) 920.00

Button, pinback, 1960s New York Yankees, round w/photographs of the heads of Mickey Mantle, Bill Skowron, Yogi Berra & Roger Maris around the edges & a stylized baseball printed "N.Y. Yankees" in the center, near mint, 3" d............3,220.00

Ty Cobb Candy Box

Candy box, cov., cardboard, the top printed w/red, blue & white on a yellow ground, produced by the Benjamin Candy Company of Detroit, held 24 Ty Cobb candy bars, ca. 1920s (ILLUS.)...............1,320.00

Champagne bottle, green glass, the paper label for "Moet & Chandon" autographed by Tom Seaver in celebration of his 300th win on August 4, 1985, signed w/his name & "No. 300 - 8-4-85"..............352.00

Check, paper, a Babe Ruth-signed check dated "June 21, 1935," printed on end & signed "G.H. Ruth," drawn on the Chemical Bank & Trust Company, New York, New York, signed on front & back, near mint condition..............................1,265.00

First-day cover envelope, for the 1939 New York World's Fair, printed w/a picture of the Federal Building & inscribed "New York World's Fair - 1939 - First Day Cover," autographs by Babe Ruth & Lou Gehrig, postmarked "April 1, 1939" complete w/U.S. three cent World's Fair commemorative stamp 1,650.00

Game, "Safe T Dart Electro Big League Baseball," 1930s, mint in box..85.00

Child's Lou Gehrig-Signed Glove

Glove, child's, leather, first baseman's model signed on the top "Best Wishes, Billy, Lou Gehrig" (ILLUS.) 2,300.00

Glove, leather, game-used by Steve Carlton, Rawlings-made model HT76 left-handed model, signed in black ink by Carlton, 1986, w/letter of authenticity..............................1,100.00

Glove, leather, game-used Eddie Miksis Ken-Wel model glove, used in the late 1940s or early 1950s, signed in the pocket by Gil Hodges, Eddie Miksis & two others, signatures light but legible...................115.00

Jersey, 1940s New York Yankee grey wool flannel road version, Joe DiMaggio's w/original Wilson Sports Equipment label & name, all-original, size 44...............................41,400.00

Jersey, Dale Mitchell Brooklyn Dodgers home version, white flannel w/blue "Dodgers" across chest above a red "8," manufactured by Spalding, 1956, size 42, w/letter of authenticity from Dale Mitchell, Jr.....................................2,200.00

Letter, hand-written one-page letter from Ty Cobb to Dr. John O'Meara returning the doctor's autograph album & discussing his career & retirement, dated "January 24, 1934," on Cobb's personal stationery 1,610.00

Pants, 1960 New York Yankee flannel pin-stripe home version, worn by Yogi Berra, stitched labels, signed "Yogi Berra," folded & framed...748.00

Pencil, mechanical, model of a baseball bat, souvenir of the 1949 World Series 75.00

Pennant, blue & white felt, printed w/a large rearing elephant above "Champion 1913 Athletics," for the world champion Philadelphia Athletics, 28" l. 1,540.00

Pennant, cloth, 1961 New York Yankees team photo souvenir-type, shows a group shot of the 196l Yankees w/a roster of the players & "New York Yankees American League Champions 196l," near mint condition 1,265.00

Photograph, 1875 Providence, Rhode Island team, a group of small vignette bust photos mounted in a large mat board, each w/the player's name below the photo & the team name across the bottom 2,185.00

Photograph, 1905 Philadelphia Athletics team photo, includes team members Connie Mack, Chief Benter, Eddie Plank & Rube Waddell, embossed in lower left corner "Copyright 1905 by Jos. N. Pearce, Phila., PA," excellent to mint condition, 10¾ x 13½" 1,840.00

Photograph, 1926 New York Yankee team, long rectangular black & white group shot, printed under photo "American League 1926 Champions," mounted on foamboard.....1,210.00

Photograph, autographed black & white bust portrait of a smiling Lou Gehrig, inscribed "To Johnny, with kindest personal regards, Lou Gehrig," 8 x 10"...........................5,060.00

Plate, souvenir-type, china, gilt scrolling vine border band, printed in the center w/a standing portrait of "Charles ("Babe") Adams" flanked by crossed bats & a ball, printed across the top "The World's Series Champion Pitcher," 1909, 8" d. (ILLUS top next column) 1,320.00

1909 World's Series Plate

Press pin, 1913 World Series, metal rectangular plate at top inscribed "World Series Shibe Park Philadelphia 1913," attached to a wide blue silk ribbon printed in gold w/"PRESS" & suspending a round gold-toned metal medallion w/a blue enamel border band printed w/"American Baseball Club of Philadelphia," the center w/a raised design of an elephant standing above cross-baseball bats & a ball over "Athletics," 2 x 4½" 4,400.00

Press pin, 1923 New York Yankee World Series model, enameled gilt-metal, round w/a blue band at top & red band near the bottom & a white baseball in the center, reads "World Series - 1923 - New York," near mint 1,610.00

Press pin, 1943 St. Louis Cardinals World Series model, celluloid w/paper insert, second version, printed as a white baseball w/"Press - 1943 - St. Louis" printed in blue & two red cardinals, near mint w/unrippled paper 2,415.00

Program, 1912 World Series between the Boston Red Sox & New York Giants, the cover printed w/"Champions 1912" above a row of long stockings suspended on a clothesline & lettered "Red Sox" above "World's Series - Fenway Park - Boston - Souvenir Biography and Score Book," neatly scored & w/an action picture & individual biography of each Red Sox player 1,320.00

Program, 1923 World Series, titled "Yankees vs Giants - 1923 - Worlds Championship Series - New York City," cover w/bust photographs of Miller Huggins & John McGraw 690.00

Program, 1949 Official Chicago Cubs, Cubs vs. New York at Wrigley Field...50.00

Program-score book, 1908 World Series souvenir-type, for the fifth game of the series, plain non-illustrated cover (staples missing, minor rust spots, minor soiling & fading on covers, one interior page crimped & torn near corners, scores written in) 7,475.00

Punch board, "Old Timers," rectangular lithographed cardboard, gambling device illustrating nineteen baseball Hall of Famers across the top including Gehrig, Grove, Dickey, Hubbell, Wagner, etc., five cents per punch, completely intact, near mint, late 1930s, 10½ x 12½" 1,035.00

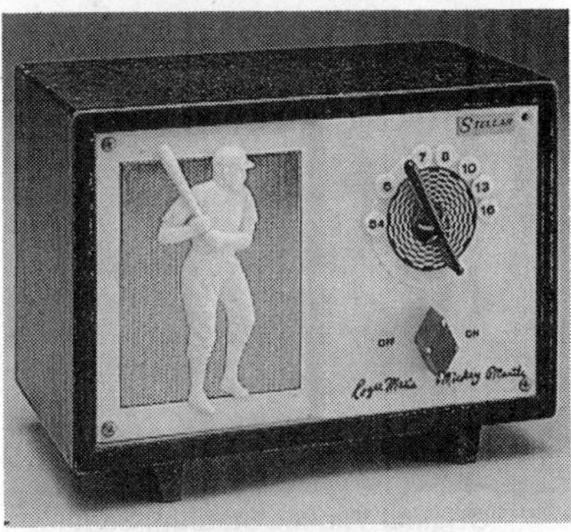

Mantle-Maris Radio

Radio, rectangular black plastic footed case, the front in white w/the relief figure of a player in a batting stance over the speaker, dial & switch on the right front, facsimile signatures of Roger Maris & Mickey Mantle on the lower right, "Steller" tag in upper right, ca. 1961 (ILLUS.) 1,035.00

Scorecard, 1880s Providence vs Boston, w/color cover picturing Arthur Irwin in an oval reserve, very good to excellent condition 575.00

Season pass, 1913 New York Giants, a flat one-bladed pocket knife incorporating at one end a Stanhope lens showing a panoramic view of the Polo Grounds & the following invitation "Baseball Evolution From Knothole To Stadium - Don' t Peek - Come In - Brush," knife case engraved on one side "Polo Grounds Thrills - For You - Season 1913 - Not Transferable - John T. Brush," the reverse printed "No. 147 Mr. Wm. T. Hodge," possibly only one known 4,600.00

Season pass, 1922 New York Giants, enameled metal, model of a cloth pennant commemorating the 1921 World Champions, worded "N.Y.

Giants 1921 - Worlds Champions," meant to wear on keyring, near mint 805.00

Sheet music, "The Cincinnati Reds Song," team photograph on the cover, commemorates the 1919 World Champion team who defeated the infamous Chicago "Black" Sox 1,380.00

Stadium seat, wood & iron, single seat from the Polo Grounds, former home of the New York Giants & New York Mets, unrestored w/original paint............................1,265.00

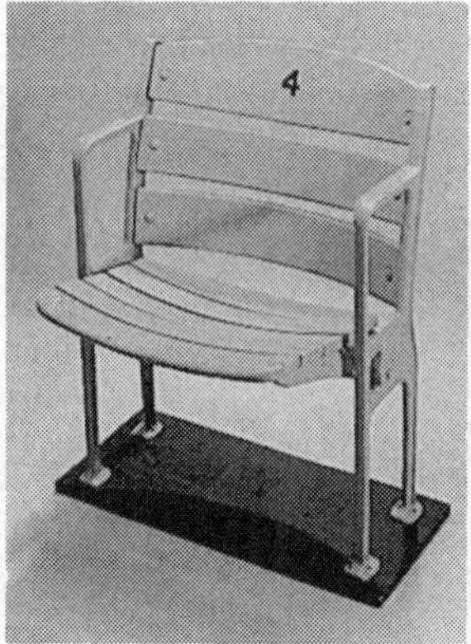

Original Yankee Stadium Seat

Stadium seat, wood & iron, original folding seat from Yankee Stadium, original blue paint, removed during 1972-73 stadium renovation (ILLUS.) 2,530.00

Tray, presentation-type, silver plate, oval, a raised finely ribbed edge & an engraved center scroll wreath framing the inscription "Presented by the members of the Cincinnati Baseball Club to Henry C. Glassford their President - July 22, 1867," 14 x 18".......................................1,150.00

Uniform, game-used by Mickey Mantle, New York Yankees uniform worn in the 1960 World Series, pin-striped flannel home uniform w/jersey & matching trousers, manufactured by Tim McAuliffe Company of Boston, jersey inscribed "To Joe - Happy Birthday - your friend, Mickey Mantle," letters of authenticity, clippings & a video included, the group 77,000.00

Uniform, 1972 New York Yankee home version white flannel jersey & pants, worn by Bobby Murcer, made by Wilson, name label in the collar, size 40 ....4,140.00

Yearbook, 1907 Detroit Tiger souvenir-type, pictorial, contains black & white individual pictures & biographies of the entire team including Cobb, Crawford & Jennings, 6 x 9" 2,530.00

BASKETS

Woven Splint Baskets

The American Indians were the first basket weavers on this continent and, of necessity, the early Colonial settlers and their descendants pursued this artistic handicraft to provide essential containers for berries, eggs and endless other items to be carried or stored. Rye straw, split willow and reeds are but a few of the wide variety of materials used. The Nantucket baskets, plainly and sturdily constructed, along with those made by other specialized groups, would seem to draw the greatest attention in an area of collecting. Also see INDIAN ARTIFACTS & JEWELRY and SHAKER ITEMS.

"Buttocks" basket, 16-rib construction, woven splint, some age, 7½ x 8", 6" h. plus bentwood handle.............$49.50

"Buttocks" basket, 20-rib construction, woven splint, weathered grey finish, 12 x 14", 7½" h. plus bentwood handle (some damage).....................49.50

"Buttocks" basket, 22-rib construction, woven splint, old worn red paint over green, 11 x 12", 5" h. plus bentwood handle (minor damage)...................275.00

"Buttocks" basket, 22-rib construction, woven splint, old worn finish, 15 x 15½", 7" h. plus bentwood handle (minor damage) 203.50

"Buttocks" basket, 22-rib construction, woven splint, 16 x 18", 8½" h. plus bentwood handle 110.00

"Buttocks" basket, 24-rib construction, woven splint, faded green & natural finish, 13 x 18", 9" h. plus bentwood handle (minor damage)...................115.50

"Buttocks" basket, 26-rib construction, woven splint, weathered patina, 13 x 17½", 7" h. plus bentwood handle (some damage)...............................126.50

"Buttocks" basket, 26-rib construction,

woven splint, good old color w/red stripe, bentwood handle marked "Rev. Clerke," 13 x 14", 7½" h. plus handle (minor damage)....................275.00

"Buttocks" basket, 28-rib construction, finely woven splint, 10 x 11", 7" h. plus bentwood handle......................220.00

"Buttocks" basket, 32-rib construction, woven splint, worn old black paint, bentwood handle, 15 x 17", 9" h. (some wear & damage) 137.50

Cheese basket, woven splint, round w/open-weave honeycomb design, 15" d...126.50

Cheese basket, woven splint in honeycomb pattern, good age & color, 21" d., 7" h. (minor damage)..275.00

Display basket, woven rye straw, circular bowl-form w/deep rounded sides & a narrow footring, 12" d., 5½" h...82.50

Field or gathering basket, woven splint, square, natural finish, 14½" sq., 12½" h. plus bentwood handle (ILLUS. left)............................71.50

Herb drying basket, woven splint, round w/open-weave bottom, bentwood rim handles, 16" d., 6¾" h. plus handles (minor damage)..236.50

Market basket, woven splint, rounded sides w/wrapped rim, fixed bentwood handle, old worn patina, 10" d., 5½" h. plus handle (minor damage)..104.50

Market basket, woven splint, round, deep rounded & slightly flaring sides, narrow wrapped rim, bentwood handle, worn patina, 13" d., 5½" h. plus handle.................60.50

Market basket, woven splint, round w/wrapped footring & wrapped rim, bentwood handle, weathered grey finish, 15" d., 8½" h. plus handle (minor damage) 104.50

Market basket, woven splint, rectangular w/oblong rim, narrow wrapped rim, old varnish finish, 9 x 17½", 10" h. plus bentwood handle (ILLUS. right)..............................126.50

"Melon" basket, woven splint, 12-rib construction, wrapped rim, bentwood handle from end to end, 14½" d., 7" h. plus handle 77.00

Nantucket basket, finely woven splint, wrapped rim, small wooden rim handles, circular wooden base, Nantucket Island, Massachusetts, 6½" d...1,100.00

Nantucket basket, woven splint, round w/wrapped rim & swing handle, incised base, Nantucket Island, Massachusetts, early 20th c., 9" d., 4¾" h..550.00

Nantucket basket, finely woven splint, wrapped rim, oval wooden base, partial paper label "A.J. Sandsbury on the South Shoal Lighthouse," 7⅛" w., 11" l. (some damage)..........825.00

Nantucket purse basket, cov., finely woven splint, wrapped rim, faux ivory engraved ship medallion on cover, (worn) leather fittings, signed "Farnum," 7¼" d., 6½" h..................258.00

Nantucket Purse Basket

Nantucket purse basket, cov., finely woven splint, oval, domed cover w/oval wooden plaque w/carved ivory dolphin in center, signed by Stanley Roop, Nantucket Island, Massachusetts, 8" h. (ILLUS.) 1,100.00

Storage basket, woven splint, oblong w/wrapped rim, red & yellow paint & natural patina, bottom w/pen & ink initials & date "M.T. 1867," 11 x 13½". 5½" h..............................132.00

Utility basket, woven splint, low foot, woven diamond at handles, 6¾" d., 3¾" h. plus bentwood handle (minor damage)..49.50

Utility basket, woven splint, square w/upright sides, natural patina & faded blue, 12" sq., 4½" h. 198.00

Utility basket, woven splint, rounded sides & wrapped rim above a corseted square base, small bentwood rim handles, old reddish brown paint, 11" d., 5½" h...............137.50

Utility basket, woven splint, round w/high kick-up, wrapped rim & bentwood handle, good brown color, 12" d., 6½" h. plus handle (some damage)..77.00

Utility basket, 24-rib construction, woven splint, oblong w/wrapped rim & low bentwood handle, old varnish finish, 15 x 16", 6½" h. plus handle..203.50

Utility basket, woven splint, round tapering sides & wrapped rim, bentwood handle, scrubbed finish, 17" d., 7¼" h. plus handle 115.50

Utility basket, woven splint, oval, well made, dark patina, 12 x 14¾", 8" h. plus bentwood handle (some damage)..247.50

Utility basket, woven splint, rectangular base on deep sides w/oval wrapped rim, bentwood handle, weathered grey finish, 11 x 16", 8½" h. plus handle 60.50

Utility basket, woven rye straw, deep rounded sides on a footring, side rim loop handles, 18" d., 9" h. (wear, one handle partially restored) 104.50

Decorative Oval Basket

Utility basket, finely woven splint, oval, Nantucket-style, scalloped tab rim & pierced border around top fastened w/small steel nails, mounted on an oval pin base w/ash swing handle, late 19th - early 20th c., 9" l., 9½" h. (ILLUS.) 1,265.00

Utility basket, woven splint, round w/deep sides & a wrapped rim w/bentwood handle, 15" d., 11" h. plus handle (some damage) 93.50

Utility basket, woven splint, round w/deep sides & wrapped rim w/bentwood rim handles, good color, 18" d., 12¾" h. (minor damages)..82.50

Utility basket, woven splint, square base w/tall straight sides to the round wrapped rim, stationary split

Tall Utility Basket

ash bentwood handle, late 19th c., 15" d., 19" h. (ILLUS.) 173.00

BELLS

Brass bell, St. Peter's, embossed figures of the twelve Apostles around skirt, cross finial, 4" d., 7¼" h..$175.00

Doorbell, brass & cast iron, round door-mounted type, marked "Taylor's Patent - 10/23/1860," w/original white porcelain knob on shaft, 5" d., 2½" h................................95.00

Figural bell, brass, full-skirted woman curtsying, wearing a bow in her hair, 2½" d., 5" h. 75.00

Figural bell, brass, full-skirted lady, two-sided w/frowning face on one side & a laughing face on the other, 2½" h., 5¼" h. 75.00

Figural bell, brass, full-skirted lady in 18th c. attire, wearing a decorative hat & holding a fan, 2¾" d., 5¾" h. 85.00

Figural bell, brass, full-skirted Colonial woman w/long hair, 3¼" d., 5¾" h. 88.00

Figural bell, brass, Jacobean head handle, embossed warriors & wording around the sides, 3¼" d., 4¼" h..125.00

Figural bell, brass, standing knight handle, embossed scene of warriors around the sides, Hemony-type, 3⅜" d., 6¾" h. 135.00

Figural bell, brass, warrior club handle, embossed scene of warriors around the sides, Hemony-type, 3¼" d., 6½" h. 135.00

Ship's bell, brass, cast w/mounting bracket, from the "California," sunk in 1887, 10" h..................................895.00

BICYCLES

Early 'Bone Shaker' Bicycle

Bone shaker-type, wood & iron, a large front & smaller back wheel in turned wood within iron bands & in an iron frame, front wheel 38" d., back wheel 32" d., third quarter 19th c. $3,000.00

Bone shaker-type, painted pine & wrought iron, a large front wheel & smaller back wheel made of turned pine, painted yellow w/black striping within a wrought-iron frame w/turned wood handle, now mounted in a black metal base, late 19th c., overall 54¼" h. (ILLUS.)...............3,575.00

Ross "Custom Flyer," lady's, red & white, working horn & lights, 1955 all-original, mint condition 500.00

Schwinn "Fleet," boy's, black & white, original excellent condition, ca. 1950s 275.00

BIG LITTLE BOOKS

Flash Gordon and the Tyrant of Mongo

The original "Big Little Books" and "Better Little Books" small format series were originated in the mid-30s by Whitman Publishing Co., Racine, Wisconsin, and covered a variety of subjects from adventure stories to tales based on comic strip characters and movie and radio stars. The publisher originally assigned each book a serial number. Most prices are now in the $25.00 - $50.00 range with scarce ones bringing more.

Billy the Kid, No. 773, 1934 ....$30.00

Blondie and Dagwood, Everybody's Happy, No. 1438, 1948 ....28.00

Blondie and Dagwood in Hot Water, No. 1410, 1946 .... 25.00

Brer Rabbit, from Disney's "Song of the South," No. 1426, 1947.............. 40.00

Bringing Up Father, No. 1133, 1936 ....25.00 to 30.00

Buck Rogers and the Depth Men of Jupiter, No. 1169, 1935 ....51.00

Buck Rogers and the Doom Comet, No. 1175, 1936 ....47.50

Buck Rogers on the Moons of Saturn, No. 1143, 1934 ....55.00 to 65.00

Bugs Bunny and the Pirate Loot, No. 1403, 1947 ....33.00

Convoy Patrol (A Thrilling U.S. Navy Story), "movie flip" page corners, No. 1446, 1942 ....25.00

Dan Dunn, Secret Operative 48 and the Dope Ring, No. 1492, 1940 ....38.50

Dick Tracy (Adventures of), No. 707, 1932, first "Big Little Book" 115.00

Dick Tracy and the Tiger Lily Gang, No. 1460, 1949 ....25.00

Dick Tracy on Voodoo Island, No. 1478, 1944 ....60.00

Dick Tracy Returns, No. 1495, 1939 ...27.50

Don Winslow of the Navy and the Secret Enemy Base, No. 1453, 1943 ....22.50

Flash Gordon and the Tyrant of Mongo, No. 1484, 1942 (ILLUS.) 55.00

Flash Gordon in the Forest Kingdom of Mongo, No. 1492, 1938 ....29.00

Gene Autry and the Red Bandit's Ghost, No. 1461, 1949 ....30.00

G-Man and the Radio Bank Robberies, No. 1434, 1937...............30.00

Jackie Cooper, Movie Star of Skippy and Sooky, No. 714, 1933 .... 20.00

Kay Darcy and the Mystery Hideout, No. 1411, 1937 ....15.00

King of the Royal Mounted, No. 1103, 1936 ....25.00

Little Lulu, Alvin and Tubby, No. 1429, 1947 ....32.50

Little Orphan Annie and Sandy, No. 716, 1933 ....32.00

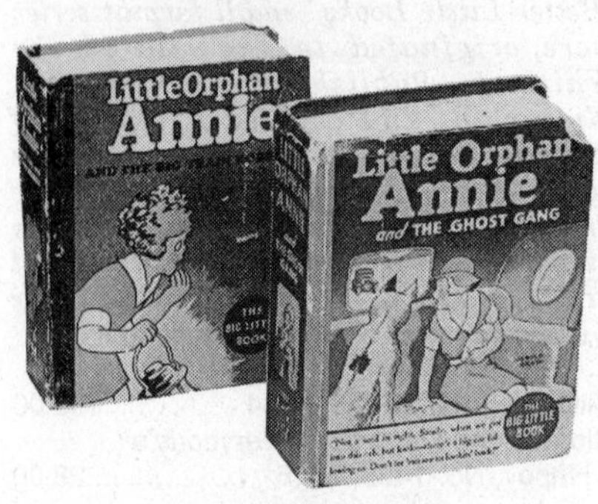

Little Orphan Annie Big Little Books

Little Orphan Annie and the Big Train Robbery, No. 1140, 1934 (ILLUS. left) 35.00
Little Orphan Annie and the Ghost Gang, No. 1154, 1935 (ILLUS. right) 26.00
Little Orphan Annie and the $1,000,000 Formula, No. 1186, 1936 ....46.50
Little Orphan Annie with the Circus, No. 1103, 1934 ....40.00
Lone Ranger and His Horse Silver, No. 1181, 1935 ....45.00
Mac of the Marines in China, No. 1400, 1938....7.50
Men of the Mounted, No. 755, 1934 ....20.00
Mickey Mouse and the Desert Palace, No. 1451, 1948 ....35.00
Mickey Mouse and the Sacred Jewel, No. 1187, 1936 ....43.00
Mickey Mouse in Blaggard Castle, No. 726, 1934 .... 47.50
Myra North Special Nurse and Foreign Spies, No. 1497, 1938 ....$14.00
Pilot Pete Dive Bomber, No. 1466, 1941....20.00
Return of the Phantom, No. 1489, 1942....20.00
Shooting Sheriffs (Sheriffs of the Wild West), No. 1195, 1936....25.00
Smilin' Jack in Wings Over The Pacific, No. 1416, 1939....20.00
Snow White and the Seven Dwarfs, No. 1460, 1938 ....50.00 to 75.00
Tarzan and the Lost Empire, No. 1442, 1948 ....35.00
Tarzan the Terrible, "movie flip" page corners, No. 1453, 1942 ....30.00
The Tarzan Twins, No. 770, 1935 ....175.00

RELATED BOOKS

Bugs Bunny and the Secret of Storm Island, Fast Action Stories, No. 13, 1942....48.00
Donald Duck, The Lost Jungle City, A Big Little Book, movie flip pages, No. 5773, 1975 (some wear) 30.00
Gene Autry and the Bandits of Silver Tip, New Better Little Books, No. 700-10, 1949 ....75.00
Houdini's Big Little Book of Magic, Cocomalt premium, from BLB No. 715, dated 1927 but actually issued in 1933....35.00
Lone Ranger and the Secret of Somber Canyon, New Better Little Books, No. 712-10, 1950 ....25.00
Long Rider and the Treasure of Vanished Man (The), Mystery and Adventure Series, hardback, No. 2317, 1946 ....20.00
Mickey Mouse, Adventures in Outer Space, A Big Little Book, No. 2020, 1968 (some wear)....25.00
Mickey Mouse, Mystery at Disney-land, A Big Little Book, No. 5770, 1977-78 (some wear)....25.00
Red Davis, The American Boy, Five Star Library, Engel-Van Wiseman Corporation, No. 20, 1935 ....15.00
Red Ryder, Acting Sheriff, New Better Little Books, No. 702-10, 1949 ....20.00
Red Ryder and the Adventure at Chimney Rock, Adventure and Mystery Series, hardback, 1940s 20.00
Red Ryder and the Mystery of the Whispering Walls, Adventure and Mystery Series, hardback, 1940s 20.00
Roy Rogers and the Snowbound Outlaws, New Better Little Books, No. 701-10, 1949 ....20.00 to 30.00
Tarzan, The Mark of the Red Hyena, A Big Little Book, No. 2005, 1967 (some wear)....35.00
Tom Mason on Top, Mascot movie w/Tom Mix, Little Big Books, Saal-field, softcover, No. 1582, 1935 ....45.00

BIRDCAGES

Paint-Decorated Birdcage

Although probably not too many people specialize in just collecting birdcages, many who keep birds as pets enjoy keeping them in old or antique cages. The shiny brass birdcages widely produced earlier in this century by firms such as Hendryx arealso popular decorative accent pieces in the homes of antiques lovers who may use them to hold a fern or potted plant rather than a live bird. Note that the very large and elaborate cages produced in the 19th century are the ones which today bring the highest prices on the collecting market.

Brass, Hendryx, patent-dated, 1906, 9" d., 13" h. $110.00

Mahogany w/bone mounting, cylindrical domed form w/domed temple crest, the sides w/columns headed by drapery swags, w/paneled door to the front, on a square plinth w/drawer, George III period, ca. 1780, 16" sq., 30" h....................16,100.00

Mahogany & ivory, in the form of tempietto, w/a colonnaded circular cupola mounted w/the figure of a boy, the wire-inset cage mounted w/urn finials & spherules, the sides mounted w/swagged draperies & fitted w/a panel-carved door, the square base w/a sliding zinc-lined tray, mounted on an associated stand w/rectangular top above a shaped apron & a recess also w/a shaped apron, raised on chamfered bowed legs, George III period, third quarter 18th c., 22½ x 22½", overall 5' 10¼" h. (some replacements to cage).....................................20,700.00

Painted & grained pine, hexagonal form w/slat sides, bottom & steeply pitched roof w/turned acorn finial, painted grey w/red, green & blue graining, swing door & inside perch, New Hampshire, late 19th c., 22½" h...1,980.00

Painted pine & wirework, the rectangular cage w/domed wirework top, the sides painted w/flowering vines, foliage & perched birds in red, green & black on a yellow ground, one end w/a swing door, probably Pennsylvania, early 20th c., some paint wear & rusting, 10½ x 20", 16½" h. (ILLUS.) 920.00

Tin, cylindrical w/the sides composed of large metal bars below the domed top composed of wide straps terminating in a central ruffled cap below the wide ring handle, 19¼" h. (rust, some damage).........................49.50

Early Tin Birdcage

Tin, cylindrical sides w/tubular bars, the shaped conical top w/a cap & tin suspending ring, fitted w/a wooden perch, New England, mid-19th c., 13" d., 26" h. (ILLUS.) 288.00

Cathedral-Form Birdcage

Wirework & parcel-gilt, Colonial-style, in the form of a cathedral w/a central bell tower flanked by turrets w/an outset nave, decorated w/parcel-gilt doors & clerestory windows, Mexico, 19th c., 24" w., 26¼" h. (ILLUS.)......920.00

Wood & wire, rectangular base w/pull-out tray, arched end framework & crossbars framing the wire sides, old brownish red paint on the wood, 14" l. 330.00

BLACK AMERICANA

Over the past decade or so this field of collecting has rapidly grown and today almost anything that relates to Black culture or illustrates Black Americans is considered a desirable collectible. Although many representations of Blacks, especially on 19th and early 20th century advertising pieces and housewares, were cruel stereotypes, even these are collected as poignant reminders of how far American society has come since the dawning of the Civil Rights movement, and how far we still have to go. Other pieces related to this category will be found from time to time in such categories as Advertising Items, Banks, Character Collectibles, Kitchenwares, Cookie Jars, Signs and Signboards, Toys and several others.

Reference books dealing with Black Americana include Black Collectibles *by Lynn Morrow (1983);* Collecting Black Americana *by Dawn E. Reno (Crown Publishers, 1986); and* Black Collectibles, Mammy and her friends *by Jackie Young (Schiffer Publishing Ltd., 1988). Also see ADVERTISING ITEMS, BANKS, CHARACTER COLLECTIBLES, CHILDREN'S BOOKS, DOLLS, POSTERS, SIGNS & SIGNBOARDS and TOYS.*

Paul Robeson Movie Poster

Ashpot, china, figural, model of a black man's head w/a red wagging tongue, wearing yellow earrings, 2½ x 3½", 3½" h. $125.00

Ashtray, ceramic, "Coon Chicken Inn," w/black bellhop, 1940s, 4" d. .... 25.00 to 35.00

Book, "Little Black Sambo," Platt & Munk, 1940 .... 85.00

Book, "Turkey Trott & the Black Santa," 1942 .... 85.00

Booklet, "Simple Simon's Schoolhouse," Aunt Jemima promotional booklet from children's radio show, Chicago 36.00

Clock, electric, animated, black man shines lady's shoes as clock ticks, Lux, 4 x 4" 65.00

Creamer & cov. sugar bowl, red & yellow plastic, figure of Aunt Jemima on front of sugar bowl & Uncle Mose on creamer, F.& F. Mold & Die Works, Dayton, Ohio, 2¼" & 2½" h., pr. 95.00

Doll, cloth, "Diana," Aunt Jemima premium, 1929 .... 110.00

Drawing book, "Little Black Sambo Magic Drawing Book," artist-signed water-color cover, 1928 .... 95.00

Figurine, lead, black boy carrying pig across shoulders, 3" h. 85.00

Kitchen set: cov. cookie jar, salt & pepper shakers, syrup pitcher & spice set; plastic, figural Aunt Jemima, complete w/original metal rack depicting steamboat, F. & F. Mold & Die Works, the set 1,000.00

Lawn sprinkler, "Sprinkling Sambo," painted wood, a cut-out of a standing black boy holding a hook to support the sprinkler hose, wearing bib overalls, a striped shirt & hat, on a metal ring base, 26½" h. (minor scratches, soiling & paint nicks) 121.00

Needle book, "Aunt Jemima's Pancake Flour," paper, book-shaped w/red cover centered by the head of Aunt Jemima, ca. 1905, 2¾" l. 155.00

Photograph, pretty black woman sitting in front of old brick building, sepia tone, oak frame, 15 x 21" 75.00

Pin dish, porcelain, decorated w/a transfer of Booker T. Washington's home, made in Dresden for A.S. Danner, Tuskegee, Alabama 32.50

Poster, movie, "Big Fella," starring Paul Robeson, British Lion Film Corp., 1937, three-sheet, linen-backed, 38 x 88" (ILLUS.) 3,450.00

Prints, "Sambo's Courtship" & "Sambo's Wedding," ca. 1910, framed & matted, 10 x 12", pr. 275.00

Salt & pepper shakers, ceramic, figural Mammy & Black Chef, marked "Japan," small, pr. 28.00

Salt & pepper shakers, plastic, red, yellow & blue, figural Mammy serving coffee, Luzianne Coffee, F. & F. Mold & Die Works, ca. 1960s, pr. 175.00

Salt & pepper shakers, pottery, figural Mammy & Black Chef, McCoy Pottery, 8" h., pr. 45.00

Sheet music, "By The Watermelon Vine," 1904 .... 15.00

Sheet music, "Ev'rybody Calls Me Honey" 15.00
Sheet music, "Pullman Porter Blues," by Ulrich & Hamilton, 1921 ....20.00
Sheet music, "Sam the Old Accordion Man," by Walter Donaldson 20.00
Shot glass, "Sambo's Bar & Grill" 22.00
Souvenir program, "Aunt Jemima," from "Ladies be Seated" radio show 75.00
Syrup pitcher, red plastic, figural Aunt Jemima, F. & F. Mold & & Die Works, ca. 1949, 5½" h. 95.00
Teaspoon, embossed "Coon Chicken Inn" 35.00
Tobacco jar, cov., bisque, bust-form, black man w/balding hair, big eyes turned to the side, smiling w/teeth showing & holding a pipe in his mouth, cover forms top of head 450.00
Tray, change, "Cottolene Shortening," illustrates blacks picking cotton 98.00
Tumbler, clear glass, "Coon Chicken Inn" 38.00

BOOK ENDS

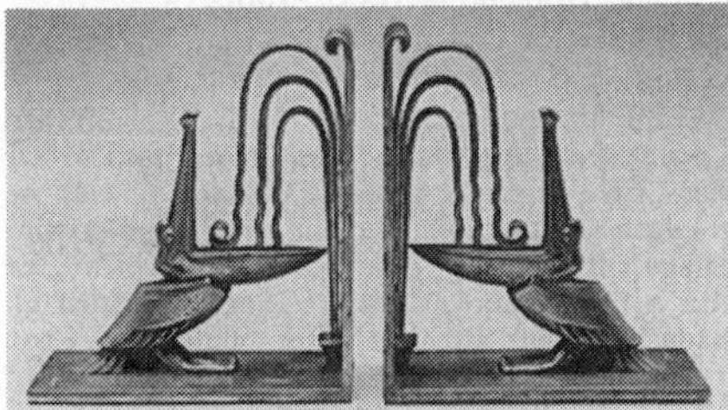

Book Ends by Edgar Brandt

Brass, model of a clipper ship, Snead & Co., pr. $35.00
Brass & Bakelite, model of a stylized elephant, the body formed by a large brass inverted "U" bar, the Bakelite block-form head w/a slender, curved brass trunk, on a rectangular brass base, Chase, ca. 1930, 4½" w., 4½" h., pr. 275.00
Bronze, cast as an arched formal doorway w/a a half-round stepped stoop, green patina, felt liner w/threaded Handel label, 7½" h., pr. 440.00
Bronze, model of setter dog at point, Artmor, pr. 150.00
Bronze, figural, two monks seated w/open book, 4½ x 7", pr. 175.00
Bronze-finished metal, bust of Shakespeare, ca. 1920s, 7" h., pr. 45.00
Bronze-finished metal, cast in relief w/the figure of a cherub, 6¼" h., pr. 247.50
Bronze-finished metal, figure of Mark Twain in seated position, pr. 55.00
Bronze-finished metal, model of "The Angelus," depicting farmers praying in the field, pr. 40.00
Cast iron, model of a camel w/rider, pr. 40.00
Cast iron, model of an elephant, patented 1930, pr. 35.00
Cast & wrought iron, thick L-form support w/tapering scrolled top, set w/a stylized fountain spewing into the open mouth of a pelican, impressed "E. BRANDT," ca. 1925, 6⅞" h., pr. (ILLUS.) 6,050.00
Chalkware, figure of a monk, 7½", pr. 35.00
Chalkware, model of an Irish Setter dog, pr. 45.00
Copper, Arts & Crafts style, hand-hammered heavy gauge w/cut-out poppy design, original dark patina, early open box mark of Dirk Van Erp, ca. 1912, 6" w., 5" h., pr. 770.00
Copper, arched backplate w/a raised design of a perched owl w/a full moon behind its head, fine dark green patina, Bradley & Hubbard, original paper label, 4½" w., 6" h., pr. 165.00
Copper, shaped rectangle w/applied metal eucalyptus pods & handmade leaves on a hammered ground, impressed logo & "OLD MISSION KOPPERKRAFT SAN FRANCISCO" on paper label, 6" w., 5" h., pr. 550.00
Gilt-bronze, "Bookmark" patt., impressed "Tiffany Studios New York 1056," 6" h., pr. 550.00
Gilt-bronze, rectangular supports cast at center w/Gothic arches & a quatrefoil reserved against a tooled ground, within a border of alternating quatrefoils & shaped oval panels, enameled in shades of blue, red, amber & green, impressed "LOUIS C. TIFFANY FURNACES, INC. - FAVRILE 607," 1918-28, 7" l., pr. 1,610.00
Gilt-metal, model of a Cocker Spaniel, on a white onyx base, pr. 65.00
Nickel-plated copper, rectangular nickel base w/a dark nickel-plated copper plaque, the vertical book holder flanked by three semi-arched supports in alternating dark & light nickel plating, designed by Walter

Von Nessen, stamped "CHASE" w/the firm's centaur logo, ca. 1930, 5¾" h., pr. 462.00
Soapstone, carved overall w/a jardiniere & ming tree decoration, China, pr. 52.50

BOOKS

(Also see CHILDREN'S BOOKS, BIG LITTLE BOOKS, CHARACTER COLLECTIBLES & DISNEY COLLECTIBLES.)

ANTIQUES RELATED

Avila, George C., "The Pairpoint Glass Story," 1968, numbered 512, autographed (no dust jacket) $125.00
Barret, Richard C., "A Collector's Handbook of Blown & Pressed American Glass," fourth printing, 1969 ....25.00
Bennett, Arnold & Judy, "The Cambridge Glass Book," color illustrations, paperback 40.00
Bishop, Robert, "American Folk Sculpture," Bonanza edition, 9 x 11" 82.50
Burroughs, Paul H., "Southern Antiques," 1931, Richmond, illustrated, original cloth binding (slight wear) 110.00
Burton, E. Milby, "Charleston Furniture," 1955, 8¾ x 11¼" (worn) 60.50
Carpenter, R.E., Jr., "The Arts and Crafts of Newport, Rhode Island, 1640-1820," 1954, Newport, inscribed by author, illustrated, original green cloth binding, limited edition of 2,000 ....462.00
Chippendale, Thomas, "The Gentleman and Cabinet-Maker's Director," 1762, London, third edition, folio, old calf gilt, 200 engraved plates (rebacked, restored, some staining) 935.00
Conningham, Frederic, "Currier & Ives Prints, An Illustrated Check List," 1949, 6¼ x 9¼" 22.00
Cripps, Wilfred, "Old English Plate," 1968, England, 5½ x 8¾" 17.50
Fauster, Carl U., "Libbey Glass Since 1818," 1979, illustrated, 415 pp. 75.00
Greaser, Paul, "Homespun Ceramics," 1973, paperback, 5¾ x 9" 100.00
Herrick, Ruth, "Greentown Glass - The Indiana Tumbler and Goblet Company and Allied Manufacturers," 1959, Printing Arts Company, Grand Rapids, Michigan, spiral-bound, illustrated 60.00
Hipkiss, Edwin J., "Eighteenth-Century American Arts. The M. and M. Karolik Collection," 1941, Boston, illustrated, original blue cloth binding (slight wear) 352.00
Hobson, R.L., "The Wares of the Ming Dynasty," 1923, London, limited to 1,500 copies, 9 x 11¼" (some wear) 93.50
Hobson, Rackham & King, "Chinese Ceramics," 1931, London, limited edition of 625, 9 x 11½" 99.00
Hornor, William, "Philadelphia Furniture" 1935, 8 x 10¾" 330.00
Jackson, Sir Charles James, "English Goldsmiths and Their Marks," 1921, London, illustrated, original green cloth binding (slight wear) 165.00
Jacobs, Carl, "Guide to American Pewter," 1957, 6½ x 9½" 71.50
Kettell, Russell Hawes, "The Pine Furniture of Early New England," 1929, New York, black & white illustrations, original gilt-labeled buckram binding (some wear) 198.00
Kirk, John, "American Furniture & the British Tradition to 1830," 1982, 9 x 12½".. 55.00
Larsen, E.B., "Staffordshire China," 1939, first edition, 8¼ x 11" 33.00
Lee, Ruth Webb, "Nineteenth Century Art Glass," 1966, front color plate, 128 pp. (no dust jacket) 35.00
Lord, Priscilla, & Foley, Daniel, "The Folk Arts & Crafts of New England," 1970, 9¼ x 12¼" 104.50
Moore, N. Hudson, "Old Pewter, Brass, Copper & Sheffield Plate," 1933, 228 pp. 25.00
Morton, Robert, "Southern Antiques and Folk Art," 1976,12¼ x 12¼" 115.50
Peck, Herbert, "Rookwood Pottery," 1968, first edition, w/dust jacket 22.00
Peters, Harry T., "Currier & Ives: Printmakers to the American People," 1942, Doubleday, hard cover (no dust jacket) 65.00
Sack, Albert, "Fine Points of Furniture," 1950, 7¾ x 10¾" 66.00
Salley, Virginia & George, "Royal Bayreuth China," 1969, sixteen color plates, softcover 30.00
Sonn, Albert H., "Early American Wrought Iron," 1928, New York, 320 illustrated plates from drawings by the author, original cloth binding, three volumes (inner joints cracked) 330.00
Thatcher, Edward, "Making Tin Toys," 1919, first edition, w/dust jacket 75.00

Van Heusden, Willem, "Ancient Chinese Bronzes," 1952, Tokyo, first limited edition, 8½ x 12" 33.00
Weatherman, Hazel Marie, "Fostoria: Its First Fifty Years," 1972, 320 pp. ...75.00
Webster, Donald, "Decorated Stoneware Pottery of North America," 1971, 8¾ x 11" 77.00

CIVIL WAR RELATED

More books have been written about the Civil War era (1861-65) than any other period in the history of our country. The following listing includes books by and about those directly involved in the fighting, overall history of the conflict and the years following.

"A History of the Sixth Iowa Infantry," 1923, from diaries, etc. 50.00
"Battle of Shiloh," by Major Reed, Washington Print Office, w/four maps 60.00
"Butler's Book," 1892, maps, engravings, photos, 1,154 pp. 75.00
"Civil War," by Frank Moore, 1889, anecdotes, poems, etc. 80.00
"General Sherman, His LIfe & Battles," by Edwin Forbes, 1886, in words of one syllable, published by McLaughlin Bros., 96 etchings...........39.00
"Harper's Pictorial History of the Civil War," 1866, uncut, Volumes 1 & 2, first edition 425.00
"History of the Civil War," by Comte De Paris, 1875-88, pictures, maps of battle areas, four vols. 90.00
"History of the 7th Rhode Island Volunteer Infantry," 1903, 543 pp. ...145.00
"Illinois in the Civil War," by V. Hicken, 1966, first edition, illustrated, w/dust jacket 25.00
"Johnny Green of the Orphan Brigade (Journal of a Confederate Soldier)," by A.D. Kirwan, 1956, author-signed 35.00
"Memoirs of General W.T. Sherman," 1891, Volumes 1 & 2, 853 pp.............110.00
"Private & Official Correspondence of General Benjamin F. Buttler," 1917, privately issued, Volumes 1, 2, 3, 4 & 5, 3,303 pp. 250.00
"Rebel Invasion of Maryland & Pennsylvania & the Battle of Gettysburg, July 1-3, 1863," by M. Jacob, Philadelphia, 1864, complete w/foldout map, 47 pp. (cover slightly faded) 75.00
"Rebellion in Missouri," by Adamson, 1961, Philadelphia, first edition, w/dust jacket..25.00
"Richmond Prisons, 1861-62," by W. Jeffrey, from records kept by the Confederate government, illustrated, 1893 ....75.00
"Roster of the Fourth Iowa Cavalry, 1861-65," Little Co., 1902.....................30.00
"War Years with Jeb Stuart," by Blackford, New York, 1946..................20.00

PRESIDENTS & HISTORICAL FIGURES

The following listing includes a wide cross-section of books by and about former Presidents of the United States and other persons of note.

"Abraham Lincoln, The War Years," by Carl Sandburg, 1939, photo illustrations, four volumes 75.00
"Anecdotes of Abraham Lincoln & Lincoln's Stories," by J. B. McClure, 1880..27.50
"Big Game Hunting in Africa," by Theodore Roosevelt, 1902...................27.00
"Citizen of New Salem - Lincoln's Early Years," by Horgan, 1961, illustrated 15.00
"How Lincoln Became President," by Wakefield, 1936, autographed by the author & number "163" 35.00
"Life & Achievements of Admiral Dewey," by Halstad, 1899 ....30.00
"Life and Times of Daniel Boone," by C.B. Hartle, 1885, illustrated 30.00
"Life & Voyages Of Christopher Columbus," Irving, 1855, leather-bound 30.00
"Life of Benjamin Harrison," by Whitelaw Reid, 1892..35.00
"The Life of David Crockett," by E.A Brainerd, 1902.......................................55.00
"Life of Jefferson Davis," by Alfriend, 1868, first edition, 645 pp. 38.00
"Life of U.S. Grant," by Dana, 1868, engravings, maps, etc. 40.00
"Lincoln, the Boy, the Man," by Morgan, 1926 ....18.00
"Lindbergh, Lone Eagle," by R.J. Beamish, 1927, World Wide Photos, first edition, w/32 illustrations, 288 pp. ..45.00
"Personal History of Grant," by Richardson, 1855, w/six maps 40.00
"Personal Memoirs of U.S. Grant," 1885, Volumes 1 & 2, 1,231 pp.......................80.00
"Teddy Roosevelt," by Thomas, 1910, signed by Roosevelt, No. 9 of 9 in special edition set..............................395.00
"The Winning of the West," by Theodore Roosevelt, published 1894-97, four volumes 95.00

STATE & LOCAL

ILLINOIS

"Elgin & Surroundings," 1891, old buildings, homes, schools, names, municipal offices, etc., 25 pictures, 40 pp. 55.00

"History of LaSalle County," 1877 ....125.00

IOWA

"Atlas of Butler & Polk Counties, Iowa," 1918 ....50.00
"Atlas of Clay County, Iowa," 1919..........60.00
"Atlas of O'Brien County, Iowa," 1911 (rebacked) 60.00
"Atlas of Sac County, Iowa," 1931 ....15.00
"Atlas of Tama County, Iowa," 1926 (hinges weakening) 55.00
"History & Foremost Citizens of Iowa," 1915, Vol. 2 ....22.00
"History of Clayton County, Iowa," 1882 (rebound)..65.00
"History of Jasper, Marshall & Grundy Counties, Iowa," leather cover, 1894.....80.00
"History of Mahaska County, Iowa," 1900 ....50.00
"History of O'Brien County, Iowa," 1897 ....55.00
"Roustabout's History of Mahaska County, Iowa" 30.00
"Ordinances of Council Bluffs, Iowa," 1907 ....12.00

MISSOURI

"Atlas of Linn County, Missouri" 40.00
"History of Jasper County, Missouri," 1901 (front hinge broken) 55.00
"History of Missouri," Belford Clark Publications, illustrated, 1889..............35.00

NEBRASKA

"Atlas of Saline County, Nebraska," 1918 ....60.00
"Atlas of Thayer County, Nebraska," 1916 ....60.00

NEW HAMPSHIRE

"History of Cheshire & Sullivan Counties, New Hampshire," 1886 ....65.00
"History of Rockingham County, New Hampshire," 1915 (spine chipped) 60.00
"History of the Town of Stratford, New Hampshire," 1925................................40.00

NEW YORK

"History of Allegheny County," 1896 (rebound)..55.00
"History of Cattargus County," 1879, 2 x 9 x 12", 512 gold-edged pages......110.00
"History of Erie County, New York," 1976 ....60.00
"History of Rochester & Monroe Counties, New York," 1908, two volumes 85.00

OHIO

"Atlas of Perry County, Ohio," 14 x 16" (some damage) 49.50
"History of Clermont & Brown Counties, Ohio," 1913...65.00
"History of Stark County, Ohio," 1881 (spine tears) 65.00

PENNSYLVANIA

"History of Chester County," 1926............20.00
"History of Lancaster County, " 1841-1941 ....25.00
"The Pennsylvania Germans of the Shenandoah Valley," published by The Pennsylvania German Folklore Society, 1964...55.00

BOTTLE OPENERS

Corkscrews were actually the first bottle openers and these may date back to the mid-18th century, but bottle openers as we know them today, are strictly a 20th century item and came into use only after Michael J. Owens invented the automatic bottle machine in 1903. Avid collectors have spurred this relatively new area of collector interest that requires only a modest investment. Our listing, by type of metal, encompasses the four basic types sought by collectors: advertising openers; full figure openers which stand alone or hang on the wall; flat figural openers such as the lady's leg shape; and openers with embossed, engraved or chased handles.

The numbers following figural openers are taken from Mike Jordan's" book Figural Bottle Openers (1981).

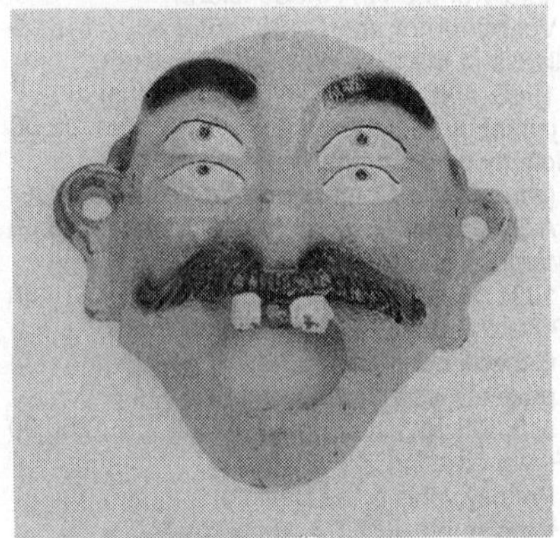

"Doubleye" Bottle Opener

Advertising, "Anheuser-Busch Malt Nutrine," figural chrome bottle w/brass label $75.00
Advertising, "Cleo Cola," metal, embossed "Ezee decapper," 1934.........35.00
Aluminum, full-figure Iroquois Indian (J-53) 35.00
Brass, model of false teeth (J-155).......80.00

Brass, model of a pretzel (J-143) 20.00
Cast iron, full figure donkey, seated w/head tilted back, John Wright Co., 3⅛" h. (J-75)..............................38.50
Cast iron, full figure drunk at lamp post, leg up, polychrome paint, John Wright Co., 4⅛" h. (J-1) 25.00
Cast iron, full figure drunk at palm tree, man w/hat leaning against tree, original polychrome paint, John Wright Co., some wear, 4" h. (J-17) 65.00
Cast iron, full figure drunk w/straw hat at signpost, John Wright Co. (J-13) 60.00
Cast iron, full figure fish, Wilton Products (J-127) 95.00
Cast iron, full figure girl standing by lamp post & sign, polychrome paint, John Wright Co., 4½" h. (J-10) ....25.00 to 30.00
Cast iron, full figure parrot (small), notched crest, John Wright Co. (J-66) 75.00
Cast iron, full figure pelican, standing w/head tilted back & large, rounded beak open, original polychrome paint, John Wright Co., some wear, 3¾" h. (J-117) ....200.00 to 225.00
Cast iron, full figure sea horse, original polychrome paint, John Wright Co., 4⅛" h. (J-119) ....100.00 to 150.00
Cast iron, full figure skunk, John Wright Co. (J-101) ....125.00 to 175.00
Cast iron, full figure squirrel, polychrome paint, John Wright Co. (J-100)...50.00
Cast iron, full figure squirrel, worn polychrome paint, John Wright Co., 3" l. (J-l00)...33.00
Cast iron, wall-mounted, four-eyed bald-headed man w/mustache, polychrome paint, paint chipping, 3¾" h. (J-169) 77.00
Cast iron, wall-mounted, four-eyed girl, "Miss Four Eyes," polychrome paint, Wilton Products, 3⅞" h. (J-167) ....100.00 to 125.00
Cast iron, wall-mounted, four-eyed lady, John Wright Co. (J-166) ....150.00 to 175.00
Cast iron, wall-mounted, four-eyed man, "Doubleye," Wilton Products, J-169 (ILLUS.) 125.00
Cast iron, wall-mounted, head of a black man, Wilton Products (J-146) ....125.00 to 150.00
Cast iron, wall-mounted, model of a bulldog's head, white w/colored trim, Wilton Products, 4" h. (J-164) ....75.00 to 100.00
Cast iron, wall-mounted, modeled as a set of false teeth, painted pink & white, Wilton Products, 3⅜" l. (J-155) ....100.00 to 125.00
Chrome, model of an auto jack, w/clip for wall mounting, Duff Norton (J-137) 25.00
Sterling silver, base-relief coat of arms, signed "Mount Royal Hotel" 55.00

BOTTLES & FLASKS

BITTERS

(Numbers with some listings below refer to those used in Carlyn Ring's For Bitters Only.) Also see DRUGSTORE & PHARMACY ITEMS.

Brown's Celebrated Herb Bitters

African Stomach Bitters, Spruance, Stanley & Co., round, light amber, 9⅝" h...$125.00
Angostura Bark Bitters, Eagle Liqueur Distiller, globe-shaped, amber, 7" h...75.00
Atwood (Moses F.) in script - None Genuine Without My Signature, round, aqua, 6¼" h. 25.00
Atwood's - Vegetable Dyspeptic - Bitters, rectangular, aqua, 6¾" h. 85.00
Baker's Orange Grove - Bitters, square w/roped corners, reddish amber, 3 x 9½" 335.00
Beggs' Dandelion Bitters, rectangular w/beveled edges, smooth base, tooled lip, yellow w/olive tone, 7¾" h...231.00
Berliner Magen Bitters Co., square, amber, 9" h. 260.00
Big Bill Best Bitters, tapering square, golden amber, ca. 1870-90, 12⅛" h...110.00
Boyce's (Dr.) Tonic Bitters, 12-sided, deep aqua, 7¾" h..45.00

Brady's (Dr.) Mandrake Bitters, Honesdale, Pennsylvania, paper label only, rectangular, smooth base, tooled lip, clear, 8⅛" h. 77.00

Brown's Celebrated Indian Herb Bitters - Patented 1867, figural Indian Queen, golden amber, 12¼" h. 605.00

Brown's Celebrated Indian Herb Bitters - Patented Feb. 11, 1868, figural Indian Queen, medium amber, 12¼" h. (ILLUS.) 550.00

Caldwells Herb Bitters (below) The Great Tonic, triangular, amber, 12⅜" h. 187.00

Caldwell's (Dr.) Herb Bitters (below) The Great Tonic, triangular, golden amber, ca. 1860-80, 12¾" h. 263.00

California Fig Bitters - California Extract of Fig Co., San Francisco, Cal., square, amber, 10" h. 88.00

California Fig & Herb Bitters - California Fig Products Co., San Francisco, Cal., square, amber, 4½" h. 195.00

California Herb Bitters, Pittsburgh, Pa., G.W. Frazier, square, amber, 9½" h. 200.00

Capuziner Stomach Bitters, Spellman Distilling Co., Peoria, Illinois, square, amber, w/paper label, qt., 8¼" h. 500.00

Celebrated Crown Bitters - F. Chevalier & Co., Sole Agents, square, light honey amber, 2¾ x 8⅞" 265.00

Clotworthy's - Oriental Tonic Bitters, square, amber, 2⅞ x 9½" 345.00

Clotworthy's - Oriental Tonic Bitters, square, honey amber, 2⅞ x 9¾" 285.00

Cole Bros. - Vegetable Bitters - Binghamton N.Y. - G.L. Cole Prop'r, rectangular, aqua, 7⅞" h. 95.00

Demuth's Stomach Bitters, Philada, square, light golden amber, 9⅜" h. ..165.00

Doyle's - Hop - Bitters - 1872 (on shoulders), square, amber, 9⅝" h......52.00

Drakes Plantation Bitters - Patented 1862, cabin-shaped, five-log, chocolate amber w/a hint of puce, 10" h. (D-109) 275.00

Drakes Plantation Bitters - Patented 1862, cabin-shaped, five-log, golden yellowish amber, 10" h. (D-106)......357.50

Drakes Plantation Bitters - Patented 1862, cabin-shaped, five-log, lemon amber, 10" h. (D-109) 175.00

Drakes Plantation Bitters - Patented 1862, cabin-shaped, five-log, strawberry puce, 10" h. (D-109).......325.00

Drakes Plantation Bitters - Patented 1862, arabesque variant, square w/six embossed logs above label panels, medium puce, 10" h. (D-102) 325.00

Drake's (S T) 1860 Plantation Bitters - Patented 1862, no "X," cabin-shaped, four-log, light honey amber (D-110) 100.00

Drake's (S T) 1860 Plantation Bitters - Patented 1862, no "X," cabin-shaped, four-log, orange amber (D-110) 60.00

Drake's (S T) 1860 Plantation Bitters - Patented 1862, no "X," cabin shaped, four-log, yellow (D-110)......475.00

Drake's (S T) 1860 Plantation Bitters - Patented 1862, no "X," cabin-shaped, six-log, deep puce, 10" h. (D-103) 160.00

Drake's (S T) 1860 Plantation X Bitters - Patented 1862, cabin-shaped, six-log, deep cherry puce, 10" h. (D-105) 93.50

Drake's (S T) 1860 Plantation X Bitters - Patented 1862, cabin-shaped, six-log, deep puce, 10" h., D-105 ....110.00

Drake's (S T) 1860 Plantation X Bitters - Patented 1862, cabin-shaped, six-log, medium amber, 10" h. (D-105) 66.00

Drake's (S T) 1860 Plantation X Bitters - Patented 1862, cabin-shaped, six-log, bright yellow w/hint of olive, 10" h. (D-108) 495.00

Drake's (S T) 1860 Plantation X Bitters - Patented 1862, cabin-shaped, six-log, dark burgundy puce, 10" h. (D-108)............165.00

Drake's (S T) 1860 Plantation X Bitters - Patented 1862, cabin-shaped, six-log, light pinkish puce, 10" h. (D-108) 395.00

Drake's (S T) 1860 Plantation X Bitters - Patented 1862, cabin-shaped, six-log, medium pinkish puce, 10" h. (D-108)............231.00

Eagle Angostura Bark Bitters, globe-shaped, amber, 4" h. 62.50

Electric Bitters - H.E. Bucklen & Co., Chicago, Ill., square, amber, 9⅞" h....30.00

"Electric" Brand Bitters - H.E. Bucklen & Co., Chicago, Ill., square, original label, amber, 8⅞" h. 25.00

Ferro Quina Bitters, D.P. Rossi, Dogliani, Italia, square, light amber, 1 x 2½" 125.00

Fischs (Doctor) Bitters - W.H. Ware, Patent 1866, figural fish, golden amber, ca. 1860-80, 11¾" h. 308.00

Fischs (Doctor) Bitters - W.H. Ware, Patent 1866, figural fish, light amber, 11¾" h. 225.00

Fischs (Doctor) Bitters - W.H. Ware, Patented 1866, figural fish, medium amber, 11¾" h. 195.00

Fish (The) Bitters - W.H. Ware, Patented 1866, figural fish, medium root beer amber, 11½" h. 165.00

Fisher's N.E. Cough Bitters, Atlanta, GA., rectangular, aqua, 5¾" h. 125.00

Genuine Bull Wild Cherry Bitters, rectangular, clear, 8¾" h. 150.00

Globe (The) Tonic - Bitters, square, golden amber, 9⅝" h. 132.00

Grand Prize Bitters, square, amber, 9¼" h. 325.00

Greeley's Bourbon Bitters, barrel-shaped, ten rings above & below center band, copper puce, 9⅜" h. 264.00

Greeley's Bourbon Bitters, barrel-shaped, ten rings above & below center band, deep wine, 9⅜" h. 412.50

Greeley's Bourbon Bitters, barrel-shaped, ten rings above & below center band, medium smoky puce, 9⅛" h. 357.50

Greeley's Bourbon Bitters, barrel-shaped, ten rings above & below center band, smoky greyish green, 9⅜" h. 1,045.00

Hall's Bitters - E.E. Hall New Haven, Established 1842, barrel-shaped, ten-rib, yellow, 9⅛" h. 210.00

Herb (H.P.) Wild Cherry Bitters, Reading, Pa., square, cabin-shaped w/cherry tree motif & roped corners, golden amber, ca. 1860-80, 10" h. 286.00

Highland Bitters and Scotch Tonic, barrel-shaped, ten-rib, light reddish amber, 9⅝" h. 1,900.00

Holtzermann's - Patent Stomach Bitters, cabin-shaped, stylized logs like hoops on barrels, golden orangish amber, 9¼" h................ 1,800.00

Holtzermans Patent Stomach Bitters

Holtzermans Patent Stomach Bitters (on shoulder), cabin-shaped w/four roofs, golden amber, w/paper label, ca. 1870-90, 9⅝" h. (ILLUS.) 330.00

Home Bitters - St. Louis, Mo. - Prepared Black - Berry Brandy, round, amber, 3¼" d., 11½" h. 250.00

Hostetter's (Dr. J.) Stomach Bitters, square, bright green, 9" h. (H-195) ..475.00

Hostetter's (Dr. J.) Stomach Bitters, square, smooth base, applied mouth, yellow, 9" h. (H-195) 165.00

Iron & Quinine Bitters - Burlington, Vt. - N.K. Brown, rectangular, aqua, 7⅛" h. 190.00

Johnson's Calisaya Bitters - Burlington, Vt., square, collared mouth w/ring, amber, 10" h. 90.00

Kelly's Old Cabin Bitters - Patd March 1870, cabin-shaped, dark root beer amber, 9¼" h. 2,420.00

Kelly's Old Cabin Bitters - Patd March 1870, cabin-shaped, medium amber, 9¼" h. 1,155.00

Kimball's Jaundice - Bitters - Troy, N.H., rectangular, yellowish amber, 7" h. ....450.00 to 550.00

King's 25 Cent Bitters, oval, aqua, 6¾" h. 110.00

King Solomon's Bitters, Seattle, Wash., rectangular, 8⅜" h. 75.00

Lacour's Bitters - Sarsapariphere, round, lettering in sunken side panels, lime green, 9" h. 5,060.00

Lacour's Bitters - Sarsapariphere, round, lettering in sunken side panels, yellowish root beer amber, 9" h. 1,650.00

Landsberg (M.G.) Chicago (bitters), square, amber, 11" h. 742.50

Landsberg (M.G.) Chicago (bitters), square, light golden amber, 11" h. ...687.50

Langley's (Dr.) Root & Herb Bitters - 76 Union St., Boston, round aqua......55.00

Leipziger Burgunder Wein Bitter, The Hockstadter Co., round, green, 11¾" h. 200.00

Litthauer Stomach Bitters

Litthauer Stomach Bitters (paper label), Hartwig Kantorowicz, Posen, Berlin, Hamburg, Germany, square case gin shape, milk white, 9½" h. (ILLUS.) 135.00

Litthauer Stomach Bitters Invented 1864 by Josef Loewenthal, Berlin, square case gin shape, milk white, 9½" h...176.00

Loew's (Dr.) Celebrated Stomach Bitters & Nerve Tonic - The Loew & Sons Co., Cleveland, O., square, emerald green, 9¼" h. 325.00

Mack's Sarsaparilla Bitters - Mack & Co. Prop'rs. San Francisco, rectangular w/concave corners, medium amber, 9¼" h.....................242.00

Mills' Bitters - A.M. Gilman - Sole Proprietor, lady's leg shape, yellowish amber, 11¼" h..............1,540.00

Moffat (John) - Phoenix Bitters - Price $1.00 - New York, rectangular w/wide beveled corners, olive green, ½ pt., 5½" h.....................................412.50

Moffat (Jno.) - Price $1 - Phoenix Bitters - New York, rectangular w/wide beveled corners, pontil scarred base, applied mouth, olive green, 5½" h. 385.00

National Bitters, embossed "Pat. Applied For" on base, figural ear of corn, amber, 12½" h. 275.00

National Bitters - Patent 1867, figural ear of corn, aqua, 12⅝" h. 3,400.00

National Bitters - Patent 1867, figural ear of corn, deep golden amber, 12⅝" h..262.00

National Bitters - Patent 1867, figural ear of corn, light shading to medium pinkish puce, 12⅝" h...................3,300.00

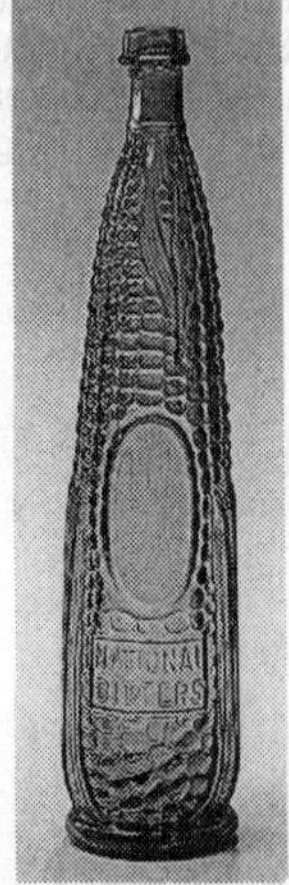

National Bitters

National Bitters - Patent 1867, figural ear of corn, yellowish amber, 12⅝" h. (ILLUS.) 1,265.00

Niagara Star (John W. Steele's), square w/roofed shoulders, three stars on roof & 1864, collared mouth w/ring, golden amber, 10" h. 715.00

Niagara Star (John W. Steele's), square w/roofed shoulders, three stars on roof & 1864, collared mouth w/ring, deep golden amber, 10¼" h...385.00

Nibol Kidney and Liver Bitters, The Best Tonic Laxative & Blood Purifier, square, amber, 9½" h. 165.00

Old Homestead Wild Cherry Bitters - Patent (on shoulders), cabin-shaped, deep strawberry puce, 9⅞" h...3,080.00

Old Homestead Wild Cherry Bitters - Patent (on shoulders), cabin-shaped w/shingles, yellowish amber, 9⅞" h..412.50

Old Sachem Bitters and Wigwam Tonic, barrel-shaped, ten-rib, bright golden amber, ca. 1860-80, 9½" h..550.00

Old Sachem Bitters and Wigwam Tonic, barrel-shaped, ten-rib, ginger ale yellow, ca. 1860-80, 9½" h..770.00

Old Sachem Bitters

Old Sachem Bitters and Wigwam Tonic, barrel-shaped, ten-rib, golden amber, ca. 1860-80, 9½" h. (ILLUS.) 175.00

Old Sachem Bitters and Wigwam Tonic, barrel-shaped, ten-rib, light yellowish amber, 9½" h...................450.00

Old Sachem Bitters and Wigwam Tonic, barrel-shaped, ten-rib, medium copper color, 9½" h. 467.50

Old Sachem Bitters and Wigwam Tonic, barrel-shaped, ten-rib, medium orangish amber, 9½" h.......742.50

Old Sachem Bitters and Wigwam

Tonic, barrel-shaped, ten-rib, medium pinkish strawberry puce, 9½" h. 715.00

Old Sachem Bitters and Wigwam Tonic, barrel-shaped, ten-rib, orangish amber, 9½" h. 325.00

Old Sachem Bitters and Wigwam Tonic, barrel-shaped, ten-rib, yellowish amber, 9½" h. 154.00

Old Sachem Bitters and Wigwam Tonic, barrel-shaped, ten-rib, aqua, 10⅛" h. 4,620.00

Original Pocahontas Bitters, Y. Ferguson, barrel-shaped w/ten horizontal ribs above & below embossing, narrow square collar, aqua, 2¼" d., 9⁵⁄₁₆" h. 2,695.00

Orruro - Bitters (on shoulders), cylindrical, green, ¾ qt., 10⅝" h. 25.00

Oxygenated for Dyspepsia, Asthma & General Debility, rectangular, aqua, ½ pt., 7⅝" h. 140.00

Pepsin Bitters - R.W. Davis Drug Co., Chicago, U.S.A., rectangular, apple green, 1⅜ x 2¼", 4⅛" h. 200.00

Pepsin Calisaya Bitters, Dr. Russell Med. Co., rectangular, green, pt., 7⅞" h. 105.00

Peruvian Bitters. w/"P.B.Co." monogram in shield, square, amber, 9¼" h. ....50.00 to 70.00

Peychaud's American Aromatic Cocktail Bitters (paper label), cylindrical, amber, 6" h. 40.00

Pierce's (Dr. Geo.) - Indian Restorative Bitters - Lowell, Mass, greenish aqua, 7⅞" h. 135.00

(Pineapple), W. & Co., N.Y., pineapple-shaped, bright yellowish green, 8⅞" h. 4,510.00

(Pineapple), W. & Co., N.Y., pineapple-shaped, medium orangish amber, 8⅞" h. 125.00

Reed's Bitters (repeated on shoulder), cylindrical, lady's leg neck, light orange amber, 12½" h. ....250.00 to 300.00

Richardson's (S.O.) - Bitters - South Reading - Mass., rectangular w/wide beveled corners, aqua, pt., 6⅞" h. ....65.00 to 85.00

Richardson's (W.L.) - Bitters - South Reading - Mass., rectangular, aqua, 7" h. 98.00

Roback's (Dr. C.W.) Stomach Bitters, Cincinnati, O, barrel-shaped, golden amber, 9⅜" h. 231.00

Root's (John) Bitters - Buffalo, N.Y. - 1867 (on two sides), rectangular, amber, 9¾" h. 1,595.00

Royal Italian Bitters, Registered, Trade Mark, A.M.F. Gianella, Genova, round, brilliant medium amethyst, 2¾" d., 13½" h. (some minor interior wear) 484.00

Royal Italian Bitters, Registered, Trade Mark, A.M.F. Gianella, Genova, round, light to medium pinkish amethyst, 2¾" d., 13½" h. 2,640.00

Royal Italian Bitters, Registered, Trade Mark, A.M.F. Gianella, Genova, round, pinkish amethyst, 2¾" d., 13½" h. 990.00

Royce's Sherry Wine Bitters, rectangular, smooth base, aqua, 8" h. 90.00

Rush's - Bitters - A.H. Flanders M.D., New York, square, amber, 8⅞" h. 40.00

Russ' St. Domingo Bitters - New York, rectangular, light yellowish amber, 9⅞" h. 275.00

Sanborn's Kidney and Liver Vegetable Laxative Bitters, rectangular, amber, 10" h. 150.00

Sazarac Aromatic Bitters, lady's leg neck, milk white, 10⅛" h. 522.50

Sazarac Aromatic Bitters, w/"PHD & Co." monogram, lady's leg neck, milk white, 12½" h. ....225.00 to 250.00

Schroeder's Bitters, Louisville, KY - S. B. & G. Co., lady's leg neck, tooled lip, smooth base, orangish amber, 9" h. 467.50

Severa (W.F.) - Stomach Bitters, square, amber, 9⅝" h. 70.00

Simon's Centennial Bitters - Trade Mark, figural bust of Washington on pedestal, aqua, ¾ qt., 9¾" h. 650.00

Solomons' Strengthening & Invigorating Bitters - Savannah, Georgia, square, cobalt blue, ³⁄₁₆" stress crack, 9⅝" h. (S-140) 1,072.00

Specialitat Richter's Rossbacher Magen Bitter, Patentamtlich Christof Richter & Bruder, Hof in Baiern, applied mouth, smooth base, olive green, 11" h., ca. 1870-80 (tiny flake on one corner) 231.00

Swiss - Stomach Bitters - WM. F. Zoeller - Pittsburgh, PA., w/paper label, rectangular, applied mouth, smooth base, yellowish amber, 9¼" h. 220.00

Tippecanoe (birch bark & canoe motif), H.H. Warner & Co., cylindrical, amber, 9" h. (ILLUS. top next column) ...80.00 to 100.00

Tonic Bitters, J.T. Higby, Milford, Ct., square, amber, 9½" h. 55.00

Von Hopfs (Dr.) - Curacoa Bitters - Chamberlain & Co., Des Moines Iowa, rectangular, amber, w/labels, ½ pt., 7½" h. ....60.00 to 80.00

Wakefield's Strengthening Bitters, rectangular w/beveled corners, aqua, 8" h. 70.00

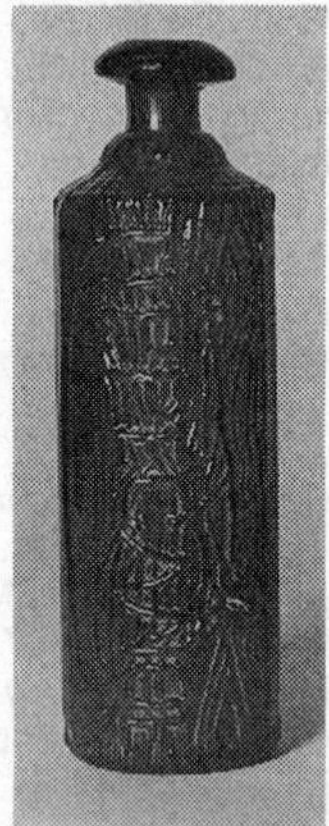

Tippecanoe Bitters

Wear & Upham & Ostrom - Julien's Imperial - Aromatic Bitters, N.Y., lady's leg-shaped, yellowish amber, 12½" h. 3,035.00

Wheeler's - Berlin - Bitters - Baltimore, hexagonal, lettering reading reversed & base to shoulder, iron pontil, yellowish olive green, 9½" h. 7,150.00

Wonser's (Dr.) U.S.A., Indian Root Bitters, round w/fluted shoulder, dark aqua, ¾ qt., 11" h. 3,080.00

Wonser's (Dr.) U.S.A., Indian Root Bitters, round w/fluted shoulder, root beer amber, ¾ qt., 11" h. 4,730.00

Yerba Buena - Bitters, S.F. Cal., flask-shaped, amber, 8½" h. 80.00

Zu Zu Bitters, square, amber, 8⅜" h. 310.00

FIGURALS

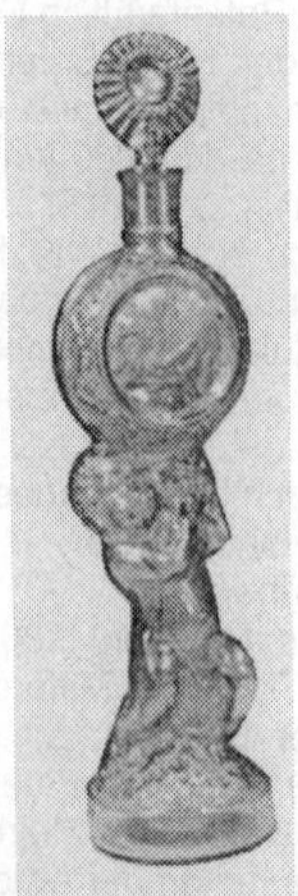

Cherub & Medallion Bottle

Bust of George Washington, applied sloping collared mouth, pontil scar, aqua, 10½" h. 27.50

Busts of three people, two men & one woman, atop of waisted paneled column, probably Europe, ca. 1880-1900, milk white cased in clear, 13½" h. 220.00

Cherub holding a medallion on his shoulder w/pressed wheel stopper in the short cylindrical neck, tooled lip, American-made, ca. 1890-1910, emerald green, 11" h. (ILLUS.) 192.50

Cherub holding a medallion on his shoulder w/pressed wheel stopper in the short cylindrical neck, tooled lip, American-made, ca. 1890-1910, medium purplish amethyst, 11" h. ...198.00

Cigar, amber glass, 5¼" l. ......25.00 to 35.00

Cigar, ground top w/screw cap, amber glass 82.50

Cucumber, horizontal ribbing, pontil scar on one end, applied knob on other, American-made, ca. 1880-1900, medium sapphire blue, 7¾" l. 77.00

Dutchman Bottle

Dutchman standing wearing baggy pants, jacket w/kerchief & hat, holding a long pipe, probably from Germany, ca. 1890-1910, amber, 11½" h.(ILLUS.) 825.00

Ham, amber glass 60.00

Klondyke gold nugget flask, milk white glass, 6" h. 62.50

Potato, sponge-daubed earthenware pottery, blue sponging on white, 8" l. 165.00

FLASKS

GI-2 - Washington bust below "General Washington" - American Eagle w/shield w/seven bars on breast, head turned to right, edges w/horizontal beading w/vertical medial rib, plain lip, pontil, aqua, pt. 245.00

GI-19 - "Washington" above bust - "Baltimore Glass Works." in semicircle around Battle Monument, Baltimore, smooth edges, plain lip, pontil, copper w/puce tones, ca. 1830-50, pt. 1,980.00

GI-22 - Washington bust (facing right) below "Baltimore X Glass Works" (all S's reversed) - classical bust facing right, three vertical ribs w/heavy medial rib, plain lip, pontil, clear, ca. 1820-40, pt. 1,210.00

GI-25 - Washington bust (facing right) below "Bridgetown New Jersey," - Classical bust below "Bridgetown New Jersey," plain lip, aqua, qt., 8¼" h., light inside haze 220.00

GI-28 -Washington bust below "Albany Glass Works," "Albany N Y" below bust - full-rigged ship sailing to right, plain lip, vertically ribbed edges, pontil, medium amber, pt. 660.00

GI-34 - "Washington" above bust (facing right) - "Jackson" above bust, plain lip, vertically ribbed edges w/heavy medial rib, pontil, light yellow olive green, ½ pt. 230.00

GI-37 - Washington bust below "The Father of His Country" - Taylor bust, "Gen. Taylor Never Surrenders, Dyottville Glass Works, Philad.a," smooth edges, plain lip, pontil, citron, qt. 375.00

GI-37 - Washington bust below "The Father of His Country" - Taylor bust, "Gen. Taylor Never Surrenders, Dyottville Glass Works, Philad.a," plain lip, smooth edge, pontil, topaz, qt. 1,450.00

GI-40 - Washington bust below "The Father of His Country" - Taylor bust, "Gen. Taylor Never Surrenders," smooth edges, sheared lip, pontil, aqua, pt. 70.00

GI-40 - Washington bust below "The Father of His Country" - Taylor bust, "Gen. Taylor Never Surrenders," smooth edges, sheared lip, pontil, bright medium green, pt. 253.00

GI-42 - Washington bust below "The Father of His Country" - Taylor bust, "A little More Grape Captain Bragg, Dyottville Glass Works, Philad.a," smooth edges, plain lip, pontil, aqua, qt. 85.00

GI-42 - Washington bust below "The Father of His Country" - Taylor bust, "A little More Grape Captain Bragg, Dyottville Glass Works, Philad.a," smooth edges, plain lip, pontil, cobalt blue, ca.1840-60, qt. 3,740.00

GI-42 - Washington bust below "The Father of His Country" - Taylor bust, "A little More Grape Captain Bragg, Dyottville Glass Works, Philad.a," smooth edges, plain lip, pontil, peacock blue, qt. 325.00

GI-43 - Washington bust below "The Father of His Country" - Taylor bust below "I Have Endeavour,d To Do My Duty," plain lip, smooth edges, pontil, dark golden amber, ca. 1840-60, qt. 1,210.00

GI-43 - Washington bust below "The Father of His Country" - Taylor bust below "I Have Endeavour,d To Do My Duty," plain lip, smooth edges, pontil, yellow w/slight olive tone, ca. 1840-60, qt. 495.00

GI-65 - "General Jackson" surrounding bust - American Eagle w/shield on oval frame, "J.T. & Co." below oval frame, thirteen small five-pointed stars above eagle, horizontal beading w/vertical medial rib, plain lip, pontil mark, aqua, 1829-32, pt. 363.00

GI-77 - Taylor bust below "Rough & Ready" - American Eagle w/shield w/eight vertical & three horizontal bars on breast, head turned left, "Masterson" above 13 five-pointed stars above eagle, plain lip, open pontil, aqua, ca. 1830-40, qt. 1,045.00

GI-80 - "Lafayette" above & "T.S." & bar below - "DeWitt Clinton" above bust & "Coventry C-T" below, plain lip, horizontally corrugated edges, pontil, light yellowish olive, ca. 1824-25, pt. 630.00

GI-80 - "Lafayette" above bust & "T.S." & bar below - "DeWitt Clinton" above bust & "Coventry C-T" below, plain lip, horizontally corrugated edges, pontil, yellowish olive, ca. 1824-25, pt. 550.00

GI-85 - "Lafayette" above bust & "Covetry (sic) - C-T" below - French liberty cap on pole & semicircle of eleven five-pointed stars above, "S & S" below, fine vertical ribbing, two horizontal ribs at base, plain lip, pontil mark, yellowish olive, ca. 1824-25, pt. 242.00

GI-86 - "Lafayette" above bust & "Coventry - C-T" below - French liberty cap on pole & semicircle of eleven five-pointed stars above, "S & S" below, fine vertical ribbing, two horizontal ribs at base, plain lip, pontil mark, yellowish olive green, ca. 1824-25, ½ pt. 440.00

GI-92 - Lafayette bust facing right below Masonic Arch & a fleur-de-lis, "Genl Lafayette" along sides - American Eagle w/shield on breast below seven stars all in an oval & "Wheeling" in semicircle above upper part of panel & "Knox & McKee" in semicircle around lower panel, smooth edges, plain lip, pontil mark, brilliant pale green, ca. 1820-40, pt. 4,070.00

GI-95 - Franklin bust below "Benjamin Franklin" - Dyott bust below "T.W. Dyott, M.D.," three vertical ribs w/heavy medial rib, plain lip, pontil mark, aqua, ca. 1820-40, pt. 242.00

GI-96 - Franklin bust below "Benjamin Franklin" - Dyott bust below "T.W. Dyott, M.D.," edges embossed "Eripuit Coelo Fulmen. Sceptrumque Tyrannis" and "Kensington Glass Works, Philadelphia," plain lip, pontil, aqua, qt. 200.00

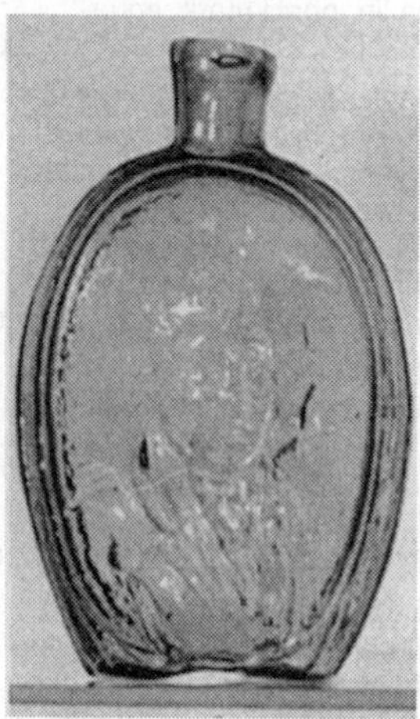

Benjamin Franklin Flask

GI-98 - Franklin bust below "Benjamin Franklin" - "Wheeling Glassworks" in semi-circle above bust of Thomas Dyott, vertically ribbed edges, plain neck, aqua, pt. (ILLUS.) 2,750.00

GI-104 - "Jeny (sic) Lind" above bust - View of Glasshouse, calabash, vertically ribbed edges, rounded collar, pontil, brilliant light powder blue, ca. 1845-60, qt. 396.00

GI-113 - "Kossuth" above bust - tall tree in foliage, calabash, smooth edges, iron pontil, light greyish blue, ca. 1840-60, qt. 495.00

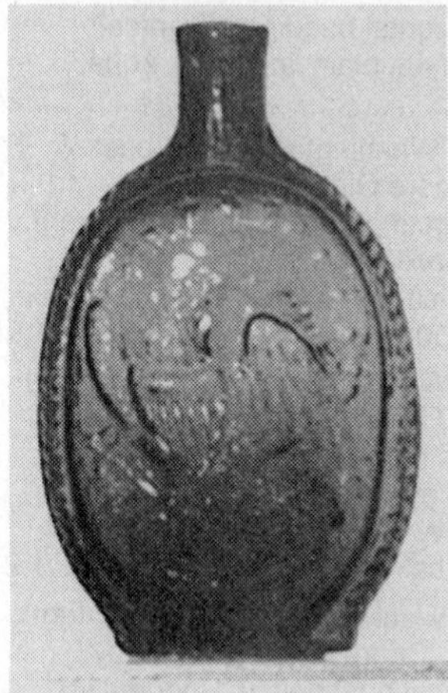

American Eagle Flask

GII-1a - American Eagle on oval, head turned to right & 10 stars in semi-circle above eagle (eight 5-pointed stars & two 6-pointed stars) obverse & reverse, beaded edges w/narrow vertical medial rib, plain sheared lip, open pontil, amber, pt. (ILLUS.) 23,650.00

GII-6 - American Eagle w/head turned right on oval w/inner band of tiny pearls, nine pearls above eagle - large Cornucopia with Produce, horizontally ribbed edges, plain lip, greenish aqua, pt. 250.00

GII-18 - American Eagle w/head turned to right above oval frame enclosing "Zanes - Ville" - Cornucopia with Produce, vertically ribbed edges, plain lip, pontil mark, aqua, ½ pt. 30.50

GII-23 - American Eagle above oval, ribbon & two semi-circular rows of stars above, oval w/elongated eight-point star - large floral medallion above oval containing an elongated eight-pointed star, edges corrugated horizontally w/vertical medial rib, plain lip, pontil, aqua, ca. 1850-55, pt. 495.00

GII-26 - American Eagle above stellar motif obverse & reverse, horizontally corrugated edges, plain lip, aqua, qt. 115.00

GII-30 - American Eagle in a small circular medallion obverse & reverse, overall heavy vertical ribbing except for medallions, plain lip, pontil, brilliant aqua, ca. 1855-60, ½ pt. 374.00

GII-31 - American Eagle in large oval medallion obverse & reverse, overall heavy vertical ribbing except for medallions, pontil, aqua, qt. 180.00

GII-48 - American Eagle on oval - American flag w/"Coffin & Hay." above & "Hammonton" below, vertically ribbed edges, plain lip, pontil, aqua, qt. 190.00

GII-61 - American Eagle below "Liberty" - inscribed in four lines, "Willington - Glass, Co - West Willington - Conn," smooth edges, deep olive green, qt. 187.00

GII-61 - American Eagle below "Liberty" - inscribed in four lines, "Willington - Glass, Co - West Willington - Conn," smooth edges, orange amber, ca. 1860-72, qt. 209.00

GII-62 - American Eagle below "Liberty" - "Willington Glass, Co West, Willington Conn," smooth edges, plain lip, emerald green, ca. 1860-72, pt. 330.00

GII-62 - American Eagle below "Liberty" - "Willington Glass, Co West, Willington Conn," smooth edges, plain lip, reddish amber, pt...308.00

GII-63 - American Eagle below "Liberty" - inscription in five lines, "Willington - Glass - Co - West Willington - Conn.," smooth edges, plain lip, deep reddish amber, ½ pt. 198.00

GII-64 - American Eagle below "Liberty" - inscription in four lines, "Willington - Glass, Co - West Willington - Conn," smooth edges, plain lip, pontil, golden amber, pt. 187.00

GII-65 - American Eagle below "Liberty" - inscribed in five lines "Westford - Glass - Co - Westford - Conn.," smooth edges, plain lip, deep yellowish olive, ca. 1860-73, ½ pt. 253.00

GII-67 - American Eagle below nine five-pointed stars standing on large laurel wreath - large anchor w/"New London" in a banner above & "Glass Works" in a banner below, smooth edges, plain lip, pontil, aqua, ca. 1860-66, ½ pt. 286.00

GII-67 - American Eagle below nine five-pointed stars standing on large laurel wreath - large anchor w/"New London" in a banner above & "Glass Works" in a banner below, smooth edges, plain lip, pontil, medium orangish amber, ½ pt. 467.50

GII-68 - American Eagle in flight below seven five-pointed stars - large anchor w/"New London" in a banner above & "Glass Works" in a banner below, smooth edges, plain lip, pontil, bright orangish amber, ca. 1860-66, pt. 467.50

GII-70 - American Eagle lengthwise obverse & reverse, vertically ribbed edges, plain lip, pontil, yellowish olive, ca. 1830-48, pt. 165.00

GII-71 - American Eagle lengthwise obverse & reverse, vertically ribbed edges, plain lip, pontil, bright yellowish olive, ½ pt. 176.00

GII-73 - American Eagle w/head turned to the right & standing on rocks - Cornucopia with Produce & "X" on left, vertically ribbed edges, plain lip, pontil, deep golden yellow, pt. 220.00

GII-105 - American Eagle above oval obverse & reverse, w/"Pittsburgh, Pa." in oval obverse & reverse, narrow vertical ribbing on edges, sheared lip w/applied flat collar, smooth base, deep green, pt. 250.00

GII-106 - American Eagle above oval obverse & reverse, w/"Pittsburgh, PA" in oval on obverse, narrow vertical rib on edges, honey amber, pt. 185.00

GII-115 - American Eagle above oval obverse & reverse, w/"Louisville KY." in oval obverse & "Glass Works" in oval on reverse, narrow vertical ribbing on edges, applied rounded collar & seamed base w/depression, aqua, pt. 195.00

GIII-1 - Cornucopia with Produce surrounded by an oval beaded panel - large circular beaded medallion enclosing a star-shaped design w/six ribbed points & a small eight-petaled rosette center, above a symmetrical palm motif, edges w/horizontal beading, plain lip, pontil mark, pale yellowish green, ca. 1820-40, ½ pt. 412.50

GIII-2 - Cornucopia with Produce obverse & reverse, vertically ribbed edges, sheared, tooled lip, pontil, aqua, ½ pt. 105.00

GIII-4 - Cornucopia with Produce - Urn with Produce, vertically ribbed edges, plain lip, pontil, bright medium green, pt. (some exterior high point wear, inner mouth flake)..319.00

GIII-7 - Cornucopia with Produce - Urn with Produce, vertically ribbed edges, sheared lip, pontil, aqua, ½ pt. 126.50

GIII-12 - Cornucopia with Produce & curled to right - Urn with Produce, plain lip, vertically ribbed edges, pontil, yellowish olive, ½ pt. 88.00

GIII-16 - Cornucopia with Produce & curled to right - Urn with Produce & w/"Lancaster.Glass.Works N.Y" above, sheared mouth, vertically ribbed edges, iron pontil, yellowish olive amber, pt. 770.00

GIV-1 - Masonic Emblems - American Eagle w/ribbon reading "E Pluribus Unum" above & "IP" (old-fashioned J) below in oval frame, tooled mouth, five vertical ribs, bright bluish green, pt. ....275.00 to 300.00

GIV-1 - Masonic Emblems - American Eagle w/ribbon reading "E Pluribus Unum" above & "IP" (old-fashioned J) below in oval frame, tooled mouth, five vertical ribs, medium bluish green, pt. 192.50

GIV-3 - Masonic Emblems - American Eagle w/heavily crimped ribbon above & "J.K. - B." below in oval frame, tooled lip, five vertical ribs, light bluish green, pt. 412.50

GIV-7 - Masonic Arch - American Eagle holding shield w/twelve dots (representing stars), open pennant ribbon above, oval frame w/eight-pointed star below, vertically ribbed sides, pontil, aqua, pt. 220.00

GIV-14 - Masonic Arch, pillars & pavement w/Masonic emblems inside the arch - American Eagle above oval frame w/elongated eight-pointed star, plain rim, vertically ribbed sides, light green, ½ pt. 440.00

GIV-17 - Masonic Arch, pillars & pavement w/Masonic emblems - American Eagle w/oval frame enclosing "KEENE" below, edges smooth w/single vertical rib, plain lip, pontil, olive green, pt. 187.50

GIV-20 - Masonic Arch, pillars & pavement w/Masonic emblems - American Eagle w/"KCCNC" in oval frame below, edges w/single vertical rib, plain lip, pontil, yellowish olive, pt. 165.00

GIV-24 - Masonic Arch, pillars & pavement w/Masonic emblems - American Eagle grasping large balls in talons & without shield on breast, plain oval frame below, smooth edges w/single medial rib, plain lip, pontil, bright light yellow amber, ½ pt. 132.00

GIV-24 - Masonic Arch, pillars & pavement w/Masonic emblems - American Eagle grasping large balls in talons & without shield on breast, plain oval frame below, smooth edges w/single medial rib, plain lip, pontil, light yellowish olive green, ½ pt. 187.00

GIV-27 - Masonic Arch, pillars & pavement w/Masonic emblems & radiating triangle enclosing the letter "G" - American Eagle w/"NEG Co" in oval frame below, vertically ribbed edges, tooled lip, pontil mark, light green, pt. 325.00

GIV-32 - Masonic Arch w/"Farmer's Arms," sheaf of rye & farm implements within arch - American Eagle, w/shield w/seven bars on breast, head turned to right, "Zanesville" above, eagle stands on oval frame w/"Ohio" inside & "J. Shepard & Co." beneath, vertically ribbed edges, open pontil, amber, pt. 330.00

GIV-32 - Masonic Arch w/"Farmer's Arms," sheaf of rye & farm implements within arch - American Eagle, w/shield w/seven bars on breast, head turned to right, "Zanesville" above, eagle stands on oval frame w/"Ohio" inside & "J. Shepard & Co." beneath, vertically ribbed edge, open pontil, aqua, pt. ....225.00 to 250.00

GIV-32 - Masonic Arch w/"Farmer's Arms," sheaf of rye & farm implements within arch - American Eagle w/shield w/seven bars on breast, head turned to right, "Zanesville" above, eagle stands on oval frame w/"Ohio" inside & "J. Shepard & Co." beneath, vertically ribbed edge, open pontil, golden yellow w/olive tone, ca. 1820-30, pt. 1,980.00

GIV-34 - Masonic Arch w/"Farmer's Arms," sheaf of rye & farm implements within arch & "Kensington Glass Works Philadelphia" around edge - Sailing frigate above "Franklin" w/"Free Trade and Sailors Rights" around edge, aqua, pt. 192.50

GIV-36 - Masonic Arch w/"Farmer's Arms," sheaf of rye & farm implements within arch - full rigged frigate sailing to right, "Franklin" below, edges horizontally beaded w/medial rib, plain lip, pontil, aqua, pt. 550.00

GV-3 - "Success to the Railroad" around embossed horse pulling cart - similar reverse, sheared lip, pontil, yellowish olive amber, pt. 132.00

GV-3 - "Success to the Railroad" around embossed horse pulling cart - similar reverse, sheared lip, pontil, yellowish olive green, pt. 627.00

GV-5 - "Success to the Railroad" around embossed horse pulling cart - similar reverse, plain lip, pontil, vertically ribbed edges, aqua, ca. 1840-60, pt. 374.00

GV-5 - "Success to the Railroad" around embossed horse pulling cart

- similar reverse, plain lip, pontil, vertically ribbed edges, forest green, ca. 1840-60, pt. 247.50

GV-6 - "Success to the Railroad" around embossed horse pulling cart obverse & reverse, w/"Success" above scene, plain lip, pontil, vertically ribbed edges, golden amber, ca. 1840-60, pt. 198.00

GV-6 - "Success to the Railroad" around embossed horse pulling cart obverse & reverse, w/"Success" above scene, plain lip, pontil, vertically ribbed edges, olive amber, pt. 192.50

GV-6 - "Success to the Railroad" around embossed horse pulling cart obverse & reverse, w/"Success" above scene, plain lip, pontil, vertically ribbed edges, yellowish olive ca. 1830-48, pt. 253.00

GV-8 - "Success to the Railroad" around embossed horse pulling cart - large American Eagle w/head turned left & holding a shield w/seven vertical & two horizontal bars on breast, seventeen large five-pointed stars surround eagle, three vertically ribbed edges w/heavy medial rib, plain lip, pontil mark, yellowish olive amber, pt. 165.00

GV-9 - "Success to the Railroad" around embossed horse pulling cart - large eagle & seventeen five-pointed stars, vertically ribbed edges w/heavy medial rib, plain lip, pontil mark, bright yellowish olive, pt. 264.00

GV-9 - "Success to the Railroad" around embossed horse pulling cart - large eagle & seventeen five-pointed stars, vertically ribbed, heavy medial rib, plain lip, pontil mark, deep olive green, pt. 192.50

GV-9 - "Success to the Railroad" around embossed horse pulling cart - large eagle & seventeen five-pointed stars, vertically ribbed, heavy medial rib, plain lip, pontil mark, medium olive amber, pt. 176.00

GV-10 - "Railroad" above horse-drawn cart on rail & "Lowell" below - American Eagle lengthwise & 13 five-point stars, vertically ribbed edges , sheared lip, pontil , yellowish olive, ½ pt. 253.00

GVI-2 - "Balto" below monument - "Fells" above & "Point" below a small sloop w/pennant flying & sailing to the right, vertically ribbed edges w/three heavy medial ribs, plain lip, pontil mark, pale aqua, ½ pt. 247.50

GVI-4a - Washington Monument in large oval panel - "Corn For The World" in semicircle above ear of corn, plain lip, smooth edges, aqua, qt. (flake on mouth) 275.00

GVIII-2 - Sunburst w/twenty-four triangular sectioned rays obverse & reverse, plain lip, pontil, clear, ca. 1826-30, pt. 687.50

GVIII-2 - Sunburst w/twenty-four triangular sectioned rays obverse & reverse, plain lip, pontil, light green, ca. 1815-30, pt. 440.00

Scarce Sunburst Flask

GVIII-3 - Sunburst w/twenty-four rounded rays obverse & reverse, horizontal corrugated edges, plain lip, pontil mark, olive amber, pt. (ILLUS.) 605.00

GVIII-5 - Sunburst w/twenty-four rounded rays obverse & reverse, horizontal corrugated edges, plain lip, pontil mark, bright yellowish olive, ca. 1815-30, pt 880.00

GVIII-8 - Sunburst w/twenty-eight triangular sectioned rays obverse & reverse, center raised oval w/"KEEN" on obverse & w/"P & W" on reverse, pontil, yellowish olive, pt. 247.50

GVIII-9 - Sunburst w/twenty-nine triangular sectioned rays obverse & reverse, center raised oval w/"KEEN" reading from top to bottom on obverse & w/"P & W" on reverse, sheared lip, pontil, olive green, ½ pt......................250.00 to 300.00

GVIII-9 - Sunburst w/twenty-nine triangular sectioned rays obverse & reverse, center raised oval w/"KEEN" reading from top to bottom on obverse & w/"P & W" on reverse, sheared lip, pontil, yellowish olive, ca. 1815-30, ½ pt. ...258.50

GVIII-16 - Sunburst w/twenty-one triangular sectioned rays obverse &

reverse, plain lip, open pontil, bright yellowish olive green, ca. 1815-30, ½ pt. 286.00

GVIII-18 - Sunburst w/twenty-four rounded rays obverse & reverse, horizontal corrugated edges, plain lip, pontil mark, olive green, ½ pt. 275.00

GVIII-18 - Sunburst w/twenty-four rounded rays obverse & reverse, horizontal corrugated edges, plain lip, pontil mark, yellowish olive amber, ca. 1815-30, ½ pt. 577.50

GVIII-18 - Sunburst w/twenty-four rounded rays obverse & reverse, horizontal corrugated edges, plain lip, pontil mark, yellowish olive green, ½ pt. 302.50

GVIII-22 - Sunburst w/thirty-six slender rays forming a scalloped ellipse w/five small oval ornaments in center obverse & reverse, smooth sides, pontil, pale green, pt. 159.50

GVIII-25 - Sunburst w/twenty-four slender rays tapering to rounded ends obverse & reverse, five oval-shaped ornaments forming five-petaled flower in middle of sunburst, plain lip, pontil, aqua, ½ pt. 192.50

GVIII-25 - Sunburst w/twenty-four slender rays tapering to rounded ends obverse & reverse, five oval-shaped ornaments forming five-petaled flower in middle of sun-burst, plain lip, pontil, medium to deep burgundy, ½ pt. 3,960.00

GVIII-28 - Sunburst w/sixteen rays obverse & reverse, rays converging to a definite point at center & covering entire side of flask, horizontally corrugated edges, plain lip, open pontil, light aqua, ½ pt. 220.00

GVIII-29 - Sunburst in small sunken oval w/twelve rays obverse & reverse, panel w/band of tiny ornaments around inner edge, entire flask except panels covered w/heavy, narrow widely spaced vertical ribbing, pontil, deep aqua, ¾ pt. ....300.00 to 315.00

GVIII-29 - Sunburst in small sunken oval w/twelve rays obverse & reverse, panel w/band of tiny ornaments around inner edge, entire flask except panels covered w/heavy, narrow widely spaced vertical ribbing, pontil, greenish aqua, ¾ pt. 140.00

GVIII-29 - Sunburst in small sunken oval w/twelve rays obverse & reverse, panel w/band of tiny ornaments around inner edge, entire flask except panels covered w/heavy, narrow, widely spaced vertical ribbing, pontil, medium bluish green, ¾ pt. ....165.00 to 185.00

GIX-2 - Scroll w/two six-point stars obverse & reverse, vertical medial rib, long neck w/plain lip, deep sapphire blue, qt., 9" h. (small mouth flake) 2,310.00

GIX-6 - Scroll w/two six-point stars obverse & reverse, one side w/"Louisville KY," the other w/"Glassworks," vertical medial rib, plain lip, pontil mark, light yellowish green, qt. 269.50

GIX-10 - Scroll w/two eight-point stars obverse & reverse, golden amber, ca. 1840-60, pt. 352.00

GIX-10 - Scroll w/two eight-point stars obverse & reverse, golden amber w/olive tones, ca. 1840-60, pt. 385.00

GIX-10c - Scroll w/two eight-point stars, a small one in upper space & medium sized one in midspace obverse - seven-point upper star reverse, vertical medial rib, plain neck, bluish green, ½ pt. 352.00

GIX-11 - Scroll w/two eight-point stars obverse & reverse, emerald green, pt. (minor interior stain) 935.00

GIX-11 - Scroll w/two eight-point stars obverse & reverse, golden amber, pt. 319.00

GIX-11 - Scroll w/two eight-point stars obverse & reverse, sapphire blue, pt. (pinpoint flakes) 1,760.00

GIX-12 - Scroll w/two seven-point stars above "Louisville" in straight line near base obverse & reverse, vertical medial rib, plain neck, bright medium olive green, ca. 1840-60, pt. 605.00

GIX-14 - Scroll w/two six-pointed stars above seven-pointed star obverse & reverse, vertical medial on edge, plain lip, pontil, aqua, pt. 82.50

GIX-20 - Scroll w/large oval ornament above large eight-point star above large six-petaled flower obverse & reverse, vertical medial rib, plain lip, pontil, medium green, pt. ...192.50

GIX-27 - Scroll w/two eight-point large stars in upper & mid-space w/slightly sunken rectangular panel near base obverse - a large nine-point star above large eight-point star reverse, vertical medial rib, plain neck, aqua, pt. 660.00

GIX-34 - Scroll w/large eight-point star above a large pearl over a large fleur-de-lis obverse & reverse, vertical medial rib on edge, tooled broad rounded collar w/lower bevel, iron pontil, aqua, ½ pt., rough lip, 5⅝" h. ((ILLUS. left) 55.00

Early Scroll Flasks

GIX-34a - Scroll w/large eight-point star above a medium-sized pearl over a large fleur-de-lis similar to obverse w/very small pearl, vertical medial rib, plain lip, aqua, ½ pt. 104.50

GIX-36 - Scroll w/medium-sized eight-point star above a large fleur-de-lis & a medium-sized pearl below obverse & reverse, vertical medial rib on edge, tooled broad collar w/lower bevel, iron pontil, aqua, ½ pt., 5⅞" h. (ILLUS. right) 93.50

GIX-39 - Scroll w/knobbed shoulder & nine-petaled flower at top & embossed initials "BP & B" near bottom obverse & reverse, vertical medial rib, plain lip, clear, ca. 1845-60, ½ pt. 495.00

GIX-43 - Scrolls w/large pearl below each curved line at base of inner frame, above a long oval finial containing a large pearl above "JR & SON" & two large pearls below scrolls at top of outer frame - fleur-de-lis w/two large pearls below top scroll left & right, vertical medial rib, plain lip, pontil mark, aqua, pt. ...495.00

GIX-45 - Scroll w/elaborate scroll decoration forming acanthus leaves w/four-petal flower at the top & diamond at center obverse & reverse, vertical medial ribs, bluish aqua, pt. 330.00

GIX-47 - Scroll w/four graduated finger-like ribs following the pear-shaped contour, large eight-point star in upper center & "R. Knowles & Co." (follow left rib), "Union Factory" (follow right rib) & "South Wheeling" in circle around "VA" - similar scroll w/large fleur-de-lis between inner ribs, plain lip, pontil mark, aqua, pt. 852.50

GX-2 - Stag standing above "Good" & "Game" at right of stag - Weeping willow tree, vertically ribbed edges, plain lip, aqua, ½ pt. 332.50

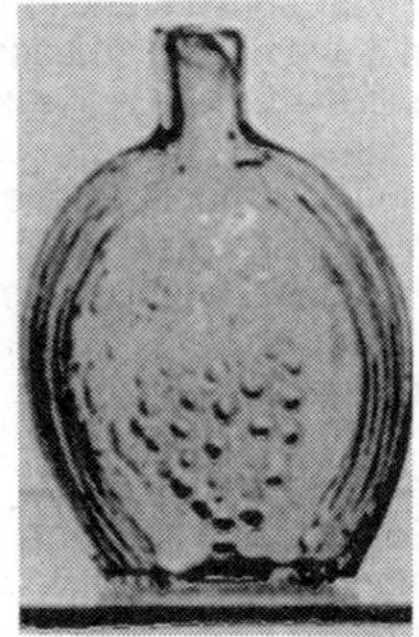

Sheaf of Rye Flask

GX-3 - Sheaf of Rye - Bunch of Grapes w/stem & three large leaves, vertically ribbed edges, sheared lip, pontil, aqua, ½ pt. (ILLUS.) 140.00

GX-4 - Cannon, "Genl Taylor Never Surrenders" inscribed in semicircle around cannon - vine & grape form a semicircular frame containing the inscription "A Little More Grape Capt Bragg," vertically ribbed w/heavy medial ribbing, plain lip, pontil, aqua, pt. 302.50

GX-4 - Cannon, "Genl Taylor Never Surrenders" inscribed in semicircle around cannon - vine & grape form a semicircular frame containing the inscription "A Little More Grape Capt Bragg," vertically ribbed w/heavy medial ribbing, plain lip, pontil, olive green, pt. 2,805.00

GX-8A - Sailboat (sloop) w/pennant on waves surrounded w/large oval frame - eight-point star w/three-pointed ornaments surrounded w/large oval frame, smooth edges, plain lip, pontil, aqua, ½ pt. 220.00

GX-14 - "Murdock" in semi-circle - "& - Cassel" in two straight lines, beneath rectangular band of heavy diagonal ribbing & below that a wider band of heavy vertical ribs extend to the base - "Zanesville" in semi-circle & "Ohio" in straight line, below ribbing similar to obverse, vertically ribbed edges w/narrow medial rib, plain lip, pontil, light bluish green, ca. 1830-37, pt. 1,760.00

GX-15 - "Summer" Tree - "Winter" Tree, plain lip, smooth edges, pontil, light olive green, pt. 324.50

GX-19 - Summer Tree - Winter Tree, plain lip, smooth edges, pontil, golden olive amber, qt. 770.00

GX-21 - Early American steamboat

w/paddle wheel & "The American" above & "System" below in the water - "Use Me But Do Not Abuse Me" in semicircle above sheaf of grain, herringbone ribbing on edges, plain lip, pontil mark, pale yellowish green, pt. 4,180.00

GXI-11 - Prospector w/tools & cane standing on oblong frame - American Eagle w/pennant above oval frame, aqua, pt. 70.00

GXI-22 - "For Pike's Peak" above prospector w/short staff & pack standing on oblong frame - American Eagle w/long pennant above oblong frame, aqua, pt. 82.50

GXI-50 - "For Pike's Peak" above prospector w/tools & cane - Hunter shooting stag, molded collar, plain edges, olive green, pt. 550.00

GXII-2 - Clasped hands, all inside shield, w/ "Waterford" above - American Eagle above oval frame, light yellow w/an olive tone, qt. 852.50

GXII-6 - Clasped hands above oval, all inside shield - American Eagle above oval frame, yellowish green, qt. 137.50

GXII-15 - Clasped hands above oval, all inside shield, w"Union" above - American Eagle above frame w/"E. Wormser C ("o" of Co just outside frame), flat collar, narrow beveled edge, aqua, qt. 110.00

GXII-31 - Clasped hands above oval, all inside shield - American Eagle above oval, golden amber, ½ pt. 154.00

GXII-37 - Clasped hands above oval all inside shield w/ "Union" above shield obverse & reverse, aqua, qt. ...55.00

GXII-38 - Clasped hands above oval, all inside shield w/ "Union" above - large cannon & American flag, smooth base, collared lip, aqua, qt. 52.50

GXII-40 - Clasped hands above oval w/ "FA & Co.," all inside shield w/"Union" above - Small cannon & large American flag, smooth base, aqua, pt. 90.00

GXII-43 - Clasped hands above square & compass above oval w/"Union" all inside shield - American Eagle, calabash, round collar, deep golden amber, qt. 242.00

GXIII-3 - Girl wearing a full-length skirt & hat & riding a bicycle - American Eagle w/head turned right above oval frame embossed w/"A & DH.C," smooth edges, collared lip, aqua, qt. 137.50

GXIII-8 - Sailor dancing a hornpipe on an eight-board hatch cover, above a long rectangular bar - banjo player sitting on a long bench, smooth edges, plain lip, pontil mark, aqua, ½ pt. 115.00

GXIII-13 - Soldier wearing a spiked helmet - rectangular frame enclosing "Balt. MD." below, smooth edges, plain lip, pontil mark, yellowish olive green, ca. 1860-80, pt. 825.00

GXIII-22 - Flora Temple obverse, plain reverse, smooth edges, small handle, ginger ale w/olive tone, ca. 1860-80, pt. 467.50

GXIII-35 - Sheaf of Grain w/rake & pitchfork crossed behind sheaf - "Westford Glass Co., Westford Conn," smooth sides, reddish amber, pt. 110.00

GXIII-35 - Sheaf of Grain w/rake & pitchfork crossed behind sheaf - "Westford Glass Co., Westford Conn," plain lip, smooth edges, yellowish amber, ca. 1860-72, pt. 132.00

GXIII-36 - Sheaf of Grain w/rake & pitchfork crossed behind sheaf & five-pointed star centered between rake & pitchfork handles - "Westford Glass Co., Westford Conn," plain lip, smooth edges, reddish amber, pt. ...143.00

GXIII-37 - Sheaf of Grain w/rake & pitchfork crossed behind sheaf - "Westford Glass Co., Westford Conn," smooth sides, deep yellowish olive, ca. 1857-60, ½ pt. 907.50

GXIII-37 - Sheaf of Grain w/rake & pitchfork crossed behind sheaf - "Westford Glass Co., Westford Conn," smooth sides, deep golden amber, ca. 1860-73, ½ pt. 121.00

GXIII-55 - Anchor w/fork-ended pennants inscribed "Isabella" & "Glass Works" on obverse - three-quarter view of glasshouse, plain lip, smooth edges, aqua, qt. 121.00

GXIII-64 - Anchor w/cable - plain reverse, smooth edges, round collar w/lower bevel, amber, qt. 55.00

GXIII-75 - Key at center, plain reverse, wide bevel each side to mold seam, narrow round collar, aqua, pt. 65.00

GXIV-1 - "Traveler's Companion" arched above & below star formed by a circle of eight small triangles - Sheaf of Grain w/rake & pitchfork crossed behind, applied flat collar, seamed base, deep golden amber, ca. 1860-72, qt. 132.00

GXIV-1 - "Traveler's Companion" arched above & below star formed by a circle of eight small triangles - Sheaf of Grain w/rake & pitchfork crossed behind, crude sloping collared mouth, smooth base, olive amber, qt.......................................104.50

GXIV-1 - "Traveler's Companion" arched above & below star formed by a circle of eight small triangles - Sheaf of Grain w/rake & pitchfork crossed behind, applied flat collar, seamed base, yellowish olive, ca. 1860-73, qt...............................143.00

GXIV-2 - "Traveler's Companion" arched above & below star formed by a circle of eight small triangles - Star like obverse & "Ravenna" above & "Glass Co" below, applied flat collar, brilliant golden amber, qt...852.00

GXIV-3 - "Traveler's Companion" arched above & below star formed by a circle of eight small triangles - Sheaf of Grain w/rake & pitchfork crossed behind, deep aqua, pt....................................110.00 to 160.00

GXIV-8 - "Traveler's" arched above & "Companion" arched below - plain reverse, plain lip, aqua, ½ pt...........165.00

GXV-7 - "Granite - Glass - Co." inscribed in three lines - "Stoddard - NH" inscribed in two lines, smooth edges, plain lip w/applied double collar, smooth base, golden amber, ca. 1860-70, pt...............................176.00

GXV-7 - "Granite - Glass - Co." inscribed in three lines - "Stoddard - NH" inscribed in two lines, smooth edges, plain lip w/applied double collar, smooth base, golden olive amber, pt...90.00

GXV-23 - "Union Glass Works" in an arc & - "New London - Ct" in straight lines below, plain reverse, round collar w/lower bevel, smooth base, light bluish green, ca. 1815-30, pt....473.00

Chestnut, forest green, free-blown, applied mouth, pontil, New England, ca. 1780-1830, 8⅝" h......................187.00

Chestnut, yellowish olive, collared mouth, pontil, New England, ca. 1780-1830, 5¾" h. 132.00

Chestnut, yellowish olive, collared mouth, pontil, New England, ca. 1780-1830, 9⅝" h. 154.00

Chestnut, ten-diamond, amber, short cylindrical neck w/flat flared rim, Zanesville, Ohio, 4¾" h. 3,410.00

Chestnut, ten-diamond, amber, short flaring cylindrical neck, fire polished pontil, 4⅝" h. 1,210.00

Chestnut, ten-diamond, light green, short flaring cylindrical neck, sheared lip, fire polished pontil, 4⅝" h. (ILLUS.) 3,410.00

Ten-Diamond Chestnut Flask

Chestnut, 16 swirled ribs, aqua, Mantua Ohio, 6" h. 165.00

Chestnut, 16 vertical ribs, aqua, 5⅝" h...137.50

Chestnut, 18 swirled ribs, pale green, Midwestern, 6½" h. 192.50

Ribbed Chestnut Flask

Chestnut, 18 vertical ribs, pale green, sheared lip, Midwestern, minor stains, wear & scratches, 7" h. (ILLUS.) 126.50

Chestnut, 24 broken swirled ribs, amber, applied lip, pontil, 7¼" h.......660.00

Chestnut, 24 swirled ribs, red amber, sheared lip, 4⅞" h. 130.00

Chestnut, 24 swirled ribs, aqua, Zanesville, Ohio, 7½" h. 550.00

Chestnut, 24 swirled ribs, golden honey amber, applied lip, pontil, 8" h...1,760.00

Chestnut, 24 vertical ribs, deep amber, sheared lip, Zanesville, Ohio, 4⅞" h. 247.50

Chestnut, 24 vertical ribs, dark amber brown, sheared & fire polished lip, pontil, 6½" h. 275.00

Chestnut, 24 vertical ribs, golden amber, Zanesville, Ohio, 4¾" h........275.00

Chestnut, checkered diamond design, clear, sheared lip, 6⅞" h. 1,100.00

Pitkin, 16 slightly swirled ribs, amber, half post neck w/sheared lip, pontil, 5½" h. 275.00

Pitkin, 24 vertical ribs, golden amber, sheared mouth, pontil, Midwestern, 1820-40, 5" h. 209.00

Pitkin, 24 vertical ribs, light olive brown, sheared mouth, pontil scar, Zanesville, 7⅞" h. 385.00

Pitkin, 30 broken ribs swirled to the left, yellowish olive green, slightly flared sheared mouth, pontil, 7¼" h. 357.50

Pitkin, 30 broken ribs swirled to the right, light bluish green, sheared neck, pontil, New England, ca. 1780-1830, 5⅛" h. (some light interior base stain, tiny mouth flake) 286.00

Pitkin, 32 broken ribs swirled to the right, bright medium green, sheared neck, pontil, ca. 1800-30, 6⅝" h. 467.50

Pitkin, 35 broken ribs swirled, pale green, sheared lip, pontil, Midwestern, ca. 1800-30, 7⅛" h. 330.00

Ribbed Pitkin Flask

Pitkin, 36 broken swirled ribs, amber, half post neck w/sheared & fire polished lip, tubular pontil, 6" h. (ILLUS.) 770.00

Pitkin, 36 broken swirled ribs, golden olive amber, half post neck w/sheared & fire polished lip, pontil, 5¾" h. 880.00

Pitkin, 36 broken ribs swirled to the left, yellowish olive, sheared lip, pontil, New England, ca. 1780-1830, 5⅛" h. 506.00

Pitkin, 36 broken ribs swirled to the left, yellowish olive green, sheared lip, 5¼" h. 440.00

Pitkin, 36 broken ribs swirled to the right, bright olive green, sheared lip, pontil, New England, ca. 1780-1830, 5¹⁄₁₆" h. 357.50

Pitkin, 36 broken ribs swirled to the right, yellow olive, sheared lip, pontil, New England, ca. 1780-1830, 5⅛" h. 385.00

Pitkin, 36 broken ribs swirled to the right, bright yellowish olive, sheared lip, pontil, New England, ca. 1780-1830, 6⅜" h. 341.00

Pitkin, 36 broken ribs swirled to the right, olive green, sheared lip, pontil, New England, ca. 1780-1830, 6⅝" h. 330.00

Pitkin, 36 broken swirled ribs, olive, half-post neck, ½ pt., 4⅞" h. 313.50

INKS

Bulbous Master Ink Bottle

Bulbous, master ink, clear glass nearly spherical body w/raised rings flanking the paper label w/"Paul's Safety Ink...," tall stick neck w/tooled rim & original pour spout, ca. 1880-1900, 8¼" h. (ILLUS.) 110.00

Cathedral, six Gothic arch panels, cobalt blue glass, embossed "Carter" around bottom edge, smooth base, qt., 9¾" h. 110.00

Cylindrical, medium sapphire blue, embossed "Harrison's Columbian Ink," applied flared mouth, 1¹³⁄₁₆" d., 4⅛" h. 577.50

Cylindrical, medium green glass, embossed "S. Fine, Blk Ink," inward rolled mouth & pontil scar, ca. 1830-50, 2⅞" h. 467.50

Cylindrical, master size, light to medium bluish green glass, rounded shoulder embossed "Hover - Phila.," cylindrical neck w/flared lip, 6" h. (professionally cleaned) 176.00

Domed octagonal w/offset neck, aqua glass, "Harrisons - Columbian - Ink," sheared & tooled lip, dug, ca. 1860-75, 1½" h. (light outside & inside content stain) 176.00

Domed w/central neck, medium amber glass, sheared & ground lip, ca. 1870-80, 1⅞" h. (tiny iridescent bruise on inside of lip) 132.00

Domed w/central neck, olive amber, mold blown glass, embossed "Bertinguiot," 2½" d., 2" h. 154.00

House-shaped, aqua glass, embossed "NE - Plus - Ultra - Fluid" on the roof, crudely sheared mouth, pontil, ca. 1860-80, 2⅝" h. 385.00

Octagonal, yellowish olive glass, tooled collared mouth, pontil scar, New England, ca. 1780-1830, 2⅜" d., 2¼" h. 242.00

Square w/central neck, clear glass, "Tinta - American," tooled & rolled lip, ca. 1840-55, 1¾" h. 253.00

Teakettle-type fountain inkwell w/neck extending up at angle from base, cobalt blue glass, ground mouth w/original lid, smooth base, 2" h. 550.00

Teakettle-type fountain inkwell w/neck extending up at angle from base, lime sherbet clambroth opaque glass, ground mouth, smooth base, 3½" d., 2¼" h. 715.00

Teakettle-type fountain inkwell w/neck extending up at angle from base of the tapering hexagonal body, ground lip, deep amethyst glass, ca. 1870-90, 2" h. (two flat chips on lip) 412.50

Teakettle-type fountain inkwell w/neck extending at angle from base of the tapering domical mushroom-form body w/six panels w/bull's-eyes divided by thin ribs, medium yellowish green glass, ground lip w/original metal neck ring, ca. 1870-90, 2¾" h. 935.00

Teakettle-type fountain inkwell w/angled neck extending from base of double-stepped domical octagonal body, attributed to Boston & Sandwich Glass Co., ca. 1870, opaque lime green glass, 2" h. 715.00

Rare Cut Teakettle-form Inkwell

Teakettle-type fountain inkwell w/neck extending up at angle from base of tapering hexagonal body, each panel cut & polished w/a diamond design, ground lip w/original brass lid, turquoise blue glass, ca. 1875-90, 2⅜" h. (ILLUS.) 715.00

Umbrella-type (8-panel cone shape), amber glass, sheared lip, open pontil, ca. 1830-50, 2½" h. 175.00

Umbrella-type (8-panel cone shape), medium amber glass, rolled lip, open pontil, ca. 1840-55, 2⅜" h. (few spots of haze) 132.00

Eight-Sided Umbrella Ink

Umbrella-type (8-panel cone shape), yellow w/amber tone glass, rolled lip, pontil-scarred base, ca. 1840-55, minor spotty stain inside, partially open discolored bubble on base edge, 2⅜" h. (ILLUS.) 825.00

Umbrella-type (8-panel cone shape), yellowish olive glass, rolled lip, open pontil, ca. 1830-50, 2⅜" h. 357.50

Twelve-Sided Umbrella Ink

Umbrella-type (12-panel cone shape), light green glass, rolled lip, open pontil, ca. 1840-55, few minor spots of inside haze, 2⅝" h. (ILLUS.) 242.00

MEDICINES

American (embossed bottle) Compound - Phila, rectangular w/paneled sides, aqua, applied mouth, open pontil, ca. 1845-55, 5⅞" h. (lightly cleaned) 93.50

Angell's (Dr. N.) Rheumatic Gun,

rectangular, deep aqua, applied mouth, pontiled base, ca. 1850-60, 7⅜" h. (light spotty interior haze) 302.50

Baker's (Dr.) - Pain Panacea, rectangular, pontil, aqua, 5" h. 100.00

Balsam of Honey, rounded, aqua, 3⅛" h.......................................55.00

Barnett (E.I.) Magic Cure Liniment, Easton, PA, rectangular, aqua, 6⅜" h.......................................26.00

Barrell's Indian Liniment - H.G.O. Cary, rectangular, aqua, 1 x 1⁹⁄₁₆ x 4¾"....................................70.00

Bears Oil, pictures walking bear above "Oil," flared lip, open pontil, rectangular, aqua, 2¾" h.................450.00

Bennett's (Dr.) Quick Cure - A.L. Scovill & Co, rectangular, rolled lip, aqua, 4⅝" h.......................................31.00

Dr. Blendigo's Celery Tonic

Blendigo's (Dr.) Celery Tonic - Peptonized - John Schweyer & Co., Sole Distributors, Chicago, Ill., rectangular w/paneled sides, amber, tooled lip, ca. 1880-1900, 9½" h. (ILLUS.) 255.00

Brinkerhoff's Health Restorative, New York, rectangular, pontil, emerald green, 7" h. 650.00

Brown's (F.) Ess of Jamaica Ginger Philada., oval, aqua, 5½" h. 25.00

Brown's Blood Cure - Philadelphia - M.B.W., U.S.A., yellowish green, 6⅛" h.......................................130.00

Brunet's Universal Remedy - Philada, cylindrical, aqua, applied mouth, open pontil, overall interior stain, ca. 1845-60, 8" h. (ILLUS.) 264.00

Brunet's (Dr.) Worm Syrup, rectangular w/beveled corners, aqua, applied mouth, open pontil, ca. 1840-55, 6¾" h. (some faint inside haze) 275.00

Brunet's Universal Remedy

Burton's (Dr. W.) Syrup - Philada, cylindrical, pale green, applied mouth, pontiled base, ca. 1845-60, 6¼" h. (light inside haze spots)........440.00

Callan's (Prof.) World Renowned Brazillian (sic) Gum," rectangular, orangish amber, 4¼" h.......................35.00

Cann's Kidney Cure, 1876, clear, 8½" h.......................................24.00

Celery Compound - Compound (over a stack of celery), square w/paneled sides, yellowish amber, tooled lip, ca. 1880-90, 10" h.............................88.00

Clarke's World Famed Blood Mixture, blue 65.00

Davis' (Perry) Pain Killer, rectangular, pontil, aqua, 8¼" h............................25.00

Davis Vegetable Pain Killer, rectangular, aqua, 4⅝" h...................35.00

Dewitts Colic & Cholera Cure - E. C. Dewitt & Co., Chicago, U.S.A., aqua, paper label, 4⅞" h....................30.00

Dewitts (Dr.) Eclectic Cure, W J Parker & Co, Baltimore, MD, rectangular, 5⅝" h.............................26.00

Fahrney's (Dr.) Health Restorer, Hagerstown, MD., amber, 7⅛" h........17.50

Fenner's (Dr. M.M.) Kidney & Backache Cure, oval, amber, 90% label, 10⅜" h. 68.00

Fenner's (Dr. M.M.) Peoples Remedies - Fredonia, N.Y. - U.S.A. 1872-1891, rectangular, blown in mold, aqua, 1¼ x 2¼ x 7¾" 32.00

Foley's Kidney & Bladder Cure - Foley & Co. - Chicago, U.S.A., rectangular, amber, paper label, 9½" h........38.00

Folger's Olosaonian - (Dr Robt. B. - New-York, rectangular w/deeply beveled corners, pontil, aqua, 1½ x 2½ x 7¾" 55.00

Freeman's (Dr. Clarkson) Indian Specific, square, aqua, 5" h. 125.00

Gesteria (Dr. J.), Regulator Gesteria, amber, 5" h. 20.00

Gould (L.A.), Portland, ME., paper label w/"White Clover Cream for Chapped Hands, Sunburn, etc...," rectangular, clear, 4½" h. 16.00

Grove's (Dr.) Anodyne for Infants, Philada., rectangular, aqua, 5½" h. (w/paper label) 22.00

Hagan's Magnolia Balm, rectangular, milk white, 5" h. 9.00

Hall's Balsam for the Lungs, John F. Henry & Co., New York, rectangular, aqua, 7¾" h. 25.00

Hall's Catarrh Cure, round, aqua, 1⅝" d., 4⅝" h. 15.00

Hanford's (Dr.) Celery Cure or Nerve Food Cures Rheumatism - Neuralgia - Insomnia - & C & C, rectangular w/beveled corners, rolled lip, pontil, aqua, 1¾ x 2½", 7⅝" h. 45.00

Healy & Bigelow's Kickapoo Cough Syrup, cylindrical, aqua, 1¼" d., 6¼" h. 20.00

Hills (embossed H w/arrow) Trade Mark Dys Pep Cu, Cures Chronic Dyspepsia, Indiana Drug Specialty Co., St. Louis & Indianapolis, rectangular w/fluted corners, amber, 8⅛" h. 110.00

Hobensack's Medicated Worm Syrup, Philada., rectangular w/indented panels, aqua, 4½" h. 39.00

Hollis' (Thomas) Balm of America, round, aqua, 5" h. 18.00

Hooker's (Dr.) Cough and Croup Syrup, round, aqua, 5⅝" h. 89.00

Hough's (Dr.) Anti Scrofula Syrup, rectangular, aqua, applied mouth, open pontil, ca. 1845-60, 9½" h. (light inside stain, small stress fissure in neck) 176.00

Hunter's (H.C.) Palm Lotion, Marlboro, Mass., paper label reading "Chapped Hands, Sunburn, Chafing & ...," rectangular, amber, 5¼" h. 38.00

Hyatt's - Infallible - Life Balsam, N.Y., rectangular w/beveled corners, smooth base, deep aqua, 9½" h. (minor lip bruise) 140.00

James' (Dr.) Cherry Tar Syrup, Pittsburgh, Penna, U.S.A., aqua, 5¾" h. 12.50

James (Dr. H.) Cannabis Indica, Crabbock & Co., Proprietors, No. 1032 Pace St. Phila. Pa., cylindrical, aqua, applied lip, 7¾" h. 302.50

Kauffman's (Dr. J.) Angeline Internal Rheumatism Cure, Hamilton, Ohio, deep amethyst, 7⅝" h. 25.00

Kilmer's (Dr.) Female Remedy, Binghamton, N.Y., rectangular, aqua, w/paper label & contents, 8⅜" h. 300.00

Kilmer's (Dr.) Indian Cough Remedy Consumption Oil, Binghamton, N.Y. U.S.A., rectangular, aqua, 5½" h. 25.00

Kilmer's (Dr.) Ocean Weed Heart Remedy, The Blood Specific, rectangular, embossed heart, aqua, 8½" h. 175.00

Kilmer's (Dr.) Swamp-Root Kidney Cure, Binghamton, N.Y., Sample Bottle, cylindrical, aqua, 3⅛" h. 20.00

Kilmer's (Dr.) Swamp-Root Kidney, Liver & Bladder Cure, Binghamton, N.Y., Sample Bottle, round, 3¼" h. 12.00

Kilmer's (Dr.) Swamp-Root Kidney, Liver & Bladder Cure, London, E.C., rectangular w/beveled corners, aqua, 7" h. 25.00

Kilmer's (Dr.) Swamp-Root Kidney, Liver & Bladder Cure, rectangular, amethyst, 7" h. 45.00

K.K. Cures Bright's Disease and Cystitis, rectangular, aqua, 7½" h. 25.00

Lindsey's - Blood + Searcher - Hollidaysburg (Pennsylvania), rectangular, aqua, qt. 89.00

Lorman's (Prof.) Indian Oil Philada., PA., rectangular, aqua, 5¼" h. 21.00

Low's (Prof.) Magnetic Liniment, Philada, Pa., rectangular, aqua, 6⅛" h. 18.00

McLean's (Dr. J.H.) Strengthening Cordial & Blood Purifier, oval, aqua, 8" h. 45.00

Miles' (Dr.) Restorative Nervine, aqua, 8½" h. 15.00

Dr. Myers Bilious King

Myers (Dr.) Bilious King - Smith Myers & Co., square w/beveled corners, amber, applied mouth, ca. 1870-80, 9" h. (ILLUS.) 93.50

National Remedy Company, New York, rectangular, amber, w/paper label, 7⅝" h. 25.00

Pierce's (Dr.) Anuric Tablets for Kidneys and Backache, cylindrical, aqua, 3½" h. 15.00

Pierce's (Dr.) Golden Medical Discovery - R.V. Pierce, M.D. - Buffalo, N.Y., rectangular, amber, 8⅜" h. 40.00

Polar Star Cough Cure, embossed star, aqua 25.00

Ransom's Hive Syrup & Tolu, square, aqua, 3½" h. 15.00

Rheumatic Syrup

Rheumatic (embossed tree) Trade Mark Syrup 1882 - R.S. Co., Rochester, N.Y., rectangular w/paneled sides, medium amber, slightly tilted applied mouth, ca. 1870-80, 9¾" h. (ILLUS.) 176.00

Richter (F.A.) & Co., New York (embossed anchor) Pain-Expeller, Reg. U.S. Patt. Off. For Rheumatism, Gout, Neuralgia, Colds, etc., rectangular w/beveled corners, aqua, 4⅞" h. 12.50

Rowand's - Tonic Mixture - Vegetable - Febrifuge - Philad, six-sided, open pontil, aqua, 5¾" h. ....140.00 to 180.00

Schrage's Rheumatic Cure, Swanson Rheumatic Cure Company, Chicago, aqua....................................39.00

Seabury's Cough Balsam, open pontil, aqua, 1¼" d., 4¾" h...40.00 to 50.00

Simonds Pain Cure, rectangular, aqua, 4¾" h. 15.00

Sparks Perfect Health (embossed man) for Kidney & Liver Diseases, amber, 9⅜" h. 50.00

Swaim's Vermifuge - Fever - Dysentery - Cholera Morbus - Dyspepsia, paneled sides, aqua, thin flared lip, open pontil, ca. 1835-45, 4¼" h. 247.50

Sykes' (Dr.) Sure Cure For Catarrh, medium apple green, 6⅝" h. 65.00

Thatcher's (Dr.) Liver & Blood Syrup, Chattanooga, Tenn., amber, sample size, 3" h. 28.00

Thatcher's (Dr.) Liver & Blood Syrup, Chattanooga, Tenn., amber, 8⅜" h....45.00

Thomson's - Compound - Syrup of Tar for Consumption - Philada, rectangular w/paneled sides, aqua, applied mouth, open pontil, ca. 1840-55, 5¾" h. 60.50

Turlington's (Robt.) Balsam of Life, paneled pear-shape, flared lip, open pontil, aqua, England, 2⅝" h. 93.50

(Warner's) Log Cabin - Extract, Rochester, NY., three indented panels on front, flat back, dark yellow amber, 8⅛" h. 95.00

Warner's Safe Cure, London, emerald green, ½ pt., 7½" h. 80.00

Warner's Safe Cure, Melbourne, w/safe, oval tooled blob lip, smooth base, amber, 1880-90, 7" h. 85.00

Warner's Safe Cure, Melbourne, w/safe, reddish amber, 9½" h. 45.00

Warner's Safe Cure (safe) Pressburg, oval, olive green, 9½" h. 1,925.00

Warner's Safe Diabetes Cure

Warner's Safe Diabetes Cure - Pressburg, w/safe, amber, applied mouth, tiny lip ding, 9½" h. (ILLUS.) 2,640.00

Warner's Safe Kidney & Liver Cure, Rochester, N.Y., w/reversed (or "left-handed") picture of safe, oval, amber, 9¾" h. 80.00

Warner's Safe Nervine, Frankfurt A/M, w/safe, oval, amber, applied mouth, 9¼" h. 1,375.00

Warner's Safe Rheumatic Cure Rochester, NY., U.S.A., w/safe, oval, light yellow, 9½" h. (spotty haze) 40.00

Wishart's (L.Q.C.) - Pine Tree Tar Cordial Phila. - (embossed pine tree) Patent 1859, square w/beveled corners, emerald green, 8" h. 242.00

Wishart's Pine Tree Tar Cordial

Wishart's (L.Q.C.) - Pine Tree Tar Cordial Phila. - (embossed pine tree) Patent 1859, square w/beveled corners, medium bluish green, 8" h. (ILLUS.) 100.00

Wishart's (L.Q.C.) - Pine Tree Tar Cordial Phila. - (embossed pine tree) Patent 1859, square w/beveled corners, yellowish green, 8" h. 121.00

Wishart's (L.Q.C.) Pine Tree Tar Cordial Phila. - Trade (embossed pine tree) Mark, square w/beveled corners, sapphire blue, tooled lip, 9¾" h. (some light scratching on back panel) 797.50

Wistar's (Dr.) - Balsam of - Wild Cherry - John D. Park - Cincinnati, Ohio, octagonal, deep aqua, 6½" h. 30.00

Wynkoop's Katharismic Sarsaparilla

Wynkoop's Katharismic Sarsaparilla - New York, rectangular, medium sapphire blue, applied mouth, iron pontil, lightly cleaned, ca. 1845-60, 10" h. (ILLUS.) 7,150.00

Zollickoffer's Anti Rheumatic Cordial - Philada, rectangular w/paneled sides, yellowish olive amber, applied mouth, open pontil, ca. 1840-50, 6⅜" h. 1,595.00

MILK

Individual Cream-Size Bottles

Amber, embossed "Golden Royal," ½" gal. 8.50

Brilliant grass green, embossed "Return to - H.B. Day," tapering cylindrical-form w/tooled square collared mouth, smooth base, 10¼" h. 198.00

Clear, individual cream-size, enameled "Blanding's - Greenville, Mich. (ILLUS. left) 21.00

Clear, individual cream-size, enameled "Country Club Dairy" (ILLUS. right) 24.00

McDonald's & Suncrest Bottles

Clear, individual cream-size, enameled "McDonald's White House Dairy" (ILLUS. left) 21.00

Clear, individual cream-size, enameled "Suncrest Farms and Mowrer's, Inc." (ILLUS. right) 26.00

Clear, "Maui - Haleakala Dairy," qt. 30.00

Clear, "Oahu - Moanaloa Dairy," 12 oz. 12.00

Clear, embossed "Registered Strictly Pure Milk - Bottled by the Empire State Dairy Company (state seal) - 502 & 506 Broadway, Brooklyn - Trade Mark," tooled lip, smooth base, ca. 1900-20, qt., 9" h. 66.00

Robinson & Woolworth Bottle

Clear, embossed "Robinson & Woolworth - 1667 B'way, N.Y. - This Bottle to be Washed and Returned Not to be Bought or Sold," base w/"Whiteman Maker - 144 Chamber St., New York," tooled lip w/original metal lid stamped "Jan. 5.1875, Patd. April 3.1889," wire closure, smooth base, qt., 8½" h. (ILLUS.)......99.00

Clear, embossed "F.K. Wards - Milk Preserving Jar - Sealed Stopper - Patents 1890 & 1892 - When Empty Return to - Ward's Alderney Milk P & C Association - Washington, D.C. - Wash Clean When Empty," embossed on smooth base "This Jar Has Been Stolen If Offered For Sale" & on lip "Refuse A Broken Seal" & cow's head, w/original glass lid & wire bail, ca. 1890-95, pt. 1,155.00

Clear, embossed "Woodrow Wilson Dairy, Palmyria, WI.," pt. 10.00

Clear, "Your Dairy New London, WI," red paint, qt. 10.00

MINERAL WATERS

Caladonia (sic) Spring, Wheelock, Vt., Saratoga-type, yellowish amber, qt., 9½" h. 660.00

Congress & Empire Spring Co., Hotchkiss' Sons, "C," New York, Saratoga, N.Y., Congress Water, smooth base, applied mouth, emerald green, ca. 1865-75, pt., 7¾" h. (ILLUS.) 170.00

Congress & Empire Spring Co.

Congress & Empire Spring Co., "C," Saratoga, N.Y., Congress Water, smooth base, applied mouth, deep emerald green, ca. 1865-75, pt. 7⅝" h. (dug, fair amount of scratching & scuffing on the outside) 121.00

Geyser Spring. Saratoga Springs. State of New York. - "The Saratoga" Spouting Spring, smooth base, applied mouth, bluish aqua, ca. 1865-75, qt., 9⅜" h. 99.00

Highrock Congress Spring - motif of rock - C & W, Saratoga, N.Y., smooth base, applied mouth, teal blue, ca. 1850-70, pt., 7⅝" h. 253.00

Hutchinson & Co., Celebrated Mineral Water, Chicago, iron pontil, applied mouth, medium cobalt blue w/tiny seed bubbles, ca. 1845-55, 7¼" h. 253.00

Knowlton (D.A.), Saratoga, N.Y., smooth base, applied mouth, deep olive amber, ca. 1860-70, qt. 110.00

John Ryan Excelsior Mineral Water

Meincke & Ebberwein, 1882, Savannah, Geo., Mineral "M&E," Water, smooth base, applied mouth, electric cobalt blue, ca. 1865-75, 7⅞" h. (lightly cleaned) 66.00

Ryan (John) Excelsior Mineral Water, Savannah, Ga., 1859, Union Glass Works, Phila. This bottle is never sold, smooth base, applied mouth, cobalt blue, lightly cleaned, ca. 1865-75, 7⅛" h. (ILLUS. bottom of previous page) 121.00

Weston (G.W.) & Co., Saratoga, N.Y., pontil mark, applied mouth, olive green, ca. 1855-65, qt., 9⅝" h. 187.00

NURSING

Blown Nursing Bottle

Aqua, mold-blown glass w/eighteen swirled ribs, Midwestern, 6½" l...........66.00

Aqua, mold-blown glass w/twelve vertical ribs, flattened ovoid shape tapering at base, slightly flared lip, Midwestern, 8¼" l. 60.50

Aqua, pressed glass, "Burr - Boston," embossed medallion..........................82.50

Clear, mold-blown glass, thick & heavy flask-form, pontil mark, sheared lip, 6¾" h. 55.00

Clear, pressed glass, "Corning - Pyrex," 4 oz., w/original wrapper 10.00

Clear, pressed glass, tilted neck, embossed "Empire," ca. 1910..........12.00

Clear, pressed glass, embosssed "Rexall" & w/a stork..........................15.00

Deep cobalt blue, mold-blown glass, flask-form, pontil mark, sheared lip, America, ca. 1830-50, 7¼" h. (ILLUS.) 231.00

Greenish aqua, mold-blown glass, flask-form, diamond pattern, pontil mark, sheared lip, America, ca. 1830-50, 6½" h. 88.00

Pale green, mold-blown glass w/expanded ogival pattern, flattened ovoid shape tapering at base, slightly flared lip, Midwestern, 6¼" l. 27.50

Pale green, mold-blown glass w/twenty vertical ribs, flattened ovoid shape tapering at base, slightly flared lip, Midwestern, 7" l. 192.50

Yellowish green w/black amber neck & shoulder, mold-blown glass, flattened ovoid shape tapering at base, slightly flared lip, sheared & fire polished lip, 7⅛" l. 225.50

PICKLE BOTTLES & JARS

Cathedral Pickle with Lattice Windows

Aqua, four-sided, cathedral-type w/Gothic arch windows, rolled lip, smooth base, Willington Glass Works, West Willington, Connecticut, ca. 1860-72, 11⅞" h. (light interior haze) 247.50

Aqua, four-sided, cathedral-type w/Gothic arch windows w/diamond lattice, smooth base, rolled lip, America, ca. 1865-75, small open bubble on one corner at base, 13¾" h. (ILLUS.) 203.50

Barrel-Shaped Pickle Jar

Bright yellow green, barrel-shaped w/embossed rows of rings at top & base, pontil mark, tooled lip, America, ca. 1860-70, 9½" h. (ILLUS.) 148.50
Clear, cathedral-type, 13" h. 165.00
Deep aqua, four-sided, cathedral-type w/Gothic arch windows w/diamond lattice, smooth base, rolled lip, America, ca. 1865-75, 11" h. (overall milky stain inside) 198.00
Deep aqua, four-sided, cathedral-type w/Gothic arch windows w/diamond lattice, smooth base, rolled lip, America, ca. 1865-75, 13¾" h. 275.00

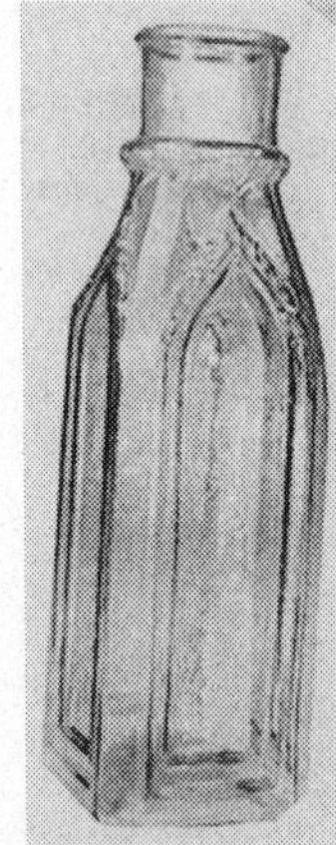

Large Cathedral Pickle Jar

Greenish aqua, four-sided, cathedral-type w/Gothic arch windows, smooth base, rolled lip, America, ca. 1865-75, 8¾" h. (ILLUS.) 143.00
Light green, four-sided, cathedral-type w/Gothic arch windows, iron pontil, rolled lip, America, ca. 1855-65, 11½" h. 297.00
Medium green, four-sided, cathedral-type w/Gothic arch windows, rolled collared mouth, pontil scar, Willington Glass Works, West Willington, Connecticut, ca. 1840-60, 13⅝" h. 2,310.00

POISONS

Clear, blown half post w/hobnails, applied flared lip, 4¾" h. (ILLUS. top next column) 27.50
Clear, flattened flask shape w/overall small square raised knobs, sheared mouth, pontil, pint, ca. 1850............231.00
Cobalt blue, six-sided, embossed "POISON" & ribbed design, 3½" h. 28.00
Cobalt blue, six-sided, embossed "POISON" & ribbed design, 5½" h. 29.00

Poison Bottle with Hobnails

Cobalt blue, rectangular, embossed "POISON" & ribbed design, 6" h. 29.00
Green, six-sided, embossed "POISON" & ribbed design, 3¼" h. 21.00
Green, six-sided, embossed "POISON" & ribbed design, 6" h. 24.00

WHISKEY & OTHER SPIRITS

Black Label Beer

Beer, "American Brewing Co., Bennett, PA," embossed w/eagle & flags, blob top, light amber, pt...........25.00
Beer, "Black Label Beer," slightly rounded cylindrical form w/tapering neck, paper label, w/screw cap, amber, 18" h. (ILLUS.) 5.50
Beer, "Bunker Hill Lager, Charlestown, Mass.," w/lightning stopper, golden amber, pt. 20.00
Beer, "Golden Gate Bottling Works, San Francisco," embossed bear holding a glass, blob top, reddish amber, ½ pt.......................................240.00
Beer, "Gold Medal, C. Maurer," applied lip, golden amber, ½ pt.........85.00

Heineken Lager Beer

Beer, "Heineken Lager Beer," green w/paper labels, 18" h. (ILLUS.) 5.50

Beer, "Hinckel Brewing, Albany, Manchester, Boston" embossed in script, smoky golden amber, pt. 25.00

Beer, "Kerns (E.L.)," w/embossed moose head, greenish aqua, pt. 25.00

Beer, D. Lagrange, Moravia, NY.," whittled neck, lightning stopper, honey amber, pt. 20.00

Beer, "Norfolk Brewing Co., Boston," amber, pt. 25.00

Beer, "Rainier Beer, Seattle," blob top, light amber, miniature bottle 80.00

Beer, "Seitz Bros., Easton PA," embossed w/large "S" on back, blob top, light amber, pt. 20.00

Bourbon, "Old Crow Bourbon Rawlins Wyoming Robt. Freedman," flask-shape, amber, pt. 300.00

Bourbon, "Phoenix Old Bourbon, Naber, Alfs and Brune, San Francisco, Sole Proprts," & an embossed eagle, orangish amber, ½ pt. 200.00

Case gin, "Wistar's Club House," iron pontil, single collared lip, red puce, qt. 750.00

Case gin, blown half post, polychrome floral enameling, light olive green, pewter lip & cap, 6⅝" h. (minor stain)..495.00

Case gin, dip-molded, square tapered-form, mushroom mouth, pontil scar, yellowish olive, ca. 1780-1830, 9½" h. 104.50

Case gin, dip-molded, tapering square-form, w/rolled & flared mouth, pontil, deep yellow olive, 5¼" d., 16⅞" h......770.00

Gin, "London Jockey Club House Gin," embossed horse & jockey, square w/beveled corners, sloping collared mouth, smooth base, bright green, 9" h. 275.00

Gin, "Olive Tree," tapered square-form, crude sloping collared mouth, smooth base, Netherlands, olive green, ca. 1860-80, 9¾" h. 242.00

Schnapps, "Udolpho Wolfe's," yellowish amber 35.00

Schnapps, "Udolpho Wolfe's - Aromatic - Schnapps - Schiedam," Stoddard-type, open pontil, crude, sandy amber, qt. 65.00

Spirits, applied seal w/"David Provost 1723," squat onion-form, free blown, applied collar, olive green, 7⅜" h. 1,925.00

Spirits, demijohn,"Saml Bowne 1759" on applied seal, pontil, applied lip, olive green, 8¾" h. (rough lip, minor wear & scratches)...880.00

Spirits, free-blown, bladder-shaped, "Thomas Morley 1730" on applied seal, green...................................1,500.00

Globular Spirits Bottles

Spirits, globular, tall neck, twenty-four swirled ribs, pontil mark, applied lip, Zanesville, Ohio, amber, 7¼" h. (ILLUS. left)..660.00

Spirits, globular, tall neck, twenty-four swirled ribs, pontil mark, applied lip, Zanesville, Ohio, golden honey amber, 8" h. (ILLUS. right) 1,760.00

Spirits, pumpkin seed, marked "Union Pacific Tea Company 1873" & embossed w/two men on an elephant, clear, ½ pt. 135.00

Spirits, rectangular w/beveled corners, ground mouth w/pewter collar & cap, pontil scar, clear ground decorated w/red, blue, yellow & white enameled bird & florals, 5½" h. 313.50

Spirits, squat, cylindrical-form w/sheared mouth w/string rim, free-blown, pontil scar, olive green, Netherlands, 1700-30, 4½" d., 5⅝" h...385.00

Spirits, squat onion-form, free-blown, sheared mouth w/string rim, pontil scar, dark yellowish olive, England, ca. 1700-30, 6" d., 6" h. 418.00

Spirits, squat onion-form, free-blown,

tooled mouth w/an applied wide neck ring, pontil scar, yellowish olive, Netherlands, 1700-30, 5½" d., 7⅛" h. 2,530.00

Whiskey, "Ambrosial" on applied seal, flattened chestnut-form w/applied mouth w/ring, pontil scar, golden amber, 9" h. (interior stain spots throughout) 132.00

Whiskey, "E.G. Booz's Old Cabin Whiskey," cabin-shaped, golden amber, 7⅞" h. 440.00

Whiskey, "Chapin & Gore Chicago Sour Mash 1867," barrel-shaped, inside threaded neck, amber (no stopper) 125.00

Whiskey, "Chestnut Grove," chestnut flask-shaped w/applied handle, open pontil, dark amber 170.00

Whiskey, "Chestnut Grove Whiskey," flattened globular-form, pontil, applied mouth ring & handle, golden amber, 8⅞" h. 143.00

Whiskey, "Cyrus Eaton Denver - One Quart You Bet," blob top, light amber, qt. 750.00

Whiskey, Goodman (Geo.) Wholesale, Paducah, KY, embossed w/sign of the Red Rock, clear, ½ gal. 90.00

Whiskey, Pierce (S.S.) Co., Est., 1831, Inc. 1891, Boston, embossed shield w/lion & eagle logo, clear, ½ gal. 45.00

Whiskey, mold-blown, globular form, 14 swirled ribs, light blue, Zanesville, Ohio, 8¼" h. 605.00

Whiskey, mold-blown, globular form, 16 swirled ribs, aqua, Midwestern, 7⅛" h. 148.50

Whiskey, mold-blown, globular form, 24 melon ribs, aqua, Zanesville, Ohio, 7½" h. 192.50

Whiskey, mold-blown, globular form, 24 swirled ribs, amber, Zanesville, Ohio, 7¼" h. 660.00

Whiskey, mold-blown, globular form, 24 swirled ribs, cornflower blue, Zanesville, Ohio, 8¼" h. 5,170.00

Whiskey, mold-blown, globular form, 24 swirled ribs, golden honey amber, Zanesville, Ohio, 8" h. 1,760.00

(End of Bottles Section)

BOXES

Band box, wallpaper-covered, oval, "Drapery Swag with Three Roses" patt., America, ca. 1830, 10½" h. $495.00

Band box, wallpaper-covered, oval, brick house & farmyard printed in red & brown on a blue ground, America, ca. 1830, 11" h. (minor imperfections) 880.00

Band box, wallpaper-covered cardboard, oval, covered w/a glazed wallpaper featuring "The Clayton's Ascent" showing a balloon ascension above a village, in tones of bright blue, green, pink & white, attributed to Putnam & Roff, Hartford, Connecticut, ca. 1830, 12¾ x 17", 11" h. 3,220.00

Band box, wallpaper-covered, oval, the paper w/a large continuous swag & tassel pattern in color, lined w/copies of the "Patriot Marine Journal" dated 1833 & 1834, 19½" l., 12" h. 259.00

Rare Band Box with Railway Scene

Band box, wallpaper-covered, oval, paper printed w/an early railroad scene entitled "B. & O. Carroll of Carroll," printed in blue, yellow & red, lined w/a newspaper dated "Newburyport June 7, 1833," some water stains & stitch repairs, 16" l., 13½" h. (ILLUS.) 11,000.00

Band box, printed wallpaper on bentwood, original paper w/florals framing a bowl of fruit & foliage in white, brown, black & faded red on a blue ground, interior lined w/an 1835 newspaper & printed label reading "Warranted Nailed Band-Boxes - Made by Hannah Davis, Jaffrey, N.H.," 20" l. (some wear, edge damage & lid banding damaged) 687.50

Bible box, William & Mary style, walnut, molded rectangular top above a conforming dovetailed case, the top opening to reveal a single compartment, the front inlaid w/line-and-berry design emanating from a central basket, inlaid w/the initials "SR," on flared, flattened ball-turned feet, Chester County, Pennsylvania, 18th c., 12½ x 18", 8¾" h....................................4,370.00

Brass, copper & glass box, the hinged rectangular boxwood box decorated w/hammered brass on the exterior w/stylized floral designs, inset w/glass cabochons in pink, green, turquoise, opalescent & cobalt blue, designed by Alfred Daguet, manufactured for Samuel Bing, signed "ALF. DAGUET, '02" & "LES CUIVRES S. BING," dated 1902, 4½ x 5½", 3⅜" h..........................1,150.00

Early Decorated Bride's Box

Bride's box, bentwood oval w/fitted lid, the lid painted w/the figures of a bride & groom below a sunfface, flowers & leafage below & surrounded by an inscription in ornamental German script, the sides boldly painted w/orange, yellow & green flowers & geometric designs, probably Europe, early 19th c., 9 x 12", 6" h. (ILLUS.) 1,150.00

Bride's box, bentwood oval w/original stylized floral decoration in red, green, yellow & white on a brown & black ground, 17½" l. (bottom board is a well-executed replacement, minor wear & edge damage) 467.50

Bride's box, painted bentwood, the flat fitted lid decorated w/a full-length portrait of a lady, the sides w/trailing tulips, Northern Europe, early 19th c., 11 x 18", 6½" h..................489.00

Candle box, pine, dovetailed construction, rectangular w/siding lid, old mellow refinishing, 10" l. 137.50

Candle box, painted & decorated pine, rectangular w/a sliding lid, the top, front, back & sides decorated w/freely drawn stylized tulips in white, red, yellow & green, on a varnished ground, southeastern Pennsylvania, late 18th c., 8 x 14", 6" h...1,495.00

Candle box, painted pine, rectangular w/canted sides, old red paint, 15" l. (minor crack in lid) 330.00

Document box, painted & decorated basswood, domed hinged lid opening to a deep well incorporating a secret drawer, the top painted w/a spread-winged American eagle grasping a banner in its beak, arrows in its talons w/the United States shield on its breast, the corners w/stylized quarter-fan devices, the front boldly painted in tones of red, green & yellow centering the initials "AB," the sides w/stylized flowerheads in red & yellow on a green ground outlined w/stylized spirals, probably Albany, New York, early 19th c., 6¾ x 12", 6¼" h...29,900.00

Document box, mahogany, Chippendale style, rectangular top lifting above a well, dovetailed sides on a molded base w/ogee bracket feet, Massachusetts, old finish, ca. 1790, 11 x 20", 10½" h.................3,575.00

Glass box, round w/lift-off cover, black amethyst decorated overall w/sanded white enamel leaves & small red enameled strawberries & blossoms, 3⅜" d., 2⅛" h. 75.00

Glass box, round w/lift-off cover, emerald green decorated overall w/dainty white & pink daisy-like flowers & green & brown leaves, 2¾" d., 2⅝" h. 55.00

Glass box, round w/metal-hinged cover, clear frosted & slight mother-of-pearl iridescence, fine acid-cut-back squiggly design overall, decorated w/enameled lavender & yellow flowers & green leaves on cover, 6⅝" d., 3½" h.........................225.00

Glass box, round w/metal-hinged cover & rim mounts, amber decorated w/coral fuchsias & green leaves on the cover, blue & pink daisies w/white accents & green leaves
around the sides, 4" d., 3⅝" h. 165.00

Glass box, round w/metal-hinged cover, ruby red, top w/white enameled bird swimming in water, rushes around bird, gold edge band, sides covered w/lacy gold flowers, leaves & scrolls, on brass feet, 3⅜" d., 3¾" h. 165.00

Knife boxes. brass-mounted satinwood, urn-form, each surmounted by a pointed ball finial above a domed lid sliding on a wooden rod & opening to pierced cutlery supports, the tapered sides continuing to a turned standard & square plinth base, on block feet, Regency period, England, first quarter 19th c., 26" h., pr. 3,450.00

Knife boxes, inlaid mahogany, each w/rectangular top & shaped slant-lid w/oval inlay centering a basket of flowers opening to an interior inlaid w/stringing & a compass star & fitted for cutlery, over a conforming base w/a shield-shaped escutcheon, America, 1790-1810, 9¼" w., 11½" deep, 15" h., pr. 7,700.00

Lace maker's box, burl walnut, rectangular w/low sides, brass carrying handles & a satinwood interior, England, second half 19th c., 17 x 22½" 1,840.00

Leather-covered box, rectangular, red & black leather w/decoration of hearts & other geometric devices worked in brass studs, brass bail handle & iron & brass lock w/hasp, interior lined w/marbleized paper w/label "Robert Burr, Trunks, Boston," 8" l. 192.50

Painted & decorated box, poplar, the rectangular hinged lid decorated w/yellow-painted border & large central abstracted yellow & red floral design flanked by four smaller floral designs at each corner on a black ground, opening to a single conforming compartment, the front also decorated w/yellow-painted border & yellow- & red-painted central fan flower, probably mid-Atlantic, 19th c., 5¼ x 8¾", 5¼" h. 6,900.00

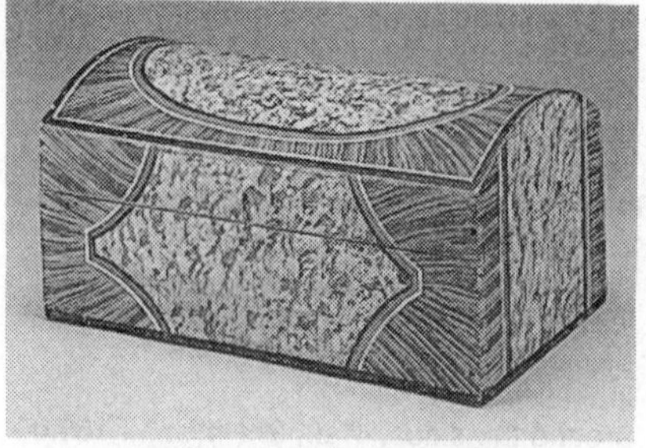

Painted & Decorated Box

Painted & decorated box, rectangular w/hinged domed lid opening to a compartment, inscribed on the interior of the lid, the exterior decorated w/grain-painted inlays of faux tiger stripe maple & faux bird's-eye maple, mid-19th c., 8¼ x 13⅛", 6½" h. (ILLUS.) 3,080.00

Pantry box, cov., painted round bentwood, fitted lid painted overall w/vinegar graining to simulate bird's-eye maple w/yellow-brown dots on a salmon-pink ground, New England, ca. 1830, 8¼" d., 5¼" h.................2,300.00

Pill box, gold (14k red) & gems, circular, plain polished body, the lid set w/a leaf containing a diamond, ruby & sapphire...............................287.00

Pipe box, birch, scroll-cut sides & backplate pierced for hanging, single fan-carved small drawer w/brass pull below, 4½ x 5¼", 19¼" h..3,163.00

Silver box, oval w/stepped base, hinged cover, the finial formed as two addorsed swans w/filigree wings, the interior fitted w/a silk lining, numbered "160," Georg Jensen Silversmithy, Copenhagen, Denmark, 1919 - ca. 1927, 9⅞" l. 6,325.00

Sweet gum box, decorated soft wood, book-shaped, decorated w/chip-caving, inlay & red & black painted designs w/old varnish, 5" l. 148.50

Sweet gum box, fruitwood, book-shaped, decorated w/simple inlay & scrubbed carved designs, soft refinishing, 4" l. 137.50

Sweet gum box, walnut, book-shaped, chip-carving & inlaid decoration, old finish, 3" l. 280.50

Tobacco box, brass, pierced & engraved decoration depicting the return of the prodigal son, Holland, 18th c., 6" l. (repaired) 1,100.00

Wall box, carved pine, a tall tapering backplate w/a flat round knob top pierced for hanging, flat sides w/a shaped top & pierced in the middle w/a starburst design, the wide front w/a scroll-cut top edge above an elaborately pierce-carved design of scallops, hearts, diamonds & a central pinwheel, molded base, covered in a brown varnish, initials "CC," probably Pennsylvania, 19th c., 4⅜ x 9¾", 18½" h. 920.00

Wall box, painted & carved wood, scrolled crest, lift lid above single sectioned drawer, painted red w/mustard & green floral decoration, America, 19th c., 6⅜ x 9½", 14½" h...880.00

Wall box, paper-covered wood, the rectangular backboard w/canted corners & downswept sides w/conforming canted front forming open storage compartments, covered in variously block-printed papers depicting white Georgian houses & a church on a blue ground, blue garlands & swags on a cream ground & figures watching garden theatricals, America, late 18th - early 19th c., 4¾ x 15", 19" h. 1,980.00

Wall box, walnut, high cut-out scrolled crest above open pocket, dovetailed construction, old finish, 12½" w., 13" h. 935.00

BREWERIANA

Early Beer Glasses

Beer is still popular in this counry but the number of breweries has greatly diminished. More than 1,900 breweries were in operation in the 1870s but we find fewer than 40 supplying the demands of the country a century later. The small local brewery has either been absorbed by a larger company or forced to close, unable to meet the competition. Advertising items used to promote the various breweries, especially those issued prior to Prohibition, now attract an ever growing number of collectors. The breweriana items listed are a sampling of the many items available. Also see BOTTLES, SIGNS & SIGN-BOARDS and TRAYS.

Ashtray, enamelware, advertising "Dow Ale" $8.00

Beer cart, push-type, "Obermeyer & Liebmann's Bottled Beers," shallow rectangular wooden platform painted black w/yellow lettering, upswept metal handles w/wooden handgrip at back, large wire wheels at the sides & a smaller one in front, interior painted pale green, marked on back edge "The New York - Made by - Willets Mfg. Co. - 590 Bedford Ave., Near Myrtle - Brooklyn, N.Y.," late 19th - early 20th c., 16" l., 43" h. (overall minor wear) 1,650.00

Beer glass, "Albany Brewery, Albany, Oregon," etched w/logo & florals, pre-Prohibition (ILLUS. left) 12.00

Beer glass, "Bartholomay," etched 24.00

Beer glass, "Breunigs, Rice Lake, Wisconsin," etched 25.00

Beer glass, "Budweiser Pilsner" & eagle decoration, etched 165.00

Early 1900s Beer Glasses

Beer glass, "Buffalo Brewing Co. - Sacramento, CA - Buffalo Lager," etched, horseshoe logo in center, early 1900s (ILLUS. left) 165.00

Beer glass, "Effinger Lager, Baraboo, Wisconsin," etched 25.00

Beer glass, "G. Burkhardt & Son, Hudson Road Brewery - Menomonie, Wis.," etched w/bottle, flowers & wheat in center, early 1900s (ILLUS. right)........................330.00

Fauerbach & Springfield Beer Glasses

Beer glass, "Fauerbach Brewing Co., - Madison, Wis.," etched, logo & florals in the center, early 1900s (ILLUS. left)....................................356.00

Beer glass, "Fresno Brewing Co.," etched 60.00

Beer glasses, "Hamm Excelsior, St. Paul, Minn.," etched w/eagle & logo, pre-Prohibition (ILLUS. right) 72.00

Beer glass, "Hussa Brewing Co.," etched, 5" h. 225.00

Enameled Beer Glasses

Beer glass, "Jax Beer - 'The Drink of Friendship,'" enameled, New Orleans, Louisiana (ILLUS. left) 28.00

Beer glass, "Kiewel's Beer," enameled w/"White Seal" seal in center, Little Falls, Minnesota (ILLUS. right) 26.00

Beer glass, "Lithia Beer, West Bend, Wisconsin," etched 25.00

Beer glass, "1952 Centennial, Potosi, Wisconsin" 25.00

Beer glass, "Peoples Brew, Oshkosh, Wisconsin," etched 17.00

Red Ribbon & Schmidt Glasses

Beer glass, "Red Ribbon Beer - Wausau, Wis.," enameled, half-length portrait of cavalier w/stein in center (ILLUS. left)..........................132.00

Beer glass, "Schmidt City Club Beer - St. Paul, Minn.," enameled, star logo in center (ILLUS. right).......................44.00

Beer glass, "The Rising Sun Brewing Co. - Seeber Special - Elizabeth, N.J.," etched, w/"Compliments of" at the top & a rising sun in the middle, pre-Prohibition (ILLUS. next col.).....165.00

Etched Pre-Prohibition Glass

Beer glass, "Springfield, Mo. - Brewing Co.," etched, landscape scene in the center, early 1900s (ILLUS. right) 189.00

Upper Peninsula Glass

Beer glass, "Upper Peninsula Brewing Co. - Marquette, Mich.," etched, wheat & flowers w/logo in center, pre-Prohibition (ILLUS.) 159.00

Book, "Brewed in America, History of Beer & Ale in the United States," by Baron 45.00

Can, cone-top, "Fehr's Beer" 27.00

Can, cone-top, "Fitzgerald Pale Ale," 12 oz. ....75.00 to 95.00

Can, cone-top, "Fort Schuyler Ale," 12 oz. 95.00

Can, cone-top, "Iroquois Indian Head Beer," 12 oz. 175.00

Can, cone-top, "Kruger Cream Ale," 32 oz. 110.00

Can, cone-top, "Old Topper Snappy Ale," crowntainer, 12 oz. 45.00

Can, cone-top, "Schmids Light Beer," 32 oz. 65.00

Can, flat-top, "Feigenspan Beer" 45.00

Can, flat-top, "Utica Club Cream Ale" ...55.00

Clock, electric, wall-type, "DuBois Budweiser," round w/Arabic numerals & glass front, metal casing, printed in red & black on the dial "Enjoy - DuBois - Budweiser - DuBois Brewing Co., DuBois, Pa.," 15" d. (paint flaking & cracked, glass scratched) 220.00

Clock, electric, hanging revolving-type, "Schlitz Beer," four-sided, one side w/clock, one side illustrates woman holding mug & two sides w/advertising, each side panel 18" l., 28" h. 290.00

Counter display figure, "Anteek Beer," composition figure of a mustached standing bartender, one arm raised to shoulder to hold a beer, other down from his side, brown & tan figure w/red lettering on his apron, 22½" h. (paint wear, hole under side of hand) 330.00

Counter display figure, carved wood, figure of King Gambrinus (King of Beer), original paint, American, 1870s 6,850.00

Counter display figure, "Hampden Ale," figure of a man singing & playing accordion, standing on ale barrel..35.00

Budweiser Beer Mugs

Mug, pottery, Budweiser, tall cylindrical body w/raised lettering "Prosit - Drink Budweiser" w/raised Anheuser-Busch logo in center, ca. 1940s (ILLUS. right).......................101.00

Mug, pottery, Budweiser, "Ye Old Moustache Mug," w/comic 'Bud Man' in center of ring, produced by Budweiser (ILLUS. left)..................143.00

Mug, blue-glazed stoneware, oversized, "Duquesne Pilsner," 11" h...120.00

Mug, pottery, "Leisy Brewing Co.," depicts Egyptian scene of camels, people, pyramids & palm trees, 5½" h...95.00

Mug, stoneware, "Royal Beer Brewing Co.," barrel-shaped, poem on back, label & gilt in good condition, 4" h. (stress crack on handle) 78.50

Photograph, "Seipp's," close-up of workers loading trucks, on cardboard backing, ca. early 1900s, 11 x 14"...85.00

Plaque, "Fred Krug Brewing Co.," colorful china, scene of owner & brewery, 1909 ....95.00

Salt & pepper shakers, "Schlitz," amber glass, bottle-shaped, w/labels, 4" h., pr. 20.00

Sign, neon, counter-type, "Duquesne Pilsener," a long rectangular box w/an upright band w/plastic letters outlined in green neon against a black ground, 24½" l., 6" h. (minor rust & water spots)............................93.50

Neon Beer Sign

Sign, neon, window-type, "E & O Beer - Early and Often," rectangular, red neon, center bar lights up w/blue lettering on red ground, window supports at bottom missing rubber, 26" l., 16" h. (ILLUS.) 467.50

Sign, "Jacob Ruppert's - Knickerbocker - Beer," painted tin, New York, New York, late 19th - early 20th c., 97½" w., 26" h.................1,100.00

Collectible Budweiser Steins

Stein, pottery, "Budweiser," cylindrical body w/embossed design of a beer label, ca. 1980s, CS 18 (ILLUS. left) 553.00

Stein, pottery, "Budweiser," printed

wording around label flanked by "1876 - 1976," CS 22 (ILLUS. right) 350.00

Steins by Budweiser

Stein, pottery, Budweiser, printed design w/"Imported German Beer - Wutzburger - Hofbrau," produced by Budweiser, CS 39 (ILLUS. left) 385.00

Stein, pottery, "Budweiser, " tall swelled cylindrical body w/embossed paneled scene of beer wagon w/green cases in a landscape, ca. 1980s, CS 50 (ILLUS. right) 610.00

Pre-Prohibition Steins

Stein, stoneware, "Cherokee Brewery Co. - St. Louis," relief-molded Indian w/bow & arrow, raised bands at top & bottom, blue trim, pre-Prohibition (ILLUS. left) 235.00

Stein, pottery, "F.D. Radeke Brewing Co. - Kankakee, Ill." printed decoration w/logo about name, pre-Prohibition (ILLUS. right) 194.00

Tap head, "Pabst Blue Ribbon" 25.00

BROWNIE COLLECTIBLES

The Brownies were creatures of fantasy created by Palmer Cox, artist-author, in 1887. Early in this century numerous articles with depictions of or in the shape of Brownies appeared.

Book, "The Brownies Around the World," by Palmer Cox, 1922..........$35.00

Cup & saucer, porcelain, color scene of five Brownies participating in sports 45.00

Doll, "Irishman," stuffed cloth, Arnold Print Works, 1892 ....110.00

Doll, "Uncle Sam," stuffed cloth, Arnold Print Works, 1892 ....110.00

Humidor, cov., ceramic, figural Brownie "Turk" wearing fez, 6" h......300.00

Humidor, cov., ceramic, figural Brownie "Uncle Sam," 6" h..............475.00

Napkin ring w/vase, silver plate, oval base w/full figural Brownie pushing ring, trumpet vase atop ring, signed 245.00

Paper doll, "Frenchman," Lion Coffee advertising insert...............................18.00

Paper doll, "Student," Lion Coffee advertising insert...............................18.00

Photo album, leather covers, ca. 1920s 18.00

Statue, metal, Brownie figure, advertising "Brownie Baking Co., Spokane, WA"..................................45.00

BUCKLES

Belt Buckle with Circus Theme

Belt buckle, bronze, rectangular plaque w/relief-cast clown faces framing a balloon reading "Barnum & Bailey's Greatest Show on Earth Season 1908," rear marked "Tiffany Studio - New York," fantasy piece produced in the early 1970s, 2¾ x 4" (ILLUS.) $38.50

Belt buckle, gold (18k yellow), designed as an oval twisted rope, w/base metal clips, French hallmarks 165.00

Belt buckle, gold (18k yellow), polished finish, signed "Cartier" 330.00

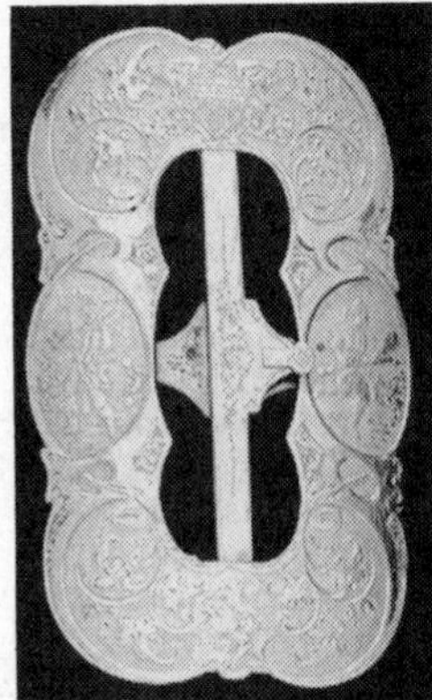

Rare American Gold Buckle

Belt buckle, gold, patent-type, shaped rectangular form w/scalloped border, each end chased w/panels of foliate scrolls & flowerheads on a matted ground, at the top an American eagle & shield, at the bottom a California bear holding a star, each side w/a panel chased w/Civil War soldiers in a landscape, maker's mark of William U. Bohm, San Francisco, California, patented in 1863, 2½" l. (ILLUS.)................1,870.00

Fabergé Belt Buckle

Belt buckle, enamel, silver & gold, oval, enameled in translucent mauve over a *guilloché* ground, the borders chased w/leaftips, marked "K. Fabergé" in Cyrillic w/Imperial warrant & 88 standard, Moscow, Russia, ca. 1900, w/original fitted holly case, 2¼" l. (ILLUS.) 3,163.00

Belt buckle, *pate-de-verre* & silver, rectangular w/rounded ends, in grey glass molded in low-relief w/a masque of a faun amid swirling foliage, in red, blue & purple, simple hammered silver mount, glass molded "G. A-R" & "G. ARGY-ROUSSEAU," silver impressed "G. A-R FRANCE," ca. 1925, 2½" w., 4⅛" l. 2,013.00

Belt buckle, silver-gilt, oval w/pointed ends, blue enamel decoration, London hallmarks, 2¼" l. 27.50

Art Nouveau Belt Buckle

Belt buckle, silver-gilt & mother-of-pearl, Art Nouveau style, elongated floriform, each reticulated petal enclosing a flower on a leafy stem, the center set w/three irregularly shaped mother-of-pearl cabochons, marked "Vantine's - STERLING," ca. 1900, 3⅛" l. (ILLUS.) 403.00

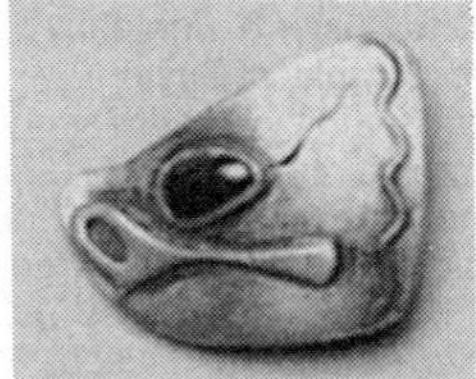

Modern Style Belt Buckle

Belt buckle, silver, copper & garnet, amorphous triangular form set w/a garnet cabochon, by Ed Wiener, ca. 1950, unsigned, 2¼" l. (ILLUS.) 460.00

Belt buckle, sterling silver, head of an Art Nouveau lady w/flowing hair, dated 1901 ....115.00

Belt buckle, white jade, two-part, each section of oval form, reticulated w/a *chilong* w/bifurcated tail, a *lingzhi* trailing from its mouth, one side w/dragonhead terminal, the second pierced to receive a terminal, the reverse of each w/a knop for attachment, China, 19th c., 4¼" l. 1,035.00

Cloak buckle, bronze, two-part, each oval section molded w/a foliate design enhanced by polychrome enamel, each impressed "L.C.T. - EL 265," Louis Tiffany, overall 3¼" l. 1,879.00

Shoe buckles, steel, oval w/bright-cut design, pr. 55.00

BUSTER BROWN

Buster Brown was a comic strip created by Richard Outcault in the New York Herald *in 1902. It was subsequently syndicated and numerous objects depicting Buster (and often his dog, Tige) were produced.*

Buster Brown Poster

Bill hook, metal, wall-type $27.00
Blotter, depicts Buster & Tige,early 35.00
Book, "Autobiography of Buster Brown," illustrated by Richard Outcault, premium book, 1914...........95.00
Cigar w/band, ca. 1920.............................8.00
Clicker, depicts Buster Brown & Tige & "5 (star) Buster Brown Shoes"........39.50
Finger puppet, cardboard, unused, 8" h...20.00
Fork, silver, Buster Brown & Tige depicted, 1910 ....36.00
Kite, "Buster Brown Shoes," paper, 1950s 28.00
Paper dolls, Buster Brown & Tige, in original envelope, J. Ottman Litho Co. 125.00
Pencil box, lacquered, scene of Buster Brown & Tige, Germany 50.00
Pinback button, gold-tone metal, bust of Buster & Tige 55.00
Playing cards, miniature, 1906 (box worn) 65.00

Buster Brown Poster

Poster, cloth-backed, "Melville B. Raymond presents the newest novelty in musical comedy creations" w/picture of George Ali, "The world's greatest animal impersonator and pantomimist," Tige pictured looking up at Ali, beside "Buster Brown," red, black, yellow & blue lettering, fold creases & line creasing & touch-up overall, 27" w., 40⅞" h. (ILLUS.) 357.50
Poster, pictures Buster standing beside Tige, Buster wearing a red suit & hat, yellow background, foil marks, minor soiling, framed, 22½ x 28½" (ILLUS.) 77.00
Sales slip hook, celluloid & metal, a round celluloid disc w/the head of Buster & Tige & Buster Brown Vacation Days Carnival, a small metal hanging hook at top & a long hook below for the slips, disc w/yellow ground, Tige in brown & Buster's cap in red, disc 2" d. (some rust)..22.00
Shoe horn, metal 12.50
Shoe trees, plastic, figural busts of Buster Brown & Tige at one end, expandable arm for inserting into shoes, pr. 40.00
Toy, pressed steel bell toy, "Buster Brown & Goldie," the two figures on a wheeled platform & ringing a series of four bells by swinging from side to side when pulled along, Watrous, ca. 1900, 13½" l................115.00
Trade card, "The Brown Shoe Co.," photo of Buster Brown & Tige below a heading "The Real, Live Buster Brown and Tige - at The World's Fair," released at the St. Louis World's Fair of 1904, brownish violet & white, advertising on the reverse....71.50
Valentine, large, framed 55.00

BUTTER MOLDS & STAMPS

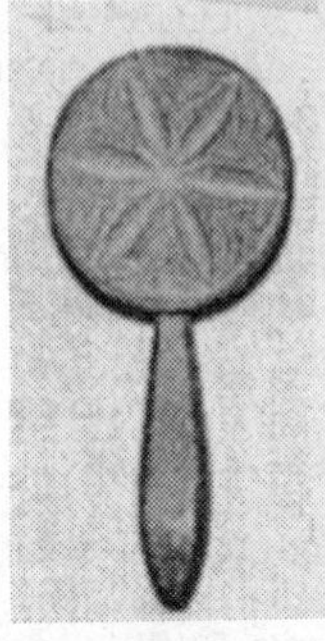

Starflower "Lollipop" Stamp

While they are sometimes found made of other materials, it is primarily the two-piece wooden butter mold and one-piece butter stamp that attract collectors. The molds are found in two basic styles, rounded cup form and rectangular box form. Butter stamps are usually round with a protruding knob handle on the back. Many were factory made items with the print design made by forcing a metal die into the wood under great pressure, while others had the design chiseled out by hand. For listing of other types of molds see MOLDS - CANDY, FOOD & MISC. category.

Acorn & leaves stamp, round w/two large, curved leaves above an elongated acorn, one-piece turned handle, old worn patina, 3¾" d. $220.00

Basket of fruit stamp, carved wood, rope carved border, turned elongated handle, scrubbed, w/pleasant dark stains, 4" d. 330.00

Cow mold, carved wood, central figure of a cow on a grassy ground beneath "Doll," one-piece turned handle, old patina, 3" d. 275.00

Cow stamp, crudely carved animal below a leaf sprig, notced rim, inserted turned handle, scubbed finish, 2½" d. 137.50

Cow stamp, primitive carved animal standing beneath an arching leafy branch, blades of grass below, notced rim, one-piece turned handle, old soft dark finish, 4½" d....330.00

Cow stamp, carved wood, standing cow facing left by a fence, tufts of grass on the ground, single stalk of grain at top, carved edge, old patina, turned handle, 4¾" d.......................325.00

Cow stamp, carved wood, standing cow w/trees & flowers, scrubbed finish, w/one piece turned handle, 5¼" d. (worn holes).........................148.50

Deer, tree, stars, etc., mold, miniature cased-type, four small tapering rectangular sides each w/a different design to be attached by wire staple hinges to a small square center panel, faint signature on bottom, good old patina, 2" h. (hinges missing) 192.50

Eagle stamp, carved wood, large stylized eagle w/leafy branch beneath one wing & flower above to one side, carved border, one-piece turned handle, scrubbed finish, 4⅜" d. (old small edge repair)..........220.00

Eagle stamp, stylized spread-winged bird facing right, old dark patina, one-piece turned handle, 4½" d. (age cracks, some edge wear) 220.00

Eagle & shield stamp, carved wood, dark finish, w/one-piece turned handle, 3⅞" d.................................137.50

Fish stamp, carved wood, elongated one-piece turned handle, old patina, 2¾" d., 5¾" l...................................192.50

Floral cased mold, carved wood, square w/overall flowers & leaves design, two-part, 6" sq. 55.00

Floral stamp, carved wood, central stylized floral design flanked by feathery fronds, one-piece turned handle, old patina, 3½" d. 110.00

Hearts & compass star stamp, popular, rectangular w/a pair of hearts at each end & a compass star at the center, good dark patina, 3½ x 5"...165.00

Pinapple stamp, carved wood, stylized deeply crosshatched pineapple flanked by feathery foliage, chip-carved border, one-piece turned handle, scrubbed finish, 4½" d. 165.00

Pomegranate stamp, carved wood, concave surface w/well-carved pomegranate & foliage, narrow reeded rim, one-piece turned handle, old patina, 5⅛" d. 247.50

Sheaf of wheat stamp, carved wood, deeply carved central design against a carved background, chip-carved border, one-piece turned handle, old yellow patina, 4¼" d. 330.00

Sheaf of wheat stamp, half-round, old worn patina, inserted turned handle, 7" l. (one corner chewed up).............82.50

Starflower "lollipop" stamp, carved wood, round head w/incised six-point star, shaped handle, good worn patina, 7⅜" l. (ILLUS.).............302.50

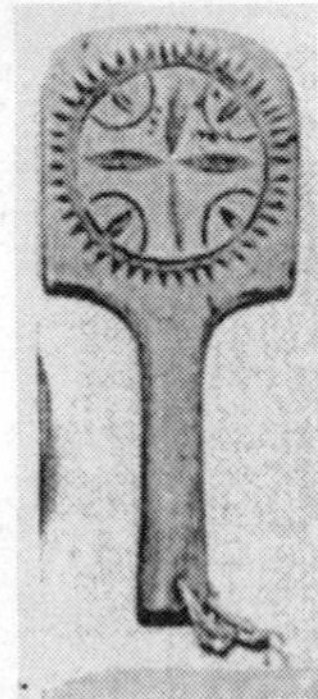

Primitive Starflower Stamp

Starflower "lollipop" stamp, carved wood, rounded paddle-form head carved w/a primitive four-point star w/arches between each & framed by a serrated border band, flat handle w/hole for hanging cord, 9" l. (ILLUS.) 110.00

Starflower stamp, carved wood, simple starflower w/small starflower between each petal, fat turned handle, dark patina, 5½" d. (age cracks) 126.50

BUTTONS

Early Enameled Button

Brass, "US Marine," Serial No. 2-76, Officer, 1" d., set of 2 ....$18.00

Enamel, h.p. primitive landscape of a tower & building in a lakeshore landscape scene, in blue, green, yellow & dark maroon, in a narrow brass frame, 18th c., 1 7/16" d. (ILLUS.) 775.00

Enamel & silver, Art Nouveau style, transparent green enamel over a *guilloché* ground, in original fitted box, set of 6 (some enamel loss).......82.50

Rare Early Button

Engraving under glass, an engraved bust portrait of a young early Victorian lady w/long curls, wearing a low-cut gown, hand-tinted brown hair, green bow & red gown w/lace collar, wide pewter frame, 1 9/16" d. (ILLUS.) 285.00

Glass, sulphide, swan, 7/8" d. 75.00

Ivory Under Glass Button

Ivory under glass, h.p. bust portrait of a young 18th c. woman w/an ornate hairdo trimmed w/lace & yellow ribbon, narrow metal frame, 1 5/16" d. (ILLUS.) 450.00

CALENDAR PLATES

Panama Canal Calendar Plate

Calendar plates have been produced in this country since the turn of the century, primarily of porcelain and earthenwares but also of glass and tin. They were made earlier in England. The majority were issued after 1909, largely intended as advertising items.

1908, cat center, Chattanooga, Tennessee advertising....................$35.00
1910, boys jumping into stream & James Whitcomb Riley quote, souvenir of Tyndall, South Dakota, marked "Dresden"..........................35.00
1910, "Old Rose Distilling Co." advertising 55.00
1915, Panama Canal map center (ILLUS.) 35.00
1917, deer, ducks & birds center, advertising "Gately & Fritzerald Furniture Co., Johnstown, PA," marked "D.E. McNicol, East Liverpool, OH," signed "Edwin McGargee," 7" d...............................20.00
1923, hunting scene center 35.00

CANDLESTICKS & CANDLEHOLDERS

Art Deco Candleholders

Also see METALS, ROYCROFT ITEMS and SANDWICH under Glass.

Candelabra, girandole-type, cast metal, three-light, a tall central leafy scroll-trimmed shaft w/flaring candle socket above a pair of ornate leafy scrolling arms w/candle sockets & conjoined at the middle & raised on a double-scroll base set on a rectangular white marble foot, the front of the base also cast w/the figure of a standing American Indian brave w/his extended arm leaning on a longrifle, mid-19th c., 17¾" h., pr...$935.00

Candelabra, ormolu & cut glass, two-light, each candlearm hung w/faceted lustres & supported on a diamond-cut domed base, early 19th c., 10½" h., pr. (some slight imperfections) 1,380.00

Candelabra, ormolu & bronze, three-light, Neoclassical style, standing draped patinated bronze female figure supporting an urn on her head continuing to a shaft decorated w/berried foliage & eagles' heads, the curved candle branches cast w/foliate motifs, eagles' heads & berries, raised on a circular pedestal cast w/anthemion & flowerheads, above a square base, Continental, early 19th c., 20" h., pr. 8,050.00

Candelabrum, glass & bronze, two-light, the circular foot w/undulating rim issuing a slender shaft supporting an adjustable two-arm section, each arm w/elongated reticulated holder w/blown green glass & detachable beaded bobeche, stamped "TIFFANY STUDIOS NEW YORK 10079," 18½" h...4,370.00

Candleholder, floor model, wrought iron & tole, two candlearms each w/a cylindrical candle socket in a dished toleware drop pan, the curved projecting arms adjusting on a tall slender tapering rod on an arched tripod base w/pad feet, probably New England, 1760-90, 19" w., 4' 1½" h. 5,175.00

Candleholder, hammered pewter, three-light, the three candle nozzles fitting into a shaped rectangular section resting on a domical base, Harald Buchrucher, impressed maker's mark & numbers, ca. 1930, 10¼" l., 3" h......................................173.00

Candleholders, brass, tapered cylindrical form w/angular handle & everted rim, enclosing bobeche, marked "Jarvie," Robert Jarvie, 6" h., pr. 1,725.00

Candleholders, bronze, Art Deco style, curved & tapering upright 'wings' framing a spherical candle socket, raised on a stepped, round disc base, original green patina, impressed marks of Carl Sorensen, ca. 1925, 4½" h., pr. (ILLUS.) 412.50

Candlestand, turned maple & birch, screw standard supporting a double candlearm, a circular plateau below w/molded edge, the circular base supported on three turned splayed legs, New England, 18th c., 15" d., 37½" h...1,725.00

Candlestick, bronze, tall slender standard supporting a bulbous candle socket issuing from a slightly domed circular base cast w/fan palm fronds, mottled green patina, impressed "B&H - 153," Bradley & Hubbard, ca. 1900, 23" h. 489.00

Candlestick, cast iron, stepped circular base, low standard w/medial ring, short candlecup w/flaring rim, decorated w/an ivy & leaf design, dark patina, 4⅝" h. 137.50

Candlestick, Favrile glass & bronze, the tripod base w/fluted tapered feet w/a sinuous, twisted vine about the bottom, supporting a ribbed iridescent glass holder w/green & gold pulled feather motif, w/removable bobeche, stamped "TIFFANY STUDIOS NEW YORK 1228," 11" h. 2,875.00

Candlestick, pressed flint glass, Dolphin patt., a hexagonal tulip-shaped socket above the figural dolphin standard on a hexagonal foot w/incurved edges, translucent blue, Pittsburgh area, ca. 1850, 6½" h. (tiny flakes on rim of socket) 770.00

Candlestick, pressed flint glass, round base, hexagonal knopped stem, clear, Pittsburgh, 9⅝" h. (pewter insert missing)....................192.50

Candlestick, pressed flint glass, hexagonal base, crucifix-form standard, canary yellow, New England, 9¾" h. (pinpoint flakes) 115.50

Candlestick, pressed flint glass, crucifix-form on stepped hexagonal base, socket attached w/a wafer of glass, milk white, ca. 1870, 11¼" h. (heat checks in base)........................82.50

Candlestick, silver & rock crystal, the domed rock crystal base raised on four lion supports, the silver stem in the form of a female saint supporting a petal-form rock crystal bobeche & paneled candle nozzle, Continental, late 19th c., 11" h. 2,128.00

Candlestick, wrought iron, 'hog scraper' type, slightly domed foot, cylindrical standard w/push-up marked "Shaw," w/lip hanger, 6⅝" h...165.00

Candlestick, wrought iron, Arts & Crafts style, the tripod base wrought w/fleur-de-lys, the cylindrical standard applied w/and terminating in scrolls, raising a cylindrical candleholder & drip pan, Samuel Yellin, impressed w/maker's mark, 26" h..3,565.00

Candlestick, wrought iron & wood, turned wooden base supporting cylindrical standard w/spiral push-up, w/lip hanger, 8½" h. 192.50

Candlestick, wrought steel, 'hog scraper' type, cylindrical shaft w/pushup marked "Birmh.," lip hanger, old black paint, Birmingham, England, 19th c., 5" h......................170.50

Candlestick, wrought steel w/tin wash, 'hog scraper' type w/push-up & lip hanger, 5¼" h. 115.50

Candlesticks, blown & pressed olive green flint glass, the blown socket w/a bulbous knop below the tall flattened flaring rim, attached w/a wafer to the pressed tiered & flaring standard, Pittsburgh, ca. 1830-45, 9¹⁄₁₆" h., pr. (one socket w/tiny crack off a piece of cullet in socket & a 1½" l. hairline in the same socket) 3,025.00

Candlesticks, brass, a cylindrical socket w/wide, flat rim above a double-knopped stem on a stepped round foot, w/push-up rod, England, 19th c., 9¼" h., pr..............................374.00

Candlesticks, brass, tall ring- and rod-turned graduated shaft on a wide, domed round foot, w/interior push-up, England, late 19th c., 10½" h., pr...209.00

Candlesticks, brass, William & Mary style, tall cylindrical ring-turned candle socket above a wide disc drip-pan above a slender knob- and ring-turned standard on a domed ring-turned round foot, probably Holland, ca. 1700, 10½" h., pr. (one bent) 3,335.00

Candlesticks, brass, "Queen of Diamonds" patt., w/pushups, 19th c., 11½" h., pr. 386.00

Candlesticks, brass, "King of Diamonds" patt., w/pushups, 19th c., 12⅜" h., pr. 275.00

Candlesticks, bronze, cylindrical standard w/flaring integral bobeche decorated w/wavy ring turnings above a domical base, dark brown patina, stamped "EVAN JENSEN - COPENHAGEN - 1937, BRONZE, GRAND PRIX - BARCELONA, 310 - 2," dated 1937, 10¾" h., pr. 1,955.00

Candlesticks, bronze, vasiform candle socket on three-prong support, tall slender standard & swirl-molded circular base, speckled copper patina, impressed "TIFFANY STUDIOS - NEW YORK - 1213," early 20th c., 11⅞" h. 1,035.00

Candlesticks, bronze & Favrile glass, the blown reticulated green glass elongated candle socket raised on a very tall thin standard on a round disc foot, brownish green patina, impressed "TIFFANY STUDIOS - NEW YORK - 1213," early 20th c., 19¾" h., pr. (bobeches missing) ...3,163.00

Candlesticks, earthenware, silver form w/a cylindrical stem rising from a flaring circular foot & supporting a campaniform candle socket w/a flaring drip pan, the whole splashed in green & marbleized w/veins of

English Earthenware Candlesticks

iron-red & black, England, mid-19th c., one w/two very small foot-rim chips, 8 11/16" h., pr. (ILLUS.) 978.00

Candlesticks, enameled bronze, the low square foot raised on tiny feet enameled around the edge w/squares, rectangles & triangles in yellow, cream, blue & red, the square standard w/square candle nozzle & rim, impressed "LOUIS C. TIFFANY FURNACES INC. - 368," after 1918, 7¾" h., pr. 920.00

Baroque-Style Candlesticks

Candlesticks, pricket-type, pewter, baroque-style, wide dished pricket holder above a tall slender baluster- and knob-turned standard supported by a three-lobed shaped & scroll-cast base on knob feet, Europe, 19th c., 25" h., pr. (ILLUS.) 357.50

Candlesticks, silvered-bronze, a palmette-cast bobeche above an acanthus-cast candle socket above the circular tapered standard w/berried leaf decoration raised on a

Silvered-Bronze Candlesticks

circular domed base cast w/palmette & bellflower decoration within a leaftip border, Louis-Philippe period, France, mid-19th c., 12" h., pr. (ILLUS.) 4,888.00

Candlesitcks, sterling silver, Chrysanthemum patt., shaped circular spreading foot applied w/chrysanthemum decoration & engraved w/a monogram, the baluster-form stem & socket w/similar chrysanthemum, the removable nozzles w/chrysanthemum rim, Tiffany & Co., 1907-47, 9½" h., pr. 4,400.00

Candlesticks, sterling silver, the ovoid socket w/flattened dished rim raised on a ribbed baluster-form shaft on a plain round foot, designed by Herbert A. Taylor for Arthur Stone (Stone Associates), Gardner, Massachusetts, monogrammed & dated inside foot, ca. 1918, 11" h., pr. 2,200.00

Chamberstick, brass, flaring base w/angular handle supporting a semi-ovoid top section, original patina, hand-incised "Jarvie" signature, early 20th c., 5" d., 6" h. 550.00

Chamberstick, tole, circular dished form w/ring handle, painted w/bold red, yellow & green floral designs on a black asphaltum ground heightened w/yellow scallops, Pennsylvania, mid-19th c., 6¼" d. 4,888.00

Rush light holder, wrought iron, twisted detail w/candle socket counterweight, on a squared wooden base, 16½" h. 467.50

Taper jack, silver plate, w/urn finial & snuffer on chain, marked "Exeter," w/red taper, 5½" h. (silver worn) 275.00

Tinder-lighter, flintlock-type, walnut, brass & steel, signed & engraved w/trophies-of-arms, brass pan, brass box for tinder w/hinged door, fitted w/a brass turned candleholder on the left, flat-sided walnut pistol grip butt & steel trigger-guard, now on a mahogany base, J & W. Richards, London, England, late 18th - early 19th c., 7½" l. 690.00

CANDY CONTAINERS (Glass)

Rocking Horse Candy Container

**Indicates the container might not have held candy originally. +Indicates this container might also be found as a reproduction. ‡Indicates this container was also made as a bank. All containers are clear glass unless otherwise indicated. Any candy container that retains the original paint is very desirable and readers should follow descriptions carefully realizing that an identical candy container that lacks the original paint will be less valuable. Also see HOLIDAY COLLECTIBLES.*

Airplane - "US P-51," Victory Glass Co., 1944-45, bottom closure of waxed cardboard, wingspread 4¼", 5" l., 1¾" h. $55.00

*Benjamin Franklin, star & circle pattern, original pewter top, perforated (may be salt shaker), 2½" base, 4" h. 270.00

Boat - Battleship on waves, w/tin closure, Cambridge Glass Co., ca. 1916, 5¼" l. 98.00

Boot - Santa Claus, original label, 3¼" h. 20.00

Bureau - w/real mirror above, original paint, w/tin closure, ca. 1913, 3⅞" h. 160.00

Clock - mantel-type, painted decoration, paper dial inside, tin closure on top, ca. 1913, 2⅞" w., 3¾" h. 125.00

Dog by Barrel - painted dog, marked "L.E. Smith Co.,...," on base of barrel, w/tin closure on barrel slotted for use as bank, ca. 1915, 3¼" h. 260.00

Happifat Boy on Drum (Fat Boy on Drum), good original paint, original tin closure, marked "HAPPY FAT - U.S. DES. PAT. GEO. BORGFELDT & CO. N.Y.C. SOLE LICENSEE," ca. 1915, 4⅜" h. 225.00

+Kewpie by Barrel - painted figure, marked "Geo. Borgfeldt & Co.,...," under barrel, w/tin closure slotted for use as bank, ca. 1915......................120.00

Lantern - square w/beveled panels, w/tin slide closure at top, original gilt paint, ca. 1910, 4⅛" h. 90.00

+Locomotive - engine marked "1028" below windows on cab, w/cow-catcher at front, marked "Victory Glass Co." on cardboard closure, 5⅛" l. 30.00

Rabbit - running on log, original paint, tin closure on base, Victory Glass Co., 4¼" l. 195.00

Rocking Horse - clear, heavy glass w/fine details w/tin closure inside base, ca. 1915-20, 4½" l. (ILLUS.)...275.00

Santa Claus - descending brick chimney, "V.G." monogram on side, Santa originally painted, w/metal screw cap on base, ca. 1927, 5" h.....92.50

Windmill - Dutch-type, heavy 6-sided tower w/original tin arms, cardboard closure marked "Pla-Toy Co.," 1940s, 4⅞" h. 100.00

Suitcase - milk white, w/painted decal-type decoration of two brown bears w/tin slide closure, ca. 1908, 2½" h. 155.00

Suitcase - original closure, ca. 1910, 3⅝" l., 2½" h. 80.00

Tank - w/man in turret, cardboard closure on base, 1942, 4¼" l. 45.00

Telephone - Millstein's "Tot," desk type w/plastic receiver, w/cardboard closure, ca. 1945, 2⅜" h. 55.00

Trunk, "Souvenir of Green Bay," clear glass, tin slide on base, 2 x 2¾", 2⅛" h. 80.00

Rabbit Eating Carrot, ca. 1947, 4⅜" h. (no closure) 30.00

Rabbit in Egg Shell - gilt-painted rabbit, marked "V.G., etc.," w/metal screw-on cap closure, 1920s, 5⅛" h. .95.00

Rabbit - "Peter Rabbit," by Millstein, w/cardboard closure, ca. 1947, 6¼" h. 35.00

CANES & WALKING STICKS

Ash walking stick, the slender shaft relief-carved overall w/stylized leafy vines, acorns & crosshatched stems as well as Masonic emblems & a presentation inscription dated "1920," old varnish finish, 35½" l....$330.00

Bamboo walking stick, movable celluloid turtle in handle 95.00

Bamboo walking stick, silver gilded white metal knob w/smiling comic head, 35" l. 27.50

Carved root walking stick, the knob end carved as a man's head, gnarled root shaft, 27½" l. (age cracks, some edge damage to carving) 181.50

Ebonized wood walking stick, silver-plate knob handle w/engraved decoration, 32" l. 71.50

Ebonized wood walking stick, gold knob handle w/floral engraving & a presentation inscription dated "1881," 35½" l. 165.00

Ebonized wood walking stick, gold knob handle w/engraved florals & monogram, maker's mark "T.D. & V.," 36" l. (dent in knob) 104.50

Ebonized wood walking stick, ivory knob handle w/silver ferrule, handle inscribed "Rev. Theobald - Concord, New Hampshire" 185.00

Ebonized wood walking stick, sterling silver curved handle, English hallmarks 175.00

Ebony walking stick, ivory knob w/gold inlaid medallion w/presentation inscription, 34" l. (tip missing) ...170.50

Glass cane, aqua w/curved handle w/twisted design, 54½" l. 77.00

Glass cane, parade-type, clear w/red & blue spirals, found in Utica, Ohio, 49" l. 192.50

Hardwood cane, the handle carved as a figural bird, the upper half of the shaft carved w/detailed animals, birds & flowers, silver-colored oval metal medallion w/engraved monogram, old varnish finish, 35" l. (minor chip to one leaf) 385.00

Hardwood cane, nickel-plated brass trim & horn tip, crosshatched carving, dark finish, 35½" l. 71.50

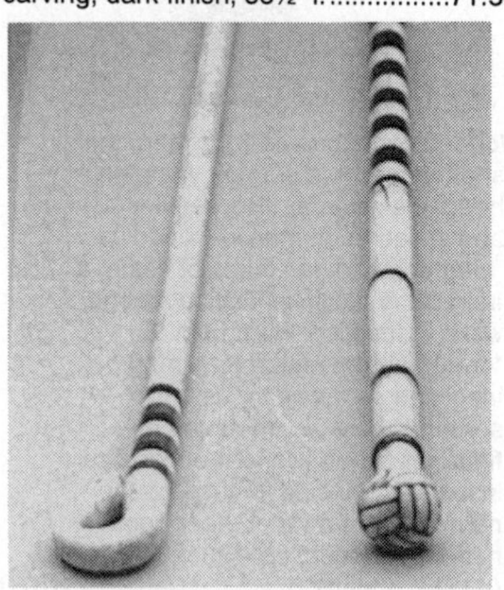

Ivory Walking Sticks

Ivory walking stick, carved walrus ivory w/the crook handle carved as a serpent w/inlaid eyes above the tapering whalebone shaft, 19th c., large cracks, 34½" l. (ILLUS. left) 990.00

Ivory walking stick, the knop handle carved as a monkey's fist, ring-incised shaft w/ebony spacers, 19th c., age cracks, 34½" l. (ILLUS. right) 1,210.00

Ivory-headed walking stick, presentation-type, the ivory knob handle inset w/a silver disc engraved "Dr. W. Harris from Dr. Irvine," two silver plaques on the wooden shaft, one engraved "We have met the enemy and they are ours," the other reads "Taken from the flag ship - Lawrence. March AD 1836," 36¼" l. (tip slightly worn).......253.00

Cane with Lady's Leg Handle

Maple cane, carved & painted, carved in relief w/a series of brown-painted turtles, running dogs, birds, a horseshoe, arrow & the stylized head of a man, the angular handle carved in the form of a lady's leg & boot, late 19th c., 36" l. (ILLUS. of part) 3,080.00

Narwhal ivory cane, the carved handgrip w/baleen rims above a tapering shaft decorated w/reeding & hatchwork over spiral & cylindrical turnings, in a gilt case w/glass cover, 19th c., 34¾" l. 2,860.00

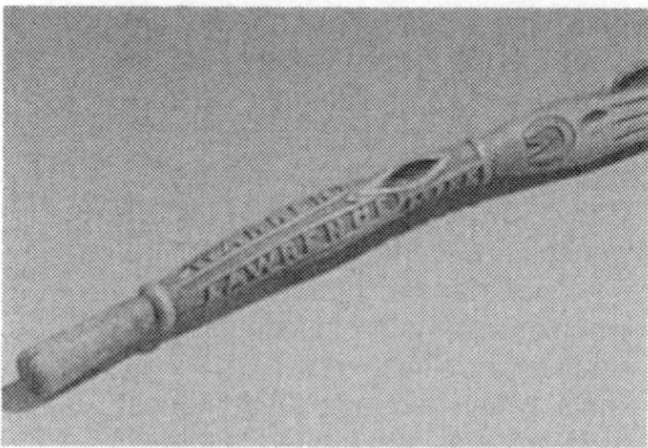

Carved & Painted Cane

Pine cane, carved & painted, the tapering shaft w/turned pine handle elaborately relief-carved w/an open hand w/silver nails centering a horseshoe on the back, the face of a monster w/silvered teeth & staring eyes & a serpent along w/relief-carved fish & a bird & the names "Warren Lawrence Mike - Orion," w/details picked out in silver & gold paint, probably Pennsylvania, late 19th - early 20th c., 34½" l. (ILLUS. of part) 3,450.00

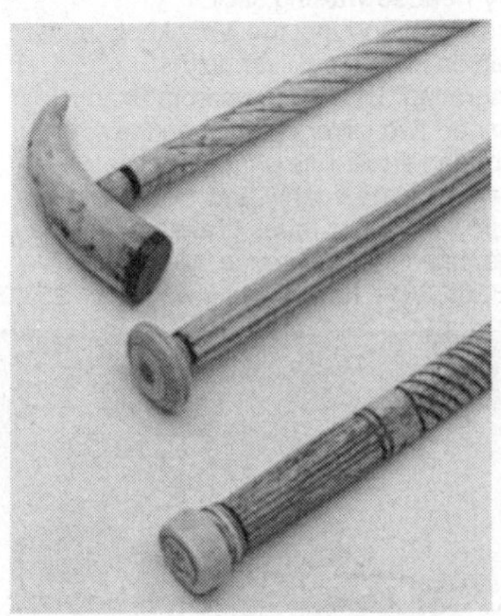

Whalebone Cane & Walking Sticks

Whalebone cane, the slender shaft incised w/a spiral twist design, w/a whale's tooth handle, 19th c., age crack, 30½" l. (ILLUS. top) 330.00

Whalebone walking stick, the shaft incised w/a spiral twist design, the flattened knob handle inset w/a metal disc initialed "AG," 19th c., 32¾" l. (ILLUS. bottom) 550.00

Whalebone walking stick, turned & incised knop, 19th c., 38½" l. 357.50

Whalebone & ivory walking stick, the slender reeded shaft topped by a flattened disc w/baleen spacer, 19th c., 33" l. (ILLUS. center)...........440.00

Whale ivory walking stick, the handle carved in the form of a sailor leaning on a tree stump holding a pipe in one hand, the shaft w/baleen spacers above a whalebone shaft, 19th c., 36" l. 1,495.00

Wooden chair-cane, in two parts: the T-shaped handle continuing to an irregular shaft w/ink inscriptions continuing unfinished w/bark & knots, w/finished tapered cylindrical base; the slat seat hinged to mid--point, also w/ink inscriptions, carved by Josiah Hayden, Union County, Liberty, Indiana, late 19th c., 45½" l. (ILLUS. of part) 2,860.00

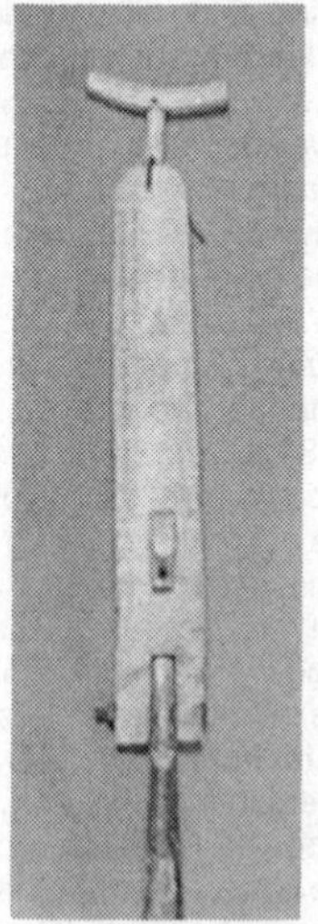

Wooden Chair

Unusual Carved Cane

Wooden cane, carved & painted, the shaft carved w/a serpent w/a man's head, identified as "Rockefeller" above figures of men identified as "the people" over figures of cattle, a train car & a chicken laying an egg, w/the inscription "Beef trust" & "profit," another figure of a man identified as "Lawson" as the serpent's back, surmounted by a figure of a man w/an American flag inscribed "frenzied finance," & the name "W.H. Lawson," deer hoof handle, America, ca. 1905, 34" l. (ILLUS. of part) 2,310.00

Wooden cane, curved handle

continuing down to a knobby sapling shaft carved in low-relief w/a model of an alligator near the base of the handle, two-tone finish, 34" l. 49.50

Wooden cane, the curved handle carved w/a small figure of an alligator, on a natural knobby shaft, old worn finish & paint, the alligator w/small metallic eyes, 35½" l. 104.50

Wooden cane, carved & painted, the cylindrical handle joining a vertical carved & decorated shaft depicting a variety of game animals, patriotic motifs, foliage, a hunter & his dog above an entwined snake, all on punched ground, w/metal tip, America, third quarter 19th c., 36" l. 990.00

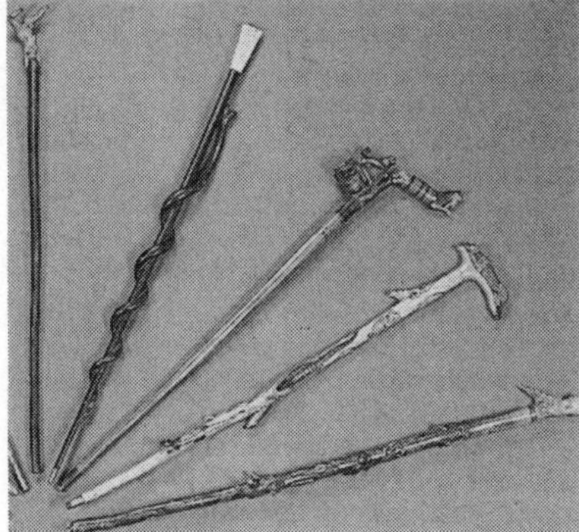

Carved Canes & Walking Sticks

Wooden cane, carved & painted, the shaped handle w/carved painted reclining hunting dog above a vertical tapering irregular shaft w/various carved & painted animals, reptiles, animal heads & running dogs, w/metal tip, America, third quarter 19th c., 36¼" l. (ILLUS. second from right)........................1,650.00

Wooden cane, the handle carved as a large upright bird, the shaft carved w/a dragon highlighted in black, 36¾" l. (some edge damage)..........185.00

Wooden cane, the carved & painted handle depicting a keg flanked by a ram's torso & dog's head, continuing to a vertical shaft w/applied figure sitting on a keg, above "Elias. H. Gilbert" in raised gilt lettering, w/metal tip, America, third quarter 19th c., 37¼" l. (ILLUS. third from right)..2,860.00

Wooden walking stick, carved & painted, handle carved in the form of a nude female w/legs in air & hands grasping the irregular tapering shaft, America, third quarter 19th c., 34" l. (ILLUS. far left) 3,520.00

Wooden walking stick, carved, the handle carved in the form of a stylized man's head, the tapering shaft carved in relief w/figures of a donkey, horse, birds, potted plants, hammer, horseshoe & snake, initialed "MM," America, late 19th - early 20th c., 35" l. 1,320.00

Wooden walking stick, carved & painted, the abstracted leaf-carved globular knob w/Masonic symbol on top, continuing to a shaped, carved shaft depicting snakes, rabbits, dogs, cheetahs, elephants, tortoises, owls & alligators, w/metal tip, America, third quarter 19th c., 36" l. 1,760.00

Wooden walking stick, the circular knop over a spiral-turned capital over a series of tapering cylindrical spiral- and ring-turned registers decorated w/relief-carved motifs of the Grand Army of the Republic, as well as the relief-carved inscriptions "Lincoln," "Gettysburg - July 1, 2, 3, 1863," "Gen Meade," "Wood from Devil's Den" &"Gen Lee," as well as relief-carved military motifs, America, probably fourth quarter 19th c., 36¾" l. 1,380.00

Wooden walking stick, tapering oval bone knob continuing to a tapering cylindrical shaft carved w/an entwined snake, metal tip, America, third quarter 19th c., 36¾" l. (ILLUS. second from left) 990.00

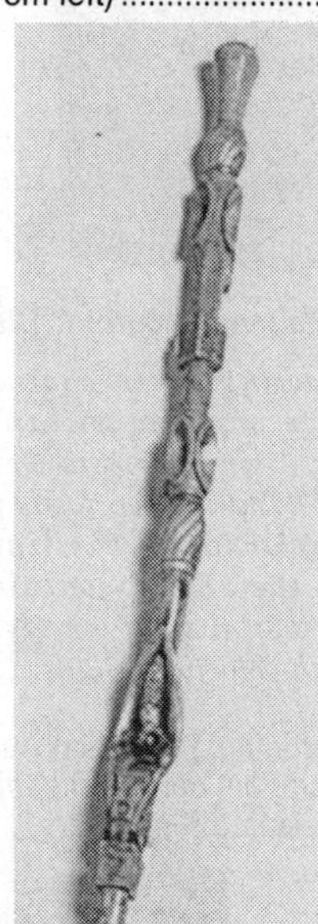

Ornately Carved Walking Stick

Wooden walking stick, carved,

painted & decorated, the rounded knop tapering w/several decorated registers including bulging fluted & gilded barrels, a circle of dished ellipses & foliate-carved decoration, all above a clerical figure set in a pulpit w/a figure behind, by H.A. Nims, Wasta, South Dakota, ca. 1917, minor losses to gilding & pigmentation, 37" l. (ILLUS. of part) 920.00

Wooden walking stick, carved, the handle carved in the form of a man's fist clutching a keg, the tapering shaft w/two intertwined snakes, probably southern United States, late 19th - early 20th c., 38½" l. 1,320.00

Wooden walking stick, carved bone handle depicting a human face, continuing to a wooden tapering irregular shaft punctuated w/animal & human faces, w/ink inscription & accents, America, third quarter 19th c., 39" l. (ILLUS. far right) 2,860.00

CANS & CONTAINERS

Huntley & Palmers "Marble" Biscuit Tin

The collecting of tin containers has become quite popular within the past several years. Air-tight tins were at first produced by hand to keep foods fresh and, after the invention of the tin-printing machine in the 1870s, containers were manufactured in a wide variety of shapes and sizes with colorful designs.

Automotive product, Protection Auto Top Preserver tin, early dome top, depicts antelope, bright colors, w/contents....................$20.00

Automobile polish, Whiz tin, w/lithograph of an auto 32.00

Axle grease, Purity Castor Oil tin..........23.00

Baking powder, Gold Label tin.............12.50

Baking powder, Jewel Tea tin, 1930s, w/contents....................35.00

Baking powder, Royal 6 oz. tin, w/paper label 18.00

Baking powder, Snow King tin, w/paper label, pictures Snow King.....35.00

Biscuit, Huntley & Palmers "Bell," inscribed "When Ye Doe Ringe" etc., 1912 ....132.00

Biscuit, Huntley & Palmers Chinese teak jewelry case w/relief dragon on lid 90.00

Biscuit, Huntley & Palmers "Lantern," 1911-13....................225.00

Biscuit, Huntley & Palmers "Marble," replica of a marble pillar w/female figure within an arch on sides, 1909, 7¼" h. (ILLUS.) 220.00

Biscuit, Ivin's Butter Jumble tin 11.00

Biscuit, Loose-Wiles tin, basketweave patt. 40.00

Biscuits, Sunshine octagonal tin, Liberty Bell pictured 40.00

Blasting caps, Du Pont tin 42.00

Blasting caps, Hercules tin, depicts a strongman....................35.00

Blasting caps, M.C. Manufacturing Works tin....................25.00

Candied fruit, Francisco tin, lithographed 145.00

Candy, Bunte tin, Art Deco style, tall 20.00

Candy, Filler Toffee tin, depicts King George VI & his family, 5½ x 9" 50.00

Candy, Hollingsworth box, "Memories of the Old South," w/hinged lid, five pictures, three depict black people, 4½ x 6½"....................35.00

Candy, Peter Paul Cream Mints tin, pictures an elf 15.00

Candy, Sharp's Toffee tin, Santa, w/golliwogs on side, England..........65.00

Candy, Thorne's English Toffee tin, depicts Steeplechase Racing 48.00

Candy, Uncle Wiggily pail....................800.00

Candy, Walters' Palm Toffee tin, colorful tropical birds depicted 16.00

Candy, Whitman's Air Bons 6 oz. tin, depicts a hot air balloon, 1950..........15.00

Carbonate of Ammonia 5 lb. can, wide cylindrical form w/pry-off lid, yellow w/green letters, a U.S. flag on the left & a baker on the right flanking center advertising for "Excelsior Carbonate of Ammonia," 7⅞" d., 4½" h. (soiled, paint loss on lid, dents & scratches) 11.00

Cherries, Blue Boys 30 lb. tin 46.00

Chewing tobacco, Pilot 10c Plug tin, depicts old style aeroplane 130.00

Chili powder, Mexene can, depicts devil 18.00

Cigarettes, Black Cat tin, color lithograph 25.00

Cigarettes, Camel flat fifties tin............30.00
Cigarettes, Cavalier one hundreds, tin oval 3 x 4"..19.00
Cigarettes, Craven flat fifties tin............15.00
Cigarettes, English Ovals flat fifties tin..45.00
Cigarettes, Fatima tin, gold on tan, 2 x 3 x 7"...50.00
Cigarettes, Horma flat fifties tin 15.00
Cigarettes, Lucky Strike flat fifties "Christmas" box 52.00
Cigarettes, Lucky Strike, round one hundreds tin 52.50
Cigarettes, McGill's flat fifties tin...........15.00
Cigarettes, Nestor tin..........................175.00
Cigarettes, Pall Mall flat fifties tin..........50.00
Cigarettes, Sweet Caporal flat fifties tin..21.00
Cigarettes, Will's Gold Flake flat fifties tin..15.00
Cigars, Banquet Hall flat tin..................25.00
Cigars, Little Chancellor tin..................10.00
Cigars, Madam Butterfly tin 290.00
Cigars, Portage 5c tin box 28.00

Possum Cigar Canister

Cigars, Possum canister, "Am Good and Sweet," possum, 5¼" d., 5¼" h. (ILLUS.) 150.00
Cigars, Scotty tin, pictures a scottie dog wearing an ascot & smoking a cigar 35.00
Cigars, Tango Stogies box 55.00
Cigars, Tom Keene tin...........................45.00
Clams, Underwood can 35.00
Cocoa, Bonn's tin, three colorful scenes, early...65.00
Cocoa, Stollwerk tin...............................25.00
Coconut, IGA tin 115.00
Coconut, Schepp's "cake box," one-shelf, original yellow w/black transfers, Goethe's "Lili, Lotte & Doretha," 11½ x 13", 14" h..............350.00
Coffee, Acme Vacuum Packed tin.........37.00
Coffee, Breakfast 3 lb. tin 20.00
Coffee, Bunker Hill 1 lb. can 110.00
Coffee, Caswell's 2½ lb. tin 20.00
Coffee, CDM (Café du Monde) 3 lb. pail, slip top 35.00

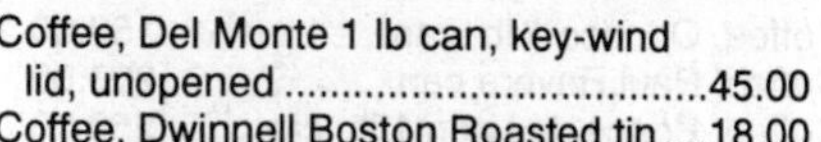

Coffee, Del Monte 1 lb can, key-wind lid, unopened 45.00
Coffee, Dwinnell Boston Roasted tin....18.00

Fischer's Coffees Bin

Coffee, Fischer's New York Coffees store bin, B. Fischer & Co., Importers - New York, sea green & blue w/gold & cream lettering & gold highlights, overall scratches & soiling, minor paint chipping, 13 x 19¼", 20¼" h. (ILLUS.) 154.00
Coffee, Folger's ½ lb. tin.......................13.50
Coffee, Fort Western can 175.00
Coffee, French Market 5 lb. pail 70.00
Coffee, Golden Rule Blend 10 lb. store bin 100.00
Coffee, Horn & Hardart 1 lb. can 45.00
Coffee, Ideal 3 lb. tin, Amish depicted..47.50
Coffee, Jefferson Park can 165.00
Coffee, Lipton 1 lb. container, screw-on lid, yellow label..........................125.00
Coffee, Market Brand 1 lb. tin, w/screw-on lid 48.00
Coffee, Mexican Java sample pail, cov., gold & red, Sherer Bros., Chicago, 2⅝" h. 300.00
Coffee, MJB 15 lb. can 35.00
Coffee, Monarch 1 lb can, key-wind lid 28.00

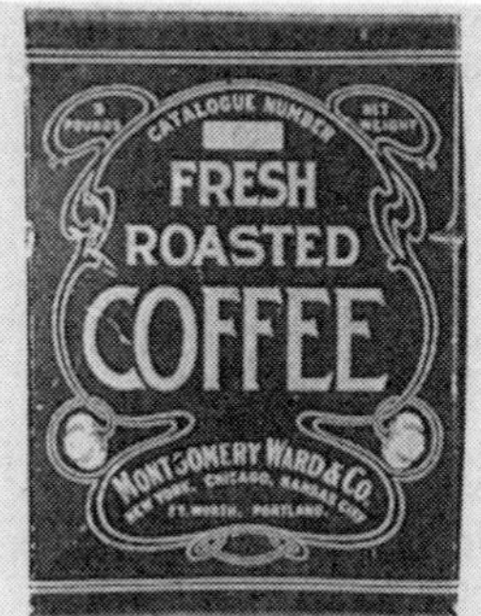

Montgomery Ward Coffee Can

Coffee, Montgomery Ward & Co. Fresh Roasted 5 lb. cardboard & metal container, blue w/cream lettering, minor soiling (ILLUS.) 93.50

Coffee, Orinoco 1 lb. can....................150.00
Coffee, Paul Revere can 200.00
Coffee, Ponce de Leon 1 lb. can 250.00
Coffee, Premier can..............................30.00
Coffee, Turkey Brand 3 lb can, ca. 1910...400.00
Coffee, Venizelos 1 lb. can.................650.00
Coffee, Wampum 2 lb. can, good colors 20.00
Coffee, Wish Bone 4 lb. pail 100.00
Cookies, Hoopees Golden Bear Cookie Co. tin, Berkeley, California..35.00
Cotter pins, Ford tin, green w/black lettering, embossed lettering on lid, "Ford Motor Company of Canada Limited" near bottom, 2¼" d., 1⅝" h. (minor dent to lid, scratches) 55.00

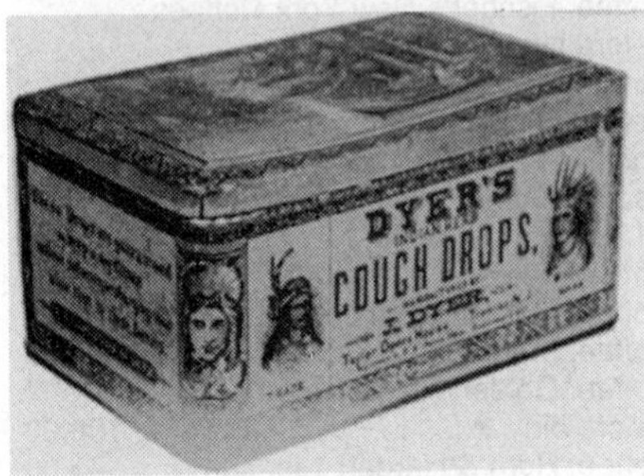

Dyer's Indian Herb Cough Drops

Cough drops, Dyer's Indian Herb rectangular container, red background w/black printing & small Indian portraits, some paint chipping on front (ILLUS.) 290.00
Crayons, Old King Cole tin, ca. 1930s...25.00
Crayons, Priscilla tin, w/most contents in good condition, ca. 1930...............45.00
Danger lights, Hitts tall cylindrical can, red & cream lettering on dark blue ground, blue lettering on white band at center, opens at middle above scene of red devil in a cream cloud over a red car w/man changing tire & flagging down people, copyright 1931 by Hitt Fireworks Co., 2¼" d., 13" h. (soiling & minor scratches) 16.50
Dusting powder, Richard Hudnut tin, Maytime Jasmine, Art Deco style floral design 45.00
Foot remedy, In Step sample tin, "For Aching Feet - Free Sample," ca. 1920s..8.00
Gum, Garwood's Peppermint Gum tin, 1906...35.00
Gun oil, Winchester tin, red & yellow....39.00
Gun powder, Illinois Powder Blasting Caps tin...20.00

Hair product, Sweet Georgia Brown Pomade sample tin 12.00

Cleanzum Hand Cleaner Can

Hand cleaner, Cleanzum can, depicting the face of a man wearing an orange cap w/"Cleanzum" across the top, No. 3 size w/removable lid, scratched, 4" d., 6¼" h. (ILLUS.) 66.00
Hand cleaner, Whiz Roadside 12 fl. oz. can, blue w/yellow triangle bordered in red, white & black lettering "The R.M. Hollingshead Co.," back w/colorful scene of man holding cleanser & car full of people on a country side road, 5¼" h. (minor rust & soiling) 38.50
Insect powder, Doctor Legear's tin.......19.00
Lard, Family pail, depicts pigs 95.00
Lighter fluid, Red Devil can, depicts devil on front 24.00
Machine oil, Firestone can, red & cream ground w/white & black lettering & red "F," 4 fl. oz., 5¼" h. (minor soiling) 16.50
Malted milk, Horlick's 25 lb. can, 15" h. (some minor nicks) 45.00
Marshmallows, Angelus 5 lb. container 30.00
Marshmallows, Bunte 5 lb. can, key-wind 375.00
Marshmallows, Whitman's, flying storks decoration 110.00
Motor oil, Aero Eastern 1 qt. can, black ground w/red & white lettering, oval reserve in the center w/a white & red airplane, 4" d., 5½" h. (rust spotting on back) 231.00
Motor oil, Grand Champion 1 qt. can, cartoon race track scene w/cars & drivers down the center, red & white background w/white lettering, red, green & blue cars, 4" d., 5½" h. (minor scratches, rust & denting).....357.50
Motor oil, Marathon 5 qt. can, yellow ground w/green & orange Greek key center band & an oval center reserve w/a nude Olympic runner, 6½" d., 9½" h. (cut on top, fading, scratches) 165.00

Motor oil, Mohawk 1 qt. can, Indian head profile on front, red & orange w/white lettering outlined in black, 4" d., 5½" h. (paint loss to front).......148.50

Motor oil, Mother Penn quart can, oval reserve w/bust portrait of Mother Penn at the top front, white w/red, white & blue, w/contents, 4" d., 5½" h. (very minor dents & scratches) 60.50

Penn-Air Motor Oil Can

Motor oil, Penn-Air 5 qt. can, yellow & green ground w/a large bi-plane flying at the top, "Penn-Air" in black under the plane, black lower half w/yellow lettering "100% Pennsylvania Motor Oil," top cut out, scratches, rust, dents, 6½" d., 9½" h. (ILLUS.) 302.50

Motor oil, Red Indian 5 qt. can, bust profile of an Indian chief wearing a large feathered headdress in red & black, black & white background, 6½" d., 9½" h. (top cut out, rust, scratches, dents) 550.00

Motor oil, Texaco Ursa 1 qt. can, white upper two-thirds above curved black & white striped lower section, black, red & white lettering & details, 4" d., 5½" h. (minor soiling)...............11.00

Tiger Motor Oil Can

Motor oil, Tiger 1 qt. can, yellow tiger, white w/yellow lines & yellow & black lettering, 4" d., 5½" h. (ILLUS.) 715.00

Motor oil, Trinton 1 qt. can, blue & white w/"Triton" in blue & "Motor Oil" in red, 4" d., 5½" h. (minor denting & scratches)...27.50

Nuts, Superior Salted Nuts 10 lb. canister, cream w/orange & black background, palm trees in the foreground w/an ocean liner in the distance, early 20th c., 7½" d., 11" h. (minor denting & scratches overall)..165.00

Ointment, Soothene tin, ornate design, made by Our Husbands Co., Lyndon, Vermont, early.....................................20.00

Texaco Outboard Gear Oil Can

Outboard gear oil, Texaco 2 lb. can, green & cream w/red, black & cream boats, red star w/green "T" logo, very minor scratches, 2¾ x 4¼", 6½" h. (ILLUS.) 99.00

Outboard motor oil, Duplex 1 qt. can, green & blue w/red boat, blue & green lettering, 2½ x 4½", 8" h. (minor denting & scratches)...............22.00

Outboard motor oil, Texaco can, rectangular, green & white w/white, black & red lettering, logo in white w/red star & green "T," 7½" h. (very minor scratches) 50.00

Oysters, "A & P" tin..............................20.00

Oysters, Moonlight Bay tin, scene of boy in half shell boat.......................150.00

Oysters, Sailor Boy 1 gal. can, blue on a white ground w/a cartoon figure of a sailor, late, 6½" d., 7½" h. 47.50

Patent medicine, Dr. Hobson's Witch Hazel & Glycerine Salve tin, 2¾" h. ...18.00

Patent medicine, Dr. Whetzel's Powder for Paroxysms of Asthma tin, 4" h...12.00

Peanut butter, Boy Scout 1 lb. pail 450.00

Peanut butter, Canadian 1 lb. pail 200.00

Peanut butter, Nash 1 lb. pail 30.00

Peanut butter, Peter Pan 25 lb. can, beige lettering on black outlined in grey, flanked by Peter Pan in orange w/black highlights on beige ground

Peter Pan Peanut Butter Can

& orange border, minor rust spotting overall & scratches, 10½" d., 10" h. (ILLUS.) 165.00

Peanut butter, Sultana 1 lb. pail, orange ground w/red & black lettering, seated children flank the central printing, pry-off lid, 4" h. (overall scratches) 33.00

Peanut butter, Sunset 25 lb. tin 13.00

Peanut butter, Toyland 1 lb. pail.........140.00

Bunnies Salted Peanuts Can

Peanuts, Bunnies Salted 10 lb can, rabbit dressed in blue & red holding a package of product, blue & yellow lettering, minor scratches & denting, 7¾" d., 11" h. (ILLUS.) 231.00

Peanuts, Harvard 10 lb. canister, gold ground w/red pennant w/gold lettering outlined in black above further red & black lettering, 8" d., 10" h. (minor scratches, rust & denting overall) 121.00

Peanuts, Jackie Coogan Salted Nut Meats 10 lb. canister, black ground w/black lithographed picture of Jackie Coogan on an elephant, black lettering, ca. 1920s, 8" d., 11" h., minor denting & rust spotting, (ILLUS. top next column) ..302.50

Jackie Coogan Canister

Peanuts, Planters Pennant Brand 10 lb. can, cylindrical, dark blue ground w/metallic red lettering & pennant outlined in black, 8½" d., 9¾" h. (dents, scratches) 33.00

Peanuts, Star Maid Salted Peanuts 10 lb. canister, cream ground w/blue lettering shadowed in silver & white, the center w/a girl's head & hands holding a tray w/peanuts in the center of a large star, blue & white dress, silver star, early 20th c., 7½" d., 11¼" h. (minor overall scratches) 231.00

Poison, McCormic Bee Brand, pictures red skull & crossbones, w/contents.......................................15.00

Popcorn, Dickinson's Big Buster Brand 10 lb. canister, drum major beating his drum in yellow & red against a blue ground, 6" d., 9½" h. (top missing, rust) 137.50

Talcum powder, American Ideal tin 125.00

Talcum powder, Sweetheart 3 oz. tin, picture of a lady 28.00

Talcum powder, Vantine's Wisteria (Oriental) tin 95.00

Tea, Premier tin, early metallic lithograph 45.00

Theatrical makeup, M. Stein Co. tin, round, top depicts a stage scene, 4" d., 2" h. 40.00

Tobacco, Abbey pocket tin 210.00

Tobacco, Brotherhood pocket tin........295.00

Tobacco, Buckingham upright can 85.00

Tobacco, Calabash tin, flat & round 32.50

Tobacco, Cannon's Irish Sliced Plug Flake - Aromatic pocket tin 165.00

Tobacco, City Club pocket tin, tall 350.00

Tobacco, Dill's Best Sliced Cut Plug tin 20.00

Tobacco, Dixie Kid pocket tin 375.00

Tobacco, Eden Cube Cut pocket tin 1,200.00

Tobacco, Edgeworth canister, curved side, knob lid 37.00

Tobacco, Electric Mixture box, 2 x 3 x 4" 145.00
Tobacco, Embassy pocket tin..............25.00
Tobacco, Forest & Stream Pocket tin, fisherman 155.00
Tobacco, Forest & Stream Pocket tin, mallard duck 87.00
Tobacco, Gail & Ax Navy lunch box ...195.00
Tobacco, Game Fine Cut box, w/wild game, 8 x 12" 250.00
Tobacco, Gibson Girl pocket tin 450.00
Tobacco, Granulated 54 fat pocket tin 87.50
Tobacco, Hand Made pocket tin ....350.00 to 400.00
Tobacco, Hindoo Granulated Plug pocket tin 1,500.00
Tobacco, Hi-Plane pocket tin, single-engine plane ....60.00 to 70.00
Tobacco, Hi-Plane pocket tin, 4-engine plane ....350.00 to 400.00
Tobacco, Holiday pocket tin 34.00
Tobacco, Jule Carrs tin, depicts railroad car, 1875............................300.00
Tobacco, Kentucky Club 7 oz. tin 6.00
Tobacco, Lucky Strike sample size pocket tin 78.00
Tobacco, Lucky Strike sliced plug can, tall 45.00
Tobacco, Model pocket tin, 15 cents 55.00

Nigger Hair Pail

Tobacco, Nigger Hair pail, red & black (ILLUS.) 225.00
Tobacco, Penny Post lunch box.........185.00
Tobacco, Pinkussohn's Potpourri pocket tin 86.00
Tobacco, Puritan Crushed Plug Mixture pocket tin..............................475.00
Tobacco, Q-Boid Granulated Plug pocket tin, concave 225.00
Tobacco, Q-Boid Granulated Plug pocket tin, convex............................260.00
Tobacco, Revelation sample size pocket tin 65.00
Tobacco, Snake Charmer pocket tin ..175.00
Tobacco, Sunset Trail pocket tin 120.00
Tobacco, Sweet Cuba lunch box, silver & green.......................................60.00

Tobacco, Taxi pocket tin, driver in taxi w/top-hatted gentleman..............................4,000.00 to 5,000.00
Tobacco, Union Leader pocket tin, w/Uncle Sam...65.00
Tobacco, Velvet sample tin 40.00
Tobacco, Wild Fruit (Bagley's) lunch box..200.00
Tobacco, Winner pocket tin 225.00
Tobacco, Winner Cut Plug lunch box, racing car scene on side 210.00
Tractor oil, Agricastral can, square w/peaked top, green ground w/pink & black lettering, two cream-colored sheaves of wheat, depicts tractor plowing fields, 21" h. (scratches & paint chipping) 55.00
Typewriter ribbon, Carter's Midnight tin, blue 20.00
Typewriter ribbon, Eureka tin...............20.00
Typewriter ribbon, Fine Service tin, pictures an airplane 15.00
Typewriter ribbon, Panama Beaver Super Superb tin, depicts beaver 35.00
Veterinary medicine, Mehlos Udder Salve tin, 4" h...7.00

CASH REGISTERS

National Model 130

James Ritty of Dayton, Ohio, is credited with inventing the first cash register. In 1882, he sold the business to a Cincinnati salesman, Jacob H. Eckert, who subsequently invited others into the business by selling stock. One of the purchasers of an early cash register, John J. Patterson, was so impressed with the savings his model brought to his company, he bought 25 shares of stock and became a director of the company in 1884, eventually buying a controlling interest in the

National Manufacturing Company. Patterson thoroughly organized the company, conducted sales classes, prepared sales manuals and established salesman's territories. The success of the National Cash Register Company is due as much to these well organized origins as to the efficiency of its machines. Early "National" cash registers, as well as other models, are deemed highly collectible today.

Brass, "American," Model No. 1, detail adder $2,650.00
Brass, "National," Model No. 2, very early wide scroll detail-adder w/glass sign 2,200.00
Brass, "National," Model No. 3, Serial #69516, restored 2,900.00
Brass, "National," Model No. 5, candy store model, narrow scroll design w/glass top sign 2,750.00
Brass, "National," Model No. 8, candy store model w/clock 650.00
Brass, "National," Model No. 50, Renaissance design cabinet w/original clock 2,500.00
Brass, "National," Model No. 52, Renaissance design cabinet, extended base, original clock, raised letters on lid that match drawer tag 3,800.00
Brass, "National," Model No. 52¼, Dolphin design cabinet, extended base 2,200.00
Brass, "National," Model No. 130, Art Nouveau style cabinet (ILLUS.) 495.00
Brass, "National," Model No. 211, antique copper finish 1,900.00
Brass, "National," Model No. 216, candy store model 1,695.00
Brass, "National," Model No. 226, w/original bilingual top sign 700.00
Brass, "National," Model No. 324 ....1,050.00
Brass, "National," Model No. 332 ....225.00 to 250.00
Brass, "National," Model No. 337, Dolphin design cabinet 925.00
Brass, "National," Model No. 441, Empire design cabinet w/quartered oak base 1,675.00
Brass, "National," Model No. 442, oak drawer base 275.00
Brass, "National," Model No. 442-E-L, illuminated top sign w/etched glass, quartered oak base 2,750.00
Brass, "National," Model No. 452, Empire design cabinet 1,800.00
Wooden, "Monitor," Model No. 1, original finish & decals 650.00
Wooden, "National," Model No. 3, early wood deep-drawer inlaid mahogany cabinet 4,500.00

CASTORS & CASTOR SETS

Tiffany Castor set

Castor bottles were made to hold condiments for table use. Some were produced in sets of several bottles housed in silver plated frames. The word also is sometimes spelled "Caster."

Castor set, 2-bottle, clear glass, openwork silver stand, George III period, R. Hennell I, London, England, 1779-80 ....$467.50
Castor set, 4-bottle, clear etched glass bottles w/original cut stoppers, revolving silver plate frame w/elaborate fretwork bail handle, late 19th c., 14½" h. 165.00
Castor set, 4-bottle, clear flint glass bottles, Gothic patt., ornate silver plate frame, signed 225.00
Castor set, 4-bottle, cobalt blue glass bottles w/silver plated tops fitted in an oval galleried silver plate frame w/four columns supporting a pierced cupola, together w/a similar salt dip w/blue glass liner, Germany, ca. 1795, 14½" h. 4,675.00
Castor set, 4-bottle, opalescent glass bottles w/horizontal ribbing & a vertical band in front enameled w/colored flowers, original ornate silver plate footed & handled frame, marked Simpson, Hall, Miller & Co. 245.00
Castor set, 4-bottle, square cranberry shading to clear pressed glass bottles, simple silver plate stand raised on four ball feet, curving overhead handle 425.00
Castor set, 5-bottle, clear etched glass bottles, fancy silver plate frame 125.00
Castor set, 5-bottle, cranberry glass Inverted Thumbprint patt. bottles, silver plate frame marked "Pairpoint" 615.00
Castor set, 6-bottle, clear facet-cut

glass bottles fitted in a sterling silver navette-shaped stand w/Greek key borders & bifurated loop handles, the frame raised on four paw feet headed by shells & foliate scrolls, the central reeded loop handle issuing from bearded masks, three bottles w/silver covers, three w/cut glass stoppers, Tiffany & Company, New York, 1854-70, 10½" l. (ILLUS.) 2,090.00

Pickle castor, amber glass Inverted Thumbprint patt. insert, enameled floral decoration, ornate silver plate frame, marked Aurora 300.00

Pickle castor, blue glass Inverted Thumbprint patt. insert w/enameled floral decoration, resilvered footed silver plate frame, 11½" h. 555.00

Pickle castor, blue opalescent glass insert, Swirled Windows patt., original resilvered frame & tongs 345.00

Pickle castor, clear pressed glass Cane patt. insert, ornate silver plate footed frame & three-finger forks, marked Meriden, 12½" h. 95.00

Pickle castor, cobalt blue glass spherical insert w/gold trim & gold enameled decoration, resilvered silver plate frame w/tongs, marked Benedict Mfg. Co. 395.00

Pickle castor, cranberry glass bulbous insert decorated w/tiny enameled flowers & white dotting around the top & bottom, resilvered frame & cover accented w/filigree work, marked Reed & Barton 425.00

Pickle castor, cranberry glass Honeycomb patt. insert enameled w/florals & berries, footed silver plate frame w/beaded base in Maltese cross shape, beaded handle & ornate cut-out feet, marked Forbes Silver Company 325.00

Pickle castor, cranberry glass Inverted Thumbprint patt. insert, decorated w/blue enameled flowers, ornate silver plate frame w/large leaves down side, marked Webster 400.00

Pickle castor, cranberry glass Inverted Thumbprint patt. w/Coralene beading insert, silver plate frame decorated w/large leaves & two pickles, bird decoration on lid 675.00

Pickle castor, cranberry glass Inverted Thumbprint patt. insert, decorated w/gold foliage, ornate silver plate frame, marked Simpson, Hall & Miller 395.00

Pickle castor, cranberry glass Inverted Thumbprint patt. barrel-shaped insert, decorated w/yellow roses, footed silver plate frame, 10¾" h. 500.00

Pickle castor, cranberry opalescent glass Daisy & Fern patt. Parian Swirl mold insert, original ornate silver plate frame on pedestal base w/ornate feet 375.00

Pickle castor, cranberry opalescent glass Hobnail patt. insert, ornate silver plate frame, marked Tufts 450.00

Pickle castor, cranberry satin glass mother-of-pearl Diamond Quilted patt. insert, enameled w/mums & gold leaves decoration, ornate silver plate frame & cover w/seahorse finial, marked Pairpoint 400.00

Pickle castor, pink crackle glass squatty w/floral decoration insert, silver plate frame w/figural pickles where handle attaches to base, 9" h. 410.00

Pickle castor, rose mother-of-pearl satin glass Diamond Quilted patt. insert w/white lining, ornate silver plate frame w/cut-out gallery, decorated pedestal base & decorated oval handle, marked Reed & Barton 345.00

Pickle castor, Rubina glass insert w/enameled floral decoration, silver plate frame 425.00

Pickle castor, sapphire blue glass paneled Optic patt. insert, h.p. w/enameled white & orange blossoms, ornate silver plate frame w/spatula feet & tongs, marked Pairpoint..325.00

Pickle castor, small breakfast-size, emerald green glass Inverted Thumbprint patt. insert w/heavy enameling of white daisies & pale blue buds, silver plate footed frame w/piecrust rim base, marked Pairpoint 295.00

Pickle castor, yellow to white opalescent satin finish glass pear-shaped insert, decorated w/pink roses, ornate silver plate frame w/small birds on front & back, 11¾" h. 765.00

CAT COLLECTIBLES

General

Andirons, cast iron, figural, swell-bodied stylized model of a cat seated facing the fire, American-made, early 20th c., 15½" h., pr. (ILLUS. top next page)...............$2,530.00

Figural Cat Andirons

Ashtrays, pottery, modeled in the form of a black cat, set of four stacked on a base, together w/a waving black cat toothpick holder, unmarked, 6¼" l., 3¼" h., the set 55.00

Calendar, 1933, "Don't Pull My Leg, Pull My Whiskers," whiskers are matches, has match striker 25.00

Condiment set: salt & pepper shakers & mustard jar w/spoon; Felix the Cat, 1930s, the set.....................1,000.00

Coverlet, crib-size, the story of "The Three Little Kittens Who Lost Their Mittens" worked in cross-stitch, 35 x 52" 110.00

Creamer, ceramic, creamy white w/green neck, orange lip & figural black cat handle, marked "Goldcastle, Made in Japan," 4¼" h...35.00

"Kitten" Doll

Doll, "Kitten" girl, modeled to resemble a little girl w/human-type features & curly hair, wearing a floor-length dress, ca. 1920, 16" (ILLUS.)............65.00

Kitchen set: cov. cookie jar, sugar bowl, creamer & salt & pepper shakers; ceramic, modeled in the form of a cat, marked "Lefton," 5 pcs. 200.00

Letter holder, pottery, modeled in the form of a black cat w/a pen forming the tail, mint paint, marked "Japan," 6½" l. 30.00

Models of cats:

Bisque, white cat on green pillow, Cappe, Italy, ca. 1981, discontinued, 3" h. 190.00

Ceramic, white cat w/green bow, wearing a yellow hat w/pink rose, incised "Cordelia," Corde-lia China Co., Ohio, ca. 1940, 4¾" h. 29.50

Ceramic, kittens: one lying on its back (HN 2579), another sitting & licking its hind paw(HN 2580), the other sleeping (HN 2581); brown & white, Royal Doulton, discontinued 1986, each 60.00

Ceramic, Siamese in seated position, HN 2862, Royal Doulton, discontinued, 4½" h.....290.00

Ceramic, bust of an Egyptian-type cat, mosaic tile effect in aqua, gold & cream on a medium brown ground, signed "Sascha B" (Sascha Brastoff, California), 7¾" h. 200.00

Porcelain, Siamese cat looking at a brown mouse, on an oval base lettered "Watch It," marked "Beswick," England, 1956-75 .....135.00

Wade Figure of "Tom"

Pottery, "Tom" & "Jerry," marked "Wade," England, 1956-60, 3¾" h., pr. (ILLUS. of "Tom") 98.00

Nodding figure, ceramic, Detroit Tigers cat uniform, souvenir dated "1967," w/Japan paper label "Sports Specialties '67," mint condition, 7¼" h...95.00

Planter, ceramic, green leafy spray w/smiling grey kitten climbing up the side, marked "Made in U.S.A.," 4" l., 4¼" h..22.50

Planter, pottery, light blue cat, Uhl Pottery, Indiana.................................120.00

Rattle w/whistle, sterling silver & wood, reclining cat, marked "Pussy,"

six bells attached, ca. 1900, 8" l. 275.00
Salt & pepper shakers, porcelain, one-piece, green dog (salt) & orange cat (pepper), marked "Bavaria" w/incised numerals & "D.R.G.M.," 2½" h. 35.00
Teapot, cov., china, figural black cat w/yellow eyes & large red bow, 7" h. 45.00
Tray, fruitwood marquetry & mother-of-pearl inlay, oblong w/pointed sides, the center inlaid w/a scene of three cats lapping milk flanked by end panels each inlaid w/a large butterfly w/mother-of-pearl body, signed in marquetry "Galle," ca. 1900, 28½" l. 6,325.00
Wall hanger, pottery, model of a cat in reclining pose w/front legs apart & back legs in position to leap, dark yellow decorated w/blue & white hearts & polka dots, green glass eyes, marked, probably Wemyssware, made at Fife Pottery, Kirkcaldy, Scotland, 19" l. 632.50

Original Artwork:

"Kittens in a Basket"

Oil on board, "Kittens in a Basket," signed "A. Augusta Talboys, R.W.A." (British, 1908-1920s), framed, 18 x 20" (ILLUS.) 4,800.00
Oil on canvas, "En Famille," signed by Daniel Merlin (France, 1861-1933), framed, 28 x 31½"......................20,000.00
Oil on canvas, "Le Dessus du Panier" (The Pick of the Basket), signed by Jules Leroy (France,1833-65), framed, 15⅛ x 22"......................14,000.00
Water-color, "Krazy Kat," by George Herriman, w/a dedication to Western artist Maynard Dixon.................13,000.00

CELLULOID

Celluloid was our first commercial plastic and early examples are now "antique" in their own right, having been produced as early as 1868 after the perfection of celluloid by John Wesley Hyatt. Earlier in this century other related "plastics" were also introduced and some examples of these items are also included.

Business card, salesman's, Wanamaker, engraving of beautiful lady, ca. 1880s...............................$28.00
Calendar/stamp holder, transportation supply company advertising, 1912 ....20.00
Cuff box, cov., painted lady & flowers on cover, brocade trim, Victorian...105.00
Dresser set, green w/roses trim, w/clock, 14 pcs. 195.00
Dresser set, pink w/black trim, w/clock & picture frame, ca. 1930, 18 pcs. ..250.00
Powder box, cov., the cover molded overall w/cherries in low-relief, lid molded "R. LALIQUE," ca. 1925, 3" sq...920.00
Powder box, decorated w/Art Nouveau lady, pink, "Evry Ann" 45.00
Shoe horn & brush w/handle, peach marbleized 12.00
Stamp holder, book-form, w/Washington, D.C. advertisement for "A Modern Dental Chair" 45.00
Tape measure, model of a basket of flowers 55.00
Tape measure, model of a dog............80.00

CERAMICS

For additional listings, see Antique Trader Books CERAMICS - POTTERY & PORCELAIN PRICE GUIDE.

ABINGDON

"Mother Goose" Cookie Jar

From about 1934 until 1950, Abingdon Pottery Company, Abingdon, Illinois manufactured decorative pottery, mainly cookie jars, flowerpots and vases. Decorated with various glazes, these items are becoming popular with collectors who are especially attracted to Abingdon's novelty cookie jars.

Book ends, model of a horse head, black glaze, pr. $100.00
Compote, open, pink glaze, No. 568 ....30.00
Console bowl, round, blue, 9" d. 8.00
Console bowl, grey-green, 9 x 14" 18.00
Console bowl, oval, white, 18" l. 18.00
Console set: No. 564 scalloped bowl & pair of No. 575 scalloped candlesticks; floral decoration, No. 33, on white ground, lavish gold trim, 3 pcs. 75.00
Cookie jar, "Aramis Bear" 25.00
Cookie jar, "Bo Peep" ....200.00 to 250.00
Cookie jar, "Choo Choo," engine ....125.00 to 150.00
Cookie jar, "Clock" (Cookie Time) 110.00
Cookie jar, "Daisy," w/"Cookies" on side 55.00
Cookie jar, "Fat Boy" 450.00
Cookie jar, "Hobby Horse" 210.00
Cookie jar, "Humpty Dumpty" ....250.00 to 300.00
Cookie jar, "Jack-in-the-Box" ....250.00 to 275.00
Cookie jar, "Little Girl," w/'O's' in "Cooky" forming her eyes ....100.00 to 120.00
Cookie jar, "Little Old Lady," black woman 800.00
Cookie jar, "Little Old Lady," white......200.00
Cookie jar, "Little Old Lady," pink 225.00
Cookie jar, "Miss Muffet".....250.00 to 300.00
Cookie jar, "Money Bag" 80.00
Cookie jar, "Mother Goose" (ILLUS.) ....300.00 to 350.00
Cookie jar, "Pineapple" 65.00
Cookie jar, "Pumpkin" (Jack o'Lantern) ....350.00 to 400.00
Cookie jar, "Windmill" ....300.00 to 400.00
Cornucopia-vase, blue glaze, 8½" w., 4¾" h. 25.00
Figurine, kneeling nude, No. 3903, pink w/decoration 178.00
Jardiniere, pink glaze w/decoration, No. 558 ....35.00
Model of a duck 18.50
Urn, small side handles, square foot, top w/vertical ribs, relief-molded leaf wreath decoration, rose, No. 538.........9.50
Vase, 8" h., model of a tulip, yellow......22.00
Vase/flower holder, fan-shaped, white, holder built inside lip, horizontal ribs at base, fan & scroll design, No. 491, 5 x 5 x 7" 22.00
Wall pocket, Lily patt., blue, No. 377 ....25.00
Wall shelf, yellow, cherub face, wings & neck support semi-circular shelf, No. 587, 4¼ x 7¾", 4½" h. 30.00

ADAMS

Adams' Rose Plate

Members of the Adams family have been potters in England since 1650. Three William Adamses made pottery, all of it collectible. Most Adams pottery easily accessible today was made in the 19th century and is impressed or marked variously ADAMS, W. ADAMS, ADAMS TUNSTALL, W. ADAMS & SONS, or W. ADAMS & CO. with the word "England" or the phrase "Made in England" added after 1891. Wm. Adams & Son, Ltd. continues in operation today. Also see HISTORICAL & COMMEMORATIVE WARES and STAFFORDSHIRE TRANSFER WARES.

Cup & saucer, handleless, Adams' Rose patt., impressed "A" (minor roughness) $165.00
Plate, 7" d., Palestine patt., blue 45.00
Plate, 8¼" d., Dickensware series, transfer-printed scene titled "Mrs. Gumage casts a damp on our departure" 15.00
Plate, 8¾" d., blue transfer-printed scene entitled "Hawthornden, Edinburghshire," impressed "Adams" (small flakes & minor scratches) 115.00
Plate, 9" d., dark blue transfer-printed center design of a cupid & a maiden, floral border, impressed mark, ca. 1830 ....159.50
Plate, 9½" d., Adams' Rose patt., free-hand red & green w/black trim, impressed "Adams" (ILLUS.) 148.50

Platter, 15¾" l., oval, Genoa patt., light blue, impressed mark (minor stains) 137.50
Soup plate w/flanged rim, Adams' Rose patt., red, green & black, 10¾" d. (rim repair)............................93.50

AUSTRIAN

Decorated Austrian Pitcher

Numerous potteries in Austria produced good-quality ceramic wares over many years. Some factories were established by American entrepreneurs, particularly in the Carlsbad area, and other factories made china under special brand names for American importers. Marks on various pieces are indicated in many listings. Also see ROYAL VIENNA.

Basket, long rectangular body w/anangular handle at midsection, raised on six tapering square feet, molded in low-relief w/a grid of squares about the rim & handle, glazed in mottled blue & emerald green, impressed factory mark, numbered "4990 – Austria," ca. 1920, 11¾" l., overall 5¼" h........$2,300.00
Bowl, 10" d., decorated w/red & white roses (M.Z. Austria) 150.00
Cake plate, handled, scalloped rim, scrolled relief at handles, decorated w/spray of pink & blue flowers, gold trim, 9½" d. (urn mark) 24.00
Chocolate pot, cov., decorated w/sprays of blossoms in rose, lavender & purple, enhanced w/lavish gold latticework & scrolling devices, matte finish (Carlsbad) 125.00
Cracker jar, cov., decorated w/white water lilies on green band of leaves, gold trim (M.Z. Austria) 125.00
Dessert set: 11½" d. charger & four 8½" d. plates; decorated w/a trellis bower of clustered green roses & yellow leaves in a center spray on a white ground, gold ribbon rim, 5 pcs. (Victoria Carlsbad) 115.00
Game platter, buck & four does in woodland scene, gold trim, 11¾ x 17½" 185.00
Pitcher, 5⅝" h., 6" d., porcelain, wide bulbous body tapering to a flat rim w/pinched spout, angled handle, h.p. top band w/clusters of oranges & pink blossoms divided by "H" designs, base, marked "Vienna Austria," early 20th c. (ILLUS.) 145.00
Pitcher, 10" h., left-handed type, h.p. w/multicolored floral & leaves decoration w/gold tracery, cream ground (Victoria Carlsbad).................75.00
Pitcher, pillow-shaped, 4¾ x 9", 16" h., four-footed, decorated w/giant molded scrolls & h.p. irises front & back, gold outlining, sponging & trim, reticulated handle, ivory ground, pink & gold neck spout, handle & feet (Carlsbad Austria)......360.00
Plate, 8¼" d., center decoration of children & lambs, scalloped edge, medium blue & gold border (Carlsbad Austria)..............................45.00
Plate, 8½" d., red poppies decoration, curved & scalloped rim 45.00
Plate, 8½" d., decorated w/spruce branches & flowers (M.Z. Austria) 55.00
Plate, 13" d., pierced to hang, h.p. head of a St. Bernard dog in black, brown & white against a shaded blue to cream to green ground, irregular scalloped & scroll-molded gilt edge, artist-signed, marked 225.00
Vase, 5½" h., two-handled, allegorical scenes on front & back in soft pastels (beehive mark)...................................60.00
Vase, 7½" h., continuous allegorical scenes w/ladies, men, cherub & flowers (beehive mark Austria) 100.00
Vase, 10" h., handled, decorated w/colorful court scenes (Victoria Carlsbad Austria) 45.00
Vase, 13½" h., 5" w. at base, four-footed, narrow neck w/flared scalloped mouth, high slender double shoulder handles, decorated w/h.p. red, yellow & white carnations, gold outlining on shaded beige-ivory ground, stylized relief-molded leaves at rim & neck, vertical ribs at base, gold trim (crown & seal "RH" Austria) 210.00
Vase, 16" h., 7" d., two-handled, swelled cylindrical body decorated w/h.p. purple violets, heavy gilt, artist-signed (crown & wreath mark)..290.00

BELLEEK

Belleek china has been made in Ireland's County Fermanagh for many years. It is exceedingly thin porcelain. Several marks were used, including a hound and harp (1865-1880), and a hound, harp and castle (1863-1891). A printed hound, harp and castle with the words "Co. Fermanagh Ireland" constitutes the mark from 1891. Belleek-type china also was made in the United States last century by several firms, including Ceramic Art Company, Columbian Art Pottery, Lenox Inc., Ott & Brewer and Willets Manufacturing Co. Also see LENOX.

AMERICAN

Bowl, 7½" square, decorated w/h.p. flowers & berries (Willets) $250.00

Bowl, 8" d., 1" h., scroll decoration in silver on white ground (Willets)..........90.00

Candy dish, fluted, white w/pink interior, 3½ x 4½" (Ceramic Art Company) 95.00

Chocolate cup & saucer, decorated w/a purple "W" monogram on white, gold trim & gold dragon handle (Willets) 37.00

Creamer, applied 'fishnet' decoration, knotted handle, all-white, 3¼" h. (Knowles, Taylor & Knowles)...........285.00

Cups, demitasse, Orient patt. (Morgan), set of four 175.00

Cup & saucer, demitasse, shell-shaped, gilded twig handle & trim (Ott & Brewer) 155.00

Dish, triple shell-shaped, pale pink pearlescent glaze w/blue coral center handle, Ott & Brewer (faint hairline on one shell).....................225.00

Mug, barrel-shaped, decorated w/h.p. leaves & nut pods, palette mark, 5" h., (Ceramic Art Company – Lenox) 145.00

Mug, decorated w/apples & leaves, ca. 1906, 6" h. (Ceramic Art Company) 90.00

Plate, 10½" d., floral decoration w/gold rim, marked "Coxon No. S-115" (Coxon)..........................200.00

Rose bowl, tri-footed, gold, green & brown leaves & vines decoration, beaded berries, 3¾" h. (Knowles, Taylor & Knowles)...............................145.00

Salt & pepper shakers, cov., blue stylized flower decoration & gold trim on pearlized ground, pr. (Willets) 165.00

Vase, miniature, 2¾" h., blue stylized flowers & gold trim on pearlized ground (Willets) 145.00

Vase, 8" h., decorated w/bluebirds & berries, artist-signed, ca. 1906, green palette mark (Lenox)..............195.00

Vase, 10" h., decorated w/black spider webs & yellow, pink, blue & orange butterflies, white pearlized ground, ca. 1906-24 (Lenox) 225.00

Vase, 12½" h., pedestal base, bulbous body w/slender neck flared at top, two gold handles at neck, yellow roses on pastel pink ground, ca. 1889 (Ceramic Art Company) 295.00

IRISH

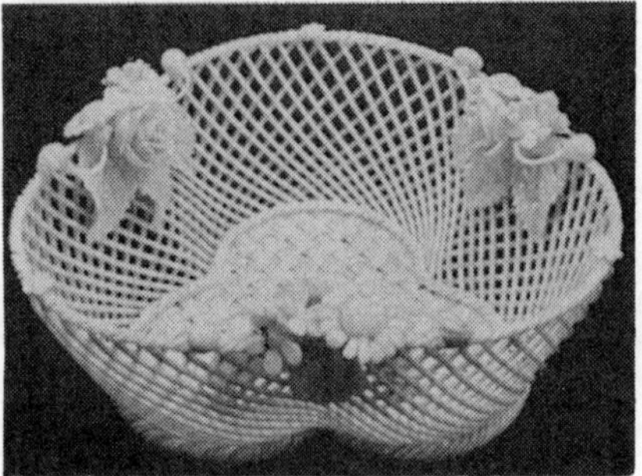

Irish Belleek Basket

Basket, Shamrock-type, four-strand, three-lobed sides w/three applied flower clusters at the rim, 6" w. (ILLUS.) ....425.00 to 475.00

Bread (or cake) plate, Neptune patt., 10" d., 3rd black mark........................95.00

Bread (or cake) plate, open-handled, Shamrock-Basketweave patt., 9" d., 2nd black mark ....100.00 to 125.00

Coffee set, demitasse: cov. coffeepot, creamer, open sugar bowl & six cups & saucers; Limpet patt., 3rd black mark, 15 pcs....................850.00

Creamer, Ivy patt., 5" h., 3rd black mark 65.00

Creamer, jug-shaped w/rope handle, 5" h., 1st black mark 450.00

Creamer, Limpet patt., 3rd black mark...95.00

Lotus Creamer

Creamer, Lotus patt., 3rd black mark (ILLUS.) 50.00

Creamer, Shamrock-Basketweave patt., large, 3" h., 3rd black mark.......65.00

Creamer, Undine patt., 2nd green mark 45.00
Creamer & open sugar bowl, Cleary patt., 2nd black mark, pr. 130.00
Creamer & open sugar bowl, Irish Pot pat., 3rd black mark, pr. 65.00
Creamer & open sugar bowl, Ribbon patt., 3rd black mark, pr. 125.00
Creamer & open sugar bowl, Toy Shell patt., 1st green mark, pr. 55.00
Cup & saucer, demitasse, Fan patt., w/pink trim, 2nd black mark 150.00
Cup & saucer, New Shell patt., 2nd green mark 25.00
Cup & saucer, Shamrock-Basketweave patt., 3rd black mark....85.00
Cup & saucer, Tridacna patt., 2nd black mark ....75.00 to 89.00

Cardium on Coral Dish

Dish, Cardium on Coral patt., shell-shaped, 3½" h., 1st black mark (ILLUS.) 300.00
Flower holder, Nautilus on Coral patt., 9½" h., 1st black mark 750.00
Holy water font, Cherub patt., figure of a winged cherub head, 8" h., 3rd black mark 185.00
Model of a harp, decorated w/shamrocks, 8" h., 2nd green mark 225.00
Model of a pig, 3" h., 2nd black mark 230.00
Model of a swan, 3½" h., 3rd green mark 55.00
Pitcher, milk, 6" h., Shamrock-Basketweave patt., 3rd black mark..198.00
Plate, 7" d., Harp-Shamrock patt., green mark 60.00
Plate, 7" d., Hexagon patt., pink trim, 2nd black mark 30.00
Plate, 7" d., Mask patt., 3rd black mark 30.00
Plate, 7" d., New Shell patt., 1st green mark 60.00
Salt dip, Cleary patt., 3rd black mark....49.00
Salt dip, Hexagon patt., 2nd black mark 175.00
Salt dip, shell-shaped, Limpet patt., 1st green mark 25.00
Salt dip, Shamrock-Basketweave patt., 3rd black mark 35.00
Spill vase, Rock patt., small, 3rd black mark 75.00
Spill vase, Rock patt., large, 3rd green mark 95.00
Tea kettle, cov., Hexagon patt., 2nd black mark 250.00

Harp-Shamrock Teapot

Teapot, cov., Harp-Shamrock patt., green mark (ILLUS.) 135.00
Teapot, cov., Shamrock-Basketweave patt., 2nd black mark 250.00
Trinket box, cov., Cherub patt., 3½" w., 3" h., 3rd green mark 65.00
Vase, 7⅛" h., 4⅛" d., Rathmore patt., 3rd green mark 55.00
Vase, 8" h., 4½" d., Ribbon patt., applied flowers, 3rd black mark 225.00

BENNINGTON

Various Bennington Wares

Bennington wares, which ranged from stoneware to parian and porcelain, were made in Bennington, Vermont, primarily in two potteries, one in which Captain John Norton and his descendants were principals, and the other in which Christopher Webber Fenton (also once associated with the Nortons) was a principal. Various marks are found on the wares made in the two major potteries, including J. & E. Norton, E. & L.P. Norton, L. Norton & Co., Norton & Fenton, Edward Norton, Lyman Fenton & Co., Fenton's Works, United States Pottery Co., U.S.P. and others.

The popular pottery with the mottled brown on yelloware glaze was also produced in Bennington, but such wares should be referred to as "Rockingham" or "Bennington-type" unless they can be specifically attributed to a Bennington, Vermont factory.

Book flasks, one w/binding impressed "Kossoth," the other impressed "7," the first w/a mottled Flint Enamel glaze, the other w/a mottled brown Rockingham glaze, attributed to Lyman Fenton & Co., ca. 1850, one w/a chipped corner, 5" & 5½" h., 2 pcs. (ILLUS. left) $357.50

Bottle, figural, barrel-shaped standing Mr. Toby, mottled dark brown Rockingham glaze, embossed "All For James Crow," impressed "1849" mark, 9" h. 395.00

Candlestick, slender columnar form w/flared round base, mottled dark brown Rockingham glaze, 9⅝" h. ...412.50

Curtain tie-backs, rosette-form, mottled brown Rockingham glaze, attributed to Lyman Fenton & Co., mid-19th c., 4¼ & 4½" d., 2 pr. 165.00

Flowerpot, cylindrical w/slightly flaring rim, incised horizontal lines, mottled Flint Enamel glaze, attributed to Lyman Fenton & Co., star crack, 19th c., 4½" h. (ILLUS. right) 715.00

Inkwell, cylindrical base, the lid sloping up to a ringed domed top, mottled brown Rockingham glaze, attributed to Lyman Fenton & Co., 19th c. 165.00

Rare Bennington Jar

Jar, cov., stoneware, wide ovoid body tapering to a flaring rim flanked by eared handles, inset cover, slip-quilled cobalt blue decoration of a large stag standing between a stump & a stylized fir tree w/grass below, impressed mark of J. Norton & Co., Bennington & "2," minor crack at rim, 2 gal., 11½" h. (ILLUS.) 4,600.00

Models of poodles, standing animal holding a basket in its mouth, the tail curled over the back, applied coleslaw on the shoulders, front legs & ears, free-standing, mottled brown Rockingham glaze, attributed to Lyman Fenton & Co., 8" h., facing pair (minute losses to coleslaw).....................11,000.00

Bennington Lion

Models of lions, each standing w/front paw on a ball, the tail curled over the back, w/an applied coleslaw mane, on a stepped rectangular base, mottled Flint Enamel glaze, each marked "Lyman Fenton & Co., patented 1849, Bennington, Vermont," imperfections, 11" l., 9" h., facing pair (ILLUS. of one)...11,000.00

Pitcher, 7½" h., cylindrical base beneath a slightly waisted neck, mottled brown Rockingham glaze, attributed to Lyman Fenton & Co., mid-19th c. (ILLUS. center).............330.00

BISQUE

Bisque Animal Dishes

Bisque is biscuit china, fired a single time but not glazed. Some bisque is decorated with colors. Most abundant from the Victorian era are figures and groups, but other pieces from busts to vases were made by numerous potteries in the U.S. and abroad. Reproductions have been produced for many years so care must be taken when seeking antique originals.

Animal covered dish, a realistic model of a chick in brown w/its broken shell on the domed green grass cover, white basketweave base (ILLUS. left) $500.00

Animal covered dish, two realistic chicks, one in tan & the other in tan & black, w/their shells on the domed green grass cover, pale yellow basketweave base (ILLUS. right) 625.00

Animal covered dish, dog reclining on a green blanket on the lid, the white shaggy animal w/brown & black head & tail, on an oval gold basketweave base, blue bisque maker's seal under the lid, France, 19th c., 5¾ x 8¼", 5⅜" h. 550.00

Bust of Victorian girl leaning on log, chin held in hand, playful flirting expression, deep molded sculpturing, Heubach "sunburst" mark, 6" h. 595.00

Bust of "Winter," modeled as a young girl w/lavender scarf on her head, wearing a sad look, on a socle base, signed "L. Kley," France, 9½" h. 350.00

Figure of a Bathing Beauty, Germany, 3½" l. 120.00

Figure of baby lying on its back w/toe in mouth, lying in glazed bathtub, Heubach mark, 4½" l., 3½" h. 395.00

Figure, Happifat boy, Germany, 3½" h. 375.00

Figure of a monk, standing wearing brown robe, holding a snuff box in one hand & a pinch of snuff in the other, a jug behind him, 3" w., 7" h. 79.00

Figure of a girl dressed in bunny costume, eyes turned to the side, hands outstretched, standing in front of large pink egg, marked "Heubach," 7½" h. 595.00

Figure of pouty character, intaglio eyes, No. 7602, Heubach "sunburst" mark, 10" h. 395.00

Figure of a young woman w/lovely serene face, holding a small book, marked "Heubach," 10¼" h. 295.00

Figure of 18th century man, Heubach "sunburst" mark, 12" h. 375.00

Figure of little blond-haired boy holding rabbit in arms & by ear, marked "Heubach," 12" h. 395.00

Blue Boy Bisque Figure

Figure of a young boy standing and wearing a Van Dyke-style pale blue outfit w/lavender florals & gold trim, holding a feathered hat to his side, he carries posies in one hand, on a round base, 3¼" d., 12" h. (ILLUS.) 175.00

Figure of young boy wearing lavender suit & holding a monkey on his arm w/hand outstretched as if begging, Heubach mark, 13" h. 375.00

Figure of a toddler standing in a small attached bisque tub, signed "Heubach," 15" h. 1,795.00

Figures of a blond-haired man & woman in pink & blue floral-decorated Empire era costumes, Germany, 18" h., pr. 475.00

Figure group, Dutch boy & girl in brown & green clothes, standing back to back, signed "Heubach," 5" h. 275.00

Figure group, a little girl holding two kittens in her skirt, a dog & cat flanking her on each side, 8½" h. 145.00

Game dish, cover & underplate, the cover modeled w/two white rabbits on a grassy mound, round basketweave base on a separate underplate, underplate minor chip, underplate 9" d., dish 7¼" d., 7¼" h., the set 470.00

Piano baby, lying on tummy holding dog in arm, Handwerck mark, 5½" h. 125.00

Piano baby, lying w/head on pillow & pacifier in its mouth, a dog reclining on its back, Handwerck mark, 6½" h. 175.00

Piano baby, crawling on tummy, wearing a white gown w/blue bow, head turned to side, Heubach "sunburst" mark, 8" h. 495.00

Snow baby & girl wearing a skirt on a sled 235.00
Snow baby on ice skates....210.00
Snow baby on skis....175.00
Snow baby riding a polar bear....185.00
Snow baby seated w/candleholder, 1" h....165.00
Snow baby, girl w/brown Snow bear on sled 285.00

BLUE & WHITE POTTERY

Dutch Children Kissing Pitcher

The category of blue and white or blue and grey pottery includes a wide variety of pottery, earthenware and stoneware items widely produced in this country in the late19th century right through the 1930s. Originally marketed as inexpensive wares, most pieces featured a white or grey body molded with a fruit, flower or geometric design and then trimmed with bands or splashes of blue to highlight the molded pattern. Pitchers, butter crocks and salt boxes are among the numerous items produced but other kitchenwares and chamber sets are also found. Values vary depending on the rarity of the embossed pattern and the depth of color of the blue trim; the darker the blue, the better. The pattern names used with our listings are taken from two references, Blue & White Stoneware, Pottery, Crockery *by Edith Harbin (Collector Books, 1977) and* Blue & White Stoneware *by Kathryn McNerney (Collector Books, 1981).*

Bowl, 9" d., embossed Apricots w/Honeycomb patt. ....$85.00 to 125.00
Butter crock, cov., embossed Butterfly patt. 96.00
Butter crock, cov., embossed Draped Windows patt., w/bail handle, 9" d., 8" h....165.00 to 195.00
Canister, cov., embossed Basketweave patt., "Tea"....150.00
Cuspidor, embossed Peacock (at Fountain) patt....345.00
Mug, embossed Basketweave patt.....150.00
Mug, embossed Windy City patt., marked on bottom "Robinson Clay Pottery Co., Akron, Ohio," 5½" h....225.00 to 250.00
Pitcher, 7¾" h., 6½" d., cylindrical, embossed Peacock patt. 550.00
Pitcher, 8" h., embossed Grape Cluster on Trellis patt. ....175.00 to 200.00
Pitcher, 8½" h., embossed Cow patt....150.00 to 175.00
Pitcher, 9" h., 6½" d., embossed Columns & Arches patt. 350.00
Pitcher, 9" h., embossed Good Luck (Swastika)....200.00 to 250.00
Pitcher, 9" h., 6" d., embossed Dutch Children Kissing patt. (ILLUS.) ....150.00 to 200.00
Pitcher, 9" h., embossed Windmill & Bush patt. 235.00
Pitcher, embossed Windy City (Fannie Flagg) patt., Robertson Co., Ohio....375.00 to 425.00
Rolling pin, blue band decoration 150.00
Rolling pin, swirl design w/diffused blues 675.00

Wildflower Pattern Rolling Pin

Rolling pin, printed Wildflower patt., 7" l. (ILLUS.) 190.00
Salt box, cov., hanging-type, embossed Apricot patt. 200.00
Salt box, cov., hanging-type, embossed Eagle w/Shield & Arrows patt....300.00
Soap dish, embossed Cat's Head patt....125.00 to 150.00
Soap dish, embossed Rose patt....125.00
Toothpick holder, figural Swan patt. 60.00

BLUE RIDGE DINNERWARES

The small town of Erwin, Tennessee was the home of the Southern Potteries, Inc., originally founded by E.J. Owen in 1917 and first called the Clinchfield Pottery.

In the early 1920s Charles W. Foreman purchased the plant and he revolutionized the company's output, developing the popular line of hand-painted wares sold as "Blue Ridge" dinnerwares. Free-hand painted by women from the surrounding hills, these colorful dishes in many patterns, continued in production until the plant's closing in 1957.

Greenbriar Pattern Plate

Bonbon, flat shell-shape, Easter Parade patt. $50.00
Bowl, cereal, Sunny patt., Colonial shape 8.00
Box, cov., Dimity patt., Sherman Lily shape 395.00
Butter pat, Valley Violet patt....................35.00
Cake plate, maple leaf-shaped, Calico patt. 40.00
Cake plate, maple leaf-shaped, Chintz patt. 75.00
Candy box, cov., Rose Marie patt 128.00
Casserole, cov., Julie patt. 35.00
Celery dish, leaf-shaped, Chintz patt....46.00
Celery dish, leaf-shaped, French Peasant patt....................90.00
Creamer & open sugar bowl, pedestal foot, French Peasant patt., pr. 240.00
Cup & saucer, demitasse, Tulip Row patt. 25.00
Cup & saucer, Christmas Tree patt. 40.00
Cup & saucer, Valley Violet patt. 20.00
Egg cup, double, Valley Violet patt.......30.00
Egg plate, Rooster patt....................78.50
Pitcher, 6" h., vitreous china, figural chick, floral decoration 87.50
Pitcher, 8¼" h., vitreous china, Chintz patt., Milady shape....................125.00
Pitcher, 8½" h., French Peasant patt., Milady shape....................229.00
Pitcher, jug-type, Paul Revere patt.....600.00
Plate, 8½" d., Blackbird patt., Songbirds series, Astor shape 75.00
Plates, 8½" d., County Fair patt., red rim, set of 4....................35.00
Plate, dinner, 9¼" d., Greenbriar patt. (ILLUS.) 7.50
Plate, 9½" d., Fruit Fantasy patt. 6.00
Plate, 10" d., Christmas Tree patt.........65.00
Plate, 10" d., Mickey patt. 7.00
Platter, 15" l., Bluebell Bouquet patt. 16.00
Platter, 15" oval, French Peasant patt. 195.00
Platter, Thanksgiving Turkey patt. 165.00
Relish dish, vitreous china, heart-shaped, Buttons & Forget-Me-Nots patt. 30.00
Relish dish, deep, shell-shaped, Chintz patt. 60.00
Relish dish, leaf-shaped w/loop handle, Serenade patt. 48.50
Salt & pepper shakers, Blossom Time patt., pr. 32.00
Salt & pepper shakers, Calico patt., Blossom Top shape, pr. 30.00
Salt & pepper shakers, figural chickens, model of a hen & rooster, hen 4" h., rooster 4¾" h., pr. 120.00
Salt & pepper shakers, tall, footed, Paper Roses patt., pr. 40.00
Salt & pepper shakers, Valley Violet patt., Blossom Top shape, pr. 35.00
Smoking set: cov. cigarette box & four ashtrays; Rooster patt., 5 pcs. 150.00
Smoking set: cov. cigarette box & four ashtrays; Sailboat patt., 5 pcs. 150.00
Sugar bowl, open, breakfast size, Valley Violet patt. 40.00
Sugar bowl, cov., w/pedestal base, French Peasant patt. 68.50
Teapot, cov., Crab Apple patt., Colonial shape, brown trim 60.00
Teapot, cov., Delta Daisy patt., Colonial shape 50.00
Teapot, cov., Sunbright patt. 75.00
Toast plate, cov., Valley Violet patt. 85.00
Vase, 8" h., boot-shaped, Gladys patt. 95.00
Vase, 9" h., ruffled rim, tapered, Delphine patt. 60.00
Vegetable bowl, open, round, French Peasant patt. 67.50

BOCH FRERES

The Belgian firm, founded in 1841 and still in production, first produced stoneware art pottery of mediocre quality, attempting to upgrade their wares through the years. In 1907, Charles Catteau became the art director of the pottery and slowly the influence of his work was absorbed by the artisans surrounding him. All through the 1920s wares were decorated in distinctive Art Deco designs and are now eagerly sought along with the hand-thrown gourd-form vessels coated with earthtone glazes that were produced during the same time. Almost all Boch Freres pottery is marked, but the finest wares also carry the signature of Charles Catteau in addition to the pottery mark

Boch Freres Jardiniere

Jardiniere, wide ovoid body w/flared mouth, decorated w/a wide band of stylized cream blossoms outlined in black against a shaded brown opaque-glazed ground, cobalt blue & cream highlights, Gres Keramis marks, ca 1890, 11" d., 9⅜" h. (ILLUS.)....$825.00

Pitcher, 4½" h., white w/black & red geometric decoration 35.00

Vase, 6¼" h., 4¾" d., wide ovoid shouldered body w/a short flaring neck, decorated w/a band of stylized antelope in blue & green against an ivory crackled background, marked 302.50

Vase, 6¾" h ., 4" d., semi-ovoid shouldered body w/short neck, incised yellow, orange & green fruit w/brown foliage against a thick white crackled ground, marked "MADE IN BELGIUM, BOCH Fes, LA LOUVIERE, FABRICATION BELGE, D. 745, ct." 192.50

Vase, 9½" h., stylized leaves in matte yellow, blue & white on a black ground, designed by Charles Catteau, artist-signed, stamp mark, ca. 1925 ....467.50

Vase, 12⅝" h., slender ovoid body tapering to a small neck w/widely flared rim, decorated w/stripes of stylized leaf & berry bands up the sides in safron yellow, ochre & white against a ground of alternating cobalt blue & copper green horizontal bands, designed by Charles Catteau, stamped company mark & facsimile signature, ca. 1930 ....1,035.00

Vase, 18" h., tall baluster-shaped body, crackled glaze decorated w/floral medallions in greens & blues, designed by Charles Catteau, printed company mark & painted "Ch. Catteau MADE IN BELGIUM" 230.00

BRAYTON LAGUNA POTTERY

Durlin E. Brayton began his operation in Laguna Beach, California in 1927. After his marriage a short time later to Ellen Webster Grieve, who also became his business partner, the venture became a successful endeavor. One of the most popular lines was the Childrens' series *which featured a rubber stamp-like mark with the first name of the child followed underneath with a line which separates the words "Brayton Pottery." Both white clay and pink clay were used during Brayton's production. More than 150 people, including approximately twenty designers, were employed by Brayton. Sometimes on items too small for a full mark, designers would incise their initials. It was not until after World War II and the mass importation of pottery products into the United States that Brayton's business declined. Operations ceased in 1968.*

Ashtray, w/one cigarette rest, round, turquoise glaze, incised 'Brayton Laguna Pottery,' 4¼" d. $12.00

Candleholder, figural, Blackamoor in seated position, colorful glazes w/lots of gold trim, designed by Ruth Peabody, 5" h. 75.00

Cookie jar, figural black Mammy, bright blue dress, white apron w/yellow, black, green & blue trim, red bandana on head, yellow earrings, marked examples only (being reproduced), 12⅝" h. 425.00

Creamer & open sugar bowl, round, eggplant glaze, incised mark, 2½" h., pr. 27.00

Figure of a black baby w/diaper, sitting, 3¾" h. 25.00

Figure of a black baby w/diaper, crawling, 4¼" l. 30.00

Figure, Childrens' series, "Ann," girl seated w/legs apart, knees bent, 4" h. 100.00

Figure, Childrens' series, "Butch," boy standing w/present under each arm, short pants w/suspenders, 7½" h.......70.00

Figure, Childrens' series, "Dorothy," girl seated w/legs together &

straight, hands by her sides, hair w/pigtails & tied w/ribbons, 4¼" l., 4" h. 95.00

Figure, Childrens' series, "Ellen," girl standing w/pigtails & a hat tied at neck, arms bent & palms forward, one leg slightly twisted, 7¼" h. 75.00

Figure, Childrens' series, "Jon," boy standing & carrying basket in one hand, rooster in other, 8¼" h. 75.00

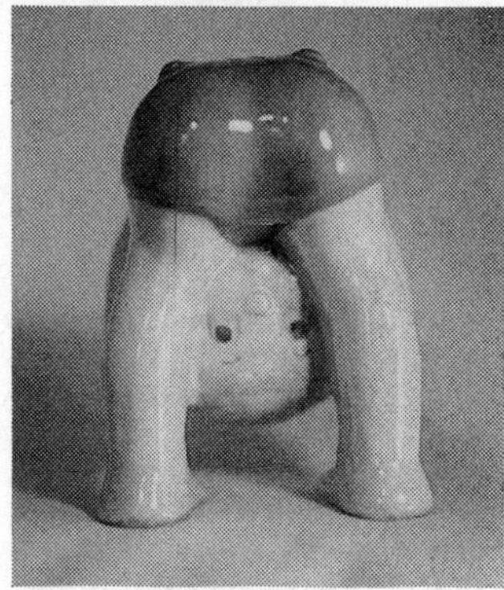

Brayton Laguna "Millie" Figure

Figure, Childrens' series, "Millie," girl bent over w/legs apart, head between legs, scarce, 3¾" h. (ILLUS.) 155.00

Figure, Childrens' series, "Miranda," girl standing, wearing coat & hat, decorations on shoes, many assorted glazes available, sometimes unmarked, 6½" h. 55.00

Figure, Childrens' series, "Pat," girl standing, freckles on her face, wearing a hat w/tie around neck & short dress, holding full-sized doll in back between her legs, 7" h. (hard to find) 85.00

Figure, Childrens' series, "Petunia," black girl standing w/basket of flowers, wearing a pinafore, 6¼" h. 130.00

Figure, Childrens' series, "Sambo," black boy standing w/chicken under one arm, 7½" h. 145.00

Figure, Gay Nineties lady, holding up her dress w/one hand, umbrella in other hand, ruffled flowing skirt, hat, high-top shoes, ca. 1930, 9½" h. 105.00

Figure, "Tweedle Dee," character from Alice in Wonderland, non-Disney, 3" h. 28.00

Figures of dice players w/dice, black boys on hands & knees, 4¾" l., 3½" h., set of 3 ....195.00

Flower holder, figural, "Francis," girl standing & holding small planter in front, blonde hair w/snood & flower, 8" h. 35.00

Model of a bear, seated, light blue, underglaze mark 'Brayton's Laguna, Cal.,' Model No. T-1, 3½" h. 18.00

Model of a duck, textured bisque body, glossy glazed green face, Model No. 4138, 5½" l., 5" h. 35.00

Model of a swan, grey & white glossy glaze, marked 'Copyright 1940 By Brayton Laguna Pottery,' 6" l., 4½" h. 20.00

Planter, figural, Dutch girl pushing a cart, girl w/yellow hair, blue dress, white apron & hat, black shoes, grey cart, ca. 1950, 8" h. 15.00

Salt & pepper shakers, figural man & woman, he w/hands in his pockets, she w/arms folded across her waist, he wears a brown jacket & pants trimmed w/yellow & white hearts & flowers, she wears a white scarf over her head & white apron, touches of yellow & green hearts & flowers, both w/brown stained faces & hands, Model No. K26, 6½" h., pr. 45.00

Tile, decorated w/a Mexican man taking a siesta under tree w/cacti nearby, blue, green, white, incised mark, ca. 1928, 6½" sq. 95.00

BUFFALO POTTERY

Buffalo Pottery was established in 1902 in Buffalo, New York, to supply pottery for the Larkin Company. Most desirable today is Deldare Ware, introduced in 1908 in two patterns, "The Fallowfield Hunt" and "Ye Olden Days," which featured central English scenes and a continuous border. Emerald Deldare, introduced in 1911, was banded with stylized flowers and geometric designs and had varied central scenes, the most popular being from "The Tours of Dr. Syntax." Reorganized in 1940, the company now specializes in hotel china.

DELDARE

Bowl, cereal, 6½" d., The Fallowfield Hunt $275.00

Bowl, fruit, 9" d., 3¾" h., Ye Village Tavern ....450.00 to 500.00

Bowl, fruit, 9" d., The Fallowfield Hunt - The Death 550.00

Bowl, soup, 9" d., The Fallowfield Hunt 495.00

Bowl, soup, 9" d., Ye Olden Days - Ye Village Street 475.00

Candleholder, shield-back, Village Scenes, 7" h. (ILLUS. top next column) 895.00

Deldare Candleholder

Candlesticks, Ye Olden Days - Ye Village Street, 9½" h., pr. 1,000.00

Card tray, tab handles, Mr. Pickwick Addresses the Club, 7" d. 900.00

Card tray, The Fallowfield Hunt - The Return, 7¾" d. ....350.00 to 375.00

Card tray, Ye Olden Days - Ye Village Street, 7¾" d. 495.00

Creamer, hexagonal, The Fallowfield Hunt - Breaking Cover 200.00

Cup & saucer, The Fallowfield Hunt - The Return......................................250.00

Cup & saucer, Ye Olden Days - Ye Village Street ....250.00 to 300.00

Dresser tray, Dancing Ye Minuet, 1909, 9 x 12" 650.00

Fern bowl, Ye Olden Days - Ye Village Street, 8" d. 675.00

Hair receiver, cov., Ye Village Street ....350.00 to 400.00

Humidor, cov., bulbous, There was an Old Sailor, etc., 8" h. 1,250.00

Humidor, cov., octagonal, Ye Lion Inn, artist-signed, 1909, 7" h. 800.00

Mug, The Fallowfield Hunt, 2½" h. ....500.00 to 550.00

Mug, The Fallowfield Hunt, 3½" h. ....350.00 to 400.00

Mug, The Fallowfield Hunt, artist-signed, 4½" h. ....450.00 to 500.00

Mug, Ye Olden Days - Ye Lion Inn, 4½" h. ....400.00 to 425.00

Nut bowl, Ye Lion Inn, 1909, 8" d., 3¼" h. 700.00

Pin tray, Ye Olden Days, 3½ x 6¼" 250.00

Pitcher, 6" h., octagonal, The Fallowfield Hunt, artist-signed, ca. 1908 ....775.00

Pitcher, 6" h., octagonal, Their Manner of Telling Stories - Which He Returned with a Curtsey ....450.00 to 550.00

Pitcher, 7" h., The Fallowfield Hunt - Breaking Cover ....450.00 to 500.00

Pitcher, 7" h., octagonal, To Spare an Old, Broken Soldier - To Advise Me in a Whisper, 1923 ....550.00 to 600.00

Pitcher, 8" h., octagonal, The Fallowfield Hunt - The Return.......................700.00 to 800.00

Deldare Octagonal Pitcher

Pitcher, 9" h., octagonal, With a Cane Superior Air - This Amazed Me (ILLUS.) 775.00

Pitcher, tankard, 12½" h., The Fallowfield Hunt - The Hunt Supper ....900.00 to 950.00

Pitcher, tankard, 12½" h., Vicar of Wakefield, All you have to do to teach the Dutchman English - The Great Controversy ....1,000.00 to 1,500.00

Plaque, pierced to hang, The Fallowfield Hunt - Breakfast at the Three Pigeons, 12" d. ....600.00 to 650.00

Plate, 7¼" d., Ye Village Street, 1908 ....125.00 to 175.00

Plate, 8¼" d., Ye Town Crier 175.00

Plate, 9½" d., Ye Olden Times, artist-signed, 1909 ....175.00 to 200.00

Plate, 10" d., The Fallowfield Hunt - Breaking Cover, artist-signed 325.00

Plate, 10" d., Ye Village Gossips ....150.00 to 175.00

Plate, chop, 14" d., An Evening at Ye Lion Inn, artist-signed, ca. 1908 ....700.00 to 800.00

Plate, chop, 14" d., The Fallowfield Hunt - The Start ....900.00 to 950.00

Powder jar, cov., Ye Village Street ....450.00 to 500.00

Relish tray, Ye Olden Times, artist-signed, 1908, 6½ x 12" 695.00

Sugar bowl, cov., The Fallowfield Hunt - Breaking Cover ....250.00 to 300.00

Teapot, cov., The Fallowfield Hunt - Breaking Cover ....350.00 to 400.00

Teapot, cov., Scenes of Village Life in Ye Olden Days, 5¾" h. ....400.00 to 450.00

Tea tile, The Fallowfield Hunt - Breaking Cover, artist-signed, 6" d. 295.00

Tea tray, Heirlooms, 1908, 10½ x12" ....700.00 to 750.00

EMERALD DELDARE

Bowl, fruit, 9" d., 3¾" h., Dr. Syntax Reading His Tour............850.00 to 900.00

Bowl, fruit & undertray, octagonal, Art Nouveau floral & geometric designs, tray 14" w., bowl 10" w., 6¾" h., 2 pcs. 1,450.00

Card tray, handled, Dr. Syntax Robbed of his Property, 7" d. 550.00

Cup & saucer, Dr. Syntax at Liverpool, 1911 ....650.00

Humidor, cov., Doctor Syntax returned Home, artist-signed, 1911, 6¼" d., 7" h. 1,750.00

Mug, Dr. Syntax scenes, "I give to the law that are owing, etc.," 2¼" h........795.00

Mug, Dr. Syntax again filled up his glass ..., 4¼" h. ....675.00 to 700.00

Plate, 7¼" d., Dr. Syntax Soliloquising....................595.00

Plate, 8¼" d., Art Nouveau stylized geometric designs....................465.00

Plate, 8½" d., Dr. Syntax - Misfortune at Tulip Hall....450.00 to 550.00

Plate, 10" d., Dr. Syntax Making a Discovery 1,100.00

MISCELLANEOUS

Campbell Kids Feeding Dish

Bowl, 4" d., 2¼" h., Blue Willow patt., design on interior & exterior 5.00

Bowl, 5" d., Blue Willow patt. 5.00

Christmas plate, 1955..........................48.00

Christmas plate, 1960..........................35.00

Christmas plate, 1962, designed for the exclusive use of Hample Equipment Company, Elmira, New York 250.00

Creamer, Abino Ware........................635.00

Cup & saucer, Blue Willow patt., 1905 ....35.00

Cup & saucer, Gaudy Willow patt.........80.00

Feeding dish, Campbell Kids decoration, Grace Drayton design, 7¾" d. (ILLUS.) 85.00

Fish set, platter & six fish plates, artist-signed 295.00

Mug, Abino Ware, sailboat decoration, ca. 1912, 4¼" h. 395.00

Mug, Abino Ware, windmill & boat decoration, artist-signed, 1913, 4¼" h. 875.00

Buffalo Hunt Pitcher

Pitcher, jug-type, 6" h., The Buffalo Hunt (ILLUS.) 325.00

Pitcher, jug-type, 6" h., Holland patt., scenes of Dutch children around the body, rural landscape band around the rim 345.00

Pitcher, jug-type, 6" h., Whaling City, souvenir of New Bedford, Massachusetts, 1907 ....650.00

Pitcher, 7" h., jug-type, Gaudy Willow patt. 335.00

Pitcher, jug-type, 7½" h., George Washington, blue decoration, gold trim, 1905 ....565.00

Pitcher, 9¼" h., waisted tankard shape, two sailors on one side, lighthouse on rocky shore reverse, blue decoration, 1906 ....500.00

Plate, 7½" d., commemorative, Faneuil Hall, Boston, blue-green 30.00

Plate, 8¼" d., Gaudy Willow patt., ca. 1908 ....90.00

Plate, 9" d., scalloped rim, The Gunner scene, deep blue-green 125.00

Plate, 9¼" d., Arts & Crafts style stylized rose decoration in cobalt blue on a white ground, ink stamped "BUFFALO POTTERY CO." (minor surface nicks)....................77.00

Plate, 10" d., Abino Ware, windmill scene 925.00

Plate, 12" d., Rouge Ware, Breakfast at the Three Pigeons, 1930s...........595.00

Platter, 12" l., Lune Ware, Cairo patt., blue 55.00
Platter, 11 x 14" rectangle, buffalo hunting scene 425.00
Platter, 14" l., Blue Willow patt., oval 145.00
Relish dish, Vienna patt. 34.00
Tray, Abino Ware, scenic decoration of windmill & boat, artist-signed, 1911, 10½ x 13¾" .....1,000.00 to 1,500.00

CALIENTE POTTERY

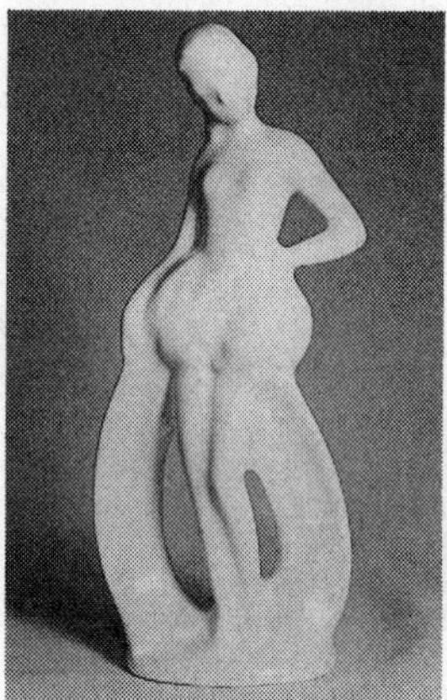

Caliente Dancing Lady

Virgil K. Haldeman opened his pottery in Burbank, California in 1933. He created satin matte glazes and blended colors while Andrew Hazelhurst, chief designer until 1941, used his talents to produce a variety of merchandise. The business moved to Calabasas, California in 1947 and closed in 1953.

Early pieces have a strong Catalina Pottery influence, probably because Virgil Haldeman worked about three years for that company. Molded pieces (numbers under 100), hand-made pieces (200 numbers), figures, mostly animals and fowl (300 numbers), dancing girls (400 numbers), a continuation of hand-made pieces (500-549), and molded pieces with roses added (550 and over numbers) were created. Since incised numbers are on many of the Caliente pieces, this system aids in their identification. Almost without exception, Caliente items have a solid bottom. A few dancing girls, especially the #401, have been reproduced. The reproductions have a hole *in the bottom, are lighter weight and many have hand-painted flowers on the dresses.*

Caliente used several marks over the years with the "Made in California" mark in block letters the most commonly found. A mold number was included on many of the pieces. Paper labels were also used.

Candleholder, model of a lily pad, pale green glaze, 5" l., 2" h. $10.00
Figure of a dancing lady, head tilted, back arched, left arm holding up edge of her dress, right arm across body touching left elbow, deep green glaze, script incised on white clay "Calif. 401," 6¾" h. 40.00
Figure of a dancing girl in bloomers, a scarf in each hand & draping to the floor, head bent & slightly tilted, face features indistinct, left hand resting on waist, Model No. 406, hard-to-find, 6½" h. (ILLUS.) 65.00
Figure of a dancing girl on base, right elbow pointed upward w/hand resting under chin, left leg bent back w/left hand holding up edge of her dress, right leg straight w/foot on tiptoes, ivory glaze, face features indistinct, weighs less than 4 ounces, Model No. 400, 4½" h. 60.00
Flower frog, model of a sailboat, white w/light blue glaze, Model No. 73, 5" h. 25.00
Model of a deer, standing, four legs separated & on an oval base, right front leg slightly bent, ivory glaze w/five tan brushed spots on body, Model No. 351, 5" h. 26.00
Model of a goose, head up, light green, Model No.303, 4¼" h. 15.00
Model of a Scottie dog & fire hydrant, dog standing w/left rear leg raised, tail up, black glaze, Model No. 311, 3½" h.; hydrant, black glaze, Model No. 352, 3½" h., set of two.................55.00
Vase, 3½" h., 3¼" d., globular shape, trefoil opening, in-relief leaves on both sides of a single rose 34.00
Vase, 5¾" h., Art Deco design, rectangular base w/two buttresses on each side flaring upward to a thin lip 30.00

CANTON PORCELAIN

This ware has been decorated for nearly two centuries in factories near Canton, China. Intended for export sale, much of it was originally inexpensive blue-and-white hand decorated ware. Late 18th and early 19th century pieces are superior to later ones and fetch higher prices.

Basket & undertray, deep oval flaring

reticulated sides, on a conforming undertray, 19th c., basket 10¾" l., 2 pcs. (ILLUS. of part)....................$920.00

Bowl, 7¼" d., shallow scalloped sides, 19th c. 550.00

Creamer, baluster-form body on a circular foot, 19th c., 3½" h. 207.00

Dinner service: fifty 7¾" & 9¾" plates, four small dishes & 14 soup spoons; each piece decorated w/variations of the river landscape scene w/pagodas, figures, bridges & boats, 19th c., 68 pcs. (chips, hairlines) 2,588.00

Dish, cov., almond-shaped w/flared sides & flat rim, low domed cover w/knob finial, faintly marked on base "China," 10½" l. (minor edge flakes) 93.50

Dish, elongated oval w/shaped sides, 10¾" l. 495.00

Pitcher, 7½" h., wide ovoid body tapering to a flaring rim w/a wide arched spout, slender highly arched strap handle, 19th c. 935.00

Pitcher, 15¾" h., footed tall ovoid body tapering to a wide arched spout, long arched C-scroll handle, 19th c...1,155.00

Canton Sauce Tureen

Sauce tureen, cover & undertray, the oblong squared deep body w/boar's head handles, the low domed cover w/stem finial, on a conforming dished undertray, 19th c., tureen 6½" l. (ILLUS. of tureen) 550.00

Serving dish, cov., oblong almond-shaped w/a flanged rim, low domed cover w/pine cone finial, 19th c., 11¼" l..467.50

Soup tureen, cov., rectangular, 19th c., 12¼" l. 1,265.00

Sugar bowl, cov., wide cylindrical body w/twisted loop handles, the domed cover w/a fruit finial, 19th c., 6" h...495.00

Teapot, cov., footed ovoid pear-shaped body w/C-form handle & swan's neck spout, the domed cover w/flanged rim & knob finial, 19th c., 8" h..522.50

Tile, square, 19th c., 4¾" w...............357.50

Tureen, cover & undertray, deep oval flaring sides above a flaring foot & w/boar's head handles, the domed cover w/stem finial, on a conforming undertray, 19th c., tureen 10¼" l......770.00

Umbrella stand, tall cylinder decorated w/large Chinese landscapes, 19th c., 24½" h..........1,430.00

Vegetable dish, cov., almond-shaped, 10¼" l. 330.00

CERAMIC ARTS STUDIO OF MADISON

Founded in Madison, Wisconsin in 1941 by two young men, Lawrence Rabbitt and Reuben Sand, this company began as a "studio" pottery. In early 1942 they met an amateur clay sculptor, Betty Harrington and, recognizing her talent for modeling in clay, they eventually hired her as their chief designer. Over the next few years Betty designed over 460 different pieces for their production. Charming figurines of children and animals were a main focus of their output in addition to models of adults in varied costumes and poses, wall plaques, vases and figural salt and pepper shakers.

Business boomed during the years of World War II when foreign imports were cut off and, at its peak, the company employed some 100 people to produce the carefully hand-decorated pieces.

After World War II many poor-quality copies of Ceramic Arts Studio figurines appeared and when, in the early 1950s, foreign imported figurines began flooding the market, the company found they could no longer compete. They finally closed their doors in 1955.

Since not all Ceramic Arts Studio pieces are marked, it takes careful study to determine which items are from their production.

Bank, figural, Mr. Blankety Bank $85.00

Bank, figural, Mrs. Blankety Bank, green dress (ILLUS. top next page)...65.00

Bell, figural, Lillibelle 50.00

Candleholder, two-light, figural Triad woman kneeling...................................69.50

Figurine, Accordion Boy, 5" h. 45.00

Figurine, Angel, praying on knees, 4½" h..35.00

Figurine, Aphrodite, black & tan, 7¾" h. 120.00

Mrs. Blankety-Blank Bank

Figurine, Bali-Gong, 5½" h. 35.00
Figurine, Balinese Dancer, 9½" h. 42.00
Figurine, Beth, modern dancer 20.00
Figurine, Cuban girl, shades of green 32.50
Figurine, Drummer Girl, 4¼" h. 78.00
Figurine, Gay 90 Woman, No. 1, artist-signed, 6½" h. 52.00
Figurine, Girl in Chair, 2¼" h. 15.00
Figurine, Guitar Boy, 5" h. 45.00
Figurine, Isaac, 10½" h..........................79.00
Figurine, Jill, 4¾" h. 18.00
Figurine, Little Jack Horner, 4½" h. 58.00
Figurine, Miss Muffet 45.00
Figurine, Pioneer Susie, standing girl w/broom, 5½" h. 35.00
Figurine, Pixie Boy, riding worm ....25.00 to 30.00
Figurine, Pixie Girl, kneeling, 2½" h......28.00
Figurine, Saxophone Boy, blue, 5½" h. 35.00
Figurine, Shadow Dancer, 7" h. 65.00
Figurine, Shepherdess, 8½" h. 40.00
Figurine, Southern Belle, blue, 7" h. 24.00
Figurine, Spanish Dance Woman 48.00
Figurine, Sultan on pillow, 4¾" h. 29.00
Figurine, Summer Sally 62.00
Figurine, Winter Willie, kneeling boy w/snowball 50.00
Figurines, Beth & Bruce, dancers, 5" & 6½" h., pr. 60.00
Figurines, Black Sambo & Tiger, 5" l., 3½" h., pr. 150.00
Figurines, Cinderella & her Prince, green costume, pr. 150.00
Figurines, Peter Pan & Wendy, on bases w/tall leafy plants, pr. 60.00
Figurines, Polish Boy & Girl, orange pants, skirt & caps, unmarked, 5½" h., pr. 50.00
Figurines, Spanish Dancers, Man & Woman, 7" & 7½" h., pr. 140.00
Figurines, Square Dance Boy & Girl, 6" & 6½" , pr. 55.00
Figurines, Temple Dancer, gold trim, pr. 178.50
Figurine, shelf-sitter, Farmer Girl, blue clothes 35.00
Figurines, shelf-sitters, Fishing Boy & Farm Girl, pr. ....85.00 to 90.00
Figure group, Hansel & Gretel, 7" h. 30.00
Lamps, Fire Man & Fire Woman, on bases, pr. 250.00
Model of Archibald the Dragon 125.00
Model of a cat, kitten playing w/ball of yarn 25.00
Model of a cat, kitten scratching, white, 2" h. 15.00
Model of a hare, 1¾" h. 15.00
Model of lovebirds , joined, pr. 25.00
Model of a skunk, Baby Boy 22.00
Models of Mother Skunk & Baby, pr. 45.00
Pitcher, jug-type, Adam & Eve, boy & girl w/apple...30.00
Pitcher, jug-type, 5½" h., brown w/monk decoration, artist-signed 400.00
Planters, models of heads, Manchu & Lotus, pr. 160.00
Salt & pepper shakers, figural Chihuahua & dog house, pr. 78.00
Salt & pepper shakers, figural deer & fawn, pr. 50.00
Salt & pepper shakers, figural Dutch boy & girl, pr. 32.00
Salt & pepper shakers, figural elephants, pr. 45.00
Salt & pepper shakers, figural Gingham Dog & Calico Cat, pr. 65.00
Salt & pepper shakers, figural Mr. & Mrs. Penguin, pr. 50.00
Salt & pepper shakers, figural monkeys, pr. 60.00
Salt & pepper shakers, figural mother & baby cow, pr. 70.00
Salt & pepper shakers, figural mother & baby polar bears, pr. 55.00
Salt & pepper shakers, figural mouse & cheese, pr. 25.00
Salt & pepper shakers, figural native boy on an alligator, pr. 180.00
Salt & pepper shakers, figural ram & ewe, polka dot decoration, pr. 60.00
Salt & pepper shakers, figural Wee Chinese Boy & Girl, pr. 28.00
Salt & pepper shakers, figural Wee Elephants, pr. 47.00
Salt & pepper shakers, figural Wee Eskimos, pr. 37.00
Salt & pepper shakers, figural Wee French Boy & Girl, pr. 48.00
Salt & pepper shakers, figural Wee Indians, pr. 47.50
Salt & pepper shakers, figural Wee Pigs, pr. 48.00
Salt & pepper shakers, figural Wee Scots boy & girl, black & yellow outfits, 3½" h., pr. (ILLUS. top next column) 45.00

Figural Salt & Pepper Shakers

Salt & pepper shakers, model of covered wagon & oxen, pr. 50.00

Vases, triple-bud, figures of Lu-Tang & Wing-Sang standing in front of bamboo-form cylinders, pr. 52.00

Wall plaque, pierced to hang, figural ballet dancer, Greg 47.50

Wall plaque, pierced to hang, model of a cockatoo 39.50

Wall plaques, pierced to hang, figural ballerinas, Arabesque & Attitude, pr...98.00

Wall plaques, pierced to hang, figural Dutch boy & girl dancing, pr..............72.00

Wall plaques, pierced to hang, figural Harlequin & Columbine, pr..............112.50

Wall plaques, pierced to hang, figural Zor & Zorina, pr.................................95.00

CHINESE EXPORT

Large quantities of porcelain have been made in China for export to America from the 1780s, much of it shipped from the ports of Canton and Nanking. A major source of this porcelain was Ching-te-Chen in the Kiangsi province but the wares were also made elsewhere. The largest quantities were blue and white. Prices fluctuate considerably depending on age, condition, decoration, etc.

CANTON and ROSE MEDALLION export wares are listed separately.

Basket, blue "Fitzhugh" patt., oval w/deep reticulated sides, the interior decorated w/pine cone, dragon & trellis diaper medallion within a border of spearheads & dumbbells & surrounded by four clusters of flowers & precious objects, the sides pierced w/fretwork & the rim w/a trellis diaper border edged in spearheads & dumbbells & interrupted by underglaze-blue upright scroll handles (one w/repaired chip, the other repaired), ca. 1810-20, 9 7/16" l. $1,035.00

Baskets, miniature, horizontally ribbed & painted w/a border of pink rose sprays, the interiors w/flowering branches in iron-red & gilt, gilt-striped ropetwist handles, ca. 1760, 2 7/8" h., pr. (slight rubbing)............2,420.00

Bowl, 10 3/8" d., deep rounded sides raised on a wide footring, *famille rose* palette, painted w/an iron-red bird flying toward another perched on a salmon & *grisaille* rock amid brown-stemmed pink & green peonies & green leaves beneath a *grisaille* & gold foliate-scroll & blossom border around the rim, ca. 1745...1,093.00

Fitzhugh Pattern Bowl

Bowl, 10 9/16" d., blue "Fitzhugh" patt., shallow sides w/a scalloped rim, the interior decorated w/four flowers & precious objects panels within a trellis diaper border edged in spearheads & dumbbells, late 19th c. (ILLUS.)................................920.00

Box, cov., 'clobbered' blue "Fitzhugh" patt., rectangular w/flat cover, the cover w/a central medallion surrounded by four clusters of flowers & precious objects washed in worn gilding & painted between Canton *famille rose* enamels & sprigs of flowers & fruits, the sides of the base w/a gilt-trimmed trellis diaper border repeated around the cover edge, the base also w/a band of spearheads & dumbbells & further enameled w/a border of butterflies, flowers & fruit, the interior w/a central divider, ca. 1875, 7 1/4" l.........345.00

Candleholders, modeled in the form of a reclining lap dog, looking forward w/open mouth & pink tongue, spotted fur markings in sepia w/gilt details, the tall nozzle decorated w/green & iron-red leaf tips, ca. 1800, 6¼" l., pr. (slight wear) 5,500.00

Charger, *famille rose* palette, painted in rose, yellow, blue, turquoise, green, brown & gold in the center w/a basket of peonies on the cavetto w/a brown & gold trellis diaper border reserved w/four floral panels, & on the rim within a pink trellis diaper band interrupted w/yellow & blue demiflowerheads, ca. 1740, 14⅛" d. 1,840.00

Creamer, helmet-shaped, w/flaring lip decorated w/sepia & gilt banding w/meandering bead & flower over a polychrome arms of the State of New York above a spreading circular foot, w/tapering bamboo-molded handle, ca. 1790-1810, 5" h. 825.00

Dinner service: eight dinner plates, nine dessert plates, a 12¾" oval platter, 11¾" oval platter, pair of scalloped sauceboats, circular potted meat dish & cover, & two soup plates; Nanking 'Two Birds' patt., each piece decorated w/a central landscape scene of a sampan on a river between banks w/pagodas, the cavetto w/a cell diaper border & rim w/a trellis diaper border edged in spearheads & dumbbells, late 18th - early 19th c., 24 pcs. (various small chips, repairs & hairlines) 3,738.00

Egg cup, blue "Fitzhugh" patt., the U-shaped bowl painted on the front & back w/a pine cone, dragon & trellis diaper medallion edged w/spear-heads & dashes, on either side w/two clusters of flowers & precious objects & on the interior w/a trellis diaper band beneath the gilt edge, the conical base w/four swastikas above a base band, 19th c., 2⅜" h. 403.00

Fish bowl, a wide ovoid body w/a flattened molded rim, decorated around the exterior w/two scaly dragons in pursuit of the flaming pearls amid clouds above a lappet border around the base & beneath a border of *ruyi* heads & prunus blossoms & a Greek key band below the rim, the flat top of the rim w/a demi-prunus blossoms border, 16$\frac{1}{16}$" d., 13½" h. (ILLUS. top next column) 1,495.00

Chinese Export Fish Bowl

Fruit basket & undertray, reticulated basket w/flaring sides & raised rim handles, sepia "Fitzhugh" patt., 10½" l., 5½" h. 935.00

Garden seat, hexagonal, blue "Fitzhugh" patt., the slightly swelling body painted on four sides with the characteristic medallion within four clusters of flowers & precious objects, & on the other two sides w/two similar clusters beneath a pair of pierced cash medallions, all between diaper bands edged in spearheads & dumbbells within molded bosses & floral lappet borders around the rim (chip) & footrim, the top w/another pierced cash medallion surrounded by four clusters of flowers & precious objects within a trellis diaper border edged in spearheads & dumbbells, late 19th c., 18⅜" h. 2,875.00

Hot water dish, cov., Nanking "Inclined Pines" patt., the deep sided oval dish w/end spouts, decorated in underglaze-blue w/a central landscape scene of a Chinese man crossing a bridge near another in a sampan on a river w/numerous buildings on the banks interrupted at the top of the base & on either side of the pine cone finial of the domed cover w/the gilt initial "P" within a beribboned oval, the cavetto of the base w/a trellis diaper border repeated on the rim of each within a band of spearheads & dumbbells, the base w/lotus & peony sprigs, ca. 1810-20, cover slightly small & w/repaired edge chips, 18$\frac{13}{16}$" l. (ILLUS. front top next column) 1,495.00

Jardinieres & undertrays, hexagonal, each piece decorated w/a continuous landscape scene of a Chinese man & his water buffalo crossing a bridge toward other

Nanking Hot Water Dish & Platter

figures & buildings on a river bank w/sampans plying the waters before distant hills, the flat rims decorated w/foliate scrolls & dots within the molded edge, 19th c., 7⅞" h., pr. 2,875.00

Model of a hawk, *famille rose* palette, perched on blue rockwork w/head cocked, his breast & head iron-red w/gilt feather details, his folded wings richly enameled w/overlapping feathers in pink, yellow, iron-red, black, blue, sepia & green, Qianlong period, 6½" h. (slight flaking to enamels of beak & feathers)......................................6,050.00

Pitchers, cov., toddy, 10¹³⁄₁₆" h., blue "Fitzhugh" patt., barrel-shaped, each painted beneath the spout (one w/a chip issuing a hairline) w/a pine cone, dragon & trellis diaper medallion bordered in spearheads & dumbbells & flanked by four clusters of flowers & precious objects, the underglaze-blue reeded entwined strap handle w/gilt trim, the low domed cover w/further decoration & a gilt recumbent kylin figural finial, one finial w/chipped tail, ca. 1810-20, pr. 5,175.00

Plate, 9¾" d., orange "Fitzhugh" patt., large spread-winged eagle w/shield in the center, 19th c. (ILLUS. top next column) 4,180.00

Platter, 9⅞ x 12⅞", armorial-type, green "Fitzhugh" patt., 19th c........1,760.00

Platter, 14⅝ x 17⅜", armorial-type, green "Fitzhugh" patt., w/reticulated insert, 19th c., 2 pcs. (rim repair on platter)..2,090.00

Platter, 21⅜" l., oval, Nanking "Inclined Pines" patt., decorated w/a

Fitzhugh Plate with Eagle

central landscape of a Chinese man carrying a parasol across a bridge near another in a sampan on a river w/various buildings on the banks, the cavetto w/a trellis diaper border interrupted by four panels of be-ribboned objects, the rim w/a trellis diaper border edged in spearheads & dumbells, ca. 1810-20 (ILLUS. back) 1,035.00

Soup plates, blue "Fitzhugh" patt., decorated w/the usual central medallion surrounded by four flower & precious objects panels all within a spearhead & dumbbell border, three w/worn gilt rims, 9¾" d., set of 15 (most w/hairlines, chips, & one w/rim repair) 575.00

Soup tureen, cover & undertray, *Mandarin palette*, oblong w/chamfered corners, the tureen w/deep rounded sides above a wide flaring foot & rabbit-head end handles, each piece painted on either side or in the center w/a scene of Mandarin figures in a fenced garden in a hilly river landscape within black scroll-edged panels between similarly edged floral or bird panels & iron-red landscape vignettes, all reserved on an iron-red, black & gold Y-diaper ground, the cover surmounted by an iron-red, turqoise & gilt floral sprig knop (losses & restoration), & the tureen & cover rims (all w/small chips & fritting) edged in iron-red, ca. 1785, 13½" & 13¹¹⁄₁₆" l., the set 4,600.00

Sugar bowl, cov., the molded bowl of globular form w/symmetric applied interlaced handles, blue banding at neck & foot centering gilt & sepia floral decoration, the molded domed lid w/shaped rim & waving band of blue enamel & gilt stars & husk band centering a strawberry finial, ca. 1790-1810, 6" w., 5¾" h. 132.00

Teapot, cov., the molded cylindrical body w/gilt & blue enamel banding & decoration at neck, tapering shoulders & center polychrome arms of the State of New York on both sides, the molded circular lid centering a gilt strawberry finial, w/gilt & blue enamel banding & decoration at edge, w/applied interlacing handle & tapering spout, ca. 1790-1810, 6" h. 1,210.00

Tureen, cov., oval, blue "Fitzhugh" patt., decorated w/the crest of the Beale family, 19th c., 10¾" l. 1,980.00

Umbrella stand, cylindrical, green "Fitzhugh" patt., painted on both sides in the upper third w/a peony, beast & trellis diaper medallion encircled by spearheads & dumbbells flanked by pairs of clusters of flowers & precious objects between characteristic borders around the rim & around the mid-section above two rows of four further clusters of flowers & precious objects, the base (star crack) w/a trellis diaper border, late 19th - early20th c., hairline in body, 23½" h. 1,438.00

Vases, 11¼" h., square bottle-form, blue & white, each side painted w/a court scene, including dancers performing before noblewomen & mounted huntresses outside a fortress, borders of crosshatch & diaper, flowering branches on the square neck, ribbon-tied artemesia leaf marks in recessed squares on the base, Kangxi period, pr. (one neck w/restoration, some fritting) 3,300.00

Vases, cov., 13½" h., wide baluster-form body w/a short cylindrical neck topped by a domed cover w/flanged rim & pointed ball finial, decorated w/a continuous scene of Chinese figures in pastel tones, 19th c., pr. 1,438.00

Vegetable dishes, cov., blue "Fitzhugh" patt., the oval body w/a wide flat flanged rim w/chamfered corners, the domed cover w/entwined branch handle, the interior & either side of the cover decorated w/a medallion & w/a wide border band of spearheads & diaper, the covers w/gilt trim, some fritting, chip on underside of one rim, gilt worn, ca. 1810, 14⅜" l., pr. 2,300.00

CLARICE CLIFF DESIGNS

Clarice Cliff Centerpiece

Clarice Cliff was a designer for A.J. Wilkinson, Ltd., Royal Staffordshire Pottery, Burslem, England when they acquired the adjoining Newport Pottery Company whose warehouses were filled with undecorated bowls and vases. About 1925 her flair with the Art Deco style was incorporated into designs appropriately named "Bizarre" and "Fantasque" and the warehouse stockpile was decorated in vivid colors. These hand-painted earthenwares, all bearing the printed signature of designer Clarice Cliff, were produced until World War II and are now finding enormous favor with collectors.

Note: Reproductions of the Clarice Cliff "Bizarre" marking have been appearing on the market recently.

Bowl, 6¼" d., octagonal flanged rim on the rounded body, Woodland patt., stylized landscape w/trees in orange, green, black, blue, purple & yellow, marked $253.00

Bowl, 8" d., 3¾" h., "Bizarre" ware, deep gently rounded sides tapering to a foot ring, Original Bizarre patt., a wide band of block & triangles around the upper half in blue, orange, ivory & purple, purple band around the bottom section, marked 440.00

Bowl, 9" d., deep rounded sides, the upper half w/a wide band in polychrome featuring large stylized cottages w/pointed orange roofs beneath arching trees, lime green banding, marked 322.00

Butter dish, cov., "Bizarre" ware, Crocus patt., a wide shallow base w/low, upright sides fitted w/a shallow, flat-sided cover w/a slightly domed top & flat button finial, the top decorated w/purple, blue & orange blossoms on an ivory ground, marked, 4" d., 2¾" h. 302.50

Candleholders, figural, modeled as a kneeling woman w/her arms raised high holding the candle socket modeled as a basket of flowers, My Garden patt., orange dress & polychrome trim, marked, 7¼" h., facing pr. 403.00

Candlestick, loop-handled, Tonquin patt., red 30.00

Centerpiece, "Bizarre" ware, model of a stylized Viking longboat, raised on trestle supports & w/a frog insert, glazed in orange, yellow, brown & black on a cream ground, printed factory marks, ca. 1925, restored, 15¾" l., 9⅝" h., 2 pcs. (ILLUS.) 345.00

Coffee service: cov. coffeepot, creamer, open sugar bowl, five cake plates & six cups & saucers; Ravel patt., creamer & sugar w/pointed conical bodies supported by buttress legs, other serving pieces w/flaring cylindrical bodies, marked, coffeepot 6" h., the set 748.00

Cup & saucer, "Bizarre" ware, Autumn Crocus patt., Athens shape 175.00

Demitasse set: cov. cylindrical coffeepot, creamer, open sugar bowl & six cylindrical demitasse cups & saucers; "Honey-glaze," each body in deep orange, the angled handles in black & dark green, all marked, coffeepot 6" d., 6¼" h., the set (chip inside pot cover, minor flake on sugar bowl) 3,190.00

Figures, "Bizarre" ware, flat cup-outs, comprising two groups of musicians & two groups of dancing couples, all highly stylized & glazed in red-orange, yellow, lime green, cream & black, printed factory marks "HAND PAINTED - Bizarre - by - Clarice Cliff - A. J. Wilkinson Ltd. - NEWPORT POTTERY - ENGLAND," ca. 1925, 5⅝" to 7" h., 4 pcs. 18,400.00

Jam pot, cov., Blue Firs patt., flat-sided round form on small log feet, domed cover w/flat round knob, stylized landscape w/trees, marked, 4¼" h. 253.00

Jardiniere, "Fantasque" line, Melon patt., Dover shape, deep cylindrical sides on three small tab feet, decorated w/Cubist-style fruits in orange, yellow, blue, green & amber against a cream ground, orange base & rim bands, marked, 6¼" d., 6¼" h. (minor inside paint wear) 1,540.00

Lemonade set: 8" h. tankard pitcher & four cylindrical tumblers; each decorated in an abstract geometric pattern in orange, blue, purple, green & yellow, marked, the set 690.00

Pitcher, 5¾" h., "Fantasque" line, Melon patt., wide conical body w/solid triangular handle, orange & thin black bands flanking a wide central band of stylized melons in yellow, blue, green & orange, marked, ca. 1930 (tiny glaze nicks at rim & base, faint scratch in lower orange band) 715.00

Pitcher, jug-type, 7" h., 6" d., "Bizarre" ware, Lotus shape, Coral Firs patt., wide ovoid body w/a wide flat rim, heavy applied loop handle, decorated w/a wide landscape band in brown, orange, yellow, brown & grey on an ivory ground, marked 770.00

Lotus Pitcher with Sunrise Pattern

Pitcher, 12" h., jug-type w/ovoid body w/overall fine molded banding, Lotus shape, Sunrise patt., decorated in bright yellow & orange, marked (ILLUS.) 920.00

Plate, 9¾" d., Forest Glen patt., a stylized cottage in a woodland scene in orange, ivory & green, die-stamped "Clarice Cliff - Newport Pottery - England" 550.00

Plate, 10¾" d., rounded w/four double-lobe protrusions around the sides, Sunrise patt., colorful center stylized sunrise design banded in orange & green, marked 253.00

Sugar shaker, Autumn patt., sharply pointed conical shape w/rows of small holes pierced around the top, decorated in pastel autumn colors, marked, 5½" h. 368.00

Tumbler, Sunray patt., conical form, polychrome decoration of a stylized sun, orange banding, marked, 3" h. 230.00

Vase, 6¼" h., 3¼" d., "Fantasque" line, Shape No. 196, Trees and House patt., a cylindrical body w/a widely flaring & rolled rim, decorated w/a wide central landscape band in black, orange & green against an ivory ground, marked 880.00

Vase, 9" h., 4½" d., "Bizarre" ware, baluster-shaped w/a short, wide slightly flaring neck, decorated on the upper half w/a wide band of triangles alternating w/quadrilateral blocks in blue, yellow & purple on an orange ground, Shape No. 14D, marked.......................................1,430.00

Vase, 11¾" h., 10" d., "Bizarre" ware, Lotus shape, Geometric patt., urn-form, handled, decorated w/a wide maroon base band & wide green neck band flanking a wide central band of triangular devices in a row in cream, purple, blue, maroon & green, black, blue & cream rim bands & cream handles, marked.......................................2,200.00

CLEMINSON

Cleminson Comic Mug

Betty Cleminson began her home-based business, named "Cleminson Clay" in 1941. Within two years it was necessary to move to larger facilities in El Monte, California and the name was changed to "The California Cleminsons." Originally, Mrs. Cleminson concentrated on creating butter dishes, canisters, cookie jars - mostly kitchen related items. After the move, and with up to 150 employees, she was able to expand her lines with giftware such as vases, wall plaques, cups and saucers, cleanser shakers and a full line of tableware called Distlefink. The incised, stylistic "BC" mark was the first mark used; the California Cleminson mark can be found with or without the boy and girl on each side. The company went out of business in 1963.

Ashtray, model of a fish, two cigarette rests at bottom edge, hole for eye, light & dark ocean blue inside w/pale grey outside, second mark without boy & girl, ca. 1950, 7½" d., 2¾" h...$24.00

Butter dish, cov., figural, model of a Distlefink sitting in an oblong base, bird's head turned toward back, brown glossy glaze w/dark brown & rust accents, 7½" l., 5¾" h. 35.00

Cleanser shaker, figure of a woman standing, yellow hair, pink scarf over head, pink & white dress w/grey trim, five holes in top of head, 6½" h..18.00

Mug, cov., man's face w/hangover expression, model of water bag forms cover, irregular shaped mug & rim, reverse of mug w/lettering "Morning after" & inside bottom of mug lettering, "Never again," white mug w/blue, dark pink, green & black accents, grey water bag bottom w/black rim & yellow top, second mark without boy & girl, 4½" d., 5" h. (ILLUS.)........................26.00

Pie bird, figural, model of a bird, white body decorated in pink, green & blue, first mark, ca. 1941, 4½" h. 22.00

Pitcher, 10½" h., figural, model of a Distlefink, beak forms head, tail is handle, white body w/brown & green accents 30.00

Plate, 7" d., scalloped pale blue edge, pink & purple flowers, green leaves, light & dark pink butterflies, two holes for hanging, second mark without boy & girl 15.00

Razor blade holder, model of a man's face w/hand holding razor, slot in top for used blades, solid unglazed bottom w/stamped mark, 3¼" d., 3¼" h..18.00

Soup mug, juvenile, straight sides w/one round knob on each side at rim, Native American boy & his dog playing & encircled by a white ring, pale pink body w/green, brown & white glazes for dog & boy, second mark w/boy & girl on each side, 4" d., 4¼ h. 36.00

Tea bag holder, model of a teapot w/words, "Let me hold the bag," yellow, blue & black glazes over white body, teapot open handle can be used for hanging, stamped mark, 4¼" h..10.00

Wall plaque, h.p. girl w/green, white & brown dress holding bouquet of flowers, butterflies, two holes at top for hanging, first mark, ca. 1941, 3½" d., 4¾" h. 15.00

Wall pocket, model of a teapot, pale

green body w/dark green lid, heart-shaped motif w/words "Kitchen bright & a singing kettle make home the place you want to settle," bail handle w/round wood center decorated w/painted flowers, 9" d., 6" h. 24.00

Wall pocket, model of a kettle w/three feet, black body w/white heart decorated w/words, "The kitchen is the heart of the home," bail handle, 4½" d., 4¼" h. 22.00

COPELAND & SPODE

Early Spode Dinner Service

W.T. Copeland & Sons, Ltd., have operated the Spode Works at Stoke, England, from 1847 to the present. The name Spode was used on some of its productions. Its predecessor, Spode, was founded by Josiah Spode about 1784 and became Copeland & Garrett in 1843, continuing under that name until 1847. Listings dated prior to 1843 should be attributed to Spode.

Bouillon cups & underplates, red, navy & green floral decoration, ribbed body, scalloped rims, ca. 1900-10, four sets, 8 pcs. $200.00

Cake plate, pedestal base, Spode's Tower patt., pink 125.00

Coffeepot, cov., Queen's Bird patt......140.00

Coffeepot, cov., straight-sided, Spode's Italian patt., blue, 9" h. 175.00

Cup & saucer, demitasse, Mayflower patt., decorated w/mulberry flowers & scrolls on the exterior, h.p. red flowers decoration on the interior, ornate handle, gadrooned rim, marked "Copeland - Spode - England - Mayflower" 23.00

Dinner service: 14⅝" l. oval soup tureen, cover & 17³⁄₁₆" l. undertray, a pair of 9⅜" w. square cov. vegetable dishes, an 18⁷⁄₁₆" l. chamfered rectangular platter, a 16¹¹⁄₁₆" l. platter, a pair of 14⅝" platters, a pair of 12⁷⁄₁₆" l. platters, an 11¹⁄₁₆" l. platter & a 10¼" l. platter & a 15" l. pierced oval strainer, a pair of oval sauce tureens, underplates & one cover, eight octagonal soup plates, 20 octagonal dinner plates & 16 octagonal dessert plates; pearlware, Italian patt., blue transfer-printed landscape design, impressed "SPODE" marks, ca. 1820, together w/a modern milk pitcher, three breakfast cups & saucers, a teabowl & seven teacups & saucers marked "COPELAND - SPODE'S ITALIAN - ENGLAND," & a similar early sauce-boat, various damages, the set (ILLUS. of part) 4,313.00

Ginger jar, cov., Spode's Tower patt., pink 300.00

Plate, 8¼" w., cabinet-type, squared w/notched corners, painted in the center in shades of rose, iron-red, purple, yellow & green w/an arrangement of flowers in a yellow urn behind a sprig of pink roses on a brown marbleized ledge against a shaded brown ground, the cavetto w/a gilt band, & the gilt-edged rim w/a tooled gilt border of flower-filled baskets alternating w/pairs of eagles flanking a flaming torch & all conjoined by foliate scrollwork, marked "SPODE" in worn gilt, ca. 1825 ....1,495.00

Plate, 10½" d., decorated w/basket of colorful flowers & fruit, marked "Copeland - England" 90.00

Punch bowl, Spode's Tower patt., blue, 15½" d. 200.00

Soup plates, ironstone, dark blue transfer-printed floral bouquet in the center & six floral clusters around the rim, overall polychrome enamel & gilt trim, marked "Copeland," 9" d., set of 6 (one w/rim chip) 132.00

Teapot, cov., Spode's Tower patt., pink 400.00

CORDEY

Founded by Boleslaw Cybis in Trenton, New Jersey, the Cordey China Company was the forerunner of the Cybis Studio, renowned for its fine porcelain sculptures. A native of Poland, Boleslaw Cybis was commissioned by his government to paint "al fresco" murals for the 1939 New York World's Fair. Already a renowned sculptor and painter, he elected to remain and become a citizen of this country. In 1942, under his guidance, Cordey China Company began producing appealing busts and figurines, some decorated by applying real lace dipped in liquid clay prior to firing in the kiln. Cordey figures were assigned numbers that were printed or pressed on the base. The Cordey line was eventually phased out of production during the 1950s as the porcelain sculptures of the Cybis Studios became widely acclaimed.

Candleholder, three-light, a slender arched scroll-molded strip applied w/flowers, applied w/three upright flower spirals staggered along the arch & serving as the candleholders, lavender & other colors w/gold trim, No. 8013, 12" l. $80.00

Figure of a Chinese goddess, tall standing female w/a tall purple headdress w/blue trim & red roses w/cinnamon leaves & yellow lace, lavender long outer gown w/dark figure work & a big blue medallion, flat blue lace trim on the long open sleeves, inner gown w/panels of gold over quilting & green & yellow flat lace, one shoe pokes out, on a high scroll-molded & gilt-trimmed base, No. 5073, 12" h. 125.00

Figure of a male harvester, standing wearing a mauve & cherry red hat & vest, mauve shirt & orange britches, No. 305, 16" h. 80.00

Figure of a man, standing wearing a large hat w/four pink leaves & white lace trimmed w/gold in bows & streamers, a long pink lace cape w/drapes & folds & white lace top ruffle & shoulder drape, a creamy figured blouse w/many gathers & turned-back cuffs & gold-trimmed pink lace streamer down the front, skin-tight pink britches flared & w/bows just below the knees, scrolled uprights on the round base trimmed w/flowers & leaves, No. 4153, 14" h. (one cape fold w/tiny crack, one leaf point off) 115.00

Figure of a Yorkshire girl, standing & balancing a jug on her left shoulder & holding grapes in the folds of her skirt w/her right hand, lace-like sleeves & skirt ruffles, nicely decorated, No. 5047, 10" h. 85.00

Figures of a lady & gentleman, standing & wearing 18th c. costumes, she w/a low-cut blouse w/ruffles, bustle & petticoat w/ruffles & a hat w/bow, holding a fan, decorated in shades of green w/some mauve, he wearing a waistcoat & shirt w/ruffles, a hat & pantaloons & holding a bouquet of flowers, same colors as the lady, lady No. 300, 15½" h., pr. 145.00

Figure group, courting couple, a lady & gentleman in ornate costumes, he standing & holding a mandolin, she seated, his outfit w/profuse folds of pink lace at the top, elbows & knees, she w/ringlets in her hair & her entire skirt & bodice trimmed w/ornate lace, the base applied w/flowers & leaves, gold trim, No. 4129A, 6¼" d., 11" h. (minor lace damage).............275.00

Lamp base, a bust of Madame DuBarry, her piled hair w/large center-part curls & a long curl down one shoulder, all trimmed w/applied flowers & ribbons, wearing a swagged lace-trimmed bodice w/a large applied ribbon at one shoulder, raised on a tall, angled scroll-molded base & set on a separate lamp base, lovely colors & gold trim, No. 8039, bust 14¼" h. 225.00

Model of a bird on a pedestal-form stump base, the chubby bird w/a black neck & head w/a short, sharp beak, russet breast & grey & black body w/long black folded wings, the stump base w/applied green leaves & pink trim, gold banding on the base, No, 2037, 8½" h. 110.00

Model of a lamb, ears extended, on a scrolled base w/a tree stump & applied leaves & flowers, No. 6025 .....135.00

Wall shelf, model of a cornucopia, half-round, flat shelf above the twisted & curled horn applied w/a large cupid figure on one side & applied blossoms, lavender scrolls, mauve roses, green leaves & buds & gilt trim, No. 7028, 8" h. 95.00

DEDHAM

Crackleware Center Bowl

This pottery was organized in 1866 by Alexander W. Robertson in Chelsea, Massachusetts, and became A. W. & H. Robertson in 1868. In 1872, the name was changed to Chelsea Keramic Art Works and in 1891 to Chelsea Pottery, U.S.A.

About 1895, the pottery was moved to Dedham, Massachusetts, and was renamed Dedham Pottery. Production ceased in 1943. High-fired colored wares and crackle ware were specialties. The rabbit is said to have been the most popular decoration on crackle ware in blue.

Since 1977, the Potting Shed, Concord, Massachusetts, has produced quality reproductions of early Dedham wares. These pieces are carefully marked to avoid confusion with original examples.

Ashtray, square w/indentations in each side, Rabbit patt., marked & dated "1943," 6" w. $1,540.00

Bell, curved conical form w/knob top, Rabbit patt., unsigned, 4" d., 4" h. ...770.00

Candle snuffer, tapering cylinder w/flattened ball end, Rabbit patt., 2" h. 660.00

Center bowl, Crackle Ware, oval w/deep scallop on sides & toothed scallops at each end, decorated w/h.p. blue flowers against a white ground, blue "registered" mark, 4 x 8¾" (ILLUS.) 660.00

Coffeepot, cov., conical body, domed cover, angled handle, Rabbit patt., inscribed "first one made," dated "4/1/14," blue stamp mark & exhibition label, 8½" h. 1,430.00

Cracker jar, cov., wide ovoid body w/a flared rim inset w/a low-domed cover w/a wide knob handle, Poppy patt., marked & dated "1931," 6¼" h. 3,300.00

Creamer & cov. sugar bowl, Rabbit patt., No. 1, stamped mark, bowl overall 4¾" h., pr. 357.50

Cup plates, one Elephant patt., one Azalea patt., two Horsechestnut patt., marked, 4⅜" d., set of 4 ....660.00

Demitasse cups & saucers, Rabbit patt., marked, saucer 4½" d., cup 2¼" h., set of 6 ....550.00

Flower frog, figural, a model of a standing rabbit atop a domed base pierced w/holes, stamped mark & dated "1931," 6¼" h. 880.00

Humidor, cov., decorated w/two elephants, clamp-type fastener, inscribed "Dedham Pottery - May 1917 - #79," 7" h. 1,980.00

Knife rests, figural, model of a rabbit, marked, 3½" l., pr. (one w/glaze roughness) 660.00

Model of a boot, miniature, high-topped & low-heeled w/blue band around top, unmarked, 2¼" h. 550.00

Paperweight, figural, model of an elephant standing on a flat oval foot, stamped mark & exhibition label, 6" l., 4" h. 7,700.00

Pitcher, 8⅜" h., Rabbit patt., w/one rabbit leaping over lower handle, No. 3, initialed "P," impressed & stamp mark 1,320.00

Plate, 6" d., Dolphin in Surf patt., marked & exhibition label 330.00

Plate, 6¼" d., Dolphin patt., marked 1,100.00

Plate, 6½" d., Chick patt., marked....2,530.00

Plate, 7½" d., Crab patt., marked 357.50

Plate, child's, 7¾" d., Rabbit patt., stamped mark & exhibition label...1,650.00

Plate, 8⅜" d., Reverse Poppy patt., marked 495.00

Plate, 8½" d., Iris patt. 175.00

Plate, 8½" d., raised Pineapple patt., impressed "CPUS - EE - X" 275.00

Plate, 8⅞" d., scalloped rim, molded Putti & Goat patt., marked 605.00

Plate, 9¾" d., Azalea patt., marked 440.00

Plate, 9¾" d., Rose Spray patt., inscribed on back "From Nature - by HR," decorated by Hugh C. Robertson, exhibition label (surface glaze burst) 1,430.00

Plate, 10" d., Elephant patt., marked 715.00

Plate, chop, 12" d., Rabbit patt., impressed mark twice & stamp........275.00

Plates, 8¾" d., Lobster patt., impressed & stamped mark, set of 5 (foot chip) 1,650.00

Platter, 12" d., Sailing Ship patt. in center, by Charles F. Davenport, marked & dated "1927," w/exhibition label 2,640.00

Tea tile, round, Rabbit patt., 6" d. 235.00

Tureen, cov., 9" d., 5½" h., Rabbit patt., figural rabbit finial on cover, marked & exhibition label (minor staining & peppering) 935.00

Vase, 7" h., 4¼" d., 'Volcanic' glaze, cylindrical, covered in a sage green glaze dripping over a metallic copper colored base, restoration to hairline at rim, incised "Dedham Pottery - HCR" 1,760.00

Vase, 7½" h., ovoid body tapering toward the base & to a flat rim, experimental iridescent oxblood drip glaze, by Hugh C. Robertson, incised "Dedham Pottery" & artist's initials 880.00

Vase, 8" h., 5¼" d., swollen-form, covered in a multicolored mottled lustered glaze, by Hugh Robertson, hand-incised "Dedham Pottery - HCR" 2,970.00

Vase, 8¼" h., 5" d., Crackle Ware, slightly swollen cylinder, decorated w/large blue poppy blossoms & pods against a white ground, painted "Dedham III - 15" 2,860.00

Vase, 10" h., 5" d., ovoid base w/wide short neck, 'Volcanic' glaze, covered in a thick brown glaze dripping over an olive green base, full of bubbles, by Hugh Robertson, hand-incised "Dedham Pottery - B.W. - HCR" 1,980.00

DELFT

English Delft Charger

In the early 17th century Italian potters settled in Holland and began producing tin-glazed earthenwares, often decorated with pseudo-Oriental designs based on Chinese porcelain wares. The city of Delft became the center of this pottery production and several firms produced the wares throughout the 17th and early 18th century. A majority of the pieces featured blue on white designs, but polychrome wares were also made. The Dutch Delftwares were also shipped to England and eventually the English copied them at potteries in such cities as Bristol, Lambeth and Liverpool. Although still produced today, Delft peaked in popularity by the mid-18th century.

Bowl, 6½" d., wide rounded body w/flattened rim, decorated in polychrome w/a scene of a house in a landscape w/a fence, trees & rocks within an iron-red & blue scale band & a border band of ovals & diamonds, Lambeth, England, ca. 1730 (cracked) $2,640.00

Bowl, 8¾" d., deep rounded sides on a thick footring, decorated in polychrome w/iron-red flowers w/green leaves & blue tendrils beneath an iron-red & blue scalloped diaper border band suspending tassels, the interior w/a blue flowerhead, Bristol, England, ca. 1730 (cracks at rim, chips on footring) 2,420.00

Charger, Tulip patt., painted in blue, green, yellow & iron-red w/a large central tulip, two flanking buds & tall leaves within blue lines around the top & bottom of the cavetto, the flanged rim w/five leaves alternating w/five stylized bud sprigs, Bristol, England, 1730-40, repaired rim w/restored chips, 13" d. (ILLUS.) 863.00

Flower brick, upright rectangular form w/three rows of round holes & two rectangular openings in the top edge, painted in blue on white on the front & back w/a landscape scene of a man in a punt on a river before two buildings & trees, & on the ends w/another building, raised on short bracket feet w/traces of cold gilding, Bristol, England, 1750-60, 5 13/16" l. (chip on one corner) 575.00

Loving cup, cov., footed bulbous body tapering to a flaring neck flanked by large loop handles, the high domed cover w/flanged rim & flattened disc finial, painted in blue, iron-red & yellow on the front & back of the body & around the cover finial w/panels of stylized flowering plants, the neck w/an iron-red & blue border of leaves, the cover rim w/a chain border, the handles w/blue stripes, Bristol, England, 1720-30, various wear, chips & hairlines, 7 7/16" h. ...5,175.00

Plate, 8¼" w., octagonal, decorated in blue on white w/a round central reserve of a couple in period costume having tea in a garden, the wide edge border w/a stylized Fitzhugh-like design, the back inscribed "E/WQ," Bristol, England, ca. 1770 (rim chips) 3,850.00

Plate, 10¼" d., decorated at one side in blue on white w/the initials "B/FM - 1698" within a tasseled cartouche, Holland (rim chip, slight flaking).......825.00

Posset pot, cov., squatty bulbous body tapering to a flared rim, C-scroll applied handle & a swan's-neck spout, the domed cover w/a flat button finial, decorated in blue on white in the 'Transitional' style w/Chinamen seated in landscapes w/trees, Lambeth, England, ca. 1690, 6¾" h. (base cracked, rim chips, cover rim restored) 6,600.00

Punch bowl, *bianco-sopra-bianco* (white-on-white) style, deep flaring rounded sides on a thick footring, decorated w/manganese & blue Chinese pavilions in a landscape on the exterior, the interior w/white-on-white diaper & floral panels, the center w/manganese flowers issuing from rocks, Bristol, England, ca. 1760, 11¾" d. (rim chips, hairline crack) 3,080.00

Wall pockets, modeled as a fish in blue & green w/iron-red spines, fins & tails & green seaplants flanking the head, Liverpool, England, ca. 1770, one cracked & reglued, some glaze flaking, 8" h., pr. 8,800.00

DOULTON & ROYAL DOULTON

Doulton & Co., Ltd., was founded in Lambeth, London, about 1858. It was operated there till 1956 and often incorporated the words "Doulton" and "Lambeth" in its marks. Pinder Bourne & Co., Burslem was purchased by the Doultons in 1878 and in 1882 became Doulton & Co., Ltd. It added porcelain to its earthenware production in 1884. The "Royal Doulton" mark has been used since 1902 by this factory, which is still in production. Character jugs and figurines are commanding great attention from collectors at the present time.

ANIMALS

Royal Doulton Dogs

Cat, sitting licking hind paw, HN 2580......................................$60.00

Cat, kitten sitting, surprised, tan, HN 2584..50.00

Cat, Siamese, sitting, HN 2655 ....110.00

Dog, Airedale, "Cotsford Topsail," HN 1023, medium..........................140.00

Dog, Bulldog, HN 1075.......................275.00

Dog, Bulldog Pup, sitting, K 2, 1¾" h.................................75.00 to 100.00

Dog, Cocker Spaniel, HN 1000 ....400.00

Dog, Cocker Spaniel, "Lucky Star of Ware," black,HN 1020, 5"......................................80.00 to 100.00

Dog, Cocker Spaniel, dark brown spots & ears, HN 1036, 6¾" l., 5¼" h. (ILLUS. right) 165.00

Dog, Cocker Spaniel, liver & white, HN 1037, small 75.00

Dog, Cocker Spaniel puppy in basket, HN 2585, 2" h. 60.00

Dog, Cocker Spaniel & Pheasant, red & white, HN 1029, small 135.00

Dog, Collie, "Ashstead Applause," HN 1059, 3½" 125.00

Dog, Dachshund, "Shrewd Saint" HN 1128, 4" ....125.00 to 150.00

Dog, French Poodle, HN 2631, 5¼"...................................125.00 to 150.00

Dog, Irish setter, HN 1056, small ....100.00 to 130.00

Dog, Pekinese, "Biddee of Ifield," HN 1012, small...................................98.00

Dog, Pekinese, HN 1040, brown & tan w/black trim, 3⅛" h., 3¾" l. (ILLUS. left) 195.00

Dog, Pekinese, sitting, K 6, miniature, 2" h.....................................50.00 to 75.00

Fox, "Huntsman," HN 6448, 1½" 135.00

Salmon, leaping, "Veined Sung Flambé" glaze, 12¼" h....................220.00

CHARACTER JUGS

The Cavalier Jug

'Ard of 'Earing, small, 3½" h..............................600.00 to 700.00

'Arriet, "A" mark, miniature, 2¼" h...135.00

'Arriet, small, 3½" h.............................95.00

'Arriet, large, 6" h. ....175.00 to 200.00

'Arry, "A" mark, miniature, 2¼" h. 165.00

'Arry, miniature, 2¼" h. 57.50

'Arry, small, 3½" h.............................100.00

Athos, large, 6" h. 95.00

Auld Mac, "A" mark, miniature, 2¼" h...38.50

Auld Mac, miniature, 2¼" h...................40.00

Auld Mac, "A" mark, small, 3½" h. 42.00
Auld Mac, "A" mark, large, 6¾" h..........89.00
Bacchus, small, 3½" h. 55.00
Beefeater, small, w/GR on handle, 3½" h. 60.00
Blacksmith, large, 6" h. 75.00
(Sergeant) Buz Fuz, small, 3½" h. 80.00
Cap'n Cuttle, "A" mark, small, 3½" h. 95.00
Cap'n Cuttle, small, 3½" h. 97.00
Capt. Ahab, small, 3½" h. 45.00
Captain Henry Morgan, small, 3½" h. 40.00
Captain Henry Morgan, large, 6" h. 75.00
Captain Hook, miniature, 2¼ h. 365.00
Captain Hook, large, 6" h., No. D6597 ....525.00
Cardinal, miniature, 2¼" h. 50.00
Cardinal, "A" mark, miniature, 2¼" h. 57.00
Cardinal, "A" mark, small, 3½" h. 85.00
Cavalier, "A" mark, small, 3½" h. 77.50
Cavalier, small, 3½" h. 65.00
Cavalier, large, 6" h. (ILLUS.) ....125.00 to 150.00
Cliff Cornell, blue, large ......275.00 to 300.00
Cliff Cornell, brown, large 400.00
Dick Turpin, mask on face, horse handle, small, 3½" h. 65.00
Dick Turpin, mask on hat, gun handle, "A" mark, miniature, 2¼" h. 65.00
Drake, small, 3½" h. 75.00
Drake, large, 5⅝" h. 340.00
Farmer John, small, 3½" h. 92.50
Farmer John, "A" mark, large, 6" h. 95.00
Fat Boy, tiny, 1¼" h. ....75.00 to 100.00
Fat Boy, small, 3½" h. 115.00
Fortune Teller, miniature, 2¼" h. ....325.00 to 350.00
Fortune Teller, small, 3½" h. 340.00
Friar Tuck, large, 6" h. 375.00
Gaoler, small, 3½" h. 68.00
Gaoler, large, 6" h. 120.00
Gardener, large, 6" h. 175.00
Gondolier, large, 6" h. 650.00
Gone Away, large, 6" h. 125.00
Granny, large, 6¼" h. 80.00
Guardsman, small, 3½" h. 50.00
Gulliver, miniature, 2¼" h. 365.00
Gulliver, small, 3½" h. 350.00
Gunsmith, miniature, 2¼" h. 48.00
Jarge, small, 3½" h. 225.00
Jarge, large, 6½" h. ....325.00 to 350.00
Jockey, large, 6" h. ....350.00 to 400.00
John Barleycorn, small 70.00
John Barleycorn, "A" mark, large 175.00
Johnny Appleseed, large, 6" h. ....300.00 to 325.00
John Peel, tiny, 1¼" h. 200.00
John Peel, miniature, 2¼" h. 50.00
John Peel, small, 3½" h. 85.00

Lumberjack Jug

Lumberjack, small, 3½" h. (ILLUS.) 55.00
Lumberjack, large, 6" h. 105.00
Mad Hatter, large, 6" h. 110.00
Mine Host, miniature, 2¼" h. 30.00
Mine Host, small, 3½" h. 42.00
Mine Host, large, 6" h. 80.00
Mr. Micawber, tiny, 1¼" h. 95.00
Mr. Micawber, "A" mark, miniature, 2¼" h. 55.00
Mr. Micawber, small, 3½" h. 70.00
Mr. Pickwick, tiny, 1¼" h. .....200.00 to 225.00
Mr. Pickwick, "A" mark, small, 3½" h. 95.00
Old Charley, "A" mark, miniature, 2¼" h. 65.00
Old Charley, "A" mark, small, 3½" h. 55.00
Old Charley, small, 3½" h. 52.00
Old Charley, "A" mark, large, 6" h. 72.50
Old King Cole, large, 6" h. 350.00
Paddy, tiny, 1¼" h. 75.00
Paddy, "A" mark, large, 6" h. 160.00
Paddy, large, 6" h. 130.00
Parson Brown, "A" mark, large, 6" h. ..175.00
Pied Piper, small, 3½" h. 47.00
Punch & Judy Man, small, 3½" h. ....300.00 to 350.00
Sairey Gamp, tiny, 1¼" h. 95.00
Sairey Gamp, "A" mark, miniature, 2¼" h. 55.00
Sairey Gamp, "A" mark, small, 3½" h. 62.50
Sairey Gamp, "A" mark, large, 6" h. ....100.00 to 125.00
Sam Weller, tiny, 1¼" h. 100.00
Sam Weller, small, 3½" h. ....125.00 to 150.00
Sam Weller, "A" mark, large, 6" h. 130.00
Sam Weller, large, 6" h. 150.00
Sancho Panza, large 70.00
Santa Claus, doll & drum handle, large 100.00
Santa Claus, reindeer handle, large ...110.00
Scaramouche, small, 3½" h. 415.00
Simon the Cellarer, large, 6" h. 130.00
Smuggler, small, 3½" h. 58.00

Tam O'Shanter, miniature, 2¼" h. 45.00
Tam O'Shanter, small, 3½" h...............55.00
Tam O'Shanter, large 125.00
Toby Philpots, miniature, 2¼" h...........45.00
Toby Philpots, "A" mark, small, 3½" h...65.00
Tony Weller, "A" mark, miniature, 2¼" h...55.00
Tony Weller, miniature, 2¼" h. 50.00
Tony Weller, "A" mark, small, 3½" h...95.00
Tony Weller, "A" mark, large..............200.00
Tony Weller, extra large 275.00
Touchstone, "A" mark, large, 6" h.......205.00
Town Crier, small, 3½" h. .....75.00 to 100.00
Trapper, small, 3½" h. 55.00
Trapper, large, 6" h..............................90.00
Veteran Motorist, small, 3½" h..............55.00
Vicar of Bray, "A" mark, large 225.00
Viking, large, 6" h. ....175.00 to 200.00
Walrus & Carpenter, small, 3½" h. 50.00
Walrus & Carpenter, large, 6" h..110.00W.C. Fields, large, 6" h.............................125.00
Yachtsman, large, 6" h. 125.00

FIGURINES

Autumn Breezes

Afternoon Tea, HN 1747, pink dress, 1935-82......................................350.00
Alexandra, HN 2398, 1970-76..........................150.00 to 185.00
Aragorn, HN 2916, tan costume, 1981-84...100.00
Artful Dodger, M 55, 1932-83 ....70.00
Autumn Breezes, HN 1911, peach dress, green jacket, 1939-76 (ILLUS.) 250.00
Autumn Breezes, HN 1913, green dress, blue jacket, 1939-71...........................200.00 to 250.00
Ballerina, HN 2116, 1953-73 ....265.00
Balloon Seller (The), HN 583, green shawl, cream dress, 1923-49...........650.00
Basket Weaver (The), HN 2245, 1959-62...........................350.00 to 375.00
Belle O' the Ball, HN 1997, 1947-79...300.00
Bernice, HN 2071, 1951-53 ....1,050.00
Biddy, HN 1513, red dress, blue shawl, 1932-51 ....225.00 to 250.00
Blacksmith of Williamsburg, HN 2240, white shirt, brown hat, 1960-83..........................200.00 to 250.00
Blithe Morning, HN 2021, blue & pink dress, 1949-71 ....150.00 to 200.00
Blithe Morning, HN 2065, red dress, 1950-73...235.00
Bride (The), HN 2166, pale pink dress, 1956-76................175.00 to 200.00
Bridesmaid (The Little), M 12, multicolor gown, 1932-45................370.00
Bridesmaid (The LIttle), HN 2196, white dress, pink trim, 1960-76........125.00
Broken Lance (The), HN 2041, 1949-75..400.00
Bunny, HN 2214, 1960-75 ....150.00
Camellia, HN 2222, 1960-71 ....200.00
Carpet Seller (The), HN 1464, 1931-69...........................275.00 to 325.00
Child from Williamsburg, HN 2154, blue dress, 1964-83 ....135.00
Claribel, HN 1951, red dress, 1940-49..550.00
Cookie, HN 2218, 1958-75 ....185.00
Curly Locks, HN 2049, 1949-53...........................350.00 to 375.00
Dainty May, M 67, pink skirt, blue overdress, 1935-49..........................400.00
Delight, HN 1772, red dress, 1936-67..150.00
Delphine, HN 2136, 1954-67...........................250.00 to 275.00
Dulcie, HN 2305, white skirt, white bodice w/ red, yellow & white designs, trimmed in blue, 1981-84...250.00
Enchantment, HN 2178, 1957-82.......160.00
First Steps, HN 2242, 1959-65 ....275.00
Forty Winks, HN 1974, 1945-73...........................175.00 to 200.00
Gaffer (The), HN 2053, 1950-59..445.00

Giselle, The Forest Glade

Giselle, The Forest Glade, HN 2140, 1954-65 (ILLUS.) 360.00
Good Morning, HN 2671, 1974-76 .....190.00

Grand Manner, HN 2723, 1975-81 ......200.00 to 225.00
Granny's Shawl, HN 1647, red cape, 1934-49 ......385.00
Harmony, HN 2824, grey dress, 1978-84 ......170.00
He Loves Me, HN 2046, 1949-62 ......145.00
Honey, HN 1910, green dress, blue jacket, 1939-49 ......760.00
Ibrahim, HN 2095, earthenware, 1952-55 ......600.00
Innocence, HN 2842, 1979-83 ......135.00
Irene, HN 1621, pale yellow dress, 1934-51 ......225.00
Ivy, HN 1768, pink hat, lavender dress, 1936-79 ......85.00
Jack, HN 2060, 1950-71 ......125.00
Janet, M 69, pale green skirt, green overdress, 1936-49 ......340.00
Janice, HN 2022, green dress, 1949-55 ......350.00 to 400.00
Jersey Milkmaid (The), HN 2057,1950-59 ......250.00 to 275.00
Jill, HN 2061, 1950-71 ......125.00 to 150.00
Julia, HN 2705, 1975-90 ......150.00 to 175.00
Karen, HN 1994, red dress, 1947-55 ......450.00
Kate, HN 2789, white dress, 1978-87 ......225.00
Katrina, HN 2327, 1965-69 ......225.00 to 250.00
Ko-Ko, HN 2898, yellow & blue, 1980-85 ......475.00
Lady April, HN 1958, red dress, 1940-59 ......275.00 to 300.00
Lady Charmian, HN 1948, green dress, red shawl, 1940-73 ......195.00
Lady Charmian, HN 1949, red dress, green shawl, 1940-75 ......235.00
Lady from Williamsburg, HN 2228, 1960-83 ......160.00
Lady Jester, HN 1222, 1927-38, black & white 1,300.00
Lady of the Georgian Period (A), HN 41, gold & blue, 1914-38 ......1,250.00
Lambing Time, HN 1890, 1938-80 ......190.00
Leading Lady, HN 2269, 1965-76 ......190.00
Legolas, HN 2917, 1981-84 ......67.00
Leisure Hour (The), HN 2055, mottled green & peach dress, 1950-65 (ILLUS. top next column) ...440.00
Lights Out, HN 2662, blue trousers & yellow spotted shirt, 1965-69 ......276.00
Lilac Time, HN 2137, 1954-69 ......225.00 to 250.00
Lily, HN 1798, white shawl, pink dress, 1936-49 ......125.00 to 150.00
Lisa, HN 2310, violet & white dress, 1969-82 ......120.00
Loretta, HN 2337, rose-red dress, yellow shawl, 1966-80 ......125.00 to 150.00

The Leisure Hour

Lorna, HN 2311, green dress, apricot shawl, 1965-85 ......125.00 to 150.00
Love Letter, HN 2149, pink & white dress, blue dress, 1958-76 ......335.00
Lucy Ann, HN 1502, red gown, 1932-51 ......150.00
Lucy Locket, HN 524, yellow dress, 1921-49 ......425.00
Lunchtime, HN 2485, 1973-80 ......150.00
Madonna of the Square, HN 2034, light green-blue costume, 1949-51 ..650.00
Margaret, HN 1989, 1947-59 ......350.00 to 375.00
Marguerite, HN 1928, pink dress, 1940-59 ......350.00 to 400.00
Marietta, HN 1314, black costume, red cape, 1929-49 ......795.00
Marjorie, HN 2788, blue & white dress, 1980-84 ......225.00
Mary Mary, HN 2044, 1949-73 ......125.00
Masque, HN 2554, 1973-82 ......175.00
Maureen, HN 1770, red dress, 1936-59 ......275.00 to 300.00
Mayor (The), HN 2280, 1963-71 ......400.00 to 450.00
Melanie, HN 2271, 1965-81 ......165.00
Melody, HN 2202, 1957-62 ......195.00
Memories, HN 2030, green & red dress, 1949-59 ......400.00 to 450.00
Meriel, HN 1931, pink dress, 1940-49 ......1,300.00
Midsummer Noon, HN 2033, 1949-55 ......595.00
Minuet, HN 2019, white dress, floral print, 1949-71 ......250.00 to 300.00
Miss Muffet, HN 1936, red coat, 1940-67 ......200.00 to 225.00
Mr. Pickwick, HN 1894, 1938-42 ......195.00
Mrs. Fitzherbert, HN 2007, 1948-53 ...725.00
Monica, M 66, shaded pink skirt, blue blouse, 1935-49 ......425.00
Nina, HN 2347, 1969-76 ......135.00 to 165.00

Noelle, HN 2179, 1957-67 ....365.00
Old King Cole, HN 2217, 1963-67 ......300.00
Olga, HN 2463, 1972-75.....................179.00
Omar Khayyam, HN 2247, 1965-83 ...140.00
Once Upon a Time, HN 2047, pink dotted dress, 1949-55 ....330.00
Orange Lady (The), HN 1759, pink skirt, 1936-75 ....210.00
Orange Lady (The), HN 1953, light green dress, green shawl, 1940-75...........................200.00 to 250.00
Orange Vendor (An), HN 1966, purple cloak, 1941-49 ....800.00
Paisley Shawl, M 4, green dress, dark green shawl, black bonnet w/red feather & ribbons, 1932-45 ....300.00
Paisley Shawl, HN 1392, white dress, red shawl, 1930-49 ....485.00
Paisley Shawl, HN 1987, cream dress, red shawl, 1946-59 ....190.00
Paisley Shawl, HN 1988, cream & yellow skirt, red hat, 1946-75...........170.00
Pantalettes, M 16, red skirt, red tie on hat, 1932-45.....................................280.00
Pearly Boy, HN 1482, red jacket, 1931-49...310.00
Pearly Boy, HN 2035, red jacket, w/hands clasped, 1949-59..............150.00
Pearly Girl, HN 1483, red jacket, 1931-49...275.00
Pecksniff, HN 2098, black & brown, 1952-67...175.00
Peggy, HN 2038, red dress, green trim, 1949-79......................................100.00
Pensive Moments, HN 2704, blue dress, 1975-81 ....175.00
Pied Piper (The), NH 2102, brown cloak, grey hat & boots, 1953-76 .....275.00
Polka (The), HN 2156, pale pink dress, 1955-69...............275.00 to 325.00
Polly Peachum, HN 550, red dress, 1922-49...350.00
Regal Lady, HN 2709, 1975-83 ....150.00
Reverie, HN 2306, peach dress, 1964-81 ....225.00 to 275.00
Rosabell, HN 1620, 1934-38 ....1,450.00
Rosamund, M 32, yellow dress tinged w/blue, 1932-45 ....450.00
Royal Governor's Cook, HN 2233, 1960-83, dark blue, white & brown ..400.00
St. George, No. 2051, 1950-85 ....400.00
St. George, HN 2067, purple, red & orange blanket, 1950-79 (ILLUS. top next column) 3,150.00
Sairey Gamp, HN 2100, white dress, green cape, 1952-67.......................275.00
Samwise, HN 2925, 1982-84..............425.00
Silversmith of Williamsburg, HN 2008, green jerkin, 1960-83.......125.00 to 150.00
Skater (The), HN 2117, red & white dress, 1953-71 ....325.00
Sleepyhead, HN 2114, 1953-55........................950.00 to 1,000.00

St. George

Soiree, HN 2312, white dress, green overskirt, 1967-84 ....150.00 to 175.00
Spring Flower, HN 1807, green skirt, grey-blue overskirt, 1937-59............................275.00 to 300.00
Stephanie, HN 2807, yellow gown, 1977-82...200.00
Stitch in Time (A), HN 2352, 1966-80...125.00
Summer, HN 2086, red gown, 1952-59...350.00
Summer's Day, HN 2181, 1957-62.....275.00
Suzette, HN 2026, 1949-59 290.00
Sweet & Twenty, HN 1298, red & pink dress, 1928-69................250.00 to 300.00
Sweet Anne, M 5, cream to red skirt, shaded red & blue jacket, 1932-45..255.00
Sweet Anne, HN 1496, pink & purple dress & hat, 1932-67 ....210.00
Sweeting, HN 1935, pink dress, 1940-73 ....140.00
Sweet Sixteen, HN 2231, 1958-65 .....260.00
Thanksgiving, HN 2446, blue overalls, 1972-76...250.00
Top O' the Hill, HN 1833, green dress,1937-71 ....175.00 to 200.00
Toymaker (The), HN 2250, 1959-73...265.00
Uriah Heep, HN 554, black jacket & trousers, 1923-39............................600.00
Victorian Lady, M 1, red-tinged dress, light green shawl, 1932-45...............385.00
Victorian Lady (A), HN 728, red skirt, purple shawl, 1925-52 .....275.00 to 300.00
Virginia, HN 1693, yellow dress, 1935-49...500.00
Votes For Women, HN 2816, 1978-81...140.00
Windflower, M 79, blue & green, 1939-49...550.00
Winsome, HN 2220, red dress, 1960-85...165.00
Winter, HN 2088, shaded blue skirt, 1952-59...335.00

MISCELLANEOUS

Ashpot, figural bust, Auld Mac ....100.00 to 125.00

Ashpot, figural bust, Farmer John 95.00

Ashtrays, figural bust, Artful Dodger, Sam Weller, Mr. Micawber & Tony Weller, 1⅞ x 2⅝", set of 4................150.00

Bowl, 8½" d., 5½" h., stoneware, squatty bulbous body on a footring, the rounded sides tapering to narrow molded rim bands & a sterling silver rim flanked by angled loop handles, decorated w/a wide band of floral clusters flanked by narrower bands of scallops, all in earthtones, marked "Doulton Lambeth - 1880" 440.00

Bowl, 9"d., Shakespeare Characters series, "Romeo" 125.00

Bowl, 10" d., Gaffers series, "Zunday Zmocks" 145.00

Bowl, 10½" d., Shakespeare Characters series, "Juliet"...............100.00

Jackdaw of Rheims Charger

Charger, Jackdaw of Rheims series, 13½" d. (ILLUS.) 175.00

Creamer, stoneware, wide flat-bottomed tapering ovoid body w/a flared short neck, decorated w/a small band of stylized florals on a mottled ground, in shades of blue & brown, marked "Doulton Lambeth - 1876," 4³⁄₁₆" h. 220.00

Cup & saucer, demitasse, Granthan patt., No. D5477.................................15.00

Cup & saucer, Coaching Days series...50.00

Flask, "Dewars," Kingsware, bust of Night Watchman, 8" h.......................150.00

Humidor, cov., Chang Ware, the squat lidded jar molded w/four ribs about the sides, flat inset lid w/large domical finial, glazed in brilliant shades of red, blue, yellow & white w/thick cracqueler, designed by Charles Noke, signed in overglaze "Chang - Royal - Doulton" & "NOKE" w/monogram, ca. 1925 ....1,955.00

Jardiniere, stoneware, bulbous body on a flaring foot & tapering to a narrow flared rim, the body decorated w/ a band of line-drawn farm animals between brightly decorated incised bands in cobalt blue, brown & ivory, by Hannah Barlow, marked "Doulton-Lambeth 1883, BHB 346, JLB 391, EM, Ob," 9" d., 7" h. 1,210.00

Jardiniere, flow blue, Babes in the Woods series, mother & child w/basket picking flowers, 9½" d., 8" h...695.00

Jardiniere, decorated w/blue daffodils on white ground, gold rim, ca. 1890s, Doulton - Burslem mark, 10" h..300.00

Jugs, squared upright body w/rounded shoulder to a small flaring neck, an angled handle from rim to shoulder, molded ribbing in brown around sides w/blue & white molded bands around the shoulder, one handle initialed "I.W.," the other "S.W.," molded base mark "Doulton Lambeth - 1882," 7¾" h., pr. 451.00

Pitcher, 6" h., Coaching Days series, "Innkeeper Talks to Driver" 195.00

Pitcher, 6" h., flow blue, Babes in the Woods series, scene of a girl holding a guitar 285.00

Pitcher, 6" h., Shakespeare Characters series, "Wolsey" 165.00

Pitcher, 10½" h., tankard-type, stoneware, incised cobalt blue & bluish grey floral decoration on tan ground, initialed "H.B." (Hannah Barlow), dated 1875, Doulton - Lambeth mark.................................700.00

Plate, 6¾" d., Coaching Days series 75.00

Plate, 7½" d., Robin Hood series (Under the Greenwood Tree), scene of Robin Hood 60.00

Plate, 8½" d., flow blue, Babes in the Woods series, girl w/ basket......485.00

Plate, 10" d., Gaffers series, "Zunday Zmocks" 65.00

Plate, 10" d., Historic England series, "Henry VIII" 55.00

Plate, 10" d., Monks series, "Fishing, Tomorrow will be Friday," signed "Noke" & dated "1911" 165.00

Plate, 10" d., Sir Roger deCoverly series 85.00

Plate, 10" d., rack-type, "The Doctor" ...65.00

Plate, 10" d., rack-type, "The Mayor" 65.00

Plate, 10" d., rack-type, "The Parson"...65.00

Plate, 10" d., rack-type, "Sir Francis Drake" 55.00

Plate, 10" d., rack-type, "The Squire"....95.00

Plate, 10½" d., Night Watchman series, watchman in blue-grey w/blue boots, tan background w/fine speckling, "With compliments of P. McIntosh & Co. Grocers," on back ...100.00

Royal Doulton Punch Bowl

Punch bowl, deep rounded bowl on a pedestal foot, decorated around the upper half w/a continuous comical scene of late 18th c. figures ice skating, titled "Pryde Goeth Before A Fall," 16" d. (ILLUS.) 385.00

Tray, Robin Hood (Under the Greenwood Tree), "King of Archers" scene, 6 x 7¾" 125.00

Tumbler, stoneware, slightly tapering cylindrical form, molded w/taverns & hunt scenes around the sides, dark brown glazed rim band above a tan body, applied sterling silver rim band w/a London hallmark, late 19th c., 4⅝" h...110.00

Vase, 4¼" h., 3¼" d., footed ovoid body w/swelled neck, decorated w/white flowers, berries & green leaves, tan & beige shaded ground, gold feet & trim on sides, Doulton - Burslem mark....................................95.00

Vase, 4¼" h., 3¼" d., ovoid body w/ruffled, flaring rim, supported by gilt scroll feet, decorated w/white flowers, black berries & green leaves on a shaded tan & beige ground, Doulton Burslem mark..........95.00

Vase, 5⅞" h., stoneware, footed bulbous ovoid body tapering to a short wide flaring neck, applied on one side w/a large branch of white cherry blossoms, the other side w/applied geese, sparrows, fish & snakes, all on a light tan ground, Doulton Lambeth mark, ca. 1890.....330.00

Vase, 6" h., Chang Ware, footed very squatty bulbous base w/the wide shoulder tapering to a short cylindrical neck, glazed in rich ruby decorated w/thick white crackle glaze trimmed w/ochre & blue, signed "Chang - Royal - Doulton - ENGLAND - Noke," original paper label, ca. 1925 ....2,588.00

Vase, 6¼" h., flow blue, Babes in the Woods series, children playing Blind Man's Buff 495.00

Vase, 6½" h., flow blue, Babes in the Woods series, girls under tree ...535.00

Vase, 7¾" h., 3" d., tapering cylindrical body w/flared rim, bands of green & periwinkle blue beading & short ribs around the top half w/mottled green on the lower half, stamped "Royal Doulton England - MW - 8128" 302.50

Vase, 8" h., Rouge Flambé glaze, landscape decoration.......................495.00

Vase, 8¼" h., 5½" d., Rouge Flambé glaze, ovoid body tapering to a short cylindrical neck, large ship on the front & back...........................195.00

Vase, 10½" h., handled, flow blue, Babes in the Woods series, mother & child scene, ornate gold handles 750.00

Vase, 11½" h., two-handled, decorated w/gold-outlined flowers in yellow, brown & pale blue, artist-initialed, Doulton - Burslem mark.....190.00

Vase, 13½" h., Chang Ware, slightly swelled cylindrical body tapering to a flared rim, brilliant flambé red glaze decorated w/white, yellow, blue & green textured overglaze, printed factory marks & "Chang" & "NOKE," ca. 1925 ....2,588.00

Fine Doulton Vase

Vase, 20" h., wide baluster-form body w/a short rolled neck, raised on a short pedestal on a square foot, decorated w/delicate birds & flowering branches on a creamy ground, ca. 1880 (ILLUS.) 715.00

Vases, 4" h., Silicon Ware, decorated w/ornate relief-molded design in white, aqua & chocolate brown on tan ground, pr. (one w/tiny firing crack) 110.00

DRESDEN

Figural Dresden Compote

Dresden-type porcelain evolved from wares made at the nearby Meissen Porcelain Works early in the 18th century. "Dresden" and "Meissen" are often used interchangeably for later wares. "Dresden" has become a generic name for the kind of porcelains produced in Dresden and certain other areas of Germany but perhaps should be confined to the wares made in the city of Dresden.

Bowl, 9" d., h.p. pink & lavender wildflowers $100.00

Bowl, 9¼" d., 2¼" h., wide reticulated sides decorated overall w/small flowers, Dresden patt. in the center, signed "Schumann" only, early 95.00

Bowl, 10½" d., three dolphin feet, reticulated sides, tiny h.p. pastel floral decoration in center 395.00

Candelabra, two-light, the candle-sockets supported by ornately scroll-molded arms raised on a tall conical pedestal base ornately molded w/scrolls & trimmed w/applied pink & yellow roses, the whole w/gilt trim, 10" h., pr. 395.00

Card tray, footed, applied flowers, cupid & cornucopia decoration, 10" sq...550.00

Charger, ornate reticulated border, tiny h.p. pastel floral decoration in center on white ground, ca. 1893, 11½" d...395.00

Clock, table model, a circular enameled dial within a scrolled rococo-style case w/four applied putti representing the four seasons, glazed in pale blue & pink, the putti brightly decorated, ca. 1880, 18" h. (minor breakage to extremities, age lines) 825.00

Compote, open, 12¼" h., circular bowl w/flaring reticulated scalloped rim, raised base w/full-figure men & women in peasant attire encircling the flower-decorated standard, late 19th c. (ILLUS.)................................605.00

Dessert plates, reticulated edges, decorated w/florals & gilt trim, 7¼" d., set of 4................................121.00

Ewer, ovoid, openwork maroon lustre & gold base & top, one side decorated w/a h.p. scene of two ladies in a garden w/cupid, the reverse w/a scene of children playing blindman's buff, elaborate openwork handle in lavish dull gold, marked "Wissman Dresden," ca. 1890, 5½" d., 11¾" h...695.00

Figure of a ballerina wearing a lace dress w/applied flowers, 3¼" h. 110.00

Figure of a ballerina w/outstretched arms, brown hair, wearing blue ruffled lace dress w/applied flowers, white bodice w/lace trim, gold slippers, marked "Dresden" in blue, crown & "T & K," 6" h. 145.00

Figure of a ballerina wearing an ornate tiered lacy dress, shown standing w/one leg forward & one hand holding her skirt as she bows, her other arm extended back, raised on an oval plinth base, "Dresden" mark under base, ca. 1890, 11" h....525.00

Figure group, a couple in 18th c. dress, the lady sitting on a settee holding a music book, the gentleman behind her playing a violin & wearing a green coat, on an oblong scroll-molded base, 10½" l., 10" h...850.00

Lamp, table-type, waisted lower portion surmounted by a baluster-form upper portion, applied w/figural cupids holding birds & flowers, the whole decorated w/applied flowers, electrified, unmarked, 16" h. plus base fittings....................................450.00

Plate, 9" d., reticulated cobalt & gold border w/center scene of a Victorian couple 195.00

Plates, 6½" d., reticulated rim, center w/polychrome floral decoration, marked "Dresden, Germany," set of 6...115.50

Vases, 9½" h., bulbous body w/straight top, two white figural panels & two gold panels w/floral decoration, ca. 1860, entwined "AP" mark, pr...250.00

FIESTA

Fiesta dinnerware was made by the Homer Laughlin China Company of

Newell, West Virginia, from the 1930s until the early 1970s. The brilliant colors of this inexpensive pottery have attracted numerous collectors. On February 28, 1986, Laughlin reintroduced the popular Fiesta line with minor changes in the shapes of a few pieces and a contemporary color range. The effect of this new production on the Fiesta collecting market is yet to be determined.

Fiesta Fruit Bowl

Ashtray
- chartreuse $52.00
- cobalt blue 38.00
- red 41.00
- turquoise 33.00
- yellow 32.00

Bowl, individual, 4¾" d.
- cobalt blue 21.50
- forest green 20.00
- ivory 19.50
- rose 23.50

Bowl, individual fruit, 5½" d.
- forest green 28.00
- light green 19.50
- yellow (ILLUS.) 16.50

Bowl, dessert, 6" d.
- chartreuse 37.00
- cobalt blue 33.00
- ivory 33.50
- rose 38.00

Bowl, individual salad, 7½" d.
- turquoise 55.00
- yellow 55.00

Bowl, nappy, 8½" d.
- grey 38.50
- light green 23.00
- medium green 79.00
- red 39.00

Bowl, nappy, 9½" d.
- cobalt blue 40.00
- rose 50.00
- yellow 38.50

Bowl, salad, 9½" d.
- ivory 28.00
- turquoise 27.50

Bowl, fruit, 11¾" d.
- cobalt blue 116.00
- turquoise 150.00

Bowl, cream soup
- forest green 45.00
- grey 58.00
- medium green 46.50
- red 43.50

Bowl, salad, large, footed
- ivory 240.00
- red 280.00
- yellow 140.00

Cake plate, 10" d.
- turquoise 605.00

Candleholders, bulb-type, pr.
- light green 57.00
- red 79.00

Candleholders, tripod-type, pr.
- cobalt blue 392.00
- ivory 236.00
- light green 340.00
- yellow 262.00

Carafe, cov.
- turquoise 160.00
- yellow 151.00

Casserole, cov., two-handled, 10" d.
- chartreuse 177.00
- forest green 231.00
- light green 94.00
- medium green 440.00
- turquoise 100.00

Coffeepot, cov., demitasse, stick handle
- cobalt blue 305.00
- ivory 289.00
- light green 200.00
- red 230.00

Coffeepot, cov.
- cobalt blue 150.00
- forest green 210.00
- grey 200.00
- ivory 120.00
- yellow 92.00

Compote, 12" d., low, footed
- cobalt blue 132.00
- red 120.00
- turquoise 111.00

Compote. sweetmeat, high stand
- light green 37.50
- red 64.00
- yellow 40.00

Creamer, individual size
- red 138.00

Creamer, stick handle
- ivory 25.00
- turquoise 35.00
- yellow 24.00

Creamer
- grey 23.00
- ivory 14.00
- light green 13.50
- rose 23.50

Cup & saucer, demitasse, stick handle
- cobalt blue 55.00
- grey 273.00
- ivory 54.00

turquoise 52.50
Cup & saucer, ring handle
chartreuse 31.00
forest green 34.50
medium green 46.00
red 29.00
yellow 19.00
Egg cup
cobalt blue 49.00
light green..................................32.00
rose 100.00
yellow 33.00
Fork (Kitchen Kraft)
red 56.00

Fiesta French Casserole

French casserole, cov., stick handle
yellow (ILLUS.). 162.00
Gravy boat
chartreuse 50.00
cobalt blue..................................41.00
grey 59.00
ivory..................................38.00
Lid for mixing bowl, size No. 1
light green..................................695.00
Marmalade jar, cov.
cobalt blue 160.00
red 186.00
Mixing bowl, nest-type
Size No. 1, 5" d.
ivory..................................Ï55.00
turquoise..................................50.00
Size No. 2, 6" d.
cobalt blue 69.00
red 67.50
Size No. 3, 7" d.
light green..................................60.00
turquoise..................................75.00
Size No. 4, 8" d.
ivory..................................65.00
turquoise..................................60.00
Size No. 5, 9" d.
light green..................................91.00
yellow 81.00
Size No. 6, 10" d.
ivory..................................106.00
yellow 90.00
Size No. 7, 11½" d.
turquoise..................................141.00
Mug
chartreuse 56.00
grey 65.00
light green..................................42.00
Mug, Tom & Jerry style
forest green 58.00

ivory/gold 55.00
light green..................................42.00
yellow 38.00
Mustard jar, cov.
cobalt blue 175.00
light green..................................150.00
yellow..................................132.00
Onion soup bowl, cov.
light green..................................425.00
red 650.00
Pie server, (Kitchen Kraft)
light green..................................45.00
red 85.00

Fiesta Two-Pint Pitcher

Pitcher, jug-type, 2 pt.
chartreuse 96.00
ivory..................................48.00
red 75.00
turquoise (ILLUS.) 40.00
yellow 42.50
Pitcher, juice, disc-type, 30 oz.
light green..................................90.00
red 392.00
yellow 37.50
Pitcher, water, disc-type
cobalt blue 152.00
grey 200.00
ivory..................................95.00
medium green 725.00
red 118.00
rose 177.00
yellow 85.00
Pitcher, w/ice lip, globular, 2 qt.
ivory..................................85.00
light green..................................80.00
yellow 85.00
Plate, 6" d.
cobalt blue 8.00
grey 8.00
light green..................................5.00
medium green 14.00
red 7.00
rose 8.00
yellow 4.00
Plate, 7" d.
chartreuse 11.00
forest green 9.00
ivory..................................6.50
light green..................................8.50
medium green 22.50

red 8.00
rose 10.00

Plate, 9" d.
chartreuse 16.00
forest green 14.00
ivory 11.00
light green 9.50
medium green 40.00
rose 18.00
turquoise 8.50
yellow 9.00

Plate, 10" d.
chartreuse 34.00
grey 48.00
ivory 22.50
light green 20.00
medium green 80.00
yellow 22.00

Plate, grill, 10½" d.
cobalt blue 35.00
light green 23.00
red 50.00
rose 45.00
turquoise 20.00

Plate, grill, 11½" d.
cobalt blue 50.00
light green 38.00

Plate, chop, 13" d.
chartreuse 50.00
grey 50.00
ivory 23.00
red 85.00
turquoise 26.00
yellow 22.50

Plate, chop, 15" d.
chartreuse 100.00
forest green 60.00
ivory 35.00
light green 35.00
red 48.00
yellow 28.00

Platter, 12" oval
chartreuse 40.00
cobalt blue 24.00
grey 40.00
light green 20.00
red 60.00
yellow 19.00

Relish tray w/five inserts
ivory 100.00
multi-colored ....150.00 to 200.00
turquoise 185.00
yellow 165.00

Salt & pepper shakers, pr.
forest green 40.00
grey 32.00
light green 18.00
medium green 105.00
turquoise 16.00
yellow 14.50

Soup plate w/flanged rim, 8" d.
cobalt blue 33.00
forest green 35.00
light green 28.00
red 46.00
rose 35.00
yellow 24.50

Spoon (Kitchen Kraft)
red 85.00

Sugar bowl, cov.
chartreuse 37.00
cobalt blue 47.00
grey 44.50
light green 26.00
red 37.00
rose 42.00
yellow 25.00

Syrup pitcher w/original lid
cobalt blue ....225.00 to 250.00
light green ....175.00 to 200.00
red 220.00
turquoise 222.00

Teapot, cov., medium size (6 cup)
chartreuse 180.00
ivory 150.00
light green 112.00
red 138.00
rose 325.00
turquoise 101.00

Teapot, cov., large size (8 cup)
red 156.00
turquoise 105.00
yellow 45.00

Tray, Figure 8
turquoise 250.00

Tumbler, juice, 5 oz.
cobalt blue 31.00
grey 250.00
light green 27.00
turquoise 19.50
yellow 25.00

Tumbler, water, 10 oz
cobalt blue 49.00
ivory 42.00
light green 41.00
turquoise 47.00
yellow 42.00

Utility tray
ivory 27.50
light green 28.00
red 32.00
turquoise 21.50
yellow 20.00

Vase, bud, 6½" h.
ivory 46.00
light green 43.00
yellow 50.00

Vase, 8" h.
cobalt blue 422.00
ivory ....275.00 to 300.00
light green 310.00
turquoise 334.00
yellow 325.00

Vase, 10" h.
cobalt blue 475.00
light green ....400.00 to 425.00
red 600.00

Vase, 12" h.
cobalt blue ....550.00 to 600.00
red ....500.00 to 600.00

FLORENCE CERAMICS

Florence "Memories" Figure

Florence Ward began her successful enterprise in 1939. By 1946 she had moved her home workshop into a small plant in Pasadena, California. About three years later it was again necessary to move to larger facilities in the area. Semi-porcelain figurines, some with actual lace dipped in slip, were made. Figurines, such as fictional characters and historical couples, were the backbone of her business. To date, almost two hundred figurines have been documented. For about two years, in the mid-1950s, Betty D. Ford created what the company called 'stylized sculptures from the Florence wonderland of birds and animals.' Included were about a half dozen assorted doves, several cats, foxes, dogs and rabbits. Several marks were used over the years with the most common being the circle with 'semi-porcelain' outside the circle. The name of the figurine was almost always included with a mark. A "Floraline" mark was used on floral containers and related items. There was also a script mark and a block lettered mark as well as paper labels. The company was sold to Scripto Corporation in 1964 but only advertising pieces were made such as mugs for the Tournament of Roses in Pasadena, California. The company ceased all operations in 1977.

Candlestick, feathered effect overall in white w/gold trim, marked "Floraline by Florence Ceramics Pasadena, CA," Model No. R6, 6" h. $20.00

Figure of a boy, "Mike," standing w/head thrown back & arms straight up & back, palms up, 6½" h. 125.00

Figure of a boy, standing w/legs apart & right leg slightly bent, holding a package in right hand, white shoes, jacket & shirt, pale blue socks, pants & hat, brown hair, 6¼" h. 105.00

Figure of a girl, "Joy," standing w/green hat, yellow dress w/white & green collor, 6" h. 85.00

Figure of a girl standing in front of rectangular planter w/left arm resting on top of planter, blond hair, green & brown hat, white coat w/green buttons, green & brown gloves, 6" h...35.00

Figure of a girl standing w/feet slightly apart, sand pail in right hand & left arm bent at elbow holding shovel to shoulder, black bathing suit w/yellow polka-dots, matching scarf tied around her short blond hair w/bow at top, 7" h...85.00

Figure of a Grandmother sitting in chair reading, "Memories," white w/22k gold trim (ILLUS.) 155.00

Figure of a mermaid, "Jane," shelf sitter-type w/arms at shoulders, elbows bent, Model No. M2, 7" h. 170.00

Figure of a woman, "Amelia," standing w/left elbow bent & right hand at waist, red brocade floor length dress w/low scalloped neckline & short sleeves, Model No. F204, 7½" h. 155.00

Figure of a woman, "Roberta," standing, one arm behind back, one hand holding skirt, head tilted, blonde hair in an upsweep, yellow floor length dress, brown gloves, 8¾" h.............135.00

Model of a dove on a base, flying position w/tail up, wings back, head down, porcelain bisque, brown w/white, designed by Betty Davenport Ford, Model No. B-6, 8" l., 11" h..95.00

Wall plaque, rectangular w/scalloped edges, molded-in-relief full-sized girl holding fan, beige plaque w/green clothing, Model No. P-3, 6½" l. 9" h......................................115.00

FLOW BLUE

Flowing Bue wares, usually shortened to Flow Blue, were made at numerous potteries in Staffordshire, England and elsewhere. They are decorated with a blue that smudged lightly or ran in the firing. The same type of color flow is also found in certain wares decorated in green, purple and sepia. Patterns were given specific names, which accompany the listings here.

ACME (Probably Sampson Hancock & Sons, ca. 1900)

Bowl, 8½ x 11", 2" h., scalloped gilt edge $150.00
Bowl, 11" d., scalloped rim 125.00
Creamer & sugar bowl, pr. 110.00
Pitcher, milk 95.00
Sauce ladle 195.00
Tea tile 95.00

AMOY (Davenport, dated 1844)

Amoy Plate

Bowl, cereal, 7¼" d. 120.00
Chamber pot 195.00
Creamer (professional repair) 475.00
Cup, handleless 95.00
Cup & saucer, handleless 150.00
Cup plate 110.00
Honey dish 75.00
Pitcher, 7¼" h., bulbous, 1½ qt. (minor professional repair) ....700.00 to 750.00
Plate, 7½" d. 85.00
Plate, 8¼" d. (ILLUS.) 97.50
Plate, 9" d. 125.00
Plate, 9¾" d. 130.00
Plate, 10½" d. 160.00
Platter, 16" l. 495.00
Platter, 20" l. (professional repair) 995.00
Sauce dish, 5" d. 75.00
Soup plate w/flanged rim, 9" d. 145.00
Soup plate w/flanged rim, 10½" d. 195.00
Sugar bowl, cov. (professional repair) 625.00
Teapot, cov. (professional repair) 625.00
Vegetable bowl, cov., 12" d. 1,195.00
Vegetable bowl, open, 10½" d. 425.00
Waste bowl, large (edge flakes) 345.00

ARGYLE (W.H. Grindley, ca. 1896)

Bowl, soup, 8¾" d. 62.50
Butter pat 35.00
Charger, 15" d. 165.00
Creamer 225.00
Gravy boat & undertray, 2 pcs. 275.00
Plate, 7" d. 37.50
Plate, 8¾" d. 75.00

Argyle Platter

Platter, 8¾ x 12¾" (ILLUS.) 250.00
Platter, 12 x 17½" 395.00
Platter, 13¼ x 19" 545.00
Sauce dish 38.00
Soup plate w/flanged rim, 8¾" d. 75.00
Toothbrush holder 295.00
Vegetable bowl, cov. 325.00

CARLTON (Samuel Alcock, 1850)

Compote, fruit 795.00
Creamer 390.00
Plate, 7¼" d. 73.00
Plate, 8½" d. 90.00
Plate, 9½" d. 125.00
Platter, 8½ x 11" 250.00
Sauce dish 60.00
Sauce tureen, cover & underplate, 3 pcs. 495.00
Vegetable bowl, open, 9¼" d. 250.00

CASHMERE (Ridgway & Morley, G.L. Ashworth, et al., 1840s on)

Cashmere Soup Plate

Compote, sauce (professional repair) 825.00
Plate, 9½" d. (under rim chip) 140.00
Plate, dinner, 10½" d. 250.00
Soup plate w/flanged rim, 10½" d. (ILLUS.) 260.00

Vegetable bowl, open, 6½ x 8½" 775.00
Waste bowl 875.00

CHAPOO (John Wedge Wood, ca. 1850)
Creamer........550.00
Plate, 7¼" d. 95.00
Plate, 8½" d. 125.00
Plate, 9½" d. 140.00

Chapoo Platter

Platter, professional repair, 10½ x13½" (ILLUS.) 350.00
Platter, 16" l. 500.00
Platter, 17¾" l. 795.00
Teapot, cov. (minor flaw) 895.00

DELAMERE (Henry Alcock, ca. 1900)
Bowl, 9"' d., 2" h. 100.00
Butter pat 25.00
Cup & saucer........75.00
Plate, 6¾" d. 30.00
Plate, 7¾" d. 38.00
Plate, 8" d. 45.00
Plate, 9" d. 60.00
Platter, 16" l. 295.00
Sauce dish........28.00
Vegetable bowl, cov. 210.00

FAIRY VILLAS - 3 Styles (W. Adams, ca. 1891)

Fairy Villas Plate

Bone dish........110.00
Butter pat........35.00

Creamer........130.00
Cup & saucer........95.00
Gravy boat........95.00
Plate, 9" d. (ILLUS.)........87.50
Platter, 5 x 8¼"........120.00
Platter, 15" l. 185.00
Sauce dish, 5" d........32.00
Soup plate w/flanged rim, 8¾" d. 75.00
Vegetable bowl, cov. ....450.00 to 500.00
Vegetable bowl open, 9" d........125.00
Vegetable bowl, open, 10" d........95.00

GAINSBOROUGH (Ridgways, ca. 1905)
Bowl, 9½" d........110.00
Butter pat........34.00
Gravy boat........80.00
Plate, 9" d. 85.00
Platter, 12 x 16" 135.00
Tureen, cov., octagonal 325.00

GIRONDE (W.H. Grindley, ca. 1891)

Gironde Cup & Saucer

Bone dish........45.00
Bowl, soup, 7¾" d. 40.00
Cup & saucer (ILLUS.) 70.00
Gravy boat & undertray, 2 pcs........145.00
Pitcher, milk........225.00
Plate, 6½" d. 35.00
Plate, 8" d. 45.00
Plate, 9" d. 55.00
Plate, 10" d. 70.00
Platter, 10¾ x 15¼"........150.00
Platter, 12 x 17" 265.00
Sauce dish........30.00
Soup tureen, cov. 300.00
Vegetable bowl, cov. 230.00
Vegetable bowl open, 9" d........85.00

HOFBURG, THE (W.H. Grindley, ca. 1891)
Bone dish........30.00
Dinner service, twelve each dinner plates, salad plates, soup bowls, cups & saucers, butter pats, eleven berry bowls, one each gravy boat & underplate, cov. butter dish w/drainer, oval vegetable bowl, 10" platter & 16" platter, the set (vegetable bowl chipped) 4,500.00
Gravy boat........45.00
Plate, 10" d. 52.00

HOLLAND, THE (Alfred Meakin, ca. 1891)

Bone dish....35.00
Bowl, cereal....25.00
Chocolate cups, pedestal base, set of 5....225.00
Plate, 8" d....40.00
Plate, 9" d....45.00
Plate, 10" d....75.00
Platter, 12½" l....128.00
Platter, 14" l....145.00
Sauce dish, 5" d....10.00
Soup plate w/flanged rim, 7¾" d....35.00

HOLLAND (Johnson Bros., ca. 1891)

Holland Plate

Cake plate, 10½" d....165.00
Creamer & cov. sugar bowl, pr....300.00
Egg cup....105.00
Gravy boat....110.00
Plate, 6½" d....35.00
Plate, 9" d....47.00
Plate, 10" d. (ILLUS.)....78.00
Sauce dish, 4¾" d....30.00
Soup tureen, cov....395.00
Vegetable bowl, open, 8½" d....95.00
Vegetable bowl, open, 9½" oval....65.00

IDRIS (W.H. Grindley, ca. 1910)

Idris Cup & Saucer

Butter pat....18.00
Cup & saucer (ILLUS.)....65.00
Pitcher, milk....185.00
Plates, 6" d., set of four....80.00
Plate, 10" d....38.00
Vegetable bowl, cov....150.00

JANETTE (W.H. Grindley, ca. 1897)

Janette Sugar Bowl

Butter pat....30.00
Plate, 8¾" d....45.00
Sugar bowl, cov., 6½" h. (ILLUS.)....130.00
Vegetable dish, 4¼ x 6"....35.00
Vegetable tureen, cov....225.00

KAOLIN (Podmore & Walker, ca. 1850)

Plate, 7½" d....55.00
Plate, 9¼" d....75.00
Teapot, cov. (minor professional repair to spout tip)....750.00

KYBER (John Meir & Son, ca. 1870; W. Adams & Co., ca. 1891)

Kyber Plate

Pitcher, 7" h., 1 qt....425.00
Pitcher & bowl set, 2 pcs....2,250.00
Plate, 7" d....35.00
Plate, 8" d. (ILLUS.)....80.00
Plate, 9" to 10" d....75.00 to 95.00
Platter, 10" l....160.00
Platter, 11 x 14½"....275.00
Sauce dish....45.00
Vegetable bowl, open, 9" d....135.00

LA BELLE (Wheeling Pottery, ca. 1900)

La Belle Chop Plate

Bowl, 9" sq., 2" h. 125.00
Bowl, 13½" d., helmet-shaped...........395.00
Butter pat...45.00
Celery dish..210.00
Charger, 12¾" d...................................335.00
Pitcher, 5" h. design at top only 95.00
Pitcher, 7" h 450.00
Plate, 6¼" d. 30.00
Plate, chop, 11½" d. (ILLUS.)............165.00
Platter, 18⅜" l.....................................375.00
Sauce dish...30.00
Soup plate w/flanged rim, 9½" d...........45.00
Syrup pitcher & underplate, 2 pcs. 325.00
Vegetable bowl open, leaf-shaped, 9" l...195.00

LORNE (W.H. Grindley, ca. 1900)

Bowl, soup 65.00
Butter pat..33.00
Gravy boat 92.00
Plate, 6½" d. 25.00
Plate, 8" d. 40.00
Plate, 8¾" d...55.00
Plate, 10" d. 70.00
Platter, 7 x 10" 110.00
Platter, 8 x 11" 130.00
Platter, 9 x 12" 155.00
Platter, 11½ x 16⅛" 225.00
Relish tray, 9" l.......................................98.00
Soup plate w/flanged rim, 7¾" d. 40.00
Soup tureen, cov. (professional repair) 650.00
Sugar bowl, cov. 155.00
Vegetable bowl, cov., oval...................295.00
Vegetable bowl, open, 7 x 9¾" 110.00
Waste bowl 55.00

LORRAINE (Ridgways, ca. 1905)

Bone dish...30.00
Butter pat...25.00
Mush cup & saucer 185.00
Plate, 9¾" d..45.00
Waste bowl 75.00

MADRAS (Doulton & Co., ca. 1900)

Cup & saucer 75.00
Dinner service: six 10½" d. plates, six 9½" d. plates, six 7½" d. plates, 13 x 15¼" platter, 10" d. open vegetable bowl, oblong cov. vegetable bowl, round cov. vegetable bowl & two 9" d. cake plates, 25 pcs.............................1,500.00
Gravy boat 82.50
Pitcher, 7" h. 195.00
Plate, 5½" to 6½" d. ....35.00 to 45.00
Plate, 7" d. 45.00
Plate, 8½" d. 80.00
Plate, 9½" to 10½" d. 85.00
Platter, 13¾" l. 150.00
Platter, 15¾" l. 255.00
Sauce dish, 4¾" d. 35.00
Sauce dish, 5¾" d. 38.00
Vegetable bowl, cov., oblong.................200.00
Vegetable bowl, cov., round 215.00
Vegetable bowl, open, 8½" oval 120.00

MARECHAL NIEL (W.H. Grindley, ca. 1895)

Bone dish..42.50
Butter pat..37.00
Cup & saucer 55.00
Gravy boat 135.00
Plate, 10" d. 95.00
Platter, 11¾" x 15½" 225.00
Platter, 18" l. 325.00
Sauce dish...37.00
Soup plate w/flanged rim 50.00
Vegetable bowl, cov., oval 285.00

MELBOURNE (W.H. Grindley, ca. 1900)

Bowl, 6¼" d..36.00
Butter dish, cov. 225.00
Butter pat 30.00
Creamer..155.00
Cup & saucer 65.00
Gravy boat & underplate, 2 pcs. 125.00
Plate, 6¾" d...40.00
Plate, 8" to 9" d. ....45.00 to 55.00
Plate, 10" d. 78.00
Platter, 8½ x 12" 130.00
Platter, 10 x 14" 140.00
Platter, 11½ x 16½" 205.00
Saucer, 5¾" d...15.00
Soup plate w/flanged rim, 10" d. 85.00
Sugar bowl, cov. 225.00
Vegetable bowl, cov., 12¼" oval...........295.00
Vegetable bowl, open, 9" oval 95.00
Vegetable bowl, open, 9¾" oval 115.00

MONGOLIA (Johnson Bros., ca. 1900)

Cup & saucer 75.00
Gravy boat, 3 x 4" 70.00
Plate, 7¼" d. 50.00
Plate, 9" d. 65.00
Platter, 12 x 16 oval 300.00
Soup plate w/flanged rim, 10" d.............55.00

MURIEL (Upper Hanley Potteries, ca. 1895)

Creamer..115.00
Gravy boat 95.00

Plate, 10" d. 75.00
Vegetable bowl, open, 10" d..............115.00

NANKIN (Ashworth, ca. 1865)

Cake plate 150.00
Plate, 8" d. 65.00
Platter, 21½" l., w/well & tree (professional repair)........................790.00
Sauce tureen w/underplate................425.00

NEOPOLITAN (Johnson Bros., ca. 1900)

Bone dish..35.00
Butter pat..30.00
Dinner service, eight each 10", 9" & 7" d. plates, butter pats, bone dishes & cups & saucers, seven sauce dishes & one each cov. butter dish w/drain insert, round cov. vegetable bowl, oval cov. vegetable bowl, 9" d. open vegetable bowl, cov. sauce tureen w/underplate, relish dish, 8 x 10½" platter, 9 x 12¼" platter & 11 x 14¼" platter, the set...........2,975.00
Plate 10" d. 70.00
Platter, 10½ x 14" 150.00

NON PAREIL (Burgess & Leigh, ca. 1891)

Non Pareil Plate

Bowl, 6½" d...47.00
Butter dish, cov. (base hairline) 275.00
Butter pat..35.00
Cake plate, 11" d. 245.00
Creamer, 5" h. 235.00
Cup & saucer.......................................105.00
Egg cup 195.00
Gravy boat 160.00
Ladle holder..225.00
Pitcher, 1 qt. 475.00
Plate, 7¾" d...50.00
Plate, 8½" d. 56.00
Plate, 9¾" d. (ILLUS.) 90.00
Plate, 11" d., two-handled 210.00
Platter, 13¾" l.......................................295.00
Platter, 12¼ x 15½" 370.00
Sauce tureen, cover & undertray, the set (professional repair to finial).......750.00
Saucer 18.00

Sauce ladle..475.00
Soup plate w/flanged rim, 8¾" d. 65.00
Sugar bowl, cov. 295.00
Teapot, cov. 375.00
Vegetable bowl, cov., rectangular 390.00
Vegetable bowl, cov., octagonal.........390.00
Vegetable bowl, open, 8½" d. 115.00
Waste bowl 110.00

OSBORNE (W.H. Grindley, ca. 1900)

Bone dish...45.00
Bouillon cup & saucer..........................85.00
Butter pat 32.00
Cup & saucer..85.00
Gravy boat & underplate, 2 pcs. 125.00
Platter, 10½" l. 55.00
Platter, 12½" l. 90.00
Platter, 13½" x 18" 395.00
Vegetable bowl, cov. 200.00
Vegetable bowl, open, 8¼" oval 60.00
Vegetable bowl, open, 10" oval 48.00

OSBORNE (Ridgways, ca. 1905)

Bone dish...40.00
Bouillon cup & saucer...........................85.00
Butter pat 42.00
Plate, 9½" d. 60.00
Relish dish, 9" oval 95.00
Soup plate w/flanged rim, 9" d. 50.00
Soup tureen, cov. 450.00
Vegetable bowl, cov., clover-shaped..240.00
Vegetable bowl, open, 8¼" oval 72.00
Vegetable bowl, open, 7¼ x 9½" 80.00
Vegetable bowl, open, 10" oval 60.00

PELEW (E. Challinor, ca. 1840)

Creamer...425.00
Cup & saucer, handleless...................175.00
Plate, 9¾" d. 130.00
Platter, 16" l. 495.00
Sauce dish 70.00
Vegetable bowl, cov. 795.00

SAVOY (Johnson Bros., ca. 1900)

Savoy Plate

Butter pat 35.00

Creamer..175.00
Cup & saucer...70.00
Plate, 7" d. 35.00
Plate, 9" d. (ILLUS.)...................................55.00
Plates, 10½" d., set of 4..........................220.00
Platter, 12¼ x 16" 155.00
Sauce dish, 5⅛" d.......................................31.00

SCINDE (J. & G. Alcock, ca. 1840 and Thomas Walker, ca. 1847)

Scinde Plate

Bowl, 6½" d., 3¾" h. 195.00
Bowl, 10½" d. 200.00
Butter dish, cover & liner (professional repair to finial) 1,275.00
Cake plate, scalloped rim, 10½" d. 70.00
Cup & saucer, handleless..................195.00
Gravy boat 405.00
Ladle holder..175.00
Plate, 7" d. 50.00
Plate, 8¼" d. 65.00
Plate, 9" d. 85.00
Plate, 10½" d. (ILLUS.).............................205.00
Platter, 9¾" l. 215.00
Platter, 11" l. 395.00
Platter, 10¼ x 13½" 450.00
Platter, 15½" l. ....675.00 to 725.00
Platter, 14 x 18" 890.00
Relish dish, mitten-shaped 295.00
Sauce tureen, cov. 895.00
Sugar bowl, cov. ....600.00 to 650.00
Teapot, cov. 985.00
Undertray for sauce tureen 325.00
Vegetable bowl, cov., 10 x 13" (minor professional repair) 795.00
Vegetable bowl open, 10¾" octagon 225.00

SPINACH (Libertas, ca. 1900, brush-painted)

Bowl, 8" d. (ILLUS. top next column) 65.00
Cup & saucer...75.00
Plate, 7¾" d. 55.00
Sauce dish 40.00

Spinach Bowl

Waste bowl 150.00

TOGO (F. Winkle, ca. 1900)

Togo Plate

Gravy boat 69.00
Plate, 10" d. (ILLUS.)...................................55.00
Platter, 9 x 12" 110.00
Platter, 14½" l. 195.00
Tray, 5 x 6¼" 52.00

TONQUIN (W. Adams & Son., ca. 1845)

Plate, 7½" x 8½" d. 75.00
Plate, 9¾" d. 125.00
Teapot, cov. (professional repair).......925.00
Waste bowl 150.00

TONQUIN (Joseph Heath, ca. 1850)

Creamer..475.00
Plate, 8½" d. 50.00
Plate, 9½" d. (some glaze wear)..........85.00
Platter, 10 x 13¼" 365.00
Platter, 16" l. 595.00
Vegetable bowl, cov. 975.00

TOURAINE (Henry Alcock, ca. 1898 and Stanley Pottery, ca. 1898)

Bone dish...84.00
Butter dish, cov. 515.00
Butter pat 47.00
Creamer & cov. sugar bowl, pr. 480.00
Cup & saucer........................85.00 to 100.00

Gravy boat & underplate, 2 pcs. 235.00
Pitcher, 6" h. 395.00
Pitcher, 6½" h. 475.00
Pitcher, 8" h. 750.00
Pitcher, 2 qt. 695.00
Plate, 6½" d. 40.00
Plate, 7½" d. 45.00
Plate, 8¾" d. 60.00

Touraine Plate

Plate, 10" d. (ILLUS.)...............................85.00
Platter, 9 x 10" 225.00
Platter, 12½" l. 150.00
Platter, 15" l. 250.00
Salt dip..48.00
Sauce dish, 6¼" d.....................................52.00
Saucer 20.00
Soup plate w/flanged rim, 7½" d. 80.00
Sugar bowl, cov. 300.00
Vegetable bowl, cov., 11¾" d. 375.00
Vegetable bowl, open, 9¼" d. 135.00
Vegetable bowl, open, 9" oval 125.00
Vegetable bowl, open, 10" d. 92.50
Waste bowl 175.00

WALDORF (New Wharf Pottery, ca. 1892)

Waldorf Cup & Saucer

Bacon platter, oval 135.00
Bowls, cereal, 6" d., set of four 140.00
Bowl, 9" d. 85.00
Creamer...150.00
Cup & saucer (ILLUS.) 85.00
Plate, 6" d. 35.00
Plate, 9" d. 70.00
Plate, 10" d. 80.00
Platter, 9 x 10¾" 110.00
Potato bowl 9" d.....................................100.00
Sauce dish 38.00
Soup plate w/flanged rim 110.00
Vegetable bowl, open, 9" d......................87.50
Vegetable bowl, open, 10" d. 125.00
Waste bowl 160.00

WATTEAU (Doulton & Co., ca. 1900)

Bowl, cereal 35.00
Butter pat 25.00
Egg cup 100.00
Ewer, 12½" h. 500.00
Plate, 6½" d. 35.00
Plate, 9½" d. 50.00
Plate, 10½" d. 72.00
Platter, 14 x 17½" 375.00
Soup plate w/flanged rim 75.00

WATTEAU (New Wharf Pottery, ca. 1891)

Bowl, 10¼" d. 185.00
Cup & saucer 75.00
Plate, 9" d. 45.00
Platter, 8 x 11" 100.00
Platter, 9 x 10¾", scalloped rim 235.00
Vegetable bowl, open, 9" d. 75.00

YEDO (Ashworth & Bros. Ltd., ca. 1870)

Plate, dinner, 10⅜" d. 95.00
Platter, 9¼ x 10¼" oval 115.00
Soup plate w/flanged rim, 10¼" d. 110.00

(End of Flow Blue Section)

FRANCISCAN WARE

Desert Rose Butter Dish

A product of Gladding, McBean & Company of Glendale and Los Angeles, California, Franciscan Ware was one of a number of lines produced by that firm over its long history. Introduced in 1934 as a pottery dinnerware, Franciscan Ware was produced in many patterns including "Desert Rose," introduced in 1941 and reportedly the most popular dinnerware pattern ever made in this country. Beginning in 1942 some vitrified china patterns were produced under the Franciscan name also.

After a merger in 1963 the company name was changed to Interpace Corporation and in 1979 Josiah Wedgwood & Sons purchased the Gladding, McBean & Co. plant from Interpace. American production ceased in 1984.

Bowl, salad, 4½ x 8", crescent-shaped, Apple patt., ca. 1940 ....$22.00
Bowl, fruit, 5¼" d., Desert Rose patt., ca. 1941 ....8.00
Bowl, soup, 5½" d., 2¼" h., footed, Desert Rose patt., ca. 1941 ....21.00
Bowl, cereal or soup, 6" d., Cafe Royal patt. 15.00
Bowl, cereal or soup, 6" d., Desert Rose patt., ca. 1941 ....10.00
Bowl, cereal, El Patio Table Ware, 1934-54 ....10.00
Bowl, cereal, Hacienda patt., green glaze, ca. 1964 ....5.00
Bowl, 7" d., Madeira patt., ca. 1967 ....6.00
Bowl, 7¾" d., Coronado Table Ware, ivory glaze, 1936-56 ....9.00
Bowl, salad, 10" d., 3¼" h., Desert Rose patt., ca. 1941 ....65.00
Bowl, salad, 11" d., Coronado Table Ware, coral satin glaze, 1936-56 ....30.00
Bowl, salad, 11¼" d., Ivy patt., ca. 1948 ....95.00
Butter dish, cov., Apple patt., ca. 1940, ¼ lb. 35.00
Butter dish, cov., Cafe Royal patt., ¼ lb. 35.00
Butter dish, cov., Coronado Table Ware, ivory glaze, 1936-56 ....65.00
Butter dish, cov., Desert Rose patt., ¼ lb. (ILLUS.) 45.00
Butter dish, cov., El Patio Table Ware, 1934-54 ....45.00
Butter dish, cov., Ivy patt., ca. 1948, ¼ lb. 40.00
Butter dish, cov., Tiempo patt., ca. 1949 ....40.00
Candleholders, Desert Rose patt., ca. 1941, 3" h., pr. 76.00
Casserole, cov., round, handled, Apple patt., ca. 1940, 1½" qt., 6¾" d., 3" h. 75.00
Casserole, cov., round, handled, Ivy patt., ca. 1948, 1½ qt., 8" d., 4" h. 110.00
Coffeepot, cov., demitasse, Coronado Table Ware, ivory glaze, 1936-56 ....125.00
Coffeepot, cov., Apple patt., ca. 1940, 7½" h. 110.00
Coffeepot, cov., Desert Rose patt., ca. 1941 ....88.00
Compote, open, footed, Coronado Table Ware, ivory glaze, 1936-56 ....45.00
Cookie jar, cov., Apple patt., ca. 1940, 9¼" h. ....150.00 to 200.00
Cookie jar, cov., Desert Rose patt., ca. 1941, 9¼" h. ....200.00 to 250.00
Creamer, Coronado Table Ware, golden glow satin glaze, 1936-56 ....12.50
Creamer, El Patio Table Ware, redwood brown glaze, 1934-54 ....8.00
Creamer, Ivy patt., ca. 1948, 4" h. 15.00
Cup & saucer, demitasse, Desert Rose patt., ca. 1941 ....37.50
Cup & saucer, demitasse, El Patio Table Ware, 1934-54 ....25.00
Cup & saucer, Apple patt., ca. 1940 ....12.00
Cup & saucer, Cafe Royal patt. 18.00
Cup & saucer, Desert Rose patt., ca. 1941 ....14.00
Cup & saucer, El Patio Table Ware, 1934-54 ....11.00
Cup & saucer, Madeira patt., ca. 1967 ....6.00
Cup & saucer, Oasis patt., ca. 1954 ....7.50
Egg cup, Apple patt., ca. 1940, 3¾" h. 15.00
Egg cup, Desert Rose patt., ca. 1941, 3¾" h. 20.00
Ginger jar, cov., Cafe Royal patt. 85.00
Gravy boat w/attached undertray, Apple patt., ca. 1940, 8¼" l., 3½" h. 35.00
Gravy boat w/attached undertray, Desert Rose patt. 35.00
Gravy boat, footed, El Patio Table Ware, golden glow gloss glaze, 1934-54 ....20.00
Gravy boat w/attached undertray, Ivy patt., ca. 1948, 9" l., 5" h. 35.00
Gravy boat w/attached undertray, Starburst patt., ca. 1954 ....25.00
Ladle, Apple patt., ca. 1940, 10" l. 20.00
Marmalade jar, cov., Desert Rose patt., ca. 1941 ....85.00
Mixing bowl, Apple patt., ca. 1940, 7½" d., 4¼" h. 22.00
Mug, Apple patt., ca. 1940, 12 oz., 4¼" h. 35.00
Mug, Desert Rose patt., ca. 1941, 12 oz. 58.00
Napkin ring, Desert Rose patt., ca. 1941, 1½" h. 25.00
Napkin rings, Cafe Royal patt., set of four in original box 85.00
Pepper mill, Apple patt., ca. 1940 ....67.00
Pitcher, milk, 6½" h., Apple patt., ca. 1940, 1 qt. ....75.00 to 85.00
Pitcher, 7¼" h., Starburst patt., ca. 1954 ....30.00
Pitcher, syrup, 6¼" h., Desert Rose patt., ca. 1941, 1 pt. 65.00
Pitcher, water, 8¾" h., Desert Rose patt., ca. 1941, 2½ qt. 125.00
Plate, 6" d., Coronado Table Ware, yellow satin, ca. 1936 ....4.00
Plate, 6¼" d., Coronado Table Ware, ivory glaze, 1936-56 ....3.00

Plate, bread & butter, 6¼" d., Ivy patt., ca. 1948 ....8.00
Plate, bread & butter, 6½" d., Apple patt., ca. 1940 ....10.00
Plate, 7" d., Oasis patt., ca. 1954 ....6.00
Plate, salad, 4½ x 8", crescent-shaped, Apple patt., ca. 1940 ....35.00
Plate, salad, 4½ x 8", crescent-shaped, Desert Rose patt., ca. 1941 ....24.00
Plate, 8¼" d., El Patio Table Ware, coral satin glaze, 1934-54 ....6.00
Plate, salad, 8½" d., Apple patt., ca. 1940 ....7.50
Plate, salad, 8½" d., Cafe Royal patt....14.00
Plate, luncheon, 9¼" d., Ivy patt., ca. 1948 ....16.00
Plate, luncheon, 9½" d., Apple patt., ca. 1940 ....8.00
Plate, 9½" d., Coronado patt., turquoise 8.00
Plate, luncheon, 9½" d., Desert Rose patt., ca. 1941 ....10.00
Plate, 9½" d., Coronado Table Ware, maroon gloss glaze, 1936-56 ....8.00
Plate, 10" d., Oasis patt., ca. 1954 ....8.00
Plate, dinner, 10¼" d., Ivy patt., ca. 1948 ....12.00
Plate, dinner, 10½" d., Apple patt., ca. 1940 ....16.50
Plate, dinner, 10½" d., Cafe Royal patt. 20.00
Plate, dinner, 10½" d., Desert Rose patt., ca. 1941 ....12.50
Plate, dinner, 10½" d., El Patio Table Ware, coral satin glaze, 1934-54 ....9.00
Plate, dinner, 10½" d., Hacienda patt., green glaze, ca. 1965 ....7.00
Plate, dinner, 10½" d., Madeira patt., ca. 1967 ....7.00
Plate, grill, 10⅞" d., Apple patt., ca. 1940 ....55.00
Plate, buffet, 11" d., Ivy patt., ca. 1948 ....24.50
Plate, chop, 12" d., Apple patt., ca. 1940 ....55.00
Plate, chop, 12" d., Cafe Royal patt. 40.00
Plate, cake, 13" d., Ivy patt., ca. 1948 ....35.00
Plate, chop, 14" d., Apple patt., ca. 1940 ....125.00
Plate, chop, 14" d., Ivy patt., ca. 1948 ....125.00
Platter, 11" l., oval, coupe steak, Desert Rose patt., ca. 1941 ....42.00
Platter, 11½" l., oval, Ivy patt., ca. 1948 ....35.00
Platter, 8½ x 12¾" oval, Apple patt., ca. 1940 ....30.00
Platter, 8½ x 12¾" oval, Desert Rose patt., ca. 1941 ....20.00
Platter, 13" l., oval, Coronado Table Ware, ivory satin glaze, 1936-56 ....16.50
Platter, 13" l., oval, El Patio Table Ware, 1934-54 ....18.00
Platter, 13" l., oval, Starburst patt., ca. 1954 ....40.00
Platter, 10¼ x 14" oval, Apple patt., ca. 1940 ....30.00
Platter, 10¼ x 14" oval, Cafe Royal patt. 45.00
Platter, 13¼ x 19" oval, Apple patt., ca. 1940 ....185.00 to 200.00
Relish dish, oblong, three-part, Apple patt., ca. 1940, 11¾" l. 30.00
Relish dish, oblong w/end handle, Coronado Table Ware, ivory glaze, 1936-56, 9" l. 15.00
Relish dish, oval, three-part, Desert Rose patt., ca. 1941, 12" l. 60.00
Salt & pepper shakers, Apple patt., ca. 1940, tall, 6¼" h., pr. 45.00
Salt & pepper shakers, Desert Rose patt., ca. 1941, tall, 6¼" h., pr. 35.00
Salt & pepper shakers, Madeira patt., ca. 1967, pr. 10.00
Sherbet, footed, Desert Rose patt., ca. 1941, 2½" h. 20.00
Soup plate w/flanged rim, Apple patt., ca. 1940, 8½" d. 16.00
Soup plate w/flanged rim, Desert Rose patt., ca. 1941, 8¼" d. 20.00
Soup plate w/flanged rim, Ivy patt., ca. 1948, 8½" d. 21.00
Soup tureen, cov., three-footed, Apple patt., ca. 1940, 7½" d., 5¼" h. 325.00
Sugar bowl, cov., Coronado Table Ware, yellow glaze, 1936-56 ....15.00
Sugar bowl, cov., El Patio Table Ware, maroon gloss glaze, 1934-54 ....18.00
Sugar bowl, open, individual, Desert Rose patt., ca. 1941, 2" h. 21.00
Teapot, cov., Apple patt., ca. 1940, 4¾" h. 85.00
Teapot, cov., Desert Rose patt., ca. 1941 ....85.00
Tidbit tray, two-tier, Ivy patt., ca. 1948 ....75.00
Tumbler, Ivy patt., ca. 1948, 10 oz., 5¼" h. 28.00
Tumbler, water, Apple patt., ca. 1940, 10 oz., 5¼" h. 25.00
Vase, bud, 6" h., Cafe Royal patt., w/original box 95.00
Vegetable bowl, open, round, Apple patt., ca. 1940, 7¾" d., 2" h. 40.00
Vegetable bowl, open, oval, divided, Cafe Royal patt., 7 x 10¾" 40.00
Vegetable bowl, open, round, Desert Rose patt., ca. 1941, 8" d., 2¼" h. 20.00
Vegetable bowl, open, round, Desert Rose patt., ca. 1941, 9" d. 32.00
Vegetable bowl, open, round, El Patio Table Ware, lettuce green gloss glaze, 1934-54, 8½" d. 20.00

Vegetable bowl, open, oval, divided, Ivy patt., ca. 1948, 12" l. 60.00
Vegetable bowl, oval, Starburst patt., ca. 1954 ....15.00
Vegetable dish, cov., Apple patt. 65.00

FRANKOMA

1978 Republican Elephant Mug

John Frank began producing and selling pottery on a part-time basis during the summer of 1933 while he was still teaching art and pottery classes at the University of Oklahoma. In 1934, Frankoma Pottery became an incorporated business that was successful enough to allow him to leave his teaching position in 1936 to devote full time to its growth. The pottery was moved to Sapulpa, Oklahoma in 1938 and a full range of art pottery and dinnerwares were eventually offered. In 1953 Frankoma switched from Ada clay to clay found in Sapulpa. Since John Frank's death in 1973, the pottery has been directed by his daughter, Joniece. In early 1991 Richard Bernstein became owner and president of Frankoma Pottery which was renamed Frankoma Industries. Joniece Frank serves as vice president and general manager. The early wares and limited editions are becoming increasingly popular with collectors today.

Book ends, Bucking Bronco, No. 423, Prairie Green glaze, 5½" h., pr. $175.00
Bottle-vase, V-6, 1974, aqua glaze, 13" h. 55.00
Bottle-vase, V-7, 1975, Desert Gold glaze w/Coffee colored cover & base, 13" h. 60.00
Bottle-vase, No. V-8, 1976, Freedom Red & white, 13" h. 60.00
Bottle-vase, No. V-9, 1977, white w/black base & stopper, 13" h. 60.00
Bottle-vase, V-14, 1982, Flame Red body on black base, 11" h. 60.00
Bowl, 10½" d., Wagon Wheel patt., Prairie Green glaze 12.00
Candleholders, double, No. 304, pr. 22.00
Candleholders, Oral Roberts, "Christ the Light of the World," pr. 18.50
Centerpiece bowl, green & brown glaze, scalloped, leaf forms center medallion, No. 200, 8¾ x 13" oval 22.00
Christmas card, 1965 ....70.00
Christmas card, 1967 ....42.50
Christmas card, 1968 ....42.50
Christmas card, 1969 ....30.00
Christmas card, 1970 ....22.50
Christmas card, 1971, profile of Franks portraits ....20.00 to 30.00
Christmas card, 1972 ....25.00
Christmas card, 1973 ....22.00
Christmas card, 1974 ....28.00
Christmas card, 1976 ....20.00
Christmas card, 1977 ....15.50
Christmas card, 1978 ....20.00
Christmas card, 1979 ....19.00
Christmas card, 1980 ....18.50
Christmas card, 1981 ....20.00
Christmas card, 1982 ....18.50
Christmas card, 1983 ....15.50
Christmas card, 1984 ....15.50
Cornucopia-vase, No. 56, Ada clay, 7" h. 25.00
Cornucopia-vase, green glaze, No. 57, 9½" l. 12.00
Creamer, Wagon Wheel patt., Prairie Green glaze 8.00
Creamer & cov. sugar bowl, Mayan-Aztec patt., grey & brown, Nos. 7A & 7B, 3⅝" h., pr. 15.00
Cup & saucer, Mayan-Aztec patt., Woodland Moss glaze 4.50
Cup & saucer, Wagon Wheel patt., Prairie Green glaze 9.00
Dish, clover-shaped, Plainsman patt., bronze glaze, No. 223, 6½" d. 6.50
Dish, leaf-shaped, Prairie Green glaze, 12½" l. 12.00
Figure of a Fan Dancer, No. 113, green on red brick clay, 1955, 8½ x 13½" ....200.00 to 225.00
Figure, Indian Chief, No. 142, brown matte glaze, 8" h. 15.50
Figures, Dreamer Girl, No. 427, Onyx Black glaze, Ada clay, 5⅜" h., pr. 182.00
Flask, Mayan-Aztec patt., green & brown, leather thong through ceramic loops, 2 x 6 x 6¼" 18.00
Flower holder, model of an elephant, No. 180, 1942, 3½" h. 89.50
Model of a circus horse, No. 138, Desert Gold glaze, 4½" h. 75.00
Model of a puma, seated, No. 114, Ada clay, green glaze, 7½" h. 69.50
Model of a swan, miniature, No. 168, black glaze, 3" h. 38.00
Model of a swan, miniature, No. 168, Desert Gold glaze, 3" h. 35.00

Mug, 1968 (Republican) elephant, Prairie Green glaze 12.00

Mug, 1969 (Republican) elephant, Nixon-Agnew, flame-red glaze 80.00

Mug, 1970 (Republican) elephant, blue glaze 35.00

Mug, 1973 (Republican) elephant, Nixon-Agnew, Desert Gold glaze.......30.00

Mug, 1975 (Democratic) donkey, Autumn Yellow glaze 19.00

Mug, 1977 (Democratic) donkey, "Carter-Mondale," pink glaze 21.50

Mug, 1978 (Democratic) donkey, blue glaze 16.50

Mug, 1978 (Republican) elephant, Prairie Green glaze (ILLUS.) 22.00

Mug, 1979 (Republican) elephant, brown satin glaze w/white interior......15.00

Mug, 1980 (Democratic) donkey, terra cotta glaze 18.50

Mug, 1980 (Republican) elephant, terra cotta glaze 15.00

Mug, 1981 (Republican) elephant, "Reagan-Bush," Celery Green glaze 20.00

Mug, 1982 (Republican) elephant, robin's egg blue glaze 25.00

Mug, Plainsman patt., Desert Gold glaze, 16 oz., 5⅜" h. 6.00

Mug, Woodland Moss glaze, No. C5, 3¾" h. 5.00

Pitcher, jug-type, 7" h., Plainsman patt., Desert Gold glaze, No. 8 ....8.50

Planter, boat-shaped, white glaze, No. 211, 5 x 12½" 12.00

Plate, 6½" d., scalloped, Plainsman patt., Woodland Moss glaze 2.50

Plate, 6½" d., Wagon Wheel patt., Prairie Green glaze 5.00

Plate, 7" d., Mayan-Aztec patt., Woodland Moss glaze 3.50

Plate, 7½" d., "Easter," made for Oral Roberts, 1972 ....15.00

Plate, 8½" d., Christmas, 1965, "Good Will Towards Men," depicts Mary, Joseph & Jesus 225.00

Plate, 8½" d., Christmas, 1968, "Flight Into Egypt" 26.00

Plate, 8½" d., Christmas, 1972, "Seeking The Christ Child" 22.50

Plate, 8½" d., Christmas, 1973, "The Annunciation" 22.50

Plate, 10" d., Wagon Wheel patt., Prairie Green glaze 8.00

Sugar bowl, cov., Mayan-Aztec patt., Woodland Moss glaze 8.50

Sugar bowl, cov., Wagon Wheel patt., Prairie Green glaze 13.00

Teapot, cov., Wagon Wheel patt., Prairie Green glaze, small, 2 cup.......15.00

Tea set: cov. teapot, creamer & cov. sugar bowl; Plainsman patt., gold-bronze, teapot, No. 5T, creamer & sugar bowl, Nos. 5A & 5B, w/original label, 3 pcs 32.00

Trivet, round, "Seals of the Five Civilized Tribes of Indians in Oklahoma," 1971-79 ....10.00 to 15.00

Vase, 6" h., figural Flower Girl, No. 700, 1942-51, blue glaze 35.00

Vase, 7⅜" h., 2⅞ x 5" rectangular, Mayan-Aztec patt., Woodland Moss glaze, No. 63Z 20.00

Vase, 8½" h., fan-shaped, green-bronze leaf forms, No. 74 ....30.00

Wall masks, bust of Indian Maiden, No. 132, ivory glaze, Ada clay, w/original sticker, 4⅛" h. 60.00

Wall masks, bust of Afro Man, No. 125, & Afro woman, No. 124, black glaze, man 6¾" h., woman 6½" h.,pr. 145.00

Wall masks, bust of Afro Man, No. 125, & Afro woman, No. 124, ivory glaze, man 6¾" h., woman 6½" h., pr. 145.00

Wall pocket, model of a cowboy boot, No. 133, white glaze, unmarked, 6½" h. ....10.00 to 20.00

Wall pocket, Wagon Wheel patt., Prairie Green glaze, Ada clay 35.00

Wash bowl & pitcher, blue & brown glaze, oval bowl 1½ x 5 x 6", pitcher 4½" h., No. 40B, 2 pcs. 10.00

FULPER

Exceptional Fulper Articles

The Fulper Pottery was founded in Flemington, New Jersey, in 1805 and operated until 1935, although operations were curtailed in 1929 when its main plant was destroyed by fire. The name was changed in 1929 to Stangl Pottery, which continued in operation until July of 1978, when Pfaltzgraff, a division of Susquehanna Broadcasting Company of

York, Pennsylvania, purchased the assets of the Stangl Pottery, including the name.

Book ends, mission bell-type, modeled as upright double-tiered mission bell towers in taupe over black & w/two figural bells in mustard yellow,unmarked, ca. 1915, 7¾" h., pr. $605.00

Bowl, 6½" d., 3¼" h., deep flaring sides molded as a large morning glory blossom, glossy grey, cobalt blue & caramel flambé interior glaze, grey, bluish purple & rose flambé matte exterior glaze, rectangular ink mark..467.50

Bowl-vase, 'Norse' design, three scrolled handles holding a vessel w/'hammered' surface, copper dust crystalline glaze, raised vertical mark, 11½" w., 11" h. (ILLUS. right)...3,575.00

Candle sconce, matte blue glaze w/blue, yellow & green leaded slag glass inserts, oval vertical ink stamp, 5" w., 10¾" h. (ILLUS. left)...........1,045.00

Candlesticks, round cushion foot tapering to a slender swelled shaft below the flared socket, leopard skin glaze, vertical box ink mark, 6" d. foot, 8½" h., pr. 357.50

Centerpiece, a round shallow bowl w/inverted rim supported by three effigy figures kneeling on a stepped disc base, the bowl w/a glossy dark blue, khaki & lavender flambé glaze, the base w/a matte green & blue glaze, vertical ink mark, 10¼" d., 7¼" h..550.00

Doorstop, figural, Bulldog in seated position w/open front legs, blue & caramel flambé glaze, unmarked, 10½" w., 7½" h. (minor restoration).....................................715.00

Dresser box, cov., figural, the cylindrical base w/a low, domed cover mounted w/a large figure of a kneeling Egyptian maiden w/hand-decorated trim, matte glaze, impressed marks, overall 8½" h.......302.50

Flower frog, model of a scarab, ochre & green glaze...................................75.00

Jardiniere, footed, matte green glaze, early ink mark, 5" h...............125.00

Perfume lamp, figural lady, pink glaze 235.00

Vase, 5¾" h., 8" d., slightly rounded sides tapering toward the top, angular handles from midsection to rim, wisteria matte mottled purple glaze over a grey ground, vertical incised mark....................................715.00

Vase, 6½" h., 8½" d., a low foot supporting a very wide squatty bulbous body tapering to a short cylindrical neck flanked by three small loop handles, overall fine leopard skin crystalline glaze, incised vertical oval mark................605.00

Vase, 9½" h., 4½" d., tall cylindrical body w/two square cut-out windows in the sides above a relief-molded base band of stylized mushrooms, finely shaded ivory to elephant's breath flambé glaze, vertical ink mark & paper label..........................825.00

Vase, 11" h., 5¼" d., six-sided baluster-form, milky blue, purple, ochre & green crystalline flambé glaze, No. 660, incised vertical oval mark...550.00

Vase, 12¼" h., 11" d., wide ovoid body tapering to a rounded, stepping neck w/a flat rim, mirrored black to sky blue flambé glaze, raised vertical oval mark 2,200.00

Vase, 13" h., 7½" d., squatty bulbous base on footring below a tall trumpet-form neck, mottled glossy brown, purple & mint green flambé glaze, oval incised mark & two paper labels.......................................935.00

Vase, 15½" h., 5" d., tall slender cylindrical body slightly swelled at the top & tapering to a flat rim, fine semi-matte light green to light yellow flambé glaze, raised vertical mark 1,320.00

Wall pocket, Art Deco design, brown & caramel glaze, vertical stamp 375.00

GOLDSCHEIDER

Goldscheider Dancer Figure

The Goldscheider firm, manufacturers of porcelain and faience in Austria between 1885 and the present, was founded by

Friedrich Goldscheider and carried on by his widow. The firm came under the control of his sons, Walter and Marcell, in 1920. Fleeing their native Austria at the time of World War II, the Goldscheiders set up an operation in the United States. They were listed in the Trenton, New Jersey, City Directory from 1943 through 1950 and their main production seems to have been art pottery figurines.

Box, cov., the cover w/a figural finial of a large German Shepherd's head w/its tongue out, shaded green & brown glaze, 4 x 5½" $85.00

Bust of a woman, earthenware, modeled w/curly reddish orange hair & lips, a yellow blossom w/green foliage at her neck, stamped & incised marks, ca. 1925, 8" h. 357.50

Bust of a woman w/a hand holding an apple, painted in naturalistic tones, in collaboration w/Myott Sone Co., on a black base, stamped company mark, 8¼" h. 230.00

Candelabra, three-light, each in the form of a dancing maiden enclosed by a circular ring set w/three candle supports, raised on a shaped standard above an oval base, the figures in clear glaze, the supports in dark brown decorated about the base & ring w/multicolored dashes, each w/printed factory marks "Goldscheider - Wien - MADE IN AUSTRIA," impressed "5366/148/11" & "5366/156/18" respectively, w/overglaze marks "D5/XXVIII./F." & "D.5/IV" respectively, ca. 1925, 19" h., pr. (now electrified) 3,450.00

Figure of an Art Deco lady dressed as a vamp, Austria, 18" h. 880.00

Figure of a dancer, a female dancer in Arabian-inspired costume, glazed in lavender, yellow, red, blue & green, printed, inscribed & impressed factory marks, ca. 1925, 17⅞" h. (ILLUS.) 2,300.00

Figure of Juliet w/doves, rose, grey, cobalt & pale blue, 12¼" h. 225.00

Figure of a lady w/muff, wearing plumed green & lavender hat, flowered cream underskirt, incised "BCV," impressed "802/5/10," 8¼" h. 90.00

Figure of a nude female dancer, one arm extended forward, the other backward, all-white on a domed black-glazed round base, after a design by Lorenzl, impressed mark "Goldscheider - Wein - MADE IN AUSTRIA - Lorenzl" & "5802 -464," ca. 1925, 11" h. 805.00

Figure of Sing Lo, young Oriental lady holds bird up, fancy yellow tunic, green trousers, long queue, w/pagoda & birdhouse, 7¼" h. 32.00

Figure group, modeled as a woman in plaid sunsuit w/straw hat over her shoulders & holding her wire-haired terrier by the front paws as if dancing w/him, glazed in shades of maroon, white, yellow, brown & black, raised on a black oval base, after a design by Dakon, impressed "Goldscheider - Wein - MADE IN AUSTRIA - Dakon" & "7194/66/19," ca. 1925, 12½" h. 4,025.00

Lamp base, figural, a belly dancer leaning against a composite column, raised on a rectangular base w/rounded corners, printed "Goldscheider" & "MADE IN AUSTRIA," ca. 1930s, 16¾" h. 1,035.00

Mask, hanging-type, modeled as a woman's head, a hand holding an orange-glazed eye mask, the face glazed in white & the hair in bluish green, stamped company mark & "MADE IN AUSTRIA," 10½" h. 345.00

Plaque, pierced to hang, figural, modeled as the stylized head of a woman turned to the left & holding a rose blossom in her hand, glazed in white, green, orange & yellow, factory mark & "4490," repaired, ca. 1925, 10½" h. 690.00

Plaques, pierced to hang, allegorical, rectangular w/crown-form crest above a low-relief landscape centered by a high-relief female figure, one representing Summer & the other Winter, titled at the base "HIVER" or "ÉTÉ," painted in shades of amber, ochre, green & ivory, decorated by Chere, one impressed "REPRODUCTION RESERVÉE - Frederich Goldscheider - Wien," Austria, ca. 1900, drill holes, 28½" h., pr. 2,300.00

GRUEBY

Some fine art pottery was produced by the Grueby Faience and Tile Company, established in Boston in 1891. Choice pieces were created with molded designs on a semi-porcelain body. The ware is marked and often bears the initials of the decorators. The pottery closed in 1907.

Bowl, 5¼" d., 2¼" h., squatty bulbous sides w/a wide shoulder to a rolled rim, molded w/wide, rounded leaves, matte green glaze, artist-initialed & dated "1906" $467.50

Bowl-vase, squatty bulbous body on a small footring, the wide shoulder tapering to a short, flared mouth, lightly molded w/wide ribs, covered in an organic matte yellow glaze, 9" d., 6½" h. 1,980.00

Candleholder, shallow dished base w/a low, flaring candle socket in the center joined to the rim by two arched handles, dark matte blue glaze, circular impressed mark & original paper label, 6" d., 2" h. 357.50

Humidor, cov., tall slightly waisted cylindrical body w/a flat inset cover w/knob finial, decorated around the rim w/a narrow band of oyster white blossoms against a French blue ground, impressed "Grueby Pottery, Boston USA - F.E. - 4-21-07," 4½" d., 8¼" h. (minor chips inside cover) 1,430.00

Grueby Jardiniere

Jardiniere, slightly canted sides, narrow shoulder & rounded rim, decorated w/tooled & applied flowers & curled leaves, thick matte green glaze, horizontal "Boston" mark, minor glaze flecks to rim & high points, 8¼" h., 8" d. (ILLUS.) 1,650.00

Lamp base, cylindrical, long tooled & applied leaves under a fine matte green glaze, impressed circular mark "GRUEBY FAIENCE - BOSTON U.S.A.," 7½" d., 12¼" h...3,300.00

Paperweight, model of a scarab beetle, leathery deep blue glaze, impressed "Grueby Pottery Boston USA," 2¼" l., 3¼" h. (very minor base nick) 247.50

Vase, 4½" h., 5" d., squatty bulbous footed body tapering to a short, flared neck, tooled & applied wide leaves under an organic matte cucumber green glaze interspersed w/yellow lily blossoms around the neck, impressed circular mark "Grueby Pottery Boston USA - FH - 17-6" 2,530.00

Vase, 5¾" h., 6¾" d., squatty bulbous body w/a wide shoulder tapering to a short cylindrical neck, wide lightly molded leaves around the sides, dark green matte glaze, unsigned 880.00

Vase, 7½" h., 4¾" d., bulbous base tapering to a short neck, tooled & applied broad leaves w/curled-up edges, interspersed w/buds on tall stems, fine matte green glaze, designed by Ruth Erickson, marked "GRUEBY POTTERY, BOSTON U.S.A., RE." 1,540.00

Vase, 8½" h., 5" d., slightly expanding cylinder w/flat narrow shoulder, covered w/ superimposed full-length tooled & applied leaves, under a rich tactile & uneven matte green glaze, by Florence Liley, impressed circular mark "GRUEBY FAIENCE CO. BOSTON U.S.A." 2,320.00

Vase, 12" h., 6¼" d., tall ovoid body, molded w/wide, tall pointed leaves up the sides to the narrow shoulder & the short, flaring neck, leaves alternate w/slender stems topped by small yellow buds around the shoulder, veined matte green glaze, incised medallion mark & "255" 3,850.00

Vase, 13" h., 8½" d., gourd-shaped, clear glaze over a curdled cobalt to light blue dripping over a light grey flambé glaze, showing a buff body, impressed circular mark "GRUEBY POTTERY BOSTON U.S.A." 6,050.00

HALL

Founded in 1903 in East Liverpool, Ohio, this still-operating company at first produced mostly utilitarian wares. It was in 1911 that Robert T. Hall, son of the company founder, developed a special single-fire, lead-free glaze which proved to be strong, hard and non-porous. In the 1920s the firm became well known for their extensive line of teapots (still a major product) and in 1932 they introduced kitchenwares followed by dinnerwares in 1936 and refrigerator wares in 1938.

The imaginative designs and wide range of glaze colors and decal decorations have led to the growing appeal of Hall wares with collectors, especially people who like Art Deco and Art Moderne design. One of the firm's most famous patterns was the "Autumn Leaf" line, produced as premiums for the Jewel Tea Company. For listings of this ware see "Jewel Tea Autumn Leaf."

Helpful books on Hall include , The Collector's Guide to Hall China *by Margaret & Kenn Whitmyer, and* Superior Quality Hall China - A Guide for Collectors *by Harvey Duke (An ELO Book, 1977).*

Hall Royal Rose Casserole

Batter pitcher, Sundial shape, Blue Blossom patt. $165.00
Batter pitcher, Sundial shape, Blue Garden patt. ....150.00 to 175.00
Bean pot, cov., single handle, Crocus patt. 225.00
Bean pot, cov., single handle, Orange Poppy patt. 70.00
Bowl, cereal, 6" d., Red Poppy patt., Radiance shape 12.00
Bowl, 8" d., straight-sided, Silhouette (Taverne) patt. 24.00
Bowl, salad, 9" d., Rose Parade patt. 30.00
Bowl, salad, 9" d., Royal Rose patt. 16.50
Bowl, salad, 9" d., Silhouette (Taverne) patt. 23.00
Butter dish, cov., Zephyr shape, Blue Garden patt. 300.00
Canisters, cov., Radiance shape, Orange Poppy patt., set of three ...1,200.00
Casserole, cov., Clover patt., w/gold trim 28.50
Casserole, cov., Radiance shape, Pastel Morning Glory patt. 35.00
Casserole, cov., Sundial shape, No. 4, Chinese Red, 8" d. 25.00
Casserole, cov., Thick Rim shape, Royal Rose patt. (ILLUS.) 38.50
Casserole, cov., Westinghouse line, canary yellow 20.00
Casserole, cov., Pert shape, Rose White patt. 40.00
Coffeepot, cov., Drip-o-lator, Cactus patt. 55.00
Coffeepot, cov., drip-type, all-china, Pert shape, Tulip patt., complete 100.00
Coffeepot, cov., w/insert, china, Wildfire patt. 50.00
Cookie jar, Sundial (Saf-Handle) shape, marine blue 325.00
Cup & saucer, Orange Poppy patt. 32.00
Custard cup, Crocus patt. 30.00
Custard cup, straight-sided, Pert patt., Chinese Red 9.00
Drip jar, cov., Clover patt. 40.00
Leftover dish, cov., Crocus patt., square 60.00
Mug, Silhouette (Taverne) patt. 35.00
Pepper shaker, handled, Blue Blossom patt. 10.00
Pie baker, Red Poppy patt. 32.00
Pitcher, 5" h., Five Band shape, Chinese Red 16.00
Pitcher, 6¼" h., Radiance shape, Red Poppy patt., No. 5 ....35.00
Pitcher, ball-type, Pastel Morning Glory patt. 40.00
Pitcher, ball-type, Silhouette (Taverne) patt., maroon, No. 5 ....24.00
Plate, 7" d., Orange Poppy patt. 15.00
Plate, 9" d., Crocus patt. 12.00

Crocus Pattern Platter

Platter, 10½ x 13¾" oval, Crocus patt. (ILLUS.) 25.00
Pretzel jar, cov., china, Crocus patt. 215.00
Pretzel jar, cov., Pastel Morning Glory patt. 100.00
Pretzel jar, cov., Silhouette (Taverne) patt. 85.00
Punch set: footed punch bowl, twelve cups & ladle; Old Crow patt., mint in box, 14 pcs. 125.00
Salt & pepper shakers, loop handles, Orange Poppy patt., pr. 45.00
Salt & pepper shakers, handled, Radiance shape, Red Poppy patt., pr. 30.00
Salt & pepper shakers, Pert shape, Rose White patt., large, pr. 22.00
Teapot, cov., Airflow shape, blue w/gold 60.00
Teapot, cov., Aladdin shape, turquoise, 6-cup size, w/infuser 75.00

Teapot, cov., Aladdin shape, yellow w/gold 35.00
Teapot, cov., Automobile shape, ivory w/gold trim 750.00
Teapot, cov., Cleveland shape, forest green....................45.00
Teapot, cov., Doughnut shape, Chinese Red 150.00
Teapot, cov., Doughnut shape, cobalt blue 125.00
Teapot, cov., Globe shape, dripless, w/turn-down spout, Addison grey & gold, 6-cup size....................35.00
Teapot, cov., Kansas shape, yellow w/gold trim 190.00
Teapot, cov., Los Angeles shape, yellow, black & white....................30.00
Teapot, cov., Manhattan shape, green....................39.50
Teapot, cov., Melody shape, Orange Poppy patt....................175.00
Teapot, cov., Nautilus shape, maroon, 6-cup size 275.00
Teapot, cov., Parade shape, canary yellow w/gold trim 55.00
Teapot, cov., Parade shape, Delphinium Blue....................40.00
Teapot, cov., Pert shape, Rose Parade patt., 6-cup size....................30.00
Teapot, cov., Star decoration, yellow & gold....................79.00
Teapot, cov., Streamline shape canary yellow....................19.00
Teapot, cov., Sundial (Saf-Handle) shape, cobalt blue....................165.00
Teapot, cov., Sundial (Saf-Handle) shape, turquoise 125.00
Teapot, cov., Surfside shape, emerald green....................135.00
Teapot, cov., T-Ball, silver, round....................125.00 to 150.00
Teapot, cov., Twin-spout shape, black & gold....................79.00
Teapot, cov., Windshield shape, maroon w/gold trim 35.00
Tea tile, Silhouette (Taverne) patt., round....................120.00

HARLEQUIN

The Homer Laughlin China Company, makers of the popular "Fiesta" pottery line, also introduced in 1938 a less expensive and thinner ware which was sold under the "Harlequin" name. It did not carry the maker's trade-mark and was marketed exclusively through F.W. Woolworth Company. It was produced in a wide range of dinnerwares in assorted colors until 1964. Out of production for a number of years, in 1979 Woolworth requested the line be reintroduced using an ironstone body and with a limited range of pieces and colors offered. Collectors also seek out a series of miniature animal figures produced in the Harlequin line in the 1930s and 1940s.

Ashtray, basketweave, turquoise....................$21.00
Bowl, 36s, 4½" d., red....................12.00
Bowl, 36s, 4½" d., rose....................12.00
Bowl, fruit, 5½" d., maroon 8.00
Bowl, fruit, 5½" d., red 8.00
Bowl, fruit, 5½" d., rose....................8.00
Bowl, oatmeal, 6½" d., chartreuse....................20.00
Bowl, individual salad, 7" d., blue 22.00
Bowl, individual salad, 7" d., turquoise 20.00
Bowl, individual salad, 7" d., yellow....................20.00
Butter dish, cov., red....................95.00
Candleholders, yellow, pr. 155.00
Casserole, cov., maroon....................135.00
Creamer, individual size, spruce green....................17.00
Creamer, forest green 12.00
Creamer, red 15.00
Creamer, turquoise....................6.00
Creamer, novelty, ball-shaped, maroon....................48.00
Creamer, novelty, ball-shaped, red 30.00
Creamer, novelty, ball-shaped, rose....................38.00
Creamer & cov. sugar bowl, yellow, pr....................25.00
Cream soup, handled, blue 21.00
Cream soup, handled, grey 12.00
Cream soup, handled, light green 11.00
Cream soup, handled, rose 10.00
Cream soup, handled, turquoise 14.00
Cup, demitasse, light green....................45.00
Cup & saucer, demitasse, blue....................65.00
Cup & saucer, demitasse, chartreuse 135.00
Cup & saucer, demitasse, maroon 165.00
Cup & saucer, demitasse, red 125.00
Cup & saucer, demitasse, rose 65.00
Cup & saucer, demitasse, spruce green....................165.00
Cup & saucer, demitasse, turquoise....................45.00
Cup & saucer, demitasse, yellow 45.00
Cup & saucer, grey....................10.50
Cup & saucer, medium green....................25.00
Cup & saucer, rose....................6.00
Cup & saucer, turquoise....................6.00
Cup & saucer, yellow....................6.00
Egg cup, single, blue 21.50
Egg cup, single, grey....................19.00
Egg cup, single, maroon....................22.50
Egg cup, single, spruce green....................30.00
Egg cup, single, turquoise 20.00
Egg cup, double, forest green 20.00
Egg cup, double, grey....................28.00
Gravy boat, blue 15.00
Gravy boat, maroon....................25.00

Marmalade jar, cov., turquoise 155.00
Nappy, 9" d., red....................................16.00
Nappy, yellow 30.00
Nut dish, individual size, basketweave interior, red..9.00
Nut dish, individual size, basketweave interior, turquoise 7.00
Nut dish, individual size, basketweave interior, yellow......................................7.00
Pitcher, 9" h., ball-shaped w/ice lip, red...54.00
Pitcher, 9" h., ball-shaped w/ice lip, spruce green.....................75.00 to 100.00
Pitcher, 9" h., ball-shaped w/ice lip, turquoise 35.00
Pitcher, 9" h., ball-shaped w/ice lip, yellow...45.00
Pitcher, cylindrical, 22 oz., chartreuse..40.00
Pitcher, cylindrical, 22 oz., grey...........54.00
Pitcher, cylindrical, 22 oz., light green..37.00
Pitcher, cylindrical, 22 oz., red.............37.00
Pitcher, cylindrical, 22 oz., rose...........39.50
Plate, 7" d., grey 6.50
Plate, 9" d., grey 11.00
Plate, 9" d., medium green 28.50
Plate, 9" d., yellow 10.00
Platter, 11" l., oval, turquoise................13.00
Platter, 13" l., oval, red 22.00
Spoon rest, turquoise 172.50
Sugar bowl, cov., rose 15.00
Sugar bowl, cov., turquoise 15.00
Sugar bowl, cov., yellow........................15.00
Teapot, cov., chartreuse.......................110.00
Teapot, cov., forest green......................72.00
Teapot, cov., red.....................................58.00
Teapot, cov., rose................75.00 to 100.00
Tumbler, blue..35.00
Tumbler, red 38.00
Tumbler, turquoise..................................35.00
Tumbler, yellow 25.00

HARLEQUIN ANIMALS

Model of a cat, maroon.........................125.00
Model of a donkey, maroon 75.00
Model of a duck, gold 24.00
Model of a fish, maroon......100.00 to 125.00
Model of a fish, yellow 72.00
Model of a penguin, yellow....................85.00

HAVILAND

Haviland porcelain was originated by Americans in Limoges, France, shortly before the mid-19th century and continues in production. Some Haviland was made by Theodore Haviland in the United States during the last World War. Numerous other factories also made china in Limoges, which see.

Haviland Demitasse Set

Bone Dish, No. 1 Ranson blank $20.00
Bone dish, decorated w/lavender & pink roses, gold trim, Blank No. 22......8.00
Bouillon cup & saucer, two-handled, No. 1 Ranson blank 18.50
Bouillon cup & saucer, two-handled, Rosalinde patt., Theodore Haviland 30.00
Bowl, 9", serving-type, unusual shape, Baltimore Rose patt. 75.00
Bowl, cream soup, handled, w/underplate, Yale patt., Blank No. 103, 2 pcs. 35.00
Bowl, oyster, Clover Leaf patt., Blank No. 98C..65.00
Box, cov., figural, modeled in the form of a recumbent fox, his ears outspread, glazed in chocolate brown against a white ground, designed by Gérard Sandoz, ca. 1925, enameled factory marks & "G.M. Sandoz SC," & incised numerals, 6¼" d. 690.00
Butter pat, decorated w/lavender & pink roses, gold trim, Blank No. 22 ....15.00
Butter pat, Princess patt. 15.00
Butter pat, Silver Anniversary patt., Blank No. 19 ....12.00
Cake plate, open-handled, decorated w/sprays of vivid red & pink roses, gold scallops, embossed mark, 16" d...125.00
Chocolate pot, cov., Silver Anniversary patt. 200.00
Chocolate set: cov. chocolate pot & six cups & saucers; Baltimore Rose patt., 13 pcs........................1,500.00
Chocolate set: tankared-shaped cov. chocolate pot & six cups & saucers; embossed & decorated w/tiny pink roses & green leaves, gold handles & trim, 13 pcs...............................295.00
Coffeepot, cov., Autumn Leaf patt., gold trim 225.00
Creamer & cov. sugar bowl, Springtime patt., pr. 115.00
Creamer & cov. sugar bowl, Yale patt., Blank No. 103, pr. 95.00

Cup & saucer, demitasse, decorated w/blue flowers & green leaves, gold rims, marked "CFH-GDM"..................20.00
Cup & saucer, demitasse, Clover Leaf patt., Blank No. 113..........................25.00
Cup & saucer, demitasse, Ranson blank, pale pink & blue flowers (ILLUS.)..25.00
Cup & saucer, demitasse, decorated w/royal blue & yellow flowers, pale blue leaves & royal blue medallions, cream ground, gold handles & trim, Blank No. 561..................................25.00
Cup & saucer, demitasse, figural butterfly handle, factory-decorated....42.50
Cups & saucers, demitasse, pink morning glories decoration, gold brushed trim, set of 6......................125.00
Cups & saucers, demitasse, applied gold handles, cream ground decorated w/pale blue leaves & royal blue & yellow flowers, set of 8..350.00
Cup & saucer, Athena patt. 45.00
Cup & saucer, Charonne patt., Blank No. 501...35.00
Cup & saucer, decorated w/lavender & pink roses, gold trim, Blank No. 22..22.00
Cup & saucer, No. 1 Ranson blank......30.00
Cup & saucer, Silver Anniversary patt., Blank No. 19............................34.00
Cup & saucer, Yale patt., Blank No. 103...32.50
Dinner service: including soup tureen, cov. butter, cov. vegetable bowl, platters; decorated w/large morning glories in shades of pink & lavender, 34 pcs. 850.00
Dinner service for 12 & extra pieces, Auberge patt., 63 pieces.................875.00
Dish, leaf-shaped, decorated w/pink roses, green leaves, gold trimmed edge, Limoges, France, 7" l. 29.00
Fish set: 24" l. platter, twelve 7½" sq. plates & gravy boat w/underplate; h.p. fish decoration on each piece, the set (two plates w/minor rim chips, gravy boat w/hairline)............450.00
Game plate, h.p. game bird center, gold decorated border, 9¾" d. 30.00
Gravy boat w/attached underplate, octagonal, interior decorated w/gold parrots on cobalt blue ground, gold trim, Theodore Haviland (speck of gold missing on edge).........................75.00
Gravy boat w/attached underplate, double pouring spouts, decorated w/pink flower sprays, marked "Theodore Haviland, Limoges - France"...65.00
Gravy boat, Yale patt., Blank No. 103..95.00
Oyster plate, decorated w/sprays of blue flowers, rose, wine, brown, pink lustre accent shells, marked "H.C.-L." 105.00
Oyster plate, factory decorated w/small yellow roses, brown leaves & stems, gold trim, four oyster wells, round, Charles Field Haviland - GDM 45.00
Plate, bread & butter, 5" d., No. 24 Ranson blank w/gold............................16.50
Plate, dessert, 5½" d., decorated w/lavender & pink roses, gold trim, Blank No. 22..7.00
Plate, 6¼" d., decorated w/lavender & pink roses, gold trim, Blank No. 22......7.00
Plate, salad, 7½" d., No. 24 Ranson blank w/gold.......................................18.50
Plate, salad, 7½" d., Silver Anniversary patt., Blank No. 19....................16.50
Plate, salad, 7½" d., Yale patt., Blank No. 103..16.50
Plate, luncheon, 8½" d., No. 1 Ranson blank 14.50
Plate, luncheon, 8½" d., No. 24 Ranson blank w/gold 16.00
Plate, dinner, 9½" d., Athena patt.........45.00
Plate, dinner, 9½" d., Princess patt. 28.00
Plate, dinner, 9½" d., No. 1 Ranson blank 19.00
Plate, dinner, 9½" d., No. 24 Ranson blank w/gold.......................................22.00
Plate, dinner, 9½" d., Silver Anniversary patt., Blank No. 19....................18.50
Plate, dinner, 9½" d., Yale patt., Blank No. 103..18.50
Plate, 11½" d., Drop Rose patt...........275.00
Plate, chop, 12½" d., self-handled, decorated w/bouquets of tiny pink roses, Ranson gold border, gold trimmed handles 115.00
Platter, 11½" l., Yale patt., Blank No. 103 ....40.00
Platter, 10 x 13¾", self-handled, Autumn Leaf patt., scalloped, gold handles 95.00
Platter, 14" l., Athena patt..................195.00
Platter, 14" l., decorated w/lavender & pink roses, gold trim, Blank No. 22....45.00
Platter, 16" l., decorated w/relief-molded sprays of bamboo & leaves, scalloped, lavish gold trim................125.00
Sauce tureen, cov., decorated w/butterflies & birds, ca. 1890s........150.00
Soup bowl & underplate, bowl w/applied handles, Rosalinde patt., the set..75.00
Soup plate w/flanged rim, Silver Anniversary patt., Blank No. 19 ....24.00
Soup tureen, Drop Rose patt., lavender & gold...............................225.00
Vegetable dish, cov., decorated w/butterflies & birds, ca. 1890s, 12" l...150.00

Vegetable dish, cov., round, Yale patt., Blank No. 103 ....90.00
Vegetable dish, open, Athena patt. 135.00
Vegetable dish, open, oval, Yale patt., Blank No. 103 ....60.00

HEDI SCHOOP

Cowboy & Lady Figure Group

Hedi Schoop began producing ceramics in 1940 in Hollywood, California. Practically all figurines from then until 1958, when a fire resulted in the closing of the pottery, were designed and modeled by Hedi Schoop even though almost fifty decorators worked at her studio. A variety of items was made including animals, ashtrays, bowls, boxes with lids, candlesticks, figurines, lamps, planters, and wall plaques. Hedi Schoop products range from those with crude characteristics to those with intricate details to others with delicate, fragile traits. Almost all items are marked. There were a variety of marks ranging from the stamped or incised Schoop signature to the hard-to-find Hedi Schoop sticker. The words "Hollywood, Cal." or "California" can also be found in conjunction with the Hedi Schoop name.

Bowl, 10½" l., 6" h., figural, duck sitting w/body forming bowl, dark brown w/gold trim $45.00
Bowl, 10¾" d., 3" h., low round sides w/fluted edges, woman sitting in middle w/one flower in her hands, dress sleeves have h.p. flowers, hair w/rough texture 75.00
Bust of a child, angel-like w/finger at mouth indicating 'quiet,' pink, white, blue decorations, 8" h. 45.00
Figure of a ballet dancer, pink w/platinum trim, platinum ring on each arm, one leg extended, other slightly bent, 10" h. 155.00
Figure of a clown standing, legs crossed, one hand to head, other hand to mouth, bucket & mop at his side, 10½" h. 95.00
Figure of a clown w/legs apart, one hand over head holding barbell, other hand on waist, turquoise & pink w/platinum trim, 13" h. 110.00
Figure of a girl standing, bell-shaped skirt w/scalloped edges, sunflower-shaped face & yellow hair, green blouse, yellow skirt, Model No. 703, 9" h. 38.00
Figure group, cowboy & lady, dancing, bisque faces & hands, he has hat & kerchief, she is holding up her long ruffled dress w/right hand & has bow in hair at back, green, black & yellow glazes,11" h. (ILLUS.) 175.00
Figure group, girl & tree on a base, girl w/head up looking at top of tree w/her arms raised, rough texture, mint green w/white glaze, brown leaves on girl's skirt, 7½" l., 11½" h. 105.00
Lamp, figural, TV-type, Comedy & Tragedy masks on a base w/full Comedy, part Tragedy conjoined, dark green w/gold trim, ca. 1954, 10¾" l., 12" h. 325.00
Model of a cat, reclining, two bells in-relief on collar, bow on collar forms two small pots at side of head, rough textured white w/dark brown pots & yellow bells, 7¼" l., 5¾" h. 50.00

HISTORICAL & COMMEMORATIVE WARES

Numerous potteries, especially in England and the United States, made various porcelain and earthenware pieces to commemorate people, places and events. Scarce English historical wares with American views command highest prices. Objects are listed here alphabetically by title of view.

Most pieces listed here will date between about 1820 and 1850. The maker's name is noted in parenthesis at the end of each entry. Also see ADAMS, and RIDGWAY.

Arms of Delaware platter, flowers & vines border, spoked wheels equidistant around border, dark blue, 16¾" l., T. Mayer, faint scratches $1,650.00

Arms of Georgia platter, flowers & vines border, spoked wheels equidistant around border, dark blue, 12¾" l., T. Mayer (restored crack, reglazed) 4,125.00

Arms of Massachusetts Platter

Arms of Massachusetts platter, flowers & vines border, spoked wheels equidistant around border, dark blue, 9½" l., T. Mayer (ILLUS.) 4,675.00

Arms of Maryland punch bowl, flowers & vines border, spoked wheels equidistant around border, dark blue, 11¾" d., 5" h., T. Mayer 9,350.00

Arms of New York plate, flowers & vines border w/spoked wheels equidistant around, dark blue, 10" d. (Mayer) 660.00

Arms of North Carolina platter, flowers & vines border, spoked wheels equidistant around border, dark blue, 14½", T. Mayer (restored, reglazed) 2,420.00

Arms of Virginia compote, flowers & vines border, spoked wheels equidistant around border, dark blue, 4½ x 12¼" oval, T. Mayer (restored, reglazed) 4,125.00

Baltimore & Ohio Railroad (Inclined) plate, shell border, dark blue, 9⅛" d. (Enoch Wood & Sons) 660.00

Battle Monument, Baltimore plate, long-stemmed roses border, purple, 9" d. (Jackson) 85.00

Belleville on the Passaic River soup tureen, cov., shell border & circular center w/trailing vine around outer edge of center, dark blue, 14½" w. (Enoch Wood & Sons) 4,675.00

Boston State House bath pitcher, floral border, dark blue, pouring handle under spout, 11" d., 13" h., John Rogers (restored, spider crack in base) 1,045.00

Boston State House plate, flowers & leaves border, medium blue, 10" d., Rogers (chip on rim back) 220.00

Capitol, Washington Platter

Capitol, Washington platter, flowers within medallions border, dark blue, 20½" l., J. & W. Ridgway (ILLUS.) 2,200.00

Castle Garden, Battery, New York cup plate, abbreviated border, dark blue, 3¾" d. (Wood) 357.50

Castle Garden, Battery, New York cup plate, shells border, circular center w/trailing vine around outer edge of center, dark blue, 3⅝" d. (Wood) 413.00

Cattskill (sic) Mountain House plate, flowers, shells & scrolls border, red, 10⅜" d., Adams (minor glaze flakes on rim) 170.50

City Hall, New York plate, flowers within medallions border, dark blue, 10" d. (Ridgway) ....200.00 to 225.00

City Hall, New York plate, long-stemmed roses border, black, 10½" d., Jackson (chips on table ring) 110.00

City Hotel, New York plate, acorns & oak leaves border, dark blue, 8½" d. (Stevenson) 302.50

Clarence Terrace, Regents Park (London, England) platter, wide vintage grape border, dark blue, 10¾" l. 412.50

Columbus (Ohio) platter, groups of flowers & scrolls border, dark blue, 14½" l., Clews (old chips & hairline, minor wear & stains) 880.00

Commodore MacDonnough's Victory plate, shell border, dark blue, 6½"d., Enoch Wood & Sons (minor wear & stains, pinpoint flakes) 330.00

Commodore MacDonnough's Victory plate, shell border, dark blue, 8" d., Enoch Wood (wear, stains, scratches & pinpoint flakes) 412.50

Commodore MacDonnough's Victory plate, shell border w/irregular center, dark blue, 10" d., Enoch Wood & Sons (imperfections) 137.50

Commodore MacDonnough's Victory sugar bowl, cov., floral border, irregular center, dark blue, 6⅞" h., Enoch Wood & Sons (chips) 660.00

Deaf and Dumb Asylum, Hartford, Connecticut pitcher & bowl set, bowl w/Lawrence Mansion, Boston, vining leaf border, dark blue, bowl 14" d., pitcher 10" h., the set, R. Stevenson 2,760.00

Denton Park, Yorkshire (England) pitcher, dark blue, early 19th c., 6¾" h., John & Richard Riley (wear, chips, stains) 247.50

Detroit platter, flower & scroll border, dark blue, 18½" l. (Clews).............3,500.00

Diorama View of Houghton Conquest House, Bedfordshire (England) platter, wide floral border, dark blue, 21¼" l. (minor wear, stains) 687.50

Doctor Syntax Taking Possession of His Living plate, floral border, dark blue, ca. 1830, 10¼" d.. (Clews)......175.00

Errand Boy (The) cup plate, flowers & scrolls border, dark blue, Wilkies Designs series, ca. 1830, 3½" d. (Clews)..302.50

Fair Mount Near Philadelphia plate, spread eagles amid flowers & scrolls border, medium blue, 10" d., Stubbs (table ring chips, wear, stains) 165.00

General W. H. Harrison, Hero of the Thames 1813 plate, black, Philadelphia importer's mark, 9½" d. ...2,365.00

General W. H. Harrison, Hero of the Thames 1813 plate, green, Philadelphia importer's mark (stains)....1,980.00

General Jackson, Hero of New Orleans plate, molded feather edge w/pink lustre trim, black, 8¾" d. (minor wear)...................................1,155.00

Hartford, Connecticut soup plates, long-stemmed roses border, red, 10½" d., Jackson, set of 4 (two w/very minor flakes on table rings) ..440.00

Hartford State House custard cup, handled, flowers & leaves border, medium dark blue, Andrew Stevenson (minute flake on rim) 1,400.00

Harvard Hall, Massachusetts plate, floral border, brown, 6¾" d. (Jackson) 90.00

Hawthornden, Edinburghshire (England) plate, dark blue, ca. 1830, 8¾" d., Adams (small flakes & minor scratches) 115.00

Lafayette at Franklin's Tomb coffeepot, cov., baluster-form w/scrolled handle & spout, domed lid w/beehive knop, floral border, dark blue, overall 12" h., Wood, short hairline, small chips, finial reglued 770.00

Lafayette at Franklin's Tomb pitcher, floral border, dark blue, 9½" h., Enoch Wood & Sons (imperfections) 770.00

Lafayette at Franklin's Tomb teapot, cov., floral border, dark blue, 7½" h., Enoch Wood (foot chips, finial reglued)...1,045.00

Landing of General Lafayette at Castle Garden, New York, 16 August, 1824 tray, floral & vine border, dark blue, rectangular w/rounded corners & end handles, 6" l., Clews (chips on table ring & back of one handle) 1,237.50

Landing of General Lafayette at Castle Garden, New York, 16 August, 1824 covered tureen, floral & vine border, oval w/flared rim & scrolled end handles, the stepped, domed cover w/florette finial, dark blue, 14¾" l., Clews (flakes) 4,675.00

Landing of General Lafayette at Castle Garden, New York, 16 August, 1824 open vegetable dish, floral & vine border, dark blue, 10 x 12", Clews (wear, scratches, old chips on back) 412.50

Letter of Introduction platter, flowers & scrolls border, blue, Wilkies Designs series, 12⅜" l., Clews (glaze wear & flakes on edge of rim) 577.50

Library, Philadelphia plate, flowers within medallions border, dark blue, 8" d., Ridgway (minor stains, crazing, pinpoint flakes) 170.50

Log Cabin cup & saucer, handleless, saucer border w/oval medallions of Major General Wm. H. Harrison alternating w/floral urns, red, Adams (small flakes & short hairline in saucer)...385.00

Mitchell & Freeman's China and Glass Warehouse, Chatham Street, Boston plate, foliage border, dark blue, 10" d. (Adams) 770.00

Montevideo, Connecticut, U.S. plate, flowers, shells & scrolls border, pink, 7" d. (Adams) 80.00

Mount Pleasant Classical Institution, Amherst, Mass. plate, flowers w/large scrolls border, dark blue, 10½" d. (Clews) 8,000.00

Peace & Plenty platter, oval, wide band of fruit & flowers border, dark blue, 19" l., Clews (small surface flakes, minor wear) 880.00

Penn's Treaty plate, latticework design border, Penn standing, attendant kneeling, Indians standing, medium blue, 8¼" d. (Thomas Green)...125.00

Portrait Medallion pitcher, oval portraits of Washington, Jefferson, Lafayette & Clinton, floral border, dark blue, R. Stevenson & Williamson (ILLUS. top next page).........12,100.00

Portrait Medallion Pitcher

The Rabbit on the Wall platter, large flowers & scrolls border, dark blue, Wilkies Designs series, 10¾" l., Clews (minor edge wear) 880.00

Residence of the Late Richard Jordan, New Jersey platter, flowers or dual line border, purple, 19½" l., J. Heath & Co. (minor spot of glaze wear) 962.50

States series plate, building & fishermen w/net, names of states in festoons separated by five-point stars border, dark blue, 10½" d. Clews (minor hairline) 247.50

States Series Plate

States series plate, building & fishermen w/net scene, names of fifteen states in festoons on border separated by five- or eight-point stars, dark blue, 10½" d., Clews (ILLUS.) 300.00

States series plate, building, sheep on lawn, names of fifteen states in festoons on border, separated by five- or eight-point stars, dark blue, 8¾" d., Clews (minor wear, hairline, pinpoint flakes on table ring) 220.00

Texian Campaigne - Battle of Chapultepec plate, symbols of war & a "goddess-type" seated border, mulberry, 9½" d. (Shaw) 350.00

Union Line plate, shells border, dark blue, 10½" d., Wood (minor glaze wear) 440.00

Valentine (The) plate, flowers & scrolls border, dark blue, Wilkies Designs series, ca. 1830, 9" d. (Clews) 290.00

View of Liverpool (England) soup plate, shell border, dark blue, 8⅜" d. (Wood) 275.00

View of New York from Weehawk platter, flowers between leafy scrolls border, dark blue, 18½" l. (Andrew Stevenson) 2,640.00

View Near Conway N. Hampshire, U.S. plate, floral wreath border, red, 9" d. (Adams) 85.00

Villa in the Regents Park, London (England) plate, leafy trees frame center scene, dark blue, 10" d., Adams (minor edge flakes) 115.00

Washington & Lafayette plate, flower & scroll border, dark blue, 10⅛" d., Stevenson & Williams (tiny rim flake) 1,300.00

Welcome Lafayette the Nation's Guest and Our Country's Glory plate, flowers & scrolls border, blue, 8¾" d., Clews (minor wear & pinpoint flakes) 632.50

West Point, Hudson River plate, scrolls & flowers border, Picturesque Views series, brown, 7⅞" d., Clews (wear, minor stains, pinpoint flakes) 104.50

Windsor Castle, Berkshire (England) platter, floral border, dark blue, 18¾" l., William Adams, minor imperfections 715.00

HULL

This pottery was made by the Hull Pottery Company, Crooksville, Ohio, beginning in 1905. Art Pottery was made until 1950 when the company was converted to utilitarian wares. All production ceased in 1986.

Reference books for collectors include Roberts' Ultimate Encyclopedia of Hull Pottery *by Brenda Roberts (Walsworth Publishing Company, 1992), and* Collector's Guide to Hull Pottery - The Dinnerware Lines *by Barbara Loveless Gick-Burke (Collector Books, 1993).*

Ashtray, Serenade patt., pink, No. S23, 10½ x 13" $70.00

Baker, cov., oval "nest" base w/figural hen cover, dark brown glaze, House 'n Garden line, 13⅜" l., 11" h. 50.00

Bank, figural Corky Pig, blue & pink, 5" h. 70.00
Bank, figural pig, pink bow, 7" l. 70.00
Bank, figural pig, orange w/a bright blue bow, 14" l. 100.00

Little Red Riding Hood Standing Bank

Bank, standing-type, Little Red Riding Hood patt., 7" h. (ILLUS.) 615.00
Bank, wall-type, Little Red Riding Hood patt., 9" h. 1,100.00
Basket, Blossom Flite patt., No. T-2, 6" h. 32.00
Basket, Blossom Flite patt., No. T-8, 8¼ x 9¼" 65.00
Basket, Bow-Knot patt., blue to pink, No. B-25-6½", 6½" 160.00
Basket, Bow-Knot patt., pink & blue, No. B-12-10½", 10½" h. 525.00
Basket, Butterfly patt., cream & turquoise, No. B13, 8 x 8" 85.00
Basket, triple-handle, Butterfly patt., matte glaze, No. B 17, 10½" h. 265.00
Basket, Capri patt., mottled maroon & dark green, No. 48, 6 x 12¼" 50.00
Basket, Continental patt., persimmon glossy glaze, No. C55, 12½" h. 81.00
Basket, Dogwood patt., center handle, blue & pink, No. 501-7½", 7½" 175.00
Basket, Ebb Tide patt., model of a large shell w/long fish handle, No. E-11, 16½" l. 175.00
Basket, Magnolia Gloss patt., No. H-14-10½", 10½" 145.00
Basket, Magnolia matte patt., No. 10-10½", 10½" h. 120.00
Basket, Mardi Gras (Granada) patt., No. 32-8", 8" l. 110.00
Basket, Mardi Gras patt., No. 65-8, 8" h. 135.00
Basket, Parchment & Pine patt., No. S-3, 6" l. 42.50
Basket, Parchment & Pine patt., No. S-8, 16½" l. 60.00
Basket, Rosella patt., No. R-12-7", 7" h. 140.00
Basket, Royal Woodland patt., turquoise, W22, 10½" l. 70.00
Basket, Tokay patt., No. 6, 8" h. 55.00
Basket, Tokay patt., round "Moon" form, white, No. 11, 10½" h. 95.00
Basket, Tulip patt., pink & blue, No. 102-33-6", 6" h. 160.00
Basket, Water Lily patt., No. L14-10½", 10½" h. 175.00
Basket, hanging-type, footed bulbous body, Woodland patt., rose & cream, No. W12-7½", 7½" h. 350.00

Woodland Gloss Basket

Basket, Woodland Gloss patt., No. W9-8¾", 8¾" h. (ILLUS.) 168.00
Basket, fan-shaped, Woodland Gloss patt., yellow & pink, No. W22-10½", 10½" h. 125.00
Batter pitcher, side pour, Little Red Riding Hood patt., 7" h. 370.00
Bean pot, cov., House 'n Garden Ware, 6½" h. 20.00
Book ends, Orchid patt., pink & blue, No. 316-7", pr. 1,050.00
Bowl, 6¼" d., 3" h., Imperial patt., relief-molded leaf decoration, dark green, No. F8 ....8.00
Bowl, 6½ x 8½", Imperial patt., pink, melon ribbed, No. 154-8½" 12.00
Bowl, 9" d., Imperial patt., dark green, basketweave, No. 117 ....12.00
Bowl, fruit, 10 x 11½", 7" h., pedestal base, two upturned sides, Serenade patt., pink, No. S-15-11½" 100.00
Butter dish, cov., House 'n Garden Ware 7.00
Butter dish, cov., Little Red Riding Hood patt. 315.00
Candleholder, Bow-Knot patt., cornucopia-form, No. B17, 4" h. 75.00
Candleholder, Butterfly patt., glossy white, No. B22, 2½" h. 22.00
Candleholders, Dogwood patt., cornucopia-form, peach & turquoise, No. 512, 3¾" h., pr. 115.00
Candleholders, Ebb Tide patt., No. E-13, 2¾", pr. 50.00
Candleholders, Magnolia Matte patt., No. 27-4", 4" h., pr. 125.00

Candleholders, Open Rose patt., model of a dove, No. 117-6½", 6½" h., pr. 215.00

Candleholders, Water Lily patt., glossy white, No. L-22, 4½" h., pr. 55.00

Candleholders, Wildflower patt., No. W-22, 2½" h., pr. 95.00

Candy dish, urn-shaped, Butterfly patt., No. B6, 5½" h. 55.00

Canister, cov., "Flour," Little Red Riding Hood patt. ....650.00 to 700.00

Canister, cov., "Nutmeg," Little Red Riding Hood patt. 875.00

Console bowl, Blossom Flite patt., No. T10, 16½" l. 135.00

Console bowl, Bow-Knot patt., No. B-16-13½", 13½" l. 215.00

Console bowl, three-footed, Butterfly patt., No. B21, 10" d. 75.00

Console bowl, Magnolia Gloss patt., pink, No. H-23-13", 13" l. 47.50

Console bowl, Orchid patt., No. 314-13", 13" l. 250.00

Console bowl, Water Lily patt., No. L-21-13½", 13½" l. 200.00

Console set: console bowl & pair of candleholders; Ebb Tide patt., bowl No. E12-15½", candleholders No. E-13, deep wine, 3 pcs. 200.00

Cookie jar, cov., Barefoot Boy, made for Hull by Gem Refractories, 13" h. ....350.00 to 375.00

Cookie jar, cov., figural apple, Novelty Line 40.00

Cookie jar, Little Red Riding Hood 365.00

Cornucopia-vase, Bow-Knot patt., No. B-5-7½", 7½" h. 115.00

Cornucopia-vase, double, Bow-Knot patt., No. B-13-13", 13" h. 210.00

Cornucopia-vase, double, Water Lily patt., No. L27-12", 12" l. 100.00

Cornucopia-vase, Wildflower patt., matte finish, No. W10-8½", 8½" h. 75.00

Cracker jar, cov., Little Red Riding Hood patt., 8½" h. 560.00

Creamer, Bow-Knot patt., blue & pink, B-21-4", 4" h. 85.00

Creamer, House 'n Garden Ware 7.00

Creamer, side pour, Little Red Riding Hood patt. 125.00

Creamer & cov. sugar bowl, House 'n Garden Ware, pr. 14.00

Creamer & cov. sugar bowl, Little Red Riding Hood patt., head pour creamer, pr. 650.00

Cup & saucer, House 'n Garden Ware ...9.00

Dish, leaf-shaped, Capri patt., No. C63, 10½ x 14" 35.00

Dish, leaf-shaped, Tuscany patt., No. 19, 14" l. 28.00

Dish, pedestal base, Imperial patt., dark green, 4¼ x 6½", 2½" h., No. F53 ....8.00

Ewer, Blossom Flite patt., No. T13, 13½" h. 95.00

Bow-Knot Ewer

Ewer, Bow-Knot patt., No. B-1-5½", 5½" h. (ILLUS.) 110.00

Ewer, Butterfly patt., No. B15-13½", 13½" h. 100.00

Ewer, Calla Lily patt., No. 506-10", 10¾" h. 235.00

Ewer, Classic patt., No. 6-6", 6" h. 17.00

Ewer, Open Rose patt., No. 105-7", 7" h. 195.00

Ewer, Pine Cone patt., green, 13½" h. 95.00

Ewer, Tulip patt., blue, No. 109-8", 8" h. 195.00

Ewer, Tuscany patt., No. 21, 14" h. 135.00

Ewer, Wildflower patt., W-11-8½", 8½" h. 115.00

Ewer, Wildflower patt., pink & blue, No. W-19-13½", 13½" h. 316.00

Flower dish, Continental patt., green, No. 51, 15½" l. 38.00

Flowerpot w/attached saucer, Bow-Knot patt., No. B-6-6½", 6½" h. 87.00

Flowerpot w/attached saucer, Sueno Tulip patt., blue, No. 116-33-6", 6" h. 95.00

Gravy boat, House 'n Garden Ware, dark brown glaze 14.00

Grease jar, cov., figural apple, Novelty Line 15.00

Jardiniere, two-handled, Orchid patt., No. 310-9½", 9½" h. 350.00

Jardiniere, Sueno Tulip patt., No. 117-30-5", 5" h. 95.00

Lamp, Little Red Riding Hood patt. ....2,000.00 to 2,500.00

Lamp-planter, model of a seated kitten beside a cylindrical flowerpot, ca. 1948 ....80.00

Lavabo & base, Butterfly patt., Nos. B24 & B25, overall 16" h. 125.00

Match box, hanging-type, Little Red Riding Hood patt., 5¼" h. 700.00

Mug, barrel-shaped, embossed "Happy Days Are Here Again," green glaze, No. 497, 5" h. 22.50

Mug, House 'n Garden Ware, No. 526, 16 oz. 7.00

Pie baker, Nuline Bak-Serve patt., blue 20.00
Pie plate, House 'n Garden Ware, 9¼" d. 20.00
Pitcher, milk, 6¾" h., House 'n Garden Ware 22.00
Pitcher, milk, 8" h., Little Red Riding Hood patt. 250.00

Madonna & Child Planter

Planter, bust of the Madonna & Child, pink, No. 26, 7" h. (ILLUS.) 25.00
Planter, Imperial patt,. four-footed, vertical rib, yellow, No. F39, 4½ x 7" oval 8.50
Planter, Imperial line, goblet-shaped, bead stem, dark green spiral bowl, No. F5, 4¾" h. 7.50
Planter, wall-type, Little Red Riding Hood patt., 9" h. 415.00
Plate, dessert, 6½" d., House 'n Garden Ware 4.00
Salt & pepper shakers, figural apple, Novelty Line, pr. 15.00
Salt & pepper shakers, mushroom-shaped, House 'n Garden Ware, 3¾" h., pr. 15.00
Salt & pepper shakers, Little Red Riding Hood patt., medium, 4½" h., pr. 800.00
Salt & pepper shakers, Little Red Riding Hood patt., large, 5½" h., pr. ....125.00 to 150.00
Salt & pepper shakers, Sunglow patt., pink, No. 54, pr. 18.00
Spice jar, cov, "Cinnamon," Little Red Riding Hood patt. 675.00
Steak platter, House & Garden Serving Ware, w/well & tree 25.00
Steins, Early Utility, Alpine drinking scene, No. 492, 6¼" h., set of 5 ....125.00
String holder, Little Red Riding Hood patt., 9" h. 2,550.00
Sugar bowl, cov., Cinderella Kitchenware, Blossom patt., No. 27-4½", 4½" h. 22.00
Sugar bowl, cov., Crescent Kitchenware, pink & maroon, No. B14, 4½" h. 12.00
Sugar bowl, open, crawling figure, Little Red Riding Hood patt. 215.00
Teapot, cov., Butterfly patt., No. B18 ....95.00
Teapot, cov., Little Red Riding Hood patt., 8" h. ....300.00 to 350.00
Teapot, cov., Serenade patt., pink, No. S17 ....110.00
Tea set: cov. teapot, creamer & cov. sugar bowl; Ebb Tide patt., 3 pcs. ...135.00
Tea set: cov. teapot, creamer & cov. sugar bowl; Magnolia Matte patt., yellow & brown, 3 pcs. 250.00
Tea set: cov. teapot, creamer & cov. sugar bowl; Serenade patt., pink glaze, 3 pcs. 275.00
Tea set: cov. teapot, creamer & cov. sugar bowl; Water Lily patt., 3 pcs. 145.00
Vase, 5" h., Calla Lily patt., chocolate brown, No. 530/33-5" 58.00
Vase, 6½" h., Bow-Knot patt., pink & blue, No. B-3-6½" 95.00
Vase, 6½" h., Parchment & Pine patt., green, No. S-1 ....15.00
Vase, 6½" h., Water Lily patt., No. L-4-6½" 40.00

Hull Wild Flower Vase

Vase, 6½" h., Wild Flower patt., No. 54 (ILLUS.) 65.00
Vase, 7" h., twin fish, Ebb Tide patt., green & pink, No. E-2-7" 55.00
Vase, 8" h., Sunglow patt., No. 94-8" ...30.00
Vase, double bud, 8" h., Woodland Gloss patt., No. W15-8" 62.00
Vase, 8½" h., two-handled, Magnolia Matte patt., pink & blue, No. 3-8½" 50.00
Vase, 8½" h., Magnolia Matte patt., pink & blue, No. 7-8½" 115.00
Vase, 8½" h., Morning Glory patt., No. 61-8½" 200.00
Vase, 8½" h., model of a hand holding a fan-shaped vase, Open Rose (Camellia) patt., No. 126-8½" (ILLUS. top next page) 125.00
Vase, 9½" h., Wildflower patt., No. W-12 ....100.00

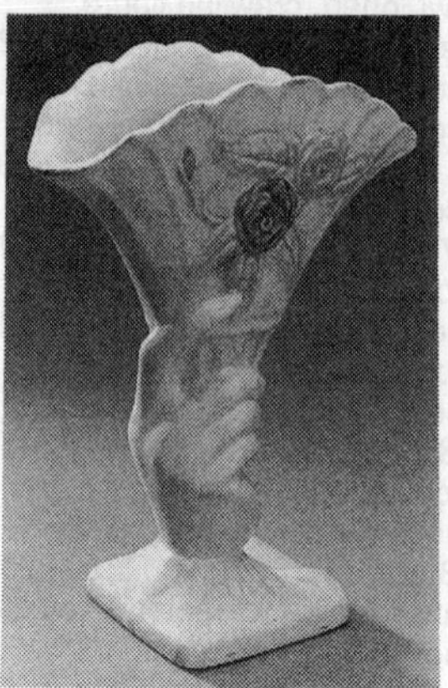

Open Rose Hand Vase

Vase, 9½" h., Wildflower patt., No. W-13-9½" 135.00
Vase, 10" h., Orchid patt., No. 302-10" ....250.00 to 275.00
Vase, 10" h., Sueno Tulip patt., blue, No. 100-33-10" 150.00
Vase, 10½" h., Bow-Knot patt., pink & blue, No. 10-10½" 315.00
Vase-candleholders, Continental patt., orange & gold, 10¼" h., pr. 60.00
Wall pocket, model of a sad iron, Bow-Knot patt., No. B-23, 6¼" h...............................175.00 to 200.00
Wall pocket, Bow-Knot patt., model of a whisk broom, blue, No. B-27-8", 8" h...115.00
Wall pocket, Woodland Gloss patt., No. W-13-7½", 7½" h. 55.00
Window box, Butterfly patt., glossy glaze, No. B-8, 4¾ x 12¾" 27.50
Window box, Dogwood patt., No. 508-10½" l. 105.00
Window box, Imperial line, "Fantasy," scalloped, glossy blue exterior, yellow interior, No. 153, 12½" l. 25.00

HUMMEL FIGURINES & COLLECTIBLES

The Goebel Company of Oeslau, Germany, first produced these porcelain figurines in 1934 having obtained the rights to adapt the beautiful pastel sketches of children by Sister Maria Innocentia (Berta) Hummel. Every design by the Goebel artisans was approved by the nun until her death in 1946. Though not antique, these figurines with the "M.I. Hummel" signature, especially those bearing the Goebel Company factory mark used from 1934 and into the early 1940s, are being sought by collectors though interest may have peaked some years ago.

"Boots"

Accordion Boy, full bee mark,1940-57, 5" h. $185.00
Accordion Boy, stylized bee mark, 1956-68, 5" h. 118.00
Accordion Boy, last bee mark, 1972-79, 5" h. 100.00
Adoration, crown mark, 1934-49, 6¼" h. ....600.00 to 750.00
Adoration, 1972-79, 6¼" h.......................150.00
Adoration, 1956-68, 9" h.........................410.00
Angel Cloud font,1940-57, 2¼ x 4¾".......................................375.00
Angel Duet candleholder, 1940-57, 5" h. 250.00
Angel Duet candleholder, 1972-79, 5" h 105.00
Angelic Song, 1934-49, 4" h. 330.00
Apple Tree Boy, 1934-49, 4" h. 225.00
Apple Tree Boy, 1940-57, 4" h. 160.00
Apple Tree Boy, 1956-68, 4" h. 80.00
Apple Tree Boy, 1972-79, 4" h. 58.00
Apple Tree Boy, 1972-79, 6" h. 125.00
Apple Tree Girl, 1934-49, 4" h...........255.00
Apple Tree Girl, 1934-49, 6" h............380.00
Apple Tree Girl, 1940-57, 6" h............275.00
Apple Tree Girl, 1956-68, 6" h............175.00
Apple Tree Girl, 1972-79, 10" h..........625.00
Apple Tree Girl table lamp, 1940-57, 7½" h. 360.00
Apple Tree Boy & Girl, 1956-68, 4" h., pr...210.00
Artist (The), 1963-71, 5½" h..............................350.00 to 425.00
Artist (The), 1972-79, 5½" h. 130.00
Auf Wiedersehen, 1934-49, 5" h. 725.00
Baker, 1963-71, 4¾" h.........................120.00
Baker, 1972-79, 4¾" h.........................100.00
Barnyard Hero, 1940-57, 4" h...................................150.00 to 175.00
Barnyard Hero, 1956-68, 4" h............110.00
Barnyard Hero, 1963-71, 5½" h...........170.00
Begging His Share, 1940-57, 5½" h...............................300.00 to 350.00

Begging His Share, w/candle hole, 1956-68, 5½" h. 185.00
Begging His Share, without candle hole,1956-68, 5½" h........................155.00
Begging His Share, 1972-79, 5½" h. ..115.00
Birthday Serenade table lamp, 1972-79, 7½" h. 215.00
Birthday Serenade table lamp, 1972-79, 9¾" h. 290.00
Blessed Event, 1963-71, 5½" h. 280.00
Blessed Event, 1972-79, 5½" h. 175.00
Book Worm, 1956-68, 4" h. 165.00
Book Worm, 1972-79, 4" h. 125.00
Book Worm, 1956-68, 8" h.................................750.00 to 850.00
Book Worm, 1972-79, 8" h.................................625.00 to 700.00
Book Worm book end, 1940-57, 5½" h...300.00
Book Worm book end, 1956-68, 5½" h...150.00
Book Worm book end, 1972-79, 5½" h...120.00
Boots, 1934-49, 5½" h. (ILLUS.) ....375.00 to 475.00
Boots, 1940-57, 5½" h.........................185.00
Boots, 1956-68, 5½" h.........................115.00
Boots, 1972-79, 6½" h.........................125.00
Boy with Horse, 1972 -79, 3½" h. 38.50
Boy with Toothache, 1963-71, 5½" h...130.00
Brother, 1956-68, 5½" h. 120.00
Brother, 1972-79, 5½" h. ....100.00 to 125.00
Carnival, 1963-71, 6" h. 165.00
Carnival, 1972-79, 6" h........................110.00
Celestial Musician, 1956-68, 7" h. 200.00
Celestial Musician, 1963-71, 7" h. 170.00
Chef, Hello, 1940-57, 6¼" h................................225.00 to 275.00
Chef, Hello, 1956-68, 6¼" h................................150.00 to 175.00
Chef, Hello, 1972-79, 6¼" h. 110.00
Chef, Hello, 1940-57, 7" h. 350.00
Chick Girl, 1934-49, 3½" h................................375.00 to 425.00
Child in Bed plaque, 1940-57, 2¾" d. 125.00
Chimney Sweep, 1956-68, 4" h..................................75.00 to 125.00
Close Harmony, 1963-71, 5½" h. (ILLUS. top next column) ....225.00 to 250.00
Confidentially, 1940-57, 5½" h.........5,000.00
Congratulations (no socks), 1940-57, 6" h. 220.00
Congratulations (w/socks), 1956-68, 6" h. 95.00
Congratulations (no socks), 1956-68, 6" h. 165.00
Congratulations (w/socks), 1972-79, 6" h. 100.00
Congratulations, 1934-49, 8¼" h.....6,500.00

"Close Harmony"

Congratulations, 1956-68, 8¼" h. 3,900.00
Doctor, 1940-57, 4¾" h.......................175.00
Doctor, 1956-68, 4¾" h.......100.00 to 125.00
Doll Bath, 1963-71, 5" h......................165.00
Doll Bath, 1972-79, 5" h......................115.00
Doll Mother, 1940-57, 4¾" h...............................275.00 to 350.00
Doll Mother, 1972-79, 4¾" h..............120.00
Duet, 1940-57, 5" h. ....225.00 to 275.00
Duet, 1972-79, 5" h. 140.00
Eventide, 1940-57, 4¼ x 4¾"...............................350.00 to 450.00
Feeding Time, 1956-68, 4¼" h. 135.00
Feeding Time, 1963-71, 4¼" h. 125.00
Festival Harmony, w/mandolin, 1934-49, 11" h. 1,100.00
Flitting Butterfly plaque, 1940-57, 2½ x 2½"..125.00
Flower Madonna, white, 1940-57, 13" h...............................250.00 to 300.00
Good Friends table lamp, 1972-79, 7½" h...195.00
Good Friends & She Loves Me, She Loves Me Not book ends, 1956-68, 5¼" h., pr. 210.00
Good Hunting, 1956-68, 5¼" h. 630.00
Good Shepherd, 1940-57, 6¼" h.........195.00
Good Shepherd, 1940-57, 7½" h......6,000.00
Goose Girl, 1956-68, 4¾" h. 145.00
Goose Girl, 1972-79, 4¾" h. 125.00
Goose Girl, 1972-79, 7½" h. 280.00
Guardian Angel font, 1934-49, 2½ x 5⅝," 1,300.00
Happiness, 1956-68,4¾" h. 92.00
Happy Days, 1940-57, 4¼" h...............210.00
Happy Days, 1972-79, 4¼" h.................83.00
Happy Days, 1972-79, 6" h.................255.00
Happy Days table lamp, 1972-79, 7¾" h.............................200.00 to 250.00
Happy Days table lamp, 1940-57, 9¾" h...700.00
Happy Pastime candy box, 1956-68, 6" h. 125.00
Hear Ye, Hear Ye, 1940-57, 5" h...............................175.00 to 200.00

Hear Ye, Hear Ye, 1972-79, 5" h.....100.00 to 125.00
Heavenly Song candleholder, 1934-49, 3½ x 4¾".....7,000.00
Herald Angels candleholder, 1934-49, 2¼ x 4".....495.00
Herald Angels candleholder, 1940-57, 2¼ x 4".....175.00
Home From Market, 1940-57, 5¾" h. 265.00
Joyful ashtray, 1940-57, 3½ x 6".....205.00
Joyous News, 1934-49, 4¼ x 4¾"...1,750.00
Joyous News, Angel w/accordion candleholder, 1940-57, 2¾" h.....120.00
Joyous News, Angel w/accordion candleholder, 1956-68, 2¾" h.....32.00
Just Resting, 1963-71, 4" h. 105.00
Just Resting, 1963-71, 5" h. 145.00
Just Resting table lamp, 1972-79, 9½" h.....225.00
Latest News, 1940-57, inscribed "Panama American," 5¼" h.....1,500.00
Little Bookkeeper, 1963-71, 4¾" h. 185.00
Little Bookkeeper, 1972-79, 4¾" h. 125.00
Little Cellist, 1934-49, 6" h.....400.00 to 450.00
Little Cellist, 1940-57, 6" h.....220.00
Little Cellist, 1956-68, 6" h.....145.00
Little Cellist, 1963-71, 6" h.....135.00
Little Drummer, 1972-79, 4¼" h.....82.50
Little Fiddler, 1934-49, 4¾" h.....330.00
Little Fiddler, 1963-71, 4¾" h.....175.00
Little Gardener, 1934-49, 5" h. 200.00
Little Goat Herder, 1956-68, 4½" h.....130.00
Little Goat Herder, 1963-71, 4¾" h.....110.00
Little Goat Herder, 1956-68, 5½" h.....160.00
Little Goat Herder, 1963-71, 5½" h.....140.00
Little Guardian, 1956-68, 4" h.....100.00
Little Hiker, 1940-57, 4¼" h. 110.00
Little Pharmacist, 1963-71, 6" h.....265.00
Little Scholar, 1940-57, 5½" h. 200.00
Little Scholar, 1956-68, 5½" h. 130.00
Lullaby candleholder, 1972-79 6 x 8".....230.00
Madonna, seated, brown cloak, 1940-57, 12" h. 9,500.00
The Mail is Here, 1963-71, 4¼ x 6" 360.00
March Winds, 1972-79, 5" h. 88.00
Max & Moritz, 1940-57, 5" h. 240.00
Meditation, 1972-79, 4¼" h. (ILLUS. top next column) 70.00
Meditation, 1956-68, 5¼" h.....110.00
Meditation, 1972-79, 5" h.....110.00
Merry Wanderer, 1956-68, 4¾" h. 115.00
Merry Wanderer, 1956-68, 6¼" h. 135.00
Merry Wanderer plaque, 1956-68, 4¾ x 5⅛".....110.00
Nativity set, 1972-79, 12 pcs. 950.00
Not for You, 1963-71, 6" h.....150.00
Out of Danger, 1956-68, 6¼" h.....220.00
Out of Danger table lamp, 1963-71, 9½" h.....225.00

"Meditation"

Photographer, 1972-79, 5¼" h. 125.00
Playmates, 1940-57, 4" h. 165.00
Playmates, 1956-68, 4" h. ..100.00 to 125.00
Playmates candy box, 1972-79, 6¼" h.....115.00
Prayer Before Battle, 1956-68, 4¼" h.....115.00
Puppy Love, 1956-68, 5" h. 200.00
Retreat to Safety, 1972-79, 4" h. 80.00
Retreat to Safety, 1934-49, 5½" h. 575.00
Retreat to Safety,1940-57, 5½" h.....350.00 to 400.00
Retreat to Safety plaque, 1972-79, 4¾ x 5" 110.00

"Ring Around the Rosie"

Ring Around the Rosie, 1956-68, 6¾" h. (ILLUS.) .....2,500.00 to 3,000.00
School Boy, 1940-57, 4" h.....130.00
School Boy, 1956-68, 5½" h. 116.00
School Boys, 1963-71, 7½" h.....775.00 to 850.00
School Girl, 1956-68, 4¼" h. (ILLUS. top next column) 110.00
School Girl, 1972-79, 4¼" h.....70.00
School Girls, 1956-68, 7½" h. .....750.00 to 850.00
Sensitive Hunter, 1972-79, 5½" h. .....100.00 to 125.00
Sensitive Hunter, 1940-57, 7½" h. 610.00
Sensitive Hunter, 1972-79, 7½" h. 185.00
Serenade, 1934-49, 4¾" h. 280.00

"School Girl"

Signs of Spring, 1963-71, 5½" h.........135.00
Signs of Spring, 1972-79, 5½" h.........145.00
Silent Night candleholder, w/black child at left, 1940-57, 5½" l., 4¾" h...9,000.00
Silent Night candleholder, 1963-71, 5½" l., 4¾" h.................................180.00

"Singing Lesson"

Singing Lesson, 1940-57, 2¾" h. (ILLUS.) ....125.00 to 150.00
Singing Lesson candy box, 1956-68, 5¼" h..125.00
Sister, 1940-57, 5½" h.........................140.00
Sister, 1956-68, 5½" h...........................135.00
Smiling Through plaque,1972-79, 5¾" d. 82.00

Star Gazer, 1963-71, 4¾" h...............135.00
Stitch in Time, 1956-68, 6¾" h. 190.00
Street Singer, 1972-79, 5" h..................................100.00 to 125.00
Strolling Along, 1956-68, 4¾" h. 150.00
Telling Her Secret, 1940-57, 5¼" h..............................300.00 to 350.00
Telling Her Secret, 1963-71, 5¼" h. 165.00
To Market, 1940-57, 5½" h. 250.00
Trumpet Boy, 1956-68, 4¾" h............110.00

Tuneful Goodnight plaque, 1956-68, 4¾ x 5"..200.00
Umbrella Boy, 1956-68, 4¾" h...........475.00
Umbrella Boy, 1972-79, 4¾" h...........260.00
Umbrella Boy & Umbrella Girl, 1956-68, 4¾" h., pr. 900.00
Umbrella Girl, 1963-71, 4¾" h.............................350.00 to 400.00
Valentine Gift, 1972-79, 5¾" h...........380.00
Valentine Joy, 1972-79, 5¼" h...........160.00
Village Boy, 1934-49, 4" h. 175.00
Village Boy, 1956-68, 5" h. 80.00
Volunteers, 1940-57, 5" h. 285.00
Waiter, 1972-79, 7" h..........................145.00
Wall vase, Boy, 1956-68, 4½ x 6¼"....190.00
Wall vase, Girl, 1956-68, 4½ x 6¼"...190.00
Wash Day, 1963-71, 5¾" h.................165.00
Wash Day, 1972-79, 5¾" h.................125.00
Wayside Devotion, 1940-57, 7½" h..............................400.00 to 475.00
Wayside Harmony, 1963-71, 3¾" h......96.00
Wayside Harmony, 1956-68, 5" h.......150.00
Wayside Harmony, 1972-79, 5" h.......140.00
Wayside Harmony lamp, 1963-71, 7½" h..210.00
Wayside Harmony lamp,1972-79, 9½" h..225.00

"Which Hand?"

Which Hand?, 1963-71, 5¼" h. (ILLUS.) 130.00
Whitsuntide, 1934-49, 7¼" h. 1,050.00
Whitsuntide, 1972-79, 7¼" h. 170.00

IRONSTONE

The first successful ironstone was patented in 1813 by C.J. Mason in England. The body contains iron slag incorporated with the clay. Other potters imitated Mason's ware and today much hard, thick ware is lumped under the term ironstone. Earlier it was called by various names, including graniteware. Both plain white and decorated wares were made throughout the 19th century. Tea Leaf Lustre ironstone was made by several firms.

Turner's Patent Bowl

GENERAL

Bowl, 11" d., deep rounded & slightly flaring sides on a thick footring, decorated in the 'Japan' patt., painted in underglaze-blue, iron-red, green, brown, yellow, rose & gold around the exterior w/sprays of stylized Oriental flowers & scrolling foliage, decorated on the interior w/a central Kakiemon-style chrysanthemum & wheat sheaf design beneath a wide underglaze-blue border patterned w/gilt diaperwork & reserved w/four trefoils of flowering plants, printed "Turner's Patent" mark, early 19th c., gilt wear on edge (ILLUS.) $1,840.00

Creamer, bulbous paneled base & tall paneled & flaring neck, "gaudy" Imari-style decoration, molded serpent handle, marked "Mason's Patent Ironstone," ca. 1850 (wear)...148.50

Cup & saucer, handleless, miniature, paneled sides, "gaudy" Urn patt. in polychrome, mid-19th c...............231.00

Cup & saucer, handleless "gaudy" Seeing Eye patt. 165.00

Cup & saucer, handleless, paneled sides, "gaudy" decoration of an urn & blossoms in underglaze-blue trimmed w/polychrome enamel & lustre, ca. 1850 ....192.50

Cup plate, "gaudy" Urn patt. 375.00

Gravy tureen, cov., two-handled, footed, paneled sides, red, blue & copper lustre decoration, 7" h. (minor stains) 104.50

Mug, paneled cylindrical sides w/flaring base & molded serpent handle, "gaudy" Imari-style floral decoration w/pink lustre trim, marked "Ironstone China," mid-19th c., 3⅞" h.................................269.00

Plate, 8¼" w., ten-sided, "gaudy" floral decoration 165.00

Plate, 8⅜" w., 12-sided, "gaudy" decoration of colorful blossoms & large underglaze-blue leaves w/lustre trim, impressed "Ironstone," ca. 1850 (wear)...............................115.00

Plate, 8½" w., paneled sides, "gaudy" Strawberry patt., underglaze-blue w/polychrome & lustre trim, ca. 1850 (wear, chip on footring) 148.50

Plate, 8⅝" d., free-hand blue Morning Glory patt., mid-19th c. (wear) 104.50

Plate, 8¾" d., polychrome transfer scene of rural England, blue rim, marked "Pratt & Co., Fenton" (rim worn)..27.50

Platter, 16" w., 20½" l., transfer-printed w/an architectural & figural landscape in an Imari palette, Mason's, early 19th c......................495.00

Punch bowl on collared base, Lily of the Valley patt., all-white, marked "W.E. Corn," 8" d., 6" h. 150.00

Sugar bowl, cov., transfer-printed blue Canton-style Oriental decoration, Mason's, 6" d., 5¾" h. 60.00

Syrup pitcher, cov., h.p. pale apricot wild rose & foliage, white body, ornate pewter top, Knowles, Taylor, Knowles mark 95.00

Teapot, cov., transfer-printed blue Canton-style Oriental decoration, Mason's, 19th c., 9½" d., 6" h. (minor nick inside rim, minor spout roughness).......................................80.00

Large Mason's Tureen

Tureens, covers & undertrays, hexagonal, each piece decorated in underglaze-blue, iron-red, green, turquoise, yellow & gold w/stylized Oriental flowers repeated as borders on the orange lustre-edged scalloped & barbed rims, the handles formed as underglaze-blue & gilt dragons' heads & scrolls & on the cover finial molded as a floral sprig, the undertrays impressed "MASON'S PATENT IRONSTONE CHINA," ca. 1820-25, reglued chip on one undertray, small chip on one handle, one finial w/small chip, undertray 11¾" w., 11$^{15}/_{16}$" h., pr. (ILLUS. of one) 6,325.00

Vase, cov., 30½" h., octagonal baluster-form w/gilt-trimmed yellow dragon-scroll handles at the sides of the neck & similarly decorated double-dolphin knop finial, each part transfer-printed in underglaze-blue & decorated in yellow & gold w/overall rococo scrolling foliage & patterned panels surrounding on the front & back of the vase an urn of lilies on a pedestal, all against a bright blue ground, the rims gilt-edged, marked w/a pattern number "5742," ca. 1835-50 (knop finial repaired, gilt wear) 2,013.00

Vegetable bowl, cov., shallow oval flaring bowl on a scalloped flaring raised foot, the domed cover w/a loop handle, Victoria patt., brown transfer-printed design w/polychrome & gilt trim, 19th c., 11½" l. 93.50

TEA LEAF IRONSTONE

Tea Leaf Crescent-Shaped Bone Dish

Apple bowl, footed, Alfred Meakin 450.00

Baker, oval, Lily of the Valley patt., Anthony Shaw, 9" l. 60.00

Baker, rectangular, Mellor, Taylor & Co., 7 x 9½", 2½" h. 40.00

Bone dish, crescent-shaped, Red Cliff, ca. 1960s 45.00

Bone dish, scalloped rim, Anthony Shaw 70.00

Bone dishes, scalloped crescent shape, Alfred Meakin, set of 3 (ILLUS. of one) 90.00

Bowl, serving, 10" w. hexagonal, Anthony Shaw 95.00

Brush box, cov., oblong, Lily of the Valley patt., Anthony Shaw 725.00

Brush box, cov., oblong, Red Cliff, ca. 1960s 135.00

Butter dish, cov., rectangular, Iona patt., gold lustre, Powell & Bishop 50.00

Butter dish, cover & liner, Fish Hook patt., Alfred Meakin, 3 pcs. 80.00

Butter dish, cover & liner, Iona patt., gold lustre, Powell & Bishop, 3 pcs. 100.00

Cake plate, handled, square, Daisy patt., Arthur Wilkinson 120.00

Cake plate, round, scroll-embossed handles, Thomas Furnival & Sons 90.00

Cake plate, open-handled, square on square pedestal base, Red Cliff, ca. 1960s 150.00

Cake stand, Edge Malkin 250.00

Canister, cov., footed spherical body, Kitchen Kraft line, Homer Laughlin, ca. 1930s 7½" d. 60.00

Chamber pot, cov., Lion's Head patt.,Mellor, Taylor & Co. (cover hairline) 175.00

Chamber pot, cov., Square Ridged patt., Mellor, Taylor & Co. 155.00

Coffeepot, cov., Bamboo patt., Alfred Meakin 110.00

Coffeepot, cov., Plain Round shape, W. & W. Corn 200.00

Compote, open, 10" w., square shallow bowl on square pedestal w/squared domed base, Alfred Meakin 300.00

Compote, open, 10" w., Square Ridged patt., Henry Burgess 90.00

Creamer, child's, Mellor, Taylor & Co. ..95.00

Creamer, demitasse size, Empress patt., Micratex by Adams, ca. 1960s 120.00

Creamer, Basketweave patt., Anthony Shaw 130.00

Creamer, Chelsea patt., Johnson Bros. 140.00

Tea Leaf Fish Hook Creamer

Creamer, Fish Hook patt.,Alfred Meakin (ILLUS.) 60.00

Creamer, Square Ridged patt., Wedgwood & Co., 6" h. 150.00

Creamer & cov. sugar bowl, Square Ridged patt., Red Cliff, ca. 1960s 95.00

Cup & saucer, child's, Lily of the Valley patt., Anthony Shaw (slight flake on saucer base rim) 350.00

Cup plates, Anthony Shaw, set of 3 ....120.00
Dish, Square Ridged patt., Arthur Wilkinson, 19" w. 55.00
Doughnut stand, round, pedestal base, Anthony Shaw 185.00
Gravy boat, Chelsea patt., Johnson Bros. 55.00
Gravy boat, Chelsea patt., Alfred Meakin 60.00
Gravy boat, Daisy patt., Arthur Wilkinson 45.00
Gravy boat, Fish Hook patt., Alfred Meakin 60.00
Ladle, sauce, gold lustre, Powell & Bishop 100.00
Mixing bowl, Kitchen Kraft line, Homer Laughlin, ca. 1930s, 8¾" d. 45.00
Mush bowl, footed, Alfred Meakin 70.00
Pitcher, 7" h., Bamboo patt., Alfred Meakin 130.00
Pitcher, 7" h., embossed design, Cartwright Bros. 60.00
Pitcher, hot water, Edge Malkin (rim flake) 525.00
Plate, 6" d., Wilkinson 5.00
Plate, 8" sq., Alfred Meakin 45.00
Plate, 9" d., Alfred Meakin 10.00
Plates, child's, Knowles, Taylor & Knowles, set of 3 ....100.00
Plates, child's, Mellor, Taylor & Co., set of 5 ....190.00
Platter, 11" l., rectangular, Alfred Meakin 15.00
Platter, 10 x 14", rectangular, Wedgwood & Co. 40.00
Posset cup, footed, Lily of the Valley patt., Anthony Shaw 400.00
Punch bowl, footed, Alfred Meakin (hairlines) 600.00
Punch bowl, deep rounded bowl on low domed base, Anthony Shaw 537.50
Relish dish, mitten-shaped, Cable patt., Thomas Furnival & Sons 50.00
Relish dish, rectangular, handled, Fish Hook patt., Alfred Meakin 20.00
Relish dish, rectangular, Square Ridged patt., Wedgwood & Co. 60.00
Salt & pepper shakers, Empress patt., Micratex by Adams, ca. 1960s, pr. ..250.00
Salt & pepper shakers, footed spherical body, Kitchen Kraft line by Homer Laughlin, ca. 1930s, pr. 70.00
Sauce dishes, square scalloped shape, Anthony Shaw, set of 4 ....60.00
Sauce tureen, cover & ladle, Bullet patt., Anthony Shaw, 3 pcs. (leg nick) 250.00
Sauce tureen, cover, undertray & ladle, Bamboo patt., Alfred Meakin, the set 325.00
Shaving mug, Chinese patt., Anthony Shaw (ILLUS. top next column) 150.00

Tea Leaf Chinese Shaving Mug

Shaving mug, Lily of the Valley patt., Anthony Shaw 215.00
Soap dish, cov., Victory (Dolphin) patt., John Edwards 155.00
Soap dish, cover & liner, Square Ridged patt., Mellor, Taylor & Co., 3 pcs. (manufacturer's defect) 110.00
Soup plate, child's, Lily of the Valley patt., Anthony Shaw 100.00
Soup plates w/flanged rims, Alfred Meakin, set of 6 ....120.00
Soup plates w/flanged rims, Red Cliff, ca. 1960s, set of 6 ....160.00
Soup tureen, cover, ladle & undertray, gold lustre, Henry Burgess, 3 pcs. ...450.00
Sugar bowl, cov., child's, Knowles, Taylor & Knowles 110.00
Sugar bowl, cov., demitasse size, Empress patt., Micratex by Adams, ca. 1960s 50.00
Sugar bowl, cov., Bamboo patt., Alfred Meakin 65.00
Sugar bowl, cov., Simple Square patt., Wedgwood & Co. 90.00
Sugar bowl, cov., Simple Square patt., Arthur Wilkinson 80.00
Sugar bowl, cov., Square Ridged patt., Henry Burgess 110.00
Teapot, cov., child's, Knowles, Taylor & Knowles 60.00
Teapot, cov., Chinese patt., Anthony Shaw 425.00
Teapot, cov., Fish Hook patt., Alfred Meakin, small 100.00
Teapot. cov., Simple Square patt., Wedgwood & Co 120.00
Toothbrush holder, upright square footed form, Anthony Shaw 200.00
Tureen, cover, underplate & ladle, Iona patt., gold lustre, Powell & Bishop, the set 90.00
Vegetable dish, cov., Iona patt., gold lustre, Powell & Bishop, 6¾" l. 90.00
Vegetable dish, cov., square, Iona patt., gold lustre, Powell & Bishop, 7¼" w. 60.00
Vegetable dish, cov., Simple Square patt., gold lustre, Powell & Bishop, 8½" w. 45.00

Vegetable dish, cov., rectangular, Bamboo patt., Alfred Meakin, 9" l. 65.00
Vegetable dish, cov., rectangular, Fish Hook patt., Alfred Meakin, 10" l. 95.00
Vegetable dish, cov., Gentle Square patt., Thomas Furnival & Sons, 10" l. 80.00
Vegetable dish, cov., oval, Lily of the Valley patt., Anthony Shaw, 10" l. 280.00
Vegetable dish, cov., rectangular, Lion's Head patt., Mellor, Taylor & Co., 10" l. 80.00
Vegetable dish, cov., rectangular, ribbed base, Iona patt., gold lustre, Powell & Bishop, 11¼" l. 55.00
Vegetable dish, open, footed square ribbed shape w/handles, gold lustre, Powell & Bishop, 10" w. 20.00
Washbowl & pitcher set, Bamboo patt., Alfred Meakin, 2 pcs. (rim flakes on bowl) 275.00
Wash pitcher, Square Ridged patt., Bishop & Stonier 90.00
Waste bowl, child's, Mellor, Taylor & Co. 160.00
Waste bowl, ribbed base, Grindley & Co. 130.00

TEA LEAF VARIANTS

Bowl, serving, fluted, Teaberry patt., J. Clementson 230.00
Coffeepot, cov., Pepper Leaf patt. 200.00
Creamer, miniature, porcelain, Cloverleaf patt., gold lustre 45.00
Creamer, porcelain, footed ovoid body, Cloverleaf patt., gold lustre 30.00
Creamer, Gothic shape, Lustre Band decoration, Red Cliff, ca. 1960s 70.00
Creamer, high spout, Morning Glory patt., Elsmore & Forster (hairline) 220.00
Creamer, Gothic shape, Pinwheel patt., 6½" h. 150.00
Creamer, simple ovoid body, lustre trim on embossed handle scrolls, Teaberry patt., J. Clementson 475.00
Cups & saucers, handleless, Ceres patt., Lustre Band trim, Elsmore & Forster, two sets 140.00
Cup plate, Laurel Wreath patt., lustre trim, Elsmore & Forster 160.00
Cuspidor, Tobacco Leaf patt., Elsmore & Forster (professional rim repair) 525.00
Egg cup, porcelain, Cloverleaf patt., gold lustre, Three Crown China 40.00
Egg cup, Teaberry patt. 475.00
Pitcher, 8" h., ovoid body, angled handle, Pepper Leaf patt. 140.00
Pitcher, 9" h., Morning Glory patt., Elsmore & Forster (spout flake) 290.00
Platter, 10 x 14" oval, Teaberry patt., J. Clementson 80.00

Punch bowl, footed, simple rounded bowl w/Lustre Band trim, J. Clementson 260.00
Punch bowl, footed, loop handles w/lustre trim, Teaberry patt., J. Clementson (hairline) 1,700.00
Relish dish, oblong diamond shape, Pepper Leaf patt. 130.00
Shaving mug, Tobacco Leaf patt. 400.00
Soup plate w/flanged rim, Teaberry patt., New York shape, J. Clementson 55.00
Sugar bowl, cov., Square Ridged patt., Henry Burgess 80.00
Sugar bowl, cov., simple ovoid shape w/domed cover, lustre trim on handles & cover, Teaberry patt., J. Clementson 185.00
Teapot, cov., porcelain, ovoid body, Cloverleaf patt., gold lustre 40.00
Teapot, cov., Morning Glory patt. 250.00
Washbowl, Morning Glory patt., Elsmore & Forster 195.00
Washbowl, Tobacco Leaf patt., Elsmore & Forster 150.00

JASPER WARE (Non–Wedgwood)

German Jasper Ware Plaque

Jasper ware is fine-grained exceedingly hard stoneware made by including barium sulphate in the clay and was first devised by Josiah Wedgwood, who utilized it for the body of many of his fine cameo blue-and-white and green-and-white pieces. It was subsequently produced by other potters in England and Germany, notably William Adams & Sons, and is in production at the present. Also see WEDGWOOD - JASPER.

Creamer, bulbous body w/short cylindrical neck, band of white relief classical figures on a dark blue ground, marked "Adams," 3¼" h. $44.00

Plaque, pierced to hang, round, white relief figure of lady & mandolin on green, white relief floral border, Germany, 4⅝" d. 40.00

Jasper Ware Plaque with Cupid

Plaque, pierced to hang, round, white relief figure of cupid holding an umbrella over a bird on a blue ground, white relief small white leaf border, Germany, 4⅝" d. (ILLUS.)......55.00

Plaque, pierced to hang, oblong, white relief figure of seated lady w/guitar, man placing wreath on her head on blue ground , Germany, 3⅝ x 5½" 45.00

Plaque, pierced to hang, round, white relief bust of Psyche w/a figure of Cupid on green ground, wide white relief floral border, Germany, 6" d. 75.00

Plaque with Game Bird

Plaque, pierced to hang, round w/deeply scalloped scroll-molded rim, white relief center scene w/a large wild game bird perched in a tree on a green ground, white relief scroll border, 6⅜" d. (ILLUS.) 70.00

Vase, 5" h., white relief scene of man, woman & dog on green ground 50.00

JEWEL TEA AUTUMN LEAF

Though not antique this ware has a devoted following. The Hall China Company of East Liverpool, Ohio, made the first pieces of Autumn Leaf pattern ware to be given as premiums by the Jewel Tea Company in 1933. The premiums were an immediate success and thousands of new customers, all eager to acquire a piece of the durable Autumn Leaf pattern ware, began purchasing Jewel Tea products. Though the pattern was eventually used to decorate linens, glasswares and tinwares, we include only the Hall China Company items in our listing.

Open Soufflé Casserole

Bean pot, two-handled, 2¼ qt. ....$100.00 to 120.00

Bowl, fruit, 5½" d...5.50

Bowl, cereal, 6½" d...10.50

Bowl, salad, 9" d. 16.00

Bowl, cream soup, two-handled 22.50

Bowls, stacking-type, 18, 24 & 34 ounce, w/cover, 10" h., set of 3 ....95.00

Butter dish, cov., ¼ lb. ....175.00 to 225.00

Butter dish, cov., 1 lb. 310.00

Cake plate, 9½" d. ....20.00 to 25.00

Candy dish w/"Goldenray" metal base ....425.00 to 525.00

Casserole, cov., round, 1½ qt. ....30.00 to 35.00

Casserole, open, swirled soufflé, 3 pt. (ILLUS.) 18.50

Coffee maker, cov., all-china, 5 cup 300.00

Coffeepot, cov., dripolator-type, 4 pcs. 45.00

Cookie jar, cov., large eared handles, Ziesel, 1957-69.............................150.00 to 175.00

Creamer & cov. sugar bowl, pre-1940 ....38.00

Cup & saucer...10.00

Cup & saucer, St. Denis style 32.50

Gravy boat...22.00

Marmalade jar, cov., w/spoon, 3 pcs. ...50.00
Mixing (or utility) bowl, nest-type, "Radiance," 6½" d. ...10.00
Mixing (or utility) bowl, nest-type, "Radiance," 9" d. ...15.00
Mixing utility or bowls, nest-type, "Radiance," set of 3 ...45.00
Pickle dish, oval, 9" l. ...28.00
Pitcher w/ice lip, ball-type, 5½ pt. ...40.00 to 55.00
Plate, 9" d. ...7.50
Platter, 13½" l. ...20.00
Range set: handled salt & peppershakers & cov. grease jar; pre-1940, 3 pcs. ...58.00
Salt & pepper shakers, bell-shaped, small, pr. ...24.00
Salt & pepper shakers, handled, range size, pr. ...32.00
Sugar bowl, cov., new style ...10.50
Teapot, cov., Aladdin lamp shape ...73.00
Teapot, cov., Newport style ...150.00 to 175.00
Vegetable bowl, open, divided, oval, 10½" l. ...68.00

KAY FINCH CERAMICS

Figure of a Madonna

Kay Finch Ceramics began in 1939 in Corona del Mar, California. Animals were always the mainstay of the enterprise which employed over twenty-five decorators, all trained by the owner, Katherine Finch. George Finch, son of Katherine and Braden Finch, designed and modeled most of the utilitarian items such as ashtrays, bowls, planters, and vases. It was in 1963, following Braden's death, that the business ceased operations. The Freeman-McFarlin Potteries purchased Mrs. Finch's molds and in the mid-seventies commisioned her to model dog figurines. This arrangement lasted until 1980. Collectors will find varying marks such as incised, impressed, ink-stamped and hand-painted. Kay Finch died on June 21, 1993 at the age of eighty-nine.

Figure of lady standing, head down, Godey fashion attire, blue skirt w/purple dots around edge & flowers in front, pink w/dark pink flower at bottom in back, white cape w/rose neck closure & white muff w/rose, pink hat w/purple deco-ration, incised "K. Finch Calif.," 7¼" h. ...$70.00
Figure of a man standing, slightly turned head, one arm behind him & other arm over waist holding bouquet of flowers, Godey fashion attire, mauve trousers w/purple stripe on each side, pink & purple hat, deep purple shoes, 8" h. ...75.00
Figure of a Madonna kneeling, hands together on chest w/head bowed, blonde hair, overall pink clay, blue & purple mantilla w/flowers over her head & shoulders, incised "K. Finch" & stamped in script "Kay Finch" w/"California" in block letters, 6½" h. (ILLUS.) ...95.00
Model of a bird, perched on a branch w/two leaves in-relief at right foot, head turned to left, feathers out slightly & tail down, matte white, incised "Kay Finch," ca. early 1950s, 4" h. ...45.00
Model of a camel, walking, ivory body w/grey & tan accents, 5¼" l., 5" h. ...85.00

Model Of A Cat

Model of a cat, standing, stylized w/sgraffito-type decorations, head turned slightly, brown glossy glaze, incised "K. Finch," 5" l., 5" h. (ILLUS.) ...75.00
Model of a dog, poodle in playful

pose, crouching on front legs, back legs almost straight, mouth open, light & dark grey w/gold trim, 11" l., 7½" h. 280.00

Model of a duck, sitting, white high glaze body w/medium green tail & top of head, dark green front feet, bill, eyes & a few back feathers, marked "Kay Finch California," 3¾" l., 3" h. 34.00

Model of a hen, "Biddy," white body w/green accents, Model No. 176, 5" l., 5½" h. 75.00

Model of a lamb, kneeling, pink body, white & dark pink accents, 2½" l., 2¼" h. 27.00

Model of a pig, "Winkie," tail & right ear up, right eye winking, left ear down, 4" l., 3¾" h. 50.00

Planter, egg w/irregular rim depicting 'broken' egg, mint matte green, 3¼" d., 4" h. 18.00

Plate, 6½" d., Santa face, 1st edition, 1950, pale pink background, white beard, dark pink hat 85.00

Powder jar w/lid, cherry blossom in-relief on lid, sea green body, 3½" d., 3" h. 25.00

Wall plaque, goldfish, light blue matte w/gold, 7¼" l., 6¾" h. 55.00

LIMOGES

Numerous factories produced china in Limoges, France, with major production in the 19th century. Some pieces listed below are identified by the name of the maker or the mark of the factory. Although the famed Haviland Company was located in Limoges, wares bearing their marks are not included in this listing. Also see HAVILAND.

An excellent reference is The Collector's Encyclopedia of Limoges Porcelain, Second Edition, *by Mary Frank Gaston (Collector Books, 1992).*

Bowl, 8⅝" d., 1¾" h., fluted body w/scalloped rim, h.p. flowers on ivory ground, further decorated w/gold scrolls & sponging, L S & S Limoges, France $35.00

Bowl, 8½" d., ramekin-type & 11½" d. matching underplate, lavish pink roses decoration on green ground, 2 pcs., T & V (Tresseman & Vogt) ... 110.00

Bowl, 9⅜" d., 4½" h., interior w/h.p. red strawberries & yellow & green

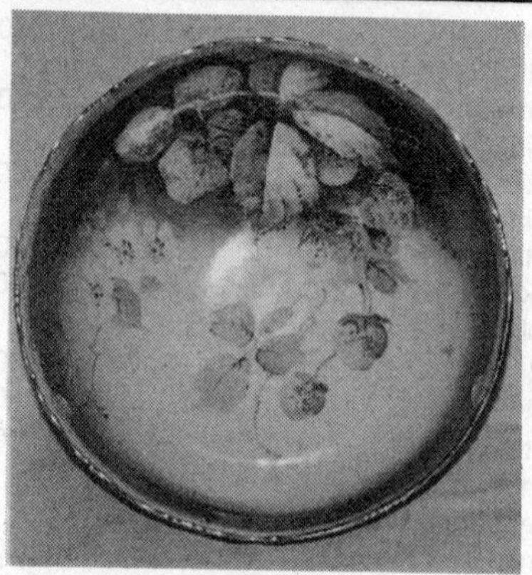

Hand-Painted Limoges Bowl

leaves against a cream & rust ground, exterior similarly dec-orated, heavy gold edge & foot, artist signed, Julius Brauer Co. (ILLUS.) .325.00

Bowl, 9½" d., 5¼" h., footed, h.p. strawberries against cream & rust ground, heavy gold scalloped edge, gold pedestal foot, artist-signed 325.00

Box, cov., purple violets decoration on gold, 8½" w. 225.00

Butter pat, decorated w/lavender floral sprays (Charles Ahrenfeldt - France) 10.00

Cake plate, h.p. orange poppies decoration, artist-signed, 10½" d., T & V 45.00

Cake plate, open-handled, decorated w/spray of mountain laurel blossoms, gold handles, artist-signed, 13" d. T & V - Limoges 95.00

Cake plate, open-handled, decorated w/giant speckled orchids, lavish gold scrolls, dated "1898," J.P.L. (Jean Pouyat - Limoges) 95.00

Center bowl, open-handled, paneled, decorated w/pink flowers & lily pads, scenic center panel, heavy gold handles, 14" d. 350.00

Charger, decorated w/giant pink h.p. roses w/green foliage on a pastel ground, scalloped rim w/rococo gilded leaf scrolls, 12¾" d., T & V Limoges 185.00

Chocolate pot, cov., decorated w/flowers & butterflies, wide gold ribbons entwine handle Ï145.00

Chocolate set: cov. chocolate pot & six cups & saucers; decorated in cobalt blue, gold & white, Jean Pouyat mark, ca. 1910, 13 pcs. 450.00

Chocolate set: cov. chocolate pot & eight cups & saucers; decorated w/blue starlings in flight against a white ground, gold handles, 17 pcs. 425.00

Cider set: 8" h., 6" d. pitcher & five cups; berries & leaves decoration, gold trim, 6 pcs. 165.00

Cracker jar, cov., branch handle, decorated w/yellow mums & brushed gold 110.00

Cup & saucer, demitasse, blue floral sprays, gold trim, A/L - Limoges, France & anchor mark 26.00

Cup & saucer, demitasse, gilded cup interior & handles, embossed gilt around saucer & cup rims, cobalt blue ground, artist-signed 50.00

Decanter, whiskey, w/original stopper, factory-decorated w/pink & red roses highlighted w/gold trim, artist-signed, 6⅜" h., T & V 195.00

Dessert set: cov. coffeepot, creamer, cov. sugar bowl, six 7¼" d. plates & six cups & saucers; h.p. sprays of tea roses against a two-toned pastel ground, further decoration on cup interiors, artist-signed, 21 pcs. T & V 700.00

Dinner service: fifteen 8¾" d. plates & a large oval tray; decorated w/different pairs of birds within peach colored & gilt borders, tray 18" l., the set 880.00

Dish, leaf-shaped, multicolored h.p. floral center, gold scrolls, matte pink border, gold rim & stem, Limoges, France, 4½ x 5" 18.00

Dish, three-section, single heavy gold branch handle from center to rim, russet shading to white w/heavy gold branches & flowers in each section, scalloped gold edge, 11½" d., marked Limoges, France...165.00

Dish, three-section w/center handle, irregular gold edge, each section decorated w/pink roses & green leaves outlined in fine gold, ornate gold handle, 13" d., 4½" h. 165.00

Dresser jar, cov., h.p. purple pansies against a light green ground 85.00

Dresser tray, h.p. courting scene of elegantly dressed Colonial couple, reticulated border w/raised pink lustre grapes, 8 x 13" 165.00

Dresser tray, rectangular, decorated w/large h.p. sprays of light blue flowers, green leaves, pink buds on shaded pastel ground, beaded scalloped blank, artist-signed, 8¼ x 10½", W. G. & Co., Limoges, France (William Guerin) 60.00

Dresser tray, handled, shaded purple decorated w/violets, 13¾" d. 150.00

Fish set: 23" l. platter & twelve 8" plates; h.p. fish decoration, gold scalloped rim, artist-signed, 9 pcs. ..475.00

Game plate, pierced to hang, h.p. deer & dog, artist-signed, 10" d. 115.00

Game plate, pierced to hang, h.p. colorful male pheasant w/female pheasant against grassy ground, heavy dull Roman gold irregular scalloped edge, artist-signed, 10" d., Coronet 195.00

Game platter, fowl & chick, gold rim, artist-signed, 12 x 19", Coronet 225.00

Game platters, h.p. large quail on one & colorful male pheasant on the other, each against a pastel natural setting w/flowers & foliage, heavy dull Roman gold edges, artist-signed, 10¾ x 16¼", pr., Limoges, France 450.00

Game set: twelve plates & matching deep platter; h.p. bird on each, artist-signed, 13 pcs., red wreath circle mark 1,450.00

Ice cream set: 16" serving plate & five individual plates; gold floral branches on a white ground, scalloped rims decorated w/cobalt blue & light blue, ca. 1891, decorators marks for A. Lanternier, 6 pcs. 595.00

Letter holder, desk-type, four gold feet, h.p. forest scene on one side, full lion face on other side, green ground, stationary gold ring handle on each side, France, 3½ x 6½ x 8½" h. 70.00

Mug, decorated w/h.p. green grapes, leaves & brown vines on pastel green to tan ground, gold handle, 4" d., 5⅝" h., T & V - Limoges - France 95.00

Pitcher, cider, 5½" h., 6½" d., h.p. red cherries & leaves on pastel ground, gold handle & trim, artist-signed, marked "Limoges - France" 165.00

Pitcher, tankard, 13½" h., twisted scroll handle, decorated w/h.p. bunches of cherries & foliate branches in ivory, gold & shades of red, wide gold bands at top & bottom, J.P. L. - France 390.00

Plaque with Grapes & Peaches

Plaque, pierced to hang, h.p. purple grapes & peaches w/green leaves against a dark & light green ground, heavy gold irregular border, artist-signed, 10¼" d., Coronet, Limoges (ILLUS.) 125.00

Plaques, pierced to hang, decorated w/French landscape scenes w/buildings on pastel backgrounds, heavy irregular Roman gold edges, unmarked, 13⅜" d., pr. 395.00

Plaques, pierced to hang, h.p. w/hunter leaning on gun visiting w/a pretty maiden sitting on a wall, a dog in the foreground, against a wooded landscape, the other w/a man holding a fishing pole talking to a girl seated on a wall, against a wood landscape, in brilliant blues, golds, greens & browns, heavy gold scalloped edges, facing pair, 13¾" d., pr. 495.00

Plate, 9" d., ornate scrolled gilt rim, decorated w/roses, artist-signed, T & V 125.00

Plate, serving, 9½" d., fancy decoration of bright flowers & gold trim, Royal Limoges 45.00

Plate, 10¼" d., decorated w/apples, berries & leaves, gold rococo rim, artist-signed 85.00

Plate, 10¼" d., two pheasants decoration, gold rococo rim, artist-signed 125.00

Plates, dessert, 9" d., floral decoration on pink & white ground, set of 6, Elite 150.00

Plates, 10¼" d., decorated w/bright colored flowers, dark blue border, ca. 1919, set of 12 ....250.00

Plates, 11¼" d., wide gold encrusted floral design rim, center filled w/polychrome flowers against a white ground, marked "Limoges, France," set of 12....................146.00

Platter, 14" l., decorated w/gold, cream & yellow roses & green leaves, T & V - Limoges....................70.00

Powder jar, cov., decorated w/stylized gold leaf fronds & lines on eggshell ground, Limoges, France 30.00

Punch bowl, h.p. violets on white ground interior & exterior, w/gold trim,12½" d., T & V - Limoges - France....................450.00

Teapot, cov., oval body, h.p. floral decoration, 9" h., T & V....................65.00

Tip tray, Perrier advertisement w/scene of girl on bar stool 75.00

Tray, handled, ornate gilt scalloped rim, decorated w/roses, artist-signed, 11" l., T & V 195.00

Trivet, three button feet, decorated w/h.p. yellow roses & foliage on pastel ground, artist-signed, 6½" d., T & V Limoges 48.00

Vase, pillow-type, 3 x 6½ x 9", gold twig feet w/encrusted berries, gold shoulder handles w/molded flowers & berries, gold rim, h.p. orange blossoms on one side & violet clusters on other, artist-signed, ca. 1882-96....................350.00

Vase, 12" h., decorated w/dahlias & chrysanthemums in pastels on a dark green ground 385.00

Vase, 13" h., portrait of woman w/long brown hair wearing sheer pink gown, light green lustre ground 550.00

Vase, 13½" h., h.p. bird & tree w/foliage on front, green, brown & light grey ground, T & V....................300.00

LIVERPOOL

Early 19th Century Liverpool Pitcher

Liverpool is most often used as a generic term for fine earthenware products, usually of creamware or pearlware, produced at numerous potteries in this English city during the late 18th and early 19th centuries. Many examples, especially pitchers, were decorated with transfer-printed patriotic designs aimed specifically at the American buying public.

Mug, cylindrical, a sepia transfer-printed design of a central oval reserve w/inscription below crossed flags centered by a Liberty cap & above a banner inscribed "Independence," early 19th c., 5" h. (flakes on base) $1,540.00

Pitcher, jug-type, 4⅞" h., black transfer-printed Seal of the United States, silver lustre highlights (some slight crazing)....................3,250.00

Pitcher, jug-type, 7⅝" h., creamware, black transfer-printed & enamel-trimmed portraits of "proscribed patriots" Samuel Adams & John Hancock, the reverse w/a three-masted sailing ship & "Success to Trade," under the spout an American eagle & the date "1802," trimmed in blue, red, yellow & green enamel, early 19th c. (repaired spout & minor imperfections) 2,750.00

Pitcher, jug-type, 8⅜" h., creamware, black transfer-printed portrait of Washington w/inscription "He In Glory & America In Tears," the other side w/George Washington memorial urn encircled w/verse, beneath the spout, "A Man Without Example - A Patriot Without Reproach," black line border (professional restoration to base, the side [into the Washington transfer], the handle and the base rim) 1,700.00

Pitcher, jug-type, 9" h., creamware, the ovoid body decorated on one side w/a transfer-printed monument to George Washington, the obverse w/an eagle w/a shield at its breast under sixteen stars within a floral wreath, under the spout inscribed "Pretty Dick," early 19th c. (glaze imperfections, flake at spout, crack at handle) 550.00

Pitcher, jug-type, 9⅛" h., creamware, one side w/a black transfer-printed oval reserve w/a scene of Classical figures flanking L'Enfant's "Plan of the City of Washington," the other side w/"Peace, Plenty and Independence," the American eagle under the spout, wear at spout, small base flakes (ILLUS.)...........2,860.00

Pitcher, jug-type, 10" h., creamware, black transfer-printed scene entitled "Defense of Stonington, Connecticut," the reverse w/"American Eagle" & cypher "GLP," a wreath beneath the spout, old repair, break to spout, flakes & spider cracks, early 19th c. 7,700.00

Pitcher, jug-type, 10" h., creamware, one side w/an oval transfer-printed reserve w/Classical figures flanking a bust of George Washington over the inscription "First President of The U.S. of America, " the other side w/a scene of the three-masted sailing ship 'Amelia' flying an American flag & trimmed w/green, yellow, red, blue & black enamel above the inscription "Amelia of New York - William S. Brooks, Commander of New-York," a wreathed monogram under the spout, early 19th c. 4,950.00

Teapot, cov., slightly ovoid body painted in shades of rose, blue, iron-red, purple & green on either side w/an Oriental-style floral spray & scattered sprigs beneath an iron-red scalloped line around the neck repeated on the cover rim beneath further floral sprays & sprigs, the spout rim & knop dashed in iron-red, Pennington's factory, ca. 1780, 6⅝" h. (small footrim chip, small hairlines & chips in cover flange) 345.00

LONGWY

Longwy Charger

This faience factory was established in 1798 in the town of Longwy, France and is noted for its enameled pottery which resembles cloisonne. Utilitarian wares were the first production here but by the 1870s an Oriental style art pottery that imitated "cloisonne" was created through the use of heavy enamels in relief. By 1912, a modern Art Deco style became part of Longwy's production and these wares, together with the Oriental style pieces, have made this art pottery popular with collectors today. As interest in Art Deco has soared in recent years, values of Longwy's modern style wares have risen sharply.

Box, cov., footed, decorated w/colorful enameled flowers & gold trim, 5" sq. $125.00

Bowl, 14¾" d., round flaring sides, white crackled glaze decorated w/Cubist stylized vine in blue, green, yellow & grey, the exterior glazed in blue, stamped "PRIMAVERA LONGWY FRANCE" & artist's signature, ca. 1920s 528.00

Center bowl, a twelve-sided flaring bowl on a conforming base, glazed in turquoise blue crackle w/stylized floral borders in pink, brick red & cobalt blue, trimmed in gold, printed factory mark, ca. 1925, 13⅜" d., 6" h. 1,495.00

Charger, the shallow circular dish molded in low-relief w/stylized black & white nude ladies in a tropical beach landscape in eggplant, mustard yellow & shades of blue, stamped "PRIMAVERA LONGWY FRANCE," 14½" d. 1,650.00

Charger, circular, painted w/a white stork surrounded by yellow, pink & salmon blossoms against a blue & green ground, decorated by R. Rizzi, stamped company mark & "DECOR de R. Rizzi," numbered "33/60," ca. 1920s, 14¾" d. 660.00

Charger, round, decorated in the Limoges-style, large pink & white roses w/green leaves on a blue ground w/gold highlights, the work of E. Killiert, incised signature & impressed mark "Longwy D - 1182" in a circle, 17" d. (ILLUS.) 880.00

Plaque w/hanger, cloisonne-style enamel decoration of a spread-winged parrot on colorful blossoming branches against a blue ground, 9" d. 275.00

Tray, Art Nouveau design, w/enameled black nude figure decoration, artist-signed, made for W.W. Atelier d'Art Bon Marche, 4⅞ x 6¼" 75.00

Trivet in metal mount decorated w/sparrow on floral branch, early marks, 6½" sq. ....150.00 to 200.00

Vases, 6½" h., 3" d., baluster-form, decorated in the Chinese style w/multicolored flowers & foliage enameled against a Chinese Blue ground, stamped "Decore A La Main - Longwy France - Made In France," w/original price tags from La Samaritaine, pr. 225.00

Vase, 9" h., tubular shape, enameled florals in blue, yellow & red 300.00

Vase, 11½" h., gourd-shaped, decorated w/stylized naked women on a waterside among stylized vegetation, in various tones of blue trimmed w/green & black, stamped "PRIMAVERA LONGWY FRANCE," ca. 1920s 2,640.00

Vase, 13⅜" h., bell-shaped, a band of stylized flowers & fruits in mustard & cherry around the lower portion, the octagonal upper portion w/defined ribbing ascending to rim, over a crackled glaze, stamped "SOCIETE DES FAIENCERIES LONGWY FRANCE" w/company logo 935.00

LUSTRE WARES

Lustred wares in imitation of copper, gold, silver and other colors were produced in England in the early 19th century and onward. Gold, copper or platinum oxides were painted on glazed objects which were then fired, giving them a lustred effect. Various forms of lustre wares include plain lustre – with the entire object coated to obtain a metallic effect, bands of lustre decoration and painted lustre designs. Particularly appealing is the pink or purple "splash lustre" sometimes referred to as "Sunderland" lustre in the mistaken belief it was confined to the production of Sunderland area potteries. Objects decorated in silver lustre by the "resist" process, wherein parts of the objects to be left free from lustre decoration were treated with wax, are referred to as "silver resist."

Wares formerly called "Canary Yellow Lustre" are now referred to as "Yellow-Glazed Earthenwares" which see.

COPPER

Copper Lustre Pitcher

Creamer, canary yellow band w/white reserves decorated w/brown transfer scenes of woman & children highlighted in polychrome enamel, 4¾" h. (some wear) $165.00

Pitcher, 5¾" h., globular lower section, wide neck, C-scroll handle, overall polychrome floral decoration (minor wear) 71.50

Pitcher, 6½" h., commemorative, footed bulbous body w/a flaring cylindrical neck w/long spout, C-scroll handle, a wide canary yellow middle band w/white oval reserves printed in black, one w/"LaFayette," the other w/"Cornwallis," early 19th c. (spout chip) 385.00

Pitcher, 6¾" h., jug-type, tapered body on a short foot, a raised beaded band around the rim, squared handle, a wide yellow band around the middle decorated w/a black transfer-printed bust portrait of Andrew Jackson on both sides, titled "General Jackson - The Hero of New Orleans"..............................1,100.00

Pitcher, 7¼" h., cylindrical w/narrow neck & flaring top, decorated w/polychrome floral enameling (some wear)..................................137.50

Pitcher, 7½" h., footed bowl-form lower body below a sloping shoulder to the high cylindrical neck w/arched mask spout & angled & scalloped serpent handle, painted blue bands around the lower body & a wide blue band around the neck w/molded blossoms decorated in polychrome 126.50

Pitcher, 8⅞" h., footed conical body w/a narrow angled shoulder to the short cylindrical neck w/long arched spout & angled handle, the middle w/a wide blue band w/an applied scene of cherubs in a chariot trimmed in polychrome enamels & purple lustre (ILLUS.)......................220.00

Sugar bowl, cov., urn-shaped w/saucer base, ram's head handles, 5¼" h..104.50

Teapot, cov., floral spray decoration w/blue trim, 6" h. 250.00

SILVER & SILVER RESIST

Bowl, 9¼" d., 4¼" h., deep rounded sides on thick footring, silver lustre resist w/large grape clusters & leaves spaced along wavy band, early 19th c. (wear, hairlines in foot)..165.00

Creamer, wide ovoid body w/a short wide cylindrical rim & angled handle, silver resist decoration of a large bird in a tree, 4⅝" h. (wear) 132.00

Pitcher, 5½" h., jug-type, bulbous ovoid body tapering to a flat rim w/pinched spout, angled handle, silver lustre resist w/a neck band of grapevines, the body w/a large "farmer's arms" design (wear)..........137.50

Pitcher, 5⅝" h., pearlware, jug-form w/wide ovoid body & angled handle, silver resist decoration w/scenes of a Dalmatian dog & dog in a flowery landscape, early 19th c. (wear, scratches, chip on spout)................104.50

Pitcher, 5¾" h., jug-type, spherical w/shaped rectangular handle, canary yellow w/wide silver resist band of stylized florals & foliage 660.00

Pitcher, 5⅞" h., jug-type, molded mask sides, canary yellow ground decorated w/polychrome highlighted w/silver resist accents.....................495.00

SUNDERLAND PINK & OTHERS

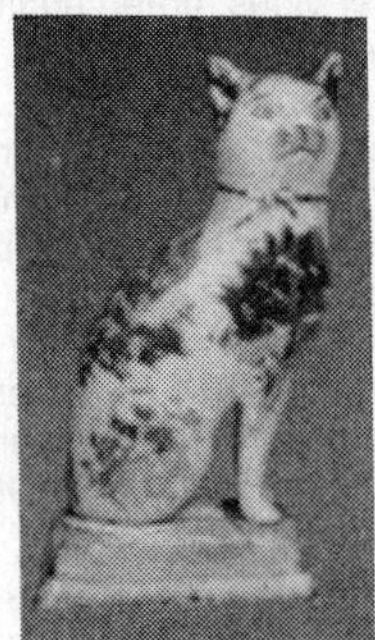

Cat Figure with Pink Lustre

Bowl, 8½" d., 4¼" h., deep rounded sides above a wide footring, black transfer-printed hunt scenes & verse on one side & a bridge scene titled "Cast iron Bridge over the River Wear" on the other, polychrome enamel trim & Sunderland lustre ground, impressed mark "Moore & Co.," 19th c. (minor wear & stains) 203.50

Butter tub w/attached undertray, cov., wide & low cylindrical body, the sides & edge of undertray w/wide white bands between thin pink lustre bands, lavish gold florals & trim, scalloped rim, marked "C.T." w/an eagle in blue, Germany, 6½" d., 4½" h...125.00

Creamer, bulbous ovoid body tapering to a short cylindrical neck, C-scroll handle, brown transfer-printed front inscription "Ladies all I pray make free - and tell me how you like your tea," red & green enamel & pink lustre trim & a Sunderland lustre band around the neck, early 19th c., 2⅞" h. (small chips) 71.50

Jar, cov., wide cylindrical body w/applied horizontal loop side handles, low domed cover w/button finial, decorated w/a black transfer-printed scene w/polychrome trim titled "Sailors Farewell," pink lustre trim, 5½" d., 4½" h. (wear, stains, pinpoint flakes)................................148.50

Models of cats, seated white animal decorated w/splotches of pink lustre, England, 19th c., 7" h., pr. (ILLUS. of one)..467.50

Pitcher, 4½" h., jug-type, wide bulbous body w/a wide cylindrical neck & angled handle, pink lustre resist w/a vintage grape design & blue rim & base stripes (chips) 220.00

Pitcher, 4¾" h., jug-type w/wide ovoid body & C-scroll handle, molded in relief around the body w/a hunting scene w/a large dog below an upper band of flower vines, green enamel & pink lustre trim, early 19th c. (wear, chips & enamel flakes)..........104.50

Pitcher, 6⅝" h., pearlware, jug-form w/wide ovoid body & angled handle, h.p. w/a wide upper band of stylized florals w/large round blossoms enclosing four petals alternating w/large serrated leaves & scattered small leaves in red, yellow, green & black w/pink lustre trim, early 19th c. (wear, minor stains & enamel flakes) 115.50

Pitcher, 7⅛" h., jug-type, commemorative, wide ovoid body w/a short cylindrical neck, simple "C" handle, each side w/a large oval reserve transfer-printed in dark brown, one w/"Iron Bridge at Sunderland," the other w/a scene of two sailors drinking, the scenes trimmed in polychrome, the background w/splashed pink lustre, early 19th c. (wear, hairlines & small chips) 385.00

Pitcher, 11½" h., black transfer-print of "Ship Caroline" on one side & "The Shipwright Arms" on the other, pink lustre trim 137.50

Plaque, pierced to hang, scroll-molded shaped rim w/pink lustre trim forming a shadow box effect & framing a black transfer scene highlighted w/polychrome enameling, marked "Waverley, S. Moore & Co., Sunderland," 7⅞ x 8½" 255.00

MAJOLICA

Majolica, a tin-enameled glazed pottery, has been produced for centuries. It originally took its name from the island of Majorca, a source of figuline (potter's clay). Subsequently it was widely produced in England, Europe and the United States. Etruscan majolica, now avidly sought, was made by Griffen, Smith & Hill, Phoenixville, Pa., in the last quarter of the 19th century. Most majolica advertised today is 19th or 20th century. Once scorned by most collectors, interest in this colorful ware so popular during the Victorian era has now revived and prices have risen dramatically in the past few years. Also see SARREGUEMINES and WEDGWOOD,.

Reference books which collectors will find useful include: The Collector's Encyclopedia of Majolica, *by Mariann Katz-Marks (Collector Books, 1992);* American Majolica, 1850-1900, *by M. Charles Rebert (Wallace-Homestead Book Co., 1981);* Majolica, American & European Wares, *by Jeffrey B. Snyder & Leslie Bockol (Schiffer Publishing, Ltd., 1994); and* Majolica, British, Continental and American Wares, 1851-1915, *by Victoria Bergesen (Barrie & Jenkins, Ltd., London, England, 1989).*

ETRUSCAN

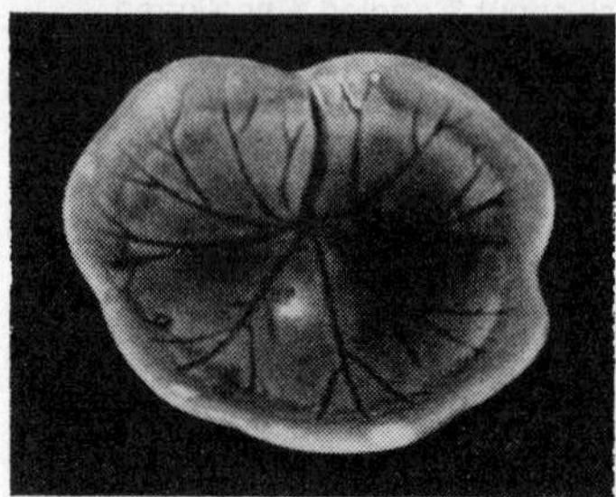

Geranium Pattern Butter Pat

Bowl, 8½" d., Shell & Seaweed patt. $275.00

Butter pat, Geranium patt., green & brown (ILLUS.)..................................70.00

Coffeepot, cov., Shell & Seaweed patt................................650.00 to 700.00

Creamer, Corn patt............................110.00

Pitcher, 4½" h., Bamboo patt.............165.00

Pitcher, 8½" h., Corn patt. 170.00

Plate, 5½" d., Cauliflower patt. 55.00

Plate, 7½" d., Cauliflower patt. 98.00

Saucer, 6" d., Albino, Shell & Seaweed patt.......................................50.00

Strawberry serving set: spade-shaped undertray-dish w/a small open sugar bowl & creamer; strawberry blossoms & leaf sprig on a lavender ground, rope borders, the set 900.00

Teapot, cov., Shell & Seaweed patt.................................525.00 to 550.00

GENERAL

Majolica Blackberries Plate

Basket, slightly canted sides, decorated w/white flowers & green leaves against a basketweave ground, the twisted handle w/bows at the terminals, 8½" l., 8" h. 425.00

Bottle, model of a duck w/straight neck, beak forms pouring spout, France, 14" h. 100.00

Bowl, 8" d., 2½" h., footed, Pond Lily patt., George Jones, England 500.00

Bowl, 11" d., Pond Lily patt., J. Holdcroft, England 250.00

Bowl, lemonade, 12" d., footed, Avalon Ware, Blackberry patt., D.F. Haynes & Co., Baltimore 180.00

Bulb bowls, the sides molded as brown wooden planks covered w/green rose vines, a gold band around the sides tying the planks together, blue interior, Minton, England, ca. 1870, 2¼ x 10½", 2" h., pr. 900.00

Butter pat, Aster patt., Wedgwood, England 130.00

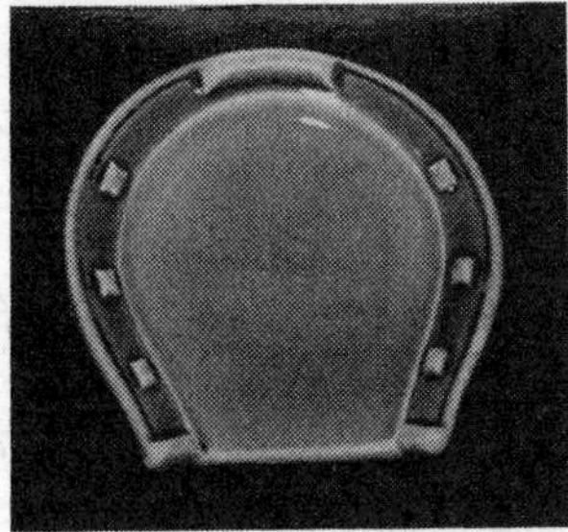

Horseshoe Pattern Butter Pat

Butter pat, Horseshoe patt., Wedgwood, England (ILLUS.) 225.00

Charger, 12" d., decorated w/fruit on gold leaf ground, Sarreguemines.......85.00

George Jones Cheese Keeper

Cheese keeper, cov., Dogwood & Woven Fence patt., George Jones, England, 11½" d., 10½" h. (ILLUS.) 2,500.00

Cheese keeper, cov., domed cover molded w/large grey & pink trout on a cobalt blue ground, arched fish handle on top, possibly J. Roth, London, England, chip on underplate 1,700.00

Compote, open, two-handled, Flower & Basketweave patt. 185.00

Creamer, birds & grapevines decoration on blue ground 15.00

Creamer, Corn patt., 4" h.......................30.00

Cup, Shell & Seaweed patt.................150.00

Cuspidor, Basketweave & Fern patt...165.00

Dessert dish, fan-shaped, Fan & Bow patt., 6½" l. 125.00

Dessert set: large open-handled platter & four matching plates; hibiscus flower decoration on a basketweave ground, incised number, Germany, 5 pcs. 375.00

Dish, Cabbage Leaf patt., Sarreguemines, France, 6½" l. 35.00

Ewer, cov., Art Nouveau w/white flowers & green leaves on a dark olive green ground, hinged pewter cover, 10" h. 350.00

Ewer, molded flower in scrolled reserves in cobalt blue, brown & yellow against a molded fishscale ground, England 280.00

Figure group, tavern scene w/a seated gentleman at a table looking across at a standing barmaid, on a rectangular footed platform base, 21" h. 880.00

Game Dish by George Jones

Game dish, cov., two-handled, game bird nestled in a grassy setting on cover, the sides decorated w/rabbits amid ferns, restored, white glazed liner, George Jones, England, 13" w., 7" h. (ILLUS.) 4,000.00

Humidor, cov., figural, model of a Pug dog, brown glaze, 9" h. 895.00

Jardiniere & stand, Art Nouveau style, globular swirl-molded jardiniere w/ornate molded leaf & flower design around rim & pierced handles, the tripod stand w/twist-molded legs & ornate molding at top & base, Dressler, Austria, 15½" d., overall 42¼" h., 2 pcs. 1,600.00

Model of a Whippet dog, the handsome animal modeled in a seated position w/collar around its neck, amber & white glaze, repairs, 31" h. 1,870.00
Pedestal, scrolled triangular form above a baluster body, decorated w/floral cartouches reserved on a cobalt ground w/yellow & gold floral sprays, impressed mark, England, 19th c., 40½" h. 742.50
Pitcher, 4½" h., Corn patt. 75.00
Pitcher, 4½" h., Dogwood patt. 70.00
Pitcher, 5½" h., Pineapple patt. 100.00
Pitcher, 5¾" h., pink & white flowers w/green leaves on a turquoise ground, registration mark on base (minor roughness at base)...............110.00
Pitcher, 6" h., floral decoration on basketweave ground.........................65.00
Pitcher, 6" h., bulbous, Wild Rose on Tree Bark patt. 70.00
Pitcher, water, 8" h., decorated w/pink flowers & green leaves 80.00

Figural Fish Pitcher

Pitcher, 11" h., figural fish, tail forms handle, lavender interior, attributed to Morley & Co., Wellsville, Ohio (ILLUS.) 175.00
Pitcher, cov. tankard, 12½" h., 5¼" d., footed cylindrical body w/applied handle, green & gold raised circles on a brown ground, hinged pewter cover 245.00
Planter, hour glass-shaped, Corn patt., 6" h..120.00
Plaque, pierced to hang, depicting a castle scene, 6½" h...........................88.00
Plate, 7" d., fruit decoration, Sarreguemines 65.00
Plate, 7½" d., blossoms & leaf decoration 85.00
Plate, 7½" d., U.S. Eagle decoration, green...55.00
Plate, 8" d., decorated w/scene of birds on branches, light blue ground, Germany 35.00
Plate, 8" d., dog & deer decoration.....110.00
Plate, 8" d., figural maple leaf...............90.00
Plate, 8" d., Pond Lily patt., George Jones 300.00
Plate, 8½"d., Lettuce Leaf patt., New Milford Pottery "Lettuce Leaf" mark...55.00
Plate, 9" d., scenic decoration of a cottage in the forest, Zell, Germany...45.00
Plate, 9" d., Water Lily patt., Zell, Germany 55.00
Plate, 10" d., Blackberry patt. 110.00
Plate, 10" d., decorated w/an apple, grapes & gold leaves 30.00
Plate, 10½" d., blackberries, blossoms & leaves on a creamy basketweave ground, unmarked (ILLUS.) 190.00
Plate, 11¼" d., decorated w/maple leaves on branch 75.00
Plates, 9" d., Bird & Fan patt., artist-signed & dated, set of 6 ....795.00
Smoking set, figural brown lion w/white ruff & chest standing in front of cups for cigarettes and matches, striker on side, green ground 250.00
Syrup pitcher, Albion Ware, morning glory design on sides, ca. 1885, Bennet's Patent, 6¼" h. 175.00
Teapot, cov., globular w/straight spout & wedge-shaped handle, four scrolled feet, sides decorated w/relief-molded swallows 140.00
Teapot, cov., wild rose decoration on gold ground, gold overglaze accents, 4½" h. 175.00
Trivet, Art Nouveau style, the tile decorated w/blue & white flowers on a green vine against a bluish green ground, Hampshire Pottery, in wire frame..90.00
Urn, Palissy-type, ovoid w/slender open-work neck, figural snake handles rising from shoulders to rim, body decorated w/relief-molded frogs, lizards, bees & beetles, 14" h..550.00
Vase, 4⅜" h., Buttercup patt., Avalon line, Haynes & Co., Baltimore 60.00
Vase, 5½" h., double-handled, Art Nouveau style, decorated w/pink flowers 45.00

MARBLEHEAD

This pottery was organized in 1904 by Dr. Herbert J. Hall as a therapeutic aid to patients in a sanitarium he ran in Marblehead, Massachusetts. It was later separated from the sanitarium and directed by Arthur E. Baggs, a fine artist and designer, who bought out the factory in 1916 and operated it until its closing in 1936. Most wares were hand-thrown and decorated and carry the company mark of a stylized sailing vessel flanked by the letters "M" and "P."

Marblehead Bowl with Indian Design

Bowl, 3¼" d., 1¾" h., bulbous form tapering gently to a wide, flat rim, smooth matte dark blue glaze, w/separate matching flower frog, bowl w/ship mark & paper label, 2 pcs. $220.00

Bowl, 5½" d., 3½" h., rounded base below flat cylindrical sides, decorated w/an incised wide band of abstract U-form devices in black against a fine shimmering matte green ground, impressed ship mark 1,210.00

Bowl, 7¼" d., 3¾" h., squatty bulbous body gently tapering to a flat mouth, matte sand-colored ground incised w/an Indian scroll design in brown, artist-initialed & impressed mark (ILLUS.) 1,870.00

Bowl, 8¾" d., 4½" h., deep flaring sides, smooth matte speckled grey glaze, impressed mark 302.50

Candlesticks, cylindrical standard w/broad flaring base & flaring rim, smooth matte speckled green glaze, impressed ship mark & paper label, 6" d.,14¼" h., pr. 1,870.00

Cider set: pitcher & four mugs; slightly tapering cylindrical form w/angled handles, smooth speckled matte green ground w/black handle & incised stripe, incised "MP" w/ship & "AB/T/MADE FOR H.P. HUGHES AUG. '07," by Arthur Baggs, 1907, pitcher 8½" h., 8¼" d., the set.......1,210.00

Lamp base, tapering base & closed-in rim, dripping satin dark blue & green glaze, factory drilled hole, 7" d., 11½" h. 770.00

impressed mark, ca. 1907 ....440.00

Vase, 3¼" h., 4¾" d., spherical body w/flat rim, decorated w/stylized swirling grey flower sprigs against a smooth matte speckled grey ground, by Hannah Tutt & Arthur Baggs, impressed ship mark & artists' initials 1,045.00

Vase, 5¼" h., wide ovoid body w/a wide flat mouth, a deep yellow ground decorated w/a spaced band of stylized trees w/double slender brown trunks & ruffled green tops, marked, ca. 1917 (small glaze bubble on side, tiny glaze skip at base) 1,760.00

Vase, 6¼" h., 5¼" d., tapering ovoid body w/rolled rim, decorated w/a wide band of stylized blossoms on twig branches in varied shades of bluish grey against a lighter grey speckled ground, impressed ship mark & paper label....................2,090.00

Vase, 7" h., 4" d., slightly ovoid, decorated w/a repeated pattern of stylized grape vines w/green leaves, blue berries & brown narrow tree trunks against a smooth speckled matte ochre ground, artist-initialed "HT," Hannah Tutt, & impressed ship mark w/"M/P" 4,950.00

Vase, 11" h., 4½" d., slightly ovoid, decorated around the top portion w/incised stylized pine cones in dark brown against a matte olive ground, "M" crossed by seagull mark, A. Baggs monogram 7,700.00

MARTIN BROTHERS POTTERY

Martinware, the term used for this pottery, dates from 1873 and is the product of the Martin brothers - Robert, Wallace, Edwin, Walter and Charles - often considered the first British studio potters. From first to final stages, their hand-thrown pottery was completely the work of the team. The early wares may be simple and conventional, but the Martin brothers built up their reputation by producing ornately engraved, incised or carved designs as well as rather bizarre figural wares. The amusing face-jugs are considered some of their finest work. After 1910, the work of the pottery declined and can be considered finished by 1915, though some attempts were made to fire pottery as late as the 1920s.

Jar, cov., modeled as a strange whimsical bird w/very expressive face, the cover formed by the head, glazed in bluish green & brown tones, mounted on a wooden base, incised on base & head "Martin Bros - London T Southhall - 11-1889," dated 1889, bird 3¾" d., 9" h. $7,000.00

Martin Brothers Jar

Jar, cov., modeled as a grotesque bird, the head w/closed eyes & a laughing expression to the open beak, glazed in browns, beige & deep blues, signed & dated "7-1892" (head) & "10-1891" (body), minor nick on beak, 4¼" w., 10½" h. (ILLUS.) 6,875.00

Jar, cov., modeled as a strange bird, the cover formed by the head, naturalistic coloring, the base & cover incised "Martin Bros. London Southall RW," & base "71890," & cover "7V890," 15" h. (beak restored) 7,475.00

Model of a grotesque bird, standing w/molded wings & feathers, blue & brown glaze, artist-signed, dated 1893 (or 98), 3" h. 715.00

Pitcher, 8⅛" h., jug-type, bulbous ovoid body w/short neck, pulled spout & applied handle, molded in low-relief w/a smiling grotesque face & incised w/clusters of grapes pendent from leafy vines, further decorated in black, chrome green & iron slips under a rich textured salt glaze, inscribed "Martin Bros - London & Southall - 2-1892," dated 1892....................................3,575.00

Pitcher, 8⅝" h., jug-type, the bulbous ovoid body w/short cylindrical neck, pulled spout & applied handle, molded in low-relief w/a smiling grotesque face amid incised clusters of raspberries & leafage, decorated in black slip under textured salt glaze, inscribed "Martin Bros. - London & Southall - 2-1892," dated 1892..3,850.00

Martin Brothers 'Sun' Pitcher

Pitcher, 9½" h., jug-type, the spherical body tapering at one side of the top to a raised spout opposite a long loop handle, molded in relief on each side w/a smiling 'Sun' face w/radiating rays glazed in pale olive, the face in dark reddish brown, inscribed "Martin Bros - London & Southall - 6-1897," ca. 1897 (ILLUS.) 6,038.00

Vase, 5¼" h., 3½" d., ovoid lobed body w/a short, molded neck, overall semi-gloss speckled brown glaze, marked "Martin Bro. - London & Southall - 1x2 - 1-1901"..................412.50

Vase, 5¾" h., 2¼" d., cylindrical body, incised decoration of two bluebirds on a branch against a beige ground, marked "R. W. Martin, Southall 11. 1877," 1877 (line around underside of base)...550.00

Vase, 8⅛" h., footed bulbous ovoid body tapering to a short flared neck, decorated w/several small flying & perched birds on flowering branches in shades of brown, tan, grey & white, all against a speckled & shaded brown & tan ground, base incised "4-1887-R-W Martin & Bros London & Southall," dated 1887 ....2,530.00

Vase, 9" h., 4" d., slightly tapering cylindrical body w/a short neck w/squared rim, upturned loop handles at the shoulder, decorated w/coral-like branches in sgraffito on a brown ground, script mark & "N5 - 7-1903" 1,210.00

MC COY

Collectors are now seeking the art wares of two McCoy potteries. One was founded in Roseville, Ohio, in the late 19th century as the J.W. McCoy Pottery, subsequently becoming Brush-McCoy Pottery Co., later Brush Pottery. The other was founded also in Roseville in 1910 as Nelson McCoy Sanitary Stoneware Co., later becoming Nelson McCoy Pottery. In 1967 the pottery was sold to D.T. Chase of the Mount Clemens Pottery Co. who sold his interest to the Lancaster Colony Corp. in 1974. The pottery shop closed in 1985. Cookie jars are especially collectible today.

A helpful reference book is The Collector's Encyclopedia of McCoy Pottery, *by the Huxfords (Collector Books), and* McCoy Cookie Jars From the First to the Latest, *by Harold Nichols (Nichols Publishing, 1987).*

Caboose Cookie Jar

Ale set: tankard pitcher & two mugs; relief-molded Buccaneer figure on sides, green glaze, 3 pcs. $55.00

Bank, barrel-shaped, "Drydock Savings Bank, That's my Bank" 22.00

Bank, Bowery money chest, green glaze, unsigned 25.00

Bank, figural sailor w/large duffle bag over his shoulder, "Seaman's Bank for Savings" 32.00

Bank, figural, model of a spread-winged American eagle on a rectangular base, made for Immigrant Industrial Savings Bank 29.00

Bank, model of an owl, Woodsy Owl ....55.00 to 65.00

Barbeque set: cov. coffee server w/warmer, four cups, chuck wagon cov. food warmer & candle, iced tea dispenser & soup tureen w/sombrero cover; El Rancho Bar-B-Que line, ca. 1960s, 8 pcs. 950.00

Basket, hanging-type, round relief-molded loop handles, basketweave design on turquoise ground, 4¼" h. 35.00

Basket, hanging-type, half-round shape, molded ivy leaves around the sides on a finely ribbed ground, pale green glaze, ca. 1950 ....18.00

Basket, hanging-type, spherical body w/wide flat rim & three-toed base, shaded brown & green matte glaze, Nelson McCoy Sanitary Stoneware Co., ca. 1926 ....20.00

Bulb bowl, oblong, horizontal ripple rim band above wide vertical ribs, white glaze, 3¾ x 4½" 4.00

Candleholder-book end, upright cluster of molded leaves, white glaze, ca. 1940, 5½" h. 15.00

Cookie jar, Apple, red, 1950-64 ....62.50

Cookie jar, Apple, yellow or green, 1950-64, each 30.00

Cookie jar, Apollo, 1970-71 ....900.00 to 950.00

Cookie jar, Asparagus, 1977 ....37.00

Cookie jar, Astronaut, 1963 ....650.00

Cookie jar, Barnum's Animals (Nabisco Wagon), 1972-74 ....300.00 to 325.00

Cookie jar, Barrel w/"Cookies" on finial, black, 1969-72 ....27.00

Cookie jar, Basket of Potatoes, 1978-80 ....35.00

Cookie jar, Bear (Cookie in Vest), 1943-45 ....75.00

Cookie jar, Bean Pot, black, 1939-43 ....40.00

Cookie jar, Bear (Hamm's Bear), 1972 ....200.00 to 225.00

Cookie jar, Bear & Beehive, 1978-86 ....50.00 to 60.00

Cookie Jar, Betsy Baker, 1975-76 ....350.00 to 400.00

Cookie jar, Bobby the Baker, 1974-79 ....40.00 to 60.00

Cookie jar, Boy on Baseball, 1978 ....250.00 to 300.00

Cookie jar, Boy on Football, 1978 ....275.00

Cookie jar, Bunch of Bananas, 1948-52 ....80.00 to 100.00

Cookie jar, Caboose, "Cookie Special," 1961 (ILLUS.) 145.00

Cookie jar, Chef (Bust), w/"Cookies" on hat band, 1962-64.......100.00 to 125.00

Cookie jar, Chilly Willy, 1986-87 ....55.00

Cookie jar, Chinese Lantern ("Fortune Cookies") 1967 ....52.00

Cookie jar, Chipmunk, 1960-61 ....100.00

Cookie jar, Christmas Tree, 1959....1,100.00

Cookie jar, Circus Horse, black, 1961 ....175.00 to 200.00

Cookie jar, Clown bust, 1945-47 ....52.00

Cookie jar, Clown in Barrel, 1953-56 ....75.00 to 100.00

Cookie jar, Clyde Dog, 1974 ....150.00 to 175.00

Cookie jar, Coalby Cat, 1967-68 ....350.00 to 400.00

Cookie jar, Coffee Grinder, brown, 1961-68 ....30.00

Cookie jar, Coffee Mug, 1963-66..........45.00
Cookie jar, Coke Jug, 1986..................60.00
Cookie jar, Colonial Fireplace, 1967-68..............................85.00 to 95.00
Cookie jar, Cookie Cabin (log cabin),1956-60.................................60.00
Cookie jar, Cookie Churn, 1977-87......29.00
Cookie jar, Cookie House, 1958-60...100.00
Cookie jar, Country Stove (Pot Belly Stove), black, 1963...........................33.00
Cookie jar, Country Stove (Pot Belly Stove), white, 1970-72......................50.00
Cookie jar, Covered Wagon (Cookie Wagon), 1959-62.............................75.00
Cookie jar, Davy Crockett, 1957...............................500.00 to 550.00
Cookie jar, Dog on Basketweave, 1956-57...55.00
Cookie jar, Duck, w/leaf in bill, 1964...110.00
Cookie jar, Dutch Boy, 1946................45.00
Cookie jar, Early American (Frontier Family), plain knob finial, 1964-71.....48.00
Cookie jar, Early American Chest (Chiffonier), 1965-68..........................72.00
Cookie jar, Elephant, whole trunk, 1953...............................100.00 to 125.00
Cookie jar, Engine, black, 1962-64..........................125.00 to 150.00
Cookie jar, Forbidden Fruit, 1967-68...65.00

Globe Cookie Jar

Cookie jar, Globe, 1960 (ILLUS.).........................200.00 to 225.00
Cookie jar, Grandma, white w/color trim, 1974-75...................................80.00
Cookie jar, Happy Face, 1972-79........35.00
Cookie jar, Hen on Nest, 1958-59........85.00
Cookie jar, Hobby Horse, 1948-53..........................150.00 to 200.00
Cookie jar, Hobnail pattern, almost heart-shaped, w/flat sides, 7-pint, 1940....................................450.00
Cookie jar, Hocus Rabbit, 1978-79.......69.00
Cookie jar, Holly Hobbie, 1980............45.00
Cookie jar, Honey Bear (on Side of Tree), 1953-55...................75.00 to 100.00
Cookie jar, House (two story), No. 161, 1980s..............................395.00
Cookie jar, Hot Air Balloon, 1985-86....28.00
Cookie jar, Hound Dog (Thinking Puppy), 1977-79..............................27.50
Cookie jar, Indian Head, 1954-56..........................325.00 to 350.00
Cookie jar, Kangaroo w/Joey in pouch, matte blue finish, after 1965...............................200.00 to 250.00
Cookie jar, Kangaroo w/Joey in pouch, tan finish, 1965..................450.00
Cookie jar, Keebler Tree House, 1986-87.............................50.00 to 75.00
Cookie jar, Kettle, hammered bronze finish, 1961-67.................................35.00
Cookie jar, Kitten on a Coal Bucket, 1983...350.00
Cookie jar, Kittens (Two) in a Low Basket, 1950s................................800.00
Cookie jar, Kittens (Three) on Ball of Yarn, 1954-55................................110.00
Cookie jar, Koala Bear, 1960-77............................75.00 to 100.00
Cookie jar, Kookie Kettle, 1960-77..............................15.00 to 20.00
Cookie jar, Lamb on Basketweave, white w/brown, 1956-57.....................48.00
Cookie jar, Lamp (Lantern), 1962-63....50.00
Cookie jar, Lazy Pig, 1978-79..............40.00
Cookie jar, Lollipops, 1958-60..............65.00
Cookie jar, "Mac" Dog, 1967-68...........83.00
Cookie jar, Mammy, "Cookies" only, decorated dress, 1948-57...............177.00
Cookie jar, Mammy, "Cookies" only, overall aqua glaze, 1948-57...........295.00
Cookie jar, Mammy, "Cookies" only, yellow dress, 1948-57......500.00 to 550.00
Cookie jar, Mammy with Cauliflower, 1939..........................1,100.00 to 1,300.00
Cookie jar, Mary, Mary, Quite Contrary, 1970.................................45.00
Cookie jar, Milk Can, w/Gingham Flowers, No. 333...............................75.00
Cookie jar, Monk ("Thou Shalt Not Steal"), 1968-73................................30.00
Cookie jar, Mother Goose, brown, 1948-52...165.00
Cookie jar, Mushrooms on Stump, 1972...65.00
Cookie jar, Oaken Bucket, 1961-71..25.00
Cookie jar, Old Fashioned Auto (Touring Car), 1962-64........70.00 to 80.00
Cookie jar, Owls (Mr. & Mrs. Owl), 1953-55.............................75.00 to 100.00
Cookie jar, Panda Bear (Upside Down Bear), 1978-79.....................................35.00
Cookie jar, Peanut, 1976-77.................30.00
Cookie jar, Pear, yellow, 1952-57.........45.00
Cookie jar, Penguin, white, 1940-43...60.00

Cookie jar, Pepper, green, 1972-75....25.00 to 30.00
Cookie jar, Pepper, yellow, 1972-80....32.50
Cookie jar, Picnic Basket, 1962-63....45.00
Cookie jar, Pineapple, natural colors, 1955-57....73.00
Cookie jar, Pine Cones on Basketweave, 1957....40.00
Cookie jar, Pirate's Chest, 1970....135.00
Cookie jar, Popeye, cylinder w/decal, 1971-72....180.00
Cookie jar, Pumpkin (Jack-O-Lantern), 1955....650.00 to 850.00
Cookie jar, Puppy (holding cookie sign), 1961-62....85.00
Cookie jar, Rabbit w/Cookie on stump, 1971....60.00
Cookie jar, Rag Doll (Raggedy Ann), 1972-75....75.00 to 100.00
Cookie jar, Rocking Chair (Dalmatians), 1961....400.00 to 425.00
Cookie jar, Snoopy on Doghouse, 1970....237.00
Cookie jar, Snow Bear, 1965....40.00
Cookie jar, Spaceship (Friendship 7), 1962-63....125.00 to 150.00
Cookie jar, Stagecoach, 1956....1,000.00 to 1,500.00
Cookie jar, Stove (Cook Stove), black, 1962-64....25.00
Cookie jar, Stove (Cook Stove), white, 1962-64....35.00
Cookie jar, Strawberry, white drip glaze, 1955-57....30.00
Cookie jar, Teddy Bear & Friend, 1986-87....40.00

Tepee Cookie Jar

Cookie jar, Teepee, 1956-59 (ILLUS.)....300.00 to 350.00
Cookie jar, Time for Cookies (Mouse on Clock), 1968-73....35.00
Cookie jar, Turkey, brown, 1960....175.00 to 200.00
Cookie jar, Turkey, green, 1960....275.00 to 300.00
Cookie jar, W.C. Fields, 1972-74....157.00
Cookie jar, Wedding Jar, 1961....80.00
Cookie jar, Winking Pig, 1972....350.00
Cookie jar, Wishing Well, 1961-70....28.00
Cookie jar, Woodsy Owl, 1973-74....200.00 to 250.00
Cookie jar, Wren House w/brown bird on top, 1958-60....75.00 to 100.00
Cookie jar, Wren House w/pink bird on top, 1958-60....150.00 to 200.00
Cookie jar, Yosemite Sam, cylinder w/decal, 1971-72....100.00 to 125.00
Creamer, Daisy patt., matte pink & turquoise glaze....6.50
Creamer, Pine Cone patt....10.00
Decanter, Apollo series, Astronaut,marked "Thomas 'n Sims Distillery," 1968....190.00
Decanter, Apollo series, missile, 1968....225.00
Decanter set, train locomotive, coal car marked "Jupiter" & two cars, 1969, the set....90.00
Fern box, oblong Butterfly patt., greenish-brown, glaze, 1940, 4½ x 8¾", 3¼" h....9.00
Flower holder, ball-shaped, scalloped top, green glaze, 1943....6.50
Flowerpot & saucer, embossed double beetle rim band decoration, orange glaze, 1961, 5" h., 2 pcs....6.00
Flowerpot w/attached saucer, embossed icicle band around upper half above finely ribbed lower section, green & cream glaze, 1957, 3¾" h....3.50
Flowerpot w/attached saucer, Greek Key band decoration, green glaze, 1954, 4" h....5.00
Food warmer, El Rancho Bar-B-Que line, model of a Chuck Wagon w/rack,1960....150.00 to 175.00
Iced tea server, El Rancho Bar-B-Que line, barrel-shaped, 1960....175.00 to 200.00
Jardiniere, underglaze slip-painted tulips, brown glaze, marked "Loy-Nel-Art," 5" h....165.00
Jardiniere, relief-molded flying birds around sides, ca. 1935, 7½" h....18.00
Jardiniere, footed bulbous body w/fluted rim & foot, glossy dark green, 1959, 7¼" d., 5¼" h.,....7.00
Lamp base, modeled as a pair of cowboy boots, brown glaze, ca. 1956, small size....65.00
Mug, barrel-shaped, brown glaze, Nelson McCoy, 1926....4.00
Mugs, coffee, El Rancho Bar-B-Que line, 1960, set of 4....80.00
Planter, Arcature line, bird & foliage framed in base, 1951, 6½" h....28.00

Planter, Banana Boat, Calypso line, man holding banjo standing by boat, tan glaze 80.00
Planter, Chinese Man w/Wheelbarrow, yellow, 1950..........................10.00
Planter, model of frog & lotus blossom, gold trim, 1943...................22.00
Planter, model of a pheasant in grass, 1959..50.00

Quail Planter

Planter, model of two adult quail w/chick, brown & green glaze, 1955 (ILLUS.) 32.00
Planter, model of a rocking chair, 1954 ....38.00
Planter, model of a rolling pin w/Boy Blue seated on one end, 1952...........60.00
Planter, model of a rooster, grey glaze, red comb, ca. 1951, 7½" h. 25.00
Planter, model of a swan, rose glaze, 1943, 4⅝ x 6"..................................16.00
Planter, model of a wishing well, brown & green glaze, 7" h.................16.00
Planter, rodeo cowboy roping steer, tan & green, ca. 1950s....................65.00
Planter, triple lily-type, three upright white blossoms above green leaves & a brown log, ca. 1950 ....22.00
Planter, Village Smithy, blacksmith standing under tree lettered "Under the spreading chestnut tree," horse standing to one side, ca. 1954 ....22.00
Planters, model of the Stretch horse, yellow glaze, pr. 200.00
Salt & pepper shakers, model of a head of cabbage, pr. 40.00
Soup tureen, cov., El Rancho Bar-B-Que line, model of a sombrero, 1960, 5 qt..........................350.00 to 450.00
Sugar bowl, open, Daisy patt.................7.00
Sugar bowl, open, Pine Cone patt..........8.00
Teapot, cov. Daisy patt.........................32.50
Tea set: cov. teapot, creamer & sugar bowl; Pine Cone patt., 3 pcs. (ILLUS. top next column) 65.00
Vase, bud, 6⅛" h., onyx glaze, streaked green, black & gold 28.00

Pine Cone Tea Set

Vase, double bud, 8½" h., a side by side large & small hexagonal upright on an oval base, white glaze, 1940...18.00
Wall pocket, conical, Mexican patt., molded peasant figures, bluish green glaze, ca. 1941, 7½" l. 25.00
Wall pocket, model of a lily, 1940, 6" h..22.00

MEISSEN

The secret of true hard paste porcelain, known long before to the Chinese, was "discovered" accidentally in Meissen, Germany, by J.F. Bottger, an alchemist working with E.W. Tschirnhausen. The first European true porcelain was made in the Meissen Porcelain Works, organized about 1709. Meissen marks have been widely copied by other factories. Some pieces listed here are recent.

Basket, reticulated oval sides w/twisted handles, floral decoration & gilt trim, 19th c., 9¾" l..................$605.00
Bowl, 9" sq., the shaped square decorated w/floral sprays, 19th c. 330.00
Butter dish, cov., ornate mold, Blue Onion patt., crossed swords mark ...325.00
Butter pat, Blue Onion patt., crossed swords mark 45.00
Candelabra, three-light, the shaped circular base supporting an ornate standard w/floral encrustations, each curved arm terminating w/a candle socket resting on a leafy base, 11½" h., pr. 715.00
Charger, decorated overall w/raised gold flowers & foliage against a soft green ground, blue crossed swords mark, 11" d...275.00
Coffee cup & saucer, each piece w/a scale-patterned ground formed of overlapping puce quatrefoils & reserved on the front or in the center w/a rococo cartouche of yellow,

blue, purple & green scrollwork heightened in gilding, issuing small floral sprigs, & colorfully painted w/a cluster of fruit (slight scratching on saucer) & flowers, the rim w/a gilt dentil edge, the elaborate scroll handle on the cup heightened in gilding, crossed swords marks in underglaze-blue, the saucer impressed "63," ca. 1750., 5 5/16" d., 2⅝" h. 575.00

Compote, 8¾" h., reticulated border, Indian Purple patt., blue crossed swords mark 550.00

Cup & saucer, demitasse, delicate, Blue Onion patt., crossed swords mark 65.00

Dish, figural, shell-shaped w/figure of a young boy glazed in white, further decorated w/a green branch covered w/pale green flowers, marked on base "M-447," 7½" w., 8¾" h. 125.00

Figure of a blackamoor, the exotic figure dressed in flowing robes, seated before a leafy bush w/one leg under him & the other fully extended to one side, a parrot perched on his right hand, glazed in pastel tones, modeled by Prof. Paul Scheurich, underglaze-blue crossed swords mark, incised "A1068," impressed "1530," 1922, 8½" h.....1,650.00

Figure of a cherub holding a scythe & wheat, blue crossed swords mark, ca. 1890s, 5" h. 575.00

Lady with Fan Figure

Figure of a lady, the Flapper modeled in full relief wearing a low-cut gown w/side slit opposite long ruffles & w/her arms crossed holding a large feather fan, standing on a rectangular base, decorated in shades of gold, brown, pink, green & black, designed by Paul Scheurich, ca. 1929, marked "SCHEURICH 29," crossed swords & "A 1224 - 930," minor repair, 18¼" h. (ILLUS.)..7,475.00

Figure of a young gardener, modeled as a girl w/yellow bow (small chips) in her hair & on her shoulders, wearing a pink bodice w/a puce-striped stomacher above a turquoise-lined bustled blue skirt & a yellow-edged & turquoise-ruched blue underskirt, carrying a tan basket of colorful flowers over her right arm, her left hand (fingertips touched up) raised before her, & standing amid iron-red & yellow florettes & green leaves on a small mound base, crossed swords mark in underglaze-blue & impressed "14," ca. 1760, 4 11/16" h. 920.00

Figure group, allegorical, composed of a craggy mountain background fitted along the slopes w/eleven separate classical male & female figures as well as model of Pegasus above a cascading spring, all raised on a scroll-molded base, late 19th c., 38" l., 27" h.....................34,500.00

Model of a lady's shoe, slipper-type, turquoise, crossed swords mark, ca. 1860, 6" l...285.00

Colorful Meissen Model of a Bird

Models of birds, colorful specimens perched on tall stumps, late 19th c., 15½" h., pr. (ILLUS. of one) 2,875.00

Plaque, pierced to hang, scene of cavalier pouring wine, No. 2621, 7⅝" d..150.00

Plate, 8 9/16" d., *famille verte* palette, painted in iron-red, green, turquoise, blue, shades of puce, black & touches of gilding w/a songbird in flight near a chrysanthemum plant growing from swirling stylized rocks, the cavetto encircled by two iron-red lines & the rim w/three flowering chrysanthemum branches, crossed swords mark in underglaze-blue &

impressed former's double-circle mark for Johann Kuhnel, Sr., ca. 1730...12,650.00

Plate, 9" d., Blue Onion patt., 19th c. ...50.00

Plate, 9½" d., center decorated w/scene of the Goddess Diana, seated on a stone bench, carrying a club & wearing a boarskin & draped in a green & white toga, red & green w/gilt borders in a classical design, underglaze-blue crossed swords mark 935.00

Platter, 20" l., Blue Onion patt. 250.00

Sauce boat w/attached undertray, Blue Onion patt., crossed swords mark...200.00

Sauce boat w/attached underplate, double-spouted, decorated w/birds & insects, 10¼" l. 104.50

Tea set: cov. teapot, cov. sugar bowl, creamer, five cups, six saucers & 19" l. oval tray; white w/heavy gilt design at midsection & rim of each piece, gilt handles,15 pcs. 797.50

Tea tile, Blue Onion patt., crossed swords mark 195.00

Tureen, oval, Blue Onion patt., underglaze-blue crossed swords mark, 19th c., 9½ x 14", 10¼" h................550.00

Vase, 6¾" h., Art Nouveau style, a wide flattened round base tapering to a tall very slender stick neck, a pale blue ground decorated w/white & grey *pate-sur-pate* poppy blossoms around the bottom w/the stems up the neck, blue crossed swords mark & stamped numbers, ca. 1898.....................................1,320.00

Vegetable dish, cov., round, Blue Onion patt., crossed swords mark ...300.00

Whistle, porcelain, Blue Onion patt., ca.1870 ....190.00

METLOX POTTERIES

Metlox Potteries was established in 1927 in Manhattan Beach, California. In 1932, dinnerware was introduced and within two years a complete line of Poppytrail was available. Carl Romanelli joined Metlox as an artware designer and became well-known for his miniature animals and novelties. However, it is the Romanelli figurines, especially nudes and nudes with vases, that are eagerly sought by collectors. After World War II, Evan K. Shaw bought Metlox and dinnerware became a staple for the success of the business. Poppets by Poppytrail are piquing the interest of collectors in today's market. They are stoneware flower-holders and planters created in doll-like fashion by Helen Slater. Metlox produced them during the 1960s and 1970s. The shelf sitters and the individual Salvation Army band figures are among the most popular. In 1989, Metlox ceased operations.

Figure of "Conchita"

Cookie jar, model of the head & tall hat of a drummer boy or toy soldier, red collar, white face, black brim on hat & chin strap, blue hat, red knob on top, 10¾" h.....................$115.00

Cookie jar, model of an owl, dark & pale blue, 10½" h. 45.00

Figure, Poppets' series, "Conchita," Mexican girl w/serape draped over her shoulders, open pot on her head & another pot beside her, open holes for her eyes, rough textured w/sand colored body, black hair, 8¾" h. (ILLUS.) 18.00

Figure, Poppets' series, "Effie" standing w/her cymbals together, blue Salvation Army hat & coat, white skirt, yellow cymbals, 7¾" h...20.00

Figure, Poppets' series, "Huck," boy shelf sitter fishing, w/feet crossed, blue pants, brown shirt, yellow hat, 6½" h..26.00

Figure, Poppets' series, "Jenny," shelf sitter w/legs crossed at knees, yellow dress & bow in hair, 8¾" h...28.00

Figure, Poppets' series, "Nellie," bird on her head, holding vase, holes for eyes & five holes around top of her hair, black hair & blouse w/black & turquoise circles on skirt, turquoise bird & vase 8¼" h.............20.00

Flower holder, figural, woman standing on square base w/her arms behind her & wrapped around a cornucopia w/three openings, satin ivory woman w/satin pink cornucopia outside & satin green & brown inside, "C. Romanelli" signed on base rim & "Metlox Made in U.S.A. Des. Patent 122409" in stamped mark under the glaze, 8¼" h. 115.00

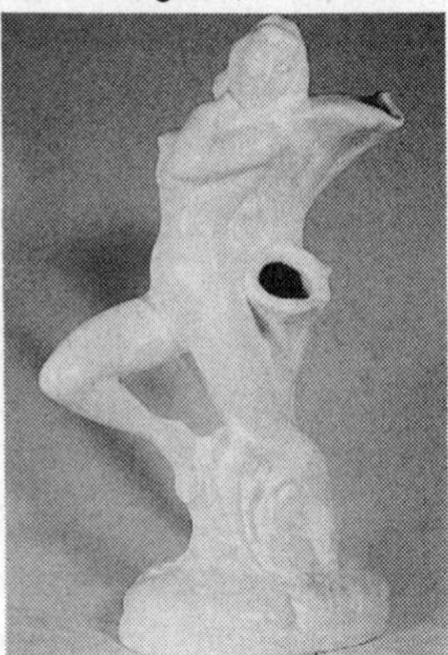

Metlox Figural Flower Holder

Flower holder, figural, nude woman standing on oval base, right leg out in front & bent at knee, right hand under left breast, left arm bent w/hand at neck, head turned to left, vase w/three openings behind her, satin ivory glaze, "C. Romanelli" signed on base rim & also incised in script on bottom, "Poppytrail Made in Californi.." incised on bottom, design patent No. 125593, Model No. 1806, 9¼" h. (ILLUS.)...............175.00

Figure of a woman standing on a stylized ovoid base & holding an urn to the right side of her head & her left arm over her head touching the urn, left leg slightly bent at knee & in front of right leg, satin ivory glaze, "C. Romanelli" signed on base rim & "patent no. 125594" on bottom, Model No. 1816, 9" h. 150.00

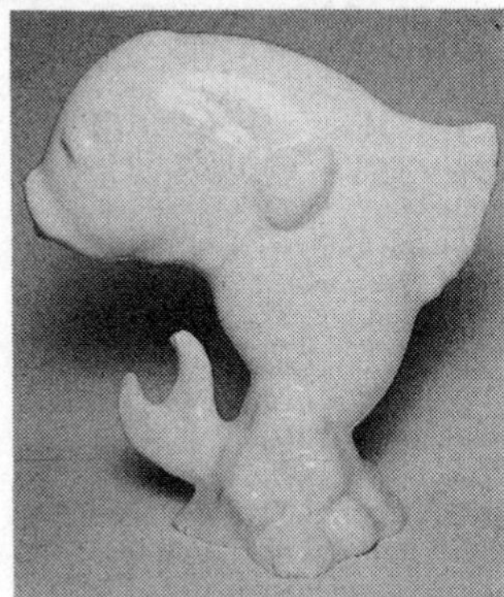

Miniature Model of a Fish

Model of a fish on a base, satin ivory glaze, paper label shows "Miniatures by Metlox Manhattan Beach, California," 4¼" h. (ILLUS.) 75.00

Metlox Model of a Stork

Model of a stork on a base, satin ivory glaze, stamp mark, "Metlox Made in U.S.A.," 6½" h. (ILLUS.)......................65.00

Planter, model of a seal w/two front flippers hugging a round planter, pale blue satin matte, Model No. 456, 5¼" h. 18.00

METTLACH

Mettlach Plaque with Knight Scene

Ceramics with the name Mettlach were produced by Villeroy & Boch and other potteries in the Mettlach area of Germany. Villeroy and Boch's finest years of production are thought to be from about 1890 to 1910.

Ale set: 12" h., 9" d. jug-type pitcher & four tumblers; Art Nouveau floral decoration, No. 2098 pitcher & No. 2834 tumblers, 5 pcs. $1,650.00

Beaker, PUG, scene of gnomes drinking, No. 1032, ¼ liter..................75.00

Charger, Art Nouveau style decoration w/floral cluster 'trees' in blue & gold around the rim separated by white leaf-shaped reserves around a central stylized 'flower-head' in gold & blue, No. 2960, 14⅞" d. 440.00

Pitcher, 8½" h., birch handle, green leaves in relief on grey, ca. 1890 .....245.00

Pitchers, 12" h., Phanolith dancing scene, white on green ground, No. 7012, pr. 1,800.00

Plaque, pierced to hang, etched scene of a cavalier pouring wine, ca. 1903, No. 2621, 7½" d. 250.00

Plaque, pierced to hang, etched scene of a cavalier holding glass, blue ground, signed "Quidenus," No. 2622, 7½" d. 295.00

Plaque, pierced to hang, etched scene depicting cavalier dressed in blue playing mandolin, brick color ground, No. 2625, 7½" d. 295.00

Plaque, pierced to hang, Phanolith, white relief bust of a lady on green, No. 7032, ca. 1900, 7½ x 8¾" oval 485.00

Plaque, pierced to hang, rectangular, cameo, white relief detailed scene of two boys, one w/flute, one w/mandolin, playing for a girl holding a fan on green ground, No. 2445, ca. 1898, 7¼ x 10¼" 650.00

Plaque, pierced to hang, PUG, Oriental lady in yellow kimono, pink floral decoration on grey background, No. 1044, 14" d. 295.00

Plaque, pierced to hang, etched scene of a knight carrying a weapon, signed "Schultz," dated 1910, No. 1385, 14½" d. (ILLUS.) 1,195.00

Plaque, pierced to hang, etched scene of man & woman on horseback, jumping fence, signed "Stocke," No. 2041, 15" d. 800.00

Plaque, pierced to hang, etched scene of Bismarck on horseback, No. 2142, 15" d. 950.00

Plaque, pierced to hang, etched scene of knight trying to kiss a maiden & being pushed away, No. 2322, 15" d. 1,195.00

Plaque, pierced to hang, Phanolith, rectangular, decorated w/white relief-molded figures in a scene from "The Flying Dutchman," No. 7046, mate to No. 7047, artist-initialed "JS," ca. 1901, w/original frame, 12¹⁄₁₆ x 15¼" 1,250.00

Plaque, pierced to hang, Phanolith, rectangular, decorated w/white relief-molded figures in a scene from "The Flying Dutchman," No. 7047, w/original frame, 12³⁄₁₆ x 15⁵⁄₁₆" 1,250.00

Plaque, pierced to hang, Phanolith, white relief-molded scene from the

Mettlach "Lohengrin" Scene Plaque

opera "Lohengrin," signed "Stahl," No. 7026, framed, 12 x 15½" (ILLUS.) 1,045.00

Plaque, pierced to hang, the center incised & decorated w/a profile bust of a young lady w/long brown hair w/a deep forest in the background, a border band of stylized flowers on a white ground, artist-signed, No. 2547, 15¾" d. 880.00

Plaque, pierced to hang, etched scene of castle above the Rhine River, gold edge, dated 1895, No. 1108, 17" d. 1,400.00

Plaque, pierced to hang, decorated w/the incised bust portrait of a young woman w/long curling brown hair amid large pink & brown lilies w/green leafage & against a bluish grey ground, matte glaze, artist-signed, No. 2549, 17½" d. 990.00

Plaque, pierced to hang, etched scene depicting an Art Nouveau woman sniffing a yellow rose, signed "R. Fournier," No. 2544, 19½" d. 805.00

Vase, 7¼" h., Mosaic, footed ovoid body tapering to a ringed trumpet neck, the body w/tapering stripes of stylized blossomhead alternating w/panels of an overall small diaper design, in shades of brown & blue, No. 1728 ....302.50

Vase, 7⅝" h., wide ovoid body w/a rounded shoulder to the short flaring neck, decorated w/two bands of confronting serrated leaf-form lappets flanking a narrow center band in shades of green, rust & blue w/similar bands of smaller lappets around the shoulder & base, all against a brick orange ground, ca. 1905, No. 1596 ....550.00

Vase, 8¾" h., ovoid body tapering to a short, wide neck w/flared rim, decorated w/a dark blue background glaze highlighted by small scattered leaf sprigs & tiny blossomheads in light blues & gold, the neck w/a brick orange band applied w/dark blue "jewels," ca. 1910, No. 2868 ....495.00

Vase, 13½" h., tall baluster-form body w/a cylindrical neck w/flared rim flanked by long loop handles from rim to shoulder, etched, large swirled scrolling leaves in soft colors on a blue ground, No. 2414 ....385.00

Vase, 13¾" h., 4½" d., tapering cylinder w/narrow shoulder & short collared neck, decorated w/incised flower pods in peacock blue & gold on a white ground, No. 2913, die-stamped marks 400.00

Vase, 14½" h., 5½" d., tapering cylinder w/narrow shoulder & scalloped rim, decorated w/large incised blossoms on tall stems, pink, ochre, brown & sage green on a bone ground, No. 2976, incised marks 700.00

Vase, 18⅞" h., tall slender baluster-form body, the tall neck decorated w/palmettes & looped band, the body w/a continuous design of exotic birds in bamboo, done in shades of blue & beige, No. 2457...............................522.50

MOCHA

Mocha Bowl with Seaweed Decoration

Mocha decoration is found on basically utilitarian creamware or yellowware articles and is achieved by a simple chemical reaction. A color pigment of brown, blue, green or black is given an acid nature by infusion of tobacco or hops. When this acid nature colorant is applied in blobs to an alkaline ground color, it reacts by spreading in feathery seaweed designs. This type of decoration is usually accompanied by horizontal bands of light color slip. Produced in numerous Staffordshire potteries from the late 18th until the late 19th centuries, its name is derived from the similar markings found on mocha quartz. In addition to the seaweed decoration, mocha wares are also seen with Earthworm and Cat's Eye patterns or a marbleized effect.

Bowl, 6" d., deep flaring & slightly rounded sides, wide center band decorated w/an undulating Earthworm patt. band, narrow dark bands at top & base, 19th c. (some discoloration) $550.00

Bowl, 6¼" d., 3¼" h., pearlware, a short wide pedestal base below the deep gently rounded sides, a wide blue band decorated w/brown Earthworm patt., narrow tan, white & brown bands around the top & embossed beaded bands, early 19th c., (small broken interior blister, small rim flake) 352.00

Bowl, 7¼" d., 3¾" h., deep flaring sides tapering to a high foot, bluish grey wide center band decorated w/a double-spiral Earthworm patt. in brown, tan & white, narrow blue stripe above & below center band (wear, small chips & hairlines) 412.50

Bowl, 11" d., 5" h., footed, a wide white center band decorated w/brown Earthworm patt., narrow green stripes at top & bottom, East Liverpool, Ohio, late 19th - early 20th c. (wear, stains) 687.50

Bowl, 12¼" d., 6" h., flaring sides w/rolled rim, wide white band w/seaweed decoration, flanked by blue stripes, minor wear (ILLUS.) 357.50

Bowl, 12½" d., 6¼" h., deep flaring rounded sides resting on a thick footring, a heavy molded rim, wide white band around the top half w/blue seaweed decoration & flanked by thin blue stripes (wear, small flakes)....................................275.00

Chamber pot, miniature, footed bulbous body w/a flattened flaring rim, yellowware w/a wide white center band decorated w/red seaweed design & flanked by narrow brown stripes, 6" d., 4" h. (edge wear, hairlines) 192.50

Creamer, jug-type, a wide white upper band w/green seaweed decoration & flanked by thin double brown stripes, another band of double brown stripes lower on the body, 4" h. (hairline in base of handle, chip on base)...412.50

Cup, footed rounded bowl w/molded rim, loop handle, white center band w/seaweed decoration in blue, on yellowware, 4¼" d. (hairline)............214.50

Flowerpots, flaring cylindrical body w/flattened rim, wide blue band flanked by narrow stripes of ochre &

brown & decorated w/a looping Earthworm patt. in blue, white, brown & ochre, tooled blue rim, 4¼" h., pr. (wear, small chips & minor hairlines) 3,190.00

Mug, squatty bulbous body w/small footring, C-scroll leaftip handle, a wide grey band flanked by orange stripes & decorated w/overlapping dot bands in white, brown & blue, tooled w/green glaze, 4¼" d. (chips on footring, wear, stains, hairline in handle) 522.50

Mug, cylindrical, ironstone w/blue & teal green bands w/black seaweed decoration divided by black stripes, marked "Pint," 4⅞" h. 357.50

Mug, cylindrical w/a wide pale orange band decorated w/several large striped white, tan & brown fan-shaped leaves, molded leaftip handle, 4⅞" h. (wear, chips) 2,200.00

Mustard pot, cov., baluster-form body tapering to a flat rim & low-domed cover w/button finial, C-scroll handle, decorated w/thin stripes of orange, chocolate brown & white w/an embossed green band, leaftip handle, 3⅝" h. (chips, repair) 467.50

Pitcher, 4¾" h., tapering cylindrical ironstone body decorated w/a wide dark blue center band w/black seaweed designs, thick white, teal blue & black edge & base bands, impressed "Pint" (minor wear) 192.50

Pitcher, 6½" h., three bands of Cat's Eye patt. around the body on a banded ground, narrow dark bands around the top & base, 19th c. (imperfections) 1,210.00

Early 19th Century Mocha Pitcher

Pitcher, 8" h., wide footed ovoid body tapering slightly toward the wide flat rim w/pointed spout, C-scroll handle, decorated w/incised green bands enclosing central bands of butternut, brown & white w/twig, wave & cat's eye decoration, molded foliate spout & handle, imperfections, early 19th c. (ILLUS.) 2,750.00

Pitcher, jug-type, 9¼" h., a wide white band around the shoulder decorated w/bold brown seaweed decoration & flanked by thin double brown stripes, another wide white band below decorated w/bands of thin brown stripes 1,210.00

Salt dip, Earthworm patt. in blue & brown on an ochre ground, 2¾" d., 2⅛" h. (flake on rim) 137.50

Salt dip, shallow cylindrical bowl raised on a short pedestal base, the sides w/a wide white band decorated w/green seaweed design, wear & stains, 2¾" d., 2⅛" h. 357.50

Shaker, cov., the footed cylindrical body tapering to a short flared neck fitted w/a pierced domed top, a wide blue band around the body flanked by black stripes & decorated in brown, white & black Earthworm patt., blue on the top, 4⅞" h. (chips) 632.50

Sugar bowl, cov., bulbous footed body tapering to a wide, rolled rim w/inset cover, a wide white center band decorated w/black seaweed design & flanked by thin blue bands, small chips, stains, 5¾" h. 990.00

Waste bowl, footed w/deep flaring sides, wide blue band flanked by pairs of black stripes & decorated w/the Cat's Eye patt. in black, brown & white, 4½" d., 2½" h. (minor wear, pinpoint foot flakes) 550.00

MOORCROFT

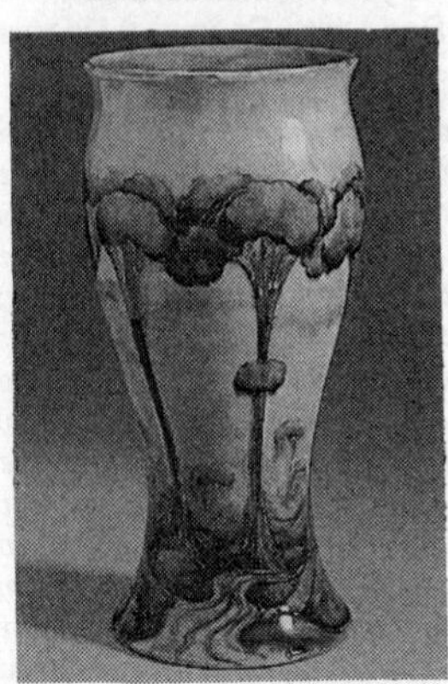

Hazledene Pattern Vase

William Moorcroft became a designer for James Macintyre & Co. in 1897 and was put in charge of their art pottery production. Moorcroft developed a number of popular designs, including Florian Ware *while with Macintyre and continued with that firm until 1913 when they discontinued the production of art pottery.*

After leaving Macintyre in 1913, Moorcroft set up his own pottery in Burslem and continued producing the art wares he had designed earlier as well as introducing new patterns. After William's death in 1945, the pottery was operated by his son, Walter.

Basket w/silver plate handle, decorated w/multicolored pomegranates on blue ground, 4" h. $365.00

Bowl, cov., 6½" d., pink & purple floral decoration on deep blue ground, signed 300.00

Bowl, 12" d., wide shallow rounded sides, the interior decorated w/the African Lily patt. w/pink & yellow flowers & green foliage against a shaded green to blue ground, marked 220.00

Box, cov., Poppy patt., 3¾" h. 215.00

Creamer & sugar bowl, Pansy patt., cobalt blue ground, Macintyre period, ca. 1897-1913, creamer 3" h., sugar bowl 3¼" d., pr. 640.00

Jar, cov., wide ovoid body w/a short cylindrical neck fitted w/a domed cover, Wisteria patt., yellow, purple & warm red blossoms on a cobalt blue ground, marked "MOORCROFT - 269 - MADE IN ENGLAND," 6" d., 8¼" h. 715.00

Jar, cov., bulbous ovoid shouldered body w/a domed cover, decorated in low-relief w/stylized trees w/a red flambé glaze, impressed mark "MOORCROFT MADE IN ENGLAND 766" & glazed "MOORCROFT," 10½" h. 6,325.00

Lamp base, table model, tall ovoid body, Pomegranate patt., decorated w/red fruit w/cobalt centers & brown foliage against a cobalt blue ground, fitted for electricity, signed, 3½" d., 7½" h. 220.00

Loving cup, wide slightly flaring cylindrical bowl flanked by long upright loop handles & raised on a short flaring pedestal foot, a round center medallion w/a swirled cloisonné design in blue & green on a glossy green ground, script signature mark, 7" w., 5¼" h. 165.00

Urn, decorated w/red & purple berries, large green, red, yellow leaves, dark teal green ground, artist-signed 225.00

Vase, 4⅛" h., compressed globular form w/short slightly flaring neck, decorated w/large magnolia blossoms in pink, green & brown on a cobalt blue ground, signature & impressed marks 220.00

Vase, 4½" h., Moonlit Blue line, landscape decoration, Macintyre period, ca. 1897-1913 ....1,120.00

Vase, 5" h., Claremont patt., large mushrooms decoration, retailed by Liberty & Co., ca. 1910 ....1,895.00

Vase, 6" h., decorated w/red poppies & blue forget-me-nots, ruffled rim, Macintyre period, ca. 1897-1913 ....1,320.00

Vase, 7½" h., baluster-form, Hazledene patt., tall trees w/clusters of foliage at the tops in shades of blue & green, printed factory marks, signed in green, retailed by Liberty & Co. (ILLUS.) 978.00

Vase, 9" h., 5¾" d., baluster-form w/two small round handles, "Tudor Rose" patt., decorated in cloisonné-style w/round blue roses against a turquoise blue ground, ink signature "W. Moorcroft, des. - Rd. No. 431157," ca. 1904 (tight hairlines to base) 770.00

Vase, 13" h., ovoid body tapering to a short, rolled rim, decorated in low-relief w/a large band of fruits & leaves in deep orange & burgundy against a very dark blue ground, impressed & glazed "Moorcroft" marks 3,680.00

Vase, 16¼" h., baluster-form, incised w/undulating iris blossoms & leafage & glazed in shades of green & blue, signed "W. Moorcroft" in green, early 20th c. 1,955.00

MULBERRY

Mulberry Jeddo Pattern Plate

Mulberry or Flow Mulberry wares were produced in the Staffordshire district of England in the period between 1835 and 1855 at many of the same factories which produced its close "cousin," Flow Blue china. In fact, some of the early Flow Blue patterns were also decorated with the purplish mulberry coloration and feature the same heavy smearing or "flown" effect. Produced on sturdy ironstone bodies, quite a bit of this ware is still to be found and it is becoming increasingly sought-after by collectors although presently its values lag somewhat behind similar Flow Blue pieces. The standard reference to Mulberry wares is Petra Williams' book, Flow Blue China and Mulberry Ware, Similarity and Value Guide.

Bowl, 10" l., rectangular, Rose patt., Edward Challinor $150.00
Chamber pot, cov., Udina patt., J. Clementson....................350.00
Coffeepot, cov., Medina patt., Jacob Furnival 325.00
Coffeepot, cov., Montezuma patt., J. Godwin....................295.00
Coffeepot, cov., Rhone Scenery patt., T.J. & J. Mayer....................275.00
Coffeepot, cov., Vincennes patt., Samuel Alcock (finial replaced) 325.00
Creamer, Abbey patt., Wm. Adams & Sons....................150.00
Creamer, Cyprus patt., Davenport......225.00
Creamer, Flora patt., Hulme & Booth 165.00
Creamer, Panama patt., Edward Challinor....................225.00
Creamer, Rose patt., Thomas Walker....................225.00
Creamer, Sydenhan patt., J. Clementson....................190.00
Creamer, Vincennes patt., Samuel Alcock 275.00
Creamer, Washington Vase patt., Podmore, Walker & Co. 210.00
Creamer & cov. sugar bowl, Genoa patt., Davenport, pr. 395.00
Cup & saucer, large, Corean patt. 95.00
Cup & saucer, handleless, Jeddo patt., Wm. Adams & Sons....................75.00
Cup & saucer, handleless, Montezuma patt., J. Godwin 75.00
Cup & saucer, handleless, Neva patt., Edward Challinor 55.00
Cup & saucer, handleless, Peruvian patt., John Wedge Wood 98.00
Cup & saucer, Rhone Scenery patt., Podmore, Walker & Co. 75.00
Cup & saucer, Tonquin patt., Heath 65.00
Cup plate, Athens patt., Wm. Adams & Sons 65.00
Cup plate, Corean patt., Podmore, Walker & Co....................60.00
Cup plate, Shapoo patt., Boote 65.00
Cup plate, Vincennes patt., Samuel Alcock 65.00
Gravy boat, Jeddo patt., Wm. Adams & Sons 175.00
Honey dish, Cyprus patt., Davenport....65.00
Honey dish, Peruvian patt., John Wedge Wood 75.00
Ladle holder, Sydenhan patt., J. Clementson....................95.00
Pitcher, 6¾" h., 1½ pt., Corean patt., Podmore, Walker & Co. 275.00
Pitcher, 8" h., Castle Scenery patt., J. Furnival (tiny repaired flake) 325.00
Pitcher, 8¼" h., Dresden patt., Edward Challinor 275.00
Pitcher, 9⅞" h., Hong patt., Thomas Walker, 2 qt....................425.00
Pitcher & bowl set, Corean patt., Podmore, Walker & Co., 2 pcs. (tiny nick on pitcher & ¾" fine hairline under bowl rim) 875.00
Plate, child's, 4⅛" d., Jeddo patt., Wm. Adams & Sons....................95.00
Plate, 6½" d., Washington Vase patt., Podmore, Walker & Co. 65.00
Plate, 7" d., Alleghany patt., T. Goodfellow 35.00
Plate, 7" d., Corean patt., Podmore, Walker & Co....................50.00
Plate, 7" d., Washington Vase patt., Podmore, Walker & Co. 52.00
Plate, 8" d., Corean patt., Podmore, Walker & Co....................45.00
Plate, 8" d., Temple patt., Podmore, Walker & Co....................45.00
Plate, 8½" d., Jeddo patt., Wm. Adams & Sons (ILLUS.)....................60.00
Plate, 8½" d., Neva patt., Edward Challinor....................45.00
Plate, 8½" d., Pelew patt., Edward Challinor....................50.00
Plate, 9" d., Peruvian patt., John Wedge Wood 55.00
Plate, 9" d., Washington Vase patt., Podmore, Walker & Co. 60.00
Plate, 9½" d., Peruvian patt., John Wedge Wood 89.00
Plate, 9½" d., Rose patt., Thomas Walker....................75.00
Plate, 9½" d., Tonquin patt., Heath.......50.00
Plate, 9⅞" d., Corean patt., Podmore, Walker & Co....................85.00
Plate, 10" d., Bochara patt., John Edwards 75.00
Plate, 10½" d., Cyprus patt., Davenport....................75.00
Plate, 10½" d., Pelew patt., Edward Challinor....................65.00
Platter, 10" l., Neva patt., Edward Challinor....................95.00
Platter, 10 x 13½", Washington Vase patt., Podmore, Walker & Co. 150.00

Platter, 10½" l., Tonquin patt., Heath....75.00

Platter, 12 x 15½", Rhone Scenery patt., T.J. & J. Mayer........................225.00

Platter, 13½" l., Heath's Flower patt., T. Heath 295.00

Platter, 14" l., Washington Vase patt., Podmore, Walker & Co. 150.00

Platter, 15¼" l., Bochara patt., John Edwards.......................................195.00

Platter, 15½" l., Athens patt., Charles Meigh 175.00

Relish dish, large, Vincennes patt., Samuel Alcock 195.00

Sauce boat, Corean patt., Podmore, Walker & Co. (hairlines) 95.00

Sauce dish, Alleghany patt., Thomas Goodfellow, 6½" d.................................40.00

Sauce dish, Pelew patt., Edward Challinor, 4½" d. 55.00

Sauce dish, Pelew patt., Edward Challinor, 5¼" d. 65.00

Sauce dish, Rhone Scenery patt., T.J. & J. Mayer, 4½" d. 55.00

Sauce tureen, Corean patt., Podmore, Walker & Co.......................................295.00

Sauce tureen, cover & underplate, Bochara patt., John Edwards, the set...525.00

Sauce tureen, cover & underplate, Vincennes patt., Samuel Alcock, the set (finial reset & professional repair) 525.00

Soup plate w/flanged rim, Washington Vase patt., Podmore, Walker & Co., 9½" d., ...55.00

Sugar bowl, cov., Castle Scenery patt., Thomas Furnival 275.00

Sugar bowl, cov., hexagonal, Corean patt., Podmore, Walker & Co. 350.00

Sugar bowl, cov., hexagonal, Hyson patt., J. Clementson.........................275.00

Sugar bowl, cov., Jeddo patt., Wm. Adams & Sons 175.00

Teapot, cov., Corean patt., Podmore, Walker & Co. (finial reset) 490.00

Teapot, cov., Foliage patt., E. Walley (finial reset)..375.00

Teapot, cov., Jeddo patt., Wm. Adams & Sons 465.00

Tea set: cov. teapot, cov. sugar bowl & creamer; Jeddo patt., Wm. Adams & Sons, 3 pcs.......................................595.00

Vegetable bowl, cov., Corean patt., Podmore, Walker & Co. 550.00

Vegetable bowl, cov., Cyprus patt., Davenport (finial reset) 450.00

Vegetable bowl, cov., Jeddo patt., Wm. Adams & Sons.........................495.00

Vegetable bowl, open, Pelew patt., Edward Challinor, 9¼" d. 175.00

Vegetable bowl, open, Temple patt., Podmore, Walker & Co., 7" d...........145.00

Waste bowl, Corean patt., Podmore, Walker & Co., 4 x 6½" (tiny faint hairline) 195.00

Waste bowl, Washington Vase patt., Podmore, Walker & Co. (tiny edge flake) 195.00

NEWCOMB COLLEGE POTTERY

Newcomb College Scenic Plaque

This pottery was established in the art department of Newcomb College, New Orleans, Louisiana, in 1897. Each piece was hand-thrown and bore the potter's mark and decorator's monogram on the base. It was always a studio business and never operated as a factory and its pieces are therefore scarce, with the early wares being eagerly sought. The pottery closed in 1940.

Bowl, 4" d., 3" h., decorated w/a band of green abstract foliage against a blue ground, matte finish, Sadie Irvine, 1933 ....$660.00

Bowl, 8¼" d., 3" h., wide squatty bulbous form w/a flat bottom, decorated around the upper half w/a continuous garland of large white stylized gardenias against a deep bluish green body, by Henrietta Bailey, probably sold at the 1904 Louisiana Purchase Exposition, incised mark "NC - HB - JM - W - CX21" 4,675.00

Box, cov., round cylindrical low sides w/a flared rim & inset slightly domed cover w/button finial, decorated w/the Espanol patt., blue stripes & blue & white swags around the body, decorated by Sadie Irvine, 1925, 2¾" h. (firing separation at finial) 1,100.00

Candlestick, a wide squatty cushion base tapering sharply to a slender standard below a cupped drip pan & cylindrical candle socket, matte bluish green speckled glaze dripping over a matte blue ground, incised "NC - JM," 6½" d., 11" h....................412.50

Creamer, spherical body decorated w/thin blue stripes on a pale blue ground, the short cylindrical neck molded w/a band of small inverted pineapples in blue, dark blue angled handle, potted by Joseph Meyer, decorated by Alice R. Urquhart, 1904, 3⅝" h......................................935.00

Jar, cov., wide bulbous ovoid body tapering slightly to a wide, low domed cover, the base w/a wide incised band of stylized sweet peas in pale blue against a deep blue ground, the cover w/the motto "Here are sweet peas on the tip toe for a flight" around a large central white blossom, glossy glaze, by Mazie T. Ryan, 1904, 6" d., 7¾" h.........10,450.00

Mug, cylindrical body flaring at the base, angled handle, decorated w/a wide upper band of stylized ivory flowers w/green stems above a cobalt blue band over the green base, cobalt blue handle, by Leona Nicholson, 1906, 3" d., 3" h...........1,870.00

Pitcher, tankard, 6⅞" h., tall tapering cylindrical body w/pinched spout & long round strap handle, decorated w/a stylized band of bluebell blossoms & leaves suspended from the rim in dark blue & bluish green against a pale blue ground, potted by Joseph Meyer, decorated by Sarah B. Levy, 1903 (dark line inside rim does not come through) 2,750.00

Plaque, rectangular, "Palms," scene w/large palm trees in the foreground, the foliage in bluish green, trees & border in blue, the lower sky a pale pink changing to light blue, matte glaze, kiln particles, framed, incised & painted "NC," impressed "84," incised artist's cipher, "Shape No. 514" on reverse & paper label, ca. 1915, 5¾ x 9¾" (ILLUS.).........4,400.00

Vase, miniature, 2" h., 3" d., wide tapering cylindrical body molded in relief around the sides w/a band of stylized foliate design in mauve, green & grey matte glaze on a blue ground, incised "NC Sa 14 12" & artist's initials 715.00

Vase, 4½" h., 5" d., squatty bulbous ovoid body tapering to a wide, flat mouth, decorated w/a night landscape w/a full moon shining through oak trees hung w/Spanish moss, in shades of light & dark blue w/a white moon, by Sadie Irvine, 1931 ....1,320.00

Vase, 5½" h., globular w/short wide neck, matte bluish green glaze w/blue background at neck & shoulder, decorated w/pale blue & yellow poppy blossoms, green & yellow leafy stems & buds, impressed "JM," "176" & "B" in a circle, inscribed "GH27" & incised artist's cipher, Cynthia Littlejohn, ca.1912 ....1,870.00

Vase, 6¼" h., 6¼" d., spherical body w/short rim, upper portion decorated in high glaze w/large yellow freesia blossoms & bluish green foliage against an ivory ground, over a light green base, incised or ink marks "NC - M.W.B - UU97 - JM - X - Q," by M.W. Butler, 1904 ....7,150.00

Vase, 7" h., 6½" d., spherical body tapering to a short flat neck, glossy glaze decorated w/a large band of floral sprigs w/ochre flowers framed by sage green leafy branches all on a white ground, possibly by Mary Reinfort, impressed mark "NC - X - J59 - MR," 1902 (hairline in rim).......4,400.00

Early Newcomb College Vase

Vase, 8¼" h., 5½" d., tapering ovoid body w/wide closed mouth, decorated w/a band of large stylized trees w/green foliage outlined in cobalt blue & w/blue trunks, by Grace Blethen, 1902, signed "NC - JM - V46 - Q" (ILLUS.) 5,775.00

Vase, 10½" h., 6" d., wide ovoid body tapering slightly to a wide, flat mouth, decorated around the shoulder w/large pink pine cones & green needles against a matte blue ground, by H. Bailey, 1919 ....3,960.00

Vase, 12⅛" h., tall slender ovoid body decorated w/a band of tall, slender oak trees in greenish blue against a cream & green ground, potted by Joseph Meyer, decorated by Maria de Hoa LeBlanc, 1909 ......25,300.00

NILOAK

This pottery was made in Benton, Arkansas, and featured hand-thrown varicolored swirled clay decoration in objects of classic forms. Designated Mission Ware, this line is the most desirable of Niloak's production which was begun early in this century. Less expensive to produce, the cast Hywood Line, finished with either high gloss or semi-matte glazes, was introduced during the economic depression of the 1930s. The pottery ceased operation about 1946.

Niloak Candlesticks

Candlesticks, Mission Ware, wide flaring base tapering to a segmented shaft, bowl-shaped candlecup, swirled clays, marked & w/paper labels, 5½" d., 8¼" h., pr. (ILLUS.) $220.00

Candlesticks, Mission Ware, widely flaring base tapering to a slender shaft ending in a wide, rounded candlecup, swirled clays, 9" h., pr....275.00

Candy jar, cov., Mission Ware, marbleized swirls, w/paper label, 8½" h...2,550.00

Cornucopia-vase, feathered rim & crest, fluted tail, glossy light blue glaze, 7 x 8" 20.00

Cornucopia-vase, Hywood Line, pink glaze 12.00

Hatpin holder, Mission Ware, marbleized swirls, 6" h. 925.00

Jardiniere, Mission Ware, marbleized swirls, 7 x 8½" 225.00

Jardiniere, Mission Ware, marbleized swirls, 8½ x 9½" 400.00

Pitcher, 5" h., bulbous w/rim spout, tannish ivory glaze 8.50

Planter, Hywood line, model of a camel, green glaze 40.00

Planter, Hywood Line, model of a canoe, brown glaze, 8" l.....................30.00

Planter, Hywood Line, model of an elephant, matte maroon glaze 35.00

Planter, Hywood Line, model of a monkey, pink glaze 22.00

Planter, Hywood Line, model of a rabbit, green glaze 25.00

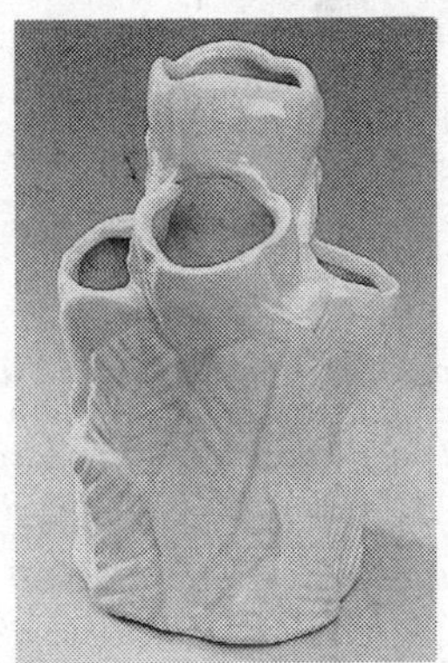

Niloak Strawberry Pot-Vase

Strawberry pot-vase, relief-molded w/staggered tulip-like blossoms & veined leaves, light blue glaze, 6½" h. (ILLUS.) 25.00

Vase, 4¾" h., Mission Ware, rolled rim, blue, brown & cream marbleized swirls 55.00

Vase, 5" h., Mission Ware, burnt orange ground w/blue & brown marbleized swirls 145.00

Vase, 6" h., 3½" d., flared rim w/wing shoulder handles, rose glaze, relief-molded mark 10.00

Vase, 6" h., 4" d., Mission Ware, marbleized shades of tan...................85.00

Vase, 6¼" h., Mission Ware, marbleized swirls of brown & blue, unmarked 125.00

Vase, 6½" h., bulbous melon-ribbed body w/a spiral twist neck w/scalloped rim, wing side handles, pea green glaze 10.00

Vase, 8" h., Mission Ware, blue & cream marbleized swirls 395.00

Vase, 8¾" h., 4½" d., Mission Ware, ovoid body tapering to a short neck w/a widely flaring rim, marbleized blue, brown & ivory clays, marked...165.00

Vase, 10¼" h., 5" d., Mission Ware, tall baluster-form body w/cupped rim, swirled multicolored clays, marked 220.00

NIPPON

Ornate Nippon Jar

"Nippon" is a term which is used to describe a wide range of porcelain wares produced in Japan from the late 19th century until about 1921. It was in 1891 that the U.S. implemented the McKinley Tariff Act which required that all wares exported to the United States carry a marking indicating the country of origin. The Japanese chose to use "Nippon," their name for Japan. In 1921 the import laws were revised and the words "Made in" had to be added to the markings. Japan was also required to replace the "Nippon" with the English name "Japan" on all wares sent to the U.S.

Many Japanese factories produced Nippon porcelains and much of it was hand-painted with ornate floral or landscape decoration and heavy gold decoration, applied beading and slip-trailed designs referred to as "moriage." We indicate the specific marking used on a piece, when known, at the end of each listing below. Be aware that a number of Nippon markings have been reproduced and used on new porcelain wares.

Important reference books on Nippon include: The Collector's Encyclopedia of Nippon Porcelain, Series One through Three, *by Joan F. Van Patten (Collector Books, Paducah, Kentucky) and* The Wonderful World of Nippon Porcelain, 1891-1921 *by Kathy Wojciechowski (Schiffer Publishing, Ltd., Atglen, Pennsylvania).*

Ashtray, rounded triangular form w/swelled sides, decorated on the interior w/sailboats, 5½" w. (green "M" in wreath mark)......................$85.00

Basket w/overhead handle, pink roses on gold stippled ground, 7¾" d., 7½" h..285.00

Bowl, 5¼" sq., decorated w/a leafy branch heavily laden w/peaches, trimmed w/jeweled black tracery........65.00

Bowl, 7½" d., footed, relief-molded nuts decoration 145.00

Bowl, 7½" l., two-handled, footed, decorated w/h.p. pink roses, moriage border 30.00

Bowl, 8¾" d., two-handled, floral & geometric decoration, gold trim 65.00

Bowl, 9" d., turned-up gold handles, decorated w/a landscape scene, red & gold border 95.00

Bowl, 9½" d., ornate mold, "gaudy" floral decoration & lavish gold..........135.00

Bowl, 9½" d., two-handled, roses decoration w/gold trim & gold handles 55.00

Bowl, 9½" d., two-handled, decorated w/scene of house & tree beside a lake, gold handles 58.00

Bowl, 10" d., 2" h., white & raised gold chrysanthemums on pale peach & yellow ground, scalloped rim w/elaborate geometric decoration, gold beading, unmarked 75.00

Box, cov., decorated w/violets, 5" d. (green "M" in Wreath mark)................25.00

Butter bowl, cover & strainer, white w/light blue & green floral decoration, gold trim around rims, handles & finial (China E-OH mark)...60.00

Cake set: open-handled 9¾" d. plate & six matching 6½" d. plates; windmill & sunset scene, 7 pcs. 120.00

Casserole, cov., decorated w/small pink flowers, 7½ x 10" oval 125.00

Celery set: oval handled tray & six tiny oval trays; h.p. plums on branch in almond, greens & brown w/geometric border design, 7 pcs. (green "M" in Wreath mark)................................150.00 to 170.00

Cheese & cracker plate, blossom decoration w/gold trim, 8½" d. 44.00

Chocolate pot, cov., decorated w/water lilies & pads, trim & jewels in shades of purple & lavender w/gold accents, bud finial on cover..175.00

Chocolate set: cov. chocolate pot & five cups; decorated w/azaleas & lavish gold trim, 6 pcs. 185.00

Creamer & cov. sugar bowl, Nile River scene decoration, pr. 85.00

Demitasse set: cov. pot, creamer, cov. sugar bowl & four cups & saucers; decorated w/trees in a meadow, 11 pcs...................................85.00

Dessert set: six cake plates, four cups & saucers, creamer, sugar bowl & 4" d. nut dish; gold tracery decoration on white ground, 17 pcs. 120.00

Dish, divided w/center basket handle, floral decoration, gold beading & trim, 5" d. 85.00

Dresser set: 4½ x 6½" tray w/attached hatpin holder, stickpin holder & ring tree; decorated w/pastel green, yellow & orange florals, gold trim, unmarked 95.00

Ferner, quadrilobed body w/rim handles, h.p. desert scene of Arab on camel at an oasis, gold handles & feet, 10¾" w. across handles, 5¾" h. 310.00

Hatpin holder, woodland scene, 4¾" h. (blue Maple Leaf mark).........295.00

Hatpin holder, decorated w/green flowers around top, gold & white ground..65.00

Humidor, cov., h.p. Victorian coaching scene around the sides, moriage Greek key rim band, 5½" h., Maple Leaf mark 525.00

Humidor, cov., barrel-shaped, sailboat scene around the sides, 6" h. (green "M" in Wreath mark) 350.00

Humidor, cov., cylindrical w/flared base & rim, decorated w/a three-quarter length portrait of an old accordion player against a shaded dark brown ground, 6" h. (green "M" in Wreath mark) 575.00

Jar, cov., squatty bulbous body on three short legs, wide domed cover w/gold berry finail, three gold loop handles on shoulder, h.p. yellow flowers & green leaves w/gold trim, 6¼" d., 5½" h. green "M" in Wreath mark (ILLUS.) 125.00

Lemonade set: 7" h., 5¾" d. pitcher & three 3⅝" h. mugs; lakeside scene w/jeweled brown rims, 4 pcs. 115.00

Mustard jar, cover & underplate, h.p. river scene, lavish gold trim (green "M" in Wreath mark)..........................50.00

Mustard jar & cover on attached undertray, h.p. lakeside sunset scene & gold beading 75.00

Pitcher, 9" h., jug-type, coralene design of roses on cobalt blue ground..425.00

Plaque, pierced to hang, decorated w/h.p. head of a dog, moriage decoration in blue on border, 8½" d. (green "M" in Wreath Mark).............425.00

Plaque, pierced to hang, rural road scene w/apple tree in foreground, 9" d. (green "M" in Wreath mark) 225.00

Plaque, pierced to hang, decorated w/pink wild roses, 9" d. 75.00

Plaque, pierced to hang, decorated w/matte-glazed windmill scene, narrow brown border, 10" d., (green "M" in Wreath mark) 120.00

Plate, 10½" d., handled, hunt scene decoration (Maple Leaf mark) 120.00

Plates, 6½" d., decorated w/roses & gold beading, set of 6 ....60.00

Powder jar, cov., three-footed, elaborate gold scrolls & beaded medallions w/beaded green swags, gold trim, 3 x 4½" (blue Maple Leaf mark)...80.00

Sugar shaker, decorated w/grapes & gold leaves on a white ground (blue Maple Leaf mark) 55.00

Syrup pitcher, cover & underplate, decorated w/gold flowers & leaves, raised gold outlining & beading on white & ivory ground, 4¼" h., the set (Royal Nippon mark) 90.00

Tea set: cov. teapot, creamer, cov. sugar bowl & four cups & saucers; moriage dragon decoration, 11 pcs. 200.00

Tea set: cov. teapot, creamer, cov. sugar bowl, four tea plates & four cups & saucers; decorated w/jewels & gold butterflies, ornate butterfly finials, 15 pcs. 115.00

Toothpick holder, three-handled, sailboats decoration, 2" h................150.00

Toothpick holder, cylindrical w/three loop handles, lakeside landscape decoration, 2¼" h. (green "M" in Wreath mark) 60.00

Vase, 4½" h., 2½" d., flattened ovoid body on a funnel-form foot, tapering at the top w/a short flared neck flanked by D-form loop handles, central four-lobed reserve decorated w/a pink rose & surrounded by overall moriage loops & beading in blue, pink & green on a greyish green ground, unmarked 65.00

Vase, 5½" h., 4½" d., footed bulbous melon-lobed body tapering to a short ruffled neck flanked by small loop handles on the shoulder, h.p. large pink rose & green leaves on a shaded pink & blue ground, moriage trim around the neck, Cherry Blossom mark 110.00

Vase, 6" h., 4¾" d., decorated w/h.p. lavender flowers & leaves on yellow, stylized raised black enamel flowers & leaves outlined in gold & gold trim (green "M" in Wreath mark).............110.00

Vase, 7" h., squatty bulbous body tapering to a short flared neck, overall relief-molded acorns & leaves (blue Maple Leaf mark) 450.00

Nippon Vase with Molded Strawberries

Vase, 9¾" h., tall ovoid body tapering to a small short flared neck, overall relief-molded red strawberries & green leaves decoration, green "M" in Wreath mark (ILLUS.) 460.00

Vase, 11¼" h., tall cylindrical body w/flared foot & scroll-molded & scalloped rim issuing long scrolling loop handles, decorated w/long clusters of purple & white wisteria against a shaded tan ground (Maple Leaf mark)....................250.00

Vase, 15¼" h., 7½" d., h.p. woodland scene w/grouse, base & rim borders decorated w/relief gold pattern (green Maple Leaf mark) 325.00

NORITAKE

Noritake Spoon Holder

Noritake china, still in production in Japan, has been exported in large quantities to this country since early in this century. Though the Noritake Company first registered in 1904, it did not use "Noritake" as part of its backstamp until 1918. Interest in Noritake has escalated as collectors now seek out pieces made between the "Nippon" era and World War II (1921-41). The Azalea pattern is also popular with collectors.

Ashtray, hexagonal, Art Deco style dancing couple in center, tan lustre ground, artist-signed, 3 x 3½" $125.00

Ashtray, figural pelican, blue on orange & white ground....................145.00

Basket, Tree in Meadow patt., "Dolly Varden," No. 213, 2½ x 4⅜", overall 4" h. ....75.00 to 100.00

Berry set: 10½" d. master bowl w/ pierced handles & six 5¼" d. sauce dishes; Tree in Meadow patt., 7 pcs. 150.00

Bouillon cup & saucer, Azalea patt., No. 124 ....22.00

Bowl, cream soup, 5⅛" d., Azalea patt., No. 363 ....150.00

Bowl, 5¼" d., handled, Art Deco style, center medallion w/colorful Art Deco lady feeding parrot a cracker, scalloped black trimmed rim, tan lustre ground, artist-signed 160.00

Bowl, 7" d., footed, Art Deco style, flower-shaped, decorated w/lavender flowers in orange circular panel, black diamond-shaped outlining 42.00

Breakfast set: sugar shaker & syrup pitcher on matching trivet; decorated w/colorful exotic birds on orange lustre ground, 3 pcs. 110.00

Butter (or cheese) dish, cov., Azalea patt., No. 314 ....125.00

Butter dish, cov., pearlized w/gold trim & handle, Nippon mark 60.00

Butter pat, Azalea patt., No. 312 ....85.00

Butter tub, Azalea patt., No. 54 ....40.00

Cake plate, handled, sunset scene w/tree, boat, water, purple sage & mountain, 8" d. (green "M" in Wreath mark)....................45.00

Cake plate, colorful florals on lustre ground, 9½" d. 58.00

Candlesticks, flaring base w/cylindrical standard, sunset scene w/tree & water, 6½" h., pr. (green "M" in Wreath mark) 105.00

Candlesticks, decorated w/gold flowers & bird on blue lustre ground, 7½" h., pr. (green "M" in Wreath mark)....................125.00

Candy dish, cov., stylized floral decoration on turquoise ground, 6½" d....................90.00

Coffee set, demitasse: cov. demitasse pot, creamer, cov. sugar bowl, four cups & saucers; Tree in Meadow patt.,11 pcs. 275.00

Compote, 6½" d., 2¾" h., Azalea patt., No. 170 ....85.00

Condiment set: salt & pepper shakers & cov. mustard jar w/spoon on handled tray; Tree in Meadow patt., No. 49, the set 45.00

Creamer & sugar bowl w/basket handle, Art Deco style, decorated w/two Japanese lanterns on a cobalt blue ground, pr.....................................40.00

Creamer & sugar shaker, Azalea patt., No. 122, creamer 5¾" h., shaker 6½" h., pr.............125.00 to 150.00

Cruet w/original stopper, Azalea patt., No. 190 ....180.00

Cruet set w/original stoppers, oil & vinegar, the two globular bottles at angles & joined at the base w/a covered handle joining them at the shoulder, Tree in Meadow patt., No. 319, tip to tip 6½" 125.00

Dessert set: large cake plate & five individual plates; cobalt blue & gold decoration on white, 6 pcs. 85.00

Dresser set: cov. powder jar, pin tray, pair of candlesticks & large tray; geometric design in turquoise & gold, 5 pcs. 165.00

Dresser tray, handled, flamboyantly dressed Art Deco-style lady decoration, blue & green lustre finish, gold handles 275.00

Egg cup, Azalea patt., No. 120............50.00

Hair receiver, cov., Art Deco style, geometric design on gold lustre ground, 3¼" h., 3½" d. (green "M" in Wreath mark) 50.00

Humidor, cov., cigar & matches decoration, 5½" h. (green "M" in Wreath mark) 250.00

Loving cup, pedestal base, scenic decoration in front medallion, enameling & moriage trim 95.00

Mustard jar, cov., parrot decoration on pearlized ground 40.00

Mustard jar, cov., w/attached liner, decorated w/flowers, beading & gold 65.00

Napkin ring, Art Deco style, decorated w/a bust portrait of a girl in red fur-trimmed outfit, blue lustre ground, 2½" w. 40.00

Pitcher, milk, 5⅝" h., jug-type, Azalea patt., No. 100, 1 qt. 100.00

Place card holders, blue lustre base w/white stripe & figural butterfly, pr. (green "M" in Wreath mark)................35.00

Plaque, pierced to hang, relief-molded w/three brown & white dog heads....595.00

Plate, bread & butter, 6½" d., Azalea patt., No. 8 ....9.00

Plate, 6" d., Tree in Meadow patt. 9.00

Plate, 8½" d., Azalea patt., No. 98..........15.00

Plate, dinner, 9¾" d., Azalea patt., No. 13 ....26.00

Plates, 7½" d., Tree in Meadow patt., No. 44, set of 6 ....75.00

Platter, 14" l., Azalea patt., No. 17........98.00

Platter, turkey, 16" l., Azalea patt., No. 186 ....300.00 to 325.00

Refreshment set: shaped plate & cup; Azalea patt., No. 39, 2 pcs................35.00

Refreshment set: tray w/cup; Tree in Meadow patt., 2 pcs...........................25.00

Relish dish, two-lobed form w/center handle, Azalea patt., No. 450, 7½" l. 30.00

Relish dish, oval, Azalea patt., No. 18, 8¼" l. 20.00

Relish dish, w/figural orange bird in center (green"M" in Wreath mark)......95.00

Sandwich server w/center handle, decorated w/stylized fruit basket designs 58.00

Soup plate, Azalea patt., No. 19...........25.00

Spoon holder, narrow oblong shape w/gold angular end handles, bright orange ground w/colored Oriental landscape scenes (ILLUS.)................57.50

Sugar bowl, basket-shaped, scenic decoration 38.00

Sugar bowl, cov., Azalea patt., No. 7 ...22.50

Syrup pitcher, cov., pansy decoration 25.00

Teapot, cov., Azalea patt., 5-cup size, No. 15, 4½" h. 175.00

Tea set, child's: cov. teapot, creamer, sugar bowl, two cups & saucers, six 4¼" d. plates; parrots on swing decoration, 13 pcs. 175.00

Tea set: cov. teapot, creamer, sugar bowl & six cups & saucers; Tree in Meadow patt., 15 pcs.........................225.00

Tea tile, round, Azalea patt., No. 169 ....40.00

Tray, handled, center decoration of rose & mauve flowers, cobalt blue border w/lavish gold beading & gold handles, 11¼" l. 85.00

Tray, Art Deco style, decorated w/a portrait of a brunette lady wearing a white dress w/blue design & a spray of pink flowers, orange lustre ground w/blue trim (green"M" in Wreath mark)..165.00

Vase, 5" h., gold lustre ground decorated w/scarlet birds & flowers in ovals, 1930s...................................35.00

Vase, double, 7" h., gate-form, two scalloped tapering tubes joined by two bars, a colorful orange parrot perched on the top bar.....................225.00

Vegetable dish, cov., Art Deco style, decorated w/orange & black floral design on lustre ground, 9" d. (green "M" in Wreath mark) 40.00

Vegetable bowl, cov., Azalea patt., 10" d., No. 101 ....60.00

Wall pocket, Art Deco vase filled w/flowers decoration, blue lustre ground, slight wear on bottom (green "M" in Wreath mark)................65.00

OHR (George) POTTERY

Tall Ohr Mug

George Ohr, the eccentric potter of Biloxi, Mississippi, worked from about 1883 to 1906. Some think him to be one of the most expert throwers the craft will ever see. The majority of his works were hand-thrown, exceedingly thin-walled items, some of which have a crushed or folded appearance. He considered himself the foremost potter in the world and declined to sell much of his production, instead accumulating a great horde to leave as a legacy to his children. In 1972 this collection was purchased for resale by an antiques dealer.

Bowl, 4½" d., 2¼" h., the squatty rounded footed body tapering to a widely flaring rolled, pinched & lobed rim, pink exterior w/green & blue sponged decoration, olive green interior, die-stamped mark "G.E. OHR - Biloxi, Miss." $1,320.00

Bowl, 8¾" w., 4" h., a footed, rounded body below a deeply folded & twisted rim, unglazed light beige clay, script signature 1,760.00

Candleholder, consisting of a floriform four-lobed ruffled receptacle covered in a gun-metal black glaze, on a flat square scalloped base covered in clear glaze, underneath is a die-stamped poem "A BILOXI WELCOME . . . .," die-stamped "G.E. OHR - Biloxi, Miss.," 1¾ x 4½" 880.00

Cup, two-handled, tall modified double gourd-form flanked by two dissimilar ear-shaped handles, dripping gun-metal & clear brownish green glaze, script signature, 6¼" w., 4½" h. 1,980.00

Inkwell, modeled in buff clay as a perfectly detailed log cabin, covered in an olive green glossy glaze, die-stamped "G.E. OHR - BILOXI," 2¼ x 3¼" ....

Mug, tall cylindrical body w/a band of pinched indentations around the middle & a deep twist the height of the sides, an angled loop handle, dead-matte dark green & black glaze, script signature, 4½" d., 4¾" h. (ILLUS.) 1,540.00

Pen holder, figural, a flat rectangular plaque incised w/squiggly lines & mounted w/a figural long-eared mule head w/a pen hole at the top of the head, overall mottled black glaze, base stamped "Geo. E. Ohr Biloxi, Miss.," 2⅝" l. (minor firing separation in base) 660.00

Pitcher, 3¼" h., 5" w., footed, pinched spout, cut-out handle, covered in a light mottled clear green glaze w/sponged gun-metal accents, die-stamped "G.E. OHR - Biloxi, Miss" 1,650.00

Pitcher, puzzle-type, 8¼" h., 8" d., w/groups of holes near the top, incised w/a gulf shore scene under a clear caramel glaze, script signature & die-stamped "Biloxi Miss - 1899" 2,970.00

Puzzle mug, slightly waisted cylindrical body pierced w/two rows of small holes near the rim, angled handle w/thin banding, clear brown speckled & gun-metal glaze, script signature, 5" w., 4" h. 605.00

Teapot, cov., spherical body w/a deep in-body twist band around the lower body, a deep galleried rim w/inset cover, swan's-neck spout & C-loop handle, clear dark blue glaze over an orange clay body, die-stamped mark "G.E. OHR - BILOXI," 7" l., 4¼" h. 3,300.00

Vase, 3½" h., 4¼" w., bulbous body w/full-length folds & dimples around the sides, gun-metal brown glaze, die-stamped mark "G.E. OHR - Biloxi, Miss." 1,980.00

Vase, 4¾" h., cylindrical body w/a bulbous swelled shoulder below the wide symmetrically folded & crimped flaring neck, glossy mottled black & brown glaze, base incised "GE Ohr" 990.00

Vase, 5½" h., 6" d., ovoid body w/the sides crumpled & the rim flared & pinched, superior leathery matte green, purple & red mottled glaze, script signature, restored (ILLUS. top next column) 9,350.00

Vase, 6½" h., 4" d., spherical base, cylindrical neck & deep flaring mouth, covered in a pigeon-feathered red & gun-metal brown

Bulbous Vase by Ohr

glaze against a honey brown base, incised "OHR - BILOXI" 3,640.00

Vase, 7" h., 4¾" d., barrel-shaped, short neck w/very deep in-body twist & cupped mouth, covered in clear glaze w/densely packed gun-metal brown speckles, die-stamped "G.E. OHR - Biloxi" 4,000.00

Vase, 8½" h., 5½" d., slightly globular w/large dimples in the sides & collapsed rim, covered in a pigeon-feathered olive, green, dark blue, rose & mustard glaze, clear glossy interior, marked "GEO. E. OHR - BILOXI, MISS." 14,300.00

OLD IVORY

Old Ivory china was produced in Silesia, Germany, in the late 1800s and takes its name from the soft white background coloring. A wide range of table pieces was made with the various patterns usually identified by a number rather than a name.

Old Ivory No. 16 Cracker Jar

Bacon platter, Thistle patt. $175.00

Berry set: master bowl & six sauce dishes; No. 15, 7 pcs. 295.00

Bowl, master berry, 9½" d., No. 75 ....75.00 to 100.00

Bowl, master berry, 9½" d., No. 84 ....100.00 to 125.00

Bun tray, No. 84 ....125.00

Cake plate, open-handled, No. 10, 9½" d. 92.50

Cake plate, open-handled, No. 11, 10" d. 60.00

Cake plate, open-handled, No. 15, 10" d. ....125.00 to 150.00

Cake plate, open-handled, No. 84, 10" d. 95.00

Cake set: 10" d., cake plate & nine dessert plates; No. 16, 10 pcs. 250.00

Chocolate pot, cov., No. 16, 10" h. 495.00

Chocolate set: cov. chocolate pot & six cups & saucers; No. 15, pot, 10" h., 13 pcs. 825.00

Cracker jar, cov., No. 16 (ILLUS.) 400.00

Creamer, No. 118 ....85.00

Creamer & cov. sugar bowl, No. 16, pr. ....125.00 to 150.00

Cup & saucer, No. 16 ....65.00

Dresser tray, La Touraine patt., lily of the valley blossoms in shades of green w/gold trim, artist-signed, 6 x 11½" 165.00

Plate, 6" d., No. 16 ....22.50

Plate, 7½" d., No. 15 ....25.00 to 50.00

Plate, 7½" d., No. 16 ....30.00

Plate, 7½" d., No. 84 ....50.00

Plate, 8" d., No. 84 ....55.00

Plate, 8¼" d., No. 16 ....35.00

Plate, 8½" d., No. 28 ....65.00

Plate, dinner, 9¾" d., No. 7 ....70.00

Plate, chop, 13" d., No. 11 ....185.00

Plate, chop, 13" d., No. 15 ....295.00

Plate, chop, 13" d., No. 16 ....150.00

Platter, cold meat, 8 x 11½", open-handled, No. 15 ....115.00

Platter, 11¾" oval, No. 16...135.00 to 165.00

Platter, cold meat, oval, No. 21 ....95.00

Relish dish, oval, handled, No. 15, 4¼ x 6½" 45.00

Relish dish, No. 84, 8½" l. ....75.00 to 100.00

Salt & pepper shakers, No. 16, pr. 135.00

Sauce dish, No. 16, 5½" d. 48.00

Sauce dish, No. 84, 5" d. 65.00

Tea tile, No. 16 ....145.00

Toothpick holder, No. 16 ....250.00 to 300.00

Toothpick holder, No. 84 ....250.00 to 275.00

Tureen, cov., No. 84 ....700.00

OLD SLEEPY EYE

Sleepy Eye, Minnesota, was named after an Indian chief. The Sleepy Eye Milling Co. had stoneware and pottery premiums made at the turn of the century first by the Weir Pottery Company and subsequently by Western Stoneware Co., Monmouth, Illinois. On these items the trademark Indian head was signed beneath "Old Sleepy Eye," The colors were Flemish blue on grey. Later pieces by Western Stoneware to 1937 were not made for Sleepy Eye Milling Co. but for other businesses. They bear the same Indian head but "Old Sleepy Eye" does not appear below. They have a reverse design of tepees and trees and may or may not be marked Western Stoneware on the base. These items are usually found in cobalt blue on cream and are rarer in other colors. In 1952, Western Stoneware made a 22 oz. and 40 oz. stein with a chestnut brown glaze. This mold was redesigned in 1968. From 1968 to 1973 a limited number of 40 oz. steins were produced for the Board of Directors of Western Stoneware. These were marked and dated and never sold as production items. Beginning with the first convention of the Old Sleepy Eye Club in 1976, Western Stoneware has made a souvenir which each person attending receives. These items are marked with the convention site and date. It should also be noted that there have been some reproduction items made in recent years.

Sleepy Eye Pitcher

Butter jar, Flemish blue on grey stoneware, Weir Pottery Co., 1903 ....$450.00 to 500.00

Pitcher, 4" h., cobalt blue on white, w/small Indian head on handle, Western Stoneware Co., 1906-37 (half pint) 190.00

Pitcher, 5¼" h., cobalt blue on white, w/small Indian head on handle, Western Stoneware Co., 1906-37 (pint) 250.00

Pitcher, 6¼" h., cobalt blue on white, w/small Indian head on handle, Western Stoneware Co., 1906-37, quart (ILLUS.) 325.00

Pitcher, 7¾" h., cobalt blue on white, w/small Indian head on handle, Western Stoneware Co., 1906-37 (half-gallon) ....225.00 to 275.00

Stein, brown on yellow, Western Stoneware Co., 7¾" h......................900.00

Stein, blue on white, Western Stoneware Co., 1906-37, 7¾" h.......600.00

Stein, Flemish blue on grey stoneware, Weir Pottery Co., 8" h....500.00

Vase, 9" h., Flemish blue on grey stoneware, Indian head signed, dragonfly, frog & bulrushes reverse, Weir Pottery Co., 1903 ....350.00 to 375.00

PACIFIC CLAY PRODUCTS

Pacific Clay Candleholder

At the beginning of the 1920s William Lacy merged several southern California potteries to form the Pacific Clay Products Company in Los Angeles. However, it was not until the early 1930s that Pacific began producing tableware and artware that has piqued the interest of today's collectors. Ceramic engineer, Frank McCann, and designer and head of the art department, Matthew Lattie, were largely responsible for Pacific's success. Pottery production ceased in 1942. Today the company has a plant in Corona, California specializing in roofing tiles.

Candleholder, double, rectangular base w/rounded corners, curved pedestal the length of base arching upward at one end w/a round holder on the top, then slanting down to the base w/a low round holder, jade green, 4½" h., 6" l. (ILLUS.) $33.00

Plate, 10¼" d., pie w/rim, deep blue without clip-on handles 32.00

Platter, 15" d., round w/numerous rings, tab handles, yellow glaze.........40.00

Vase, 3¼" h., 3" d., model of a miniature cornucopia on a base w/six rings near middle of body & w/six rings at the narrow end, maroon glossy glaze, Model No. 3010, ca. 1930s 18.00

Vase, 4¼" h., baluster shape w/elongated molded handles from center to under rim, maroon glaze.....20.00

Vase, 5" h., 6" d., bulbous body w/three horizontal rings near bottom & three horizontal rings at middle, jade green, Model No. 1500, raised circular mark, ca. late 1930s.............55.00

Vase, 6½" h., oval base, straight sides flaring gently to pleated & tiered rim, Model No. 3050, ca. 1938.................35.00

Vase, 7¼" h., 2¾" d., bottle shaped w/molded handles on each side near middle, mint green, Model No. 886 ....28.00

PARIAN

Parian Figure of John A. Andrews

Parian is unglazed porcelain in the biscuit stage, and takes its name from its resemblance to Parian marble used for statuary. Parian wares were made in this country and abroad through much of the last century and continue to be made.

Bust of Charles Dickens, 10¼" h......$200.00

Bust of Lord Byron, raised on a socle base, late 19th c., 8⅛" h. 66.00

Bust of a young woman, looking down w/a pensive expression, scalloped edge, raised on a low footed base, base marked "C. Delpeoh Art Union of London 1855," 13" h. (minor edge chips) 330.00

Figure of John A. Andrews, standing stocky gentleman wearing a long cloak over his suit, atop a square base w/cut corners, printed verse on the back on the base, impressed marks "M. Milmore Sc." & "Publishers - J. McD & S Boston -copyright," England, ca. 1867, chips on base, 21" h. (ILLUS.) 1,210.00

Figure of Daniel Webster, full-bodied, standing upright w/right hand in coat next to a fabric-draped half pillar w/books propped below, on a square base w/fringed floor cover, marked on reverse "T. Ball, Sculptor, Boston, MA 1853 - Patent Assigned to G.W. Nichols, Boston," 26" h...2,300.00

Figure group, a young woman in classical garb seated on a mound & holding a basket of fish, a young child seated at her side, 7¼" w., 6½" h. 175.00

Pitcher, 5½" h., the body molded in relief w/holly berries & leaves, a twisted twig handle, Minton, 19th c. 110.00

Pitcher, 8" h., footed ovoid body tapering to a low arched spout, strap handle, the sides w/relief-molded foliage framing oval medallions w/figural representations of day and night, 19th c. 137.50

Pitcher, cov., 9⅛" h., molded leaf & grain design w/green & yellow enameling, pewter lid, English registry mark 181.50

Planter, oblong, molded in high-relief w/a young girl & two turkeys & chicks, 10½" l., 6" h.........................200.00

PARIS & OLD PARIS

China known by the generic name of Paris and Old Paris was made by several Parisian factories from the 18th through the 19th century; some of it is marked and some is not. Much of it was handsomely decorated.

Paris Porcelain Centerpiece

Centerpiece, a round flaring reticulated basket set atop a pedestal surrounded by kneeling figures of angels holding ring wreaths above a round ormolu base w/raised scrolls & lions' masks & raised on paw feet, artist-signed, ca.1810 (ILLUS.) $29,700.00

Ecuelle & cover, each colorfully painted between gilt bands w/a wide border of birds beneath chaplets of roses suspending from their beaks gilt floral swags further suspended from foliate scrolls & octagonal panels framing smaller gold-ground panels of pink rose sprigs above further leaf scrolls suspending green laurel swags below the birds, the leaf-molded angular handles & loop knop heightened in gilding, ca. 1790, 7⅞ w. 460.00

Pots de creme (custard cups), cov., a pink border band decorated w/entwined ribbons & floral reserves, h.p. cups on scrolls in the center, by Boyer - Rue de la Paix, late 19th c., 3" h., set of 12 .... 920.00

Urns, octagonal body, the neck decorated w/flowers above a panel boss base flanked by mask handles above a circular socle; raised on a step plinth decorated w/wreaths & the initial "B," mid-19th c., 14½" h., pr. (restorations) 1,150.00

Vases, 11¾" h., blue-ground ovoid body decorated around the shoulder w/a wide tooled gilt border of floral paterae between beads & leafage issuing whorls suspending grape clusters & blossoms interrupted at the sides by gilt swan-form handles, the lower body w/a further dot-and oval border above the gilt waisted foot & integral square base (slight wear), the trumpet-form neck fully gilded, incised numerals "6" & "11" or "S," ca. 1825, pr. 2,588.00

Vases, 14⅜" h., gold ground reserved on the front of the ovoid body w/a rectangular panel colorfully painted w/a cluster of flowers on a russet & white marble ledge against a shaded brown ground within a tooled foliate surround, the reverse tooled w/Gothic arches & tracery between tooled floral & foliate borders on the lower body (one w/three tiny chips), shoulder & trumpet-form neck, the sides w/gilt loop handles molded w/foliate scrolls (one w/tiny chip) & paterae, the circular foot on an integral square base molded around the

Paris Porcelain Vases

edges w/blossoms & foliage, Darte Freres, Palais Royal No. 21 marks stenciled in iron-red, ca. 1820, 14⅜" h., pr. (ILLUS.) 19,550.00

Vases, 17" h., decorated w/a central floral panel surrounded by a scrolling gilt border on a cobalt blue ground flanked by scrolled handles, artist-signed, mid-19th c., pr. 2,875.00

PAUL REVERE POTTERY

Paul Revere Pottery Bowl

This pottery was established in Boston, Massachusetts, in 1906, by a group of philanthropists seeking to establish better conditions for underprivileged young girls of the area. Edith Brown served as supervisor of the small "Saturday Evening Girls Club" pottery operation which was moved, in 1912, to a house close to the Old North Church where Paul Revere's signal lanterns had been placed. The wares were mostly hand decorated in mineral colors and both sgraffito and molded decorations were employed. Although it became popular, it was never a profitable operation and always depended on financial contributions to operate. After the death of Edith Brown in 1932, the pottery foundered and finally closed in 1942.

Bowl, 6" d., 3¾" h., slightly canted sides & gently rounded shoulder, wide band at top of stylized incised blossoms in oyster white w/green foliage against an orange ground above a blue speckled body, ink marked "339-12-11 - S.E.G. - S.G., Sara Galner, 1911 ....$1,650.00

Bowl, 8½" d., 3" h., green-glazed w/sgraffito interior border of yellow nasturtium blossoms outlined in black below off-white band at rim, signed on base "S.E.G." & "SG" in circle (ILLUS.) 935.00

Box, cov., wide squatty bulbous body w/closed rim, low-domed cover w/button finial, overall bluish green glaze, dated "7/9/26," 5½" d., 4¼" h. 137.50

Canister, cov., upright hexagonal form w/low, flat cover, a blue band around the top & shoulder above a matte cream ground decorated w/a monogrammed round medallion in yellow & green w/a cream-colored rabbit, inscribed marks & artist-initialed, 4½" h. 550.00

Luncheon set: five mug-style cups, five dessert plates & five luncheon plates; cream ground decorated around the rim w/a repeating band of trees & sky in green & blue, designs outlined in black, signed & numbered, the set........................1,650.00

Mug, incised tree-filled landscape & solitary nightingale over the inscription "In the forest must always be a nightingale and in the soul a faith so faithful that it comes back even after it has been slain," glazed in greens, brown, blue, cream & yellow, decorated by Sara Galner, inscribed artist's initials & marks, ca. 1915, 4" h. 1,430.00

Pitcher, tankard, 7¾" h., incised & decorated w/stylized yellow tulips & brown leaves outlined in black on yellow ground w/a white horizontal ring below spout, spout loss & hairline, signed "SEG/AM" 660.00

Plate, 8½" d., incised center monogram "HOS" in a circle for Helen Osbourne Storrow, the border decorated w/a band of running pigs in brown, yellow & green, signed "SEG - F.L." & numbered.............1,870.00

Vase, 4¼" h., 3¾" d., wide ovoid body w/closed rim, overall green volcanic glaze, impressed mark & "5/25" 220.00

Vase, 6½" h., 3½" d., slightly swelled cylindrical body w/a flat rim, decorated around the upper half w/a banded landscape of broad stylized trees in ochre & brown against a white ground & above the ochre lower body, marked 825.00

Vase, 9" h., 4¾" d., swelled cylindrical body w/wide flat mouth, decorated w/stylized yellow tulips against a dark, light & teal blue mottled matte glaze, marked 2,200.00

Vase, 10½" h., 5½" d., tall ovoid body tapering to a wide flat mouth, glossy blue to teal blue drip glaze, impressed circular mark 385.00

PEWABIC

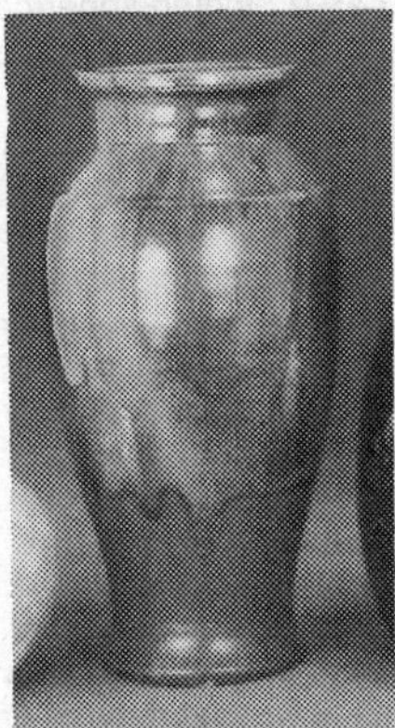

Fine Pewabic Vase

Mary Chase Perry (Stratton) and Horace J. Caulkins were partners in this Detroit, Michigan pottery. Established in 1903, Pewabic Pottery evolved from their Revelation Pottery, "Pewabic" meaning "clay with copper color" in the language of Michigan's Chippewa Indians. Caulkins attended to the clay formulas and Mary Perry Stratton was the artistic creator of forms & glaze formulas, eventually developing a wide range of colors for her finely textured glazes. The pottery's reputation for fine wares and architectural tiles enabled it to survive the depression years of the 1930s. After Caulkins died in 1923, Mrs. Stratton continued to be active in the pottery until her death, at age ninety-four, in 1961. Her contributions to the art pottery field are numerous.

Bowl, 1⅜" h., wide flat bottom & low incurved sides, a mottled glossy black glaze around the top half above a silvery green iridescent lower glaze, impressed mark & paper label w/original "$2.00" price $220.00

Bowl-vase, spherical body tapering to a low, flat molded rim, overall iridescent greyish blue glaze, impressed mark, ca. 1910, 3⅛" h. 302.50

Vase, miniature, 2¼" h., bulbous ovoid body w/a short cylindrical neck, overall mottled silver, grey, purple & blue iridescent glazing, marked on base 220.00

Vase, 3¾" h., 4¾" d., squatty bulbous body w/a wide shoulder to a short slightly flaring neck, matte cobalt blue glaze, incised mark 467.50

Vase, 4¾" h., 4" d., squatty bulbous base w/tapering cylindrical neck, mottled green & burgundy iridescent glaze, faint traces of impressed mark 550.00

Vase, 6" h., 4½" d., footed spherical body tapering to a short flaring neck, deep eggplant gun-metal glaze, impressed mark 990.00

Vase, 6¾" h., 3¾" d., ovoid body tapering to a flaring neck, iridescent burgundy & green glaze, w/paper label 715.00

Vase, 9" h., 7½" d., bulbous ovoid body tapering to a short wide & slightly flaring neck w/molded rim, iridescent copper glaze dripping over a cobalt blue body, w/paper label (restoration to rim)...............1,210.00

Vase, 10½" h., 5" d., baluster-form body w/sloping shoulder to a short cylindrical neck w/a flat molded rim, covered in a vibrant thick gold lustered glaze dripping over a matte dark blue body, die-stamped circular mark w/"PEWABIC - DETROIT" (ILLUS.) 3,850.00

PHOENIX BIRD & FLYING TURKEY PORCELAIN

The phoenix bird, a symbol of immortality and spiritual rebirth, has been handed down through Egyptian mythology as a bird that consumed itself by fire after 500 years and then rose again, renewed, from its ashes. This bird has been used to decorate Japanese porcelain designed for export for more than 100 years. The pattern incorporates a blue design of the bird, variously known as the "Flying Phoenix," the "Flying Turkey" or the "Ho-o," stamped on a white ground. It became popular with collectors because there was an abundant supply since the ware was produced for a long period of time. Pieces can be found marked with Japanese characters, with a "Nippon" mark, or a "Made in Japan" or "Occupied Japan" mark. Though there are several variations to the pattern and border, we have lumped them together since values seem to be quite comparable. A word of caution to the collectors, Phoenix Bird pattern is still being produced.

Phoenix Bird Plate

Casserole, cov., Phoenix Bird $45.00

Creamer, Phoenix Bird 12.50

Egg cup, Phoenix Bird............................16.00

Plate, 7" d., Phoenix Bird (ILLUS.) 12.00

Plate, dinner, 10" d., Phoenix Bird 30.00

Sugar bowl, cov., Phoenix Bird 18.50

Teapot, cov., one-cup size, Flying Turkey 35.00

PICKARD

Pickard, Inc., making fine hand-colored china today in Antioch, Illinois, was founded in Chicago in 1894 by Wilder A. Pickard. The company now makes its own blanks but once only decorated those bought from other potteries, primarily from the Havilands and others in Limoges, France.

Bowl, 6¼" d., 2¼" h., flowers & berries decoration, artist-initialed, pre-1915 mark $135.00

Bowl, 4½ x 7¼", 1¾" h., decorated w/nasturtiums & trailing stems, Haviland blank, ca. 1898 ....87.50

Bowl, 9" d., shallow, single open handle, pastel scenic decoration w/two fully-leaved trees & bush in foreground, leafless woods in background w/meandering stream, wide gold border, ca. 1912, artist-signed 295.00

Bowl, 9¼" d., 4¾" h., pedestal base, Modern Conventional patt., artist-signed 300.00

Cake plate, open-handled, decorated w/gold-outlined multi-colored leaves, artist-signed 95.00

Candy dish, round, ball-footed, decorated w/currants & lavish gold trim, artist-signed, Willets Belleek blank, ca. 1905 ....135.00

Celery tray, oval, center decoration of bunches of grapes hanging down from each side, yellow & purple w/green, blue & yellow leaves on cream ground, heavy gold edge band w/maroon design, artist-signed, 1898-1904 mark, 6⅝ x 14", 2½" h. 225.00

Charger, h.p. scenic decoration w/farm & stream, gold trim, artist-signed, 12" d. 250.00

Chocolate pot, cov., white w/gold trim, gold initials "C.E.," w/blue trim, ca. 1905 ....175.00

Coffeepot, cov., demitasse, Art Deco style, wide band of pastel water lilies, blue flowers & gold trim, artist-signed, Willets Belleek blank 195.00

Condensed milk can holder & underplate, h.p. iris decoration, gold trim, 6½" h., 2 pcs. (some gold wear) 78.00

Creamer, h.p. scenic decoration, artist-signed, 2¾" h. 125.00

Creamer & cov. sugar bowl, decorated w/violets, artist-signed, ca. 1898-1904, Silesia blank, pr. 325.00

Creamer, sugar bowl & tray, overall gold decoration, No. 486, 3 pcs. 75.00

Dresser set: 12" oval tray, 6" h. cov. powder jar, 5" d. hair receiver, 4" d. cov. jewelry box; decorated w/violets, tendrils, leaves, heavy gold trim, artist-signed, 1905-12 mark, impressed "B," Tresseman & Vogt, Limoges blank, the set 850.00

Dish, oval w/deep sides, h.p. daffodils, Limoges blank, ca. 1908, 12" l. 95.00

Gravy boat, decorated w/acorns, ca. 1905-10, artist-signed, M & Z - Austria blank 295.00

Jug w/original flat-topped stopper, tall waisted cylindrical body tapering to a short small neck, sharply angled handle from the neck to the shoulder, decorated w/ears of corn outlined in gold on a burgundy ground, 10¾" h. 550.00

Marmalade jar, cov., h.p. strawberries decoration w/gold trim & handles, ca. 1905 (slight wear on handles) 95.00

Mug, decorated w/strawberries & foliage, artist-signed, 1910 mark, 6" h. (gold wear on handle) 90.00

Nappy, scalloped rim, ring handle, decorated w/a center reserve of blackberries & blackberry blossoms framed by wide gold sides, artist-signed, ca. 1915, 9" d. 135.00

Pitcher, 4" h., "Aura Argenta Linear" patt., artist-signed 115.00

Pickard Pitcher with Cherries

Pitcher, 5¾" h., 7½" d., squatty bulbous shouldered body w/an angled handle, the wide shoulder band in gold decorated w/green & purple leaves & beige & gold flowers & a large cluster of yellow cherries w/green & purple leaves overhanging the lower body on a dark green satin ground, gold handles, artist-signed, ca. 1905-10 (ILLUS.) 395.00

Pitcher, 7½" h., 8½" d., overall decoration of lavender, yellow & orange spider mums, gold trim, artist-signed, ca. 1905-1910, Limoges blank.................................400.00

Pitcher, tankard, 16" h., tall footed tapering hexagonal body w/a high spout & long angular handle, each panel decorated w/tall stylized chrysanthemums in shades of purple w/gold stems & white leaves all against a deep reddish orange ground, gold rim, handle & base band, artist-signed 550.00

Plate, 6" d., decorated w/currants & foliage, artist-signed, ca. 1910...........75.00

Plate, 8" d., decorated w/walnuts, almonds & filberts in brown tones, artist-signed 145.00

Plate, 8" d., pastel Western landscape scene, artist-signed...........................95.00

Plate, 8½" d., colorful tulips decoration, heavy gold trim, circle mark 95.00

Plate, 8¾" d., decorated w/Easter lilies, artist-signed 138.00

Plate, 8¾" d., decorated w/red carnations, artist-signed, ca. 1905............185.00

Plate, 9" d., decorated w/purple plums, artist-signed, ca. 1905-10.....175.00

Plate, 12" d., decorated w/a landscape w/house, trees & lake, artist-signed 550.00

Relish dish, decorated w/floral decoration & gold trim, 9½" d.............85.00

Sugar bowl, cov., stylized Art Deco design, artist-signed...........................65.00

Sugar bowl, cov., decorated w/roses, artist-signed 85.00

Tray, two-handled, decorated w/stylized flowers, gilt border, 9½" l. 40.00

Tray, handled, decorated w/garden scene, heavy gold trim, artist-signed, 15½" l. 245.00

Vase, 5½" h., scenic decoration of two mallards in flight, artist-signed 375.00

Vase, 7½" h., tiger lilies decoration on black ground, gold trim 125.00

Vase, 8½" h., decorated w/yellow roses & green leaves on blue ground, gold collar & gold band at base, artist-signed, ca. 1905-1910..410.00

Vase, 12" h., handled, poinsettias & daisies decoration w/heavily decorated wide band of gold around top & scalloped free-form rim w/gold twisted handles, artist-signed, ca. 1905..325.00

PICTORIAL SOUVENIRS

Souvenir Mug With Pig

These small ceramic wares, expressly made to be sold as a souvenir of a town or resort, are decorated with a pictorial scene which is usually titled. Made in profusion in Germany, Austria, Bavaria, and England, they were distributed by several American firms including C.E. Wheelock & Co., John H. Roth (Jonroth), Jones, McDuffee & Co., Stratton Co., and others. Because people seldom traveled in the early years of this century, a small souvenir tray or dish, picturing the resort or a town scene, afforded an excellent, inexpensive gift for family or friends when returning from a vacation trip. Seldom used and carefully packed away later, there is an abundant supply of these small wares available today at moderate prices. Their values are likely to rise.

Bowl, 5¼" d., reticulated rim, gold trim, "Prospect Point, Niagara Falls," Schwarzenburg, Bavaria blank $14.00

Dish, "New Meadow Inn, Bath, Maine," cut-out corners folded back, Wheelock, Germany blank, 4¾" d. 14.00

Model of "Ann Hathaway's Cottage," Goss, England, 6" w., 4¼" h. 40.00

Mug, footed bulbous body w/rolled rim, a small gold figural pig applied to the inner rim, oval color scene of "Court House and Soldiers' Monument - Peoria, Ill.," pale yellow iridized grund, marked "Made in Germany," 2¼ h. (ILLUS.)................29.50

Pitcher, "Boldt Castle on Heart Island, Alexandria Bay, 1000 Islands, New York," h.p. scene on bluish-green lustre, Germany (shows light wear) 8.00

Plate, 6" d., "Cooper Bldg., Newton, Kansas," Wheelock, Austria blank.....10.00

Plate, 6½" d., "Village Free Library, West Gouldsboro, Maine," scalloped & beaded scroll purple lustre rim, gold tracery trim 15.00

Plate, 7½" d., "Plymouth, Massachusetts," six historical scenes in medallions, crown & circle marks, Jonroth, England blank 16.00

Plate, 9⅞" sq., "Rainbow Falls, Watkins Glen, New York," h.p. on ivory, thistle & camellia border decoration, scalloped corners, Jonroth, Adams England blank 19.00

Plate, "Methodist Church, Forest Grove, Oregon," Homer Laughlin blank 20.00

Vase, 4¼" h., 2¾" d., pinched neck flanked by high handles, "Life Saving Station, South Haven, Michigan," h.p. scene medallion on cobalt blue ground 16.50

Vase, 4⅝" h., "Grand Canyon National Park, Arizona," colored scene on cream ground, Jonroth, Royal Winton, England blank.............17.00

PIERCE (Howard) CERAMICS

Stylized Figure of an Eskimo Man

Howard Pierce began his studio in 1941 in Claremont, California. By 1950, he had national representation for all his products. From the beginning, wildlife and animals were the major output of Pierce's artware. In the early years, Pierce produced some polyurethane pieces but an allergic reaction forced him to stop using it. He also created a small amount of merchandise in a Wedgwood Jasper ware style. A few years later, Pierce designed porcelain bisque animals and plants that were placed in or near the open areas of high-glazed vases. When Mt. St. Helens volcano erupted, Pierce obtained a small quantity of the ash and developed a sandy, rough-textured glaze. There was also a 'lava' glaze unrelated to the Mt. St. Helens treatment. Mr. Pierce described 'lava' as "...bubbling up from the bottom." He created a few pieces in gold leaf; however, there was a 'gold' treatment of the 1950s which became known as 'Sears gold.' Sears, Roebuck & Company ordered a large quantity of assorted Pierce products but wanted them done in an overall gold color. Only a few of these pieces have the Howard Pierce mark. In the late 1970s, Mr. Pierce began incising a number in the clay of experimentally glazed products. From this numbering system he was successfully able to create various glazes in blues, deep greens, pinks, purples, yellows, and blacks which are highly collectible. In November 1992, due to health problems, Howard and Ellen Pierce destroyed all the molds they had created over the years. In 1993, Mr. Pierce began work on a very limited basis creating smaller versions of past porcelain items. These pieces are simply stamped "Pierce." Howard Pierce passed away in February, 1994.

Bowl, 9" d., 2½" h., round base w/flared, deep sides, dark brown outside, brown & white 'lava' treatment inside, signed in script "Pierce" $65.00

Bowl, nut, 5" l., 1¾" h., rectangular shape w/an irregular rim, glossy light green interior, mauve exterior, incised mark, "Howard Pierce P-6, Calif" 15.00

Figure of an Eskimo man, standing, crude face features, arms indistinct against body, brown face & feet over white body, Model No. 206P, ca. 1953, 7" h. (ILLUS.) 85.00

Figure of a girl, kneeling w/bowl in left hand, right arm extended, palm raised & open, 'Sears gold,' no mark, 7" h. 15.00

Figure group of a black boy & girl holding hands, white glossy glaze, ca. 1985, 4½" h. 30.00

Model of a circus horse, head down, tail straight, leaping position w/middle of body attached to small, round center base, experimental blue, 7½" l., 6½" h. 85.00

Model of an egret, standing, feet & legs obscured by leaf base, neck long & curved, 9½" h. 75.00

Model of an elephant, seated, trunk raised, 'Mt. St. Helens' ash treatment, 4¾" h. 28.00

Model of a fawn, sitting, head & ears up, legs folded under body, dark brown eyes, experimental tan glaze, ca. 1985, 5½" h. 32.00

Model of a giraffe, head turned to side, modernistic design, legs slightly apart, no base, 12½" h. 42.00

Model of a goose, seated w/head stretched upward, mouth open, 'Sears gold,' no mark, 3¾" h. 7.00

Model of a panther, pacing position, black glaze, 11½" l., 2¾" h. 75.00

Model of a raccoon, seated, head turned slightly, full face, brown glaze w/four stripes around tail, 9" l., 3½" h. 55.00

Model of a roadrunner, standing on wire legs, tail pointed upward, head held high, polyurethane, 8" h. 155.00

Model of a tiger, pacing position, cream body, brown hand-painted stripes, limited production, 11½" l., 2¾" h. 315.00

Pencil holder, nude women in relief around outside, one year limited production, 1980, 3½" d., 4¼" h. 25.00

Sign, dealer advertising, smooth surface, triangular shape, 'Pierce' at top in 1½" block letters, 'Porcelain' underneath Pierce in ½" letters, 6" l., 2½" h. 110.00

Sign, dealer advertising, rough surface resembling tree bark, 'Howard Pierce' in script on upper line, "Porcelain' in block letters on second line, gold leaf, 6" l., 2½" h. 80.00

Sign, dealer, advertising, rough surface resembling tree bark, 'Howard Pierce' in script on upper line, 'Porcelain' in block letters on second line, grey or brown glaze, 6" l., 2½" h. 65.00

Vase, 7½" h., rectangular black base w/straight-sided glossy vase on one end, white porcelain bisque fawn & tree on other end w/three tree branches attached to vase, underside of recessed base divided in half w/one side incised in script underglaze 'Howard Pierce' & the other side incised '302P Claremont, Calif.' 125.00

Whistle, bird shape w/hole at tail, brown w/white glaze, 3½" h. 20.00

PISGAH FOREST

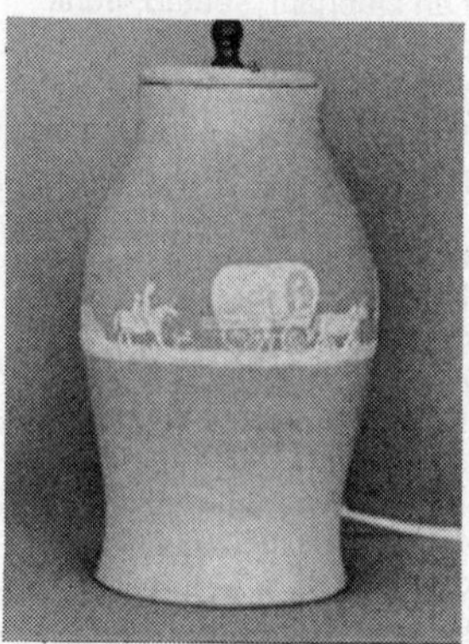

Pisgah Forest Lamp Base

Walter Stephen experimented with making pottery shortly after 1900 with his parents in Tennessee. After their deaths in 1910, he eventually moved to the foot of Mt. Pisgah in North Carolina where he became a partner of C.P. Ryman. Together they built a kiln and a shop but this partnership was dissolved in 1916. During 1920 Stephen again began to experiment with pottery and by 1926 had his own pottery and equipment. Pieces are usually marked and may also be signed "W. Stephen" and dated. Walter Stephen died in 1961 but work at the pottery still continues, although on a part-time basis.

Creamer, Cameo ware, scene of a mountain man, his dog, a cabin & mountains $350.00

Cups & saucers, turquoise glaze, ca. 1950s, four sets 120.00

Lamp base, Cameo ware, baluster-form body decorated w/a white relief band of pioneers & covered wagons against a powder blue ground, signed "STEPHEN," 6" d., 10¾" h. (ILLUS.) 450.00

Pitcher, milk, 6" h., 4½" d., Cameo ware, covered wagon scene, matte green top & glossy glaze blue bottom, signed "Stephen" on side & "Cameo Stephen, Longpine, Arden, N.C., 195?" 425.00

Sugar bowl, cov., turquoise & pink glaze, 3½ x 3½" 25.00

Vase, 5" h., 3½" d., bell-shaped, light green crystalline glaze, pink interior ..75.00

Vase, 4" h., bulbous, blue crystalline glaze w/pink interior, dated "1938" 50.00

Vase, 5¼" h., Cameo ware, wide baluster-form body w/a flaring mouth, Wedgwood blue ground decorated w/a white-relief central band of pioneers in covered wagons, marked, dated "1951" 550.00

Vase, 7" h., 4¾" d., Cameo ware, ovoid body below the wide slightly waisted neck, the neck decorated in white relief w/an Indian buffalo hunt scene on a dark green ground, a white crystalline lower body, rose pink interior, raised mark 1,210.00

Vase, 7¼" h., 4½" d., ovoid body tapering to a short slightly flared neck, covered in a glaze of tightly packed medium sized blue crystals against a clear sea green body, raised mark 770.00

Vase, 8½" h., 5¼" d., ovoid body w/a rounded shoulder to the short cylindrical neck w/flat wide mouth, lustre glaze in blue & bluish green crystals over a gold body, rose pink interior, raised mark, 1943 ....550.00

Vase, 10" h., 4¾" d., tall ovoid body tapering to a gently flared neck, overall tiger's-eye flambé glaze, rose pink interior, raised mark 220.00

Vase, 13¼" h., 7¾" d., Cameo ware, tall ovoid body tapering to a short cylindrical neck, a dark green band around the neck & shoulder decorated w/a white relief covered wagon scene, the lower body w/a periwinkle blue crystalline glaze, marked, artist-signed & dated 1939 ....1,430.00

PRATT WARES

The earliest ware now classified as Pratt ware was made by Felix Pratt at his pottery in Fenton, England from about 1810. He made earthenware with bright glazes, relief sporting jugs, toby mugs and commercial pots and jars whose lids bore multicolored transfer prints. The F. & R. Pratt mark is mid-19th century. The name Pratt ware is also applied today to mid and late 19th century English ware of the same general type as that made by Felix Pratt.

Prattware Model of a Cockerel

Creamer, slightly squared form, molded & decorated w/children in hearts, one side lettered "Sportive Innocence" & the other "Mischievious Sport," all in polychrome enamels, 4⅞" h. (small edge chips) $434.50

Figure of a lady, standing & wearing a brown hat & gloves & a brown-dotted dress, holding two sprigs of ochre roses & green leaves, standing barefooted on a green mound base dashed in ochre & brown, ca. 1815, 8⅛" h. (hat brim touched up, base footrim chips).......575.00

Model of a cockerel, the stylized bird w/ochre comb & wattles, a brown beak & eyes, incised plumage sponged or feathered in yellow, brown, ochre & blue, modeled perched astride a grassy scroll on a circular mound base washed in green, ca. 1800, 8¼" h. (ILLUS.) ..2,013.00

Mug, portrait-type, modeled as the head of a smiling officer wearing a yellow-edged dark brown tricorn hat, a light brown collar above a ruffled jabot, a white waistcoat, ochre sash over a blue coat w/yellow & ochre frogging & epaulets, the brown queue of his hair looping up to form the handle, ca. 1800-10, 6$\frac{3}{16}$" h. (small chips on hat, repaired hairline in handle) 633.00

Pratt Fox & Swan Sauceboat

Sauceboats, each modeled as the head of an ochre fox w/an open mouth forming the spout & w/pricked ears (very small chips), conjoined w/the spread-winged body of a white swan w/an arched neck & yellow-beaked head forming the handle, the neck & wings (one repaired) lightly sponged in brown & interrupting at the back of the oval base a border of green & yellow leaves (one chipped) molded against a dimpled ground between blue bands, the rim (one chipped) also edged in blue, ca. 1800, 6⅞" & 7" l., pr. (ILLUS. of one) 805.00

QUIMPER

This French earthenware pottery has been made in France since the end of the 17th century and is still in production today. Because the colorful decoration on this ware, predominantly of Breton peasant figures, is all hand-painted and each piece is unique, it has become increasingly popular with collectors in recent years. Most pieces offered today date from about the mid-19th century to the present. Modern potteries continue to operate today and contemporary examples are available in gift shops.

Figure of the Madonna & Child, titled on the round base "Ste. Vierge," decorated in cobalt blue, yellow & orange, decorated by Adolphe Porquier, Henriot, France, ca.

Madonna & Child Figure

1930s, small chips on base, age lines, 10½" h. (ILLUS.)....................$302.50

Pitcher, 4⅛" h., cylindrical body w/flat rim & angled handle, the front decorated w/three vertical rectangular panels, the center h.p. w/the bust portrait of a sailor, the two flanking w/the heads of young ladies in costume, in shades of blue & white against a dark green ground, marked "HB Quimper Odetta 453-1145," ca. 1930s....................302.50

Plaque, pierced to hang, "Les Filets Bleus," in blue, orange & black central decoration & rim, inscribed marks, 12⅜" d....................357.50

Plate, 9½" d., h.p. polychrome center scene of a standing soldier framed by floral sprigs, paired sprigs on the wide border w/scalloped rim, titled "Vive la Nation - 1789," marked "Henriot - Quimper, France" (edge chips)....................165.00

REDWARE

Unique Redware Figure Group

Red earthenware pottery was made in the American colonies from the late 1600s. Bowls, crocks and all types of utilitarian wares were turned out in great abundance to supplement the pewter and handmade treenware. The ready availability of the clay, the same used in making bricks and roof tiles, accounted for the vast production. The lead-glazed redware retained its reddish color though a variety of colors could be obtained by adding various metals to the glaze. Interesting effects occurred accidentally through unsuspected impurities in the clay or uneven temperatures in the firing kiln which sometimes resulted in streaks or mottled splotches.

Redware pottery was seldom marked by the maker.

Bowl, 8¼" d., 5¼" h., squatty bulbous body on a thin footring, the sides tapering to a widely flaring rim, applied ribbed strap handles at the shoulders, brown sponged glaze (wear, glaze flakes & chips)....................$104.50

Cup, squatty wide bulbous body w/flared rim resting on a narrow footring, applied C-scroll handle, brown splotches on reddish ground, 5¼" d., 3½" h. (edge wear, chips)....110.00

Figure group, the small-scale grouping including a log cabin w/shingled roof & chimney, a bearded man w/whiskey flask & dog seated before them, all mounted on a shaped rectangular base, the roof inscribed "Sovineer (sic) of Strasburg, VA," J. Eberly & Co., Strasburg, Virginia, ca. 1894, 6½ x 9¼", 5½" h. (ILLUS.)....................29,900.00

Flowerpot w/attached saucer base, finger crimped rims, tooled foliate band, greenish amber glaze, 5½" h. (wear & chips)....................137.50

Jar, ovoid body tapering to a slightly flared rim, side strap handle, dark amber glaze w/brown splotches, 5⅞" h. (small flakes)....................93.50

Jar, ovoid body w/a wide molded rim, greenish orange pebbly glaze, Galena, Illinois-type, 6¼" h. (hairline in base)....................181.50

Jar, ovoid body tapering to a wide upright molded rim band, greenish amber glaze w/olive green speckled dots, Galena, Illinois-type, 7¼" h. (wear, chips)....................192.50

Jar, ovoid, eared shoulder handles, tooled lines around shoulder, clear glaze w/dark brown splotches, 9" h. (wear, glaze chips & hairline)..........165.00

Jar, cov., wide bulbous body tapering

to a wide mouth w/molded gallery rim w/side spout, side ribbed strap handle, tooled shoulder ring, wide brown sponged stripes down the sides, 9" h. (minor chips on pot, chipped mismatched cover) 467.50

Model of a chest of drawers, miniature, a rectangular top overhanging a case w/three pairs of small drawers over the scalloped apron & bracket feet, yellow slip glaze w/overall brown speckles, the back incised "Annie Maria Marsden, 1884," 5¾ x 11¼", 10¼" h. (very minor edge chips) 825.00

Pitcher, miniature, 3¼" h., simple ovoid body tapering to a flared rim w/pinched spout, applied loop handle, incised on base "W.W.C. 1906" 93.50

Pitcher, 5¾" h., wide ovoid body tapering to a flared rim w/pinched spout, small ribbed loop handle, yellowish glaze w/amber spots (minor edge wear)............................55.00

Pitcher, 10½" h., bulbous ovoid body tapering to a wide flaring neck w/pinched spout, small strap handle, clear glaze w/dark scattered manganese splotches, 19th c. (imperfections) 357.50

Rare Redware Sugar Bowl

Sugar bowl, cov., squatty bulbous body on a small footring & w/eared handles flanking the flaring rim, high stepped & domed cover w/ball finial, decorated overall w/marbleized white & black slip on a red ground, Pennsylvania, first half 19th c., cover & base cracked, 12" h. (ILLUS.) 4,600.00

RED WING

Various potteries operated in Red Wing, Minnesota from 1868, the most successful being the Red Wing Stoneware Co., organized in 1878. Merged with other local potteries through the years, it became known as Red Wing Union Stoneware Co. in 1894, and was one of the largest producers of utilitarian stoneware items in the United States. After a decline in the popularity of stoneware products, an art pottery line was introduced to compensate for the loss and this was reflected in a new name for the company, Red Wing Potteries, Inc., in 1930. Stoneware production ceased entirely in 1947, but vases, planters, cookie jars and dinnerwares of art pottery quality continued in production until 1967 when the pottery ceased operation altogether.

BRUSHED & GLAZED WARES

Red Wing Lion Vase

Lobby (sand) jar or umbrella stand, Brushed Ware, cylindrical, embossed stag & doe in mountainous landscape, shaded green glaze, 12" d., 15" h. $1,500.00

Vase, 10" h., Glazed Ware, embossed lion in landscape decoration, tan & grey glaze (ILLUS.) 80.00

Vase, 12" h., expanding cylinder w/squared handles rising from narrow shoulder to mouth, Grecian design, No. 155...............................80.00

Vase, 12½" h., squared handles, tapering cylinder, marked w/pre-1936 ink mark, No. 163......................75.00

DINNERWARES & NOVELTIES

Bean pot, cov., Village Green patt........25.00

Bowl, 5¼" d., Tampico patt.......................6.00

Bowl, salad, 6" d., Bob White patt. 35.00

Bowl, 8" d., Vintage patt. 10.00

Bowl, 9" d., two-handled, Bob White patt..25.00

Bowl, 12" d., salad, Bob White patt., deep 45.00

Butter dish, cov., Bob White patt. 62.00

Butter dish, cov., Lute Song 32.50
Butter dish, cov., Vintage patt., ¼ lb.....15.00
Cake stand, pedestal base, Tampico patt. 35.00
Casserole, cov., Village Green patt., 1 qt. 12.00
Console bowl, Magnolia patt. 60.00
Cookie jar, cov., Bob White patt. ....125.00 to 145.00
Cookie jar, cov., figural French Chef, blue or yellow glaze, h.p. details, stamped wing mark & "Red Wing Pottery," each 80.00
Cookie jar, cov., figural Katrina (or Dutch Girl), blue or yellow glaze, impressed "Red Wing U.S.A.," each 70.00
Cookie jar, cov., figural Monk, "Thou Shalt Not Steal," yellow or blue glaze, each 95.00
Creamer, Merrileaf patt. 8.00
Cup & saucer, Bob White patt. 19.00
Cup & saucer, Tampico patt. 12.50
Cup & saucer, Vintage patt. 7.00
Ewer, Magnolia patt., No. 1028 ....45.00
Figure of a lute player, deep maroon glaze, No. 2507 ....125.00
Figure of an Oriental man, standing wearing a tall hat & long robes w/long sleeves, green glaze, No. 1309, 10" h. 125.00
Gravy boat, cov., handled, Vintage patt. 15.00
Hors d'oeuvre holder, Bob White patt., model of a bird pierced for picks 40.00
Model of a badger on football, stump base, signed "Red Wing Potteries" & dated 1939 ....110.00
Model of a gopher on football, "Minnesota," dated 1939 ....85.00
Mug, cylindrical w/embossed banner reading "Hamm's Krug Klub" over embossed scene of a bird & animals in the forest around the body, brown glaze 70.00
Mug, Village Green patt. 9.00
Pitcher, 7" h., Bob White patt., 60 oz. ...18.00
Pitcher, 12" h., Bob White patt., 112 oz. (ILLUS. top next column ....35.00 to 40.00
Planter, model of a cornucopia, yellow outside, salmon pink inside, artist-signed 38.50
Plate, bread & butter, 6½" d., Bob White patt. 7.50
Plate, salad, 7½" d., Round Up patt. 17.50
Plate, dinner, 10" d., Vintage patt. 9.00
Plate, dinner, 10¼" d., Lute Song patt. 8.50
Plate, dinner, 10½" d., Bob White patt. 12.50
Plate, dinner, 10½" d., Round Up patt. 60.00

Tall Bob White Pitcher

Plate, 11" d., Capistrano patt. 7.50
Platter, 12¾" oval, Vintage patt. 15.00
Platter, 13" oval, Bob White patt. 25.00
Relish dish, three-part, handled, Bob White patt. 18.00
Salt & pepper shakers, figural birds, Bob White patt., pr. 30.00
Salt & pepper shakers, tall, hourglass shape, Bob White patt., 6" h., pr. 20.00
Salt & pepper shakers Village Green patt., pr. 20.00
Sugar bowl, cov., Bob White patt. 22.50
Sugar bowl, cov., Rodeo patt. 65.00
Sugar bowl, cov., Vintage patt. 8.00
Teapot, cov., Bob White patt. 65.00
Toothpick holder, model of a gopher on a log, signed "Red Wing Potteries" & dated 120. 00
Vegetable bowl, open, divided & angled, Bob White patt. 35.00
Vegetable bowl, oval, divided, Lute Song patt. 20.00
Vegetable bowl, divided, Vintage patt., 12" d. 14.00
Wall pocket, model of a guitar, green glaze, No. M1484 ....35.00
Water jar, cover & stand, Bob White patt., 2 gal. 375.00

STONEWARE & UTILITY WARES

Red Wing Spongeware Bowl

Bowl, 6" d., Grey Line stoneware 165.00

Bowl, 6" d., paneled sides, spongeware (ILLUS.)....................................90.00

Bowl, 7" d., paneled sides, blue banding, spongeware 98.00

Bowl, 7" d., Grey Line, stoneware w/spongeband decoration, w/Wisconsin advertising 195.00

Bowl, 8" d., Grey Line, stoneware, w/ advertising..................................185.00

Bowl, 9" d., Grey Line, stoneware w/paneled sides & blue sponge band decoration ....100.00 to 125.00

Fruit jar w/screw-on lid, "Stone Mason Fruit Jar, Union Stoneware Co., Red Wing, Minn." printed in black on stoneware, qt. 185.00

Fruit jar w/screw-on zinc lid, "Stone Mason Fruit Jar, Union Stoneware Co., Red Wing, Minn." printed in black (or blue) on stoneware, half gal. 190.00

Jug, miniature, beehive shape, copy of the "little brown jug," symbol of football rivalry between Minnesota & Michigan, brown top half, grey bottom half printed in blue w/"Who Will Win?".......................................195.00

Pitcher, 5" h., spongeware, rust & green daubing on stoneware, unmarked...80.00

Pitcher, milk, 8" h., stoneware w/dark blue edging & crimped lip, logo on front...235.00

Pitcher, 8½" h., (so-called Russian milk pitcher without pouring spout), brown glaze, 1 gal............................75.00

Red Wing Poultry Feeder

Poultry feeder (or waterer), stoneware, "Ko - Rec Feeder," half gal. (ILLUS.) 125.00

Refrigerator jar w/bail handle, white-glazed stoneware w/blue bands, No. 5 ....200.00

RIDGWAYS

Ridgway Ale Set

There were numerous Ridgways among English potters. The firm J. & W. Ridgway operated in Shelton from 1814 to 1930 and produced many pieces with scenes of historical interest. William Ridgway operated in Shelton from 1830 to 1865. Most wares marked Ridgway that have been offered in this country were made by one of these two firms, or by Ridgway Potteries, Ltd., still in operation. Also see HISTORICAL & COMMEMORATIVE WARES

Ale set: 9½" h. tankard pitcher & six 4½" h. mugs on a 12¼" d., tray; Coaching Days & Ways series, caramel ground w/black transfer-printed coaching scenes, silver lustre rims & handles, 8 pcs. (ILLUS.) $295.00

Bowl, 10" d., Coaching Days & Ways series 50.00

Dessert service: a pair of shaped oval dishes, a pr. of shaped square dishes, three cruciform dishes & nine plates; each piece transfer-printed in green & trimmed in gilt w/an overall design of blossom clusters & berried branches within a gilt-edge scalloped & wave-molded rim, the dishes molded at either end w/a row of five gilt-trimmed rose blossoms, pattern number 323l, ca. 1835, dishes 9¾", 10½" & 11½" l., the set (some gilt wear) 1,035.00

Gravy boat, Coaching Days & Ways series, "Old England Ware," ca. 1920-50..25.00

Mug, Coaching Days & Ways series, 4" h...25.00

Mug, Coaching Days & Ways series, silver lustre trim, 4½" h. 38.00

Pitcher, 7½" h., Coaching Days & Ways series 80.00

Pitcher, 9" h., relief-molded stoneware, the sides molded w/a scene from "Tam O'Shanter," ca. 1835 ....150.00

Pitchers, jug-type, graduated set, 4¼" h., 4¾" d., 5" h., 5" d., 5½" h., 5½" d., Coaching Days & Ways series, scenes in black on caramel background, silver lustre trim, "Racing the Mall," "Henry the Eighth" & "The Abbot of Reading," set of 3 ....135.00

Plate, 9" d., Coaching Days & Ways series, marked "Old England Ware," ca. 1920-50..30.00

Plate, 10¼" d., "View from Ruggles House Newburgh," blue transfer-printed scene 55.00

Soup plate w/flanged rim, "Harper's Ferry from the American Side," blue transfer-printed scene, 9" d...............65.00

Tea set: cov. teapot, open handled sugar bowl & creamer; spherical bodies, rich deep caramel background w/scenes in black, silver lustre top bands & handle trim, scenes based on Dickens' Mr. Pickwick character, teapot 4" d., 4½" h., sugar bowl 5½" d., 2⅜" h., creamer 3⅛" d., 2⅝" h., 3 pcs..........145.00

Tray, oval, Coaching Days & Ways series, 12½" l. 80.00

ROCKINGHAM WARES

Rockingham-Glazed Bowl

An earthenware pottery was first established on the estate of the Marquis of Rockingham in England's Yorkshire district about 1745 and occupied by a succession of potters. The famous Rockingham glaze of mottled brown, somewhat resembling tortoise shell, was introduced about 1788 by the Brameld Brothers, and was well received. During the 1820s, porcelain manufacture was added to the production and fine quality china was turned out until the pottery closed in 1842. The popular Rockingham glaze was subsequently produced elsewhere, including Bennington, Vermont, and at numerous other U.S. potteries. We list herein not only wares produced at the Rockingham potteries in England, distinguishing porcelain wares from the more plentiful earthenware productions, but also include items from other potteries with the Rockingham glaze.

Bowl, 8½" d., 3½" h., deep rounded sides on a footring & flaring to a wide flattened rim, mottled brown glaze $60.50

Bowl, 9½" d., 4¼" h., deep rounded sides on a footring & a molded rim, tan & white horizontal bands beneath overall mottled dark brown glaze 132.00

Bowl, 11" d., 2¾" h., a wide round flat bottom & wide gently sloping low sides, mottled dark brown glaze 93.50

Bowl, 11" d., 4¾" h., deep rounded & flaring sides on a thick footring, a flaring rolled rim, mottled dark brown glaze, some wear (ILLUS.) 71.50

Bowl, 11½" d., 3¼" h., wide canted sides, overall mottled dark brown glaze 126.50

Bowl,11½" d., 3¼" h., wide flat bottom w/widely canted sides, mottled dark brown glaze (minor wear) 82.50

Cuspidor, hand-held, cylindrical mug-form w/strap handle, mottled dark brown glaze, 3½" h. 181.50

Dish, round flat bottom w/low flared sides, mottled dark brown glaze, 5" d..44.00

Dish, squared & ruffled flaring sides w/the rounded corners molded w/ribbing, scroll bands at the rims, mottled dark brown glaze, 9" w..........44.00

Jar, cov., cylindrical sides w/a molded base band & wide flaring top, domed cover w/button finial, mottled dark brown glaze, 8" d. (chip on cover) 88.00

Lamp base, modeled in the form of a seated dog, mottled dark brown glaze, drilled at top & base for fittings, 8¼" h. 253.00

Models of lambs, reclining animal w/light curly coat, on a cobalt blue glazed oval base, 5½" l., pr.............495.00

Mug, cylindrical w/molded base, C-scroll handle, mottled dark brown glaze, 3" h...44.00

Pie plate, wide round flat bottom w/low sloping sides, mottled dark brown glaze, 9" d. 82.50

Pie plate, wide flat bottom w/low flared sides, mottled dark brown glaze, 9½" d.....................................49.50

Pie plate, wide round flat bottom w/low sloping sides, mottled dark brown glaze, 10" d. ....75.00 to 100.00

Pie plate, wide flat bottom w/flat, flared sides, mottled dark brown glaze, 11¼" d. 93.50

Pitcher, 6⅜" h., footed bulbous base tapering to cylindrical sides, high arched spout & angled handle, molded Gothic Arch design on sides, mottled dark brown glaze 60.50

Pitcher, 8⅝" h., footed bulbous octagonal body w/incurved panels to the short neck w/scalloped rim & wide, arched spout, angled handle, overall mottled & streaky flint enamel glaze, mid-19th c. (small chips) 192.50

Pitcher, 9" h., footed bulbous ovoid body tapering to a flat rim w/arched spout, S-scroll handle, relief-molded deer & hanging game designs on the sides, mottled dark brown glaze 165.00

Pot, cov., a bulbous ovoid flat-bottomed container tapering to a wide flat rim w/large spout & a long stick handle to the side, the low domed cover w/a button finial, mottled dark brown glaze, 4⅝" h. 280.50

Soap dish, oval, mottled dark brown glaze, 4⅞" l. 49.50

Soap dish, deep rounded tapering sides w/molded rim, mottled dark brown glaze, 5¼" d. 38.50

Vegetable dish, open, oval, shallow flaring sides w/rolled rim, mottled dark brown glaze, 10" l. 71.50

Vegetable dish, open, octagonal w/wide flanged rim, boldly mottled dark brown glaze, 13½" l. 170.50

ROOKWOOD

Considered America's foremost art pottery, the Rookwood Pottery Company was established in Cincinnati, Ohio in 1880, by Mrs. Maria Nichols Longworth Storer. To accurately record its development, each piece carried the Rookwood insignia, or mark, was dated, and, if individually decorated, was usually signed by the artist. The pottery remained in Cincinnati until 1959 when it was sold to Herschede Hall Clock Company and moved to Starkville, Mississippi, where it continued in operation until 1967.

A private company is now producing a limited variety of pieces using original Rookwood molds.

Book ends, figure of an Oriental lady seated in the lotus position, stepped sides on the back plate, matte brown glaze, No. 2362, 1919, William P. McDonald, 5¼" w., 7¾" h., pr. (minor roughness to top of headdresses) $220.00

Book ends, figural, model of an elephant, trunk up, glossy ivory glaze, No. 6124, 1957, pr. 350.00

Book ends, figural, model of an owl, matte blue glaze, No. 2655, 1935, pr. 350.00

Bowl-vase, squatty bulbous body w/a closed rim, decorated w/large clusters of yellow roses on a dark brown ground, Standard glaze, No. 214C, 1903, Edith Noonan, 5½" d., 2¾" h. (crazing) 302.50

Bowl-vase, very compressed squatty bulbous body w/the wide shoulder tapering to a wide flat rim, decorated w/deep red, ochre & blue blossoms & green foliage on a dark purple & raspberry butterfat ground, Wax Matte glaze, No. 923, 1922, E. Lincoln, 6¼" d., 2½" h. 935.00

Dish, low swirled sides, Uncle Remus series, center w/a line drawing of a man & child, lettered "Miss Sally Callin' - Better Run Along" on a pumpkin ground, gilded edge, No. 87G, 1885, E.P. Cranch, 6½" d. ...440.00

Dish, shallow rounded form molded on one side w/a large model of a frog, fine leathery matte peacock green glaze, No 2606, 1922, 7" l., 4" h. 330.00

Ewer, flattened disc-form base tapering to a slender tall neck w/a trilobed rolled rim, loop handle from neck to shoulder, decorated w/orange nasturtiums on a bright orange shaded to dark brown ground, Standard glaze, No. 715E, 1898, 4½" d., 5" h. 165.00

Rookwood Ewer with Flowers

Ewer, squatty spherical body on a

narrow footring w/a tall, slender cylindrical neck w/tricorner rim & long strap handle, decorated w/exotic yellow & white flowers on brown leafy stems, green Standard glaze, No. 101C, 1885, Matt Daly, crazing, 8½" h. (ILLUS.)....................385.00

Ewer, squatty bulbous base below a tall slender neck w/a trilobed rim & S-shaped handle, the base w/silver overlay Art Nouveau flowers & scrolling foliage, silver overlay on the rim & handle, the background h.p. w/sprigs of orange flowers & green foliage on a shaded brown ground, Standard glaze, No. 468CC, 1893, Josephine Zettel, silver marked "Gorham," 5½" d., 8½" h. 3,475.00

Jar. cov., Limoges-type, globular body w/dimpled sides & low collared neck, decorated w/snails & insects on a rust, sand & deep blue ground w/green foliage & gilded accents, 1882, Maria Longworth Nichols, 5" d., 6" h. (tight hairline in side) ...1,650.00

Mug, bisque, tapering sides w/three incised lines near base & top, temperance-oriented, "Wild Oats, Thistles," decorated w/drawn allegory of men drinking & its consequences, No. 587W, 1892, E.P. Cranch, 5½" d., 4½" h. 550.00

Paperweight, model of an elephant, green glaze, No. 6490, 1946 ....110.00

Pitcher, 4¼" h., 5" d., rounded tapering triangular body w/three pinched spouts, decorated around the lower half w/stylized red blossoms on a green ground, Matte glaze, No. 341E, 1902, A. R. Valentien...385.00

Pitcher, 6⅜" h., simple ovoid body tapering to a short cylindrical neck w/long pinched spout, angled handle, decorated w/a long holly sprig in green & brown w/red berries highlighted in white against a shaded bluish grey ground w/ivory rim & interior, Standard glaze, No. 18, 1890, Edward Abel..............605.00

Rookwood Scenic Plaque

Plaque, rectangular, decorated w/a beach scene in half-light w/a blue sky, turquoise water & pink sand, in original wide, flat oak frame, 1916, Lenore Asbury, 5¼ x 8¼" (ILLUS.) 2,310.00

Vase, 4¾" h., 4¼" w., hexagonal body on small tab feet, lightly molded in each panel w/a facing pair of small birds above a basket of fruit, dark bluish green Matte glaze, 1920, Arthur Conant 165.00

Vase, 5¾" h., 4¾" d., bulbous ovoid shouldered body tapering to a short cylindrical neck, decorated around the top half w/a continuous branch of white & celadon green dogwood flowers & leaves on a shaded pink, cream & teal blue ground, Iris glaze, No. 531E, 1908, K. Van Horn 1,210.00

Vase, 6" h., 3½ d., waisted cylindrical form, molded around the top w/a band of stylized chickens in purple, green & ochre, Matte glaze, No. 1358F, 1912, W. Hentschel.......550.00

Vase, 8⅛" h., slightly cylindrical body tapering to a flat rim, decorated w/a landscape in shades of green, blue, cream & brown, Vellum glaze, 1921, Frederick Rothenbusch.................1,495.00

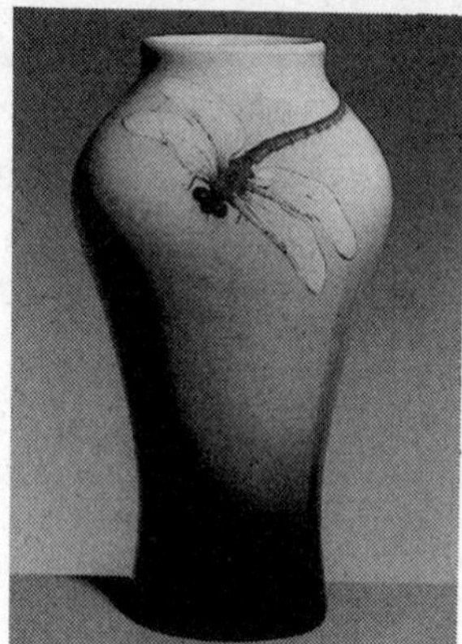

Rare Iris Glaze Vase

Vase, 10" h., baluster-form body swelled near the top, decorated w/a large dragonfly, Iris glaze, Carl Schmidt (ILLUS.) 15,400.00

Vase, 11¾" h., 5" d., expanding cylinder w/narrow flared rim, decorated w/golden daffodils & green foliage against a shaded pink ground, Wax Matte glaze, No. 2790, 1928, Sallie Coyne 1,540.00

Vase, 14½" h., baluster-form w/everted rim, decorated w/chrysanthemums in amber, green, ochre & dark brown, Standard glaze, No. 816B, 1899, Amelia Sprague Browne..1,380.00

Water jug, ovoid w/strap handle at top & circular spout at shoulder, Limoges-type, decorated w/gilded incised Moorish designs at shoulder & base & painted roses & insects in tones of brown & blue against a beige ground, die-stamped "ROOKWOOD 1883 - Y41," dated 1883, 7" d., 9¾" h. 660.00

ROSELANE POTTERY

Roselane Pottery began in the home of William "Doc" Fields and his wife, Georgia, in 1938. In 1940 the Fields moved the operation to Pasadena, California. The pottery successfully manufactured such items as vases, ashtrays, figurines, covered boxes, candlesticks, bowls, sculptured animals on wood bases, "Sparklers" and wallpockets. Roselane moved again in 1968 to Baldwin Park, California where it remained for six years. In 1977, the business closed. Several marks were used as well as paper labels.

Roselane Figure of a Boy

Bowl, 9" d., 2" h., high-glaze grey underneath, pink inside w/sgraffito-type grey "snowflakes" design, scroll mark, Model No. A-9........................$35.00

Bowl, 15" d., 8" w., shallow rectangle form w/butterfly, bird, tulip & marigold in each corner in-relief underglaze & "Chinese Modern" footed base, deep purple inside w/light purple on decorations, scroll mark, Model No. 52 ....60.00

Candleholder, double "Chinese Modern" openwork base w/two lily shaped holders, one slightly higher than the other, deep purple glaze, 6½" l., 5¼" h.......................................35.00

Figure of a boy, seated & holding open cookie jar w/cookies in it & left hand holding one cookie near mouth, legs folded under body w/right foot showing, satin matte beige & brown glaze, incised "Roselane U.S.A." w/copyright symbol, 3½" h. (ILLUS.)....................24.00

Figure of a girl, kneeling, arms folded over chest w/hands together in prayer, head slightly raised, eyes closed, reverse of girl shows pony-tail & bottoms of feet & toes, satin matte beige & brown glaze, incised "Roselane U.S.A." w/copyright symbol, 4½" h. 22.00

Figure of a newsboy, standing, left hand in pocket, newspaper tucked under right arm, knee patch on left trouser, beige & brown, incised on back bottom of left pant leg, "Roselane" & incised on right pant leg bottom "USA" w/copyright symbol, 5" h. 26.00

Model of a bear, seated, head facing forward & tilted slightly, ears up, arms & hands in front of body but not touching, rough textured, light to dark brown glaze, Model No. 2635, 5½" h..28.00

Model of a bulldog, seated, glossy beige, brown, light blue, w/pink plastic eyes, "Sparkler" series, 2½" h..23.00

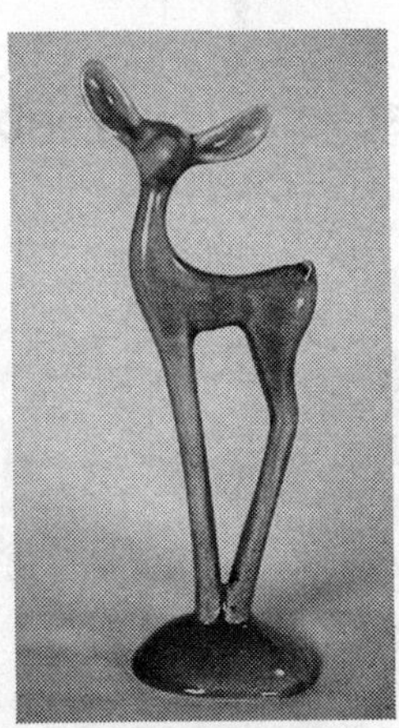

Roselane Deer

Model of a deer on oval base, stylized design, standing w/back legs together & bent, front legs together & straight, head turned, ears straight, weighs two ounces, glossy green glaze, 5" h. (ILLUS.) 35.00

Model of a duck, standing on round base, wings back w/4" wing span,

head turned to right, glossy light brown glaze, Model No. 126, 4" h. 18.00
Model of a goose, seated w/head & neck over back w/bill touching back, light & dark grey satin-matte glaze, incised "USA" w/copyright symbol, 2¼" l., 3½" h. 16.00
Model of an owl, modernistic design w/large head & tapering body, plastic eyes, semi-porcelain, "Sparkler" series, 6" h. 45.00
Model of a giraffe, seated, two front legs folded under, back legs not visible, tail up & over back, long neck twisted w/head turned to look behind, glossy cream glaze w/dark brown spots, Model No. 264, ca. 1960, 4¾" l., 9" h. 35.00
Model of a horse standing on oval base, stylized, light grey w/brown glaze, ca. 1949-53, 8½" h. 32.00
Model of a raccoon, seated, head turned, tail up, semi-porcelain w/brown & black glaze, "Sparkler" series, 4¼" h. 25.00
Sign, dealer advertising, scroll design, glossy light grey glaze, 12½" l., 3" h. 145.00
Vase, 6½" h., "Chinese Modern," openwork on small square base rising to straight sides w/tiny flare at rim, glossy grey exterior, maroon interior 15.00

ROSE MEDALLION - ROSE CANTON

Rose Mandarin Platter

The lovely Chinese ware known as Rose Medallion was made through the past century and into the present one. It features alternating panels of people and flowers or insects with most pieces having four medallions with a central rose or peony medallion. The ware is called Rose Canton if flowers and birds or insects fill all the panels. Unless otherwise noted, our listing is for Rose Medallion ware.

Basin, decorated w/panels of long-tailed birds & peony alternating w/figural court scenes, 19th c., 18½" d. $1,150.00
Bowl, 5¾" d. 71.50
Bowl, 9" d., 3⅝" h. 187.00
Bowl, 9¼" d., shallow 195.00
Bowl, 11⅛" d., decorated w/a profusion of fruit, flower & bird panels alternating w/figural panels, 19th c. 518.00
Bowl, 11¼" d., Rose Mandarin variant, richly decorated w/a scene of mounted hunters before the chase & treeing the fox, a deep border & a hunting vignette on the interior, ca. 1785 ....1,093.00
Bowl, 11¾" d., 4½" h., flaring sides 495.00
Bowl, 13½" d., 5½" h. 1,045.00
Creamer, helmet-shaped 225.00
Creamer, Rose Canton, helmet-shaped, 4" h. 93.50
Dish, cov., oval, 8" l. 550.00
Dish, hexagonal, footed, 11" w. 302.50
Flowerpot, hexagonal, 4¾" h. 220.00
Plate, 7¾" d., Rose Canton, bird & butterfly border 148.50
Plate, 8½" d., Rose Canton, bird & butterfly border 148.50
Plates, 5¾" d., octagonal, set of 8 ....275.00
Platter, 15" l., orange peel glaze 412.50
Platter, 14¾ x 18" oval, Rose Mandarin variant, three figural & three floral panel reserves around the sides, 19th c. (ILLUS.) 522.50
Punch bowl, deep rounded sides, decorated w/colorful panels of pavilions, flowers, birds & insects, w/wooden base, 16" d. 1,540.00
Soap dish, cover & drain insert, Rose Mandarin variant, 19th c., 4" w., 5½" l., 3 pcs. (imperfections) 412.50
Teapot, cov., Rose Mandarin variant the sides decorated w/figures in a lakeside garden viewing a passing junk flying a large banner, ca. 1785 ....403.00
Umbrella stand, 19th c., 24" h. 1,540.00
Vase, 8½" h., decorated w/two lizards, gold trim 265.00
Vase, 14¼" h., baluster-form, the wide cylindrical neck w/a flaring rim & flanked by a pair of molded animal-head handles, 19th c. 440.00
Vase, 15½" h., flaring base, bulbous midsection & cylindrical top w/collared rim 489.50
Vegetable dish, cov., Rose Mandarin variant, 19th c., 8¼" w., 9½" l. 715.00

ROSEVILLE

Roseville Pottery Company operated in Zanesville, Ohio from 1898 to 1954 after having been in business for six years prior to that in Muskingum County, Ohio. Art wares similar to those of Owens and Weller Potteries were produced. Items listed here are by patterns or lines.

APPLE BLOSSOM (1948)

White apple blossoms in relief on blue, green or pink ground; brown tree branch handles.

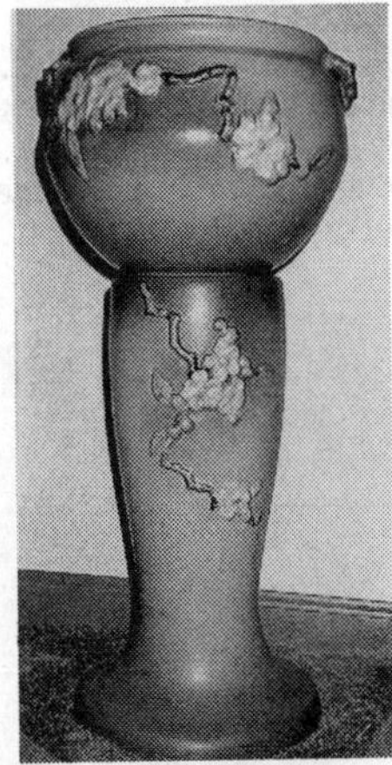

Apple Blossom Jardiniere & Pedestal

Basket w/low overhead handle, blue or green ground, No. 310-10", 10" h, each ....$175.00 to 225.00
Basket, hanging-type, pink ground 125.00
Bowl, 6½" d., 2½" h., flat handles, blue or green ground, No. 326-6", each ....85.00 to 95.00
Candlesticks, pink ground, No. 352-4½", 4½" h., pr. 95.00
Console bowl, blue ground, No. 333-14", 8 x 18" oval 125.00
Console bowl, pink ground, No. 331-12", 12" l. 135.00
Cornucopia-vase, green ground, No. 321-6", 6" h. ....50.00 to 70.00
Creamer & open sugar bowl, blue ground, pr. 85.00
Ewer, pink ground, No. 318-15", 15" h. 395.00
Jardiniere, two-handled, No. 302-5", 5" h. 65.00
Jardiniere, pink ground, No. 302-10", 10" h. 395.00
Jardiniere & pedestal base, pink ground, No. 302-8" & No. 305-8", overall 24½" h., 2 pcs. (ILLUS.) 785.00
Jardiniere & pedestal base, green ground, No. 306-10", overall 31" h., 2 pcs. ....1,100.00 to 1,275.00
Vase, 6" h., pink ground, No. 342-6" 95.00
Vase, 7" h., green ground, No. 373-7" 80.00
Vase, bud, 7" h., base handles, flaring rim, blue, green or pink ground, No. 379-7", each ....60.00 to 75.00
Vase, 9½" h., 5" d., asymmetrical handles, cylindrical w/disc base, green ground, No. 387-9" 90.00
Vase, 10" h., two-handled, blue ground, No. 389-10" 140.00
Vase, 12½" h., base handles, blue ground, No. 390-12" 145.00
Wall pocket, conical w/overhead handle, pink ground, No. 366-8¼",8½" h. ....125.00 to 150.00
Window box, end handles, green or pink ground, No. 368-8", 2½ x 10½", each ....60.00 to 70.00
Window box, end handles, pink ground, No. 369-12", 12" l. ....125.00 to 150.00

BANEDA (1933)

Band of embossed pods, blossoms and leaves on green or raspberry pink ground.

Bowl, 8" d., 2½" h., two-handled, green ground 255.00
Bowl, 9" d., 3¾" h., two-handled, green ground 295.00
Bowl, 10" d., 3½" h., two-handled, raspberry pink ground 270.00
Candlesticks, handles rising from flaring base to nozzle, green ground, pr. ....400.00 to 425.00
Jardiniere, green ground, 7" h. 485.00
Jardiniere, raspberry pink ground, 9½" h. 750.00
Jardiniere & pedestal base, raspberry pink ground, 8" h. jardiniere, 2 pcs. 1,850.00
Vase, 4½" h., tiny rim handles, sharply canted sides, raspberry pink ground, No. 603-4" 280.00
Vase, 6" h., two-handled, tapering cylinder w/short collared neck, green ground 225.00
Vase, 7" h., two-handles at shoulder, cylindrical, green ground 250.00
Vase, 7" h., two-handled, bulbous, green ground, No. 605-7" 360.00
Vase, 8½" h., green ground 200.00
Wall pocket, flaring sides, raspberry pink ground, 8" h. 1,200.00

BLEEDING HEART

Pink blossoms and green leaves on shaded blue, green or pink ground.

Basket w/circular handle, blue ground, No. 360-10", 10" h. 250.00

Candlesticks, conical base, curved handles rising from base to midsection, blue ground, No. 1139-4½", 5" h., pr. 80.00

Cornucopia-vase, blue ground, No. 141-6", 6" h. 60.00

Cornucopia-vase, blue ground, No. 142-8", 8" h. 160.00

Ewer, pink ground, No. 963-6", 6" h. ..165.00

Jardiniere, small pointed shoulder handles, blue ground, No. 651-3", 3" h. 65.00

Bleeding Heart Vase

Vase, 8" h., base handles, blue ground, No. 969-8" (ILLUS.) 180.00

Vase, 15" h., two-handled, flaring hexagonal mouth, green ground, No. 976-15" 375.00

Wall pocket, angular pointed overhead handle rising from midsection, blue ground, No. 1287-8", 8½" h. 250.00

BUSHBERRY (1948)

Berries and leaves on blue, green or russet bark-textured ground; brown or green branch handles.

Basket w/asymmetrical overhead handle, russet ground, No. 369, 6½" h. 170.00

Basket w/asymmetrical overhead handle, blue, green or russet ground, No. 370-8", 8" h., each ....125.00 to 150.00

Basket w/low overhead handle, asymmetric rim, blue ground, No. 372-11", 12" h. 185.00

Beverage set: 8½" h. ice lip pitcher & four 3½" h. handled mugs; blue ground, pitcher No. 1325, mugs No. 1-3½", 5 pcs. 600.00

Bowl, 4" h., two-handled, globular, blue ground, No. 411-4" 65.00

Bowl, 6" d., russet ground, No. 412-6" 115.00

Candleholders, large flaring handles, russet ground, No. 1147, 2" h., pr. 58.00

Console bowl, two-handled, russet ground, No. 414-10", 10" d. 130.00

Console bowl, russet ground, No. 415-10", 10" d. 125.00

Ewer, blue ground, No. 1-6", 6" h. 65.00

Ewer, cut-out rim, russet ground, No. 3-15", 15" h. 285.00

Flowerpot w/saucer, green ground, No. 658-5", 5" h. 60.00

Jardiniere, russet ground, No. 657-6", 6" h. 245.00

Jardiniere & pedestal base, blue ground, No. 657-8", 2 pcs. 975.00

Mug, russet ground, No. 1-3½", 3½" h. 90.00

Planter, handled, russet ground, No. 384-8", 8" l. 90.00

Tea set: cov. teapot, creamer & sugar bowl; russet ground, No. 2, 3 pcs. ...275.00

Small Bushberry Vase

Vase, 4" h., conical w/tiny rim handles, blue ground, No. 28-4" (ILLUS.) 40.00

Vase, double bud, 4½" h., gate-form,blue ground, No. 158-4½" 70.00

Vase, 6" h., two-handled, blue or green ground, No. 30-6", each ....75.00 to 85.00

Vase, 7" h., two-handled, blue ground, No. 31-7" 90.00

Vase, bud, 7½" h., asymmetrical base handles, cylindrical body, russet ground, No. 152-7" 90.00

Vase, 18" h., floor-type, green or russet ground 450.00

Wall pocket, high-low handles, green or russet ground, No. 1291-8", 8" h. ....170.00 to 200.00

CARNELIAN I (1910-15)

Matte glaze with a combination of two colors or two shades of the same color with the darker dripping over the lighter tone or heavy and textured glaze with intermingled colors and some running.

Candleholders, simple disc base w/incised rings at base of candle nozzle, deep green & light green, 2½" h., pr. 40.00
Flower frog or candleholder, blue & rose, 3½" h. 55.00
Lamp, factory drilled w/original fittings, two-handled, mottled olive green & pink 425.00
Urn, light blue & dark blue, 7" h. 95.00
Vase, double bud, 5" h., thick olive green & blue 150.00
Vase, 6" h., pillow-type, light blue & dark blue 55.00
Vase, 7" h., deep green & light green...57.50
Vase, 8" h., two-handled, ovoid base & ringed neck, deep green & light green....................................55.00
Vase, 10" h., semi-ovoid base & long wide neck w/rolled rim, ornate handles, dark blue & light blue...........60.00

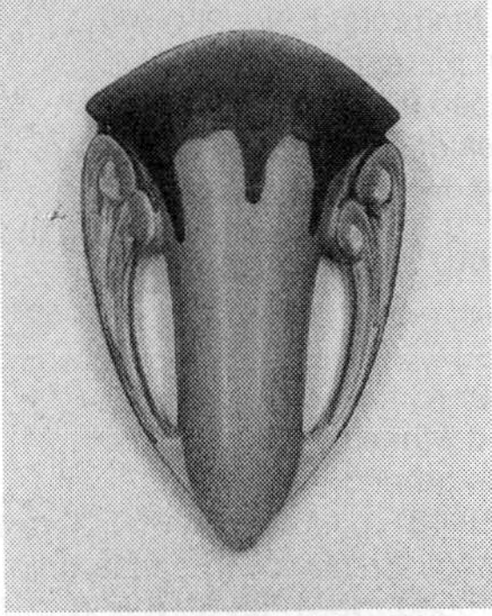

Carnelian I Wall Pocket

Wall pocket, ornate side handles, flaring rim, dark blue & grey, 8" h. (ILLUS.) 95.00

CHLORON (1907)

Molded in high-relief in the manner of early Roman and Greek artifacts. Solid matte green glaze, sometimes combined with ivory. Very similar in form to Egypto.

Jardiniere & pedestal base, the wide ovoid jardiniere w/a molded band of dancing classical ladies around the top, the trumpet-form pedestal tapering toward the base then flaring to a tripod base w/blocky buttress feet, fine matte green glaze, chip to base, jardiniere 14½" d., overall 42½" h., 2 pcs. (ILLUS. top next column) 880.00

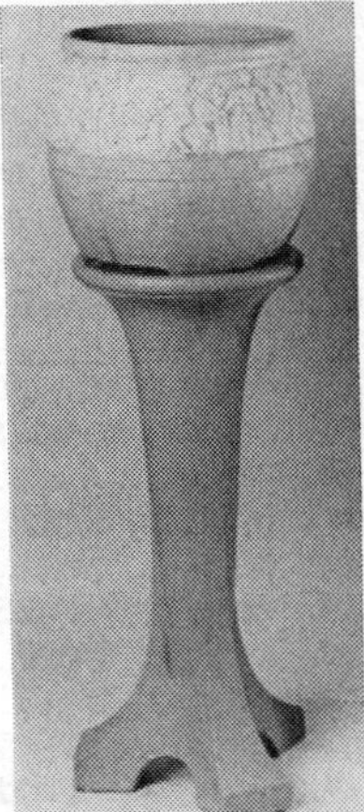

Chloron Jardiniere & Pedestal

Planter, eared handles, relief-molded heart-shaped leaves in groups of three, matte green glaze, 7" d., 3" h. 225.00
Umbrella stand, relief-molded poppies decoration, matte green ground, 22" h. 750.00
Umbrella stand, octagonal, each panel decorated w/a relief-molded iris blossom, 23¼" h. 275.00

CLEMATIS (1944)

Clematis blossoms and heart-shaped green leaves against a vertically textured ground - white blossoms on blue, rose-pink blossoms on green and ivory blossoms on golden brown.

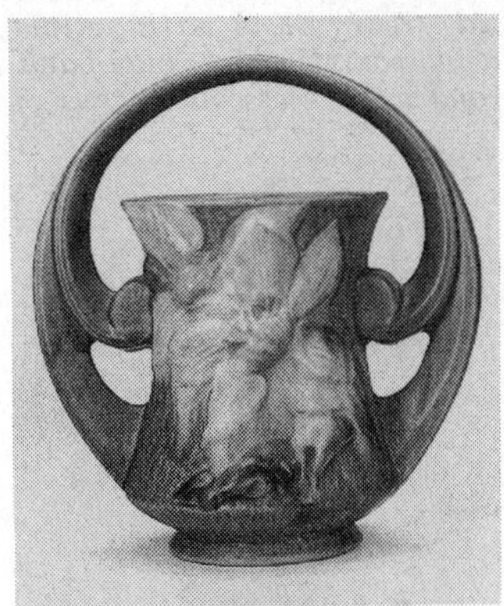

Clematis Basket

Basket w/ornate circular handle, waisted cylindrical body, brown ground, No. 387-7", 7" h. (ILLUS.) ...115.00
Bowl, 10" d., two-handled, green ground, No. 6-10" 65.00
Console bowl, end handles, blue ground, No. 456-6", 9" l. 75.00

Cornucopia-vase, brown ground, No. 190-6", 6" h....65.00
Creamer & sugar bowl, blue ground, Nos. 5C & 5S, pr....110.00
Ewer, squatty, brown ground, No. 16-6", 6" h....75.00
Ewer, blue ground, No. 17-10", 10" h....125.00
Flower arranger, base handles, three openings for flowers, brown ground, No. 102-5", 5½" h....55.00
Flowerpot w/saucer, blue ground, No. 688-5", 5½" h....75.00
Rose bowl, brown ground, No. 455-4", 4" d....35.00
Vase, 5" h., green ground, No. 192-5"....70.00
Vase, double bud, 5" h., two cylinders joined by a single clematis blossom, blue ground, No. 194-5"....65.00
Vase, 6" h., two-handled, urn-form, blue ground, No. 188-6"....75.00
Vase, 6" h., two-handled, urn-form, brown or green ground, No. 188-6", each....50.00 to 65.00
Vase, 8" h., two-handled, blue ground, No. 107-8"....82.50
Vase, 8" h., two-handled, globular base w/high collared neck, green ground, No. 108-8"....70.00
Vase, 10" h., two-handled, blue or brown ground, No. 111-10", each....145.00
Wall pocket, angular side handles, green ground, No. 1295-8", 8½" h....120.00

COSMOS (1940)

Embossed blossoms against a wavy horizontal ridged band on a textured ground - ivory band with yellow and orchid blossoms on blue, blue band with white and orchid blossoms on green or tan.

Cosmos Vase

Basket w/pointed overhead handle, pedestal base, tan ground, No. 358-12", 12" h....285.00
Basket, hanging-type, handles rising from midsection to rim, blue ground, No. 361-5", 7"....275.00
Bowl, 6" d., two-handled, shaped rim, green ground, No. 369-6"....65.00
Candlesticks, loop handles rising from disc base, slightly tapering candle nozzle, tan ground, No. 1137-4½", 4½" h., pr....95.00
Console bowl, end handles rising from base to rim, shaped rim, tan ground, No. 372-10", 10" l....60.00
Flower frog, pierced globular body w/asymmetrical overhead handle, blue ground, No. 39, 3½" h....60.00
Planter, rectangular w/shaped rim, blue ground, No. 381-9", 3 x 3½ x 9"....375.00
Vase, 4" h., two-handled, globular base & wide neck, blue ground, No. 944-4"....60.00
Vase, bud, 7" h., slender, slightly tapering cylinder w/large loop handles at base, blue ground, No. 959-7"....82.50
Vase, 8" h., two-handled, cut-out top edge, tan ground, No. 950-8"....185.00
Vase, 9" h., tapering cylinder w/shaped flaring mouth, curved handles at midsection, blue or tan ground, No. 953-9", each....175.00 to 200.00
Vase, 12½" h., ovoid w/large loop handles, green ground, No. 956-12" (ILLUS.)....350.00
Vase, 18" h., floor-type, trumpet-shaped w/handles rising to flaring rim, tan ground, No. 958-18"....650.00 to 750.00
Wall pocket, circular overhead handle, blue ground, No. 1285-6", 6½" h....300.00
Window box, tan ground, No. 381-9", 9" l....165.00

DAHLROSE (1924-28)

Dahlrose Jardiniere & Pedestal

Band of ivory daisy-like blossoms and green leaves against a mottled tan ground.

Basket, hanging-type, 7½".................175.00
Bowl, 6" d..............................115.00
Bowl, 10" d., two-handled.................195.00
Console bowl, 9" d........................82.50
Jardiniere, tiny rim handles, 7" d., 4" h.........................160.00
Jardiniere, tiny rim handles, 6" h. 150.00
Jardiniere, tiny rim handles, 8" h. 225.00
Jardiniere, 10" h..........................365.00
Jardiniere & pedestal base, overall 25" h., 2 pcs. (ILLUS.)..................675.00
Vase, 5" h., 7" w., pillow-shaped 100.00
Vase, double bud, 6" h., gate-form 100.00
Vase, triple bud, 6½" h., expanding cylinder flanked by tusk-form tubes ....100.00 to 125.00
Vase, bud, 8" h., ornate curving asymmetrical handle, mound base ..125.00
Vase, 8" h., two handles rising from midsection to rim............................125.00
Vase, 9" h., No. 65-9" 175.00
Vase, 10" h., two-handled, ovoid w/wide flaring rim 165.00
Wall pocket, tiny rim handles, 9" h......155.00
Wall pocket, two-handled, conical, 10" h...175.00
Window box, 6 x 12½" 240.00

DELLA ROBBIA, ROZANE (1906)

Incised designs with an overall high-gloss glaze in colors ranging from soft pastel tints to heavy earth tones and brilliant intense colors.

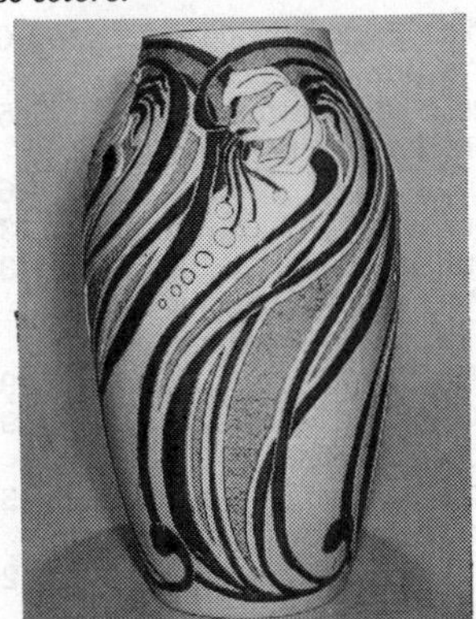

Monumental Della Robbia Vase

Teapot, cov., footed, compressed base & incurving tapered sides, high pointed handle, decorated in sgraffito w/stylized roses under a caramel & brown glaze, 5¼ x 8½" (small chip under lid).......................605.00
Teapot, cov., tall tapering hexagonal body w/long graceful spout & loop handle, domed cover w/pointed finial, each panel carved w/an abstract design of roses & leaves in greyish green against dark bluish grey, wafer mark, 7" w., 8¼" h. 1,100.00
Vase, 8½" h., 6½" d., globular w/short neck, carved overall decoration of green tear-shaped medallions encompassing lavender stylized flowers, excised bands of stylized spades at top & bottom, a band of yellow crocuses around the rim, against a glossy burnt orange ground, Frederick Rhead, 1906, unmarked.....................................5,225.00
Vase, 11½" h., 4" d., footed & buttressed tapering cylindrical body, intricate incised & excised Wiener Werkstatte style design of a stylized cityscape in brown, yellow, pink & grey w/tall square trees in grey w/yellow buds against a honed khaki ground, decorator-initialed by Frederick Rhead, 1906 ....10,450.00
Vase, 15⅝" h., decorated w/deeply cut back, incised & painted flowers in the Art Nouveau style, in shades of bluish grey, navy blue & peach, artist-initialed (ILLUS.) 14,850.00

DOGWOOD (1916-18)

White dogwood blossoms and brown branches against a textured green ground.

Bowl, 5" d...75.00
Bowl, 6½" d.......................................125.00
Jardiniere, 10" h.................................270.00
Jardiniere, 12" d., 12" h. 295.00
Vase, 6½" h. 70.00
Wall pocket, cone-shaped, 9½" h. 155.00

DONATELLO (1915)

Deeply fluted ivory and green body with wide tan band embossed with cherubs at various pursuits in pastoral settings.

Donatello Wall Pocket

Basket w/high pointed overhead handle, globular body, 15" h. 450.00

Basket, hanging-type, 7" d., 5" h.....................................175.00 to 200.00
Bowl, 8" d., 3½" h. 135.00
Bowl, 10" d., 3" h., rolled rim 65.00
Console bowl, oval, No. 60-8", 8" l. 85.00
Flower frog, No. 14-2½", 2½" d. 15.00
Flower frog, No. 14-3½", 3½" d. 18.00
Flowerpot w/saucer, flaring sides, 5" h...115.00
Flowerpot w/saucer, 7" h. 135.00
Jardiniere, No. 575-4", 4" h. 45.00
Jardiniere, 7" d., 6" h. 75.00
Jardiniere & pedestal base, 8" h. jardiniere & 15" h. pedestal, 2 pcs. 650.00
Jardiniere & pedestal base, 10" h. jardiniere, overall 29" h., 2 pcs.........750.00
Pitcher, 6½" h. ....250.00 to 300.00
Plate, 8" d. 275.00
Vase, bud, 7" h. 55.00
Vase, 8" h., cylindrical 50.00
Vase, 8½" h., slightly canted lower section, cylindrical top half.................85.00
Vase, 9" h., two-handled 160.00
Vase, bud, 10" h., bottle-form, No. 115-10"..225.00
Wall pocket, ovoid, 9" h. (ILLUS.).......140.00
Window box, No. 60-12", 6 x 12"........135.00

FERRELLA (1930)

Impressed shell design alternating with small cut-outs at top and base; mottled brown or turquoise and red glaze.

Bowl, 9½" d., 4¼" h., deep flaring sides w/rolled rim, on a flared foot, the bowl rim w/a band of small pierced triangles above a band of larger pierced ovals, pierced triangles also around the foot, turquoise & red glaze, w/flower frog, 2 pcs. 275.00
Console bowl w/attached flower frog, brown glaze, No. 87-8", 8" d. 250.00
Console set: 9½" d. bowl w/flower frog & pair of 4½" h. goblet-form candlesticks; turquoise & red glaze, the set 522.50
Urn-vase, compressed globular form w/tiny handles at midsection, recticulated foot & rim, turquoise & red glaze, No. 505-6", 6" h..............315.00
Vase, 4" h., squatty base w/exaggerated handles & narrow neck, turquoise & red glaze, No. 497-4".......................................265.00
Vase, 4" h., angular handles, bulbous, turquoise & red glaze, No. 498-4"....250.00
Vase, 6" h., handles rising from shoulder of compressed globular base to beneath the rim of the long tapering neck, brown glaze, No. 502-6".......................................250.00
Vase, 9" h., sharply compressed globular base, large handles rising from midsection to below rim, brown glaze 405.00
Vase, 10" h., 6¼" d., ovoid body on flaring foot & tapering to a widely flaring mouth, low angular handles down the sides, the foot pierced w/a band of small squares, the mouth pierced w/two bands of small rectangles, brown glaze, No. 511-10" 550.00

FLORENTINE (1924-28)

Bark-textured panels alternating with embossed garlands of cascading fruit and florals; ivory with tan and green, beige with brown and green or brown with beige and green glaze.

Florentine Wall Pocket

Bowl, 8" d., shallow, beige...................68.00
Bowl, 9" d., low, beige 47.50
Compote, 5" d., brown 50.00
Jardiniere, brown, No. 130-4", 7" d., 4" h...63.00
Jardiniere, ivory, 8" d., 6¼" h.............130.00
Jardiniere, 14" h.................................435.00
Vase, 8" h., squared handles rising above rim, ovoid w/collared neck, ivory, No. 255-8" 95.00
Vase, 10" h., 6" d., footed, beige..........98.00
Wall pocket, conical, beige, 7" h.................................100.00 to 150.00
Wall pocket, semi-ovoid, brown, 9½" h. (ILLUS.) ....100.00 to 125.00
Wall pocket, tapering cylinder, brown, 12½" h. 140.00

FOXGLOVE (1940s)

Sprays of pink and white blossoms embossed against a shaded matte finish ground.

Basket w/circular overhead handle, green ground, No. 373-8", 8" h. 175.00

Basket, hanging-type, blue or green ground, No. 466-5", 6½", each ....225.00 to 250.00
Book ends, pink ground, No. 10, pr. ...250.00
Console bowl, green ground, No. 421-10", 10" l. 95.00
Console set: 12" l. bowl & pair of 2½" h. candleholders; pink ground, Nos. 423-12" & 1149-2½", 3 pcs......195.00

Foxglove Cornucopia-vase

Cornucopia-vase, snail shell-type, blue ground, No. 166-6" (ILLUS.) 70.00
Ewer, blue ground, No. 6-15", 15" h. ....300.00 to 325.00
Model of a conch shell, blue ground, No. 426-6", 6" l. 78.00
Vase, bud, 5" h., pink ground, No. 159-5" 75.00
Vase, 7" h., handled, pink ground, No. 45-7" 65.00
Vase, 14" h., conical w/flaring mouth, four handles rising from disc base, blue ground, No. 53-14" 250.00
Vase, 18" h., floor-type, blue ground ..625.00
Wall pocket, two-handled, blue ground, No. 1292-8", 8" h. 185.00

FREESIA (1945)

Trumpet-shaped blossoms and long slender green leaves against wavy impressed lines - white and lavender blossoms on blended green; white and yellow blossoms on shaded blue or terra cotta and brown.

Basket w/low overhead handle, terra cotta ground, No. 390-7", 7" h. 75.00
Basket w/overhead handle, blueground, No. 391-8", 8" h. (ILLUS. top next column) 110.00
Bowl, 10" d., green ground, No. 467-10" 135.00
Bowl, 16½" l., two-handled, blue ground, No. 469-14" 110.00
Candleholders, tiny pointed handles, domed base, blue ground, No. 1160-2", 2" h., pr. 75.00

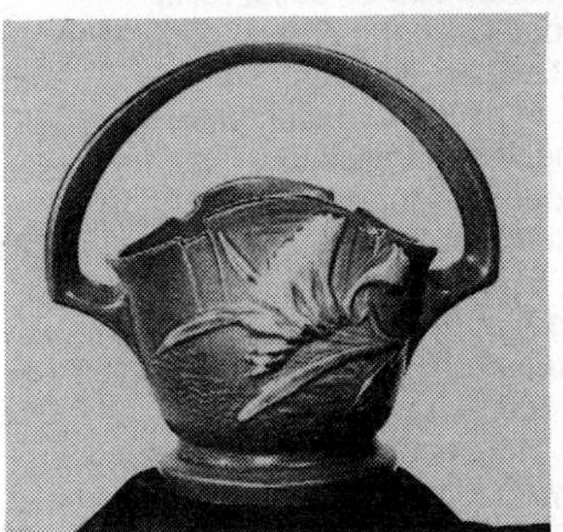

Freesia Basket

Ewer, terra cotta ground, No. 21-15", 15" h. 300.00
Flowerpot w/attached saucer, blue ground, No. 670-5", 5½" h. 125.00
Jardiniere, tiny rim handles, terra cotta ground, No. 669-4", 4" h. 45.00
Pitcher, 10" h., swollen cylinder, green or terra cotta ground, No. 20-10", each ....110.00 to 125.00
Vase, 7" h., base handles, long cylindrical neck, blue ground, No. 119-7" 95.00
Vase, 7" h., two-handled, slightly expanding cylinder, green ground, No. 120-7" 100.00
Vase, 7" h., two-handled, fan-shaped, green, No. 200-7" 100.00
Vase, 8" h., two-handled, green ground, No. 121-8" 95.00
Vase, 9½" h., pointed handles at midsection, terra cotta ground, No. 123-9" ....85.00 to 95.00
Vase, 10" h., blue ground, No. 126-10" ....125.00 to 150.00
Vase, 15" h., two-handled, blue ground, No. 128-15" 265.00
Vase, 18" h., blue ground, No. 129-18" 315.00
Wall pocket, angular handles, green or terra cotta ground, No. 1296-8", 8½" h., each ....130.00 to 160.00

FUTURA (1928)

Varied line with shapes ranging from Art Deco geometrics to futuristic. Matte glaze is typical although an occasional piece may be high gloss.

Bowl, 8" d., collared base, shaped flaring sides w/relief decoration, rose glaze, No. 187-8" 285.00
Jardiniere, angular handles rising from wide sloping shoulders to rim, sharply canted sides, tan w/multi-colored leaves, No. 616-7", 7" h. 440.00
Pot, square body w/canted sides on a

low footed square base, relief-molded flowering branch decoration, mottled blue & green, 3½" h. 230.00

Vase, 5" h., 6" w., rectangular, elongated triangles forming a fan-shaped design on sides in shades of blue, No. 81-5" 285.00

Vase, 6" h., stepped shoulders, square body w/canted sides, grey w/green & blue elongated triangles, No. 380-6" 265.00

Vase, 6" h., octagonal cone-shaped body on a conforming low base, bluish green, No. 397-6" 325.00

Vase, 6" h., squared buttressed form, mottled grey, No. 423-6" 260.00

Vase, 8" h., ovoid w/short collared neck, lightly embossed floral branch at shoulder, incised rings at mid-section, deep rosy beige shading to sand white & back to beige w/touch of blue at branch, No. 428-8" 350.00

Futura Vase

Vase, 8¼" h., 5" d., conical body on flat disc base, buttressed sides, orange w/green buttresses & blue base, No. 401-8" (ILLUS.)...............375.00

Vase, 10¼" h., 5¼" d., small buttressed handles at disc base, slightly swollen cylindrical lower portion flaring to a wide mouth, decorated w/blue flowers on green stems against a shaded orange body, No. 431-10" 600.00

Vase, 14" h., 5½" d., two large handles at lower half, squat stacked base & faceted squared neck, matte glaze in three shades of brown, No. 411-14" 1,540.00

Wall pocket, canted sides, angular rim handles, geometric design in blue, yellow, green & lavender on brown ground, 6" w., 8¼" h.........................315.00

IRIS (1938)

White or yellow blossoms and green leaves on rose blending with green, light blue deepening to a darker blue or tan shading to green or brown.

Basket w/pointed overhead handle, compressed ball form, blue or rose ground, No. 354-8", each................250.00

Bowl, 14" l., end handles, shaped rim, tan ground, No. 364-14"..................150.00

Candlesticks, flat disc base, cylindrical nozzle flanked by elongated open handles, tan ground, No. 1135-4½", 4½" h., pr. 150.00

Jardiniere, two-handled, rose ground, No. 647-3", 3" h...................................65.00

Jardiniere, two-handled, tan ground, No. 647-4", 4" h...................................95.00

Rose bowl, tan or blue ground, No. 357-4", 4" h., each.......................95.00

Pot, globular body w/wide mouth & tiny handles, on small circular foot, rose or tan ground, No. 647-3", 3" h., each...65.00

Vase, 4" h., base handles, tan ground, No. 914-4" 60.00

IXIA (1930s)

Embossed spray of tiny bell-shaped flowers and slender leaves - white blossoms on pink ground; lavender blossoms on green or yellow ground.

Ixia Centerpiece

Bowl, 7" d., pink or yellow ground, No. 329-7", each...............................65.00

Candleholder, two-light, green ground, No. 1127, 3" h.......................50.00

Centerpiece, one-piece console set w/six candleholders attached to center bowl, green ground, 13" l. (ILLUS.) 170.00

Flower frog, pink ground, No. 34 ....60.00

Flowerpot w/saucer, green ground, No. 641-5", 5" h.................................65.00

Vase, 7" h., closed handles, ovoid, green ground, No. 854-7" 75.00

Vase, 10½" h., closed pointed handles at shoulder, cylindrical w/short neck, green ground, No. 862-10".....130.00

JONQUIL (1931)

White jonquil blossoms and green leaves in relief against textured tan ground; green lining.

Basket w/pointed overhead handle rising from base, waisted body, No. 323-7", 7" h. 325.00
Basket w/tall pointed overhead handle, bulbous body, No. 324-8", 8" h. 315.00
Basket, hanging-type 345.00
Bowl, 3" h., large down-turned handles, No. 523-3" 85.00
Jardiniere, two-handled, No. 621-9", 9" h. 300.00

Jonquil Jardiniere & Pedestal

Jardiniere & pedestal base, overall 29" h., 2 pcs. (ILLUS.) 1,045.00
Urn, 5½" h. 135.00
Vase, 4½" h., globular, No. 93-4½" 175.00
Vase, 7" h., base handles 150.00
Vase, 8" h., tapering cylinder w/elongated side handles, No. 528-8" 200.00

JUVENILE (1916 on)

Transfer-printed and painted on creamware with nursery rhyme characters, cute animals and other motifs appealing to children.

Juvenile Feeding Dish

Dinner set: four 8¼" d. plates, four 6¾" d. plates, four mugs, one cereal bowl & one creamer; sitting rabbit, 14 pcs. (tight hairline to bowl) 440.00
Feeding dish w/rolled edge, chicks, 7" d. 81.00
Feeding dish w/rolled edge, chicks, 8" d. 90.00
Feeding dish w/rolled edge, seated dog, 8" d. 95.00
Feeding dish w/rolled edge, sitting rabbits, 8" d. (ILLUS.) 100.00
Pitcher, 3½" h., sunbonnet girl 105.00
Plate, 8" d., chicks 69.00

MAGNOLIA (1943)

Large white blossoms with rose centers and black stems in relief against a blue, green or tan textured ground.

Basket w/ornate overhead handle, green ground, No. 384-7", 7" h. 85.00
Basket w/fan-shaped overhead handle, blue ground, No. 384-8", 8" h. 125.00
Basket, hanging-type, green ground, No. 469-5" 125.00
Bowl, 10" d., two-handled, tan ground, No. 450-10", 10" l. 110.00
Candlesticks, angular handles rising from flat base to midsection of stem, tan ground, No. 1157-4½", 5" h., pr. 90.00
Cornucopia-vase, blue or tan ground, No. 184-6", 6" h., each ....55.00 to 75.00
Ewer, blue or green ground, No. 13-6", 6" h., each ....85.00 to 95.00
Ewer, green ground, No. 15-15", 15" h. 275.00

Magnolia Jardiniere & Pedestal

Jardiniere & pedestal base, blue ground, 2 pcs. (ILLUS.) ....725.00 to 825.00
Pedestal base, green ground, 16" h. ..300.00

Planter, shell-shaped w/angular base handles, green ground, No. 183-6", 6" l. 66.00
Planter, rectangular w/angular end handles, green ground, No. 388-6", 8" l. 57.00
Rose bowl, tan ground, No. 446-4", 4" d. ....55.00 to 65.00
Vase, 6" h., two-handled, green ground, No. 87-6" 65.00
Vase, 6" h., angular pointed handles from base to midsection, blue or green ground, No. 88-6" 67.00
Vase, 8" h., two-handled, green ground, No. 91-8" 155.00
Vase, 9" h., two-handled, blue ground, No. 93-9" 135.00

MING TREE (1949)

Embossed twisted bonsai tree topped with puffy foliage — pink-topped trees on mint green ground, green tops on white ground and white tops on blue ground; handles in the form of gnarled branches.

Basket w/overhead branch handle, rounded body w/shaped rim, blue or white ground, No. 508-8", 8" h., each ....85.00 to 100.00
Candleholders, squat melon-ribbed body w/angular branch handles at shoulder, blue ground, No. 551, pr. ...45.00
Console set: 10" l. bowl & pair of candleholders, No. 551; blue ground, 3 pcs. 180.00
Ewer, green or white ground, No. 516-10", 10" h., each 125.00
Vase, 8" h., asymmetrical branch handles, green ground, No. 582-8" 85.00

MOSS (1930s)

Spanish moss draped over a brown branch with green leaves against a background of ivory, pink or tan shading to blue.

Basket, hanging-type, tan ground, No. 353-5" 325.00
Bowl, 6" d., tan ground, No. 291-6" 145.00
Console set: 10" d. bowl & pair of 4½" h. candlesticks; pink ground, bowl No. 193-10", 3 pcs. 195.00
Vase, 6" h., large open angular handles, tan ground, No. 774-6" 90.00
Vase, 7" h., ivory ground, No. 777-7" 150.00
Wall pocket, bucket-shaped, pink ground, No. 1279, 10" h. 475.00

MOSTIQUE (1915)

Incised Indian-type design of stylized flowers, leaves or geometric shapes glazed in bright high-gloss colors against a heavy, pebbled ground.

Bowl, 7" d., low rounded sides, floral design, sandy beige ground 67.50
Jardiniere, geometric design, tan ground, 18" h. 175.00
Vase, 6" h., glossy yellow stylized flowers, grey ground, green glazed interior 50.00

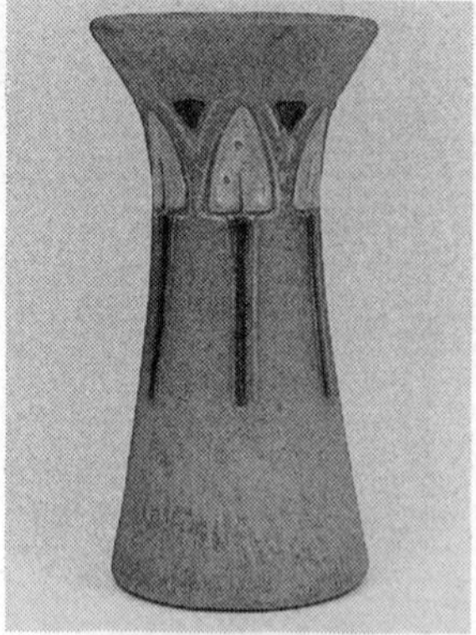

Mostique Vase

Vase, 10" h., slightly waisted cylinder w/flaring mouth, arrowhead designs, grey ground (ILLUS.) 80.00
Vase, 15" h., corset-shaped, geometric floral design, grey ground 275.00

PANEL (1920)

Recessed panels decorated with embossed naturalistic or stylized florals or female nudes.

Candleholders, dark brown ground, 2½" h., pr. 125.00
Urn, dark green ground, 4" h. 65.00
Vase, 6" h., pillow-shaped, small rim handles, orchid blossoms decoration, dark green ground 105.00
Vase, 6" h., cylindrical w/short collared neck, stylized florals, dark brown ground 92.00
Vase, 6" h., pillow-shaped, dark brown ground 120.00

PEONY (1942)

Peony blossoms in relief against a textured swirling ground — yellow blossoms against rose shading to green, brown shading to gold or gold with green; white blossoms against green.

Basket w/overhead handle, gold ground, No. 377-8", 8" h. 85.00

Basket, hanging-type, green ground, No. 467-5" 120.00

Book ends, gold ground, No. 11, 5½" h., pr. 135.00

Bowl, 13" d., rose ground, No. 432-12" 95.00

Peony Double Candleholders

Candleholders, double, green ground, No. 1153, 5" h., pr. (ILLUS.) 55.00

Candlesticks, gold or green ground, No. 1152-4½", 4½" h., each pr..........60.00

Cornucopia-vase, rose ground, No. 171-8", 8" h.................................76.00

Ewer, gold ground, No. 8-10", 10" h...135.00

Ewer, gold or rose ground, No. 9-15", 15" h., each.....................250.00 to 300.00

Flower frog, fan-shaped w/angular base handles, rose ground, No. 47-4", 4" h.......................................58.00

Jardiniere, rose ground, No. 661-4", 4" h...65.00

Jardiniere & pedestal base, rose ground, overall 30" h., 2 pcs. 725.00

Pedestal base, gold ground, 20½" h............................300.00 to 325.00

Planter, rectangular w/angular end handles, slightly canted sides, green ground, No. 387-8", 10" l....................85.00

Rose bowl, two-handled, gold ground, No. 427-6", 6" d..............................135.00

Teapot, cov., gold ground, No. 3 ....135.00

Tray, single rim handle, rose ground, 8" sq....................................55.00 to 65.00

Vase, 8" h., urn-form, rose ground, No. 169-8" 100.00

Vase, 9" h., green ground, No. 65-9"..190.00

Vase, 14" h., angular handles at midsection, rose ground, No. 68-14" 235.00

Vase, 15" h., floor-type, gold ground, No. 69-15" 335.00

Wall pocket, two-handled, green ground, No. 1293-8", 8" h. 265.00

Water set: ice lip pitcher & 4 mugs; green ground, No. 1326-7½ & No. 2-3½, 5 pcs. 275.00

PINE CONE (1931)

Realistic embossed brown pine cones and green pine needles on shaded blue, brown or green ground. (Pink extremely rare.)

Ashtray, blue or green ground, No. 499, 4½" l., each ....85.00 to 95.00

Basket w/overhead branch handle, brown ground, No. 409-8", 8" h................................425.00 to 450.00

Basket w/overhead branch handle rising from midsection of cylindrical body w/shaped base, disc foot, brown ground, No. 353-11", 11" h....325.00

Bowl, 4½" h., two-handled, shaped rim, brown ground, No. 320-5" 75.00

Pine Cone Bowl

Bowl, 6¼ x 9½", 4" h., oval w/pleated ends, twig handles, green ground, No. 279-9" (ILLUS.) 125.00

Candleholders, flat disc base supporting candle nozzle in the form of a pine cone flanked by needles on one side & branch handle on the other, blue ground, No. 1123, 2½" h., pr. 235.00

Cornucopia-vase, blue ground, No. 126-6", 6" h.............................100.00

Ewer, brown ground, No. 851-15", 15" h...500.00

Flower frog, blue ground, No. 20-4"....150.00

Flower frog, brown or green ground, No. 21-5", each 175.00

Jardiniere, two-handled, globular, blue or green ground, No. 632-5", 5" h., each ....325.00 to 350.00

Jardiniere, two-handled, blue or green ground, No. 632-6", 9" d., 6½" h., each ....225.00 to 250.00

Jardiniere & pedestal base, green ground, overall 25" h., 2 pcs. 950.00

Pedestal, blue ground, No. 406-10" ...800.00

Planter, single side handle rising from base, blue or brown ground, No. 124-5", 5" h., each.......80.00 to 100.00

Planter, green ground, No. 456-6", 6" l...95.00

Rose bowl, green ground, No. 278-4", 4" h...225.00

Tray, double, center handle in the form of pine needles & cone, blue, brown or green ground, 6½ x 13", each ....250.00 to 275.00

Tumbler, green ground, No. 414, 5" h...130.00

Urn, blue ground, No. 745-7", 7" h. 275.00

Vase, 6" h., brown ground, No. 838-6" 110.00

Vase, 7" h., brown or green ground, No. 704-7"...........................150.00 to 175.00

Vase, 7" h., spherical body w/flat

mouth, raised on a small square foot, small loop twig handles, green ground, No. 745-7" 165.00

Vase, 8" h., pillow-type, green ground, No. 845-8" 225.00

Vase, 12" h., brown ground, No. 911-12" 325.00

Vase, 18½" h., floor-type, two-handled, low foot, ovoid w/short neck & flaring rim, No. 913-18" 660.00

Wall pocket, double, brown or green ground, No. 1273-8", 8½" h., each .... 275.00 to 300.00

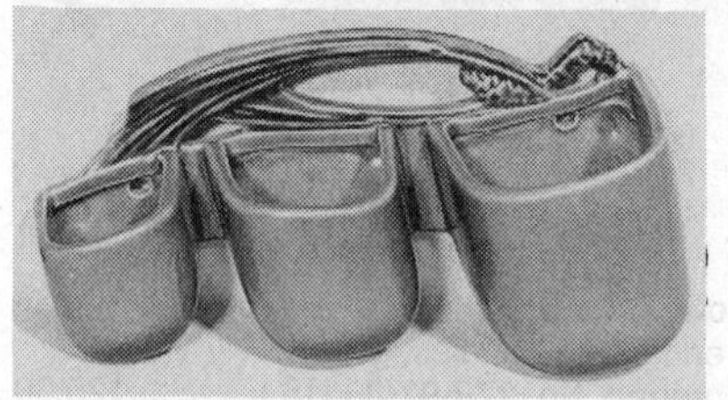

Triple Pine Cone Wall Pocket

Wall pocket, triple, green ground, No. 466-8½", 8½" w. (ILLUS.) 350.00

POPPY (1930)

Embossed full-blown poppy blossoms, buds and foliage — yellow blossoms on green, white blossoms on blue or soft pink blossoms on a deeper pink.

Poppy Rose Bowl

Basket w/pointed overhead handle, slender ovoid body on disc base, green ground, No. 348-12", 12½" h. 215.00

Bowl, 5" d., two-handled, pink ground, No. 336-5" 110.00

Bowl, 8" d., two-handled, irregular rim, blue ground, No. 337-8" 100.00

Ewer, ornate cut-out lip, green or pink ground, No. 876-10", 10" h., each .... 150.00 to 175.00

Flower frog, pink ground, No. 35 .... 105.00

Jardiniere, tiny handles at rim, pink ground, No. 642-4", 4" h. 80.00

Jardiniere & pedestal base, green ground, 8" h. jardiniere, 2 pcs. 825.00

Rose bowl, two-handled, pink ground, No. 334-4", 4" h. (ILLUS.) 72.50

Vase, 7½" h., two-handled, green ground, No. 869-7" 105.00

Vase, 7½" h., two-handled, expanding cylinder w/slightly waisted neck & wide mouth, green ground, No. 868-7" 65.00

Vase, 10" h., two-handled, semi-ovoid, cut-out rim, green ground, No. 875-10" 225.00

Wall pocket, triple, tapering center section flanked by small tapering cylinders, green ground, No. 1281-8", 8½" h. 310.00

RAYMOR (1952)

Modernistic design oven-proof dinnerware.

Raymor Dinnerware

Bean pot, cov., individual size, Contemporary white, No. 195 .... 35.00

Bowl, soup, lug-type, Autumn brown, No. 155 .... 18.00

Celery & olive dish, Beach gray, No. 177 .... 35.00

Coffee tumbler, handled, Beach gray, No. 179 (small inner rim flake) 18.00

Coffee tumbler, handled, Terra Cotta, No. 179 .... 30.00

Corn servers, individual size, long slender form w/section for butter, one each Autumn brown, Avocado green, Terra Cotta, Beach gray & Contemporary white, 12½" l., set of 5 .... 200.00

Cup, Autumn brown, No. 150 .... 12.00

Cup & saucer, Autumn brown, Nos. 150 & 151, set 18.00

Cup & saucer, Beach gray, Nos. 150 & 151, set 25.00

Dinner service for five: dinner plates, cov. ramekins & cups & saucers; Beach gray, 20 pcs. 200.00

Plate, bread & butter, Autumn brown, No. 154 .... 6.50

Plate, salad, Beach gray, No. 154 .... 15.00

Plate, salad, Terra Cotta, No. 154 .... 15.00

Platter, rectangular, Avocado green, No. 163 .... 50.00

Teapot, cov., black, No. 174 .... 125.00

ROZANE (early 1900s)

Underglaze slip-painted decoration on dark blended backgrounds.

Rozane Vase with Dog Portrait

Jardiniere, squeeze bag decoration of flying geese & stylized trees, artist-signed, 10" d., 6" h. 605.00

Jug, floral decoration, artist-signed, No. 888, 4½" h. 215.00

Vase, 8¼" h., 5" d., tall ovoid body, decorated w/burnt orange poppies on green stems & w/green leaves in a glossy glaze against a creamy bisque ground, glossy-glazed interior 1,540.00

Vase, 9" h., 6" d., ovoid w/tiny mouth, decorated w/pink, white & green raspberries w/green foliage against a shaded brown ground, artist-signed 425.00

Vase, 9½" h., pillow-type w/scalloped rim, decorated w/a scene of a hunting dog w/a pheasant in its mouth, artist-signed (ILLUS.) 660.00

Vase, 10¼" h., 6¼" d., a wide domed base on tab feet tapering sharply to a bulbous knob at the base of the tall slender cylindrical neck w/a widely flaring rim, slender straight handles running from rim to top of knob, squeeze-bag decoration w/dark bands trimmed in delicate scrolls around the base & on the knob, the base further decorated w/a large cluster of chestnuts & leaves in bluish grey & brown against a light ground, artist-signed (two tight horizontal hairlines in handles) 1,320.00

Vase, 10½" h., 4" d., tall waisted cylindrical form w/short flared neck, decorated w/sprigs of white & grey flowers against a shaded greyish green ground, artist-signed & numbered "36" 440.00

Vase, 13" h., 6" d., tall footed ovoid body tapering to a short wide slightly flaring neck, decorated w/a bust portrait of an Indian warrior against a dark shaded ground, artist-signed & die-stamped "A (?) PPC - D" 660.00

Vase, 13½" h., decorated w/a dog portrait against a dark shaded ground, signed M. Timberlake 1,400.00

Vase, 18" h., blueberry decoration against a grey ground 1,870.00

Vase, 21¼" h., 12" d., floor-type, tall footed ovoid body tapering to a short narrow neck w/flared rim, golden & brown irises on a dark brown ground, artist-signed (very minor rim chip) 1,320.00

Vase, 22" h., portrait of Indian in full headdress, signed A. Dunlavy 5,225.00

SILHOUETTE (1952)

Recessed shaped panels decorated with floral designs or exotic female nudes against a combed background.

Ashtray, square w/indentations at corners, rose, No. 799 ....45.00

Basket w/asymmetrical rim & overhead handle, florals, rose, tan or white w/turquoise blue panel, No. 709-8", 8" h., each ....90.00 to 110.00

Basket w/curved rim & asymmetrical handle, florals, white w/turquoise blue panel, No. 710-10", 10" h. 125.00

Basket, hanging-type, florals, turquoise blue ....80.00 to 110.00

Bowl, 10" d., florals, white, No. 730-10" 70.00

Bowl, 12" l., florals, tan, No. 729-12" 75.00

Ewer, bulging base, florals, turquoise blue, No. 716-6", 6" h. 55.00

Planter, florals, turquoise blue, No. 769-9", 9" l. 80.00

Rose bowl, female nudes, rose or tan, No. 742-6", 6" h., each ....285.00 to 315.00

Urn, female nudes, rose, No. 763-8", 8" h. 400.00

Vase, 7" h., florals, double wing-shaped handles above low footed base, cylindrical w/asymmetrical rim, white, No. 782-7" 95.00

Vase, 7" h., fan-shaped, florals, white w/turquoise blue panel, No. 783-7" 230.00

Vase, 8" h., urn-form, tapering ovoid body raised on four angled feet on a round disc base, wide slightly flaring mouth, turquoise blue, No. 763-8" 330.00

Vase, 9" h., flat closed handles between domed base & body, florals, white, No. 785-9" 165.00

Vase, 12" h., florals, turquoise blue, No. 788-12" 125.00

Vase, 12" h., florals, white, No. 788-12" 125.00

Wall pocket, bullet-shaped w/angular pierced handles, florals, white w/turquoise blue panel, No. 766-8", 8" h. 120.00

SNOWBERRY (1946)

Clusters of white berries on brown stems with green foliage over oblique scalloping, against a blue, green or rose background.

Snowberry Sugar Bowl

Basket w/low pointed overhead handle, shaded blue ground, No. 1BK7", 7" h. 115.00

Basket w/curved overhead handle, disc base, shaded rose ground, No. 1BK-10", 10" h. 150.00

Basket w/overhead handle curving from base to beneath rim on opposite side, curved rim, shaded rose ground, No. 1BK-12", 12½" h. 195.00

Basket, hanging-type, shaded rose ground, No. 1HB5", 5" h. 175.00

Book ends, shaded blue or rose ground, No. 1BE, each pr. 145.00

Bowl, 6" d., shaded blue ground, No. 1BL2-6" 75.00

Bowl, 10" d., footed, shaded blue ground, No. 1FB-10" 145.00

Bowl, 14" d., green ground, No. 1BL14" 65.00

Candlesticks, angular side handles, shaded rose ground, No. 1CS2-4½", 4½" h., pr. 75.00

Console bowl, pointed end handles, shaded rose ground, No. 1BL1-10", 10" l. 75.00

Console set: 12" l. bowl & pair of candleholders; shaded blue ground, No. 1BL2-12", 3 pcs. 175.00

Cornucopia-vase, shaded blue, green or rose ground, No. 1CC-6", 6" h., each 48.00

Cornucopia-vase, shaded blue ground, No. 1CC-8", 8" h. 115.00

Creamer & sugar bowl, angular side handles, shaded blue ground, Nos. 1C & 1S, pr. (ILLUS. of sugar bowl) 95.00

Ewer, sharply compressed base w/long conical neck, shaded blue ground, No. 1TK-10", 10" h. 145.00

Ewer, flaring base, oval body, shaded green or rose ground, No. 1TK-15", 16" h., each ....250.00 to 300.00

Flower holder, shaded blue ground, No. 1FH-7", 7" h. 85.00

Jardiniere, two-handled, shaded rose ground, No. 1J-4", 4" h. 62.00

Jardiniere, shaded rose ground, No. 1J-6", 6" h. 115.00

Jardiniere & pedestal base, shaded blue ground, overall 25" h., 2 pcs. 600.00

Vase, 6½" h., pillow-type, shaded blue ground, No. 1FH-6" 100.00

Vase, bud, 7" h., single base handle, asymmetrical rim, shaded green ground, No. 1BV-7" 52.50

Vase, 9" h., base handles, shaded rose ground, No. 1V1-9" 95.00

Vase, 18" h., shaded blue ground, No. 1V-18" ....575.00 to 600.00

Window box, shaded blue or rose ground, No. 1WX-8", 8" l. 75.00

SUNFLOWER (1930)

Long-stemmed yellow sunflower blossoms framed in green leaves against a mottled green textured ground.

Sunflower Vase

Candlestick, 4" h. 250.00

Urn, globular w/small rim handles, 4" h. 210.00

Urn, straight sided, 5" h. 280.00

Vase, 5" h., two-handled, bulbous (ILLUS.) 240.00

Vase, 5½" h., 5½" d., bulbous ovoid body tapering to a wide flat mouth, small loop handles at the shoulder 385.00

Vase, 6" h., cylindrical w/tiny rim handles 235.00

Wall pocket, curved openwork double handle, 7½" h. 600.00

THORN APPLE (1930s)

White trumpet flower and foliage one side, reverse with thorny pod and foliage against shaded blue, brown or pink ground.

Basket w/pointed overhead handle, conical w/low foot, shaded brown ground, No. 342-10", 10" h. 135.00
Basket, hanging-type, shaded brown ground, No. 355-5", 7" d.................................175.00 to 225.00
Bowl, 7" d., 3" h., pointed handles, shaded pink ground, No. 308-7" 145.00
Jardiniere, shaded blue ground, No. 638-5", 5" h...............................55.00
Urn, stepped handles, disc foot, shaded pink ground, No. 305-6", 6½" h...200.00
Vase, 6" h., shaded blue ground, No. 810-6"..70.00
Vase, 6" h., shaded blue or pink ground, No. 811-6", each..................75.00
Vase, 7" h., shaded pink ground, No. 815-7"..75.00
Vase, 8½" h., semi-ovoid body flanked by slender columns, on low disc base, shaded pink ground, No. 816-8"......................115.00 to 135.00
Vase, 10" h., shaded pink ground, No. 821-10"....................................175.00
Vase, 12" h., curved base handles, flaring cylinder, shaded pink ground, No. 823-12"....................................250.00
Vase, 15" h., floor-type, shaded pink ground, No. 824-15".......................350.00
Wall pocket, triple, shaded blue or brown ground, No. 1280-8", 8" h., each ....275.00 to 300.00

TUSCANY (1927)

Gently curving handles terminating in blue grape clusters and green leaves.

Bowl, 7" d., two-handled, mottled pink 54.00
Candlesticks, domed base w/open handles rising from rim to beneath candle nozzle, mottled grey or pink, 3" h., each pr.....................................87.50
Console bowl, mottled grey, 14½" l. 85.00
Flower arranger, pedestal base, flaring body, open handles, mottled pink, 5" h. 80.00
Flower frog, mottled pink, 3" h. 32.50
Urn-vase, mottled pink or grey, 5" h.......................................60.00 to 75.00
Vase, 8" h., two-handled, mottled grey 135.00
Vase, 10" h., shoulder handles, bulbous, mottled pink.......................100.00
Wall pocket, long open handles, rounded rim, mottled pink, 8" h. 175.00

VELMOSS (1935)

Embossed clusters of long slender green leaves extending down from the top and crossing three wavy horizontal lines. Some pieces reverse the design with the leaves rising from the base.

Velmoss Vase

Cornucopia-vase, double, mottled blue, No. 117-8", 8½" h...................100.00
Urn-vase, angular pointed side handles, mottled blue, No. 264-5", 8½" d., 5" h. 110.00
Urn-vase, angular pointed side handles, mottled pink, No. 265-6", 6" h...175.00
Vase, 5" h., angular handles, mottled green...65.00
Vase, 6" h., cylindrical w/angular pointed handles, mottled green, No. 714-6"...........................50.00 to 60.00
Vase, 7" h., angular side handles at midsection, cylindrical w/low foot, mottled blue or raspberry red, No. 715-7", each.............135.00 to 150.00
Vase, 8" h., angular pointed handles at midsection, footed, mottled raspberry red, No. 717-8" 160.00
Vase, 9½" h., angular handles, mottled green, No. 719-9" (ILLUS.) 250.00

WATER LILY (1940s)

Water lily blossoms and pads against a horizontally ridged ground. White lilies on green lily pads against a blended blue ground, pink lilies on a pink shading to green ground or yellow lilies against a gold shading to brown ground.

Basket, hanging-type, gold shading to brown ground, No. 468-5", 9" h.......160.00
Bowl, 6" d., blended blue ground, No. 439-6"...75.00
Console bowl, pointed end handles, blended blue ground, No. 443-12", 12" l. 118.00

Water Lily Cookie Jar

Cookie jar, cov., angular handles, blended blue ground, No. 1-8", 8" h. (ILLUS.) ....250.00 to 300.00

Ewer, flared bottom, blended blue ground, No. 10-6", 6" h. 92.00

Ewer, compressed globular base, pink shading to green ground, No. 11-10", 10" h. 150.00

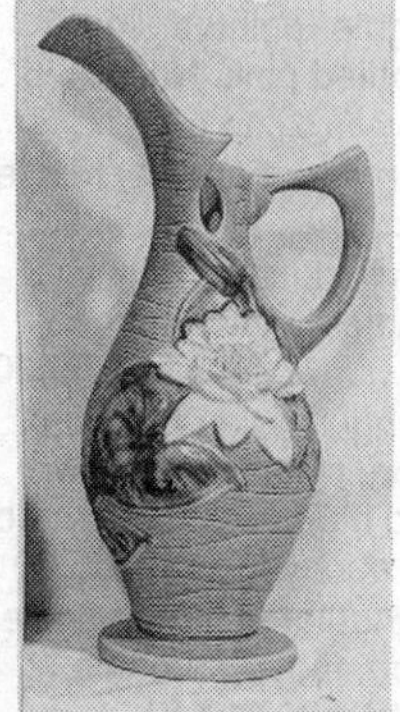

Large Water Lily Ewer

Ewer, swollen cylindrical form on flat base, blended blue ground, No. 12-15", 15" h. (ILLUS.) 260.00

Flower holder, two-handled, fan-shaped body, gold shading to brown or pink shading to green ground, No. 48, 4½" h., each ....45.00 to 50.00

Jardiniere, two-handled, gold shading to brown ground, No. 663-3", 3" h......45.00

Jardiniere & pedestal base, blended blue ground, 2 pcs. 895.00

Model of a conch shell, gold shading to brown or pink shading to green ground, No. 438-8", 8" h., each........150.00

Pedestal base, blended blue ground, 17" h. 275.00

Rose bowl, two-handled, gold shading to brown or pink shading to green ground, No. 437-4", 4" h., each ....50.00 to 75.00

Rose bowl, two-handled, gold shading to brown ground, No. 437-6", 6" d....100.00

Urn-vase, pink shading to green ground, No. 175-8", 8" h. 80.00

Vase, 4" h., blended blue ground, No. 71-4" 47.00

Vase, 8" h., two-handled, blended blue ground, No. 76-8" 80.00

Vase, 14" h., angular side handles, gold shading to brown or pink shading to green ground, No. 82-14", each ....250.00 to 275.00

Vase, 15" h., gold shading to brown ground, No. 83-15" 200.00

WHITE ROSE (1940)

White roses and green leaves against a vertically combed ground of blended blue, brown shading to green or pink shading to green.

Basket w/low pointed overhead handle, blended blue ground, No. 362-8", 7½" h. 125.00

Basket w/low pointed overhead handle, pink shading to green ground, No. 362-8", 7½" h. 150.00

Basket w/pointed circular handle, blended blue ground, No. 363-10", 10" h. 195.00

Basket w/pointed circular handle, brown shading to green or pink shading to green ground, No. 363-10", 10" h., each ....135.00 to 165.00

Basket w/sweeping handle rising from base to rim at opposite side, blended blue ground, No. 364-12", 12" h. 190.00

Basket, hanging-type, blended blue, brown shading to green or pink shading to green ground, No. 463-5", each ....150.00 to 175.00

Book ends, blended blue ground, No. 7, pr. ....165.00 to 195.00

Bowl, 10" d., two-handled, blended blue ground, No. 392-10" 100.00

Console bowl, elongated pointed handles, pink shading to green ground, No. 393-12", 16½" l. 125.00

Console set: bowl, pair of candle-holders & flower frog w/overhead handle; pink shading to green ground, No. 392-10", No. 1141 & No. 41, the set 245.00

Ewer, compressed globular base, blended blue or pink shading to green ground, No. 981-6", 6" h., each ....65.00 to 75.00

Jardiniere, two-handled, blended blue ground, No. 653-3", 3" h. 60.00

Jardiniere, brown shading to green ground, No. 653-5", 5" h. 80.00

Jardiniere & pedestal base, pink shading to green ground, 10" h. jardiniere, 2 pcs. (minor chips)......1,095.00
Vase, 4" h., cylindrical w/slightly sloping shoulder, blended blue ground, No. 978-4"............................30.00
Vase, double bud, 4½" h., two cylinders joined by an arched bridge, blended blue ground, No. 148 ....115.00
Vase, 6" h., cylindrical w/short collared neck, angular handles at shoulder, blended blue or pink shading to green ground, No. 979-6", each...75.00
Vase, 7" h., pink shading to green ground, No. 983-7"...........................65.00
Vase, 8" h., base handles, brown shading to green ground, No. 984-8"..100.00
Vase, 8½" h., handles rising from globular base to rim, blended blue, No. 985-8"..125.00
Vase, 9" h., blended blue ground, No. 986-9"..135.00
Vase, 18" h., two-handled, blended blue ground, No. 994-18"................465.00
Wall pocket, swirled handle, flaring rim, pink shading to green ground, No. 1288-6", 6½" h..........................175.00

WINCRAFT (1948)

Shapes from older lines such as Pine Cone, Cremona, Primrose and others, vases with an animal motif, and contemporary shapes. High gloss glaze in bright shades of blue, tan, yellow, turquoise, apricot and grey.

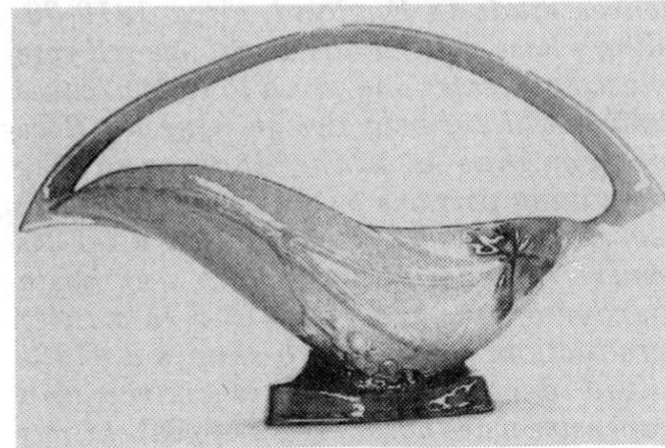

Wincraft Basket

Basket w/low overhead handle, shaped rim, narcissus-type blossoms & foliage in relief on blue ground, No. 208-8", 8" h.................105.00
Basket w/low overhead handle, shaped rim, berries & foliage in relief on green ground, No. 209-12", 12" h. (ILLUS.) 85.00
Basket, hanging-type, lime green or tan, 8" h., each..............................110.00
Book ends, yellow, No. 259, 6½" h., pr...60.00
Bowl, 8" d., blue, No. 226-8"..................75.00
Candleholders, brown, No. 251, pr.......92.50
Cigarette box, cov., rectangular, blue, No. 240, 4½" l. 95.00
Console bowl, brown, No. 228-12", 12" l..165.00
Ewer, stepped lower portion & long slender neck w/flaring mouth, leaves in relief on shaded lime green ground, No. 218-18", 18" h. 350.00
Vase, 6" h., asymmetrical fan shape, pine cones & needles in relief on shaded blue or brown ground, No. 272-6", each 75.00
Vase, 10" h., cylindrical, tab handles, black panther & green palm trees in relief on shaded green ground, No. 290-10"...435.00
Vase, 12" h., tan, No. 275-12" 160.00
Vase, 18" h., floor-type, blue, No. 289-18"......................400.00 to 425.00
Wall pocket, horizontally ribbed square body, shaded brown, No. 266-4, 8½" h.............................125.00

WISTERIA (1933)

Lavender wisteria blossoms and green vines against a roughly textured brown shading to deep blue ground, rarely found in only brown.

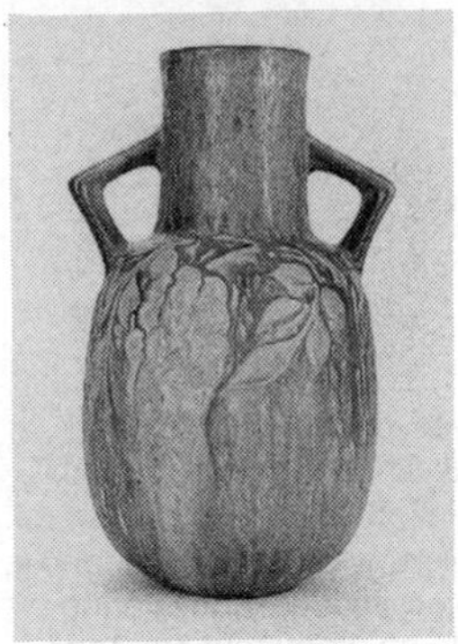

Wisteria Vase

Bowl, 4" h., angular rim handles, brown ground, No. 242-4"................145.00
Candleholders, high domed base w/angular pointed handles, No. 1091-4", 4" h., pr. 450.00
Planter, rectangular w/angular end handles, brown ground, No. 243, 5 x 9"..225.00
Vase, 4" h., squatty, angular handles on sharply canted shoulder, No. 629-4"...195.00
Vase, 6" h., two-handled, pear-shaped w/wide mouth, No. 631-6"...235.00
Vase, 6½" h., globular w/angular rim handles, No. 637-6½" 430.00

Vase, 7" h., angular handles at shoulder, brown ground, No. 634-7" 210.00
Vase, 8" h., 6½" d., wide tapering cylindrical body w/small angled handles flanking the flat rim, No. 633-8" 450.00
Vase, 8½" h., slender base handles, conical body bulging slightly below rim, brown ground, No. 635-8" ....275.00 to 325.00
Vase, 9½" h., cylindrical body w/angular handles rising from shoulder to midsection of slender cylindrical neck, No. 638-9" (ILLUS.) 450.00
Wall pocket, flaring rim, 8" h. 575.00

ZEPHYR LILY (1946)

Deeply embossed day lilies against a swirl-textured ground. White and yellow lilies on a blended blue ground; rose and yellow lilies on a green ground; yellow lilies on terra cotta shading to olive green ground.

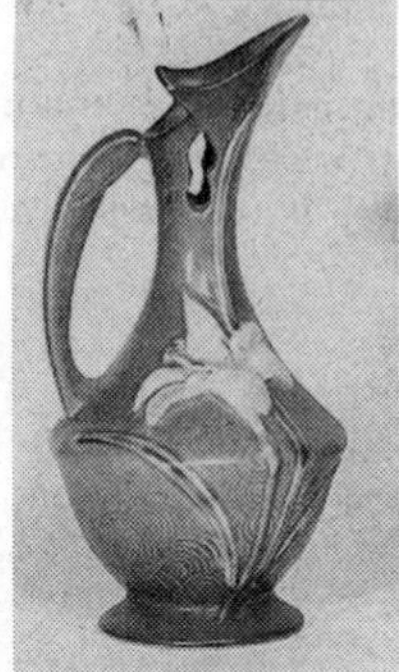

Zephyr Lily Ewer

Basket w/asymmetrical overhead handle & rim, terra cotta ground, No. 394-8", 8" h. 115.00
Basket w/low, wide overhead handle, disc foot, cylindrical body flaring slightly to an ornate cut rim, terra cotta ground, No. 395-10", 10" h. 175.00
Basket, hanging-type, blue, green or terra cotta ground, No. 472-5", 7½", each ....125.00 to 150.00
Book ends, green ground, No. 16, pr. 135.00
Bowl, 8" d., terra cotta ground, No. 474-8" 80.00
Candlesticks, terra cotta ground, No. 1163-4½", 4½" h., pr. ....75.00 to 95.00
Console bowl, end handles, terra cotta ground, No. 474-8", 8" l. 80.00
Cornucopia-vase, blue ground, No. 204-8", 8½" h. ....75.00 to 85.00
Creamer, blue or terra cotta ground, No. 7-C, each ....50.00 to 60.00
Ewer, terra cotta ground, No. 23-10", 10" h. (ILLUS.) 110.00
Jardiniere, two-handled, terra cotta ground, No. 671-4", 4" h. 80.00
Tea set: cov. teapot, creamer & sugar bowl; green ground, Nos. 7C, S & T, 3 pcs. 225.00
Vase, 6½" h., fan-shaped, base handles, blue ground, No. 205-6" 85.00
Vase, bud, 7½" h., handles rising from conical base, slender expanding cylinder w/flaring rim, blue ground, No. 201-7" 95.00
Vase, 8" h., green ground, No. 134-8" 85.00
Vase, 8½" h., handles rising from flat disc base to midsection of cylindrical body, No. 133-8" 135.00
Vase, 9" h., green or terra cotta ground, No. 136-9", each ....125.00 to 150.00
Vase, 12" h., conical w/base handles, green ground, No. 139-12" 125.00
Vase, 18" h., terra cotta ground, No. 142-17" 350.00

(End of Roseville Section)

ROSE WARES

Three different gaudy-type patterns of rose-decorated wares, once popular with the Pennsylvania "Deutsch" (Germans) that settled in the southeastern part of that state, are sought out by collectors who are willing to pay high prices for these early wares made in England, circa 1810-30. King's Rose pattern has an orange-red rose placed off center and green to yellow leaves and is quite a bold design. Queen's Rose pattern has a pink bloom and the remaining portions of the design are more delicate. Adams' Rose, named after its maker, William Adams (which see), has a border of two red roses and is a later production. The superb shapes and the vivid decoration of this scarce and expensive ware has a cheery appeal entirely its own.

Creamer, footed boat-shaped body w/C-scroll handle, molded ribs at front & back, King's Rose patt., 4¾" h. (minor stains & wear) $187.00
Cup & saucer, handleless, King's Rose patt. (wear, pinpoint flakes) 82.50
Cup plate, King's Rose patt., solid pink border, 3½" d. (wear, small old chips) 110.00
Plate, 7¼" d., King's Rose patt. (wear, flaking & pinpoint flakes) 159.50
Plate, 8½" d., King's Rose patt. 165.00

Teapot, cov., footed boat-shaped body w/molded ribs at front & back & on base of spout, angled handle, inset domed cover w/knob finial, King's Rose patt., 6" h. (professional repair) 302.50

Toddy plate, King's Rose patt., solid border, 5¼" d. 93.50

ROYAL BAYREUTH

Good china in numerous patterns and designs has been made at the Royal Bayreuth factory in Tettau, Germany, since 1794. Listings below are by the company's lines, plus miscellaneous pieces. Interest in this china remains at a peak and prices continue to rise. Pieces listed carry the company's blue mark except where noted otherwise.

CORINTHIAN

Box, cov., curved front, classical figures on black ground, 4" sq. $40.00

Creamer, classical figures on black ground..52.50

Mug, classical figures, 4¾" h. 55.00

Pitcher, 5½" h., classical figures on orange ground 65.00

Corinthian Pitcher

Pitcher, 5½" h., classical figures on black ground, yellow bands w/leaf decoration around neck & base (ILLUS.) 75.00

Pitcher, 7⅛" h., 4⅜" d., classical figures on black ground 135.00

Smoke set: cov. cigarette jar, a jar w/striker for matches, a jar for spent matches & kidney-shaped tray; 4 pcs. 195.00

Tea set: cov. teapot, creamer & open sugar bowl; classical figures on red ground, 3 pcs. 150.00

Toothpick holder, classical figures on black ground 100.00

Vase, 3½" h., classical figures on green ground 125.00

DEVIL & CARDS

Devil & Cards Candy Dish

Ashtray, full-figure devil 450.00

Ashtray, figural devil's head, red.................................550.00 to 650.00

Ashtray w/match holder & striker.....1,000.00

Candleholder, low.............350.00 to 400.00

Candlestick, 8" h.............................3,000.00

Candy dish, 7" d. (ILLUS.) ..300.00 to 350.00

Creamer, 4" h. ....225.00 to 275.00

Dresser tray ....500.00 to 600.00

Match holder, wall-type.......................525.00

Match holder, wall-type, full figure-style 1,800.00

Mug, beer-type 425.00

Pitcher, milk, 5" h...............350.00 to 400.00

Pitcher, water, 7¼" h. ....550.00 to 600.00

Stamp box, cov., 3½" l.........................800.00

MOTHER-OF-PEARL FINISH

Bowl, 9" d., conch shell mold, pearlized white w/black highlights.............50.00

Bowl, nut, poppy mold, pearlized finish 110.00

Cracker jar, cov., grape cluster mold, pearlized white finish ....425.00 to 450.00

Creamer, grape cluster mold, pearlized finish..................................145.00

Creamer, Oyster & Pearl mold 335.00

Creamer, poppy mold, lavender pearlized finish..................................150.00

Gravy boat & underplate, conch shell mold, pearlized white w/black highlights, 2 pcs. 60.00

Hatpin holder, octagonal, scalloped rim w/gold scroll trim, pearlized finish 135.00

Marmalade jar, cov., grape cluster

mold, pearlized yellow finish 350.00
Nappy, Oyster & Pearl mold, large.....250.00
Pitcher, 4" h., 2¾ x 6¼", Murex Shell patt., pearlized finish exterior (unmarked) 79.00
Plate, 5½" d., oak leaf mold..................80.00
Platter, 5 x 7", grape & leaf mold, white pearlized finish 135.00
Salt & pepper shakers, figural grape cluster, white satin finish, pr.............120.00
Salt & pepper shakers, grape cluster mold, pearlized red finish, pr............160.00
Sugar bowl, cov., grape cluster mold, pearlized finish................................165.00
Sugar bowl, cov., poppy mold, white pearlized finish................................575.00

ROSE TAPESTRY

Rose Tapestry Dresser Tray

Basket, three-color roses, 4½" w., 4" h...285.00
Basket, two-color roses, 4¼" w., 3¾" h...............................350.00 to 375.00
Basket, footed, drapery chain of buds on base w/handle & base cut-outs, 5½" h...455.00
Bell w/wooden clapper, pink roses decoration on white background, gold handle 395.00
Box, cov., oval, one-color roses, 4" l..235.00
Box, cov., three-color roses, 2½" sq..275.00
Box, cov., two-color roses, 3¼" d., 2¼" h...275.00
Cake plate, three-color roses, free-form fancy rim w/gold beading, 9½" w. 365.00
Cake plate, pierced gold handles, three-color roses, 10½" d.................450.00
Chocolate pot, cov., footed, four-color roses, gold trim, 8½" h. 2,000.00
Clock, two-color roses, German works (runs) 1,200.00
Creamer, pinched spout, three-color roses, 3" h...195.00
Creamer, three-color roses, 3¼" h. 175.00
Creamer, pinched spout, two-color roses, 3½" h..195.00
Creamer, corset-shaped, three-color roses, 3¾" h...195.00
Creamer, pinched spout, three-color roses, 4" h...275.00
Dish, leaf-shaped, three-color roses...195.00
Dresser tray, rectangular, two-color roses, 10" l..325.00
Dresser tray, rectangular, three-color roses, 8 x 11½" (ILLUS.).................350.00
Hair receiver, cov., one-color rose......225.00

Rose Tapestry Hair Receiver

Hair receiver, cov., three-color roses (ILLUS.) ....250.00 to 300.00
Hatpin holder, two-color roses, scrolled base, 4½" h. 275.00
Hatpin holder, three-color roses, scrolled base, 4½" h. ....400.00 to 450.00
Pitcher, milk, 4" h., three-color roses..185.00
Pitcher, 4¼" h., pinched spout, three-color roses 285.00
Pitcher, water, 5⅞" h., pinched spout, three-color roses 610.00
Plate, 6" d., red roses & daisies..........125.00
Plate, 6" d., three-color roses 180.00
Powder box, cov., one-color rose, 4" d..................................175.00 to 200.00
Sauce dishes, red roses & green & yellow leaves, 5¾" d., pr. 250.00

SAND BABIES

Creamer, spherical body w/narrow, short neck, decorated w/three children running, pastel ground, gold handle, 2¼" d. 3" h.............................75.00
Dish, clover-shaped, 4¼" w. 159.00
Dish, diamond-shaped, 4¼" w...........135.00
Dish, star-shaped, 4¼" w...................155.00
Feeding dish, 7¼" d............................145.00
Plate 125.00
Vase, miniature, 3" h., babies running, silver collar..98.00

SNOW BABIES

Candleholder, shield-back, handled...........................225.00 to 250.00
Creamer, squatty 135.00
Inkwell, cov., w/original paper label....375.00

Nappy, handled, curled-in sides, 3½ x 5" 110.00
Plate, 9" d. 140.00
Sugar shaker, scene of children sledding 125.00
Teapot, cov. 225.00
Vase, 3¼" h., footed, shell-molded around top 100.00
Vase, 3¾" h., three-handled, silver rim 130.00

SUNBONNET BABIES

Sunbonnet Babies Plate

Candlestick, babies mending, 4¼" h. 325.00
Candy dish, 5" d. 265.00
Creamer, babies ironing, 4" h. ....150.00 to 175.00
Creamer, babies mending, 4" h. 200.00
Creamer, babies washing, 4" h. ....150.00 to 175.00
Creamer, tankard-type, babies washing, 4" h. 290.00
Creamer & open sugar bowl, babies washing & mending, pr. 395.00
Dish, cov., club-shaped, babies fishing 265.00
Hatpin holder, bulbous body w/saucer base, babies cleaning 495.00
Mug, babies cleaning, 2¾" h. 195.00
Pin tray, babies cleaning, 4" sq. 15.00
Plate, 6" d., babies cleaning 110.00
Plate, 8¼" d., babies washing (ILLUS.) 100.00

TOMATO ITEMS

Tomato box, cov., 3¾" d. 51.00
Tomato box, cov., 4½" d. 45.00
Tomato creamer, cov., small 65.00
Tomato creamer, cov., large 115.00
Tomato cup, demitasse 65.00
Tomato gravy boat 95.00
Tomato mustard jar, cov. 85.00
Tomato mustard jar, cover, leaf-shaped, spoon & underplate, 4 pcs. 150.00
Tomato pitcher, water 425.00
Tomato salt & pepper shakers, pr. 110.00

Tomato Sugar Bowl

Tomato sugar bowl, cov. (ILLUS.) 70.00
Tomato teapot, cov., large 195.00
Tomato teapot, cov., small ....250.00 to 275.00
Tomato tea set: large cov. teapot, creamer & cov. sugar bowl; footed, 3 pcs. ....325.00 to 375.00

MISCELLANEOUS

Figural Lobster Bowl

Ashtray, cows in pasture decoration, 5½" d. 95.00
Ashtray, figural clown ....325.00 to 350.00
Ashtray, figural eagle w/talons extending upward, grey 525.00
Ashtray, figural elk ....175.00 to 200.00
Ashtray, flying goose holding a frog in its mouth decoration, blues & orange, unmarked 475.00
Ashtray, round, hunt scene w/woman riding a horse & hounds, naturalistic colors, 4⅝" d. 55.00
Basket, "tapestry," scenic decoration of mountain, cove & cottage, 4½" d., 5" h. 395.00

Bell, girl w/dog scene....198.00
Bowl, 5½" d., "tapestry," lady portrait, gold trim....145.00
Bowl, 4¾ x 8", figural red lobster (ILLUS.)....350.00 to 450.00
Bowl, 9" d., figural pansy....295.00
Bowl, 10½" d., figural orchid, decorated w/fuchsia, yellow & gold trim....165.00
Box, cov., egg-shaped w/a four-footed ring base, scenic decoration of mountain buildings & a waterfall, unmarked, 2¾" w., 4" l., 2½" h....150.00
Boxes, cov., spade-shaped, fox hunt scene w/man & woman....195.00
Cake plate, open handles, figural orange poppy, 10½" d....395.00
Calling card holder, figural clown, red, 6 x 7"....125.00
Candleholder, figural basset hound, black w/red trim....450.00
Candleholder w/tray, figural owl....1,000.00
Candlestick, figural clown in seated position, red....1,900.00
Candlestick, figural monk in grey robes holding a jug & candle, unmarked....1,200.00
Candlestick, figural red poppy....850.00
Candlestick, handled, Jack & the Beanstalk decoration....150.00
Candy dish, figural clown....395.00
Chamberstick, cows in field decoration on green ground....110.00
Chamberstick, shield-back, Ring Around the Rosy decoration....225.00
Chamberstick w/center grip handle & three-footed base, shaded green & yellow ground decorated w/large orange roses....195.00
Charger, Cavalier Musicians decoration, grey ground, 14" d....425.00
Charger, stag & does winter scene decoration, 12¾" d....185.00
Chocolate pot, cov., decorated w/man & dog hunting scene....275.00
Creamer, two-handled, Brittany Girl decoration, 4" h....175.00
Creamer, cows scene decoration....75.00 to 100.00
Creamer, scene of schooner on ocean, black ground, gold handle....195.00
Creamer, pinched spout, goats decoration, 4" h....210.00
Creamer, hunting scene decoration, 4½" h....115.00
Creamer, corset-shaped, rooster & hen decoration, 5" h....125.00
Creamer, figural alligator....350.00 to 400.00
Creamer, figural apple....150.00 to 175.00
Creamer, figural bear, brown....700.00 to 750.00
Creamer, figural bellringer..250.00 to 300.00
Creamer, figural Bird of Paradise....250.00 to 300.00
Creamer, figural bull's head, brown & white....240.00
Creamer, figural bull's head, grey....175.00 to 200.00
Creamer, figural butterfly w/closed wings....425.00 to 475.00
Creamer, figural butterfly w/open wings....350.00 to 400.00
Creamer, figural cat, black....175.00 to 200.00
Creamer, figural cat handle....250.00 to 300.00
Creamer, figural chimpanzee, black w/rose beige face, crossed arms & interior....700.00

Figural Chimpanzee Creamer

Creamer, figural chimpanzee, grey (ILLUS.)....425.00 to 475.00
Creamer, figural chrysanthemum....395.00
Creamer, figural clown, red w/black buttons....225.00
Creamer, figural coachman wearing red coat....250.00 to 300.00
Creamer, figural cockatoo....550.00
Creamer, figural cow, grey....225.00 to 250.00
Creamer, figural cow, red....275.00
Creamer, figural crow, black w/red beak....200.00 to 250.00
Creamer, figural crow, black w/yellow beak....300.00

Figural Fish Head Creamer

Creamer, figural Dachshund dog....200.00

Creamer, figural duck ....150.00 to 200.00
Creamer, figural eagle, black ....300.00 to 325.00
Creamer, figural eagle, brown ....150.00 to 175.00
Creamer, figural elk head, shades of brown & cream, 3½" d., 4¼" h. 125.00
Creamer, figural fish head (ILLUS.) ....175.00 to 200.00
Creamer, figural flounder...................450.00
Creamer, figural frog...........175.00 to 200.00
Creamer, figural geranium..................495.00
Creamer, figural girl w/basket ....750.00 to 850.00
Creamer, figural girl w/pitcher, blue ....700.00 to 750.00
Creamer, figural grape cluster, green...125.00
Creamer, figural grape cluster, purple..............................100.00 to 125.00
Creamer, stirrup-type, figural ibex head..700.00
Creamer, figural iris 950.00
Creamer, figural ladybug 675.00
Creamer, figural lamplighter, green, 5½" h...............................300.00 to 325.00
Creamer, figural lemon.......150.00 to 200.00
Creamer, figural lettuce leaf w/figural lobster handle, unmarked 150.00
Creamer, figural lobster .....100.00 to 125.00
Creamer, figural maple leaf 350.00
Creamer, figural melon w/morning glory 350.00

Figural Monk Creamer

Creamer, figural monk, brown (ILLUS.)................800.00 to 825.00
Creamer, figural monkey, brown ....375.00 to 400.00
Creamer, figural monkey, green..............................450.00 to 475.00
Creamer, figural mountain goat................................300.00 to 375.00
Creamer, figural oak leaf 300.00
Creamer, figural Old Man of the Mountain ....75.00 to 100.00
Creamer, figural orange......200.00 to 250.00
Creamer, figural owl ....375.00 to 400.00
Creamer, figural pansy, dark pink.......250.00
Creamer, figural penguin....450.00 to 500.00
Creamer, figural pig, grey 650.00
Creamer, figural pig, red, unmarked...700.00
Creamer, figural platypus ....900.00 to 1,000.00
Creamer, figural Poodle dog ....200.00 to 225.00
Creamer, figural poppy, pink 195.00
Creamer, figural poppy, red.................................150.00 to 175.00
Creamer, figural red parrot handle, 5" h...250.00
Creamer, cov., figural rose, pink ....400.00 to 450.00
Creamer, figural St. Bernard dog.................................175.00 to 200.00
Creamer, figural Santa Claus 2,900.00
Creamer, figural seal ....325.00 to 350.00
Creamer, figural seashell w/coral handle, tall ....125.00 to 150.00
Creamer, figural trout, 4" h. 175.00
Creamer, figural turtle.........................600.00
Creamer, figural water buffalo, grey ....225.00 to 275.00
Creamer, figural water buffalo, black w/orange horns & trim, 3½ x 6", 4" h...150.00
Creamer & cov. sugar bowl, figural pansy, lavender, pr. 375.00
Creamer & cov. sugar bowl, figural parrot, pr. 265.00
Creamer & cov. sugar bowl, Brittany Girl decoration, pr. 85.00
Creamer & cov. sugar bowl, cows decoration on shaded lavender ground, pr. 125.00
Cup & saucer, demitasse, figural rose, gold ....400.00 to 475.00
Cup & saucer, demitasse, figural shell 150.00
Cup & saucer, stag & doe in winter scene 65.00
Dish, cov., figural turtle, 6"..................325.00
Dish, canoe-shaped, handled, stag & doe in winter scene, 9½" l.................95.00
Dish, spade-shaped, stag & doe in winter scene, 5¼" l.............................65.00
Dresser tray, "tapestry," raging waterfall scene, 7 x 11"....................550.00
Ewer, bulbous base tapering to small mouth, scenic design of four sheep on hillside, green background, 4" h....95.00
Ewer, "tapestry," scene of castle on mountain w/ladies by pond at mountain base, blue & green ground, gold trim, unmarked, 2¼" d., 3½" h. 225.00
Humidor, cov., "tapestry," scene of a woman leaning on horse, 6½" h..1,675.00
Match holder, hanging-type, figural red clown ....300.00 to 325.00

Match holder w/striker, figural Santa Claus (slight damage) 2,200.00
Match holder, hanging-type, man working w/two horses scene on cup, cottage scene background..............150.00
Match holder, hanging-type, "tapestry," Cavalier Musicians scene.........345.00
Mayonnaise dish, cover & underplate, figural red poppy, the set 525.00
Model of a lady's shoe, "tapestry," decorated w/violets, original shoe lace 750.00

Figural Elk Beer Mug

Mug, beer, figural elk, 5¾" h. (ILLUS.) 650.00
Mug, nursery rhyme scene w/Jack and the Beanstalk 95.00
Mustard jar, cov., figural apple, green...............................200.00 to 225.00
Mustard jar, cov., figural lobster 165.00
Mustard jar, cov., figural shell.............145.00
Nappy, clover-shaped, ring handled, "tapestry," scene of cottage, waterfall w/rocks, mountains, gold trim.....235.00
Nappy, handled, spade-shaped, nursery rhyme scene w/Little Jack Horner..135.00
Nut cup, master size, figural poppy 150.00
Pin dish, figural turtle 500.00
Pin tray, Brittany Girl decoration, 3½ x 5"...50.00
Pin tray, rectangular w/cut corners, Hunt scene w/rider & hounds, 3½ x 5"..50.00
Pitcher, 2¾" h., 2¼" d., ovoid body w/short cylindrical neck, gold handle, scene of Dutch boy flying kite w/dog at his heels, blue & brown ground.......................................55.00
Pitcher, 3⅜" h., 1⅛" d., tapering cylindrical body, double-handled, scene of lady in purple dress walking w/gentleman, pastel cream, blue & green ground 55.00
Pitcher, 4" h., Brittany Girl decoration...95.00
Pitcher, 5½" h., stork decoration on yellow ground......................................75.00
Pitcher, 5½" h., decorated w/a scene of hounds pursuing a stag in a marshy landscape against a green ground...185.00
Pitcher, lemonade, 7¾" h., figural lemon 395.00
Pitcher, milk, figural alligator..............550.00
Pitcher, milk, figural apple 225.00
Pitcher, milk, figural coachman...........775.00
Pitcher, milk, 4½" h., figural clown, yellow ....600.00 to 650.00
Pitcher, milk, figural elk.......................235.00
Pitcher, milk, 4" h., figural owl ....400.00 to 500.00
Pitcher, milk, 5¼" h., figural Santa Claus 3,500.00
Pitcher, milk, figural St. Bernard dog, unmarked 300.00
Pitcher, milk, figural strawberry 325.00

Cavalier Musicians Pitcher

Pitcher, milk, Cavalier Musicians scene decoration (ILLUS.) 225.00
Pitcher, milk, 5½" h., Hunt scene decoration 165.00
Pitcher, water, 6" h., figural apple.......875.00
Pitcher, water, 6½" h., figural clown ...895.00
Pitcher, water, figural coachman ....750.00 to 800.00
Pitcher, water, 7" h., figural orange..............................700.00 to 800.00
Pitcher, water, 6½" h., figural red parrot handle...................................550.00
Pitcher, water, 6½" h., figural poppy...795.00
Pitcher, water, 7" h., figural Santa Claus...3,100.00
Pitcher, water, 7" h., Jester pictured & "Never say die - Up man and try".....375.00
Pitcher, water, 8" h., three cows & calf scene 295.00
Pitcher, 8" h., pinched spout, Hunt scene decoration w/rider & hounds 110.00
Planter, "tapestry," woodland & mountain scene w/deer in a stream & gazebo in background, small........175.00
Plate, 4½" d., full figure red devil against a black clock face...............575.00

Plate, 4½" d., full figure red devil against a white clock face w/black Roman numerals 575.00

Plate, 6" d., Hunt scene decoration 75.00

Plate, dessert, 6" d., stag & doe in winter scene 45.00

Plate, 6½" d., nursery rhyme scene w/Little Bo Peep & rhyme 125.00

Plate, 7" d., ring-handled, figural apple leaf in green w/yellow blossoms at edge 33.00

Plate, 9" d., scenic decoration of man resting w/draft horse 110.00

Plate, 10½" d., pierced handles, stag & doe winter scene 165.00

Ramekins w/underplates, decorated w/pink roses w/leaves, wide embossed gold trim, six sets, 12 pcs. 175.00

Relish dish, open-handled, courtship scene decoration, 4 x 8¼" 200.00

Salt & pepper shakers, figural apple, pr. 75.00

Salt & pepper shakers, figural elk head, pr. 160.00

Salt & pepper shakers, figural radish, pr. 185.00

Salt & pepper shakers, figural seashell, multicolored glaze, pr. 170.00

Salt dip, figural pansy ....100.00 to 125.00

Salt dip, figural lobster claw................90.00

Salt shaker, figural lemon (unmarked) 85.00

Shaving mug, figural elk .....450.00 to 550.00

Stirrup cup, figural elk head 550.00

Rooster String Holder

String holder, hanging-type, figural rooster head (ILLUS.) 350.00

Sugar bowl, cov., figural apple, 3½" h. 100.00

Sugar bowl, cov., figural grape cluster, purple ....125.00 to 150.00

Sugar bowl, cov., figural pansy...........235.00

Table set: creamer, cov. sugar bowl, salt & pepper shakers; figural grape cluster, purple, artist-signed, 4 pcs. 325.00

Teapot, cov., "tapestry," Arab & horses scene, blue ground, 5" h. 149.00

Teapot, cov., scene of girl w/dog on leash, 5½" h. 180.00

Teapot, cov., scenic decoration of hunter w/turkeys 95.00

Tea tray, nursery rhyme scene w/Little Boy Blue, verse & holly border, 7¾ x 11" 325.00

Toothpick holder, basket-shaped w/square mouth & overhead handle, Dutch children in sailboat scene 145.00

Toothpick holder, figural elk head..............................125.00 to 175.00

Toothpick holder, Goose Girl decoration (unmarked)....................125.00

Toothpick holder, pedestal base, decorated w/lavender roses & butterflies 145.00

Toothpick holder, three-handled, Goose Girl decoration......................145.00

Tumbler, "tapestry," castle by the lake scene, 3¾" h. 200.00

Tumbler, "tapestry," wooded scene w/deer in stream & gazebo in background 225.00

Small Royal Bayreuth Vases

Vase, 3" h., 2⅝" d., conical body tapering to a silver rim, small loop handles at the shoulder, decorated w/a scene of a Dutch lady carrying a basket, a sailboat in the distance, shaded blue to white to brown ground (ILLUS.) 55.00

Vase, 4" h., 4½" d., squatty bulbous base flanked by small loop handles, a tall slender swelled cylindrical neck w/silver rim, scene of two sheep on a shaded green to grey ground (ILLUS. left) 60.00

Vase, 4" h., bulbous base, "tapestry" castle scene.....................................110.00

Vase, 4¼" h., nursery rhyme scene w/Little Boy Blue decoration 160.00

Vase, 6" h., handled, "tapestry," castle scene decoration 310.00

Wall pocket, figural grape cluster, pink 175.00

Wall pocket, pictures a jester & "Penny in Pocket," 9" h.......................550.00

ROYAL BONN & BONN

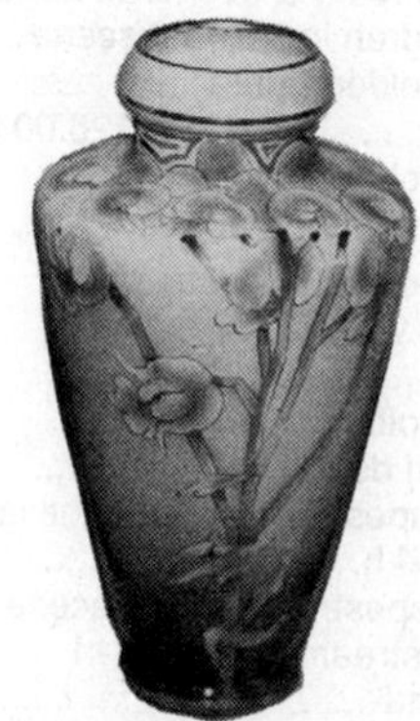

Floral Decorated Royal Bonn Vase

Bonn and subsequently Royal Bonn china were produced in Bonn, Germany, in a manufactory established in 1755. Later wares made there are often marked Mehlem or bear the initials FM or a castle mark. Most wares were of the hand-painted type. Clock cases were also made in Bonn.

Ewer, scrolled gold handle, decorated w/large multicolored flowers on front & back, raised gold veins & outlining, 4" d., 10½" h.......................$155.00

Ewer, decorated w/pink & blue flowers & gold tracery on a cream ground, gold trim around neck & handle, 13" h...485.00

Pitcher, 6½" h., decorated w/pink & gold flowers & leaves 65.00

Sardine box, cov., floral decoration w/figural sardine handle 75.00

Umbrella stand, cylindrical w/flaring base, decorated w/large iris blossoms & foliage in shades of blue, yellow & green base & top relief-molded w/a scrolling foliate design, 11" d., 18" h. (professional touch-up)..395.00

Vase, 6⅝" h., tapering rounded cylindrical body w/low molded rim, decorated overall w/Art Nouveau stylized colorful floral sprigs in red, orange, yellow & green against a pale blue & reddish orange ground, ca. 1905, base marked "Royal Bonn Old Dutch Germany - 265 - 1997 - 12"...385.00

Vase, 7½" h., 4" d., tapering ovoid body w/a short closed neck, soft gold flowers on a pale blue & pink ground, gold trim, late 19th c. 75.00

Vase, 8" h., 3⅞" d., expanding cylinder w/sharply angled shoulder, short wide neck, decorated w/golden yellow flowers against a pink shading to blue ground, gold trim (ILLUS.) 65.00

Vase, 11¼" h., decorated w/pink & yellow roses against a green & yellow ground, gold trim, ca. 1900, red crown mark, Franz Anton Mehlem Porcelain Factory 275.00

Vase, 27" h., baluster-form body w/applied gilt dragon handles, raised on molded gilt scroll feet, decorated w/a scene of three gentlemen observing an artist painting in his studio, the reverse w/a formal garden landscape w/a marble stairway, artist-signed 1,980.00

Vase, 50" h., slender elongated baluster-form body w/a tall flaring neck, the bottom fitted into a leafy petal-form gilt cup above a short pedestal w/an everted ring over the flaring foot set in a gilt molded base w/four scroll feet, a flaring & scroll-molded rim on the neck & applied, knotted cord gilt handles on the shoulder, the sides decorated w/large pink & yellow roses against a shaded green ground, artist-signed, late 19th c. 3,300.00

ROYAL CROWN POTTERY

The Royal Crown Pottery and Porcelain Company, Merry Oak, North Carolina was in business from 1939-1942. Victor and Henry Obler were Russian immigrants who became silversmiths in New York but it was Victor who pursued the pottery business. Despite the name of his company, there have been no records found proving that any porcelain products were made and no examples have been found. However, Victor was able to create some remarkable glazes for his pottery with the help of Jack Kiser, Charlie Craven and Leslie Stanley. Many colors were used: black, blue, Colonial cream, enamel green, golden brown, maroon, moss green, Spanish moss, turquoise, white, and yellow. Harder to find glazes are light blue or pink and also 'rainbow' finishes on blue, white, turquoise or black backgrounds. Vases were the biggest money maker for Royal Crown due, in part, to Obler furnishing vases to the New York Florist Association. Some of Obler's vases, especially the handled pieces, are similar to George Ohr products. Catalogs have been found indicating Royal Crown also made miniatures but, because they were probably not marked, none have been attributed to this company. Almost all the other pottery items were marked.

Basket, footed, flared sides w/crimped rim ends, center handle, yellow glaze, 8½" d., 11" h. $68.00

Bowl, 10" d., 2½" h., round w/oblong handles, yellow glaze, Model No. 34 .... 34.00

Bowl, 14" d., 4" h., deep sides w/crimped edges, moss green glaze 85.00

Ewer, bulbous body tapering to short neck w/three bands, twig handle from center of body & rising slightly above rim, Colonial cream glaze, 16" h. 185.00

Pitcher, milk, 6" h., bulbous, maroon glaze 27.00

Royal Crown Vase

Vase, 5" h., bulbous body tapering gently to a short neck w/scalloped rim, moss green glaze (ILLUS.) 45.00

Vase, 7" h., conical w/handles at bottom, maroon glaze 38.00

Vase, 9" h., 4½" d., classic shape w/four rings at base tapering to a tall neck, handles from center of body to rim, Model No. 1210 .... 85.00

Vase, 11" h., globular w/thin, flat rim, molded ring handles, rainbow finish 125.00

Vase, 15" h., 5½" d., baluster shape, twisted shoulder handles 110.00

Vase, 16" h., 7" d., baluster shape w/shoulder to rim handles, golden brown glaze 95.00

ROYAL DUX

This factory in Bohemia was noted for the figural porcelain wares in the Art Nouveau style which were exported around the turn of the century. Other notable figural pieces were produced through the 1930s and the factory was nationalized after World War II.

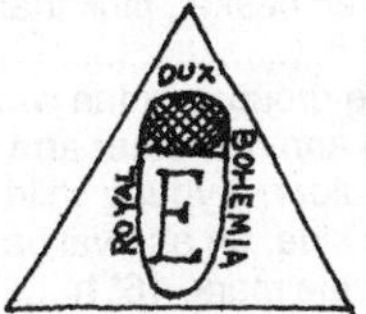

Bust of a Victorian woman, lavish lace trim on hat & dress, pastel decoration, parian finish, 16" h. $550.00

Centerpiece, figural, the oblong bulbous bowl molded in high-relief pods w/long undulating leaves, centered by a large full-figure model of a seated classical maiden w/a dove on one arm, pierced branch-form base band, glazed in solid olive green & pink w/gold & beige trim, triangular tag & impressed marks, ca. 1900, 13¼" h. 880.00

Centerpiece, figural, a large oblong shell-form shallow bowl fitted at one end w/a large seated figure of an Art Nouveau maiden w/flowing hair & robe, raised on a blossom & branch pedestal base w/another full-figure maiden clinging to one side, cream glaze trimmed in gold & grey, triangular tag & impressed marks, ca. 1900, 15" h. 770.00

Centerpiece, figural, cast as a young maiden seated on the edge of a large shell carried by two long-haired tritons over cresting waves & water foliage, glazed in tones of olive green, pale puce & ivory trimmed w/gold, applied triangular mark & impressed numbers, ca. 1900, 23¼" h. 1,725.00

Dish, figural, molded as a harem lady in an elaborate costume w/decorated bodice, openwork midriff & flaring skirt, her arms lifted as she dances on tip-toe, long lengths of ribbons trailing into the clover leaf-form dish below, its edges molded in full-relief w/clusters of blossoms, glazed in tones of mustard yellow, cotton-candy pink, lavender, charcoal grey & ivory, trimmed w/gilt, applied triangular mark & impressed & incised numbers, ca. 1900, 10⅞" h. 690.00

Figure of a girl at a waterfall, the lovely young woman dressed in flowing robes, pink triangle mark, 12½" h. 995.00

Figure of a sheepherder, pink triangle mark, 16½" h. 895.00

Figure of Cupid, bisque, depicted w/his arm in a sling, 21" h. 550.00

Figure group, mother w/child near woven basket, pink triangle mark, 8½" h. 425.00

Figure group, woman w/basket on one arm, the other arm raised to her shoulder, a young child standing to one side, on an oval base, pink triangle mark, 16" h. 695.00

Figure group, model of a sea shell w/a woman seated at the top & another clinging to the side of the shell, 17½" 500.00

Figure group, cloaked Harlequin male dancer enfolding matching female, artist-signed, No. 294/72, 15 x 20" 875.00

Model of a cockatoo on limb, white w/pink head, marked, 15" h. 175.00

Model of a dog, German Shepherd, pink triangle mark, No. 458, 8¼" h. 119.00

Model of a dog, Setter, w/pheasant in mouth, "Sportsman's Dream," pink triangle mark, 19" h. 350.00

Model of a polar bear, 10½ x 12½".....575.00

Vase, 14⅜" h., figural, a long-haired maiden nude but for a flowing length of dusty-rose drapery falling from her neck, astride a moss green & pale pink conch shell, sea-foam green waves & pale pink, ivory & green lotus blossoms & leaves swirling below, applied triangular mark & impressed & incised numbers, ca. 1900 ....920.00

Vases, 15½" h., ovoid body w/square foot, Art Nouveau style, molded olive tree swirling branches forming two levels of handles, pink triangle mark, pr. 437.00

Vide poche (figural dish), the standing figure of a maiden w/arms folded across her breast wearing a voluminous green gown continuing to form a dish at her feet, glazed in pink & cream, heightened in gilt, impressed applied factory mark, numbered "1313," ca. 1900, 14¾" h. 920.00

ROYAL VIENNA

The second factory in Europe to make hard paste porcelain was established in Vienna in 1719 by Claud Innocentius de Paquier. The factory underwent various changes of administration through the years and finally closed in 1865. Since then, however, the porcelain has been reproduced by various factories in Austria and Germany, many of which have reproduced also the early beehive mark. Early pieces, naturally, bring far higher prices than the later ones or the reproductions.

Royal Vienna Covered Urn

Candlesticks, scenic medallions on maroon & gold ground, signed "Angelica Kauffmann," blue beehive mark, 5½" h., pr. $550.00

Charger, cupid & a maiden surrounded by six cherubs, pseudo beehive mark in black enamel & stamped "CARL KNOLL CARLSBAD 29," ca. 1900, 16½" d. 1,725.00

Cup, three-handled, urn-shaped w/undulating gilt rim, decorated w/children at play within three gilt-dot rimmed medallions on a cream ground, dark green & gilt-patterned foot, applied gilt scroll handles, 20th c., 4" h. 88.00

Demitasse set: cov. pot, cov. creamer, cov. sugar bowl, cups w/deep saucers & a rectangular tray w/cut corners; each of cylindrical form w/angled handles, white decorated w/delicate floral bouquets & wavy ribbon edge bands, late 19th c., tray 11" l., the set 660.00

Figure group, two cherubs representing the Arts studying & reading beneath a palm tree, 12½" h. 302.50

Plaque, decorated w/h.p. white water lilies on shaded ground, narrow gold rim, gold palette mark & green crown mark, 9½" d. 45.00
Plate. 9½" w., octagonal, decorated in the center w/a scene of Venus & Adonis, the maroon & gilt patterned paneled rim w/small classical nymphs, artist-signed....................467.50
Plates, 6⅛" d., chocolate brown, gold, blue & pink lustre w/center decoration of two cherubs, beehive mark, Austria, set of 6....................300.00
Urns, cov., each decorated w/a continuous allegorical band surmounted by a removable waisted neck & domed cover, raised on triform legs ending in paw feet, pseudo shield mark in blue enamel, 17½" h., pr. (ILLUS. of one) 5,463.00
Urns, cov., one entitled "Romischer Siegeszug" (Rome under Siege), the other "Romischer Triumphzug" (Rome Triumphant), the foot, neck & lid adorned w/gilt scrolls & animal figures on wine red ground, lionesque applied ormolu handles & pineapple finial, each scene finely painted on a gilt-dot ground, on ormolu mounted square base on four paw feet, each decorated by K. Willnert, 27" h., pr. 17,000.00
Vase, 5" h., 4½" w., triangular, decorated w/a brown bird perched on the corner, green foliate decoration on the front, against a beige satin ground, gold trim, marked "Turn" 95.00
Vase, 21½" h., ovoid w/short neck & flaring rim, decorated w/a continuous allegorical scene against a cream ground, the neck & base heightened w/gilt, signed "Gorney," pseudo beehive mark in blue enamel & title in black enamel, late 19th c. 4,025.00
Vase, 38" h., "Bachantan," ovoid body raised on a pedestal base, slender neck w/flaring rim, decorated w/a scene of a classically garbed reclining woman on front, the reverse a scene of putti in a garden, gilt decorated dark green lustre ground, 19th c. 18,700.00

ROYAL WORCESTER

This porcelain has been made by the Royal Worcester Porcelain Co. at Worcester, England, from 1862 to the present. For earlier porcelain made in Worcester, see WORCESTER. Royal Worcester is distinguished from those wares made at Worcester between 1751 and 1862 that are referred to as only Worcester by collectors.

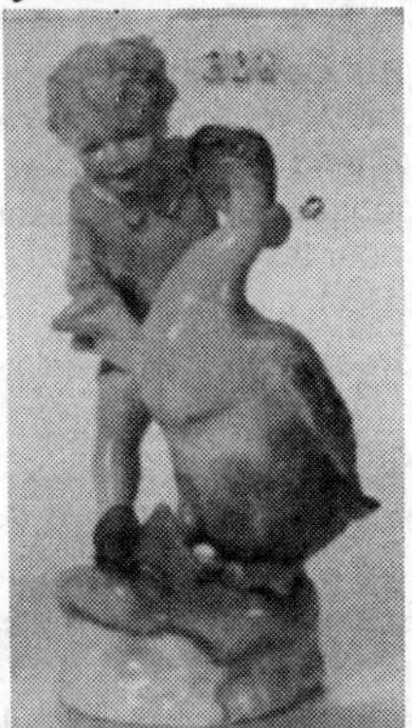

"Goosie Goosie Gander"

Candle snuffer, figural monk............$115.00
Celery tray, decorated w/apples & purple grapes, gold border, artist-signed, 4¼ x 10" 275.00
Cracker jar, cov., cobalt blue leaves on a white molded bamboo background, matching cover, 5¾" d., 7" h. 355.00
Creamer & sugar bowl w/gold wreathed lyres, beribboned lanterns & scrolls, ca. 1906, 4" d., pr. 24.00
Cup & saucer, demitasse, h.p. gold scenes commemorating the state of Maryland against a cream ground, No. RD 117963 ....195.00
Cup & saucer, decorated w/pink, yellow & blue flowers w/gold trim on beige satin ground, cup 3⅜" d., 2½" h., saucer 5⅝" d. 85.00
Dish, square, decorated w/apples & purple grapes, gold border, artist-signed, 5 x 7" 225.00
Ewer, melon-form, decorated w/applied gold leaves, gold spout & handle, 7" h. 435.00
Ewer, tusk-form w/closed spout & branched antler-form handle, decorated w/gilt & iron-red chrysanthemums & gilt bands, No. 1116, artist-initialed, 11" h. 330.00
Ewer, salamander handle, decorated w/pastel pink blossoms, ivory ground shading to green, impressed mark, No. 226/6 ....175.00
Figure, "The Dandelion," 4¼" h. 100.00
Figure, "Duchess's Dress," designed by F. Doughty, No. 3106....................300.00
Figure, "January" 175.00
Figure, "Sir Walter Raleigh," tan, lavender & ecru, dated 1885, 6½" h. 190.00

Figure, "Tommy," designed by F. Doughty, No. 2913, 4½" h. 110.00

Figures, a Mideastern lady playing a tambourine & a companion man w/a stringed instrument, each signed "Hadley," 12½" h., pr. 825.00

Figure group, "Goosie Goosie Gander," playful young curly-haired child w/one hand on the goose's neck, the goose w/one wing raised & its beak near the child's face, 5½" h. (ILLUS.) 150.00

Model of a Great Tit, No. 335, artist-signed 50.00

Model of a Kingfisher, No. 2666 .... 125.00

Model of a Nuthatch, No. 3334, artist-signed 50.00

Model of a Sparrow, No. 3236, artist-signed 50.00

Pitcher w/ice lip, 5¾" h., chased gold w/floral decoration, ca. 1887 .... 235.00

Royal Worcester Melon-Form Pitcher

Pitcher, 8½" h., melon-form body w/a wide cylindrical leaf-molded neck & spout, gilt leaves continuing to vine handle, the body decorated w/pastel floral sprigs, No. 1369, ca. 1889 (ILLUS.) .... 400.00 to 450.00

Pitcher, ice water, 10" h., tusk-form, yellow ground w/stylized gilt florals, No. 1116, ca. 1885 .... 265.00

Plate, 9⅛" d., h.p. bird decoration w/red & gold embossed gilded border, artist-signed, No. W-202, ca. 1880 .... 75.00

Plate, 10¾" d., h.p. Tewkesbury village scene, artist-signed, ca. 1953 .... 225.00

Plates, 8" d., Granada patt., set of 7 .. 100.00

Platter, 12½" l., Blue Willow patt. 75.00

Spill vase, Japanese-style, square tapering sides applied w/a model of a climbing frog & molded w/ivy vines, No. 499, ca. 1875, 3½" h. 295.00

Teapot, cov., molded melon-form in the Japanese taste, the lobed creamy body decorated w/gilt & iron-red leaf & stalk forms, 6" h. 247.50

Vase, 2½" h., miniature, decorated w/flowers & gold enameling, cranberry ground 85.00

Vase, 4" h., center decoration of bird in flight, beige ground w/black enamel borders, artist-signed 375.00

Vase, 6½" h., two-handled, reticulated sides w/floral decoration, artist's initials on base, No. 982, ca. 1883 .... 225.00

Vase, 7¾" h., ovoid body molded w/a basketweave design & decorated w/applied leafy vines in gold & iron-red, Crown & Circle mark 302.50

Vase, 13¾" h., bulbous body supporting a cylindrical neck w/reticulated lip, applied gilt handles, decorated w/purple & lavender flowers on gilt branches, Crown & Circle mark, artist-initialed 825.00

R.S. PRUSSIA & RELATED WARES

Ornately decorated china marked "R.S. Germany" and "R.S. Prussia" continues to grow in popularity. According to Clifford J. Schlegelmilch in his book, Handbook of Erdmann and Reinhold Schlegelmilch — Prussia – Germany and Oscar Schlegelmilch – Germany, *Erdmann Schlegelmilch established a porcelain factory in the Germanic provinces at Suhl, in 1861. Reinhold, his younger brother, worked with him until 1869 when he established another porcelain factory in Tillowitz, upper Silesia. China bearing the name of this town is credited to Reinhold Schlegelmilch. It customarily bears also the phrase "R.S. Germany." Now collectors seek additional marks including E.S. Germany, R.S. Poland and R.S. Suhl. Prices are high and collectors should beware the forgeries that sometimes find their way to the market . Mold names and numbers are taken from Mary Frank Gaston's books on R.S. Prussia.*

We illustrate three typical markings, however, there are several others. The "R.S. Prussia" mark has been reproduced in decal form so buy with care.

R.S. GERMANY

Bowl, 9½" d., Cabbage or Lettuce mold (Mold 126), rose decoration on a green ground $225.00

Bowl, 7 x 10½" oval, floral decoration... 55.00

Celery tray, Bird of Paradise decoration, 10½" l. 195.00

Celery tray, two-handled, floral decoration, 13" l. 32.50
Cracker jar, cov., handled, decorated w/yellow roses & greenery, 5" h.......115.00
Creamer & cov. sugar bowl, cobalt blue floral decoration w/gold highlights, 3" h., pr. 75.00
Creamer & cov. sugar bowl, cream & apricot shaded feathery tulips on beige to grey blended ground w/gold trim, pr...47.50
Dessert set: master bowl & six 7" d. matching bowls; Lettuce mold (Mold 12), interior floral decoration, pearlized lustre finish, 7 pcs. 165.00
Dresser tray, snowball floral decoration, gold trim, 8½" d. 100.00
Hatpin holder, Mold 777, decorated w/pink & white roses on earthtone ground, 4½" h. 60.00
Hatpin holder, pussy willow decoration 90.00
Mustard pot, cov., white floral decoration on pastel ground, 3" h. 28.00
Pitcher, tankard, 11½" h., Mold 520, h.p. pink & yellow roses 495.00
Snack set: tray w/cup; parrot decoration, 6¼ x 7½" 150.00
Snack set: tray w/cup; pheasants decoration, 9½" l., 2 pcs. 135.00
Vase, 4" h., scenic decoration of windmill w/stream, house in trees, boy walking in the grass, shadow leaves in background 125.00

R.S. PRUSSIA

Basket, Scallop & Fan mold, triple handle, nine scalloped feet w/each further scalloped, roses decoration, glossy finish, 8½" d., 8" h..................450.00
Berry set: 9" l. leaf-shaped master bowl & six sauce dishes; Leaf mold (Mold 10), decorated w/flowers, unmarked, 7 pcs. 495.00
Berry set: 10½" d. master bowl & six sauce dishes; Acorn or Nut mold, pink & red roses decoration, 7 pcs. 495.00
Bowl, 7" d., three-footed, Carnation mold (Mold 28), ivory, blue & pink florals 165.00
Bowl, 8½" d., Icicle mold (Mold 7), decorated w/pears, grapes & plums 300.00
Bowl, 9½" d., Fleur-de-lis mold (Mold 9), fruit decoration..................175.00
Bowl, 10" d., Iris mold (Mold 25), Summer Season decoration 4,600.00
Bowl, 10" d., Mold 90, fruit decoration...275.00
Bowl, 10¼" d., 3" h., Mold 95, center decorated w/pink poppies, cobalt blue florals surround the sides.........965.00
Bowl, 10½" d., Mold 105, Countess Potocka portrait in center.............1,050.00
Bowl, 10½" d., Mold 252, Swans & Gazebo decoration 775.00
Bowl, 10¾" d., Mold 53, Reflecting Water Lilies decoration, satin finish 345.00
Bowl, 11" d., Mold 405, Swans & Evergreens decoration on a shaded lavender ground..............................395.00
Bowl, 8 x 12½" oval, Mold 343, center floral decoration w/beaded rim, cobalt blue ground, unmarked 450.00
Bun tray, Icicle mold (Mold 7), Sitting Basket decoration 200.00
Cake plate, open-handled, Mold 155, barnyard decoration w/swallows, chickens & duck, 9¾" d.................1,005.00
Cake plate, open-handled, Icicle mold (Mold 7), swan decoration, 10" d. 600.00
Cake plate, open-handled, Mold 259, pink & white roses w/lavender Tiffany coloring, 10" d. 300.00
Cake plate, open-handled, Mold 82, decorated w/flowers on a blue ground, 10¼" d. 175.00
Cake plate, open-handled, decorated w/floral center & Tiffany finish on border & inner ring, six cupids on border & two scenes of reclining women w/cupids, 10½" d. (unmarked)...475.00
Cake plate, open-handled, Fleur-de-lis mold (Mold 9), Spring Season decoration, 11" d...........................1,400.00
Cake plate, open-handled, Lily mold (Mold 29), large Madame Recamier portrait, green ground w/gold trim, 11" d...1,095.00
Cake plate, open-handled, Mold 276, decorated w/yellow & brown roses, 11½" d...50.00
Celery tray, Stippled Floral mold (Mold 23), decorated w/roses, 12" l..80.00
Celery tray, Mold 304, Man in the Mountain decoration, 6 x 12" 795.00
Celery tray, Lily mold (Mold 29), decorated w/florals, 12½" l..............150.00
Celery tray, Plume mold (Mold 16), Reflecting Poppies & Daisies decoration, green shading, 12½" l. 80.00
Celery tray, Medallion mold (Mold 14), Reflecting Poppies & Daisies decoration, portraits of Diana the Huntress & Flora on each side, 7" w., 14" l. 650.00
Chocolate pot, cov., Iris mold (Mold 25), decorated w/poppies 160.00
Chocolate pot., cov., Mold 454, decorated w/green roses on yellow ground, 11" h. 295.00

ground, 11" h. 295.00

Chocolate pot., cov., Mold 501, decorated w/blue florals on a white ground, 10" h. 195.00

Chocolate pot., cov., Mold 520, white snowballs & pink roses decoration on a pale green ground, 10½" h. 325.00

Mold 644 Chocolate Pot

Chocolate pot., cov., Mold 644, floral decoration, 11" h. (ILLUS.) 595.00

Coffeepot, cov., Mold 474, floral decoration, 9" h. (unsigned) 375.00

Cracker jar, cov., Lily mold (Mold 29), decorated w/pink & yellow roses (unmarked) 295.00

Cracker jar, cov., Sunflower mold (Mold 626), footed, pearly white w/green trim, 6½" h. 275.00

Cracker jar, cov., Mold 933, decorated w/white roses on a fuchsia ground...295.00

Creamer & cov. sugar bowl, Mold 452, swans decoration, satin finish, pr...600.00

Dessert set, child's: six cups & saucers & handled cookie plate; Mold 550, pink & white floral decoration on pastel blue & white ground (unsigned)..........................135.00

Dresser tray, Stippled Floral mold (Mold 23), rectangular, decorated in the center w/a large cluster of pink & red roses & green leaves against a shaded green ground, white & yellow border band, 7⅛ x 10¾" 195.00

Dresser tray, Icicle mold (Mold 7), swans in lake decoration, 7 x 11½" 485.00

Dresser tray, Icicle mold (Mold 7), heavy gold tapestry w/hanging baskets in relief, 7½ x 11½" 595.00

Dresser tray, Ribbon & Jewel mold (Mold 18), Melon Eaters & Dice Players decoration, 12" l. 1,375.00

Dresser tray, Mold 78, floral decoration, 7½ x 12" 75.00

Dresser tray, Mold 327, rose floral decoration, 12" l. 80.00

Ewer, Mold 640, roses decoration, artist-signed, 5" h. 125.00

Nut set: 5¾" d., 3" h. master bowl & seven 1½" h. individual bowls; Mold 107 variation, decorated w/peach-colored roses, 8 pcs. 560.00

Pitcher, tankard, 11½" h., Carnation mold (Mold 526), roses decora tion 895.00

Pitcher, tankard, 11½" h., Mold 508, decorated w/red & white roses, satin finish (unmarked) 495.00

Pitcher, tankard, 12½" h., Carnation mold (Mold 526), decorated w/pink roses 650.00

Pitcher, tankard, 13½" h., Carnation mold (Mold 526), poppies decoration, satin finish..........................960.00

Plate, 7" d., Icicle mold (Mold 7), water lily decoration 60.00

Plate, 8½" d., Mold 90, mill scene decoration 425.00

Plate, 8½" d., Mold 300, Castle scene 425.00

Plate, 8½" d., Mold 303, swan decoration, lavender & blue satin finish (unmarked) 195.00

Plate, 9" d., Carnation mold (Mold 28), decorated w/roses on teal blue ground..165.00

Plate, 10" d., Point & Clover mold (Mold 82), Melon Eaters & Dice Players decoration 950.00

Lily Mold Plate

Plate, 12" d., Lily mold (Mold 29), large center portrait of Madame Recamier against a shaded yellow to dark green ground, Tiffany finish greenish bronze panels around the border (ILLUS.) 1,650.00

Shaving mug w/beveled mirror, Stippled Floral mold (Mold 525), roses decoration on green ground...550.00

Tea set, child's: cov. teapot, creamer, cov. sugar bowl, five cups & saucers & five 6" d. plates; Mold 517, decorated w/pink poppies w/blue trim, 18 pcs. 2,150.00

Urn, cov., ovoid body on a pedestal base, two large gold loop handles, Mold 932, molded jewels & scrolls & rope chains w/small jewels around the shoulder, decorated w/Melon Eaters & Dice Throwers scenes, 7" d., 12" h. 3,000.00

Vase, 4½" h., handled, scene of a girl & a boy..450.00

Vase, 4½" h., Melon Eaters decoration w/mountain background.........495.00

Vase, 4½" h., Mold 914, woman in swing decoration............................550.00

Vase, 5" h., two-handled, cartouches w/small pink roses, unusual gold handles, cobalt blue ground............425.00

Vase, bud, 6⅛" h., multicolored floral decoration on "tapestry" body 195.00

Vase, 6½" h., baluster-shaped, decorated w/landscape of swans in the foreground & Old Man of the Mountain in the distance.................695.00

Vase, 9½" h., tall urn-form body w/swelled top & serrated, jeweled rim flanked by long loop handles, raised on a domed & jeweled pedestal base, decorated w/rose florals & lovely colors w/a satin finish 575.00

OTHER MARKS

Bowl, 10" d., cameo portrait of lady holding roses, green w/gold trim (E.S. Germany) 130.00

Celery tray, Chief Spotted Horse decoration, 5½ x 12" (E.S. Germany - Royal Saxe) 225.00

Celery tray, decorated w/roses, 12½" l. (P. K. Silesia) 95.00

Coffee set: 9" h. cov. coffeepot, creamer, sugar bowl & six cups & saucers; figural scenes on all pieces, some marked "Angelica Kauffmann," 15 pcs. (R.S. Suhl) ...1,675.00

Creamer, Mold 645, molded swags & jewels, barnyard animals scene (Wheelock)....................................400.00

Cuspidor, decorated w/roses (E.S. Germany - Prove. Saxe) 395.00

Ewer, Lebrun portrait, red & pink decoration on pale cream ground, 6½" h. (O.S. St. Kilian)...................145.00

Ewer, lady w/swallows decoration, pink & lavender iridescent finish, 7⅜" h. (Prov. Saxe - E.S. Germany) 250.00

Hair receiver, cov., Ribbon & Jewel mold (Mold 8), water lilies decoration (Wheelock Prussia) 200.00

Ice cream set: tray & five plates; pheasant decoration, 6 pcs. (E.S. Germany) 195.00

Jar, cov., floral "tapestry" decoration (E.S. Germany) 875.00

Plate, 7½" d., the Cage scene, cobalt blue ground w/lavish gold trim (R.S. Suhl) 695.00

Plate, 8¼" d., full frontal portrait of Queen Louise, iridescent w/gold decoration (E.S. Germany) 195.00

Shaving mug, scene of swallows over mountain & lake (E.S. Germany) 85.00

Vase, 5⅜" h., parrot decoration on a lavender ground w/lavish gold (Prove. Saxe - E.S. Germany) 295.00

Vase, 10½" h., swallows on cream ground w/gold highlights (E.S. Germany).......................................165.00

Vase, 11" h., decorated w/poppies, green leaves & gold trim on dark green ground (R.S. Poland) 295.00

RUSSEL WRIGHT DESIGNS

The innovative dinnerwares designed by Russel Wright and produced by various companies beginning in the late 1930s were an immediate success with a society that was turning to a more casual and informal lifestyle. His designs, with their flowing lines and unconventional shapes, were produced in many different colors which allowed the hostess to arrange a creative table. Although not antique, these designs, which we list below by line and manufacturer, are highly collectible. In addition to dinnerwares, Wright was also known as a trend-setter in the design of furniture, glassware, lamps, fabrics and a multitude of other household goods.

AMERICAN MODERN (Steubenville Pottery Company)

Ashtray, coaster-type, seafoam blue ..$10.00

Ashtray, coaster-type, white 21.00

Bowl, fruit, lug handle, bean brown 20.00

Bowl, fruit, lug handle, coral 10.00

Bowl, salad, cedar green 65.00

Bowl, salad, chartreuse 50.00

Bowl, salad, coral 45.00

Bowl, salad, granite grey 51.00

Bowl, soup, lug handle, cedar green 26.00

Bowl, soup, lug handle, chartreuse 7.00

Carafe w/stopper, bean brown 200.00

Bowl, soup, lug handle, cedar green....26.00
Bowl, soup, lug handle, chartreuse........7.00
Carafe w/stopper, bean brown..........200.00
Carafe w/stopper, granite grey...........140.00
Casserole, cov., stick handle, black chutney (deep brown)......................71.00
Casserole, cov., stick handle, coral......46.00
Casserole, cov., stick handle, glacier blue..145.00
Casserole, cov., stick handle, seafoam blue..................................51.00
Celery tray, slender oblong shape w/asymmetrical incurved sides, bean brown, 13" l...............................60.00
Celery tray, slender oblong shape w/asymmetrical incurved sides, black chutney, 13" l..........................36.00
Celery tray, slender oblong shape w/asymmetrical incurved sides, cedar green, 13" l............................18.00
Coffeepot, cov., demitasse, black chutney 90.00
Coffeepot, cov., demitasse, chartreuse..60.00
Coffeepot, cov., chartreuse 65.00
Coffeepot, cov., granite grey 100.00
Creamer, chartreuse.................................7.00
Cup & saucer, demitasse, chartreuse..23.00
Cup & saucer, demitasse, coral...........19.00
Cup & saucer, demitasse, granite grey...20.00
Cup & saucer, granite grey....................9.00
Gravy boat, black chutney....................15.00
Gravy boat & underplate, coral, 2 pcs. 30.00
Hostess set w/cup, chartreuse 62.00
Hostess set w/cup, white........................85.00
Mug, white 85.00
Pickle dish, black chutney 18.00
Pitcher, water, 12" h., black chutney 67.00
Pitcher, water, 12" h., chartreuse 55.00
Pitcher, water, 12" h., coral..................75.00
Plate, salad, 8¼" d., granite grey............8.00
Plate, dinner, 10" d., black chutney 16.00
Plate, dinner, 10" d., cedar green.........12.00
Plate, dinner, 10" d., glacier blue..........20.00
Plate, chop, 13" sq., bean brown..........45.00
Plate, chop, 13" sq., black chutney 31.00
Plate, chop, 13" sq., seafoam blue.......30.00
Platter, 13¾" l., oblong, coral................14.00
Ramekin, cov., black chutney.............165.00
Ramekin, cov., chartreuse..................145.00
Refrigerator jar, cov., chartreuse 195.00
Relish dish, divided, bean brown........250.00
Salt & pepper shakers, black chutney, pr...15.00
Salt & pepper shakers, granite grey, pr...12.00
Salt & pepper shakers, seafoam blue, pr...10.00
Teapot, cov., bean brown 135.00
Teapot, cov., coral 55.00
Teapot, cov., granite grey......................65.00
Teapot, cov., seafoam blue 40.00
Vegetable bowl, cov., coral, 12" l..........45.00
Vegetable bowl, open, oval, black chutney, 10" l. 21.00
Vegetable bowl, open, oval, coral, 10" l...17.00
Vegetable dish, divided, charteuse......50.00
Vegetable dish, divided, coral.............55.00
Vegetable dish, divided, granite grey...60.00
Vegetable dish, divided, white 87.50

CASUAL CHINA (Iroquois China Company)

Bowl, cereal, 5" d., avocado yellow 6.00
Bowl, cereal, 5" d., canteloupe (orange) 14.00
Bowl, cereal, 5" d., pink sherbet 6.00
Bowl, fruit, 5½" d., pink sherbet.............6.00
Butter dish, cov., avocado yellow 40.00
Butter dish, cov., lettuce green (chartreuse) 60.00
Butter dish, cov., pink sherbet...............67.00
Butter dish, cov., ripe apricot 60.00
Carafe, cov., avocado yellow, 10" h..125.00
Carafe, cov., ice blue, 10" h.................105.00
Carafe, cov., lettuce green, 10" h. 92.00
Carafe, cov., sugar white, 10" h..........150.00
Casserole, cov., divided, nutmeg brown, 1½ qt.......................................45.00
Creamer, pink sherbet...........................12.00
Creamer, stack-type, avocado yellow.....5.00
Creamer, restyled, sugar white.............24.00
Creamer & sugar bowl, stack-type, cantaloupe, pr....................................31.00
Creamer & sugar bowl, stack-type, pink sherbet, pr. 25.00
Creamer & sugar bowl, stack-type, sugar white, pr. 55.00
Cup & saucer, restyled, canteloupe.......20.00
Cup & saucer, tea, avocado yellow 8.00
Cup & saucer, tea, oyster grey 10.00
Cup & saucer, tea, pink sherbet 9.00
Gumbo soup bowl, handled, charcoal ..22.00
Gumbo soup bowl, handled, ice blue ...25.00
Gumbo soup bowl, handled, sugar white 20.00
Mug, nutmeg brown, 13 oz. 50.00
Mug, restyled, ice blue..........................40.00
Mug, restyled, pink sherbet 48.00
Plate, salad, 7½" d., lemon yellow..........4.00
Plate, salad, 7½" d., pink sherbet...........8.00
Plate, luncheon, 9" d., ice blue 5.00
Plate, dinner, 10" d., avocado yellow......6.00
Plate, dinner, 10" d., sugar white..........12.00
Platter, 12¾" l., oval, aqua...................30.00
Platter, 12¾" l., oval, nutmeg brown......16.00
Platter, 14" l., oval, forest green 18.00
Salt & pepper shakers, stack-type, ice blue, pr. 16.00
Soup bowl, cov., canteloupe................10.00
Sugar bowl, cov., restyled, nutmeg brown 12.00

Teapot, cov., restyled, sherbet pink......95.00

Teapot, cov., restyled, sugar white.....150.00

Vegetable bowl, open, canteloupe, 8" d...36.00

Vegetable bowl, open, lettuce green, 8" d...13.50

Vegetable bowl, open, divided, lettuce green, 10" d. 24.00

SAN ILDEFONSO (Maria) POTTERY

Dish by Maria & Julian

A thin-walled and crudely polished blackware has been made at most Rio Grande Pueblos. Around 1918 a San Ildefonso Pueblo woman, Maria Montoya Martinez and her husband, Julian, began making a thicker walled blackware with a finely polished gun-metal black sheen. It was fired in the traditional manner using manure to smother the firing process and produce the black coloration. The following is a chronology of Maria's varied signatures: Marie, mid to late teens-1934; Marie & Julian, 1934-43; Maria & Santana, 1943-56; Maria & Popovi, 1956-71 and Maria Poveka, used on undecorated wares after 1956. Maria died in July of 1980. Rosalia, Tonita, Blue Corn and other signatures might also be found on pottery made at the San Ildefonso Pueblo. Considered a true artistic achievement, early items signed by Maria, or her contemporaries, command good prices. It should be noted that the strong pottery tradition is being carried on by current potters.

Dish, shallow, blackware w/matte geometric design around the rim, glossy center, signed "Maria & Julian," 5¾" d. (ILLUS.)..................$550.00

Jar, squatty bulbous form w/a sloping shoulder, blackware w/a matte & shiny spearhead design on the upper half, signed "Marie & Julian," ca. 1940, 4⅝" d., 2⅞ " h. (minor wear)..313.50

Jar, ovoid body w/a wide, flat mouth, blackware w/a finely polished feature design around the upper half, signed "Donicia Tafoya," 4⅜" d., 3¼" h. (faint rub line at shoulder).......93.50

Jar, blackware, wide rounded base below a tapering funnel-shaped upper half, finely polished w/a feather design around the shoulder, signed "Pauline," Pauline Martinez, granddaughter of Maria, 3¼" d., 3½" h...104.50

Jar, squatty bulbous form w/steeply angled shoulder to flat mouth, black on black w/a geometric avian design around the shoulder, signed "Mama-Popovi 669," ca. 1960s, 5" d., 4" h. (small repaired rim chips) 286.00

Jar, blackware, squatty glossy globular body w/three matte lines, the sloping shoulder decorated in a glossy & matte feather design, signed "Santana & Adam" 2,970.00

Plate, 5¾" d., black on black w/a feather border design, signed "Maria & Santana" (very minor wear).........192.50

SARREGUEMINES

Sarreguemines Majolica Pitcher

This factory was established in Lorraine, France, about 1770. Subsequently Wedgwood-type pieces were produced as was Mocha ware. In the 19th century, the factory turned to pottery and stoneware.

Basket, Etna line, leopard skin crystals, quilted green ground, marked "Etna," 9" h. $215.00

Cup & saucer, majolica, cup modeled in the form of an orange, leafy saucer 125.00
Dish, cov., majolica, strawberries in basket decoration 175.00
Humidor, cov., molded high-relief figures & forest scene around body....125.00
Pitcher, 5⅜" h., 4⅜" d., majolica, figural bulbous man's head, color trim w/red cheeks & nose, aqua lining, marked (ILLUS.) 65.00
Plate, 7½" d., majolica, molded grapes & leaves 50.00
Plate, pierced to hang, French peasant scene, F. Richard, marked "PV" 40.00
Stein, w/pewter top, decorated w/colored scene of men drinking beer on front, cream exterior & white interior, 9½" h. 195.00
Vase, 5" h., Etna line, the squatty bulbous body tapering to a wide cupped rim, overall green crystalline glaze w/the crystals forming concentric circles, marked on base "Sarreguemines - Etna - 4072 - 227 - G - E," early 20th c. 605.00
Vase, 6½" h., squatty bulbous base tapering to a tall trumpet-form neck, shaded amber to rich brown glaze, blue-glazed interior, impressed mark 33.00

SASCHA BRASTOFF

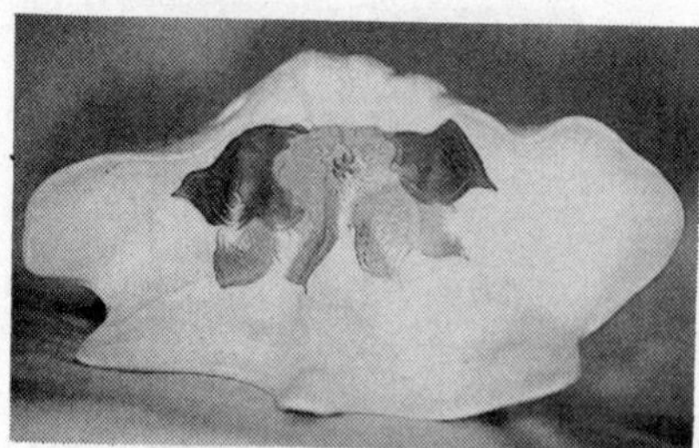

Sascha Brastoff Bowl

Even though Sascha Brastoff experimented with different materials and had a natural talent for sculpting, it was not until November, 1953 that he felt his unique ability in ceramic design was recognized. His friend, Winthrop Rockefeller, backed him in a large, newly constructed showplace encompassing a full block on Olympic Boulevard in downtown Los Angeles, California. Brastoff designed each piece personally and the Brastoff-trained employees produced them. He created a full line of hand-painted china in about twelve designs. A pottery dinnerware line named 'Surf Ballet,' a marbleized treatment usually in gold and pink or silver and blue, was marketed. Artware items with patterns such as 'Star Steed,' a leaping fantasy horse and 'Rooftops,' a village scene with a batik look, are popular items. Hard-to-find resin items are an example of Brastoff's diversified talents. A line of enamels on copper was also made. Pieces signed "Sascha B." were done by his artisans; those with the full "Sascha Brastoff" signature were personally hand-painted by him. The chanticleer was a Brastoff trademark used as a backstamp in conjunction with the signature marks. Because of health problems Brastoff left his company in 1963; it would be another ten years before the business closed. Sascha Brastoff died February 4, 1993.

Ashtray, rectangular w/six cigarette rests at one end, house motif in black, grey, maroon & white glaze, 7½" w., 10" l. $65.00
Bowl, 3½" d., 5" h., three small round feet, "Surf Ballet," blue & silver marbleized glaze....20.00
Bowl, 12" d., 4½" h., shell-shaped white matte glaze w/gold & platinum glossy leaves in bottom of shell (ILLUS.) 95.00
Candleholder, yellow resin, 4" d., 7¼" h....27.00
Cigarette holder, pipe-shaped, overall gold glaze, Model No. 080, 4¼" h....45.00
Cigarette holder, round w/straight sides, turquoise w/abstract flower design, 2½" h. 22.00
Cigarette lighter, white w/pink glaze w/blue & purple flowers, 2" h. 25.00
Cup & saucer, peacock design w/tan, gold, light blue & white over brown background, saucer 5½" d., cup 3½" d., 3" h. 25.00
Model of a bear, seated w/legs straight, head slightly raised, arms across chest, dark green resin, 10½" h....250.00
Obelisk w/lid, horizontal stripes in brown, blue & tan over white background, full signature, 22" h. 310.00
Pitcher, 6" h., 5½" d., bulbous ovoid body tapering to a rim slightly raised forming angular spout, brown glossy background w/tan & rust fruits & leaves trimmed in green & gold 95.00
Sugar bowl, cov., "Surf Ballet," pink & gold marbleized glaze, 4½" d., 3¾" h....40.00
Tray, angular free-form shape, white background, platinum & gold flowers & leaves, Model No. F3, 9¾" l., 5½" w. 35.00

Tray, shallow oval, enamel on copper, abstract design w/blue, black, yellow & green glazes, 4" l., 3½" w. 28.00

Vase, 9" h., figural model of a high-buttoned shoe, blue, brown, tan stripes over white background, ca. 1959 ....85.00

SATSUMA

Miniature Satsuma Bowl

These decorated wares have been produced in Japan since the end of the 18th century. The early pieces are scarce and high-priced. Later Satsuma wares are plentiful and, with prices rising, as highly collectible as earlier pieces.

Bowl, miniature, 4" d., flattened form, decorated w/mon, flowers & foliage in colors & gilt, signed "Kinkozan," early 20th c. (ILLUS.)$1,000.00 to 1,500.00

Bowl, 4" w., squared form, the interior decorated w/Kannon flying & holding a lotus blossom amid clouds, each interior side decorated w/a flying crane, a small applied figure on the exterior peeks over the corner of the rim, the exterior decorated w/fan & heart-shaped panels depicting geisha, dancers & samurai, a fluted leaf border near the base, signed 330.00

Bowl, 6" d., lotus-form, polychrome & gilt design of Rakan & their attributes, late 19th c. ....400.00 to 600.00

Bowl, 6¾" d., decorated on the exterior w/a scene of men in a two-story pavilion w/mountains & a waterfall in the background, the interior rim decorated w/flying cranes 220.00

Bowl, 15½" d., deep, the center depicting a pair of cockerels & hens in a garden w/blooming wisteria & bellflowers, the scene surrounded by a border of alternating patterned panels beneath the barbed rim edged in gilt, the exterior painted w/beribboned cash designs & paulownia crests, on a later carved wood stand, late 19th c. (slightly rubbed) 1,725.00

Box, cov., cover w/Foo dog finial, decorated overall w/beautiful ladies & scholars, w/stamped signature, 3 x 3¼" 650.00

Box, cov., square form w/canted corners, decorated w/a procession of samurai reserved on a ground of chrysanthemums, the interior decorated w/irises, 3¼" w. 330.00

Buttons, floraform w/designs of butterflies, 1¼" d., ca. 1925, set of 7 ....100.00 to 175.00

Dish, motif of Kannon astride a dragon, signed "Kinkozan," ca. 1910, 10" d. (repairs to rim) ....1,050.00 to 1,500.00

Figure of a man seated on a tatami mat & holding a pipe, late 19th c., 6" l. ....1,200.00 to 1,500.00

Jar, cov., wide ovoid body w/a four-lobed scalloped base, figural drum handles on the shoulders flanking the short flaring neck supporting a high domed & reticulated cover w/a double pod finial, the sides decorated overall w/Immortals & attendants on a ground of gold dots, signed, 11¼" h. 825.00

Koro (censer), globular, Rakan & dragon in relief, three stump feet, 7" h. (finial restored).........400.00 to 600.00

Plates, 7" d., h.p. scene of geisha & master, moriage trim, ca. 1920s, set of 5 ....150.00

Sake cup, 1000 Butterflies patt., exterior w/panels of flowers, ca. 1900, 2" d.........................500.00 to 600.00

Sake pot, teapot-shaped, floral decoration w/lappets, 19th c., 2½" h........675.00

Teapot, cov., overall decoration of irises in colors & gilt, ca. 1920, 4½" h..............................400.00 to 600.00

Vase, 4¼" h., baluster-form w/dragon handles, decorated w/Ebisu & panels of flowers, gilt & colors, signed "Dai Nihon Satsuma Hozan," ca. 1910 ....800.00 to 1,000.00

Vase, 5½" h., globular form w/panels of Samurai, late 19th c. ....500.00 to 700.00

Vase, 6" h., black ground w/gold scenic decoration, signed "Satsumayaki," ca. 1930 ....200,00 to 300.00

Vase, 9" h., gourd-shape, design of cranes & flowers below a lappet border, colors & gilt, ca. 1910 ....800.00 to 1,200.00

Vase, cov., 11" h., three-footed, decorated w/scene of warriors, Foo dog handles & finial 85.00

Vase, 11½" h., figural medallions on brocade ground, colors & gilt late 19th c. ....800.00 to 1,200.00

Vase, 14½" h., ovoid, four panels w/birds on flowering branches, ca. 1910, signed "Satsuma yaki" ....1,000.00 to 1,500.00

SCHAFER & VATER

Founded in Rudolstadt, Thuringia, Germany in 1890, the Schafer and Vater Porcelain Factory specialized in decorative pieces of porcelain usually in white or colored bisque. They produced many novelty figural items such as creamers, toothpick holders, boxes and hatpin holders and also produced a line of jasper ware with white relief decoration in imitation of the famous Wedgwood jasper wares. The firm also decorated white ware blanks.

The company ceased production in 1962 and collectors now seek out their charming pieces which may be marked with a crown over a starburst containing the script letter "R."

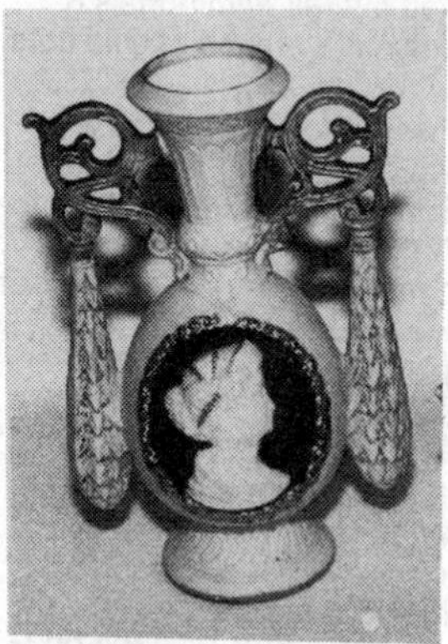

Schafer & Vater Vase

Box, cov., cameo-like white relief bust profile of Art Nouveau lady, No. 3177, 4" d. $115.00

Creamer, bisque, figural orange 35.00

Hatpin holder, bisque, figural, Egyptian woman's head, pink, 4½" h. 170.00

Humidor, cov., man w/pipe decoration, lavender 550.00

Match holder w/attached tray, jasper ware, white relief roses on a light green ground 50.00

Pitcher, 3½" h., figural maid w/jug & keys, multicolor trim 98.00

Pitcher, 5½" h., figural Mother Goose, blue trim 98.00

Pitcher, milk, 6½" h., figural cow dressed as a woman.........................195.00

Vase, 4¾" h., 3" d., bisque, balusterform w/the tall trumpet neck flanked by looped scroll handles suspending long pendent swags, the front centered by an oval reserve w/a white relief cameo portrait of a classical lady against a dark green ground, the body & handles washed in pale green (ILLUS.)......................55.00

Vase, 6½" h., jasper ware, white relief scene of a man, woman & cupid against a blue ground, No. 593........150.00

Wall pocket, jasper ware, decorated w/white relief roses on green ground...48.00

SEVRES & SEVRES-STYLE

Sevres-Style Candelabra

Some of the more desirable porcelain ever produced was made at the Sevres factory, originally established at Vincennes, France, and transferred, through permission of Madame de Pompadour, to Sevres as the Royal Manufactory about the middle of the 18th century. King Louis XV took sole responsibility for the works in 1759 when production of hard paste began. Between 1850 and 1900, many biscuit and soft-paste porcelains were again made. Fine early pieces are scarce and high-priced. Many of those available today are late productions. The various Sevres marks have been copied and pieces listed as "Sevres-Style" are similar to actual Sevres wares, but not necessarily from that factory. Three of the many Sevres marks are illustrated below.

Cache-pots, Sevres-Style, gilt-bronze mounted, the cylindrical sides decorated w/a figural panel of lovers in a garden, framed by gilt scrolling, the reverse w/a floral panel, all on a *bleu celeste* ground, mounted at the top w/a pierced flaring gilt-bronze band, fitted at the sides w/lion mask handles w/rings & raised on a round tapered gilt-bronze base w/scrolled feet, late 19th c., 11½" h., pr.......$6,325.00

Candelabrum, Sevres-Style, six-light, each of vase-form painted w/a figural panel on the obverse & birds & flowers on the reverse, on a cobalt ground w/gilt highlights, raised on a gilt-bronze square base fitted w/painted porcelain plaques & supporting tiers of foliate-scrolled branches, late 19th c., 28¾" h., pr. (ILLUS. of one) 6,900.00

Centerpieces, Sevres-Style, oval bowl w/figural panels flanked by ram's heads, the rim & base fitted w/foliate scrolled mounts, late 19th c., 13" l., 10" h., pr. 3,163.00

Cup & saucer, Sevres-Style, cobalt blue decorated w/scenic panels of young lovers & landscapes, gilt trim 60.00

Tea service: cov. teapot, cov. sugar bowl, creamer, six cups & saucers; Sevres-Style, each decorated w/figural panels on a cobalt blue ground, w/circular "sevres," crowned interlacing "L" mark & Chateau mark, late 19th c., teapot 18" h., 15 pcs. 4,313.00

Urn, cov., Sevres-Style, gilt-bronze mounted, the tall baluster-form body decorated on the front w/a large oval panel depicting the coronation of Napoleon based on the David painting, the reverse w/a panel of a landscape scene, each panel within gilt laurel border, the flaring neck decorated w/a spread-winged eagle & the domed cover w/a gilt crown, the base decorated w/gilt athenium & scrolls, all against a cobalt blue ground, fitted w/gilt-bronze mounts & a bracket plinth, artist-signed, late 19th c., pseudo "Mre. Imple de Sevres" mark in red, 4' 10" h.......36,800.00

Vase, 13½" h., commemorative, tall ovoid body tapering to a short cylindrical neck, the waist w/four *pate-sur-pate* roundels enclosing athletes at various pursuits in white slip on grey within lime green borders reserved against a rich blue ground trimmed w/gilt laurel leaves, made to commemorate the 1924 Olympic Games in Paris, factory marks, artist-signed 10,350.00

Vase, cov., 15" h., Sevres-Style, slender ovoid body w/flaring trumpet neck & pointed cover, slender pedestal base w/gilt metal foot, large decorated reserve w/full-length portrait of woman & cupid in garden, background of blue & gold, artist-signed 495.00

SHAWNEE

Dutch Girl Cookie Jar

The Shawnee pottery operated in Zanesville, Ohio, from 1937 until 1961. Much of the early production was sold to chain stores and mail-order houses including Sears, Roebuck, Woolworth and others. Planters, cookie jars and vases, along with the popular "Corn King" oven ware line, are among the collectible items which are plentiful and still reasonably priced. Reference numbers used here are taken from Mark E. Supnick's book, Collecting Shawnee Pottery, The Collector's Guide to Shawnee Pottery *by Duane and Janice Vanderbilt, or* Shawnee Pottery - An Identification & Value Guide *by Jim and Bev Mangus.*

Ashtray/coasters, heart-shaped w/three-section interior, No. 411, various colors, set of 4 ....$38.00

Bank, figural Bulldog..........................125.00

Bank-cookie jar combination, figural Smiley Pig, No. 61 ....325.00

Bank-cookie jar combination, figural Winnie Pig, chocolate-colored base 395.00

Bank-cookie jar combination, figural Winnie Pig, caramel-colored base ...550.00

Batter pitcher, embossed Snowflake patt., yellow glaze 50.00

Bowl, 6" d., "Corn King" line, No. 92.....32.50

Bowl, soup or cereal, "Corn King" line, No. 94 ....32.50

Bowl, 9" d., "Corn King" line, No. 95.....45.00

Bowls, nest-type, "Corn King" line, set of 3 .... 85.00

Butter dish, cov., "Corn King" line, No. 72 .... 52.50

Casserole, individual size, "Corn King" line, No. 73, 9 oz. 55.00

Casserole, cov., "Corn King" line, 1½ qt., No. 74 .... 62.00

Casserole, cov., model of fruit basket, No. 81, 5½" h. 40.00

Cookie jar, "Corn King" line, figural ear of corn, No. 66 .... 145.00

Cookie jar, "Corn Queen" line, figural ear of corn, No. 66 .... 195.00

Cookie jar, figural Cottage, "USA 6" .... 1,000.00 to 1,500.00

Cookie jar, figural Dutch boy, blue tie, striped pants .... 100.00 to 150.00

Cookie jar, figural Dutch Girl, marked "Great Northern, No. 1026" (ILLUS.) 150.00

Cookie jar, figural Dutch Girl, decorated w/a tulip 114.00

Cookie jar, figural Elephant, marked "Lucky" on the front, w/gold trim & floral decals 695.00

Cookie jar, Fernware line, octagonal, green glaze 75.00

Cookie jar, figural Jug, blue glaze 150.00

Cookie jar, Little Chef patt., hexagonal w/molded chefs in three panels & "Cookies" in others, cream ground 65.00

Cookie jar, figural Mugsey Dog, w/blue bow .... 350.00 to 450.00

Cookie jar, figural Owl .... 125.00 to 175.00

Cookie jar, figural Owl, gold trim .... 250.00 to 300.00

Cookie jar, figural Puss 'n Boots 145.00

Cookie jar, figural Puss 'n Boots, gold trim .... 500.00 to 550.00

Cookie jar, figural Sailor Boy .... 100.00 to 125.00

Cookie jar, figural Sailor boy, gold trim & decals 295.00

Cookie jar, figural Smiley Pig, blue collar, gold trim 348.00

Cookie jar, figural Smiley Pig, decorated w/pink flowers & gold trim, red kerchief .... 275.00 to 325.00

Cookie jar, figural Winnie Pig, decorated w/clover leaves 290.00

Corn King Salt & Pepper & Creamer

Creamer, "Corn King" line, No. 70, 5" h. (ILLUS. right) 29.00

Creamer, "Corn Queen" line, No. 70, 5" h. 25.00

Creamer, figural Elephant, gold trim .... 125.00 to 150.00

Creamer, figural Puss 'n Boots, white w/color trim, 5" h. 45.00

Creamer, figural Smiley Pig, colored trim 40.00

Creamer, Heart & Tulip patt. 45.00

Creamer, embossed Snowflake patt., green glaze 15.00

Ewer, tall slender footed ovoid body, angled handle w/gold trim, No. 1168, 8" h. 15.00

Figurine, model of a Pekinese dog 39.50

Figurine, model of a puppy dog 39.50

Mixing bowl, "Corn King" line, No. 5, 5" d. 45.00

Mixing bowl, "Corn King" line, No. 6, 6½" d. 37.50

Model of a gazelle, recumbent, mottled brown glaze 50.00

Pie bird, pink glaze, 5¼" h. .... 35.00 to 40.00

Pitcher, tankard, "Corn King" line, 1 qt., No. 71 .... 76.00

Pitcher, 5½" h., ball-shaped, embossed Flower & Fern patt., yellow glaze 45.00

Pitcher, ball-type, Fruit patt., No. 80 .... 65.00

Pitcher, ball-type, Pennsylvania Dutch patt. .... 150.00 to 175.00

Pitcher, ball-type, Sunflower patt. .... 50.00 to 75.00

Pitcher, ball-type, Valencia line, yellow glaze, 2 pt. 60.00

Pitcher, figural Chanticleer Rooster, w/flower decals & gold trim 125.00

Pitcher, figural Little Bo Peep, peach trim .... 50.00 to 75.00

Pitcher, figural Little Boy Blue, No. 46 .... 90.00

Pitcher, figural Smiley Pig, red clover decoration .... 150.00 to 175.00

Planter, figural, boy standing beside stump, wearing a pale turquoise cap & shorts & a large bow tie, No. 533 .... 12.00

Planter, figural clown lying on his back, w/gold trim, No. 607 .... 19.00

Planter, model of an alarm clock, No. 1262 .... 12.00

Planter, model of a bull, brown glaze, No. 668 .... 45.00

Planter, model of a large chick pulling a spherical cart, No. 720 .... 19.00

Planter, model of a doe & log, lime green base, No. 766, 7" h. 28.00

Planter, model of a fish w/wide open mouth, tail curled up & touching back of head, blue glaze 40.00

Planter, model of a frog on lily pad, No. 726 .... 59.00

Planter, model of gazelle & baby heads, glossy black glaze, No. 841 .... 48.00

Planter, model of a globe, 7" h. 25.00

Planter, model of a goose flying, No. 820 ....25.00
Planter, model of a horse, standing, red glaze w/white mane & tail, No. 506 ....20.00
Planter, model of a hound & Pekinese, No. 611 ....18.00
Planter, model of a hound next to green keg, No. 610 ....12.00
Planter, model of a pig, No. 760 ....16.00
Planter, model of a ribbed conch shell, No. 655 ....10.00
Planter, model of an upright piano, No. 528 ....25.00
Planter, model of a watering can, 5½ x 8" 10.00
Planter, model of a windmill, white w/gold trim, No. 715 ....35.00

Train Planter Set

Planters, train set composed of locomotive, coal car, box car & caboose, 4 pcs. (ILLUS.) 99.00
Plate, 8" oval, "Corn King" line, No. 93 ....26.00
Plate, 10" d., "Corn King" line, No. 65 ....37.00
Plate, 10" oval, "Corn King" line, No. 68 ....36.50
Platter, 12" oval, "Corn King" line, No. 96 ....45.00
Relish tray, "Corn King" line, No. 79 ....35.00
Relish tray, "Corn Queen" line, No. 79 ....18.00
Salt & pepper shakers, Basket of Fruit line, No. 82, small, pr. 19.00
Salt & pepper shakers, Basket of Fruit line, No. 82, large, pr. 35.00
Salt & pepper shakers, "Corn King" line, No. 76, 3¼" h., pr.(ILLUS. left) 20.00
Salt & pepper shakers, "Corn King" line, large range size, No. 77, 5¼" h., pr. 28.00
Salt & pepper shakers, embossed Fernware line, green glaze, large, pr. 28.00
Salt & pepper shakers, Sunflower patt., large, 5" h., pr. 45.00
Salt & pepper shakers, figural Chanticleer Rooster, small, pr. 35.00
Salt & pepper shakers, figural Chanticleer Rooster, gold-decorated, large, pr. 45.00
Salt & pepper shakers, figural duck, 3¼" h., pr. 35.00
Salt & pepper shakers, figural Dutch Boy & Girl, small, pr. 45.00
Salt & pepper shakers, figural Dutch Boy & Girl, large, pr. 60.00
Salt & pepper shakers, figural lobster claw, Lobster Ware, Kenwood Line, pr 35.00
Salt & pepper shakers, figural Little Bo Peep, pr. 15.00
Salt & pepper shakers, figural Mugsey Dog, small, pr. 48.00
Salt & pepper shakers, figural Mugsey Dog, large, pr. 108.00
Salt & pepper shakers, figural Owl, pr. 35.00
Salt & pepper shakers, figural Sailor Boy, 3½" h., pr. 15.00
Salt & pepper shakers, figural Smiley Pig, green scarf, small, pr 30.00
Salt & pepper shakers, figural Swiss Boy & Girl, large, pr. 45.00
Salt & pepper shakers, figural Winnie & Smiley Pig, large, 5" h., pr. ....100.00 to 115.00
Sugar bowl, cov., Clover Flower patt. 75.00
Sugar bowl, cov., "Corn King" line, No. 78 ....40.00
Sugar bowl, cov., "Corn Queen" line, No. 78 ....38.00
Sugar bowl, cov., figural water bucket ..25.00
Sugar bowl, cov., Lobster Ware, Kenwood line, domed white cover w/red lobster finial 30.00
Teapot, cov., Blue Leaves patt. 39.00
Teapot, cov., "Corn King" line, 30 oz., No. 75 ....77.00
Teapot, cov., embossed Flower & Fern patt., green glaze 38.00
Teapot, cov., Embossed Rose patt. 48.00
Teapot, cov., embossed Snowflake patt., blue glaze, small 35.00
Teapot, cov., embossed Snowflake patt., blue glaze, medium 45.00
Teapot, cov., embossed Snowflake patt., green glaze 25.00
Teapot, cov., Fernware line, yellow glaze 19.00
Teapot, cov., Pennsylvania Dutch patt. 45.00
Teapot, cov., Sunflower patt., 6½" h. 44.00
Teapot, cov., figural Granny Ann, coral apron 85.00
Utility jar, cov., Basketweave patt., green trim 58.50
Vase, bud, 8" h., tall cylindrical footed body w/gold trimmed handles, No. 1178 ....18.00
Vase, bulbous body tapering to a flaring neck flanked by short open handles, overall diamond-quilted embossed design w/small flowers, grey glaze, No. 287 ....25.00

Vegetable bowl, open, "Corn King" line, 9" oval, No. 95 ....45.00
Wall pocket, model of a birdhouse & birds, No. 830 ....28.00

Shawnee Bow Wall Pocket

Wall pocket, model of a large bow, yellow & rose glaze (ILLUS.) 11.00
Wall pocket, model of a bowknot, No. 434 ....22.00
Wall pocket, model of a grandfather clock, No. 1261 ....25.00

SHELLEY

Shelley Cake Plate

Members of the Shelley family were in the pottery business in England as early as the 18th century. In 1872 Joseph Shelley formed a partnership with James Wileman of Wileman & Co. who operated the Foley China Works. The Wileman & Co. name was used for the firm for the next fifty years, and between 1890 and 1910 the words "The Foley" appeared above conjoined "WC" initials.

Beginning in 1910 the Shelley family name in a shield appeared on wares, although the firm's official name was still Wileman & Co. The company's name was finally changed to Shelley in 1925 and then Shelley China Ltd. after 1965. The firm changed hands in the 1960s and became part of the Doulton Group in 1971.

At first only average quality earthenwares were produced but in the late 1890s new shapes and better quality decorations were used.

Bone china was introduced at Shelley before World War I and these fine dinnerwares became very popular in the United States and are increasingly popular today with collectors. Thin "eggshell china" teawares, miniatures and souvenir items were widely marketed during the 1920s and 1930s and are sought-after today.

Bouillon cup,Old Sevres patt. $55.00
Cake plate, Regency patt., 9½" d. 65.00
Cheese dish, cov., Rosebud patt. 90.00
Coffeepot, cov., Regency patt., 8½" h. 125.00
Coffee set: large cov. coffeepot, creamer & cov. sugar bowl; Dainty White patt., 3 pcs. 250.00
Creamer & sugar bowl, demitasse, Regency patt., pr. 30.00
Creamer & cov. sugar bowl, all white w/gold trim, Dainty shape, small, pr. 80.00
Creamer & cov. sugar bowl, Dainty Blue patt., small, pr. 78.00
Creamer & cov. sugar bowl, Pansy patt., Dainty shape, medium, pr. 85.00
Creamer & cov. sugar bowl, Regency patt., pr. 45.00
Cup & saucer, demitasse, Begonia patt. 45.00
Cup & saucer, demitasse, Blue Rock patt., six-flute shape 38.00
Cup & saucer, demitasse, Harebell patt., blue & white 55.00
Cup & saucer, demitasse, Rosebud patt. 45.00
Cup & saucer, demitasse, The Georgian patt. 20.00
Cup & saucer, demitasse, Thistle patt. 50.00
Cup & saucer, Begonia patt., six-flute shape 45.00
Cup & saucer, Bridal Wreath patt. 48.00
Cup & saucer, Charm patt. 48.00
Cup & saucer, Dainty Blue patt., six-flute shape 45.00
Cup & saucer, Dainty White patt. 35.00
Cup & saucer, Daffodil Time patt. 32.50
Cup & saucer, Fantasy patt. 45.00
Cup & saucer, Harebell patt. 43.00
Cup & saucer, Lilac patt., six-flute shape 46.50
Cup & saucer, Lily of the Valley patt. 35.00
Cup & saucer, Old Mill patt. 45.00
Cup & saucer, Oleander shape 50.00
Cup & saucer, Polka Dot patt., aqua 48.00
Cup & saucer, Rambler Rose patt. 48.00

Cup & saucer, Regency patt., Dainty shape 35.00
Cup & saucer, Rock Garden patt. 55.00
Cup & saucer, Shamrock patt., six-flute shape 44.00
Cup & saucer, Stocks patt. 35.00
Cup & saucer, Wildflowers patt. 45.00
Cup & saucer, Woodland patt. 28.00
Dessert set: cup & saucer & dessert plate; Red Daisies patt., 3 pcs. 75.00
Dessert set: cup, saucer & 5" d. plate; Stocks patt., 3 pcs. 65.00
Dessert set: cake plate, four dessert plates, cups & saucers; Queen Anne shape, 13 pcs. 350.00
Dessert set: large creamer, sugar bowl, cake plate, four dessert plates & cups & saucers; Gainsborough shape, 15 pcs. 370.00
Dessert set: 8 x 9½" cake plate, six 6¼" d. plates, six cups & saucers; Tall Trees & Sunrise patt., 19 pc. (ILLUS. of cake plate) 650.00
Egg cup, Rosebud patt., six-flute shape, small 42.50
Jam jar, cov., Rosebud patt., six-flute shape 70.00
Luncheon set: 8" plate, cup & saucer; Bridal Rose patt., 3 pcs. 125.00
Luncheon set: 8" plate, cup & saucer; Daffodil Time patt., 3 pcs. 110.00
Luncheon set: 8" plate, cup & saucer; Rosebud patt., 3 pcs. 80.00
Mug, Rosebud patt., six-flute shape, 4" h. 60.00
Mustard jar, cov. & underplate, Dainty Pink patt., 2 pcs. 80.00
Nut dish, Regency patt. 15.00
Plate, 6" d., Dainty Blue patt., six-flute shape 22.50
Plate, 7" d., Wildflowers patt. 22.00
Plate, 7¾" d., Dainty Blue patt., six-flute shape 35.00
Plate, 8" d., Old Sevres patt. 90.00
Plate, 9½" d., Wildflowers patt. 30.00
Plate, dinner, 10½" d., Dainty Blue patt., six-flute shape 50.00
Plates, 8" d., Begonia patt., six-flute shape, set of 6 ....150.00
Plates, luncheon, Dainty White patt., six-flute shape, set of 6 ....195.00
Saucer, 5½" d., Dainty Blue patt., six-flute shape 13.50
Sugar bowl, cov., handleless, Dainty Blue patt., six-flute shape 22.50
Teapot, cov., Dainty White patt. 300.00
Teapot, cov., Regency patt., small 75.00
Tea set: cov. teapot, creamer & sugar bowl; Daffodil Time patt., 3 pcs. 350.00
Tea set: cov. teapot, creamer & sugar bowl; Woodland patt., 3 pcs. 395.00
Vase, 7½" h., stylized butterflies decoration on black glaze 110.00

SLIPWARE

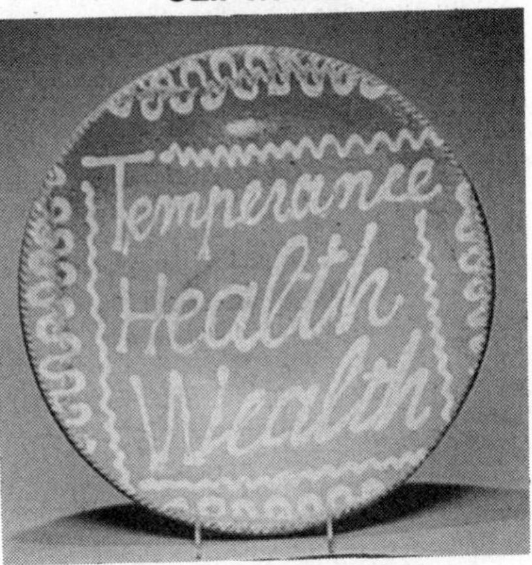

Slipware-Inscribed Charger

This term refers to ceramics, primarily redware, decorated by the application of slip, or semi-liquid paste made of clay. Such wares were made for decades in England and Germany and elsewhere on the Continent, and in the Pennsylvania Dutch country and elsewhere in the United States. Today, contemporary copies of early Slipware items are featured in numerous decorator magazines and offered for sale in gift catalogs.

Charger, redware w/a stylized petaled flower center, dash border, in yellow, pale orange & brown, 11½" d., (wear, flakes, hairlines & small old rim repairs) $632.00
Charger, round dished form w/crimped rim, the interior decorated w/a yellow slip inscription reading "Temperance - Health - Wealth" flanked by squiggled lines in yellow & green slip, New England, 19th c., 13¾" d. (ILLUS.) 19,500.00
Dish, round w/shallow canted sides, the interior decorated w/a single blossomhead in the center & angled bands extending from the rim, all in rust slip on the yellow ground, scattered green splotches, Pennsylvania, 19th c., 6" d. (rim flakes) 1,495.00
Dish, round w/deep double-tapered sides, the interior decorated w/sgraffito-incised tulips, flowers & leaves on a yellow ground w/green splotches, Pennsylvania, ca. 1800, 11¼" d. (some minor flakes) 9,775.00
Flask, footed spherical form w/flattened front & back sides, small flaring mouth, each flat side decorated w/a yellow slip bull's-eye design on orangish red, Pennsylvania, 3¾" h. (two minor flakes) 1,035.00

Jug, flattened cylindrical sides tapering to a wide slightly flared mouth, each side w/a yellow slip inscription "JS(?) 1794" flanked by leafy vines up the edges, Pennsylvania, 8½" h. (numerous chips, handle missing) 1,265.00

Loaf dish, rectangular w/rounded corners, crimped edge, the center decorated w/an abstract design of trailed & scrolled slip in shades of green & yellow on an orangish red ground, Pennsylvania, 19th c., 10½ x 13⅞" 6,325.00

Milk bowl, shallow rounded sides, greenish amber glaze w/white slip bands around the interior, 9" d., 3" h. (old surface chips) 247.50

Pie plate, round w/crimped rim, decorated w/eight bold yellow slip lines across the middle flanked by wavy trailed slip bands, scattered green splotches, Pennsylvania, ca. 1850, 9¼" d. 8,050.00

Pie plate, coggled edge, decorated w/small scattered yellow slip "pine tree" devices, 9⅝" d. (small chips) ...385.00

Pie plate, round w/coggled rim, decorated w/a row of triple-line yellow slip "S" scrolls, rim chips, Pennsylvania, mid-19th c., 10⅝" d. 805.00

Pie plate, shallow round form w/crimped edge, the interior decorated w/an incised depiction of a man on horseback, possibly George Washington, shown holding a sword & horn, the border decorated w/stylized leaves, the whole glazed in green, blue & red on a yellow ground, attributed to Johannes Neesz, Tyler's Port, Montgomery County, Pennsylvania, ca. 1800, 10⅝" d. (two very minor flakes) 24,150.00

Pie plate, oval w/crimped edge, the interior decorated w/trailed slip in green, yellow & brown on a rust ground, Pennsylvania, 19th c., 10¾" l. (minor glaze flake) 5,750.00

SPATTERWARE

This ceramic ware takes its name from the "spattered" decoration, in various colors, generally used to trim pieces hand-painted with rustic center designs of flowers, birds, houses, etc. Popular in the early 19th century, most was imported from England.

Related wares, called "stick spatter," had free-hand designs applied with pieces of cut sponge attached to sticks, hence the name. Examples date from the 19th and early 20th century and were produced in England, Europe and America.

Some early spatter-decorated wares were marked by the manufacturers, but not many. 20th century reproductions are also sometimes marked, including those produced by Boleslaw Cybis in the 1940s which sometimes have "CYBIS" impressed.

Creamer, squatty bulbous footed body tapering to a wide arched shoulder, C-scroll handle, Rose patt., free-hand blossom in red, black & green, brown & black spatter ground, 4" h. $247.50

Creamer, tall footed waisted & paneled body w/a wide arched spout & C-scroll handle, Rose & Cornflower patt., free-hand flowers in red, blue, green & black, red & blue spatter ground, 5⅜" h. (stains, hairlines) 143.00

Cup, handleless, Vine & Berry patt., free-hand red berries on a yellow vine, green spatter ground 357.50

Cup & saucer, handleless, Peafowl patt., free-hand bird in red, blue, yellow & black, red spatter borders..412.50

Rooster Cup & Saucer

Cup & saucer, handleless, Rooster patt., free-hand bird in blue, red, black & yellow ochre, blue spatter rims, stains & minor wear, small flakes on table ring of cup, saucer marked "T" (ILLUS.) 440.00

Cup & saucer, handleless, Tulip patt., free-hand red, green & black flower, yellow spatter borders (minor stains & pinpoint flakes, short hairline in cup) 852.50

Pitcher, 7⅝" h., footed bulbous ribbed body tapering to a flaring rim w/high arched spout, S-scroll handle, free-hand daisy-like flower in yellow, green, pink & black within a squared bordered reserve on the side surrounded by blue spatter (stains, wear) 330.00

Pitcher & bowl set, footed tall paneled tapering pitcher w/high arched spout & angled handle & matching bowl, Rose patt., free-hand flowers & leaves in red, green & black w/blue spatter background, bowl 13¾" d., pitcher 12" h., pr. (hairlines, small chips & stains) 880.00

Plate, 8⅝" d., Rainbow spatter, a red & blue spatter blossom-form cross in the center & alternating bands of red & blue spatter around the border (wear, small flakes) 302.50

Plate, 8¾" d., Peafowl patt., free-hand bird in blue, green, yellow ochre & black, red spatter border 467.50

Plate, 9½" d., Star patt., free-hand six-point star in red, blue & green in the center, blue spatter border band......440.00

Toddy plate, Peafowl patt., free-hand bird in red, yellow, blue & black, yellow spatter background, 6" d. (professional repair) 467.50

Toddy plate, Thistle patt., free-hand thistle in red & green, yellow spatter border, 6¼" d. 1,595.00

STICK OR CUT-SPONGE SPATTER

Bowl, 9" d., shallow, center decorated w/large, gaudy blossoms within a border of cut-sponge design, blue & white, marked "Villeroy & Boch".......137.50

Creamer & cov. sugar bowl, bulbous body w/loop handle, each decorated w/a band of cut-sponge blue blossoms above a wide band of free-hand yellow & green leaves w/small blue cut-sponge blossoms, marked "Maastricht," Holland, early 20th c., pr. 165.00

Cup & saucer, handleless, miniature, a band of paired leaves in blue around the rim of the cup & saucer, flanked by red pinstripes, impressed mark "Tunstall" (stains) 71.50

Cup & saucer, handleless, rounded cup & deep bowl each w/free-hand green leaf sprigs w/triple cut-sponge red blossoms, black trim 38.50

Mug, miniature, cylindrical, decorated w/a free-hand colorful flower & leaf band w/small cut-sponge blossoms, 2¼" h....................................38.50

Mug, decorated w/green & yellow striping over a central band of black cut-sponge diamond design, 3" h. ...110.00

Rabbit Pattern Stick Spatter

Mug, slightly tapering cylindrical body, Rabbit patt. transfer-printed top & bottom bands flanking a wide center band w/free-hand & cut-sponge polychrome flowers & leaves, edge chips, 5½" h. (ILLUS. center)........1,210.00

Plate, 7¾" d., ten-sided, decorated w/three tightly packed rows of diamonds w/dots, diamond-petaled flowerhead in the center, in red, blue & green (underrim chip) 104.50

Plate, 9¼" d., Rabbit patt., transfer-printed center design, a wide border band w/polychrome free-hand leaves & large & scattered small cut-sponge blossoms (ILLUS. left).........467.50

Plate, 9¼" d., Rabbit patt., transfer-printed center design w/a wide border band of free-hand poly-chrome leaf bands & large blossoms & clusters of three small cut-sponge blossoms, stains, rim hairlines (ILLUS. right) 440.00

Plate, 9¼" d., Rabbit patt. transfer-printed border center design w/a wide border band of free-hand polychrome leaf & cut-sponge blossoms, circle of small cut-sponge blossoms in the very center (rim hairline) 330.00

Platter, 14" l., oval, a wide "chain" design border band, the center w/large polychrome leafy sprigs w/small cut-sponge blossoms, marked on back "Auld Heather Ware, Scotland" 412.50

SPONGEWARE

Spongeware Crock

Spongeware's designs were spattered, sponged or daubed on in colors, sometimes with a piece of cloth. Blue on white was the most common type, but mottled tans, browns and greens on yellowware were also popular. Spongeware generally has an overall pattern with a coarser look than Spatterwares, to which it is loosely related. These wares were extensively produced in England and America well into the 20th century.

Bowl, 13" d., 6½" h., deep rounded sides w/molded rim band, overall blue on white (crazing, hairline) $192.50

Cheese keeper, cov., Cockscomb patt., red, brown, blue & yellow..........85.00

Creamer, octagonal, grape leaf decoration on panels, scalloped rim, sponged rim & handle, blue on white, 3" h. 54.00

Crock, straight-sided, overall coarse blue sponging on white, rim chip & hairline, 10¾" d., 15" h. (ILLUS.) 440.00

Cup & saucer, ring-handled, oversized, heavy dark blue on white.......390.50

Pitcher, milk, 6" h., bulbous body tapering to a shaped rim w/wide arched spout, C-form handle, overall heavy dark blue on white (minor stains) 247.50

Pitcher, 6¾" h., cylindrical body w/pointed rim spout, squared handle, overall blue on white (minor hairline, tiny flakes) 247.50

Pitcher, 7¾" h., bulbous ovoid body tapering to a wide tall spout, C-form handle, a narrow blue center band flanked by narrow white bands & surrounded by overall blue on white (short hairline & crow's foot) 385.00

Pitcher, 8½" h., tall barrel-shaped body w/small rim spout, C-form handle, overall heavy blue on white (rim chips) 302.50

Pitcher, 8⅞" h., cylindrical w/pinched rim spout & C-form handle, relief-molded flower sprig on the sides highlighted in dark blue, coarse blue sponged bands at the rim & base, white ground (small chips) 495.00

Pitcher, 9" h., ovoid body tapering to a flat rim w/a pinched spout, C-form handle, overall coarse blue sponging on white, dark brown Albany slip interior (surface & edge chips) 330.00

Pitcher, 9¼" h., bulbous body tapering to a wide, flaring neck w/pinched spout, small C-form handle, overall finely spattered blue on white, dark brown Albany slip interior 385.00

Pitcher, 10" h., 7" d., cylindrical, embossed Old Fashioned Garden Rose patt., blue on white 750.00

Pitcher, 11⅜" h., footed baluster-form body w/a high & wide arched spout & long S-scroll handle, overall coarse light blue sponging on white (stain, chips on base).......................385.00

Pitcher, embossed decoration of girl & dog, blue on white...........................445.00

Slop jar, cov., slightly waisted form, wire bail handle w/wooden grip, blue band near base flanked by white bands, repeated on cover, overall blue on white, hairline & chips, 12½" h...247.50

Syrup jug, bulbous ovoid body w/rim spout & filler opening, wire bail handle w/wooden hand grip, blue on white w/oval reserve on the front printed "GRANDMOTHER'S MAPLE SYRUP OF 50 YEARS AGO," 7" d., 6½" h...800.00

Tray, rectangular w/rounded corners & slightly flared edges, heavy blue on white, 10½" l. (small edge chips) 137.50

STAFFORDSHIRE FIGURES

Equestrian Figure of St. George

Small figures and groups made of pottery were produced by the majority of the Staffordshire, England potters in the 19th century and were used as mantel decorations or "chimney ornaments," as they were sometimes called. Pairs of dogs were favorites and were turned out by the carload, and 19th century pieces are still available. Well-painted reproductions also abound and collectors are urged to exercise caution before investing.

Cat, miniature in seated position, white coat w/orange & black spots, green trim, 2⅞" h. $181.50

Cat, miniature, in seated position w/bow around neck, white & orange w/blue & green trim, 3⅞" h. (small edge flakes) 247.50

Cat, standing animal w/tail curled over its back, black & tan sponging, glass eyes, 5¼" h. 275.00

Cat, seated, large black spots on white w/painted facial features, on a green & red pillow w/a rectangular base, gilt trim, 19th c., 7¼" h. (enamel wear) 357.50

Cats, seated w/tail curled around legs, brown spatter decoration w/black & yellow trim, 5⅛" h., pr. (hairline, small chips) 715.00

Dog, Pug, miniature, creamware, seated animal w/a brown muzzle & eyes & a streaky brown & ochre coat wearing a collar fastened at the back w/an incised florette, seated on a mound base washed in green, ca. 1770-80, 3" h. (tail restored) 1,265.00

Dog, hound w/a slender body seated on a stepped oval base, creamware splashed w/brown & green spots, ca. 1760, 8¾" h. (chip on base)..11,000.00

Dog, Spaniel, miniature, in seated position & holding the handle of a small basket in its mouth, sanded coat w/worn gilt trim, 3" h. 192.50

Dog, Spaniel in seated position, white w/sanded coat & black & yellow enameling, 3⅝" h. 143.00

Dog, Spaniel in seated position, molded fur, white w/black & yellow, worn gilt trim, 14¾" h. 275.00

Dogs, Pekingese, orange & white, 9" h., pr. 835.00

Dogs, Spaniel, white w/brown muzzle, 10" h., pr. 450.00

Equestrian figure, miniature, man in soldier's uniform astride a prancing white horse, on oval base, polychrome enamel trim, 4⅝" h. (wear to paint) 258.00

Equestrian figure, St. George, his plumed helmet splashed in ochre & green w/green drapery, yellow tack on his brown-spotted horse, a green dragon at his feet, Ralph Wood-type, spear broken, chips to right foot, his left foot & horse's tail restuck, ca. 1780, 11" h. (ILLUS.) 2,090.00

Equestrian figure, man w/plumed hat astride a horse w/head down & left front leg raised, ca. 1850, 13¾" h. ...325.00

Equestrian figure, creamware, William III or the Duke of Cumberland, the man wearing classical garb w/a blue cloak, green & blue armor, astride a rearing brown charger supported by moss-encrusted rockwork on a waisted rectangular base w/green laurel, ca. 1785, 14¾" h. (one hoof missing, his left foot reglued, chip to reins) 13,200.00

Equestrian figures, Scotsman on horseback, late 19th c., 14½" h., pr. ....467.50.

Ewe & lamb, creamware, the recumbent ewe splashed in brown, her lamb at her side on a shaped base molded & applied w/flowers splashed in green & brown, ca. 1775, 6" l. (ears, tail & three flowers restored, cracked) 880.00

Figure of "The Lion Slayer," man in Scots outfit holding a dead lion by one rear paw, oval base w/title molded, late 19th c., 16¼" h. 357.50

Figure of a woman standing & holding a rose to her bosom, wearing a large feathered hat & a long dark blue coat & ruffle-trimmed gown, polychrome detailing, 19th c., 5½" h. 192.50

Figure group, pearlware, bull-baiting scene, the iron-red-spotted salmon bull (right rear leg hair cracked) w/grey head & horns (left restored), spine, tail tuft (repaired), hooves & tether (touched up), tossing a black-spotted white dog (repainted & extremities restored) over his shoulder while another yellow-spotted dog (feet & tail restored) barks at the bull's head & a showman (reconstructed in plaster) wearing a russet jacket, grey waistcoat & yellow breeches stands to one side, one a green serpentine-fronted rectangular base above a black-sponged apron molded on the front w/an iron-red, blue & green floral garland & raised on four ridged bracket feet, Obadiah Sherratt-type, ca. 1830, 11¼" l. 1,725.00

Figure group, a girl wearing flowered dress & small hat seated on a large, horned goat w/shaggy fur, oval base, late 19th c., 12" h. 605.00

Figure group, Highland lad & lassie w/deer, bright polychrome enameling, 7⅝" h. (minor wear & flaking) 275.00

Figure group, "St. John" depicted w/goose, white w/enamel & gilt trim, 11¼" h. (crazed) 214.50

Goat, recumbent animal on an oval base, polychrome enamel trim, 2¾" l. 137.50

Hen on nest, polychrome feather detail, yellow basketweave base, 9¾" l. (minor chips & wear).............225.50

Hen on nest, white hen on a basket-weave base, trimmed in orange, green & black, 3¼" h. 110.00

Hen on nest, large white hen w/red comb & black eyes on a green grass & brown basket base, 10½" l. 302.50

Horses, earthenware, bocage-type, modeled affronté, one w/black spots (legs hair cracked & left ear chipped), the other w/brown spots, each standing before a leafy green tree (first partially missing) applied w/yellow-centered iron-red & blue blossoms, on a bright green mound base (first hair cracked) decorated at the front w/blue dashes, 1820-30, 5½" h., pr. 4,888.00

Lamb, white animal w/sanded coat on four free-standing legs, 2¼" h. 258.50

Rabbit, reclining black & white animal on a red & green "coleslaw" grass base above an underglaze-blue band, 3½" l. (crazed, hairlines) 247.50

Rooster, jar, cov., the removable head forming the cover & decorated w/iron-red comb & wattles & yellow beak, his body & arched tail in yellow, iron-red & grey & his wings & tail in shades of grey, perched on a turquoise grassy scroll on a green & brown mottled mound base applied w/small mounds of 'moss,' ca. 1820-30, 8⅜" h. (enamel chips, restoration to neck rims, flange & right spur) 920.00

Sheep, standing animal on an oval base, polychrome enamel trim, 3" h. 159.50

Staffordshire Pearlware Squirrel

Squirrel, pearlware, modeled nibbling a nut, his incised coat spotted all over in mocha- and chocolate brown, seated on a chamfered rectangular base streaked in green, chips, some restored, two small hair cracks on the base & left ear tip restored, 1790-1800, 6¾" h. (ILLUS.) 1,955.00

Vase, 8¾" h., figural, maiden & deer above a rockwork arch enclosing a swan in front of a tree trunk vase, polychrome trim 255.50

Vase, spill-type, 11" h., figural Robert Burns & his Mary 375.00

Vases, 10¾" h., model of a cow w/a nursing calf standing in front of a tree stump vase, on a grassy mound base, pr. 935.00

STAFFORDSHIRE TRANSFER WARES

Palestine Pattern Plate

The process of transfer-printing designs on earthenwares developed in England in the late 18th century and by the mid-19th century most common ceramic wares were decorated in this manner, most often with romantic European or Oriental landscape scenes, animals or flowers. The earliest such wares were printed in dark blue but a little later light blue, pink, purple, red, black, green and brown were used. A majority of these wares were produced at various English potteries right up till the turn of the century but French and other European firms also made similar pieces and all are quite collectible. The best reference on this area is Petra Williams' book Staffordshire Romantic Transfer Patterns - Cup Plates and Early Victorian China *(Fountain House East, 1978). Also see ADAMS, and other makers and HISTORICAL & COMMEMORATIVE WARES. Also see ABC PLATES.*

Basket & undertray, deep oval flaring reticulated sides w/end loop handles, light blue design of Roman ruins, matching oval underplate, impressed "Rogers," ca. 1840, 9¾" l., 2 pcs. $852.50

Basket & undertray, the basket w/reticulated oval loops forming the sides below a flaring rim w/end handles, the oval undertray w/a reticulated rim, each decorated w/English country landscapes w/a vintage border, medium blue, ca. 1830, tray 10¼" l., 2 pcs. 632.50

Coffeepot, cov., Italia patt., blue, Davenport 165.00

Coffeepot, cov., Scroll Frond Border patt., blue, Charles Meigh & Son, 1850s 350.00

Creamer & cov. sugar bowl, Coysh patt., blue, Spode, pr. 135.00

Cup & saucer, handleless, Cologne patt., red...49.50

Cup & saucer, handleless, oversized, large basket of flowers design, dark blue (wear, small colored-in rim flakes) 181.50

Cup & saucer, Roselle patt., blue, John Meir & Son 75.00

Cup & saucer, handleless, pearlware, Salopian polychrome enameled transfer of birds & flowers, early 19th c., chips on saucer, wear on cup 93.50

Cup & saucer, handleless, scene entitled "Washington," red (minor edge flakes) 137.50

Cup plate, Canova patt., brown 35.00

Cup plate, central scene of a landscape w/a large lake & arched bridge in the distance, dark blue, impressed "Wood," 3¾" d. 159.50

Cup plate, Oriental scenery, Fakeer's Rock, fruit & flower border, dark blue, Hall & Sons, 4¼" d. 140.00

Ladle holder, Columbia patt., blue, J. Wedgwood, ca, 1845 ....95.00

Mug, cylindrical, pearlware, black scene of a military surrender titled "Cornwallis," pink lustre trim, 2⅛" h. (wear, small chips) 467.50

Mug, motto-type, black transfer-printed scene illustrating "Dr. Franklin - Poor Richard" maxim "Constant dropping wears away stones...." 2½" h. (wear, chip on bottom)...104.50

Pitcher, 8" h., Medici patt., blue, Mellor, Venables & Co., ca. 1835-50.....195.00

Pitcher, 11¼" h., Roselle patt., blue, John Meir & Son 350.00

Pitcher, 12¼" h., Lausanne Villa patt., blue 295.00

Pitcher & bowl set, tall paneled tapering pitcher w/scalloped rim & angled handle, matching bowl, Byzantium patt., light blue, bowl 13" d., pitcher 10" h., 2 pcs. (stains, hairlines) 275.00

Plate, 5⅞" w., octagonal, black transfer-printed center scene titled "Robinson Crusoe" & trimmed in polychrome enamel, ca. 1830 (small edge flakes) 93.50

Plate, 6⅜" d., Quadrupeds patt., dog depicted, dark blue 165.00

Plate, 7" d., Palestine patt., blue, Adams, ca. 1850 (ILLUS.) 45.00

Plate, 7⅛" d., black center scene entitled "The Sluggard," enhanced w/blue, orange, yellow & green enamel, purple lustre rim 104.50

Plate, 7⅞" d., Oriental scenes, dark blue, Clews 60.50

Plate, 8" d., Wild Rose patt., dark blue (wear)..55.00

Plate, 8¼" d., Siam patt., blue, J. Clementson, mid-19th c....................45.00

Plate, 8⅞" d., Castle of Furstenfel scene, dark blue 115.50

Plate, 8⅞" d., English river scene w/fishermen, dark blue, Clews (very minor wear) 170.00

Plate, 9" d., Clyde Scenery patt., purple, ca. 1840 ....38.50

Plate, 9½" d., Florentine patt., blue, T. Mayer..65.00

Plate, 9½" d., a central scene of an Indian landscape w/elephant & temple, floral border, light medium blue, ca. 1840 (wear) 93.50

Plate, 10" d., Castle Scenery patt., blue, J. Furnival 75.00

Plate, 10" d., Lozere patt., blue, E. Challinor...75.00

Plate, 10" d., central round reserve w/a large fruit cluster, wide border w/flower & leaf reserves, dark blue, marked "Stubbs," ca. 1830s (small flakes on table ring) 132.00

Plate, 10½" d., Cambrian patt., black, George Phillips 72.00

Plate, 10½" d., Delaware patt., blue, Ridgways 25.00

Plate, 10½" d., Palestine patt., dark blue, R. Stevenson, ca. 1830s...........82.50

Platter, 7¼ x 10", Isola Bella patt., blue, W. Adams 125.00

Platter, 9¾ x 12½", Florentine patt, blue, T. Mayer......................................225.00

Platter, 10¼ x 13½", Montilla patt., blue, Davenport 250.00

Platter, 10¾ x 13", Pantheon patt., polychrome center scene w/green transfer border, Ridgway & Morley, ca. 1840 ....150.00

Platter, 13½" oval, an overall scene of rabbit hunters on horseback, design runs to outer border, medium blue, ca. 1840 (minor stains) 225.00

Platter, 14" l., Oriental patt., Ridgway 175.00

Platter, 11 x 14", Cypress patt., mulberry, anchor mark, Davenport ..200.00
Platter, 12 x 15½", Ontario Lake Scenery patt., blue, Heath, ca. 1845-53...350.00
Platter, 15¾ l., oval, Canova patt., light blue (stains)...............................192.50
Platter, 17" l., oval, India Temple patt., blue, J. & W. Ridgway, first quarter 19th c. 247.50
Platter, 14½ x 17", Canova patt., blue, T. Mayer...325.00
Platter, 17¼ l. oval, lightly scalloped rim, Oriental patt., green w/gilt rim, ca. 1840 ....165.00
Platter, 20" l. oval, Lucerne patt., light blue, ca. 1840 (wear, glaze chips on back) 187.00
Soup plate w/flanged rim, a center scene of a fisherman w/his wife & child, a wide floral border, medium blue, 10" d...82.50
Soup plate, Palestine patt., medium blue, 10¼" d.......................................38.50
Soup plates, pastoral design w/cows in a meadow, grapevine border, dark blue, William Adams, early 19th c., 10¼" d., set of 5 (minor imperfections) 825.00
Sugar bowl, cov., oblong boat-shaped body w/raised & angled rim, angled end handles, slightly domed inset cover w/knob finial, medium blue design of a hunter w/two dogs, ca. 1830, 4⅞" h. (minor chips inside cover, hairline in one handle)...........148.50
Sugar bowl, cov., oblong bulbous body w/closed rim & inset domed cover w/knob finial, Salopian polychrome transfer of a lad grooming a cow in a landscape, ca. 1800, 5" h. (stains, inner flange chipped) 302.50
Toddy plate, Cologne patt., lavender, ca. 1830s 60.00
Toddy plate, the center w/a design of a young woman & a goat, a wide looped design around the rim, brown, ca. 1830, 5" d. 82.50
Tureen, cov., deep bulbous oblong body w/loop end handles & tapering to small pad feet, the wide flat rim supporting a stepped, domed cover w/loop handle, decorated w/European castle scenes, blue, ca. 1840, 13½" l. (hairline in cover handle & some damage).................220.00
Vegetable bowl, cov., Dorothy patt., Johnson Bros.....................................150.00
Vegetable dish, cov., Spoletto patt., dark blue, 13" l. (minor stains) 137.50
Waste bowl, Cobridge patt., blue, Brownfield, ca. 1850 ....125.00
Waste bowl, footed, overall florals, dark blue, 6¼" d. (wear, small flakes) 137.50

STANGL POTTERY

Johann Martin Stangl, who first came to work for the Fulper Pottery in 1910 as a ceramic chemist and plant superintendent, acquired a financial interest and became president of the company in 1926. The name of the firm was changed to Stangl Pottery in 1929 and at that time much of the production was devoted to a high grade dinnerware to enable the company to survive the Depression years. One of the earliest solid-color dinnerware patterns was their Colonial *line, introduced in 1926. In the 1930s it was joined by their* Americana *pattern. After 1942 these early patterns were followed by a wide range of hand-decorated patterns featuring flowers and fruits with a few decorated with animals or human figures.*

Around 1940 a very limited edition of porcelain birds, patterned after the illustrations in John James Audubon's "Birds of America," was issued. Stangl subsequently began production of less expensive ceramic birds and these proved to be popular during the war years, 1940-46. Each bird was handpainted and each was well marked with impressed, painted or stamped numerals which indicated the species and the size.

All operations ceased at the Trenton, New Jersey plant in 1978.

Two reference books which collectors will find helpful are The Collectors Handbook of Stangl Pottery *by Norma Rehl (The Democrat Press, 1979), and* Stangl Pottery *by Harvey Duke (Wallace-Homestead, 1994).*

BIRDS

Bird of Paradise, No. 3408, 5½" h.............................$100.00 to 125.00
Bluebird, No. 3276-S, 5" h......85.00 to 90.00
Blue-Headed Vireo, No. 3448, 4¼" h...75.00
Bobolink, No. 3595, 4¾" h. 135.00
Brewer's Blackbird, No. 3591, 3½" h...............................125.00 to 150.00
Broadbill Hummingbird, No. 3629, 6½" l., 4½" h.....................100.00 to 125.00
Canary facing right - Rose Flower, No. 3746, 6¼" h...............................150.00
Cardinal, No. 3444, 6" h. ....100.00 to 125.00
Chat, No. 3590, 4¼" h. ....100.00 to 150.00

Chestnut-Backed Chickadee, No. 3811, 5" h. ....50.00 to 70.00
Chestnut-Sided Warbler, No. 3812.......95.00
Cockatoo, No. 3405-S, 6" h. 52.00

Stangl Cockatoo

Cockatoo, No. 3484, 11⅜" h. (ILLUS.) 275.00
Cock Pheasant, No. 3492, 6¼ x 11"..........................155.00 to 175.00
Double Wren, No. 3410D .....75.00 to 100.00
Drinking Duck, No, 3250-E, 3¾" h.......75.00
Feeding Duck, No. 3250-C, 1¾" h.......40.00
Flying Duck, No. 3443, 9" h..................................225.00 to 275.00
Gazing Duck, No. 3250-D, 3¾" h. 60.00
Golden Crowned Kinglet, No. 3848, 4" h..92.50
Goldfinch, No. 3849..............................92.50
Grosbeak, No. 3813, 5" h. ..100.00 to 125.00
Group of Goldfinches, No. 3635, 4 x 11½"..........................200.00 to 225.00
Hummingbirds, pr., 3599-D, 8 x 10½" 215.00
Indigo Bunting, No. 3589, 3¼" h...........60.00
Kingfisher, No. 3406, 3½" h...................65.00
Kingfisher, No. 3406-S, 3½" h. 80.00
Oriole, No. 3402-S, 3¼" h......................55.00
Painted Bunting, No. 3452, 5" h. 90.00
Pair of Hummingbirds, No. 3599-D, 8 x 10½"..........................225.00 to 250.00
Pair of Love Birds, N0. 3404-D, 4½" h..............................100.00 to 125.00
Pair of Parakeets, No. 3582, 7" h. 245.00
Pair of Wrens, No. 3401-D, 8" h..................................100.00 to 125.00
Paraquet, No. 3449, 5½" h. 125.00
Preening Duck, No. 3250-B, 2¼" h.......85.00
Quacking Duck, No. 3250-F, 2¼" h......60.00
Red-Breasted Nuthatch, No. 3851 ....50.00
Red-Headed Woodpecker (Double), No. 3752-D, 7¾" h. ....300.00 to 350.00
Rieffers Hummingbird, No. 3628, 4½" h..125.00
Rivoli Hummingbird, No. 3627, 6" h....150.00
Rooster, yellow, No. 3445, 9" h. 185.00
Rufous Hummingbird, No. 3585, 3" h...35.00
Scarlet Tanager (Double), No. 3750-D, 8" h. 395.00
Wren, No. 3401, 3½" h. 60.00
Wren, No. 3401S 42.00
Yellow Warbler, No. 3850.......................65.00

DINNERWARES & ARTWARES

Ashtray, Cosmos patt., 5½" d. 25.00
Ashtray, square, Mallard Duck patt., Sportsmen's Giftware line, 9" sq. 45.00
Ashtray, oval, Mallard Duck patt., Sportsmen's Giftware line, No. 3921, 10⅝" oval 38.00
Ashtray, oval, Pheasant patt., Sportsmen's Giftware line, No. 3926 ....50.00 to 60.00
Ashtray, oval, Quail patt., Sportsmen's Giftware line, No. 3926...........49.00
Ashtray, crescent-shaped, Tropical Fish patt., Sportsmen's Giftware line, No. 3927..................................55.00
Ashtray, Tulip patt., 4" d. 15.00
Ashtray/coaster, Blossom Time patt., No. 3886 ....12.00
Bowl, cereal, 5½" d., Apple Delight patt. 10.00
Bowl, cereal, 5½" d., Fruits & Flowers patt. 6.00
Bowl, cereal, 5½" d., Starflower patt.....10.00
Bowl, cereal, 5½" d., Thistle patt. 12.00
Bowl, 6¼" d., Bittersweet patt.................7.00
Bowl, 8" d., Country Garden patt. 30.00
Bowl, soup, w/lug handles, Americana patt., red..4.00
Bowl, soup, 5¼" d., w/lug handles, Apple Delight patt. 12.00
Bowl, soup, w/lug handles, Blueberry patt. 15.00
Bowl, soup, w/lug handles, Thistle patt. 18.00
Bread tray, Thistle patt., 15¼" l. 22.00
Butter dish, cov., Thistle patt. 32.00
Candy dish, cov., Terra Rose patt. 22.00
Celery tray, Wild Rose patt. 18.00
Chamberstick, ring handle, motto around base, medium blue flambé glaze, artist-signed, 5¼" h. 35.00
Cigarette box, cov., Blossom Time patt., No. 3886 ....38.00
Cigarette box, cov., Garden Flower patt., 4 x 5"..36.00
Coaster, Country Garden patt., 5" d. 7.00
Coaster, Orchard Song patt., 5" d. 5.00
Coffeepot, cov., Blue Tulip patt., Terra Rose finish, 8-cup 65.00
Coffee server, cov., Amber Glo patt..................................40.00 to 50.00
Coffee warmer, Golden Harvest patt. ...12.00
Creamer, Fruits & Flowers patt...............6.00
Creamer, Thistle patt. 4.50
Creamer, Wild Rose patt. 10.00

Creamer & cov. sugar bowl, Bittersweet patt., pr. 15.00
Creamer & cov. sugar bowl, Golden Harvest patt., pr. 10.00
Cup & saucer, Apple Delight patt. 13.00
Cup & saucer, Bittersweet patt. 10.00
Cup & saucer, Country Garden patt. 10.00
Cup & saucer, Dahlia patt., blue, green & white 4.50
Cup & saucer, Fruits & Flowers patt.....10.00
Cup & saucer, Golden Harvest patt........7.50
Cup & saucer, Provincial patt. 10.00
Cup & saucer, Thistle patt. 11.00
Egg cup, Golden Blossom patt. 8.00
Gravyboat & underplate, Thistle patt., 2 pcs. 32.00
Mug, Pheasant patt., Sportsmen's Giftware line, large, 2 cup 30.00
Pitcher, cov., Colonial patt., aqua glaze 40.00
Pitcher, Chicory patt., 2 qt. 40.00
Plate, 6" d., Apple Delight patt. 5.00
Plate, 6" d., Blueberry patt. 7.00
Plate, 6" d., Dahlia patt. 2.00
Plate, 6" d., Fruit & Flowers patt. 4.00
Plate, 6" d., Golden Harvest patt. 3.00
Plate, 6" d., Orchard Song patt. 2.00
Plate, 6" d., Starflower patt. 4.00
Plate, 6¼" d., Thistle patt. 6.00
Plate, 8" d., Blueberry patt. 6.00
Plate, 8" d., Blue Daisy patt. 6.50
Plate, 8" d., Fruits & Flowers patt. 8.00
Plate, 8" d., Golden Blossom patt. 5.00
Plate, 8" d., Rooster patt. 28.00
Plate, 8" d., Town & Country patt., blue glaze 20.00
Plate, luncheon, 8¼" d., Apple Delight patt. 3.50
Plate, 9" d., Little Bo Peep patt., Kiddieware line 78.00
Plate, 9" d., Star Flower patt. 7.00
Plate, dinner, 10" d., Apple Delight patt. 15.00
Plate, dinner, 10" d., Blue Daisy patt. 8.00
Plate, dinner, 10" d., Fruits & Flowers patt. 10.00
Plate, dinner, 10" d., Golden Harvest patt. 7.50
Plate, dinner, 10" d., Magnolia patt. 8.00
Plate, dinner, 10" d., Star Flower patt...10.00
Plate, chop, 12½" d., Colonial patt., blue glaze 12.00
Salt & pepper shakers, Bittersweet patt., pr. 8.00
Salt & pepper shakers, Country Garden patt., pr. 14.00
Salt & pepper shakers, Thistle patt., pr. 14.00
Server, center-handled, Bella Rosa patt. 10.00
Server, center-handled, Fairlawn patt. 10.00
Server, center-handled, Orchard Song patt. 2.00
Smoke set: cov. cigarette box & round ashtray; Mallard patt., Sportsmen's Giftware line, the set 110.00
Snack set: cup & saucer & 8" d. plate; Orchard Song patt., 3 pcs. 6.00
Sugar bowl, cov., Carnival patt. 22.00
Sugar bowl, cov., Thistle patt. 15.00
Vase, Tulip patt., Terra Rose line, yellow glaze, No. 3613 ....50.00
Vegetable bowl, open, divided, Country Garden patt. 24.00
Vegetable bowl, open, divided, Thistle patt., 10½" l. 32.00
Wig stand, stylized lady's head, brown hair, No. 5168, w/ceramic base, 15" h. 425.00

STONEWARE

Stoneware Crock with Bird

Stoneware is essentially a vitreous pottery, impervious to water even in its unglazed state, that has been produced by potteries all over the world for centuries. Utilitarian wares such as crocks, jugs, churns and the like, were the most common productions in the numerous potteries that sprang into existence in the United States during the 19th century. These items were often enhanced by the application of a cobalt blue oxide decoration. In addition to the coarse, primarily salt-glazed stonewares, there are other categories of stoneware known by such special names as basalt, jasper and others.

Bank, model of a seated spaniel dog, molded fur & details, covered w/a dark cobalt blue glaze, coin slot in underside, 19th c., 9" h. $4,025.00
Batter jug, ovoid w/short wide neck, brushed cobalt blue floral & foliate decoration & impressed label "Cowden & Wilcox, Harrisburg," wire

bail handle w/wooden handgrip & tin lids, 9" h. (in the making hairline in base) 1,705.00

Batter jug, cylindrical body w/rounded top, incised label "James Holloway" highlighted in cobalt blue w/blue feather foliate designs & incised rope spiral handle, glaze has dark drips of brown glaze, 10⅜" h. (rare filler hole lid is glued, minor chips & blue has bubbled) 1,320.00

Bird feeder, beehive form w/an arched & hooded side opening, a ball final on the top, decorated around the hood & the top w/brushed cobalt blue leaf sprigs, impressed mark of Richard C. Remmey, Philadelphia, late 19th c., 10" h. (two small flakes near base) 2,530.00

Bottle, miniature gemel-type, the conjoined ovoid bottles tapering to small mouths, a wide applied strap handle centered at the back, splotches of cobalt blue on the necks, impressed "NEW - HAVEN," possibly from the shop of Absalom Stedman, New Haven, Connecticut, ca. 1830, 3" h. 3,163.00

Bottle, figural, molded as a spread-winged eagle, the body tapering down to a round foot, decorated on its breast w/an American shield, blue & mahogany glazes, impressed mark "M & W, Gr," head-form cap, 10½" h. (small chips on base of head) 330.00

Butter churn, wide semi-ovoid body w/molded flared rim & eared handles, slip-quilled cobalt blue large crested peacock-like bird perched on a stump, impressed label "Cowden & Wilcox, Harrisburg, PA," ca. 1860, 14½" h. (cracked, some chips) 9,200.00

Butter churn, semi-ovoid body w/molded rim & eared handles, slip-quilled cobalt blue scene of a Gothic-style cottage flanked by fir trees & w/a picket fence in the yard, marked by Haxton Edmund & Co., Fort Edward, New York, ca. 1860, w/Albany slip-covered cover, 19" h. (cover cracked & chipped) 12,650.00

Butter crock, cov., wide cylindrical form w/eared handles & molded rim, low domed cover w/flat button finial, brushed cobalt blue stylized leaf & blossom band, impressed "1½," 19th c., 1½ gal., 12" d. (hairline in base, minor chip inside lid flange) ...412.50

Butter crock, slightly swelled cylindrical sides, upturned loop handles at sides, brushed cobalt blue blossom & leaf cluster, blue trim on handles, New York, 19th c., 12½" d., 7" h. 242.00

Chicken waterer, high domed shape w/button finial at top, molded w/a large oval opening, white glaze, 5½" h. 137.50

Crock, slightly waisted cylindrical body w/molded rim & eared handles, impressed label. "F.-----& Son, Taunton, Mass" over brushed cobalt blue florals, 8" d., 7" h. 247.50

Crock, slightly tapering cylindrical body w/protruding lip & applied eared handles, the front decorated w/a slip-quilled cobalt blue pecking chicken, all on a rosy-beige ground, America, late 19th c., 8¾" d., 8" h....575.00

Crock, cylindrical w/eared handles & molded rim, brushed cobalt blue stylized bird on leafy scroll branch, impressed label at top "C.L. & A.K. Ballard - Burlington, VT - 2," second half 19th c., 2 gal., 8¼" h. (cracked) 633.00

Crock, cylindrical w/rolled lip & eared handles, decorated on the front w/a slip-quilled cobalt blue bird perched on a flowering branch, indistinctly stamped w/the maker's name & "3," America, 19th c., 3 gal., 11¼" d., 10¼" h. (some cracks) 575.00

Crock, ovoid w/flared mouth & eared handles, slip-quilled cobalt blue stylized flower w/a bulbous upright blossom on a horizontal leafy stem, impressed "John B. Caire & Co., Main St., Po-keepsie, NY," 1845-52, 10½" h. (flakes) 330.00

Crock, tall cylindrical body w/rounded shoulders tapering to a low molded rim, brushed cobalt blue large leafy sprig w/a droopy flowerhead, late 19th c., now mounted as a lamp, 10⅝" h. 288.00

Crock, cylindrical w/molded rim & eared handles, slip-quilled cobalt blue bird on a large scalloped leaf, stamped mark "Fulper Bros. - Flemington, NJ 4," late 19th c., 4 gal., old rim chips, 11½" d., 11¼" h. (ILLUS.) 460.00

Crock, cylindrical w/eared handles, slip-quilled cobalt blue decoration of a rooster eating, mid-19th c., 12" h. 230.00

Crock, cylindrical body tapering in slightly to the molded rim, eared handles, slip-quilled cobalt blue bird on branch, impressed label "White & Wood - Binghamton, N.Y. - 4," 1882-88, 4 gal., 13¾" h. (hairlines) 412.50

Rare Stoneware Crock

Crock, wide ovoid body w/ringed neck & applied strap handles, incised & cobalt blue- and ochre-decorated large flower & leaf bouquet w/a butterfly, impressed rim mark "N. Clark & Co. Lyons," Lyons, New York, ca. 1845, minor spider crack on side, 14½" h. (ILLUS.)............16,500.00

Crock, tall cylindrical sides w/eared handles & molded rim, stenciled cobalt blue large label "8 - E.S. & B. - Newbrighton - PA," late 19th c., 8 gal., 16" h....................................126.50

Cuspidor, cylindrical waisted sides, top center opening & oblong drainage hole at top of one side, grey salt glaze w/brown highlights, 19th c., 8½" d. (minor chips) 55.00

Food mold, Turk's turban-form, interior w/molded fluted design w/a decorative border & brown Albany slip, exterior w/grey salt glaze, 12¾" d..330.00

Jar, wide ovoid body w/molded rim & small side strap handle, brushed cobalt blue stylized floral design on the front, 8¾" d., 7" h. 412.50

Jar, wide ovoid body w/a wide molded rim, brushed cobalt blue large lobed leaf, impressed label "Sipe Nichols & Co., Williamsport, Pa.," 8" h. (surface flakes) 275.00

Jar, ovoid w/molded rim, cobalt blue brushed wavy & straight lines & "1½," 1½ gal., 9" h. 220.00

Jar, ovoid body tapering to a short, flared rim, overall two-tone grey & brown banded glaze, impressed mark "Boston 1804," attributed to Frederich Carpenter, 9½" h. (minor firing chips) 1,210.00

Jar, ovoid body swelling to a wide molded rim, cobalt blue stenciled label w/"A.P. Donaghho - Frederickstown, Pa." above a stenciled spread-winged eagle, late 19th c., 9¾" h. 962.50

Jar, ovoid body w/wide, molded mouth, eared handles, brushed cobalt blue large leaf sprig & blossom, impressed label "Cowden & Wilcox 2," Harrisburg, Pennsylvania, 1870-81, 2 gal., 10" h. 440.00

Jar, slender cylindrical body w/sloping shoulders tapering to a flaring rim, brushed cobalt blue humorous anthropomorphic bird w/oversized head & a flowering tree, Indiana, mid-19th c., now mounted as a lamp, 10¼" h. 978.00

Jar, slightly ovoid w/molded rim, eared handles, slip-quilled cobalt blue stylized floral design, impressed "2," 2 gal., 10¾" h. 247.50

Jar, cylindrical sides tapering gently to a thick flaring rim, brushed cobalt blue bold leaf sprig w/two large stylized blossoms, late 19th c., now mounted as a lamp, 11" h. 345.00

Jar, cylindrical slightly tapering sides w/a flat, flared mouth, brushed cobalt blue bands around the top & a "2" & lines at the base, the center stenciled in cobalt blue w/a very large marking reading "Hamilton & Jones - Star Pottery - Greensboro - PA" & centered by a star, late 19th c., now mounted as a lamp, 2 gal., 11¾" h. (some cracks) 518.00

Jar, ovoid w/molded rim & eared handles, cobalt blue brushed tulip & leaves, impressed "T. Reed 3," Ohio, mid-19th c., 3 gal., 13¼" h. 550.00

Jar, semi-ovoid w/eared handles, brushed & stenciled cobalt blue label "Hamilton & Jones, Greensboro, Pa. 3," late 19th c., 3 gal., 13¾" h...330.00

Jar, cylindrical w/tooled lines beneath molded rim, eared handles, cobalt blue stenciled label "Jas Hamilton & Co, Greensboro, Pa 4," 4 gal., 15" h. (hairlines) 181.50

Jar, ovoid, stenciled cobalt blue label "Zanesville Stoneware Co., Zanesville, O. 4," late 19th c., 4 gal., 15" h. (small chips).......................................93.50

Jar, slightly ovoid w/rolled rim, eared handles, stenciled cobalt blue label w/three shields & "L.B. Milliner, New Geneva, PA 6," 6 gal., 16½" h. 715.00

Jug, squat semi-ovoid body w/strap handle, impressed label "J. Matheis" & incised bird & branch w/cobalt blue wash & "1869," blue stripes on handle, 6¼" h. (small chips & short hairline in base) 3,327.50

Jug, Bellarmine-type, bulbous ovoid body tapering to a short cylindrical neck w/molded rim, impressed bearded mask on neck & armorial medallion on the front, dark glaze, Germany, 19th c., 8½" h. 440.00

Jug, cylindrical w/canted shoulders, strap handle, cobalt blue brushed label "J.F. Weiler, Allentown, Pa., 9" h. 275.00

Jug, baluster-shaped ovoid body w/applied strap handle, brushed cobalt blue decoration on the circular base, stamped identification "Confederate Relief Bazaar - Baltimore, April 7, 1885," probably Maryland, 9¾" h. 2,760.00

Jug, ovoid, strap handle, the front decorated w/an incised & cobalt blue-washed depiction of a grotesque half-man/half-beast, possibly the devil, w/protruding belly & long tail, shown smoking a pipe w/a bubble coming from its mouth incised "MONEY," probably New York, ca. 1820, 11½" h. (minor flakes on base) 12,650.00

Jug, shouldered cylindrical body w/arched strap handle, impressed label "Ottman Bros. Fort Edward, N.Y." above cobalt blue slip-quilled foliate design w/ flourish, 11¾" h. 181.50

Jug, semi-ovoid, stenciled cobalt blue label arched at the top & bottom & reading "Amos Meller, Dealer in Groceries, etc. - Little Falls NY," impressed "White's Utica," New York, 1865-77, 12" h. 203.50

Jug, ovoid, brushed cobalt blue scalloped band around the shoulder, impressed mark "C. Crolius New York," ca. 1820-30, 2 gal., 12¾" h. 880.00

Jug, semi-ovoid w/angular strap handle, impressed label "Whites, Utica 2" & cobalt blue slip-quilled bird on a branch, 2 gal., 13½" h.......330.00

Jug, ovoid tapering to a small cylindrical neck, cobalt blue stenciled decoration of a large spread-winged eagle w/a banner in its beak reading "Star Pottery" above a brushed cobalt blue "2" near the base, Elmserdorf, Texas, 1888-1914, small chips on lip, 2 gal., 13¾" h. 1,265.00

Jug, ovoid, slip-quilled cobalt blue feathered wreath framing a "2," impressed mark "Burger Bros. & Co., Rochester," New York, 1867-71, 2 gal., 13¾" h. (some glaze flakes) 55.00

Jug, baluster-form w/molded lip, applied strap handle, Bellarmine-type w/grimacing bearded mask & beaded rondel, orange peel glaze, Continental, 18th c., 14" h. 550.00

Jug, semi-ovoid, cobalt blue script inscription "E. A. & H. Hildreth, Southampton, N.Y.," 2 gal., 14" h. 880.00

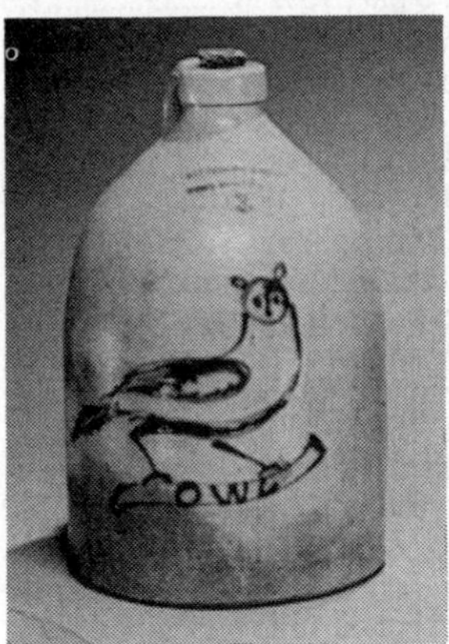

Stoneware Jug with an Owl

Jug, semi-ovoid tapering to a molded rim & strap handle, slip-quilled cobalt blue stylized owl perched on a banner w/"OWL," impressed mark for Satterlee & Mory, Fort Edward, New York above a "3," ca. 1865, 3 gal., 15" h. (ILLUS.) 3,163.00

Jug, semi-ovoid w/applied strap handle, slip-quilled cobalt blue large long-necked dotted bird perched on a long, vining scrolly-leaf branch, impressed mark "Bergan & Foy 3," 19th c., 3 gal., 15" h. 1,072.50

Jug, ovoid, brushed cobalt blue tulip design, 15½" h. (minor chips on base) 250.00

Jug, ovoid, ribbed strap handle, brushed cobalt blue stylized blossom on front shoulder, impressed mark "S.S. Perry & Co., W. Troy," ca. 1827-31, 15½" h.........247.50

Jug, ovoid w/strap handle, brushed cobalt blue stylized floral design w/"3," 3 gal., 16½" h. (chip on lip) 330.00

Jug, semi-ovoid, slip-quilled cobalt blue flower w/two large bulbous blossoms filled w/dots & raised on a single stem above a clump of long, dotted leaves, impressed mark "John Young & Co., Harrisburg, PA 3," 19th c., 3 gal., 17" h. 935.00

Jug, ovoid, brushed cobalt blue & incised fish & flower spray on the front & sides centering the inscriptions "...Addington...Utica," Samuel H. Addington, Utica, New York, ca. 1825, 18½" h. 3,163.00

Jug, slightly ovoid tapering to a molded rim & strap handle, slip-quilled cobalt blue large spread-winged eagle w/a banner in its beak reading "1876 - 1776," impressed mark of New York Stoneware Co., Fort Edward, New York below a "5," flakes, 5 gal., 19½" h. 1,540.00

Milk pan w/eared handles, deep canted sides w/a rim spout on the edge, cobalt blue brushed scroll decoration, impressed "H. Smith & Co.," 19th c., 11" d. 1,100.00

Pitcher, 7" h., bulbous body w/pinched spout, the front decorated w/an incised & cobalt blue-filled bird on a branch w/flowers & leaves, incised & blue-trimmed inscription below the handle "R.C. Remmey, 1872," Richard C. Remmey, Philadelphia, Pennsylvania 17,250.00

Pitcher, 7" h., ovoid body tapering to a wide cylindrical neck w/pinched spout, applied strap handle, brushed cobalt blue crude floral sprig, 19th c. (minor hairline) 635.00

Pitcher, 8" h., ovoid body tapering to a gently flared rim, strap handle, brushed cobalt blue stylized leaf & blossom sprig (chips on base) 715.00

Pitcher, 9½" h., ovoid body tapering to a cylindrical neck w/pinched spout, applied strap handle, brushed cobalt blue bird perched on a large leafy branch, dot clusters around the neck, Pennsylvania, ca. 1845 ....4,888.00

Pitcher, 10½" h., ovoid body tapering slightly to a tall cylindrical neck w/pinched spout, applied strap handle, brushed cobalt blue squiggly bands around all the body & neck, Pennsylvania, ca. 1860 (flakes on rim) 2,185.00

Large Stoneware Pitcher

Pitcher, 14½" h., tall wide ovoid body tapering to a cylindrical neck w/pinched spout, applied ribbed strap handle, brushed cobalt blue leafy floral band around the shoulder & wavy line around the neck (ILLUS.) 1,760.00

Pitcher, 15½" h., wide ovoid body tapering to a wide cylindrical neck w/pinched spout, applied strap handle, brushed cobalt blue leafy vines & blossoms up the front & leaf sprigs around the neck, impressed "3" at front, Pennsylvania, ca. 1850 (two small flakes on base, one flake on rim) 4,313.00

Preserving jar, slightly ovoid w/molded rim, brushed cobalt blue bands around the rim & base & cobalt blue stenciled label "J.H.---, St. Clairsville, Ohio," 6½" h. (small edge chips) 302.50

Preserving jar, slightly ovoid w/molded rim, stenciled cobalt blue label w/leaf sprigs reading "From Richard Nolan - Wheeling, W. Va.," late 19th c., 8" h. 247.50

Preserving jar, diagonal cobalt blue stenciled label "A.P. Donagho, Parkersburg, W.Va," 8¼" h. 137.50

Preserving jar, slightly ovoid body w/molded flaring rim, brushed cobalt blue bands at the top & base & a cobalt blue stenciled label reading "E.J. Miller & Co....Alexandria, Va.," 19th c., 9½" h. 412.50

Punch bowl, deep rounded bowl on a flaring foot, the sides molded w/three large shields w/cobalt blue-trimmed incised inscription "Bardwell's Root Beer," each shield separated by clusters of grapes & leaves tied w/bowknots all trimmed in blue & all on a dotted ground, the base w/a leafy band & Greek key band trimmed in blue, probably New York state, ca. 1890, 19½" d., 10½" h. 3,450.00

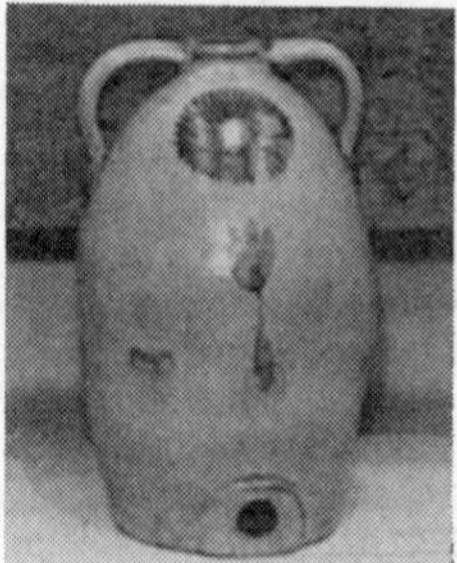

Large Stoneware Water Cooler

Water cooler, ovoid w/large eared handles & tooled lines at shoulder, impressed label "Westhafer Lambright 1865," brushed cobalt blue decoration w/daisy-like flower on one side, cockscomb-like flower on the other w/meandering line stem w/leaves & dots & repeated impressed date "1865," very minor chips, 26" h. (ILLUS.) 3,740.00

TECO POTTERY

Teco Pottery was actually the line of art pottery introduced by the American Terra Cotta and Ceramic Company of Terra Cotta (Crystal Lake), Illinois in 1902. Founded by William D. Gates in 1881, American Terra Cotta originally produced only bricks and drain tile. Because of superior facilities for experimentation, including a chemical laboratory, the company was able to develop an art pottery line, favoring a matte green glaze in the earlier years but eventually achieving a wide range of colors including a metallic lustre glaze and a crystalline glaze. Though some hand-thrown pottery was made, Gates favored a molded ware because it was less expensive to produce. By 1923, Teco Pottery was no longer being made and in 1930 American Terra Cotta and Ceramic Company was sold. A book on the topic is Teco: Art Pottery of the Prairie School, *by Sharon S. Darling (Erie Art Museum, 1990).*

Ashtray, novelty figural-type, the flattened oblong shape formed as the body of a grumpy man w/his head extending from one end & his feet from the other, his arms going down the sides, semi-gloss light green glaze, marked, 5½" l. $275.00

Bowl, 8" d., 2½" h., shallow bulbous form w/a wide scalloped & slightly angled shoulder to a wide, flat mouth, smooth matte green & black glaze, marked 467.50

Bowl, 10½" d., 2½" h., saucer-shaped body, resting on a cross-shaped foot, smooth matte green glaze, die-stamped "Teco," w/paper label & original price tag 1,540.00

Lamp base, kerosene table-type, a squatty bulbous lower body tapering in slightly to a wide cylindrical upper body molded w/four wide buttress handles from the rim to the shoulder, overall matte green glaze, w/metal kerosene canister insert, Model No. 288, ca. 1905, impressed mark, 8⅛" h. 1,650.00

Vase, 3½" h., 4" d., footed spherical body w/a small molded mouth, smooth matte green veined glaze, Model No. 246, marked 385.00

Vase, 3¾" h., 3½" d., bulbous base, stovepipe neck & angular handles, smooth matte green glaze, die stamped mark 522.50

Vase, bud, 4½" h., 3" d., footed ovoid body tapering to a tiny mouth, fine veined smooth matte green glaze, impressed mark 467.50

Vase, 5" h., 4½" d., bulbous base, wide neck w/undulating rim, matte green glaze, die-stamped mark 357.50

Vase, 5½" h., 3" d., cylindrical body contained in two full-length buttresses, smooth matte green glaze, die-stamped mark 660.00

Vase, 5½" h., 4¾" d., compressed globular base & long slender neck flaring slightly at rim, light matte green glaze, die-stamped mark & "#50" 440.00

Vase, 6" h., 8½" w., bulbous footed body pulled out at the sides to form heavy handles looping up & continuing into the flared rim of the short neck, smooth matte black & green glaze, designed by N. Forester, stamped "Teco - (2X) - 297" 605.00

Vase, 6¼" h., a wide tapering domical form w/alternating wide & narrow twisted panels up the sides, the narrow panels w/narrow grooves, the top w/a small incurvate opening, overall dark green glaze, stamped mark & paper label & number "319," ca. 1905 ....3,080.00

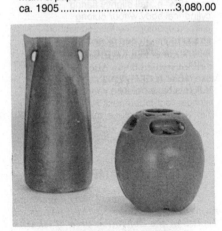

Tall & Bulbous Teco Vases

Vase, 6½" h., 5¾" d., bulbous gently melon-lobed body w/four pierced oval openings & small pierced openings flanking the short neck & flat mouth, smooth matte dark green glaze, designed by F. Albert, Shape No. 113, stamped mark, firing nick at one corner (ILLUS. right) 990.00

Vase, 6¾" h., 4" d., pear-shaped w/two square buttressed handles flush w/the rim, smooth matte green glaze, die-stamped "Teco" twice......770.00

Vase, 8½" h., a footed wide squatty bulbous body below a slender tall stick neck w/flared rim, overall mottled red, gold & black crystalline glaze, marked, ca. 1915 ....825.00

Vase, 9" h., slightly flaring cylindrical & gently lobed lower body tapering to form four elongated upright oblong knobs which extend past the top opening, an orange matte glaze on the lower half & a textured green & orange glaze on the upper half, marked, ca. 1910 (small base chip) 1,980.00

Vase, 11" h., 5" d., tall slightly tapering cylindrical body w/two full-length buttressed handles, green & black leathery matte glaze, die-stamped mark, designed by W.B. Mundy, Shape No. 266 (ILLUS. left) 935.00

Vase, 11½" h., 4¼" d., footed baluster-form body w/a trumpet-form neck, a band of narrow upright pierced leaves extending from the base to the shoulder & bent at right angles to attach to the neck, overall green glaze, stamped "Teco 85" (chip on one leaf, two touched-up nicks at top) 4,400.00

Vase, 13⅞" h., tall slightly flaring cylindrical body w/four oblong pierced openings connected w/short straps to the arched closed rim, leathery yellow matte glaze, ca. 1905 ....1,870.00

Vase, 16¾" h., 8¼" d., squatty bulbous base below a very tall slender four-lobed neck w/flaring rim, green matte glaze, marked 1,760.00

TEPLITZ - AMPHORA

These wares were produced in numerous potteries in the vicinity of Teplitz in the Bohemian area of what is now The Czech Republic during the late 19th and into the 20th century. Vases and figures, of varying quality, were the primary products of such firms as Riessner & Kessel (Amphora), Ernst Wahliss and Alfred Stellmacher. Although originally rather low-priced items, today collectors are searching out the best marked examples and prices are soaring.

Large Amphora Bust

Bust of a young woman wearing an elaborate off-the-shoulder dress in lavender & green, her hair curled & coiffed w/flowers & a large plume, Turn-Teplitz marking, 17¼" h.........$852.50

Bust of a serene maiden in a stylized medieval gown & headdress, raised on a tapering rectangular base molded w/a frieze on the front of a maiden on horseback in a forested meadow, the sides w/branching handles, all in shades of tan, brown & olive green trimmed w/gold, impressed Amphora marks & numbers, ca. 1900, minor chips, 18¾" h. (ILLUS.) 2,200.00

Candlestick, the cylindrical rib-molded stem-form shaft molded w/a thistle bud candle socket, the shaft flanked around the base w/three curled leaves looped down to the round, flaring base, overall bluish green glaze, Alfred Stellmacher company mark, early 20th c., 8¼" h. 495.00

Figure group, three cherubs struggle to carry three heavy baskets draped w/floral garlands, in pale pink & lavender glaze, impressed Amphora mark, 9½" h..385.00

Jardiniere, wide slightly tapering cylindrical body, boldly relief-molded around the sides w/a continuous scene of a man & wagon being pulled by two horses, trimmed in pale green, brown & tan, pearlized interior, Imperial - Amphora mark, 10" d., 13" h. 975.00

Model of a bird of prey, perched on a rockwork base, decorated in grey, brown & white, impressed "Amphora 38 - 17" & initialed "M.Z.," 15" h. 825.00

Pitcher, 10" h., 4¼" d., figural, modeled as a cream colored laughing cat w/grey spotting, wearing a red bow tie, black tail forms handle, marked "Amphora - Austria" 145.00

Plaque, figural, cast as the bust of a dour maiden w/flowing hair peering through a head of cabbage, glazed in cream, green & purple, heightened in gilt, impressed "AMPHORA," numbered "1270/9," "TURN-TEPLITZ-BOHEMIA - RSTK - MADE IN AUSTRIA" printed in red, inscribed "Ed. Stellmacher," ca. 1900, 8⅛" h. (chips to edges of leaves) 1,495.00

Tray, figural, the shaped rectangle cast w/the torso of a maiden at either end & decorated w/garlands of blossoms, glazed in pale blue & trimmed in gold, printed marks of Ernst Wahliss & impressed "MADE IN AUSTRIA - 4684," numbered in red overglaze "4684 - 223 - 12," ca. 1900, 11¼" l. 805.00

Vase, 5½" h., squat bottle-form w/short tiny neck, Art Nouveau style portrait & landscape decoration in olive green w/gold highlights on a cream ground, stamp, impressed numbers & "Amphora - Turn," ca. 1915..550.00

Vase, 8⅛" h., cast as a ripe ribbed melon w/vining leafy stem, a nude maiden perched on the upper edge, glazed in green & matte gilt, printed factory mark "DEPOSE' - EW - Turn Wien - Made in Austria," impressed "MADE IN AUSTRIA - 1754 - C," painted in overglaze "4755./28./7.," ca. 1900 (minor repairs to rim) 920.00

Vase, 10⅜" h., Art Deco-style, bulbous ovoid body w/a rolled thick rim, the sides decorated w/two large round reserves, one w/a polychrome scene of an old man w/a walking stick, the other w/a scene of a young woman on a white horse, the reserves joined by wide center bands w/tan Art Deco scrolls all against a pebbled bluish green ground & w/dark blue borders & rim, ink-stamped on the base "Imperial Amphora Decoré A la Main" in a shield w/"LE" above, also "Modele Deposé - Czechoslovakia" & "46 - III" 330.00

Vase, 19¼" h., tall slender ovoid body w/flat rim, decorated w/ the bust profile of a crowned maiden w/the rising sun on the horizon, against a mottled blue & green ground, her crown & head ornaments decorated w/'jewels,' the whole trimmed w/gold, impressed & printed marks of Riessner & Kessel, Turn, Teplitz (ILLUS. top next column) 4,600.00

Jeweled Amphora Vase

Vase, 21¼" h., 6¾" d., Art Deco style, tall ovoid body tapering to a small mouth flanked by heavy, small loop rim handles, carved & polychromed scene of brightly colored birds on branches against a mottled tan & white matte ground, die-stamped "Amphora - Czechoslovakia," ca. 1920s 550.00

Vide poche (figural dish), in the form of a young Art Nouveau style maiden w/flowing pale & deep blue gown, her hair cascading down her back, her hips supporting two spade-form leaves forming trays, the base further cast w/the head of another Art Nouveau style maiden, the whole heightened w/gilt, printed & impressed factory marks & numbers, ca. 1900, 20¼" h. 4,600.00

TILES

Tiles have been made by potteries in the United States and abroad for many years. Apart from small tea tiles used on tables, there are also decorative tiles for fireplaces, floors and walls and this is where present collector interest lies, especially in the late 19th century American-made art pottery tiles.

American Encaustic Tiling Company, Zanesville, Ohio, molded in low-relief w/a scene of a reclining Bacchus holding a wine goblet & clothed only in a grapevine around his waist, clear caramel glaze, marked, 6 x 16" $330.00

American Encaustic Tiling Company, multicolored scene of shepherdess, 6 x 18"...550.00

American Encaustic Tiling Company, incised scene of a woman & pig, 6" d...190.00

California Faience Company, Berkeley, California, decorated w/a blue basket w/pink & yellow flowers against a white ground, marked, 5¼" d. 77.00

California Faience Company, cloisonné decoration of a Spanish galleon, in a matte mustard & brown & glossy turquoise glaze, incised mark, 5¾" sq. 88.00

DeMorgan (William), London, England, stylized scrolling floral design in green & blue against a white ground, signed, framed, 6" sq. 385.00

DeMorgan, William, large & bold stylized floral sprays in bluish green & purple on a white ground, marked, 9" sq. 440.00

Grueby Faience & Tile Company, Boston, Massachusetts, decorated in cuenca w/a pair of brown & ivory ducks on a green water background in front of an orange setting sun & blue sky, circular mark & rectangular paper label, painted "MCM," 4" sq. 412.50

Grueby Faience & Tile Company, square, depicting a yellow tulip w/green leaves on a green ground, unmarked, 6" sq. 550.00

Grueby Faience & Tile Company, a stencil-designed figure of a monk playing the cello, rich & thick blue & ochre glaze, marked "659," 6" sq. 165.00

Grueby Faience & Tile Company, square, decorated w/a green chamberstick & a half-burnt yellow candle against a green ground, mounted in a four-footed hammered brass frame marked "HANDICRAFT SHOP, Boston, 6" sq. 990.00

Grueby Faience & Tile Company, each w/a galleon-type ship w/wind-filled sails & banners flying, polychrome on a red clay body, impressed "82," 8" sq., pr. 495.00

Grueby Faience & Tile Company, rectangular, decorated w/a group of three slip-trailed mottled brown elephants on dark greenish yellow ground & below pale blue skies, wide black wood ogee frame, paper & fabric label, artist-initialed, 5⅜ x 8½" 4,510.00

Grueby Faience & Tile Company, a two-tile frieze w/a continuous scene of a scrolling Viking-style longboat w/figure, dark ochre & gold w/scrolling cream sail, swirling cream clouds & waves w/pale green banding, blue sky, recently framed, 8½ x 17", pr. (small edge repair) 2,200.00

Low (J. & G.) Art Tile Works, Chelsea, Massachusetts, bust portrait of Shakespeare's Shylock holding a bag of coins, impressed inscription in upper corner, glossy shaded glaze, signed, framed, 6" sq. 220.00

Low (J. & G.) Art Tile Works, molded in low-relief w/a bust profile portrait of a bearded man in Renaissance costume, clear green glaze, marked "Copyright 1882," framed, overall 7½" sq. 220.00

Marblehead Pottery, Marblehead, Massachusetts, incised design of a tall sailing ship in brown & green on blue water w/light green clouds, in wide flat oak frame, rare paper label, tile 5¾" sq. 605.00

Marblehead Pottery, scene depicting a Boston house in ochre, blue & grey against a light grey speckled ground, matte finish, in an oak Arts & Crafts style frame, tile 6" sq. 1,430.00

Marblehead Pottery, incised woodland scene glazed in shades of green, impressed mark & paper label, 6⅛" sq. (chips) 385.00

Marblehead Pottery, decorated w/a scene of a white ship on blue ground 360.00

Mosaic Tile Company, Zanesville, Ohio, Medusa head, stork decoration, 4" d. 95.00

Paul Revere Pottery, Boston, Massachusetts, a round central reserve decorated w/a scene of a cottage by a lake in green, brown, white & orange outlined in black, on a light blue ground, signed & numbered, 5¾" d. 412.50

Pewabic Pottery, Detroit, Michigan, hexagonal, the center w/a stylized view of the Detroit skyline in blue & silver beige iridescent glazes, border band inscribed "Detroit," stamped mark & paper label on reverse, 2⅞" w. 220.00

Pewabic Pottery, souvenir-type, round, the center w/a stylized skyline view of Detroit in dark red & greenish blue iridescent glazes, dark red border band impressed "Detroit - GF-W-C - 1935," impressed mark on the back, 3⅛" d. 247.50

Rookwood Pottery, Cincinnati, Ohio, relief-molded stylized blossoms w/a matte purple, turquoise blue & pink glaze, framed, tile 5¾" sq. 220.00

Rookwood Pottery, oval, bas-relief design of a large kneeling putto amid blue & yellow flowers & green foliage against a burgundy ground, matte glaze, No. 9375DD, 13¾ x 23½" (two rim chips) 880.00

Spanish pottery, a bas-relief design of an old stone bridge w/rounded arches in front of a cityscape, in blues & brown, designed by Daniel Zuolagaa & impressed w/his name, Spain, framed, 6¼ x 8½" 220.00

Trent Tile Company, Trenton, New Jersey, rectangular, scenic, decorated w/a molded landscape scene of cows walking across a hillside toward a distant sunset, overall dark brownish green glossy glaze, designed by Isaac Broome, incised on the front "Broome 1882," framed, 10¼ x 12⅛" 1,100.00

Viennese Art Nouveau Tile

Viennese pottery, Art Nouveau design w/a flowing decoration of stylized blossoms, leaves & berry clusters in French blue, orange, pink & green against a white ground, Vienna, Austria, early 20th c., unmarked, framed, 10½ x 16½" (ILLUS.) 440.00

TOBY MUGS & JUGS

Ralph Wood-Type Toby

The Toby is a figural jug or mug usually delineating a robust, genial drinking man. The name has been used in England since the mid-18th century. Copies of the English mugs and jugs were made in America.

For listings of related Character Jugs see DOULTON & ROYAL DOULTON.

Evans (Alfred), Napoleon, white background w/colored decoration, marked "Napoleon Jug - Alfred Evans, Phila. Pa.," 9¾" h. (some wear & crazing) $247.50

Melba Ware Toby, Henry VIII seated, H. Wains & Sons, Ltd., England, after 1951 ....99.00

Rockingham-glazed Toby, half-length figure of Mr. Toby wearing a tricorn hat, mottled dark brown glaze, 6" h. 55.00

Staffordshire creamware Toby, seated Mr. Toby wearing a brown tricorn hat over his light brown hair & face, a blue coat, white waistcoat, yellow breeches & brown shoes, holding in his right hand a beaker, in his left a light brown jug of ale, seated on a brown chair above a brown chamfered rectangular base, England, ca. 1780, 6⅜" h. (hat & right wrist repaired, small chips on base) 575.00

Staffordshire creamware Toby, seated Mr. Toby wearing a brown tricorn hat on his greyish brown hair, a brown coat, white waistcoat, yellow breeches & brown shoes, holding a beaker in his right hand & a tan jug in his left, seated on a brown chair above a chamfered rectangular base, England, 1780-90, 6⅝" h. (hat abrasions & touch-ups, wrist repair, edge of jug rough, handle restored) 460.00

Staffordshire creamware Toby, Ralph Wood-type, seated Mr. Toby wearing a black tricorn hat, dark blue coat & yellow breeches, holding a frothing jug of ale & a beaker, a pipe between his feet, ca. 1780, pipe stem broken, 9¼" h. (ILLUS.) 1,100.00

Staffordshire creamware "Thin Man" Toby, seated man wearing a brown tricorn hat on his long brown hair, a white coat w/green cuffs & sprinkles of brown on his sleeves, a green waistcoat & brown breeches, smoking a pipe & holding a brown slip-glazed jug, seated on a green-washed & brown-sprinkled chair, brown-shod feet, on a brown-fronted base, England, ca. 1780, 9⅝" h. (hat restored, star crack in back, various repairs, cracks & regluing) 690.00

'King Hal' Toby

Staffordshire pearlware "King Hal" Toby, seated figure wearing a black tricorn hat (chip & repair) w/a yellow-plumed removable crown forming the cover (repaired), an iron-red jacket w/yellow cuffs, shoulders & slashes in the chest & sleeves, olive drab breeches, black shoes & a green belt suspending a brown scabbard (repaired) from which he draws his sword (missing), his left hand clasping a yellow shield (repaired) molded w/a royal profile portrait initialed "GR," & seated on a brown tree stump (chip, hairline) rising from a green mound base (cracked) applied around the edges w/iron-red & yellow floral clusters & green 'moss,' (some abrasions), ca. 1835, 15¼" h. (ILLUS.) 3,450.00

Staffordshire pearlware "Rodney's Sailor" or "Planter" Toby, the seated man wearing a brown flattened tricorn hat on his grey hair, a green waistcoat, manganese brown jacket, trousers & shoes, holding a beaker in his right hand & a green jug in his left supported on a manganese chest beneath his green chair, a loop handle issuing from its back, on a green-washed base molded w/rocks & grasses, England 1775-85, 11¹¹⁄₁₆" h. (repaired hat, abrasions, chip on back edge) 805.00

Staffordshire Toby, seated Mr. Toby wearing tricornered hat, decorated in underglaze blue & polychrome enamel, 8½" h. 440.00

Staffordshire yellowware Toby, seated man holding a jug in one hand, white slip decorated in black, tan, brown & blue glaze, 10¼" h. (old professional repair) 385.00

Syracuse China Toby, Herbert Hoover, ca 1928 ....115.00

TORQUAY POTTERIES

Torquay Creamer & Sugar Bowl

In the second half of the 19th century several art potteries were established in the South Devon region of England to take advantage of a belt of fine red clay. The coastal town of Torquay gives its name to this range of wares which often featured incised sgraffito *decoration or colorful country-style decoration with mottos.*

The most notable potteries operating in the Torquay area were the Watcombe Pottery, The Torquay Terracotta Company and the Aller Vale Art Pottery, which merged with Watcombe Pottery in 1901 and continued production until 1962. Other firms whose wares are collectible include Longpark Pottery and The Devonmoor Art Pottery.

Basket, round w/the sides pinched in at the middle & joined by a handle, Motto Ware, Cottage patt., "Aisy on the Sugar," 3¾ x 5¼", 4" h. $65.00

Cheese scoop, dustpan-shaped, Motto Ware, Sailboats patt., "Take a little cheese," 4¼ x 5", 2¾" h. 60.00

Creamer, bulbous ovoid body tapering to a flared rim & pinched spout, Motto Ware, Cottage patt., "Look BeforeYou Leap," 2⅜" d., 3" h. 30.00

Creamer, bulbous ovoid body tapering to a short cylindrical neck, Motto Ware, Cottage patt., "Take a Little Cream," 3" d., 3" h. 28.00

Creamer, wide slightly tapering cylindrical body w/short cylindrical neck, Motto Ware, Cottage patt., "Hope Well and Have Well," 2⅞" d., 3⅛" h. 30.00

Creamer, bulbous ovoid body tapering to a flared rim, Motto Ware, Cottage patt., "Lands End" & "Guid volks be scarce, take care o' me," 3⅜" d., 3⅛" h. (ILLUS. left) 40.00

Creamer, bulbous body tapering to a flared rim, Motto Ware, Cottage patt., "Help Yourself to cream," 3¼" d., 3¼" h. 35.00

Cup & saucer, Motto Ware, Cottage patt., "Wookey Hole" & "It's better to wear out than rust out," saucer 5⅜" d., cup 3⅜" d., 3" h. 45.00

Cup & saucer, Motto Ware, Cottage patt., "Have another cup full," saucer 6" d., cup 3⅜" d., 3¼" h. 45.00

Egg cup, Motto Ware, "Still Waters Run Deep" 35.00

Hatpin holder, Shamrock patt. 98.00

Jam dish, rounded fan-shaped ruffled bowl w/loop handle, Motto Ware, Cottage patt., "Canterbury" & "Take a little Jam," cobalt blue edging, 4⅜" w., 2⅝" h. 45.00

Jam jar, cov., cylindrical, Motto Ware, Cottage patt., "Widecombe" & "Guid volks be scarce take care of me," 3⅛" d, 4" h. 55.00

Jam jar, cov., cylindrical, Motto Ware, Cottage patt., "Isle of Wight" & "Go aisy wi' it now," 2⅞" d., 4¼" h. 55.00

Mug, cylindrical, Motto Ware, Cottage patt., "Look before you leap," 2¾" d., 3⅛" h., ...35.00

Mug, cylindrical, Motto Ware, Cottage patt., "Make hay while the sun shines," 3¼" d., 3¾" h. 45.00

Pitcher, child's, 2" h., 2" d., spherical body, Motto Ware, Cottage patt., "Castleton" & "Little Tommy Tucker" ..45.00

Pitcher, child's, 2" h., 2" d., spherical body, Motto Ware, Cottage patt., "Llandudno" & "For my dolly" 45.00

Pitcher, 4⅛" h., 3½" d., slightly tapering cylindrical body, Motto Ware, Cottage patt., "Cheddar Gorge - Help Yourself to Milk" 45.00

Plate, 8¼" d., Cottage patt., marked DMW, Made in England" 55.00

Salt & pepper shakers, footed, egg-shaped, Motto Ware, Cottage patt., "Kind words never die" on one, "Hope well have well" on other, 3" h., pr. 70.00

Sugar basin, open, bulbous body w/flared rim, Motto Ware, Cottage patt., "Be aisy with the sugar," 3⅞" d., 2¾" h. (ILLUS. right, with creamer) 40.00

Sugar bowl, open, pedestal base, Motto Ware, Cottage patt., "Do good in time of need," 3½" d., 2⅞" h. 45.00

Teapot, cov., squatty bulbous body, Motto Ware, Cottage patt., "Daunt'ee Worry but 'ave a cup of tay," 5" d., 4¾" h. 95.00

Trivet, round, Motto Ware, "Except the kettle boiling B - Filling the teapot spoils the T," Longpark mark, 5¾" d. 40.00

Vase, 6" h., relief-molded peacock on blue ground, ca. 1917 ....165.00

VAN BRIGGLE

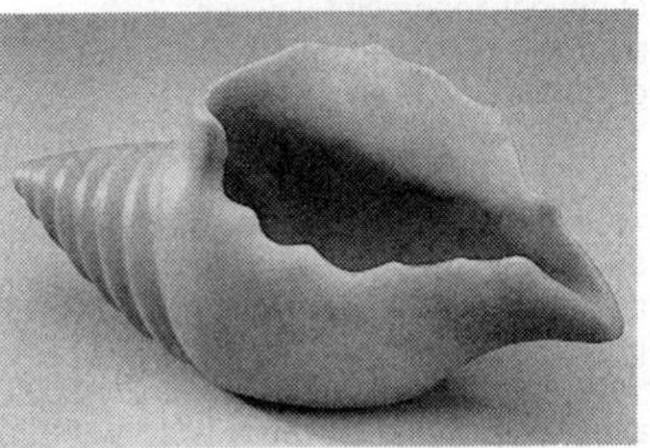

Van Briggle Conch Shell

The Van Briggle Pottery was established by Artus Van Briggle, who formerly worked for Rookwood Pottery, in Colorado Springs, Colorado, at the turn of the century. He died in 1904 but the pottery was carried on by his widow and others. From 1900 until 1920, the pieces were dated. It remains in production today, specializing in Art Pottery.

Book ends, model of a squirrel, Persian Rose glaze, ca. 1930, pr. $275.00

Bowl, 6¼" d., 3½" h., tapering sides, large embossed heart-shaped leaves under a fine thick mottled matte brown glaze, marked "AA1914," 1914 ....450.00

Bowl, 6⅜" d., 2⅛" h., molded stylized leaves, Turquoise Ming glaze, Shape No. 776, ca. 1920 ....135.00

Bowl, 8" d., 3¼" h., squatty bulbous body tapering to a small closed mouth, molded around the mouth w/a band of stylized flowers, leathery turquoise blue & purple glaze against a matte turquoise ground, Shape No. 22, incised "1902 - III 22" 935.00

Bowl-vase, spherical w/wide mouth, decorated w/embossed stylized peacock feathers under a shaded white, bluish grey to deep purple matte glaze, incised "AA - VAN BRIGGLE - 1903 - 231 - III," 6" d., 5½" h. 2,000.00

Lamp base, figural, kneeling Indian woman holding urn on shoulders, purple & lavender glaze, 19" h. 275.00

Model of a conch shell, Turquoise Ming glaze, ca. 1940-60, 9" l. (ILLUS.) 47.50

Plate, 8½" d., molded w/large poppy blossoms & swirled leaves & vines, apple green matte glaze, Shape No. 20, incised "Van Briggle 1903 - 20," 1903 ....825.00

Urn, footed bulbous spherical body tapering to a short, flared neck, loop handles angling from the shoulders, molded around the sides w/a band of upright spearpoint devices, robin's-egg blue shaded to dark blue glaze, incised "AA - 191(7)," 14" w., 11" h. 440.00

Vase, 3½" h., 4½" d., squatty w/canted sides & wide mouth, decorated w/crisply embossed crocuses, textured frog-skin matte green glaze, incised "145 - AA - 1904 - V," 1904 ....1,200.00

Vase, 4⅛" h., spherical body w/a low, molded flat rim, molded w/a repeating design of stylized rayed hearts, variegated matte green glaze, Shape No. 148, 1904 ....880.00

Vase, bud, 6¼" h., 3¾" d., squat base & long swollen neck, veined chartreuse matte glaze, incised "AA - VAN BRIGGLE - 1902 - III - 88," 1902 ....500.00

Vase, 6⅝" h., wide bulbous body w/a narrow shoulder tapering to a wide, flat mouth, molded around the shoulder w/stylized morning glory blossom clusters, the stems continuing down the sides, overall olive green matte glaze w/darker green highlights, Shape No. 284, 1905 ....825.00

Vase, 7⅞" h., slightly waisted cylindrical body molded w/narrow stripes below a squatty bulbous rim w/closed neck molded w/rounded, overlapping leaves, dark red matte glaze streaked w/green highlights, Shape No. 171, 1903....................1,760.00

Vase, 8" h., 4" d., expanding cylindrical body tapering slightly to a wide mouth, molded w/raised flowing poppies & poppy pods on swirling stems, matte raspberry glaze, incised "AA - VAN BRIGGLE - 1902," 1902 ....2,310.00

Vase, 9⅜" h., simple ovoid body tapering to a short cylindrical neck, molded around the shoulder w/a band of poppy pods atop slightly swirled stems down the sides & w/broad leaves around the base, mottled light blue glaze over red body, Shape No. 173, dated 1905......................................1,100.00

Vase, 9¾" h., 8" d., bulbous ovoid body tapering to a flat rim, molded w/large swirling poppies & stems around the sides in matte ochre against a brown & green 'hammered' ground, Shape No. 143, 1904.................................11,000.000

Vase, 10½" h., 4" d., tapering cylinder w/cup-form mouth, heavily embossed stylized narcissus blossoms & long twisting sinewy leaves, olive green to lighter green matte glaze, incised "AA - VAN BRIGGLE - 1902 - III - 40," 1902...2,300.00

Vase, 11½" h., 5" d., slightly tapering cylinder, rich mottled bluish green feathered matte glaze over heavily embossed daisies, incised "Van Briggle Colo Spgs. 10,145," 1907-12 ....1,800.00

Vase, 14" h., 5" d., tall bullet-form body, smooth burgundy matte glaze, marked "Van Briggle - 1903 - III - 134," 1903 ....1,100.00

Vase, 16¼" h., 7" d., tall conical body molded in relief w/tall yucca plants, dark blue & purple matte glaze, Shape No. 157, early 20th c. 467.50

Vase, 17" h., tall tapering cylindrical body, each side molded in relief w/a spray of three tulips, dappled blue & green glazes, incised mark "Van Briggle 1905 - V," ca. 1905 ....2,640.00

VERNON KILNS

The story of Vernon Kilns Pottery begins with the purchase by Mr. Faye Bennison of the Poxon China Company (Vernon Potteries) in July 1931. The Poxon family had run the pottery for a number of years in Vernon, California, but with the founding of Vernon Kilns the product lines were greatly expanded.

Many innovative dinnerware lines and patterns were introduced during the 1930s, including designs by such noted American artists as Rockwell Kent and Don Blanding. In the early 1940s items were designed to tie in with Walt Disney's animated features "Fantasia" and "Dumbo." Various commemorative plates, including the popular "Bits" series, were also produced over a long period of time. Vernon Kilns was taken over by Metlox Potteries in 1958 and completely ceased production in 1960.

DINNERWARES

Ashtray/coaster, Organdie patt., blue plaid, 4" d. $10.00

Ashtray/coaster, Tam O'Shanter patt 8.00

Bowl, 5½" d., Early California line, brown 3.00

Bowl, 5½" d., Gingham patt. 6.00

Bowl, 5½" d., Homespun patt. 3.00

Bowl, 5½" d., Tickled Pink patt. 7.50

Bowl, 8½" d., Gingham patt. 9.00

Bowl, 9" d., Organdie patt....................15.00
Bowl, 9" d., Tickled Pink patt. 16.00
Bowl, cereal, Heavenly Days patt...........8.50
Butter dish, cov., Tam O'Shanter patt., ¼ lb. 20.00
Butter dish, cov., Tickled Pink patt. 35.00
Carafe & stopper, Organdie patt...........35.00
Carafe & stopper, Raffia patt...............30.00
Carafe & stopper, Tam O'Shanter patt...35.00
Casserole, cov., Modern California patt., blue 200.00
Casserole, cov., Tam O'Shanter patt., 8" d..40.00
Chowder bowl, lug-handled, Vernon 1860 patt 10.00
Creamer, Heavenly Days patt. 10.00
Creamer, Native California line, yellow 10.00
Creamer, Tickled Pink patt. 9.00
Creamer & cov. sugar bowl, Homespun patt., pr. 15.50
Creamer & cov. sugar bowl, Monterey patt., pr...15.00
Creamer & cov., sugar bowl, Ultra California line, pr. 25.00
Creamer & sugar bowl, Chintz patt., pr...45.00
Creamer & sugar bowl, May Flower patt., pr. 40.00
Cup & saucer, demitasse, Early California line, red.............................25.00
Cup & saucer, demitasse, Early California line, cobalt 25.00
Cup & saucer, demitasse, Tam O'Shanter patt.......................................50.00
Cup & saucer, Gingham patt. 8.50
Cup & saucer, Homespun patt. 10.00
Cup & saucer, Tickled Pink patt. 7.00
Dinner service: complete service for eight including large platter, large round chop plate, vegetable bowl, gravy pitcher, salt & pepper shakers, creamer & cov. sugar bowl; Dolores patt., 49 pcs. 460.00
Egg cup, Homespun patt. 15.00
Gravy boat, Gingham patt. 6.00
Gravy boat, Homespun patt...................18.00
Gravy boat, May Flower patt. 45.00
Gravy boat, Raffia patt..........................16.00
Mixing bowl, Organdie patt., blue, 5⅛" d...15.00
Mixing bowl, Homespun patt., 6" d. 8.00
Mixing bowl, Homespun patt., 8" d. 10.00
Mixing bowls, Homespun patt., nested set of 3, 5", 8" & 9", the set...............75.00
Mixing bowls, Early California line, nested set of 4 ....150.00
Mixing bowls, Organdie patt., nested set of 4, 6", 7", 8" & 9", the set...........85.00
Pitcher, 5" h., Homespun patt................15.00
Pitcher, Organdie patt., 2 qt..................30.00
Plate, bread & butter, 6½" d., Early California line, brown 3.00
Plate, bread & butter, 6½" d., Vernon 1860 patt. 7.50
Plate, 7" d., Heavenly Days patt. 7.00
Plate, 7" d., Homespun patt....................4.00
Plate, 7" d., Organdie patt. 5.50
Plate, salad, 7½" d., Tickled Pink patt. ...7.00
Plate, luncheon, 9½" d., Homespun patt. 9.50
Plate, luncheon, 9½" d., Organdie patt. 8.50
Plate, dinner, 10" d., Brown Eyed Susan patt. 11.00
Plate, dinner, 10" d., Heavenly Days patt. 9.50
Plate, dinner, 10½" d., Organdie patt. 7.00
Plate, chop, 12" d., Homespun patt......12.00
Plate, chop, 12" d., Modern California line, green 25.00
Plate, chop, 12" d., Modern California line, ivory..25.00
Plate, chop, 12" d., Tam O'Shanter patt. 35.00
Plate, chop, 12" d., Ultra California line, yellow 20.00
Plate, chop, 14" d., Frontier Days (Winchester 73) patt. 145.00
Plate, chop, 14" d., Vernon 1860 patt...75.00
Plate, chop 17" d., Early California line, red 145.00
Plate, chop, 17" d., Modern California line, orchid 145.00
Platter, 10" l., Organdie patt. 12.00
Platter, 11" l., Tam O'Shanter patt........15.00
Platter, 11" l., Tickled Pink patt............18.00
Platter, 12" l., Gingham patt.................15.00
Platter, 12" l., Hibiscus patt..................25.00
Platter, 12½" l., Organdie patt. 15.00
Platter, 12¾" l., Homespun patt...........18.00
Platter, 13" l., Heavenly Days patt. 24.00
Platter, 13" l., Tam O'Shanter patt........19.00
Platter, 13" l., Tickled Pink patt............24.00
Platter, 14" l., Homespun patt...............15.50
Relish, divided, Tickled Pink patt...........22.00
Salt & pepper shakers, Chintz patt., pr...18.00
Salt & pepper shakers, Homespun patt., pr...14.00
Salt & pepper shakers, May Flower patt., pr...23.00
Salt & pepper shakers, Organdie patt., pr...10.50
Salt & pepper shakers, Raffia patt., pr...12.00
Salt & pepper shakers, Tam O'Shanter patt., pr..............................16.00
Salt & pepper shakers, Ultra California line, pr. 10.00
Salt & pepper shakers, Vernon 1860 patt., pr...12.00
Sugar bowl, cov., Gingham patt. 9.50
Sugar bowl, cov., Heavenly Days patt. 14.00
Sugar bowl, cov., Ultra California line 10.00

Teapot, cov., Arcadia patt....................65.00
Teapot, cov., Chintz patt....................110.00
Teapot, cov., Dolores patt. 28.00
Teapot, cov., Heavenly Days patt.........48.00
Teapot, cov., May Flower patt.............75.00
Teapot, cov., Tam O'Shanter patt. 45.00
Tea set: cov. teapot, creamer & sugar bowl; Chintz patt., 3 pcs....................75.00
Tea set: cov. teapot, creamer & sugar bowl; Monterey patt., 3 pcs...............75.00
Tidbit tray, three-tier, Gingham patt......35.00
Tumbler, Frontier Days (Winchester 73) patt., 5½" h. 45.00
Tumbler, Modern California line 20.00
Tumbler, Organdie patt........................18.00
Tumblers, Early California line, set of 6 ....90.00
Tureen, cover & underplate, Vernon 1860 patt., tureen 13" d., underplate 15" d., 3 pcs. 195.00
Vegetable bowl, cov., Gingham patt.....25.00
Vegetable bowl, cov., handled, Tam O'Shanter patt...................................55.00
Vegetable bowl, open, divided, Gingham patt., 11½" oval 15.00
Vegetable bowl, open, divided, Heavenly Days patt...........................18.00
Vegetable bowl, open, Native California line 9.00
Vegetable bowl, open, Organdie patt. 9.00
Vegetable bowl, open, divided, Tickled Pink patt. 20.00
Vegetable bowl, open, Vernon 1860 patt., 10" oval.....................................22.00
Vegetable bowl, open, divided, Tam O'Shanter patt., 11" d........................22.50

"BITS" SERIES

Pitcher, Bits of the Old West, "Blue Ridge Betsy" 65.00
Plate, 8½" d., Bits of Old England, No. 6 ....6.50
Plate, 8½" d., Bits of Old England, No. 8 ....20.00
Plate, 8½" d., Bits of the Old South, "The Old Mill" 12.00
Plate, 8½" d., Bits of the Old Southwest, Santa Barbara Mission 45.00
Plate, 8½" d., Bits of the Old West, "The Stage Arrival".............................30.00
Plate, 8½" d., Bits of the Old West, "The Train Robbers" 30.00
Plate, chop, 14" d., Bits of Old New England, "Tapping for Sugar" 60.00

CITIES SERIES - 10½" d.

Plate, "Atlanta, Georgia" 12.00
Plate, "Chicago, Illinois".......................15.00
Plate, "Greenville, South Carolina," blue 13.00
Plate, "Long Beach California," blue.....11.00
Plate, "Los Angeles, California"............17.00
Plate, "Memphis, Tennessee"..............15.00
Plate, "Natchez, Mississippi" 15.00
Plate, "Omaha, Nebraska"...................25.00
Plate, "Portsmouth, New Hampshire" ...15.00
Plate, "Riverside, California"...............12.00
Plate, "Rochester, Minnesota - 1954 Centennial" 35.00
Plate, "St. Augustine, Florida," red 13.00
Plate, "St. Mary's, Nevada"..................25.00
Plate, "San Francisco, California".........26.00
Plate, "Tri-Cities of Davenport, Iowa & Rock Island & Moline, Illinois," red.....13.00
Plate, "Tucson, Arizona".......................15.00
Plate, "Wichita, Kansas," blue 7.00
Plate, "Williamsburg, Virginia," multicolored 13.00
Plate, "Yakima, Washington," blue 12.50

DISNEY "FANTASIA" & OTHER ITEMS

Bowl, 10½" d., 3" h., Sprite design, blue, No. 125 ....225.00
Bowl, 12" base d., 2½" h., Winged Nymph design, pink, No. 122...........275.00
Figure of an elephant ballerina, No. 27 ....525.00
Figure of a hippopotamus ballerina, No. 32, 5½" h. 595.00
Figure of a satyr, No. 2, 4½" h...........225.00
Figure of a satyr, No. 5, 4½" h...........225.00
Pepper shaker, model of a mushroom, No. 36, 3¼" h. 75.00
Plate, 9½" d., Nutcracker patt............175.00
Vase, 10" h., Diana, Goddess of the Moon depicted in high relief, glossy white glaze, ca. 1940 (minor staining) 275.00

DON BLANDING DINNERWARES

Bowl, fruit, 5½" d., Hawaiian Flowers patt., maroon......................................12.00
Bowl, fruit, 5½" d., Leilani patt. 12.00
Chowder bowl, lug-handled, Hawaiian Flowers patt., maroon 35.00
Coffeepot, cov., Coral Reef patt., 6-cup 150.00
Cup & saucer, demitasse, Hawaiian Flowers patt., blue 18.00
Plate, 7½" d., Coral Reef patt., yellow..20.00
Plate, 9" d., Hawaiian Flowers patt., maroon..22.50
Plate, 9½" d., Coral Reef patt., blue & white 21.00
Plate, chop, 12" d., Coral Reef patt. 45.00
Plate, chop, 12" d., Hawaiian Flowers patt., blue 65.00
Plate, chop, 12" d., Leilani patt. 45.00
Plate, chop, 16½" d., Hilo patt., multicolored floral decoration 115.00
Platter, 13" l., Leilani patt......................85.00
Soup bowl w/flanged rim, Hawaiian Flowers patt., maroon 45.00

ROCKWELL KENT DESIGNS

Bowl, 8" d., Moby Dick patt.................125.00
Plate, 9½" d., Moby Dick patt. 55.00
Plate, chop, 12" d., Moby Dick patt.....155.00
Plate, chop, 16½" d., Salamina patt., ca. 1939 ....220.00
Plate, chop, 17" d., Moby Dick patt., brown 280.00

STATES SERIES - 10½" d.

Plate, "Alabama" 15.00
Plate, "Arizona" map, maroon...............16.50
Plate, "Arkansas," blue 7.00
Plate, "Colorado," red 10.00
Plate, "Connecticut," red.......................13.00
Plate, "Florida" 12.50
Plate, "Georgia, Empire State of South," blue 15.00
Plate, "Historical South Carolina," brown 13.00
Plate, "Idaho," multicolored..................11.50
Plate, "Iowa," maroon 7.00
Plate, "Maine" 8.00
Plate, "Michigan," maroon 12.00
Plate, "My Maryland," blue....................13.00
Plate, "Nevada"......................................25.00
Plate, "New Hampshire" 12.00
Plate, "North Carolina," multicolored 12.00
Plate, "Oregon," blue 21.00
Plate, "Rhode Island," brown................13.00
Plate, "Texas," blue...............................11.00
Plate, "West Virginia"............................10.00
Plate, "Wisconsin," blue..........................7.00
Plate, "Wyoming," red............................13.00

MISCELLANEOUS COMMEMORATIVES

Ashtray, "Glen Iris Inn, URC"...................8.00
Ashtray, "Michigan State College"..........12.00
Plate, 8½" d., "Baltimore Harbor," blue..11.00
Plate, 8½" d., "Carroll Mansion - Homewood," blue...............................11.00
Plate, 8½" d., "Ft. McHenry," blue 11.00
Plate, 8½" d., "Historic Baltimore, Johns Hopkins Hospital," blue 11.00
Plate, 8½" d., "Old Shot Tower"...........13.00
Plate, 8½" d., "University of Maryland School of Medicine," blue 11.00
Plate, 10½" d., "Baker's Chocolate 175th Anniversary"..............................20.00
Plate, 10½" d., "Chinatown," San Francisco, California, maroon.............7.00
Plate, 10½" d., "Knott's Berry Farm," blue 20.00
Plate, 10½" d., "Mount Rushmore Memorial," dark red & white, ca. 1950s 15.00
Plate, 10½" d., "Northwestern University," dark red & white, ca. 1950s 15.00
Plate, 10½" d., "Statue of Liberty," multicolored 25.00
Plate, 10½" d., "University of Chicago" 12.00
Plate, 10½" d., "Will Rogers," dark red & white, ca. 1950s 15.00
Plate, "Convair" airplane.......................75.00
Plate, "50th Anniversary Bluemke & Sons, Rosendale, Wisconsin," multicolored 35.00
Plate, "Seattle - Ernst Hardware," maroon...22.50
Plate, "Supreme Forest Woodman," maroon...22.50
Plate, "Virginia Truckee Railroad".........25.00
Plate, "Washington Monument," blue ...11.00
Plate, "Western Colorado Wonderland" 16.00

WARWICK

Numerous collectors have turned their attention to the productions of the Warwick China Manufacturing Company that operated in Wheeling, West Virginia, from 1887 until 1951. Prime interest would seem to lie in items produced before 1914 that were decorated with decal portraits of beautiful women, monks and Indians. Fraternal Order items, as well as floral and fruit decorated items, are also popular with collectors.

Chocolate pot, cov., decorated w/florals on a brown ground, 11" h..$125.00
Chocolate set: 10¾" h. tankard cov. chocolate pot & five matching cups & saucers; wild roses & daisies decoration, much gold & embossing, chocolate pot w/ornate handle & finial & scalloped base, 11 pcs. 245.00
Mug, decorated w/scene of a monk drinking ale, 4" h. 45.00
Mug, commemorative, "Detroit Foundry Mens Assn.," fisherman decoration 50.00
Mug, commemorative, Elk lodge emblem, 5½" h. 90.00
Pitcher, 7" h., monk decoration...........200.00
Pitcher, 7¼" h., swirl-molded body decorated w/h.p. large yellow & pink flowers, sponged gold scalloped rim & handle..55.00
Pitcher, tankard, 12" h., ornate mold, poppies decoration 165.00
Pitcher, tankard, 13" h., monk decoration, IOGA mark 185.00
Pitcher, lemonade, plums decoration, IOGA mark 135.00
Syrup pitcher w/original spring lid, decorated w/orange poppies, artist-signed (slight age crazing) 85.00
Vase, 4¾" h., pine cone decoration on light background, IOGA mark 35.00

Vase, 8" h., pillow-shaped, portrait of a young brunette girl wearing a white bonnet 145.00

Vase, 9" h., two-handled, seagulls decoration on white ground 225.00

Vase, 10½" h., twig handles, portrait of lovely lady w/blue hair ribbon in brunette hair, IOGA mark................145.00

Vegetable dish, open, decorated w/lavender roses, 10" l.......................35.00

WATT POTTERY

Apple Bean Pots

Founded in 1922, in Crooksville, Ohio, this pottery continued in operation until the factory was destroyed by fire in 1965. Although stoneware crocks and jugs were the first wares produced, by 1935 sturdy kitchen items in yellowware were the mainstay of production. Attractive lines like Kitch-N-Queen (banded) wares and the hand-painted Apple, Cherry and Pennsylvania Dutch (tulip) patterns were popular throughout the country. Today these hand-painted utilitarian wares are "hot" with collectors.

A good reference book for collectors is Watt Pottery, An Identification and Value Guide, *by Sue and Dave Morris (Collector Books, 1933).*

Apple bowl, Apple patt., No. 73, 9½" d., 4" h. $85.00

Apple bowl, Apple patt., w/advertising, No. 73, 9½" d., 4" h..........................115.00

Baker, cov., Apple patt., No. 96, 8½" d., 5¾" h. 85.00

Batter bowl, Esmond line, orange & black glaze...55.00

Bean pot, cov., tab handles, American Red Bud (Tear Drop or Bleeding Heart) patt., No. 76, 7½" d., 6½" h...132.00

Bean pot, cov., tab handles, Apple patt., No. 76, 7½" d., 6½" h. (ILLUS. left)...175.00

Bean pot, cov., tab handles, Double Apple patt., No. 76, 7½" d., 6½" h....775.00

Bean pot, cov., Apple patt., w/advertising, No. 502, rare oversized version (ILLUS. right).......................900.00

Bean pot, cov., Peedeeco line, 8" d., 6¾" h...45.00

Bean server, individual, American Red Bud (Tear Drop or Bleeding Heart) patt., No. 75, 3½" d., 2¼" h.....40.00

Watt Apple & Red Bud Bowls

Bowl, 4" d., ribbed, Apple patt., No. 04 (ILLUS. left) ....50.00 to 75.00

Bowl, cov., ribbed, 5" d., 4" h., Apple patt., No. 05 ....175.00

Bowl, 5" d., 2½" h., ribbed, Double Apple patt., No. 05..........................110.00

Bowl, 5½" d., 2" h., individual cereal, Eagle patt., No. 74..............................69.50

Bowl, 5½" d., 2" h., Mexican patt., shaded brown, No. 603......................95.00

Bowl, berry, 5¾" d., 1½" h., Starflower patt...60.00

Bowl, 6" d., ribbed, American Red Bud pat., No. 06...................................55.00

Bowl, 6" d., 3" h., Apple patt., No. 06 ...40.00

Bowl, 6" d., 3" h., ribbed, Double Apple patt., No. 06 ....110.00

Bowl, 6½" d., 2½" h., cereal or salad, Starflower patt., No. 52 ....45.00

Bowl, 3¾" h., 7" d., ribbed, American Red Bud (Tear Drop) patt., No. 07 (ILLUS. right) 65.00

Bowl, cov., 7½" d., 5½" h., Apple patt., No. 66 ....65.00

Bowl, cov., 7½" d., 5½" h., Rooster patt., No. 66 ....275.00

Bowl, cov., 7¾" d., ribbed, Apple patt., No. 600 ....135.00

Bowl, cov., 8½" d., Apple patt., No. 67 ....50.00

Bowl, cov., 8½" d., 6½" h., Rooster patt., No. 67 ....240.00

Bowl, 8½" d., Apple patt., No. 96..........35.00

Bowl, cov., 8¾" d., 6½" h., ribbed, Apple patt., No. 601 ....132.00

Bowl, cov., 8¾" d., 6½" h., ribbed, Tulip patt., No. 601 ....150.00

Bowl, salad, 9½" d., Apple patt., w/green stripe, No. 73........................85.00

Bowl, salad, 9½" d., Autumn Foliage patt., No. 73 ....70.00

Bowl, 9½" d., 4" h., brown Basketweave patt., No. 102 ....20.00

Bowl, salad, 9½" d., Double Apple patt., No. 73 ....175.00 to 200.00

Bowl, salad, 9½" d., Tulip patt., No. 73 ....150.00

Bowl, 11¾" d., Starflower patt., No. 55 ....75.00 to 100.00

Bowl, serving, 15" d., 3" h., Bull's-eye w/Cut Leaf Pansy patt....................155.00

Canister, cov., Tulip patt., No. 72, 7" d., 9½" h. 380.00

Dome-Top Apple Canister

Canister, dome-top, Apple patt., No. 91, 7½" d., 10¾" h. (ILLUS.) ..2,300.00

Canister set: four-section on wooden base, w/wooden cover; Esmond line, each section labeled: "Flour," "Sugar," "Coffee," "Tea," 6 pcs. ....250.00 to 275.00

Casserole, cov., individual, French-type w/stick handle, Apple patt., No. 18, 8" l., 4" h. ....225.00 to 275.00

Casserole, cov., individual, French-type w/stick handle, Dutch Tulip patt., No. 18, 8" l., 4" h. ....275.00 to 325.00

Casserole, cov., individual, French-type w/stick handle, Pansy (Cut Leaf) patt., No. 18, 7½" l., 3¾" h..........98.00

Casserole, cov., individual, French-type w/stick handle, raised Pansy patt., No. 18, 7½" l., 3¾" h..............................125.00 to 150.00

Casserole, cov., individual, French-type w/stick handle, Rooster patt., No. 18, 8" l., 4" h.................................295.00

Casserole, cov., individual, French-type w/stick handle, Starflower patt., No. 18, 8" l., 4" h. 180.00

Casserole, cov., individual, French-type w/stick handle, Starflower patt., green, No. 18, 8" l., 4" h.................132.00

Casserole, cov., individual, tab-handled, Starflower patt., No. 18, 5" d., 4" h. 106.00

Casserole, cov., Dutch oven-type, Apple patt., No. 73, 9½" d., 6" h.................................250.00 to 300.00

Casserole, cov., brown Basketweave patt., No. 128, 8½" d., 6½" h............40.00

Casserole, cov., Cherry patt., No. 54, 8½" d., 6" h. 95.00

Casserole, cov., oval, Rooster patt., No. 86, 10" l., 5" h........................1,400.00

Chip & dip set w/metal rack, Apple patt., No. 120 bowl, 5" d., 2" h., No.110 bowl, 8" d., 3¾" h., the set.....90.00

Chip & dip set w/metal rack, Autumn Foliage patt., No. 120 bowl, 5" d., 2" h., & No. 110 bowl, 8" d., 3¾" h., the set 179.00

Cookie jar, cov., Apple patt., No. 503, 8¼" d., 8¼" h. 325.00

Cookie jar, cov., Cherry patt., No. 21, 7" d., 7½" h. 139.00

Cookie jar, cov., marked "Goodies" on the side, No. 76, 7½" d., 6½" h. 400.00

Cookie jar, cov., Starflower patt., No. 21, 7" d., 7½" h.........175.00 to 200.00

Cookie jar, cov., Tulip patt., No. 503, 8¼" d., 8¼" h. 410.00

Cookie jar, cov., barrel-shaped, Woodgrain line, marked "Cookie Barrel," No. 617, 8" d., 11" h. 150.00

Creamer, American Red Bud (Tear Drop or Bleeding Heart) patt., No. 62, 4¼" h.................................130.00

Creamer, Apple patt., No. 62, w/advertising, 4¼" h..........................115.00

Creamer, Autumn Foliage patt., No. 62, 4¼" h. ....150.00 to 175.00

Creamer, Double Apple patt., No. 62, 4¼" h..80.00

Creamer, Pansy (Cut Leaf) patt., 6" w., 2¾" h. 130.00

Creamer, Rooster patt., No. 62, 4¼" h...............................125.00 to 150.00

Creamer, Tulip patt., No. 62, 4¼" h. ...275.00

Creamer & open sugar bowl, molded Morning Glory patt., creamer, No. 97 & sugar bowl, No. 98, creamer 4¼" h., sugar 4¼" h., pr. 385.00

Cup & saucer, Pansy (Cut Leaf) patt...265.00

Grease jar, cov., Apple patt., No. 01, 5¼" d., 5½" h. ....,...........................250.00

Ice bucket, cov., American Red Bud (Tear Drop or Bleeding Heart) patt...185.00

Ice bucket, cov., Apple patt., No. 72, 7½" d., 7¼" h. 250.00

Ice bucket, cov., Rooster patt., No. 72, 7½" d., 7¼" h.......................300.00

Ice bucket, cov., Starflower patt., No. 72, 7½" d., 7¼" h.......250.00 to 300.00

Mixing bowl, American Red Bud patt., No. 5, 5" d., 2¾" h. 55.00

Mixing bowl, Apple patt., No. 5, 5" d., 2¾" h...50.00

Mixing bowl, ribbed, Apple patt., w/advertising, No, 5, 5" d., 2¾" h.......80.00

Mixing bowl, Double Apple patt., No. 5, 5" d., 2¾" h...........................200.00

Mixing bowl, Rooster patt., No. 5, 5" d., 2¾" h. 85.00

Mixing bowl, Starflower patt., No. 5, 5" d., 2¾" h. 60.00
Mixing bowl, ribbed, Starflower patt., No. 5, green on brown, 5" d. 55.00
Mixing bowl, American Red Bud patt., No. 6, 6" d. 55.00
Mixing bowl, ribbed, Green/White Banded patt., No. 6, 6" d., 3½" h. 28.00
Mixing bowl, Rooster patt., No. 6, 6" d...95.00
Mixing bowl, ribbed, Starflower patt., No. 6, green on brown, 6" d. 55.00
Mixing bowl, Apple patt., No. 7, w/advertising, 7" d...........................40.00
Mixing bowl, ribbed, Apple patt., No. 7, 7" d., 4" h.................40.00 to 60.00
Mixing bowl, Cherry patt., No. 7, 7" d., 4" h...50.00
Mixing bowl, Rooster patt., No. 7, 7" d., 4" h. 69.00
Mixing bowl, ribbed, Rooster patt., No. 7, 7" d., 4" h..............................100.00
Mixing bowl, Starflower patt., No. 7, green on brown, 7" d.........................65.00
Mixing bowl, ribbed, Apple patt., No. 8, 8" d., 4½" h. 60.00
Mixing bowl, Apple patt., No. 8, w/advertising, 8" d., 4½" h. 100.00
Mixing bowl, Rooster patt., No. 8, 8" d., 4½" h. 150.00
Mixing bowl, Starflower patt., pink on green decoration, No. 8, 8" d., 4½" h... 90.00
Mixing bowl, Pansy (Cut Leaf) patt., No. 9, 9" d., 4½" h. 95.00
Mixing bowl, ribbed, Starflower patt., w/advertising, No. 9, 9" d., 5" h.........95.00
Mixing bowl, brown band decoration, No. 12, 12" d. 100.00
Mixing bowl, Kitch-N-Queen line, No. 14, 14" d. 75.00
Mixing bowl, Dutch Tulip patt., No. 63, 6½" d...50.00
Mixing bowl, Apple patt., No. 63, w/advertising, 6½" d..........................35.00
Mixing bowl, Rooster patt., No. 63, 6½" d...95.00
Mixing bowl, Apple (three leaf) patt., No. 64, 7½" d., 5" h..........................60.00
Mixing bowl, Starflower patt., No. 64, 7½" d., 3" h. 65.00
Mixing bowl, Apple patt., No. 65, 8½" d., 5¾" h. 90.00
Mixing bowl, Apple (two-leaf) patt., No. 65, 8½" d., 5¾" h.........................85.00
Mixing bowl, Tulip patt., No. 65, 8½" d., 5¾" h. ....125.00 to 150.00
Mug, barrel-shaped, American Red Bud (Tear Drop or Bleeding Heart) patt., No. 501, 2¾" d., 4½" h.............90.00
Mug, Starflower patt., No. 501, 4½" h..............................150.00 to 200.00
Pepper shaker, Rooster patt., hour-glass shape, w/advertising...............280.00

Pie plate, black band decoration, No. 33, 9" d. 45.00
Pie plate, Rooster patt., No. 33, 9" d...525.00
Pie plate, Starflower patt., w/advertising, No. 33, 9" d. 155.00
Pitcher, 5½" h., American Red Bud (Tear Drop or Bleeding Heart) patt., No. 15 ....56.00
Pitcher, 5½" h., Apple patt., No. 15 ....50.00 to 75.00
Pitcher, 5½" h., Autumn Foliage patt., No. 15 ....55.00
Pitcher, 5½" h., Double Apple patt., No. 15 ....425.00
Pitcher, 5½" h., Dutch Tulip patt., No. 15 ....130.00
Pitcher, 5½" h., Rooster patt., No. 15 ....75.00 to 100.00
Pitcher, 5½" h., Starflower patt., No. 15 ....75.00 to 100.00
Pitcher, 6¾" h., Apple patt., No. 16 ....125.00 to 150.00
Pitcher, 6¾" h., brown & white drip glaze, No. 16...................................59.50
Pitcher, 6¾" h., Dutch Tulip patt., No. 16 ....150.00 to 185.00
Pitcher, 6¾" h., Rooster patt., No. 16 ....125.00 to 150.00
Pitcher, 6¾" h., Rooster patt., w/advertising, No. 16 ....150.00 to 200.00
Pitcher, 6¾" h., Starflower patt., No. 16 ....100.00 to 150.00
Pitcher, 6¾" h., Tulip patt., No. 16 ....150.00 to 200.00
Pitcher, 7" h., Kla Ham'rd patt. 45.00
Pitcher w/ice lip, 8" h., Apple patt., No. 17 ....275.00 to 325.00
Pitcher w/ice lip, 8" h., Esmond line, No. 17 ....95.00
Pitcher w/ice lip, 8" h., Starflower patt., No. 17 ....275.00
Pitcher w/ice lip, 8" h., Tulip patt., No. 17 ....200.00 to 250.00
Pitcher, plain lip, 8" h., Dutch Tulip patt., No. 17 ....85.00
Pitcher w/ice lip, 8" h., molded Morning Glory patt., No. 96.............450.00
Pitcher, refrigerator-type, 8" h., Apple patt., No. 69 ....350.00 to 400.00
Pitcher, refrigerator-type, 8" h., Dutch Tulip patt., No. 69 ....625.00
Plate, dinner, 10" d., Apple patt., No. 101 ....450.00 to 550.00
Plate, dinner, 10" d., brown glaze, No. 101 ....55.00
Plate, dinner, 10" d., Pansy patt., No. 101 ....155.00
Platter, 15" d., Apple patt., No. 31 ....550.00 to 600.00
Platter, 15" d., Cherry patt., No. 31.....165.00
Platter, 15" d., Pansy (Cut Leaf) patt., No. 31 ....100.00

Platter, 15" d., Starflower patt., No. 31 ....150.00 to 175.00

Platter, 15" d., Starflower patt., green on brown, No. 31 ....110.00

Salt & pepper shakers, hour-glass shape, Apple patt., 4½" h., pr....................................250.00 to 300.00

Salt & pepper shakers, hour-glass shape, w/raised "S" & "P," Apple patt. (two-leaf), w/advertising, 2½" d., 4½" h., pr. 400.00

Salt & pepper shakers, Autumn Foliage patt., pr. 275.00

Salt & pepper shakers, barrel-shaped, Starflower patt., 4" h., pr....................................125.00 to 175.00

Spaghetti bowl, Apple patt., No. 39, 13" d., 3" h. 75.00

Spaghetti bowl, Cherry patt., No. 39, 13" d., 3" h. ....125.00 to 150.00

Spaghetti bowl, Pansy (Cut Leaf) patt., No. 39, 13" d., 3" h......................................65.00 to 85.00

Spaghetti bowl, Pansy (Old) patt., No. 39, 13" d., 3" h...........150.00 to 175.00

Spaghetti bowl, Starflower patt., No. 39, 13" d., 3" h..........................118.00

Sugar bowl, cov., Apple patt., No. 98, 4½" h..115.00

Sugar bowl, cov., Autumn Foliage patt., No. 98, w/advertising, 4½" h. 85.00

Sugar bowl, cov., Rooster patt., w/advertising, No. 98, 4½" h. 250.00

Tumbler, round-sided, Starflower patt., No. 56, 4½" h. 350.00

WEDGWOOD

Reference here is to the famous pottery established by Josiah Wedgwood in 1759 in England. Numerous types of wares have been produced through the years to the present.

CREAMWARE

Plate, 9⅛" d., "Buns! Buns! Buns!," man selling buns to lady & child h.p. center scene, gold border, artist-signed "E Lessore,".......................$395.00

Teapot, cov., Chintz patt., spherical body decorated w/four wide panels centering an iron-red & green flowerhead & purple foliage within an iron-red scalloped cartouche reserved on a black fish-red & scalework ground interrupted at the top & bottom w/iron-red, purple & yellow triangles, all between green, purple & yellow vertical bands edged w/black scalloped lines, the cover similarly decorated around the pierced ball knop, & the handle & spout patterned w/iron-red & black chevrons, possibly painted by David Rhodes, ca. 1770, 5$\frac{5}{16}$" h., (body cracked & w/restored chip, repaired chip on cover, handle terminal chipped off) 4,025.00

JASPER WARE

Jasper Ware Cracker Jar

Bowl & underplate, 4½" d., white relief classical figures on blue, underplate w/white relief floral band, 2 pcs........375.00

Candlesticks, white relief classical figures on a dark blue ground, 5½" h..175.00

Cracker jar, cov., barrel-shaped, white relief classical figures on dark blue, silver plate rim, cover & bail handle, marked "Wedgwood" only, 5" d., 6" h. (ILLUS.) 225.00

Cup & saucer, demitasse, white relief classical ladies in oval medallions on the black ground, colored enamel & gold trim, marked "Wedgwood" only, cup 2" d., 2" h., saucer 4½" d...425.00

Flowerpot, white relief garlands of grapes & leaves w/lion's heads & small figures of classical women under each lion head on dark blue, marked "Wedgwood England," 3⅝" h., 4" d. 175.00

Mug, three-handled, white relief classical figures in an oval vignette on blue, late 19th c., 4½" h. 325.00

Pitcher, 5¾" h., globular base tapering to a wide neck, white relief classical figures on salmon, marked "Wedgwood - Made in England" 192.50

Pitcher, 6" h., bulbous body, white relief classical figures on crimson, marked "Wedgwood - England" 895.00

Pitcher, 7" h., white relief classical figures on dark blue, ca. 1930 ....185.00

Pitcher w/silver plate hinged lid, 7¼" h., white relief classical figures on dark blue, lid w/engraved decoration & small lion finial, marked "Wedgwood" only 185.00

Pitcher w/pewter cov., 9" h., jug-type, white relief classical figures on blue, white relief scene of "Sacrifice to Love" on the front, late 19th c. 180.00

Plate, 10" d., white classical figures on green, marked "Wedgwood" only 325.00

Portland vase, 5" h., white relief classical figures on dark blue, marked "Wedgwood - England" 350.00

Sweetmeat jar, cov., white relief classical figures on sage green, resilvered lid, rim & handle, marked "Wedgwood" only, 4½" h., 3¾" d. 195.00

Teapot, cov., bulbous body, white classical figures on salmon, marked "Wedgwood - Made in England," 5" h..247.50

Teapot, cov., squatty bulbous body w/domed cover, white relief classical figures on dark blue, marked "Wedgwood England," 6½" h., 6½" d...295.00

Tray, octagonal, white relief classical figures on blue, early 20th c., 10½" w. 225.00

Small Jasper Ware Vase

Vase, 4⅞" h., 3¾" d., baluster-form, white relief classical ladies at altar scene around the body on dark blue, marked "Wedgwood" only (ILLUS.) ..125.00

Vases, 5¼" h., 2½" d., footed ovoid body tapering to a small flaring neck, white relief scene of man w/a dog on one side of one & a girl w/a dog on the other, both w/white relief scene of cupids on the backs, all on dark blue, marked "Wedgwood" only, pr...175.00

Vase, 6⅝" h., four-color, the tapering cylindrical body w/flared foot & wide, rolled rim, green ground applied w/four white pilasters surmounted by lion's-mask-and-ring capitals suspending yellow floral garlands & interrupting yellow ribbon-entwined ivy & cable borders between white bands, the interstices w/lilac & white oval medallions, the rim & foot w/a white foliate border, impressed mark "WEDGWOOD" only & date letters for December 1882 (small rim chips) 2,013.00

MISCELLANEOUS

Small Dragon Lustre Bowl

Bowl, 2¾" d., 1¾" h., Dragon Lustre, mottled orange exterior, blue interior 80.00

Bowl, 4½" d., 2½" h., Dragon Lustre, mottled blue w/gold dragons decoration exterior, mother-of-pearl lustre w/Three Jewels & gold trim interior, pattern No. Z4829, Portland Vase mark (ILLUS.) 195.00

Bowl, 9" w., octagonal, Dragon Lustre, gold dragons & trim on green shading to purple exterior, orange interior..545.00

Parian Bust of Milton

Bust of Milton, parian, by W.E. Wyon, bolted base, marked "Wedgwood" only, 8½" d., 14½" h. (ILLUS.) 850.00

Cup & saucer, Appledore patt. 28.00

Dish, pearlware, footed oblong form w/incurved edges & notched corners, mauve rim band h.p. w/flowers & leafy vines in green, red, yellow & black, impressed "Wedgwood" only, early 19th c., 8½ x 11" (pinpoint flakes, chip on underside of foot)............................192.50

Pin dish, center decoration of gold bull on blue ground, lustre finish, decorated gold rim, 3¾" d. 165.00

Plate, 6" d., bread & butter, Appledore patt...18.00

Plate, 7¾" d., majolica, grape leaf decoration, green.............................135.00

Plate, 9" d., scene of "Old Meeting House, Bingham, Mass.," blue & white 40.00

Plate, 10" d., pink lustre trim, Fallow Deer patt., Etruria, England 75.00

Plate, 10½" d., commemorative, "Old Ironsides," blue transfer on white 35.00

Plate, dinner, Appledore patt.................26.00

Soup plate w/flanged rim, Ivanhoe Series, "Wamba & Gurth," blue transfer on cream, ca. 1882................75.00

Tile, "April," blue transfer on white, 6" sq. 145.00

Tile, "October," brown transfer on white, framed, 6" sq.........................135.00

Toothpick holder, Butterfly Lustre, pearlized gold & orange, 3" h. 250.00

Tray, Lustre, center decoration of snake, snail & bamboo rod, scalloped, gold trimmed rim, marked "Wedgwood, England," 7 x 11¾"......285.00

WELLER

This pottery was made from 1872 to 1945 at a pottery established originally by Samuel A. Weller at Fultonham, Ohio, and moved in 1882 to Zanesville. Numerous lines were produced and listings below are by the pattern or lines.

Reference books on Weller include The Collectors Encyclopedia of Weller Pottery, *by Sharon & Bob Huxford (Collector Books, 1979) and* All About Weller *by Ann Gilbert McDonald (Antique Publications, 1989).*

AURELIAN (1898-1910)

Similar to Louwelsa line but brighter colors and a glossy glaze.

Charger, decorated w/a scene of baby chicks amid straw, brown glaze, artist-signed, 13" d. $4,400.00

Clock, the long domed case w/flattened & incurved sides tapering to a flared footed & scalloped base, decorated overall w/blackberry vines in green & gold against a shaded black, brown & gold ground, signed, 10⅞" h. (two glaze chips at edge of clock dial, minor glaze scratches).................1,320.00

Vase, 8⅞" h., squared form flaring out at base, decorated w/orange flowers 275.00

Vases, 8½" h., corseted form, flowers & leaves decoration, one unmarked, pr..485.00

Vase, 8⅞" h., tall slender squared body w/flared base, leaf decoration.......................................275.00

Tall Aurelian Vases

Vases, baluster-form, brilliant orange & yellow splashes amid similarly colored pansies & foliage, swirling on a deep brown ground, artist-signed, pr. (ILLUS.)....................12,100.00

BALDIN (about 1915-20)

Rustic designs with relief-molded apples and leaves on branches wrapped around each piece.

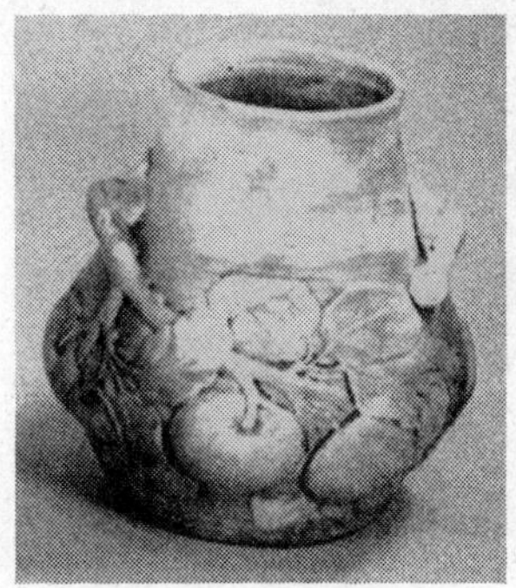

Baldin Vase

Bowl, 7½" d., 4" h., brown ground 160.00
Jardiniere & pedestal base, overall 39" h., 2 pcs. 1,250.00
Vase, 6" h., bulbous base....................45.00
Vase, 7½" h., blue ground 275.00
Vase, 9½" h., squatty base w/wide tapering neck, branches forming flat handles (ILLUS.) 600.00
Wall pocket..95.00

BLOSSOM (mid-late 1930s)

Pale pink flowers & green leaves on blue or green matte glazed ground.

Blossom Bowl-Vase

Basket, bulbous body w/uneven rim & scrolled, arched handle, 6" h. 45.00
Bowl-vase, footed squatty bulbous lobed body below a short flaring & ruffled neck, small eared handles on the shoulder, green ground, 5½" h. (ILLUS.) 35.00
Cornucopia-vase, 6" h., flared rim 25.00
Pitcher, 12½" h. 135.00
Vase, 7½" h., two-handled, blue ground..45.00

BOUQUET (late 1930s)

Various molded flowers in color against a light blue, green or ivory ground on simple shapes often accented by lightly molded ribbing.

Bouquet Vase with Tulips

Bowl, three-lobed sides, blue ground ...35.00
Pitcher, tankard, 9½" h., ivory ground ..50.00
Vase, 5" h., ovoid body w/flared rim flanked by tiny loop handles, No. B-15...25.00
Vase, 12" h., tall egg-shaped body w/four lobe rim & molded w/tall tulips issuing from the base, light green ground (ILLUS.) 125.00

CAMEO (1935 - late 1930s)

White relief-molded flower and leaf bouquets on pastel blue, green or deep buff ground.

Basket w/ornate asymmetrical overhead handle, rounded sides, low foot, buff ground, 7½" h. 30.00
Baskets, hanging-type, fluted floral form, 5" h., pr. 110.00
Bowl, 10" d..25.00
Vase, 7½" h., two-handled....................40.00
Vase, 9¾" h., green ground..................35.00
Vase, 10" h., upright square body, buff ground..20.00

CLAYWOOD (ca. 1910)

Etched designs against a light tan ground, divided by dark brown bands. Matte glaze.

Claywood Jardiniere

Basket, hanging-type, etched floral decoration, 10½" h...........................125.00
Bowl, 3" d., etched butterflies 12.50
Jardiniere, cylindrical sides tapering at the base, a series of panels each w/a different scene of a California Mission, the Mission name in a band at the top, unmarked, 9¾" d., 8" h. (ILLUS.) 137.50
Jardiniere, decorated w/a band of Greek figures, 10" h. 225.00
Jardiniere, 9½" x 11" 300.00
Mug, cylindrical, etched floral decoration, 5" h. 42.50
Vase, 3" h., etched panels of butterflies 35.00
Vase, 7½" h., etched floral decoration..65.00

COPPERTONE (late 1920s)

Various shapes with an overall mottled green glaze. Some pieces with figural frog or fish handles. Models of frogs also included

.

Candleholders, model of a turtle beside a water lily blossom, 3" h., pr....450.00 to 475.00

Console bowl, shallow oblong lily pad-form w/a figural frog seated at one end, 11" l., 4½" h....330.00

Model of a frog, 4" h. 275.00

Vase, 8¼" h., 9" w., fan-shaped top molded w/reeds above a low squatty bulbous base composed of lily pads & molded w/a pair of figural frogs on the shoulder, ink mark 700.00

Vase, 8½" h., bulbous base w/wide, flaring neck, heavy strap handles 200.00

Vase, 8½" h., 5¼" d., waisted cylinder 180.00

Watering device, model of a frog w/hole in mouth, 6" h. 565.00

DICKENSWARE 2nd LINE (1900-05)

Various incised "sgraffito" designs usually with a matte glaze.

Dickensware Turk's Head Humidor

Humidor, cov., figure of a military man's head, called "The Captain," dark blue collar & hat w/red trim, ca. 1905, 6¾" h....550.00

Humidor, cov., figural, Turk's head, dark-skinned man w/black beard & mustache wearing a multicolored turban, ca. 1905, chips on cover, turban repaired, 7⅛" h. (ILLUS.) 385.00

Mug, tapering cylindrical body w/ring-molded flaring base, etched elk head decoration, 6" h. 385.00

Pitcher, jug-type, 5½" h., scene of a bridge across a river & "The Mt Vernon Bridge Co, Mt Vernon, O"....375.00

Vase, 8½" h., bust portrait of Indian wearing full headdress, "Black Bear" 1,450.00

Vase, 9" h., 4½" d., expanding cylinder w/rolled rim, scene of golfer preparing to address the ball, against a tree-lined ground in shades of blue, green & brown, marked "DICKENSWARE - WELLER" 1,100.00

Vase, 9½" h., scene w/football players 1,250.00

Vase, 9½" h., decorated w/a bold, outlined design of a fully-rigged galleon w/crosses on the sails on a rough dark green sea & a shaded yellow to pink sky, glossy glaze, signed (minor glaze scratches) 990.00

Vase, 9½" h., 5½" d., ovoid bottle-form w/short narrow neck & tiny mouth, "Domby and Son," decorated w/the figure of a gentleman seated next to a young boy, marked "DICKENSWARE WELLER, 54(?), 12D" 440.00

Vase, 12" h., woman walking the dog scene 750.00

Vase, 16" h., decorated w/scene of four cats 2,750.00

EOCEAN (1898-1925)

Early art line with various hand-painted flowers on shaded grounds, usually with a glossy glaze

.

Pitcher, tankard-type, 12" h., decorated w/berries, artist-signed....750.00

Vase, 7⅛" h., pilgrim flask-shaped, the flattened round body raised on thick flared feet, a squared rectangular neck at the top flanked by angled handles, decorated w/a single wading white stork against a shaded grey ground w/ribbon-like clouds & ripples, artist-signed, numbered "21" & "90," ca. 1905....1,100.00

Vase, 7⅛" h., simple ovoid body tapering to a flat mouth, decorated around the middle w/a cluster of small stylized pink & yellow blossoms & large green leaves against a shaded black to pale blue ground, ca. 1920 ....247.50

Vase, 7¼" h., wide cylindrical body tapering slightly to a wide, flat mouth, decorated around the shoulder w/large cluster of Virginia creeper leaves & berries in pink, green & dark blue, a cobalt blue rim band & a pale blue ground, ca. 1925 ....550.00

Vase, 8" h., simple ovoid body w/closed flat rim, decorated w/a cluster of black berries & shaded green leaves against a shaded dark green to grey-green ground, ca. 1900 (minor glaze dimples) 412.50

Vase, 10⅛" h., wide ovoid body tapering to a short narrow neck w/flat rim, decorated w/large stylized undulating leafy vines w/berries in dark greyish blue & pink against a shaded pale greyish blue to cream ground, signed, ca. 1905 ....1,430.00

Vase, 12¼" h., wide ovoid body tapering to a short neck w/widely flaring rim, decorated w/large stylized pink blossoms & green leaves around the shoulder against a shaded dark to pale blue ground, ca. 1925 (small glaze skip at base) 440.00

FLEMISH (mid-Teens to 1928)

Clusters of pink roses and green leaves, often against a molded light brown basketweave ground. Some pieces molded with fruit or small figural birds. Matte glaze.

Chamberstick, dished base centered by a blossom socket, ring handle at edge, No. 45 ....185.00

Jardiniere, wide slightly swelled cylindrical body, the sides divided into panels w/large molded red flowers & green leaves, 7½" h. 100.00

Jardiniere, deep slightly flared sides on three short legs, pink flowers & green leaves around the base, 6" d., 8" h. 165.00

Jardiniere & pedestal, cream ground w/rose-colored flowers, 26½" h., 2 pcs. 550.00

Towel bar, a narrow horizontal oblong backplate molded in relief at the top w/two bluebirds & at the bottom center w/a cluster of red roses, a thick arched bar runs from end to end, marked, ca. 1915, 11⅝" l. 1,210.00

FOREST (mid-Teens - 1928)

Realistically molded and painted forest scene.

Basket, hanging-type, w/chains, 10" d. ....225.00 to 250.00

Jardiniere, 4½" h. ....100.00 to 125.00

Jardiniere & pedestal, the tapering cylindrical jardiniere resting upon a cylindrical pedestal flaring at the top& bottom, overall 29" h.(ILLUS. top next column) 990.00

Planter, tub-shaped, loop rim handles, 4" h. 95.00

Planter, tub-shaped, loop rim handles, 6" h. 125.00

Vase, 8" h., waisted cylinder w/flaring rim 125.00

Forest Jardiniere & Pedestal

Vase, 8" h., cylindrical w/slightly flared rim 60.00

GLENDALE (early to late 1920s)

Various relief-molded birds in their natural habitats, life-like coloring.

Vase, 8½" h., cylindrical, two parakeet-like birds on branch 325.00

Vase, 11¼" h., bulbous body tapering to a tall cylindrical neck, decorated w/a nesting marsh bird among cattails, marked 467.50

Wall vase, double bud, pierced to hang, tree trunk-form vases flank a panel w/a bird & nest w/four eggs, 7" h. 225.00

HUDSON (1917-34)

Underglaze slip-painted decoration.

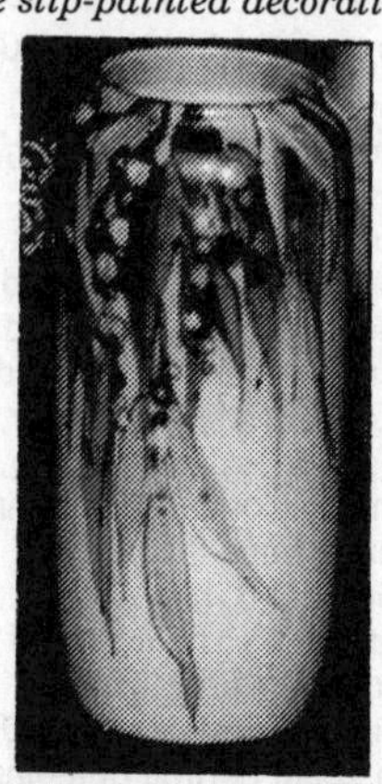

Hudson Vase with Leaves & Berries

Vase, 6" h., 3½" d., swelled cylindrical

body tapering slightly to a wide flat rim, decorated w/pink & white cherry blossoms against a shaded lavender ground, signed & artist-initialed 275.00

Vase, 6⅞" h., slightly swelled cylindrical body w/incurvate rim, decorated w/a band of long slender drooping green leaves & dark red berries suspended from the top, against a pale shaded yellow to pink ground, marked, minor glaze discoloration, ca. 1930 (ILLUS.) 605.00

Vase, 8⅜" h., plain cylindrical body w/flat rim, decorated w/a continuous landscape scene including a red-roofed cottage near a poplar tree, in shades of green, yellow, red & blue below a pastel blue & pink sky, marked & artist-signed, ca. 1925..2,200.00

Vase, 8¾" h., 4" d., gently ovoid body tapering to a small flat mouth, decorated around the upper half w/a cluster of pink & yellow roses on a shaded blue, pink & yellow ground, artist-signed & marked.....................440.00

Vase, 11⅝" h., tall hexagonal body w/a widely flaring cushion base, decorated w/delicate white dogwood blossoms & leaves around the top against a pale shaded blue to green ground, marked.................................275.00

Vase, 11⅞" h., baluster-shaped body tapering to a short neck w/rolled rim, decorated w/large pink & white rose-of-sharon on tall green leafy stalks, against a pale green shaded to yellow ground, artist-signed & marked, ca. 1930 ....990.00

Vase, 13⅞" h., wide bulbous ovoid body tapering to a short cylindrical neck w/thick rolled rim, wide strap handles from neck to sides, decorated w/a large colorful macaw on a flowering jungle vine against a shaded bluish grey to pink ground, artist-signed, ca. 1920 ....6,875.00

Vase, 15¼" h., 7" d., baluster-form, decorated w/multicolored irises in lavender, white, blue & brown against a shaded green to lavender ground, artist-initialed, ink-stamped "WELLER POTTERY"...................1,100.00

Wall pocket, decorated w/black-berries, white ground,10" h. 1,500.00

IVORY (1910 to late 1920s)

Ivory-colored body with various shallow embossed designs with rubbed-on brown highlights.

Jardiniere & pedestal, jardiniere w/angled shoulder on a tapering cylindrical body w/four raised feet,

Ivory Jardiniere & Pedestal

the sides molded w/four full-length Art Nouveau style women against stylized trees, on a matching decorated cylindrical pedestal, unsigned, 18" d., 35" h. (ILLUS.) 2,090.00

Vase, 9" h., bottle-shaped, decorated w/molded women's faces around the rim, molded fruit clusters around the base 95.00

Vase, 10" h., waisted cylindrical form, ornate winged scroll design 79.00

Vase, 10" h., cylindrical, molded w/nude caryatid figures around the top above ribbed columns & swags...125.00

L'ART NOUVEAU (1903-04)

Various figural and floral-embossed Art Nouveau designs.

Jardiniere, molded blossoms in dark green shading to light green, 8½" h...245.00

Vase, 9" h., tall slender square form flared at the base & w/a swelled rim molded w/blossoms, figures of Art Nouveau ladies on the side panels ....225.00 to 250.00

Vase, 11¾" h., tall cylindrical body swelled at the top & tapering to a closed rim, molded at the top w/ large orange poppy blossoms against a shaded grey-green ground, matte glaze, signed, ca. 1905 ....522.50

LASA (1920-25)

Various landscapes on a banded reddish and gold iridescent ground

Vase, 5¼" h., 2¾" d., stick-type, rocky

lakeside landscape w/pine trees, rose, gold, green & blue iridescent glaze 250.00

Vase, bud, 7½" h., scenic decoration of two pine trees, clouds, green, rose & gold iridescence 275.00

Vase, 9" h., 4¼" d., swelled cylindrical body tapering to a short, flaring rim, decorated w/poppies in purple & blue against a gold & orange iridescent ground (fine scratches on inside rim) 330.00

Vase, 11½" h., scenic decoration of sunset over water & trees 500.00

Vase, 11⅝" h., simple ovoid body gently tapering to a wide flat mouth, decorated w/an underwater scene of yellow & red fish among brown seaweed against a gold ground, all in iridescent glazes (few glaze scratches & rubs)............................550.00

LOUWELSA (1896-1924)

Hand-painted underglaze slip decoration on dark brown shading to yellow ground; glossy glaze.

Clock, mantel or shelf, a wide domed case flattened at the front & back, swelled sides tapering down to rounded feet & an undulating front base, the round white enameled dial w/black Arabic numerals framed by a brass bezel, the case decorated overall w/wild roses & leafy vines in shades of gold, green, orange, brown & black, marked, ca. 1905 (bit of loose glaze near dial)..................385.00

Pitcher, 5½" h., yellow floral decoration on brown ground...................125.00

Pitcher, tankard, 11½" h., decorated w/long stemmed flowers 175.00

Umbrella stand, h.p. portrait of an Indian in full headdress, artist-signed, 23" h. 1,210.00

Vase, 2⅝" h., jug-type, spherical body w/small neck, small shoulder spout opposite a loop handle, flowers on a shaded brown ground 185.00

Vase, 10" h., tall square form, decorated overall w/a dark red glaze w/a light & dark pink Virginia creeper vine & berries climbing around the sides, marked & artist-signed, ca. 1905 (minor glaze scratches, small firing flaw at base)..........................990.00

Vase, 10½" h., 7" d., wide ovoid body tapering to a short flared neck, decorated w/a large bust profile portrait of an Indian chief wearing a headdress, artist-signed 1,760.00

Vase, 16¾" h., tall ovoid body tapering to a flaring neck, decorated w/large bold dogwood blossoms & leaves in yellow, gold & burnt orange against a shaded dark brown to reddish brown ground, artist-signed, ca. 1902 ....990.00

MATT GREEN (ca. 1904)

Various shapes with slightly shaded dark green matte glaze and molded with leaves and other natural forms.

Vase, 12½" h., 5½" d., tall ovoid body molded in bold relief w/two full-length maidens embracing the sides at the top, fine mottled green glaze, unmarked....................................2,530.00

Vase, 13⅝" h., tall slightly tapering cylindrical body, a cluster of large poppy pods molded in high-relief at the rim w/a thin band & leaves wrapping around & over pierced slots near the rim, overall dark green glaze, ca. 1910, unmarked (minor griding of chips on base)..............1,540.00

MELROSE (about 1920)

Molded flowers or fruit clusters with branches on simple forms often molded with swirled ribs or indentations and with pale tan, grey or pink matte backgrounds.

Basket, 8½" h., flaring cylindrical sides w/high branch handle from rim to rim, molded grape cluster & vines 85.00

Vase, 7" h., cylindrical body w/twists below a ruffled rim, applied open branch handles wrap around the lower half & suspend apples...........150.00

MUSKOTA (1915-late 1920s)

Figural pieces with human figures, birds, animals or frogs. Matte glaze.

Figure of a seated nude lady on rocks w/a swan below ....375.00 to 400.00

Figure of a standing nude boy holding a drape across his waist, No. 107, 5¼" h...225.00

Flower frog, molded w/a dragonfly 135.00

Flower frog, model of two geese w/wings spread, 6½" h....................300.00

Flower frog, model of a lobster, 2" h...115.00

Model of a rabbit, brown, 13" l., 7¾" h...1,200.00

SICARDO (1902-07)

Various shapes with iridescent glaze of metallic shadings in greens, blues, crimson, purple or copper tones decorated with vines, flowers, stars or free-form geometric lines.

Very Large Sicardo Vase

Bowl, 2⅜" h., wide flat bottom w/low upright sides molded w/four thin buttresses, iridescent glaze w/silvery clover leafs against a dark reddish purple ground, signed, early 20th c. (small chips on base) 550.00

Bowl, 8" d., 3¾" h., waisted flaring sides w/a shaped rim, the sides molded w/stylized scrolling flowers, green & purple iridescent glaze, signed in script "Sicard Weller" 605.00

Box, cov., squatty five-pointed star shape, conforming low pyramidal cover w/button finial, overall iridescent glaze decorated w/repeating gold fleur-de-lis & random dots on a crimson & blue ground, signed, 5¼" w., 2¾" h. 550.00

Jardiniere, very wide squatty bulbous hexagonal body raised on short arcaded feet, tapering to a low flared & scalloped rim, the sides boldly embossed overall w/repeating scrolling vine & shell Moresque-style designs, reddish purple & dark bluish green iridescent glaze, signed, 12⅛" h. (small chip on one foot) 4,400.00

Plaque, rectangular, molded in relief w/a bust profile portrait of Saint Cecilia, after Donatello, iridescent glaze w/gold, reddish purple, blue & green highlights, marked, ca. 1902-07, 16½" w., 21" h. (minor chips at edge, repair to top right corner) 3,630.00

Vase, 4⅞" h., swelled base below tapering twisted cylindrical body w/a thick ruffled rim, iridescent glaze in shades of purple & dark green decorated w/stylized scrolling leaves, signed, No. 2039, ca. 1902-07 .... 770.00

Vase, 6" h., 2½" d., swollen shoulder & corseted base, decorated in a lustred glaze w/silver blue stars on a burgundy ground, signed in script "Weller Sicard" 550.00

Vase, 6⅛" h., squatty bulbous base below a tall ovoid body tapring to a flat mouth, iridescent glaze in shades of green decorated w/scattered shamrocks, marked & incised "X 453," ca. 1902-07 .... 990.00

Vase, 6¼" h., 5¼" d., corseted-form w/a broad flaring base, decorated w/a multitude of gold stars on an orange shading to green lustred ground, signed "Weller Sicard" 1,000.00

Vase, 7⅛" h., simple ovoid body tapering to a flat molded mouth, decorated w/iridescent green leafy scrolls & blossoms against a reddish purple iridescent ground, signed, ca. 1902-07 (some kiln burn & blistering near base) 660.00

Vase, 7⅜" h., gently ovoid body tapering to a wide flat rim, iridescent glaze in shades of green depicting grasses on the lower half below stylized trumpet-form blossoms on the upper half, signed 1,045.00

Vase, 9½" h., tall slender ovoid body w/a flared rim, iridescent glaze in shades of blue & green decorated w/swirling whiplash blossoms & vines, marked & incised "X 39" (minor grinding to back nicks) 1,540.00

Vase, 11⅛" h., tapering cylindrical body w/a swelled shoulder below a short cylindrical neck, molded in relief around the shoulder w/large poppy blossoms, the stems undulating down the sides, overall purple & green iridescent glaze, marked 3,850.00

Vase, 27¾" h., very large baluster-form body w/a short neck & widely flaring rim, decorated w/iridescent glazes forming wild swirling & crashing waves in blues, greens & golds against a dark reddish purple ground, signed, possibly an exhibition piece at the 1904 St. Louis World's Fair, tiny glaze nick at rim, some minor crazing (ILLUS.) 9,625.00

WILD ROSE (early to mid-1930s)

An open white rose on a light tan or green background. Matte glaze.

Basket, tan ground, 5½" h. 65.00

Basket, round bulbous footed body w/sides continuing to form strap handle across top, this handle topped by second smaller arched

Cornucopia-vase, tan ground, 5½" h.....30.00

Wild Rose Vase

Vase, 6½" h., footed gently flaring trumpet-form w/small tab handles near top, green ground (ILLUS.).........47.50

Vase, 7" h...30.00

WOODCRAFT (1917)

Rustic designs simulating the appearance of stumps, logs and tree trunks. Some pieces are adorned with owls, squirrels, dogs and other animals.

Woodcraft Planter with Foxes

Basket, hanging-type, molded fox face & apples, 9" d., 4½" h..............................225.00 to 250.00

Bowl, 7" d., 5½" h., squatty round base w/molded branch, leaves & acorns around rim & figural squirrel seated on rim 110.00

Candelabra, two-light, a curved pair of branch-like uprights joined by looping apple-laden branches, each arm w/a petal-form bobeche, a small figural owl between the sockets at the top, marked, pr..........................660.00

Jardiniere, acorn-shaped w/deep sides 170.00

Planter, cylindrical tree trunk form w/three small foxes peeking out at side, 4½" h. (ILLUS.)........................135.00

Planter, log-form w/molded leaf & narrow strap handle at top center, 9" l., 4" h............................50.00 to 75.00

Vase, 8½" h., cylindrical tree trunk form molded w/a branch of pink dogwood blossoms around the sides 110.00

Vase, 9" h., footed slender cylindrical body slightly flaring to the scalloped rim, molded w/tall slender trees w/leaf & fruit clusters around the top..120.00

Vase, 12" h., cylindrical smooth tree trunk-form w/molded leafy branch from rim down the sides & suspending cherries........................165.00

Wall pocket, conical tree trunk-form w/relief-molded branch down front & figural squirrel seated at base, 9" h.................................200.00 to 225.00

Wall pocket, conical, molded owl head in trunk opening, 10" h...............................150.00 to 195.00

ZONA (about 1920)

Zona Umbrella Stand

Red apples and green leaves on brown branches all on a cream-colored ground; some pieces with molded florals or birds with various glazes.

A line of children's dishes was also produced featuring hand-painted or molded animals. This is referred to as the "Zona Baby Line."

Comport, open, 5½" h., deep rounded bowl molded around the sides w/a band of large pink blossoms & green leaves on a wood-grained ground, raised a flaring pedestal base 125.00

Creamer, ovoid body w/twig handle, dinnerware line, 3½" h. 35.00

Pitcher, 7" h., cylindrical body, paneled splashing duck decoration 155.00

Pitcher, 8" h., cylindrical, paneled colored kingfisher decoration on a cream ground, brown branch handle 220.00
Pitcher, 8" h., cylindrical, paneled kingfisher decoration w/overall dark green glaze 125.00
Pitcher, 8" h., cylindrical body, paneled kingfisher decoration w/overall dark pink glaze, branch handle 145.00
Umbrella stand, cylindrical, decorated w/a row of tall, standing maidens in long dresses holding a continuous garland of pink roses, green ivy vines around the top, all on a cream ground, glossy glaze, 20½" h. (ILLUS.) ....1,000.00 to 1,400.00

WILLOW WARES

Blue Willow Plate

This pseudo-Chinese pattern has been used by numerous firms throughout the years. The original design is attributed to Thomas Minton about 1780 and Thomas Turner is believed to have first produced the ware during his tenure at the Caughley works. The blue underglaze transfer print pattern has never been out of production since that time. An Oriental landscape incorporating a bridge, pagoda, trees, figures and birds, supposedly tells the story of lovers fleeing a cruel father who wished to prevent their marriage. The gods, having pity on them, changed them into birds enabling them to fly away and seek their happiness together.

Also see BUFFALO POTTERY.

BLUE

Bouillon cup, Ridgway, England $25.00
Bowl, 5" d., deep, England 14.00
Bowl, 5¼" d., Homer Laughlin 3.50
Bowl, 5½" d., Royal China Co. 3.00
Bowl, cereal, 6" d., Adams, England 12.00
Bowl, cereal, 6½" d., Flair, Japan 12.00
Bowl, soup, 8½" d., Royal China Co. 8.50
Bowl, soup, 8⅞" d., Maddocks, England 22.00
Butter dish, cov., Allerton, England 190.00
Cake plate, Moriyama, Japan 125.00
Canister, cov., marked "Sugar," Japan 55.00
Compote, open, low, ca. 1880s, W.T. Copeland, England 120.00
Condiment set: oil cruet w/stopper, vinegar cruet w/stopper, cov. mustard pot & salt in wire rack, Japan, 5 pcs. 110.00
Cracker jar, cov., barrel-shaped, 9" h. 125.00
Creamer & cov. sugar bowl, Allerton, England, pr. 100.00
Creamer & cov. sugar bowl, Ridgway, England, pr. 100.00
Cup, lithophane base w/portrait of Geisha, Japan 25.00
Cup & saucer, demitasse, Booth's, England 45.00
Cup & saucer, W.T. Copeland, England 45.00
Cup & saucer, Japan 12.00
Cup & saucer, Meakin, England 12.00
Cup & saucer, Occupied Japan 15.00
Cup & saucer, Royal China Co. 5.00
Cups & saucers, demitasse, Japan, set of 6 ....100.00
Cup plate, Staffordshire, England, mid-19th c., 4" d. 33.00
Demitasse set, cov. coffeepot, creamer & six cups & saucers, 14 pcs. 175.00
Dinner set: six dinner plates, one large platter, two medium cov. vegetable bowls, open round vegetable bowl, open square vegetable bowl, two relish dishes, gravy boat, creamer & cov. butter dish w/drain; Wedgwood, England, 16 pcs. 1,400.00
Egg cup, Japan 15.00
Gravy boat, Ridgway, England 50.00
Mug, interior design & on handle, Japan 12.00
Plate, child's, 4½" d. 9.00
Plate, 5¾" d., Allerton, England 8.00
Plate, 6" d., Japan 2.00
Plate, 6¼" d., Homer Laughlin 4.00
Plate, 6" d., Meakin, England 5.00
Plate, 6⅜" d., Royal China Co. 3.00
Plate, dessert, 7" d., J. & G. Meakin.....15.00
Plate, 8" d., Maddocks, England 7.00
Plate, 8½" d., Alfred Meakin, England..15.00
Plate, 8¾" d., Japan 4.50
Plate, 9" d., Japan 8.00

Plate, 9" d., Royal China Co. 5.50
Plate, 9" d., Shenango China Co. 6.00
Plate, 9¼" d., Japan (ILLUS.) 14.00
Plate, grill, 9¾" d., Japan 12.00
Plate, 10" d., Johnson Bros., England ..12.00
Plate, 10" d., Homer Laughlin..............10.00
Plate, dinner, 10" d., J. & G. Meakin, England 30.00
Plate, 10" d., Ridgway, England 15.00
Plate, 10½" d., Wm. Adams & Sons, England, made for Fisher Bruce & Co., Philadelphia...............................30.00
Plate, 12" d., Royal China Co. 15.00
Plates, 9" d., Allerton, England, pr. 30.00
Plates, 10" d., ca. 1930s, Adderley, England, set of 4 ....180.00
Plates, 10" d., ca. 1880s W.T. Copeland, England, set of 8 ....200.00
Platter, 9⅛ x 11¼", Allerton, England..100.00
Platter, 11½" l., ca. 1880s, W.T. Copeland, England 45.00
Platter, 11½" l., Homer Laughlin..........16.00
Platter, 11½" l., Ridgway, England 65.00
Platter, 12½" l., Japan 25.00
Platter, 13" l., ca. 1880s, W.T. Copeland, England 60.00
Platter, 13" l., Ridgways, England..110.00
Platter, 15" l., Homer Laughlin..............45.00
Platter, 15 x 18", "Ye Old Willow," gold trim, Booths, England (shows a little wear) 150.00
Sauce dish, Ridgway, England...............5.00
Sauce dishes, Burleigh Ware, Burgess & Leigh, England, set of 8 ...40.00
Soup bowl, coupe-style, 7½" d., Ridgway, England..............................22.00
Soup plate w/flanged rim, J. & G. Meakin, England 15.00
Soup plate w/flanged rim, 8¾" d., Ridgway, England..............................24.00
Soup plate w/flanged rim, Allerton, England..22.00
Teapot, cov., Japan 75.00
Teapot, cov., "Ringtons Limited Teas Merchants" on base, 8" h. 85.00
Teapot, cov., Woods Ware, England....85.00
Toothpick holder, unmarked 85.00
Vegetable bowl, cov., ca. 1880s, W.T. Copeland, England 150.00
Vegetable bowl, cov., handled, Ridgway, England 60.00
Vegetable bowl, open, Allerton, England..60.00
Vegetable bowl, round, Moriyama, Japan 40.00

OTHER COLORS

Butter dish, cov., red, ca. 1890, Societe Ceramique, France 90.00
Creamer & cov. sugar bowl, Mandarin patt., red, Spode, England, pr. 150.00
Cup, red, ca. 1890, Societe Ceramique, France 20.00
Egg cup, pink, Allerton, England 25.00
Ginger jar, cov., green, Mason's Patent Ironstone China, England, made for R. Twining & Co. Ltd., London, England..................................65.00
Gravy boat w/attached undertray, red, ca. 1890, Societe Ceramique, France...125.00
Platter, 10½ x 13¾", red, ca. 1890, Societe Ceramique, France 175.00
Platter, 11½ x 16¾", red, ca. 1890, Societe Ceramique, France 225.00
Relish tray, red, ca. 1890, Societe Ceramique, France 5 x 8¾" 75.00
Salt & pepper shakers, red, pr. 20.00
Sugar bowl, cov., large, red, ca. 1890, Societe Ceramique, France 80.00
Vegetable bowl, cov., two-handled, large, red, ca. 1890, Societe Ceramique, France 275.00
Vegetable bowl, open, oval, red, ca. 1890, Societe Ceramique, France 65.00

WORCESTER

The famed English factory was established in 1751 and produced porcelains. Earthenwares were made in the 19th century. Its first period is known as the "Dr. Wall" period; that from 1783 to 1792 as the "Flight" period; that from 1792 to 1807 as the "Barr and Flight & Barr" period. The firm became Barr, Flight & Barr from 1807 to 1813; Flight, Barr & Barr from 1813 to 1840; Chamberlain & Co. from 1840 to 1852, and Kerr and Binns from 1852 to 1862. After 1862, the company became the Worcester Royal Porcelain Company, Ltd., known familiarly as Royal Worcester, which see. Also included in the following listing are examples of wares from the early Chamberlains and early Grainger factories in Worcester.

Fruit stand, the spirally-fluted dish & foot painted on the interior & exterior w/blue vines issuing gold- or black-delineated iron-red blossoms & bright green leaves forming a ground reserved in the center w/a gold- and iron-red-edged blue roundel depicting an iron-red & gold stylized kylin amid vines, & the worn gilt-edged rim w/six floral vignettes, Chamberlain's, ca. 1800, 12½" l. ...$770.00
Mug, tall footed pear-shaped body, decorated w/the "Beckoning Chinaman" patt., painted in shades

of purple, iron-red, yellow, green, rose, blue & black on one side w/a Chinaman beckoning to a young boy w/raised arms running by a stylized rock, the reverse w/an Oriental flowering branch extending to the front, the back w/a ridged loop handle, ca. 1758, 5$^{11}/_{16}$" h. (restored hole on the side) 1,955.00

Teapot, cov., chinoiserie-style, spherical footed body finely printed in black & painted in green, rose, iron-red, black, yellow, white, blue & gold on either side w/two Oriental servant ladies & a small boy standing before a table at which is seated a Chinaman beside another standing lady, a tall table behind them, the domed cover w/a reduced version of the scene flanking the rose & green floral-sprig knop, the pot shoulder & cover rim w/an iron-red & gilt scallop-and-dot border, ca. 1770, 5½" h. (two small chips on spout) 990.00

Vases, 13⅝" & 13$^{9}/_{16}$" h., bulbous ovoid body w/a cylindrical neck flanked by figural gold stag heads, raised on a short knopped pedestal on a square foot, each side of the body reserved w/a gilt-edged shaped oval cartouche colorfully painted w/a cluster of summer flowers against a drab green ground, the shoulder w/a border of gilt palmettes & foliate scrolls interrupted by the stag's head handles (some restoration to the antler tips) between molded gilt bands, the cylindrical neck w/a gilt flared rim decorated on the interior w/a bronze-ground border of gilt palmette & florette designs, the bronze-bordered square base (one w/shallow repaired chip) decorated on the upper corners w/gilt palmettes on a gilt-stippled ground, impressed crowned "FBB" marks & "Flight, Barr & Barr - Royal Porcelain Works. - Worcester - London House 1 Coventry Street," 1825-35, pr. 19,800.00

Waste bowl, deep rounded sides raised on a footring, decorated w/the "Japan" patt., the exterior painted in underglaze-blue, iron-red, green, turquoise, shades of pink & gold w/a panel of a bird & a rock in a fenced garden, a second panel of a tree & flowers in a fenced garden, & a third panel of flowers, all separated by blue-ground narrower panels patterned w/gilt trelliswork & reserved w/iron-red & gilt *mons* beneath the gilt-edged rim, incised letter "B" mark of Flight & Barr, ca. 1800, 6⅝" d. (slight rim wear) 460.00

ZSOLNAY

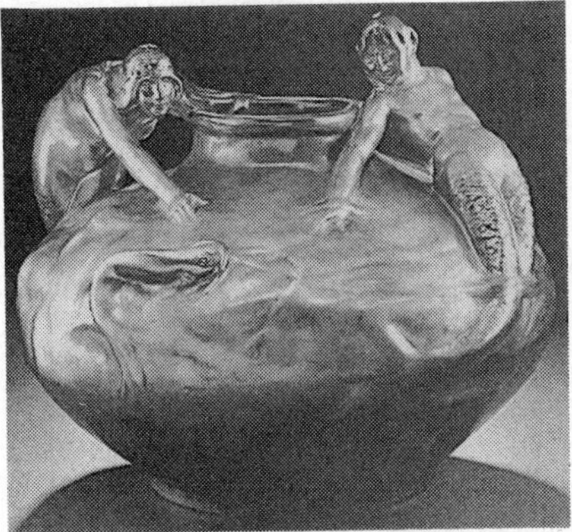

Zsolnay Figural Vase

This pottery was made in Pecs, Hungary, in a factory founded in 1862 by Vilmos Zsolnay. Utilitarian earthenware was originally produced but by the turn of the century ornamental Art Nouveau style wares with bright colors and lustre decoration were produced and these wares are especially sought today. Currently Zsolnay pieces are being made in a new factory.

Chargers, pink flowers center on a cobalt blue ground, repeated on the border amid yellow & green reticulated scrolls, 17" d., pr...........$330.00

Figure group, modeled as a seated little boy w/a cat on his shoulder eating from his plate, peacock blue iridescent glaze, stamped company mark & artist's name incised on side, 6" h. 403.00

Vase, 6⅞" h., double-gourd shape w/four molded handles, red & ochre iridescent glaze decorated w/four mice, impressed company mark & "6020" (hairline in neck) 748.00

Vase, 8⅞" h., squatty bulbous body tapering to a short neck w/molded rim, the wide shoulder molded in full relief w/a large mermaid & merman & fish, peacock blue iridescent glaze, impressed company mark & "MADE IN HUNGARY" (ILLUS.) ...1,610.00

Vase, 10½" h., wide bulbous spherical body w/incurvate rim raised on a low flaring foot, decorated w/stylized foliage in regular geometric patterns in green, gold, grey, silver &

burgundy lustres against a black ground, printed factory mark, ca. 1900 ....2,300.00

Vase, 17" h., figural, a footed cushion base w/a wide shoulder to a tall, tapering cylindrical body, the base molded w/wild waves below the tall full-figure of a standing maiden w/diaphanous gown & long hair clutching the sides, iridescent gold, green & brown glaze, raised medallion mark, ca. 1903 (minor glaze chip) 2,640.00

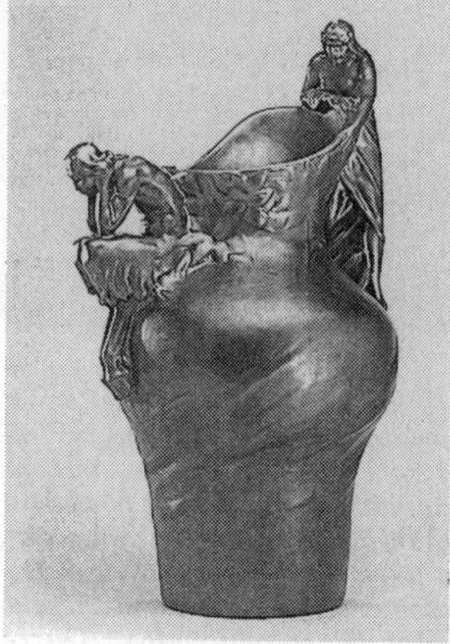

Large Zsolnay Vase

Vase, 17¾" h., baluster-form w/irregular rim, modeled w/a partially draped maiden & satyr around the rim, in a purple lustre glaze, impressed "ZSOLNAY PECS 6129 23 1" (ILLUS.) 4,025.00

(End of Ceramics Section)

CHALKWARE

So-called chalkware available today is actually made of plaster of Paris, much of it decorated in color and primarily in the form of busts, figurines and ornaments. It was produced through most of the 19th century and the majority of pieces were originally quite inexpensive when made. Today even 20th century "carnival" pieces are collectible.

Chalkware Model of a Stag

Bust of a monk, brown paint, 8¼" d., 12" h. $65.00

Bust of Pocahontas, wearing low-cut gown & elaborate necklace, ca. 1930, 19" h.....................................125.00

Figure of a Chinese girl, polychrome paint, 9" h. 147.50

Lamp, TV-type, model of a galleon, w/original glass, carnival prize 65.00

Mantel garniture, modeled as a fan-shaped cluster of fruit w/spiky leaves raised on a low pedestal w/a domed foot, decorated w/black, green, yellow & red, 19th c., 14" h. ..962.50

Mantel garnitures, model of an urn-form compote filled w/colored fruit below a pair of small facing lovebirds, 19th c., 12½" h., pr. (repainted) 550.00

Model of a bird, perched on a large ball w/a flaring rectangular base, original green, red, yellow & black paint, 5⅛" h. (paint wear) 330.00

Model of a cat, seated animal on a thick molded base, original deep yellow body w/red & black trim, 19th c., 9½" h. (possible old repair to head)...990.00

Model of a cat, reclining, original tiger stripe w/colored bow at neck, 12" l. (wear, chips & some touch-up) 93.50

Model of a cat, reclining w/head down, original black & white striping, w/colored bow at neck, 12" l. (wear, chips & splashes of paint) 165.00

Model of a dog, Spaniel-like animal seated w/the head turned facing the viewer, on a rectangular base, original red, green & brown trim, 6" h. (wear, minor edge damage).........363.00

Model of a dog holding a ball, carnival prize, 7" h...15.00

Model of a dove, polychrome decoration, 19th c., 11¼" h. (surface wear & soiling) 220.00

Model of a pig, nodder-type, standing animal w/worn black & red paint, 7½" l. (wear, stains & chips) 770.00

Model of a rabbit, nodder-type, recumbent animal w/h.p. collar, ears & facial features in yellow,black & red, 6¼" l. (minor wear) 1,100.00

Model of a rooster, colorful tail & wings in yellow, red & green, 19th c., 5⅝" h. (minor wear).....................687.50

Model of a stag, recumbent figure w/alert expression, on an oval base, minor paint loss, found in Vermont, 16" l., 16" h. (ILLUS.) 935.00

Chalkware Models of Colorful Roosters

Models of roosters, the hollow molded standing figure painted w/markings of red, yellow & black on a white ground, some paint loss, Pennsylvania, 19th c., 7⅜" h., pr. (ILLUS.) 748.00

Models of stags, recumbent animal w/red-painted ears, nose & mouth, on oval base, Pennsylvania, 19th c., 10" h., pr. 330.00

Watch hutch, modeled as a compote of fruit w/an opening for the watch face, polychrome decoration, 19th c., 14" h. (wear)...............................330.00

CHARACTER COLLECTIBLES

Numerous objects made in the likeness of or named after movie, radio, television, comic strip and comic book personalities or characters abounded from the 1920s to the present. Scores of these are now being eagerly collected and prices still vary widely. Also see ADVERTISING ITEMS, BIG LITTLE BOOKS, BROWNIES, BUSTER BROWN COLLECTIBLES, COCA-COLA ITEMS, COMIC BOOKS, DISNEY COLLECTIBLES, DOLLS, GAMES & GAMEBOARDS, GOLLIWOGS, KEWPIE COLLECTIBLES, and MOVIE MEMORABILIA.

Beatles Comic Book

Addams Family (TV) card game, Milton Bradley, 1965 ....$40.00

Addams Family cartoon, original artwork in water-color, ink & wash on cardboard, depicts Morticia, Pugsley, Wednesday & others watching Gomez test a sound system inscribed "Now... listen to the shriek run through its entire range without peaking.," signed "Chas. Addams," 15 x 18" 3,520.00

Addams Family (TV) lunch box w/thermos ....65.00 to 75.00

Admiral Ackbar (Star Wars - Return of the Jedi) costume & mask, mint in box 35.00

Alvin (The Chipmunks, TV) "Soaky" container 20.00

Amos & Andy (radio) arcade card, "Calling On The President" 14.00

Amos & Andy ashtray, ceramic, marked "Famous Artists" 125.00

Amos & Andy ashtray w/match holder, chalkware, embossed "I'se Regusted"..............................155.00

Amos & Andy figures, die-cut cardboard, stand-up type w/radio story information & radio station timetable, Pepsodent premium, w/original mailer, ca. 1930, 8½" h., pr...125.00

Amos & Andy sheet music, "Three Little Words,"' from the movie "Check & Double Check" 20.00

Andy Gump (comics) hairbrush, celluloid..40.00

Andy Gump marble, bust portrait, ⅝" d..30.00

Andy Gump sheet music, "Oh Min," 1928..30.00

Andy Panda (Woody Woodpecker, TV) paint book, 1946 ....65.00

Annie Oakley and Tagg (TV) lunchbox & thermos, rectangular, scene of Annie on rearing horse, Aladdin Industries, 1956, 2 pcs.....................220.00

Ann Sothern writing tablet, unused.......25.00

Archie Bunker (All in the Family, TV) tumbler, glass, "Archie Bunker For President" 14.00

Barbie lunch box & thermos, black vinyl, front w/a bust profile portrait of Barbie & four figures in different costumes, King Seeley Thermos, 1962, 2 pcs. (near mint)...................242.00

Barney Google (comics) figure, composition & wood, 1944, 4" h. 72.00

Barney Google original artwork, pen & ink on illustration board for a daily strip, by Billy DeBeck, January 21, 1931, 5½ x 18"............462.00

Batman (TV) bank, china, figural, 1966, 6¾" h...85.00

Batman belt buckle, ca. 1960 ....10.00

Batman (TV) man's suit, worn by the character Bruce Wayne played by Adam West, black w/maroon & green pinstripes, three-piece w/jacket, vest & pants, designed by Ideal Tailoring, jacket lining inscribed "Adam West," 1960s.........715.00

Batman mask, felt...................................22.00

Batman pen, ball-point type, w/Batman figural clip, on original display card, 1966, 2" 85.00

Batman puzzle, jigsaw-type, England, 1966, mint in box 65.00

Batman radio, wrist-type, in box 70.00

Batman tennis shoes, ca. 1966 ....65.00

Batman toy, Batmobile, battery-operated, Alps Shojo Ltd., Tokyo, Japan, 11" l., mint condition.............400.00

Batman toy, walkie-talkie, "Batman Walkie Talkie," in unopened package 50.00

Batman & Robin bowl, china, Washington Pottery, England, 1966 ....65.00

Batman & Robin mug, milk white glass w/red decal, marked "Fire-King"..35.00

Batman & Robin mug, porcelain, illustrates the dynamic flying duo, England, 1966..................................55.00

Batman & Robin scarf, w/three illustrations of Batman & Robin, England..150.00

Battlestar Galactica (TV) game, board-type, includes spinner & four colonial viper die-cut cardboard spaceships, Parker Brothers, 1978, 9 x 18" box 25.00

Beany & Cecil (TV) guitar, Mattel, 1962..60.00

Beatles billfold, red w/four signatures in white one side & their picture on the other, mint condition 80.00

Beatles comic book, No. 1, Sept. - Nov. 1964, Dell file copy, stories w/color photo pin-ups (ILLUS.) 690.00

Beatles comic book, "Yellow Submarine," w/pull-out poster, Gold Key/Whitman, 68 pp., 1968 ....45.00

Beatles Bobbing Head Figures

Beatles figures, composition, bobbing head-type, h.p. wearing greyish blue collarless suits, each playing the appropriate instrument, on gold bases w/facsimile signatures, w/original box in pristine condition, "Car Mascots Inc.," 1964, each 8" h., set of 4 (ILLUS.)............................1,725.00

Beatles figures, rubber, inflatable-type, 1964, mint in original box, set of 4...120.00

Beatles game, board-type, "Flip Your Wig," Milton Bradley, 1964..............120.00

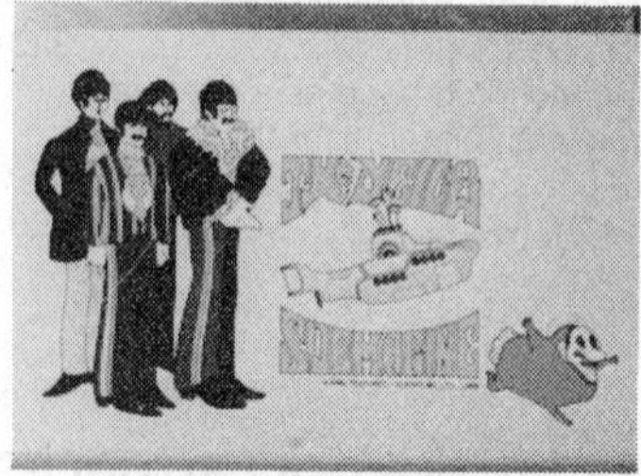

Beatles Letter Holder

Beatles letter holder, depicted standing to one side, center lettered "The Yellow Submarine" w/sketch of the sub (ILLUS.)..............................917.00

Beatles lunch bag, rectangular blue vinyl w/zipper top & black strap handle, sketch of each band member's head across the front in color, 1960s 307.00

Beatles lunch box, "Beatles," the front features a picture of each member of the band w/their signatures, a shot of a performance on the back, 1966, near mint condition 575.00

Beatles lunch box & thermos bottle, steel, "Yellow Submarine," King-Seeley, © 1968 King Features & Subafilms Ltd., 2 pcs. 325.00

Beatles magazine cover & story, "Datebook," 1966, September 15.00

Beatles magazine cover & story, "Look," January 19, 1968, pictures John Lennon on the cover & a pull-out section which includes pictures of all the Beatles 75.00

Beatles nylon stockings, in original package picturing the "Fab Four," 1960s, Holland..................................32.00

Beatles overnight bag, black vinyl, round w/flat sides & bottom, color illustration of the four below "The Beatles," black strap handle, 1960s 351.00

Beatles phonograph, blue case w/two large color pictures of the Beatles, one on the inside showing the band playing, the one on the outside w/typical portraits, original nobs inside, 1960s, 10 x 18", 6" h. (tone arm missing, minor drill holes in side, wear on turntable mat) 1,200.00

Beatles plate, blue & white china, portraits of the four, marked "Bone China England," 7" d...........................85.00

Beatles Poster

Beatles poster, "Here Come The Beatles - Candlestick Park - Monday August 29 - 8 p.m.," artwork by Wes Wilson, 1966, 17¼ x 24" (ILLUS.) 1,495.00

Beatles purse, vinyl, clutch-type, ivory w/portraits of the four in black w/facsimile autographs under each, leather pull attached to zipper at top edge, ca. 1964, 9½" w., 5½" h. 90.00

Beatles record album, 'gold' album award for "Abbey Road," the RIAA award presented to CBS-FM to commemorate the sale of more than 500,000 copies of the Capitol Records, Inc. long-playing album, matted & framed, 17 x 21" 1,265.00

Beatles store counter display w/pins, stand-up cardboard w/black & white photos of the Beatles, used to hold two dozen lapel pins, one complete set of pins attached, each pin featuring a plastic Beatle figure w/instrument, 1960s, 11 x 20" (damage along bottom edge, general wear & a tear on edges & corners)...661.00

Beatles talc canister, lithographed tin container w/pictures of the Beatles on the front & back, by Margo of Mayfair, manufactured in Great Britain, 1960s, full 320.00

Beatles towel, large size, features graphics of the Beatles wearing antique-style striped bathing costumes, 1960s (discoloration down one side) 109.00

Beatles toy, guitar, pink & red w/pictures of the heads of each band member on the body in black, Mastro, 1960s, on original illustrated display card w/original cellophane, 21" l. (some tears in cellophane) ..1,206.00

Beatles Tumblers

Beatles tumbler, glass, clear w/printed bust portrait of Paul w/his name (ILLUS. second from right).................88.00

Beatles tumblers, glass, clear w/a printed bust portrait of each member of the band w/their name, John, George & Ringo, ea. (ILLUS. left to right)...91.00

Beatles tumbler, white plastic, color picture of the four inlaid under clear plexiglass exterior, facsimile autographs, lip prints around top rim, EMS, ca. 1964, 6" h. 90.00

Beatles water color set, Yellow Submarine pictured, complete in psychedelic design colored box.........85.00

Ben Cartwright doll, American Character, near mint in box, 8" h. 240.00

Betty Boop cookie jar, ceramic, Enesco 395.00

Betty Boop coverlet, twenty-four squares separated by pink & blue floral bands, the four corner squares each embroidered w/a large bust of Betty, the remainder embroidered w/full-figure action scenes of Betty, 63 x 88" 195.00

Betty Boop doll, composition & wood, all original clothing & stickers, Steiff (Giengen, Germany), 1932, 14" h....825.00

Betty Boop figure, bisque, jointed arms, 6½" h.......................................225.00

Betty Boop string holder, ceramic, Vandor 50.00

Betty Rubble figure, bisque, posing w/prehistoric greenery, 6" h. 28.00

Beverly Hillbillies (TV) coloring book, Whitman Publishing Co., 126 pp., 1963 ....35.00

Beverly Hillbillies game, board-type, board in excellent condition, in original box w/light wear along corners & edges..................................55.00

Beverly Hillbillies (TV) lunch box w/thermos 125.00

Beverly Hillbillies puzzle, jigsaw-type, full-color photograph of family sitting in their 1921 truck, Jaymar No. 6572, 100 pcs., 17 x 22"............48.00

Bimbo (Betty Boop's dog) figure, jointed wood & composition, oversized head, painted outfit, arms & legs jointed, w/original decal, Ideal, 1930s, 9" h. 633.00

Blondie birthday card, Hallmark, 6 pp., 1942..30.00

Blondie Movie Poster

Blondie movie poster, "Blondie," Columbia, starring Penny Singleton & Arthur Lake, one-sheet, 1938, linen backed, 27 x 41" (ILLUS.) 2,420.00

Blondie & Dagwood coloring book, 1945...75.00

Bob Dylan-Signed Guitar

Bob Dylan guitar, Ibanez acoustic model, signed boldly on the front in blue marker, inscribed "To Gary, Best Wishes, Bob Dylan," w/case, 2 pcs. (ILLUS.) 3,450.00

Bobbie Benson (radio) map, w/original mailer, H-O Oats Co. premium, ca. 1930 ....60.00

Bob Hope book, "They Got Me Covered," biography, in colorful store envelope advertising "Bob Hope's Life Story," Pepsodent premium, 95 pp., 1941 ....30.00

Bonanza (TV) lunch box w/thermos, ca. 1965 ....75.00

Bonanza (TV) magazine, Vol. 1, No. 1, 1965 ....27.50

Bonny Braids (Dick Tracy) doll, miniature, attached to original card w/Dick Tracy graphics, dated 1951, 1" h. doll, 3 x 5" card.........................85.00

Bonzo toothpick holder, porcelain, figural, orange & white glaze 40.00

B.O. Plenty Drawing by Gould

B.O. Plenty drawing, water-color & India ink on illustration board, from

"Dick Tracy," signed by Chester Gould, date unknown, condition very fine, 20 x 24" (ILLUS.) 528.00

Bringing Up Father puzzles, jigsaw-type, set of 4, boxed 85.00

Brutus (Popeye) puppet, hand-type, Gund Mfg. Co., excellent condition....58.00

Buccaneer (TV) lunch box & thermos, dome-top model, pirate ship scenes, Aladdin Industries, 1957, 2 pcs........418.00

Buck Jones guitar, professional size w/steel strings 175.00

Buck Jones ring, central embossed bust portrait of Jones within a horseshoe, ca. 1937 ....80.00

Buck Rogers Magazine Story

Buck Rogers magazine stories, "Amazing Stories," August 1928 & March 1929, which marked the first & second appearances of Buck Rogers, very good condition, 2 issues (ILLUS. of August) 935.00

Buffalo Bill, Jr. (TV) coloring book, 1957 ....25.00

Bugs Bunny candy dispenser, PEZ, plastic, Warner Bros. copyright, 1978 ....25.00

Bugs Bunny figure, chalkware, 9½" h...50.00

Bugs Bunny pictures, "Bugs Magic Rub-Off Pictures," 1954, unused, in box 42.00

Bullwinkle (TV) blackboard & chalk, mint in package...............................20.00

Bullwinkle (cartoons) coin set, plastic rim w/paper insert, the set pictures members of the Bullwinkle show including Bullwinkle, Rocky, Natasha, Boris & Dudley, each coin printed in bright colors, set of 60 (ILLUS. of part top next column)......805.00

Bullwinkle Moose figure, furry figure w/white felt antlers & hands, red sweater w/green letter "B," Dakin, 1978, mint w/original tag, 12" h..........31.00

Bullwinkle Coin Set

Bullwinkle Moose (cartoons) game, quiz-type, "Bullwinkle's Electric Quiz Fun Game," cardboard light-up game, premium from General Mills, fine graphics of Bullwinkle, 1960s, w/original mailer, 11" sq. (light bulb missing) 75.00

Bullwinkle Moose (cartoons) game, board-type, "Bullwinkle Travel Adventure Game," colorful box cover w/Bullwinkle & friends, Transogram, 1970 (box edge wear, corner splits, some Rocky cards detached from insert) 75.00

Bullwinkle radio, AM figural 325.00

Bullwinkle toy, "Bullwinkle Cartoon Kit," complete in box, Colorforms, 1962....45.00

Bullwinkle Moose toy, "Bullwinkle Stamp Set," six stamps & pad, stamps include Rocky, Bullwinkle, Natasha, etc., Lido, 1965, mint on card, 6½ x 12" 75.00

Bullwinkle tumbler, pictures him w/balloons, clear glass, Pepsi-Cola collection series, 12 oz. 10.00

Captain America (comics) figure, "Bend'n Flex," Mego, 1972, 5" h., on original card 35.00

Captain Gallant of the Foreign Legion (TV) badge, brass, membership type, Heinz 57 premium 175.00

Captain Kangaroo (TV) guitar, musical windup-type 22.00

Captain Kangaroo (TV) lunch box w/thermos, vinyl ....400.00 to 450.00

Captain Marvel Club (radio) membership set, w/card, letter, flyer & envelope 195.00

Captain Marvel key chain, ca.1944-47 ....20.00

Captain Marvel movie poster, "Adventures of Captain Marvel,"

Republic serial in 12 chapters, starring Tom Tyler, six-sheet, 1941, linen backed, 81 x 81" 4,620.00

Captain Marvel push-outs, paper, ca. 1944, mint in package..................35.00

Captain Midnight (radio) decoder manual, 1945 ....105.00

Captain Midnight patch, "SQ 15th Anniversary," cloth, 1957 ....42.00

Captain Midnight pin, "Captain Midnight - Flight Commander" flying cross, Ovaltine radio premium, 1942 ....135.00

Captain Video (TV) goggles, electronic-type, w/instruction card & original mailer, ca. 1949-56 ....135.00

Captain Video ring, "Photo Ring"..........65.00

Casper, the Friendly Ghost (TV) costume, in box..................................22.00

Casper, the Friendly Ghost game, board-type, complete w/spinner, Milton Bradley, 1959 (box lid sides slightly warped 24.00

Casper, the Friendly Ghost kite, Saalfield, uncut 25.00

Casper, the Friendly Ghost thermos bottle 100.00

Charlie Brown (Peanuts) doll, rubber, United Features Syndicate, 7½" h. 22.00

Charlie Chaplin cartoon book, "Charlie Chaplin in the Movies," ca. 1917 ....68.00

Charlie Chaplin doll kit, cloth, printed front & back to be sewn together & stuffed, marked "British Mfg., Charlie Chaplin," 1930s, 13" 120.00

Charlie McCarthy birthday card, 1938..38.00

Charlie McCarthy knife, silver plate, handle w/relief figure of Charlie dressed as a cowboy 69.00

Charlie McCarthy marionette, composition, 13" h. 140.00

Charlie McCarthy pencil box, lithographed tin, 1932 ....85.00

Charlie McCarthy teaspoon, embossed "Inspector," 1938 ....32.00

Charlie McCarthy & Edgar Bergen book, "Day With Charlie McCarthy & Edgar Bergen & Hints on Ventriloquism," pictorial cover & 38 pages of movie scenes, 8½ x 13" 35.00

Chester Gump (comics) pinback button, Kellogg's "Pep" Cereal premium, 1940s 8.00

Chipmunks (TV) lunch box, vinyl 375.00

Cisco Kid (radio) pinback button, "Triple S Club," ca. 1942 ....20.00

Cisco Kid tie rack, wooden 95.00

Close Encounters of the Third Kind lunch box & thermos, scenes from the movie on the sides, 1977, 2 pcs. 143.00

Cool Cat & Daffy Duck Tumblers

Cool Cat tumbler, clear glass w/illustration of Cool Cat being shot at by a hunter, Warner Brothers Inter-action Series, Pepsi-Cola premium, 1976 (ILLUS. left).......................................35.00

Cornelius (Planet of the Apes) figure, flex & bend type, 1967, on original card 22.00

Daddy Warbucks (Orphan Annie comics) figure, chalk, h.p., wearing blue jacket & black trousers, marked "Chicago Tribune," 6" h. 20.00

Daffy Duck tumbler, clear glass w/illustration of Daffy in large pot, Warner Brothers Interaction Series, Pepsi-Cola premium, 1976 (ILLUS. right)...38.00

Daffy Duck tumbler, clear glass w/illustration & "Daffy Duck" on both sides, Warner Brothers Collector Series, Pepsi-Cola premium, 1973 ......7.00

Dale Evans book, "Angel Unaware," written by Dale Evans, 1953 ....12.00

Dale Evans book, "To My Son, Faith at Our House," written & signed by Dale Evans, 1957 ....25.00

Dale Evans book, "Story of Roy Rogers & Dale Evans Happy Trails," written by Dale Evans 20.00

Dale Evans cap gun, mint on card......250.00

Dale Evans wrist watch box, die-cut cardboard w/a figure of Dale on Buttermilk in the foreground, Roy & the ranch in the background & Dale & Roy on the back, 1950s, w/clear plastic lid, box only...........................138.00

Dale Evans & Buttermilk lamp, composition, Dale riding a rearing Buttermilk..200.00

Dale Evans & Buttermilk pencil box......45.00

Daniel Boone (TV) lunch box & thermos bottle, scene of Boone fighting Indians on one side, shooting a bear on the other, Aladdin Industries, 1965, 2 pcs........220.00

Daniel Boone (Fess Parker) thermos, 1965 ....22.00

Dark Shadows gum cards, Philly Gum, first series, complete set 275.00

Darth Vader (Star Wars movie) bust, ceramic, 10 x 12" 25.00

Dennis the Menace (TV) game, board-type, cartoon graphics on the cover, a black & white photograph of Dennis from the TV show on left side, game complete, Standard Toykraft, 1960 (corner split at seam) 57.00

Dennis the Menace growth chart, linen, 1975 ....15.00

Dennis the Menace paint set, unused, in very good box 45.00

Dennis the Menace teaspoon, Kellogg's premium, silver plate, w/original flyer 20.00

Dennis the Menace toy, battery-operated, Dennis plays the xylophone, mint in box, ...385.00

Dick Clark cuff links & tie bar set, "American Bandstand," ca. 1960, boxed, the set 38.00

Dick Tracy badge, brass enameled w/"Dick Tracy" & "Crime Stopper" & illustrates Dick, shield-shaped 90.00

Dick Tracy code book, "Secret Service Patrol Secret Code Book," Quaker Puffed Wheat or Rice premium, 1939 ....70.00

Dick Tracy decoder card, green, Post Cereal premium, unpunched, ca. 1950, 3½ x 6¾" 30.00

Dick Tracy lunch box w/thermos, Aladdin, 1967 ....125.00 to 150.00

Dick Tracy mask, paper, Motorola premium, 1953, unpunched 35.00

Dick Tracy Comic Art

Dick Tracy original artwork, ink on paper, portion of a daily strip featuring Tracy and The Brow, dated "8/23/44," 7 x 23" (ILLUS. of part) 1,035.00

Dick Tracy phonograph record, colorfully illustrated w/Dick & gangster enemies on jacket cover & cartoons to be traced on inside & back covers 85.00

Dick Tracy pocket knife, w/Crime Stopper whistle & clue detector, excellent condition 75.00

Dick Tracy ring, "Secret Compartment," brass, 1938 ....500.00

Dick Tracy "Soaky" container, plastic, wearing yellow trench coat & fedora w/black accents, 1965, 10¼" h. 81.00

Dick Tracy wrist radios, two-way electronic units, two complete stations, in original colorful box, Remco, 1950 ....95.00

Dick Tracy wrist watch, Remco, 1960, w/box 60.00

Dick Tracy & Police Chief figures, lead, excellent paint, 2" h., pr. 30.00

Dionne Quintuplets booklet, "Protecting the Dionnes," Lysol premium, 1936 ....14.00

Dionne Quintuplets calendar, 1936, 11 x 16½" 35.00

Dionne Quintuplets cereal bowl, chrome-plated, babies' faces in bottom, 6" d. 32.00

Dionne Quintuplets photograph, shows each one holding an identical doll, 1935, 12 x 16" 50.00

Dionne Quintuplets postcard, pictures the girls in sailor outfits 8.00

Dionne Quintuplets talcum powder, tin, portrait of baby Marie, pastel colors, 1930s 65.00

Dishonest John (Beany & Cecil cartoons) puppet, talking-type, 1962, mint condition 125.00

Dr. Seuss book, "Bartholomew and the Oobleck," 1949, first edition w/dust cover 35.00

Dr. Seuss book, "The King's Stilts," 1939, first edition w/dust cover 150.00

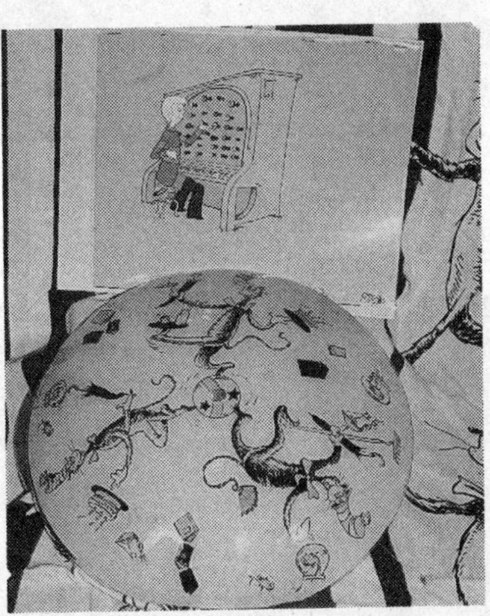

Dr. Seuss Cartoon Cel & Light Shade

Dr. Seuss book, "More Boners," 1931, first edition 50.00

Dr. Seuss book, "The 500 Hats of Bartholomew Cubbins," 1938, first edition w/dust cover 150.00

Dr. Seuss book, "How the Grinch Stole Christmas!," 1957, first edition w/dust cover......................................65.00

Dr. Seuss book, "And To Think That I Saw It On Mulberry Street," 1937, first edition w/dust cover 150.00

Dr. Seuss book, "Dr. Seuss Story-time," 1974, two volumes, each 20.00

Dr. Seuss book, "The Cat in The Hat," 1957, 1967 reprint w/dust cover 20.00

Dr. Seuss cartoon cel, original production four-cel overlay from "Pontifical Pock" (ILLUS. back) 275.00

Dr. Seuss ceiling light shade, white glass w/red, blue & black scenes of The Cat in The Hat, 1960s, 14" d. (ILLUS. front) 150.00

Dr. Seuss drawing & note, black felt tip pen note on green paper inscribed "A Special Green Egg for Sanks #2 from Dr. Seuss," w/a black & green ink drawing of an egg, matted & framed w/a picture of a typical Dr. Seuss character holding an umbrella, 13 x 17" 460.00

Dr. Seuss Lunch Box

Dr. Seuss lunch box & thermos, metal, titled "The World of Dr. Seuss," Aladdin, 1970 (ILLUS.) 100.00

Dr. Seuss Puzzle

Dr. Seuss puzzle, jigsaw-type, Essolube premium set, several in the original envelope, 1940s (ILLUS. of one)..100.00

Dr. Seuss Child's Rocker

Dr. Seuss rocking chair, child's molded plastic, figural Cat in The Hat crouching w/safety seat on its back, Coleco, 1983 (ILLUS.) 35.00

Dr. Seuss Toy Phone

Dr. Seuss toy, "Dr. Seuss Mattel-O-Phone," plastic, Mattel, 1970, sealed in original package (ILLUS.) 300.00

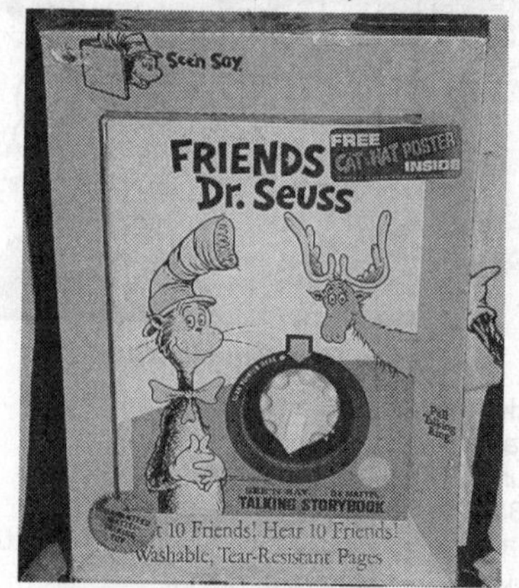

Dr. Seuss Talking Storybook

Dr. Seuss toy, "See'n Say Talking Storybook," plastic, Mattel, 1970, sealed in original package (ILLUS.) .300.00

Dudley Do-Right Lunch Box

Dudley Do-Right lunch box & thermos bottle, metal, side w/scene of Nel swooning over Dudley & his horse, Ohio Art, 1962, 2 pcs. (ILLUS.).....2,200.00

Dudley Do-Right lunch box & thermos bottle, the blue vinyl box depicting Dudley rescuing Nel from Snidley Whiplash, 1972, near mint condition, 2 pcs. 2,760.00

Eddie Cantor book, "Eddie Cantor's NBC Picture Book," Chase & Sanborn premium, 1933, opens to 18 x 23" 20.00

Eddie Cantor book, "Your Next President," 1932 ....30.00

Eddie Cantor game, board-type, "Tell It To The Judge" 75.00

Elmer Elephant (cartoons) soap, figural, Lightfoot Schultz, in original box, 1930s 115.00

Elmer Fudd (cartoons) tumbler, clear glass w/illustration & "Elmer Fudd" on both sides, Warner Brothers Collector Series, Pepsi-Cola premium, 1973......................................7.00

Elvis Presley alarm clock, windup-type, Bradley......................................45.00

Elvis Presley album award, a 'platinum' award for "Elvis in Concert," the RIAA award presented to George Parkhill to commemorate the sale of more than one million copies of the RCA Records long-playing record album, matted & framed, 17 x 21"..............................690.00

Elvis Presley album cover & records, double 45 EP-type, the cover signed in blue ball-point pen by Elvis Presley, inscribed "To Shevaunn from Elvis Presley," the two records are "Tutti Fruitti" & "Blue Suede Shoes," the set.................................690.00

Elvis Presley belt, white leather w/turquoise stones, w/silver lining & chains, made by Mike McGregor & worn by Elvis in 1970, signed by McGregor 5,463.00

Elvis Presley car key, to Elvis Presley Rolls Royce, the 'gold' key inscribed "Rolls Royce" w/Rolls Royce logo & also inscribed "Elvis Presley"........1,840.00

Elvis Presley cuff link, single engraved 'gold' cuff link w/geometric design on one side, engraved "EP" on the other, w/certificate of authenticity, 2 pcs. 920.00

Elvis Presley guitar pick, used at a concert June 23, 1973, thrown to the audience 460.00

Elvis Presley hat, 'Superfly' type, black felt w/wide removable brass band w/a large roundel at the front, w/two photos of Elvis wearing the hat in 1975-76..............................5,175.00

Elvis Presley mirror, pocket-type, pictures Elvis & his parents, 1956......25.00

Elvis Presley movie poster, "Love Me Tender," original release version w/various images of Elvis, 1956, 40 x 60" (wear on edges & corners, tear at top) 330.00

Elvis Presley Outfit

Elvis Presley outfit, stage-type, jumpsuit, cape & belt, the cream cotton jumpsuit w/zipper front, flared trousers w/lime green inserts, high collar, decorated w/green, red, gold & blue rhinestone sunburst design, w/label in the collar "Nudie's Rodeo Tailors," & tag along the zipper which has his name "Elvis Presley" & his chest size, together w/a silk-lined matching cape, finished in dazzling rhinestone design & matching belt, w/a copy of the purchaser's invoice from Nudie's, a copy of an article about Nudie & a photocopy of a picture of Elvis & Nudie, the group (ILLUS.) 17,250.00

Elvis Presley Tiger Suit

Elvis Presley outfit, two-piece suit, denim, orange stitching & orange snaps w/several images of Tigers In orange & black w/rhinestone trim, size 42, worn in late 1974, w/photocopy of a photo of Elvis wearing the suit, tagged "Faded Glory by appendasez RN 48305" (ILLUS.) 11,500.00

Elvis Presley record album, "Elvis Presley Perfect for Parties Highlight Album," full-figure drawing of Elvis on the cover, features Elvis, Tony Cabot, Tony Scott, etc., RCA, 1950s, 7" d. 155.00

Elvis Presley ring, lapis lazuli & 14k gold, large gold ring in a nugget style, w/a lapis stone mounted in the center....................................6,900.00

Elvis Presley sheet music, "Any Way You Want Me," 1950s, very fine condition 25.00

Elvis Presley sheet music, "Don't Be Cruel," 1950s, very fine condition 30.00

Elvis Presley shirt, red & white vertical candy stripe, pull-over v-neck style w/no buttons, tagged "L," probably ca. 1964 ....1,495.00

Elvis Presley souvenir photo album, the cover signed in blue ball-point pen by Elvis Presley, inscribed "yours Elvis Presley," dated "August 5, l956"..633.00

Elvis Presley sunglasses, rectangular aviator glasses w/blue tint & stainless steel frames, made in Germany w/the style "nautic / neostyle" inscribed on the inside of the frame.....................................1,380.00

Elvis Presley vest, rayon & cotton in black w/a gilt diamond tapestry pattern, by Custom Collection by Fargo, no buttons, ca. 1970..........1,955.00

Felix the Cat bank, metal, ca. 1959....250.00

Felix the Cat clicker, tin, w/"Fancy Meeting You Here Felix," Germany ...75.00

Felix the Cat figure, composition, 13" h...475.00

Felix the Cat figure, jointed wood, paint & decal in excellent condition, 1930s, 3½" h...................................143.00

Felix the Cat figure, jointed & painted wood, Felix stands on his two movable feet, w/a long tail, movable arms & an oversized smiling head complete w/leather ears, Schoenhut, ca. 1924, 7¼" h. 230.00

Felix the Cat plate, china, three images of Felix & friends, 1930s, 7" d...155.00

Felix the Cat Toy

Felix the Cat toy, windup tin, Felix in a two-wheeled cart pulled by a frisky mule (ILLUS.) 14,850.00

Flash Gordon book, pop-up type, "Flash Gordon - Tournament of Death," King Features, 1935...........150.00

Flash Gordon movie poster, "Flash Gordon Conquers the Universe," 12-part serial, starring Larry "Buster" Crabbe, Universal, 1940, one-sheet, linen-backed, 27" w., 41" h. 8,250.00

Flash Gordon movie poster, "Flash Gordon's Trip to Mars," starring Larry "Buster" Crabbe, various vignettes depicting a rocket ship, Flash Gordon, Emperor Ming & other characters, Universal, 1939, one-sheet, linen-backed, autographed by Buster Crabbe, 27 x 41" 7,820.00

Flash Gordon original artwork, color cover design for Gold Key Buck Rogers No. I, depicts Flash & Dale fighting a prehistoric monster, together w/a copy of the comic book, 19 x 25", 2 pcs. 770.00

Flash Gordon pinback button, celluloid, "Chicago Herald & Examiner," 1¼" d. 250.00

Flintstones ashtray, ceramic, shaped oblong form w/low incurved sides, features a scene of Fred & Wilma dancing in the bottom, 1960s............51.00

Flintstones bank, plastic, book-shaped 15.00

Flintstones cookie jar, cov., Fred sitting in a chair holding Pebbles on his lap, bottom impressed "c 1989 Vandor," 10" h. ...155.00

"The Rubbles" Cookie Jar

Flintstones (TV) cookie jar, cov., house-shaped w/Barney standing in the doorway & Betty looking out the window above "The Rubbles," cover w/dinosaur finial, American Bisque, impressed "USA" (ILLUS.) ...945.00

Flintstones lunch box (excellent condition) ...85.00

Flintstones paper dolls, premium in "Jack & Jill" magazine, March 1963 issued, uncut ...18.00

Flintstones postcard set, lush color set featuring the Flintstones in daily activities, cards numbered 1-9 & 6610-6612, 1964, group of 12 ...55.00

The Flying Nun (TV) costume, 1967, complete in box, fine condition ...98.00

Fonz (Happy Days - TV) paint set, paint by numbers-type, 1976, mint in box ...25.00

Fonz (Happy Days - TV) wrist watch, Time Trends, 1976 ...65.00

Foxy Grandpa toy, cast iron, Foxy Grandpa in a two-wheeled carriage painted tan, black & maroon & pulled by a tan horse, Grandpa w/oversized painted 'nodder' head, Kenton Hardware, ca. 1910, 9¾" l. ...288.00

Foxy Grandpa toy, cast iron pull-type, a small donkey pulls a large-headed nodding Foxy Grandpa in a two-wheeled cart, Hubley, ca. 1905, 6" l. (paint chipped) ...322.00

Fred Flintstone bank, vinyl, figural, Vinyl Products, 13" h. ...38.00

Fred Flintstone costume, vinyl costume & plastic mask, in original box w/cellophane window, Ben Cooper, dated 1973 (box slightly crushed on one side) ...35.00

F-Troop (TV) comic books, each shows major characters, Dell, 1966, set of 3 ...199.00

Gangbusters badge, brass w/blue enameling, "OFFICIAL Phillips H. Lord's GANGBUSTERS," minor wear ...85.00

Gene Autry belt, brown leather ...75.00

Gene Autry billfold, plastic, mint in box ...175.00

Gene Autry book, "Gene Autry Book of Adventures," hard cover, illustrated, England, 1958 ...65.00

Gene Autry cap pistol, cast iron w/orange grips, long barrel-type, 1940, mint in original box ...365.00

Gene Autry .44 cap pistol, die-cast, nickel-finish, swing-out side-loading action, revolving cylinder chambers, black horsehead grips, w/six metal bullets, 1950s, 11" l. ...275.00

Gene Autry coloring book, "Sgt. Gene Autry Sings," 1940s ...35.00

Gene Autry coloring book, 1955 ...30.00

Gene Autry comic book, "Gene Autry - March of Comics," No. 78, K.K. Publications/Western Publishing Co. ...80.00

Gene Autry cowboy outfit, consisting of chaps, vest, shirt, kerchief, lariat, hat & gun, mint condition, the set ...500.00

Gene Autry cuffs, brown leather, pr. ...150.00

Gene Autry galoshes, mint in box ...135.00

Gene Autry game, board-type, "Cowboys & Indians," Simon & Schuster, 1948 ...10.00

Gene Autry guitar, wooden, by Hemony, original case, early 1940s ...175.00 to 225.00

Gene Autry gun set: Texas Ranger double holster & two 7¾" l. guns w/inlaid grips, 3 pcs., mint in box ...700.00

Gene Autry lunch box, flat steel box w/metal handle, matching steel & glass thermos w/red cup, Universal, 1954-55 (mint condition) ...645.00

Gene Autry movie press book, "Cow Town" ...45.00

Gene Autry paper dolls, "Jimmy and Jane Visit Gene Autry at Melody Ranch," Whitman No. 1184, 1951, uncut ...150.00

Gene Autry pennant, cloth, pictures Gene riding Champion & reads "Back in the Sadde Again" ...65.00

Gene Autry pinback button, advertising "Sunbeam Bread" ...40.00

Gene Autry puzzle, jigsaw, color frame tray-type, inlay picture puzzle w/sleeve, 1950, 8 x 12" ...55.00

Gene Autry sheet music, "At Mail Call Today," pictures Gene in WWII sergeant's uniform, 1945 ...15.00

Gene Autry song book, "Gene Autry Sings," 1942 ...35.00

Gene Autry spurs, w/box, pr. ...145.00

Gene Autry writing tablet, illustration of Gene riding Champion & facsimile signature ...28.00

George Harrison (Beatles) model kit, plastic, mint & sealed in original box, Revel, 1960s 270.00

Get Smart (TV) game, board-type, color photos on the box cover, complete contents w/punched-out cards, Ideal, 1960s (one white spot on box cover) 125.00

Get Smart (TV) toy, "Get Smart Pen Radio," actual working radio, Maxwell Smart on box, Multiple Toymaker, 1960s, mint toy in original box (minor edge & surface wear on box) 178.00

Get Smart (TV) toy, Headquarters Signal Ray Gun, blue plastic gun w/Agent 86 sticker on handle, mounted on original card w/graphics of Max & reading along the bottom "The Infallible Maxwell Smart - Hero of the Get Smart TV Show!," Marx, 1960s, gun 8" l. (small red piece broken on the side of the gun) 152.00

Gilligan's Island (TV) coloring book, partially colored, Whitman, 1960s.....75.00

Gilligan's Island (TV) game, board-type, box cover illustration of the Skipper, Gilligan & Mr. Howell, Game Gems, 1960s, complete in box (tape repair on board) 600.00

Gilligan's Island (TV) game, board-type, Milton Bradley, Filmation version, 1974 ....55.00

Gonzo (Muppets) sugar bowl, cov., ceramic, Sigma, w/paper label, 1980..28.00

Grandpa Munster (TV) puppet, hand-type, vinyl, Ideal, 1964, package w/black & white cast photos, in original package...............................143.00

Green Acres (TV) game, board-type, Standard, 1960s, mint contents in original box 172.00

Green Hornet costume, Ben Cooper, mint in box 250.00

Green Hornet (TV) lunch box & thermos, scene of The Green Hornet fighting criminals, King-Seeley Thermos, 1967, 2 pcs. 418.00

Green Hornet (TV) notepad, wire spiral-bound, cardboard cover w/illus-tration of the Green Hornet & Kato, 1960s, 3 x 5"..........................136.00

Green Hornet toy, Acme Viewer, on original card 85.00

Green Hornet toy, automobile, "Black Beauty," Corgi, 1966, mint condition, 2¼ x 2¼ x 6"...................175.00 to 200.00

Gunsmoke (TV) lunch box & thermos, Matt Dillion in shoot-out on front, on horseback chasing outlaws on back, Aladdin Industries, 1959, 2 pcs. (mint condition) 690.00

Harold Lloyd (silent movies) toy, windup tin walker, a bowler-hatted figure shuffles along swinging his cane as his facial expression changes from down to all smiles, Marx, ca. 1930, 11" h. (some paint chipping) 1,725.00

Harold Teen (comic character) pinback button, Pittsburgh Post Gazette premium 28.00

Helen Trent (The Romance of Helen Trent radio show) brooch, model of an early television set, cast photo-graphs on revolving disc & appear on the screen as knob is turned.......100.00

Hogan's Heroes (TV) lunch box & thermos bottle, steel, domed, Aladdin Industries, 1966, 2 pcs. 325.00

Honey West (TV) doll, hard plastic body w/soft vinyl head & rooted blonde hair, dressed in black fabric stretch suit, Gilbert Toys, ca. 1965-66, mint in box, 11½" h. 325.00

Hopalong Cassidy badge, "Sheriff," six-pointed star, brass........................45.00

Hopalong Cassidy ballpoint pen refill, in original box...27.00

Hopalong Cassidy Barette

Hopalong Cassidy barette, brass, embossed, 2" l. (ILLUS.)...................47.50

Hopalong Cassidy bedspread, full-size, chenille ....175.00 to 250.00

Hopalong Cassidy Binoculars

Hopalong Cassidy binoculars, metal, black crinkle painted finish w/two multicolor decals, ca. 1950, 5" h. (ILLUS.) ....50.00 to 100.00

Hopalong Cassidy book (TV), pop-up type, "Hopalong Cassidy & His Young Friend Danny," Bonnie Book....................55.00

Hopalong Cassidy book, "Hopalong Cassidy Serves a Writ," by Clarence E. Mulford, Garden City Publishing Co. (cover worn)....................10.00

Hopalong Cassidy breakfast set: plate, mug & bowl; porcelain, w/colorful portraits of Hopalong & Topper on each piece, 3 pcs. 135.00

Hopalong Cassidy button, lithographed tin, "Hopalong Cassidy's Saving Rodeo" around rim w/a star & "#6-20 Foreman" in center, 1950s, 2" d....................86.00

Hopalong Cassidy coat rack, wooden, wall-type, w/three pegs, "Northland Milk" premium....................195.00

Hopalong Cassidy Pictorial Cookie Jar

Hopalong Cassidy cookie jar, cov., barrel-shaped w/picture of Hoppy & Topper within a 'rope' frame, row of cactus around bottom, cover w/saddle finial, unmarked (ILLUS.)..550.00

Hopalong Cassidy cuff links, pr. 15.00

Hopalong Cassidy drum w/drumsticks, illustration of Hoppy on both sides of the drum....................395.00

Hopalong Cassidy game, canasta, saddle-form revolving tray, set w/all cards & instructions, in original box....................250.00

Hopalong Cassidy game, "Chinese Checkers," 6-point star sheriff's badge forms board, Milton Bradley, complete....................100.00

Hopalong Cassidy game, "Target," lithographed tin, Louis Marx & Co., mint condition, 16 x 27"....................350.00

Hopalong Cassidy knife, hunting-type, in sheath, miniature, pearl-like handle, marked "Colonial Knife Co.," 4" l....................120.00

Hopalong Cassidy knife, fork & teaspoon set, stainless steel w/embossed figure of Hoppy & "Hopalong Cassidy" on each, mint in box, set of 3....................225.00

Hopalong Cassidy knife, pocket-type, Imperial Knife Co., 1950s....................95.00

Hopalong Cassidy Lamp

Hopalong Cassidy lamp, figural bullet, Aladdin Alacite glass (ILLUS.)..........250.00

Hopalong Cassidy lamp, glass, figural gun & holster, Aladdin....................425.00

Hopalong Cassidy linoleum, overall Western motif, 6' x 9'....................1,200.00

Hopalong Cassidy Lunch Box & Thermos

Hopalong Cassidy lunch box w/thermos bottle, Aladdin Industries, 1950 (ILLUS.)....................220.00

Hopalong Cassidy magazine feature, "Look," August 29, 1950....................28.00

Hopalong Cassidy manual, "Hopalong Cassidy Publicity & Exploitation Manual," contains several photographs & articles, 10 x 15"....................20.00

Hopalong Cassidy movie, "Three on a Trail," 16 mm, original box....................89.00

Hopalong Cassidy movie lobby card, "Hopalong Rides Again," color photo of Hoppy & Gabby Hayes, 1930s, 11 x 14"....................175.00

Hopalong Cassidy movie poster, "Revenge of the Sioux," full color, local theatre schedule attached, mint condition, 1940s.......175.00 to 225.00

Hopalong Cassidy mug, ceramic, multicolored bust of Hoppy, back-stamped "Hopalong Cassidy by W.S. George" in gold, 3" h. 75.00

Hopalong Cassidy pen, ballpoint-type, three-dimensional bust of Hopalong at the top, mint in box 225.00

Hopalong Cassidy pencil, mechanical-type 25.00

Hopalong Cassidy pennant, felt, black w/white lettering & picture of Hoppy on Topper, 1950 ....50.00

Hopalong Cassidy photograph album, leather w/embossed picture of Hoopy on Topper on cover, mint condition 165.00

Hopalong Cassidy Radio

Hopalong Cassidy radio, red or black metal w/silver foil design on front, Arvin, 1948 (ILLUS.) 690.00

Hopalong Cassidy record & story album, "Hopalong Cassidy & the Singing Bandit" ....100.00 to 125.00

Hopalong Cassidy record & story book album, "Hopalong Cassidy and the Square Dance Holdup," two-record set.........................100.00 to 125.00

Hopalong Cassidy Savings Club kit, in original envelope.............................225.00

Hopalong Cassidy spurs, pr. 65.00

Hopalong Cassidy stationery, 25 sheets w/envelopes in original box, lithographed, unused 65.00

Hopalong Cassidy sweater, V-neck, beige & burgandy, pictures Hopalong on front & Topper on back ....175.00 to 200.00

Hopalong Cassidy towel, cloth, "Hopalong Cassidy" above a scene of Hoppy riding a galloping Topper, name in red, 1950s, 18 x 34" 138.00

Hopalong Cassidy toy, Shooting Gallery, wind-up, Automatic Toy Co., in original box 295.00

Hopalong Cassidy Viewmaster reel, No. 955, 1950 ....14.00 to 18.00

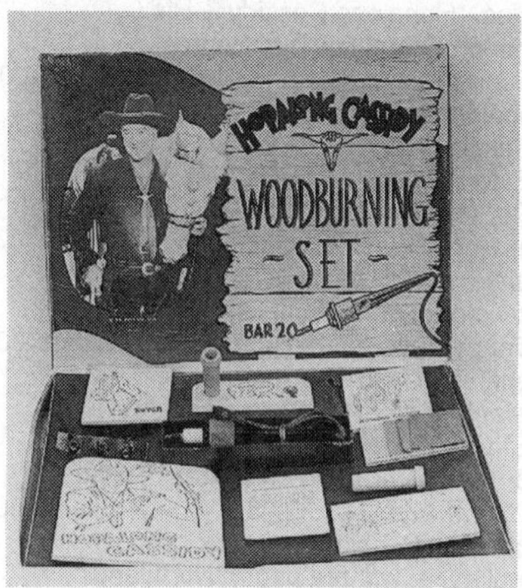

Hoppy Woodburning Set

Hopalong Cassidy woodburning set, w/electric tool & wooden plaques, American Toy Co., Chicago, 1950, in original box (ILLUS.) 250.00

Hopalong Cassidy wrist watch, large size, Bradley, 1951, w/box..............350.00

Hopalong Cassidy & Topper figures, plastic, Ideal Toys, early 1950s, Hopalong 4" h., Topper 5" h., 2 pcs. ....150.00 to 200.00

Hoss (Bonanza) doll, American Character, very fine condition, 8" h. 100.00

Howdy Doody advertising display, hanging-type, "Howdy Doody Wonder Bread," large 55.00

Howdy Doody billfold, 1950s 40.00

Howdy Doody birthday cake decorations, centerpiece & six character candleholders, mint on card...............45.00

Howdy Doody book, "Howdy Doody Fun Book," features games, puzzles & stories, 1951 ....45.00

Howdy Doody book, "Howdy Doody in the Wild West," Big Golden Book 35.00

Howdy Doody book, "Sticker Fun Book," Whitman, 1951, 10 x 12" 28.00

Howdy Doody bottle, "Welch's Grape Juice" w/Howdy's picture, 1946, 1½ pt. ....75.00 to 100.00

Howdy Doody bubble pipe, on card......55.00

Howdy Doody cap, kepi-style, complete w/pinback button on brim w/picture of Howdy 125.00

Howdy Doody card game, characters from TV show on cards, Kagran, 1950s ....25.00 to 35.00

Howdy Doody catalog. "Howdy Doody's Doodle List," 1954-55, 4 pgs. 12.00

Howdy Doody comic book, Dell No. 27, original price 10¢ 25.00

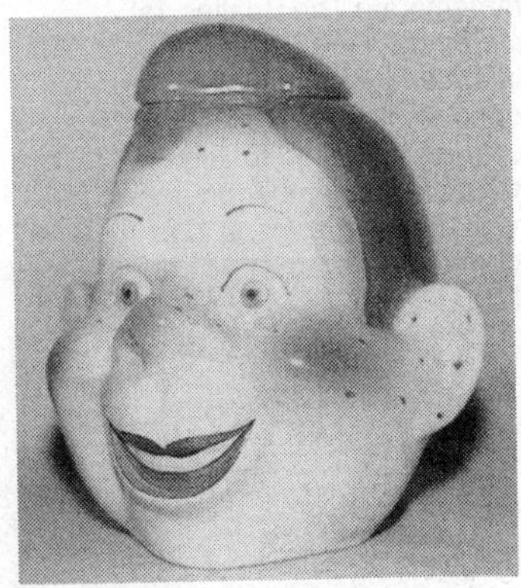

Howdy Doody Cookie Jar

Howdy Doody cookie jar, cov., head of Howdy, Purinton, early 1950s (ILLUS.) 750.00

Howdy Doody cookie jar, cov., Howdy riding in a bumper car, Vandor, 1988 ....120.00

Howdy Doody earmuffs 82.50

Howdy Doody juice jar neck tag, rectangular paper w/center hole, yellow ground featuring a colorful head of Howdy saying "Welch's is My Favorite!," 1950s, 2½ x 6" 46.00

Howdy Doody key chain, take-apart type, w/instructions 15.00

Howdy Doody mug, ceramic, 1950s, near mint 45.00

Howdy Doody night-light, figural, plastic, manufactured by Nor' east Nauticals, 7" h. ....100.00 to 150.00

Howdy Doody pencil case, Howdy "face," w/all original inside parts 120.00

Howdy Doody purse, embossed face of Howdy on front, w/shoulder strap, mint condition 145.00

Howdy Doody puzzle, jigsaw-type, "Howdy Doody's Ice Cream Shop," 11½ x 15" 15.00

Howdy Doody ring, flasher-type, cereal premium, ca. 1950 ....140.00

Howdy Doody shoe polish, w/original box 50.00

Howdy Doody sign, die-cut cardboard, illustrates Howdy promoting "Palmolive Soap" 45.00

Howdy Doody swim ring, inflatable, bright yellow w/pictures of Howdy, Clarabell & Flub-A-Dub, Ideal Novelty & Toy Corp., ca. 1950 ....75.00 to 100.00

Howdy Doody tool box, figural metal ranch house w/handle 175.00

Howdy Doody toy, windup tin, Howdy seated on open auto carriage, Nylint 350.00

Howdy Doody toy, windup tin, two-man band, Howdy tap dances as Bob Smith appears to play the highly cartooned piano, Unique Art, 1950s, 8¼" h. 690.00

Huckleberry Hound (TV) cereal bowl, plastic, Huckleberry depicted as a cowboy, jet pilot & sailor in blue against a beige ground, F & F Mold & Die Works, dated 1961, 5½" d., 2½" h. 22.00

Huckleberry Hound figure, ceramic, mint condition, 5" h. 45.00

Huckleberry Hound tie bar & cuff links, on card, the set 14.00

Huckleberry Hound Club ring, metal, 1961, very fine to excellent condition 65.00

I Dream of Jeannie (TV) Halloween costume, Ben Cooper, 1960s, excellent condition in original box 110.00

Ignatz the Mouse figure, wooden, jointed body, copyright by Geo. Herriman, 6" h. 150.00

I Love Lucy coloring book, expansive color photo cover pictures Lucy & Desi, 1954 ....110.00

Jabba the Hut (Star Wars) kit, Diorama model kit, Snap-Tite, 1983, large set, complete in fine box 35.00

Jack Armstrong (radio) flashlight, bullet-shaped 25.00

Jack Armstrong game, "Magic Answer Box," radio premium, 1938, w/original mailer 50.00

Jack Armstrong newspaper, "Tru-Flite News-Newspaper," Vol. 1, No. 1, 1944 ....30.00

Jack Armstrong telescope, "Explorer" 30.00

Jack Armstrong token, bronze, illustrates a dragon on one side & embossed "Jack Armstrong, Adventures with the Dragon" on the other side 275.00

Jack Webb (Dragnet TV) whistle 25.00

Jackie Coogan Peanut Butter Pail

Jackie Coogan pail, tin, "Peanut Butter," photo picture of Jackie on the front, w/wire bail handle, some light wear (ILLUS.) ....300.00 to 350.00

James Bond game, broad-type, "Thunderball," 1960s, w/box 65.00

James Bond lunch box & thermos, the black box w/scene depicting Bond driving a car & shooting at Dr. No, the thermos features an underwater fight scene, 1966, the set.................690.00

James Bond phonograph record album, "Goldfinger," in sleeve w/James Bond juxtaposed against golden statue on cover, Shirley Bassey, United Artists........................45.00

James Bond phonograph record album, "Thunderball," performed by Tom Jones, in sleeve w/Sean Connery as Bond & undersea battle on cover, United Artists.....................55.00

James Bond toy, automobile, "James Bond's Aston-Martin," battery-operated, complete w/packing tag & instruction sheet, mint in box 595.00

Jerry Mahoney (Paul Winchell's) pencil, w/hard rubber figural cap........30.00

Jetsons (TV) game, "Fun Pad," w/original box, 1963..........................95.00

Jetsons (TV) game, board-type, "Out Of This World," 1962.........................95.00

Jetsons (TV) lunch box & thermos, cartoon scenes, Aladdin Industries, 1963, 2 pcs. 1,200.00

Jetsons (TV) paper dolls, 1963, in original colorful folder........................45.00

Jetsons (TV) toy, "Jetsons Crayon by Number and Stencil Set," great graphics of the whole family, box in very good condition, Transogram, 1962, complete 80.00

Jimmie Allen (radio) whistle, "Secret Signal" type..45.00

Joe Palooka (comics) lunch box w/thermos, 1948 ....150.00 to 175.00

John Lennon Record Award

John Lennon award, brass, flat apple-shaped award inscribed "To Commemorate The Beatles 1st Apple Single 'Hey Jude' 4th September 1968," mounted on a wooden block base w/plaque inscribed "Presented to John Lennon," serial number on back, 4" h. (ILLUS.) 3,105.00

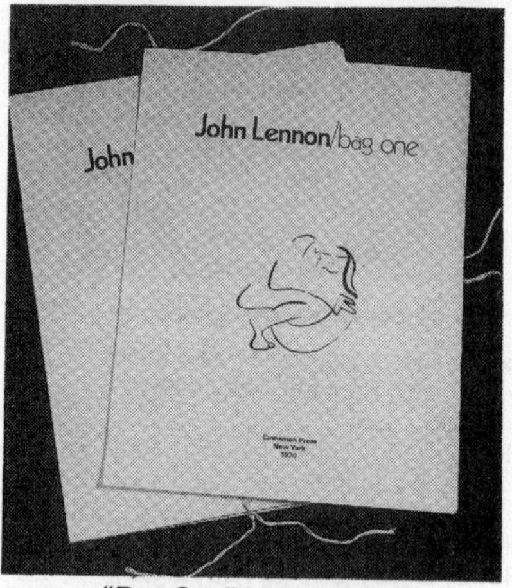

"Bag One" Lithographs

John Lennon lithographs, "Bag One," numbered limited edition comprising 13 reproductions of drawings in sepia & ink, a poem, frontispiece & explanatory page, each sheet numbered in pencil & 15 sheets w/pencil signatures of John Lennon, in white portfolio, 1970, 23 x 30", the set (ILLUS.)................................18,400.00

Jonny Quest (TV) game, board-type, nice graphics on box of Jonny talking on a walkie-talkie while Race hits a frogman, Transogram, 1964 (1 chest & 3 boats missing) 184.00

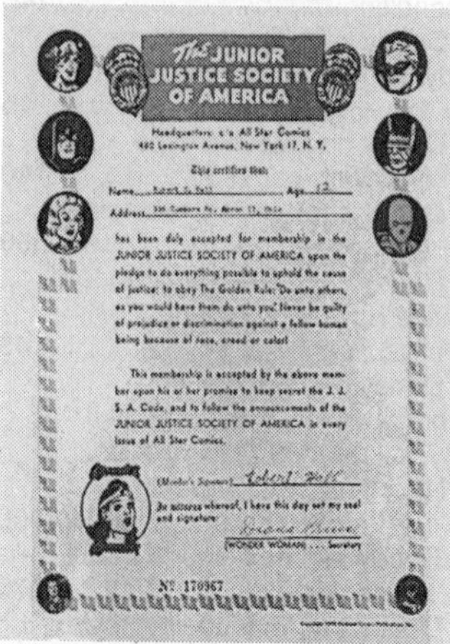
The JUNIOR JUSTICE SOCIETY OF AMERICA

Headquarters: c/o All Star Comics
480 Lexington Avenue, New York 17, N. Y.

This certifies that

Name ________ Age ____

Address ________

has been duly accepted for membership in the JUNIOR JUSTICE SOCIETY OF AMERICA upon the pledge to do everything possible to uphold the cause of justice: to obey The Golden Rule: "Do unto others, as you would have them do unto you!" Never be guilty of prejudice or discrimination against a fellow human being because of race, creed or color!

This membership is accepted by the above member upon his or her promise to keep secret the J. J. S. A. Code, and to follow the announcements of the JUNIOR JUSTICE SOCIETY OF AMERICA in every issue of All Star Comics.

(Member's Signature) ________

In witness whereof, I have this day set my seal and signature

WONDER WOMAN . . . Secretary

No. 170967

Junior Justice Society Certificate

Junior Justice Society membership kit, includes certificate, secret code, cover letter, 1½" d. metal pin & original mailing envelope, also an advertising mechanical for the Junior Justice Society membership kit scheduled to appear in *Wonder Woman #47*, 1948, the group (ILLUS. of part) 1,840.00

Kit Carson (TV) costume, 1950s 155.00

Krazy Kat Artwork

Krazy Kat original artwork, pen & ink on paper, original art for a Sunday page, features Ignatz, Krazy Kat & Ofissa Pupp, dated "9/28/41," 17 x 24½" (ILLUS.) 5,060.00

Laugh-In (TV) lunch box & thermos, front w/various cast members' faces, back w/Arte Johnson riding a tricycle, Aladdin Industries, 1970, 2 pcs. (mint condition)......................220.00

Lawman (TV) lunch box & thermos bottle, scene of two lawmen w/guns drawn, King-Seeley Thermos, 1961, 2 pcs. (mint condition).....................275.00

Liberace Jacket

Liberace outfit, stage-type, a gold & blue raised-nap jacket embellished w/clear rhinestones in a swirling leaf pattern, the lapels & border trimmed in gold lamé, a green silk dolphin lining throughout, w/a white rayon dress shirt w/velcro front closures & removable sleeves trimmed w/white lace & gold bugle beads & w/rhinestone cuff buttons, also a black beaded clip bow tie, jacket designed by Acuna, the group (ILLUS. of jacket) 1,035,00

Li'l Abner greeting cards, 1950s, set of 15, in original package..................25.00

Li'l Abner tumbler set: includes illustrations of Abner, Daisy Mae, Mammy Yokum, Pappy Yokum, Lonesome Polecat, Schmoos, Unwashable Jones; clear glass, United Features Syndicate, 1949, 4¾" h., set of 7...............................145.00

Li'l Abner wrist watch, Li'l Abner saluting a waving American flag on face, New Haven Clock Co., ca. 1947, w/original box.........375.00 to 400.00

Lily Munster (TV) doll, vinyl, Remco, 1960s, mint & sealed in original box 431.00

Little Annie Rooney & Zero tea set: cov. teapot & four cups & saucers; authorized by King Features Syndicate Inc., marked "Japan," 1935, 9 pcs. 195.00

Little Joe (Bonanza) doll, American Character, near mint condition, 8" h..165.00

Little Lulu (cartoons) bank, vinyl, small 25.00

Little Lulu coloring book, 1944..............18.00

Little Lulu (cartoons) doll, cloth, Lulu wearing a red dress trimmed w/white rick-rack & wearing a floppy hat, matching labeled purse, Georgene Novelties, ca. 1944, 13½" h...403.00

Little Lulu paint book, 1946..................32.00

Little Lulu puzzle, jigsaw-type, 1958.....35.00

Lone Ranger badge, "Deputy," w/secret compartment, 1949 ....95.00

Lone Ranger Bandana

Lone Ranger bandana, red, black & white linen, ca. 1940, 21 x 23" (ILLUS.) ....45.00 to 60.00

Lone Ranger belt, leather, 1950s 75.00

Lone Ranger bib overalls, child's, 1938 ....300.00

Lone Ranger book, "The Lone Ranger & the Secret of Somber Cavern," 1950, excellent condition 45.00

Lone Ranger cereal bowl, ceramic, embossed "Good Luck - From Lone Ranger" 55.00

Lone Ranger clothes brush, 1938 ....38.00

Lone Ranger comic book, Dell No. 125, 1940, fine condition 30.00

Lone Ranger comic book, entitled "His Mask & How He Met Tonto," 1954.....15.00

Lone Ranger egg cup, cream-colored porcelain, pictures Clayton Moore as the Lone Ranger, ca. 1950 ....40.00 to 60.00

Lone Ranger Chalk Figure

Lone Ranger figure, chalkware, carnival-type, 15" h. ....100.00 to 140.00

Lone Ranger figure, molded plastic, blue shirt & pants, Hartland, 1950s, 7" h. (wear on nose, minor scratches on body) 35.00

Lone Ranger First Aid Kit

Lone Ranger "First Aid" kit, tin, manufactured by The American White Cross Labs, Inc., dated 1938, w/contents, 4 x 4" (ILLUS.) 125.00

Lone Ranger flashlight, "Signal Siren," w/silver bullet code, original box ....100.00 to 150.00

Lone Ranger flashlight-ring, complete in box w/instructions ....90.00 to 100.00

Lone Ranger Target Game

Lone Ranger game, "Target," square tin board, red metal gun, two darts, Marx, 1938, 9½ x 9½" board, w/box (ILLUS.) 135.00

Lone Ranger guitar, 1940s, w/original box ....125.00 to 175.00

Lone Ranger Hairbrush

Lone Ranger hairbrush, wood w/color decal of the Lone Ranger on Silver, 1939, mint in box (ILLUS.) 145.00

Lone Ranger lunch box w/thermos bottle, 1950s ....150.00 to 225.00

Lone Ranger membership card, "U.S. Savings Bond Peace Patrol," w/picture of Clayton Moore, unused 20.00

Lone Ranger membership kit, "Legend of the Lone Ranger," Cheerios premium, 1980 ....40.00

Lone Ranger movie viewer, w/boxed films, original display box, 1948.......145.00

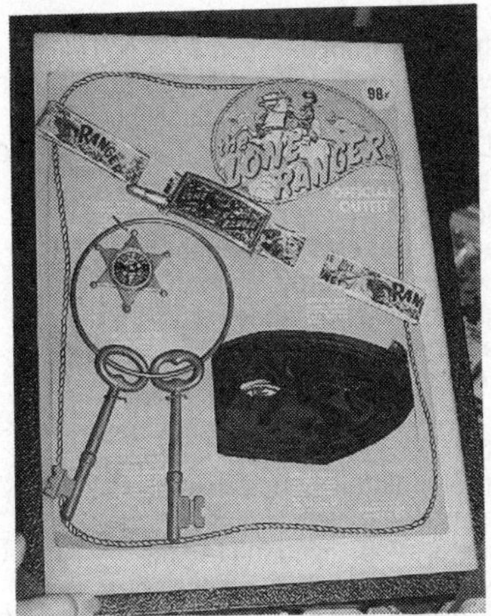

Lone Ranger Outfit

Lone Ranger outfit, consisting of a mask, two jail keys on a ring, badge, key chain & belt, mint on card w/scene of the Lone Ranger & Silver in one corner & lettered "The Lone Ranger Official Outfit," framed (ILLUS.) 350.00

Lone Ranger paint book, 1938, unused, 11 x 14" ....30.00 to 40.00

Lone Ranger paper premium, a full color scene of the Lone Ranger on a rearing Silver, based on a painting by Sheffield, possibly a bread company premium, 1943, 10 x 13" (folds, creases) 120.00

Lone ranger pedometer, 1943, Kix Cereal premium, mint in box ....25.00 to 55.00

Lone Ranger pen, ballpoint, "Silver Bullet Secret Code," 1950s, mint on card 45.00

Lone Ranger pencil box, 1940s, 4 x 8" 50.00

Lone Ranger pinback button, "Lone Ranger Safety Club Cobakco," metal 75.00

Lone Ranger pinback button, red & blue enamel on gold-tone metal, "Silvercup Bread" premium, reads "Safety Scout Membership Badge," mint condition 90.00

Lone Ranger play set, "Rodeo Ranch," including figures, horses, fencing, wagon, trees, cactus & instructions, w/original box & bags 435.00

Lone Ranger postcard, from "Bond Bread," offering membership in the Lone Ranger Safety Club, 1939, unused 50.00

Lone Ranger rifle, plastic, "Lone Ranger Cap Shooting Carbine Rifle," silver plastic w/metal cap loading trigger, box top w/fine illustration of the Lone Ranger & Tonto & the rifle, rifle stock embossed "The Lone Ranger," Marx, 1950s, 25" l. (box w/damaged corners) 197.00

Lone Ranger ring, film strip-type, w/film, 1940s ....125.00 to 150.00

Lone Ranger sheet music, "Hi-Yo Silver," Chappell Music Co., 1938 copyright 38.00

Lone Ranger snow dome, 3" d. clear glass dome containing figures of Lone Ranger & small calf, plastic base w/decal lettered "Lone Ranger Round-up," 1950s, 4" h. .....80.00 to 100.00

Lone Ranger Telescope

Lone Ranger telescope, yellow & green tube w/scene of the Lone Ranger on Silver, w/original box (ILLUS.) 264.00

Lone Ranger tent w/original box.........300.00

Lone Ranger toy, "Lone Ranger - An Authentic Punch-Out set," includes sturdy cardboard punch-out figures of the Lone Ranger & Tonto, their horses & Western gear, fine graphics of the Lone Ranger on the box cover, DeJournette Mfg., 1930s, complete (fence part punched out) ..200.00

Lone Ranger toy, windup tin, the masked man seated on a rearing Silver, when wound the lariat swirls & Silver circles, Marx, 7½" h. 375.00

Lone Ranger & Silver figure, composition, the Lone Ranger posed on a rearing Silver, marked "1938 L. Ranger Ent.," 4½" h. 60.00

Lone Ranger & Silver figures, plastic, Gabriel, 1973, Lone Ranger 10" h. & Silver 11" h., 2 pcs. 160.00

Looney Tunes pen set, figural, includes Coyote, Road Runner, Pepe Lepew & Tasmanian Devil, set of 4, mint condition...........................30.00

Lost in Space (TV) doll, vinyl, representing the character Judy, cloth clothes, plastic boots, insert card w/color photo of the cast, Japan, in tall clear cylinder container, 1960s, doll 9½" h. (boots discolored, slight damage to plastic case) 258.00

Lost in Space (TV) game, board-type, Milton Bradley, 1960s, complete in original box 46.00

Louis Armstrong toy, wind-up, w/trumpet sound, Japan 350.00

Lum & Abner's (radio) Family Almanac, 1936....................15.00 to 20.00

Madonna Leather Bracelet

Madonna bracelet, pink leather, covered w/spikes & studs, worn on stage, w/a March 4, I985 issue of *Time* magazine w/a picture of Madonna wearing the bracelet, 2 pcs. (ILLUS.) 1,380.00

Maggie (Bringing Up Father comics) charm, full-figure, silver finish (somewhat tarnished) 18.00

Maggie & Jiggs salt & pepper shakers, figural, porcelain, Japan, pr. 95.00

Mandrake the Magician (comics) magic kit, King Features Syndicate, 1949, w/original box........................160.00

Man from U.N.C.L.E. (TV) coloring book, 1967 ....65.00

Man from U.N.C.L.E. (TV) game, board-type, w/original box.................65.00

Man from U.N.C.L.E. (TV) game, "Secret Code Wheel Pinball Game," pinball-style bagatelle device w/code wheel in center & marbles, Marx Toys, 1966, 10 x 11 x 22" 160.00

Man from U.N.C.L.E. (TV) magazine, "TV Week," black & white cover photo of actor Robert Vaughn, November 15, 1964, story inside 30.00

Mary Marvel (comics) wrist watch, Bradley, 1948, w/plastic box 375.00

Matt Dillion (Gunsmoke - TV) shirt & chaps, 1950s 160.00

Maverick (TV) masquerade costume, 1959, in original box.......................195.00

Michael Jackson leather jacket, bright red w/the "Marc Laurent Paris" label inside, covered w/many zippers & metal mesh design at the shoulder, worn by Jackson in the video for the song "Beat It," together w/two photos, one of Jackson wearing the jacket, the other of Jackson w/the boy to whom he gave it, note of authenticity from Jackson & newspaper article, the group 7,763.00

Mighty Mouse (cartoons) doll, vinyl, by Dakin, mint in package, 6" h. 27.00

Mighty Mouse doll, stuffed cloth, molded soft vinyl face & black plush head & outer ears, inner ears & hands pink corduroy, uniform of bright yellow slick fabric w/red shorts & feet, cape red slick fabric w/name in yellow, Ideal Toys, mid-1950s, 14" h..100.00

Mighty Mouse toy, rubber, squeeze-type, standing w/hands clenched at sides of chest, yellow outfit w/red shorts & shoes, wearing red felt cape, "Mighty Mouse" across chest, early 1950s, 9¼" h. 80.00

Mr. Ed (TV) puppet, "Mr. Ed Talking Plush Hand Puppet," Mattel, 1962, mint & sealed in original box...........109.00

Mr. Magoo toy, automobile, tin, "Crazy Car," battery-operated, Hubley, mint ....275.00 to 295.00

Mr. Spock Tunic

Mr. Spock (Star Trek) tunic, a Starship Enterprise tunic worn on the television show "Star Trek," blue velour side-zippered tunic w/a black knit collar, gold brocade on cuffs & insignia on upper left chest, inside tunic is a Western Costume Company tag reading "No. 2207-1 Leonard Nimoy" (ILLUS.) 5,280.00

Monkees playing cards, full deck..........40.00

Mummy (The) toy, paddle ball, distributed by Universal Pictures, mint on card 35.00

Munsters (TV) game, board-type, "Munsters Drag Race Game," box cover cartoon graphics of Herman driving a dragster, inside pieces assembled & complete, Hasbro, 1965 (surface & edge wear on box, tape mark & some writing in one corner) 569.00

Munsters (TV) toy, "The Munsters Cartoon Kit," Colorforms, box cover signed by Butch Patrick, mint contents, 1960s 103.00

Munsters (TV) toy, "Munster Koach," plastic, AMT, unassembled in original box, 1960s 103.00

Munsters (TV) toy, "Munsters Rub-Ons, " partially used in original box, complete contents, Hasbro, 1960s (minor box surface & edge wear) 322.00

Munsters (TV) toy, "Munster's Stardust Touch of Velvet Art Set," partially used, contents 95% complete, Hasbro, 1960s (minor edge wear) 201.00

Mutt & Jeff (comics) comic book, "The Adventures of Mutt & Jeff," by Bud Fisher, published by Cupples & Leon Co., ca. 1930 .... 175.00

My Favorite Martian (TV) magic set, Gilbert, 1964, unused in very fine box 150.00

My Favorite Martian (TV) toy, "My Favorite Martian Plastic Palette Coloring Set," nice box graphics, Standard Toykraft, 1960s, near mint contents in original box (side seam splits on box) 103.00

Myrt & Marge (radio) record, Wrigley's Gum premium, radio drama on one side & reverse side shows radio station broadcasting the program & shows gum box, 4" d. 55.00

Olive Oyl charm, full-figure, silver finish (somewhat tarnished) 18.00

Olive Oyl pony tail holder, mint on card 65.00

Orphan Annie bank, dime register 90.00

Orphan Annie book, "Orphan Annie Captain's Secrets," 1942 .... 30.00

Orphan Annie book, pop-up type, "The 'Pop-Up' Little Orphan Annie and Jumbo the Circus Elephant," ca. 1930 .... 100.00 to 130.00

Orphan Annie cane, carnival-type, china head 100.00

Orphan Annie decoder, 1935, Ovaltine premium 35.00

Orphan Annie decoder, 1936, w/secret compartment, excellent condition 50.00

Orphan Annie decoder, 1939, Ovaltine premium 38.00

Orphan Annie decoder, Speedomatic, 1940 .... 75.00 to 100.00

Orphan Annie decoder w/Secret Society manual, in original mailer, 1939, 2 pcs. 175.00

Orphan Annie decoder manual, 1936 .... 75.00 to 85.00

Orphan Annie figure, wood-jointed, stamped "Harold Gray," 4¾" h. 95.00

Orphan Annie map of Simmons Corners, Tucker County, 1936, 19 x 24" 120.00

Orphan Annie Mug

Orphan Annie mug, creamware pottery, w/decal picture of Annie & Sandy, Ovaltine premium, signed "Harold Gray" (ILLUS.) .... 40.00 to 50.00

Orphan Annie pinback button, Kellogg's Pep cereal premium 15.00

Orphan Annie pinback button "Secret Society" 25.00

Orphan Annie puzzle, "Tucker County Race Puzzle," 1933 .... 50.00

Orphan Annie ring, "Look Around," near mint condition 70.00

Orphan Annie ring, two-initial signet-type, 1937 .... 135.00

Orphan Annie rope maker kit, complete w/partially made rope, 1930s 90.00

Orphan Annie token, "Good Luck" coin, "Radio Secret Society" 30.00

Orphan Annie toy, electric stove, tin, green & tan w/good decals, w/three pots, 8½ x 9½" .... 50.00 to 70.00

Orphan Annie whistle, tin, 1942 .... 60.00

Orphan Annie wrist watch, colorful full-figure Annie on watch face, dark blue band, New Haven Clock Co., ca. 1947, w/original box ... 300.00 to 325.00

Orphan Annie & Sandy ashtray, figural, china, lustre finish, marked by Famous Artists Syndicate .... 100.00 to 120.00

Orphan Annie & Sandy wall pocket vase, china, Annie & Sandy on white ground, tan pearlized trim, marked "Licensed by Famous Artists Syndicate, Made in Japan," 3" top d., 5¼" h. 95.00

Oswald Rabbit Cel

Oswald the Lucky Rabbit cartoon cel, black & white, depicting a determined Oswald carrying a football, gouache on celluloid, ca. 1930, framed, 8½ x 12" (ILLUS.) 920.00

Outer Limits (TV) game, board-type, interesting monsters on the cover, Milton Bradley, 1960s, complete in original box 126.00

Paladin (Have Gun -- Will Travel, TV) clock, wall-type, mint in box 45.00

Paladin (Have Gun -- Will Travel, TV) lunch box, 1960 ....65.00

Partridge Family (TV) paper dolls, 1973, cut but complete 25.00

Patty Duke (TV) game, board-type, 1963 ....35.00 to 45.00

Paul McCartney (Beatles) Halloween costume, flocked hair on mask, soft cloth costume w/button illustration of the Beatles, 1960s (minor crack in chin of mask, minor tear in trousers) 126.00

Paul McCartney (Beatles) Soakie container, molded plastic, in original open-faced box w/a picture of the Beatles on the back, 1960s, 10" h. ..166.00

Peanuts Gang megaphone, lithographed tin, Chein Mfg. (some light scratches) 25.00

Peanuts Artwork

Peanuts original artwork, pen & ink on paper, a daily strip featuring Lucy, dated "9/7/79," 7 x 24" (ILLUS. of part) 483.00

Petticoat Junction (TV) coloring book, partially colored, Whitman, 1960s......63.00

Phantom (The) (comics) game, three-game board set, unpunched, complete in box, 1956......................125.00

Pogo Comic Art

Pogo (comic strip) original comic art, pen & ink on paper, from a daily strip dated "4/13/54," featuring Pogo & Albert, 4½ x 16" (ILLUS. of part) 1,150.00

Popeye Auto Magic Picture Gun, together w/six films, instructions & screen, dated 1938 ....165.00

Popeye bank, ceramic, Popeye bust w/original pipe, American Bisque Pottery ....400.00 to 450.00

Popeye bank, chalkware, bust-shaped 125.00

Popeye bank, dime register, metal w/slide trap, King Features Syndicate, 1929, 2½" sq. 95.00

Popeye book, "Popeye & The Pirates," animated, illustrated by Sagendorf, 1945, spiral-bound..................................95.00

Popeye card game, Whitman, 1934, w/box 35.00

Popeye Christmas card, 1934, Hallmark...35.00

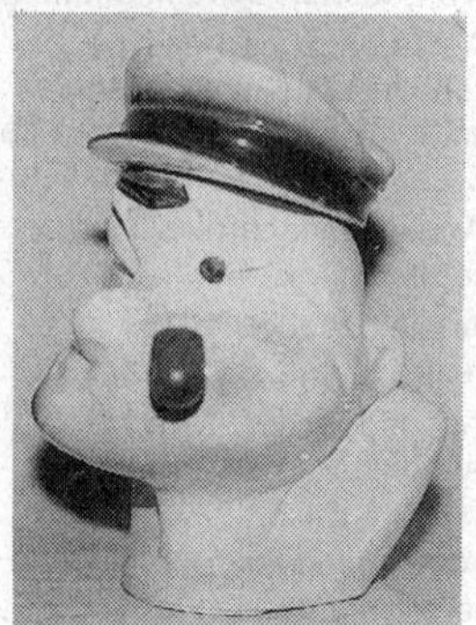

Popeye Cookie Jar

Popeye cookie jar, cov., ceramic, bust of Popeye, American Bisque Co., marked "USA" (ILLUS.) ....1,000.00 to 1,200.00

Popeye cookie jar, cov., ceramic, bust of Popeye, Vandor, "Copyright 1980 King Features Syndicate, Inc." paper label, 8½" h. 485.00

Popeye doll, cloth, marked "King Features Syndicate," 1930s, 16" h...148.00

Popeye figure, Fun-E-Flex, hollow celluloid, pre-war, 3½" h. 125.00

Popeye game, pinball-type, lithographed w/Popeye surrounded by various foods, each marked w/a score, in original box, 23" h.............425.00

Popeye game, "Pin the Pipe on Popeye," 1937, mint condition 65.00

Popeye game, "Pipe Toss," Rosebud Art Co., 1935, original box 95.00

Popeye game, "Popeye the Juggler" bead game, glass covered, 1929 copyright, 3½ x 5" 45.00

Popeye game, "Where's Me Pipe ," 1937, w/original box............50.00 to 75.00

Popeye gumball machine, Hasbro Mfg., 1968...40.00

Popeye napkin ring, Bakelite 45.00

Popeye pencil, Eagle Pencil Co., New York, 1929, mint in box, 10¾" l. 95.00

Popeye phonograph record, entitled "Favorite Sea Songs," 1959..............28.00

Popeye phonograph record player, Emerson, 1950s..............100.00 to 125.00

Popeye pinback button, enameled picture, 1930s 65.00

Popeye pipe, whistle-type, Northwestern Products, 1930s 115.00

Popeye pipe/kazoo, tin & cardboard, 1934, 3" l. ....50.00 to 60.00

Popeye play set, "Popeye the Printer" set, 1935, w/original box 85.00

Popeye pocketknife, simulated mother-of-pearl handle w/an applied blue full-figured Popeye, two blades, marked "King Features Syndicate," ca. 1940 ....120.00

Popeye "Soaky" container, plastic, 1960s, excellent condition, 10" h. 30.00

Popeye toy, pull-type, lithographed paper on wood, "Boom-Boom Popeye," Popeye w/Swee' Pea beating out a tune on a drum, on wheeled base, Fisher-Price, 7½" l. ....325.00 to 350.00

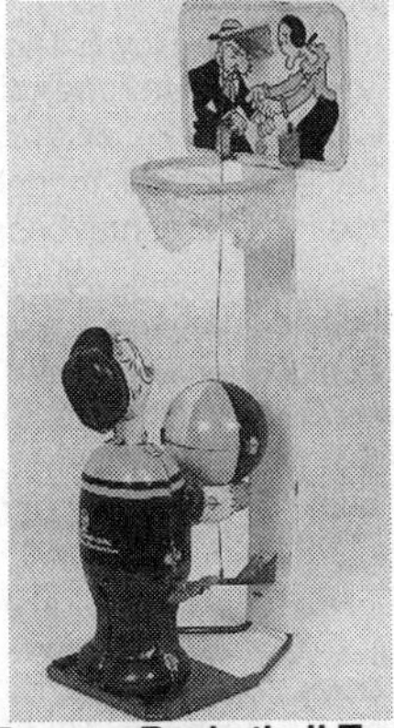

Popeye Basketball Toy

Popeye toy, windup tin, Popeye the basketball player, featuring a lithographed figure who shoots a basketball into the net above, Line Mar, 9" h. (ILLUS.) 1,045.00

Popeye Drummer Toy

Popeye toy, windup tin, Popeye standing & playing a drum, red, white & blue outfit & red & white drum, J. Chein, some wear, 7⅛" h. (ILLUS.) 1,045.00

"Popeye Express" Toy

Popeye toy, windup tin, "Popeye Express" walker, Popeye figure pushing a wheelbarrow containing a steamer trunk w/pop-up parrot, Marx, ca. 1937, 8¼" h. (ILLUS.) ....500.00 to 600.00

Popeye toy, windup tin, Popeye w/upright punching bag, featuring Popeye standing on lithographed green base working out on an orange punching bag, Chein, ca. 1932, 7½" h..................900.00 to 1,000.00

Popeye toy, windup tin, Popeye carrying parrot cages, Marx, 1935, 8½" h...............................450.00 to 500.00

Popeye toy, windup tin, Popeye on a tricycle, featuring a lithographed figure w/celluloid arms pedaling his tricycle, Line Mar, 4½" h.............................775.00 to 850.00

Popeye writing tablet, picturing Popeye w/no hat, Olive Oyl & Wimpy looking on, King Features Syndicate, 1929 (unused).................18.00

Popeye & Olive Oyl figures, plastic, 1957, mint in package, each 3" h., pr...10.00

Popeye & Olive Oyl toy, windup tin, lithographed Popeye dances on the rooftop, as Olive sways & appears to play the accordion, Louis Marx, ca. 1935, w/original red & black lithographed box, 9½" h........................1,000.00 to 1,500.00

Popeye & Wimpy "Walk-A-Way," Marx, 1964, mint in box....................90.00

Porky Pig lamp, composition, table-type, colorful, 1940.........................295.00

Porky Pig lunch box, scene depicting Porky's lunch wagon w/a variety of Warner Brothers characters waiting for lunch prepared by Porky, near mint, 1959......................................552.00

Porky Pig wrist watch, the face featuring Porky whose arms are the hands of the watch, brown band, Ingraham Co., ca. 1949, in original lithographed box.............500.00 to 575.00

Prince Valiant (comic strip) bank, dime register, marked "King Features Syn.," 1954.......150.00 to 200.00

Princess SummerFall/WinterSpring (Howdy Doody, TV) toy, puppet, push-type, 1950s, near mint, 6" h...68.00

Quick Draw McGraw (TV cartoons) cartoon cel, depicting Quick Draw in front of train tracks, gouache on full celluloid applied to a water-color production background, unframed, Hanna-Barbera Studios, ca. 1960s, 7 x 9"...253.00

Quick Draw McGraw (TV) magazine, "TV Week," black & white picture of Quick Draw on the cover, story inside, May 22, 1960.........................25.00

Raggedy Ann & Andy rocking horse w/bench seat for toddlers..................90.00

Rat Patrol (TV) game, "Rat Patrol Spin to Win Game," Pressman, 1967 (box wear)..............................40.00

Red Ryder BB Gun, Daisy Mfg., 1950s...125.00

Red Ryder paint book, 1941................45.00

Ricochet Rabbit (TV) book, "Showdown at Gopher Gulch Bakery," authorized by Hanna-Barbera..10.00

Ringo Starr (Beatles) figure, chalkware, nodder-type, 7½" h...75.00

Ringo Starr (Beatles) Soakie container, molded plastic, in original open-faced box, picture of the Beatles on the box back, 1960s, 10" h...174.00

Rin Tin Tin (TV) pen, rifle-shaped, premium, w/original mailer, mint condition ....50.00 to 75.00

Rin Tin Tin (TV) pinback button, w/sepia tone photograph, ½" d. 20.00

Rin Tin Tin (TV) scrapbook, spiral-bound, unused...................................35.00

Rin Tin Tin (TV) toy, "Rin Tin Tin 3-D Viewer" & cards, cereal premium, in original box 100.00

Robin (Batman's partner) bank, ceramic, 1966 ....65.00 to 75.00

Robin (Batman's partner) wrist watch, his picture on the face w/the Batman logo behind him, Timex, 1978 ....150.00

Rocky & Bullwinkle cartoon cel, publicity-type, gouache on celluloid depicting Bullwinkle standing next to Rocky Squirrel, holding a 'Rocky Fan Club - Bullwinkle Moose, President' sign which Boris Badenov is busy sawing, much to the delight of Natasha Fatale, ca. 1960, 8½ x 11" 1,035.00

Rocky & Bullwinkle (TV cartoon) game, board-type, "Rocky & Bullwinkle Magic Dot Game," colorful Rocky & Bullwinkle on the box cover, includes gameboard, spinner & magic crayons, Whitman, 1962 (tissues missing).......................75.00

Rowan and Martin's "Laugh-In" (TV) coloring book, Saalfield, 1968, unused 65.00

Roy Rogers alarm clock, animated, Ingraham, 1951...............250.00 to 300.00

Roy Rogers bandana, red w/lariat design around border, Roy & Trigger pictured, "Roy Rogers" in rope-print script 75.00

Roy Rogers bank, pot metal, model of a cowboy boot on horseshoe base, 6" h.......................................50.00 to 75.00

Roy Rogers billfold, leather 45.00

Roy Rogers book, "Roy Rogers & The Gopher Creek Gunman," worn dust jacket, 1945 ....20.00

Roy Rogers book, "Roy Rogers and the Raiders of Sawtooth Ridge," hard cover, illustrated, w/dust jacket, 1946..20.00

Roy Rogers book, "Roy Rogers, King of the Cowboys," Whitman, 1956.......65.00

Roy Rogers Book Bag

Roy Rogers book bag, brown leatherette, 13" w., 10" h. (ILLUS.) 145.00

Roy Rogers coloring book, 1951, mint 40.00

Roy Rogers crayon set w/stencils, unused 195.00

Roy Rogers cuff links & tie bar set, figural boots & saddle , on original card 35.00

Roy Rogers Horseshoe Set

Roy Rogers game, "Horseshoe Set," two tin targets w/sticks & four vinyl horseshoes, Ohio Art Co., 7¼ x 14" box (ILLUS.) 145.00

Roy Rogers guitar, cardboard & wood, Jefferson, in original illustrated cardboard shipping box ....150.00 to 200.00

Roy Rogers guitar, red plastic, in original guitar-shaped box, mint condition, 2 pcs. 250.00

Roy Rogers harmonica, on original card 95.00

Roy Rogers hat, tan felt..........50.00 to 60.00

Roy Rogers knife scabbard, vinyl, worn on belt, excellent condition........35.00

Roy Rogers lantern, tin, battery-operated, Ohio Art Co., w/box, 12" h. ....125.00 to 150.00

Roy Rogers "Lucky" Horseshoe

Roy Rogers "lucky" horseshoe, hard rubber (ILLUS.) ....25.00 to 35.00

Roy Rogers lunch box w/thermos, "Chow Wagon" ....125.00 to 150.00

Roy Rogers lunch box w/thermos bottle, "Double R Bar Ranch" metal box, ca. 1960 ....125.00

Roy Rogers lunch box, tan vinyl, "Saddlebag," pictures Roy & Trigger, King-Seeley Thermos, 1960, mint condition 195.00

Roy Rogers movie poster, "Down Dakota Way," 1949 ....175.00 to 225.00

Roy Rogers movie poster, "Man From Oklahoma," 1940s 175.00

Roy Rogers Mug

Roy Rogers mug, hard plastic, modeled in the form of Roy wearing a cowboy hat, Quaker Oats premium, ca. 1950, 4½" h. (ILLUS.) 65.00

Roy Rogers notebook, loose leaf-type, w/zipper 135.00

Roy Rogers paint set, Sugar Crisp premium, 1954, complete 45.00

Roy Rogers paper dolls, "Roy Rogers Corral," uncut 95.00

Roy Rogers puzzle, jigsaw-type, color scene of Roy standing at the top of stairs, Whitman, 1950s, complete in box 25.00

Roy Rogers raincoat, yellow slicker w/black trim, original tag ..200.00 to 275.00

Roy Rogers rifle, "Big Game Rifle," cap-firing replica of a .348 caliber game rifle, Marx, mid-1950s, 34" l. ..140.00

Roy Rogers ring, "Microscope," ca. 1949 ....125.00 to 150.00

Roy Rogers saddle, child's size....400.00

Roy Rogers saddle blanket 250.00

Roy Rogers shirt, Western-style, w/original Roy Rogers label & tag, near mint....75.00 to 100.00

Roy Rogers spurs, George Schmidt Co., 1949, pr. 20.00

Roy Rogers toy,"Fix-It Stagecoach," w/two horses, all parts in original display box, Hartland 195.00

Roy Rogers toy, play set, "Roy Rogers Fix-It Chuck Wagon & Jeep," plastic, includes seated figures of Roy, Dale & Pat Brady, a horse-drawn chuck wagon w/accessories & "Nellybelle" jeep, Ideal (Brooklyn, NY), mint in original box, the set....225.00

Roy Rogers wrist watch, w/unusual goldtone case & matching band, Bradley, 1951 ....375.00

Roy Rogers wrist watch, green face w/picture of Roy & Trigger, original brown leather band, Ingraham, 1951, w/box ....250.00 to 300.00

Roy Rogers & Dale Evans bedspread, shown riding in a jeep 175.00

Roy Rogers & Dale Evans lunch box & thermos, the box w/a blue band, the front depicts Roy riding Trigger w/Dale waving to him from the Double R Bar Ranch, the thermos depicts all three, mint condition, 1954 ....299.00

Roy Rogers & Dale Evans record album, "Songs of the Old West," w/original album cover 28.00

Roy Rogers, Dale Evans & Buttermilk figural soap set, Roy bust, Dale posed on rearing Buttermilk, original box, Hartland, the set 420.00

Roy Rogers & Trigger bank, porcelain, Roy riding Trigger rearing, signed "Roy Rogers & Trigger," mint condition 245.00

Roy Rogers & Trigger box-type camera, w/original box....125.00

Roy Rogers on Trigger lamp, figural, plastic w/plaster base, very good original shade, base 12½" h....200.00 to 300.00

Roy Rogers & Trigger peanut machine, coin-operated, bunkhouse shape w/decal of Roy & Trigger, 1950s 175.00

Roy Rogers & Trigger postcard 7.00

Scrappy (cartoons) doll, cloth & composition, the little boy w/molded hair, side-glancing eyes & open smiling mouth wearing a beige shirt & black two-button shorts & oversized molded brown shoes & cap, E.D. & T.C. Co., w/original tag, ca. 1935, 14½" h. 230.00

Sergeant Preston cards, "Yukon Adventure," ca. 1950, original envelope, set of 36 ....70.00

Sergeant Preston flashlight, secret two-way signal type 65.00

Sergeant Preston gold ore detector, complete w/instructions, w/box....145.00

Sergeant Preston pedometer, in original mailer w/instructions ....45.00 to 50.00

The Shadow Cape & Hat

The Shadow (radio) cape & hat, black material w/red trim & collar on the cape w/a red logo medallion on front, offered for Christmas, 1940, 2 pcs. (ILLUS.) 1,035.00

The Shadow coloring book, No. 4636, Saalfield, 1974 ....65.00

The Shadow ring, crocodile, plastic w/black stone, Carey Salt premium, 1947 ....900.00

Shari Lewis toy, Colorform set, 1960s 22.00

Sherman (Bullwinkle TV) bank, ceramic, figural, 1960 ....345.00

Shirley Temple book, "How I Raised Shirley Temple," by her mother, 1935, Saalfield, #945, 40 pp. ....75.00 to 100.00

Shirley Temple book, "My Young Life," 1945, Garden City Publishing Co. 35.00

Shirley Temple book, "Shirley Temple and The Screaming Spector," Whitman, No. 2311, 1946 ....30.00

Shirley Temple book, "The Shirley

Temple Edition of Captain January & The Little Colonel," 1959, Random House, No. X-5 ....18.00 to 20.00

Shirley Temple book, "The Shirley Temple Edition of Susannah of the Mounties," 1959, Random House, No. X-4................................25.00 to 30.00

Shirley Temple book, "Shirley Temple - Little Playmate," Saalfield Publishing Co., a 'Little Movie Book,' No. 1730-A, 1936.................15.00 to 20.00

Shirley Temple book, "Shirley Temple in Heidi," Saalfield Publishing Co., No. 1771, 1937 ....35.00 to 45.00

Shirley Temple book, "Shirley Temple in Susannah of the Mounties," Saalfield Publishing Co., No. 1786, 1936, w/dust jacket 30.00

Shirley Temple book, "Shirley Temple in the Little Colonel," 'Big Little Book,' Saalfield Publishing Co., No. 1095 ....25.00 to 35.00

Shirley Temple book, "Shirley Temple in The Little Princess," Saalfield Publishing Co., No. 1783, 1938 ....45.00

Shirley Temple book, "Shirley Temple in The Littlest Rebel" 'Big Little Book,' Saalfield Publishing Co., No. 1115, w/dust jacket ....25.00 to 35.00

Shirley Temple book, "Shirley Temple in Wee Willie Winkie," Saalfield Publishing Co., No. 1769, 1937, 9½ x 10" 37.50

Shirley Temple book, "Shirley Temple's Favorite Poems," Saalfield Publishing Co., No. 1720, 1936.........45.00

Shirley Temple book, "The Real Little Girl," Saalfield Publishing Co., 1938 ....50.00

Shirley Temple coloring book, "Great Big Coloring Book," 1936 ....65.00 to 75.00

Shirley Temple coloring book, "The Little Princess Coloring Book," Saalfield Publishing Co., No. 1784, 1936 ....110.00

Shirley Temple figure, chalkware, carnival-type, colorful, 13" h..............95.00

Shirley Temple fountain pen, brown w/glittery gold threads.........................95.00

Shirley Temple magazine cover, "Modern Screen," March 30, 1942.....15.00

Shirley Temple mirror, pocket-type, photo on pink ground, Fox Films, 1935, 1¾" d...30.00

Shirley Temple mirror, pocket-type, shades of brown & pink, imprinted "Shirley Temple, America's Sweetheart, Heidi, Copyright 1937, Fox Film," 2¼" d...............................40.00

Shirley Temple pin, enameled, "Shirley Temple League," English premium, 1930s 85.00

Shirley Temple pitcher, cobalt blue glass, w/white decal portrait of Shirley ....40.00 to 50.00

Shirley Temple postcard, "Little Colonel," 1930s, England (mint) 20.00

Shirley Temple ring, sterling silver, w/picture of Shirley ....225.00 to 275.00

Shirley Temple sewing machine, Linstrom Electric Co.........................155.00

Shirley Temple soap figure...................65.00

Shirley Temple song book, "Shirley's Favorite Songs," 1937 ....45.00

Shmoo (Li'l Abner comic) bank, plastic, figural, on original card....................................60.00 to 75.00

Skeezix (comics) card game, complete in original box, 1930s 45.00

Skippy (comics) figure, celluloid, w/jointed arms, 1930s, 5½" h..............................250.00 to 275.00

Skippy (comics) toothbrush holder, bisque, movable arms, 5¾" h...............................125.00 to 175.00

Sky King (TV) ring, "Electronic TV Ring," w/pictures ....75.00 to 125.00

Sky King (radio) ring, "Magni-Glo Writing Ring," Peter Pan Peanut Butter premium, 1940s ......80.00 to 100.00

Sky King (radio) ring, "Navajo Treasure"..160.00

Sky King (radio) ring, "Teleblinker," Peter Pan Peanut Butter premium, 1940s ....75.00 to 125.00

Smitty (comic strip) cane, carnival-type, china head 100.00

Smokey the Bear ranger hat, felt, mint condition 20.00

Snoopy (comics) bowl & plate, ceramic, yellow background w/red & blue rings in bowl center, matching plate, marked "Iroquois," 1970s, plate 7" d., 2 pcs. 28.00

Snoopy cookie jar, Snoopy lying on doghouse, McCoy, marked "USA," 1970 ....245.00

Snoopy figure, composition, bobbing head-type, 1970, mint on card, 4" h..25.00

Snoopy figure, "Snoopy Daredevil Flyer," mint in box 32.00

Snoopy mug, ceramic, Taylor International 18.00

Snoopy play set, "Snoopy Sno-Kone Machine," mint in box.........................27.00

Snoopy toy, roll-type, hard plastic w/bell inside 22.00

Snuffy Smith (Barney Google comics) charm, full-figure, silver finish (somewhat tarnished) 18.00

Snuffy Smith pinback button, Kellogg's Pep cereal premium ....8.00 to 12.00

Sonja Henie book, "Wings on My Feet," 1940 ....35.00

Sonja Henie ice skates, mint w/original box, pr.............................200.00

Sonja Henie souvenir book, "Hollywood Ice Review," flocked & embossed cover, 1946 ....34.00

Sonny & Cher Movie Poster

Sonny & Cher movie poster, "Good Times," Columbia Pictures, three-sheet, linen backed, 1967, 41 x 81" (ILLUS.) 575.00

Space Patrol (TV) Space-O-Phones, w/original box & instructions 75.00

Sparkle Plenty (Dick Tracy comics) toy, washing machine (mint condition) 165.00

Spider-Man puppet, hand-type, Ideal, 1966, mint condition..........................125.00

Starsky (Starsky & Hutch TV) costume, complete in box, 1977 ....25.00

Star Trek coloring book, 1967 ....22.50

Star Trek comic book, No. 2, 1968 ....40.00

Star Trek (TV) game, board-type, Ideal, 1967, complete in original box (some surface & edge wear on box)..101.00

Star Trek game, Super Phaser II Target game, Mego, Paramount Pictures, unused in original box, 1976..55.00

Star Wars, Empire Strikes Back photo cards, 1980, set of 37 ....90.00

Star Wars puzzle, jigsaw-type, "Space Battle," 1977 ....20.00

Star Wars (movie) figure, Storm-trooper, plastic, mint in box, 12" h....125.00

Straight Arrow (radio) bandana, pictures Straight Arrow, Steve Adams, Packy & Fury ....50.00 to 75.00

Street Hawk lunch box & thermos bottle, based on the TV show, features Street Hawk on his motorcycle on the front & a scene of him communicating w/his command center on the reverse, the thermos depicts action shots from the show, 1984, mint condition, 2 pcs. 288.00

Superman automobile set, die cast, Corgi Toys, set of 5, mint in box 75.00

Superman bank, dime register, tinplate, 1940s ....100.00 to 125.00

Superman candy cigarettes, in original package.................................40.00

Superman cookie jar, depicts Superman in telephone booth, California Originals ....350.00 to 425.00

Superman costume, illustrated box, Ben Cooper, 1976...............................30.00

Superman game, board-type, "Calling Superman," complete in box...........120.00

Superman movie poster, "Superman and the Mole Men," starring George Reeves & Phyllis Coates, Lippert Pictures, 1951, one-sheet, linen backed, 27 x 41"..............................3,300.00

Superman pinback button, Kellogg's "Pep" cereal premium ....15.00 to 20.00

Superman radio, transistor-type, 1973, mint in box 55.00

Superman toothbrush, battery-operated, Janex Corp., 1970s 30.00

Superman toy, swim fins, "Kiddie Paddlers," in original box, pr......................................125.00 to 150.00

Sweet Pea (Popeye comic) bank, ceramic, Vandor...............................150.00

Tarzan Bracelet

Tarzan (radio & comics) bracelet, enameled metal, green & black jungle scenes against an orange ground around the sides w/a central oval panel incised "Tarzan Radio Club - Drink More Milk" (ILLUS.)....1,829.00

Tarzan mask, cardboard, "Wheaties" premium, 1950s, 13 x 15"................75.00

Tarzan toy, Colorforms set, 1960s 22.00

Terry & the Pirates (comics) ring, "Gold Ore"..80.00

Three Stooges puppets, finger-type, set of 3...10.00

Time Tunnel (TV) coloring book, Saalfield, copyright 1966, 8¼ x 11" ...18.00

Tom & Jerry (cartoons) dolls, cloth, Tom the cat wearing a blue hunter's cap & carrying a wooden gun at the end of which clings Jerry the mouse, Lars-of-Italy, ca. 1950, 18½" h., pr...276.00

Tom Corbett, Space Cadet (TV) book, "Danger In Deep Space," 1953..........20.00

Tom Corbett, Space Cadet (TV) book, "Treachery in Outer Space," hardcover 20.00

Tom Corbett, Space Cadet (TV) coloring book, 1950s....40.00 to 45.00

Tom Corbett, Space Cadet (TV) lunch box, steel, red w/full color picture on one side, Aladdin, 1952....125.00 to 150.00

Tom Corbett, Space Cadet (TV) membership button....150.00

Tom Corbett, Space Cadet (TV) official outfit, Yankee Boy, complete, excellent in near mint box....600.00

Tom Corbett, Space Cadet (TV) shoulder patch, from membership kit....150.00

Tom Corbett, Space Cadet (TV) toy, atomic rifle, plastic, excellent condition, 21" l. 175.00

Tom Mix arrowhead, signal-type, Lucite, radio premium....55.00 to 60.00

Tom Mix belt, "Straight Shooter's Belt"....175.00

Tom Mix book, miniature, "Rider of Death Valley," Universal Pictures premium, 1934....25.00

Tom Mix catalog, Straight Shooter's Premium Catalog, 4 pp. ....25.00 to 30.00

Tom Mix comic book, "The Life of Tom Mix," radio premium w/original mailer....98.00

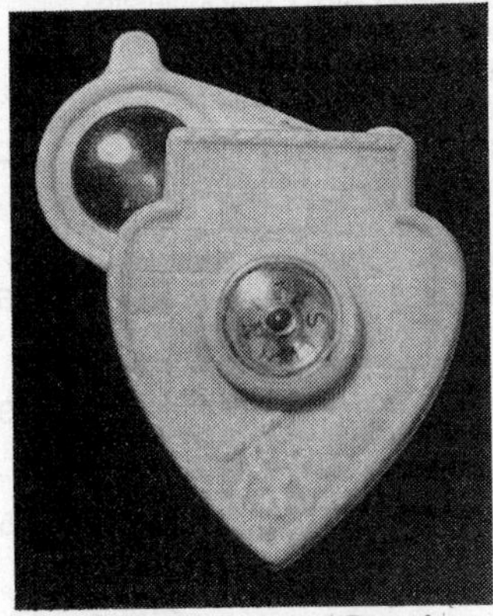

Tom Mix Arrowhead Premium

Tom Mix compass & magnifying glass, glow-in-the-dark arrowhead,"Straight Shooters" Ralston premium, 1947 (ILLUS.) ......40.00 to 50.00

Tom Mix game, card-type, "Wild Cat," 1935, excellent condition....48.00

Tom Mix "I.D." bracelet....95.00

Tom Mix manual, "Secret Manual," Ralston premium, 1944....50.00

Tom Mix Bandana

Tom Mix neckerchief or bandana, 16 x 16" (ILLUS.)....85.00

Tom Mix periscope, w/original mailer....90.00

Tom Mix postal telegraph signal set, Ralston premium, w/mailer....50.00

Tom Mix ring, "Magic-Light Tiger-Eye" type, plastic, simulated cabochon stone setting, Ralston premium, 1950....200.00 to 250.00

Tom Mix ring, "Magnet," Ralston premium, 1930s-40s....50.00 to 75.00

Tom Mix ring, signature-type, rectangular top w/a copy of his signature engraved, 1942....175.00 to 200.00

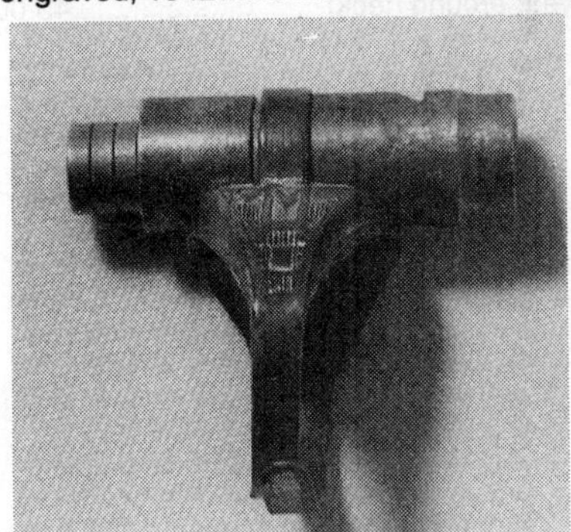

Tom Mix Ring

Tom Mix ring, sliding whistle-type, Ralston premium, 1949 (ILLUS.)....50.00 to 75.00

Tom Mix toy, "Postal Telegraph Signal Set," blue, Ralston premium, 1938, near mint in box....60.00

Tom Mix watch fob, gold-ore-type, 1940 (ILLUS top next page)...50.00 to 75.00

Tonto & Scout figures, plastic, Gabriel, 1973, Tonto 10" h. & Scout 11" h., 2 pcs. 135.00

Tom Mix Gold Ore Watch Fob

Tony the Tiger cookie jar, soft plastic, "Kellogg's" premium, 1968...............160.00

Toonerville Trolley (comics) toy, windup tin, motorman driving the trolley on a wobbly course, Fischer, 1920s, good condition, 5" l...............431.00

Toonerville Trolley toy, windup tin, comic trolley piloted by the Skipper, running on eccentric wheels, NIfty, ca. 1925, w/original box, 6½" h........650.00

Topo Gigio (little mouse from Ed Sullivan TV Show) bank, ceramic, bobbing head-type, coin slot in back of red apple, paper foil label on base "Rossini Japan" (some paint wear around neck)............................45.00

Tubby Tom Tumbler

Tubby Tom (Little Lulu comics) tumbler, clear glass w/printed picture of Tom walking, Flipper the dog on reverse, 1940s, 4¾" h. (ILLUS.) 66.00

Uncle Walt (Gasoline Alley comic strip) pinback button, "Pittsburgh Post Gazette" premium......................28.00

Uncle Wiggily book, "Uncle Wiggily Storybook," 1947, mint.......................30.00

Uncle Wiggily Mug

Uncle Wiggily mug, pottery, Ovaltine premium, embossed 1924 Fred A. Wish Inc., Sebring Pottery Co., manufactured for The Wonder Co., 3" h. (ILLUS.) ....50.00 to 60.00

Underdog (cartoons) plate, plastic, picture of Underdog rescuing Polly from an alligator, 1960s, 7" d. 40.00

Underdog (cartoons) punching bag, inflatable, 1982, mint in box, 24" l. 32.50

Untouchables (TV) game, target-type, "The Official Untouchables Target Game," consists of a 13½" l. tapered clear hard plastic dome over a lithographed tin target that features a windup rotating disk depicting a gangster car & gangster head, the opposite end w/6" l. black plastic pistol that fires small metal ball bearings at target, box features a photograph of Robert Stack, Louis Marx, early 1960s, mint in box...........70.00

Voyage to the Bottom of the Sea (TV) lunch box & thermos bottle, scenes aboard the submarine, Aladdin Industries, 1967, 2 pcs....................385.00

Wild Bill Hickock & Jingles (TV) play set, Western bunkhouse, 42 pcs. in original envelope, mint condition 48.00

Wild Bill Hickock & Jingles (TV) poster, color portraits, Vornado premium, ca. 1950 ....35.00

Winnie's Twins (Winnie Winkle comic strip) pinback button, Kellogg's "Pep" cereal premium 20.00

Wonder Woman wrist watch, Dabs "Supertime," 1977, mint in box w/color insert & warranty papers 175.00

Woody Woodpecker clock, animated, shows Woody riding horse, 1959.....290.00

Woody Woodpecker coloring book, Whitman, over 200 pp., mint.............20.00

Woody Woodpecker lunch box...........100.00

Woody Woodpecker toy, "Bubble Machine" 25.00

Woody Woodpecker toy, talking kazoo, figural, mint in box..................40.00

Wyatt Earp (TV) cap gun, 9" l. 60.00

Wyatt Earp (TV) coloring book, Hugh O'Brian on cover,Whitman, 1958, unused, 8½ x 11" 35.00

Wyatt Earp play set: figure of Wyatt w/cowboy hat & guns w/horse, plastic, Hartland Plastics, 1960-61, in original box.................................275.00

Yellow Kid (early comics) game, punchout board-type, illustrates Kid holding an umbrella, never used......195.00

CHILDREN'S BOOKS

The most collectible children's books today tend to be those printed after the 1850s and, while age is not completely irrelevant, illustrations play a far more important role in determining the values. While first editions are highly esteemed, it is the beautiful illustrated books that most collectors seek. The following books, all in good to fine condition, are listed alphabetically. Also see BLACK AMERICANA, BIG LITTLE BOOKS, CHARACTER COLLECTIBLES, COMIC BOOKS and DISNEY COLLECTIBLES.

"A Connecticut Yankee in King Arthur's Court," by Mark Twain, 1917, Harper's $35.00

"A Child's Garden of Verses," by Robert Louis Stevenson, 1905, w/12 full color pen & ink illustrations by Jessie Willcox Smith ....100.00 to 125.00

"A Cup of Tea," by E.S. Tucker, 1892, Worthington Co., New York, book of dolls & verse, hard cover, 8 x 11" 45.00

"Adventures of Unc' Billy Possum," by Thornton Burgess, 1919 ....15.00

"Alice's Adventures in Wonderland," by Lewis Carroll, illustrated by Tenniel, A. Whitman & Co., 1928 ......45.00

"All About Peter Rabbit," by Beatrix Potter, illustrated by Dick Hartley, 1914..25.00

"Animated Antics in Playland," by Julian Wehr, 1946............................55.00

"An Old Fashioned Girl," by Louisa May Alcott, 1911 ....25.00

"Bambi," by Felix Salten, 1931, translated by Whittaker Chambers, illustrated by Kurt Wiese 35.00

"Billy Whiskers Twins," by Frances Montgomery, 1911, Saalfield 16.00

"Bird Children," by Elizabeth Gordon, 1912..............................100.00 to 125.00

"Bonny Bairns," by Ida Waugh, 1888, many full page color illustrations of children, 48 pp. 250.00

"Bunnie Cottontail," by M. Blair, color illustrations by M. Posts, McLoughlin Bros., 1920, 10 x 12½" 25.00

"Campfire Girls in the Outside World," by Winston, 1914 ....15.00

"Dale Evans and the Lost Gold Mine," Little Golden Book, 1954, No. 213.....15.00

"Dame Trot & Her Comical Cat," Pleasewell series, McLoughlin Bros., 1890 ....18.00

"Dick Hamilton's Steam Yacht," by Goris, 1913 ....5.00

"Doctor Dan, The Bandage Man," Little Golden Book, 1950, No. 111 .....11.00

"Goldilocks and the Three Bears," published by Saalfield Publishing, 1919..25.00

"Grandmother Goose's Nursery Rhymes," published by McLoughlin Bros., 1890 ....125.00

"Gunsmoke," Little Golden Book, 1958, No. 320 ....12.00

"Hans Brinker or The Silver Skates," by Mary Mapes Dodge, 1931, color illustrations by Alice Carsey..................30.00

"Howdy Doody's Lucky Trip," Little Golden Book, 1st edition,1953, No. 171 ....22.00

"Jack & the Beanstalk and Other Stories," illustrated by John Neill, 1908..15.00

"Just So Stories," by Rudyard Kipling, 1912, illustrated in color & black & white, 247 pp. 25.00

"Kitty Cat Stories," published by Saalfield, 1930, Frances Brundage cover illustration depicts mother cat rocking kittens in a cradle 35.00

"Lady & the Tramp (Walt Disney's)," Little Golden Book, 1954 ....7.00

"Little Black Sambo," by Ethel Hays, 1942..79.00

"Little Mr. Thimblefinger," by Joel Chandler Harris, 1922.........................18.00

"Little Red Riding Hood," published by Blue Ribbon Press, pop-up type, 1934..140.00

"Little Red Riding Hood," linen-type, published by Whitman, 1955 ....20.00

"Little Red Riding Hood," Little Golden Book, illustrated by Sharon Koester, 1959, w/uncut paper dolls, No. A34...38.00

"Little Susie Sunbonnet," by Uncle Milton, 1907 ....150.00

"Little Women," by Louisa May Alcott, illustrated by Jessie Willcox Smith, Little, Brown & Co., 1929 ....25.00

"Mickey Mouse and His Spaceship," Little Golden Book, 1952, No. D29 ....12.00

"Miss Sniff, the Fuzzy Cat," by Curry, 1945...20.00

"Mother Goose," published by Whitman, punch-out, stand-up book, 1939..48.00

"New Little Black Sambo," published by Whitman, 1939, illustrated by Juanita Bennett, full-color, 8 x 10", 12 pp. 25.00
"Nice Puppy!," by Martha Paulsen, 1943, color illustrations by Mabel Hatt, Saalfield 35.00
"Nobody's Boy," by Hector Malot, illustrated by Johnny Gruelle, 1916....25.00
"Old Mr. Toad," by Thornton Burgess, 1919, Boston, illustrated, w/dust jacket 23.50
"Penrod & Sam," by Booth Tarkington, 1931, illustrated by Grant....25.00
"Peter Rabbit & Jimmy Chipmunk," by V. Albert, 1918, picture boards, twelve full page color illustrations, w/dust jacket....25.00
"Pets," published by Saalfield, 1917, linen cover, 8½ x 10" 25.00
"Pinocchio," by C. Collodi, 1916, Whitman, color illustrations by Alice Carsey 35.00
"Raggedy Ann & Andy and the Camel with the Wrinkled Knees," by Johnny Gruelle, 1924 ....25.00
"Raggedy Ann's Alphabet Book," by Johnny Gruelle, 1925....18.00
"Raggedy Ann's Wishing Pebble," by Johnny Gruelle, 1925, first edition 35.00
"Rebecca of Sunnybrook Farm," by Kate D. Wiggin, 1903, first edition 40.00
"Snow White & Rose Red," 1929, illustrated by Frances Brundage 40.00
"Stories From Uncle Remus," by Joel Chandler Harris, 1941, illustrated by A.B. Frost, 16 pp., hard cover, 7¾ x 10¼"....40.00
"Sunny Rhymes for Happy Children," by Olive Beaupre Miller, 1917, B.F. Volland Co., illustrated by Carmen L. Browne....25.00
"Swiss Family Robinson (Walt Disney)," Little Golden Book, 1961, No. D95....7.00
"Tale of Paddy Muskrat," by Bailey, 1916....9.00
"Tarzan & the Jewels of Opar," by Edgar Rice Burroughs, 1919, A.C. McClurg & Co. 150.00
"Teenie Weenie Neighbors," by William Donahey, 1945, vivid color plates, 68 pp. 55.00
"The Angora Twinnies," by Margaret Evans Price, 1919....20.00
"The Book of Bow Wows," by Elizabeth Gordon, 1913....25.00
"The Emerald City of Oz," by L. Frank Baum, illustrated by John R. Neill, 1910, first edition 135.00
"The Favorite Book of Fables," published by Thomas Nelson & Sons, London, 1891, illustrated (spine & edge show some wear)....35.00
"The Flintstones," Little Golden Book, 1961, No. 450 ....18.00
"The Funny Froggy Bubble Book," illustrated "Book That Sings," Harper Bros. & Columbia Graphophone Co., complete w/5½" records playing "A Frog He Would A-Wooing Go" & others, 1919....125.00
"The Hole Book," by Peter Newell, 1908....85.00
"The Jolly Jump-Ups Vacation Trip," by Clyne, pop-up book, 1942....59.00
"The King's Stilts," by Dr. Seuss, 1939....195.00
"The Little Postcard Painter," published by McLoughlin Bros., 1904, 16 postcards to paint, 7 x 11", soft cover....45.00
"The Little Red Hen," Little Golden Book, illustrated by Rudolf Freund, 1942, No. 6 ....15.00
"The Magic Aeroplane," illustrated by Emile Nelson w/Christmas & winter scenes, 1911 ....125.00
"The Motor Boys On the Wing," Motor Boys Series, 1911....7.50
"The Rover Boys In The Air," by Arthur Winfield, 1912 ....5.00
"The Patchwork Girl of Oz," by L. Frank Baum, 1913, Reilly Britton, first edition 125.00
"The Prince & The Pauper," by Mark Twain, 1917, illustrated by Booth....40.00
"The Talking Clock & Other Rhymes for Children," 1880, colorful lithograph illustrations, soft cover, 5 x 5"..45.00
"Travels of Babar," by De Brunhoff, 1934....18.00
"Tom Swift and His Ocean Airport," by Victor Appleton, Grosset, 1934, first edition, orange binding 40.00
"Treasure Island," by Robert L. Stevenson, illustrated by N.C. Wyeth, 1911, Scribner's Publications 10.00
"Water Babies," by Charles Kingsley, 1903....85.00

CHILDREN'S DISHES

During the reign of Queen Victoria, dollhouses and accessories became more popular and as the century progressed, there was greater demand for toys which would subtly train a little girl in the art of homemaking. Also see CHARACTER COLLECTIBLES and DISNEY COLLECTIBLES and, under Glass, AKRO AGATE, DEPRESSION GLASS and PATTERN GLASS.

Oval Star Butter Dish

Berry set: 4" d. master bowl & six 2¼" d. sauce dishes; pressed glass, Lacy Daisy patt., clear, U.S. Glass Co., ca. 1900, 7 pcs. $65.00

Bowl, individual berry, pressed glass, Pattee Cross patt., clear, 2" d. 10.00

Breakfast set: cup & saucer & plate; china, brown transfer decoration of Punch & Judy, Staffordshire, England, 19th c., 3 pcs. 55.00

Butter dish, cov., pressed glass, Beaded Swirl patt., clear....................60.00

Butter dish, cov., pressed glass, Colonial patt.,Cambridge Glass Co., olive green 35.00

Butter dish, cov., pressed glass, Doyle's 500 patt., clear 55.00

Butter dish, cov., pressed glass, Michigan patt., w/gold decorated edges 125.00

Butter dish, cov., pressed glass, Oval Star patt., clear (ILLUS.) 32.50

Butter dish, cov., pressed glass, Pert patt., clear 150.00

Castor set, fancy braided wire footed frame w/high center handle, holds three plain clear glass bottles, the set 125.00

Cracker jar, cov., china w/woven wicker handle, caramel & blue lustre glaze, decorated w/flowers, marked "Japan"...85.00

Creamer, porcelain, decorated w/a scene of an elephant juggling 35.00

Creamer, ironstone china, ovoid shape w/loop handle, brown transfer-printed scene of a girl sowing seed, marked "Staffordshire, England," late 19th c., 3¼" h..............60.50

Creamer, pressed glass, Amazon patt., clear 34.00

Creamer, pressed glass, Clear & Diamond Panels patt., blue...............40.00

Creamer, pressed glass, Doyle's 500 patt., amber 75.00

Creamer, pressed glass, Hobnail patt., Northwood, white opalescent....45.00

Creamer, pressed glass, Rexford patt., clear 13.50

Creamer, pressed glass, Sweetheart patt., Cambridge Glass Co., clear......15.00

Creamer, pressed glass, Thumbelina patt., clear 20.00

Cup & saucer, china, Nursery Rhyme patt., cup decorated w/Little Jack Horner, saucer decorated w/Little Miss Muffet, marked "Germany" 35.00

Dinner set: 6" oval handled tureen, 4½" oval cov. vegetable dish, 6 x 9¾" meat platter, 4¾" sq. open vegetable dish, six 6½" d. dinner plates, six 6¼" d. deep soup plates & six 5¼" salad plates; china, embossed beading, decorated w/Dutch children w/windmill scenes & florals, marked "Germany," 22 pcs. (unseen mark under the glaze on tureen)......425.00

Mug, pressed glass, Bird on Branch patt., blue 52.50

Mug, pressed glass, Doyle's 500 patt., clear 20.00

Mug, pressed glass, Rabbit patt., branch handle, amber.......................45.00

Pitcher, water, pressed glass, Galloway patt., clear 28.50

Pitcher, water, pressed glass, Michigan patt., clear..........................38.00

Pitcher, water, pressed glass, Nursery Rhyme patt., clear, 4½" h. 90.00

Plate, china, Little Bo Peep decoration, Shenango China 40.00

Punch bowl, pressed glass, Thumbelina patt., clear 20.00

Punch bowl, pressed glass, Tulip & Honeycomb patt., clear......................25.00

Punch bowl, pressed glass, Wild Rose patt., milk white.........................50.00

Punch cup, Wheat Sheaf patt., Cambridge Glass Co.,clear.................9.00

Punch set: punch bowl & four cups; pressed glass, Whirligig patt., clear, 5 pcs. 95.00

Punch set: punch bowl & six cups; pressed glass, Inverted Strawberry patt., Cambridge Glass Co., clear, 7 pcs. 215.00

Spooner, pressed glass, Amazon patt., clear 32.50

Spooner, pressed glass, Doyle's 500 patt., amber...40.00

Spooner, pressed glass, Horizontal Threads patt., ruby-stained 37.00

Spooner, pressed glass, Lion patt., clear 80.00

Spooner, pressed glass, Rex (Fancy Cut) patt., clear 50.00

Spooner, pressed glass, Sawtooth Band patt., Heisey, clear...................40.00

Sugar bowl, cov., pressed glass, Doyle's 500 patt., clear 75.00

Sugar bowl, cov., pressed glass, Hobnail patt., Northwood, white opalescent 134.00
Sugar bowl, cov., pressed glass, Hobnail w/Thumbprint Base patt., blue 48.00

Liberty Bell Sugar Bowl

Sugar bowl, cov., pressed glass, Liberty Bell patt., clear (ILLUS.) ....150.00 to 175.00
Sugar bowl, cov., pressed glass, Mardi Gras patt., clear 60.00
Sugar bowl, cov., pressed glass, Menagerie patt., figural bear, clear 150.00
Sugar bowl, cov., pressed glass, Wee Branches patt., clear..........................60.00
Table set: cov. butter dish, cov. sugar bowl, creamer & spooner; pressed glass, Acorn patt., clear, 4 pcs.........600.00
Table set, pressed glass, Oval Star patt., clear, 4 pcs. 125.00
Table set, pressed glass, Tulip & Honeycomb patt., clear, 4 pcs. ....75.00 to 100.00
Tea set: cov. teapot, creamer, cov. sugar bowl, four cups & saucers; china, Blue Willow patt., 11 pcs. 68.00
Tea set: cov. teapot, cov. sugar bowl, creamer & four cups & saucers; ball-shaped pieces w/robin's egg blue shaded to white bodies, decorated w/little bouquets of roses & snowball flowers, ruffled rims on covered pieces, unsigned R.S. Prussia, 11 pcs. 250.00
Tea set: cov. teapot, cov. sugar bowl, creamer, waste bowl, two 5" d. plates & four cups & saucers; Staffordshire earthenware, bulbous footed bodies w/flared rims & scroll handles, light blue transfer-printed tree design, marked "Forest - Florentine China," ca. 1850-70, the set (teapot finial reglued & chips, chip on creamer).............................302.50
Tea set: cov. teapot, cov. sugar bowl, creamer, four cups & saucers, four tea plates & an oval handled cake plate; china, decorated w/bands of roses, signed "Edwin Knowles," ca. 1910, 16 pcs. 145.00
Tea set: cov. teapot, cov. sugar bowl, creamer, six cups & saucers & six tea plates; china, tan to blue pearl lustre glaze decorated w/silhouetted cupid w/butterfly wing & holding a bird, signed "Silesia-Germany," ca. 1900, 21 pcs. 375.00
Tea set: tray, eight plates, eight cups & saucers & two creamers; tin, Mother Goose patt., Ohio Art, 27 pcs. (one creamer missing handle) 44.00
Tumbler, pressed glass, Oval Star patt., clear 10.00
Tumbler, pressed glass, Rex (Fancy Cut) patt., clear 16.00
Water set: pitcher & four tumblers; pressed glass, Nursery Rhyme patt., clear, 5 pcs. 135.00

CHILDREN'S MUGS

The small sized mugs used by children first attempting to drink from a cup appeal to many collectors. Because they were made of such diverse materials as china, glass, pottery, graniteware, plated silver and sterling silver, the collector can assemble a diversified collection or single out a particular type around which to base a collection. Also see CHILDREN'S DISHES and PATTERN GLASS..

Pressed glass, Beads In Relief patt., milk white $35.00
Pressed glass, Butterfly patt., amber, 2½" h...48.00
Pressed glass, Ceres patt., opaque turquoise 35.00
Pressed glass, Dutch Mill patt., clear ...30.00
Pressed glass, Elephant patt., blue 165.00
Pressed glass, Hobnail patt., clear, 2⅜" h..15.00
Pressed glass, Horned Devil patt., milk white 35.00
Pressed glass, Monkey & Vines patt., milk white 55.00
Pressed glass, Our Boy & Jester w/Pig patt., amber, polished base......55.00
Pressed glass, Peacock & Heron patt., clear 65.00
Pressed glass, Robin patt., black amethyst 45.00
Pressed glass, Scampering Lamb patt., amethyst 55.00

Pressed glass, Two Fighting Cats patt., clear, small....................40.00
Pressed glass, Waterfowl patt., clear ...35.00
Pressed glass, Wheat & Barley patt., amber, large....................30.00
Silver plate, embossed buffalo decoration....................15.00
Staffordshire pottery, pearlware, cylindrical, black transfer-printed bird titled "A Pretty Bird," polychrome enamel trim, 2" h. (wear, small chips, short hairline in base)....................99.00
Staffordshire pottery, cylindrical, brown transfer-printed scene of a lumberjack kneeling & surveying felled trees, scene titled "Franklin Maxims - Little Strokes Fell Great Oaks," polychrome enamel trim, 2½" h. (glaze wear on handle) 170.50
Staffordshire pottery, cylindrical, transfer-printed large & small "A" & "B" against a landscape background in brown w/red enamel trim, 2½" h. (hairline in handle, old repair on bottom edge)....................165.00
Staffordshire pottery, cylindrical, black transfer-printed design of a boy riding a large dog & a sheep, titled "Boy and Dog" & "Sheep," 2½" h. (pinpoint flakes) 132.00
Staffordshire pottery, cylindrical, black transfer-printed large "I" on one side & "J" on the other w/an interior scene of a workman in the center, green & orange enamel trim, 2½" h....................170.50
Staffordshire pottery, cylindrical, black transfer-printed design of a child in a dog cart, polychrome enamel trim, 19th c., 2⅝" h....................137.50

CHRISTMAS TREE LIGHTS

Along with a host of other Christmas-related items, early Christmas tree lights are attracting a growing number of collectors. Comic characters seem to be the most popular form among the wide variety of figural lights available, most of which were manufactured between 1920 and World War II in Germany, Japan and the United States. Figural bulbs are generally painted clear or milk white glass unless otherwise noted.

BULBS

Betty Boop....................$70.00
Bird, red & yellow....................25.00
Bulldog....................30.00
Cat, googly-eyed 45.00
Clown....................20.00
Dick Tracy & Smitty, pr. 95.00
Little Jack Horner....................145.00
Punch & Judy, Germany, pr. 395.00
Santa Claus, full-figure, 5½" h. 95.00
Star, cobalt blue glass, in tin frame, Nippon 25.00

CANDLE LIGHTS

Mold-blown glass, bell-shaped w/diamond quilted patt., molded rim, deep red, 3¾" h. (pinpoint rim flakes) 93.50
Mold-blown glass, bell-shaped w/diamond quilted patt., folded rim, cobalt blue, 3¾" h. 170.50
Mold-blown glass, bell-shaped w/diamond quilted patt., folded rim, emerald green, 3" h. 137.50
Mold-blown glass, bell-shaped w/large overall hobnail design, red, 3¾" h. (slight rim roughness) 192.50

SETS

Mazda Disney characters, Mickey Mouse & friends, in original colorful display box, ca. 1930s 235.00
NOMA Disney Mickey Mouse lights, 1930s, excellent condition in original box....................245.00
NOMA Santa & Winter Wonderland, cover & pop-up display, 1927, in original box 65.00
NOMA "Whirl-Glo," revolving, in original box, 1936 ....25.00

CHRISTMAS TREE ORNAMENTS

The German blown glass Christmas tree ornaments and other commercially-made ornaments of wax, cardboard and cotton batting were popular from the time they were first offered for sale in the United States in the 1870s. Prior to that time, Christmas trees had been decorated with homemade ornaments that usually were edible. Now nostalgic collectors who seek out ornaments that sold for pennies in stores across the country in the early years of this century are willing to pay some rather hefty prices for unusual or early ornaments.

Angel w/lighted halo, tree-top, composition....................$28.00
Angel, tree-top, spun glass, w/gold wings & stars, 8" d. 78.00
Angel, wax, gold wings & human hair, 5" h....................60.00
Baby shoe, Dresden-type cardboard, w/original bag....................350.00

Bird, blown glass w/spun glass tail 12.00
Boy on sled, blown glass 145.00
Camel, Dresden-type cardboard 30.00
Cat riding on frog, pressed cotton 165.00
Champagne bottle w/paper label, blown glass 75.00
Champagne bottle, pressed cotton.......75.00
Deer, blown glass, cobalt blue & silvered 45.00
Ear of corn, blown glass, golden yellow, 3½" l. 30.00
Elephant, Dresden-type cardboard.....265.00
French horn, blown glass, 2 x 4" 45.00
Girl, pressed cotton w/die-cut face 125.00
Girl sitting on flower, two-sided, blown glass 150.00
Grape cluster, blown glass, green, brass hanger, 5⅛" l. 440.00
Heart, blown glass, silver, puffy 20.00
Horn, blown glass, 4½" h. 25.00
House, blown glass, silver w/red roof ...15.00
Kugel, gold, w/brass hanger, 3" d. 82.00
Kugel, silver, w/brass hanger, 5" d. 145.00
Owl, blown glass, cream graduating to blue at bottom, yellow & black eyes, ca. 1930, 3½" h. (minor wear, top hook loose) 16.50
Santa Claus head, blown glass ....35.00 to 50.00
Skeezix, blown glass, Germany 200.00
Snowman, pressed cotton, w/tin foil hat, Occupied Japan, 4" h. 45.00
Snowmen, each playing a different musical instrument, papier-mache, Japan, each 5" h., set of 7 ....85.00
Tomato, blown glass, large..................95.00
World globe, Dresden-type cardboard, 3½" d. 155.00

HALLMARK KEEPSAKE ORNAMENTS

Note: These must be "Mint in box" to bring top prices.

A Matchless Christmas, "Little Trimmers" ornaments, 1979 ....50.00
Angel, "Crown Classics" ornaments, 1981 ....15.00
Behold the Star, "Decorative Ball" ornaments, 1979.............................10.00
Bellringer, "Twirl-About" collection, 1977 ....40.00
Bellswinger, "Bellringer" series, first edition, 1979 ....175.00
Betsey Clark, "Adorable Adornments" ornaments, 1975..............................225.00
Betsey Clark, "Betsey Clark's Christmas" shadow box ornament, "Property" ornament, 1980.............25.00
California Quail, "Holiday Wildlife" series, fourth edition, 1985 ....30.00
Canadian Mountie, "Clothespin Soldiers Collectibles" series, 1984.....35.00
Caught Napping, "Norman Rockwell" series, fifth edition, 1984 ....28.00
Checking Up, "Norman Rockwell" series, seventh edition, 1986 ....25.00
Chris Mouse Dreams, "Keepsake Magic" series, 1986 ....45.00
Christmas Fantasy, "Handcrafted" ornaments, 1981 ....60.00
Christmas Heart, "Handcrafted" ornaments, 1979 ....70.00
Christmas Treats, "Traditional" ornaments, 1985...............................10.00
Cinnamon Teddy, "Porcelain Bear" series, first edition, 1983...................70.00
Cloisonne Angel, "Handcrafted" ornaments, 1982...............................65.00
Drummer Boy, "Nostalgia Collection" ornaments, 1975.............................150.00
Early American, "Clothespin Soldiers Collectibles" series, 1983................30.00
Elfin Artist, "Bellringer" series, sixth edition, 1984 ....30.00
Feliz Navidad, "Windows of the World" series, first edition, 1985....................68.00
Frosty Friends, "Frosty Friends" series, third edition, 1982.......................................75.00 to 100.00
Heart Full of Love, "Commemorative" ornaments, 1985...............................25.00
House on Main Street, "Nostalgic Houses & Shops" series, fourth edition, 1987...55.00
Husband, "Commemorative" ornaments, 1987.................................5.00
Ice-Hockey Holiday, SNOOPY and Friends" series, first edition, 1979.....95.00
Ice Sculptor, "Handcrafted" ornaments, 1981 ....72.00
Jack-in-the-Box, "Yesteryears" ornaments, 1977..................................75.00
Joy, "Colors of Christmas" ornaments, 1980 ....15.00
Magical Unicorn, "Limited Edition" ornaments, 1986...............................85.00
Miss Piggy, "Property" ornaments, 1983 ....20.00
Nativity, "Colors of Christmas" ornaments, 1982...............................30.00
Panorama Ball, "Handcrafted" ornaments, 1978..................................75.00
Pinecone Home, "Handcrafted" ornaments, 1982...............................90.00
Rocking horse, Appaloosa, "Rocking Horse" series, fourth edition, 1984.....40.00
Rocking horse, Dappled, "Rocking Horse" series, first edition, 1981 ....325.00 to 350.00
Rocking horse, Russett, "Rocking Horse" series, third edition, 1983...................................125.00 to 150.00
Santa & Sleigh, "Nostalgia Collection" ornaments, 1975...............................250.00
Santa's Flight, "Colors of Chirstmas" ornaments, 1982..............................35.00

Santa Star, "Holiday Humor" ornaments, 1984 .... 25.00

Shall We Dance, "Mr. & Mrs. Claus" series, third edition, 1988 .... 38.00

Snow Goose, "Holiday Wildlife" series, sixth edition, 1987 .... 25.00

Thimble Angel, "Thimble" series, seventh edition, 1984 .... 30.00

Tin Locomotive, "Tin Locomotive" series, first edition, 1982 .... 40.00

Tin Locomotive, "Tin Locomotive" series, third edition, 1984 .... 67.00

Tin Locomotive, "Tin Locomotive" series, seventh edition, 1988 .... 40.00

Tin Soldier, "Handcrafted" ornaments, 1982 .... 30.00

Two Angels, "Bellringer" series, second edition, 1980 .... 45.00

Uncle Sam, "Traditional" ornaments, 1984 .... 30.00

Vrolyk Kerstfeest, "Windows of the World" series, second edition, 1986 .... 37.00

Wooden Reindeer, "Wood Childhood" ornaments, 1986 .... 12.00

CIGAR & CIGARETTE CASES, HOLDERS & LIGHTERS

Russian Silver & Enamel Cigarette Case

Cigar box, sterling silver, rectangular, applied w/etched strapwork to simulate a medieval iron-bound chest, engraved w/contemporary initials, marked on base & numbered "21119Z-9020" stamped "SPECIAL HAND WORK," Tiffany & Co., New York, ca. 1930, 11½" l. $16,100.00

Cigar box, sterling silver, rectangular w/radially fluted top & sides, gilt interior, marked "STERLING" below a stylized monogram, early 20th c., 11¼" l. 4,025.00

Cigarette box, gold-inlaid silver, rectangular, the hinged cover w/reeding & square gold plaque engraved w/letters "G P R U" & "ChS R M K," applied w/silver thumbpiece, the inside lined w/rosewood, the base lined w/leather, marked by Cartier, Paris, ca. 1930, 8⅝" l. 5,750.00

Cigarette case, Bakelite, composed of black & white Bakelite strips, opening to reveal individual cigarette compartments 115.00

Cigarette case, gold (9k) & enamel, engine-turned, the interior of the cover enameled w/a horse & jockey & w/a presentation inscription, Birmingham, England, 1934, 3¾" l. 863.00

Cigarette case, gold, ivory, enamel & diamond, rectangular gold body w/rounded sides, the ivory fields framed by rose-cut diamond borders & black enamel ends, 3¾" l. 1,035.00

Cigarette case, gold (14k yellow) & gems, as engraved floral design centered by a diamond & synthetic saphite center w/small monogram, 2½ x 3½" (minor damage) 660.00

Cigarette case, gold (14k yellow), sapphire & diamond, set on top w/bezel-set sapphires & diamond initials "MPH," marked "BS & F-G" 1,100.00

Cigarette case, goldtone metal,Chicago motor Club emblem on front in black, white & red, w/green cloth pouch & original box, Elgin American, 3½ x 5½" (minor wear & watermarks to box, fading to pouch) 300.00

Cigarette case, mother-of-pearl highlighted w/glitter, Marhill 30.00

Cigarette case, silver & enamel, the rectangular top decorated w/an enamel plaque of a winged female figure above a row of three polar bears over a field of stylized raised flowers, the surrounded enamel blue & green, w/a green hardstone thumbpiece, Russia, ca. 1910, 4⅜" l. (ILLUS.) 2,588.00

Cigarette case, silver & shaded enamel, the cover enameled *en plein* w/a winter scene, the reverse enameled w/a castle & a sunrise, the surrounds colorfully enameled w/scrolling flowering foliage on a deep green ground, The Sixth Artel, Moscow, Russia, ca. 1910, ca. 1910, 4½" l. 3,450.00

Cigarette case, silver-gilt & shaded enamel, one side enameled w/a richly plumed bird among colorful foliage, the other side enameled w/a sea creature, borders of white beads Vasili Agafonov, Moscow, Russia, ca. 1900 ....1,495.00

Cigarette holder, brass & black enamel, ca. 1920, 14" l. 20.00

Cigarette lighter, chrome-plated, Masonic Emblem, Zippo 25.00

Cigarette lighter, souvenir, "University of Nortre Dame," Zippo 28.00

Cigarette lighter, souvenir, "Shawnee on Delaware" w/arrowhead, Zippo.....30.00

Cigarette lighter, gold (14k yellow), black enamel & engraved accents, "Dunhill," retailed by Tiffany & Co. ...467.50

Cigarette lighter, 18k yellow gold, rectangular fluted gold jacket w/metal interior, w/flip top, signed "Dunhill" 345.00

Cigarette lighter, "Kool Cigarettes," model of a penguin, hinged head opens to reveal lighter, ca. 1930s, 4½" h...195.00

Cigarette lighter, silvertone metal top w/clear plastic base containing dice, Scripto..24.00

CIGAR & TOBACCO CUTTERS

Caswell Club Cutter & Ashtray

Both counter-type and individual cigar ad plug tobacco cutters were in widespread use last century and earlier in this century. Some counter types were made in combination with lighters and vending machines and were used to promote various tobacco packaging companies.

Counter-type, cast iron, plug cutter, Griswold #3, Triumph "Star" model $80.00

Counter-type, cast iron, "The Erie Griswold," used by "Shenkberg Co., Sioux City, IA" & so marked, dated 1883..127.00

Counter-type, sheet iron, a silhouetted figure of a stepping horse above an iron blade, w/a pine handle, on a pine base, 19th c., 11½" l. 385.00

Counter-type cutter & ashtray combination, nickel-plated brass, embossed lettering & decoration, minor tarnish, 7" h. (ILLUS.) 300.00

CIRCUS COLLECTIBLES

The romance of the "Big Top," stirred by memories of sawdust, spangles, thrills and chills, has captured the imagination of the American public for over 100 years. Though the heyday of the traveling circus is now past, dedicated collectors and fans of all ages eagerly seek out choice memorabilia from the late 19th and early 20th centuries, the "golden age" of circuses.

Book, "Circus Parades," by C.P. Fox, 1953, concerns circus wagons, their makers & carvers, etc., w/dust jacket $65.00

Paint book, "Circus Animal Painting Book," colorful die-cut cover w/majestic circus animals in ornate cage, 1921 ....40.00

Paint book, "Clowns from Circusland Cutout and Paint Book," complete w/crayons...65.00

Poster, Cristiani Bros. Circus, "The Greatest Riding Troupe of All Time," ca. 1960, 21 x 28" 60.00

Poster, King Bros. & Cristiani Combined Circus, shows three laughing clowns w/a pig, ca. 1945, 28 x 41"...165.00

Poster, Parker & Watts Circus, pictures Kit Carson, Jr., ca. 1930, 28 x 40" 175.00

Poster, Ringling Bros. & Barnum & Baily Combined Shows, features "Prairie Bill & His Congress of Rough Riders of the World," ca. 1930, 20 x 28"...200.00

Program, "Hagenbeck-Wallace & Sells Bro.," 1935 ....45.00

Program, "Robbins Bros. Circus," Hoot Gibson pictured on the cover, 1930s 45.00

Ticket, "Cole Bros. Circus," ca. 1930s, unused 17.00

CLOCKS

Gilbert Rohde Alarm Clock

Also see ADVERTISING ITEMS, ART NOUVEAU, BREWERIANA and COCA-COLA ITEMS.

Alarm, Gilbert Rohde, chromed-metal & glass, the clock face w/simple black dots denoting numerals, enclosed by a circular wooden frame w/a simple rectangular foot supported by a chromed-metal side bracket, manufactured by Herman Miller Company, ca. 1933, wood stamped "404 B," 8⅛" l. (ILLUS.) $3,680.00

Animated, Lux Clock Company, Waterbury, Connecticut, black shoe shine boy polishing lady's shoes, ca. 1930s ....300.00 to 350.00

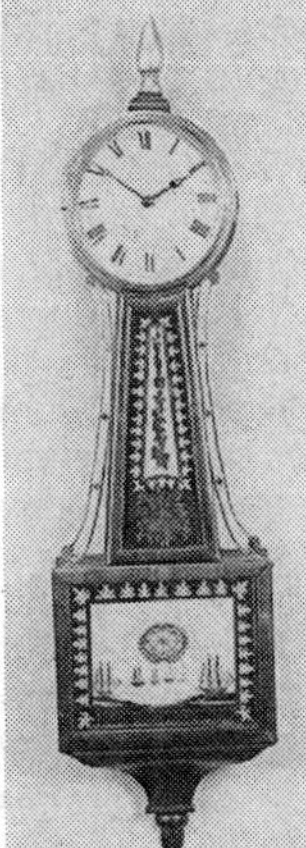

Banjo Clock by Simon Willard

Banjo, Simon Willard, Roxbury, Massachusetts, Federal mahogany case, the circular glazed dial door w/brass bezel enclosing a white-painted dial w/Roman numeral chapter ring signed "Simon Willard, Roxbury Mass" above a tapering throat w/an eglomisé panel decorated w/gilt pendant foliate vine w/fruit over a basket of fruit & flanked by curved pierced brass sidearms above a rectangular base w/eglomisé cupboard door decorated w/a central medallion above five sailing vessels over a shaped base w/pendant, ca. 1820, 3¾ x 10", 35" h. (ILLUS.) 1,430.00

Banjo, attributed to Simon Willard, Roxbury, Massachusetts, Federal case, acorn finial above a circular brass bezel opening to a white-painted dial w/Arabic chapter ring over a tapering throat w/eglomisé panel inscribed "Patent" centering a thermometer above a box base w/an eglomisé panel, ca. 1805, 33½" h. 5,280.00

Bracket clock, J. Bertrand, Paris, France, Louis XV style, the circular white enamel dial w/black Roman & Arabic numerals inscribed, together w/the backplate, "J. PH. BERT-RAND A PARIS," the move-ment striking on two bells w/pull repeat, contained within a green lacquered cartouche-shaped case outlined w/elaborate ormolu borders cast & chiselled w/scrolling foliage, shell & wave motifs, the top centered by a flower-filled vase entwined w/a dragon above a fantastic mask, the corners marked w/stylized dragons, the glazed hinged door fitted w/ormolu branches flanked by dragons perched at each side, the whole raised on ormolu leaf-cast feet, mid-19th c., 22" h. 7,475.00

Late 18th Century Bracket Clock

Bracket clock, Thomas Lindhorst, Philadelphia, Chippendale brass-mounted mahogany case, the late 18th c. imported English case w/an arched hood fitted w/a brass bail handle above an arched glazed hinged door opening to a white-painted dial w/"strike-silent" mechanism & seconds register inscribed "T. LINDHORST, PHILADA.," the molded base on brass ogee bracket feet, some retouching to name on dial, ca. 1795, 6¾ x 10¼", 17" h. (ILLUS.) 3,450.00

Grandfather, John Adamson, London, England, Charles II style walnut case, the case w/a flat top rising hood, the molded cornice supported by twist columns flanking a square glazed door opening to a 10½" square dial w/applied signature "John Adamson London," the silver chapter ring w/fleur-de-lis half hour marks ring enclosing shuttered winding holes, date aperture & seconds ring in the matted center, cherub & scroll spandrels, above a trunk door w/oval-inlaid panels & glazed lenticle, w/similarly inlaid plinth & later skirting, the movement w/latched pillars, restored bolt & shutter maintaining power, well-formed anchor & crutch striking the hours by means of inside count wheel, 6' 7" h. 6,900.00

Grandfather, Jacob Eby, Manheim, Pennsylvania, Federal inlaid cherry case, the hood w/swan's-neck pediment ending in pinwheel-carved terminals centering three turned urn finials, the glazed hinged door opening to a white-painted dial w/Roman numerals, phases of the moon & inscribed "Jacob Eby, MAN*HEIM," the case w/an inlaid spread-winged eagle clutching arrows & a branch w/banner in its beak w/the inscription "E Pluribus Unum," the shaped hinged long narrow door below flanked by inlaid canted corners, the quarter-fan-inlaid base on bracket feet, ca. 1815, 11 x 19¾", 7' 11" h. (slight repair to veneers) 44,850.00

Grandfather, Chr. Gould, London, England, William & Mary style walnut & marquetry case, the case w/flat top hood supported on spiral-turned columns flanking a square glazed door opening to an 11" square dial bearing the signature "Chr. Gould London Fecit" beneath the silvered chapter ring w/matted center, date aperture & subsidiary seconds ring, ringed winding holes & winged cherub spandrels, above a rectangular trunk door w/lenticle & inlaid w/bird & floral marquetry within shaped panels, w/similar marquetry to the plinth & later skirting, the five-pillar movement w/anchor escapement & outside countwheel strike on bell, 6' 9" h. 10,925.00

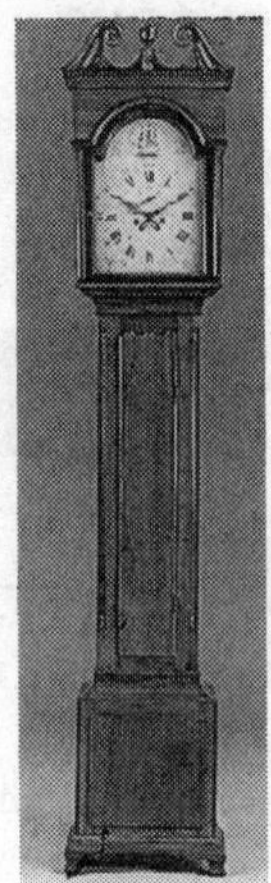

Chippendale Grandfather Clock

Grandfather, Leslie & Williams, New Brunswick, New Jersey, Chippendale cherry case, the hood w/swan's-neck pediment centering an urn finial & dentil-carved tympanum, the arched glazed door below opening to a white-painted dial w/Roman numerals, calendar, date & second register, inscribed "LESLIE & WIL-LIAMS, NEW BRUNSWICK," the tall, narrow lower door w/shaped top flanked by quarter-columns down the sides, the paneled & rope-car-ved base on ogee bracket feet, feet & saddleboard replaced, ca. 1780, 10 x 20½", 8' 1¼" h. (ILLUS.) 6,613.00

Grandfather, Elnathan Taber, Roxbury, Massachusetts, Federal style inlaid mahogany case, the hood w/pierced fretwork crest surmounted by three brass ball-and-steeple finials above an arched glazed door opening to a white-painted dial w/Roman numerals, phases of the moon, calendar date & seconds registers, inscribed w/the maker's name, brass stop-fluted colonettes flanking, the tall waisted case w/fan-inlaid door flanked by brass stop-fluted quarter columns, the fan-inlaid & cross-banded base w/a shaped skirt below continuing to flared French feet, ca. 1800, 9¾ x 18½", 7' 4½" h. 33,350.00

Grandfather, David Williams, Newport & Providence, Rhode Island, Federal style mahogany case, the hood w/three reeded plinths surmounted by ball-and-spire brass finials centering pierced fretwork above an arched molded cornice over a glazed door opening to a white-painted dial w/Roman & Arabic chapter ring enclosing a sweep seconds & calendar day ring, the spandrels embellished w/painted roses, surmounted by a lunar dial, signed "D. Williams, Newport," flanked by two reeded colonettes w/brass capitals & bases over waisted case flanked by reeded quarter columns w/brass capitals & bases over a rectangular base, on bracket feet, ca. 1825, 11½ x 21½", 7' 9¼" h. 9,900.00

Shelf, or mantel, Ansonia Clock Co., New York, Royal Bonn molded china case, decorated w/h.p. rose & yellow poppies against a yellow, blue & green ground, 14" h. 695.00

French Bisque Figural Clock

Shelf, or mantel, Barrancourt, Paris, France, figural, ormolu, bisque & white marble, the central enamel dial signed "Barrancourt A Paris," w/symmetrical winding holes, bell striking movement w/flat bottomed plate & anchor escapement, the bisque rocky outcrop case flanked by waterfalls & surmounted by a scantily draped maiden, on a molded oval white marble base faced w/a frieze depicting putti studying astronomy, ca. 1785, 18½" h. (ILLUS.) 6,325.00

Shelf, or mantel, Hotchkiss & Benedict, Auburn, New York, classical-style mahogany carved case w/an arched & scalloped crestboard between block finials above a square glazed door opening to a white-painted dial w/Roman numerals & floral painted corners over a long mirrored door flanked by flat pilasters w/acanthus leaf gilt-plaster capitals, flat base, marked "A Munger's Patent," ca. 1830, 37¾" h. (minor imperfections).......1,100.00

Shelf, or mantel, Leslie & Price, Philadelphia, Pennsylvania, Chippendale brass-mounted mahogany case, the arched top fitted w/brass bail handle above a glazed arched hinged door opening to a brass-engraved dial centering a "strike-silent" indicator & calendar date register, inscribed "Leslie & Price, Philadelphia," raised on brass ogee bracket feet, the backplate engraved & inscribed as the dial, 1793-99, 7 x 10¼", 17¼" h...7,150.00

Ornate Classical Shelf Clock

Shelf, or mantel, Benjamin Torrey, Hanover, Massachusetts, Classical (American Empire) mahogany & eglomisé case, two-part construction: the hood w/scrolled pediment above a rectangular top over an eglomisé panel embellished w/gilt harps above an oval reserve inscribed "Benjamin D. Torrey, Hanover 1829" opening to a white-painted dish dial w/Roman chapter ring enclosing inscription "Warranted for Joshua Whitmarsh," the case w/rectangular panel depicting a shepherd & sheep over a molded base, on brass paw feet, 1829, 6½ x 14", 32" h. (ILLUS.) 7,700.00

Table clock, brass, partial copper plated & enamel, "Zephyr," the rectangular copper-finished metal body w/rounded corners decorated w/brass bands, w/a digital face, designed by Kem Weber for the Lawson Time Inc., w/the firm's tag & "Model No. 304," ca. 1934, 3¼ x 8", 3½" h.................................880.00

Mid-20th Century Electric Table Clock

Table clock, electric, circular body on a tripod base, protected by a semi-spherical plastic shell, designed by George Nelson, Howard Miller Clock Co., mid-20th c., 8⅞" h. (ILLUS.).....690.00

Wall clock, iron case w/a tooled brass facade, the arched crest embossed w/a scene of ploughing above the round white enameled dial w/black Roman numerals, dial labeled "Bezancon a Charny," brass hands w/decorative sunbursts, France, 19th c., 15¼" h. plus pendulum (back plate replaced, pendulum & weights modern replacements)........275.00

Wall regulator, E. Howard & Co., Boston, Massachusetts, mahogany, the long figure-eight form body w/a small top crest w/bull's-eye over the round dial w/Roman numerals over the long waist w/a conforming glass panel above round glass panel at the bottom trimmed w/another small crest, ca. 1870, 34" l. 2,860.00

CLOISONNE & RELATED WARES

Cloisonné work features enameled designs on a metal ground. There are several types of this work, the best-known utilizing cells of wire on the body of the object into which the enamel is placed. In the plique-a-jour form of cloisonné, the base is removed leaving translucent enamel windows. The champlevé technique entails filling in, with enamels, a design which is cast or carved in the base. "Pigeon Blood" (akasuke) cloisonné includes a type where foil is enclosed within colored enamel walls. Cloisonné is said to have been invented by the Chinese and brought to perfection by the Japanese.

CLOISONNE

Cloisonne Tripod Censer

Censer, tripod *ding*-form, decorated around the sides w/eight multicolored lotus blooms on a continuous scrolling foliate vine, w/two upright pierced handles, all raised on gilt monster-mask legs, restorations, Ming period, China, 17th c., to top of handles 4½" h. (ILLUS.) $4,600.00

Incense burner, modeled in the form of a quail w/removable wings forming the cover, standing on gilt-bronze legs w/clawed feet, the beaked head held up opposite long overlapping tail feathers, enameled in turquoise & cobalt blue w/details picked out in green, vermillion, yellow, white & black, China, 18th c., 6 ¾" h. (typical pitting) 5,750.00

Jardiniere, rectangular w/rounded sides flaring at the rim, each side mounted w/a gilt-metal plaque in high-relief of figures in leisurely, fishing & agricultural pursuits, reserved on a deep blue ground w/a foliate scroll, divided on the corners by foliate dragon panels, the everted rim w/*shou* medallions & floral cartouches, raised on four short cylindrical legs, 9½ x 14¾" (typical pitting) 575.00

Rhyton, modeled in the form of an elephant's head, the dark green ground decorated w/iron-red, turquoise, maroon & blue dragons amid white, pink, yellow & turquoise scrolls, & molded w/gilt-copper trappings applied w/florettes, the curled trunk & tusks (one repaired) forming supports on which to stand the cup, the interior washed in gilding, China, 5⅜" h. (gilding worn) 518.00

Vases, baluster-form raised on a flaring foot, colorfully decorated w/four lotus roundels all reserved on a turquoise ground strewn w/lotus blossoms borne on continuous scrolling vines, continuing on to the splayed base & waisted neck mounted w/two large *ruyi*-shaped handles suspending loose rings beneath the flared neck, six-character Qianlong mark on the rim, China, Qianlong Dynasty, 14" h., pr. 23,000.00

RELATED WARES

Champlevé & silver-gilt bowl & stand, enameled in colorful stylized foliate forms, w/geometric borders on a black ground, Ovchinnikov, Moscow, Russia, 1876, stand 7" d., 2 pcs. ..2,300.00

Plique-a-jour & silver-gilt serving plate, enameled w/colorful flowering scrolling foliage, w/shaped border, the center in the form of a translucent stained glass window, Antip Kuzmichev, Moscow, Russia, 1892, 9" d. 3,450.00

Plique-a-jour & silver-gilt tankard, cov., the octagonal base decorated in plique-a-jour enamel w/the Russian Imperial Eagle, the circular cover decorated w/plique-a-jour foliate designs, the lower part of the body w/reserves enameled w/colorful scrolling flowering foliage on grounds of blue & green, Ovchinnikov, Moscow, Russia, ca.1890, 6½" h. 21,850.00

CLOTHING

Recent interest in period clothing, uniforms and accessories from the 18th, 19th and through the 20th century compels us to include this category in our compilation. While style and fabric play an important role in the values of older garments of previous centuries, designer dresses of the 1920s and 30s, especially evening gowns, are enhanced by the original label of a noted couturier such as Worth, or Adrian. Prices vary widely for these garments which we list by type, with infant's and children's apparel so designated. Also see MOVIE MEMORABILIA.

"Domino" Cape by Fortuny

Belt, ivory celluloid, five panels of black cameos w/alternating black & cream rings $195.00

Blouse, black& white beadwork, size 10, ca. 1912 ....100.00

Bolero, cream silk faille, sharply cropped over the shoulders & densely embroi-dered w/black sequins & bugle beads, w label "BALENCIAGA 10 AVENUE GEORGE V, PARIS," 1946 ....2,760.00

Boots, young boy's leather, inlaid w/white butterfly, w /riding heel, well worn, ca. 1940s, pr. 165.00

Bunting, baby's, pink silk, ca. 1900 ......90.00

Cape, rose pink silk velvet, "Domino" style, stenciled w/a Renaissance-style multicolored design of pomegranates surrounded by garlands of rosehips, pinecones & foliage, the lappet hood w/extended dagges trimmed w/silk-covered wooden beads, lined in green gilt-stenciled silk & gilt-stenciled brown velvet facings, Fortuny, Italy, 1930s (ILLUS.) 34,500.00

Christening gown, full-length panels of lace & tucks, lace hem, collar & sleeves, 36" l. 85.00

Christening gown, heavily tucked, further decorated w/broiderie anglaise,drawstring neck, high waist 65.00

Coat, lady's, brown silk velvet, gilt-stencil-ed w/intertwining flowering vines, edges w/stenciled green velvet facing & trim at the short sleeves, lined in rust silk, w/label "Mariano Fortuny Venice," Italy.....4,025.00

Coat, lady's, emerald green tweed wool, straight cut w/half-sleeves gathered at the cuff bands, w/label "BALENCIAGA 10 AVENUE GEORGE V, PARIS"........................552.00

Coat, lady's, sapphire blue wool, three-quarter length, double-breasted, w/large notched lapel collar, w/label "Yves St. Laurent, Paris," 1984 ....483.00

Coat, man's heavy wool, three-quarter length, belted, plaid lining, size 44 regular, ca. 1940s 65.00

Cocktail dress, black lace, chemise-style w/self-ruffle trim at the hem, w/label "BALENCIAGA 10 AVENUE GEORGE V, PARIS"........................460.00

Cocktail dress, chocolate brown panne velvet, heavily beaded silk yoke, size 9, ca. 1930s 65.00

Corset, peach fabric, "Dolly" 22.00

Cowboy outfit, child's, includes felt hat, leather & denim vest & chaps, the set 105.00

Dress, black silk pongee, the sleeveless bodice w/scoop neckline & gathered waist, w/label "BALENCIAGA 10 AVENUE GEORGE V, PARIS"........................345.00

Dress, blue & white w/violet lace panel & flounce, tiny tucking & lace trims, long skirt, 1900.....................95.00

Dress, flapper era, bittersweet silk pongee, long dropped waist, scalloped hem outlined w/rows of crystal & bittersweet beading in floral panels, same beading motif on front & back of skirt & bodice, all around vertical rows of beading.......225.00

Dress, grey wool, straight-cut w/accordion pleated skirt front, center pocket on the high-necked, straight sleeved bodice, the black leather belt w/chrome & glass disk buckle, w/label "PIERRE CARDIN, PARIS," ca. 1969 ....4,600.00

Dress, flapper era, grey velvet w/chinchilla trim, low chiffon insert at neckline outlined in bugle beads, rhinestones & large crystals, 1920s 125.00

Dress, tomato red wool, the A-line front trimmed w/trapunto stitching, split & draped at the back w/self-bow in the center over a shorter underskirt, w/label "PIERRE CARDIN PARIS," 1970 ....3,680.00

Dress, mourning-type, two-piece, black silk w/black beading, Victorian era...200.00

Dress, topaz lace w/chiffon sleeves & skirt inserts, some beading, ca. 1920s 125.00

Dress & jacket ensemble, navy blue slubbed silk, the dress w/three button V-neck bodice, cap sleeves & self-belt, the smock-style jacket w/dolman sleeves gathered at the cuffs, patch pockets & white pique collar, w/label "BALENCIAGA 10 AVENUE GEORGE V, PARIS," 1953 ....920.00

Evening coat, ivory slubbed silk satin, the buttonless tent-cut coat w/bias-rolled collar & three-quarter sleeves, w/label "BALENCIAGA 10 AVENUE GEORGE V, PARIS," 1953...........1,035.00

Evening dress, navy blue silk cloque, the fitted bodice & A-line skirt trimmed w/filigree buttons, over a full underskirt of matching fabric & silk taffeta ruched "bustle" back, designed by Karl Lagerfeld, w/"Chanel" label, 1984 ....3,680.00

Evening dress, 'Tango,' orange crepe, boat-shaped neckline, bias-cut "furi-sode" sleeves trimmed w/diamond-shap-ed medallions in pink & silver sequins, two splits to the front of the skirt, un-labeled Jeanne Lanvin design, France, ca. 1938 (some sequins lacking) 880.00

Evening dress & jacket, blue bugle beading overall, the dress w/camisole bodice & mid-calf A-line skirt, the short V-neck jacket w/elbow-length shaped sleeves & a black-painted wooden butterfly form clasp, Elsa Schiaparelli, w/firm's label (relined, w/original lining on the side) 3,680.00

Evening gown, black hammered satin, bias-cut in pointed pieces at the waistline, the sleeveless bodice w/keyhole back closure, self-belt trimmed w/a rhinestone clasp, Madeleine Vionnet, ca. 1932 ....4,830.00

Evening gown, navy blue "treebark" wool crepe, the narrow bias-cut gown w/sunburn back, shocking pink & purple off-the-shoulder cape collar, trimmed w/purple satin at the hem, Elsa Schiaparelli 4,370.00

Evening jacket, ivory satin, the full cut collarless three-quarter length coat w/gold leather applique, bugle bead & diamante embroidery in an eighteenth century style foliate design, w/label "BALENCIAGA 10 AVENUE GEORGE V, PARIS".....3,450.00

Evening suit, black satin, double-breasted box-cut jacket & straight skirt slightly gathered at the waistband, each linedin black silk, the jacket w/label "BALEN-CIAGA 10 AVENUE GEORGE V PARIS" 690.00

Evening suit, black silk velvet, the long fitted jacket w/slightly gathered shoulders, self-belt w/rhinestone buckle, the bias-cut skirt w/satin waistband, each lined in silk, the jacket w/label "Modele cree par Yves Saint Laurent, Paris reproduit sous Licence" 403.00

Garters, man's lavender, elegant Art Deco style, "Paris," in original colorful box 48.00

Gloves, lady's French fashion-type, white kid leather w/black stitching, pr...110.00

Gown, magenta pleated silk, "Delphos" style, sleeveless, trimmed w/silk cord & brown Venetian glass beads, inseam printed "Made in Italy, Fabriqué en Italie, Fortuny Deposé" 3,680.00

Gown, peach pleated silk, "Peplos" style, the long-sleeved tunic-style bodice trimmed w/silk ribbon stenciled w/a leaf pattern & w/yellow & brown Venetian glass beads at the shoulders, w/separate under-skirt, Fortuny, Italy 2,070.00

Gown, peach silk net w/green velvet belt & rhinestone buckle, ca. 1930s...65.00

Gym bloomers, lady's, black wool 30.00

Hat, lady's, Flapper era, cloche, navy blue fine textured straw......................45.00

Hat, lady's, black velvet bowler w/velvet ties, w/label "BALENCIAGA 10 AVENUE GEORGE V, PARIS" 403.00

Hat, lady's, cream lace, w/wide, turned-back brim, the net ground appliqued w/large embroidered flowers, w/label "Christian Dior, modele export Exclusif Pour I. Magnin & Co., Made in USA"...........552.00

Hat, lady's, ruffled black lace, velvet banding, Schiaparelli, large 55.00

Hat, man's, top hat, beaver, large, never worn 60.00

Hat, man's, Panama fedora, size 7¼, 1930s, w/original box 62.00

Jacket, lady's, copper silk velvet, stenciled in green w/a mosaic pattern, w/short sleeves & grey-green satin lining, w/label "Mariano Fortuny Venice," Italy 4,370.00

Parasol, child's, wood, brass, ivory & taffeta, Victorian, 20" d. 85.00

Parasol, lady's, black & white swirled pattern, long metal tip, black wooden handle w/silver ferrules & rhinestone band 37.50

Parasol, lady's, white linen, w/daisy embroidery, Edwardian 98.00

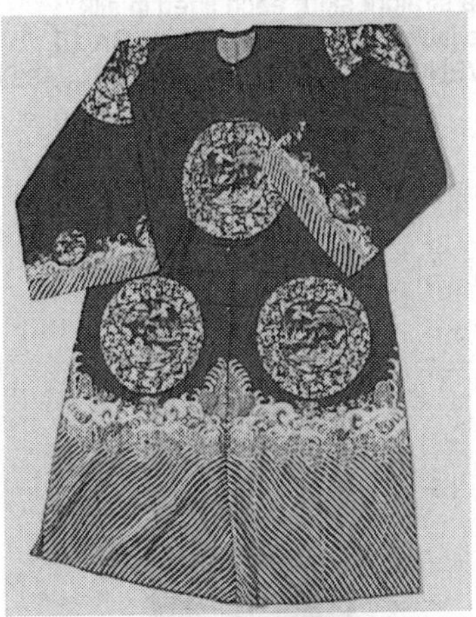

Chinese Black Silk Robe

Robe, black silk, informal-type, satin-stitched w/figurative rondels depicting cranes & bats flying above pavilions & river landscapes w/*lishui* stripe & wave pattern borders, China, 19th c., 53" l. (ILLUS.) 2,310.00

Shawl, black & white twill-woven check design w/plaid border, Victorian, square 467.50

Shawl, silk, pale orange decorated w/large embroidered florals, 16" l. fringe 95.00

Shoes, baby's, high button-type, white leather, ca. 1930s, size 3, pr. (some wear) 10.00

Shoes, baby's, two-tone leather, high button-type, pr...65.00

Shoes, child's, black leather Mary Janes, pr 50.00

Shoes, lady's, black fabric w/leather overlay, ca. 1930, pr 40.00

Shoes, lady's, high-top, black & brown leather, Victorian, pr.........................125.00

Shoes, lady's, lace-up style, black suede, Victorian, pr 100.00

Shoes, lady's, Lucite, high heels w/rhinestones & ankle straps, size 5-5½, 1950s, pr 22.00

Skirt, white lace, long & full, hand-made, ca. 1900 ....75.00

Spats, black wool, button-up style, pr 17.00

Suit, lady's, cream wool, the box-cut jacket w/gilt braid trim & double C buttons, the skirt w/front side pleats, each lined w/cream silk & labeled "CHANEL BOUTIQUE," France 863.00

Suit, lady's, dove grey tweed linen, the fitted double-breasted jacket trimmed in white grosgrain ribbon, w/a straight skirt, each lined in silk, the jacket w/label "BALENCIAGA 10 AVENUE GEORGE V, PARIS"........483.00

Balenciaga Silk Suit

Suit, lady's, two-piece, black textured silk, woven w/a dot pattern resembling matelassé fabric, comprising a short fitted jacket w/elbow-length sleeves & gently gathered skirt, the jacket labeled "BALENCIAGA 10 AVENUE GEORGES V, PARIS"(ILLUS.) 920.00

Suit, man's, ecru silk, size 42L, ca. 1950s 100.00

Vest, man's, brocade, printed cotton lining, ca. 1880s 35.00

Waistcoat, embroidered silk, a long-waisted style w/flared flaps at the bottom w/pocket flaps, embroidered in chain-stitch w/scattered dots & floral sprigs along the bottom edges w/polychrome silk threads, late 18th c. (some discoloration)............605.00

Waistcoat, man's, embroidered silk, trimmed in embroidered chain-stitch w/polychrome silk threads, late 18th c., minor discoloration, let-out back 660.00

Walking suit, lady's, burgundy taffeta, ca. 1885 ....500.00

Wedding dress, creamy white silk, w/lace over the bodice & skirt, trimmed w/beads & pearls, early 1900s 185.00

COCA-COLA ITEMS

Coca-Cola promotion has been achieved through the issuance of scores of small objects through the years. These, together with trays, signs, and other articles bearing the name of this soft drink, are now sought by many collectors.

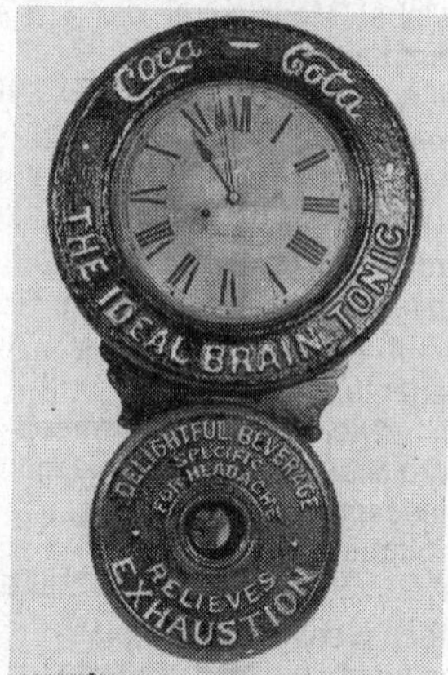

Coca-Cola Clock by Baird

Bank, tin, model of a cooler, ca. 1948..$175.00

Blotter, 1934, "Thirst come - thirst served," newsboy drinking from bottle 97.00

Blotter, 1942, beautiful girl lying down reading a magazine 13.50

Blotter, 1942, pictures a girl at the beach beside a boat 8.00

Book cover, illustrated w/the Sprite boy & a bottle...18.00

Booklet, "Romance of Coca-Cola," 1916, 16 pp...85.00

Bottle carrier, cardboard, 1930, 24-bottle size..60.00

Bottle carton-carrier, cardboard, w/Christmas sleeve, ca. 1940, 6-pack 85.00

Bottle holder for shopping cart, two-bottle iron wire rack w/metal plaque "Enjoy Coca-Cola While You Shop - Place Bottles Here," ca. 1940 ....50.00

Bowl, green glass, slightly pinched-in sides, embossed "Drink Coca-Cola" alternating w/"Ice Cold" under rim, 1930s ....450.00 to 500.00

Calendar, 1899, picture of Hilda Clark sitting at a table & "Coca-Cola Relieves Mental and Physical Exhaustion" in the upper right corner, 7⅜ x 13" 4,400.00

Calendar, 1927, elegant young lady seated holding a glass of Coca-Cola, full pad 1,760.00

Calendar, 1928, beautiful lady seated in armchair w/fur-collared garment about shoulders, small folio, full pad, 7½ x 13" 1,150.00

Calendar, 1932, Norman Rockwell

depiction of a young boy seated on the edge of a rockwork well, his dog sitting up in a begging position, full pad & cover sheet...............................695.00

Coca-Cola Door Plates

Calendar, 1937, N.C. Wyeth's boy w/fishing pole & dog, "It's the Refreshing Thing To Do," full pad..................................500.00 to 600.00

Calendar, 1940, pretty girl holding a bottle of Coca-Cola & a glass 145.00

Calendar, 1941, girl ice skater seated on a snowy log holding a bottle of Coca-Cola & "Thirst knows no season" 175.00

Calendar, 1943, Army nurse w/cape over her shoulders holding a bottle of Coca-Cola..................................150.00

Calendar, 1957, beautiful girl holding ski poles under one arm & a bottle of Coca-Cola in the other hand, "The pause that refreshes"........................75.00

Calendar, 1959, "American Birds," home calendar presented by the bottler, 6 x 7"...................................100.00

Calendar, 1968, pretty teen-aged girl holding phonograph records & a bottle of Coca-Cola, couple dancing in the background, "Coke has the taste you never get tired of"..............65.00

Calendar holder, round metal disc w/hook, white lettering on red ground, 1950...................................100.00

Can w/original opener: large diamond can & opener w/script logo; produced for Japan Airlines, unopened can, 2 pcs. 440.00

Cigarette lighter, bottle-shaped, opens at the center, tin cap w/"Coca-Cola" logo, 2½" h.......................................49.50

Cigarette lighter, musical-type, white background, red logo circle w/white lettering "Drink Coca-Cola," 1970 ....250.00

Clock, wall-type, Baird Clock Co., papier-maché "figure eight" case, face a bit dark, repainted, 1896 (ILLUS.) 3,500.00

Clock, wall regulator, Gilbert Clock Co., wooden case, "Drink Coca-Cola" in script on glass front, 1916-20...850.00

Comic book, "Refreshment through the ages," 1950s 7.50

Doll, Santa Claus standing holding bottle of Coca-Cola, cloth stuffed body, white boots, ca. 1950-60..........55.00

Door push & pull plates, aluminum, NJ Aluminum, Co., Newark, NJ, ca. 1905, now mounted on black in a shadow box frame, push plate 3 x 8", pull plate 2¼ x 8", pr. (ILLUS.) 1,233.00

Fan, cardboard, "Quality Carries On - Drink Coca-Cola," illustrates a hand holding bottle of Coca-Cola 40.00

Game, Checkers, "Dragon Checkers" on box, black & white wooden pieces embossed w/"Coca-Cola" logo, ca. 1930, in original box 50.00

Ice pick, wooden handle, 1930s 24.00

Mailer card for Kit Carson Kerchief, 1953 ....20.00

Menu board, wood & Masonite, Art Deco style, "Drink Coca-Cola" & the silhouette of a girl at the bottom of the frame, 1939..............................450.00

Menu board, wood, "Drink Coca-Cola," late 1950s.............................160.00

Mirror, pocket-type, 1907, pretty lady in low-cut dress holding a glass of Coca-Cola...515.00

Mirror, pocket-type, 1909, girl at table w/glass of Coca-Cola, "J.B. Carroll Chicago" etc., on rim, oval 450.00

Mirror, pocket-type, 1910, Coca-Cola Girl, "J.B. Carroll Chicago" etc., on rim, oval 300.00

Coca-Cola Bottle-Shaped Radio

Mirror, pocket-type, 1920, Garden Girl, "Bastian Bros. Co." etc., on rim, oval 550.00

Music box, model of a cooler, 1950s 150.00

Nature Study Cards, Series I through VIII, ca. 1928-33, total of 96 cards 45.00

Needle case, w/Party Girl on heavy paper cover, 1924-25, 2 x 3" 65.00

Playing cards, Airplane Spotter, World War II, full deck 85.00

Playing cards, 1943, Stewardess 45.00

Radio, Bakelite, model of a bottle, Crosley, ca. 1931-34, 7½" d., 24" h. (ILLUS. previous page) 4,598.00

Ruler, wooden, "Delicious & Refreshing," ca. 1930, 7" l. 30.00

Sandwich plate, china, shows bottle & glass & "Drink Coca-Cola - Refresh Yourself" around the rim, American Chinaware Corp., 1931, 7⅜" d. 275.00

Seltzer bottle w/metal top, glass, applied color label "Susanville Coca-Cola Bottling Co., Susanville, Calif.," top stamped "Coca-Cola" 130.00

Sign, aluminum, "Drink Coca-Cola In Bottles," for front of truck, 1920s......400.00

Sign, cardboard, rectangular, depicting a pretty girl holding an umbrella & standing by a dispenser that reads "Drink Coca-Cola - Ice Cold" & the top reads "Refreshment right out of the bottle,"1941, 16 x 27" 425.00

Sign, cardboard, rectangular, pictures a pretty girl in a swimsuit & "Yes - Coca-Cola," 1946, 16 x 27" 525.00

Sign, cardboard, rectangular, pictures a pretty girl in a swimsuit, "Drink Coca-Cola - Delicious and Refreshing" within a circle, 1939, 29 x 50" 400.00

Sign, cardboard, rectangular, green ground w/yellow lettering reading "For people on the go" above a soldier walking beside a young woman in a white halter-top swim outfit, the Coca-Cola disc logo in the lower left, ca. 1944, 29½ x 50" (edge tears, nail holes, tear in the word 'people,' watermark on edges).........770.00

Sign, cardboard, rectangular, green background w/yellow lettering to left reading "Refreshment you go for," a girl on a bicycle w/Coca-Cola in her basket & wearing a cream blouse & brown plaid skirt, round red disc to far right reads "Drink Coca-Cola - Delicious and Refreshing," ca. 1944, 27½ x 56¼" (scratches, edge tears, small pieces missing at edges, stain on skirt) 401.50

Sign, cardboard, rectangular, illustrates a winter scene & a pretty girl wearing ice skates & holding a bottle of Coke, "Drink Coca-Cola - Delicious and Refreshing" within a circle & "The year-round answer to thirst" across the bottom, 1941, 29 x 50" 675.00

Sign, chrome, "Drink Coca-Cola In Bottles" in script, for vehicle radiator, 17" l. 425.00

Sign, metal, w/flange, "Drink Coca-Cola" w/bottle on yellow dot below, 1940s 375.00

Sign, porcelain, rectangular, "Drink Coca-Cola - Fountain Service," 1950s, 12 x 28" 325.00

Sign, tin, bottle-shaped, 1950s, 17" h. 100.00

Coca-Cola Tin Sign

Sign, tin, oval, dark green & gold w/pretty girl offering a glass of Coke superimposed on "Coca-Cola," 1926, 13 x 19" (ILLUS.) 6,500.00

Sign, tin, rectangular, "Drink Coca-Cola - Delicious & refreshing," pictures the new Betty, 1941, 19 x 54" 300.00

Sign, tin, rectangular, "Fishtail" logo, "Drink Coca-Cola - Enjoy that Refreshing New Feeling" & bottle of Coke illustrated, 1963, 20 x 28" 115.00

Syrup bottle, clear glass w/enameled label, "Drink Coca-Cola" within wreath, 1920s 850.00

Thermometer, metal, "Drink Coca-Cola Delicious and Refreshing" on red ground circle above thermometer & black-on-white silhouette of girl drinking from bottle in circle below, 1939 ....285.00

Thermometer, metal w/glass front, round, "Things go better with Coke," 1964, 12" d. 150.00

Toy railroad boxcar, "Tyco," yellow w/red lettering "Drink Coca-Cola" & "The Pause That Refreshes" & bottle in red dot 85.00

Toy train set, "Lionel Trains," engine marked "Drink Coca-Cola," cars marked "Sprite" & "Fanta," and caboose marked "Drink Coca-Cola," includes track & transformer, 1975, mint in original box 400.00

Buddy-L Toy Coca-Cola Truck

Toy truck, "Buddy-L," wood, ca. 1940, 19" l. (ILLUS.) 4,174.00

Toy truck & semi-trailer, "Matchbox," red & white, "Drink Coca-Cola" on side panels of trailer, ca. 1970 ....45.00

Training kit for route salesman, films, records & meeting guides, Volume I, 1955, together w/17 x 19" case w/handle 1,500.00

Tray, change, 1909, Beautiful Girl at table w/glass of Coca-Cola (once called St. Louis World Fair Girl), 4¼ x 6" oval ....425.00 to 475.00

Early Glass Coca-Cola Tray

Tray, glass, 1907, "Drink Coca-Cola 5¢" center w/scrolling design above & below, some minor flaking (ILLUS.) 3,200.00

Tray, 1910, Coca-Cola Girl, 10½ x 13¼" rectangle 250.00

Tray, 1917, 8½ x 19 oblong ....250.00 to 350.00

Tray, 1924, Smiling Girl, 10½ x 13¼" oblong 435.00

Tray, 1925, Girl at Party, 10½ x 13¼" oblong 285.00

Tray, 1927, lady w/bottle, green, 10½ x 13¾" 385.00

Tray, 1932, Girl in Yellow Swimsuit, 10½ x 13¼" oblong 325.00

Tray, 1934, Johnny Weissmuller & Maureen O'Sullivan (Tarzan & Jane), 10½ x 13¼" rectangle ....350.00 to 400.00

Tray, 1937, Running Girl in Swimsuit, 10½ x 13¼" oblong ....200.00 to 250.00

Tray, 1941, Girl Ice Skater, 10½ x 13¼" rectangle 185.00

Vending machine, "Cavalier 44," coin-operated 1,650.00

Vending machine, "Vendalator 27" w/stand (restored) 2,100.00

Vending machine, "Vendo 27" w/original stand & rack, restored ..2,200.00

Vending machine, "Vendo 44" 2,300.00

Whistle, tin, yellow w/red lettering, 1930s 175.00

COFFEE GRINDERS

Colorful Tin Coffee Grinder

Most coffee grinders collected are lap or table and wall types used in many homes in the late 19th and early 20th centuries. However, large store-sized grinders have recently been traded.

Lap-type, cast iron & lithographed tin, colorful scenes on sides of "Old Glory," cavalry officers, crossed flags, etc. in red & blue on a pale green ground, lacy iron dome top, high center crank w/wooden knob, labeled "The Bronson-Walton Co, Cleveland, O," 8" h. plus handle (ILLUS.) $550.00

Lap-type, cherry box w/dovetailed construction & a single nailed drawer, pewter hopper w/iron crank handle, 8½" h. (age cracks, hopper battered, wooden handle knob replaced) 82.50

Lap-type, cherry dovetailed box w/drawer w/porcelain pull, pewter hopper, wrought-iron handle, on low stepped scalloped base, marked "E. Nagle, Maker," overall 10" h. 165.00

Lap-type, tin, "Peugeot Freres" 50.00

Lap-type, wooden case, dovetailed

construction, w/drawer, lacy iron dome top w/high center crank handle, ca. mid-1800s 69.00

Lap-type, wood w/brass bowl, w/manufacturer's nameplate 90.00

Lap-type, wood, tin & brass, a scalloped square wooden top w/a footed brass cup & iron crank handle w/wooden grip, baluster-turned wood corner posts & square base framing flat tin sides & a single drawer, tin panels w/worn dark gold paint & traces of paper labels, 19th c., 11" h. (brass cup battered) 82.50

Store counter model, two-wheel, cast iron, "Enterprise No. 3" 695.00

Store counter model, two-wheel, cast iron, "Star Mill," very good original red, navy & gold paint, dated 1885 ....375.00

Wall-type, cast iron & glass, "Arcade Crystal," clear glass jar 80.00

Wall-type, black metal, "Regal I F & C-NO 44," all original (no cup) 75.00

Wall-type, cast iron, "Parker Pat No. 90," w/original tin lid, 11 x 11", 11" l. handle 175.00

Wall-type, cast iron & wood, "Golden Rule" 230.00

COMIC BOOKS

Comic books, especially first, or early issues of a series, are avidly collected today. Prices for some of the scarce ones have reached extremely high levels. Prices listed below are for copies in fine to mint condition.

The Incredible Hulk No. 1

All Star Comics, National Periodical No. 19 ....$200.00

Animal Comics, Dell Publishing No. 23, October-November 1946 ....12.00

Barbie and Ken, Dell Nos. 1-5, 1962-, Dell file copies, near mint, set of 5 ....920.00

Batman, National Periodical Publications No. 38, Penguin cover 125.00

Beany and Cecil, Dell Nos. 1-5, 1955-, Dell file copies, mint & near mint, set of 5 ....920.00

Beware the Creeper, National Periodical Publications No. 1, 1968 ....20.00

Blackhawk, Comic Magazines No. 76, 1954 ....35.00

Charlie McCarthy, True Comics, July 1942 ....30.00

Christmas with Mother Goose, by Walt Kelly, Four Color, Dell Publishing No. 172, 1947 ....35.00

Cisco Kid, Dell Publishing No. 9, 1958 ....15.00

Daredevil Battles Hitler, Lev Gleason Publications, July 1941, file copy, w/letter of authenticity (apparent restoration) 1,380.00

Detective Comics, National Periodical Publications/DC Comics No. 41, Robin's first solo 250.00

Detective Comics, National Periodical Publications/DC Comics No. 45, first Joker story in Detective (tape repair to front cover) 225.00

Flash (The), DC Comics No. 1, March 1959, first issue w/his own title (apparent restoration) 1,295.00

Fox and the Crow, National Periodicals Nos. 1-4, 1951, set of 4 ....863.00

Get Smart, Dell Publishing Co. No. 5 ....12.00

Gumps (The), Dell Publishing Co. No. 4 ....20.00

Gunsmoke, Dell Publishing Co./Gold Key No. 24 ....9.00

Hopalong Cassidy, Fawcett Publications No. 41 ....10.00

I Dream of Jeannie, Dell Publishing Co. No. 2...6.00

Incredible Hulk (The), Marvel Comics Group No. 1, 1962, very fine condition (ILLUS.) 7,130.00

I Spy, Gold Key No. 1, August 1966...40.00

Lois Lane, DC Comics No. 1, April 1958, very fine 4,830.00

Lone Ranger (The), Dell Publishing Co. No. 90...7.00

Man from U.N.C.L.E. (The), Gold Key No. 9 ....15.00

Man from U.N.C.L.E. (The), Gold Key No.11 ....10.00
Marvel Mystery, Timely Publications Nos. 7 & 8, 1940, No. 8 features battle between the Human Torch & Sub-Mariner, 2 pcs. 770.00
Negro Romances, Charlton Comics No. 4, 1955, near mint 518.00

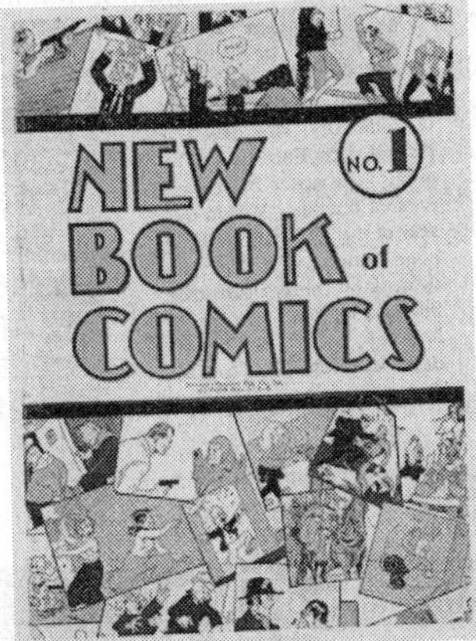

New Book of Comics No. 1

New Book of Comics, National Periodical Publications No. 1, 1937, fine condition (ILLUS.) 4,485.00
Outer Limits (The), Dell Publishing Co. No. 1 ....30.00
Rat Patrol (The), Dell Publishing Co. No. 1, March 1967 ....22.00
Rat Patrol (The), Dell Publishing Co. No. 2 ....15.00
Red Ryder, Dell Publishing Co. No. 36 ....45.00

Superman No. 1

Red Ryder, Dell Publishing Co. No. 43 ....25.00
Silver Kid Western, Key/Stanmore Publications Vol. 1, No. 1, October, 1954 ....15.00
Spirit (The), No. 1, June 2, 1940 ....400.00
Spirit (The), August 3, 1952 ....200.00
Superman, DC Comics No. 1, 1939, restored fine condition (ILLUS.) ..10,350.00
Twilight Zone (The), Dell Publishing Co. No. 1 ....42.00
Walt Disney Comics & Stories, Vol. 12, No. 3, December 1951 ....60.00
Wild, Wild West (The), Gold Key No. 2 ....17.00
Wings Comics, Fiction House Magazines No. 113, 1951 ....10.00

COMMEMORATIVE PLATES

Limited edition commemorative and collector plates rank high on the list of collectible items. The oldest and best-known of these plates, those of Bing & Grondahl and Royal Copenhagen, retain leadership in the field, but other companies are turning out a variety of designs, some of which have been widely embraced by the growing numbers who have made plate collecting a hobby. Plates listed below are a representative selection of fine porcelain, glass and other plates available to collectors.

ANRI
Christmas

1971, St. Jakob in Groden $41.00
1972, Pipers at Alberobello 45.00
1973, Alpine Horn 100.00
1974, Young Man & Girl 56.00
1975, Christmas in Ireland 70.00
1976, Alpine Christmas 95.00
1977, Legend of Heiligenblut 83.00
1978, The Klockler Singers 83.00
1979, The Moss Gatherers of Villnoess 65.00
1980, Wintry Church-going in Santa Christina 80.00
1981, Santa Claus in Tyrol 105.00
1982, Star Singers 116.00
1983, Unto Us a Child Is Born 133.00
1984, Yuletide in the Valley 88.00
1985, Good Morning, Good Cheer ....75.00 to 100.00

BAREUTHER
Christmas

1967, Stiftskirche ....50.00 to 70.00
1968, Kappl 13.50

1969, Christkindlesmarkt 9.00
1970, Chapel in Oberndorf 8.50

1971 Bareuther Christmas Plate

1971, Toys for Sale (ILLUS.) 8.00
1972, Christmas in Munich 18.50
1973, Christmas Sleigh Ride 7.00
1974, Church in the Black Forest 9.50
1975, Snowman 22.00
1976, Chapel in the Hills 13.50
1977, Story Time 13.00
1978, Mittenwald 9.50
1979, Winter Day 10.00
1980, Miltenberg 21.00
1981, Walk in the Forest 16.00
1982, Bad Wimpfen 25.00
1983, The Night Before Christmas 25.50
1984, Zeil on the River Main 24.50
1985, Winter Wonderland 27.50
1986, Market Place in Forchheim 26.50

Father's Day

1969, Castle Neuschwanstein 17.00
1970, Castle Pfalz 9.00
1971, Castle Heidelberg 13.00
1972, Castle Hohenschwangau 11.50
1973, Castle Katz 10.50
1974, Wurzburg Castle 16.00
1975, Castle Lichtenstein 21.00
1976, Castle Hohenzollern 27.00
1977, Castle Eltz 27.00
1978, Castle Falkenstein 30.00
1979, Castle Rheinstein 25.00
1980, Castle Cochem 22.00
1981, Castle Gutenfels 35.50
1982, Castle Zwingenberg 25.50
1983, Castle Lauenstein 25.50
1984, Castle Neuenstein 19.00
1985, Castle Wartburg Near Eisenach 30.50
1986, Castle Hardegg 29.50
1987, Castle Buerresheim 20.00

Mother's Day

1969, Dancing 21.00
1970, Mother & Children 9.00
1971, Doing the Laundry 11.50
1972, Baby's First Step 10.00
1973, Mother Kissing Baby 18.50
1974, Musical Children 13.00
1975, Spring Outing 9.50
1976, Rocking Cradle 13.00
1977, Noon Feeding 15.00
1978, Blind Man's Bluff 20.00
1979, Mother's Love 13.00
1980, First Cherries 15.00
1981, Playtime 15.50
1982, Suppertime 16.50
1983, On Farm 16.00
1984, Village Children 25.00
1985, Sunrise 21.00

BELLEEK
Christmas

1970 Belleek Christmas Plate

1970, Castle Caldwell (ILLUS.) 78.00
1971, Celtic Cross 48.00
1972, Flight of the Earls 31.00
1973, Tribute to W. B. Yeats 31.00
1974, Devenish Island 200.00
1975, The Celtic Cross 55.00
1976, Dove of Peace 50.00
1977, Wren 55.00

Irish Wildlife Christmas

1978, A Leaping Salmon 47.00
1979, Hare at Rest 47.00
1980, Hedgehog 50.00
1981, Red Squirrel 50.00

BING & GRONDAHL
Christmas

1895 .... 5,495.00 to 5,595.00
1896 .... 1,642.00
1897 .... 1,621.00

1898....................................610.00
1899....................................1,299.00
1900....................................855.00
1901....................................339.00
1902....................................288.00
1903....................................280.00
1904....................................109.00
1905....................................107.00
1906....................................67.00
1907....................................68.00
1908....................................57.00
1909....................................65.00
1910....................................63.00
1911....................................60.00
1912....................................62.00
1913....................................63.00
1914....................................55.00
1915....................................94.00
1916....................................57.00

1917 Bing & Grondahl Christmas Plate

1917 (ILLUS.)....................................56.00
1918....................................56.00
1919....................................50.00
1920....................................54.00
1921....................................52.00
1922....................................47.00
1923....................................47.00
1924....................................50.00
1925....................................50.00
1926....................................50.00
1927....................................66.00
1928....................................51.00
1929....................................46.00
1930....................................64.00
1931....................................58.00
1932....................................59.00
1933....................................49.00
1934....................................53.00
1935....................................48.00
1936....................................51.00
1937....................................56.00
1938....................................98.00
1939....................................115.00
1940....................................121.00
1941....................................179.00
1942....................................139.00
1943....................................121.00
1944....................................72.00
1945....................................92.00
1946....................................52.00
1947....................................67.00
1948....................................54.00
1949....................................52.00
1950....................................78.00
1951....................................64.00
1952....................................62.00
1953....................................57.00
1954....................................58.00
1955....................................64.00
1956....................................95.00
1957....................................101.00
1958....................................69.00
1959....................................88.00
1960....................................100.00
1961....................................72.00
1962....................................46.00
1963....................................64.00
1964....................................24.00
1965....................................28.00
1966....................................23.00
1967....................................23.00
1968....................................18.00
1969....................................12.00
1970....................................12.00
1971....................................10.00
1972....................................9.00
1973....................................11.50
1974....................................10.50
1975....................................14.00
1976....................................12.00
1977....................................11.50
1978....................................13.00
1979....................................15.50
1980....................................17.00
1981....................................18.50
1982....................................24.00
1983....................................26.00
1984....................................21.00
1985....................................21.00

Mother's Day

1969, Dog & Puppies....................................337.00
1970, Birds & Chicks....................................12.00
1971, Cat & Kitten....................................8.00
1972, Mare & Foal....................................8.00
1973, Duck & Ducklings....................................9.00
1974, Bear & Cubs....................................8.50
1975, Doe & Fawns....................................12.00
1976, Swan Family....................................12.00

1977, Squirrel & Young 12.00
1978, Heron....................11.00
1979, Fox & Cubs....................16.00
1980, Woodpecker & Young....................20.00
1981, Hare & Young....................22.00
1982, Lioness & Cubs 19.50
1983, Raccoon & Young....................23.00
1984, Stork & Nestlings....................23.00

Jubilee

1915, Frozen Window....................114.00
1920, Church Bells 45.00
1925, Dog Outside Window....................85.00
1930, The Old Organist 109.00
1935, Little Match Girl....................568.00
1940, Three Wise Men 1,525.00
1945, Royal Guard Amalienborg Castle....................117.00
1950, Eskimos....................122.00
1955, Dybbol Mill....................123.00
1960, Kronborg Castle....................89.00
1965, Churchgoers....................44.00
1970, Amalienborg Castle 11.00
1975, Horses Enjoying Meal....................22.00
1980, Happiness over Yule Tree....................23.00

FENTON (Glass)
Christmas

1970, Little Brown Church, blue satin...17.00
1970, Little Brown Church, carnival......20.00
1971, Old Brick Church, blue satin.......16.00
1971, Old Brick Church, carnival..........22.00
1972, Two Horned Church, carnival.....20.00
1972, Two Horned Church, white satin....................30.00
1973, St. Mary's, carnival 22.50
1974, Nation's Church, carnival............23.00
1974, Nation's Church, white satin.......12.50
1975, Birthplace of Liberty, blue satin ..24.50
1975, Birthplace of Liberty, carnival 19.00
1975, Birthplace of Liberty, white satin....................14.50
1976, Old North Church, carnival 17.50
1977, San Carlos Borromeo, carnival...15.00
1977, San Carlos Borromeo, white satin....................14.50
1978, Church of Holy Trinity, blue satin....................15.00
1978, Church of Holy Trinity, carnival...15.00
1978, Church of Holy Trinity, white satin....................14.50
1979, San Jose y Miguel de Aguayo, blue satin 15.00
1979, San Jose y Miguel de Aguayo, carnival 12.50
1979, San Jose y Miguel de Aguayo, white satin....................9.00
1980, Christ Church, carnival 15.00
1981, Mission of San Xavier del Bac, carnival 16.00

Mother's Day

1971, Madonna with Sleeping Child, blue satin 17.00
1971, Madonna with Sleeping Child, carnival 20.00
1972, Madonna of the Goldfinch, blue satin 13.50
1972, Madonna of the Goldfinch, carnival 8.00
1972, Madonna of the Goldfinch, white satin....................20.00
1973, Cowper Madonna, blue satin......60.00
1973, Cowper Madonna, carnival.........10.50
1974, Madonna of the Grotto, blue satin 12.00
1974, Madonna of the Grotto, carnival 8.00
1974, Madonna of the Grotto, white satin 14.50
1975, Taddei Madonna, blue satin 60.00
1975, Taddei Madonna, carnival 15.00
1976, Holy Night, carnival....................11.50
1977, Madonna & Child, blue satin.......17.00
1977, Madonna & Child, carnival..........12.50
1978, Madonnina, carnival 9.50
1978, Madonnina, white satin....................15.00
1979, Madonna of the Rose Hedge, carnival 12.00

FERRANDIZ, JUAN
Christmas - Anri (Wood)

1972, Christ in Manger 139.00
1973, Boy with Lamb....................70.00
1974, Nativity....................169.00
1975, Flight into Egypt....................75.00
1976, Mary & Joseph Pray 127.00
1977, Girl with Tree 45.00
1978, Leading the Way....................65.00
1979, Drummer Boy 86.00
1980, Rejoice....................95.00
1981, Spreading Word....................73.50
1982, Shepherd Family 75.00
1983, Peace Attend Thee....................80.00

Mother & Child - Schmid (Porcelain)

1977, Orchard Mother 47.00
1978, Pastoral Mother 38.00
1979, Floral Mother 49.00
1980, Avian Mother 50.00

Mother's Day - Anri (Wood)

1972, Mother Sewing....................112.00
1973, Mother & Child....................62.00
1974, Mother & Child....................79.00
1975, Mother Holding Dove....................79.00

1976, Mother & Child..............50.00 to 75.00
1977, Girl with Flowers........................59.00
1978, Beginning..................................65.00
1979, All Hearts..................................80.00
1980, Spring Arrivals..........................101.00
1981, Harmony....................................77.00
1982, With Love...................................75.00

FRANKLIN MINT (STERLING SILVER)
Norman Rockwell Christmas Series

1970 Rockwell Christmas Plate

1970, Bringing Home the Tree (ILLUS.) 183.00
1971, Under the Mistletoe 100.00
1972, The Carolers..............................80.00
1973, Trimming the Tree 80.00
1974, Hanging the Wreath..................108.00
1975, Home for Christmas..................136.00

FRANKOMA
Christmas

1965, Goodwill Toward Men...............207.00
1966, Bethlehem Shepherds................89.00
1967, Gifts for the Christ Child 60.00
1968, Flight into Egypt..........................18.50
1969, Laid in a Manger.........................27.00
1970, King of Kings 20.00
1971, No Room in the Inn......................12.00
1972, Seeking the Christ Child.............15.00
1973, The Annunciation..........................9.50
1974, She Loved & Cared 16.00
1975, Peace on Earth...........................17.50
1976, Gift of Love 18.00
1977, Birth of Eternal Life 18.50
1978, All Nature Rejoiced....................22.50
1979, Star of Hope 15.00
1980, Unto Us a Child Is Born 12.50
1981, O Come Let Us Adore Him.........15.00
1982, Wise Men Rejoice......................13.00
1983, Wise Men Bring Gifts..................14.00
1984, Faith, Hope & Love....................14.50
1985, The Angels Watched 13.50

FURSTENBERG
Christmas

1971, Rabbits 19.00
1972, Snowy Village 19.00
1973, Christmas Eve 23.50
1975, Deer Family 12.00
1976, Winter Birds 22.00

Mother's Day

1972, Hummingbird 21.00
1973, Hedgehogs 12.00
1974, Doe with Fawn............................14.00

GORHAM - NORMAN ROCKWELL
Christmas

1974, Tiny Tim......................................24.00
1975, Good Deeds 24.00
1976, Christmas Trio 19.00
1978, Planning Christmas Visits..........18.50
1979, Santa's Helpers 15.00
1980, Letter to Santa 22.50
1981, Santa Plans His Visit..................19.00
1982, The Jolly Coachman...................19.50
1983, Christmas Dancers.....................28.00
1984, Christmas Medley.......................28.00
1985, Home for the Holidays................25.00
1987, The Homecoming 25.00

Four Seasons

1971, A Boy & His Dog, set of 4.........225.00
1972, Young Love, set of 4.................................150.00 to 200.00
1973, The Ages of Love, set of 4........167.00
1974, Grandpa & Me, set of 4 ....91.00
1975, Me & My Pal, set of 4 ....132.00
1976, Grand Pals, set of 4.................122.00
1977, Going on Sixteen, set of 4 ....71.00
1978, The Tender Years, set of 4.........63.00
1979, A Helping Hand, set of 4.............50.00
1980, Dad's Boy, set of 4 ....111.00
1980, Landscape Series, set of 4.........95.00
1981, Old Timers, set of 4 ....72.00
1982, Life with Father, set of 4 ....50.00
1983, Old Buddies, set of 4 ....75.00

HAVILAND & CO.
Christmas

1970, A Partridge in a Pear Tree..........42.50
1971, Two Turtle Doves 20.00
1972, Three French Hens......................20.00
1973, Four Colly Birds 19.00
1974, Five Golden Rings 18.00
1975, Six Geese A'Laying 20.00
1976, Seven Swans A'Swimming.........25.00
1977, Eight Maids A'Milking 25.00
1978, Nine Ladies Dancing 43.00

1979, Ten Lords A'Leaping 32.00
1980, Eleven Pipers Piping 45.50
1981, Twelve Drummers Drumming.....42.00

HAVILAND & PARLON
Christmas
1972, Madonna & Child (Raphael) 25.00
1973, Madonnina (Feruzzi)...................50.00
1974, Cowper Madonna & Child (Raphael) 35.00
1975, Madonna & Child (Murillo)..........28.00
1976, Madonna & Child (Botticelli) 28.00
1977, Madonna & Child (Bellini) 30.00
1978, Madonna & Child (Fra Filippo Lippi) 30.00
1979, Madonna of the Eucharist (Botticelli) 90.00

Mother's Day
1975, Laura & Child..............................15.00
1976, Pinky & Baby 9.50
1977, Amy & Snoopy...........................10.00

Tapestry Series

Haviland & Parlon 1971 Unicorn Plate

1971, The Unicorn in Captivity (ILLUS.) 71.00
1972, Start of the Hunt 26.00
1973, Chase of the Unicorn..................55.00
1974, End of the Hunt...........................60.00
1975, The Unicorn Surrounded 52.00
1976, The Unicorn is Brought to the Castle...40.00

The Lady & The Unicorn
1977, To My Only Desire.......................20.00
1978, Sight 24.00
1979, Sound 25.00
1980, Touch..27.00
1981, Scent 25.00
1982, Taste...32.00

HUMMEL (GOEBEL WORKS)
Annual
1971, Heavenly Angel 476.00
1972, Hear Ye, Hear Ye 44.00

1973 Goebel Hummel Christmas

1973, Globe Trotter (ILLUS.) 78.00
1974, Goose Girl 44.00
1975, Ride into Christmas 50.00
1976, Apple Tree Girl 47.00
1977, Apple Tree Boy...........................49.00
1978, Happy Pastime 44.00
1979, Singing Lesson 34.00
1980, School Girl 47.50
1981, Umbrella Boy 54.00
1982, Umbrella Girl...............................92.00
1983, The Postman 145.00
1984, Little Helper 58.00
1985, Chick Girl....................................64.50
1986, Playmates.................................109.00
1987, Feeding Time............................179.00
1988..81.00

Anniversary
1975, Stormy Weather..........................80.00
1980, Spring Dance...............................59.00
1985, Auf Wiedersehen 158.00

KAISER
Christmas
1970, Waiting for Santa Claus..............14.00
1971, Silent Night 13.50
1972, Welcome Home 19.50
1973, Holy Night...................................23.50
1974, Christmas Carolers......................15.50
1975, Bringing Home the Christmas Tree 15.00
1976, Christ the Saviour is Born............13.50
1977, The Three Kings 14.00
1978, Shepherds in the Field................14.50
1979, Christmas Eve 22.00
1980, Joys of Winter.............................22.50
1981, Most Holy Night 27.50
1982, Bringing Home the Christmas Tree 25.00

Mother's Day

1971, Mare & Foal 14.00
1972, Flowers for Mother......................11.00
1973, Cat & Kitten 23.00
1974, Fox & Young................................23.00
1975, German Shepherd with Pups 30.00
1976, Swan & Cygnets 19.00
1977, Mother Rabbit & Young 23.00
1978, Hen & Chicks..............................21.50
1979, A Mother's Devotion 20.00
1980, Raccoon Family...........................22.00
1981, Safe Near Mother 26.50
1982, Pheasant Family..........................25.00
1983, Tender Care 27.50

Anniversary

1972, Love Birds...................................13.00
1973, In the Park 13.00
1974, Canoeing Down River.................16.00
1975, Tender Moment 13.50
1976, Serenade for Lovers 14.50
1977, A Simple Gift...............................13.00
1978, Viking Toast................................18.50
1979, Romantic Interlude 19.50
1980, Love at Play.................................25.50
1981, Rendezvous..................................27.00
1982, Betrothal 27.00

LALIQUE (Glass)

1967 Lalique Plate

Annual

1965, Deux Oiseaux (Two Birds)........900.00
1966, Rose de Songerie (Dream Rose) ....75.00 to 100.00
1967, Ballet de Poisson (Fish Ballet) [ILLUS.] 105.00
1968, Gazelle Fantaisie (Gazelle Fantasy) 64.00
1969, Papillon (Butterfly) ....50.00 to 75.00
1970, Paon (Peacock) 65.00
1971, Hibou (Owl).................................60.00
1972, Coquillage (Shell) 55.00
1973, Petit Geai (Jayling) 76.00
1974, Sous d'Argent (Silver Pennies)...73.50
1975, Duo de Poisson (Fish Duet) 100.00
1976, Aigle (Eagle) 85.00

LENOX

Boehm Bird Series

1970, Wood Thrush ....100.00 to 125.00
1971, Goldfinch 80.00
1972, Mountain Bluebird.......................32.00
1973, Meadowlark 24.00
1974, Rufous Hummingbird...................39.00
1975, American Redstart.......................33.50
1976, Cardinals 43.00
1977, Robins 47.00
1978, Mockingbirds ....50.00 to 75.00
1979, Golden-Crowned Kinglets..........85.00
1980, Black-Throated Blue Warblers....95.00
1981, Eastern Phoebes 95.00

Boehm Woodland Wildlife Series

1973, Raccoons......................................38.00
1974, Red Foxes 33.00
1975, Cottontail Rabbits 44.00
1976, Eastern Chipmunks 34.00
1977, Beaver 55.00
1978, Whitetail Deer 46.00
1979, Squirrels 72.50
1980, Bobcats...68.50
1981, Martens...88.50
1982, Otters 103.00

LIHS-LINDNER

Christmas

1972, Little Drummer Boy.....................15.50
1973, Little Carolers 9.00
1974, Peace on Earth................................9.00
1975, Christmas Cheer..............................9.00
1976, Joy of Christmas..........................11.00
1977, Holly-jolly Christmas 19.00
1978, Holy Night 10.00

LLADRO

Christmas

1971, Caroling 100.00
1972, Carolers 21.00
1973, Boy & Girl 55.00
1974, Carolers 45.00
1975, Cherubs 45.00
1976, Christ Child 70.00
1977, Nativity Scene................................80.00

Mother's Day

1971, Kiss of the Child............................37.00
1972, Bird & Chicks 30.00
1973, Mother & Children.........................20.00
1974, Mother Nursing ....50.00 to 75.00
1975, Mother & Child 24.00
1976, Tender Vigil 24.00

1977, Mother & Daughter......................24.50

Annual Cathedral Series

1970, Notre Dame Cathedral................20.00
1971, Westminster Abbey 30.00
1972, Basilica di San Marco 25.00
1973, Cologne Cathedral......................61.00
1974, Temple Rue de la Victoire, Paris...49.00
1975, Basilica di San Pietro, Rome......36.00
1976, Christ Church, Philadelphia........36.00
1977, Masjid-E-Shah 81.00
1978, Santiago de Compostela 56.50

Mother's Day

1971, Flowers for Mother.....................17.50
1972, Mother & Children......................17.00
1973, Mother & Child...........................16.00
1974, Mother & Child...........................15.00
1975, Child's First Steps......................45.50
1976, Children & Puppy.......................17.50
1977, Child & Dove..............................17.50
1978, Mother & Child...........................17.50

PORSGRUND

Christmas

1968, Church Scene..............50.00 to 75.00
1969, Three Kings 7.00
1970, Road to Bethlehem......................7.00
1971, A Child is Born............................8.00
1972, Hark, the Herald Angels Sing 7.00
1973, Promise of the Savior 9.00
1984, The Stepherds 6.00
1975, Jesus on the Road to the Temple..9.00
1976, Jesus & the Elders.......................7.00
1977, Draught of the Fish 8.00

Traditional Norwegian Christmas

1978, Guests Are Coming 8.50
1979, Home for Christmas.....................9.00
1980, Preparing for Christmas.............10.00
1981, Christmas Skating 11.00
1982, White Christmas 13.00

Father's Day

1971, Fishing.......................................10.00
1972, Cookout 8.00
1973, Sledding.......................................5.00
1974, Father & Son 3.50
1975, Skating..6.00
1976, Skiing...5.00
1977, Soccer 5.00
1978, Canoeing 5.00
1979, Father & Daughter.......................8.00
1980, Sailing..4.00
1981, Building a Ship.............................5.00
1982, Father & Daughter.......................6.50
1983, Father's Day 6.00
1984, Tree Planting 8.00

Mother's Day

1970, Mare & Foal..................................7.00
1971, Boy & Geese 7.00
1972, Doe & Fawn..................................6.50
1973, Cat & Kittens................................3.50
1974, Boy & Goats 4.50
1975, Dog & Puppies..............................5.50
1976, Girl & Calf 7.50
1977, Boy & Chickens 7.50
1978, Girl & Pigs.....................................5.50
1979, Boy & Reindeer 6.00
1980, Girl & Lambs...............................10.00
1981, Boy & Birds...................................6.00
1982, Girl & Rabbits 12.00

RED SKELTON

Freddie the Freeloader Series (Crown Parian)

1979, Freddie in the Bathtub 165.00
1980, Freddie's Shack..........................75.00
1981, Freddie on the Green 56.00
1982, Love That Freddie 37.50

Famous Clowns Series (Fairmont)

Freddie the Freeloader Plate

1976, Freddie the Freeloader (ILLUS.) 348.00
1977, W. C. Fields 61.00
1978, Happy 67.00
1979, The Pledge 58.00

Freddie's Adventures Series (Crown Parian)

1981, Captain Freddie 48.00
1982, Bronco Freddie 45.00
1983, Sir Freddie 46.00
1984, Gertrude & Heathcliffe 45.00

Single Releases

1983, Seventy Years Young (Armstrong's/Crown Parian) 52.00

1984, Freddie the Torchbearer (Armstrong's/Crown Parian) 50.00

RORSTRAND

Christmas

1968, Bringing Home the Tree ..... 300.00 to 350.00
1969, Fisherman Sailing Home 16.00
1970, Nils with His Geese 11.00
1971, Nils in Lapland 24.00
1972, Dalecarlian Fiddler 9.00
1973, Farm in Smaland 50.00
1974, Vadstena 40.00
1975, Nils in Vastmanland 16.00
1976, Nils in Uppland 19.00
1977, Nils in Varmland 16.00
1978, Nils in Fjallbacka 22.00
1979, Nils in Vaestergoetland 25.00
1980, Nils in Halland 30.00
1981, Nils in Gotland 28.00
1982, Nils at Skansen in Stockholm 33.00
1983, Nils in Oland 32.00
1984, Nils in Angermanland 37.00
1985, Nils in Jamtland 40.00

Father's Day

1971, Father & Child 9.50
1972, Meal at Home 6.50
1973, Tilling Fields 6.50
1974, Fishing 7.00
1975, Painting 6.50
1976, Plowing 6.00
1977, Sawing 7.00
1978, Self-Portrait 15.00
1979, Bridge 15.50
1980, My Etch-Nook 15.00

ROSENTHAL

1931 Rosenthal Christmas Plate

Christmas

1910 ..... 370.00
1911 ..... 148.00
1913 ..... 110.00
1915 ..... 119.00
1916 ..... 160.00
1923 ..... 90.00
1926 ..... 115.00
1927 ..... 108.00
1928 ..... 110.00
1929 ..... 135.00
1930 ..... 69.00
1931 (ILLUS.) 152.00
1933 ..... 125.00
1934 ..... 125.00
1935 ..... 110.00
1936 ..... 107.00
1937 ..... 110.00
1938 ..... 110.00 to 115.00
1939 ..... 110.00
1942 ..... 200.00
1944 ..... 176.00
1945 ..... 240.00
1946 ..... 150.00
1949 ..... 110.00
1950 ..... 110.00
1951 ..... 250.00
1952 ..... 115.00
1953 ..... 120.00
1954 ..... 120.00
1955 ..... 118.00
1956 ..... 124.00
1957 ..... 115.00
1958 ..... 115.00
1959 ..... 110.00
1960 ..... 115.00
1961 ..... 96.00
1962 ..... 87.00
1963 ..... 93.00
1964 ..... 115.00
1965 ..... 87.00
1966 ..... 147.00
1967 ..... 95.00
1968 ..... 107.00
1969 ..... 103.00
1970 ..... 84.00
1971 ..... 53.00
1972 ..... 52.00
1973 ..... 57.00
1974 ..... 52.00
1975 ..... 58.00

Wiinblad Christmas

1971, Maria & Child 600.00
1972, King Caspar ..... 175.00 to 200.00
1973, King Melchior 186.00
1974, King Balthazar 258.00
1975, The Annunciation 138.00
1976, Angel with Trumpet 118.00
1977, Adoration of the Shepherds 132.00

1978, Angel with Harp....................121.00
1979, Exodus from Egypt....................129.00
1980, Angel with Glockenspiel 131.00
1981, Christ Child Visits Temple 148.00
1982, Christening of Christ.................143.00

Hibel Nobility of Children Series
1976, La Contessa Isabella...................78.00
1977, La Marquis Maurice-Pierre 78.00
1978, Baronesse Johanna-Maryke Van Vollendam Tot Marken 95.00
1979, Chief Red Feather 101.00

ROYAL BAYREUTH
Christmas
1972, Carriage in the Village ..25.00 to 30.00
1973, Snow Scene 15.00
1974, Old Mill.......................................12.50
1975, Forest Chalet "Serenity" 8.50
1976, Christmas in the Country.............9.50
1977, Peace on Earth...............................8.00
1978, Peaceful Interlude.......................25.00
1979, Homeward Bound........................17.50

Mother's Day
1973, Consolation...................................20.00
1974, Young Americans 79.00
1975, Young Americans II 25.00
1976, Young Americans III 40.00
1977, Young Americans IV.....................25.00
1978, Young Americans V......................16.00
1979, Young Americans VI......................30.00
1980, Young Americans VII....................33.00
1981, Young Americans VIII...................22.50
1982, Young Americans IX.....................27.00

ROYAL COPENHAGEN

1921 Royal Copenhagen Christmas Plate

Christmas
1908...3,487.00
1909..131.00
1910..99.00
1911...115.00
1912...122.50
1913...117.00
1914...115.00
1915...120.00
1916...78.00
1917...71.00
1918...75.00
1919...75.00
1920...70.00
1921 (ILLUS.) 65.00
1922...58.00
1923...59.00
1924...78.00
1925...63.00
1926...65.00
1927...109.00
1928...65.00
1929...64.00
1930...85.00
1931...84.00
1932...74.00
1933...122.00
1934...111.00
1935...158.00
1936...128.00
1937...179.00
1938...233.00
1939...293.00
1940...303.00
1941...261.00
1942...285.00
1943...411.00
1944...195.00
1945...307.00
1946...136.00
1947...189.00
1948...160.00
1949...172.00
1950...178.00
1951...268.00
1952...97.00
1953...99.00
1954...100.00
1955...141.00
1956...136.00
1957...71.00
1958...87.00
1959...86.00
1960...103.00
1961...107.00
1962...153.00
1963...64.00
1964...40.00
1965...41.00
1966...23.00
1967...24.00
1968...17.50

1969....................19.00
1970....................26.00
1971....................12.00
1972....................13.00
1973....................12.00
1974....................16.00
1975....................11.00
1976....................15.50
1977....................20.00
1978....................20.00
1979....................27.00
1980....................30.00
1981....................20.00
1982....................32.00
1983....................30.00
1984....................32.00
1985....................44.00

Mother's Day

1971, American Mother....................12.00
1972, Oriental Mother....................9.00
1973, Danish Mother....................9.00
1974, Greenland Mother....................9.00
1975, Bird in Nest....................8.00
1976, Mermaids....................7.50
1977, The Twins....................6.50
1978, Mother & Child....................6.50
1979, A Loving Mother....................8.00
1980, An Outing with Mother....................14.00
1981, Reunion....................14.50
1982, Children's Hour....................13.50

Motherhood Series

1982, Mother Robin & Her Young Ones....................18.00
1983, Mother Cat & Kitten....................20.00
1984, Mare with Foal....................17.00
1985, Mother Rabbit with Bunny....................23.00
1986, Dog & Puppies....................26.00
1987, Goat & Kid....................33.00

ROYAL DOULTON

Beswick Christmas Series

1972, Christmas in England....................22.50
1973, Christmas in Mexico....................24.00
1974, Christmas in Bulgaria....................32.50
1975, Christmas in Norway....................45.00
1976, Christmas in Holland....................46.00
1977, Christmas in Poland....................38.50
1978, Christmas in America....................27.00

Victorian Christmas

1977, Skater....................13.00
1978, Victorian Girl....................13.00
1979, Sleigh Ride....................14.00
1980, Santa's Visit....................17.50
1981, Carolers....................16.50
1982, Santa's Visit....................17.00

Mother & Child Series

1973, Colette & Child....................278.00
1974, Sayuri & Child....................92.00
1975, Kristina & Child....................42.50
1976, Marilyn & Child....................50.00
1977, Lucia & Child....................44.00
1978, Kathleen & Child....................39.00

SCHMID HUMMEL

1971 Schmid Hummel Christmas Plate

Christmas

1971, Angel (ILLUS.)....................15.00
1972, Angel with Flute....................11.00
1973, The Nativity....................57.00
1974, The Guardian Angel....................9.00
1975, Christmas Child....................11.00
1976, Sacred Journey....................10.00
1977, Herald Angel....................9.50
1978, Heavenly Trio....................9.00
1979, Starlight Angel....................9.00
1980, Parade into Toyland....................19.50
1981, A Time to Remember....................15.00
1982, Angelic Procession....................19.00
1983, Angelic Messenger....................22.00
1984, A Gift from Heaven....................26.00
1985, Heavenly Light....................17.00

Mother's Day

1972, Playing Hooky....................8.00
1973, Little Fisherman....................38.00
1974, Bumblebee....................8.00
1975, Message of Love....................15.00
1976, Devotion for Mother....................10.00
1977, Moonlight Return....................15.50
1978, Afternoon Stroll....................15.00
1979, Cherub's Gift....................15.00
1980, Mother's Little Helpers....................17.00
1981, Playtime....................11.00
1982, The Flower Basket....................16.00
1983, Spring bouquet....................20.00
1984, A Joy to Share....................23.00
1985, A Mother's Journey....................20.00

SPODE

Christmas

1970, Partridge in a Pear Tree 20.00
1971, In Heaven the Angels Singing 16.00
1972, We Saw Three Ships A'Sailing...18.00
1973, We Three Kings of Orient Are 33.00
1974, Deck the Halls 35.00
1975, Christbaum 34.50
1976, Good King Wenceslas 16.50
1977, The Holly & the Ivy 21.00
1978, While Shepherds Watched 24.50
1979, Away in a Manger.......................21.00
1980, Bringing in the Boar's Head........25.00
1981, Make We Merry 47.00

VAL ST. LAMBERT (Glass)

1970 DaVinci Plate

Old Masters Series

1968, Rubens & Rembrandt, pr............53.00
1969, Van Gogh & Van Dyck, pr. 38.00
1970, DaVinci & Michelangelo, pr. (ILLUS. of one) 62.00
1971, El Greco & Goya, pr. 61.00
1972, Reynolds & Gainsborough, pr. ...54.00

WEDGWOOD

Christmas

1969, Windsor Castle 78.00
1970, Christmas in Trafalgar Square....17.00
1971, Picadilly Circus, London 20.00
1972, St. Paul's Cathedral....................24.00
1973, Tower of London.........................41.00
1974, Houses of Parliament 22.00
1975, Tower Bridge 28.00
1976, Hampton Court 19.00
1977, Westminster Abbey 30.00
1978, Horse Guards 24.00
1979, Buckingham Palace....................32.00
1980, St. James Palace........................29.00
1981, Marble Arch 26.00
1982, Lambeth Palace..........................59.00
1983, All Souls, Langham Palace.........55.00
1984, Constitution Hill...........................45.00
1985, The Tate Gallery.........................53.00
1986, Albert Memorial 135.00
1987, Guildhall......................................75.00
1988, The Observatory, Greenwich......70.00

Mother's Day

1971, Sportive Love..............................20.00
1972, Sewing Lesson 10.00
1973, Baptism of Achilles 14.00
1974, Domestic Employment................23.00
1975, Mother & Child............................19.50
1976, The Spinner 13.00
1977, Leisure Time...............................24.00
1978, Swan & Cygnets 19.00
1979, Deer & Fawn...............................29.00
1980, Birds 28.50
1981, Mare & Foal 30.00
1982, Cherubs with Swing....................20.50
1983, Cupid & Butterfly.........................19.00
1984, Cupid & Music 23.00
1985, Cupid & Doves............................30.50

COMPACTS & VANITY CASES

Bakelite compact, intricate design w/Art Deco women & glittered background on cover, Christian Dior, ca. 1920 ....$225.00

Brass compact w/scenic transfer on celluloid lid, "Yardley," ca. 1935 ....75.00

Brass-plated compact, round, overall engraved design centering a relief shield, 2" d. 15.00

Celluloid compact, tortoiseshell-type finish, 5¼" d. 25.00

Enameled compact, ten-sided, decorated w/flowers in shades of blue, w/matching lavender over brass comb case, Stratton, England, compact 3¼" w., 2 pcs. 35.00

Enameled compact, flap jack form, red w/rhinestones, depicting the Statue of Liberty...............................45.00

Enameled compact, red w/gold crown, Prince Matchabelli, No. 701, 1¾ x 2¼"..15.00

Enameled compact, square, black decorated w/paisley-type florals 25.00

Gold (14k yellow) compact, octagonal w/engine-turned design & chased edge, centered w/engraved initials, marked "Tiffany & Co," 247.50

Gold (14k yellow), diamond & sapphire compact, rectangular-form w/engine-turned decoration, ornamented w/a Retro-style three-tone gold stylized ribbon clasp set w/diamonds & sapphires,2 x 2⅞" 1,840.00

Gold (14k two-color) & enamel compact, engine-turned, circular w/bombé sides, the hinged cover & base w/a narrow border of green enamel leaftips, marked w/the initials of workmaster Henrick Wigstrom, "Fabergé" in Cyrillic & 56 standard, containing a powder puff, in the original fitted holly wood case, St. Petersburg, Russia, ca. 1910, 1⅝" d. 11,500.00

Gold-plated (24k) compact, flapjack-type, engraved floral decoration, Rex, 4" d. 50.00

Goldtone compact w/three red & white enameled ballerinas, "Stratto," 3" 68.00

Goldtone compact, w/petit point scene of ladies w/parasols, Vogel, 2¼" sq. 75.00

Goldtone vanity case, decorated w/multicolored intaglio-cut designs, a cameo center surrounded w/prong-set rhinestones, w/tassel & chain, France 350.00

Mother-of-pearl compact, checker-board-type design, "Elgin American" 30.00

Plastic compact, figural Army hat 40.00

Silver compact, embossed Art Nouveau style lady & two peacocks, Fitch 95.00

Silver compact, w/miniature painting on ivory of Princess de Lamballe, front pierced w/florals & back engraved w/plumes, 3 x 3" 225.00

Silver-plated compact, silhouette of a lady on lid, w/decorative silver chain, ca. 1920 ....40.00

Silver-plated compact w/engraved flowers & blue leaves, contains Evening in Paris, Bourgois rouge & powder, 2¼ x 3¼" 60.00

Silver-plated vanity case, decorated w/relief nymphs, marked "Djer-Kiss" & dated May 19, 1925 ....150.00

Sterling silver minaudiere, the envelope-type body of flattened ovoid cylindrical form, w/an overall Florentined finish, accented w/yellow gold overlaid clasp & compartment pulls, opening to reveal a mirror, comb holder, lipstick, powder well & cigarette container, signed "Gucci," 6 ¾" l. 316.00

Wood compact, top decorated w/enameled white & black Scottie dogs, large 135.00

Wood compact w/brass trim, 2¾" d. 50.00

COOKIE CUTTERS

Stag Cookie Cutter

Recently there has been an accelerated interest in old tin cookie cutters. For the most part, these were made by tinsmiths who shaped primitive designs of tin strips and then soldered them to a backplate, pierced to allow air to enter and prevent a suction from holding the rolled cookie dough in the form. Sometimes an additional handle was soldered to the back. Cookie cutters were also manufactured in great quantities in an outline form that could depict animals, birds, stars and other forms, including the plain round that sometimes carried embossed advertising for flour or other products on the handle. Aluminum cookie cutters were made after 1920. All cutters listed are tin unless otherwise noted.

Animals, "Nagley Noah's Ark Cake Cutters," boxed set of 9, 7¾ x 9¾" $38.50

Bird, large stylized songbird, flat backplate pierced w/three holes, 6" l. 71.50

Cow, stylized walking animal, flat backplate pierced w/three small holes, 5¼" l. 77.00

Dog, large animal w/tail up & curled over, flat backplate pierced w/single hole, 6" 82.50

Dutchman w/large head, flat back-plate pierced w/single hole, 7¼" 170.50

Goose, stylized bird w/oblong body w/pointed tail, the straight neck w/long-beaked head, solid backplate, 5" h. 38.50

Heart, open-topped w/narrow strap handle from side to side, 4½" w. 115.50

Heart in hand, pierced flat backplate, 4¼" (handle missing, soldered repair & traces of japanning) 258.50

Horse, stylized prancing animal w/stubby legs & bobbed tail, flat backplate pierced w/two holes, 6½" l. 170.50

Razorback pig, flat backplate pierced w/single hole, 4¼" l. 41.00

Rooster, flat backplate pierced w/four holes 4½" (handle missing) 148.50

Stag, standing animal w/prominent antlers, flat backplate, one seam in hind quarters loose, 8¼" h. (ILLUS.) 341.00

Special Focus:

Metlox and Twin Winton Cookie Jars

by Joyce Roerig

1Cookie jar collecting continues to grow in popularity. As the older well-known jars disappear into collections, aficionados are assuaging their appetites with more accessible and, hopefully, more affordable jars. The jars most in demand today are from two companies that were once thriving California potteries, Metlox and Twin Winton.

Much remains to be learned about the wares of these companies that are finally gaining well-deserved recognition. Metlox closed June 1, 1989. Many of their jars, marked only with paper labels, are very difficult to identify because the labels are no longer intact. The *Collector's Encyclopedia of California Pottery* by Jack Chipman gives a brief in-depth history of Metlox. *The Collector's Encyclopedia of Cookie Jars* by Fred Roerig and Joyce Herndon Roerig colorfully highlights twenty-nine Metlox cookie jars in addition to the jars featured in the eleven original catalog sheets. This should be a great help to collectors. *The Collector's Encyclopedia of Cookie Jars Book II* adds even greater insight to Metlox cookie jars. Many of the jars previously featured in catalog sheets are photographed and valued in *Book II.* Also included are six different catalog sheets. Hopefully, 1994 will broaden our knowledge on this subject. Carl Gibbs is currently working with Collector Books on a manuscript devoted solely to Metlox Pottery.

One major breakthrough for collectors occurred with the identification of the Metlox *Scrub Woman* (previously referred to as the *Washtub Mammy*). Brandon MacNeal, the former Director of Marketing for Metlox, set the record straight in the September/October 1992 issue of *Cookie Jarrin,'* The Cookie Jar Newsletter. In addition, he identified the *Debutante* as being Metlox. Both jars have enclosed lids with small vent holes in the bottom. Melinda Shaw Avery, daughter of the late Evan K. Shaw (owner of Metlox), verified this information. The *Scrub Woman* is probably the single most sought after of all Metlox jars. She was in demand before anyone knew she was Metlox.

Many think of Metlox as being fully glazed jars with three stilt marks on the bottom (marks left by the stilt holding the piece away from the bottom or shelf of the kiln). This is not always the case. The *Cookie Boy* and *Candy Girl* (names assigned by Metlox), *Kangaroo,* and *Scrub Woman* all have a dry foot, or unglazed ring of pottery on the bottom that also keeps the glazed piece from touching the surface of the kiln. The unmarked *Cookie Boy* and *Candy Girl* are often found with the cold paint (enamel applied over the glaze) missing. *Candy Girl* should have aqua blue dots on the bow in her hair, and aqua blouse showing between the edges of her collar. *Cookie Boy* has a red button and bill on his cap, and red stripes on his shirt visible between the collar edges. The mother *Kangaroo,* in natural colors, wears a yellow plaid apron over her pouch. The outside brim of her bonnet has the same plaid. A yellow tie holds the bonnet in place. "Joey" has a yellow bow around his neck. There is an in-mold "MADE IN USA" on the bottom of our *Kangaroo,* as well as a gold and brown circular foil label.

Perhaps *Little Red Riding Hood* is the second most sought after Metlox jar. Or is it *Uncle Sam's Bear*? *Uncle Sam* is clad in patriotic colors of red (in reality burgundy), white, and blue. Red and blue stars encircle the top hat. A red bow tie sets off his blue trimmed jacket. The brightly striped trousers again pick up the red. The umbrella tucked by his side readies him for any "political" storm. Where would the elusive *Kangaroo* (11¼" tall, produced in 1960) fit in? She has to be among the top ten. Where do we place the *Cub* and *Brownie Scouts, Drummer Boy, Jolly Chef,* and *Happy the Clown*? I found the *Jolly Chef* (company assigned name) in Portland, Oregon while a guest at the December, 1990 Don Wirfs show. He had a damaged lid, but I knew the moment I saw him he was special. Simply done, he has a white chef's hat, a white collar, black eyes, brows, handlebar mustache, goatee, and bow tie. Rosy highlights accent the cheeks and nose on his flesh-colored face. I remember telling some friends at the show that I felt the jar was Metlox. About a year later we found another with the paper label still intact. I now have two *Jolly Chefs*, one with dark blue eyes, and one with black.

Happy the Clown (company assigned name) appears to have a collar made of ribbon candy. An aqua blue pompon balances on top of his head. The yellow pompons look like earmuffs. Aqua is also used for the eyebrows and lashes. His clown face is painted on with red cold paint. *Happy* is another unmarked Metlox.

The Daughters of Charity of St. Vincent de Paul *Nun* is yet another outstanding Metlox jar. The grand motherly looking figure appears to be the epitome of kindness. A white apron trimmed in blue protects her white habit. She holds a plate of chocolate chip cookies. The pink *Rose* and yellow *Tulip* are both highly coveted. The *Tulip* is by far the rarer of the two flowers. The *Mammy* with red polka dots is extremely hard to locate. The matching salt and pepper shaker sets are next to impossible. Competition among the factions increases when an item fits into more than one collectible category.

Metlox was bountiful in fruits and vegetables. The *Boy on Pumpkin* is difficult to locate. The realistic *Grapes, Watermelon,* and *Squash* are a little easier, but not much. There are Metlox collectors, cookie jar collectors, and fruit and vegetable collectors all after a limited harvest.

Metlox made several canister sets. One of the cutest is *Beau Bear* made in three graduated sizes, each wearing a different color bow, burgundy, blue or yellow. There are *Owls* in three sizes, 1½, 2, and 2½ quarts, and *Strawberries* in 2½, 3, and 3½ quart sizes.

Animal lovers seek the Jersey *Calf Head*, sometimes called Beulah. She is *not* a licensed member of Elsie's entourage, even though she wears a garland of daisies around her neck. She is hard to find with the crier intact, but even harder to find with one that still says "moo."

Humpty Dumpty comes in two models. The older unmarked egg-shaped version wears yellow striped pants and blue belt with a gold-colored buckle. He has a very large pink nose, and pink blush on each cheek. His hat with blue brim is the lid. A yellow knob forms a finial for easy access. The newer version sits on a brick wall, and is well marked. Again, a pink nose, blue collar and cuffs, yellow buttons and tie, with a yellow hat band on the cover.

The *Space Ship* is wonderful-another top Metlox jar. The resemblance to the Napco version is startling. Not to worry, the Metlox version is bigger, heavier and marked "MADE IN USA." Will we someday find such friendly beings in outer space?

Sunbonnet clad *Francine Duck* ("METLOX CALIF USA") has her ducklings (salt and pepper shakers) on parade. She is much more difficult to find than her mate *Sir Francis Drake.* I am sure he felt she would capture the limelight and limited production.

Little Pig, or *Pig, Little* as he is listed in the catalog sheet, is far from small. He stands over twelve inches tall! He is marked "METLOX CALIF U.S.A." so if you find him you will know you have the real thing. *Little Pig* is a Yorkshire (all white) with soft pink hooves and snout. Black eyes are the only other color added.

Metlox jars continue to surface. They did contract and specialty jobs, so it could take years before most are identified and documented.

Jack Chipman expands the knowledge of the early years of the Canadian born twin brothers, Don and Ross Winton in the *Collector's Encyclopedia of California Pottery.* He records the earliest formal business venture as Burke-Winton of Pasadena, California in 1936. Burke was the last name of Helen Burke, a ceramic decorator. This partnership lasted three years before the twin brothers went solo. World War II interrupted their fledgling careers. After the war the Wintons returned to the Pasadena area to make their mark in history.

It amazes me how collectors could ever make the statement "Who wants those old brown things!" Our first cookie jar purchase, after realizing we were indeed collectors of cookie jars, was the Twin Winton *Sheriff Bear.* Granted, he was in the Collector's Series, but he would have had a home even if he had been one of those "old brown jars." The wood-finish (brown) and Collector's Series remain our favorites. Many are gathering examples from the Twin Winton color division established in 1970. Most of the solid color pieces have no accent painting. Simply based in avocado, pineapple, orange, grey, and red, they were antiqued to give dimension. High gloss examples were available from 1964 through 1977. The Collector's Series started in 1974 with eighteen examples available at that time.

The rarest and most valuable Winton jar recorded to date is the *Howard Johnson's Restaurant*. This was a contract item of very limited production. Marked "Twin Winton ©," the bright orange roof and turquoise steeple bring instant recognition to the cross-country chain. The figures on the front appear to be a man in chef's clothing handing an ice cream cone to a small boy with his dog. Grey stone trims the right side of the building, and grey shutters stand out against the white building. Well-groomed shrubs in planter boxes complete the picture.

The glazed *Hillbilly* line was produced from 1946 through 1950. The rather extensive line included punch bowls and cups, tankards, pitchers, mugs, pretzel bowls, salt and pepper shakers, pour spouts, lamps, ashtrays, etc. The rail fence designed to advertise Hillbilly pour spouts is in heavy demand; few have surfaced. Our favorite hillbilly items are the *Outhouse* and *Ice Buckets* (four, that we know of to date) done primarily in wood-finish with glazed accents (hands, faces, feet, water, patches, etc.). The *Ice Buckets*, designed for fun and to accent bars, appeared in the 1960s catalogs as *Bottoms Up, Suspenders, Bathing,* and *With Jug*. All but *Bathing* were 7½ x 14" and sold for five dollars wholesale. *Bathing* was 7½ x 16", and sold for six dollars. Each came with liners.

Our *Outhouse* is marked only with the distinct artistry of Don Winton. We knew it was Winton even before verification as his brand of humor is unmistakable. Who else would put a badger in an outhouse with the occupant? A "Sale" catalog hangs outside the door just within reach.

Water related designs that fit into key Winton collectibles are the *Snail, Lighthouse, Frog, Tommy Turtle, Tugboat,* and *Walrus*. There could be matching shakers for each jar. We know for certain there are *Frogs* and *Tommy Turtles*.

The *Snail,* in wood-finish, is carrying a passenger, a little gnome forming the finial. The unmarked 8 x 9" *Frog* on a log, has dark green spots, pink tongue, and protruding black eyes. The crouched shakers appear ready to jump. The *Lighthouse* is another unmarked Winton. Familiar characters peek out the windows or float in the waves. Glazed touches of blue and yellow accent everything just right. *Tommy Turtle* (8 x 13") made his first public appearance in Ermagene Westfall's *An Illustrated Value Guide to Cookie Jars* in 1983. We looked for him until the summer of 1991. The matching shakers arrived in October 1993. These items are not plentiful.

The rotund *Walrus* is also elusive. Amazingly, he brought $360.00 at public auction in Freeman, Missouri in February 1993. Talk about supply and demand, or a serious case of "auction fever." The happiest *Tugboat* in the whole U.S.A. is captained by a bear, with a duck passenger and a bunny stowaway along for the ride.

There are at least two Winton *Grandma's*. We are featuring one very similar in design to the popular Alberta's Molds, Inc. version. It is similar because Don Winton also designed Alberta's Grandma. Picture Grandma in the *Two-Story House* with matching shakers. Green shrubs decorate the corners of the House and salt shaker. The pepper shaker has one shrub, a door and window. No House would be complete with a *Clock*. A friend found the perfect example, complete with pink feet. The wonderful *Dog* with pink-trimmed bow would never make a guard dog. He was probably intended to be a companion to the playful kittens on grandma's *Churn*.

The 7 x 10" *Ole King Cole* is delightful. You will find carved into the back of his throne images of a bowl, pipe and fiddlers three. Yellow glazed fleur-de-lis decorate his robe. The 8 x 13" *Modern Head* lends a simple degree of elegance. Perched on a box of cookies, Magilla (?) *Gorilla* is in a league of his own. His tie is outlined in the same soft blue found on the band of his derby hat. Yellow buckles match the buttons on his galluses. Pink and yellow iced cookies adorn the box.

The *Dinosaur* is not extinct! He was "dug" up by a friend, and now guards my computer. This cutsie reptile has scales outlined in yellow with mint green spots. His outstanding black eyes are framed with black lashes. Black nails complete the decorating accent on the wood-finish body. Interestingly enough, at almost exactly the same time one friend discovered the cookie jar, another found the matching shakers. Now we can open our own *Jurassic Park* when we talk her out of the shakers.

The *Pirate Fox* is an excellent example of the Collector's Series. In most instances the jar is based in pineapple with orange and blue accent. The entire jar is then antiqued, giving it a rustic appearance. Sometimes the blue or orange is the prominent color, depending upon which color is appropriate.

Wood-finish display plaques or counter signs were provided to customers with their initial orders. They have become a prize to avid Winton collectors.

Don Winton is the father of cookie jars. He has designed for practically everyone, whether or not he received the deserved acclaim. Designs for Brush ('50s through '60s) resemble closely Twin Winton designs, only the coloring and finish sets them apart. He has left his signature, you simply must learn to read it.

It is interesting to know both Evan K. Shaw and Don Winton were affiliated with Disney. Shaw's California-based American Pottery was licensed by Disney to produce figurines based on cartoon characters. His purchase of Metlox enabled him to continue production until 1956. Many of his famous pieces were produced by the Metlox staff.

Don Winton still has close ties with Disney. Most recently he created *Rolly Dalmatian* for Treasure Craft. He designed forty to fifty commemorative coins of Mickey, Minnie, Donald, Daisy, Goofy, etc., and coins of the theme parks and coin albums with sixty to eighty coins for each album of *Fantasia, Pinocchio,* and six Disney movie classics struck by the Franklin Mint. He designed ten 4½" figures to be done in crystal for the Disney stores. He designed the rare beloved figures of *Dumbo, Figaro,* and *Practical Pig* as banks and cookie jars for Hagen-Renaker in the 1950s.

Evan Shaw had Helen MacIntosh, a former Disney designer, in his employ for many years. I feel it is more than coincidental that two companies, Metlox and Twin Winton, both generated loving, happy figures which have become high demand items. When you can look at your purchase and smile or even laugh, and feel satisfied with every aspect - these history making potters have achieved their joyful, creative purpose in life.

ABOUT THE AUTHOR: Joyce Herndon Roerig is co-author with her husband, Fred, of The Collector's Encyclopedia of Cookie Jars *(Collector Books) published in 1991. Their new* Collector's Encyclopedia of Cookie Jars, Book 2 *was recently released and contains over 400 pages of material not included in their first book. Ms. Roerig also produces* Cookie Jarrin' with Joyce: THE Cookie Jar Newsletter.

PRICE LISTINGS:

METLOX

Calf Head..........................$200.00 to 225.00

Candy Girl..........................300.00 to 350.00

Cookie Boy)......................300.00 to 350.00

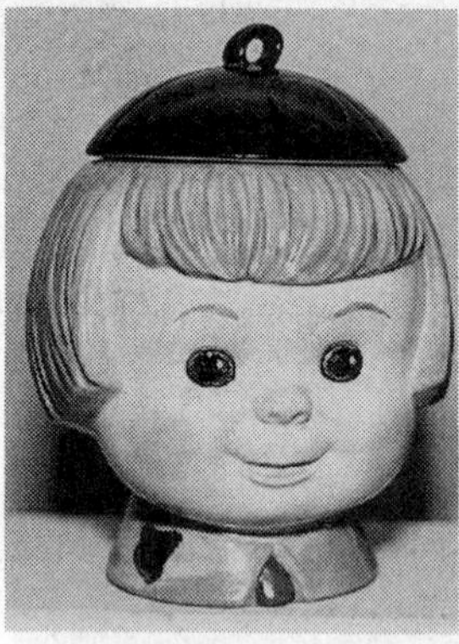

Cub Scout (top) & Brownie (bottom) each....................365.00 to 375.00

Drummer Boy ....225.00 to 250.00

Francine Duck ....125.00 to 175.00
Duckling salt & pepper shakers, each..30.00

Grapes...............................125.00 to 225.00

Watermelon ....200.00 to 225.00

Happy the Clown ....325.00 to 375.00

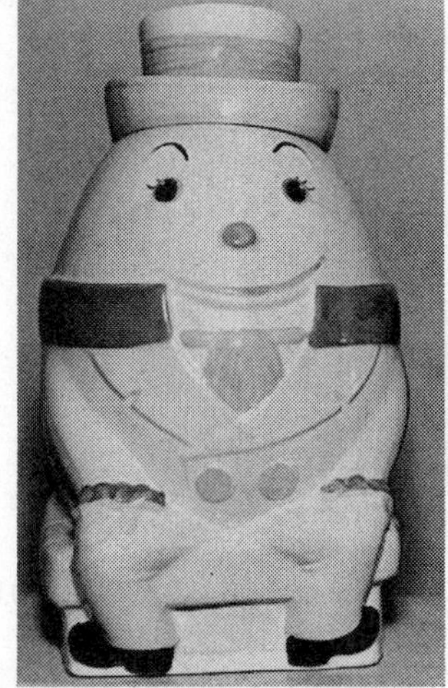

Humpty Dumpty, seated ....125.00 to 150.00

Humpty Dumpty, plain, older version ....300.00 to 350.00

Kangaroo..500.00+

Little Pig.............................150.00 to 175.00

Nun..300.00+

Pumpkin, plain........................35.00 to 45.00

Pumpkin, with boy on lid...................400.00+

Red Polka Dot Mammy ....375.00+

Matching salt & pepper shakers, each..150.00

Rose ....275.00 to 300.00

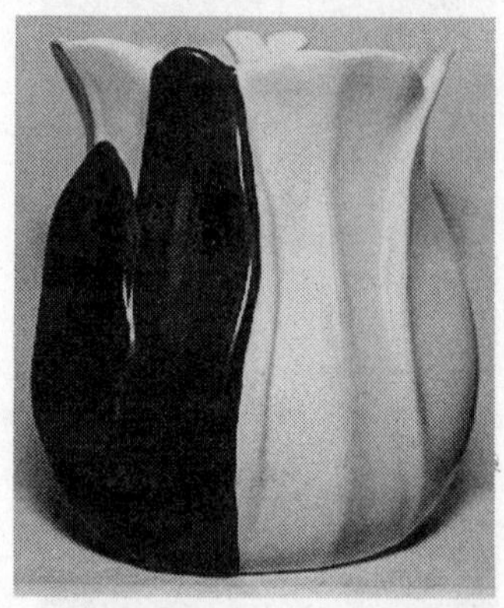

Tulip ....300.00+

Scrub Woman...............................1,200.00+

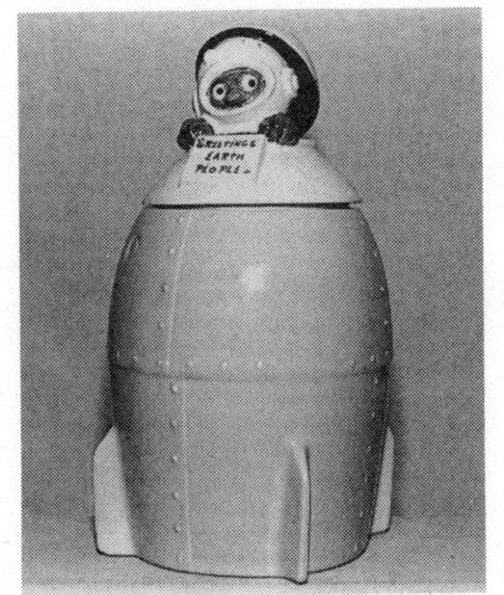

Spaceship..400.00+

Squash ....125.00 to 150.00

TWIN WINTON

Churn & Kittens ....60.00 to 80.00

Clock..................................125.00 to 175.00

Collector's Series - Pirate
Fox..................................125.00 to 175.00

Cookie Tug ....85.00 to 95.00

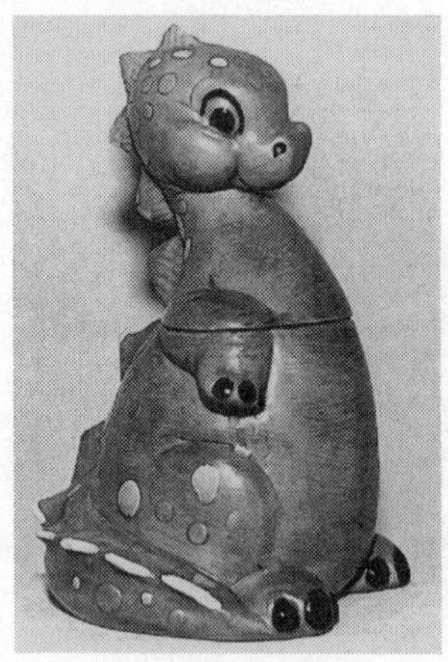

Dinosaur 300.00

Gorilla ....250.00 to 300.00

Dog with Bow......................100.00 to 125.00

Grandma..125.00

Frog ....90.00 to 125.00
Matching shaker, each ...40.00 to 60.00

Hillbilly ice bucket -
Bathing............................175.00 to 200.00

Hillbilly ice bucket - Bottoms Up ....125.00 to 150.00

Howard Johnson's ....750.00+

Hillbilly ice bucket - Suspenders......................125.00 to 150.00

Lighthouse ....175.00 to 200.00

Hillbilly ice bucket - With Jug ....125.00 to 150.00

Modern Head...................................250.00+

Ole King Cole ....150.00 to 175.00

Two-Story House................125.00 to 175.00
Matching shaker, each ...40.00 to 60.00

Snail....................................125.00 to 150.00

Walrus ....150.00 to 175.00

(End of Speical Focus)

Turtle ....70.00 to 90.00
Matching shaker, each 30.00

COOKIE JARS

All sorts of charming and whimsical cookie jars have been produced in recent decades and these are increasingly collectible today. Many well known American potteries such as McCoy, Hull and Abingdon, produced cookie jars and their products are included in those listings. Below we are listing cookie jars produced by other companies.

Current reference books for collectors include: The Collector's Encyclopedia of Cookie Jars, *by Fred and Joyce Roerig (Collector Books, 1991);* Collector's Encyclopedia of Cookie Jars, Book II *by*

Fred and Joyce Roerig (Collector Books, 1994) and The Complete Cookie Jar Book *by Mike Schneider (Schiffer, Ltd., 1991).*

AMERICAN BISQUE

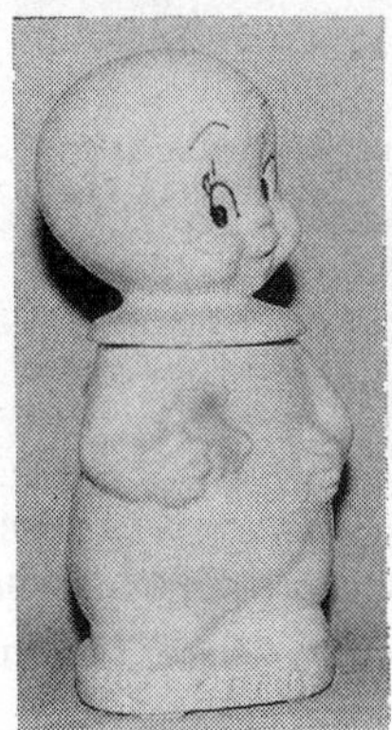

Casper Cookie Jar

Baby Elephant $105.00
Bear with Cookies 35.00
Bear with Hat 60.00
Bear with Honey, flasher-type ....350.00 to 400.00
Blackboard Boy 400.00
Blackboard Clown ....250.00 to 300.00
Blackboard Girl ....300.00 to 350.00
Boy Bear w/blue pants...........................75.00
Casper, the Friendly Ghost (ILLUS.) ..850.00
Cheerleaders, flasher-type ....275.00 to 300.00
Chef 210.00
Chick with yellow & brown coat 48.00
Churn 35.00
Clown on Stage, black curtains, flasher-type ....250.00 to 300.00
Coffeepot 25.00
Coffeepot, with "Cookies" 45.00
Collegiate Owl ....50.00 to 75.00
Cookie Barrel 35.00
Cookie Truck ....50.00 to 75.00
Cowboy Boots ....175.00 to 200.00
Davy Crockett, standing, name across chest 450.00
Dutch Boy 70.00
Dutch Girl...70.00
Elephant w/Baseball Cap .....75.00 to 100.00
Fred Flintstone, Dino finial (ILLUS. top next column) ....900.00 To 1,200.00
French Poodle, blue decoration............85.00
Girl Bear w/Cookie.................................75.00
Grandma ....100.00 to 125.00
Hot Chocolate Mug 50.00
Kids Watching TV, "Sandman Cookies," flasher-type 300.000
Kitten and Beehive 50.00
Kittens on Ball of Yarn 40.00

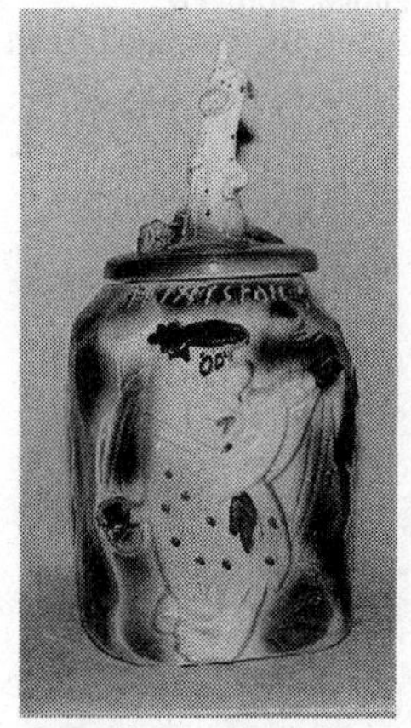

Fred Flintstone Cookie Jar

Lady Pig..85.00
Majorette ....350.00 to 400.00
Milk Wagon, with "Cookies & Milk" 95.00
Pennsylvania Dutch Girl .....350.00 to 375.00
Pig Dancer 30.00
Pig-in-Poke 65.00
Pig w/Hands in Pockets 95.00
Pig w/Straw Hat 75.00
Pinky Lee Head, blue hat 550.00
Rabbit in Hat 65.00
Recipe Jar 75.00
Ring the Bell for Cookies ....50.00 to 75.00
Rubbles House 850.00
Saddle Blackboard 165.00
Saddle, without black-board..............................200.00 to 225.00
Santa Head, laughing 300.00
Schoolhouse w/bell lid, "After School Cookies" ....40.00 to 50.00
Spaceship, w/"Cookies Out of This World" ....300.00 to 350.00
Train Engine, gold trim 195.00
Treasure Chest 110.00
Tugboat, blue, light brown & green.......95.00
Umbrella Kids ....350.00 to 375.00
Yarn Doll ....75.00 to 100.00
Yogi Bear ....350.00 to 450.00

BRAYTON - LAGUNA

Granny 389.00
Lady, floral top 645.00
Mammy, blue dress 1,200.00

BRUSH - MC COY

Cinderella Pumpkin ....175.00 to 225.00
Circus Horse, green, brown & white trim ....900.00 to 1,000.00
Clown bust ....350.00 to 400.00
Clown w/brown pants ....175.00 to 200.00
Cookie House ....50.00 to 75.00
Covered Wagon 750.00
Cow, w/Cat finial, brown ....75.00 to 100.00

Cow, w/Cat finial, purple & white ....1,200.00 to 1,400.00

Davy Crockett Cookie Jar

Davy Crockett, brown (ILLUS.) ....350.00 to 400.00
Davy Crockett, gold decoration ....875.00 to 900.00
Elephant w/Ice Cream Cone, wearing baby hat 425.00
Fish, 1971 ....550.00
Formal Pig ....250.00 to 275.00
Granny, green dress..........450.00 to 500.00
Granny, white w/blue polka dots on dress 450.00
Happy Bunny, grey ....200.00 to 250.00
Hillbilly Frog 5,000.00
Humpty Dumpty w/Beanie ..250.00 to 275.00
Humpty Dumpty w/Peaked Hat ....175.00 to 200.00
Little Red Riding Hood, large................600.00
Nite Owl ....100.00 to 150.00
Old Woman's Shoe..................................95.00
Owl, not stylized, yellow 110.00
Panda Bear...125.00
Peter Pan, large ....700.00 to 1,000.00
Peter Pumpkin Eater (Pumpkin w/Lock on Door).............300.00 to 400.00
Puppy Police.......................600.00 to 650.00
Red Riding Hood 595.00
Sitting Pig 425.00
Smiling Bear ....375.00 to 425.00
Squirrel on Log ....75.00 to 100.00
Squirrel w/Top Hat.............250.00 to 300.00
Stylized Owl, brown 350.00
Teddy Bear, feet together...100.00 to 125.00
Three Bears, tree stump finial ....75.00 to 100.00
Treasure Chest..95.00

CALIFORNIA ORIGINALS

Bert & Ernie Fine Cookies, No. 977 ....250.00 to 300.00
Big Bird, No. 976 ....100.00
Christmas Tree ....125.00 to 150.00
Cookie Monster (ILLUS. top next column) 50.00
The Count..........................450.00 to 500.00
Donald Duck & Pumpkin 275.00

Cookie Monster Cookie Jar

Dumbo's Greatest Cookies on Earth ..125.00
Eeyore 395.00
Ernie ....50.00 to 75.00
Oscar the Grouch, No. 972 ....75.00
Rabbit on Stump, No. 2620 ....65.00
Raggedy Ann...60.00
Santa Claus, standing, No. 871 ....150.00
Sheriff w/Hole in Hat..............50.00 to 70.00
Tiger 115.00
Tigger 155.00
Winnie the Pooh, No. 907.....75.00 to 100.00
Woody Woodpecker in Tree House, copyright by Walter Lantz 625.00

DORANNE OF CALIFORNIA

Cat w/Bow Tie 45.00
Cookie Cola, bottle-shaped 55.00
Cow Jumped Over the Moon..............175.00
Duck w/Basket of Corn 75.00
Elephant, seated......................................40.00
Owl, wearing mortar board hat 110.00
Pig w/Barrel of Pork.................................85.00
Pinocchio Head, non-Disney, marked "CJ46" 250.00

METLOX POTTERIES

Barrel of Apples 65.00
Bear with Bow, "Beau"..........75.00 to 100.00
Bear on Roller Skates............................125.00
Bear with Sombrero (Pancho) 85.00
Bunch of Grapes ....175.00 to 200.00
Calico Cat, lime green 85.00
Chicken (Mother Hen) 75.00
Clown, standing, black & white outfit ....150.00 to 175.00
Cookie Girl, matte glaze 125.00
Cow with Butterfly, purple...400.00 to 600.00
Daisies, globe-shaped w/pedestal base 50.00
Dinosaur, "Mona"...............150.00 to 175.00

Dog, Fido 75.00
Duck with Raincoat
(Puddles) ....75.00 to 100.00
Dutch Boy...........................150.00 to 175.00
Gingham Dog 74.00

Humpty Dumpty by Metlox

Humpty Dumpty (ILLUS.) ...250.00 to 275.00
Kitten Head w/Hat, "meows" when hat
tipped ....100.00 to 125.00
Koala Bear.........................100.00 to 125.00
Lamb's Head w/Hat 100.00
Lion, seated.......................175.00 to 200.00
Mammy, yellow polka dots 495.00
Mouse, Chef Pierre..............75.00 to 100.00
Orange..89.00
Panda Bear..100.00
Pelican Coach (U.S. Diving Team).....125.00
Penguin (Frosty) 120.00
Rabbit on Cabbage...............................154.00
Raccoon, Cookie Bandit.........................95.00
Raggedy Andy...................200.00 to 225.00
Raggedy Ann..130.00
Rose Blossom 450.00
Scottie Dog, black..............175.00 to 200.00
Sir Francis Drake (duck).......................50.00
Slenderella (pig) ....100.00 to 125.00

Metlox Spaceship

Spaceship (ILLUS.) ....400.00 to 450.00
Squirrel on Pine Cone ....75.00 to 100.00
Strawberry ....75.00 to 85.00

Topsy, blue & white polka dots...........450.00
Wheat Sheaf w/Ribbon..........................25.00

POTTERY GUILD

Balloon Lady..65.00
Dutch Boy ....60.00 to 80.00
Dutch Girl...80.00
Elsie the Cow ....275.00 to 325.00

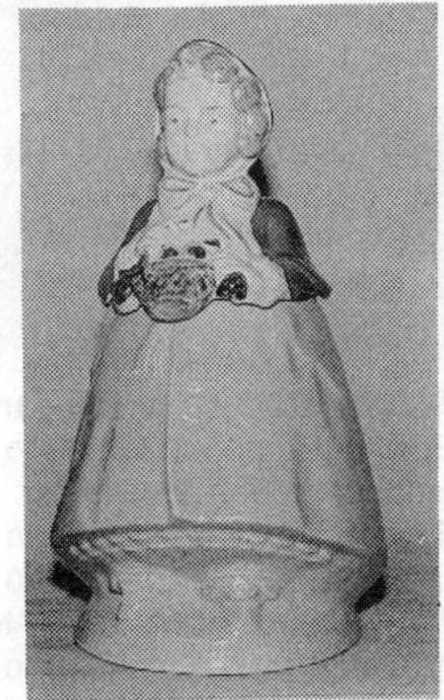

Little Red Riding Hood

Little Red Riding Hood
(ILLUS.) ....125.00 to 150.00
Rooster 75.00

REGAL CHINA

Regal Little Miss Muffet

Barn, Old MacDonald line...400.00 to 450.00
Churn Boy..275.00
Davy Crockett 375.00
French Chef........................200.00 to 250.00
Goldilocks ....300.00 to 350.00
Hubert the Lion 850.00
Humpty Dumpty.................300.00 to 350.00
Kraft-T-Bear (Kraft Marsh-
mallows)..........................200.00 to 250.00
Little Miss Muffet
(ILLUS.) ....200.00 to 250.00
Little Red Riding Hood.........................295.00
Pig in Diaper ....400.00 to 500.00
Quaker Oats Canister.........100.00 to 150.00

ROBINSON RANSBOTTOM

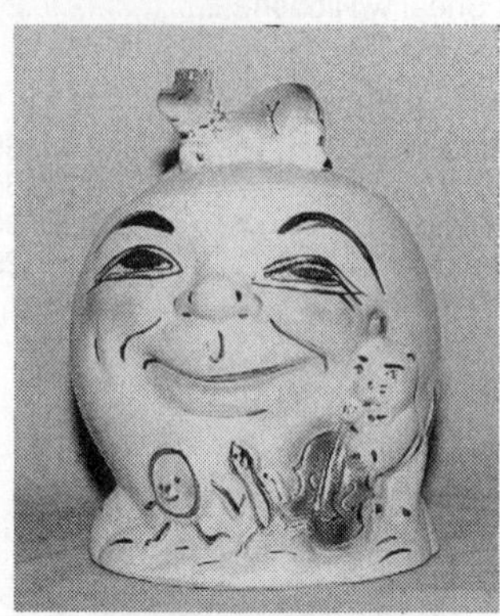

Cow Jumped Over Moon Jar

Chef with Bowl of Eggs.......200.00 to 225.00
Cow Jumped Over Moon [Hi Diddle Diddle] (ILLUS.) ....200.00 to 225.00
Dutch Girl...........................175.00 to 225.00
Hootie Owl (Wise Bird) ....50.00 to 75.00
Jocko the Monkey..............375.00 to 400.00
Sailor Jack...200.00
Sheriff Pig..........................100.00 to 115.00
World War II Soldier (Bud) ....150.00 to 200.00

TWIN WINTON

Churn & Kittens Cookie Jar

Bambi, beside stump 90.00
Barn, "Cookie Barn"...............................40.00
Churn & Kittens (ILLUS.) ....60.00 to 80.00
Chipmunk 65.00
Cookie Time Clock, button lid ....125.00 to 175.00
Cookie Time Clock, mouse on lid ....22.50 to 27.50
Cooky Catcher Truck.............................65.00
Cow ....65.00 to 75.00
Dutch Girl...............................50.00 to 75.00
Elf Bakery Tree Stump ....45.00 to 55.00
Friar Tuck 50.00
Hotei (Buddha) 175.00
Ole King Cole ....150.00 to 175.00
Persian Kitten 65.00
Raccoon 75.00
Ranger Bear ....45.00 to 55.00
Rooster...60.00
Sailor Elephant ....55.00 to 65.00
Squirrel on Nut, "Cookie Nut" ....35.00 to 45.00
Turtle, seated..........................70.00 to 90.00
Walrus 95.00

MISCELLANEOUS COMPANIES

Butler (Carol Gifford) 145.00
Daisy Mae in Barrel (Imperial Porcelain, Paul Webb design) 795.00
Dog House w/Cat on Roof (Starnes of California) 250.00
Donald Duck w/Hand in Cookie Jar (Hoan Ltd.)...75.00
Humpty Dumpty (Puriton Pottery Co.) 425.00
Kooky-K-Egg (Green Products)..........200.00
Liberty Bell (House of Webster)..............25.00
Mickey Mouse w/Chef's Hat & Rolling Pin (Hoan Ltd.)..................................50.00
Nun, "The Lord Helps Him Who Helps Himself" (Deforest of California).......275.00
Pirate on Chest (Starnes of California) 395.00

R2-D2 Cookie Jar

R2-D2, Roman Ceramics (ILLUS.) 200.00
Smoky Bear head (Norcrest) 450.00
Snoopy (Holiday Designs) 60.00
Snowman (B.C. - Made in U.S.A.)........55.00
Tasmanian Devil (Warner Bros., Inc., The Good Co.) ....300.00 to 350.00
Trolley with People (Otagiri) ...30.00 to 40.00
Young Lady, head (Lefton Co.) 75.00

COOK BOOKS

Advertising, "Chiquita Banana," 1950...15.00
Advertising, Knox Gelatin, "Dainty Deserts for Dainty People," 39 pp., 1924...12.00
Advertising, "Jewel Tea Cookbook," by Mary Dunbar, 1927 ....20.00

Advertising, "Karo Cookbook," Leyendecker cover, 47 pp., 1910 ......25.00

Advertising, "National Brewing Co.," Hans Plato illustrations, black chef on cover, 1942 ....35.00

Advertising, "Royal Baking Powder Cookbook," 1922 ....15.00

"Amy Vanderbilt's Complete Cookbook," illustrated by Andy Warhol, 1961 ....50.00

"Better Homes & Gardens Cookbook," 1952..15.00

"The Boston Cooking School Cookbook," by Fannie Merritt Farmer, 1927 ....24.00

"Dr. Oliver's Treasured Secrets," hardcover, 1894................................40.00

"French Chef," by Julia Child, 1968, first edition, w/dust jacket..................20.00

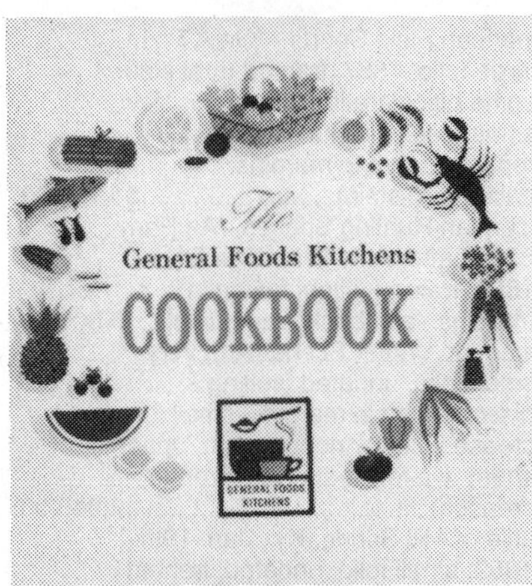

General Foods Kitchens Cookbook

"General Foods Kitchens Cookbook," by The Women of General Foods Kitchens, photography by George Lazarnick, drawings by Mary Ronin, Random House, Inc., 436 pp., 1959, 8½ x 9¼" (ILLUS.) 14.00

"Handbook of Practical Cookery," hardcover, 1888................................35.00

"James Beard's American Cookery," 1972, first edition, 877 pp. 12.50

"La Cuisine de France," by Turgeon, 1964 ....27.00

"Mrs. Appleyard's Kitchen, autographed, 1942.......................................15.00

"New Calendar of Salads," by Hiller, 365 different salads, ca. 1920s 12.00

"Old Vienna Cookbook," by Christensen, 1959..............................25.00

"Pure Food Cookbook," by Mary J. Lincoln, contains early advertising, 80 pp., 1907 ....45.00

"Southern Cookbook," depicts black person, w/dust jacket, 1935..............55.00

"Theory & Art of Bread Making," by Horsford, copyright 1863 ....12.00

"200 Years of Charleston Cooking," cloth cover, 1934 ....22.50

"Treasury of Great Recipes," by Mary & Vincent Price, Ampersand, w/dust jacket, 1965 ....38.00

"Woman's Favorite," color & black & white plates, 1906.............................25.00

CORKSCREWS

Figural Corkscrew-Bottle Opener

Advertising, pocket-type, "Anheuser-Busch," wooden handle $65.00

Advertising, pocket-type, "Arrowhead Farms," screws apart for assembly, patent-dated "8-1-23," 3" l. 25.00

Advertising, "Columbia Beer," w/wooden handle..............................28.00

Advertising, bullet-shaped, "Drink Lemps," patent-dated 1897, 3" l..........40.00

Brass, figural pair of hinged lady's legs flanking the corkscrew, each leg w/striped celluloid inlay, late 19th - early 20th c., 2⅝" l.................148.50

Cast iron, "Champion," bar-mounted, patent-dated "Sept. 7, 1897"............145.00

Cast iron, figural, "Old Snifter," caricature of Congressman Andrew Volstead, author of Prohibition legislation, w/hinged jaw bottle opener, 6¾" h. (ILLUS.) ...150.00 to 200.00

COUNTRY STORE COLLECTIBLES

Country store museums have opened across the country in an effort to recreate those slower-paced days of the late 19th and early 20th centuries when the general store served as the local meeting place for much of rural America. Here one not only purchased necessary supplies for upcoming weeks, but caught up on important news events and local gossip. With strong interest in colorful tin cans during the early 1960s came the realization that these stores and neighborhood groceries were fast disappearing, replaced by the so-called supermarkets, and collectors began buying all items associated with these early stores. Also see CANS & CONTAINERS and CASH REGISTERS.

Diamond Dyes Cabinet

Cabinet, counter-type, dyes, "Diamond Dyes," colored scene in door w/a clear diamond in the center giving off colored rays w/a circle of women from infant to elderly around the edges, "Evolution of Woman," oak cabinet, 10 x 21¼", 30" h. ....$950.00 to 1,000.00

Cabinet, counter-type, dyes, "Diamond Dyes," oak case w/lithographed tin front w/scene known as "Woman Dyeing Clothes" (ILLUS.) ....1,125.00 to 1,200.00

Display fixture, metal, contains tacks, swivels for each access to various sections, colorful signs, 20" h. 65.00

Display rack, brooms, "Blu-J," full color signs on each end, great color, holds twleve brooms, ca. 1920s 495.00

Jars, cov., pear-shaped w/high conical finials on lids, 10½" h., pr.....125.00

Paper sack holder, twisted wire, pyramidal form, 30" h.....................247.50

CURRIER & IVES

This lithographic firm was founded in 1835 by Nathaniel Currier with James M. Ives becoming a partner in 1857. Current events of the day were portrayed in the early days and the prints were hand-colored. Landscapes, vessels, sport, and hunting scenes of the West all became popular subjects. The firm was in existence until 1906. All prints listed are hand-colored unless otherwise noted.

The Celebrated Horse Dexter

American Field Sports - "On A Point," large folio, 1857, framed (mat stain, some discoloration in margins, few small tears & nicks on edges, repaired tears in margins, backboard stain) $1,150.00

American Hunting Scenes, "An Early Start," after A.F. Tait, large folio, 1863, framed (slight foxing in margins, faint backboard stain).....5,500.00

American Winter Scene (An), very small folio, undated (soiling & discoloration in margins, small crease in lower right margin, upper sheet w/a few tears & horizontal creases) 2,645.00

Battle of Mill Spring, Ky., Jan. 19th, 1862, small folio, undated, framed (small stain in bottom margin)..........150.00

Blackwells Island, East River, From Eighty-Sixth Street, New York, after F.F. Palmer, medium folio, 1862, framed (mat stain & few fox marks in margins, a few minor abrasions in sky) 1,380.00

Catching A Trout - "We Hab You Now, Sar," large folio, N. Currier, 1854, framed (small abraded split, tear in upper margin, margin corner creased & replaced, slight damp-staining) 7,475.00

Celebrated Horse Dexter (The), "The King of the Turf," large folio, 1865, few small tears in sheet edge, small abraded area in sky at top left, few surface scuffs, framed (ILLUS.) 805.00

Celebrated Horse Dexter (The), "The King of the World," large folio, 1867, (some margin repairs, pale staining & skinning) 1,093.00

Celebrated Horse George M. Patchen (The) - "The Champion of the Turf...," large folio, 1860, framed (soiling in margins, spots of foxing, small tears, reinforced w/tape on verso)....................................1,955.00

Celebrated Horse Lexington (The), N. Currier, large folio, 1855, matted & framed..990.00

Central Park, The Drive, medium folio, 1862, framed (repaired tear in left sheet edge, loss in top left corner, few tiny tears in upper sheet edge)..............................2,185.00

"Crack" Sloop in A Race to Windward (A), large folio, 1882, framed (scuff in the sky at right, small crease in the sky at left, new nicks, pinholes & small creases in extreme sheet edges)......................................1,380.00

Darktown Elopement (The), "Hurry Mr. Jonsing...," small folio, 1885, framed...137.50

Darktown Elopement (The), "Skip softly lub,...," small folio, 1885, framed (minor margin stain)............137.50

Darktown Fire Brigade (The) - To the Rescue, small folio, 1884, framed (stains & minor edge damage).........357.50

Falls of Niagara (The), "From the Canada Side," after B. Hess, large folio, 1873 (two small tears at vertical margin edges, very pale staining & surface soiling showing mostly in margins & on reverse) 990.00

Fast Trotters on Harlem Lane, N.Y., large folio, 1870, framed (mat stain, some soiling in margins, few surface scuffs & foxing, repaired tears, lower right corner re-attached)......3,738.00

Fruits of the Seasons, small folio, 1872, framed (water stains)...............93.50

Going for a Shine - "He kin knock de stuffin outen a mule," small folio, 1888, matted & framed (repaired edge tears)..126.50

Golden Fruits of California, large folio, 1869, framed (two pin holes just in the image at sides, tiny nicks in extreme sheet edges)...................1,840.00

Great Bartholdi Statue (The), Liberty Enlightening the World...," large folio, 1885, framed (two creases, backboard stain showing, laid down)...575.00

High Pressure Steamboat Mayflower, large folio, 1855, framed (minor nicks & tears at edges, minor soiling)..3,190.00

Home on the Mississippi (A), small folio, 1871, matted & framed (minor stains)...467.50

Hudson Near Coldspring (The), small folio, undated, beveled mahogany veneer frame (stains & corner tear, damage to frame)..........................165.00

Hunter's Shanty (The), In the Adirondacks, large folio, 1861, framed (minor discoloration, rubbing & a few filled in paper losses in sheet edges)..............................2,070.00

Landscape, Fruit and Flowers

Landscape, Fruit and Flowers, after F.F. Palmer, large folio, 1862, colors faded, two vertical stains at center, small unobtrusive surface scrape at bottom right, pale staining & scattered foxing mostly in margins & reverse, framed (ILLUS.)..............2,300.00

Life & Age of Man (The), N. Currier, small folio, undated, beveled cherry frame (stains, side margins trimmed)..104.50

Life of a Fireman (The), The Fire - "Now, then with a will - Shake her up, boys!," large folio, N. Currier, 1854 (repaired tears, verso somewhat soiled & rubbed)..........1,035.00

Little Kitty, small folio, undated, in cross-corner frame w/gilded liner & white porcelain buttons...................143.00

Mr. Bonner's Horse Joe Elliott, Driven by J. Bowen, after J. Cameron, large folio, 1873, framed (surface scrape in sky, margins folded back, mat staining & creases)...........................920.00

My Little White Kittie After the Goldfish, small folio, undated, framed (stains)...............................220.00

Night on the Hudson (A), "Through at Daylight," after F.F. Palmer, large folio, 1864, framed (sky a bit retouched, foxing & soiling in margins, small abrasion just below bow of the boat at left, small losses in the extreme sheet edges).........5,463.00

Preparing for Market, N. Currier, large folio, 1856, framed (few fox marks, few scrapes in sky, two pin holes in margins).......................................2,300.00

Road (The) - Summer, N. Currier, large folio, 1853, framed, good condition (scattered foxing & staining)......................................2,860.00

Silver Creek - California, small folio, undated, framed (margins slightly trimmed) 192.50

Sinking of the Cumberland by the Iron Clad "Merrimac" off Newport News, Va., small folio, 1863, framed 440.00

Smuggler & Judge Fullerton, small folio, 1876, matted & framed 385.00

A Snowy Morning

Snowy Morning (A), after F.F. Palmer, medium folio, 1864, small repaired paper loss in right sheet edge, light foxing, framed (ILLUS.) 2,645.00

Tree of Life (The), N. Currier, small folio, undated, framed (stains, colors faded) 104.50

Tree of Temperance (The), N. Currier, small folio, undated, in a beveled curly maple frame (stains) 220.00

Washington Columns (The), Yosemite Valley, small folio, undated, framed (tear in top edge, minor stains & rebacked on paper) 71.50

Yacht 'Mohawk' of New York (The), large folio, 1877, framed (few tiny abrasions in water, small tear in bottom sheet edge) 1,725.00

Young Continental (The), N. Currier, small folio, undated, walnut frame w/edge beading (stains) 165.00

DECOYS

Canvasback Drake Decoy

Decoys have been utilized for years to lure flying water fowl into target range. They have been made of carved and turned wood, papier-maché, canvas and metal, and some are in the category of outstanding folk art and command high prices.

American Brant, hollow cedar construction w/inlet bill, Cobb Island-style, worn original paint, 18" l. $715.00

Black Duck, by Ralph Malpage, carved wood w/carved feather & wing detail, original paint & glass eyes, signed "Ralph Malpage, London, Ont. May '89," Canada, 15¼" l. 71.50

Black Duck, by Gene Sullivan, carved wood in the Salisbury-style of the Ward Brothers, original paint w/modest use wear 385.00

Bluebill Drake, by Addie Nichol, Smith Falls, Ontario, Canada, carved wood, professionally restored in the style of its original maker 275.00

Bluebill Hen, preening, carved wood, original paint, Upper Chesapeake Bay, in the style of Jobes, 13¼" l. (age cracks) 148.50

Blue Goose Drake, carved wood w/good detail, original paint & glass eyes, Michigan, mid-20th c., 24½" l. 225.50

Bufflehead Duck Drake & Hen, by Jim VanBrunt, Setauket, New York, carved wood w/original paint & glass eyes, one labeled, ca. 1950s, each 8½" l., pr. 341.00

Canada Goose, hollow cedar construction w/inletted lead weight, leather thong, original paint w/feathering on back, Barnegat Bay, New Jersey, 23" l. (minor loss to weathered paint) 770.00

Canvasback Drake, oversized, carved & painted wood, w/original red, black & white paint, glass eye, leather thong, age cracks, Wisconsin, 18" l. (ILLUS.) 5,463.00

Canvasback Hen, by Madison Mitchell, carved wood, original paint, branded "D. Yundt," 16" l. 280.50

Eider Duck Drake, crudely carved wood w/original paint & incised bill carving, Friendship, Maine, area, ca. 1930 (missing one eye) 5,750.00

Sturgeon Fish Sizing Decoy

Fish, "Sturgeon," carved & painted pine, sizing-type, full figure w/protruding nails as whiskers & yellow painted tin fins, the body painted black, now mounted on a rod on a black metal base, formerly used to help fishermen determine the size & legality of sturgeon, probably Michigan, early 20th c., 35" l. (ILLUS.) 2,875.00

Goldeneye Drake, by L.E. Bernard, Hale, Michigan, carved wood, original paint & glass eyes, unsigned, branded "Hall," ca. 1940, 15¼" l. 126.50

Goldeneye Drake, by Orel LaBoeuf, St. Ancient, Quebec, Canada, carved wood, branded on the bottom (two fine hairline cracks in shoulder) 660.00

Greenwing Teal Hen & Drake, by D.W. Nichol, Smith Falls, Ontario, Canada, carved wood, mint original condition, pr. 1,210.00

Hudsonian Curlew, by Elmer Crowell, East Harwich, Massachusetts, life-sized carved wood w/rare turned neck position, original paint w/some separation & loss of filler where leg meets body, maker's rectangular stamp on base (one digit of left foot missing) 16,500.00

Loon, by Byron Bruffee, carved wood w/fine original paint, maker's name stamped in base 330.00

Mallard Drake, by Paul Arness, California, carved hollow body, original paint & glass eyes, initialed "P.A.," 19½" l (some wear)..............181.50

Mallard Drake, by Dale Drake, Pekin, Illinois, carved wood, original paint & glass eyes, unsigned, 15¾" l. 82.50

Mallard Hen, by Charles Perdew, Illinois, carved wood w/original paint & glass eyes, marked weight in base 725.00

Merganser Drake, carved solid wood construction w/relief-carved wings & old paint, Maritime Provinces, Canada, late 19th c..........................920.00

Owl, confidence-type, papier-maché w/original paint & glass eyes (two on each side), marked "Souler Swicher, Decatur, Illinois, Pat. Pend.," 14¼" h. (minor wear) 104.50

Pintail Drake, by Elmer Crowell, East Harwich, Massachusetts, carved wood w/original paint, rectangular stamp mark, early 20th c., 18" l. ...1,760.00

Redbreasted Merganser Drake, by Capt. Harry Jobes, carved wood, original paint, signed "Capt. Harry Jobes," 14¼" l. 121.00

Redbreasted Merganser Hen & Drake by Hurley Conklin, Manahawkin, New Jersey, carved wood, original paint w/some areas of exposed wood, pr. 1,210.00

Ringtail Drake, by Dave Hockman, Niles, Michigan, carved wood, old paint & glass eyes, unsigned, 14" l. ...77.00

Sanderling, by Elmer Crowell, East Harwich, Massachusetts, carved wood in life-sized preening position w/raised wing, rectangular maker's mark on base, outstanding original paint 4,400.00

Oversized Canvas Scoter Decoy

Scoter, attributed to Captain Clarence Bailey, Kingston, Massachusetts, oversized white winged canvas-covered surf scoter w/a carved wooden head w/tack eyes & much of the original black paint, from an original rig of five known to have been made by Captain Bailey, ca. 1920, 24" (ILLUS.) 2,300.00

Whistler Hen, by William Cooper, Verdun, Quebec, Canada, carved wood in turned-head position, original paint on back, head & chest, paint on sides lightly flaking to reveal original paint beneath...........412.00

Wood Duck, by Robert Kerr, Smith Falls, Ontario, Canada, carved wood in raised-wing preening position, name branded on base, 1950s, mint condition...............................3,740.00

Yellowlegs, carved wood w/applied hinged metal wings, original paint, 19th c. (crack in neck)..................1,380.00

DISNEY COLLECTIBLES

Scores of objects ranging from watches to dolls have been created showing Walt Disney's copyrighted animated cartoon characters, and an increasing number of collectors now are seeking these, made primarily by licensed manufacturers.

Alice in Wonderland book, pop-up type, published by Saalfield, No. 964, never used $250.00

(DISNEY Collectibles continued on p. 395)

IT'S ALWAYS TIME FOR CLASSIC DISNEY COLLECTIBLES

by David Longest

Probably no area of character toy collecting in America is more recognized than that of vintage Disneyana collectibles. The most desired of all early Disney character items are those fashioned in the likeness of Mickey Mouse, with Donald Duck, Minnie Mouse, Pluto and the collectibles associated with Snow White and the Seven Dwarfs and Pinocchio following a close second.

One of the reasons early Disneyana is so desired by today's collectors is its immediate recognition value. Even non-collectors have an appreciation for the strong graphic image of the 1930s Mickey Mouse. Many collectors believe that the "golden age" of Disneyana manufacturing was the period from 1928 until about 1939. This time frame includes three periods of golden age Disneyana design. The first period runs from the creation of Mickey Mouse in 1928 up until about 1931. During this short era, Mickey was often depicted in an early "ratty" looking style with a long snout, squinting eyes, and sometimes even sharp teeth. This ratty look was more often found in European designs like Bavarian china items and figurines. During the early 1930s and up through about 1937, Mickey Mouse merchandise had a very uniform look with Mickey always having pie-shaped oval eyes (with one piece cut out) and a more world-wide uniform appearance. The later years of the 1930s, from about 1937 through late 1939, found Mickey in what collectors refer to as his "transitional" period of appearance. Here, his pie-cut eyes became solid ovals and his limbs started to become more fluid, human-like, and less rigid.

Vintage Mickey items from the very earliest Mickey period are often marked "Walt E. Disney" or "Walter E. Disney." Toys from the middle period and the later period are usually all marked "© Walt Disney Enterprises" or "Walt Disney Mickey Mouse, Ltd.," the latter being the marking on toys from the English market.

With the popularity of the Disney Studio's series of short featurette cartoons known as the "Silly Symphonies" 1930s audiences were introduced to various storybook type characters and later Donald Duck and the Big Bad Wolf and the Three Pigs. Character toys associated with Snow White and the Seven Dwarfs (1937) and Pinocchio (1939) are also extremely popular with collectors because both of these early Disney feature films are often regarded as some of the best films ever produced by the studio.

The most uniform markings that all character merchandise from the vintage Disneyana era contain are the copyright notations of "Walt Disney Enterprises." This was the merchandising and marketing branch of the early days of the Disney Studio, so any toys found with this period marking are certain to have been manufactured somewhere between the early 1930s and on through 1939. It is this period of vintage Disney character merchandise that continues to lead the pack among all character toy collecting.

Like all areas of toy collecting, the vintage Disneyana market has seen its ups and downs over the years. As new collectors continually come into the market, prices can sometimes fluctuate wildly. This is particularly true if new and serious collectors have a significant bankroll behind them. During the late 1980s, a phenomenon of "overnight toy inflation" occurred when a handful of collectors made headlines on the national scope by paying fantastic sums of money for Disneyana in an attempt to buy up major collections quickly. As a result, vintage Disneyana prices soared like blue chip stocks and coastal Florida real estate! As these prices have edged back down to reality in the past three or four years, some dealers and collectors alike have suggested that interest in vintage Disneyana might be waning.

It is the opinion of most seasoned collectors that this is merely a "correction" taking place after a wildly erratic toy marketplace in the late 1980s. Interest in vintage Disneyana from 1928 through the 1930s is still extremely strong in national collector auctions and on the floor at major collectible shows.

What will help to sustain the popularity of vintage Disneyana in years to come will be the unfailing and timeless popularity of the Walt Disney Company. Mickey Mouse is not only a popular national symbol, he is also the corporate "spokesmouse" for a major U.S. corporation. Consequently, his early likeness and the memory of his early years will be fondly preserved for generations to come by his continued association as THE symbol of the Walt Disney Company and the Walt Disney Studios.

Collectors who continue to seek out "early Mickey" and the likes of 1930s long-billed Donald Duck, Minnie Mouse, Pluto, the Three Pigs, Pinocchio, and Snow White with all of the Dwarfs help preserve the integrity of our memories of the very early days of Disney. These toys are still popular among today's collectors of all ages because the characters themselves are so popular.

Mickey Mouse isn't the upstart that he once was. He is now a powerful image in the popular culture of America, and that lasting image will keep him ever on the toy shelves of devoted collectors.

A single Mickey Mouse Slate Dancer crank toy sold for $29,150 in a 1993 auction and set a new world's record for a character toy being sold at auction.

Yes, old Mickey is still *good* Mickey. With his pie-eyed, beaming presence, 1930s vintage Mickey is still popular, respected, and much sought after in the toy marketplace.

He'll be staying with us for quite a few more years!

ABOUT THE AUTHOR

David Longest is a long-time collector of early Disney collectibles and has written extensively on the subject. He has co-authored with Michael Stern The Collector's Encyclopedia of Disneyana - A Value & Identification Guide *(Collector Books, Paducah, Kentucky, 1992) and also wrote* Character Toys and Collectibles *and* Character Toys and Collectibles, Second Series, *also published by Collector Books. David is also a regular contributor to* Toy Trader *magazine, published monthly by Antique Trader Publications.*

ILLUSTRATED PRICE GUIDE

Mickey Mouse & Friends

Donald Duck Toy & Art Stamp Set

Donald Duck Art Stamp Picture Set, large boxed set w/pad & stamps, 1930s (ILLUS. back) $225.00

Donald Duck figure, bisque, jointed arm, Walt Disney Enterprises, Japan, 1930s, 6" h. (ILLUS. w/Mickey & Minnie) 800.00

Donald Duck figure, wood composition, Knickerbocker, Walt Disney Enterprises, 1930s, 10" h. (ILLUS. w/Mickey) 1,200.00

Donald Duck toy, pull-type, Donald waving, Fisher-Price, 1930s (ILLUS. center w/Mickey & Pluto) 250.00

Donald Duck toy, windup wood composition, George Borgfeldt Distributors, 1930s, 12" h. (ILLUS. above) 1,500.00

Mickey Mouse Safety Blocks

Mickey Mouse blocks, "Mickey Mouse Safety Blocks," painted wood, illustrated box, Halsam Blocks, Walt Disney Enterprises, boxed set, 1930s 275.00

Mickey Mouse Cookie Tin

Mickey Mouse cookie tin, round, color picture of Mickey, Minnie Mouse & Donald Duck on the lid, England, 1930s 350.00

Mickey Mouse Bisque Figures

Mickey Mouse figure, bisque, playing drum, Japan, 1930s, 3" h. 250.00

Mickey Mouse figure, bisque, playing French horn, Japan, 1930s, 3" h......250.00

Mickey Mouse figure, bisque, playing banjo, 1930s, 5½" h. 400.00

Mickey Mouse figure, bisque, playing drum, 1930s, 5½" h. 400.00

Mickey Mouse figure, bisque, playing French horn, 1930s, 5½" h. 400.00

Mickey Mouse Film & Figure

Mickey Mouse figure, composition, standing waving, Lionel Train Corp., 1930s 200.00

Mickey Mouse figure, bisque, standing w/hands on hips, 1930s, 5" h. (ILLUS. w/Minnie & Donald) 350.00

Mickey & Donald Knickerbocker Figures

Mickey Mouse figure, jointed wood composition w/jointed arms, Knickerbocker, 1930s 1,000.00

Mickey Mouse film, "Mickey Mouse Safety Film," W.D. Enterprises, in original box w/colorful graphics, 1930s (ILLUS. above).........................65.00

Mickey Mouse Night Light & Flashlight

Mickey Mouse flashlight, metal w/colorful scenes around the middle, by USA Light, 1930s 350.00

Mickey Mouse game, "Mickey Mouse Dominoes," in original box w/colorful comic cover, by Halsam, Walt Disney Enterprises, 1930s, complete in box (ILLUS. top next page).......................................200.00

Mickey Mouse hat rack, child's, die-cut wooden colorful figure of Mickey, 1930s, (ILLUS. next page) 300.00

Mickey Mouse night light, lithographed tin, by Micro Lite, 1930s (ILLUS. w/flashlight) 350.00

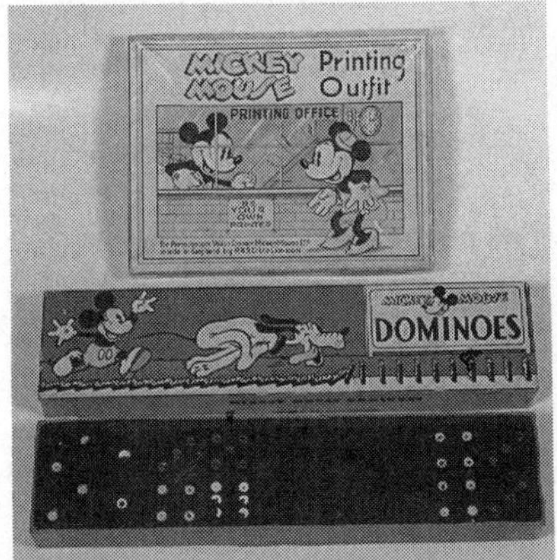

Mickey Mouse Dominoes & Printing Set

Mickey Mouse Hat Rack

Mickey Mouse printing set, "Mickey Mouse Printing Outfit," in original colorful box, Walt Disney Mickey Mouse Ltd., England, 1930s (ILLUS. w/Dominoes) 300.00

Mickey Mouse Sand Pail

Mickey Mouse sand pail, lithographed tin, tapering cylindrical body w/rounded footring, colorful picnic scene titled "Mickey Mouse Picnic," Ohio Art, 1930s, 8" h.......................550.00

Giant Mickey Mouse Sand Pail

Mickey Mouse sand pail, lithographed tin, slightly tapering cylinder, colorful beach scene w/Mickey & friends, Ohio Art, 1930s, 10" h......................700.00

Mickey Mouse Tea Set

Mickey Mouse tea set, lithographed tin, colorful scenes of Mickey, Minnie & friends, Walt Disney Enterprises, Ohio Art, 1930s, complete in original box 300.00

Mickey Mouse toothbrush holder, bisque, jointed arm, 1930s, 5" h. (ILLUS. w/Minnie Mouse) 500.00

Mickey Mouse toy, pull-type, die-cut wood & tin, Mickey playing a large drum on a wheeled platform base, Fisher-Price, 1930s, 12" h. (ILLUS. top next page) 750.00

Mickey Mouse toy, pull-type, die-cut wood, Mickey running, on small wheels, Walt Disney Enterprises, Fisher-Price, 1930s, 6" h. (ILLUS. w/Pluto & Donald) 275.00

Mickey Mouse Drummer Pull Toy

Mickey Mouse Top & Watering Can

Mickey Mouse toy, top, lithographed tin, colorful scenes of Mickey & friends around the top, early 1930s 250.00

Mickey Mouse Windup Toys

Mickey Mouse toy, windup tin, Mickey Mouse drummer, lever-activated, by Nifty, 1930s 1,500.00

Mickey Mouse toy, windup tin, Mickey & Minnie Mouse handcar, red car, Lionel, w/track, 1930s 1,100.00

Mickey Mouse watering can, lithographed tin, colorful scene of Mickey in a garden, Ohio Art, 1930s (ILLUS. w/top) 250.00

Mickey & Minnie Mouse tray, lithographed tin, oval, colorful scene of Mickey & Minnie holding hands, France, 1930s (ILLUS.) 300.00

Mickey & Minnie Mouse Tin Tray

Minnie Mouse Cup & Minnie & Mickey Toothbrush Holders

Minnie Mouse cup, porcelain, Bavaria, 1930s 275.00

Minnie, Donald & Mickey Figures

Minnie Mouse figure, bisque, hands on hips, Walt E. Disney, Japan,1930s, 5" h. 350.00

Minnie Mouse toothbrush holder, bisque, one jointed arm, 1930s, 5" h. (ILLUS. w/cup) 500.00

Pluto, Donald & Mickey Pull Toys

Pluto toy, pull-type, die-cut wood on wheels, Pluto holding a basket in his mouth, Walt Disney Enterprises, Fisher-Price, 1930s, 6" l. 250.00

Three Little Pigs Puzzle

Three Little Pigs puzzle, jigsaw-type, in box w/colorful scene of Mickey & Minnie Mouse & the Three Pigs, box marked "Mickey Mouse Vera Puzzle," France, 1930s 300.00

PINOCCHIO

Jiminy Cricket Figure, Pinocchio Bank & Figure

Jiminy Cricket figure, composition, standing on a square base, Multi Products Corp., 1940, 5" h. 250.00

Pinocchio bank, composition, Pinocchio seated on a green turtle, Crown Toy, 1939 ....400.00

Pinocchio Doll

Pinocchio doll, jointed composition, cloth clothes & hat, w/original wrist tag, Knickerbocker, 1939 ....400.00

Pinocchio Pull Toy

Pinocchio figure, composition, standing on square base, Multi Products of Chicago, 1940, 6" h. (ILLUS. with Jiminy Cricket) 250.00

Pinocchio toy, pull-type, "Pinocchio Express," Pinocchio driving a cart, platform base w/small wheels, Fisher-Price, Walt Disney Enterprises, 1939 (ILLUS.) 650.00

Pinocchio Delivery Toy

Pinocchio Walker Toy

Pinocchio toy, windup tin, "Pinocchio

Delivery," Pinocchio steering a colorful lithographed cart, Louis Marx, lever-action (ILLUS.) 900.00

Pinocchio toy, windup tin, walker-type, Pinocchio shuffles forward when wound, Walt Disney Enterprises, Louis Marx, 1939 (ILLUS.) 450.00

SNOW WHITE & THE SEVEN DWARFS

Snow White & Dwarfs Toothpick Holders

Dwarf Bashful toothpick holder, china, S. Maw and Sons, England, 1938 (ILLUS. second from right)...............275.00

Dwarf Doc toothpick holder, china, S. Maw and Sons, England, 1938, 3" h. (ILLUS. second from left)...............275.00

Dwarf Dopey & Snow White Collectibles

Dwarf Dopey night light, lithographed tin, figure of Dopey beside cylinder w/light on top, W.D. Enterprises, Micro Lite, 1930s (ILLUS. right) 300.00

Dwarf Dopey toothpick holder, china, S. Maw and Sons, England, 1938 (ILLUS. far left, above).....................275.00

Dwarf Dopey toy, windup tin, Dopey shuffles forward when wound, Walt Disney Enterprises, Louis Marx, 1930s (ILLUS. w/night light).............475.00

Dwarf Happy doll, stuffed oilcloth, Richard Krueger Co., New York, Disney Enterprises, late 1930s (ILLUS. upper left, with dolls)...........375.00

Dwarf Sleepy toothpick holder, china, S. Maw and Sons, England, 1938 (ILLUS. far, right, left column)..........275.00

Dwarf Happy, Snow White & Dwarf Sneezy Dolls

Dwarf Sleepy toothpick holder, china, S. Maw and Sons, England, 1938 (ILLUS. far right, left column)...........275.00

Dwarf Sneezy doll, stuffed oilcloth, Richard Krueger Co., New York, Disney Enterprises, late 1930s (ILLUS. right, above)........................375.00

Snow White baby rattle, celluloid, Snow White & Dwarfs around the cylindrical body, loop handle, Walt Disney Enterprises, 1938 (ILLUS. w/night light, left column) 300.00

Snow White doll, stuffed oilcloth, Ideal Toy Company, late 1930s (ILLUS. center, above) 450.00

Snow White toothpick holder, china, S. Maw and Sons, England, 1938 (ILLUS. center, left column) 275.00

Snow White Mechanical Valentines

Snow White valentine, mechanical, lithographed paper, cut-out figure of Snow White sweeping, Walt Disney Enterprises, late 1930s 35.00

Snow White valentine, mechanical, lithographed paper, heart-shaped scene of Snow White & Dwarfs dancing, verse below, 1937 ....35.00

(Disney Collectibles continued from p. 387)

Big Bad Wolf Tumbler

Alice in Wonderland coloring book, entitled "Alice in Philcoland," Philco premium, 1949, uncolored 45.00

Alice in Wonderland movie cel, gouache on full celluloid applied to a printed Disneyland background, the Caterpillar talks to a tiny Alice seated in the bowl of a spoon, unframed, 1952, 8 x 10"..................920.00

Alice in Wonderland movie cel, gouache on trimmed celluloid applied to a gouache production background, showing Alice standing among the cabbage leaves & looking up at butterflies, signed by Walt Disney on the mat & stamped "WDP," Disney Productions label on the back, 1951, framed, 9¼ x 11¼" 12,100.00

Alice in Wonderland record album, Walt Disney front & back cover art, Ginger Rogers as Alice, 1944 ....58.00

Alice in Wonderland salt & pepper shakers, ceramic, model of Alice, white w/gold trim, made by Regal China, marked "Disney," pr.............350.00

Alice in Wonderland stationery, child's set, 1951 ....95.00

Alice in Wonderland wrist watch, U.S. Time, ca. 1950, w/teacup in box 350.00

Bambi concept drawing, water-color on paper of a wintery forest scene, 1942, framed, 9½ x 11" 690.00

Bambi figure w/butterfly on tail, ceramic, American Pottery, 1947, 8" h...........................100.00 to150.00

Bambi movie cel, gouache on laminated celluloid applied to a Courvoisier airbrush & water-color background, scene of Bambi meeting Flower, 1942, unframed, 8½ x 11¼"....................................4,025.00

Bambi record album, three records, narrated by Shirley Temple, RCA, 1949..125.00

Big Bad Wolf (from "Three Little Pigs") tumbler, glass w/color transfer design, Second Dairy Series, ca. 1939, 4¾" h. (ILLUS.) ....65.00 to 75.00

Chip 'n' Dale cartoon cel, large images of Chip 'n' Dale, each character about 6½" h., gouache on celluloid w/a photocopied outline, signed by Bill Justice, ca. 1960s, framed, 8½ x 9"............................1,495.00

Cinderella movie cel, gouache on trimmed celluloid applied to a studio-prepared background featuring a long scene w/a Cinderella fleeing the ball in the pumpkin carriage drawn by four racing white horses & driven by the coachman as the magic spell ends at midnight, 1950, framed, 12½ x 31".........................19,550.00

Cinderella Movie Poster

Cinderella movie poster, featuring scenes from the movie, one-sheet, linen-backed, 27 x 41" (ILLUS.) 462.00

Cinderella song folio, colorfully illustrated scenes from the film, England, 1949, 21 pp.........................50.00

Cinderella wrist watch, w/glass slipper case, U.S. Time, 1950, mint in box..350.00

Cinderella & Prince salt & pepper shakers, ceramic, Walt Disney Productions, pr...................................95.00

Cinderella & Prince toy, windup plastic Cinderella & Prince dancing, manufactured by Irwin, copyright Walt Disney Productions, 5" h., mint in box 150.00 to175.00

Davy Crockett belt & buckle, leather.................................40.00 to 60.00

Davy Crockett billfold, mint in box 50.00

Davy Crockett cereal bowl, milk white glass w/red figures & lettering, Fire-King Ovenware, 4¾" d., 2½" h. (ILLUS. top next column) .....15.00 to 25.00

Davy Crockett chair, folding-type, aluminum w/canvas seat & back,

Davy Crockett Cereal Bowl

illustration of Davy & signature in script on back....................................30.00

Davy Crockett cookie jar, cov. American Bisque.............325.00 to 375.00

Davy Crockett cookie jar, cov., bust of Davy wearing coonskin cap & "Davy Crockett" embossed on his collar, base marked "Translucent Vitrified China, copyright, C. Miller 55-140 B," Regal China 450.00

Davy Crockett costume, girl's, includes blouse, skirt, belt & lithographed tin pin, the set................80.00

Davy Crockett horseshoe set, hard rubber, 1950s, mint in original box.....75.00

Davy Crockett mug, Brush pottery.................................40.00 to 50.00

Davy Crockett pin, "Davy Rifle Sharp Shooter," mint on original card.....................................20.00 to 25.00

Davy Crockett plate, milk white glass...16.50

Davy Crockett play set, "Davy Crockett Flying Arrows," 1955, in original package.............................42.00

Davy Crockett sunglasses, mint on card..35.00

Davy Crockett tie slide, metal, mint on card...............................10.00 to 15.00

Davy Crockett wrist watch, U.S. Time, 1954, w/powder horn case..............300.00

Disney phonograph record, "Little Toot," by Capitol Records, 1948........20.00

Disney postage stamp album, stamps & catalog, Marlen, 1986, unused.......50.00

Disney characters book, "Previews of Pictures to Come," drawings include Donald Duck & Ludwig Von Drake, Vol. 14..55.00

Disney characters card game, "Silly Symphony Mickey Snap," includes Mickey & several Disney characters, England, 1930s.............................110.00

Disney characters chamber pot, child's, ceramic, molded in relief on one side w/Mickey & Minnie Mouse running off to Dreamland & Huey, Dewey & Louie on the reverse,

Disney Characters Chamber Pot

trimmed in color, marked "141" on the bottom, 6" d. (ILLUS.) 92.00

Disney characters drum, lithographed tin, illustrates Mickey & Minnie Mouse, Donald Duck, Pluto, etc., Ohio Art Co. (Bryan, Ohio), 6½" 210.00

Disneyland game, board-type, "Haunted Mansion," mint in box.......100.00

Disneyland toy, "Disneyland Rocketship Control Board," in original box 300.00

Disneyland toy, windup-type, "Casey Jr. Train," w/black engine & one each blue, green & yellow cars, decorated w/Disney characters, 12" l., 2½" h., the set........175.00 to 225.00

Donald Duck cartoon cel, from "Donald Gets Drafted," gouache on laminated celluloid applied to a Courvoisier water-color background, shows Donald in uniform, marching, carrying a rifle & saluting, 1942, 6½ x 7" 1,430.00

Donald Duck comic strip artwork, pen & ink on illustration board for a daily strip, by Al Taliaferro, July 11, 1941, 5 x 21½" 935.00

Donald Duck cookie jar, cov.,ceramic, head-shaped, marked "Walt Disney Productions WD5" & paper label "Original Dan Brechner Exclusive Japan"..575.00

Donald Duck doll, stuffed cloth, long-billed Donald dressed, w/spats, original Knickerbocker tag, ca. 1930s, 6" h. 145.00

Donald Duck doll, stuffed cloth & felt, Donald dressed in a red bandleader's uniform w/gold trim & brass buttons, w/a "bearskin" tall black hat & wooden baton, Knickerbocker, ca. 1930s, 21" h. (ILLUS. top next column) 1,000.00

Donald Duck figure, bisque, long-billed Donald, 1930s, 1¾" h. 65.00

Large Donald Duck Doll

Donald Duck night light, General Electric Co., 1965, on original card ....45.00 to 50.00

Donald Duck paint box, Transogram, 1938 ....55.00

Donald Duck rug, shows Donald carrying Chip 'n' Dale in buckets (one in each hand), 21" w., 3' l. 100.00

Donald Duck soda straws, multicolor box of 100, Herz Mfg. Co., New York, New York, 1940s, ¾ x 3¾ x 8¾" box 20.00

Donald Duck switchplate cover, plastic, full-figure Donald behind a camera 15.00

Donald Duck tea set: cov. teapot, creamer, sugar bowl, tray & six cups, saucers & plates; tin, Ohio Art Co., Bryan, Ohio, marked "Walt Disney Productions," 1939, the set 150.00

Donald Duck toy, balancing-type, a celluloid long-billed Donald w/jointed arms standing atop an orange & white weighted base, Japan, ca. 1930s, 7" h. (small split at back of neck, arms detached but present) ...440.00

Donald Duck toy, pull-type, "Donald Duck Cart," Fisher-Price No. 500, 1951 ....225.00

Donald Duck toy, pull-type, "Donald Duck Xylophone," Fisher-Price, No. 185, 1938 ....225.00 to 275.00

Donald Duck "Dipsy Car"

Donald Duck toy, windup tin, "Disney Dipsy Car," Donald behind the wheel of a tractor-like vehicle, Line Mar, Japan, w/original box (ILLUS.) 687.50

Early Donald Duck Tumbler

Donald Duck tumbler, pictures Donald & his name, ca. 1937 (ILLUS.)...........65.00

Donald Duck & Mickey Mouse Book, "Donald Duck & Mickey Mouse Cub Scouts," Walt Disney Productions, 1950 ....20.00

Donald & Nephews Tumbler

Donald Duck & nephews tumbler, colored scene of Donald & his nephews as Boy Scouts, 1942 Series (ILLUS.) 52.00

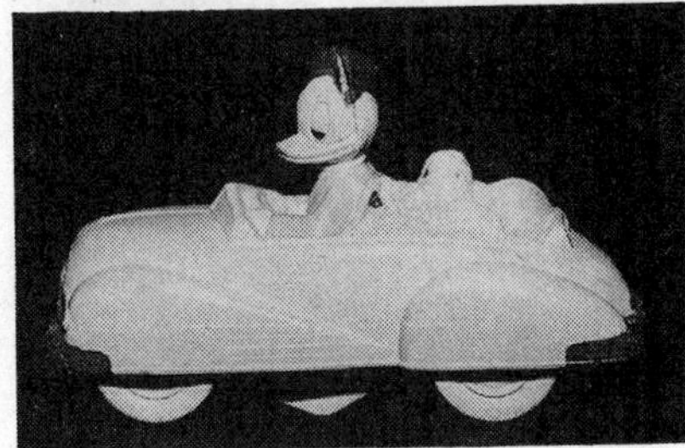

Donald & Pluto Auto

Donald Duck & Pluto toy, automobile, hard rubber, Sun Rubber Co., Barberton, Ohio, 1940s, 6½" l. (ILLUS.) 60.00

Donald Duck & Pluto toy, composition, metal & wood, h.p. figures riding a railroad flatcar on which Pluto's doghouse is placed, The Lionel Corporation, ca. 1938, w/original box, 10" l. 863.00

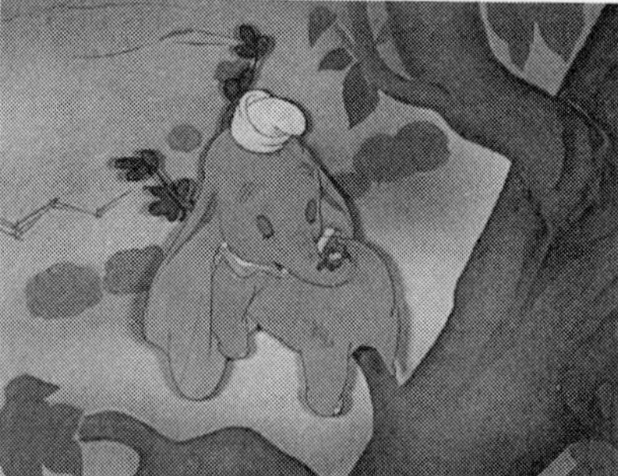

Dumbo Movie Cel

Dumbo the Elephant movie cel, gouache on celluloid applied to an airbrushed background, shows Dumbo asleep on a tree branch w/Timothy Mouse nestled in his trunk, stamped "WDP" in lower right, w/a Courvoisier Galleries label on back, 1941, framed, 7¼ x 10" (ILLUS.) 3,163.00

Dumbo the Elephant movie poster, three-sheet, color lithographed pictures of Dumbo flying above a circus train & a line of elephants, linen-backed, 1941, 41" w., 81" h. 19,800.00

Dumbo & Pluto cookie jar, turnabout, Leeds China......................150.00 to175.00

Dwarf Dopey costume & mask, by Fishbach-Spotlite, w/original box.......30.00

Dwarf Dopey Movie Cel

Dwarf Dopey movie cel, from "Snow White and the Seven Dwarfs," gouache on laminated celluloid applied to a Courvoisier Galleries wood veneer background, shows Dopey running up stairs holding a candle, 1937, unframed, 5½ x 7" 2,310.00

Dwarf Dopey movie cel, from "Snow White and the Seven Dwarfs," gouache on celluloid applied to an airbrushed wood veneer background, Dopey hitting a cymbal,1937, framed, 8 x 9" (ILLUS.) 2,875.00

Dwarf Dopey valentine card, mechanical, Walt Disney Enterprises, 1938, 3 x 4½"................60.00

Dwarf Dopey Ventriloquist Dummy

Dwarf Dopey ventriloquist dummy, composition head, hands & feet, wearing a long red robe, greyish blue pants & tan cap (ILLUS.)..........675.00

Dwarf Grumpy movie cel, from "Snow White and the Seven Dwarfs," gouache on full celluloid applied to a Courvoisier airbrush background, shows Grumpy standing & looking angry, 4½ x 5" 1,870.00

Dwarf Grumpy Tumbler

Dwarf Grumpy tumbler, Grumpy conducting, Second Dairy series, Musical Notes series, 1938 (ILLUS.) ....60.00 to 70.00

Dwarf Happy cartoon cel, from "Snow White and the Seven Dwarfs," gouache on partial celluloid applied to a Courvoisier wood veneer background, shows Happy within a circle waving, framed together w/a Walt Disney signature, 1937, 7½" sq. 3,220.00

Dwarf Sneezy valentine card, mechanical, Walt Disney Enterprises, 1938 ....28.00

Fantasia movie cel, from the Nutcracker Suite segment, gouache on celluloid, the multi-cel set-up w/special effects applied to an airbrushed background, showing a group of mushrooms dancing, stamped "WDP" at lower left & w/the Courvoisier Galleries label to back, framed, 1940, image 6 ¾ x 8" 3,738.00

Fantasia Movie Cel

Fantasia movie cel, from the Pastoral Symphony sequence, gouache on celluloid applied to an airbrushed background, depicting baby Pegasus nestled under mother Pegasus' wing, stamped "WDP" in lower right, framed, 1940, image 4", overall 9½ x 12½" (ILLUS.)......3,450.00

Fantasia movie inspirational sketch, pastel on black paper, showing the yellow Thistle Men dancing, unframed, 1940, 10 x 12".............1,380.00

Ferdinand the Bull figure, composition, jointed, signed Walt Disney Enterprises & Ideal 160.00

Ferdinand the Bull layout drawing, graphite & colored pencil on paper, showing Ferdinand riding in the back of a hay-filled farmer's wagon, 1938, unframed, 9½ x 12"............1,265.00

Ferdinand the Bull mask, canvas 65.00

Ferdinand the Bull movie cel, gouache on trimmed celluloid applied to an air-brushed background, scene depicting Ferdinand's mother eating grass amid the flowers, 1938, 8¼ x 10½"................690.00

Ferdinand the Bull Movie Cel

Ferdinand the Bull movie cel, gouache on a partial celluloid applied to a Courvoisier airbrushed & water-color background, Ferdinand depicted smiling w/his head through a floral wreath, 1938, unframed, 16 x 17¼" (ILLUS.) 1,840.00

Figaro (Pinocchio's cat) doll, mohair w/oilcloth face, ca. 1939 ....150.00

Figaro toothpick holder, porcelain 75.00

Flower the Skunk (Bambi) figure, miniature, Hagen-Reneker.................75.00

Goofy toy, windup plastic, Goofy in a convertible automobile, 5" l. 45.00

Jiminy Cricket (Pinocchio) figure, wood-jointed, 9" h. 225.00

Jiminy Cricket toy, windup tin, a smiling Jiminy Cricket wearing a black & white tuxedo w/blue top hat bobs up & down when wound, Line Mar, ca. 1960, 6" h...........................322.00

Jiminy Cricket wrist watch, Ingersoll, in box 110.00

Lady and The Tramp Movie Cel

Lady and The Tramp movie cel, gouache on trimmed celluloid, bust portraits of Lady & Tramp, framed, 1955, image size Lady 4¼", Tramp 6", overall 6½ x 7½ " (ILLUS.).......2,588.00

Mary Poppins carpet bag, plastic, 1960s, 9" h....................................16.00

Mary Poppins lunch box & thermos, depicting a flying Mary Poppins on both sides of the box, the thermos w/a carousel scene, near mint condition, 1965 ....104.00

Mary Poppins pencil case, vinyl, 1964..15.00

Mary Poppins spoon, silver plate, figural handle depicting Mary w/open umbrella, International Silver, 1964, near mint condition 35.00

Mary Poppins stationery, colorful carousel scene on box, England, 1964..45.00

Mickey Mouse bank, composition & tin, the still bank in the form of Mickey standing and wearing short pants & oversized shoes & resting against a large tree trunk w/curved lid & embossed studs & handles, painted trim, embossed across front of base "Walt Disney Crown," ca. 1940s, 6¼ " h. 230.00

Mickey Mouse bicycle toy, clip-on type, battery-operated, "Mickey Mouse talking Cycle Buddy," by Stelber, mint in box 100.00

Mickey Mouse book, "King Arthur's Court," pop-up type, 1933, mint condition 775.00

Mickey Mouse book, "Mickey Mouse's Mother Goose," Whitman, 1937..140.00

"Mickey Mouse Story Book"

Mickey Mouse book, "Mickey Mouse Story Book," David McKay Company, 1931 (ILLUS.) 805.00

Mickey Mouse book, "Ye Olden Days," pop-up type, Blue Ribbon Books, 1934...................................195.00

Mickey Mouse bowl, Beetleware, w/alphabet & numerals on rim, Walt Disney Ent., ca. 1930s, large...........65.00

Mickey Mouse breakfast set: plate, cereal bowl & mug; china, 3 pcs 40.00

Mickey Mouse bridge score pad, large illustration of Mickey on cover..65.00

Mickey Mouse candy container, composition Mickey head & molded cardboard body, w/original paper label, 1940s 235.00

Mickey Mouse Cartoon Cel

Mickey Mouse cartoon cel, gouache on celluloid, Mickey holds the jaws of a fearsome bear, from an unknown production, possibly a publicity cel, ca. 1930, image Mickey 3½", bear 6", overall 10 x 12" (ILLUS.) 2,300.00

Mickey Mouse coloring book, 1931, large..50.00

Mickey Mouse coloring book, "Mickey Mouse Goes To Frontierland," Dell Books, 1957 ....20.00

Mickey Mouse costume, orange w/red pants, plastic mask, ca. 1950s, child's size large 12-14, original size paper tag sewn in (mask slightly pushed in, minor soil on one arm & leg) 45.00

Mickey Mouse desk, school master-type w/flip-over blackboard, marked "Falcon Toy"...295.00

Mickey Mouse doll, stuffed cloth, cloth swivel head w/black felt 'pie' eyes, black nose, open-closed mouth, felt applied ears, cloth body w/composition orange feet, leather tail, wearing original red shorts w/white buttons, 11" (overall general fading & aging, felt eyes & leather tail replaced, small split seam in nose, right foot sole missing, left sole partially missing) 425.00

Mickey Mouse drawing, pencil on paper, a sketched head of Mickey, signed "Walt Disney - with apologies to Mickey Mouse" at the bottom & "To Christina and Fiona" at the top, ca. 1935, 15¼ x 15½" 8,050.00

Mickey Mouse figure, bisque, Mickey riding Pluto, 1930s, 3¼" h. 80.00

Mickey Mouse figure, bisque, Mickey playing a mandolin, 5" h. 435.00

Mickey Mouse figure, composition, jointed arms & head, wearing a Mexican outfit, w/sombrero & serape, 9" h. 1,495.00

Mickey Mouse figure, hard rubber, Seiberling, 1930s, 6" h. 175.00

Mickey Mouse figure, jointed wood, two decals on feet, marked "A Fun-e-Flex Toy," excellent paint, 1930s, 7" h. (minor flaking on chest decal) 650.00

Mickey Mouse Fun-e-Flex Figure

Mickey Mouse figure, jointed wood & composition, Fun-e-Flex , painted composition head & wood jointed body w/movable limbs, cloth-covered tail w/wooden knob at end, marked "Mickey Mouse Des. Pat. 82802 by Walt Disney," ca. 1930s, 9 ¼" h. (ILLUS.) 1,035.00

Mickey Mouse game, "Jacks" w/zipper case 30.00

Mickey Mouse game, "Mickey Mouse Scatterball," w/spinning wooden top & small wooden game balls, ca. 1930 ....225.00

Mickey Mouse game, "Pin the Tail on Mickey," includes 16 linen-like tails numbered consecutively & the Mickey target w/his back turned, in colorful box picturing Mickey, Minnie & the Three Pigs, marked "Walt Disney Enterprises," Marks Bros., target 17½ x 22", box 9½ x 10½" (pinkish tinge to upper quarter of target, 2 small splits in box) 155.00

Mickey Mouse game, "Quoits" (ring toss), lithographed paper on wood, England, 18½" sq. 135.00

Mickey Mouse map, "Treasure Island," 1939, Standard Oil premium, 20 x 25" 125.00

Mickey Mouse mask, paper, Dennison, 1930s, excellent condition 35.00

Mickey Mouse napkin holder, Bakelite 85.00

Mickey Mouse pail, lithographed tin, "Happynak," England, 1939 ....95.00

Mickey Mouse paint box, lithographed tin, Transogram, 1952 ....23.00

Mickey Mouse paint book, "Mickey Mouse & The Beanstalk," 1948 ....37.00

Mickey Mouse pinback button, celluloid, "Good Teeth," 1930s 115.00

Mickey Mouse pinback button, celluloid, "Mickey Mouse Club," pictures Mickey w/one hand raised & the other on his hip, marked "Copy. 1928-1930 By W.E. Disney" ....125.00 to 150.00

Mickey Mouse postcard, illustrates Mickey w/ children, unusual colorization, 1930s 30.00

Mickey Mouse puppet, hand-type, in original box, 1950, Gund 75.00

Mickey Mouse table set: cov. sugar bowl, salt & pepper shakers & tray; china, each modeled as long-nosed Mickey on a shaped triangular tray, black & white w/yellow shoes, marked "Made in Germany," mint condition, sugar bowl 4" h., the set ....2,000.00 to 2,500.00

"Mickey Mouse Slate Dancer"

Mickey Mouse toy, battery-operated, locomotive, tin & plastic, w/lights & sound, Japan, like new in nice box, ca. 1960s 350.00

Mickey Mouse toy, hand-crank type, "Mickey Mouse Slate Dancer," articulated Mickey dances whencrank is turned (ILLUS. previous page) 29,150.00

Mickey Mouse toy, windup tin, "Dipsey Car," Line Mar.................1,050.00

Mickey Mouse & Donald Duck candy box, lithographed tin, illustration of Donald painting Mickey's portrait, England, ca. 1930, 6"......................235.00

Mickey Mouse & Donald Duck cartoon color guide drawing, graphite & colored pencil on paper, Officer Mickey drives a motorcycle while Officer Donald rides in a bucket seat extending forward, from"The Dognapper," 1934, 9 x 11"..............920.00

Mickey Mouse & Donald Duck dollhouse, lithographed tin, two-story, Marx, 25" h.......................80.00

Mickey Mouse & Donald Duck lunch box, scene of Pluto pulling a cart filled w/Donald's nephews & Mickey running behind, near mint condition, 1954 ....403.00

Mickey Mouse & Donald Duck shoes, "Pals," size 2, pr...............................35.00

Mickey Mouse & Donald Duck toy, windup tin, "Mickey Mouse Handcar," painted plaster figures of Mickey & Donald on lithographed handcar w/four cast wheels, w/six lengths of track, Wells, in original colorful cardboard box, box bottom has large hole 978.00

Mickey Mouse, Donald Duck & Pluto ceiling globe, glass, all holding balloons (mint) 125.00

Mickey & Minnie Mouse cookie jar, cov., pottery, "turnabout," Leeds China Co...225.00

Mickey & Minnie Mouse horn, paper w/wooden mouthpiece, pictures of Mickey & Minnie above their names on the sides, marked "Walt Disney, Licensee, Marks Bros. Co.," 6¾" l...49.50

Mickey & Minnie Mouse paper doll set, four outfits for each including cowboy, drum major & swimming, Saalfield, 1933, 10½" h...................125.00

Mickey & Minnie Mouse toy, windup, tin & composition, handcar w/figures of Mickey & Minnie on each end of center handle, Lionel ca. 1933, w/original box ....1,100.00 to 1,500.00

Mickey & Minnie Mouse & Pluto toothbrush holder, bisque 175.00

Mickey Mouse & Pluto Toy

Mickey Mouse & Pluto toy, push-type, lithographed paper on wood, a tinplate drum & cymbal are activated by Mickey w/moving arms, on a blue four-wheeled wooden platform, No. 530, Fisher-Price Co., 1935-36, 4 x11 x 12" (ILLUS.).....................2,300.00

Mickey Mouse Club costume, Mousketeer, mint in box..................125.00

Mickey Mouse Club cowboy gloves w/fringe, w/illustrations of Spin & Marty & "Triple R Ranch," pr.............25.00

Mickey Mouse Club harmonica, 1970, in package 25.00

Mickey Mouse Club Magazine, Vol. IV, No. 1, February, 1957 ....20.00

Mickey Mouse Club Mousketeer ears 10.00

Mickey Mouse Club tray, tin, illustrates several Disney characters, 1950s, 12½ x 17" 135.00

Minnie Mouse Cartoon Cel

Minnie Mouse cartoon cel, from "The Brave Little Tailor," gouache on trimmed celluloid applied to a Courvoisier wood-veneer background, depicting Princess Minnie smiling w/delight, 1938, 6½ x 6¾" (ILLUS.) 7,130.00

Minnie Mouse doll, plush & felt, Charlotte Clark, late 1940s, 20" h..500.00

Minnie Mouse earrings, lacquered wood, 1940s 145.00

Mrs. Potts (Beauty & the Beast) cookie jar, mint in box, 10" h.............50.00

Mowgli (The Jungle Book) toy, squeak-type, soft vinyl in pastel shades of brown, Holland, dated 1967, 6" h...20.00

101 Dalmatians puzzles, 1961, set of 4..85.00

Peter Pan marionette, Peter Puppet Playthings, ca. 1952 ....195.00

Peter Pan movie cel, gouache on celluloid applied to a photographic copy of the original background, shows Peter seated cross-legged on the top of a chair back, 1953, 12½ x 17" 2,875.00

Pinocchio pinback button, celluloid, "Good Teeth," 1920s-'30s 135.00

Pinocchio cookie jar, bust of Pinocchio, pottery, marked "CJ46 - ©USA" on two lines, Doranne of California...600.00

Pinocchio cut-out circus, 1939 bread company promotion, 18 x 20", uncut 125.00

Pinocchio doll, composition, jointed, Knickerbocker, 14" h.......................350.00

Pinocchio doll, jointed wood, wearing a red suit, green tie, white gloves & a red & purple-banded hat, Ideal, ca. 1940, 19½" h. (chip to hair).............345.00

Pinocchio & Jiminy Cricket Movie Cel

Pinocchio fan, folding-type, wood w/lithographed paper showing a film scene, 1939, Spain 65.00

Pinocchio movie cel, gouache on trimmed celluloid depicting Jiminy Cricket in conversation w/Pinocchio, applied to an airbrushed background, w/Courvoisier Galleries label on back, 1940, framed 8¼ x 9½" (ILLUS.) 6,325.00

Pinocchio movie sketch, graphite & white paint on paper, scene of J. Worthington Foulfellow (Honest John) taking Pinocchio's pulse, stamp at bottom "Copyright 1939 Walt Disney Prod.," Courvoisier Galleries label on back, 1940, 10 x 12"..2,588.00

Pinocchio toothpick holder, china.........75.00

Pinocchio toy, pull-type, "Plucky Pinocchio," Pinocchio on donkey, Fisher-Price No. 494........275.00 to 325.00

Pinocchio & friends lunch pail, tin, cylindrical w/swing handle, various characters march around the sides, dated 1940, 6¼" h..........................250.00

Pluto figure, ceramic, crouching position, Brayton Laguna, unsigned, 1938-40...85.00

Pluto hand puppet, Gund, 1950s..........33.00

Pluto lamp, ceramic, soft brown tones, Leeds, marked "Walt Disney Productions" on base, late 1940s, figure 4 x 4 x 6"..............................115.00

Pluto planter, ceramic, Pluto looking over his shoulder at the cart he is pulling, Leeds...................................65.00

Pluto toy, "Mickey's Pal Pluto Pop-Up Kritter," yellow dog w/black tail, red collar & black oilcloth ears on a guitar-shaped base, Model 210, Fisher-Price, Inc., 1936, mint condition 350.00

Pluto wall hanger, wood, marked "W.D.," 1930s, excellent condition, 8" h...30.00

Pongo & Perdita (101 Dalmatians) salt & pepper shakers, authorized by "Walt Disney Productions," pr 155.00

Rolly (101 Dalmatians) cookie jar, h.p., mint in box, 13" h 50.00

Silly Symphonies advertising fan, shows all characters picnicking in richly colored scene, mint 175.00

Sleeping Beauty movie cel, gouache on trimmed celluloid applied to a water-color production background, a scene with Briar Rose looking up at a squirrel coming out of a knot in the tree that forms part of the fairy godmothers' cottage, marked along bottom margin "Prod. 2082, Seq 6, Sc 15," inscribed "To Don Da Gradi, Best Wishes, Walt Disney" in the lower right of mat, bears the WDP stamp, 1959, 11 x 12" 12,650.00

Snow White cut-out book, all characters & dwarfs' house in lustrous color graphics, 1937, 13 x 13" 150.00

Snow White & the Seven Dwarfs child's chair, leather & plush, lithograph of Snow White & the dwarfs on front trim below the seat, lithograph of forest animals on the back, marked Walt Disney Enterprises, 1938, 12" w., 15" h 650.00

Snow White & the Seven Dwarfs figures, bisque, figures range from 2" to 2¾" h., set of 8.........................140.00

Snow White & the Seven Dwarfs lamps, figural, one depicting Snow White holding the hem of her skirt up, the other Dopey w/his name on the base, one shade pictures Doc & the other shows the seven dwarfs outside their house, "Walt DIsney Enterprises" seal on bottom, 1938, pr..1,000.00

Snow White Movie Cel

Snow White & the Seven Dwarfs movie cel, gouache on trimmed celluloid w/a cel overlay applied to an airbrushed background, scene depicting the evil Queen disguised as an old hag offering the poisoned apple to Snow White, 1937, framed, 7 x 9" (ILLUS.) 14,950.00

Snow White & the Seven Dwarfs movie cel, gouache on celluloid, a multi-cel set-up applied to an airbrushed background, showing the Prince standing w/his arms around Snow White & getting ready to lift her onto his horse, four of the dwarfs look on & wave goodbye, 1937, framed, 9" sq.......................8,050.00

Snow White & the Seven Dwarfs movie poster, scene depicting Snow White & the Seven Dwarfs w/Prince Charming on a white horse, the Queen & the witch behind them w/the castle in the distance, rendered in lovely pastel tones, one-sheet, RKO, 1937, linen-backed, 27 x 41".....................................12,650.00

Snow White & the Seven Dwarfs soap figures, Kerk, 1938, mint in original box, box 11" l., set of 8 ....250.00 to 275.00

Three Caballeros record album w/promotional booklet, 1944 ....40.00

Tortoise & the Hare book, Walt Disney Studios, 1935, w/dust jacket..50.00

20,000 Leagues Under the Sea toy, windup "Nautilus," actual working submarine, w/box ....275.00 to 300.00

Winnie-the-Pooh stationery, Winnie & friends featured on colorful box, England, 1965...................................55.00

Zorro flashlight, miniature, 1950s 50.00

Zorro half-mask & wrist flashlight, in original box, 2 pcs 55.00

Zorro paint-by-number set, Walt Disney Productions, w/box 85.00

Zorro wrist watch, U.S. Time, 1957, original box ....125.00 to 175.00

(End of Disney Collectibles)

DOLL FURNITURE & ACCESSORIES

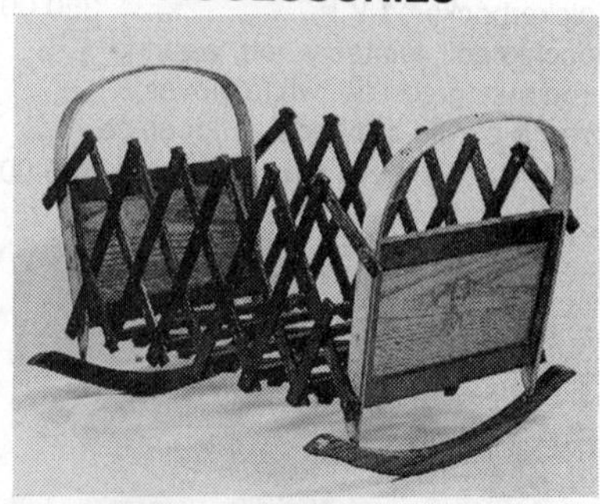

Patented Adjustable Cradle

Bed, w/canopy pole, bamboo, spindled sides w/stepped openwork at head & foot, on casters, 10½ x 21½", 13" h.........................$395.00

Bed, hardwood, chunky turned head posts centering a shaped headboard, conforming footposts, turned feet, w/mattress, bolster & old faded red & green machine-sewn quilt, 13½ x 19", 18" h.............302.50

Bucket, wooden, stave construction, worn original grey paint on a white ground w/red stenciled stars, horse, crossed flags & "Good Boy," wire bail handle w/wooden grip, 4¾" d., 3¼" h. (bottom band missing) 148.50

Buffet, Eastlake-style, ornately carved backboard w/a shelf & mirror, carved base w/drawer above two cupboard doors, 6 x 13", 20½" h......295.00

Canister set, tin, blue & white lithographed decoration of windmills, 4 pcs. 95.00

Carriage, two-wheeled cart-type, gondola-form wooden body painted dark red, wooden axle & handle for pulling, wooden wheels w/wooden spokes, black oil cloth hood w/original fringe, late19th c., overall 21" h. (oilcloth on hood lightly worn & cracks, handle repaired) 420.00

Carriage, painted wicker & wood, wooden frame trimmed w/white-painted scrolling wicker, original interior upholstery, metal-rimmed wheels, late 19th c., 23" l. (some paint wear, axle glued & repaired w/newer screws) 225.00

Carriage, white vinyl & metal, an adjustable vinyl hood above the shallow white metal boat-shaped body, metal frame & white rubber tires, w/matching vinyl cover, marked "Doucet - Made in France - Modele Depose," France, early 20th c. 400.00

Carriage, wood & iron, a flat black oilcloth fringed canopy raised on pierced metal uprights above the low sled-form wooden body painted red, raised on arched metal springs above spoked wooden wheels, red wooden handle at rear, 19th c., 22" h. (small tears in oilcloth) 350.00

Carrying case, Barbie, round w/flat bottom, black w/red writing & pictures of Barbie wearing "Evening Splendour," "Apple Sheath" & "Suburban Shopper," interior beige w/brown stars, handle, zipper & metal closure, dated 1961 (small tear in plastic on inside bottom, closure discolored)............................25.00

Chair, ladderback-style, two thin slats between heavy stiles w/knob finials, woven splint seat, old red finish, 13¼" h...82.50

Chest of drawers, cast iron, w/original paint, J. & E. Stevens Co., ca. 1875, 6½" h.............................250.00

Chest of drawers, oak, a superstructure w/mirror above a rectangular top w/a dark finish & gold swirls to imitate marble above a light finished case w/three graduated long drawers w/small wood knobs, late 19th - early 20th c., 22" h..160.00

Clothing, Barbie's "Cheerleader" outfit, includes skirt, sweater w/"M," white socks, red tennis shoes, pompons & megaphone (pompons flat w/one smaller size paper) 90.00

Clothing, Barbie's "Evening Splendour" 900 series outfit, including pale gold dress (tagged), matching coat w/fur trim, fur hat w/pearl trim, corduroy clutch purse, white hankie, short white gloves, pearl necklace, one pearl earring & brown open-toed shoes (few pin holes in coat lining) 60.00

Clothing, Barbie's "Fashion Luncheon" 1600 series outfit, includes dress, matching jacket w/diamond closure, hat w/flower accent, long white gloves & pale pink open-toed shoes (several pinholes in dress & jacket, small pull on bodice of dress) 500.00

Clothes, Barbie's "Going Hunting" outfit, complete 30.00

Clothing, Barbie's "Pajama Pow" 1800 series outfit, includes print jumpsuit, plastic dangle earrings w/gold, red & purple circles (earring stems discolored, untagged) 330.00

Clothing, Barbie's "Trail-Blazer" 1800 series outfit, includes two-piece striped corduroy suit, yellow cotton blouse w/decal, green plastic glasses w/pink stripes & lime green ankle boots (mint) 90.00

Clothing, Barbie's boyfriend Ken's "Ken in Mexico" outfit, includes felt jacket w/braid trim, matching pants, hat w/chin strap & green adjusting bead sash, tie on rubberband, black boots (hat top is flat, ends of braid trim on clothing beginning to fray)......45.00

Clothing, Barbie's friend Francie's "Silver Cage" outfit, includes pink nylon dress w/silver fishnet overdress, silver/pink fishnet stockings, silver clutch purse & pink bow shoes (mint) 60.00

Clothing, Barbie's friend Francie's "Swingin' Skimmy" set, includes cotton dress, yellow cotton hood, red cotton knit hose & red ankle boots (several pulls on dress trim)...110.00

Clothing, G.I. Joe "Deep Sea Diver" outfit, includes diving suit, mittens, double breast plate, diver's helmet, weighted shoes & belt, rubber hose & signal float (diving suit stained & elastic pulled) 30.00

Corner chair, turned & painted wood, canted ring-turned back stiles w/bobbin-turned finials flanking a ring-turned crestrail over plain spindles, round seat on three ring-turned legs joined by plain stretchers, dark finish w/gold-painted finials & gold metal decoration on middle spindle, late 19th c., 10" h. (finish cracking & somewhat worn) 150.00

Cradle, painted pine, angular hood, simple straight sides, on rockers, old brown graining, 19" l. (one edge of hood has damage)...........................165.00

Cradle, painted & decorated pine, hooded, on rockers, old red flame graining, late wire nail construction, 25" l. (edge damage) 104.50

Cradle, painted & decorated poplar, rectangular w/low, shaped & canted sides w/base molding above the rockers, original brown vinegar graining, 19th c., 14¾" l...................192.50

Cradle, painted poplar, low shaped & canted sides on rockers, original dark red paint w/white & yellow striping, 19½" l. (some wear) 99.00

Cradle, wooden paneled head- & footboards w/bentwood open crests, accordion-type open adjustable sides, on rockers, patented by C.A. Fenner, Mystic River, Connecticut, open 20" l. (ILLUS.) 350.00

Cupboard, Empire (American) country-style, black-painted wood framing glazed cupboard doors & sides, one shelf, 6 x 15 x 16¾" 85.00

Dining room set, wooden, Strombecker No. 872, boxed........................45.00

Early Bliss Dollhouse

Dollhouse, printed paper on wood, on two floors, the exterior w/white stone lower floor & white clapboard w/yellow details, the front porch w/turned wood corner supports, balcony on upper level, two-room interior, blue-stained deeply pitched roof, front steps, Bliss, early 20th c., some interior paper replaced, some paper loss on exterior, 16" h. (ILLUS.) 805.00

Small Bliss Dollhouse

Dollhouse, printed paper on wood, a tiled roof, front porch, opening door, the exterior w/yellow shingles & blue clapboard, hinged front, Bliss, late 19th c., original interior papers, some paper loss at sides, 16⅛" h. (ILLUS.) 460.00

Large Bliss Dollhouse

Dollhouse, printed paper on wood, the lower floor exterior finished as stone, w/full-width porch supported on six columns, the upper floor exterior w/a timbered & stucco design, two front bay windows upstairs topped by small gable roofs, slate roof, stairs to front porch, the interior w/four rooms w/original wallpapers, kitchen w/half wood paneling, tiled floor, paper-applied internal opening doors, Bliss, early 20th c., signs of play wear, roof papers poor & worn, 21¼" h. (ILLUS.) 920.00

Dollhouse, carpenter-made, exterior painted as cream stone on lower floor, mustard brick upper floor, balcony above at long glazed windows, steps to central front door, hinged facade, four internal rooms, three w/contemporary wallpaper, back wall of each room w/chimney breast & fireplace, later crudely wired for electric light, probably England, early 20th c., fair condition, 22½" h. 403.00

Dollhouse carriage, cast iron, Kilgore 65.00

Dollhouse crib, cast iron, Kilgore 65.00

Dollhouse family, mother, father, girl, boy & baby, plastic, Renwal, 5 pcs. 75.00

Dollhouse grand piano w/bench, plastic, Renwal, Model L-75..............65.00

Dollhouse potty chair, cast iron, Kilgore 55.00

Dollhouse rocking chair, cast iron, Kilgore 45.00

Dollhouse sink, cast iron, pedestal-type w/wooden tub & commode, Arcade, 3 pcs. 75.00

Hoosier cupboard, tri-tone paint & stenciling, 39" h. 695.00

Tent set, G.I. Joe "Bivouac Deluxe Pup Tent" set, includes tent w/metal supports, machine gun w/tripod, ammo box & entrenching tool 25.00

Trunk, camel back style, original blue liner & lithographs, w/trays, 10 x 10 x 16" 350.00

Waffle iron, cast iron, "E.C. Simmons," wooden handles, unusual interior design 225.00

Waffle iron, cast iron, "Stover Junior No. 08" 225.00

Wicker set: couch, chair, rocker w/cushions & table; painted blue, the set 100.00

DOLLS

Also see ADVERTISING ITEMS, CHARACTER COLLECTIBLES and DISNEY COLLECTIBLES.

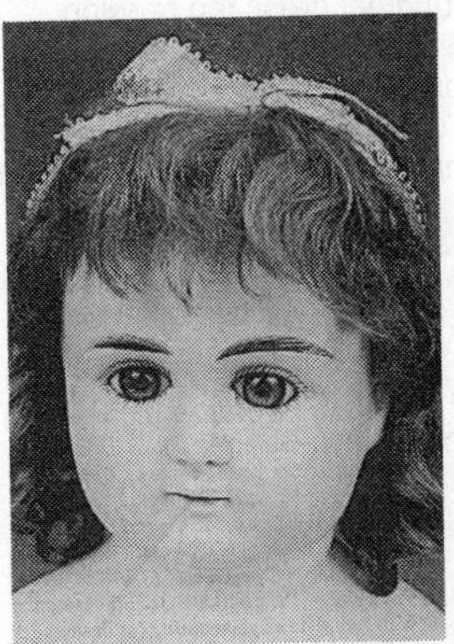

Alt, Beck & Gottschalck Bisque Head Girl

A.B.G. (Alt, Beck & Gottschalck) bisque socket head girl marked "ABG - 1362 - Made in Germany - 0.5," blue sleep eyes w/real lashes, replaced blonde human hair (h.h.) wig, pierced ears, open mouth w/four upper teeth, jointed wood & composition body, wearing an antique white eyelet dress, under-clothing, socks & shoes, 15" (tiny rub on left cheek, small crack on left side of body, minor repair on knees) $350.00

A.B.G. bisque shoulder head girl marked "1125 (crosshatch) 19," set brown eyes, brown h.h. wig, open mouth w/two upper square teeth & one lower square tooth, kid body w/bisque lower arms, rivet joints at elbows, gussets at hips & knees, wearing an antique white dress, underclothing, socks & shoes, 24" (kid damaged by back shoulder plate, patches on body) 400.00

A.B.G. bisque head girl marked "1008/11," fixed threaded blue eyes lined in black, closed painted mouth, molded blonde curly hair, fabric body w/bisque lower arms, wearing an old blue silk gown, cotton under-wear, 26" 440.00

A.B.G. bisque shoulder head girl marked "10 - 1123½ - Germany," set blue eyes, brown mohair wig, open mouth w/six upper teeth, kid body covered w/cloth, bisque lower arms, wearing possibly original clothing, underclothing, old socks & shoes, (inherent firing line on seam of head, short line on upper lid, replaced lower legs, 26" (ILLUS.) 400.00

Alexander (Madame) Cowgirl, hard plastic head w/blue sleep eyes w/molded lashes, original synthetic blonde wig, hard plastic child body jointed at the shoulders, hips &

knees, original dress tag reading "Cow Girl by Madame Alexander New York USA," wearing original cowgirl outfit, panties & boots, mint in original box, 8" 175.00

Alexander Elise Ballerina

Alexander (Madame) Elise Ballerina, hard plastic head w/blue sleep eyes w/real lashes, closed mouth, pierced ears, original synthetic brown wig, hard plastic body w/vinyl arms, jointed at shoulders, elbows, hips, knees & ankles, wearing original gold ballerina tutu, gold crown, stockings & slippers, 15" (ILLUS.) ...430.00

Alexander (Madame) Fairy Princess, composition head w/brown sleep eyes w/real lashes, original blonde h.h. (human hair) wig, closed mouth, five-piece composition body, wearing tagged pink satin dress, original underclothing, socks, shoes, 'crown' & necklace, 17" 375.00

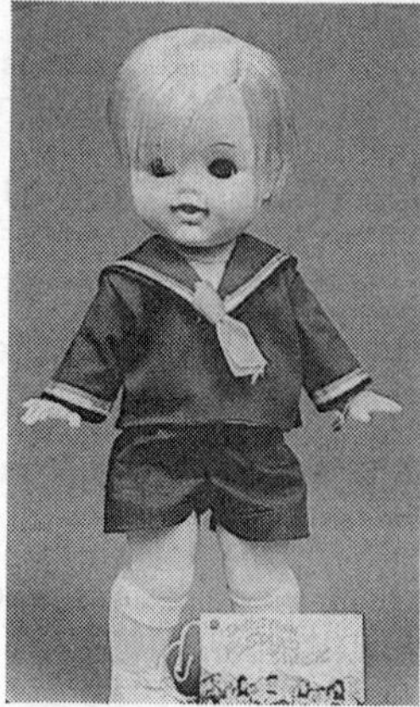

Madame Alexander Kurt

Alexander (Madame) Kurt, from 'Sound of Music,' vinyl head w/blue sleep eyes w/real lashes, open-closed mouth, rooted synthetic blond hair, five-piece vinyl body, wearing original tagged sailor suit outfit w/socks & shoes, unplayed-with condition, 11" (ILLUS.) 435.00

Alexander (Madame) Margaret Rose, hard plastic head w/blue sleep eyes w/real lashes, closed mouth, brown mohair wig, five-piece plastic body, wearing original tagged dress, panties, socks, shoes & straw hat, 17" (clothing washed) 250.00

Alexander (Madame) Renoir Portrette, hard plastic head w/blue sleep eyes & molded lashes, closed mouth, original brown synthetic wig, hard plastic body jointed at shoulders, hips & knees, original wrist tag, original dress tag reading "Renoir by Madame Alexander - New York U.S.A.," wearing original navy blue taffeta dress, underclothing, shoes, stockings, red taffeta hat, mint in original box, 9" 325.00

Alexander (Madame) Wendy Ann, hard plastic head w/blue sleep eyes w/real lashes, closed mouth, original blonde floss wig, five-piece hard plastic body, wearing tagged light blue taffeta dress w/red roses, original underclothing, blue coat, socks, shoes & gold purse, 14" (one brow a bit worn) 350.00

All-bisque lady w/swivel neck, set blue glass eyes, closed mouth, original blonde mohair wig, molded & painted socks & two-strap shoes, wearing original European ethnic clothing, 4½" (silk skirt deteriorated)..185.00

All-bisque Oriental man, head w/stiff neck, painted brown eyes, black mustache, closed mouth, molded & painted hair w/brush strokes around face, all-bisque body jointed at shoulders & hips, molded & painted shoes, wearing original military uniform & hat, 2½" (left leg shorter than right)..110.00

Amberg (Louis) bisque flange head "Newborn Babe" marked "©L.Amberg & Son - Germany 886/8", blue sleep eyes, softly blushed hair, closed mouth, cloth body w/composition hands, wearing old blue taffeta baby dress w/embroidered flowers, matching bonnet, slip & booties, 21" (some body flaking) 375.00

A.M. (Armand Marseille) bisque socket head Oriental boy marked "A.M. - Germany - 353/6/0 - K," dark painted head w/set brown eyes, painted black hair, closed mouth, five-piece composition body, wearing original Oriental outfit w/pants, patterned shirt, wide hat & w/a stick shoulder harness suspending wooden jugs, 7" 275.00

A.M. bisque shoulder head character girl marked "640 - A. 2/0 M. - Germany," blue sleep eyes, blonde mohair wig, closed slightly smiling mouth, kid body w/bisque lower arms, gussets at elbows, hips & knees, redressed in new white dress w/lace trim, slip, stockings & shoes, 13" (short firing line on back of head, minor repair on kid on arm, little finger on left hand missing)..............425.00

A.M. bisque socket head baby marked "Germany - G. 327 B. - A. 6 M. - D.R.G.M. 259," brown sleep eyes, brown h.h. wig, open mouth w/two lower teeth, five-piece composition baby body, wearing white eyelet dress, underclothing, socks & shoes, 15" (minor rub on left cheek, body repainted) 350.00

A.M. bisque socket head girl marked "1894 - A.M. 3 DEP - made in Germany," set brown eyes, synthetic brown wig, open mouth w/four upper teeth, jointed wood & composition body w/straight wrists, redressed in antique white dress w/lace trim & tucks, underclothing, original socks & shoes, 16½" (few strips of paint missing on upper arms & legs) 325.00

A.M. bisque socket head boy marked "1894 - A.M. 5 DEP," brown sleep eyes, blond mohair wig, open mouth w/four upper teeth, crude jointed wood & composition body, wearing a sweater, shorts & knit cap, 18" (minor inherent split on rear rim)......425.00

A.M. bisque socket head girl marked "Armand Marseille - Germany - 390 - A.15 M.," brown sleep eyes w/real lashes, original brown h.h. wig, open mouth w/four upper teeth, jointed wood & composition body, redressed in fancy peach-colored outfit, 31" (two inherent splits in rim, minor wear) 700.00

A.M. bisque socket head girl marked "Armand Marseille - Germany - 390 - A. 15 M.," blue sleep eyes w/real lashes, brown mohair wig, open mouth w/four upper teeth, jointed wood & composition body, wearing fine antique white dress trimmed w/lace, underclothing, replaced shoes & socks, 33" (small rub on left cheek, slight roughness at neck opening, repair & repaint on right upper arm) 675.00

A.M. bisque socket head girl marked "Duchess, A. 17 M., Made in Germany," set blue eyes, heavy molded & feathered brows, painted lashes, h.h. wig, open mouth w/four upper teeth, jointed wood & composition body, dressed, replaced stockings & shoes, 36" (small firing flaws on rim of head, uneven coloring on back of head, minute lines on back of head & behind left ear, crazing & crack on lower torso, body repainted) 1,200.00

A.M. bisque socket head girl marked "A 14 M," blue sleep eyes, blonde mohair wig, open mouth w/four upper teeth, jointed wood & composition body, wearing an antique white dress, slip, socks & shoes, 31" (eyes replaced, neck socket repaired, hands crazed & flaking) 550.00

Averill (Georgene) "Bonnie Babe" marked "Copr. by Georgene Averill - 1005/3652," bisque flange head w/brown sleep eyes, lightly molded & painted hair, open mouth w/two lower teeth & wobble tongue, cloth body w/composition lower arms & legs, wearing antique white long baby dress & underclothing, 15" (small chip upper left eyelid, inherent line in corner of mouth, tiny rub on back of head, general crazing & paint flaking on body, right hand finger ends chipped) 550.00

Averill (Georgene) bisque head "Bonnie Babe," blue glass sleep eyes, cloth body w/composition arms and legs, 17" 995.00

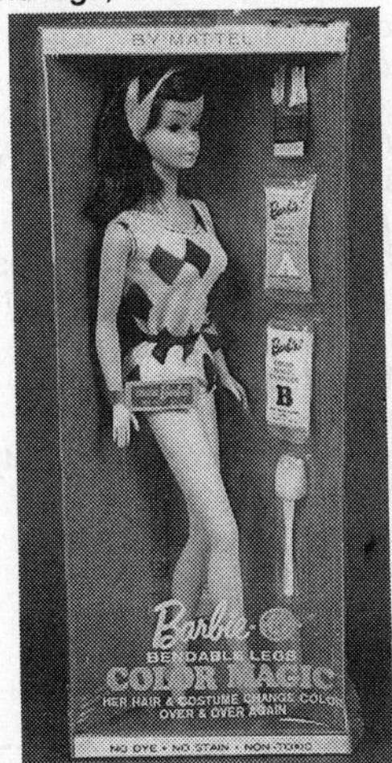

Rare Color Magic Barbie

Barbie, "American Girl Barbie," ash blonde hair, pink lips, bent leg, wearing original swimsuit, in box (faded stain on right foot, box worn) 875.00

Barbie, "American Girl Barbie," light brown hair, full dark pink lips, bent leg, wearing original swimsuit (slight eyelash rubs, legs w/faint blue spots on front & sides, slight roughness top of left hand) 650.00

Barbie, ash blonde swirl ponytail hairstyle, full beige lips w/faded pink coloring, pearl earrings, wearing red nylon swimsuit, w/original box 180.00

Barbie, "Bubble Cut Barbie," auburn hair, No. 850, mint in original box, 1964 ....195.00

Barbie, "Color Magic Barbie," midnight black hair, near mint in original box (ILLUS. previous page) 4,300.00

"Color Magic Barbie"

Barbie, "Color Magic Barbie," golden flame - scarlet flame hair, tan lips, bent leg, wearing original swimsuit w/hairband & aqua open-toe shoes, in clear plastic box w/booklet, color changer A & B, net, hair ribbons & barrettes, slight discoloration on lips, wrist tag split on side (ILLUS.) 1,000.00

Barbie, No. 1, ponytail model w/brunette hair, fleshtone coloring, original hoop earrings & shoes (ILLUS. top next column) 4,100.00

Barbie, No. 3, brunette ponytail, red lips, straight leg, wearing black & white swimsuit (body white w/tan coloration on torso & legs, hair retied & bottom w/loose curls, rectangular spot on back from sticker) 300.00

Barbie, No. 4, pale blonde, w/original topknot, coral lips, straight leg, wearing red nylon swimsuit (several loose hair strands on top & bottom

Original Barbie No. 1

w/fuzzy curls, lips repainted, couple of ink stains, left arm finish rough) ...155.00

Barbie, No. 5 together w/"Mix 'n Match" set, blonde hair in original set, red lips, wrist tag, straight leg, wearing black & white swimsuit, in box w/stand, booklet, glasses & black open-toed shoes in cellophane, outfit pieces to Winter Holiday, Resort Set, checked bodyshirt w/jeans, grey skirt, striped bodyblouse, blue bra & panties (mint, original cellophane over outfits w/one side seam split, original overall covering replaced, box slightly discolored) 800.00

Barbie, "Twist 'N' Turn Barbie," blonde, rooted eyelashes, bent leg, wearing original swimsuit w/net cover-up, hair bow, plastic hair covering, part of wrist band attached & remaining tag present, 1967 (slight roughness on lower lip) 190.00

Fashion Lady by Barrois

Barrois (E.) bisque shoulder head Fashion lady marked "E. 7. B," cobalt blue eyes, original blonde mohair wig, closed mouth w/accented lips, pierced ears, kid body w/gussets at elbows, hips & knees, individually stitched fingers, redressed in antique fabrics, hat & shoes, 24" (ILLUS.) 4,700.00

Bebe Mascotte bisque socket head girl marked "Mascotte - H," blue paperweight eyes, original blonde mohair wig, closed mouth w/accented lips, pierced ears, jointed wood & composition body marked on left hip "Bebe Mascotte - Paris," redressed in fancy French-style outfit made of antique fabrics, antique underclothing, socks & shoes, 18" (minor inherent flaw inside left rim, minor body wear) ... 4,300.00

Bergmann (C.M.) bisque socket head girl marked "S & H - C.M.B. - 6½," blue sleep eyes, synthetic brown wig, open mouth w/four upper teeth, pierced ears, jointed wood & composition body, redressed in pale peach organdy dress w/pinafore, antique underclothing, replaced socks & shoes, 18" (very minor inherent flaw on left forehead) 275.00

Bergmann (C.M.) bisque socket head girl marked "C.M. Bergmann - Simon & Halbig - 7," brown sleep eyes, molded & feathered brows, original blonde mohair wig, open mouth w/four upper teeth, pierced ears, jointed wood & composition body, wearing antique clothing, replaced socks & shoes, 19" (faint hairline on back of head) 240.00

Bergmann (C.M.) bisque socket head girl marked "C.M. Bergmann - Simon & Halbig - 13½," blue sleep eyes w/remnants of real lashes, molded & feathered brows, pierced ears, brown mohair wig, open mouth w/four upper teeth, jointed wood & composition body, wearing an antique white dress, underclothing, socks & high button shoes, 29" (two fingers missing & thumb chipped on one hand, toes chipped, red polish on fingers & toes) 475.00

Bergmann (C.M.) bisque socket head girl marked "C.M. Bergmann - Simon & Halbig - 14½," brown sleep eyes, molded & feathered brows, original platinum blonde mohair wig, open mouth w/four upper teeth, jointed wood & composition child body, wearing antique clothing, underclothing, stockings & child's shoes, 32" 950.00

Bergmann (C.M.) bisque socket head girl marked "C.M. Bergmann - Waltershausen - 1916 - 17," set brown eyes, blonde h.h. wig, open mouth w/four upper teeth, jointed wood & composition body, wearing an antique white dress, underclothing & socks, 38" (small inherent cut near right rear crown, minor firing line behind ear, repair at neck socket, lower right arm old replacement) 775.00

Betsy McCall vinyl character girl marked "McCall 19©61," vinyl character head w/blue sleep eyes w/real lashes, original rooted synthetic hair, closed smiling mouth, vinyl body jointed at shoulders, wrists, waist, hips & ankles, wearing original blue, green & lavender striped dress, underclothing, socks & shoes, 27" 350.00

Bru bisque head girl marked "Bru Jne R," stationary blue glass eyes, outlined open mouth, brown h.h. wig, pierced ears, composition jointed body w/jointed wrists, wearing a beige silk dress w/pink flowers & trimmed in maroon velvet, matching bonnet w/green plume, underclothes & socks, 12" 2,500.00

Bru bisque socket head girl marked "Bru Jne - No. 2," threaded pale blue paperweight eyes, pierced ears, blonde mohair wig, open-closed mouth w/accented lips & tongue, kid body w/unjointed kid upper arms, bisque lower arms, gussets at hips & knees, finely redressed in beige & rose French-style dress w/lace overlay, antique underclothing, socks & shoes, 12" (replaced kid attaching shoulderplate to body) 10,000.00

Bru bisque head girl marked "Bru Jeune 3," fixed light blue paperweight eyes, closed mouth, pierced ears, cork pate w/replaced brunette h.h. wig, gusseted kid body w/bisque lower arms, molded breast shoulderplate, wearing an old maroon satin dress w/pleated bodice & short skirt, new underclothes & cream simulated leather shoes, ca. 1890, 13½" (slightly grainy bisque, body worn in places, one earring missing) ... 11,500.00

Bru bisque socket head Fashion lady marked, "E," pale blue paperweight eyes, closed smiling mouth, replaced blonde mohair wig, pierced ears, kid body w/gussets at elbows, hips & knees, individually stitched fingers, redressed w/antique fabrics, underclothing, stockings & shoes, 18" (fused hairline on forehead, repair on bridge of nose, minor body repairs) 1,500.00

Bru Nursing Doll

Bru bisque socket head 'nursing' girl marked "Bru Jne - 5 5," bulbous brown paperweight eyes, antique blonde mohair wig, open mouth w/accented lips & nursing mechanism, kid body w/bisque lower arms & wooden lower legs, wearing fine antique lace baby dress, underclothing & bonnet, small reglued chip on earlobe, tiny flake at earring hole, 18" (ILLUS.) 5,200.00

"Circle Dot" Bru Doll

Bru bisque socket head "circle dot" girl marked "Bte SGDG 9," blue paperweight eyes, brown h.h. wig, open-closed mouth, jointed body, wearing an antique style lace-trimmed dress & cap (ILLUS.) 20,500.00

Buddy Lee boy marked "Buddy Lee," hard plastic head w/stiff neck, painted black side-glancing eyes, molded & painted hair, closed smiling mouth, hard plastic body jointed at shoulders only, molded & painted black boots, wearing original Lee bib overalls, denim shirt, red bandana & Lee denim hat, pants labeled "Union Made Lee - Sanforized - Reg. U.S. Pat. Off.," & "Lee Union Made" on front, 12" (one flaw in hair paint on top)..................225.00

Bushow & Beck celluloid head boy marked "No. 7 - 42 - Germany" & 'helmet' mark, blue painted intaglio eyes, closed mouth, molded & painted hair, jointed cloth body w/celluloid hands, wearing probably original boy's suit w/matching hat, socks & high shoes, 16"..................165.00

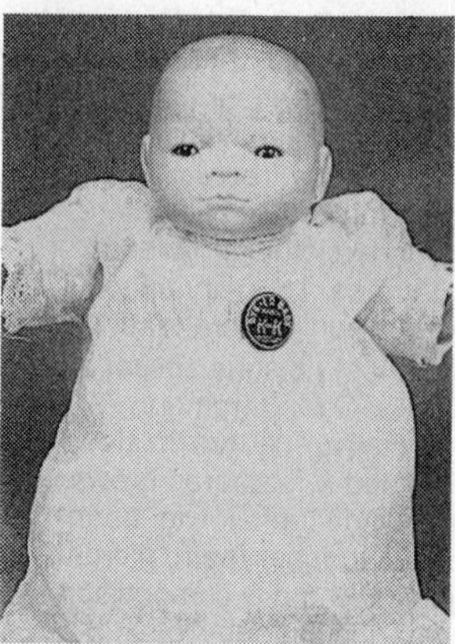

Bye-Lo Baby by Grace Putnam

Bye-Lo Baby, bisque head marked "Copr. by Grace S. Putnam," brown sleep eyes, closed mouth, softly molded & blushed hair, cloth "frog" body w/celluloid hands, wearing original tagged dress & flannel underclothing, 10" (ILLUS.).............350.00

Bye-Lo Baby, bisque flange head marked "Copr. by Grace S. Putnam," blue sleep eyes, softly blushed brows, closed mouth, softly molded & blushed hair, cloth "frog" body w/celluloid hands, wearing original tagged dress, underclothing & w/original pink blanket marked "Bye-Lo Baby" across top three times w/a stork below, 11" 550.00

Catterfelder Puppenfabrik bisque socket head girl marked "Germany - C.P. - 1100 - 3," blue sleep eyes, synthetic blonde wig, open mouth w/four upper teeth, wearing an antique white eyelet dress, underclothing, replaced socks, shoes, black corduroy coat & hat, red gloves, 21" (minor inherent head flaws, minor body repairs)...............450.00

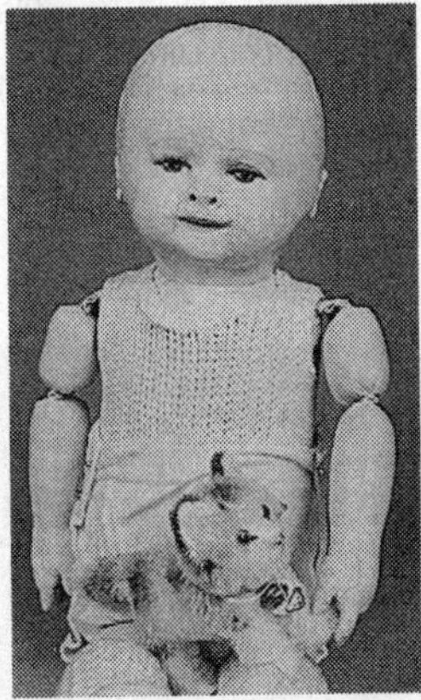

Martha Chase Hospital Baby

Chase (Martha) stockinet 'Hospital' baby, oil-painted stockinet head w/painted blue eyes, open-closed mouth, painted blonde hair, oil-painted cloth body jointed at shoulders, elbows & hips, weighted to simulate a real baby, wearing a knit shirt, flannel diaper & long cotton socks & booties, marked "Chase Hospital Doll - Trade Mark - Pawtucket, R.I. - Made in U.S.A.," 20" (ILLUS.) 550.00

Chase (Martha) stockinet girl, oil-painted head w/painted blue eyes, painted short blonde hair, pierced nostrils & ear canals, closed mouth, cloth body w/oil-painted lower arms & legs jointed at shoulders, elbows & hips, wearing possibly original dress & replaced socks, 21" (small nose rub, minor paint cracks, torso recovered, left hand backwards)......450.00

Chase (Martha) stockinet baby, oil-painted stockinet head w/painted brown eyes, single stroke brows, painted lashes, closed mouth, painted blond hair, applied ears, cloth body jointed at shoulders, elbows, hips & knees, torso padded w/cotton for realistic form, oil-painted arms & legs, redressed in two-piece boy's romper, 24" (lashes missing from left eye, light rub on nose, light wear on hands)...............500.00

Chase (Martha) stockinet boy, oil-painted head w/brown eyes, painted blond hair, closed mouth, applied ears, cloth body w/sateen-covered torso, wearing original rust-colored wool two-piece suit, hat & white shirt, body stamped "Chase Stockinet Doll - Trade Mark," 25" (crazing & flaking on hair, minor face crazing & flaking, crazing & flaking on lower arms & legs, left elbow loose at seam, moth holes in suit) ...400.00

China head girl, Alice-type, painted blue eyes w/red accent lines, molded & painted black hair pulled away from face, exposed ears, cloth body w/china lower arms, bisque lower legs, wearing a pale yellow antique dress trimmed w/blue ribbons, pinafore, slip, 11" (tiny spot of black off one back curl, cloth legs patched, legs don't match)..............300.00

China head girl, brown painted eyes w/red accent line, molded & painted center-part blonde hair w/exposed ears, closed mouth w/accent line between lips, felt body w/china lower arms, gussets at hips & knees, wearing a pink velvet dress trimmed w/white lace, underclothing, stockings, 12"...................................325.00

China head lady marked "5" on back of shoulder plate, painted blue eyes, closed mouth, blonde mohair wig, cloth body w/china lower arms & legs, wearing an antique gold two-piece outfit & slip, 13" (small paint flake on right eye, body & legs heavily patched)..............................350.00

China head lady, solid dome shoulder-head w/painted blue eyes w/red accent line, closed mouth w/white space between lips, original brown h.h. wig w/a braided bun, cloth body w/china lower arms & legs, wearing a pink taffeta dress trimmed in black lace & beaded braid, 15" (light imperfection on tip of nose, replaced body & possibly lower legs) 420.00

China Head Dolls

China shoulder head lady, painted blue eyes w/red accent line, closed smiling mouth w/accent line between lips, molded & blonde painted vertical curls around face, cloth body w/bisque lower arms & legs w/molded boots, wearing a two-piece antique outfit & underclothing, lower arms & legs possibly replaced, minor chips on toes, 17" (ILLUS. left, previous page) 475.00

China shoulder head 'flat-top' lady, painted blue eyes w/red accent line, closed mouth, molded & black painted center part hair, cloth body w/leather lower arms, wearing a possibly original brown print dress, pinafore, underclothing, socks & leather shoes, individual fingers split, wear on shoes, 18" (ILLUS. right, previous page) 195.00

China head lady, 'flat-top' style w/black molded & painted hair w/side curls, painted blue eyes w/red accent line, closed smiling mouth, cloth body w/leather lower arms & individually stitched fingers, wearing an antique red sprigged dress & underclothing, 23" 240.00

China head lady, painted blue eyes, single stroke brows, accent line over eyes, molded & painted curly center-part hairdo, closed mouth, original cloth body w/leather lower arms, blue & white striped lower legs to indicate socks, leather boots for the feet, dressed in original underclothing & dress, 19" (very minor wear on back of head) 220.00

China head lady, black 'flat top' center-parted hairdo w/tight side curls, painted blue eyes w/black & red lines over eyes, closed mouth w/accent lines, cloth body w/china lower arms & legs, wearing possibly original antique underclothing, 21" (body replaced, minor wear on back of head) 175.00

China head Highland Mary lady, painted blue eyes, molded & painted blonde hair, kid body w/china lower arms & legs, wearing an old beige lace dress w/lavender underdress & layers of underclothing, 22" 695.00

China head lady, 'flat top' molded & center-parted black hairdo w/molded side curls, painted blue eyes, closed mouth, cloth body w/china lower arms, red leather boots over lower legs, wearing original-looking underclothing & a dress made of antique fabrics, 36" (upper arms possibly replaced, leather of right foot deteriorated & taped) 475.00

China shoulder head 'low brow' lady, molded blonde hair, blue painted eyes, rosy cheeks, on a jointed cloth body w/bisque lower arms & legs, wearing an elaborate black & ecru lace gown w/wine-colored velvet ribbon trim & a matching reticule, 17" 180.00

'High Brow' China Head Doll

China shoulder head 'high brow' lady, painted blue eyes w/red lines, molded center-part black hair w/curls at forehead & molded curls low toward the back of the head, closed mouth, kid body w/gussets at elbows, hips & knees, individually stitched fingers, redressed in plaid two-piece outfit, underclothing & socks, light color wear on back of head, 17" (ILLUS.) 165.00

China shoulder head girl, painted blue eyes w/red accent line, single stroke brows, molded & painted curly black hair, closed mouth,cloth body w/leather hands, dressed in period clothing, 19" (minor wear on back of head, kiln speck on front shoulder plate, inherent flaw on back of neck, hands polished & worn) 200.00

China shoulder head lady, black 'covered wagon' center-parted hair w/molded curls over the ears, painted blue eyes w/red accent lines, closed mouth, cloth body w/china lower arms, redressed in fancy lace-trimmed gown made w/old fabric, underclothing, replaced stockings & shoes, 22" (minor wear on back of head, slight scratch on left cheek, replaced upper arms) 225.00

Cloth "Mammy" doll, black hand-painted cloth head w/brown eyes, closed smiling mouth & a plaid kerchief, cloth body w/jointed shoulders, hips & knees, wearing original navy blue & white striped dress, navy blue & white checked apron, red plaid shawl & kerchief & underclothing, 12" (ILLUS.)..............425.00

Cloth Mammy Doll

Cloth "rag" black girl, brown cloth body w/oil-painted facial features, brown oil cloth feet, dressed in a brown & white checked dress, 18"..2,250.00

Cloth "rag" doll, embroidered face & brown yarn hair in pigtails, dressed in red, green, white & blue plaid long dress w/red rick rack trim, 22"............49.50

Columbia bisque shoulder head girl marked "Columbia (in diamond) - 2½," brown sleep eyes, blonde mohair wig, open mouth w/four upper teeth, kid body w/bisque lower arms, cloth lower legs, gussets at hips & knees, redressed in pink floral-print dress trimmed w/ribbon, straw bonnet, underclothing, socks & shoes, 18½" (questionable line on left shoulder, light rub on left cheek, finger repaired) 165.00

Composition flange head soldier, painted light blue eyes, molded & painted hair, open-closed mouth, cloth body w/composition lower arms, jointed at shoulders & hips, wearing original soldier's uniform w/jacket, pants, belt, boots & hat, jacket labeled "Tipperary Tommy - Reg. U.S. Pat. Off. No. 82,999," 16" (some light wear, feet of boots crazed)...175.00

Composition Oriental boy, flange head w/painted brown eyes, painted hair w/one center tuft of real hair, open-closed smiling mouth w/four

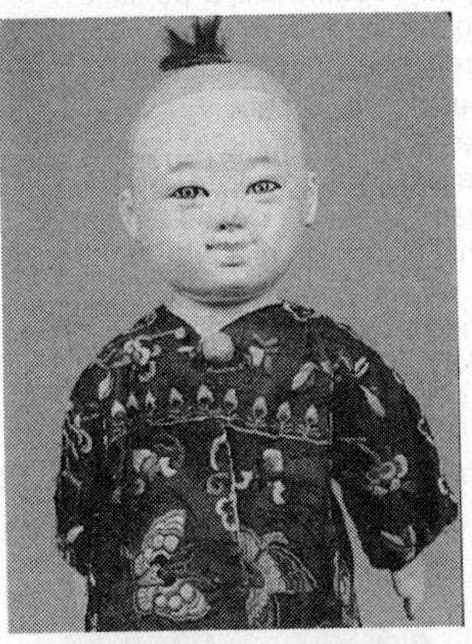

Composition Oriental Boy Doll

upper teeth, cloth body w/composition lower arms & legs, wearing original elaborately embroidered two-piece Oriental outfit, socks, shoes & crocheted hat, superficial crack on back of head, light wear & discoloration to composition, 11" (ILLUS.) 90.00

Coquette composition flange head character girl, blue intaglio side-glancing eyes, open-closed mouth w/four painted teeth, molded & painted blonde hair w/molded & painted ribbon, head slightly tilted on a cloth body w/composition hands, jointed at shoulders & hips, black shoes made on legs, wearing original checked dress & underclothing, early 20th c., 14" (light paint wear, repair on cloth torso)...85.00

Dewees Cochran latex character head girl, painted blue eyes, closed mouth, original brown h.h. wig, five-piece latex child body, wearing probably original floral sprigged organdy dress, underclothing, replaced socks & shoes, 14½" (head stuck in neck, few areas of touch-up on body)...290.00

Dollhouse man, bisque shoulder head marked "3T9 8/0," painted blue eyes, closed mouth, molded & painted mustache & hair, cloth body w/bisque lower arms & legs, wearing original ecru satin shirt, dark coat w/long tails & pants, 6¼" (body repaired on front) 150.00

Dollhouse man, bisque shoulder head marked "184 8/0," painted blue eyes, closed mouth, molded & painted mustache, beard & hair, cloth body w/bisque lower arms & legs, wearing original ecru satin shirt, dark coat w/tails & pants, 8" (minor ear flaw, body recovered, feet repaired, shirt not complete) 180.00

Dollhouse nurse & baby, nurse unmarked, baby marked "Japan," nurse w/bisque shoulder head, painted blue eyes, closed mouth, original blonde mohair wig, cloth body w/bisque lower arms & legs, wearing original black dress, white pinafore & cap, baby crude all-bisque, jointed at shoulders only, wearing original white baby dress, nurse 7", 2 pcs. 190.00

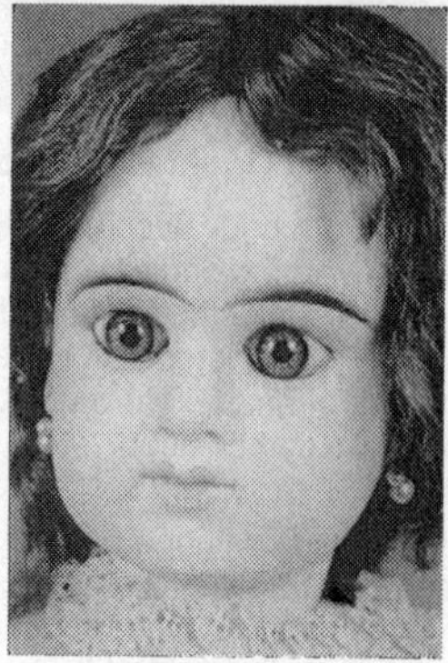

E.D. Bisque Girl Doll

E.D. bisque socket head girl marked "E - 10 - D," blue paperweight eyes, brown mohair wig, pierced ears, closed mouth, jointed wood & composition body w/jointed wrists, wearing a beige dress trimmed w/ecru lace & melon ribbon, underclothing, socks & shoes, 25" (ILLUS.) 2,250.00

Eden Bebe bisque head girl marked "Eden Bebe - Paris," blue paperweight glass eyes, brown h.h. wig, pierced ears, closed mouth, stockinette body on padded armature, wooden lower arms w/composition hands, composition lower legs, wearing an antique white silk dress, underclothing, socks & shoes, 27" (some crazing & flaking on composition of body)...............1,200.00

Effanbee "American Children" boy marked "Effanbee - USA," composition head w/painted blue eyes, blond mohair wig, closed mouth, five-piece composition body, wearing a white shirt, black & white herringbone pattern shorts & jacket, socks & shoes, paint finish on ears rough, some tiny flakes off back of head, light crazing on legs, 17" (ILLUS. left, next column) 500.00

Effanbee "American Children"

Effanbee "American Children" girl marked "Effanbee - American Children," composition head w/painted blue eyes, blonde mohair wig, closed mouth, five-piece composition body, wearing a black & white herringbone pattern dress w/lace-trimmed collar, socks & shoes, some light crazing lines on face, pale coloring, body repainted, 17" (ILLUS. right) 675.00

Effanbee "American Children" girl marked "Effanbee - American Children" on head & "Anne-Shirley" on body, composition head w/brown sleep eyes & real lashes, blonde h.h. wig, closed mouth, composition five-piece child body, wearing an old white dress w/print, original undercloths, socks & shoes, blue wool coat w/hood, metal heart bracelet, 20" 550.00

Effanbee "Baby Tinyette" Dutch Twins, composition head w/painted blue side-glancing eyes, closed mouth, molded & painted hair, on five-piece composition child body, the boy wearing original Dutch outfit w/red hat & shirt, black pants & wooden shoes, the girl wearing a dress w/blue bodice & red print skirt, red, white & blue apron, white organdy hat & wooden shoes, 8", pr. (some paint flaking, unplayed-with) 275.00

Effanbee "Patsy Mae," composition head w/brown sleep eyes w/real lashes, original blonde h.h. wig, rosebud mouth, cloth body w/composition arms & lower legs, wearing a dotted Swiss nylon dress, underclothing, replaced socks & shoes, 30" (glassene eyes cracked, slightly yellowed around eyes & nose, very light body crazing & flaking, non-working cryer)..............700.00

Effanbee "Sweetie Pie," composition flange head w/brown sleep eyes & real lashes, original skin wig, closed mouth, cloth body w/composition arms & lower legs, wearing original red-dotted white Swiss dress, pink crocheted bonnet, white organdy pinafore, underclothing, socks & shoes, paper wrist tag & label on box end reads "I Am Sweetie Pie - with Moving Eyes - An Effanbee Durable Doll," 19"............................250.00

Effanbee "Wee Patsy," composition head w/stiff neck, painted blue eyes, molded & painted hair, closed mouth, composition child body jointed at shoulders & hips, molded & painted socks & shoes, wearing original spotted dress & fitted in original suitcase box marked "Fairy Princess - The Colleen Moore Doll House Doll," complete w/three extra dresses & panties, 6" (very minor crazing, one dress probably a replacement, box lid loose).............500.00

Effanbee "Whistling Jim" character boy, composition head w/blue intaglio eyes, molded & painted hair, open mouth w/whistle hole, cloth body w/composition lower arms, wearing original red & white striped shirt, blue bib pants w/brown trim, black shoes made as part of feet, 15" (minor crazing)..........................350.00

Emma Clear bisque head lady, molded & painted blonde hair w/molded blue scarf around the head & on the front shoulder, set blue glass eyes, closed mouth, cloth body w/bisque lower arms & legs, wearing a blue brocade dress, underclothing including pants & corset, 17".......................................260.00

Emma Clear bisque head George & Martha Washington portraits, Martha w/painted brown eyes, closed mouth, molded & painted hair & mob cap & wearing a beige satin dress trimmed in lace, George w/painted blue eyes, closed mouth, molded & painted hair, wearing a beige satin vest, rust velvet two-piece suit trimmed in lace, black velvet hat, both w/a cloth body w/bisque lower arms & legs w/molded & painted shoes, each 27", pr. (little finger off Martha's left hand)..........................600.00

Fam Lee composition head girl marked "Pat. Apr. 12, 1921," head screws onto body, painted blue eyes, blonde mohair wig, closed mouth, cloth body w/composition lower arms & legs, wearing original pink organdy dress, underclothing, bonnet, socks & shoes, body marked "Fam Lee Doll, New York," in original compartmented box w/two interchangeable heads & extra outfits & instructions, 16" (minor wear, flaking on original head, other heads w/minor cracks & flaking)......450.00

Fine French Fashion Doll

French Fashion, bisque socket head marked "3," set cobalt blue glass eyes, pierced ears, blonde h.h. wig, closed mouth, kid body w/gussets at elbows, hips & knees, individually stitched fingers, wearing an antique brown taffeta two-piece outfit w/blue ribbon trim, underclothing, stockings & red leather shoes, dark firing crack low on right socket seam, 17" (ILLUS.) 1,600.00

Gaultier (F.) bisque swivel head lady marked "F.G.," blonde wig, blue paperweight eyes, pierced ears & a closed mouth, kid body, dressed in white cotton blouse & lavender print skirt & underclothes, 11"...............1,295.00

Gaultier (F.) bisque socket head Fashion lady marked "8 - FG," deep blue paperweight eyes, feathered brows, pierced ears, brown h.h. wig, closed mouth, kid body w/individually stitched fingers & toes, wearing fine two-piece outfit in antique fabric, underclothing, stockings & high button shoes, 29" (minor firing line behind ear, small patches on body & body lightly painted) 3,000.00

Gebruder Kuhnlenz bisque shoulder head girl marked "38-27," threaded blue paperweight eyes, pierced ears, blonde mohair wig, closed mouth, kid body w/bisque lower arms, gussets at elbows, hips & knees, wearing an antique white blouse, plaid wool skirt, underclothing, crocheted booties, blue wool cape w/feather stitching, 18" (right earring hole chipped & cracked, two fingers missing, one chipped) 500.00

Goebel bisque socket head girl toddler marked "W over G - B5 - 3 3/4 - Germany," blue sleep eyes, blonde mohair wig, open mouth w/two upper teeth, jointed wood & composition toddler body w/jointed knees, wearing white fancy dress & matching bonnet, underclothing, socks & shoes, 16" (lower left arm cracked) 450.00

Greiner Papier-Maché Head Lady

Greiner papier-maché head lady marked "Greiner's Patent Heads, Pat. No. 8 March 30th '58," on label on back of shoulder plate, painted blue eyes, single stroke brows, painted upper lashes, exposed ears, cloth body w/leather arms, dressed in purple & white dress, underclothing, socks & shoes, touch-up on nose, light touch-up added to original color on face, light wear on hair, body recovered, old replaced leather arms, old age hairline in shoulder plate, 25" (ILLUS.).............400.00

Handwerck (Heinrich) bisque socket head girl marked "Heinrich Handwerck - Simon & Halbig - 1 - Germany," brown sleep eyes, pierced ears, synthetic brown wig, open mouth w/four upper teeth, jointed wood & composition body, wearing an antique white dress, underclothing, socks & high button shoes, 18" (minor rubbing, little finger missing on left hand).............400.00

Handwerck (Heinrich) bisque socket head girl marked "11 1/2 99 - DEP - Germany," brown sleep eyes, pierced ears, brown h.h. wig, open mouth w/four upper teeth, jointed wood & composition body, wearing a factory chemise, pants, replaced socks & shoes, 20" (replaced teeth, torso cut for missing cryer, one finger replaced) 400.00

Handwerck (Heinrich) bisque socket head girl marked "Handwerck -109-11 - Germany - Halbig - 2½," brown sleep eyes, blonde mohair wig, pierced ears, open mouth w/four upper teeth, jointed wood & composition body, wearing an antique white dress, underclothing, socks & shoes, 21" (tiny flake upper right eye, tiny flake right earring hole, three fingers repaired) 450.00

Handwerck (Heinrich) bisque head girl marked "Heinrich Handwerck - Simon & Halbig - Germany - 4½," blue sleep eyes w/real lashes, molded & feathered brows, open mouth w/four upper teeth, pierced ears, synthetic wig, jointed wood & composition body, wearing an antique white dress, underclothing, replaced socks & old shoes, 27"......450.00

Handwerck (Heinrich) bisque socket head girl marked "109-15 - DEP - Germany - Handwerck - Halbig - 6," brown sleep eyes, brown h.h. wig, open mouth w/four upper teeth, pierced ears, jointed wood & composition body, wearing a lime green white dotted Swiss dress, underclothing, replaced socks & shoes, 30" (short firing line near right ear, minor repair on arm socket) 700.00

Handwerck 99 Girl Doll

Handwerck (Heinrich) bisque head girl marked "16 - 99 - DEP - Germany - H 7," brown sleep eyes, brown h.h. wig in braids, open mouth w/four upper teeth, jointed wood & composition body, wearing an antique white dress, under-clothing, socks & slippers, tiny flake at earring hole, body repainted, hands may be replaced, 35" (ILLUS.) 850.00

Handwerck (Max) bisque head socket girl marked "421 - 19, Handwerck, 7 1 - 2," large weighted brown eyes, open mouth w/upper teeth, pierced ears, dimpled chin, replaced brown h.h. wig, jointed wood & composition body, redressed in blue dotted cotton Victorian-style gown & underwear, ca. 1910, 34".............1,265.00

Hertel, Schwab & Co. bisque head baby marked "150 - 6," blue sleep eyes, original blond skin wig, open-closed mouth, five-piece bent-limb baby body, wearing an antique white baby dress, underclothing, booties, 15" (short hairline near inside corner of right eye, repair & slight damage to repainted body) 300.00

Hertel, Schwab & Co. bisque socket head baby marked "151 - 10," solid dome head w/blue sleep eyes, brush-stroked hair, open mouth w/molded tongue & two painted upper teeth, five-piece bent-limb baby body, wearing an antique white long baby dress & slip, 17" (minor neck chip & firing line, missing fingers)...650.00

Hertel, Schwab & Co. bisque head character baby marked "152 - 13," weighted blue eyes, open mouth, dimpled chin & cheeks, replaced brown h.h. wig, curved limb composition body, redressed, ca. 1912, 22".......................................460.00

Heubach (Ernst) - Koppelsdorf bisque head baby marked "Heubach Koppelsdorf - 339," blue sleep eyes, painted hair, cloth body w/celluloid hands, white lace nursing gown & cap, 15"..595.00

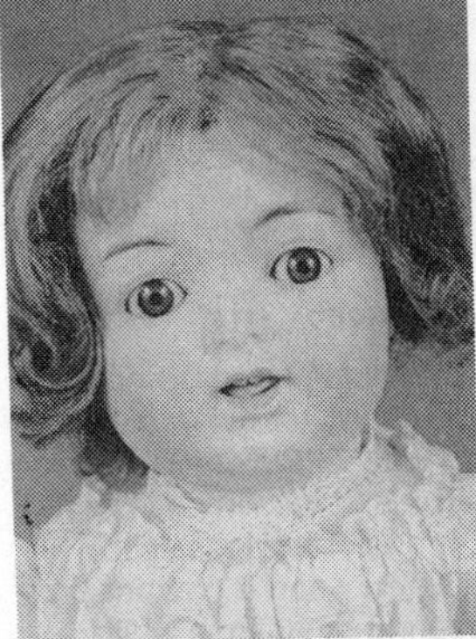

Ernst Heubach Toddler

Heubach (Ernst) - Koppelsdorf bisque socket head toddler marked "Heubach-Koppelsdorf, 342.8, Germany" on back of head, blue sleep eyes, feathered brows, painted lashes, accented nostrils, open mouth w/two upper teeth & wobble tongue, h.h. wig, five-piece toddler body w/diagonal hip joints, dressed in pink & white dress, white pinafore, pants & baby shoes, wig pulls near crown, light rub on left cheek, finish worn at top of torso & arms, chip on lower rear torso, toes chipped on each foot, 23" (ILLUS.) 500.00

Heubach (Ernst) - Koppelsdorf bisque socket head baby marked "Heubach - Koppelsdorf - 342.8 - Germany," blue sleep eyes w/real lashes, brown mohair wig, open mouth w/two upper teeth & wobble tongue, composition bent-limb baby body, wearing a new blue two-piece outfit, socks & shoes, 23" (lashes missing on left eye, partially missing on right eye, torso cut for missing cryer).......400.00

Gebruder Heubach Character Girl

Heubach (Gebruder) bisque shoulder head character girl, molded & painted brown hair w/pink ribbons, tilted head w/side-glancing eyes, open-closed mouth w/upper teeth, jointed bisque body w/molded & painted shoes & socks, wearing a lace-trimmed dress, 9" h. (ILLUS.) 1,900.00

Heubach (Gebruder) bisque shoulder head character boy marked "0 - 77 - Germany - 29," blue intaglio eyes, molded & painted blond hair, open-closed mouth w/two lower teeth, kid body w/bisque lower arms, cloth lower legs, gussets at hips & knees, wearing a black two-piece boy's suit, socks & shoes, 10" 350.00

Heubach (Gebruder) bisque socket head girl marked "8550 - Heubach - Germany," glass sleep eyes, open-closed mouth w/teeth & tongue showing, in small wicker basket w/three outfits, handmade pillows & quilts, 13" 1,295.00

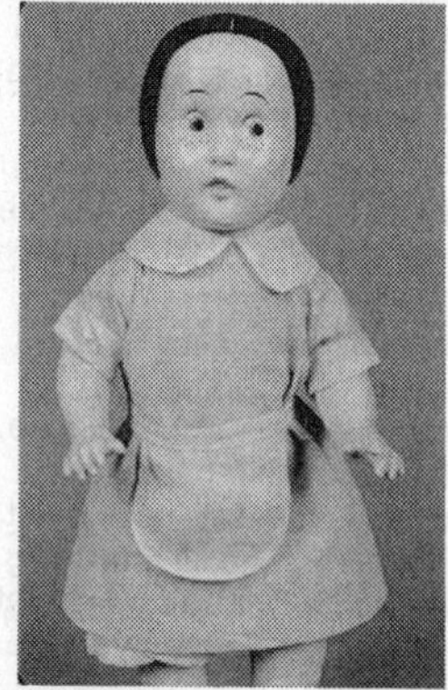

Horsman "Ella Cinders" Doll

Ideal Deanna Durbin

Horsman "Ella Cinders," marked "©, 1925, M.N.S." on back of head, "Ella Cinders, Trade Mark Reg. U.S. Pat. Off., Copyright 1923, Metropolitan Newspaper Service" on tag on sleeve, "Horsman Doll, M'f'd in U.S.A." on tag on back of dress, composition flange head, painted blue eyes glancing to side, single stroke brows, painted upper lashes, painted freckles, accented nostrils, open-closed mouth, molded & painted black hair, cloth body w/composition arms & lower legs, dressed in original tagged clothing, underclothing, socks & shoes, very fine light crazing on face, light paint flaking off back of head, deep cracks in finish of arms, legs very well repainted, 17" (ILLUS.) 375.00

Ideal Novelty & Toy Co. "Deanna Durbin" marked "Deanna Durbin - Ideal Doll" on composition head, green sleep eyes w/real lashes, original brown h.h. wig, open mouth w/six upper teeth, five-piece composition body, wearing original tagged patterned dress, underclothing, shoes & socks, some tiny craze lines, tiny crack above right eye, pale face coloring, minor flaking & cracks, 24" (ILLUS.) 280.00

Ilfelder & Co. bisque head girl marked "101 - 11 B.I. & Co. My Sweetheart," weighted blue glass eyes, open mouth, dimpled chin, red h.h. wig, jointed wood & composition body, redressed in long pink gauze gown, underwear & old cream shoes, ca. 1915, 23"..345.00

Jumeau (E.) bisque head girl marked "Size 12" in red on back of head, brown paperweight eyes, dark blonde h.h. wig, pierced ears, open mouth w/molded upper teeth, jointed composition body, dressed in old light beige wool dress w/intricate embroidery work, beige bonnet w/plume, underclothes, socks & French shoes, 27" 2,500.00

Jumeau "Triste" Doll

Jumeau (E.) bisque head "Princess Elizabeth" character girl marked "Unis France - 71 306 149 - Jumeau - 1938 - Paris," blue flirty eyes w/tin eyelids, brown h.h. wig, closed mouth, jointed wood & composition body, wearing an antique white dress, jacket, underclothing, socks &

shoes, 33" (eyelashes missing, crack in right eye, minor touch-up on lips, body checking & flaking, wood showing on arms) 950.00

Jumeau (E.) bisque head 'long-faced' girl, Carrier-Belleuse 'triste' type, paperweight eyes, brown h.h. wig, closed mouth, wearing fine antique-style costume (ILLUS. previous page)...17,000.00

K (star) R (Kammer & Reinhard) bisque head "Gretchen" character girl, painted blue eyes, pouty mouth, original blonde hair w/rolled bun braids, jointed composition body, dressed in old cream crocheted dress w/matching hat, shoes & stockings, 11"...............................3,000.00

K (star) R bisque socket head baby marked "36 - K★R - 100," painted blue eyes, lightly molded & brush-stroked hair, open-closed mouth, five-piece bent-limb baby body, wearing an antique white baby dress, underclothing, 15" (minor body cracks) 600.00

K (star) R bisque socket head girl marked "K★R - Simon & Halbig - Germany," blue sleep eyes w/real lashes, brown mohair wig, open mouth w/four upper teeth, jointed wood & composition body w/walking mechanism, wearing a factory-made dress, stockings & shoes, replaced underclothing, 15" (very slight nose rub, minor finish cracks & finger repairs)..550.00

K★R Character Children

K (star) R bisque socket head character children marked "K★R - 101," Marie & Peter each have a good wig, painted blue eyes, closed mouth & jointed composition body, wearing color-coordinated clothing, each is missing one finger, Peter's legs replaced, together w/a detailed trunk, trunk 9½ x 10 x 19½", dolls 15", the group (ILLUS.) 4,600.00

K (star) R socket head baby marked "K★R - Simon & Halbig - 122 - 42," brown sleep eyes, blond mohair wig, open mouth w/two upper teeth & tongue, composition bent-limb baby body, wearing an antique white baby dress, under-clothing & baby shoes, 16" (two fingers missing on left hand)..675.00

K (star) R bisque head Scottish boy marked "K★R - Simon & Halbig - 3," brown sleep eyes, pierced ears, original curly brown mohair wig, open mouth w/four upper teeth, jointed wood & composition body, wearing original Scottish outfit w/shirt, kilt, jacket, hat, scarf, shoes & stockings, 17" (minor rubs & repair) 850.00

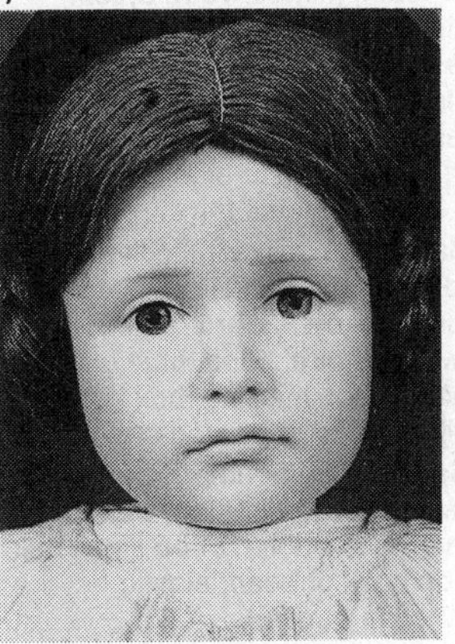

K★R Character Girl 114

K (star) R bisque socket head character girl marked "K★R 114 - 49," painted blue eyes, brown h.h. wig, closed 'pouty' mouth, jointed wood & composition body, wearing a pastel multicolored striped dress w/lace-trimmed collar, antique under-clothing, replaced shoes & socks, hairline on back of head, old body repaint, 19" (ILLUS.) 1,900.00

K (star) R bisque socket head girl marked "K★R - Simon & Halbig 126 - 46," brown flirty sleep eyes w/eyelids, brown mohair wig, open mouth w/two upper teeth & wobble tongue, jointed wood & composition toddler body w/diagonal hip joints & jointed knees, wearing antique blue romper, underclothing, socks & shoes, 20" (slight flakes & wear, hands replaced & repainted, little toe off one foot)...............................700.00

K (star) R bisque head "Mein Liebling" character head girl marked "117A," stationary blue eyes, brown h.h. wig, ball-jointed composition body, wearing a cotton shift, 24" (finger damage) 4,830.00

K (star) R bisque head baby marked "K★R - Simon & Halbig - 126," blue sleep eyes, open mouth, replaced wig, composition bent-limb baby body, ca. 1920s, 24" (repainted arms) 575.00

K (star) R bisque head girl, incised "Simon & Halbig - K★R," brown sleep eyes, brown wig, open mouth w/four teeth, pierced ears, jointed composition body, wearing a white cotton dress & straw hat, 26" 805.00

K (star) R bisque socket head girl marked "191 - 17," blue sleep eyes, brown h.h. wig, open mouth w/four upper teeth, jointed wood & composition body, wearing an antique white dress w/sailor-type top, underclothing, socks & shoes, 30" (eyelashes missing, tiny flake at corner of left eye, tiny flake at left earring hole, hands repainted) 700.00

Ken (Barbie's boyfriend), flocked blond hair, pink lips, straight leg, wearing "Campus Hero" outfit, in box w/black wire stand, blue booklet (some flocking missing, box bottom heavily stained & marked on) 45.00

Ken (Barbie's boyfriend), flocked brunette hair, straight leg, wearing original swim trunks (three small hair rubs on back of head, elastic stretched in trunks) 40.00

Kestner (J.D.) bisque socket head girl marked "Made in Germany - S 143 3," brown sleep eyes, blonde mohair wig, open mouth w/two upper teeth, jointed composition body w/straight wrists, wearing a pink organdy dress trimmed w/black velvet ribbon, underclothing, socks & shoes, 9½" (leg socket reglued) 620.00

Kestner (J.D.) bisque socket head black girl marked "b - made in Germany - 3 - 143," brown tinted head w/brown sleep eyes, black mohair wig, open mouth w/two upper teeth, jointed wood body & composition brown-tinted body, wearing a simple blue hand-made cotton dress & slip, socks & shoes, 10" (body finish damaged & possible lower leg repairs, some uneven coloring) 900.00

Kestner (J.D.) bisque head girl marked "5/148," brown sleep eyes, blonde mohair wig, open mouth w/four upper teeth, kid body w/bisque lower arms, gussets at hips & knees, cloth lower legs, wearing a white blue-sprigged dress, underclothing, socks, shoes & straw hat, 14½" (tiny color flaw on back of head, left eye glazed) 300.00

Kestner (J.D.) bisque head character baby marked "J.D.K. 235 - Made in Germany," blue sleep eyes, original brown mohair wig, open mouth w/two lower teeth, rare kid baby body w/composition lower arms & legs & remnant of original sticker, wearing the original blue & white checked baby dress & underclothing, 15" (tiny firing line in lobe of right ear, minor kid repair on knee & toes) 800.00

Kestner (J.D.) bisque socket head girl marked "149 - Made in Germany C7," brown sleep eyes, brown mohair wig, open mouth w/four upper teeth, jointed wood & composition body, wearing an antique dark blue dress w/white spots, underclothing, socks & shoes, 15" (minor flake inside corner of upper right eye lid, minor repairs & repainting) 550.00

Rare Kestner Child Doll

Kestner (J.D.) bisque head girl marked "13," set blue eyes, feathered brows, painted lashes, antique blonde mohair wig, closed mouth w/accent line, jointed composition body w/straight wrists, wearing a factory-made outfit w/white dress, blue coat w/white fur trim & matching fur hat, underclothing, stockings & shoes, replaced eyes, 19" (ILLUS.) 2,800.00

Kestner (J.D.) bisque shoulder head girl marked "Dep. 10. 154," brown sleep eyes, original brown h.h. wig, open mouth w/four upper teeth, kid body w/bisque lower arms, rivet-jointed at elbows, hips & knees, wearing possibly original rust-colored dress, underclothing, old shoes & socks, 22" (real eyelashes missing, light soil on body)..............325.00

Kestner (J.D.) bisque head character girl marked "257/57," blue sleep eyes, replaced brown mohair wig, open mouth w/two teeth, tremble tongue, curved limb composition body, wearing a lace-trimmed gown & petticoat, 22½"..............................990.00

Kestner (J.D.) bisque socket head girl marked "H ½ Made in Germany 12½ - 167," brown sleep eyes w/real lashes, original auburn mohair wig, open mouth w/four upper teeth, jointed wood & composition body, wearing antique white dress w/lace inserts, underclothing, replaced shoes & socks, 23½" (minor firing lines behind ears, eyelashes gone from left eye, sparse on right eye)..500.00

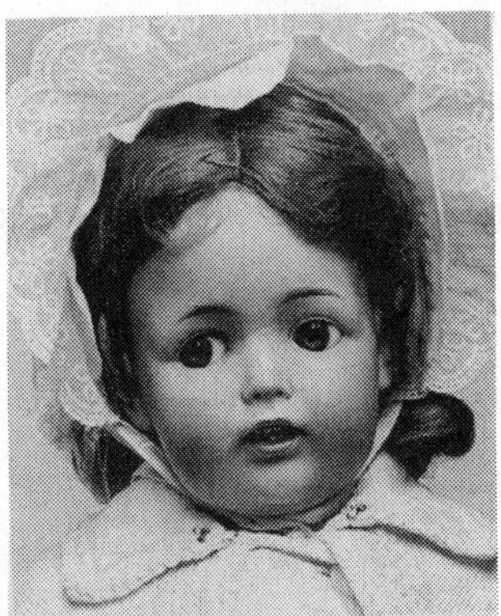

Kestner Character Girl

Kestner (J.D.) bisque head character girl marked "260/63," flirty blue glass eyes, open mouth w/upper teeth & molded tongue, dark blonde h.h. wig over replacement pate, jointed wood & composition chunky toddler body w/diagonal hip joints, redressed in blue short gown, underwear & old white corded cotton coat w/cape collar & embroidered trim, body repainted, 25" (ILLUS.) 1,093.00

Kestner (J.D.) bisque head solid dome baby marked "J.D.K. Made in 20 Germany," brown sleep eyes, molded & brush-stroked hair, open mouth w/two lower teeth, five-piece bent-limb baby body, wearing antique baby dress, 25" (arms repainted, minor firing line behind left ear)..1,300.00

Kestner (J.D.) bisque socket head girl marked "L made in Germany 15 - 164," brown sleep eyes w/real lashes, open mouth w/four upper teeth, synthetic brown wig, jointed wood & composition body, wearing an antique white dress w/lace trim, underclothing, replaced shoes & socks, 26" (small eye chip touched-up, small firing line behind right ear, rub on left eyebrow, body repainted & peeling)...450.00

Kestner (J.D.) bisque socket head girl marked "Made in Germany - 18½ - 142," blue sleep eyes w/real lashes, brown h.h. wig, open mouth w/four upper teeth, jointed wood & composition body w/label reading "Made for G.A. Schwartz, Philadelphia, Made in Germany," stamped on body "Quaker Doll Hospital, 155 No. 6th St., Philadelphia, PA. Excelsior," 34" 750.00

Rare Kewpie Girl Doll

Kewpie girl, made by Kestner, bisque head w/glass side-glancing eyes, molded & painted hair, smiling "watermelon" mouth, jointed composition body, wearing a satin dress, 14" (ILLUS.) 4,700.00

Kid-leather covered wooden head lady, painted facial features, wooden hands, wearing an early, long worn dress, 19th c., 7"..............................192.50

Kley & Hahn "Walkure" bisque socket head girl marked "250 - K.H. - Walkure - 3¼ - Germany," blue sleep eyes, synthetic brown wig, open mouth w/four upper teeth, jointed wood & composition body, wearing an older blue & white checked dress, underclothing, socks & shoes, 24"...................................300.00

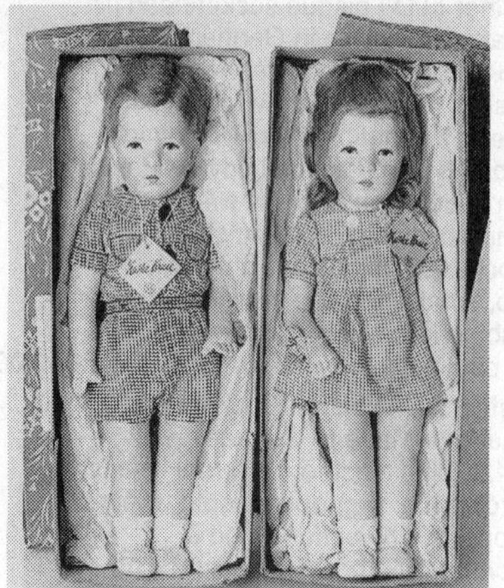

Kathe Kruse Character Dolls

Kruse (Kathe) character boy, molded felt face w/painted eyes, h.h. wig, closed mouth, molded felt body, wearing a checked pattern shirt & shorts, shoes & socks, in original box (ILLUS. left) 4,000.00

Kruse (Kathe) character girl, molded felt face w/painted eyes, h.h. wig, closed mouth, wearing a checked pattern dress, socks & shoes, molded felt body, in original box (ILLUS. right) 4,600.00

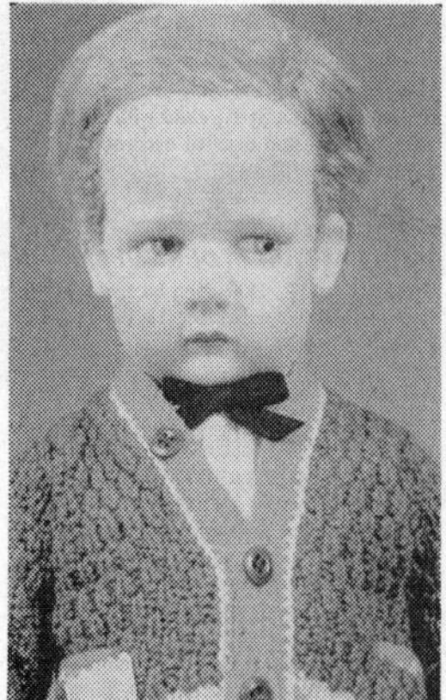

Lenci Boy Doll

Lenci boy, molded felt face w/painted brown side-glancing eyes, blond mohair wig, closed mouth, five-piece jointed felt body w/hollow torso, wearing original felt shirt & shorts, knit sweater & leggings & shoes, slightly faded w/light soil, light touch-up on face, torso pushed in, 16" (ILLUS.) 600.00

Lenci boy, pressed felt head w/sad brown painted side-glancing eyes w/shading, closed pouty mouth, applied ears, original blond mohair wig rooted in scalp, five-piece felt body, original felt shirt & shorts, knit sweater & socks w/opening in bottom, marked on bottom of feet, 16½" (light surface discoloration, one small hole in back of shorts) 600.00

Lenci lady, blonde-haired lady w/painted features, blue side-glancing eyes & long limbs, wearing a yellow & orange organdy dress, black & green hat & gloves, w/Lenci label, 20" 863.00

Lenci child, pressed felt head w/brown eyes painted looking right, light brown mohair wig, wearing mid-green felt jacket & matching hat, cream shirt, tan jodphurs buttoning down the sides of legs from knee to foot, black shoes, Model 500P, good condition overall, late 1920s - early 1930s, 21½" (missing one button from jodphurs & one from jacket) 978.00

Lenci Oriental lady, pressed felt swivel head, painted slanted & side glancing eyes, felt decorative hair style, closed mouth, felt body jointed at shoulders & hips, wearing ornate black felt Oriental costume & shoes w/high wooden soles, 22" (general fading & soil in front) 1,100.00

Lenci Lady Doll

Lenci lady, pressed felt head w/glass "googlie" side-glancing eyes, blonde hair, wide-open mouth w/a startled expression, jointed felt body, wearing unusual Victorian style gown & hat, w/original box (ILLUS.) 6,800.00

Mascotte bisque socket head girl marked "Mascotte J," blue paperweight eyes, pierced ears, blonde mohair wig, closed mouth w/accented lips, jointed wood & composition body, wearing a light green silk dress made from antique fabric, underclothing, socks, shoes & hat, 25" (small flake at each earring hole, minor flaw in bisque between eyebrows)........................2,750.00

Midge (Barbie's friend), blonde hair w/blue ribbon, pink lips, bendable legs, undressed (faded small stain on right elbow & upper left thigh)..175.00

Midge (Barbie's friend), brownette hair, pink lips, bendable legs, wearing original swimsuit, in box w/gold wire stand (box worn on outside & discolored) 400.00

Midge (Barbie's friend), titian hair , pink lips, bendable legs, wearing Tropicana dress (two small pinholes on both sides of lips, small lip rub, few indentations on ankles, dress soiled) 145.00

Papier-maché "milliner's model," papier-maché shoulder head w/painted blue eyes, molded & painted hair sweeping down over ears & back w/a coiled braid, closed mouth, wooden body w/tongue & groove joints, painted lower arms & legs w/painted shoes, wearing antique dark green dress trimmed w/light green slip, 7" (light crazing, possible touch-up on face)..............375.00

Parian head bonnet baby marked "Germany," bisque shoulder head w/painted blue eyes, single stroke brows, molded & painted white bonnet w/blue bows at sides, closed mouth, cloth body w/bisque lower arms, wearing a long white baby dress w/lace inserts, underclothing, socks, 9" 325.00

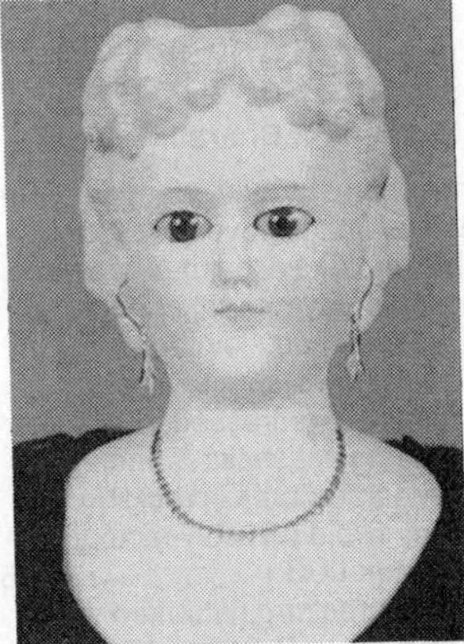

Glass-eyed Parian Lady

Parian head lady, molded blonde center-part curly hairdo w/blue ribbon, set blue glass eyes, closed mouth, molded gold necklace, cloth body w/bisque lower arms & legs, wearing a black taffeta dress & underclothing, body fragile w/many patches, replaced bisque arms & legs, 18" (ILLUS.)............................750.00

Parian shoulder head boy marked "122," painted blue eyes, blond hair, kid body w/bisque hands, wearing a brown embroidered coat, ca. 1860s, 22"...920.00

Raggedy Ann & Andy Dolls

Raggedy Ann & Andy, cloth bodies w/painted facial features, button eyes & yarn hair, original clothing, by Volland, pr. (ILLUS.) 3,100.00

Recknagel bisque socket baby marked "R.A. 28-7/0," blue intaglio eyes, molded & painted hair & bonnet, open-closed smiling mouth w/two upper teeth, crude five-piece composition baby body, wearing an antique white baby dress & underclothing, 9½" (light rubs on cheeks, repainted body) 325.00

Unusual Reynal Dolls

Reynal boy, molded cloth face w/painted side-glancing eyes, blond h.h. wig, closed mouth, jointed cloth body, wearing a sailor suit, socks & shoes, France (ILLUS. left) 1,350.00

Reynal girl, molded cloth face w/painted side-glancing eyes, blonde h.h. wig, closed mouth, jointed cloth body, wearing a white confirmation dress & veil w/a crucifix pendant, socks & shoes, France (ILLUS. right) 1,650.00

Rickey (friend of Barbie), painted red hair, straight legs, wearing original jacket & blue shorts (tiny hair rubs on front of head & behind left ear, outfit faded) 55.00

Sandy McCall vinyl character boy, vinyl character head w/blue sleep eyes w/real lashes, molded & painted hair, freckles, closed smiling mouth, five-piece vinyl child body, wearing original white shirt, bolo tie, black corduroy shorts, socks & shoes, ca. 1959, w/original wrist tag, 35" (jacket missing, body faded)..240.00

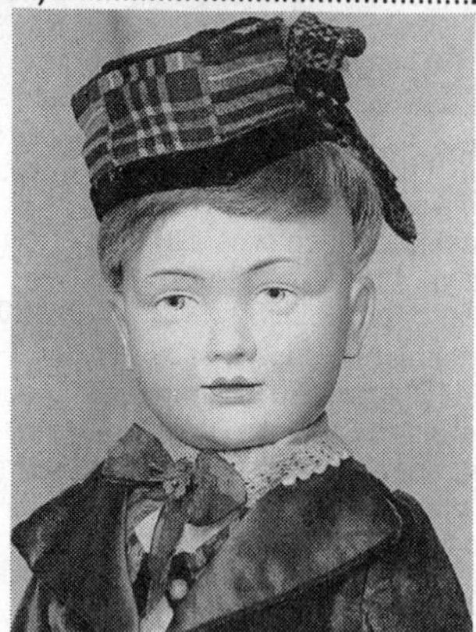

Bruno Schmidt Boy Doll

Schmidt (Bruno) bisque head character boy, Model 2025, painted eyes, h.h. wig, closed smiling mouth, jointed body, wearing an antique boy's costume w/plaid cap (ILLUS.) 4,250.00

Schmitt bisque socket head girl marked "10" (crossed hammers) & "Sch" in a shield, blue paperweight eyes, pierced ears, h.h. wig, closed mouth w/accented lips, jointed wood & composition French body w/straight wrists, redressed in ecru silk dress w/pink bows, antique underclothing, socks & shoes, 20" (minor color flaw on left cheek, firing lines around both ears, repainted non-Schmitt body).........................3,600.00

Schoenau & Hoffmeister bisque flange head baby marked "Made in Germany - S PG (star) H N.N.B.," blue sleep eyes, softly blushed hair, closed mouth, unusual kid body lacing up the back at the neck to attach head, jointed wood & composition arms, rivet joints at hips & knees, undressed, 13" (stitching apart at right shoulder)......................700.00

Schoenau & Hoffmeister bisque head girl marked "1909 - 5 1 - 2," weighted blue glass eyes, open mouth, replaced dark brown mohair wig, jointed wood & composition body, redressed, ca. 1909, 23½" (hands repainted)..............................316.00

Schoenau & Hoffmeister bisque socket head girl marked "S PB (star) H 1906 - 17 - Germany," set brown eyes w/molded & painted brows, blonde mohair wig, open mouth w/four upper teeth, jointed wood & composition body, wearing antique red wool child's dress, under-clothing, straw bonnet, socks & shoes, 38" (minor flake at hole high on left side of head, old hip repair, arms reglued, little fingers replaced).......................................1,000.00

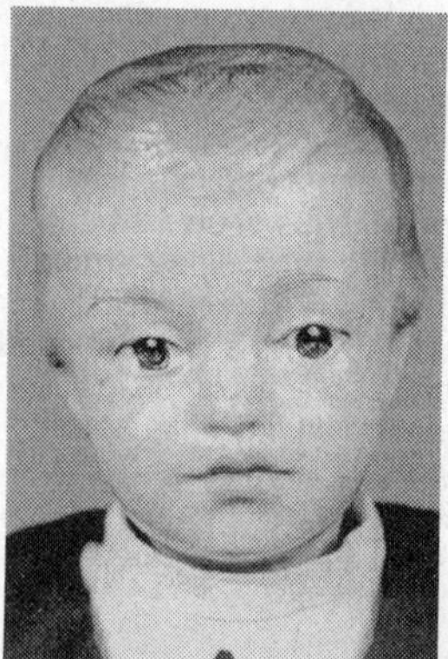

Schoenhut Character Boy

Schoenhut character boy, wooden head w/blue intaglio eyes w/white highlights, molded & painted brown hair, closed pouty mouth, spring-jointed wooden body jointed at shoulders, elbows, wrists, hips, knees & ankles, redressed in a blue sailor suit, original socks & one original shoe, few small cracks in finish, body w/old possibly factory repaint, 14" (ILLUS.) 2,250.00

Schoenhut character girl marked "Schoenhut Doll - Pat. Jan. 17-11 U.S.A. & Foreign Countries," wooden head w/blue intaglio eyes, brown h.h. wig, closed pouty mouth, spring-jointed wooden body jointed at shoulders, elbows, wrists, hips, knees & ankles, wearing an old white dress, underclothing, socks & shoes, 14" (slight color wear & fading)..550.00

Schoenhut character girl marked "Schoenhut Doll - Pat. Jan. 17-11, U.S.A. & Foreign Countries," wooden head w/blue intaglio eyes, original brown mohair wig, closed mouth, spring-jointed wooden body jointed at shoulders, elbows, wrists, hips, knees & ankles, wearing appropriate style dress made w/antique fabrics, knit underclothing, slip, socks & shoes, 14" (slight paint flaking & fading) 900.00

Schoenhut male manikin, wooden head w/brown intaglio eyes, molded & painted hair, closed mouth, spring-jointed wooden body jointed at shoulders, elbows, wrists, waist, hips, knees & ankles, wearing a copy of the original outfit w/shirt, bib overalls, socks & shoes, 19" (light crazing on face, light rub on end of nose, light flaking on body)...........3,900.00

Schoenhut "dolly face" girl marked "Schoenhut Doll - Pat. Jan. 17th-1911 U.S.A.," wooden head w/blue decal eyes, mohair wig, open-closed mouth w/four painted teeth, jointed wooden body, wearing pink Schoenhut-style dress & hat, knit underclothing, original socks & shoes, 20" (light crazing & flaking, minor repair to left eye) 400.00

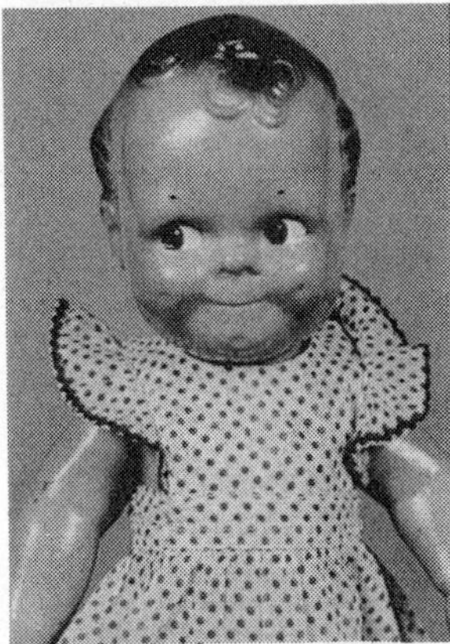

Black Scootles Doll

Scootles composition black child, brown composition head w/painted brown side-glancing eyes, molded & painted black hair, closed smiling mouth, five-piece composition body w/starfish hands, wearing old blue & white polka dot pinafore, panties, socks & shoes, light crazing on face, area of finish chipped off back of hair & stomach, some small areas of damage on body, 12" (ILLUS.) 500.00

S.F.B.J. (Societe Francaise de Fabrication de Bebes & Jouets) bisque socket head black girl marked "S.F.B.J. Paris 4," brown paperweight eyes, pierced ears, original black mohair wig, open mouth w/four upper teeth, jointed wood & composition French body, wearing original outfit of gold velour pants, white silk dickey, purple plush jacket, socks & shoes, 13½" (minor flakes on torso) 1,050.00

S.F.B.J. bisque socket head girl marked "21 S.F.B.J. - 301 - Paris - 12," blue sleep eyes w/real lashes, pierced ears, brown h.h. wig, open mouth w/six upper teeth, jointed wood & composition body, wearing an old white dress, underclothing, socks & newer shoes, 26" (minor firing line by left ear) 550.00

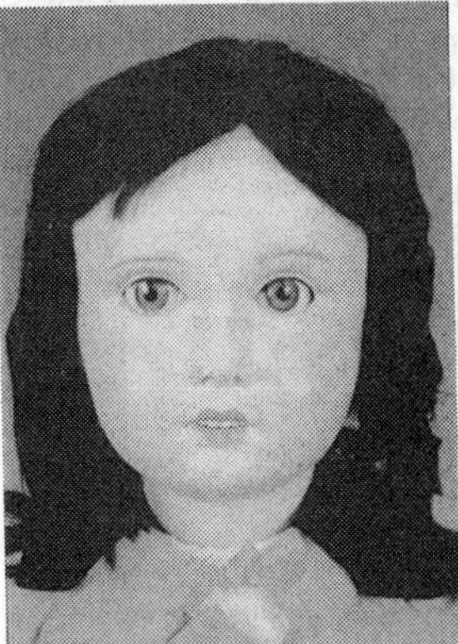

S.F.B.J. Girl

S.F.B.J. bisque socket head girl marked "24 - France - S.F.B.J. Paris - 15," set blue eyes w/real lashes, brown h.h. wig, open mouth w/six upper teeth, jointed wood & composition body w/jointed wrists, wearing old red dress trimmed w/black velvet, matching cape, underclothing, socks & shoes, short hairline on forehead from crown, left eye cracked, 33" (ILLUS.).......................850.00

Shirley Temple "Ranger," composition head w/hazel sleep eyes w/real lashes, original blonde mohair wig, open mouth w/six upper teeth, five-piece composition child body, wearing original Ranger outfit w/plaid shirt, red nylon bandana, shorts, leather chaps, holster w/gun,

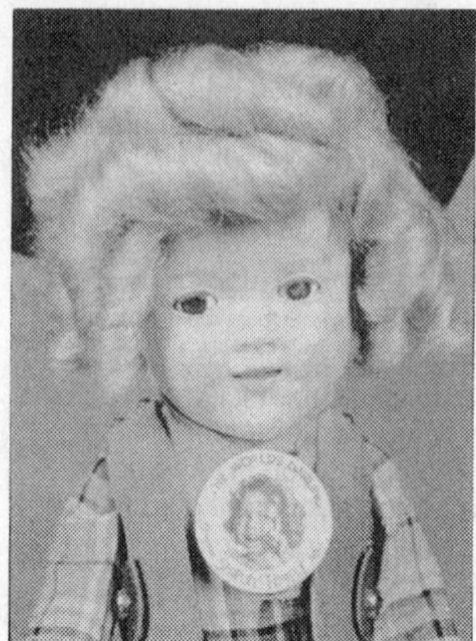

Shirley Temple "Ranger" Doll

leather vest, original Shirley Temple pin, black felt cowboy hat w/red band reading "Ride 'em Cowboy," brown boots, w/original promotion picture in box, left eye cloudy, 11" (ILLUS.) 2,500.00

Shirley Temple, composition, hazel sleep eyes w/real lashes, original mohair wig, open mouth w/six upper teeth, five-piece composition child body, wearing tagged pink organdy dress, original underclothing, socks & shoes, 17".......................................800.00

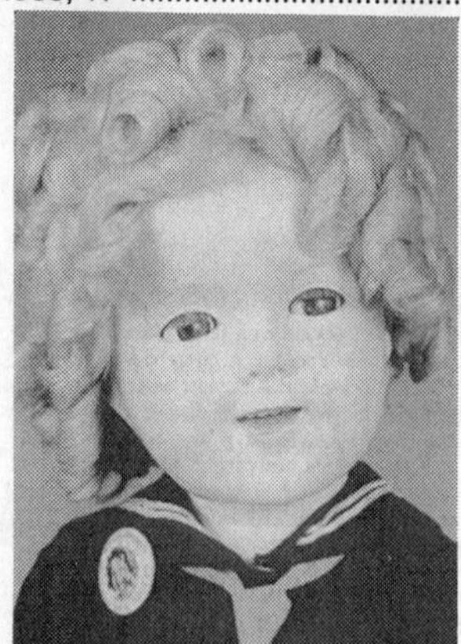

Shirley Temple Sailor Doll

Shirley Temple, composition head w/hazel flirty sleep eyes w/real lashes, original blonde mohair wig, open mouth w/six upper teeth & metal tongue, five-piece composition child body, wearing blue sailor dress tagged "27," underclothing, socks & shoes, w/original Shirley Temple pin, face coloring slightly pale, minor craze line above & below right eye, left eye cracked, 27" (ILLUS.) 1,400.00

Simon & Halbig bisque socket head girl marked "1078 - Germany - Simon & Halbig - S&H 3," brown sleep eyes, pierced ears, replaced brown h.h. wig, open mouth w/four upper teeth, jointed wood & composition body, wearing a blue & white dress, underclothing, antique shoes & socks, 12" (small flake at right earring hole, paint flaked off upper & lower arms, dark spot on right hand).......................................400.00

Simon & Halbig bisque socket head girl marked "Germany 1009 No. 8 DEP," set brown eyes, pierced ears, blonde h.h. wig, open mouth w/four upper teeth, jointed wood & composition body, wearing a blue silk dress & bonnet, underclothing, socks & shoes, 17" (finger off left hand).......................................500.00

Simon & Halbig bisque socket head girl marked "S&H 949," blue paperweight eyes, pierced ears, brown h.h. wig, closed mouth w/accented lips, kid body w/bisque lower arms, gussets at elbows, hips & knees, wearing antique white dress, underclothing, socks & shoes, 18½" 800.00

Simon & Halbig bisque socket head boy marked "S9H - 1009 - DEP," set brown eyes, pierced ears, brown mohair wig, open mouth w/four upper teeth, jointed wood & composition body, wearing boy's suit w/white shirt, 19" (lower arms don't match, right lower leg repaired) 500.00

Simon & Halbig bisque socket head girl marked "Germany - Simon & Halbig - 2½," "W" on forehead w/crown, blue sleep eyes, brown h.h. wig, open mouth w/four upper teeth, wearing a new pale blue dress, underclothing, socks & shoes, 21".......................................525.00

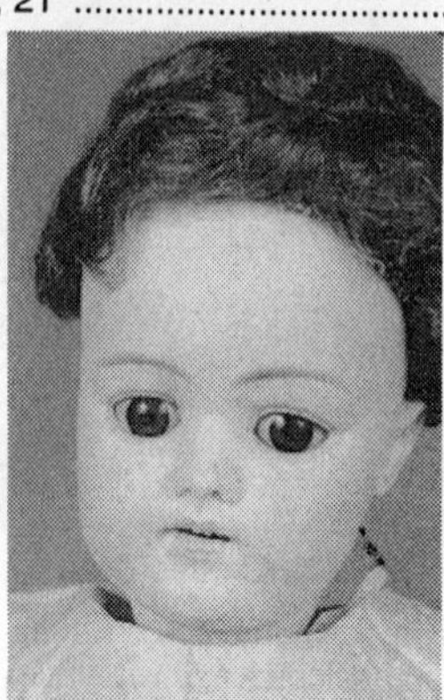

Simon & Halbig 1079 Doll

Simon & Halbig bisque socket head girl marked "S & H - 1079 DEP

Germany 12," blue sleep eyes, brown h.h. wig, open mouth w/four upper teeth, pierced ears, jointed wood & composition body, wearing an antique white dress, underclothing, replaced socks & antique high button boots, tiny flake outside corner right eye, minor firing line behind right ear, 25" (ILLUS.) 500.00

Simon & Halbig bisque head lady marked "S & H Dept - 1159 Germany 10," set brown eyes w/real lashes, pierced ears, original blonde mohair wig, open mouth w/four upper teeth, jointed wood & composition lady body, wearing possibly original ecru silk blouse, black skirt, underclothing, socks, shoes & straw hat, 26" (minor flake at each earring hole, minor firing line behind right ear, minor repair upper right leg) 1,500.00

Simon & Halbig "Santa" bisque head girl marked "S & H 1249 Dep Santa 14 ½," weighted blue glass eyes, open mouth w/upper teeth, pierced ears, replaced dark brown nylon wig, wearing an adapted old white cotton gown w/pintucked bodice & cutwork trim, old child's lace-up ankle leather boots, ca. 1914, 33"..1,380.00

Skipper with Original Box

Skipper (Barbie's sister), titian hair, beige lips, bent-leg version wearing original swimsuit & hair band, in original box w/booklet in cellophane & gold wire stand (ILLUS.)..............185.00

Steiner (Jules) bisque head girl marked "Sie., C O" & stamped in red "J. Steiner B.S.G.D.G. - Bourgoin," original blonde wig, blue sleep eyes, pierced ears, outlined closed mouth, wood & composition jointed body, wearing a period dark red wool coat, black satin dress & original cotton slip, w/a paper-covered trunk including a period crochet dress, three night shirts, two pair of cotton bloomers, two cotton blouses, two bonnets, a white cotton christening dress trimmed w/lace, a tan wool jacket trimmed in blue silk & a blue & tan cotton dress, 15", the group (hairline in back of head) 1,955.00

Figure C Steiner Doll

Steiner (Jules) Figure C bisque head girl, blonde hair, paperweight eyes, closed mouth, jointed composition Steiner body, wearing an antique style lace-trimmed dress & bonnet, 17" (ILLUS.) 6,800.00

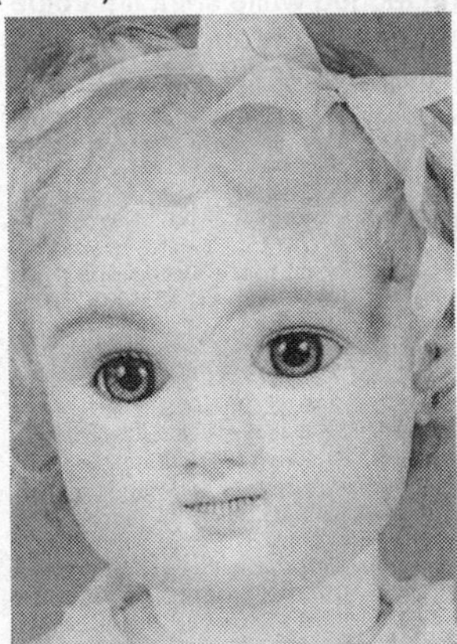

Figure B Steiner Doll

Steiner bisque socket head girl marked "Figure B No. 5 J. Steiner Bte. S.G.D.G. Paris," paperweight eyes w/mauve blush, pierced ears, original blonde mohair wig w/original purple cardboard pate, open mouth w/ten upper & lower teeth, jointed composition Steiner body w/straight wrists, wearing antique white dress, underclothing, socks & shoes, minor firing line over right ear, body repainted, 25" (ILLUS. previous page)....................................3,300.00

Swaine & Co. bisque head character baby marked "D.V. 0," weighted blue eyes, closed mouth, painted hair, curved limb baby body, wearing cream cotton gown & cap, ca. 1910, 9"...978.00

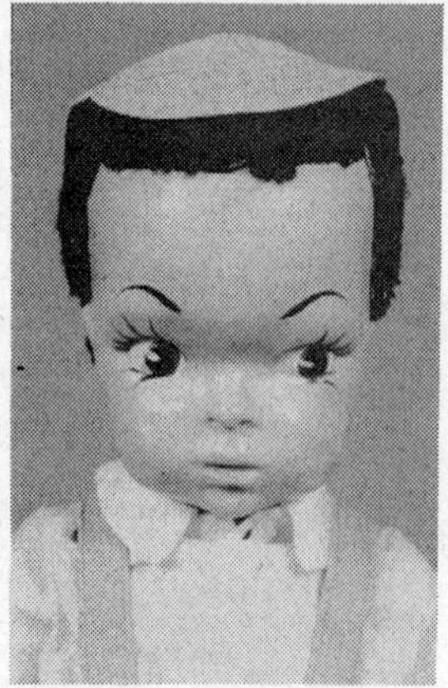

Terri Lee "Benji" Doll

Terri Lee plastic black "Benji" boy marked "Terri Lee Pat. Pending," brown hard plastic head w/painted brown side-glancing eyes, original black caracul wig, closed mouth, five-piece hard plastic child body, wearing tagged white shirt, light blue shorts & matching cap, shoes & socks, minor wear to finish, 15" (ILLUS.) 1,500.00

Vogue "Cathy" Doll

Thuillier bisque swivel head girl marked "A. 12 T.," almond-shaped blue glass paperweight inset eyes, closed mouth w/modeled tongue between the shaded & accented lips, pierced ears, brunette h.h. wig, kid gusset-jointed body w/bisque forearms & hands, wearing a multi-layered antique costume, 27" 42,000.00

Vogue "Cathy," hard plastic, sleep eyes, closed mouth, brown synthetic wig, wearing original dress, straw hat, socks & shoes, complete in original marked box (ILLUS.) 1,320.00

Wax (poured) shoulder head girl, set blue eyes, brown h.h. inserted into wax, closed mouth, cloth body w/poured wax lower limbs, wearing antique white chemise & pants, 20" (pale coloring, some stains & soil, rivet replaced in shoulder plate).......300.00

Wax over papier-maché lady, set blue glass eyes, painted upper lashes & brows, original blonde mohair wig, pierced-in ears, closed mouth, cloth body w/kid lower arms, wearing blue dress made from old fabric, under-clothing, high button boots, 27" (crack in wax at right side, minor cracks in body, lower arms replaced) 250.00

(End of Dolls Section)

DOORSTOPS

Basket of Kittens Doorstop

All doorstops listed are flat-back cast iron unless otherwise noted. Most names are taken from Doorstops - Identification & Values, *by Jeanne Bertoia (Collector Books, 1985).*

Amish man, bearded man w/green shirt, black hat, vest & pants, standing on brown base, purple shirt variation, 3¾ x 8½" $275.00

Amish woman, wearing a green blouse, mate to Amish man 275.00

Apple Blossoms, in basket, Hubley, 7⅝" h...95.00

Basket of Flowers, large polychrome blossom, in tall, tightly woven basket w/high loop handle, stepped base, Hubley, 5 x 7" 145.00

Cape Cod Cottage, colorful flowers growing up onto two-level roof, two large trees behind, Hubley, No. 444, 7¾" w., 5½" h. 250.00

Cat, full figure, tall, slender seated animal, black w/silver eyes, Hubley, 3⅜"w., 10" h. ....150.00 to 200.00

Cat, Fireside, Angora in reclining position, full figure, original grey & white paint w/pink trim, marked "Hubley," 10¾" l. 225.00

Cat, Hunchback, w/raised tail, full figure, original black paint w/green eyes & red mouth, Hubley, 10¾" h. ....125.00 to 150.00

Cat, reclining kitten, white 225.00

Cat, seated black animal w/large head, ribbon at neck, four white paws, one raised, 4½" w., 7" h. 100.00

Cat, seated w/a bow on the left side of its neck, full figure, old worn black & white repaint, 7½" h. 154.00

Cats, Basket of Kittens (3), original polychrome paint, marked "M. Rosenstein, Copyright 1932, Lancaster, PA USA," 7 x 10" (ILLUS.) 370.00

Cats, kittens, three kittens in a high button shoe, 10" h. 275.00

Chameleon, advertising, "The Sherwin Williams Paint Co.," 1¼ x 8" 150.00

Cinderella Coach w/horses and driver, polychrome paint, marked "Hubley 376-2" 325.00

Clipper ship, original polychrome paint, 11¼ x 20½" 70.00

Clipper ship on waves, brown ship w/sails on water, marked "Albany FDY." 90.00

Clown, wide ruffled collar & pointed hat, bending w/hands on knees, thin rectangular base, original polychrome paint w/red suit, 4½" w., 10" h. 1,300.00

Cockatoo, white, beautiful pastel shading, Albany & National Foundry, 5¼" w., 11¾" h. 160.00

Colonial Lawyer, orange jacket & black pants, WS in triangle mark, 9⅝" h. 400.00

Colonial Woman, pink & blue gown & hat, Littco Products & others, 5¾" w., 10¼" h. 145.00

Cottage with Fence, arch of roses over door, further colorful flowers around house, picket fence to back, red roof, National Foundry, No. 32, 8" w., 5¾" h. 165.00

Cottage, w/roses around door, Hubley & National Foundry, 7½" w., 5¾" h. 160.00

Daisy Bowl, bulbous bowl on rounded foot, Hubley, No. 232, 6" w., 7" h. ....100.00 to 150.00

Daisy Bowl, original paint, Hubley, 5⅛" w., 7½" h. 165.00

Dog, Cairn Terrier, seated animal on base, Bradley & Hubbard, 6 x 9" ....275.00 to 300.00

Dog, Cocker Spaniel, full figure, standing black animal, Hubley, 11" l., 6¾" h. 325.00

Dog, Cocker Spaniel, seated black animal marked "Va Metalcrafters, Waynesboro, Va WK, Dream Boy 18-7 1949," 7" w., 9" h. 145.00

Dog, German Shepherd, full figure, 9¾ x 13" 165.00

Dog, Japanese Spaniel, black & white animal in begging position, 4½ x 9" 250.00

Dog, Mutt & His Bone, sad looking pup seated on grassy base w/his bone at his feet, original brown & black paint, 5½" w., 8¼" h. 175.00

Dog on fence, Albany Foundry Co. 135.00

Dog, Russian Wolfhound (large), full figure, standing animal w/head slightly turned, old white paint, 16" l., 9" h. 245.00

Dog, St. Bernard, standing animal w/brandy keg at his neck, on long oval base, original metallic brown & black paint, 9¼" l. 175.00

Dog, Scottie, cream paint, marked "Wilton Products; Wrightsville, PA" ..135.00

Dog, Setter in hunting stance, full figure, original black & white paint, Hubley, 15⅞" l., 8¾" h. (pristine.) ... 250.00

Dog, Terrier, standing animal on base, polychrome paint, marked "Spencer, Guildford, Conn.," wedge in back, 5¼ x 6" 130.00

Dolphin Doorstop

Dolphin, stylized creature on a cushion plinth, Victorian, 19th c. (ILLUS.) 6,600.00

Donald Duck, standing figure holding a stop sign, © Walt Disney Productions, 5¼" w., 8⅜" h. (stop sign missing) 125.00

Drum Major, full figure, solid bright blue jacket & hat, 13½" h. 375.00

Duck, standing w/head up, old white repaint, 6½" w., 9½" h. 250.00

Duck with Top Hat, worn old polychrome paint, 7½" h. 550.00

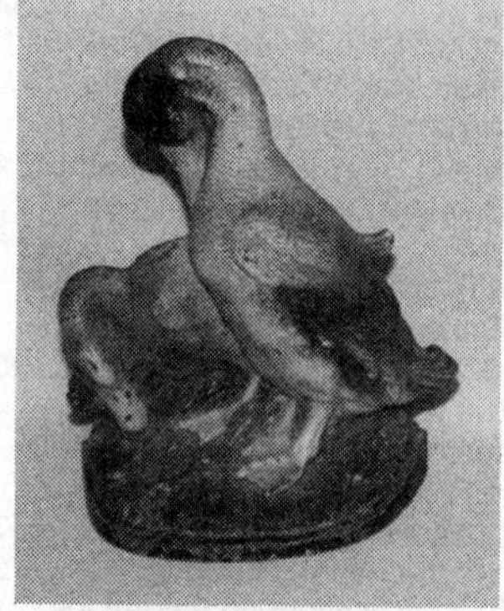

Ducks Doorstop

Ducks (two), on half-round base, Hubley, No. 291, 6¼" w., 8¼" h. (ILLUS.) 425.00

Dutch girl w/shoulder yoke & buckets, original polychrome paint, paper label "Littco Products, Howe & Fory Co.," 13" h. 300.00

Elephant, full-bodied free-standing walking animal w/trunk curled down between front legs, worn white paint, 7" l. 82.50

Fruit Basket Doorstop

Elephant on barrel, green & orange circus elephant on striped barrel, Taylor Cook series, dated 1930, 8¼" h. .... 375.00 to 400.00

Fisherman in Boat, man in yellow slicker standing at back of small boat, 4" w., 6¾" h. 275.00

French Basket, mixed bouquet in woven basket w/gently curving rim, overhead handle w/large bow, rounded base, Hubley, No. 69, 6¾" w., 11" h. 225.00

Fruit Basket, tall ribbed basket overflowing w/fruit, tall arched handle w/ribbon along one side, worn polychrome paint, 10⅛" h. (ILLUS. previous column) 250.00

Girl with Bonnet, young girl w/short dress & pantalets, holding wide-brimmed bonnet by her side, oval base, 5¼" w., 8" h. (blue dress variation) 450.00

Gladiolas, Hubley, 8" w., 10" h. 175.00

Gnome, full figure, walking figure w/beard & wearing pointed red cap, black coat, green leggings & black & green shoes, original paint, 5" w., 11" h. ....100.00 to 125.00

Grandpa Rabbit, heavy-set seated rabbit wearing red vest, 8⅝" h. 525.00

Heron, original polychrome paint, Albany Foundry, 7½" h. 145.00

Horse, full figure, standing animal w/dark brown coat w/white accents, black hooves, eyes, ears & mouth, Hubley, 11" l., 7½" h. 165.00

House, modern style one-story cottage w/floral vines across front, marked "cJo 1288," 4½ x 8⅛" ....200.00 to 225.00

Lilies of the Valley, ribbed basket w/blue bow & base, Hubley, 7½" w., 10½" h. 195.00

Li'l Red Riding Hood, standing chubby little girl w/basket, polychrome paint, signed "Grace Drayton," Hubley, 5 x 9½" 1,300.00

Li'l Red Riding Hood and Wolf, child standing beside large animal on grassy base, marked "NUYDEA Little Red Riding Hood," 9½" l., 7½" h. 1,095.00

Lion rampant, one front paw resting on a tree stump, on a waisted plinth base, unpainted, 15" h. (pitted) 80.00

Little Girl Holding Shoe, bronze figure on marble base, rubber knobs, marked "B&H" 450.00

Little Miss Muffet, little girl w/pigtails seated atop a large mushroom, 5" w., 7¾" h. 265.00

London Royal Mail Coach, coach w/figures pulled by two horses, original polychrome paint, marked "Pat. Pending," 12" l., 7" h. 110.00

Major Domo, black man standing wearing a frock coat & breeches, marked "cJo," 5⅛" w., 8⅜" h. ....225.00 to 250.00

Mammy (Medium), full figure, Hubley, 10" h. 75.00

Man in Chair, seated figure in side chair wearing a stocking cap & resting a stein on one knee, England, 5¾" w., 9½" h. 225.00

Man with Flowers, standing chubby figure w/large flower bouquet in each hand, 5¾ x 9" 550.00

Marigolds, black & white horizontally ribbed vase holding large colorful bouquet, Hubley, No. 315, 8" w., 7½" h. ....150.00 to 175.00

Monkey, full figure, seated animal w/head resting on one paw, brown paint, 4⅝" w., 8½" h. 350.00

Narcissus, a variety of narcissus in a low, half-round footed basket w/striped sides trimmed w/a slender floral swag, Hubley, No. 266, 6¾" w., 7½" h. 300.00

Nasturtiums, flowers in a wide, striped flowerpot, Hubley, 6½" w., 7¼" h. 135.00

Old Fashioned Lady, light blue dress & hat, Hubley, 4" w., 7¾" h. 550.00

"Old Salt," man wearing yellow slicker & black rain hat, hands in pockets, 6½" w., 14½" h. ....325.00 to 350.00

Old Woman, standing figure wearing bonnet & carrying a basket of flowers in one hand & a closed parasol in the other, on rectangular base, rubber knobs on back, marked "B&H 7796," 7" w., 11" h. 300.00

Organ Grinder, man cranking street organ w/monkey crouched at his feet, 5¾" w., 9⅞" h. 450.00

Penguin with Top Hat Doorstop

Oriental Girl, full figure, green & yellow, solid one-piece casting, 7½" h. 235.00

Parrot, original polychrome paint, Albany Foundry, 7½" w., 12½" h. 145.00

Parrot in Medallion, oval medallion w/relief-molded & silver painted parrot on a perch, on an ornate scrolling base w/ring handle, 5" w., 9¼" h. 150.00

Peacock, tail fanned-out, on oval base, old polychrome paint, 6¼" w., 6¼" h. 190.00

Penguin with Top Hat, full figure, original paint, 10¼" h. (ILLUS.) ....300.00 to 325.00

Peter Rabbit, Hubley, signed "Grace Drayton," 4¾" w., 9½" h. 425.00

Pied Piper, little elf in red jacket seated atop a large mushroom & playing a horn, 5" w., 7½" h. 285.00

Poinsettia, large single blossom on leafy stem in flowerpot on oblong base, red & green paint, marked "cJo 1232," 5" w., 10" h. ....325.00 to 350.00

Policeman, holding billy club in one hand, cap down over one eye, marked "Le Mur Lgt Co. PAT," 4" w., 7⅞" h. 265.00

Polly, cockatoo on perch, original polychrome paint, Hubley, 5¼" w., 8⅛" h. ....125.00 to 175.00

Poppies and Daisies, globular vase w/overall diamond design holding a colorful floral bouquet, on a stepped base, Hubley, 6" w., 7¼" h. 180.00

Poppy Basket, red poppies in brown basket w/four-sided angular handle, 9½ x 10½" ....250.00 to 300.00

Quail, two birds on grassy, round base, Hubley, No. 459, 6¼" w., 7¼" h. 400.00

Rabbit Eating Carrot, standing rabbit wearing red sweater, 8⅛" h. 210.00

Rooster, w/head up, naturalistic paint, browns, yellows & red, 8½" w., 13" h. 600.00

Snow White & the Seven Dwarfs, each painted differently, modeled after the Brothers Grimm fairy tale, Denmark, Snow White 16" h., dwarfs from 10" to 12" h., set of 8 ....4,000.00

Squirrel, seated on tree stump holding nut in paws, grey paint, 6⅜" w., 9" h. 200.00

Stagecoach, w/driver & pair of horses, Hubley, No. 376, 11¼" w., 5⅞" h. 170.00

Tiger Lilies (3) & foliage, original paint, Hubley, 10½" h. 250.00

Tulips in Pot, reddish orange blossoms & green leaves in low, cylindrical pot on base w/cut corners, marked "LA-CS 770," 5⅞" w., 10½" h. 300.00

Tulip Vase, eight multicolored blossoms in a flaring ribbed vase, on stepped pointed rectangular base, Hubley, No. 443, 8" w., 10" h. 235.00

Warrior, elf holding shield & club standing on stepped rectangular base, old polychrome paint, marked "Bradley & Hubbard No. 7795," 7¼" w., 13¼" h. ....475.00 to 500.00

Washington (George), bronze finish, 7¼ lbs., 12¼" h. 325.00

Windmill, marked "10 Cape Cod," National Foundry, 6⅞" w., 6¾" h. ....100.00 to 125.00

Windmill (variant), large structure towering above red barn & other building, Greenblatt Studios, 11½" w., 11⅞" h. 475.00

Woman with Fan, lady wearing bonnet, yellow dress & a shawl, holding a cluster of flowers in her right hand & a fan in her upraised left hand, 9½" h. 250.00

DRUGSTORE & PHARMACY ITEMS

The old-time corner drugstore, once a familiar part of every American town, has now given way to the modern, efficient pharmacy. With the streamlining and modernization of this trade many of the early tools and store adjuncts have become outdated and now fall into the realm "collectibles." Listed here are a variety of tools, bottles, display pieces and other ephemera once closely associated with the druggist's trade.

Enterprise Cork Compressor

Cork compressor, cast iron on wooden base, marked "Enterprise Mfg. Co. Phila - No. 1 Pat. Aug. 7, 1867," excellent working condition, most of the original paint intact, America, ca. 1870-90 (ILLUS.) $132.00

Display jar, milk white glass, baluster-form w/applied pedestal & foot, tooled & flared lip, polished pontil, w/original blown ground glass stopper, probably America, ca. 1870-80, 12¾" h 550.00

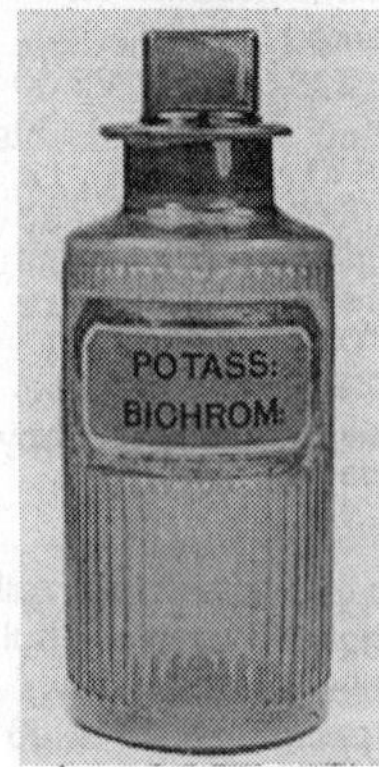

Label-Under-Glass Drug Jar

Drug jar, cov., label-under-glass type, cylindrical ribbed body w/narrow shoulder & wide mouth, gold, white, red & black label lettered "POTASS BICHROM," yellowish green, w/original ground glass stopper, probably England, ca. 1890-1900, 7¾" h. (ILLUS.) 110.00

Drug jar, cov., milk white glass, cylindrical w/low foot & sloping lid, powder blue w/multicolored h.p. floral decoration surrounding "Ong Merc. S," America or Europe ca. 1880-1910, 11¼" h 522.50

19th Century Pottery Drug Jar

Drug jar, cov., pottery, cylindrical w/outset base & top, blue w/gold label painted in black "Ex. Cannab Ind." on side, base stamped "Hawke," America or England, ca. 1870-90, 5¼" h. (ILLUS.) 1,265.00

Leech jar, cov., stoneware, cylindrical w/flat lid & metal clamp closure, stamped "AD - Patent - Leech Jar - London Pottery J. Stiff & Sons Lambeth" in oval beneath a raised band w/vertical perforated slits for ventilation, cream colored glaze, England, ca. 1840-70, qt., 6" h. (⅜" chip off side of lip) 1,850.00

Pill cutter or separator, circular wooden base tapering to one end, w/handled blade attached by a brass hinge, America, ca. 1870-90, 12½" l 209.00

Show globe, golden amber globe w/ornate clear glass lid & low pedestal base w/flared foot, America, ca. 1890-1900, overall 12½" h., 3 pcs 302.50

EGG REPLICAS

Long the symbol of rebirth, the egg has close associations with springtime and the Easter holiday. Easter eggs made in various materials were popular gifts in the late 19th and early 20th centuries in Europe and America, and especially in Russia. Since Easter is the most important religious holiday for the Eastern Orthodox Church, beautiful eggs, many in precious materials, were produced in Russia before the Revolution.

Silver-Gilt & Enamel Egg

Enamel on silver, decorated w/colorful scrolling foliage on a peach ground, the interior w/fittings for egg cups, Fyodor Ruckert, Moscow, Russia, ca. 1900, 2½" h...........................$6,325.00

Gold (14k) & translucent enamel, miniature, pendant, enameled in the form of a ladybug, the back enameled translucent red w/black dots, the underside enameled translucent lime green, marked w/Cyrillic initials of workmaster Feodor Afanassiev, Fabergé, St. Petersburg, Russia, ca. 1900, ½" l 7,763.00

Papier-maché, one side painted w/a depiction of the Descent into Hell, the other w/a church, Russia, ca. 1875, 5" h....................................1,870.00

Papier-maché & lacquer, one side painted w/the Guardian Angel, the other w/a cathedral, green ground, Russia, ca. 1875, 3¾" h...............1,210.00

Porcelain, painted w/an angel on one side, a cross against a blue ground on the other, Russia, ca. 1875, 4½"h..2,860.00

Porcelain, mottled deep blue ground applied w/the gilt-metal Imperial cypher of Alexander III, Russia, ca. 1881, 4¾" h.................................1,650.00

Porcelain, one side painted w/St. Vladimir, one hand raised in benediction, within an ornate gilt border, deep blue ground, Russia, ca. 1875, 4½" h.............................2,860.00

Silver-gilt & enamel, enameled w/colorful flowers on a gilded strippled ground, the front hinged & enameled w/a red cross, Maria Semyonova, Moscow, Russia, ca. 1910, 3⅛" h. (ILLUS.) 3,850.00

Silver-gilt & shaded enamel, enameled w/foliage & flower sprays on a robin's-egg blue ground, Moscow, Russia, ca. 1900, 2" l.....3,163.00

ENAMELS

Enamels have been used to decorate a variety of substances, particularly metals. The best-known small enameled wares, such as patch and other small boxes and napkin rings, are the Battersea Enamels made by the Battersea Enamel Works in the last half of the 18th century. However, the term is often loosely applied to other English enamels. Russian enamels, usually on a silver or gold base, are famous and expensive. Early 20th century French enamel on copper wares and those items produced in China at the turn of the century in imitation of the early Russian style are also drawing dealer and collector attention.

Beakers, silver & shaded enamel, tapered cylindrical shape w/ring foot, enameled w/multicolored flowers on a pale blue ground, the borders enameled in geometric foliate designs, Moscow, Russia, ca. 1910, 4¾" h., pr $2,588.00

Bonbonniere, modeled in the form of an apple, the skin shaded from pinkish red to white, w/three green leaves & a brown stem, gold mount, Germany, ca. 1765, 2¼" h. (mount restored) 1,955.00

Bowl, low foot, gently rounded sides, the exterior painted in shaded tones of ochre yellow, lime green, deep lilac & crimson w/large open blooms on an undulating fleshy stem issuing further intertwining leafy tendrils & smaller opening buds in colors, on a deep claire-de-lune ground, the interior bluish turquoise, the reign mark inscribed on the underside in blue w/four characters, *Kangxi yuzhi*, within a square, China, 6⅛" d. (scratches,small restored area at footring) 57,500.00

19th Century Enameled Box

Box, cov., rectangular, colorfully enameled w/a central oval panel depicting a couple & a child in a landscape, the corners & sides reserved w/floral bunches, surrounded by white scrolls & floral sprigs, on a light blue ground, cracks, France, 19th.c., 7¼" l. (ILLUS.) 1,035.00

Carafe w/original stopper, silver-gilt & enamel, bulbous base & long slender neck, enameled turquoise blue between silver filigree scrolls, w/borders of white beads, stopper similarly decorated, Gustav Klingert, Moscow, Russia, 1891, 8¼" h...................................1,150.00

Etui, cylindrical, the top in the form of a female bust, the girl wearing a flowered headdress, the lower part painted w/a basket of flowers & inscribed "Je Matche A La Plus Douce," gilt-metal mounts, Continental, late 18th c., 5⅛" l......1,840.00

Salt cellars, silver & shaded enamel, circular shape w/colorful stylized foliage on grounds of cream & green, The Sixth Artel, Moscow, Russia, ca. 1910, 2¾" d., pr..........1,150.00

Vase, copper, the cylindrical vessel enameled in dark brown shading to silver w/four stylized male profiles, signed in gilt "SAR - LAN - DIE - LIMOGES, decor de Beaumont," ca. 1930, 3⅝" h............................2,875.00

Wine pot, cov., cube-form, brightly decorated on three sides w/a *meiren* standing beneath a willow in a garden setting framed by foliate & diaper borders, divided by a pink-diaper band on the canted corners, an upright spout issuing from the fourth panel, the top decorated w/four phoenix roundels on a diaper ground, the upright handle & domed fitted cover w/matching decoration, all raised on four tab feet, the underside w/a blue *shou* medallion encircled by four pink bats, Canton, China, 19th c., 7¾" h. (chips)........1,610.00

EPERGNES

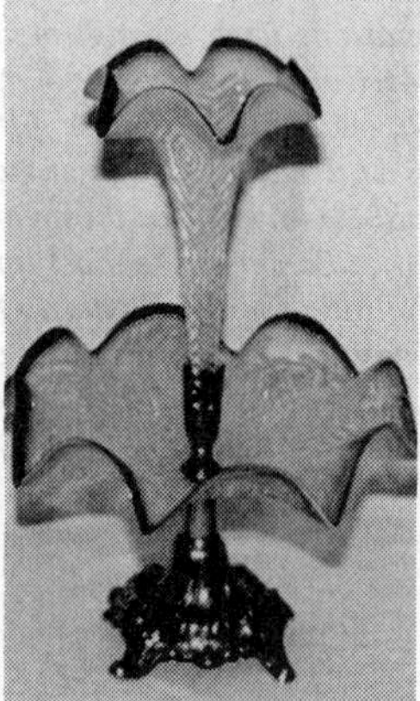

Cranberry Opalescent & Spatter Epergne

Epergnes were popular as centerpieces on tables of last century. Many have receptacles of colored glass for holding sweetmeats, fruit or flowers. Early epergnes were made entirely of metal including silver.

Amethyst swirled glass, single lily, tall trumpet-form lily w/ruffled rim, lower wide ruffled bowl, decorated w/gold enameled flowers, 12½" h $450.00

Clambroth glass w/gold decoration, single lily, ruffled rim on lily & ruffled rim on base, 6¼" h..........................225.00

Cranberry opalescent shaded to white shaded to greenish yellow spatter glass, single lily, ruffled rim tapering to a slender ribbed body set in a brass mount above the widely flaring ruffled & finely ribbed bowl, all raised on a short brass pedestal & pierced scroll-molded domed footed base, 10" d., overall 17" h. (ILLUS.) 395.00

Purple Opalescent Epergne

Purple opalescent shaded to clear w/white opalescent glass, single lily, the lily & matching lower bowl w/overall molded white opalescent 'tree bark' design, a nickel-plated mount supports the lily & a domed, scroll-cast footed nickel-plated base supports the lily & bowl, 9½" d., overall 14" h. (ILLUS.)....................295.00

Sterling Silver Epergne

Sterling silver, four-basket, the central rectangular plateau raised on a wavy domed base fitted w/four scrolled arms from which hang four swing-handle sweetmeat baskets, each on four feet for separate use, all w/baroque ornament, monogrammed, Frank W. Smith, Gardner, Massachusetts, ca. 1900, 23½" l. (ILLUS.) 6,613.00

Sterling silver, Classical Revival style, on circular base w/presentation inscription, raised on four lozenge-shaped feet topped by foliate scrolls, the stem in the form of a classical female figure holding an urn from which spring foliate scroll branches supporting a large central circular tazza & three smaller tazze w/gilt interiors, Tiffany & Co., Union Square, New York, ca. 1865, 17¾" h.......................................16,100.00

EYE CUPS

The eye cup was an early means of treating an injured or infected eye. The oval cup, filled with a medicated solution, was held over the open eye. With the advent of eye droppers and plastic dropper bottles, the eye cup became obsolete.

Clear glass, "John Bull," patent dated, "August 14, 1917" $25.00

Clear glass, squat fish bowl-shaped bowl 14.00

Cobalt blue glass, "John Bull," patent dated "August 14, 1917"...................45.00

Cobalt blue glass, paneled, marked "W.T. Co. B, USA"...........................30.00

Cobalt blue glass, marked "Wyeth Collyrium"...27.00

Green glass, "John Bull," patent dated "August 14, 1917" ....75.00 to 85.00

Green glass, pedestal base w/tulip-shaped bowl..28.00

Milk white glass, paneled bowl 15.00

FABERGE'

Fabergé Bellpush

Carl Fabergé (1846-1920) was goldsmith and jeweler to the Russian Imperial Court and his creations are recognized as the finest of their kind. He made a number of enamel fantasies, including Easter eggs, for the Imperial family and utilized precious metals and jewels in other work. Also see BUCKLES, EGG REPLICAS, OPERA GLASSES and STICKPINS.

Bell push, enamel & silver, the domed push enameled translucent rose pink over a *guilloché* ground & applied w/silver-gilt ribbon-tied swags, the push enameled translucent sky blue, marked w/Cyrillic initials of Workmaster Johan Victor Aarne, "Fabergé" in Cyrillic & 88 standard, St. Petersburg, ca. 1910, 2⅛" d. (ILLUS.) $8,050.00

Bowl, enamel & silver-gilt, the squatty

bulbous body tapering to a/wide short cylindrical neck, raised on a small foot, the sides enameled in yellow & white w/a wide band of leafy scrolls on a dark blue ground, marked w/Cyrillic initials of Workmaster Michael Merchin, also "Fabergé" in Cyrillic & 88 standard, St. Petersburg, ca. 1890, 2½" d....3,220.00

Bowl, cut glass & silver, the wide round clear cut glass bowl cut w/a wide band of alternatingly large & small pointed leaves below a diamond band, the rim mounted w/a reeded ribbon-tied silver band, silver marked "K. Fabergé" in Cyrillic w/imperial warrant & 84 standard, Moscow, ca. 1900, 8¾" d.............5,750.00

Cake dish, silver, the wide shallow shell-shaped bowl boldly chased on the interior w/long leafy scrolls & fine scalloped ribbing, on a plain disc foot, marked "K. Fabergé" in Cyrillic w/imperial warrant & 88 standard, Moscow, 1894, 10" d 1,610.00

Cigarette case, gold (14k) & jewels, the curved sides reeded overall, the cover mounted w/the Imperial Eagle set w/diamonds & a cabochon sapphire, w/cabochon sapphire thumbpiece, marked "K. Fabergé" in Cyrillic w/Imperial warrant & 56 standard, Moscow, ca. 1900, 4" l...9,775.00

Claret jug, cov., cut glass & silver, the ovoid clear cut glass body w/a wide silver neck-mount applied w/garlands of foliage, w/a silver ribbon-tied reeded handle, the hinged silver domed cover w/bud finial, silver gilded on the interior, the glass body cut w/large vesicas w/starbursts & button bands, marked "K. Fabergé" in Cyrillic w/imperial warrant & 84 standard, Moscow, ca. 1900, 10½" h...........8,050.00

Clock, desk-type, silver-gilt & translucent enamel, of Siamese inspiration, w/a domed top & spreading base, enameled translucent pale blue over a *guilloché* ground, also enameled w/a view of a monument w/a fountain in the foreground, the circular dial bordered by seed pearls, the base chased w/a border of acantuhus leaves, marked w/initials of Workmaster Henrik Wigstrom, Fabergé in Cyrillic & 91 standard, St. Petersburg, ca. 1910, 4¼" h. (lacks feet) 18,400.00

Cup & saucer, demitasse, silver & shaded enamel, the cup w/slightly tapering cylindrical sides & a wide flat handle topped w/a flaring blossom above an angled bar, the sides decorated in enamel w/a band of leafy spirals w/blossoms all on a cream ground w/geometric borders, shallow matching saucer, marked "K. Fabergé" in Cyrillic w/imperial warrant & 88 standard, Moscow, ca. 1900, saucer 3½" d......................2,875.00

Kovsh (boat-shaped dish), silver-mounted wood, the wooden bowl applied w/silver leaves & mounted w/two small chrysoprase cabochons at the prow, a high curved handle at the stern, marked "K. Fabergé" in Cyrillic w/imperial warrant & 88 standard, Moscow, ca. 1910, 7" h...2,875.00

Magnifying glass, silver & nephrite, the silver border of the glass decorated w/entwined ribbons, w/beaded border, the nephrite handle rising from entwined serpents, the heads of the serpents mounted w/faceted citrines, marked w/Cyrillic initials of Workmaster Michael Perchin, Faberge in Cyrillic & 88 standard, St. Petersburg, ca. 1890, 6¾" l..................................9,200.00

Parasol handle, nephrite, gold & diamond, of tau shape, set w/diamonds, the collar w/a a border of diamonds, marked w/initials of Workmaster Henrik Wigstrom & 56 standard, St. Petersburg, ca. 1905..4,600.00

Pin, gold & enamel, navette shape, enameled translucent pale blue over a *guilloché* ground, the center set w/a diamond, the border chased w/leaftips, marked w/initials of Workmaster Henrik Wigstrom & 56 standard, St. Petersburg, 1910, 1½" l..1,725.00

Salt cellar, enamel & silver-gilt, squatty bulbous body on small knobby feet, the exterior enameled in muted tones of green & brown w/spirals & leafy designs, each handle in the form of a rooster's head, marked "K. Fabergé" in Cyrillic w/imperial warrant & 88 standard, together w/a silver-gilt & shaded enamel spoon by The Sixth Artel, Moscow, ca. 1910, 2¼" d., 2 pcs. 2,300.00

Tea glass holder, copper, cylindrical w/slightly flared bottom rim, squared handle w/thumbrest, one side w/the Cyrillic inscription "War, 1914-15, K. Fabergé," the other side w/the Imperial Eagle, ca. 1915, 3¼" h....1,150.00

FARM COLLECTIBLES

Early Wheelbarrow

Bee skep, woven rye straw, 17" d., 17" h. $231.00

Bee smoker, tan leather bellows, from the Root Company, w/instructions 45.00

Corn husker, nickel-plated steel, two-point, marked "Clark Universal, Pat. Pend.," 5¼" l. 22.00

Egg case, wooden, "Queen City," Bangor, Maine, stenciled, 13 x 15 x 16" 47.50

Egg scale, metal, "Acme," patented 1924, unused mint condition.............35.00

Egg scale, metal, "Jiffy Way," mint condition, w/box 30.00

Implement seat, cast iron, "Deering" 65.00

Implement seat, cast iron,"Dodds"......125.00

Implement seat, cast iron, "Fuller & Johnson," cut-out letters 200.00

Implement seat, cast iron, "Jenkin".....125.00

Implement seat, cast iron, "Jones" 100.00

Pitchfork, marked "Keen Kutter" 25.00

Seed sower, "Cahoon," w/original booklet & instructions........................10.00

Wheelbarrow, painted wood, trapezoidal form w/rounded sides, painted green, the outside also painted w/a small running horse & the front w/"G.B. Tufts," tapering down-turned handles, chamfered tapering stops, a central red-painted front wheel, 19th c., 19 x 51½", 21½" h. (ILLUS.) 2,860.00

Windmill weight, cast iron, model of a buffalo, the flat silhouetted form w/incised detail mounted on a horizontal rod, America, late 19th - early 20th c., 16" w.,11½" h. 990.00

Windmill weight, cast iron, model of a standing silhouetted bull w/red, white & orange repaint, made by Fairbury, Nebraska, 24½" l. 770.00

Windmill weight, cast iron, model of a rooster, 16¾" w., 15¾" h.................495.00

Windmill weight, cast iron, model of a rooster, swell-bodied stylized bird w/molded comb, wattle & jowl detail, mounted on a clamp base, late 19th - early 20th c., 19" l., 19" h..............863.00

Windmill weight, cast iron, model of a rooster w/molded neck, wing & arched rib tail, painted red, mounted on a black metal base, late 19th c., 19" h. 3,335.00

FIREARMS

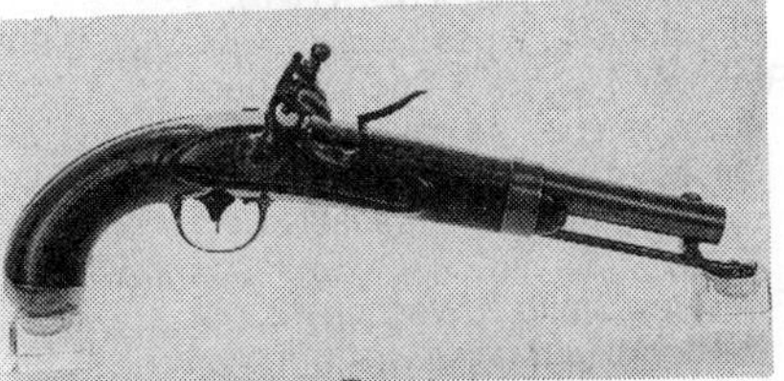

Model 1836 Flintlock Pistol

Blunderbuss, walnut stock w/well-carved shell around the breech area, octagonal to round brass stamped barrel w/a cannon-type muzzle & engraved "London," lock has been converted to percussion, engraved "Turvey," engraved nickel silver hardware w/drums, flags, etc., England, 30½" l. (breech w/damage to fore end & age cracks) $825.00

Musket, flintlock, octagon to round smoothbore barrel w/brass hardware including an engraved pineapple-type trigger guard, lock, barrel & side plate are stamped "C.P.," 40" l. (restoration w/some replacements) 550.00

Pistol, flintlock holster-type, walnut stock, lock plate marked "Ketland," brass mountings, brass barrel w/proof marks & stamped "London," England, late 18th c., 14" l 550.00

Pistol, flintlock Model 1836, by Asa Waters & Robert Johnson, marked "US - R. Johnson - MIDDn, CONN 1841" (ILLUS.) 3,500.00

Pistol, S. North Model 1816, flint-type, .54 caliber, lock has partial signature w/eagle, "U.S." & "Midln, Con," barrel shows proof stamps & stock has faint inspector's mark, iron hardware, 15" l. 550.00

Revolver, Colt Army Model, .45 caliber, single action, frame has "U.S." stamp, barrel marked "N.J.," nickel-plated, walnut grips w/faint cartouche, serial No. 113235, together w/a letter from Colt describing this piece as delivered to a U.S. inspector in 1884 & was originally blued, barrel 7½" l., 2 pcs 1,210.00

Revolver, Colt single action, .41 caliber, greyish brown metal, shows good signature & patent dates, hard rubber Colt grips (thin chip on one side), serial No. 130025, barrel 4¾" l. (minor pitting) 1,155.00

Revolver, Colt Third Model Dragoon, .44 caliber, "U.S." mark on frame, folding leaf rear sight, lightly cleaned to a grey finish, together w/matching shoulder stock, revolver serial No. 17299, stock serial No. 17918, barrel 7½" l., 2 pcs 4,400.00

Revolver, Rogers & Spencer, percussion-type, .44 caliber, bold inspector's mark on grip, all serial numbers matching, serial No. 4644 ....935.00

Revolver, Smith & Wesson #2, .32 caliber, blued finish w/some wear, rosewood grips, serial No. 25551, barrel 6" l. (small pin missing at top strap) 605.00

Revolver, Whitney Navy Model, percussion-type, .36 caliber, cylinder w/engraved scene w/eagle, ships, lion & shield, barrel & cylinder show traces of blue, lightly cleaned, serial No. 20242A, barrel 7½" l.................495.00

Rifle, Indiana half-stock, percussion-type, curly maple stock w/good dark patina & brass hardware w/some simple engraving, barrel signed "S.J. Heston," 53" l. (some pitting to barrel) 990.00

Rifle, Kentucky full-stock, curly maple stock w/brass patch box, percussion lock, overall 56" l. (damage & age cracks to stock) 522.50

Rifle, Kentucky full-stock, curly maple stock w/decorative brass patch box & oval silver medallion w/engraved eagle, percussion lock conversion from flintlock, possibly York County, Pennsylvania, overall 56" l. 1,320.00

Rifle, Kentucky full-stock, curly maple stock w/percussion lock, lock signed "H.E. Leman, Lancaster, Pa.," barrel signed "...Marker," overall 56" l. (somewood damage & age cracks) 550.00

Rifle, Kentucky half-stock, walnut w/brass & white metal inlays, percussion lock marked "Henry Parker Warrented," heavy octagonal barrel initialed "R.B.," overall 48½" l..935.00

Rifle, S. North "Common Rifle," steel hardware w/three bands & oval patchbox, lock has bold signature, town & "1829," barrel & breech have inspector's marks, "U.S." & "1829," converted to percussion, 52" l..........550.00

Rifle, Ohio half-stock, percussion-type, curly maple stock w/good color & stripe, brass hardware including a cap box, marked "G. Meissner #266," Zanesville, Ohio, 52" l........1,320.00

Rifle, long Pennsylvania swivel breech-type, Golcher percussion lock, curly walnut stock, silver flower inlay on cheek piece, brass hardware w/a three-piece pierced patch box, 54" l. (lock in need of finetuning) 1,320.00

Shotgun/rifle, barrel stamped "REM" possibly for Remington, German silver mountings, stock inlaid w/large eagle decoration, cased w/mold & accessories, case labeled "O. Churchill Albany," mid-19th c., 40" l...1,760.00

FIRE FIGHTING COLLECTIBLES

Painted Leather Fire Bucket

Belt, leather, worn original red, black & white decoration, lettered "HAMPDEN," 42" l. (some damage)...........$71.50

Belt, leather, marked "Hercules" in red & white paint, 19th c. 95.00

Belt, leather, w/ladder hook & hose spanner wrench 45.00

Bucket, painted leather, slightly bulbous cylindrical form, w/applied leather handle, painted scene on one side depicting a house on fire, a desperate figure on the second floor & firefighters running to the rescue surrounded by the motto "ADROIT FIRE CLUB - DELAY NOT - JOSEPH ROSE" & centering the date 1806 above, America, 1806, 9" d., 13" h. (ILLUS.) 16,500.00

Bucket, painted leather, tapering cylindrical form, old green repaint w/yellow label reading "No. 4, N. Tibbets 1843," swing strap handle, 13" h. (wear, rivet added to one side of handle)..412.50

Bucket, painted leather, cylindrical w/rolled & sewn lip & circular base, decorated in red, white, gold, blue & black w/an American eagle, U.S. flag, shield, military trophy & ribbon garlands, signed "1810 - J. Atherton - Northfield," Massachusetts, ca. 1810, 15" h. 575.00

Bucket, painted & decorated leather, inscribed "N° 1 Calvin Haven. 1821" in gold on a green ground, 20" h. (paint wear) 1,045.00

Fire alarm gong, oak case, "Gamewell," 6" 725.00

Fire extinguisher, copper & brass, "Elkhart," 24" l. 80.00

Fire extinguisher, copper & brass, "Guardene," 2½ gal. 20.00

Hayward's Fire Grenade

Fire extinguisher, cobalt blue glass, "Hayward's - Hand Fire - Grenade - S.F. Hayward - 407 - Broadway - New York - Patented - Aug. - 8 - 1871," squared body w/domed shoulder & slender neck w/tooled lip, smooth base, America, ca. 1875-90, w/original contents, pint, 6" h. (ILLUS.) 253.00

Fire extinguisher, cobalt blue glass, "Hayward Hand Fire Grenade Fire Extinguisher - New York " around shoulder, squared form w/diamond-shaped design around shoulder & base, smooth base, slender neck w/tooled lip, America, ca. 1880-90, w/original contents, pint, 6" h. 231.00

Fire extinguisher, green glass, "Harden Star," w/contents 195.00

Fire extinguisher, turquoise blue glass, "Star (inside star) Harden Hand Grenade - Fire Extinguisher," globular w/wide ring at midsection & vertical ribbing, smooth base, long slender neck w/ground lip, America, ca. 1885-95, w/original contents, qt., 8" h...165.00

Fire extinguisher, yellowish olive glass, "Healey's Hand Fire Extinguisher," cylindrical lower section swelling to a bulbous midsection & tapering to an applied

Healey's Hand Fire Extinguisher

mouth, smooth base, America, ca 1880-90, removable inside content stain, qt., 10¾" h. (ILLUS.)..............962.50

Fire hose nozzle, bronze & copper, incised "Elkhart Brass Mfg. Co. - No. 211," 30" l. 175.00

Fire mark, cast iron, oval, depicting fire hose & "F.A.," worn old dark green repaint, 7¼" w., 11½" h............71.50

Fire trumpet, painted tin, red w/inscription "Fire Ward," late 19th c., 17¼" l. (imperfections) 165.00

Hat shield, for leather hat, red & white decal lettered "Lieutenant - Lynnfield" w/a fire trumpet pictured, 6" h. (worn & edge damage) 33.00

Helmet, red metal w/shield front w/black lettering, "Deposit F.D.," size 7½, early 20th c. (minor wear)..170.50

Lantern, copper front w/slide-off cage, "Dietz King" 175.00

Speaking trumpet, presentation-type, nickel-plated, engraved "Present to Ex-Chief Simon Steiner by the R.V.C. F.D. Aug. 27, 1901" 650.00

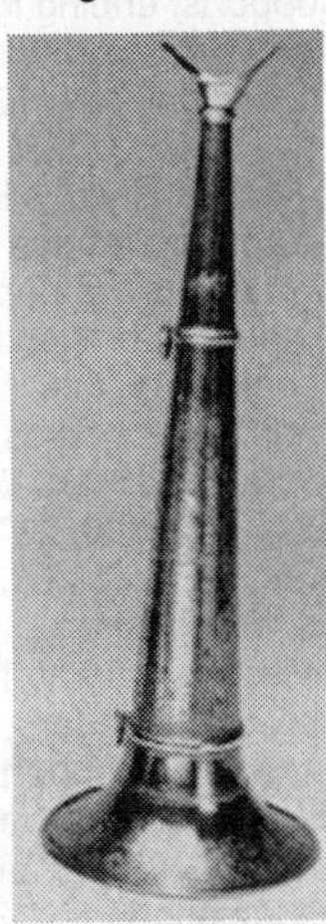

Presentation-type Speaking Trumpet

Speaking trumpet, presentation-type, silver plate, engraved "Presented to their foreman E.P. Buffinten, Esq. by the members of the Niagara Fire Co., no. 4 of Fall River...," minor imperfections, 20½" l. (ILLUS.) 1,540.00

FIREPLACE & HEARTH ITEMS

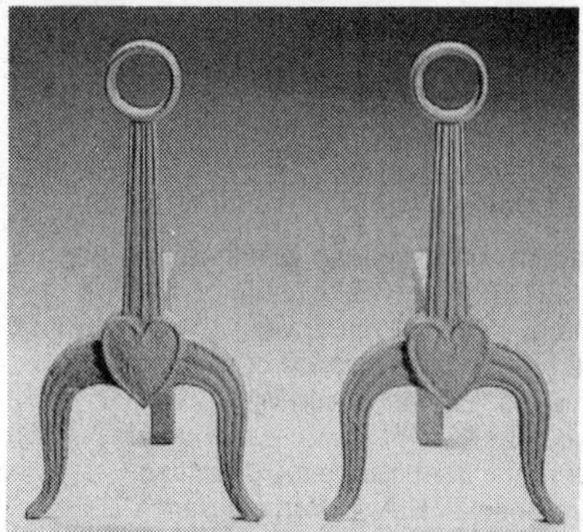

Cast-Iron Andirons with Hearts

Andirons, brass & wrought iron, Chippendale style, an urn-form finial above a tapered column standard, the plinth base w/cyma-shaped apron on spurred arched supports, ending in claw-and-ball feet, impressed "R. WITTINGHAM, N.YORK," ca. 1795, 18¼" l., 27¼" h., pr. $4,600.00

Andirons, brass & wrought iron, Chippendale style, surmounted by a gadrooned urn-and-flame twist finial above a fluted tapered column, the molded plinth base on double-spurred arch supports, ending in claw-and-ball feet, attributed to Daniel King, Philadelphia, ca. 1775, 19" l., 23" h., pr. 23,000.00

Andirons, brass, Federal style, a large faceted lemon-form finial above a flaring ringed foot above the paneled shaft raised on spurred, arched front legs ending in snake feet, the conformingly shaped log guards behind, each w/stamped mark "J. DAVIS BOSTON," ca. 1820, 23" l., 21½" h., pr. 1,955.00

Andirons, brass & wrought iron, Queen Anne style, urn & flame-form finial above a baluster standard, the molded plinth on arched supports, ending in pad feet, Boston or New York, 1740-65, 24" l., 24½" h., pr. (rear foot of one log support replaced) 1,725.00

Andirons, cast iron, an open ring finial on a flat ribbed shaft over a molded heart issuing arched & ribbed legs, American-made, early 20th c., 12½" h., pr. (ILLUS.) 460.00

Andirons, cast iron, molded in the half-round w/two small hearts under a curved & flat 'anvil' crest continuing to a tapering standard terminating in a large heart on curved supports, America, mid-19th c., 13¾" h., pr. 2,070.00

Andirons, cast iron, model of an owl perched on arched branches, cast half-round w/large pierced eyes, early 20th c., 14" h., pr. 4,888.00

Andirons, wrought iron, modeled in the form of a stylized dog w/frontward flaring ears & short curled tail, joined by a squared rod resting on the curled edge of the ears, by Edouard Schenck, ca. 1932, each 16" deep, 8½" w., 12½" h., pr. 3,450.00

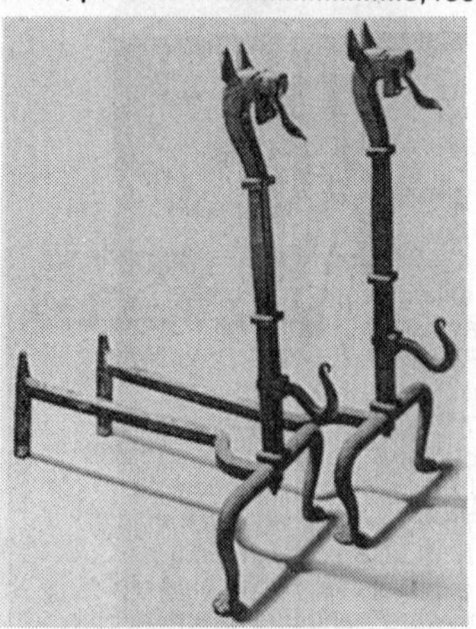

Andirons with Dogs' Heads

Andirons, wrought iron, square upright topped by the stylized head of a Great Dane dog, a hook at the base of the upright above the rounded arched legs w/paw feet, attributed to Samuel Yellin, ca. 1910, 29⅜" h., pr. (ILLUS.) 5,175.00

Andirons, wrought iron & sheet iron, faceted finial above a tapering standard continuing to an inverted heart, on arched legs ending in penny feet, New England, late 18th c., 20" h., pr. 4,888.00

Andirons & fender, brass, Federal style, the andirons w/domed & faceted cylindrical finial above a sphere w/faceted band over a ring-turned shaft on a circular ring-turned plinth on arched spurred legs w/ring-turned & ball feet; the brass & iron wire fire fender of bow form w/brass railing above a wire screen w/scrolling wire embellishment, attributed to Edward Smylie, New York City, ca. 1820, fender 51" w., andirons 12" h., 3 pcs. 2,530.00

Bellows, painted & decorated wood, the flat sides & handle grain-painted, stenciled & decorated w/an overall spotted tortoiseshell-like design, 19th c., 17¼" l. (deterioration to leather)..165.00

Bellows, turtle-back type, painted wood & leather, original yellow paint w/striping & a bowl of flowers in stenciled & free-hand red, gold & black, old worn leather, brass nozzle, 17" l. 214.50

Bellows, turtle-back type, painted & decorated pine, painted salmon w/gilt decorated flowerpot, flowers & leafage heightened w/stylized stenciled floral borders in gilding & black paint, the leather sides fastened w/brass tacks, New England, early 19th c., 19½" l. 633.00

Bellows, turtle-back type, painted yellow w/stenciled fruit-filled cornucopia & foliage in gilt-bronze w/details in green & black, leather sides fastened w/brass tacks, New England, ca. 1830, 20" l. (some wear to leather)................................403.00

Ember tongs, wrought iron, 18th c., 18⅛" l. 715.00

Fireboard, painted pine, composed of five planks w/applied breadboard ends, painted in a fanciful genre landscape w/fully rigged sailing ship & feathery trees on the surrounding banks, the sky w/billowy clouds in tones of green, yellow, orange & blue, attributed to Rufus Porter, New England, early 19th c., 46" w., 35" h...23,000.00

Fireplace fender, brass, Federal style, the serpentine brass rail centering three reeded finials over a screen composed of vertical wires w/enclosed scrolling decoration, America, ca. 1800-20, 46" w.........1,650.00

Fireplace fender, wrought iron, Art Deco style, the gently curved base molded w/egg-and-dart above the perimeter supporting a low railing centered by a cipher, flanked by stylized egrets w/scrolling openwork wings, probably France, ca. 1925, 41½" l., 25" h...............................4,600.00

Fireplace screen, wrought iron, Art Deco style, composed of four hinged panels, the center two wrought w/stylized cranes standing amid water grasses, black patina, unsigned, American-made, ca. 1925, 49½" l., 33" h.......................2,760.00

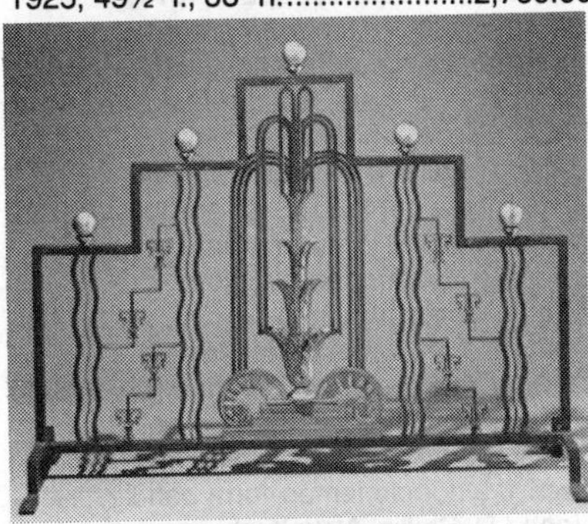

Art Deco Fireplace Screen

Fireplace screen, wrought iron, bronze & brass, Art Deco style, the stepped framework enclosing a central stylized fountain flanked by wavy vertical members & geometric designs, supported by angular feet, the top set w/five bronze spheres, possibly American-made, ca. 1925, 42" l., 34" h. (ILLUS.) 8,050.00

Fireplace set: pair of andirons, tongs & shovel; brass, Federal style, the andirons w/acorn finial w/beaded & tapering mid-band over a faceted hexagonal plinth on spurred arched legs w/ball feet, the tools w/conforming finials, firetools 30" l., andirons 17½" h., America, 1790-1810, the set........................3,850.00

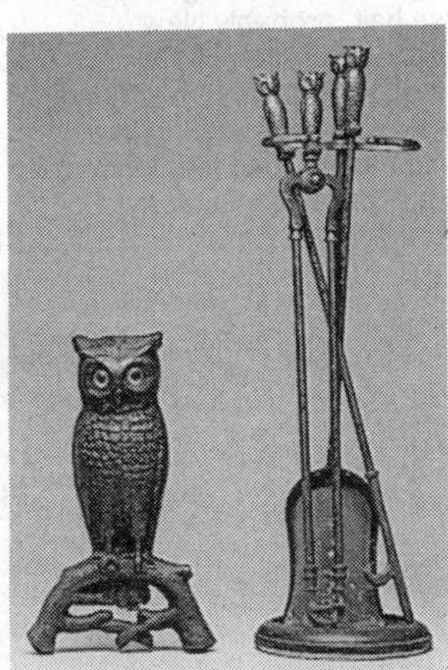

Fireplace Set with Owls

Fireplace set: pair of andirons, shovel, tongs, poker & tool holder; cast iron, the andirons topped by a fully modeled half-round owl w/ears flattened back, large yellow & black glass eyes, detailed feathers, perched on an intertwined rustic twig base, the billet bars stamped "Rostand," & owls stamped "407#," the matching fire tools w/figural owl finials on the handles, each owl w/brass bead eyes, Rostand Mfg. Co., Milford, Connecticut, early 20th c., andirons 15" h., tool holder 27½" h., the set (ILLUS. of part) ...5,750.00

Fireplace shovel, wrought iron, the elongated & rounded handle w/rams' horns terminus & D-shaped shovel, America, early 19th c., 22⅜" l. 173.00

Fireplace tools: shovel, tongs & poker; brass & wrought iron, Federal style, each w/a double lemon-form handle, signed D. Phillip, New York, ca. 1815, 29½" l. 4,313.00

Fireplace trammel, wrought iron, sawtooth-type w/decorative detail & several hooks, 31" l. (pitted) 275.00

Fireplace trammel, wrought iron, sawtooth-type, lollipop finial, 35" l....165.00

Hearth broiler, wrought iron, a wide heart-shaped rack w/five curved tines sliding on a slender upright rod above the arched tripod base w/penny feet, decorative diamond-shaped rivet on spring, 28" h. 1,100.00

Hearth brush, painted pine, the baluster- and ring-turned tapering handle delicately painted w/sprays of pink, blue & green flowers & foliage, the midsection decorated w/gilt-painted geometric motifs on a cream ground continuing to a brush of horse hair, probably New England, early 19th c., 31" l. 920.00

Hearth fork, wrought iron, two-tined, the flattened handle ending in a pierced heart-shaped terminus, probably Pennsylvania, early 19th c., 28½" l. 518.00

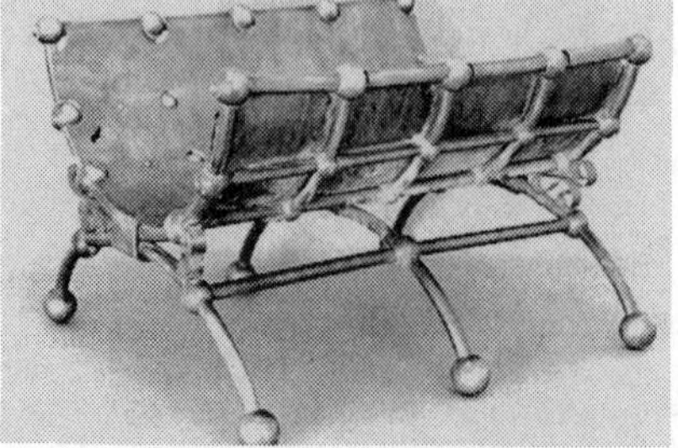

Arts & Crafts Log Holder

Log holder, brass, Arts & Crafts style, curved basket sitting on curved tubular legs, fastened w/little balls, early 20th c., some tarnishing to patina, 14 x 17 x 21½" (ILLUS.).......650.00

Pipe tongs, wrought steel, good detail, polished, 11½" l. 440.00

FISHING COLLECTIBLES

BOOKS & PAPER ITEMS

Book, "Book of Fish & Fishing," by L. Rhead, 1920 ....$45.00

Book, "Fish & Fishing in the Upper Mississippi River," by Carlander, 1954 ....5.00

Book, "Fishing in the West," by Carhart, first edition, 1950 ....20.00

Book, "Flyrod for Bass," Outdoor Life, 1942, picture wraps, 85+ pp. 10.00

Book, "Professional Fly Tying," by Herter, 1954.......................................30.00

Catalog, "Pflueger Fishing Tackle," color cover, 1938, 128 pp..................65.00

Catalog, "South Bend Fishing Tackle," color cover, 1931, 79 pp. 65.00

Catalog, "South Bend Fishing Tackle," 1934 ....37.50

Catalog, "Willmarth Tackle Co.," Roosevelt, New York,1929-30, 56 pp. 50.00

Magazine, "The Fishing Gazette," July 1909 ....15.00

LURES

Creek Chub Bait Co., "Creek Chub Wiggler," No. 101, w/advertising pamphlet 18.00

Gibbs "Cast-A-Lure," wooden, Buzzards Bay, Massachusetts, w/original box, 4½" l. 30.00

Heddon "Zig-Zag Jr.," No. 8340 series, wooden, painted red & white, mint in box 45.00

Land (Charles W.) "Minnow Harness," patented 1914, Madrid, New York 60.00

REELS

Horton Mfg. Co., "Bluegrass No. 34"..275.00

Horton Mfg. Co., "Meek No. 3" 275.00

Meisselbach (A.F.) & Bros. "Takapart No. 480," chrome 35.00

Meisselbach (A.F.) & Bros. "Takapart No. 481" 79.00

Pflueger "Model No. 1895" 18.00

Shakespeare "Model 1912" 25.00

Talbot "Comet Reel," Nevada, MO, patent date 1-22-01 ....750.00

Talbot "Star," Kansas City, MO...........650.00

Edward Vom Hofe, bass, 1896, in original leather case........................195.00

Winchester Repeating Arms Co., "No. 2336" 150.00

Winchester Repeating Arms Co., "No. 4231" 150.00

Winchester Repeating Arms Co., "No. 4331" 150.00

RODS

Winchester Repeating Arms Co. fly rod, split bamboo, w/case, ...425.00

Winchester Repeating Arms Co. fly rod & reel, bamboo rod No. 6087 & fly reel No. 1235 ....525.00

MISCELLANEOUS

License, 1937, Arkansas 12.00

License, 1937, New Jersey 30.00

License, 1940, Ohio............................20.00

Sign, model of a northern pike, reads "Winchester Fishing Lures Sold Here," colorful, 20" l. 100.00

FOOT & BED WARMERS

Bed warmer, brass pan w/tooled floral design & an "L" on the lid, turned hardwood handle w/traces of old painted graining, 42" l. $330.00

Bed warmer, brass pan w/engraved floral on cover, turned wood handle, 44" l. (pan w/edge damage & old repair where ferrule attached)..........247.50

Bed warmer, brass pan w/engraved floral design w/star on lid, pan has crown & "E.R.," turned wooden handle, refinished & polished, 45½" l. (pan battered & has small split) 275.00

Bed warmer, copper pan w/simple engraved pinwheel design on the cover, turned wooden handle w/worn old black paint, 30¾" l. 236.50

Bed warmer, copper pan w/floral pinwheel tooled brass lid, turned wooden handle w/old worn black paint, 36½" l. 159.50

Bed warmer, copper pan w/engraved & bright-cut pierced cover, turned & shaped walnut handle, probably American-made, ca. 1785, 43½" l. 1,265.00

Bed warmer, copper & brass, simple tooled design on lid, turned wooden handle w/worn black paint, 44½" l. (repairs to pan) 192.50

Foot warmer, tin & cherry, mortised frame w/turned corner posts, punched tin sides & top w/a design of circles & diamonds, 19th c., 7¾ x 9" 192.50

FOX (R. Atkinson) PRINTS

Robert Atkinson Fox (1860-1935) was an American artist whose prolific output included romantic landscapes, mountain scenes and portraits of domestic livestock & wildlife. Many of his paintings were reproduced as popular prints early in this century. Today these prints are increasingly collectible thanks in great part to the well-researched series of articles written by Rita Mortenson for The Antique Trader Weekly *beginning in 1980. This series then led to her 1985 book,* R. Atkinson Fox, His Life and Work *(Wallace-Homestead), followed by a sequel,* R. Atkinson Fox, Volume 2, *(L-W Book Sales, 1992). The numbers accompanying our listings are those assigned by Mrs. Mortenson in her works.*

"Approaching Storm (The)," framed, No. 85, 16 x 20" $135.00

"Clipper Ship," No. 75, framed, 13½ x 17½"..95.00

"Daydreams," No. 138, framed, 16 x 20"..160.00

"Dreamland," No. 41, framed, 14 x 22"..75.00

"Edge of the Meadow (The)," No. 117 ....225.00

"Enchanted Steps," No. 56, framed, 12 x 20"..55.00

"Good Ship Adventure," No. 17, framed, 9½ x 12½"..............................65.00

"Heart's Desire," No. 55, framed, 18 x 30"...60.00

"Indian Summer," No. 35, 17 x 24" 65.00

"Inspiration Inlet," No. 58, framed, 10 x 20"..60.00

"Jersey Homestead (A)," No. 124, framed...200.00

"Nature's Beauty," No. 16, framed, 10 x 20"...45.00

"Nature's Sentinels," No. 531, calendar print, 8 x 11" 45.00

"Nature's Sublime Grandeur," No. 64, framed, 14 x 18"...............................55.00

"Old-Fashioned Garden (An)," No. 12, framed, 18 x 30"...............................80.00

"Path to the Valley," No, 201, framed, 10 x 16"...60.00

"Poppies," No. 45, framed, 18 x 30" 55.00

"Promenade," No. 10, 12 x 20"................60.00

"Rose Bower," No. 46, framed, 10 x 16"..............................50.00 to 75.00

"Sunrise," No. 30, framed, 12 x 16" 185.00

"Sunset,", No. 182, framed, 9¼ x 17¼"....50.00

"Sunset Dreams," No. 23, framed, 10 x 18"..155.00

"Tom & Jerry," No. 583, horse print, 9 x 12"...40.00

FRAMES

Brass, tooled w/a Virginia creeper design, 3" w. sides, 17¼ x 20½" $93.50

Tiffany Pine Needle Frame

Bronze & glass, rectangular w/wide flat sides, the metal pierced w/the Pine Needle patt., backed w/mottled green opalescent Favrile glass, impressed mark "TIFFANY STUDIOS - NEW YORK - 947," 8 x 9½" (ILLUS.) 1,035.00

Gilded brass, rectangular w/narrow sides set w/colored stones, marked "Austria," 6 x 8" 121.00

Gilt-bronze, rectangular, the narrow flat borders cast w/meandering flowers & tendrils centered by a flower-filled urn, impressed "TIFFANY STUDIOS - NEW YORK 1611," early 20th c., 11¾" h..3,163.00

Sterling silver, oblong scalloped & scroll-rimmed design in the Rococo style, w/swing-leg back support, Tiffany & Co., New York, late 19th c., 9" h.................................1,320.00

Sterling silver, rectangular, elaborately etched w/scrolling foliate vines, flowerheads & tiger lilies enclosing the inscription "Marjorie to Papa 1899," Tiffany & Co., New York, ca. 1899, 10" h. 1,980.00

Wood, horseshoe-shaped, relief-carved detail w/pots of flowers, joined hands, starflowers, "Good Luck 1904" & scalloped border, old varnish finish, 9" w., 12" h. (some touchup on one side) 82.50

FRATERNAL ORDER COLLECTIBLES

Eastern Star lapel pin, gold, gold-filled & seed pearls, model of a star w/cross & staff, reverse side engraved "BE Tinkham," 1915.........$27.50

G.A.R. Sign

G.A.R. (Grand Army of the Republic) sign, painted & carved pine, the oblong sign w/lobed ends, the top section painted w/a gilt spread-winged eagle perched atop two crossed cannons, an American flag w/thirteen stars in white on blue & red & white stripes in the center w/a five-point gilt star at the bottom inscribed "Walter A. Wood - 294 - Post - GAR Vet" in black, all on a black ground w/gilt trim, ca. 1870, 4' 2" h. (ILLUS.) 2,300.00

Improved Order of Red Men lodge axe, tin, w/turned walnut handle, worn red & blue paint on tin, from lodge in Tuscon, Ohio, 20¼" l. 60.50

I.O.O.F. (Independent Order of Odd Fellows) collection box, poplar w/original red paint & gold & black lettering "ORPHANS FUND," Wooster, Ohio lodge, 6¼" l., ("A" scratched out, age crack in top).......467.50

I.O.O.F. Hanging Comb Box

I.O.O.F. comb box, hanging-type, painted & gilded pine, the pierced backplate carved w/a large gilt tassel & applied w/moon, stars & the all-seeing eye, the wall pocket front carved w/the three rings, book, heart & hand & the initials "F L T," painted red w/gilt highlights, New York State, late 19th c., 11½" w., 21¼" h. (ILLUS.) 3,738.00

Knights of Columbus hat, sash & sword belt, 1920s, 3 pcs.. ....150.00

Knights of Columbus sword & scabbard, 1920s, 2 pcs...................125.00

Masonic apron, white cotton w/blue printed design, green & yellow applied braid borders, 17 x 17" (stained & very worn) 71.50

Masonic cradle, presentation-type, silver, in the form of a silk-lined child's cradle supported by two silver columns & w/Masonic emblems on onyx base, also w/a silver presentation plaque inscribed "Lebanon Lodge No. 1326, presented to the wife of Bro. William J. Burton by the members of the Lodge to mark the happy event of the birth of a son during his year of office as Worshipful Master, July 1901," Birmingham maker's mark "V & S," 1901, 11" l. 1,150.00

Masonic hooked rug runner, worked in brilliant tones of red, green, yellow & blue fabric alternating areas of striped geometric patterns at center, the Masonic compass, house, cow, ducks, three entwined circles & cross compasses along w/the initials "B.F." & letter "G," probably New England, early 20th c., 23" w., 16' l. (some areas of wear) 1,380.00

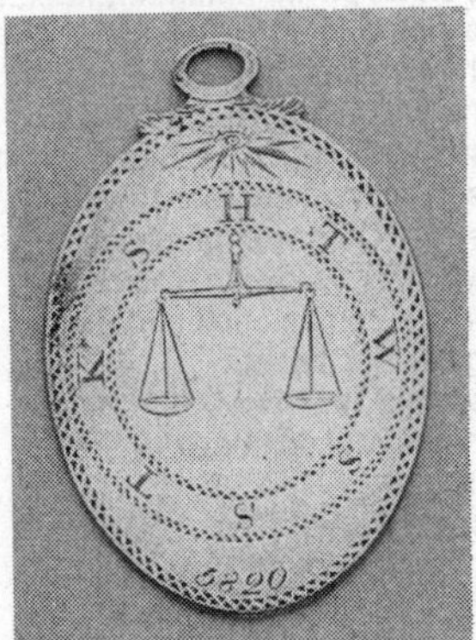

Oval Masonic 'Jewel'

Masonic 'jewel,' silver, the flat oval disc w/oval loop at top, the front engraved w/a circular cartouche enclosing a balance & scales, the border engraved w/letters "HTWSSTKS," engraved above w/a radiating eye & below the Masonic year "5280," the reverse engraved w/a compass & square enclosing script initials "CF," American-made, 1820, 2¼" l. (ILLUS.) 440.00

Ornate Masonic 'Jewel'

Masonic 'jewel,' silver, flat cartouche-form w/suspension loop at the top, the obverse engraved w/a mask above a banner w/inscription "SIT LUX ET LUX FUIT" above a burning bush surround by the inscription "Zaccheus Hovey, Temple M M Lodge," the reverse engraved w/an eye above two winged cherub heads above a ladder surrounded by script initials "HTWSSTKS," the border similarly engraved, American-made, early 19th c., 3¼" l. (ILLUS.) 575.00

Masonic Gold Pendant

Masonic lapel pin, 14k gold, model of a sword 20.00

Masonic medal, silver, bar pin suspending circle enclosing Masonic symbols, engraved "Ira E. Finfrock 1893," w/case, 3¼" h. 121.00

Masonic membership certificate,

copper-plate etched on vellum, presented to Thomas Fisher, master mason of Mount Moriah Lodge, No. 132, New York & dated April 22, 1820, w/seal of the Grand Lodge of the State of New York affixed near lower margin, in original tin covered sleeve, 14 x 17" (w/vertical & horizontal creases) 220.00

Masonic pendant, 14k yellow gold, triangle w/"32" above a perched double-headed eagle centered by an old mine-cut diamond, hinged & opening to reveal an enamel decorated Masonic emblem, the reverse bearing a cross through a crown & inscribed "IN HOC SIGNO VINCES" (ILLUS. previous page) 632.00

Masonic pendant, silver, engraved inscriptions, insignia & "Wm. Faulkner Geneva, Royal Arch Chapt No 36," 2⅞" h. 495.00

Masonic pin, 14k gold & moonstone, the Masonic emblem centered by a carved moonstone depicting a man in the moon within an elaborate frame....................220.00

Masonic ring, platinum & diamond, centered by an old mine-cut diamond & a five-point star set w/colored stones within a pierced diamond set top 110.00

Masonic shelf, hanging-type, walnut, wire nail construction, single shelf beneath cut-out work depicting Masonic symbols, lower bracket w/cut-out design, 16½" h. (bottom bracket incomplete) 38.50

Masonic trowel, sterling silver, engraved "Evergreen Lodge 259 F&AM, Riverside, California - EA Oct. 19 - FC Oct. 26 - MM Nov. 24, 1917"....................40.00

Decorated Shrine Goblet

Shrine goblet, molded glass, the ruby-stained bell-form bowl w/the Shrine emblem in gold & white, the bowl supported by gilt-trimmed scimitars above a waisted tree trunk-form stem on a black swirl-molded foot, Pittsburgh, Pennsylvania insignia on the front & "St. Paul, Minn. 1908" on the back,3" d., 5¼" h. (ILLUS.) 95.00

Shrine wine, clear glass, "1899, Syria Temple, Pittsburgh, Pa.," scimitar & shrine symbol on base, gold trim 110.00

Shrine wine, clear glass, "1900, Washington D.C.," three-sword symbol on base, gold trim 110.00

FRUIT JARS

Best Fruit Jar

Acker Merrall & Condit Company New York (front) & Cafe Deluxe (on two sides), ground lip, aluminum screw cover, amber, ½ gal. $60.50

Atlas Wholefruit Jar, smooth lip, lightning beaded neck seal, wide mouth, clear, pt. 8.00

Ball (in script, 3-L loop), "IV" on smooth base, automatic bottle machine lip, original zinc lid, aqua moonstone, ½ gal. 198.00

Ball Mason, yellowish green, ½ gal. 40.00

Ball Mason, "Ball" in script, greenish aqua w/heavy yellowish green striations, automatic bottle machine lip, original zinc lid, qt....................44.00

Ball Mason's Patent Nov. 30th, 1858, smooth rim, Mason shoulder seal, aqua, ½ gal. 33.00

Ball Mason's Patent (The), 1858, smooth base, ground lip, aqua, qt. 11.00

Ball Perfect Mason (in dual line letters), smooth lip, Mason beaded neck seal, clear, qt. 60.50

Bambergers "The Always Busy Store" Newark, smooth base, ground lip, Mason shoulder seal, zinc lid, aqua, qt. 93.50

Bennett's No. 1, cylindrical w/applied collared mouth, smooth base, aqua, qt. 396.00

Best, cylindrical, ground lip, smooth base, amber glass insert in zinc screw band, Canada, root beer amber, ca. 1900, qt. (ILLUS.) 220.00

Cassidy & CMCo monogram on reverse, ground lip, glass lid w/wire bail & a wooden slotted ramp, clear, ½ gal. 715.00

Cohansey Glass Mfg. Co., barrel-shaped, embossed hops & staves design, aqua, 7⅜" h. 110.00

Crown & crown emblem embossed on front, T. Eaton Co. Limited - Toronto and Winnipeg on back, smooth base, ground lip, glass insert & screw band, clear w/tint of amethyst, midget 99.00

Cunningham & Co., Pittsburgh, PA, (embossed on base), applied lip, smooth base, ca. 1870, deep aqua, ½ gal. (small stress crack) 121.00

Excelsior, glass lid embossed "Patd. Aug 8th. 1865," zinc screw band, smooth base, ground lip, light yellowish green, qt. 302.50

Excelsior Fruit Jar

Excelsior, tapering sides, aqua, qt., 7¼" h. (ILLUS.) 33.00

Family Fruit Jar (The), cylindrical, ground mouth w/glass lid & wire bail, clear, pt. 550.00

Fridley & Cornman's Patent Oct. 25th 1859 Ladies Choice, iron rim w/gutta percha insert, smooth base, ground lip, aqua, ½ gal. 1,320.00

Gilberds Improved (embossed star) Jar, glass lid embossed "Gilberd's Improved Jar Cap," wire clamp, smooth base, ground lip, aqua, qt. ..165.00

Globe, glass lid, wire & iron clamp, metal band around neck, smooth base, ground lip, aqua, qt. 121.00

Glocker Trademark Sanitary Pat. 1911 Others Pending, glass lid embossed "Glocker Pat. 1911 Others Pending Sanitary," rubber gasket, smooth lip, aqua, qt. 44.00

Halle (C.K.) & Co. - 121 Water St. - Cleveland. O.," cylindrical w/applied collared mouth, smooth base, aqua, ca. 1863-80, qt. 214.50

Haller (Wm. L.) Carlisle, Pa., cylindrical, applied collared mouth, smooth base, aqua, ½ gal. 319.00

Hansee's Place Home Jar, monogrammed "PH," base marked "Pat. Dec. 19 1899," glass straddle-lid seal, closed by lever w/fulcrum in wire bail, clear, qt. 88.00

Kerr "Self Sealing" Trademark Reg. Patented Mason, glass insert & screw band, cornflower blue, qt. 50.00

Lafayette (in script), glass & metal lid embossed "Patented - Sept. 2, 1884 - Aug. 4, 1885," tooled lip, smooth base, aqua, qt. 60.50

Lightning, amber, ½ gal. 80.00

Lightning, amber, ½ gal. 80.00

Lightning "Trade Mark" Jar

Lightning below arched "Trade Mark" amber, qt. (ILLUS.) 55.00

Mason Porcelain Lined, smooth base, ground lip, Mason shoulder seal, aqua, qt. 165.00

Mason's - 404 - Patent Nov 30th 1858, ground lip, smooth base, original zinc lid, aqua, midget pt. (ILLUS.) 110.00

Mason's Improved - CFJCo, ground lip, glass insert & screw band, olive green, qt. 14.00

Mason's Patent Nov 30th 58, ground lip, Mason shoulder seal, zinc lid (known as the Christmas Mason because of the lettering style), aqua, pt. 60.50

Mason's 404 Fruit Jar

Mason's Patent Nov 30th 1858, Mason shoulder seal, ground lip, original zinc lid, light to medium emerald green w/slight amber striation, qt. 192.50

Mason's (Cross) Patent Nov 30th 1858, smooth base, ground lip, zinc lid, medium yellow w/olive tone, qt. 330.00

Mason's Patent Nov 30th 1858, Mason shoulder seal, ground lip, unlined zinc lid embossed "Chases Pat. Oct. 27 1857," two vertical wrench lugs soldered on top of lid, aqua, qt. 375.00

Mason's Patent Nov. 30th 1858, smooth base, ground lip, zinc lid, aqua, midget pt. 55.00

Mason's Patent Nov. 30th 1858, smooth base, Mason shoulder seal, zinc lid, golden amber, qt. 264.00

Mason's Patent Nov. 30th 1858 & embossed moon & stars, smooth base, ground lip, zinc lid, aqua, ½ gal. 132.00

Mason's (shield) Union, smooth base, ground lip, aqua, ½ gal. (zinc lid missing) 99.00

Millville Atmospheric Fruit Jar - Whitall's Patent June 18th 1861, smooth base, applied mouth, correct glass lid w/metal yoke, highly whittled, aqua, qt. 77.00

Moore's Patent Dec 3D 1861, applied mouth, smooth base, original glass lid & metal yoke marked "Patented Dec 3D 1861," aqua, qt. 99.00

Newman's Patent Dec. 20th 1859, cylindrical, ground mouth, smooth base, aqua, ca. 1859-70, pt., 5⅝" h. 847.00

Nonpareil Patented July. 17, 1866, cylindrical, ground mouth, smooth base, aqua, qt. 330.00

Pet, glass lid embossed "Patd August 31th 1869 T.G.O.," spring wire clamp w/coil, smooth base, applied mouth, aqua, qt. 104.50

Potter & Bodine, Philadelphia, ground lip, metal lid w/soldered wire clamp, aqua, ½ gal. 319.00

Putnam (embossed on base), ground lip, light amber, qt. 35.00

Putnam (embossed on base), ground lip, light amber, ½ gal. 70.00

Reservoir (The), cylindrical, applied collared mouth, glass stopper embossed "Mrs. G.E. Haller - Pat d. Feb. 15. 73," smooth base, aqua, ½ gal. 352.00

Root Mason, w/zinc lid, aqua, qt. 12.00

Spencer's (C.F.) Patent Rochester N.Y., applied mouth, smooth base, ca. 1865-75, deep aqua, ½ gal. (metal closure missing) 77.00

Star (above star emblem), Pat'd Feb 5 1867 (on base), ground lip, glass insert w/zinc screw band, aqua, ½ gal. 88.00

Stone (A.) & Co. Philada Manufactured by Cunninghams & Co., Pittsburgh, PA, iron pontil, applied wax seal ring, aqua, qt. 850.00

Stone (A.) & Co., Philada., cylindrical, applied collared mouth w/threaded glass stopper, smooth base, aqua, qt., 8⅝" h. 352.00

Strittmatters - embossed bee - Pure Honey - Put Up By - F.J. Strittmatter & Wife - R.D. 1, Ebensburg, PA, smooth base, ABM lip, blue, pt. 38.50

Unembossed, cylindrical w/tapering shoulders embossed w/long 'petals' in the upper half, applied mouth, iron pontil, ca. 1855-65, deep bluish aqua, ½ gal. 467.50

Van Vliet Jar of 1881 (The), "Pat. May 3d 1881" on glass lid, metal yoke & wraparound wire bail, smooth base & ground lip, aqua, ½ gal. 412.50

Whitney, smooth base embossed "Whitney Glass Works, Glassboro, N.J.," ground lip, glass insert marked "Patented June 12th 1866," zinc screw band, aqua, ½ gal. 605.00

W M & P, N.Y., square w/large vertical flutes, applied rolled collared mouth, pontil scar, aqua, 7¼" h. 99.00

Woods Fruit Jar, smooth base, rolled collared mouth, aqua, pt., 7½" h. 330.00

Woods Fruit Jar, smooth base, tooled & rolled lip, aqua, qt. 176.00

Yeoman's Fruit Bottle, smooth base, applied mouth, aqua, ½ gal. 33.00

THE NEWEST "TRUE" ANTIQUES

FURNITURE OF THE 1890S

by Connie Morningstar

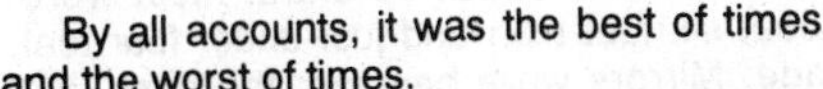

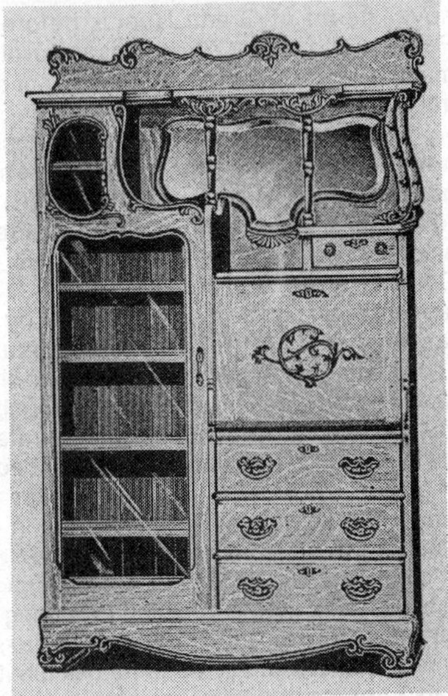

By all accounts, it was the best of times and the worst of times.

For furniture manufacturers in the 1890s, labor was cheap; prison labor more so. Oak, a preferred wood, was still in reasonable supply. Mahogany, a preferred finish, could be applied to plentiful birch. Carving machines such as the Goehring embosser, patented about 1890, could press any pattern that "could be drawn with a pencil." The Union carving machine cut designs at a rate of 50 feet an hour, producing in one day more than ten handcarvers.

Contrary to apprehensions, such machinery did not cause workers to be laid off. Increased production, in fact, created new jobs. And, at 95 cents for a double-pressed and spindle-back sidechair in 1895, the average consumer could afford well-made, inexpensive furniture.

Business boomed. Cincinnati's 150 furniture factories employed about one in four residents there in 1890. Production was valued at $9,000,000. An exposition of furniture goods took place in July of that year at the Music Hall – the first such exclusive show of its kind in the United States.

Grand Rapids enjoyed the best season in its history that spring. All factories were running at full capacity, several of them operating twelve or thirteen hours a day. In Rockford, Illinois, another active furniture-manufacturing center, plants closed only for Christmas and New Years.

The first furniture factory in Wisconsin had been established in 1846 and by 1890 there were 48 in full production, employing 3,306 workers. Their average annual wage was a respectable $400.69. Meanwhile, annual income for each of the 2,050 employees of the state's fourteen chair factories was $299.72. (*American Furniture Gazette*, Oct. 1890). Chairmakers consistently were the lowest paid in the industry.

The Panic of 1893, touched off by falling gold reserves, dropped prices, curtailed employment, and plunged the country into a severe depression that lasted about three years. Grand Rapids lost some 5,000 jobs. In Chicago, where 38 parlor frame and furniture manufacturers had been doing business in 1889, only 11 remained in the same location and under the same name in 1893. Optimism reigned in Cincinnati, however, where it was predicted that the furniture business would be the first to recover from the depression because "people must have furniture."

The magnificent World's Columbian Exposition in Chicago alleviated to a certain extent the doldrums of the 1893 Panic. But there was great bickering among the furniture people before the event. Manufacturers in New York were peeved that the Fair had been awarded to Chicago. Grand Rapids manufacturers were in a snit because they had not been given sufficient space. They were later appeased by attention from English dealers who had

This side-by-side combination secretary was one of several produced in birch by the Sheboygan Novelty Company, Sheboygan, Wisconsin, in 1895. Its flowing lines and tendril-like applied carvings suggest the popular Art Nouveau movement. Illustrated above right.

never heard of Grand Rapids before the Fair. In all, about 70 American furniture manufacturers were represented, 20 of them from Grand Rapids.

Stylewise, it was an eclectic age, then as now. Turkish or Moorish was in fashion, according to the decorators, but few Americans were inclined to set aside an alcove in their parlors to be furnished with Oriental carpets and heavily overstuffed and tasseled divans as recommended by the tastemakers. Although suites, usually consisting of a settee, armchair, sidechair, and platform rocker, were sold throughout the decade, a Springfield, Illinois, retailer claimed in mid-1896 that "There has been a change in parlor goods in the past few years. We do not sell it in suites but in odd pieces." (*Michigan Artisan*, July 1896).

Oak, which had become popular in the late 1880s, soared to prominence during the 1890s. Already in 1890, *Trade Bureau* announced that the demand for oak furniture had superseded ash, maple, and birch almost entirely and, like the walnut craze a few years before, there seemed no prospect of its abatement.

But it was not the darling everywhere. According to an article in *Michigan Artisan*, July 1896, customers in Memphis demanded walnut; so did those in Baltimore. Philadelphians preferred mahogany. Angelenos insisted on "cheap" oak. Birch did not play in Peoria but curly birch with an imitation mahogany finish did well there. The explanation: "We have a very dirty country and the grime from soft coal gets into the wood and checks it and it never can be cleaned." For the same reason, dark furniture of mahogany or fumed oak was deemed best in Pittsburgh.

Among the new pieces introduced during the 1890s was the first kitchen cabinet, the "Russell," patented January 9, 1894, by the Niemann & Weinhardt Table Company, Chicago. Actually, it was a table with bins for flour and bread, drawers for spices, and two meat or baking boards, all located below the work surface. The "Russell" was still a leader in 1898 when the *Furniture Worker* observed, "Owing to its splendid selling qualities, the company has found many imitators, but it is safe to say not one comes up to the old reliable Russell." The more familiar kitchen cabinets with a superstructure were first advertised by Kokomo Furniture Mfg. Co., Kokomo, Indiana, in 1898. The upper section held small drawers for spices. The popular "Hoosier" did not come along until after the turn of the century.

Combination pieces, such as the side-by-side secretary (dropfront desk and bookcase) also were new, or nearly so, in the Nineties. *The Rockford Furniture Journal*, April 15, 1890, noted five factories in Rockford, Illinois, alone that were turning out these units. One of them, Skandia Furniture Company, offered a "Double Library Case" (bookcases flanking the desk unit) in oak or solid mahogany.

Cook & Baker of Allegan, Michigan, forerunner of the contemporary Baker Furniture Company, began manufacturing these "combination bookcases" with 200 units in 1893. By 1895, production totaled 3,211 pieces. The price was $5 each. The 1895 Montgomery Ward catalog shows ten models of similar combination secretaries priced from $10.50 to $26.75. Most were constructed of quarter-sawed oak, but top-of-the-line models also were available in curly birch for about $3 extra. Most were about six feet high and just under four feet wide. Mirrors were beveled; the desk unit was fitted with pigeonholes and drawers; and shelves in the bookcase were adjustable. One double unit was offered at $24.75.

Three models of a combination china cabinet/sideboard were advertised in Montgomery Ward's 1897 furniture catalog. The sideboard's drawer fronts were serpentine and glass in the door was "swelled" (curved). At $43.90, this was the highest priced of the three.

Metal beds came into fashion about 1893, reaching their zenith of popularity some four years later. They were highly touted as being more hygienic than the

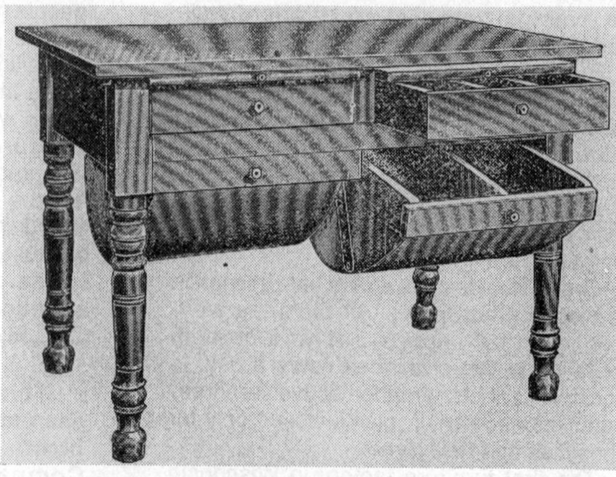

The "Russell" kitchen table was patented in 1894. Believed to be the first kitchen cabinet, it provided tin bins for flour and bread, partitioned drawers for spices, and two pull-out boards.

traditional wooden bedsteads. Accompanying pieces seemed to present a problem, however. In 1896, L.C. & W.L. Cron, Piqua, Ohio, advertised dressers and washstands finished in white enamel with gold trim as the ideal companions to metal beds. According to *Furniture World*, March 1898, bureaus, dressing tables, and chiffoniers of mahogany or birdseye maple would go well with metal bedsteads while oak and birch were not pleasing to the eye. The whole idea was an English gimmick anyhow and, the journal predicted, it would be only a matter of time before wooden bedsteads returned to favor here.

They returned in pairs. By the end of the decade, twin beds were considered suitable for the master bedroom. Again, better hygiene was the explanation. The public was less than enthusiastic, however, and twin beds did not become popular until the 1920s.

Montgomery Ward offered 50 designs of brass beds in 1897 noting that they were "always in style, always clean, never break, and most comfortable to sleep in. They are easily taken apart in case of accident. The different parts are interchangeable, and new pieces can always be had."

Iron beds, offered in the same catalog, were "graceful, seemingly slight, yet firm and strong, do not appear to fill a room as the more cumbersome wooden ones do." It was noted the beds could be draped with cretonne, sateen, or other material that was pretty and inexpensive and would become an ornament to any room. Frames were finished in white enamel with brass "knobs" (finials). The double model was "richly ornamented with brass top rods and knobs and 14 brass rosettes in head and foot end."

Beds that folded into sofas, mantels, wardrobes, or desks continued to be popular. New to the decade was "The Success," a combination bed/desk/wardrobe or bookcase, designed to turn on its base "only requiring the space it occupies against the wall to turn in." This piece received the highest award at the 1893 World's Columbian Exposition. The Henry L. Albee & Company, a manufacturer of folding beds in Boston, predicted that the "next generation will not move their beds, they being built into the walls of the house and finished in a style to match the room finish." (*Trade Bureau*, May 24, 1890).

The split-pedestal extension dining table of earlier vintage developed five or six legs during the Nineties. Legs were heavy, turned and/or fluted or reeded and, most often, paired and connected by a carved stretcher. Feet were castered, sometimes doubly so. Closed, most measured about 48x48 inches. Leaves extended these tables to 8, 10 or 12 feet.

Platform rockers had been around since the 1840s, designed, some said, to save wear and tear on carpets. They continued to be popular throughout the 1890s and beyond. The McLean Patent Swing Rocker (glider) was touted as a "first class rocker in every respect" by its manufacturer, Biver, Ernster & Company, Chicago, early in 1891. Six models of this piece were advertised in Montgomery Ward's 1895 catalog as the "most comfortable rocker made." Reproductions are marketed currently.

Variations of the subsequently very popular Roman chair began to appear toward the end of the century. Part of the Empire Revival movement, Romans were occasional or novelty pieces designed for the parlor or hall. A continuous curule seat and arms, low back, often with a curule base are distinguishing features. Mueller & Slack, Grand Rapids, was an early manufacturer of the style offering eight models of chairs and window seats in 1896. All were made of birch with a mahogany finish; all seat covering was brocatelle or silk damask.

Twenty-seven plain and fancy models of rattan and reed rockers and chairs were shown in the 1895 Montgomery Ward catalog; 19 in 1897. They were available in gold, white and gold, natural, or the "new" shellac finish. Both

Adams & Westlake Co., Chicago, advertised its #116 brass bedstead in 1892. The piece boasted solid cast brass mounts, Bessemer steel frames, best brass tubing, and finest quality lacquer. Brass casters (never porcelain) were removable and interchangeable.

One of the first manufacturers of Roman chairs, Mueller & Slack, Grand Rapids, offered this piece in 1896.

issues explained the finishes: "On account of the reed being porous we finish these goods in different colors, as it beautifies them and makes them more durable. The new and stylish finish we call shellac, which leaves a natural color to the reed."

Today, the term "Golden Oak" defines a finish and an era from the early 1890s until well into the twentieth century. Yet there is little reference to the term as such in trade journals of the 1890s. *American CabinetMaker*, January 1891, observed, "It is said the popular finish for the coming year will be the dark English finish. Antique Oak will continue to be a good seller while 16th-Century seems to have lost in the scuffle."Antique Oak seems to refer to a dark fumed finish accomplished by the use of ammonia. Ammonia is missing in the other

Several versions of the McLean Patent Swing Rocker were offered during the 1890s. This model was available in solid oak and highly polished from Montgomery Ward in 1895. Its "Cobbler" seat was made of genuine sole leather. Price was $3.40.

finishes mentioned. A 16th-Century finish was achieved by a number of ingredients including burnt sienna to provide a reddish tint. It was hand-rubbed to a high polish. "Made of solid oak and highly hand polished," a description of many dining and bedroom pieces in Montgomery Ward's 1895 catalog, seems to come closest to Golden Oak.

Finally, an advertisement in *Michigan Artisan*, June 1898, by Adams Elting Company, Chicago, promoted the use of a filler that would "make a perfect Golden Oak finish without staining."

PRICE LISTINGS:

CHAIRS

Armchair, oak, pressed-back shaped crestrail w/leafy scrolls flanked by simple turned stiles w/knob finials, bentwood arms, seven long ring-turned spindles in the back, scooped-out solid seat, turned front legs joined by double ring-turned rungs in the front & plain double rungs at the sides & back (ILLUS. right) $395.00

Dining chair, oak, line-incised back rails framing a perforated plyboard back insert w/tack trim, demi-arms above the framed slip seat, turned front legs & square back legs joined by a ring turned H-stretcher (ILLUS. top next page) 195.00

Rocking chair, platform-type, spool-turned crestrails joined by small spindles, turned stiles joining open velvet-upholstered pad back, angular spool-turned arms on angled arm frames, upholstery seat, platform base on front casters, by Dexter, Black River, New York, reupholstered in green-striped velvet 185.00

Rocking chair, platform-type, pierced & scroll-carved crest above finger-carved stiles flanking the tall tufted upholstered back, shaped open arms on bobbin-turned supports, shaped upholstered seat, platform base, new blue velvet upholstery (ILLUS. top next column) 140.00

Side chair, oak pressed-back type, slightly arched crestrail w/paired cornucopias above inverted C-scrolls above seven ring-turned spindles, simple turned stiles w/knob finials, bentwood seat braces to the rectangular seat w/caned insert (broken), simple turned legs w/triple front rungs & double rungs at sides & back 149.00

Side chairs, oak pressed-back type, fancy high pressed crest & waist separated by seven short turned spindles, full-height stiles, hip brackets on seat, splined cane seat insert, scrolled apron, set of 6 (Not Illus.) 1,800.00

CHINA CABINETS

Chippendale Revival style, fumed oak, D-shaped top above a flat door flanked by curved glass sides w/carved lion-head masks at the top of the dividing stiles, conforming apron, cabriole legs w/paw feet on casters, four shelves, mirrored-back top shelf (ILLUS.) 1,700.00

Chippendale Revival style, quarter-sawn oak, carved crestrail on the D-shaped top above a curved glass door & sides, four shelves, the top one w/mirror back, ball-and-claw feet w/casters 1,400.00

Chippendale Revival style, mahogany, D-shaped top above curved glass front & sides, four claw-and-ball feet on front, two straight rear legs 467.50

Classical Revival style, oak, D-shaped top w/wide curved cornice above a front door flanked by curved glass sides, four shelves, curved apron, four heavy bun feet (Illus.) 3,200.00

Empire Revival style, oak, carved center crest on the D-shaped top above a flat door flanked by pilasters & curved glass sides, paw front feet, straight rear feet 1,485.00

Empire Revival style, oak, center crest w/applied carving & flanked by carved griffins, D-shaped top above a curved glass door & sides separated by rope-twist pilasters, four shelves w/the top one mirror-backed, paw feet..........................2,100.00

Empire Revival style, birch, D-shaped top above a flat door flanked by ogee pilasters & curved glass sides, simple C-scroll front legs & square back legs, three shelves, refinished, smaller size (ILLUS.) 400.00

HALL TREES

Aesthetic Movement substyle, oak, flat coved crestrail above four flat stiles w/angular line-incised bands, two double-section open panels w/scroll-carved brackets at the top centered by a rectangular beveled mirror above another open area, the stiles mounted w/curved metal coathooks, a wide medial band w/triangular sunburst carving above a center lift-top box flanked by umbrella openings, ring-and-block front legs w/knob finial joined by a lower shelf, drip pans in base missing (ILLUS.) 1,695.00

Golden oak substyle, oak, carved crestrail w/three flame finials, large rectangular mirror flanked by smoothly turned posts each w/one double metal hook, lift-top bench seat, open arms w/carved griffin head ends, ball-and-claw feet.......3,100.00

Golden oak substyle, oak, oblong top section w/flat ends & applied carved scrolls at the crest above four double metal hooks arching above a large round beveled mirror, paneled flaring back to shaped flat arms above the rectangular bench lift-seat, flat outswept front legs & slightly shaped apron (ILLUS.) 1,195.00

KITCHEN CABINETS

Oak, rectangular top above a pair of single-pane glazed doors w/molded edges & arched tops opening to two shelves above an open recess above the wide working surface above two pull-out shelves over two narrow drawers over two deep pull-out bins w/bentwood bottoms, ring-turned legs (ILLUS. top next column) 1,295.00

Pine, rectangular top w/narrow cornice above a pair of single pane textured glass doors opening to a shelf above a pair of drawers over a recessed pie shelf, the wide rectangular work surface above a pair of narrow drawers over two deep bins w/tin bottoms (ILLUS.).....625.00

SIDEBOARDS

Oak, a rectangular top shelf supported by tall curved & scroll-carved S-form scrolls centered by small open shelves flanking the rectangular beveled mirror in the back, the rectangular top w/molded edge above a pair of drawers w/round brass pulls above a long drawer w/pierced brass pulls over

two flat doors centered by leaf carvings, short square legs on casters (ILLUS.)..............................675.00

Oak, wide serpentine crestrail w/applied leafy scrolls at the center above a narrow rectangular shelf w/scroll-cut brackets, wide shaped sides centered by an oblong mirror, rectangular top above a pair of serpentine-front drawers above a long serpentine-front drawer over two paneled doors w/large leaf-carving & separated by a curved leaf panel, gadroon-carved apron, short square legs, brass pulls (ILLUS.)..1,095.00

SIDE-BY-SIDE COMBINATION CUPBOARDS

Secretary, quarter-sawn oak, double-arched staggered crests w/incised scrolls, one side w/a long flat glazed door opening to three shelves, the other side w/a shaped beveled

mirror above a shelf over a flat fall-front w/incised shield device opening to a desk interior above a large flat cabinet door, simple flat shaped front feet (ILLUS.) 795.00

Secretary, oak, shaped crest w/applied carving & a heart-shaped cut-out in center above one side w/a curved glass cupboard door opening to four shelves, the opposite side w/a beveled dome-shaped mirror above a fall-front w/applied carving opening to a desk unit above three drawers 875.00

Secretary, cherry, a flat top w/gadroon edge above one side w/a flat glazed door opening to a bookcase & w/applied carving at the top corners of the door frame, the other side w/a rectangular mirror above a galleried shelf over two small drawers over a fall-front w/applied carved "Northwind" mask & opening to a desk unit, two small drawers below fall-front, reeded pilasters flank bookcase, full-width long drawer at bottom, paw feet 1,017.50

Secretary, quarter-sawn oak, one half the crest w/scroll carving, other half w/a flat crest w/small leafy scrolls, one half of cabinet w/a tall pointed-top flat glazed door opening to three shelves, the other half w/a shield-shaped beveled mirror above a narrow shelf above the fall-front opening to a desk unit w/pigeonholes & a small drawer above a cabinet door, flat shaped front legs (ILLUS. top next column) 895.00

Secretary, quarter-sawn oak, flat crestrail above one section w/a curved glass door opening to four shelves, the other section w/a square mirror setback over a shallow round-fronted drawer above the fall-front opening to a desk unit above three bombé-front drawers, paw front feet on casters 1,600.00

Sideboard-china cabinet, oak, the sideboard section w/a scrolled crest over one shelf above a large rectangular mirror, two half-width drawers, one full-width drawer & a two-door cabinet, the china cabinet section w/ogee molding around the top over a serpentine glass door opening to four shelves.................1,500.00

Secretary, quarter-sawn oak, high ornately scroll-carved crestrail pierced at the center w/a leaf crest above one section w/a plain curved glass door, the other section w/an ornately shaped beveled mirror in pierced framing above a fall-front centered by a scroll-carved cartouche opening to a desk unit above a round-fronted drawer over two flat drawers, all w/bail pulls, simple cabriole front legs (ILLUS.).1800.00

TABLES

Dining table, oak, extension-type, square top w/molded edge above a line-incised apron w/beveled corners w/incised starbursts, on six paired square ring-and-block tapering legs joined by curved stretchers w/scroll-cut crests, on casters, w/six leaves, stamped mark "James Pleukhart & Co. - Patent Knock Down - Double Frame Pillar - Extension Tables - Columbus, Ohio," 44"w.(ILLUS.) 1,300.00

Dining table, oak, extension-type, square top w/molded edge above a line-incised apron, raised on five ball-and-rod reeded legs, corner legs w/large paw feet, w/one leaf (ILLUS. top next page.).....................1,195.00

Dining table, fumed oak, extension-type, square top w/molded edge above a shaped apron, raised on five heavy round ring-and-ball-turned legs w/a pineapple-carved central section & reeded ball feet on casters, w/one leaf (LLUS. center next page) 1,195.00

Dining table, oak, extension-type, round top above a plain apron, on ring-and-rod-turned reeded legs w/ball feet on casters, w/one leaf (ILLUS. bottom next page) 495.00

Side table, oak, square top w/molded edge above a scalloped apron, on four canted knob-and-rod-turned reeded legs ending in glass ball-and-claw feet, medial shelf w/molded serpentine edges (ILLUS.)...........550.00

OTHER PIECES

Bed, brass, tubular double-plated head- & foot-boards, plain rails, headposts 4' 9" h., footposts 38" h. 1,495.00

Desk, oak, drop front-type, pressed crestrail above a mirror flanked by small open shelves, slanted drop-front w/applied carving, two full-width shelves in base, Larkin Furniture label, refinished 275.00

Side table, quarter-sawn oak, square top w/beveled edge above a beaded apron, on four canted ring-and-baluster-turned legs joined by a square shaped medial shelf 195.00

Window seat, oak, Roman-style, wide curved seat w/knob-turned rails flanking a frame w/pressed designs flanking the reupholstered seat, on baluster and-ring-turned legs w/knob feet & joined by a turned H-stretcher (ILLUS.).......... 150.00

END OF SPECIAL FOCUS

FURNITURE

Furniture made in the United States during the 18th and 19th centuries is coveted by collectors. American antique furniture has a European background, primarily English, since the influence of the Continent usually found its way to America by way of England. If the style did not originate in England, it came to America by way of England. For this reason, some American furniture styles carry the name of an English monarch or an English designer. However, we must realize that, until recently, little research has been conducted and even less published on the Spanish and French influences in the areas of the California missions and New Orleans.

After the American revolution, cabinetmakers in the United States shunned the prevailing styles in England and chose to bring the French styles of Napoleon's Empire to the United States and we have the uniquely named "American Empire" style of furniture in a country that never had an emperor.

During the Victorian period, quality furniture began to be mass-produced in this country with its rapidly growing population. So much walnut furniture was manufactured, the vast supply of walnut was virtually depleted and it was of necessity that oak furniture became fashionable as the 19th century drew to a close.

For our purposes, the general guidelines for dating furniture will be:

Pilgrim Century - 1620-85
William & Mary - 1685-1720
Queen Anne - 1720-50
Chippendale - 1750-85
Federal - 1785-1820
  Hepplewhite - 1785-1820
  Sheraton - 1800-20
American Empire (Classical) - 1815-40
Victorian - 1840-1900
  Early Victorian - 1840-50
  Gothic Revival - 1840-90
  Rococo (Louis XV) - 1845-70
  Renaissance - 1860-85
  Louis XVI - 1865-75
  Eastlake - 1870-95
  Jacobean & Turkish Revival - 1870-95
  Aesthetic Movement - 1880-1900
Art Nouveau - 1890-1918
Turn-of-the-Century - 1895-1910
Mission (Arts & Crafts movement) - 1900-15
Art Deco - 1925-40

All furniture included in this listing is American unless otherwise noted. Also see MINIATURES (Replicas), ROYCROFT ITEMS and SHAKER COLLECTIBLES.

BEDS

Country-Style Rope Bed

Art Deco bed, pallisander, mother-of-pearl & ebony marquetry, the headboard w/gently serpentine crest ending in columnar supports, the siderails supporting a similarly shaped footboard w/applied outset panel veneered in a basketweave pattern & inlaid w/a spray of stylized flowers & butterflies in ebony & mother-of-pearl, the feet & lower edge of the footboard w/gilt-bronze mount, Jules Leleu, France, ca. 1937, 56½ x 77½", headboard 36" h. $3,450.00

Art Nouveau bed, carved mahogany, the high headboard carved in a tryptych cartouche outline w/curving stems at corners, inlaid w/two flame burled walnut panels, the lower footboard similarly decorated, branded "L. Majorelle FRANCE," ca. 1900, 66¼ x 84", 5' 3½" h. 4,600.00

Country-style low poster rope bed, grain-painted, the high stepped crestrail above a paneled headboard flanked by baluster- and ring-turned headposts topped by mushroom finials, matching footboard, overall grain-painted decoration, Pennsylvania or Ohio, mid-19th c., 51" w., 47½" h. (ILLUS.) 1,320.00

Federal child's crib w/tester, mahogany, the turned head- and foot-posts centering paneled head- and footboards, the sides w/crib rails, w/serpentine tester, some patches, first half 19th c., 48½" w., 51" l., without tester 38½" h. (ILLUS. top next page) 2,990.00

Federal Crib with Tester

Federal child's tall poster canopy bed, painted cherry, the headboard w/a plain rectangular board flanked by slender turned tapering posts, plain footposts, canopy frame at the top complete w/cotton crocheted hangings, painted red, first half 19th c., 36 x 72", 47" h.................................2,990.00

Federal tall poster canopy bed, birch & maple, a plain gently arched headboard flanked by headposts w/baluster-turned legs, a columnar-turned central section & a tapering, reeded upper section, the matching footposts w/similar turning, an arched canopy frame across the top, New England, ca. 1810.................5,750.00

Federal tall poster bed, satinwood & ebony-inlaid mahogany, slender reeded & ring-turned foot- and headposts, the headposts flanking a stained pine simple arched headboard, the posts continuing to form fan- and line-inlaid square tapering legs ending in spade feet, New England, ca. 1800, 57¼ x 76", 5' 3" h...10,925.00

Federal "Pencil-Post" Bed

Federal tall poster "pencil-post" bed, maple & pine, the arched & scroll-cut headboard flanked by tall paneled & tapering posts, plain paneled footposts, square tapering legs, lacks bolts & one rail, w/two additional rails, New England, ca. 1815, 56¼ x 76½", 7' 3½" h. (ILLUS.).........................1,035.00

Gustav Stickley Twin Bed

Mission-style (Arts & Crafts movement) twin bed, oak, the high headboard w/four wide vertical slats between slightly tapering rectangular stiles, wide sideboards, footboard slightly shorter but matching headboard, original medium finish, branded Gustav Stickley mark, ca 1912, 46¾ X 79", 46¼" h. (ILLUS.).........1,725.00

Mission-style (Arts & Crafts movement) double bed, oak, the head- and footboard w/tapered rectangular uprights & curved crestrails above 13 horizontal slats, w/exposed tenon construction, red decal mark of L. & J.G. Stickley, headboard 59 x 83", 4' 7¾" h.......................................16,100.00

Mission Oak Bed

Mission-style (Arts & Crafts movement) double bed, oak, head- and footboard w/modified "V" rail over five broad vertical slats, squared tapering posts, original medium-light finish, co-joined label of L. & J.G. Stickley and Gustav Stickley, 56 x 78", 4' h. (ILLUS.)..................3,410.00

Modern style single bed, limed &

ebonized oak, the square upright tall headboard composed of eight square slats between the stiles, matching lower footboard, wide siderails, ball feet, designed by Josef Hoffmann, Vienna, Austria, ca. 1903, 39⅜ x 79⅛", 45¼" h....12,420.00

Molesworth Bed Headboard

Molesworth bed headboard, rectangular w/a hand-carved horse head framed by a hand-tooled copper plaque surrounded by original brown leather-covered wood, two applied copper & leather conchos & trimmed w/copper-hammered tacks three-quarters size, ca. 1950, 48" w., 40½" h. (ILLUS.) 3,000.00

Queen Anne-Style queen-sized tall poster bed, mahogany, the wide, gently arched headboard flanked by tall, slender turned & tapering posts topped by turned urn finials, lower footboard w/matching posts & resting on cabriole legs w/pad feet, quality 20th c. reproduction marked "Reid," 7' 5" h. 1,155.00

Victorian double bed, black-painted & parcel-gilt metal, the high arched headboard composed of ornate pierced scrolling centered by a round medallion painted w/a genre scene, slightly lower footboard of similar design, looped metal side-rails & scrolling footboard apron, spiral-twist stiles on head- and footboards, probably Portugal, 19th c., 4' h. 4,313.00

Victorian bed, Renaissance Revival substyle, walnut & burled walnut, central headboard crest bearing a carved seated cupid flanked by stylized dolphins, caryatids & urns, above arched paneled headboard, conformingly paneled footboard, attributed to John Jelliff, Newark, New Jersey, ca. 1850-60, 68½" w., 8' 7" h. (ILLUS. top next column) ..6,875.00

Victorian Renaissance Revival Bed

Rococo Half-Tester Bed

Victorian half-tester bed, Rococo substyle, walnut, the half-tester w/an arched crestrail topped by a pierced & scroll-cut crest & bulbous corner finials, supported on scroll-cut brackets above the tall quatrefoil headposts flanking the arched & paneled headboard w/a scroll-cut crest, the shaped & scroll-cut foot-board flanked by short quatrefoil footposts w/bulbous turned finials, school of Francois Seignouret, New Orleans, ca. 1850-60, 69 x 82", 9' 7" h. (ILLUS.)............................7,700.00

BENCHES

Bucket (or water) bench, painted poplar, a three-quarter gallery top w/rounded front corners on the rectangular top shelf above a lower open shelf, bootjack cut-out feet on board ends, old worn olive grey repaint, 41 x 48½", 29" h. 451.00

Bucket (or water) bench, pine, a tall superstructure w/a narrow rectangular shelf w/an arched & scroll-cut three-quarter gallery above a row of three drawers raised on cut-out sides above an open back & a stepped-out lower case w/a rectangular top above a pair of paneled cupboard doors, bracket feet, refinished, 18 x 42", 4' 6" h. ..1,760.00

Early Bucket Bench

Bucket (or water) bench, pine, the arched top & shaped sides flanking three shelves w/open backs supported by V-braces, bootjack feet, Pennsylvania, early 19th c., 15½ x 46¾", 4' 11" h. (ILLUS.) 1,495.00

Mission-Style Hall Bench

Hall bench, Mission-style (Arts & Crafts movement), oak, a slightly arched crestrail above six wide splats between stiles & open arms over a rectangular lift-seat above a compartment, original black finish, branded mark of the Limbert Furniture Co. Model No. 92, early 20th c., 17½ x 41¾", 41¼" h. (ILLUS.) 1,430.00

Modern style bench, upholstered steel, "Marshmallow" type, two rows w/nine round cushions across the back & seat, mounted on a steel frame w/straight narrow tubular legs, upholstered in bright orange fabric, designed by George Nelson for Herman Miller, ca. 1956, 30 x 51", 31" h. 9,200.00

Piano bench, oak, the rectangular top held by rounded raised rectangular ends w/cut-outs, the top supported by a stretcher w/exposed tenons, the ends joined by a similar stretcher below, w/partial paper label & red decal of Gustav Stickley, Model No. 217, ca. 1909, 12¾ x 36", 22" h. 2,530.00

Mission-Style Window Bench

Window bench, Mission-style (Arts & Crafts movement), oak, upright open ends w/through-tenons flanking a leather-upholstered rectangular seat w/tack trim, original dark finish, large red decal mark of Gustav Stickley, Model No. 178, ca. 1902, leg roughness, 18½ x 36", 26" h. (ILLUS.) 1,210.00

Window bench, Rococo, painted & parcel-gilt, rectangular upholstered seat flanked by out-curved scrolled supports, raised on scrolling leaf-carved legs joined by a scrolled X-stretcher centered by a foliate finial, Italy, mid-18th c., 95" l. 11,500.00

BOOKCASES

Art Deco bookcase, walnut & marble, inset rectangular grey & white marble top above configural case fitted w/two doors on the inset, w/a conforming plinth base, France, ca. 1930, 17¾ x 43¼", 41" h. 1,100.00

Chippendale Pine Bookcase

Chippendale bookcase, pine, two-part construction: the upper part w/molded pitched pediment centering a turned finial, a pair of hinged glazed doors below opening to brown-painted shelves; the lower section w/two pairs of hinged paneled doors opening to shelves, repairs & patches, Pennsylvania or New Jersey, 1780-1810, 14½" deep, 63" w., 7' 1" h. (ILLUS.) 5,175.00

Classical (American Empire) bookcase, mahogany, two-part construction: the upper part w/rectangular molded cornice above a pair of geometrically glazed cupboard doors enclosing shelves; the lower section w/a pair of paneled cupboard doors enclosing shelves, on paw feet headed by scrolls, New York, 1820-35, 14½ x 71", 8' 5½" h. 4,620.00

George III Bookcase

George III bookcase, mahogany, two-part construction: the upper section w/a rectangular top w/molded overhanging cornice above a pair of glazed doors w/Gothic arch molded mullions opening to a shelved interior; the projecting lower section w/a molded waist above a pair of brushing slides & two paneled doors opening to shelves, raised on a molded plinth, restoration to upper section, shelves later, England, late 18th c., 22½ x 65", 8'7½" h. (ILLUS.) 10,450.00

Hepplewhite country-style bookcase, walnut, a rectangular top w/a flaring molded cornice above a pair of tall 8-pane glazed doors opening to shelves above two pairs of short drawers across the base, raised on tall French feet, slightly curved apron, early 19th c., 12¾ x 63", 7' ¼" h. (minor pieced repairs) 4,620.00

Lifetime Open Bookcase

Mission-style (Arts & Crafts movement) open bookcase, oak, a three-quarter gallery w/rounded sides on the rectangular top w/outset front corners over brackets above the case w/three adjustable open shelves, slightly arched apron, paper label of the Lifetime Furniture Company, some restoration to the original dark finish, 12 x 44", 4' 4" h. (ILLUS.) 990.00

Mission-style (Arts & Crafts movement) bookcase, oak, a deep three-quarter gallery on the rectangular top over a pair of 6-pane glazed cupboard doors opening to shelves, flat apron, through tenons w/keys in the sides which continue to form low arched feet, original medium finish & black-finished metal hardware, red decal mark of Gustav

Gustav Stickley Bookcase

Stickley, Model No. 525, ca. 1901, two panes replaced, interior molding strip repair, 11¾ x 39", 45" h. (ILLUS.) 6,900.00

Mission-style (Arts & Crafts movement) bookcase, oak, rectangular top w/low flat gallery above a set of three 9-pane glazed doors opening to three shelves, recent dark finish, replaced back, paper label of the Lifetime Furniture Co., 12½ x 61½", 4'7" h. 1,650.00

Mission-style Book Rack

Mission-style (Arts & Crafts movement) book rack, oak, wide upright end boards w/rounded cut-out top handles flanking a top V-form shelf & a flat lower shelf, low cut-out end feet, keyed tenon construction, water marks, tenon split, red decal mark of Gustav Stickley, Model No. 74, ca. 1907, 10 x 30", 31" h. (ILLUS.) 660.00

Modern style bookcase, grey lacquered wood, the upright terraced form composed of six irregular open shelves, some w/tubular brushed

Modern Style Wood & Steel Bookcase

steel supports, Paul Frankl, 20th c., 12 x 36", 5' 9½" h. (ILLUS.) 7,475.00

Victorian Aesthetic Movement Bookcase

Victorian bookcase, Aesthetic Movement substyle, inlaid rosewood, the rectangular top above a floral-inlaid & paneled frieze, w/three floral carved glazed doors w/floral inlaid lower sections, each door flanked by a floral panel, raised on a plinth base, formerly architecturally fitted, stamped "HER... BRO'S," Herter Brothers, New York, third quarter 19th c., 69" w., 5' 6" h. (ILLUS.)....25,300.00

Victorian bookcase, Renaissance Revival substyle, carved & burl walnut, the stepped top w/three arched crests each carved w/full-figure allegorical figures, angels & Liberty Bells above a three-section case w/arched & glazed doors separated by turned columns above a stepped-out lower case w/a tall arch-paneled cupboard door flanked by smaller arched doors below small drawers, each door separated by

Unusual Renaissance Revival Bookcase

pilasters w/lion-head capitals & acanthus leaf bases, molded base, Philadelphia, ca. 1876 (ILLUS.) ..14,300.00

Renaissance Revival Bookcase

Victorian bookcase, Renaissance Revival substyle, walnut & burl walnut, a tall center section w/a rectangular hipped top above a burl band over a tall glazed door w/a carved top crest & flanked by narrow burl panels & buttons, two lower side sections w/glazed doors flanked by burl panels above a conforming base w/three paneled drawers on the molded base, ca. 1875 (ILLUS.) 2,300.00

BUREAUX PLAT

Louis XV bureau plat, mahogany, the rectangular top inset w/a leather writing surface, each side fitted w/a leather-lined writing slide, the front w/two frieze drawers, raised on square tapered legs ending in gilt metal *sabots*, France, last quarter 18th c., 25½ x 51", 30½" h...........5,750.00

Louis XV-Style bureau plat, gilt-bronze mounted tulipwood, the rectangular top w/a leather writing surface above three frieze drawers, the central one recessed, raised on cabriole legs, complete on all sides & the whole fitted w/gilt-bronze masks at the knees & ends, foliate escutcheons, hoof feet, bail handles & borders, France, late 19th c., 56" l., 30" h................................11,500.00

Louis XVI Bureau Plat

Louis XVI bureau plat, ormolu-mounted mahogany, the shaped rectangular top w/rounded corners & an inset leather writing surface within an ormolu cabochon & leaf-tip border above one frieze drawer flanked by two short drawers on one side & one deep drawer fitted w/a safe simulating two short drawers on the other, all flanked by fluted pilasters, the sides fitted w/leather-lined writing slides, raised on round tapering fluted legs headed by berried laurel capitals & ending in thimble *sabots*, the drawer fronts & sides fitted w/ormolu leaf-tip borders, fitted w/oval ribbon-tied keyhole escutcheons, France, last quarter 18th c., alterations, 27¼ x 51¾", 29¼" h. (ILLUS.).....21,850.00

CABINETS

China cabinet, Mission-style (Arts & Crafts movement), oak, rectangular top w/plate rail above a pair of glazed cupboard doors opening to adjustable shelves, arched toe board, original dark finish, unmarked Limbert Company, Model No. 1464, 15½ x 48", 4'8" h..........................1,540.00

China cabinet, Mission-style (Arts & Crafts movement), rectangular top w/three-quarter gallery above a single 16-pane glazed door, sides

Gustav Stickley China Cabinet

w/four panes in each side, three fixed shelves, marked w/paper label of Gustav Stickley, 13 x 35¾", 4' 10¼" h. (ILLUS.) 3,850.00

Stickley China Cabinet

China cabinet, Mission-style (Arts & Crafts movement), oak, a rectangular top above a pair of tall glazed doors, each w/six small panes above a large single pane, the sides w/the same glazing, arched aprons, white decal mark of L. & J.G. Stickley w/"The work of L. & J.G. Stickley," Model No. 746, 16¼ X 44", 5' 1¾" h. (ILLUS.) 3,220.00

China cabinet, Victorian Golden Oak style, a D-shaped top w/outset center section w/an ornately carved shell & scroll crest above a conforming case w/curved glass sides & a

Golden Oak China Cabinet

curved glass center door, four interior shelves, on four ball-and-claw feeton casters, ca. 1900 (ILLUS.)...........11,400.00

Louis XVI Revival Cabinet

China cabinet, Victorian Louis XVI Revival style, giltwood, the D-shaped top w/ornate arched crests carved w/rose clusers & leaf bands separated by two scroll-carved finials above a conforming case w/a palmette-carved frieze band above curved glass sides flanking a long curved glass door, each section separated by a slender reeded column w/acanthus-carved capitals & bases, three interior glass shelves, the rounded base band carved w/large florettes, a leafy scroll-carved central apron drop, four turned tapering reeded legs, American-made, late 19th c. (ILLUS.) 3,300.00

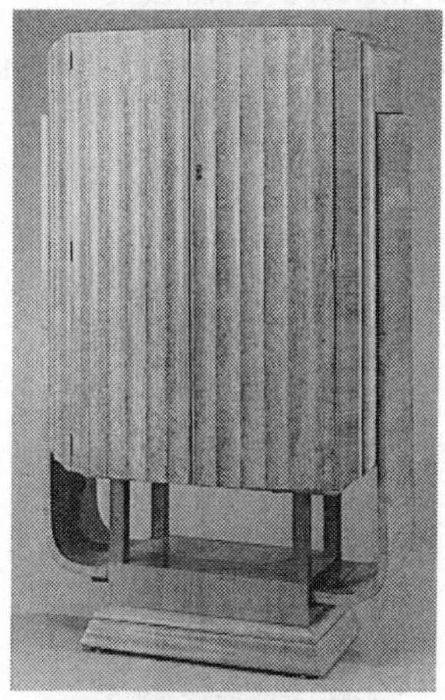

Art Deco Liquor Cabinet

Liquor cabinet, Art Deco, burled wood, the upright rectangular cabinet w/a pair of tall fluted doors opening to a mirrored fitted interior, raised on a U-form support above a molded base, England, ca. 1930, 19 x 41", 5' 7½"h. (ILLUS.) 3,680.00

Mission Oak Liquor Cabinet

Liquor cabinet, Mission-style (Arts & Crafts movement), oak, square sliding top opening to retractable bottle rack above a small drawer above a paneled cabinet door opening to a fitted shelf, original dark finish, unsigned, ca. 1910, 18¾" w., 30" h. (ILLUS.) 402.50

Music cabinet, Art Deco, mother-of-pearl inlaid mahogany, the shaped rectangular top above a single door in burled veneer & set w/a center panel inlaid w/stylized mother-of-pearl blossoms & opening onto a shelved interior, above two short

Art Deco Music Cabinet

drawers, raised on tapering paneled front legs, Louis Majorelle, France, ca. 1920, 17½ x 17¾", 47½" h. (ILLUS.) 4,888.00

Meeks Music Cabinet

Music cabinet, Victorian Rococo substyle, carved rosewood, rectangular top w/low pierced scroll-carved gallery above a beaded cornice above large door w/needlework panel, pierced scroll-carved sides, beaded base band, raised on Y-form scroll-carved end legs on a trestle base, J. & J.W. Meeks, New York, ca. 1840-50 (ILLUS.) 5,720.00

Side cabinet, Art Nouveau, carved walnut, breakfront-style, arched rectangular top above cut-out supports dividing three mirrored panels, the center w/a floral-carved crest, above open shelves above a

Art Nouveau Side Cabinet

wide outset center section w/a rectangular mirror above a curved marble top above two curved drawers over a pair of curved cupboard doors, side cabinets flanking w/floral-carved panels above half-round glazed doors opening to shelves, molded apron w/short bracket feet, Diot, France, ca. 1900, 23 x 73½", 7' 3⅝" h. (ILLUS.) 4,140.00

Gallé Vitrine Cabinet

Vitrine cabinet, Art Nouveau, inlaid mahogany & satinwood, rectangular top w/molded edge inlaid w/poppy flower buds, top overhangs a long door w/the upper section in glass above a delicately inlaid panel of poppies in blooms, each side composed of 12 square panels of burled satinwood each inlaid w/a spent poppy blossom & falling petals, engraved "Emile Gallé – Nancy," France, ca. 1900, 16⅛ x 24", 4'5"h. (ILLUS.) 2,990.00

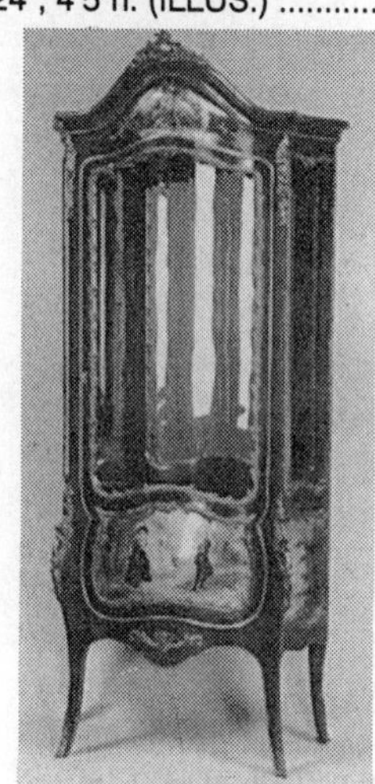

'Verni Martin' Vitrine

Vitrine cabinet, Louis XV-Style, 'Verni Martin' type, the oblong top w/a high arched front w/floral-carved crest above a conforming case w/glass sides & a curved glass *bombé* door, sides & door each w/lower panels decorated in the Verni Martin style w/scenes of landscapes w/lovers in 18th c. dress, serpentine apron w/scrolled ormolu center mount, slender tapering cabriole legs w/ormolu mounts, 19th c., 15 x 32", 5' 10"h. (ILLUS.) 2,200.00

CHAIRS

Art Nouveau Armchair

Art Nouveau parlor armchairs, heavy ornately carved curved frame, the wide crestrail carved w/sinuous Art Nouveau figures & blossoms & vines, flowering vines continuing down the arms to the short cabriole legs w/knob feet & across the seatrail, Karpen Furniture Co., early 20th c., pr. (ILLUS. of one) 5,280.00

Arts & Crafts Hall Chair

Arts & Crafts style hall chair, oak, a tall shield-shaped flat back w/a spade-form cut-out above the angular seat over flat shaped & canted solid legs w/inverted heart cut-out & bracket feet, tenon & key rungs from front to back leg, Limbert Company Model No. 80 (ILLUS.).....880.00

Wright-Designed Side Chair

Arts & Crafts style side chair, oak, a tall upright square back w/nine slender square spindles between square stiles & continuing down past the back edge of the rectangular upholstered drop-in seat, square front legs, H-stretcher, designed by Frank Lloyd Wright in collaboration w/George M. Niedecken-Wallbridge for the Avery Coonley House, Riverside, Illinois, ca. 1908, 36" h. (ILLUS.) 8,050.00

Thonet Bentwood Rocker

Bentwood lady's rocker, Jungenstil, the curved cut-out 'spindled' back between turned stiles continuing down to form base brace, oblong bentwood ovals form the arms & rockers, original finish, remnants of paper label of Thonet, Austria, early 20th c., 32"h. (ILLUS.) 1,980.00

Early American country-style child's ladder-back armchair, a pair of slightly arched slats in the back between heavy turned stiles w/elongated knob finials, rod arms from stiles to front posts w/knob finials continuing to form front legs, box stretchers, woven paper fiber seat, good turned detail, refinished, 24½" h...522.50

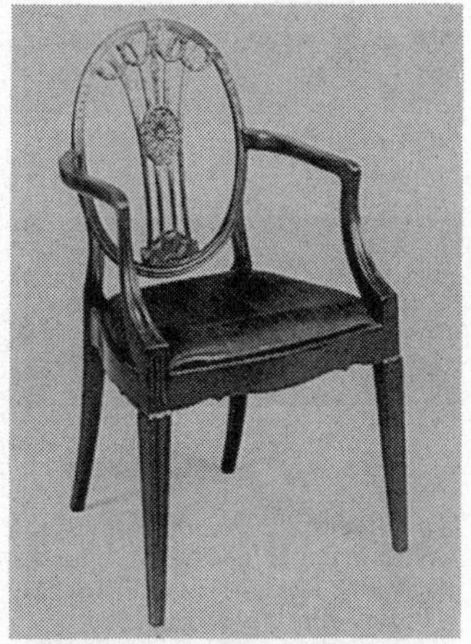

Federal Mahogany Armchair

Federal armchair, carved mahogany, the oval back centered by a pierced carved splat w/bellflowers, fans, swags & flowerheads, above shaped leaf-carved arms, the serpentine seatrail enclosing a slip seat on molded square tapering legs, prob-ably Maryland, ca. 1795, patches & repairs (ILLUS.) 3,450.00

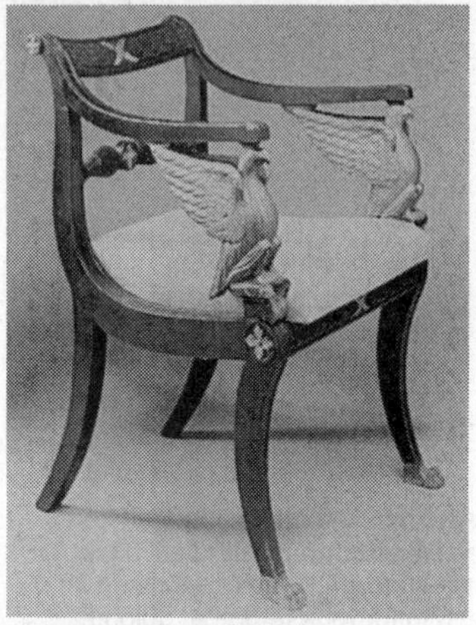

Federal Eagle-Carved Armchair

Federal armchair, mahogany, the slightly curved paneled crestrail carved w/water reeds above an acanthus- and flowerhead-carved lower back rail, the molded arms w/arm supports in the form of a gilded squatting eagle, the acanthus-carved seatrail enclosing a removable slip seat, on acanthus-carved & molded down-curving legs ending in front brass animal paw feet, probably Philadelphia, ca. 1805 (ILLUS.) 20,700.00

Federal Barrel-Back Wing Chair

Federal 'barrel-back' wing armchair, mahogany, the tall barrel-back w/rounded top upholstered & tufted into wide vertical bands, short upright outward scrolling arms, bowed seat, on square tapering molded front legs ending in spade feet, New York, ca. 1800 (ILLUS.) 29,900.00

Federal *bergere* (open-arm armchair), carved rosewood, the sloping crest above continuous arms that terminate in scrolled handholds over concave continuous arm supports, on gadroon-carved & tapering cylindrical front legs & sabre rear legs, w/casters, Boston or New York, 1800-15, 21¼" w., 35½" h...9,900.00

Federal "lolling" armchair, mahogany, the tall upholstered back w/slightly arched crest above open molded arm terminals & supports, wide upholstered seat on turned & reeded legs, probably Maryland, ca. 1815, 47" h. (minor imperfections)..........2,860.00

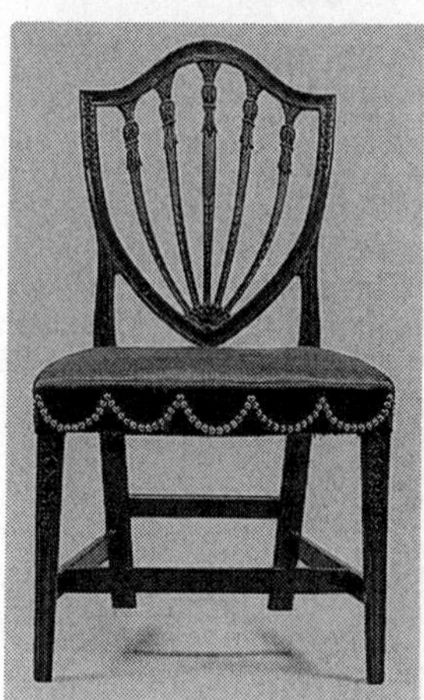

Federal Shield-Back Side Chair

Federal side chair, carved mahogany, the molded shield back w/carved trailing flowerettes along the upper stiles containing five reeded & foliate-carved banisters above an over-upholstered seat w/bowed front rail, on molded square tapering legs w/trailing flowerettes, joined by H-stretchers, Salem, Massachusetts, 1790-1810, 18¾ x 21¾", 37¾" h. (ILLUS.) 3,300.00

George III library armchairs, mahogany, curved serpentine back & seat upholstered in pale yellow embroidered floral silk, the arm supports carved w/trailing foliage, on straight chamfered legs joined by stretchers, w/brass casters, England, third quarter 18th c., restorations, partly re-railed, pr. 16,500.00

Louis XV *fauteuils a la reine* (open-arm armchairs), cartouche-shaped upholstered backrest carved w/flowerheads & leaftips, padded armrests raised on molded voluted supports, the serpentine-fronted seat carved to match the backrest & raised on cabriole legs carved at the knees w/flowerheads ending in leaf-carved toes, upholstered in multicolored foliate *gros point* needlework (worn), France, pr. (restorations) 12,650.00

Louis XVI-Style Armchairs

Louis XVI-Style *fauteuils a la reine*, carved wood, the squared upholstered back w/ribbon & floral carved frame over scrolled, padded arms above the squared upholstered seat w/a bowed seatrail on turned & fluted tapering legs, France, late 19th c., 38" h., pr. (ILLUS.) 2,640.00

Mission-Style Billiard Chair

Mission-style (Arts & Crafts movement) billiard chair, oak, a curved crestrail above five vertical slats in the raised back, flat curved arms on arm supports w/corbels continuing to form the front legs, shaped saddled seat, square wood inlay on the back stiles, tall legs w/double upper rungs & lower foot rest, original finish, some wear to foot rest, branded mark of the Limbert Company, 19¾ x 26", 45" h. (ILLUS.) 2,700.00

Mission-style (Arts & Crafts movement) child's armchair, oak, the back w/three horizontal slats flanked by square stiles continuing to form back legs, flat arms on square setback arm supports continuing to form front legs, single wide stretcher at front & back, two narrow side stretchers, square dark leather seat, Gustav Stickley red decal mark, Model No. 344, ca. 1909, 26" h. 552.00

Mission-style (Arts & Crafts movement) 'Cube' armchair, oak, the back w/fifteen square spindles & the even arms each w/sixteen spindles, cream-colored leather-upholstered cushions, Gustav Stickley Model No. 391, 26 x 27¾", 29⅛" h. 8,625.00

Limbert Dining Chairs

Mission-style (Arts & Crafts movement) dining chairs, oak, double flat crestrail above three flat vertical slats flanked by square stiles, shaped seat, square legs joined by single stretcher front & back & double stretchers on sides, original medium finish, branded mark of Limbert Company, Model No. 1921, ca. 1910, 17¼" w., 38" h., set of 6 (ILLUS. of two) 1,980.00

Mission-style (Arts & Crafts movement) Morris chair, oak, upright adjustable back w/four slats above flat arms on flat arm supports continuing to form front legs, wide

Limbert Morris Chair

side stretchers in base, arched front apron, medium finish, branded Limbert Furniture Company mark, back hinge damage, water staining on arm, no back cushion, ca. 1907, 28½" w., 37½" h. (ILLUS.) 2,990.00

'Paddle-Arm' Morris Chair

Mission-style (Arts & Crafts movement) Morris chair, paddle-arm type, oak, the upright adjustable back w/four slats above wide flat arms above corbels & arm supports forming the heavy square legs, worn original leather seat, original medium finish, unsigned L. & J.G. Stickley, Model No. 412, ca. 1910, 35" w., 41" h. (ILLUS.) 5,462.50

Mission-style (Arts & Crafts movement) rocker w/arms, oak, flat crestrail over five vertical slats, shaped flat arms over corbels over

Charles Stickley Rocker

five vertical slats, reupolstered seat, original medium finish, unsigned Charles Stickley, 28¼" w., 36½" h. (ILLUS.) 489.00

Gustav Stickley Rocking Chair

Mission-style (Arts & Crafts movement) rocking chair w/arms, oak, a V-form crestrail above seven slender tapering vertical slats in the raised back, leather-upholstered cushion seat, notched seatrail & notched arm supports continuing to form front legs, original dark finish, unsigned Gustav Stickley, Model No. 2555, ca. 1900, replaced cushion, 27½" w., 38" h. (ILLUS.) 2,640.00

Mission-style (Arts & Crafts movement) rocking chair without arms, oak, low upright back w/curved-top crestrail over five vertical slats, worn leather seat upholstery, original light - medium finish, Handcraft decal of L. & J.G. Stickley, Model No. 821,

Armless Mission Rocker

ca. 1907, dry, toned finish, 19¾" w., 31" h. (ILLUS.) 258.50

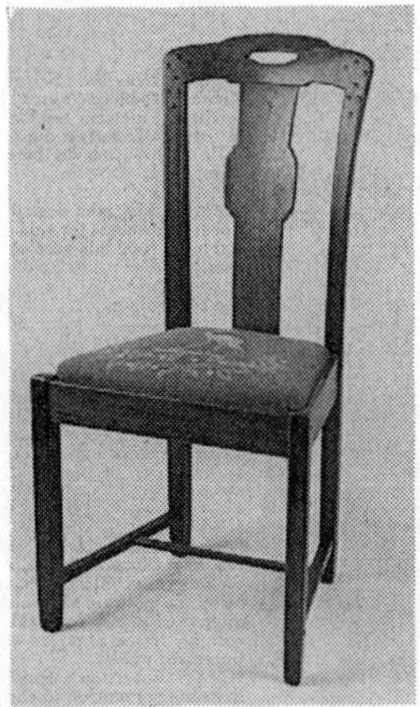

Greene and Greene Side Chair

Mission-style (Arts & Crafts movement) side chair, mahogany, a stepped & slightly arched crestrail pierced w/a hand-hole & w/ebony splines & square pegs into the out-curved stiles, a flat shaped splat above the inset upholstered seat, slightly tapering square legs joined by an H-stretcher, designed by Greene & Greene & executed by the workshop of Peter Hall for the D.B. Gamble House, Pasadena, Cali-fornia, ca. 1908, restoration, abrasion,19⅝" w., 39" h. (ILLUS.) 9,900.00

Mission-style (Arts & Crafts movement) side chairs, oak, a slightly arched crestrail above six tapering vertical slats in the raised back above the upholstered seat, arched

Mission-Style Side Chairs

seatrail over chair braces joined to the square legs joined by an H-stretcher, original medium finish, Handcraft Furniture decal of L. & J.G. Stickley, Model No. 324, ca. 1907, 18½" w., 38¼" h., set of 3 (ILLUS. of two).............................1,092.00

Fiberglass "Petal" Chair

Modern style "Petal" armchair, molded fiberglass, molded as a stylized large orchid blossom, the cream fiberglass shell seated on a circular white-painted metal base, designed by Erwine Laverne, ca. 1950s, 22 x 46", 4'2"h. (ILLUS.) 1,035.00

Modern "Mushroom" Chairs

Modern style "Mushroom" chairs, woven wicker on a rattan frame, round w/sloped top to dished interior, natural finish, designed by Eero Aarnio, decal label & manufacturer's stamp, ca. 1965, minor abrasions, 32" d., 26" h., pr. (ILLUS.) 550.00

Eames DCW Chair

Modern style side chairs, "DCW"-type, molded plywood, oblong curved back panel raised above the curved panel seat, on flat tapering canted legs, painted black, designed by Charles & Ray Eames, made by Herman Miller Evans Product Division, designed ca. 1946, pr. (ILLUS. of one) 1,610.00

"MR 10" Side Chair

Modern style side chairs, chrome & cord, "MR 10"-type, cantilevered tubular chrome frame strapped w/white plastic-coated cord on seat & back, designed by Ludwig Mies Van Der Rohe, ca. 1927, made by Bamberg Metallwerkstatten, ca. 1931, pr. (ILLUS. of one) 805.00

Modern style side chair, painted aluminum & cloth, red-painted aluminum frame w/round back panel

Wright-Designed Side Chair

raised on two supports continuing to form back legs, each conjoined to the seat by five curved stretchers, the circular sliding seat raised on a curved stretcher & circular front legs ending in stepped foot, upholstered in orange wool fabric, designed by Frank Lloyd Wright for the S.C. Johnson Wax Administration Building, Racine, Wisconsin, 1936 (ILLUS.) 13,800.00

Molesworth Armchair

Molesworth armchair, upholstered fir, heavy fir canted stiles flanked the slick yellow upholstery panel back h.p. w/a military insignia, flat upholstered arms w/hammered brass Oxford tack trim raised on fir post supports above the curved upholstered seat, turned fir post legs joined by an H-stretcher, ca. 1948, 18 x 24½", 35½" h. (ILLUS.) 750.00

Queen Anne corner chair, maple, the U-shaped back above two vase-

Queen Anne Corner Chair

form splats centering ring-turned uprights, the molded seatrail enclosing a rush seat on a frontal cabriole leg ending in a pad foot joined by a turned X-form stretcher,New England, ca. 1760 (ILLUS.) 4,025.00

Regency Dining Chair

Regency dining chairs, beech, each armchair w/reeded bobbin-turned top rail above a pierced rectangular paneled backrest mounted w/a gilt-metal flowerhead within oak leaf foliage & acorns, flanked by down-scrolling arms centering a black horsehair-upholstered loose-cushioned caned seat, raised on sabre legs, first quarter 19th c., six armchairs & six side chairs, minor repairs, set of 12 (ILLUS. of one armchair) 24,150.00

Revival Style side chair, mahogany, a scroll-cut & arched crestrail w/mahogany veneer above a wide vase-form splat w/crotch-grain mahogany veneer flanked by slender carved & tapering stiles w/knob finials above a paper woven rush seat (replaced) above a shaped front apron & cabriole front legs ending in claw-and-ball front legs joined by a swelled H-stretcher to the square canted rear legs, early 20th c., 36¾" h. (refinished)..........................137.50

Victorian armchair, Rococo substyle, carved & laminated rosewood, the wide, curved back ornately pierce-carved w/foliate scrolls incorporating dolphins' head, open scrolled arms above the upholstered seat, cabriole legs, ca. 1850, attributed to John Henry Belter, New York, 45" h. 1,100.00

Victorian "horn" armchair, the crest, arms & legs composed of curled horns, reupholstered in black leather, late 19th c., 21" deep, 29½" w., 41" h...............................467.50

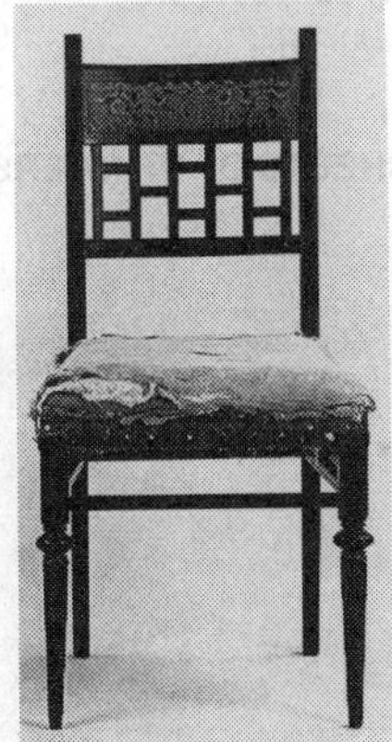

Victorian Aesthetic Side Chair

Victorian side chairs, Aesthetic Movement substyle, ebonized & inlaid wood, flat slightly curved crestrail w/inlaid stylized florals above a band of trellis flanked by square backswept stiles, rectangular upholstered seat, tapering turned front legs joined to rear legs w/high stretchers w/cut-out band at each side of the seat, Herter Bros., New York, late 19th c., pr. (ILLUS. of one)..13,200.00

Victorian parlor side chairs, Rococo substyle, carved & laminated rosewood "Cornucopia" patt., the high balloon back w/wide arched pierce-carved crest & sides w/scrolls & flower-filled cornucopias surrounding the upholstered panel, upholstered seat of serpentine seatrail w/carved flowers at center &

Victorian Rococo Side Chair

legs, on casters, attributed to John Henry Belter, ca. 1850, pr. (ILLUS.) 9,900.00

CHESTS & CHESTS OF DRAWERS

Victorian Apothecary Chest

Apothecary chest, Victorian, mahogany, rectangular top w/molded edge overhanging a case w/five rows of four drawers, each drawer w/an inset wooden knob pull, molded base w/bracket feet, by Parnall & Sons Shop Fitters, Narrow Wine St., Bristol, England, mid-19th c., 11 x 50", 30" h. (ILLUS.) 2,300.00

Blanket chest, child's, Federal country-style, walnut, rectangular stepped hinged top w/molded edge opening to a well w/till, two cockbeaded small drawers at the bottom, molded base on knob feet w/pointed ends, probably Lancaster County, Pennsylvania, ca. 1815, 9¾ x 20¼", 16" h. (ILLUS. top next column) 1,725.00

Early Child's Blanket Chest

Blanket chest, country-style, painted poplar, the hinged rectangular top w/applied edge molding opening to a compartment fitted w/a till, on bracket feet, original salmon grey paint, Darke County, Ohio, origin, 17¾ x 37", 19¾" h............................440.00

Blanket chest, Federal country-style, painted & decorated pine, rectangular top w/molded edge opening to a well, the front decorated w/large scrolling leafy branches w/blossoms flanking a rectangular panel inscribed "Mary Becht" above a small house flanked by trees done in polychrome on an orangish red ground, a lower molding above three molded overlapping drawers above the molded base on scrolled bracket feet, overall orangish red ground, Pennsylvania, ca. 1805, 23 x 51", 28" h. (feet & base molding replaced) 8,050.00

Blanket chest, painted & decorated walnut, poplar & maple, rectangular top w/molded edges opening to a deep well w/till, double panels on the front decorated w/yellow graining, the framing decorated overall w/reddish brown flame graining, on slender turned legs ending in ball feet, found in Troy, Ohio, 19th c., 16¾ x 43½", 25½" h.....................1,100.00

Blanket chest, Pilgrim Century, carved oak, the rectangular molded top opening to a well w/till, the front of the case comprising three rectangular inset panels w/carved stylized foliate curves & fleur-de-lis, a single drawer below, on ball feet, attributed to John Thurston, Medfield, Massachusetts, ca. 1685, 20 x 49½", 32" h. (top, feet & drawer restored) 3,163.00

Chippendale "block-front" chest on

Chippendale Chest-on-Chest

chest, carved mahogany, two-part construction: the upper section w/a bonnet top w/a molded swan's-neck cresting centering three spirally-turned finials above three small drawers, the deep center one fan-carved, over four long graduated drawers flanked by fluted pilasters; the lower section w/four long graduated blocked drawers above the molded base & scroll-cut bracket feet, the molded base centering a small fan-carved drop pendant, Boston, Massachusetts, ca. 1770, alterations to bonnet, skirt pendant replaced, minor foot repairs , 21 x 42", 7' 8¾" h. (ILLUS.)........................21,850.00

Chippendale chest-on-frame, walnut, two-part construction: the upper section w/rectangular top w/overhanging molded cornice above a row of three small drawers over five long graduated thumbmolded drawers flanked by quarter columns; the lower section w/mid-molding above a flattened-arch scroll-cut skirt w/central trefoil pendant, on cabriole legs w/carved shell at knees & trifid feet, apparently original butterfly brasses, Pennsylvania, 1760-80, 22½ x 43½", 5' 10½" h. 16,100.00

Chippendale chest of drawers, cherry, rectangular top w/thumb-molded edges above a case w/four long graduated drawers flanked by quarter-round colonettes at the corners, a molded base raised on ogee bracket feet, replaced simple bail pulls, late 18th c., 20½ x 41¾", 35¼" h. (feet renailed, filled crack in one end).......................................2,640.00

Classical Chest of Drawers

Classical (American Empire) chest of drawers, rectangular white marble top above a conforming case w/one long drawer over three graduated long drawers flanked by columns w/brass capitals & bases, on cylindrical & disc front feet, New York, 1830-40, 24 x 49¾", 42¾" h. (ILLUS.) 3,080.00

Empire (American) chest of drawers, painted poplar, rectangular top above four graduated drawers w/white porcelain pulls, flanked by half-round baluster- and ring-turned pilasters, paneled ends, on double knob turned feet, original red flame graining, 21¼ x 40½", 4' ¼" h. (minor wear).................................1,100.00

Federal "Bow-Front" Chest of Drawers

Federal "bow-front" chest of drawers, cherry, the rectangular top w/bowed front w/inlay along front & side edges above a conforming case w/four graduated long drawers over a molded base on shaped bracket feet w/spur returns, New England, 1790-1810, 22½ x 42¾", 34¼" h. (ILLUS.) 2,530.00

Federal "bow-front" chest of drawers, mahogany, the rectangular top w/rounded front corners, bowed front & reeded edge over a conforming case w/three graduated cockbeaded long drawers between crossbanded dividers, on ring-turned tapering legs w/paw feet, New York, 1790-1810, 20¾ x 36½", 37½" h. 13,200.00

Federal Inlaid Chest of Drawers

Federal chest of drawers, curly maple-inlaid birch, rectangular top above four long, graduated cockbeaded drawers w/oval inlaid panels, the shaped skirt continuing to shaped tall French feet, New England, ca. 1820, minor repairs, 18¾ x 41", 37" h. (ILLUS.) 2,645.00

Federal chest of drawers, mahogany, the rectangular top over a conforming case fitted w/four graduated long drawers w/cockbeaded surrounds flanked by inset fluted quarter columns over a shaped skirt w/line inlay, on French feet, probably Connecticut, 1790-1810, 18½ x 41", 37½" h. 3,300.00

Federal country-style chest of drawers, painted & decorated pine, rectangular top over a case w/four reverse graduated drawers, on bracket feet, shaped apron, the drawers painted to simulate an exotic wood w/faux mahogany crossbanded edges, the case marbleized in blue, New England, ca. 1810, 17½ x 40¾", 38½" h......4,313.00

George III "serpentine front" chest of drawers, satinwood & rosewood, the serpentine top centered by an oval panel above a conforming case w/four graduated long drawers, the uppermost fitted w/a sliding tray & various compartments w/central ratcheted mirror, on bracket feet,

George III "Serpentine Front" Chest

England, late 18th - early 19th c., 23 x 46", 35" h. (ILLUS.) 7,700.00

Hadley chest-over-drawers, carved oak, the rectangular hinged overhanging top above a conforming case decorated w/carved stylized floral motifs, the front w/three panels, the central panel carved w/the initials "S.S.," over two long drawers w/wooden pulls, the feet are continuation of the stiles, traces of red paint remain, Connecticut River Valley, Massachusetts, 1700-25, 20 x 46", 42¾"h. (feet pieced approximately 5", top pieced & reused from a blanket chest) 57,500.00

Hepplewhite country-style chest of drawers, walnut, a rectangular top above a case w/four long graduated drawers w/simple turned wood knobs & inlaid diamond keyhole escutcheons, a scalloped apron continuing into tall French feet, casters at the front feet, old worn refinishing, early 19th c., 19¾ x 39¾", 41¼" h. (some edge damage, old repair, top edge strips old replacements) 990.00

Hepplewhite country style chest of drawers, inlaid cherry, rectangular top w/an inlaid edge band of light & dark above four long graduated drawers flanked by front stiles w/line inlay, inlaid diamond keyhole escutcheons, another dark & light inlaid band above the scalloped apron, French feet, old mellow refinishing, early 19th c., replaced oval brasses, feet ended-out w/replaced brackets, 20½ x 38¾",43¼" h. (ILLUS. top next column) 2,200.00

Hepplewhite Chest of Drawers

Chestnut Chest of Drawers

Mission-style (Arts & Crafts movement) chest of drawers, chestnut, a three-quarter gallery on the rectangular top above a pair of small drawers over three long graduated drawers, all w/wood knobs, flat apron, flush mortises on the sides, original dark finish, unmarked Gustav Stickley, 21 x 36", 45½" h. (ILLUS.) 1,430.00

Mission-style (Arts & Crafts movement) chest of drawers w/mirror, oak, a large rectangular-framed mirror swiveling between bracketed uprights above the rectangular top above a pair of small drawers over two deep long drawers, all w/hammered copper plates & ring pulls, slightly arched apron, paneled sides, original medium-light finish, unmarked L. & J.G. Stickley, 21 x 42", 5'7" h. (ILLUS.) 2,530.00

Chest of Drawers with Mirror

Mission-style (Arts & Crafts movement) tall chest of drawers, oak, a rectangular top over a pair of paneled doors opening to cedar-lined cabinets over a pair of small drawers over three long graduated drawers, all w/painted wrought-iron plates & ring pulls, red decal mark of Gustav Stickley, Model No. 614, ca. 1902, 23½ x 46", 5' 1⅞" h. 24,150.00

Mule chest (box chest w/one or more drawers below a storage compartment), Federal country-style, painted & decorated pine, the rectangular top opening to a deep well above two long drawers at the bottom, drop-paneled apron, raised on high bracket feet, original reddish brown flame graining w/a pair of opposing "arches" on the top front, the drawers w/white edge banding, round brass pulls on drawers, found in New Hampshire, early 19th c., 17 x 40½", 37½" h. (replaced brasses, rehinged top, locks & escutcheons removed, minor damage).......................................1,430.00

Queen Anne country style tall chest of drawers, maple w/pine sides, rectangular top w/molded edge above two short drawers over four graduated long overlapping drawers, high bracket feet, replaced engraved brasses, 17¼ x 38¼", 4' 2¾"h...4,180.00

Queen Anne tall chest of drawers, figured walnut, rectangular top w/molded cornice above three short drawers above two short drawers over three graduated long

Queen Anne Tall Chest

drawers, on short cabriole legs ending in trifid feet, Pennsylvania, 1740-70,22½ x 41¾", 5' 1"h. (ILLUS.) 4,313.00

Sheraton tall chest of drawers, cherry & curly maple w/inlay, rectangular top above a case w/two short drawers over two graduated long drawers over a pull-out shelf above a short drawer flanked by two smaller drawers over a long drawer, the drawers w/curly maple veneer w/walnut cross banding & applied beading, paneled ends, scalloped apron, turned feet, 20½ x 40", 50¼" h. (feet ended out) 3,190.00

William & Mary Chest

William & Mary chest of drawers, inlaid walnut, the rectangular overhanging top w/geometric line-inlaid decoration above a conforming case w/two line-inlaid small drawers over three graduated line-inlaid long drawers above a molded base, on block feet, Pennsylvania, 1720-40, 23 x 38½", feet restored, 35½" h. (ILLUS.) 41,800.00

William & Mary chest of drawers, painted oak & pine, the rectangular molded top above four paneled drawers, the sides & case each w/four inset panels above a base molding, on flattened ball feet, painted w/swirls & triangles in brown on a golden-yellow ground, New England, 1700-30, 24½ x 41", 40" h. (feet & some case moldings replaced) 5,750.00

CRADLES

Early Heart-Decorated Cradle

Country-style low cradle on rockers, painted walnut, canted sides w/simple step-down from the headboard, hand-holds cut at the center of the sides, flat tops on head- & footboards, old dark greenish black paint, 19th c., 36½" l. (age crack in one end) 247.50

Country-style low cradle on rockers, painted cherry, wide canted stepped sides w/heart cut-outs & canted rounded ends w/heart cut-outs, on wide rockers, old worn red paint, 42" l. (age cracks, nailed edge repairs) 302.50

Country-style low cradle on rockers, poplar, the canted stepped sides w/cut scrolls & hand-holds dove-tailed to the canted ends, the higher headboard w/a rounded top, on shaped rockers, old worn dark finish, 19th c., 42" l. 275.00

Suspended swing-type cradle, decorated chestnut & cherry, the cradle w/canted dovetailed sides fitted w/six metal rocking knobs, heart-pierced end uprights on an arched base joined by double medial transverse, Pennsylvania, 1780-1800, 39" l., 27" h. (ILLUS.) 5,750.00

Ornate Giltwood Cradle

Suspended swing-type cradle, giltwood, formed as a stylized shell w/silk upholstery within foliate giltwood bands, the U-form support headed by cherubs above ornate carved floral drops, raised on a scroll-carved & baluster-turned trestle base, Europe, late 19th c., losses, 48" l., 4' 3" h. (ILLUS.) 5,175.00

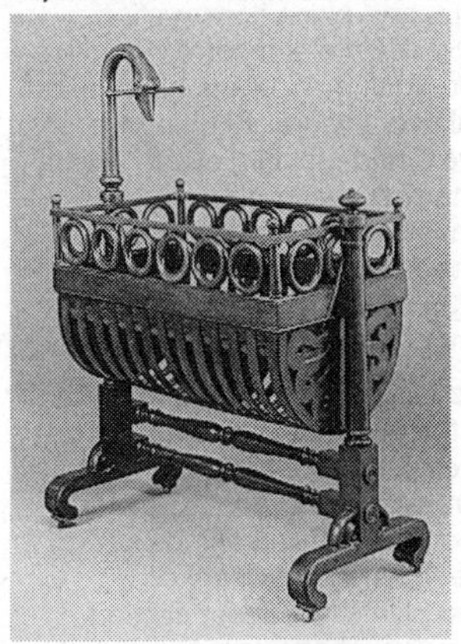

Charles X Era Cradle

Suspended swing-type cradle, mahogany, deep cradle w/a pierced band of circles above flat slat band sides suspended between turned uprights, a swan's head arched finial at one end, on a trestle base w/double baluster-turned stretchers, Charles X period, France, second quarter 19th c. (ILLUS.) 8,050.00

CUPBOARDS

Chippendale Corner Cupboard

Corner cupboard, Chippendale, walnut, the molded dentil-carved cornice above a pair of arched glazed doors opening to a green-painted interior, fluted pilasters flanking, a pair of hinged paneled doors below opening to a cream-painted shelved interior, the molded base on bracket feet, New Jersey or Pennsylvania, ca. 1795, 21 x 49½", 7' 11" h. (ILLUS.) 5,463.00

Corner cupboard, country-style, walnut, one-piece construction, the flat top w/a deep slightly flaring & stepped cornice above a pair of long paneled doors opening to shelves above a thin medial molding above a pair of short paneled doors, raised on high block feet, 47¾" w., 6' 11½" h. (some edge damage)......................................2,090.00

Corner cupboard, Federal style, cherry, one-piece construction, the molded projecting cornice above a twelve-pane glazed cupboard door opening to an interior fitted w/shelves, each shelf w/a plate groove, above a pair of raised-panel cup-board doors opening to a shelf, shaped scroll-cut apron, the sides forming front feet, Pennsylvania, first quarter 19th c., 27½ x 55¼", 7' 5½" h. (ILLUS. top next column)..4,025.00

19th Century Federal Corner

Federal Corner Cupboard

Corner cupboard, Federal, curly maple, two-part construction: the upper section w/a simple molded coved cornice above a single 12-pane glazed cupboard door opening to a green-painted shelved interior w/plate grooves; the lower section w/a pair of paneled cupboard doors opening to shelves, front sides forming feet, probably New York or Pennsylvania, ca. 1820, 23½ x 45", 7' 4¾" h. (ILLUS.)........................10,925.00

Corner cupboard, Federal, walnut, two-part construction: the upper section w/a molded & reeded cornice above a pair of glazed 8-pane cupboard doors opening to a red-painted shelved interior w/plate grooves; the lower section w/a pair of hinged double-paneled doors opening to shelves, shaped skirt, on slightly flared bracket feet, Pennsylvania or Middle Atlantic States, ca. 1810, 29½ x 51¾", 7' 5½" h. 5,225.00

Grain-Painted Corner Cupboard

Corner cupboard, Federal country-style, grain-painted, one-piece construction, the flat top w/a heavy molded cornice above a pair of long paneled doors opening to shelves above a medial band over a pair of paneled cupboard doors, heavy bracket feet, overall grain-painted finish, probably Ohio, ca. 1820, minor imperfections, 18 x 44", 6' 9¼" h. (ILLUS.).........................1,760.00

Corner cupboard, Queen Anne, walnut, one-piece construction, the top w/a molded cornice above a pair of tall, narrow double raised-panel doors w/brass H-hinges above a mid-molding over a pair of tall, narrow raised-panel doors w/brass H-hinges, scroll-cut bracket feet, Pennsylvania, ca. 1760, 21 x 35", 6" 10¼" h. (feet slightly extended) 20,700.00

Court cupboard, two-part construction: the upper section w/projecting cornice & dentil frieze mounted w/corbels above a recessed canted cupboard w/applied spindles & hinged central door flanked by turned pillars; the lower section w/one drawer above two paneled cupboard doors, feet continuous w/stiles, all decorated w/crease molding, Cambridge, Massachusetts, 1680-1700, 23 x 48⅞, 4' 8½" h. (applied ornament on doors, drawers & panels missing in part).......................................68,500.00

Painted Pine Hanging Wall Cupboard

Hanging wall cupboard, painted & decorated pine, the molded cornice above a hinged glazed door opening to shelves, the shaped & scrolled shelf below, the sides decorated w/small hex signs, retains traces of orange, yellow & green paint, Pennsylvania, ca. 1780, 13 x 31", 36½" h. (ILLUS.) 5,750.00

Hanging wall cupboard, inlaid walnut, a pitcher classical molded pediment centering an urn-form ivory finial & ivory corner button finials over a hinged door w/a narrow band of herringbone inlay framing a rectangular beveled mirror w/another inlaid edge band, a narrow drawer below the door w/two inlaid ivory diamonds flanking an inlaid keyhole escutcheon & small ivory knob, molded base banding, American-made, ca. 1890, 16¼" w., 25¾" h. 920.00

Hanging wall cupboard, pine & tulip poplar, a rectangular top w/a deep flaring molding above a single double paneled door w/rattail hinges opening to shelves & above a stepped-back narrow open shelf w/a scalloped top edge & scroll-cut sides, Pennsylvania, second half 18th c., 11½ x 22¾", 36" h. 10,925.00

Hanging wall cupboard, Queen Anne, walnut, a rectangular top w/molded cornice above a single hinged raised panel door w/rattail wrougt-iron hinges opening to shelves, two small drawers at the bottom w/shaped, raised panels, small pendants at lower front corners, some loss to lower pendant, Pennsylvania, 1750-70, 14 x 33", 39½" h. (ILLUS. top next column) 3,450.00

Queen Anne Hanging Wall Cupboard

American Empire Jelly Cupboard

Jelly cupboard, American Empire country-style, decorated walnut & poplar, two-part construction: the upper section w/a rectangular top above a large paneled cupboard door; lower section w/medial band above a single long, deep drawer w/wooden knobs, on short baluster-turned legs w/knob feet, decorated w/original dark reddish brown flame graining, inside door w/stenciled label "Jah. Hart Jan. the 4, 1847," base 24 x 39", overall 4'11¾" h. (ILLUS.) 1.705.00

Jelly cupboard, Federal, painted tulip poplar, the rectangular top w/shaped splashboard above two drawers & a pair of paneled cupboard doors opening to removable shelves on turned feet, painted apple green, Pennsylvania, ca. 1825, 20 x 42¼", 47½" h. (ILLUS. top next column) 4,313.00

Federal Painted Poplar Jelly Cupboard

Jelly cupboard, painted pine, rectangular top w/cove molded cornice above single paneled door, simple cut-out feet, old grey paint, cornice 17 x 38½", 5' 2" h. (minor edge damage)....................................880.00

Jelly cupboard, walnut, a rectangular top w/a narrow cove-molded cornice above a pair of tall paneled doors w/original brass thumb latch w/porcelain knob over a single long drawer, scalloped apron continuing to tall, slender front legs, simple turned wood drawer knobs, old dark alligatored finish, 19th c., 19 x 46¾", 5' 8½" h.......................1,540.00

Linen press, Chippendale, cherry, two-part construction: the upper section w/rectangular molded cornice above a pair of paneled cupboard doors enclosing three shelves, flanked by reeded quarter columns; the lower part w/molded waist over three graduated long drawers & a molded base, on bracket feet, Pennsylvania, 1780-1800, 19 x 46¾", 6' 5½" h.............7,700.00

Linen press, Federal, mahogany, two-part construction: the upper section w/a rectangular top over a cornice w/dentil molding above a pair of inlaid & banded cupboard doors; the lower section w/a mid-molding above a case w/three long, graduated drawers w/bail handles, molded base on bracket feet, probably New York, 1780-1810, restoration to veneer, 22½ x 45" (ILLUS. top next column) 4,600.00

Pewter cupboard, country-style, walnut, one-piece construction, the rectangular top w/a narrow flaring cornice above beaded framing

Federal Linen Press

board around the open cupboard w/three shelves above a stepped-out lower section w/a pair of raised panel cupboard doors, flat base, good old finish, 19th c., 22 x 47", 7' 2" h. (some edge damage & missing moldings) 2,530.00

Step-Back Pewter Cupboard

Pewter cupboard, step-back country-style, pine, one-piece construction, a rectangular top w/a narrow molded cornice above an open case w/three shelves & plate guards above a stepped-out lower case w/a pair of flat cupboard doors mounted w/H-hinges, wide angled bracket feet, New England, late 18th c., 6' 6" h. (ILLUS.)..............................1,430.00

Pie safe, cherry & poplar, rectangular top slightly overhanging a case w/two doors, each w/five punched tin panels w/a circle & star design, five conforming panels in each end, on low square legs, found in Indiana, top 17 x 39½", 5' 9½" h. (tins have traces of old paint & several have rust damage) 1,595.00

Tin & Pine Pie Safe

Pie safe, pine & pierced tin, a rectangular molded top above a rectangular case w/tin sides punched & pierced w/various designs including sunbursts, animals & humans on the front & stars & hearts on the sides, one side inscribed "Centennial Safe - G.H. Reed - 1876," Pennsylvania, 26 x 32½", 35½" h. (ILLUS.) 4,025.00

Pie safe, walnut w/poplar secondary wood, rectangular top w/breadboard ends over a case w/two small drawers over two hinged doors w/three punched tin panels depicting a horse & rider between two trees in each, tins retain old worn green paint, doors are on pintel hinges & are removable, simple cut-out feet, attributed to New Bremen, Ohio, 19½ x 52", 4' 8½" h. (breadboard ends replaced) 10,450.00

Pie safe, yellow pine, a flat rectangular top overhanging a pair of very tall cupboard doors each fitted w/two large rectangular punched tin panels w/a four-arm star & bull's-eye design above a pair of shorter paneled doors over a simple scalloped apron, old varnish finish, King and Queen, Virginia origin, 20 x 44", 6' 5½" h. 880.00

Step-back hutch cupboard, Chippendale, walnut, the rectangular top w/a narrow molded cornice above five wide vertical beaded tongue-and-groove backboards fronted by two open shelves w/double-beaded & rounded outer edges, each w/a double-beaded dish retainer above & flanked by shaped cut-out sides

Chippendale Hutch Cupboard

above the stepped-out lower case w/three short drawers above two fielded-panel cupboard doors opening to a common interior w/one shelf, on low bracket feet, Pennsylvania, 1750-1800, 18½ x 61", 7' 5" h. (ILLUS.)..........................15,400.00

Step-back wall cupboard, child's, painted poplar, one-piece construction, rectangular top w/narrow cornice molding above a pair of paneled cupboard doors w/turned wood knobs above an open pie shelf over the stepped-out base w/two paneled cupboard doors w/wood knobs, slightly arched apron, old red paint, 19th c., 24" h. (some repair & replaced moldings) 495.00

Step-back wall cupboard, country-style, walnut, two-piece construction: the upper section w/a rectangular top over a narrow flaring cornice above a pair of 6-pane glazed cupboard doors, each pane w/a curved mullion & opening to two shelves above an open pie shelf; the lower stepped-out section w/a pair of shallow drawers above a pair of raised-diamond paneled doors above a molded base raised on short bracket feet, old worn dark varnish finish, interior w/old green paint, early 19th c., 20¾ x 51¾", 7' 1¼" h. (brass hardware old replacement, wear & some edge damage, crack in one drawer & one pane).....................................8,250.00

Wall cupboard, country-style, painted & decorated pine, a flat rectangular top above flat sides flanking four open & backless shelves above a slightly stepped-out lower case w/a row of three small drawers w/wooden knobs above two pairs of graduated longer drawers, the framework decorated w/mustard yellow wood-graining, the drawer fronts w/burnt sienna mahogany wood-graining, New England, ca. 1820, 14⅛ x 61", 5' 11¼" h. 3,850.00

Early Pine Cupboard

Wall cupboard, country-style, painted pine, rectangular top w/a narrow molded cornice above a pair of hinged triple-paneled doors opening to shelves, molded base, the stiles forming feet, painted green, probably Canada, second half 18th c., two upper side moldings replaced, 23 x 54", 6' 6" h. (ILLUS.) 4,888.00

Wall cupboard, country-style, walnut, one-piece construction, a rectangular top above a widely flaring deep cornice above a pair of long double-paneled doors opening to shelves above a thick, rounded medial molding over a pair of paneled cupboard doors above short bracket feet, old cast-iron thumblatch on lower door, 19¼ x 47½", 7' 1" h. (replaced latch on lower doors, wear, edge damage) ...990.00

Wall cupboard, Federal country-style, painted & decorated walnut, one-piece construction, the rectangular flat top above a pair of cupboard doors each w/four panes of glass over a rectangular panel opening to shelves above two lower paneled doors opening to shelves, grain-painted overall, probably Middle Atlantic states, early 19th c., 16 x 47½", 6' 4¼" h. 1,100.00

DESKS

Anglo-Chinese "partners" desk, rosewood, the rectangular top w/scalloped edge & outset sections over three frieze drawers to each side interspersed w/stylized anthemia, each pedestal w/five drawers to each side flanked by carved flowerheads & arrows, on a scalloped plinth, China, third quarter 19th c., 37½ x 64", 32¾" h. 6,050.00

Art Deco desk, bronze inlaid, *ebene de Macassar,* the gently arched rectangular top inlaid w/bronze stringing, raised on pedestal ends, each w/a single door opening to four sliding shelves, the backs of each pedestal rounded, raised on canted plinths, the edges w/bronze surrounds, attributed to Dubre Lafon, France, ca. 1930, 29 x 75", 29" h. 8,625.00

Art Deco desk, carved & inlaid, the large rectangular top fitted w/leather writing surface above one long drawer, flanked by shorter drawers, supported on tapering cylindrical legs, the drawers w/inlay of ivory & mother-of-pearl, Maurice Dufrene, France, 31 x 58", 30" h. 3,680.00

Art Deco Fall-Front Desk

Art Deco fall-front desk, rosewood & parchment, rectangular top above a cabinet w/a parchment-covered fall-front opening to a sycamore-fitted interior, raised on rectangular column supports w/flaring rectangular feet, Maurice Dufrene, France, ca. 1930, 10½ x 34¾", 46"h. (ILLUS.) 5,175.00

Art Deco partner's desk, mahogany, rectangular top w/side extensions raised on double-sided pedestals w/four drawers on each side flanking kneehole drawers, the drawers set w/nickled-bronze cylindrical pulls, ca. 1930, w/glass top, 47 x 58¼", 31" h. 2,070.00

Art Nouveau desk, gilt-bronze-mounted mahogany & rosewood, "Aux Nénuphars," the rectangular top inset w/a tooled leather writing surface above two small drawers flanking a long center drawer over the kneehole flanked by side cabinets w/paneled doors, long gilt-bronze lily pad stems, leaves & blossoms down each corner, foliate handles, Louis Majorelle, France, ca.1900, 29 x 59", 31" h. 40,250.00

Art Nouveau desk, mahogany & gilt-bronze, the shaped rectangular top w/embossed leather writing surface, fitted w/two drawers w/elaborate gilt-bronze floral drawer pulls, surmounted by three drawers w/gilt-bronze floral drawer pulls, all supported on four curved tapering legs, the front legs w/carved buttress supports, Louis Majorelle, France, 31 x 53½", 39" h. 20,125.00

Chippendale serpentine-front desk, carved mahogany, narrow rectangular top above a hinged slant front opening to a stepped interior w/small compartments & drawers, above a serpentine-fronted case w/four graduated long drawers, ball-and-claw feet, probably original batwing brasses, Massachusetts, ca. 1770, 22 x 41½", 43" h. 9,350.00

Chippendale Slant-Front Desk

Chippendale slant-front desk, carved cherry, a narrow rectangular top above the rectangular hinged molded lid opening to an interior fitted w/valanced pigeonholes over small drawers centering a shell-carved prospect door opening to a pull-out prospect section revealing three secret drawers, fluted shell-carved document drawers flanking, all above four graduated molded long drawers flanked by fluted quarter-columns down the sides, on ogee bracket feet, Lancaster County, Pennsylvania, ca. 1780, 21¾ x 43", 46" h. (ILLUS.) 9,775.00

Classical Gentleman's Desk

Classical (American Empire) gentleman's desk, mahogany, two-part construction: the upper section w/rectangular white marble top above conforming top over scrolled supports resting on a marble slab above two blind doors opening to a compartment flanked by columns w/brass capitals & bases; the lower section w/marble top above a hinged butler's drawer which pulls out & opens to expose a fitted interior w/baize writing surface & two stacked end drawers centering an arched compartment flanked by document drawers above two blind doors opening to reveal two shelved compartments flanked by columns w/brass capitals & bases, on cylindrical disc front feet, New York, 1830-40, minor losses to veneer, 22 x 36¾", 53¾" h. (ILLUS.) 7,700.00

Country-style table-top desk, decorated butternut & poplar, rectangular slant lid opening to a compartment fitted w/pigeonholes, dovetailed case w/applied base molding, old red flame graining repaint, 31" sq., 25½" h. 220.00

Federal desk-on-stand, mahogany, a rectangular case w/a wide fold-down writing surface opening to reveal a well & three short drawers w/ivory pulls above an apron fitted w/a single cockbeaded drawer w/turned knobs, on turned reeded swelled legs in brass socket casters, Boston, Massachusetts, 1800-10, 19⅞ x 28⅞", 37" h. 3,680.00

Federal "fall-front" desk, mahogany, two-part construction: the upper section w/a rectangular top above a hinged double-paneled fall-front opening to a felt-lined writing surface backed by a pair of shelves over three small drawers; the lower section w/a rectangular top over a pair of cockbeaded short drawers w/round brass florette & ring pulls, on round reeded tapering legs ending in paw feet, New York, ca. 1810-25, 23¾ x 32", 5' ¼" h. 5,280.00

Federal Lady's Writing Desk

Federal lady's writing desk, mahogany, the rectangular top w/hinged out-folding writing slab, the interior fitted w/three short drawers & two hinged compartments, over a conforming case w/one long drawer, on four ring-turned & reeded swelled & tapering cylindrical legs w/swelled & tapered cylindrical feet, Massachusetts, 1800-15, 17¾ x 29", 33½" h. (ILLUS.) 1,650.00

George II architect's desk, mahogany, formed as two kneehole bureaux, one w/a hinged ratcheted rectangular top enclosing a pop-up section w/drawers & pigeonholes, the front w/a simulated long drawer, w/a drawer to the side, the other bureau w/molded rectangular top above a frieze drawer fitted w/a baize-lined slide, the kneeholes flanked by cupboard doors enclosing tiers of drawers w/numbered escutcheons, the ends w/hinged cupboard doors, on ogee bracket feet, England, ca. 1740, 87" w., 32" h. 22,000.00

Lifetime Furniture Desk

Mission-style (Arts & Crafts movement) desk, oak, the rectangular top above heavy legs w/through-tenons flanking a small cabinet w/paneled door beside a long drawer over a small deep drawer, all w/hammered copper hardware, the stretchers joined by a medial shelf, decal & paper label of the Lifetime Furniture Company, Model No. 927, ca. 1910, edge roughness, 30 x 54", 29½" h. (ILLUS.) 1,265.00

Gustav Stickley Desk & Chair

Mission-style (Arts & Crafts movement) desk, oak, flat rectangular top over an arrangement of a locking center drawer flanked by a pair of short drawers w/heavy copper hardware w/large oval pulls, paneled sides, together w/ladderback side chair w/tacked-on leatherette seat, original color, skinned finish, desk w/branded Gustav Stickley mark, Model No. 709, chair unmarked Model No. 306½, the set (ILLUS.) 2,200.00

Mission-style (Arts & Crafts movement) slant-front desk, oak, a narrow rectangular top above a pair of short 2-pane glazed doors above a hinged slant lid opening to a fitted interior above a pair of short drawers above a single long drawer, all drawers w/round copper ring pulls, raised on slender square legs joined by stretchers, brass tag of the Quaint Furniture Company, ca. 1908, 35" w., 4' 7" h. (refinished, escutcheon missing) 880.00

Small Writing Desk

Mission-style (Arts & Crafts movement) writing desk, oak, a high upright gallery w/boxed slots above the rectangular top over a narrow drawer w/small wooden knobs & raised on slender square legs w/thin stretchers, dark finish, unsigned, ca. 1910, gallery loss, replaced pulls, 19¼ x 28", 42" h. (ILLUS.) 144.00

Modern style desk, Macassar ebony & nickeled steel, the rectangular top over two narrow frieze drawers, raised on a slender angular steel frame, attributed to Adnet, France, ca. 1940, 25 x 66", 30" h. 2,070.00

Queen Anne "block-front" kneehole desk, carved mahogany, the oblong thumb-molded top above a blocked frieze drawer & two tiers of three blocked drawers centering a volute- and diamond-carved valance drawer & recessed paneled cupboard door, the molded base w/shaped pendant on bracket feet, Boston, Massachusetts, ca. 1760, 20 x 32¼", 29¼" h.(feet reduced)....................................21,850.00

Queen Anne slant-front desk-on-frame, painted maple, two-part construction: the upper section w/hinged molded lid opening to an interior fitted w/valanced pigeonholes over drawers, a single molded drawer below; the lower section w/shaped skirt on circular tapering legs ending in pad feet, Connecticut, ca. 1750, 17 x 32¾", 41½" h...25,875.00

Queen Anne slant-front desk-on-frame, red-stained hardwood,

Queen Anne Desk-on-Frame

narrow rectangular top above a slant-front opening to a fitted interior of valanced pigeonholes & stepped short drawers above a case w/four long graduated thumb-molded drawers w/batwing brasses, on a molded base w/short cabriole legs ending in pad feet, appears to retain original brasses, restorations to frame, New England, second half 18th c., 19 x 34½", 42¼" h. (ILLUS.) 4,620.00

Schoolmaster's desk, walnut, rectangular top w/three-quarter gallery overhanging a short apron w/single drawer, baluster- and ring-turned legs, refinished, 31¼ x 42", 29" h. plus gallery 715.00

William & Mary Table-Top Desk

William & Mary slant-front table-top desk, maple, narrow rectangular top above a hinged slant-lid w/molded edge opening to an interior fitted w/valanced pigeonholes over small drawers above a well w/a sliding lid, one long molded drawer below, molded base on flattened ball feet, patch to rear section of baseboard, Massachusetts, ca. 1720, 14¼ x 23", 20" h. (ILLUS.) 5,750.00

DINING SUITES

Modern Style Dining Suite

Art Nouveau: extension dining table & eight side chairs; "Chicoree," carved mahogany, the table w/rectangular top w/slightly swelled sides & molded edge, raised on four shaped molded legs w/carved buttressed supports, the matching chairs w/gently arched back rails raised above leaf-carved side supports enclosing a shaped cane panel, the shield-shaped cane seats on shaped legs carved w/conforming decoration, together w/two leaves, Louis Majorelle, France, ca. 1900, the table 46¾" w., extended 8' l., 30" h., 9 pcs. 23,100.00

Late Victorian: circular pedestal base table, mirrored breakfront, three-tiered server, glass-front china cabinet & one Chippendale-Style armchair & four side chairs; mahogany, the case pieces carved w/gargoyles & griffins w/scroll trim & on paw feet, ca. 1900, American-made, the set 11,550.00

Modern style: extension dining table & four side chairs; oak, the round table on four square tapering legs, the chairs each w/a rectangular back enclosing a simple splat w/diamond-shaped central section, the tapering rectangular seat upholstered in black leather w/a row of embossed nailheads around the edge, raised on square legs joined by stretchers, designed by Bruno Paul, made by Vereinigte Werkstatten F. Kunst I. Handwerk A.G., Berlin, Germany, marked, ca. 1910, table 47¼" d., 30¼" h., 5 pcs. (ILLUS.)...............2,475.00

DRY SINKS

Decorated poplar, hutch-style, the superstructure w/a pointed three-quarter gallery above a pair of short arched cupboard doors over three small drawers w/white porcelain knobs above cut-out sides above the wide zinc-lined well above a pair of large arched cupboard doors w/a cast-iron & brass thumb latch, wire nail construction, overall grain-painted decoration, late 19th c., 19 x 36", 6' 2¼" h.........................1,650.00

Painted pine, rectangular top, deep well over case w/central batten door w/replaced cast-iron latch, simple cut-out feet, traces of old blue paint, 24¾" x 44", 33¾" h. 440.00

Painted & decorated poplar, rectangular dovetailed well w/zinc liner above a wide board w/small drawer at right side over pair of paneled cupboard doors w/original cast-iron & brass thumb latches, simple cut-out feet, old worn oak graining over an earlier dark finish, 20 x 42", 35" h. (had hinged top) 555.50

Painted poplar & walnut, rectangular top well over a pair of paneled cupboard doors, old worn red repaint w/black "comma" graining & black door panels over darker blue, 19th c., 19 x 39¼", 36" h.................632.50

Pine, a small rectangular work surface at each end flanking the long well & over two small drawers w/wooden knobs above a pair of raised panel cupboard doors set in reeded frames, center drop in apron, on simple cut-out feet, old mellow refinishing, interiors & well painted blue, 19th c., 22 x 58¾", 32" h. 935.00

Poplar, hutch-style, the raised superstructure w/a low crestrail above a narrow shelf over a recessed open shelf flanked by small square end drawers all above the long rectangular zinc-lined well above a pair of paneled cupboard doors flanked by small square drawers at the ends, scroll-cut bracket feet, old dark finish, late 19th c., 21½ x 61¾", 4' 3" h. 2,200.00

Poplar, hutch-style, the superstructure w/shaped sides & high shelf above work surface at one end above a small drawer beside the rectangular well over two paneled doors, on simple cut-out feet, old replaced cast iron thumb latch, refinished, 20¾ x 48¼", 4' 6" h......................1,375.00

GARDEN & LAWN FURNITURE

(Cast iron unless otherwise noted)

Armchair, the back & arms cast w/berried oak leaves, the arm supports topped by animal heads w/animal-form legs, painted white (ILLUS.) 2,645.00

Armchairs, back composed of pierced lyre design flanked by florals, old white repaint, 32" h., pr...440.00

Armchairs, the back w/interlacing ferns continuing to scrolled arms, the seat of pierced scrolls, raised on scrolling legs, pr.......................8,050.00

Bench, aluminum, Fern patt., 55" l. 805.00

Bench, three-chairback style, center crestrail cast w/an ornate medallion over a pierced scrolling design, flanked by lower similarly decorated crestrails above matching scrollwork, old white repaint, 46" l....544.50

Bench, the back composed of roundels above a wooden slat seat, painted finish, 76" l.........................1,150.00

Ornate Garden Bench

Bench, three-chairback style, center high crestrail over an ornate lacy pierced design, flanked by lower crestrails above a scrolling pierced design, stamped "Peter Timmes Son, Brooklyn, N.Y.," late 19th c. (ILLUS.) 1,150.00

Chair, crestrail cast w/an ornate medallion over a pierced scrolling design, seat w/center medallion w/label "Mfg. by the Kramer Bros. Fdy. Co. Dayton, O," old worn white repaint, 36" h...................................440.00

Chair, the half-round base supporting a tall hooded upper section, composed of horseshoes, painted white 690.00

Oval-Back Garden Chairs

Chairs, oval back centered w/the figure of a boy, overall w/a pierced scrolled design, raised on scrolled legs headed by masks, second half 19th c., set of 4 (ILLUS. of two) 2,875.00

Garden suite: bench & armchair; aluminum, the bench comprised of interlacing flowers, the armchair w/a back composed of lily of the valley blossoms, bench 39" l., 2 pcs. 460.00

Garden suite: settee & two armchairs; Fern patt., 3 pcs.............................1,380.00

Garden suite: settee & two armchairs; each w/a fern-molded back & strapwork-scrolled seat on shaped legs, New York, possibly the Fiske or Mott foundries, 1870-1900, 3 pcs. 4,025.00

HALL RACKS & TREES

Hall rack, Art Deco, wall-type, wrought iron, a rack of bars across the top raised above a rectangular open framework centered by a rectangular beveled mirror within a hammered frame w/pierced scrolls at the upper corners & flanked by pierced narrow panels of stylized

Art Deco Wall-Mounted Hall Rack

leaves & scrolls above pairs of hooks, stamped "Mouchet," France, ca. 1925, 8 x 33½", 24" h. (ILLUS.) 1,840.00

Hall rack, wrought iron, the three-square section upright supports mounted at the top w/a circular ring set w/coat hooks, a lower circular ring also set w/coat hooks, mounted on a hexagonal base, Continental, ca. 1915, 31¼" w., 6' 5¼" h. 920.00

Large Art Deco Hall Rack

Hall rack, Art Deco, wrought iron, double-sided, the rectangular tall mirror plates w/canted upper corners flanked by openwork sections wrought w/scrolling coat hooks, the lower section w/umbrella compartments, raised on scrolling feet, attributed to Paul Kiss, ca. 1925, 25½ x 59", 6' 11" h. (ILLUS.) 4,025.00

Hall tree, Classical (American Empire), carved & painted pine, the slender baluster- and ring-turned columnar standard fitted w/angular turned Windsor-style arms, gilt-painted ball finial, supported on arched well-carved animal paw feet w/gilded acanthus leaf carving, painted brownish green w/gilt trim,

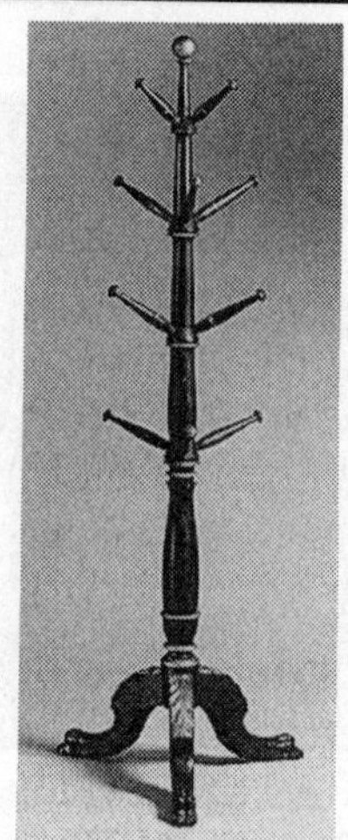

Early Classical Hall Tree

New York state, mid-19th c., 5' 4¼" h. (ILLUS.) 1,265.00

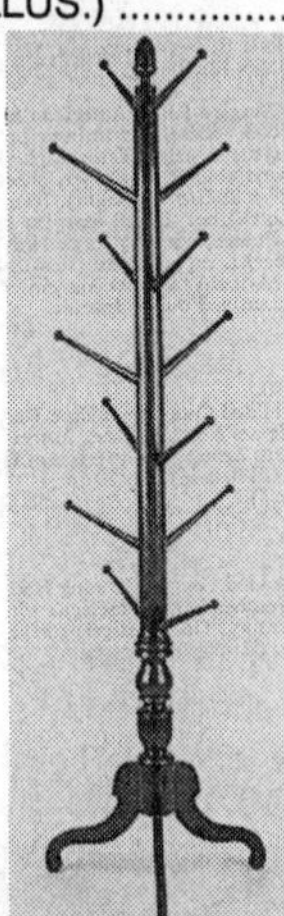

Federal Hall Tree

Hall tree, Federal, turned maple, the tall columnar standard topped w/an acorn finial & fitted w/14 slender knob-ended arms above the ring- and baluster-turned column base raised on a tripod base w/S-scroll feet, New England, 1820-30, 5' 10½" h. (ILLUS.) 1,320.00

Hall tree, turned wood, slender central post w/two groups of three turned wood spindles, on four turned splayed legs, old worn green paint, 5' 8" h. 220.00

HIGHBOYS & LOWBOYS

Highboys

Chippendale "flat-top" highboy, figured walnut, two-part

Chippendale Highboy

construction: the upper section w/molded cornice above three short drawers over two short drawers above three long graduated molded drawers; the lower section w/one long & three short molded drawers, the shaped skirt below continuing to cabriole legs ending in claw-and-ball feet, Pennsylvania, ca. 1765, 23¾ x 44⅛", 6' 7¼" h. (ILLUS.) 10,350.00

Queen Anne "Bonnet-Top" Highboy

Queen Anne "bonnet-top" highboy, cherry, two-part construction: the upper section w/a broken-arch closed bonnet top w/three flame-turned finials above a pair of small drawers flanking a deep central shell-carved drawer above a case of four long graduated drawers w/pierced batwing brasses; the lower section w/a stepped mid-molding above a long drawer over a row of three drawers, the smaller central drawer shell-carved, scalloped apron w/two acorn-turned drops, simple cabriole legs ending in pad feet on discs, refinished, old replaced brasses, Litchfield, Connecticut, 18th c., 18½ x 38½", 6' 10½" h. (ILLUS.) 41,250.00

Queen Anne "flat-top" highboy, carved cherry, two-part construction: the upper section w/molded cornice w/canted corners above two short stacked drawers centering a fan-carved drawer over four graduated drawers all thumb-molded & flanked by canted fluted pilasters above an applied mid-molding; the lower section w/mid-molding above two long drawers over three short drawers, the center drawer carved w/a shell, all thumb-molded above a serpentine & lobed skirt, flanked by canted fluted pilasters terminating in a lamb's-tongue, on cabriole legs w/slipper feet, appears to retain original hardware, Connecticut, 1740-60, 19½ x 42", 6' h. (pieced corner of first long drawer, break to one leg) 18,400.00

Queen Anne "Flat-Top" Highboy

Queen Anne "flat-top" highboy, curly maple, two-part construction: the upper section w/a rectangular top w/a molded cornice above a row of three small drawers over four long graduated drawers, all w/batwing brasses; the lower section w/a mid-molding over a long drawer above a pair of deep drawers flanking a short center drawer above the deep scalloped apron, cabriole legs ending in raised pad feet, New

England, 1750-70, patches to drawer fronts, mid-moldings replaced, 21 x 38", 6' h. (ILLUS.)..5,750.00

William & Mary Highboy

William & Mary "flat-top" highboy, walnut, maple & pine, three-part construction: the upper section w/a rectangular top w/a molded cornice above a row of three small drawers over three long graduated drawers w/batwing brasses; the lower section w/a mid-molding above a pair of cockbeaded deep drawers flanking a short cockbeaded center drawer, triple-arched cockbeaded apron on trumpet-turned legs joined by flat shaped stretchers & ending in turnip feet, Massachusetts, possibly Lynn, 1720-60, 21¾ x 39", 5' 7" h. (ILLUS.) 23,000.00

Lowboys

Philadelphia Chippendale Lowboy

Chippendale lowboy, carved & figured cherry, the oblong molded top w/notched front corners above three molded drawers, the shaped skirt below continuing to shell-carved cabriole legs ending in claw-and-ball feet, appears to retain two original brass handles, New York, 1750-65, overall 20⅜ x 34½", 28½" h. (small patch to one drawer lip) 18,400.00

Chippendale lowboy, figured walnut, rectangular top w/a thumb-molded edge & notched corners above a long drawer over a pair of small deep drawers flanking a short central drawer all flanked by fluted canted corners, the shaped skirt continuing to shell- and volute-carved cabriole legs ending in claw-and-ball feet, minor patches to drawer fronts, Philadelphia, ca. 1755, 19¾ x 33⅛", 29" h. (ILLUS.) 14,950.00

Chippendale-Style lowboy, carved mahogany, rectangular top w/molded edges & rounded front corners over a case w/a long narrow drawer w/pierced butterfly brasses above a pair of small square drawers flanking a larger central drawer w/ornate shell & leafy scroll carving, scalloped apron centered by a small carved shell & edge scrolls, cabriole legs w/leafy scroll-carved knees & ending in ball-and-claw feet, Philadelphia style, old reproduction, 20 x 34¼", 29" h......2,860.00

Queen Anne lowboy, inlaid walnut, the oblong top w/notched corners & line-inlaid border above one long & three short line-inlaid molded drawers, the shaped skirt below hung w/a pointed ball pendant continuing to angular cabriole legs ending in pointed slipper feet, Rhode Island or Coastal Connecticut, 1740-60, overall 21¼ x 31", 30" h. 57,500.00

Queen Anne lowboy, mahogany, the rectangular thumb-molded top above one long & three short molded drawers, the shaped skirt below w/turned acorn pendants continuing to angular cabriole legs ending in raised pad feet, appears to retain original brasses, pendants & finish, Boston, Massachusetts, 22⅛ x 36⅜", 30" h........................46,000.00

LOVE SEATS, SOFAS & SETTEES

Canapé (love seat), Second Empire, ormolu-mounted mahogany, the narrow rolled crestrail mounted w/decorative ormolu bosses above the two-panel upholstered back flanked by open arms raised on gilt sphinxes, the seatrail further

Second Empire "Canapé"

mounted w/ormolu bosses above three front legs headed by giltwood winged lions' heads & ending in gilt paw feet, France, late 19th c. (ILLUS.) 8,250.00

Chaise longue, Art Deco, giltwood, the outscrolled upholstered back continuing to the downscrolled upholstered seat, raised on short sabre legs, celadon & silver damask upholstery, ca. 1930, 61" l. 9,775.00

Chaise longue, Modern style, upholstery, laminated wood & metal, "Listen to Me," the curved channel upholstered seat & back raised on laminated wood legs, conjoined by circular rods & an x-form tension cable, designed by Edward Wormley, manufactured by Dunbar Furniture, ca. 1948, w/metal manufacturer's tag, 75" l. 5,175.00

Modern Style Chaise Longue

Chaise longue, Modern style, upholstery & walnut, biomorphic shape upholstered w/a mottled turquoise & cream square design wool fabric, on a walnut base w/four widely canted legs w/fluted feet, designed by Vladimir Kagan, 60" l., 32" h. (ILLUS.) 2,415.00

Chaise longue, Regency, gilt-stenciled & ebonized wood, the scrolled padded backrest & shaped side above a loose-cushioned seat, raised on square tapering splayed legs, overal gilt stenciled designs on

Regency Chaise Longue

the frame, on casters, England, ca. 1810, 51" l. (ILLUS.) 6,900.00

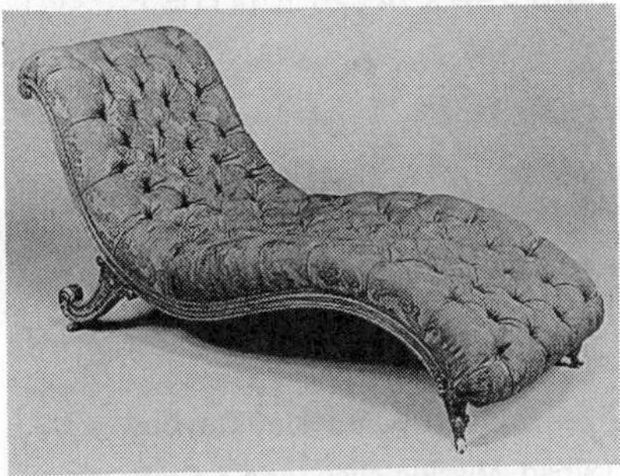

English Victorian Chaise Longue

Chaise longue, Victorian, the tufted-upholstered curvilinear seat on foliate-carved scrolled supports, England, mid-19th c., 69" l. (ILLUS.) 5,500.00

Daybed, Art Deco, "ebene-de-Macassar," the expanded U-form framework w/tapering end rails raised on large wedge-shaped feet, upholstered in peach brocade fabric, probably by Andre-Leon Arbus, France, ca. 1925, 31½" w., 90" l. ...7,475.00

Empire Iron Daybed

Daybed, Empire, silvered iron, the front rail cast w/a large rosette enclosed within spirals w/acanthus leaves & a laurel spray tapering to vitruvian scrolls cast w/berries, acanthus leaves & beading, raised on *toupie* legs, Europe, 19th c., 36 x 88½", 29" h. (ILLUS.) 6,900.00

Mission-Style Daybed

Daybed, Mission-style (Arts & Crafts movement), oak, square legs taller at one end & supporting angled brackets for the smaller cushion, the wide siderails w/elongated corbels at the headboard, leather cushions worn, corbel loss, retailer's label, ca 1910, 29½ X 74", 26" h. (ILLUS.).....330.00

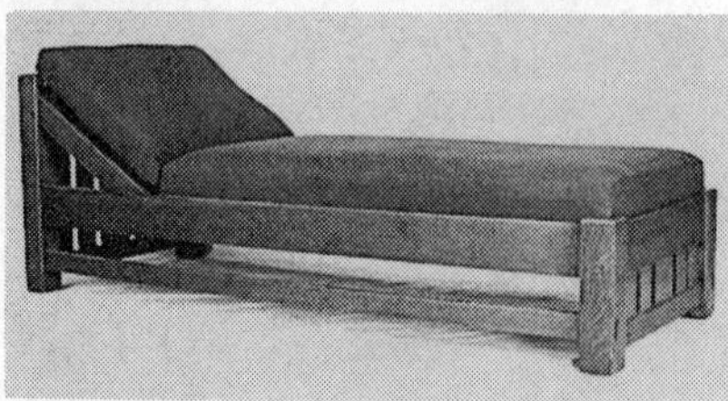

L. & J.G. Stickley Daybed

Daybed, Mission-style (Arts & Crafts movement), oak, headboard w/wide vertical slats supporting angled braces for the shorter cushion, the low footboard w/short slats, long rung below the siderails, original medium color, some loss of finish, decal label of L. & J.G. Stickley, Model No. 291, 30 x 76", 26" h. (ILLUS.) 1,100.00

Daybed, Modern style, painted wood, the black painted concave frame covered w/a hammock-style woven cord, supported by crossed tapering feet held together w/a stretcher, 1950s, 29 x 73", 20" h......................978.00

Daybed, Victorian country-style, turned maple, a narrow flat backrail above 15 simple turned spindles, turned backposts w/pointed finials, simple turned end arms on baluster-turned arm supports, slat seat w/cushion, turned legs, probably Southern, mid-19th c., old finish, 31" h. (imperfections) 345.00

Love seat, Art Nouveau, carved mahogany, the gently arched crestrail pierced & carved w/clematis vines & leafage continuing down to curved open arms continuing to form the front legs, the serpentine crestrail carved w/flowers & leafage, upholstered in dark satin fabric, Majorelle, France, ca. 1900, 51" l..6,900.00

Louis XV-Style Love Seat

Love seats, Louis XV-Style, carved & gilt walnut, the serpentine crestrail continuing to curved arms enclosing a three-section upholstered back surmounted by a carved ribbon & leafy dividing bands, the arms ending in a carved & gilt ram's head, loose long cushion above the serpentine seatrail w/suspended leafy swags, cabriole legs w/scroll feet, late 19th - early 20th c., 25 x 53", 38" h., pr. (ILLUS. of one) 1,650.00

American Classical Recamier

Recamier, Classical (American Empire), mahogany, the shaped & scroll-carved low back flanked by outswept arms of differing heights continuing down to the reeded seatrail, raised on legs headed by carved cornucopae & ending in heavy paw feet on casters, possibly by Anthony Quervelle, Philadelphia, ca. 1825 (ILLUS.)..........................7,700.00

Recamiers, Classical (American Empire), carved mahogany, each w/a molded scrolled back w/acanthus-carved crest flanked by outscrolled arms w/gadrooned convex seatrail on acanthus-carved legs ending in animal paw feet, on brass casters, Philadelphia, ca. 1825, 74" l., pr. (minor repairs) 6,038.00

Settee, Art Nouveau, two-chairback style, the framework carved w/clematis vines & blossoms, upholstered in deep geeen velvet, Louis Majorelle, France, 25" deep, 51½" l., 42" h. 3,450.00

Federal Country-Style Settee

Settee, Federal country-style, painted & decorated poplar, triple-back style w/the shaped crestrail above three wide pierced lyre-form splats flanked by S-scroll end arms on small spindles above the plank seat, raised on eight ring-turned legs joined by box stretchers, the crestrail, splats & seatrail painted w/stylized leaf & fruit clusters in polychrome on a tan ground w/black & yellow trim, Pennsylvania, ca. 1840, 72" l. (ILLUS.) 1,725.00

Settee, Federal country-style, painted & decorated, a wide flat crestrail supported on four stiles above a narrower slat rail, S-form end arms on two bobbin-turned spindles & a simple turned arm support, long plank seat on eight simple turned & canted legs joined by turned rungs, olive green paint w/dark stripings & stenciled floral decoration on the crestrail, probably Pennsylvania, ca. 1830, 16¾ x 72½", 33" h. (imperfections) 747.50

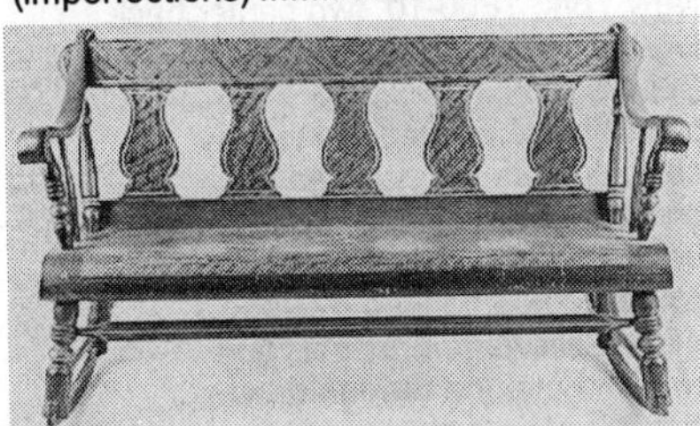

Early Decorated Settee on Rockers

Settee w/rockers, Federal country-style, painted & decorated, the wide flat crestrail above five vase-form splats flanked by baluster-turned stiles, S-scroll end arms above a spindle & ring- and knob-turned arm supports above the S-form plank seat, short ring-turned front legs joined by an arrow stretcher, integral rockers, burnt orange & black patterned graining outlined in gold striping on the crestrail & splats w/vinegar grained burnt orange graining & gold trimmed in black on the seat, natural maple arms, original finish, New England, ca. 1830-40, 50½" l., 29½" h. (ILLUS.) 9,900.00

Early Windsor Settee

Settee, Windsor, painted, the long slender U-form crestrail above numerous simple turned spindles & ending in canted baluster-turned arm supports above the simple shaped plank seat, raised on eight baluster- and ring-turned slightly canted legs joined by H-stretchers, Philadelphia area, 1760-80, 47" l., 28" h. (ILLUS.) 1,540.00

Settee, Windsor, the long U-shaped crestrail above 29 bulbous turned spindles, flat & shaped end arms above spindles & on canted baluster-turned arm supports above the long plank seat, on eight canted baluster-turned legs joined by shaped, turned stretchers, 1785-1810, 76½" l.........................5,463.00

Early English Settle

Settle, country-style, painted pine, the tall rectangular back w/four long panels flanked by shaped end arms on simple turned supports above the flat boxed seat w/central lift-lid, three panels in the front apron between the square legs, old orange, gold & dark green paint, surface imperfections, England 18th c., 52" l., 44" h...................................1,870.00

Settle, Mission-style (Arts & Crafts movement), even-arm type, oak, the crestrail over thirteen vertical slats & the even arms over five canted slats, brown leather-covered cushion seat & three back cushions, Gustav Stickley Model No. 173, 32¾ X 70", 38½" h. 17,250.00

L. & J.G. Stickley Settle

Settle, Mission-style (Arts & Crafts movement) oak, the long V crestrail above 12 vertical slats between stiles above the shaped flat arms over corbels & arm supports forming the front legs, upholstered cushion seat, original dark finish, Handcraft decal of L. & J.G. Stickley, Model No. 260, ca. 1910, 51¾" l., 38¼" h. (ILLUS.) 2,420.00

Sofa, Biedermeier, birch & flame veneer, straight crestrail w/ball finials, the high arms fronted by turned columns w/ebonized detail, Europe, 19th c., 33 x 84", 41½" h. 1,430.00

Sofa, Chippendale 'camelback,' mahogany, serpentine arched & canted back flanked by downward sloping & outward flaring scrolled arms above a straight seatrail, on tapering square molded legs joined by a medial stretcher, now on cast-ers, Philadelphia, 1765-85, 32 x 98", 38½" h. (feet slightly reduced, crest pieced) 19,800.00

American Classical Sofa

Sofa, Classical (American Empire), carved mahogany, the gadrooned flowerhead-carved curved crestrail flanked by outswept arms w/the fronts carved w/a stylized dolphin body, the molded seatrail on writhing sea serpent feet on brass casters, probably Philadelphia, ca. 1820, missing one rear caster, repair to left rear leg, 82" l. (ILLUS.) 2,185.00

Sofas, Classical (American Empire), carved mahogany, the paneled figured crestrail flanked by acanthus carving, the reeded seatrail raised on reeded sabre legs ending in brass animal paw feet, on brass casters, attributed to John Needles, Baltimore, Maryland, ca. 1825, 93" l., pr.......................................8,625.00

Federal Mahogany Sofa

Sofa, Federal, carved mahogany, the backswept crestrail centered by ribbon-tied drapery swags flanked by reeded rectangular panels over a padded back, the bowed seat flanked by reeded serpentine arms above turned tapering foliate-carved supports, on turned tapering reeded legs w/brass cup feet & casters, New York, 1800-10, two center back legs restored, 32 x 60", 36¼" h. (ILLUS.) 7,150.00

Sofa, Federal, carved mahogany cane-seated, the paneled flat crestrail carved w/three panels, the center panel w/thunderbolts tied w/a bowknot, flanked by panels carved w/swags & tassels tied w/bowknots, the reeded down-curving arms over caned panels above waterleaf-carved & reeded arm supports on reeded tapering legs ending in vaseform feet on brass casters, caned seat & back panels, attributed to Duncan Phyfe, New York, ca. 1805, 72' l. (repair to one rear leg) 51,750.00

Sofa, Mission-style (Arts & Crafts movement), oak, a wide flat crestrail above seven wide vertical slats between heavy stiles w/curved front brackets over the flat arms above

Lifetime Sofa

slats, leather-upholstered seat, original medium-dark finish, unsigned Lifetime Furniture Company, Model No. 688¾, ca. 1910, 72" l., 34" h. (ILLUS.) 2,990.00

Window seat, Classical (American Empire), carved mahogany, curule-style base, the sloping curved end crestrails carved w/central gilded lion's-head medallion flanked by leafy tendrils above curved & reeded rail centering a curule crossed back w/central carved rosette flanked by curved reeded stiles continuing into the reeded seatrails over the double curule crossed reeded legs ending in carved paw feet, the legs centering a carved & gilded lion's-head medallion & joined by baluster- and ring-turned medial stretchers, New York City, 1810-15, 18 x 69¼", 33½" h...29,900.00

MIRRORS

Art Deco Wall Mirror

Art Deco wall mirror, bronze & leaded glass, the tall mirror w/a stepped & arched top & incised at the bottom w/an arched fountain design above a cast metal Gothic arch band, the sides flanked by tall pointed double-panel faceted glass sconces composed of white leaded glass & lighted from behind, attributed to Ferrobrandt, ca. 1925, 23" w., 40" h. (depatinated)....................................7,475.00

Art Deco wall mirror, wrought iron, a pointed top w/a section of pierced scrolls at the tip, scalloped narrow sides & a base band w/further pierced scrolls, attributed to Paul Kiss, Paris, France, ca. 1925, some finish loss, 22½" w., 42" h. (ILLUS.) 1,210.00

Art Nouveau wall mirror, carved giltwood & gesso, the beveled rectangular mirror plate within a molded surround, decorated w/applied pierced & carved gesso stylized whiplash foliage & intertwining blossoms, France, ca. 1900, 32" w., 4' 4¾" h. (losses & breaks) 1,650.00

Baroque wall mirror, giltwood, a long shaped rectangular mirror within a narrow scrolled trailing vine border surmounted by a dentil cornice above an anthemion & flowerhead border flanked by winged putti masks above Corinthian pilasters, raised on a similar base cornice ending in molded feet of breakfront outline, Italy, late 17th c., 54" l., 39½" h...8,050.00

Chippendale country-style wall mirror, mahogany, high crest w/ornate scroll carving w/scroll-carved ears above a molded rectangular frame around the mirror plate, conformingly carved lower corners & bottom rail, the mirror plate w/a decorative etched border, late 18th - early 19th c., 18" h. (repair) 3,190.00

Chippendale Wall Mirror

Chippendale wall mirror, carved mahogany & gilt gesso, elaborately scrolled crest centering a spread-winged phoenix-type bird within a pierced roundel above a rectangular mirror plate within a molded frame w/gilt inner liner above a shaped & scrolled pendant, England, ca. 1770, refinished, 17¼" w., 30" h. (ILLUS.) 2,970.00

Chippendale wall mirror, mahogany veneer on pine, ornately scrolled & pierce-carved crestrail centering a phoenix, rectangular mirror plate w/gilt liner, scroll-carved base, 20½" w., 36½" h. (one top ear replaced, some damage to liner & phoenix, glass worn) 3,960.00

American Classical Mirror

Classical (American Empire) wall mirror, carved & gilded pine, the horizontal oval mirror plate surrounded by a graduated double cornucopia frame w/beaded interior edge & centering a weeping willow, the cornucopia bursting w/fruits & leafage & centering a flora-form cresting w/pendant wheat ears rising from a plinth w/relief-carved stars, probably New England, early 19th c., 28" w., 36" h. (ILLUS.) 19,550.00

Empire (American) wall mirror, painted pine, the rectangular mirror plate within a slightly canted broad horizontal frame boldly painted in red, black & gold stripes, the corners w/scrolling anthemia leafage, ca. 1850, 50" w., 41" h.......................4,313.00

Federal country-style wall mirror, pine, a flat pedimented cornice w/stepped-out corner blocks above pilasters flanking a rectangular reverse-painted scene of a colorful house above the rectangular mirror plate, stepped, molded base, old dark varnish stain, early 19th c., 15¾ x 29½" (flaking on painting & worn mirror silvering) 412.50

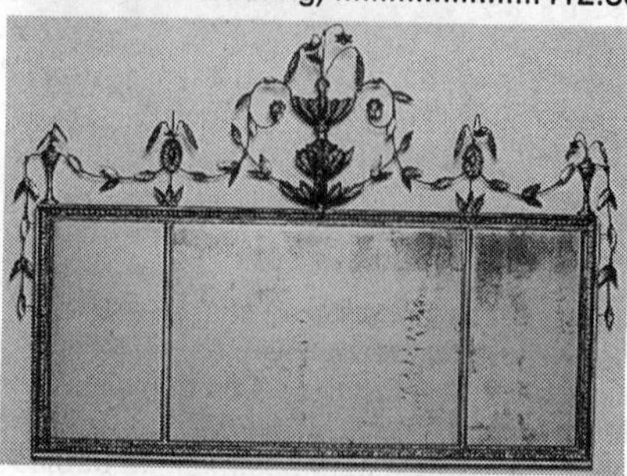

Federal Overmantel Mirror

Federal overmantel wall mirror, giltwood & gesso, rectangular in three sections w/delicate leaf-molded borders, surmounted by a delicate leaf-, urn- & wheat-molded swagged gessoed crest, 19th c., repairs, 49" l., 35½" h. (ILLUS.) 6,900.00

Federal (late) wall mirror, stenciled pine, the rectangular mirror plate within a molded frame w/gilt stenciled stylized floral & fruit motifs on a black ground, mid-19th c., 13" w., 17" h...690.00

Federal Convex Wall Mirror

Federal wall mirror, carved giltwood, a wide deep round framework surrounding a convex mirror & surmounted by a spread-winged eagle flanked by flowerheads & leaves, a fan- and bellflower-form pendant at the base, New England, early 19th c., paper label w/inscription on base, repairs, 18½" w., 35" h. (ILLUS.) 3,450.00

Federal wall mirror, carved giltwood, the flat molded cornice w/outset corners hung w/spherules over a rectangular panel w/a relief foliate

Federal Giltwood Wall Mirror

basket above the rectangular mirror plate flanked by half-round carved colonettes up the side, flat base rail w/corner blocks, probably Massachusetts, ca. 1825, minor imperfections, 21" w., 41½" h. (ILLUS.)......3,575.00

Folk Art Mirror with Sheep

Folk art wall mirror, carved mahogany, a rectangular mirror inset into a deep shaped frame w/cut scallops at the base & corner curlicues at the top centering a full-bodied figure of a sheep, American-made, 19th c., 4⅝ x 8½" (ILLUS.) 4,600.00

Folk art wall mirror, chip-carved & painted pine, a wide deeply carved & layered rectangular frame w/wide triangular cuts, painted red, dark green, black & brown, American-made, ca. 1930, 14¼ x 18¼" (ILLUS. top next column) 575.00

Louis XV wall mirror, giltwood, a rectangular divided mirror plate contained within a rectangular frame

Mirror with Chip-Carved Frame

w/serpentine edges, carved w/flowerheads, foliage & crosshatching, the arched top rail carved w/shell & wave motifs, second quarter 18th c., 29½" w., 6' h. 8,050.00

Louis XVI overmantel mirror, giltwood, (later) rectangular mirror plate within a leaf-tip border beneath an egg-and-dart fluted & foliate-carved frieze centering pendant husks, the corbel sides w/pendant berried branches, England, late 18th c., 61" w., 4' 4" h. (branches re-gilded) 16,500.00

Stickley Table-Top Mirror

Mission-style (Arts & Crafts movement) table-top mirror, oak, rectangular frame w/slightly pointed crestrail swiveling between two uprights w/shoe feet, by Gustav Stickley, ca. 1909, 21 x 25" (ILLUS.) 1,265.00

Mission-style (Arts & Crafts movement) wall mirror, oak, wide flat rectangular frame w/a slight V outline across the top, exposed tenon & pegged construction, red decal mark of Gustav Stickley, ca. 1902, 47¼" l., 32¾" h....................5,175.00

Neoclassical dressing mirror, the oval mirror plate contained within a plain frame supported & flanked by flower-filled cornucopiae ending in rams' heads, carved w/*rinceaux*, the rectangular base fitted w/a drawer at each end, raised on ball feet, Continental, first quarter 19th c., 6" deep, 21¼" w., 21¼" h. 4,600.00

Queen Anne wall mirror, mahogany, the shaped crest flanking upswept scrolled ears over a rectangular mirror plate surrounded by a conforming molded frame, over a scrolling pendant centering a shaped base, probably America, late 18th c., 11½ x 17½"....................................660.00

Queen Anne wall mirror, parcel-gilt walnut, the scrolled cresting centered by a pierced foliate spray above a cushion-molded surround w/inside & outside gilt borders centering a two-part beveled shaped rectangular mirror plate, second quarter 18th c., 24" w., 5' 7" h. (restoration to veneers & gilded surfaces, crack in upper mirror) 4,313.00

Queen Anne Wall Mirror

Queen Anne wall mirror, walnut & gilt, a high arched, pierced & scroll-cut crest centered by pierced roundel w/gilt leaves above the arched & molded framework surrounding the mirror, probably England, ca. 1750, 22 x 48" (ILLUS.)...........2,200.00

Regency wall mirror, giltwood, a round convex mirror framed by an inner fluted ebonized border, the molded recessed surround carved w/leaf-tips & hung w/spherules, w/a displayed spread-wing eagle at the top on a tablet flanked by scrolled leaves, a leaf-carved pendant at the bottom, England, ca. 1820, 26¼" w., 44" h. (ILLUS. top next column)....3,450.00

Regency Convex Wall Mirror

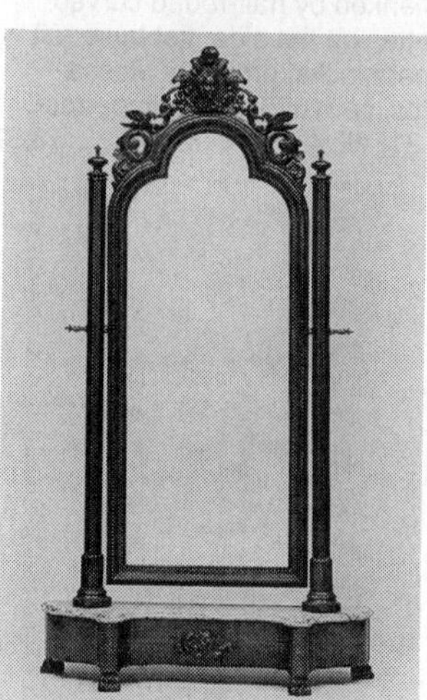

Victorian Rococo Cheval Mirror

Victorian cheval mirror, Rococo substyle, carved rosewood, the tall molded frame w/arched crestrail topped by pierced leafy scrolls w/birds & fruit & centering a bust of Washington (?), the mirror swiveling between tall slender paneled posts w/squatty urn finial & resting upon a D-shaped white marble top over a conforming base on paw feet, attributed to John Henry Belter, New York, ca. 1855 (ILLUS.) 13,200.00

Victorian wall mirror, shell-encrusted, the wide rectangular shadowbox frame encrusted w/an inner geometric design of small shells w/an outer random shell design w/shell rosettes at each corner, remnants of trade label on the back, Eng-

Shell-Encrusted Victorian Mirror

land, late 19th c., 15½ x 17½" (ILLUS.) 2,090.00

PARLOR SUITES

Empire Style Armchair

Art Deco: settee, two large armchairs & two smaller armchairs; giltwood, the settee w/rounded backrail continuing to an upholstered back flanked by tapering columnar front supports carved w/draped festoons ending in scrolled feet, the chairs *en suite,* upholstered in deep red silk moiré, France, ca. 1925, settee 50½" l.,5 pcs. 7,475.00

Art Nouveau: settee & two *bergeres* (closed-arm armchairs); *Sieges Aubépine*, fruitwood, each w/a gently rounded crestrail over the upholstered back, closed slightly outswept arms w/carved bands of stylized leaves & berries continuing into slightly canted tapering legs, undulating seatrail w/further carving, white on white silk damask upholstery, Louis Majorelle, France, ca. 1900, settee 52" l., 3 pcs.......18,400.00

Art Nouveau: settee & two side chairs; mahogany, the settee w/a rectangular upholstered back w/a flat crestrail carved at the corners w/florals, flaring upholstered arms, carved arm fronts continuing to tapering front legs flanking the flat seatrail, matching chairs, all w/beige velvet upholstery, Louis Majorelle, France, ca. 1900, settee 66½" l., 3 pcs. 4,600.00

Bentwood: settee & two armchairs; the settee w/a U-form backrail w/spindles enclosing the D-form seat & continuing to a conforming base rail, upholstered in red leather, the chairs *en suite*, designed by Josef Hoffmann, manufactured by J. & J. Kohn, Austria, ca. 1906, settee 48" l., 3 pcs. 5,750.00

Empire Style: settee, two armchairs & two side chairs; gilt-bronze mounted mahogany, each piece w/a rectangular upholstered back within a frame, decorated w/interlacing circle mounts headed by a cluster of reeds joined by gilt-bronze ribbon continuing to padded arms & upholstered seat; the apron similarly decorated, the rectangular tapering legs headed by gilt-bronze winged female busts, France, late 19th c., 5 pcs. (ILLUS. of an armchair)....25,300.00

Louis XV-Style: settee & two armchairs; giltwood, each w/upholstered oval or oblong back within a molded frame, the crest decorated w/flowers continuing to padded open arms & upholstered seat, raised on cabriole legs, upholstered in figural Aubusson tapestry, France, 19th c., 3 pcs. 8,625.00

Louis XVI-Style: settee & four open-arm armchairs; giltwood, the settee w/an oval medallion upholstered back continuing to tapering upholstered arms w/edge pads, upholstered seat on curved, molded seatrail, on spiral-turned tapering legs, the matching armchairs w/round backs, all w/small floral-carved crests on the crestrail, floral Aubusson tapestry upholstery, France, late 19th c., set of 5 ......17,250.00

Louis XVI-Style: settee, four armchairs & two side chairs; each w/a rectangular back headed by a quiver of arrows & flaming torch tied w/a ribbon, continuing to padded arms & upholstered seat, raised on circular fluted legs, front casters, upholstered in figural Aubusson tapestry, France, late 19th c., 7 pcs. (ILLUS. of an armchair top next column) 10,925.00

Louis XVI-Style Armchair

Modern style: settee & two armchairs; upholstered bentwood, each piece w/a flat crestrail curved at the ends to form the tops of the arms, upholstered & tufted back panels, the arms composed of large eye-shaped panels stretching from the top rail to a matching base rail, upholstered seat w/grey pigskin, original manufacturer's labels for Mundus, designed by Josef Hoffmann, Austria, ca. 1915, settee 53¼" l., 3 pcs. 13,225.00

Belter Parlor Suite

Victorian Rococo substyle: sofa, gentleman's armchair & a side chair; laminated & carved rosewood, "Cornstalk" patt., each piece w/a pierce-carved crestrail continuing to form the sides framing the upholstered back panel, carved w/a central floral bouquet flanked by long, leafy scrolls, shaped scroll & leaf-carved seatrails & demi-cabriole front legs, on casters, John Henry Belter, New York, ca. 1850-60, 3 pcs. (ILLUS.) 15,400.00

SCREENS

Fire screen, Art Deco style, steel & brass, the rectangular frame in black-painted steel enclosing wire mesh set w/radiating lightning bolts of polished brass, unsigned, ca. 1940, 32⅝" w., 27½" h. 1,955.00

Fire Screen Designed by Brandt

Fire screen, cast & wrought iron, the rectangular frame cast w/dentils enclosing a panel wrought w/stylized scrolling leafage centering an antelope, above a lower panel wrought w/flowerheads, raised on scrolling strap feet, impressed "E. BRANDT," ca. 1925, 30¼" h. (ILLUS.) 27,500.00

Folding screen, three-fold, mahogany & fruitwood, Art Nouveau design w/each rectangular panel carved on the upper third w/lotus blossoms & leaves above panels inlaid w/large sailing galleons, signed in marquetrie "Cutler & Girard," Italy, ca. 1902, overall 62¾" w., 5'11¼" h. 2,185.00

Lacquer & Gilt Scenic Screen

Folding screen, four-fold, lacquer & gilt, each rectangular panel lacquered in brilliant red, the whole decorated w/a scene of spotted Japanese deer grazing in a meadow w/bamboo in the distance, worked primarily in gilt, the reverse in plain red lacquer, signed "Thanhlé," one hinge loose, gilt rubbed, mid-20th c., overall 63" w., 5'1⅜" h. (ILLUS.) ...4,400.00

Folding screen, six-fold, plywood & canvas, consisting of identical plywood sections joined together by equally tall pieces of canvas sandwiched between the layers of wood, designed by Charles & Ray Eames, produced by Herman Miller, ca. 1946, overall 60" w., 5'7¾" h...2,420.00

Folding screen, ten-fold, Coromandel, depicting a continuous scene of various sages & holy men amidst fantastical beasts within an extensive landscape bordered by dragons, utensils & floral sprays, the reverse w/poetic inscription within borders of beats & panoramas, executed in polychrome lacquer against a black ground, China, dated Kangxi seventh year, corresponding to 1668, each panel 17½" w., 9'4" h. (restorations).....26,400.00

SECRETARIES

Early Classical Secretary-Bookcase

Classical (American Empire) secretary-bookcase, parcel-gilt rosewood & mahogany, three-part construction: the upper part consisting of a molded rectangular cornice; the middle part w/brass line-inlaid frieze above a pair of glazed cupboard doors w/ribbon-tied foliate muntins enclosing shelves above a pair of brass line-inlaid short drawers; the lower section w/hinged lid enclosing a fitted interior & baize-lined writing surface over a pair of graduated long drawers & faceted tapering supports above an inswept shelf, on hairy paw feet headed by foliage, probably Albany, New York, 1815-25, 24 x 43¾", 7' 1½" h. (ILLUS.) 13,200.00

Classical (American Empire) secretary-bookcase, mahogany, two-part construction: the upper section w/a scroll-cut pediment above an ogee cornice above a pair of glazed cupboard doors w/Gothic arch tops opening to three shelves; the stepped-out lower section w/a hinged writing surface above a pair of Gothic-paneled cupboard doors, on molded bracket feet, New York, 1830-40, 22¼ x 42¾", 7' 6¼" h.....1,495.00

Late Empire Secretary-Bookcase

Classical (American Empire) secretary-bookcase, tiger stripe maple, two-part construction: the upper section w/a rectangular top w/a deep ogee cornice w/rounded front corners above a tall case w/2-pane glazed cupboard doors opening to shelves; the stepped-out lower section w/rounded front corners & four long graduated drawers w/simple wood knobs, flat apron w/scroll-cut corner brackets, Ohio, mid-19th c., refinished, imperfections, 19 x 38", 6' 8" h. (ILLUS.) 2,310.00

Federal country-style secretary-bookcase, painted & decorated, two-part construction: the upper section w/a rectangular top w/a molded cornice above a pair of raised panel cupboard doors w/small wooden knobs opening to shelves; the lower section w/a hinged slant front opening to an interior fitted w/pigeonholes & small drawers above a pair of slide supports

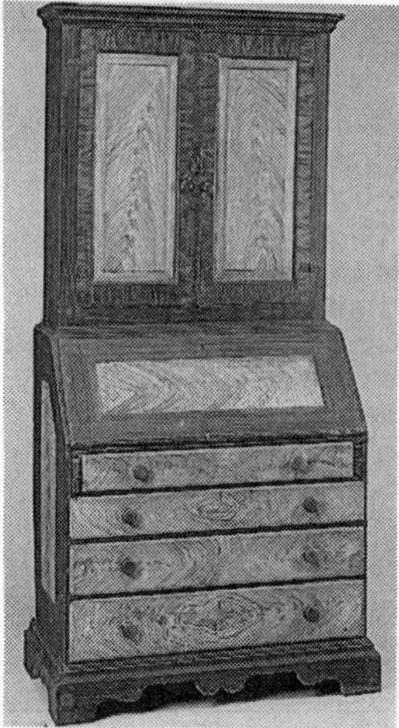

Federal Country-Style Secretary

flanking a narrow long drawer over three long graduated drawers, each w/wooden knobs, molded base w/shaped skirt & bracket feet, boldly decorated overall to simulate mahogany & flamed-birch veneers, knobs appear to be original, New England, ca. 1815, 18 x 36½", 6' 4" h. (ILLUS.)..........................14,950.00

Federal 'cylinder-front' secretary-bookcase, inlaid mahogany, two-part construction: the upper section w/a crestrail w/centered raised block w/patera inlay & blocked corners w/turned urn finials above a line-inlaid frieze band over a pair of 6-pane glazed cupboard doors w/triple Gothic arches at the top of each; the lower section stepped out w/a row of three small drawers w/pairs of round brass pulls above a cylinder-front w/round brass pulls & opening to an interior fitted above a pair of narrow drawers w/pairs of round brass pulls over two long drawers w/similar pulls, raised on bulbous ovoid feet, early 19th c., 24¼ x 42", 7 '4" h. ...2,530.00

Federal secretary-bookcase, mahogany, two-part construction: the top section w/a rectangular top w/a shaped stationary cornice w/veneered frieze above a pair of tall diamond-glazed cupboard doors opening to an interior w/seven slots for shelves; the stepped-out lower section w/a central hinged writing flap flanked by small drawers over one long drawer, all w/pressed glass pulls, above a flattened arch apron, on four turned tapering reeded legs w/ring-and-peg feet, Massachusetts, possibly Salem, ca. 1800-10, finials

Early Federal Secretary-Bookcase

& cupboard shelves missing, 20¾ x 43", 6' 6¾" h. (ILLUS.) 4,180.00

Federal secretary-bookcase, grain-painted pine, three-part construction: the top section w/a rectangular top w/a pierced circle-band gallery separated by blocks w/turned & pointed urn finials above a pair of cupboard doors w/a centered by diamond panels above a medial bar to the middle section w/a pair of narrow drawers above a pair of short, wide doors w/raised geometric banded paneling w/a center diamond; the lower section w/a fold-out writing surface above a long drawer flanked by pull-out supports above three long graduated drawers, scalloped apron & tall French feet, simple brass knobs & bail drawer pulls, probably Massachusetts, ca. 1790, 18½ x 40", 7' 9" h. (minor imperfections) 22,000.00

Late Federal secretary-bookcase, cherry, two-part construction: the upper section w/a rectangular top w/a molded cornice above a pair of paneled doors opening to shelves above a pair of short reeded doors opening to a desk interior fitted w/pigeonholes above small drawers centering a reeded prospect door opening to a pigeonhole & two small drawers; the lower stepped-out section w/a hinged writing flap above a pair of cockbeaded drawers, on ring-turned & reeded legs ending in ball feet, New York State, ca. 1820, 23 x 42½", 6' 5" h. (ILLUS. top next column) 4,600.00

Late Federal Secretary-Bookcase

Queen Anne secretary-bookcase, carved mahogany, two-part construction: the upper section w/a molded swan's-neck crest surmounted by two ribbed brass ball finials above a pair of arched paneled doors opening to a double fan-carved interior fitted w/valanced pigeonholes & two small drawers, two candle slides below; the lower section w/a hinged slant lid lined on the interior w/baise & opening to an amphitheatre interior fitted w/valanced pigeonholes above serpentine drawers centering a scalloped hinged prospect door opening to a valanced drawer & a blocked small drawer, the case below w/four blocked long drawers, each w/cockbeaded surrounds, the molded base w/shaped center pendant & continuing to bracket feet, Boston, Massachusetts, ca. 1760, 41½ x 41¾", 7' 8½" h.....134,500.00

SIDEBOARDS

Art Deco sideboard, rosewood marquetry & mother-of-pearl, the shaped rectangular top w/molded edge above a pair of central cabinet doors inlaid w/basketweave marquetry & bordered w/floral marquetry, the blossoms inlaid w/mother-of-pearl, flanked by curved side cabinets, the curved sides set w/molded consoles continuing to tapering legs ending in bronze *sabots*, inset ivory plaque signed "J. Leleu," Jules Leleu, France. ca. 1935, 24½" deep, 114" l., 41½" h...6,900.00

Art Deco Sideboard

Art Deco sideboard, mahogany, marble & ivory inlaid, the rectangular case w/a curved backsplash fitted w/a lozenge-shaped mirror above an inset marble top flanked by tall cabinets fitted w/an upper glass door above a longer door inlaid w/stylized flowers, two central drawers over two shorter doors, on round tapering legs, Europe, ca. 1930, 18 x 63", 5' 5" h. (ILLUS.) ...1,150.00

Art Moderne sideboard, bronze-mounted & lacquered, rectangular top w/rounded corners above a pair of long cabinet doors opening to a fitted interior w/open shelves & three drawers, raised on short tapering turned feet, the doors mounted in the center w/gilt-bronze shells & the doors, side panels & feet also mounted w/thin bronze moldings, lacquered in mottled chocolate brown & gold, France, ca. 1940, 19½ x 73½", 36½" h......................6,600.00

Art Nouveau server, carved red narra wood, tile, enamel & copper, the circled top rail supported on shaped upper tier, the rectangular surface & backsplash set w/mottled blue ceramic tiles, above two drawers decorated w/elaborate green enameled, cut & hammered copper key escutcheon & drawer pulls, supported on carved legs w/lower tier, by Gustave Serrurier-Bovy, ca. 1899, designed for the Paris Exposition, 1900, branded "SERURRIER LIEGE," 21¼ x 67¾", 5' 6⅞" h.................25,300.00

Biedermeier sideboard, brass-mounted mahogany, the shaped rectangular top slightly overhanging one very long drawer w/three keyholes & a smaller drawer above a wide central cupboard door flanked by smaller cupboard doors, now enclosing sliding shelves, raised on a plinth base, brass keyhole escutcheons, Europe, second quarter 19th c., 24 x 77", 45½" h. 7,150.00

Small Classical Sideboard

Classical (American Empire) sideboard, mahogany, rectangular top below a high stepped splashboard over a case w/a pair of round-front drawers w/pressed glass knobs above a pair of paneled cupboard doors flanked by engaged columns w/Ionic capitals, on short ring- and knob-turned legs, Mid-Atlantic area, 1815-30, 23¾ x 52½", 4' 6¼" h. (ILLUS.) 1,150.00

Classical (American Empire) sideboard, mahogany, the rectangular white marble top above three short drawers flanked by rectangular plaques above a pair of paneled cupboard doors enclosing a shelf centered by pairs of colonettes w/brass capitals milled w/rosettes & grapevines centering a short drawer w/scrolling foliate brackets above a kneehole backed by a mirrored plate over a molded base, New York, 1820-30, 24 x 62", 42¾" h. 6,600.00

American Classical Sideboard

Classical (American Empire) sideboard, ormolu-mounted mahogany, the rectangular white marble top above a frieze w/three drawers, each fitted w/an ormolu mount, the center mount depicting Neptune pulled by horses w/a putto blowing a horn & two mounts showing the goddess Diana being pulled in a chariot by lions, all centering flower & leaf mounts, the front supported by four tapered ormolu-mounted columns, the center of the base inset & backed by a mirror, the end plinths on acanthus-carved paw feet, New York, ca. 1810, lacks backboard, 25 x 73½", 43½" h. (ILLUS.) 5,175.00

Danish Modern Sideboard

Danish Modern sideboard, teak, rectangular top above a case w/a pair of long sliding doors opening to shelves flanking three central drawers w/lipped edge pulls, raised on four round tapering legs, ca. 1950s, 31½" h. (ILLUS.) 575.00

Ornate Edwardian Sideboard

Edwardian sideboard, inlaid satinwood & mahogany, classical style w/a tubular brass top gallery w/a high central oval & side posts mounted w/pairs of candlearms, rectangular 'breakfront' style top above a conforming case w/a band of frieze drawers w/gilt classical designs above three short central doors on tall square tapering legs flanked by a pair of tall doors above pairs of short square tapering legs, overall banded inlay, England, early 20th c. (ILLUS.) 6,325.00

Federal Country-Style Huntboard

Federal country-style huntboard, pine, rectangular top above pairs of deep end drawers w/oval brasses flanking a central paneled door, on turned tapering legs, Southern U.S., ca. 1820 (ILLUS.) 2,960.00

Federal huntboard, inlaid mahogany, the long rectangular top w/a serpentine front above a conforming apron centered by an oval figured reserve w/oval inlaid dies at the corners, the sides fitted w/drawers, on square tapering line- and bellflower-inlaid legs ending in crossbanded cuffs, Baltimore, Maryland, ca. 1795, 26¼ x 66½", 35¾" h. (drawers replaced, some veneer patches) 42,550.00

Federal Server

Federal server, mahogany, a low three-quarter gallery around the rectangular top slightly overhanging a long beaded drawer w/oval brass pulls & keyhole escutcheon raised on turned columnar supports above the galleried medial shelf on short baluster-turned legs, probably Philadelphia, ca. 1810, 17½ x 42½", 37½" h. (ILLUS.) 3,025.00

Federal serving table, mahogany & mahogany veneer, rectangular top above a pair of short drawers above a single long drawer over a medial shelf flanked by turned & reeded legs ending in cast brass paw feet, replaced pulls, refinished, New York, ca. 1800, 18 x 36", 37" h. (repairs) 4,400.00

Federal "bow-front" sideboard, satinwood & ebony-inlaid mahogany, the oblong top w/crossbanded edge above a conformingly-shaped case w/three bowed frieze drawers, the center drawer faced to simulate two working drawers, a pair of bottle drawers & a pair of hinged cupboard doors below, centering over inlaid dies on line-inlaid square tapering legs ending in crossbanded cuffs, Massachusetts, ca. 1805, 24¾ x 66", 40¼" h. (some repair to inlay) 10,350.00

Federal Serpentine-Front Sideboard

Federal "serpentine-front" sideboard, inlaid mahogany, the rectangular top w/serpentine front above a conforming case w/a pair of short end drawers flanking a long central drawer over a pair of central cupboard doors flanked by bottle drawers at each end, raised on slender square tapering legs, minor veneer repairs, probably Massachusetts, ca. 1800, 26½ x 69½", 41½" h. (ILLUS.) 6,050.00

Federal sideboard, bird's-eye maple & mahogany inlaid cherry, the oblong top w/outset corners above a frieze w/inlaid swags & tassels above a deep drawer flanked by bottle drawers, above three cockbeaded long drawers, three-quarter-round columns flanking, the shaped skirt continuing to turned front feet, probably original brasses, New England, probably Connecticut, ca. 1815, 20¼ x 46", 43⅞" h. 5,225.00

Federal sideboard, inlaid cherry, rectangular top w/a D-shaped central section above a pair of drawers flanking a D-front drawer,

Unusual Federal Sideboard

each outlined in cross-banded contrasting veneer, a pair of end cupboard doors inlaid w/facing eagles & flanking a pair of angled central doors & panels w/fan inlays & icicle inlays above quarter-fan brackets topping the square tapering legs w/inlaid cuffs, oval brass drawer pulls & small brass door knobs, Connecticut River Valley, early 19th c., imperfections, minor repairs, 23¼ x 69¼", 38½" h. (ILLUS.) 69,300.00

Federal sideboard, mahogany, the serpentine front w/rounded corners above a conforming case fitted w/a convex central cockbeaded long drawer over an arched skirt w/central curved drop flanked by concave cockbeaded doors, on square tapering legs w/spade feet, Annapolis, Maryland, 1790-1810, 25¾ x 71¼", 36¼" h......................6,900.00

Federal sideboard, inlaid walnut, the oblong top w/swelled center section w/a line-inlaid edge above a conforming case w/three frieze drawers, the center long one paneled to resemble two, over convex rounded doors flanked by a pair of hinged cupboard doors, on line-inlaid square tapering legs ending in crossbanded cuffs, Southern, ca. 1810, 24 x 69", 45⅜" h. (minor losses to inlay) 7,700.00

Hepplewhite country style huntboard, painted & decorated pine, rectangular top above a deep case w/a long drawer over a narrow pull-out work shelf above another long drawer, turned wood knobs, slender square tapering legs, old but not original alligatored brown finish w/black & gold-painted decoration, top w/old grey over a yellowed marbleized paint, early 19th c., 19½ x 30¾", 38" h. (replaced pulls on work shelf, replaced molding on bottom edge)...2,200.00

Jacobean-Style sideboard, oak, rectangular top w/outset corners

Jacobean-Style Sideboard

above a pair of long drawers ornately carved w/leafy scrolls & separated by three blocks carved w/lions' masks each above a boldly carved herm figure separating two ornately carved cupboard doors centered by a grotesque mask, stepped & molded base on short compressed grotesque mask feet, England, 19th c., 25 x 70¾", 39½" h. (ILLUS.) 1,100.00

Stickley Brothers Server

Mission-style (Arts & Crafts movement) server, oak, rectangular top w/low backrail overhanging four square legs & a medial shelf, recent dark finish, metal tag mark of Stickley Bros., Model No. 92, early 20th c., 20 x 36", 36" h. (ILLUS.) 825.00

Mission-style (Arts & Crafts movement) sideboard, oak, rectangular top w/a gallery above a pair of drawers over a pair of cupboard doors w/butterfly keys, pyramidal iron pulls on the drawers, slab sides w/exposed keyed tenons, red decal mark of Gustav Stickley, Model No. 901, ca. 1902, 23¼ x 50½", 40" h.. 16,100.00

Mission-style (Arts & Crafts movement) sideboard, oak, a raised back superstructure w/plate rail above the rectangular top above a pair of cabinet doors w/long hammered copper strap hinges flanking a pair

L. & J.G. Stickley Sideboard

of drawers w/copper plates & bail pulls over an open recess, a single long drawer across the bottom, original medium finish, minor surface dent, Handcraft Furniture decal of L. & J.G. Stickley, Model No. 708, ca. 1907, 20⅝ x 48", 44½" h. (ILLUS.) 2,760.00

Mission-style (Arts & Crafts movement) sideboard, oak, the low slightly rounded crestrail w/plate rack above the rectangular top over a pair of narrow drawers over a single long drawer over a pair of paneled cupboard doors, slightly arched apron, paneled ends, original suede drawer lining, reddish brown finish, branded mark of the Limbert Furniture Company, Model No. 1320, 19 x 45", 42½" h. (some wood replaced on plate rack) 1,430.00

Modern Style Sideboard

Modern-style sideboard, 'Janus' type, hardwood, a raised superstructure w/rectangular top over four double-panel cupboard doors mounted each w/two unique Japanese carved woodblocks above four narrow drawers over an open area above a rectangular black faux marble drop-in top over four cupboard doors w/inlaid panels over a single long drawer across the bottom, on short square legs, designed by Edward Wormley for Dunbar Furniture Corp., Model Nos. 5723 & 5724, 1957, w/manufacturer's pamphlet, 20 x 66", 6' 5½" h. (ILLUS.) 3,025.00

Regency sideboard, mahogany w/figured veneer, rectangular top w/scrolling three-quarter gallery above case w/five drawers over two large & two small paneled doors & two deep drawers w/inlaid escutcheons, turned & reeded legs on brass casters, replaced hardware, England, early 19th c., 24½ x 73½", 44¼" h. plus gallery (repair to gallery, minor edge damage to case) 1,550.00

STANDS

Chippendale 'Tilt-Top' Candlestand

Book stand, Mission-style (Arts & Crafts movement), oak, a three-quarter open gallery above the stack of four open shelves & open sides, the bottom shelf flanked on each side by three vertical slats, tenon construction, unsigned, ca. 1912, 12 x 29", 36" h. (lightly refinished) ...546.00

Candlestand, Chippendale, mahogany, the oval top tilting above an elongated ring-turned standard on a tripod base w/cabriole legs ending in snake feet, Boston, Massachusetts, ca. 1780, 15½ x 24", 27¾" h. (ILLUS.) 2,875.00

Candlestand, Federal, paint decorated maple, the oblong top w/rounded corners above a turned standard, on a tripod base, painted in shades of red, orange & yellow, New England, probably Vermont, early 19th c., 15½ x 16", 26" h....55,200.00

Candlestand, Federal, tilt-top, inlaid cherry, the oval top inlaid w/central patera & a border of trailing vine inlay flowing from a vase & tied in a bow at the apex, outlined in a band of triple inlay, the top, edged in double line inlay above cylindrical shaft w/line-inlaid turned urn, on shaped inlaid legs w/cuffs, Connecticut, 1790-1810, 16⅜ x 24½", 29" h....................................8,050.00

Candlestand, Hepplewhite, tilt-top, curly maple, rectangular top w/cut corners veneered w/cross-banded mahogany tilting above a turned column above a tripod base w/spider legs ending in spade feet, 16½ x 23¼", 31¾" h. (rectangular patch in column & latch holding top is replaced) 1.430.00

Candlestand, Queen Anne, mahogany, octagonal tilt-top over a ring- and baluster-turned pedestal on a tripod base w/cabriole legs & spade feet, Long Island, 1740-60, 18¾ x 22½", 28" h.........................1,210.00

Ornate Victorian 'Tilt-Top' Candlestand

Candlestand, Victorian, tilt-top, papier-maché & pine, the shaped circular papier-maché top w/cut-out fleur-de-lis surround tilting above a baluster- and ring-turned tapering standard on a tripod base terminating in pierced reverse scrolled legs, the top w/a papier-maché floral wreath on a grained ground, the surround highlighted w/red fleur-de-lis & black pinstriping, the standard & legs painted mustard yellow w/red & black highlights, some wear to paint, old age cracks to papier-maché, attributed to the Litchfield Manufacturing Co., Litchfield, Connecticut, mid-19th c., 17½" d., 28" h. (ILLUS.)................2,875.00

Candlestand, Windsor, hardwood, a thick round disc base raised on three turned & splayed short legs centered by a baluster-turned column below a threaded shaft supporting a round adjustable shelf & a shaped adjustable candle arm w/turned details, old worn & heavily alligatored dark green paint, 31½" h. (one leg old dowel replacement, shelf & candle arm w/frozen threads).......................................1,870.00

Canterbury (music stand), early Victorian, painted & decorated, circle & X-form dividers above a frieze drawer on turned legs & brass feet w/casters, decorated overall w/Chinese figures, pavilions & vessels in gilt on a black ground, England, ca. 1835, 13¾ x 19", 22" h...3,520.00

Classical two-drawer stand, mahogany & figured veneer, rectangular top w/biscuit corners over two drawers flanked by bulbous turning continuing to turned & rope-carved legs ending in button feet, replaced brasses, top drawer has added dividers, 18½ x 23½", 28½" h...1,485.00

Crock stand, painted oak, three-tier, semi-circular w/graduated shelves, old green repaint, 19" deep, 39" w., 43¾" h..368.50

Empire Revival-Style two-drawer stand, mahogany, rectangular top flanked by drop-leaves above a case w/two drawers, raised on an acanthus-carved pedestal w/a tripod base ending in paw feet, late 19th c., 18 x 21", 29½" h. 412.00

Federal Curly Maple Stand

Federal stand, curly maple, rectangular top above a plain apron on square tapering legs, New England, ca. 1815, 17¾ x 18", 28" h. (ILLUS.) 920.00

Fine Decorated Federal Stand

Federal one-drawer stand, painted & decorated, the rectangular top w/outset rounded turret corners & horizontal ring turnings above an apron w/one long drawer, ring- and baluster-turned legs ending in tear-drop feet, the drawer & back panel painted w/a woven green basket filled w/red apples & leafage w/red & black grain-painted ground to simulate rosewood & trimmed w/green & yellow pinstriping, the top & legs similarly decorated, the sides w/foliate decoration on a similar ground, South Paris Hill, Maine, early 19th c., 21⅛ x 23¼", 29" h. (ILLUS.) 37,950.00

Federal one-drawer stand, walnut, the rectangular top above a case w/a cockbeaded frieze drawer, on square tapering legs, early 19th c., 14¼ x 19¼", 28½" h......................1,150.00

Federal two-drawer stand, carved & figured mahogany, the rectangular top above two graduated drawers on acanthus-carved legs joined by a shaped medial shelf, on brass casters, New York, ca. 1820, 17¾ x 22¾", 29⅛" h.....................1,725.00

Federal two-drawer stand, cherry, rectangular top above two small drawers, on ring-turned legs w/ball feet, Pennsylvania, 1810-25, 19 x 22", 28¾" h.............................288.00

Magazine stand, Mission-style (Arts & Crafts movement), oak, four wide, open graduated shelves between wide canted sides w/curved tops & arched base cut-outs, lightened finish w/added lacquer & some alligatoring, branded mark of the Charles Limbert Company, Model No. 300, early 20th c., 14 x 20", 36½" h...605.00

Limbert Magazine Stand

Magazine stand, Mission-style (Arts & Crafts movement), oak, four tapering open shelves between canted & tapering sides w/incurved top & pairs of semi-circular cut-outs near the base, original dark finish, branded mark of the Limbert Company, Model No. 300, 14 x 20", 37" h. (ILLUS.) 825.00

Nightstand, Art Nouveau, carved mahogany, "Clematis" patt., the arched crestrail pierced & carved w/leafy vines above the rectangular red marble-inset top over a narrow drawer above three open shelves framed by carved clematis vines & blossoms, shaped apron & short legs further carved w/blossoms, Louis Majorelle, France, ca. 1900, 13 x 15", 41¼" h. 1,495.00

Mission-Style Oak Nightstand

Nightstand, Mission-style (Arts & Crafts movement), oak, a rectangular top between a very low gallery framed by low rounded corner posts continuing to form the legs, a single long drawer w/two wooden knobs below the top & galleried medial shelf in the base, recent finish, attributed to Stickley Brothers, early 20th c., 17 x 20½", 29" h. (ILLUS.) 605.00

Nightstand, Mission-style (Arts & Crafts movement), oak, rectangular top above two drawers w/wooden pulls raised on four square legs joined by two stretchers, L. & J.G. Stickley Model 105, early 20th c., 14 x 19⅛", 29⅜" h. 1,495.00

Plant stand, Art Nouveau, marble & brass, the oviform red marble shaft supporting a square plant holder, set within a brass mount cast w/vegetal designs, France, late 19th - early 20th c., 44" h. 2,185.00

Plant stand, Mission-style (Arts & Crafts movement), oak, square clip-cornered overhanging top on a wide apron, square flaring legs, original dark finish, red decal mark of Gustav Stickley, Model No. 660, 18" sq., 20" h. 1,320.00

Plant Stand with Grueby Tile

Plant stand, Mission-style (Arts & Crafts movement), oak, open rails above the square top inset w/a green Grueby Pottery tile w/textured glaze above deep aprons w/curved edges between the square legs joined by arched lower stretchers, unsigned, ca 1900, 13" sq., 29¾" h. (ILLUS.) 5,750.00

Plant stand, Mission-style (Arts & Crafts movement), oak, a square top widely overhanging a deep apron w/curved edge between splayed square legs w/a cross trestle base, stenciled mark of the Stickley Broth-

Stickley Brothers Plant Stand

ers, Model No. 131, ca. 1910, refinished, 12" sq., 34" h. (ILLUS.) 825.00

Plant stand, Victorian, painted & decorated pine, three-tiered, the graduated & tiered half round form w/applied cut-out heart decorations at the edges, on ring-turned baluster legs, green over old red paint, New England, mid-19th c., 22 x 43", 44" h. 4,025.00

Sheraton one-drawer stand, curly & bird's-eye maple, rectangular one-board top overhanging an apron w/a single drawer w/brass pull, slender turned legs, old mellow refinishing, 17 x 19¾", 29" h. (minor age crack in top) 935.00

Sheraton country-style two-drawer stand, cherry, square top above one fitted shallow drawer & a deeper drawer, each w/figured veneer fronts & edge beading, on slender turned legs, replaced carved pulls, refinished, 18¾ x 19", 30¾" h. (age crack in one side) 440.00

Umbrella Stand by Gallé

Umbrella stand, Art Nouveau, inlaid mahogany & bronze, the rectangular form raised on stylized frog legs, inlaid in various woods on the front w/an aquatic landscape w/water lilies & arrowroot blossoms & leafage, a small panel at upper right carved w/stylized leafage, tin liner w/bronze rim, set w/bronze handles cast as stylized frogs, signed in marquetry "Gallé," France, ca. 1900, 10¼ x 20¾, 28¾" h. (ILLUS.) 12,650.00

Federal Tambour Top Washstand

Washstand, Federal, mahogany, the arching tambour top opening above a rectangular top fitted for wash basin & bowls over a cockbeaded drawer & cupboard door, on turned tapering legs w/brass paw feet, New York, 1810-20, 20 x 20", 35" h. (ILLUS.) 5,500.00

Washstand, Federal country-style, corner-type, cherry, shaped tapering backboards w/a small shelf above a bowed top w/a large round cut-out, a medial shelf above a single small drawer flanked by two false drawers, turned top supports & raised on slender turned & tapering legs w/double-knob feet, early 19th c., 16½ x 24", 38" h. (refinished, repaired cracks, repair to bottom rail)..907.50

STOOLS

English Art Deco Stool

Art Deco stool, burr elm, oval taupe leather-upholstered top over an oval base w/tall rectangular cut-out on each side, England, ca. 1930 (ILLUS.) 2,300.00

Art Nouveau Stool

Art Nouveau stool, mahogany, a leather-upholstered seat w/the leather continuing up the outswept ends above pierced sides w/carved scrolling vines, curved open brackets under the seat, green leather upholstery, ca. 1900, 15 x 23", 22" h. (ILLUS.) 4,600.00

Classical Piano Stool

Classical (American Empire) piano stool, carved mahogany, a curved tablet crestrail above a horizontal backrail carved w/a flowerhead flanked by foliage above an adjustable trapezoidal upholstered slip seat, on a pedestal support decorated w/carved acanthus leaves over a quadripartite base w/molded hipped downswept reeded legs headed by flowerheads, brass paw feet on casters, New York, ca. 1820-35, 32½ h. (ILLUS.) 990.00

Classical (American Empire) stools, mahogany, each w/rectangular padded saddle seat on a curule base centered by turned bosses joined by a ring- and baluster-turned stretcher, on ball feet, New York, 1810-20, top 17 x 17", 17" h., pr. (repairs) 3,300.00

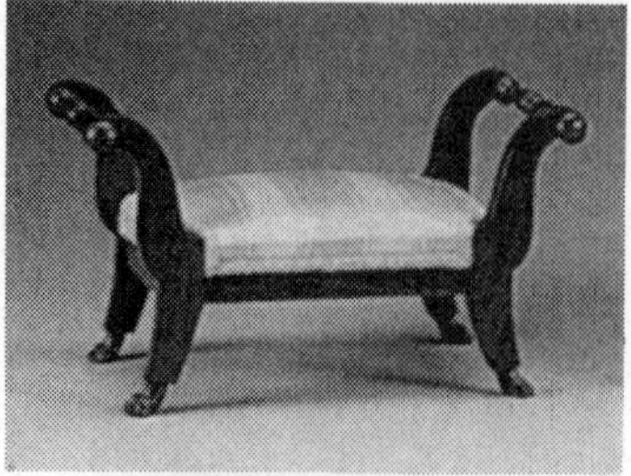

Federal Footstool

Federal footstools, mahogany, a padded upholstered rectangular top between upswept scrolling arms joined by baluster- and ring-turned stretchers, on splayed rectangular tapering legs w/paw feet, New York, 1810-25, one foot lacking a toe, 9¾ x 19¼", 10¼" h., pr. (ILLUS. of one)...1,430.00

Federal Curule Stool

Federal stools, mahogany, rectangular upholstered seat above a curule-form base, the legs joined by a turned medial stretcher, probably New York, ca. 1820, repairs to legs, pr. (ILLUS. of one) 2,875.00

Footstool, country-style, painted pine, the rectangular top made to resemble a thick closed book, on bootjack legs, old green paint, 15" l. (wear, edge damage).......................291.50

Footstool, folk art-type, painted pine, the rectangular top w/rounded corners painted w/a patriotic design of a waving American flag w/gilt finial, the sides painted w/a band of white stars on a dark blue ground, raised on shaped bracket feet, all on a coral red ground, inscribed in pencil on the bottom, "Stool made by Jack Downing, brother-in-law of H.G. Perry," ca. 1875, 10½ x 18½", 8½" h...4,600.00

Upholstered Footstool

Footstool, upholstered, the lozenge-shaped top covered w/a hooked rug worked w/the reclining figure of a spotted cat in tones of orange, brown, beige, black & white on a light blue ground, raised on turned maple 'turnip' feet, New England, ca. 1850, 28½" l., 8"h. (ILLUS.) 1,093.00

George II Stool

George II stool, walnut, the rectangular padded seat upholstered in contemporary floral needlework, on shell-carved cabriole legs ending in claw-and-ball feet, England, ca. 1730, 18 x 22", 19½" h. (ILLUS.) 9,350.00

Gustav Stickley Footstool

Mission-style (Arts & Crafts movement) footstool, oak, a rectangular hard leather top between square legs w/double end rungs framing seven slender spindles, flat side rungs, fine original finish, paper label of Gustav Stickley, Model No. 395, ca. 1906, 15 x 16 x 20" (ILLUS.) 3,190.00

Mission-style (Arts & Crafts movement) footstool, oak, rectangular rush top, four square legs w/tapering feet joined by wide flat stretchers, red decal mark of Gustav Stickley, Model No. 301, 15¾ x 17½ x 19¾" (replaced rush)...............................605.00

Mission-style (Arts & Crafts movement) rocking footstool, oak, rectangular w/original heavy leatherette-covered spring seat, flanked by square posts, arched rails, on rockers, unmarked L. & J.G. Stickley, Model No. 389, 18 x 21", 18" h...880.00

Modern style stool, beech & laminated bentwood, the square top w/rounded corners centered by a cut-out handhold & pierced holes, set into a square beech bentwood frame raised on four bentwood square w/rounded corner frames joined by aluminum studs, designed by Otto Wagner & produced by Thonet of Austria for the main Banking Hall of the Imperial Austrian Postal Savings Bank, Vienna, ca. 1906, 16½" sq., 18½" h...9,775.00

Windsor footstool, pine, thick rectangular top, splayed legs, worn original brown painted ground w/yellow & green striping & foliate detail, 13" l. (edge wear) 93.50

Painted Windsor Stool

Windsor stool, painted & decorated, oval slightly concave seat on bamboo-turned splayed legs joined by bamboo-turned stretchers, painted green, Philadelphia, ca. 1795 (ILLUS.) 1,380.00

Windsor stools, pine, each having an upholstered seat in petitpoint, one depicting a recumbent stag w/a floral border, the other a recumbent leopard having similar border, w/olive fringe border & brass tacks, on bamboo-turned tapering splayed legs joined by conformingly shaped stretchers, painted yellow w/brown highlights, New England, early 19th c., 13" d., 15" h., pr. (minor loss to paint) 18,400.00

TABLES

Art Deco center table, parchment, chromed metal & glass, round etched glass top above w/a wide white parchment pedestal on a chrome disc base, France, ca. 1930, 39¼" d., 30" h. 3,450.00

Art Deco Illuminated Table

Art Deco center table, illuminated-type, rosewood & birch, the round top w/an open center well fitted w/electric light, birch banding around the edge, on a tripart pedestal base w/coved sides & birch edge banding, ca. 1940, 47" d., 29¾" h. (ILLUS.) 2,588.00

Art Deco Coffee Table

Art Deco coffee table, Dominique macassar ebony & nickeled bronze, rectangular top above a lower shelf raised on solid curved ends mounted in nickeled bronze, unsigned, ca. 1940, 14¼ x 33½", 20" h. (ILLUS.) 6,325.00

Art Deco console table, wood & glass,

the rectangular top fitted w/black glass above three drawers, on slab legs, 13 x 45", 31½" h. 207.00

Art Deco dining table, oak, the oval top on a pedestal base w/four curving scrolled feet, Jacques-Emile Ruhlmann, France, 53 x 72", 26½" h., plus two 19½" leaves....23,000.00

Art Nouveau dining table, parcel-gilt mahogany & marquetry, the oblong top w/molded edge inlaid in various woods w/a diamond design, the apron carved w/stylized poppy blossoms & whiplash tendrils trimmed in gilt, probably Lyons, France, ca. 1900, 45 x 63", 30½" h. 8,050.00

Art Nouveau games table, carved & inlaid, the rectangular top inlaid w/a checkerboard pattern in the center, surrounded by inlay of blossoming clover, on four carved "twisted" legs, the front legs & apron carved w/clover leaves & blossoms & w/another inlaid panel in front, the table opening to form a square top w/green baize center, inlaid signature "Galle," Emile Gallé, France, 20½ x 35¼" closed, 31½" h. 3,450.00

Art Nouveau side table, fruitwood marquetry, the rectangular top w/outset rounded corners inlaid in various woods w/carnation blossoms & leaves, raised on four giant dragonfly-form legs joined by a shaped shelf inlaid w/a carnation against a stylized leaf-strewn ground, signed in marquetry "Gallé," ca. 1900, 22½ x 31¾", 29½" h. 23,000.00

Art Nouveau side table, maple & abalone inlay, rectangular top raised on square tapering legs headed by abalone roundelles & ribbon carving joined by a platform stretcher surmounted by a pierced brass gallery ending in incised brass caps, ca. 1900, 24" sq., 23½" h. 8,338.00

Art Nouveau tea table, fruitwood marquetry, three-tier, the shaped rectangular top w/molded surround inlaid w/a dragonfly in flight among withering blossoms, a larger conformingly shaped lower tier inlaid w/arrowroot leaves & blossoms, raised on shaped curved legs conjoined by a lower shelf inlaid w/bleeding hearts, signed in marquetry "Gallé," France, ca. 1900, 18½ x 28", 34" h. 5,175.00

Art Nouveau nest of tables, carved fruitwood & marquetry, four tables on carved legs, each top w/a different inlaid design: a sickle among mistletoe; oak branch & a cluster of acorns; wooded scene, spears & a boar ornamented stake; and a bird in flight below a sunburst; each signed in marquetry "Gallé," 15 x 22", tallest 28¼" h., the set ...3,450.00

Arts & Crafts style library table, drop-leaf style, inlaid mahogany, the rectangular top above an apron w/a drawer at each end & flanked by D-shaped drop leaves w/gently rounded corners featuring abstract Japonesque inlay, gate legs w/characteristic square ebony pegs, designed by Greene & Greene & executed by the workshops of Peter Hall for the Belle Barlow Bush-William T. Bolton House, Pasadena, California, branded mark "His True Mark - Greene & Greene," ca. 1907, 47¾ x 63½" extended, 29⅞" h. (alterations) 18,400.00

Baroque Console Table

Baroque console table, walnut, a long D-shaped top supported on angled H-form scroll-cut legs w/angled scroll-cut braces, Italy, late 17th c., 25¼ x 55", 30½" h. (ILLUS.) 3,850.00

Chippendale card table, carved mahogany, rectangular top w/squared outset corners opening to a baize-lined playing surface w/four scooped wells folding above a conforming apron fitted w/a single short drawer, on four cabriole legs w/shell-carved knees & carved double pendant husks & ball-and-claw feet, Newport, Rhode Island, 1750-70, 15⅝ x 30⅜", 27⅜" h. ...48,300.00

Chippendale card table, carved & inlaid mahogany, the well-figured mahogany top w/molded serpentine edges above a conformingly shaped line-inlaid frieze centering a small drawer, fan-inlaid oval dies flanking, the gadrooned skirt below continuing to Chinese pierced brackets, on square molded legs, Rhode Island, ca. 1780, small

Fine Chippendale Card Table

surface patch to leaf where hinge broke out, 15⅞ x 32¾", 28¼" h. (ILLUS.) 37,375.00

Chippendale dressing table, carved walnut, molded top above a long drawer over three short drawers & concave demilune areas in a drawer & skirt, on cabriole legs w/carved leafage on the knees ending in ball-and-claw feet, replaced brasses, refinished, probably New York, ca. 1750. 34½" w., 33" h..................20,900.00

Chippendale Dining Table

Chippendale drop-leaf dining table, mahogany, the rectangular top w/two hinged rectangular leaves above a plain frieze, on stop-fluted square legs, now on casters, Goddard-Townsend School, Newport, Rhode Island, ca. 1770, patches to top near hinges, 42" l. extended, 49" w., 30" h. (ILLUS.)..3,450.00

Chippendale 'tilt-top birdcage' tea table, carved mahogany, molded circular top tilting on a 'bird-cage' mechanism w/baluster-form supports above a columnar standard w/foliate carved ball w/punchwork & gadrooning over a tripod base w/similarly carved cabriole legs terminating in webbed ball-and-claw feet, old refinish, Lancaster County, Pennsylvania, 1750-70, 33" d., 27⅜" h.......................................45,100.00

Classical (American Empire) card table, rectangular w/a crossbanded D-shaped hinged top swiveling above a conforming apron to reveal a well lined w/marbleized paper above two columnar supports on a bracketed trestle base w/turned feet on casters, attributed to Duncan Phyfe, New York, 1820-30, 18 x 35½", 28½" h.........................3,300.00

Classical (American Empire) card table, mahogany veneer, rectangular top w/rounded corners lifting & swiveling to open above an in-curved apron raised on a carved solid lyre-form pedestal on a plinth raised on four downswept legs ending in paw feet, the knees boldly carved w/acanthus leaf scrolls decorated w/gilt, on casters, attributed to William Hook, Salem, Massachusetts, first quarter 19th c., 17½ x 35¼" closed, 29½" h. (black & gilt restored, minor wear, top w/age crack) 1,595.00

American Classical Center Table

Classical (American Empire) center table, carved mahogany, round top above an apron w/a gadrooned lower rim raised on five heavy S-scroll legs headed w/acanthus leaf carving & ending in large paw feet all resting upon a five-point star-form plinth on bulbous ribbed feet, attributed to Anthony Quervelle, Philadelphia, ca. 1825 (ILLUS.) 36,300.00

Classical (American Empire) dining table, mahogany, three-pedestal, the rectangular center section w/wide drop leaves & two D-shaped end sections each w/a wide drop leaf, each above a brass-mounted skirt on a heavy ring-turned standard continuing to shaped down-curving legs ending in brass cuffs & casters, ca. 1825, extended 187" l., 30" h. (minor repairs) 13,800.00

American Classical Dining Table

Classical (American Empire) dining table, extension-type, mahogany, the round top w/a deep apron opening on a large split clustered-column pedestal resting on a lobed squared base, w/ten leaves, ca. 1840-50, closed 54" d., 30½" h. (ILLUS.) 7,150.00

Classical (American Empire) pier table, mahogany, the rectangular top gilt stenciled w/a double-headed eagle amid fruit & foliage above a conforming frieze decorated w/fruit & a palmette border over columnar supports stenciled w/foliage backed by mirrored plates above an inswept shelf decorated w/a basket of fruit flanked by scrolling foliage, on turned feet stenciled w/leaves, New York, 1820-35, 18½ x 40", 41¼" h...3,850.00

Colonial Revival demi-lune console table, mahogany, the D-shaped top raised on legs, ca. 1900, 17½ x 36", 29" h...880.00

Country-style "harvest" table, painted pine & hardwood, long rectangular top flanked by wide single board drop leaves w/curved corners, ends of top have under edge brackets for attaching extensions, turned legs, old worn green repaint over red, 19¾ x 95½", w/13¾" leaves, 28¾" h. (one leaf w/pinned age crack, minor age cracks in top)...15,675.00

Edwardian bow-front side table, mahogany, the top w/an ebonized inlaid edge, w/two frieze drawers, on straight tapering legs, joined by a concave stretcher, signed "Waring," England, early 20th c., 24 x 34", 30" h...4,025.00

Federal card table, satinwood & mahogany, the oblong D-shaped top w/a conforming hinged leaf above a frieze centering a rectangular inlaid reserve, rectangular inlaid dies flanking, raised on slender round reeded tapering legs ending in brass caps on casters, New York, ca.

Federal Card Table

1805, some losses to veneer, 18¾ x 37½", 28¼" h. (ILLUS.) 2,875.00

Federal country-style drop-leaf dining table, cherry, rectangular flanked by wide drop leaves w/notched corners, on slender baluster- and ring-turned legs w/turned knobs at the leg ankles, first half 19th c., 17¼ x 40" plus 15¼" leaves, 29" h. (refinished) 550.00

Federal country-style "harvest" table, painted maple & pine, a long rectangular top flanked by two hinged short drop leaves, on tapering turned legs w/knob feet, painted red, first half 19th c., 36 x 72" open, 29½" h...4,602.00

Federal dining table, curly maple, the rectangular top w/two hinged rectangular leaves above a plain frieze on ring-turned legs ending in columnar feet, Mid-Atlantic States, ca. 1820, open 49½ x 77", 30½" h................5,463.00

Federal Two-Part Dining Table

Federal dining table, mahogany, two-part, comprising two D-shaped end sections, each w/a hinged rectangular leaf, the figured frieze above reeded & ring-turned tapering legs, early 19th c., extended 44 x 83", 29" h. (ILLUS.) 7,475.00

Federal Dressing Table

Federal dressing table, mahogany, a rectangular superstructure w/two small drawers topped by a high double scroll-cut crest & resting on a rectangular top w/molded edge above a single long drawer above ring-turned tapering legs, New England, ca. 1825, 18 x 33", 38½" h. (ILLUS.) 605.00

Federal drop-leaf table, mahogany, the rectangular top w/two conforming drop leaves above a plain apron w/beaded edge, on molded square tapering legs, Philadelphia, 1790-1810, 53¼" deep, open 64¼" w., 28¼" h.........4,400.00

Federal Pembroke Table

Federal Pembroke table, inlaid mahogany, the rectangular top flanked by hinged leaves w/notched corners above a single line-inlaid drawer, the back end faced to simulate a working drawer, oval inlaid dies flanking, the square tapering legs ending in crossbanded cuffs, New York, ca. 1805, appears to retain original oval brasses, repairs to inlays, extended 32 x 40½", 28¼" h.(ILLUS.) 1,840.00

Federal Revival-Style card table, inlaid mahogany, the oblong fold-over top w/bowed front & serpentine ends, above a conforming apron w/an oval satinwood panel centering the front, raised on straight square tapering line-inlaid legs, late 19th c., 18½ x 37", 30½" h........................2,860.00

Hutch (or chair) table, painted pine, the rectangular top tilting above a well w/hinged lid, on shoe feet, painted mustard yellow over original red, New England, ca. 1825, 38½ x 48¼", 27½" h......................4,313.00

Hutch (or chair) table, painted poplar & pine, rectangular two-board pine top tilting above a bench seat between single board ends w/cut-out feet, old brown graining over original red on base, old dark finish on top, 19th c., 28 x 37", 28" h. (top of base may be old replacement)..1,045.00

New England Hutch Table

Hutch (or chair) table, pine & maple, round top tilting above a rectangular seat over a deep apron, on narrow shoe feet, New England, late 18th c., 45¾" d., 27⅛" h. (ILLUS.) 2,090.00

Mission-Style Dining Table

Mission-style (Arts & Crafts movement) dining table, oak, round fixed top above a conforming apron between heavy square legs joined by cross-stretchers, original medium finish, decal mark of L. & J.G. Stickley, ca. 1910, 42" d., 29⅛" h. (ILLUS.) 1,495.00

Mission-style (Arts & Crafts movement) dining table, oak, round top above a square non-dividing pedestal w/four curved bracket feet, original medium finish, decal & crate label of Handcraft Furniture by L. & J.G. Stickley, Model No. 717, ca. 1907, 48" d., 29¾" h. 3,450.00

Mission-style (Arts & Crafts movement) library table, oval top raised on heavy square legs w/a medial shelf above two enclosed open-fronted compartments, original black finish, Michigan Chair Company, unmarked, 28 x 44", 29" h. (some finish wear) 385.00

Mission-Style Library Table

Mission-style (Arts & Crafts movement) library table, oak, rectangular top overhanging four heavy square legs on casters joined by a wide medial shelf w/keyed tenons through end stretchers, black finish, attributed to Charles Stickley, 30 x 48", 29¾" h. (ILLUS.) 402.50

Mission-style (Arts & Crafts movement) side table, oak & leather, hexagonal top covered in hard leather affixed along the edge w/round tacks, six evenly spaced stretchers join in the middle w/a faceted finial, original leather top & original finish, paper label & red decal mark of Gustav Stickley, Model No. 624, 48" w., 29" h. 11,000.00

Mission-style (Arts & Crafts movement) side table, oak, round top above four square legs joined by cross stretchers w/a round shelf, medium - dark finish, partial paper label of the Lifetime Furniture Company, Model No. 930, ca. 1910,

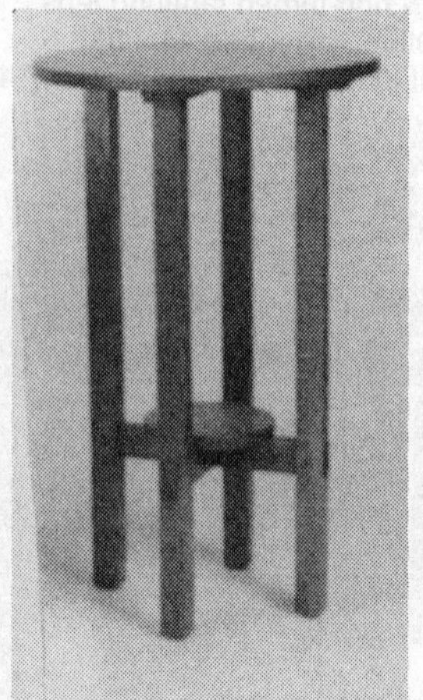

Lifetime Side Table

refinished, losses, 18" d., 29¼" h. (ILLUS.) 517.50

Tea Table with Grueby Tiles

Mission-style (Arts & Crafts movement) tea table, oak, the rectangular top composed of 12 matte green glazed Grueby Pottery tiles above an arched apron, a medial shelf below w/keyed tenons through the end stretchers, original medium finish, water stains & light toning on the top, red decal mark of Gustav Stickley, ca. 1903, 20¼ x 24", 25" h.(ILLUS.) 29,900.00

Mission-style (Arts & Crafts movement) tea table, oak, round top overhanging an apron on square legs joined by arched cross stretchers, Handcraft decal mark of L. & J.G. Stickley, ca. 1910, 25" d., 28½" h. (top separation) 605.00

Modern style coffee table, molded plywood, the dished circular top raised on molded legs, ebonized finish, designed by Charles & Ray

Eames, manufactured by Herman Miller Furniture Company, ca. 1946, 34½" d., 15¼" h. 460.00

Modern style coffee table, walnut & glass, the round glass top w/molded tapering X-frame support, raised on four walnut tapering legs ending in brass *sabots*, designed by Gio Ponti, stamped "Made in Italy," ca. 1953, 39" d., 14" h. 2,530.00

Modern style conference table, rosewood, aluminum & painted steel, the rectangular wooden top inlaid w/radiating veneers of rosewood, raised on a large metal four unit pedestal base, designed by Charles & Ray Eames, ca. 1960, 96" l., 30" h. 4,888.00

Neoclassical side table, fruitwood, the rectangular top inset w/a veined grey-green marble slab, the frieze fitted w/one long drawer, the corners marked w/ebonized diamonds fitted w/bearded masks, raised on square tapering legs ending in paw feet, Austria, early 19th c., 16¾ x 24", 31¼" h. 3,738.00

Oriental side table, cypress, rectangular top w/everted end flanges, on flared legs of rounded rectangular form, w/cloud-scroll spandrels, joined by double cross braces enclosing a scrolling cut-out design, China, 18th-19th c., 14 x 42", 35¼" h. 2,875.00

Queen Anne Breakfast Table

Queen Anne breakfast table, mahogany, oblong top w/two hinged D-shaped drop leaves above a plain skirt, on cabriole legs ending in pad feet, Boston, Massachusetts, 1740-60, 23½ x 26⅞" extended, 25½" h. (ILLUS.) 40,250.00

Queen Anne drop-leaf table, mahogany, the hinged oval top w/D-shaped drop leaves over a flat-arched apron, on turned legs w/pad feet, Rhode Island or Pennsylvania, 1740-60, 44¼" deep, open 43¾" l., 28½" h. 9,350.00

Queen Anne tavern table, country-style, painted hardwood & pine, oval one-board top over shaped apron, splayed base w/turned legs on button feet, old red paint on base, top w/old dark refinishing, 23 x 30¼", 24¾" h. (top w/repaired age cracks) 2,640.00

Queen Anne tea table, tiger maple & maple, rectangular top above plain skirt w/single drawer, cabriole legs ending in pad feet, refinished, Newport, Rhode Island, ca. 1740, 17⅝ x 27", 25¾" h. (imperfections) 29,700.00

Queen Anne tea table, mahogany, rectangular top above a plain frieze w/a shaped apron continuing to slender cabriole legs ending in pointed pad feet, New York, ca. 1740-60, 19¾ x 31", 26½" h. (top tray moldings missing) 21,850.00

Regency drum table, mahogany, the circular top inset w/a tooled morocco surface above a conforming frieze of alternating sham & functional drawers, revolving above a turned pedestal w/downswept quatrepod ending in brass castered toe caps, England, early 19th c., 41½" d., 30" h. 5,500.00

Regency Sofa Table

Regency sofa table, rosewood, the rectangular top flanked by D-shaped leaves above two long, narrow frieze drawers opposed by false drawers, raised on a parcel-gilt turned pedestal above a four-sided concave plinth w/parcel-gilt scroll feet, England, ca. 1825, restored, extended 28 x 60", 28½" h. (ILLUS.) 2,875.00

Victorian Golden Oak dining table, round divided-top raised on a split

Golden Oak Dining Table

pedestal base w/four heavy animal paw legs headed by snarling lions' heads, 54" d. (ILLUS.) 3,600.00

Renaissance Revival Dining Table

Victorian Renaissance Revival dining table, mahogany, square divided top w/an egg-and-dart carved edge band, on a heavy reeded columnar pedestal above a four-part base w/large acanthus-carved S-scrolls above the C-scroll feet, late 19th c., w/eight 15⅝" w. leaves, 54" sq., 29" h. (ILLUS.) 4,125.00

Victorian Rococo Center Table

Victorian Rococo substyle parlor center table, carved rosewood, the turtle-top inset w/white marble above a conforming apron ornately carved w/rectangular plaque at the center of each side & end & each w/a figural animal head above a turned drop, each plaque flanked by panels of leafy vines, on four heavy S-form carved legs headed by busts of children above floral clusters, each leg ending in a dolphin head, legs joined by scrolled cross stretchers centered by a large bulbous urn-form finial, attributed to Alexander Roux, New York, ca. 1850 (ILLUS.) 13,200.00

William & Mary Dining Table

William & Mary drop-leaf "gate-leg" dining table, maple, rectangular top w/rounded ends flanked by a pair of D-shaped drop leaves above an apron w/a small end drawer above baluster- and ring-turned legs w/two swing gate-legs, on ball feet, New England, ca. 1740, old surface, restored, 41¾ x 47½", 29¼" h. (ILLUS.) 2,860.00

William & Mary drop-leaf "gate-leg" dining table, turned walnut, the oblong top flanked by two hinged D-shaped drop leaves above an apron w/a single end drawer, on vase-, reel- and block-turned legs joined by blocked stretchers, probably New York, ca. 1720, 42½ x 54", 28½" h. (feet reduced in height) 10,350.00

William & Mary tavern table, carved walnut, the rectangular removable top widely overhanging a shaped deep skirt w/incised edge, each side w/a stylized shell-form pendant, fitted w/a drawer at each end & in the center of one side, on massive ring-turned vase-form legs joined by box stretchers, ending in flattened ball feet, Pennsylvania, 1740-60, 35½ x 68¾", 28¾" h....................24,150.00

WARDROBES & ARMOIRES

Armoire, Art Deco, lacquered wood, rectangular stepped top over a pair of long doors w/geometric patterned marquetry designs & opening to an interior fitted w/shelves, drawers & a garment rack, red lacquer on the top & sides & black lacquer trim, designed by Paul T. Fankl, ca. 1927, 22 x 56", 6' ½" h. (ILLUS. top next column) 2,300.00

Art Deco Armoire

Armoire, Art Nouveau, carved mahogany, "Clematis" patt., the arched central crest carved w/flowering clematis vines above a central beveled glass door flanked by two arched beveled glass doors opening to shelved interiors, raised on a shaped base w/three short drawers each w/gilt-bronze pulls cast as clover leaves, further carved blossoms & vines along the base, by Louis Majorelle, France, ca. 1900, 19 x 72", 7' 8" h. 3,850.00

Liberty & Company Armoire

Armoire, Arts & Crafts style, inlaid oak, a rectangular top w/a molded cornice above a pair of tall arched-panel doors w/stylized floral inlay of mother-of-pearl & various fruitwoods panel all above a pair of deep drawers over a deep molded base, original copper hardware, original medium finish, unsigned Liberty & Company, England, ca. 1905, one pull broken, minor abrasion, 23 x 76¼", 7' 9½" h. (ILLUS.) 2,300.00

Kas (American version of the Netherlands *Kast* or wardrobe), walnut, molded cornice w/rounded corners above pair of raised panel doors w/wrought-iron rattail hinges, brass shield-shaped escutcheons, molded base w/rounded corners, on casters, interior w/one shelf & wooden hooks, old finish, from Ohio, probably Zoar, cornice 22½ x 51", case 46¾" w., 6' 4½" h. (minor damage to ends of cornice) 1,950.00

Kas, walnut, made to disassemble, a rectangular top w/a flat, flaring cornice above a wide frieze band over a narrow molding above a pair of long doors each w/four long rectangular raised panels above another narrow molding over a pair of drawers w/batwing brasses & keyhole escutcheons, molded base w/shaped apron & bracket feet, old mellow refinishing, Pennsylvania, late 18th - early 19th c., 22¼ x 60¾", 6' 5" h. (feet replaced, minor edge damage & repair, replaced brasses) 3,850.00

Kas, grain-painted pine, made to disassemble, molded cornice above pair of three-panel doors, over two dovetailed overlapping drawers, raised panel ends, bracket feet, original red flame graining, cornice 31½ x 70¼", case 65½" w., 6' 8" h. (minor insect damage) 1,155.00

Painted Pennsylvania Schrank

Schrank, painted pine, made to disassemble, the flaring molded removable cornice above a wide flat frieze over a molding above the double raised-panel door flanked by wide side panels over a base molding above a single long drawer in the base, molded base band, Pennsylvania, 1750-70, retains traces of green & white paint, 24 x 55", 6' 8" h. (ILLUS.)............................9,200.00

Wardrobe, Classical (American Empire), mahogany, in several parts, the rectangular top w/deep removable projecting cornice centering an ormolu mount in the form of griffins above a pair of long hinged doors flanked by wide reeded pilasters w/Ionic capitals, the whole raised on ribbed, flattened ball feet, Boston, Massachusetts, ca. 1820, 25 x 66", 7' 4" h..........................10,350.00

American Classical Wardrobe

Wardrobe, Classical (American Empire), mahogany, a rectangular top w/a wide flat angled cornice above a frieze band above a pair of double-paneled long doors flanked by ormolu-mounted columns, flat apron & block feet on casters, New York, early 19th c. (ILLUS.) 5,775.00

Wardrobe, Victorian country-style, painted & decorated pine & poplar, a rectangular top w/a wide angled flaring cornice above a tall paneled door, curved apron & simple cut-out feet, overall old red flame graining, 19th c., 19¼ x 44¼", 6' 7" h. (rail over door cracked)..........................385.00

Wardrobe, Victorian Rococo substyle,carved mahogany, a rectangular top w/a deep flaring & rounded cornice above a wide frieze over a pair of tall arched-panel doors w/scroll carving, two drawers below w/scroll-carved keyhole escutcheons, molded base on bracket feet, attributed to Prudent Mallard, New Orleans, ca. 1850 (ILLUS.) 2,970.00

Prudent Mallard Wardrobe

New Orleans-Made Wardrobe

Wardrobe, Victorian Rococo substyle, carved rosewood, rectangular top w/an arched front cornice topped by a high pierced scroll- and flower-carved pediment centered by a fruit-filled urn & flanked by ribbed crown-form corner finials above a conforming arched frieze band over a beaded band framing the case w/a pair of long, mirrored doors above a single long paneled drawer at the base over an egg-and-dart carved band on the molded base w/cushion feet, attributed to Prudent Mallard, New Orleans, ca. 1860 (ILLUS.) 19,800.00

WHATNOTS & ETAGERES

Etagere, Art Nouveau, carved mahogany, the rectangular top w/a

Renaissance Revival Etagere

bowed front & pierced carved back rail above two shaped lower shelves supported by a paneled back & a branching front leg carved w/orchid blossoms & leafage, Louis Majorelle, France, ca. 1900, 17 x 21½", 4' 3" h. 3,450.00

Etagere, Federal, carved mahogany, surmounted by pointed ball-form finials centering three scalloped shelves, four X-form divider supports below, mounted on one side w/a lyre- and ribbon-carved applique, a single drawer below on turned legs, ending in brass casters, Boston area, Massachusetts, 18 x 18⅛", 5' 1" h. 4,888.00

Etagere, papier-maché ebonized & parcel gilt, top shelf painted after the "Boyar Wedding" over two open shelves, raised on octagonal straight legs & shaped feet, Russia, 14 x 20¼", 38½" h. 1,100.00

Etagere, Victorian Renaissance Revival substyle, carved rosewood, the superstructure w/a high central arched crest w/a scroll-carved pediment centered by a large roundel flanked by scrolls, four turned urn-form finials & two smaller crests flanking above a three-section mirrored back w/a tall central rectangular mirror w/pierced scroll-carved corner brackets flanked by narrower mirrors behind three-shelf open display sections joined by slender ring-turned spindles above pierced C-form base brackets above the shaped D-form white marble top resting on a conforming scalloped apron carved w/palmettes & scrolls over the four shaped legs headed by carved fruit clusters & ending in scrolls, the base backed by a square central mirror flanked by open shaped shelves & a base shelf, attributed to Alexander Roux, New York, ca. 1860 (ILLUS.) 8,250.00

Victorian Rococo Etagere

Etagere, Victorian Rococo substyle, carved rosewood, the arched & molded crestrail topped by a tall crest of pierced delicate leafy scrolls centered by a cartouche medallion, two-tier turned urn finials at the top corners, the tall three-section mirrored back w/three-shelf open units joined by ring-turned spindles flanking the central mirror section, a narrow shaped D-form white marble shelf at the base above a deep conforming apron w/carved leafy scrolls flanking bold center roundels, on a pair of short cabriole legs at the center & pierced inverted U-form legs at the sides, ca. 1850, 20 x 50", 8' 1" h. (ILLUS.) 8,880.00

GAMES & GAME BOARDS

For related items see the CHARACTER COLLECTIBLES and DISNEY COLLECTIBLES categories.

Abbott Spelling Puzzle (The), move wooden letters to make words, in original box $75.00

Autobridge, 1957, complete.................12.00

Barbie Prom Queen board game, 1960...55.00

Camouflage board game, caricatures of comedians Sid Caesar, Steve Allen, etc. on colorful box, ABC-TV, 1961, complete 25.00

Cavalcade Horse Racing board game, w/all pieces & directions, Selchow & Righter Co., worn box 40.00
Corner the Market board game, Whitman Publishing Co., 1938, w/box & instructions 30.00
Cribbage board, ivory-inlaid mahogany, a narrow rectangular board w/round tab ends inlaid w/two rows of rectangular ivory blocks & rounded ivory pieces at the ends, raised on small shoe feet, 19th c., 10¾" l., ⅞" h. 440.00
Dawn of the Dead board game, 1978, mint in sealed box.................... 40.00
Easy Money board game, Milton Bradley, 1936 ....35.00
Flinch card game, 1911, w/original box & instructions 15.00
Game board, metal, one side marked w/squares for the game of checkers, the reverse for the game of Chinese checkers, 16" 12.50
Game board, painted & decorated wood, one side painted w/faux marble playing squares within a border stenciled w/bands of paired leaf-like designs & crosses at the corners, molded painted frame, early 20th c., 18¼" sq. 440.00
Game board, painted wood, one side w/a checkerboard in two shades of red, black & green, the other side w/a parcheesi board in six colors, 16" sq. 550.00
Grimm's Fairy Tales card game, color scenes of Snow White, etc., Austria, w/box & instructions 25.00
Hee Haw board game, 1975, mint in box 38.00
Hollywood Go! board game, 1954....... 40.00
Jan Murray's TV Word Game, board-type, 1961, near mint 20.00
Life of the Party board game, figural donkey spinner, mint in octagon-shaped box 100.00
Loonykins board game, Hassenfeld Bros., complete.................... 65.00
Mah Jong, Parker Bros., wooden, Babcock rules, complete in case, 1923.................... 95.00
Monopoly board game, Parker Bros., 1936, w/metal markers 25.00
Parcheesi board game, Selchow & Righter, 1920s, w/original box & instructions 20.00
Peter Coddle Tells Of His Trip to Chicago card game, Parker Brothers, ca. 1890 ....25.00
Piggeries game, painted tin-plate pigs race to feed, ca. 1870s, mint w/box 295.00
Raggedy Ann's Magic Pebble board game, Milton Bradley 25.00
Ringmaster board game, ca. 1947, complete 45.00
Round the World With Nellie Bly board game, McLoughlin Bros., 1890 .... 350.00
Safari board game, 1950 ....40.00
77 Sunset Strip board game 65.00
Shoot-A-Loop marble game, Wolverine 45.00
Skip-Bo card game, new condition in original red flocked box 50.00
Snap card game, cards illustrated w/pictures of Roosevelt Bears, Parker Bros., 1900s, mint in box 35.00
Spell-It board game, 1937 .... 23.00
Spot Shot marble game 55.00
Tilt 'n Roll Obstacle Puzzle game, Milton Bradley, 1964 ....15.00
Ting, Tong, Tang marble game, Alox Co., St. Louis, 1939, w/marbles, board & wooden storage box (no instructions) 20.00
Trolley card game, cards & box illustrated w/trolley, original instructions, Snyder Bros. Game Co., Elmira, New York, 1904 .... 45.00
Winky Dink & You board game, 1968, unopened 20.00

Wonderful Game of Oz

Wonderful Game of Oz board game, Parker Brothers, 1921, game intact, corners torn (ILLUS.) 176.00
You Shoot marble game 55.00

GARDEN FOUNTAINS & ORNAMENTS

Ornamental garden or yard fountains, urns and figures often enhanced the formal plantings on spacious lawns of mansion-sized dwellings during the late 19th and early 20th century. While fountains were usually reserved for the lawns of estates, even modest homes often had a latticework arbor or cast-iron urn in the yard. Today garden enthusiasts look for these ornamental pieces to lend an aura of elegance to their landscaping.

Figure of a Man by Durenne

Armillary sphere, zinc, an upright metal ring fitted a wide metal ring in the center, on a cylindrical pedestal base on a round foot, traces of astrological signs, 23" d., overall 38½" h. $1,650.00

Bench, stone, simple rectangular top w/molded edge above leafy scrolled supports, 33½" h. 2,300.00

Figure of a child, marble, the young boy seated w/one leg crossed over the other, one hand extended, on a cylindrical pedestal w/square base, signed "P. GUARNERIO MILANO 18??," overall 5' 11" h. 4,313.00

Figure of a man, cast iron, the allegorical figure wearing a draped garment over one shoulder, one hand holding aloft an early grease lamp, the other hand at his waist, signed "A. Durenne," Antoine Durenne, Paris, France, late 19th c., 5' 3" h. (ILLUS.) 6,900.00

Figure of a young woman, bronze, wearing a diaphanous gown, the strap slipping off one shoulder, one hand raised holding a shallow cup to her lips, the other hand holding the hem of her skirt, on a marble pedestal base, signed "MULLER CREFIELD," 7' 1" h. 12,650.00

Figure group, bronze, depiction of Leda & the swan, the nude Leda partially draped about her lower body seated on a rockwork base, the swan on a lower rocky out-cropping by her feet, weathered patina, signed "C. Dorn - Aktien-Gesoll Schaft, H. Gladenseck John, Bildgiesseri," Carl Dorn, ca. 1897, 6' 4" 50,600.00

Font, marble, the standard w/spiral fluting ending in leaf tips, raised on a plinth base supporting a raised deeply paneled circular font, the whole raised on a stepped square base, 43" h. (restorations) 4,025.00

Fountain, cast iron & metal, cast w/two children under an umbrella, within a welled interior cast w/frogs & turtles, signed "J.W. FISKE MANUF. NEW YORK," 4' 5" h. (alterations) 3,738.00

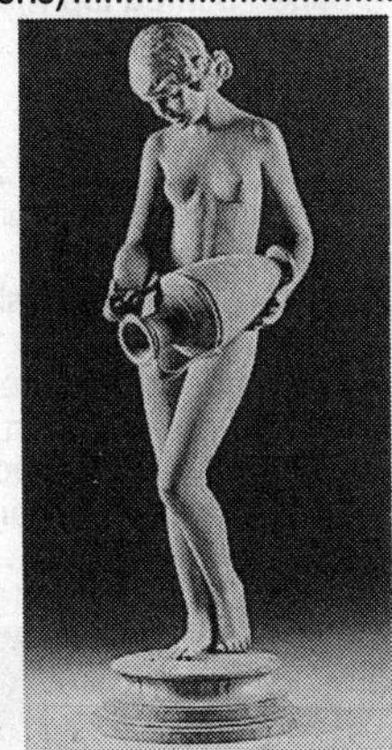

Fountain with a Female Water Bearer

Fountain, lead, depicting a nude female holding an urn in a pouring position, the urn incorporating a nozzle, signed "C.S. Paolo, 1955," 3' 7" h. (ILLUS.) 1,725.00

Marble Fountain with Putto & Dolphin

Fountain, marble, depicting a putto blowing into a conch shell while riding on the back of a dolphin immersed in waves, the whole raised on a rectangular base w/canted corners, late 19th c., 27" h. (ILLUS.) 4,600.00

Fountain, zinc, depicting a partially nude young woman holding a drape above & behind her head, another drape about her hips, two frolicking putti at her feet, after a design by J.W. Fiske, late 19th c., 5' 3" h......6,900.00

Garden seat, earthenware, barrel-shaped, decorated overall w/blue scrolling flowers against a white ground, impressed "MINTONS" & "2638," late 19th c. 805.00

Gazebo, wrought iron, arched sides supporting an open domed top w/a scrolled finial, 6' 10" h. 3,450.00

Hose guards, lead, each formed as a fish w/an upright tail, 19" h., set of 9..2,185.00

Jardinieres, marble, carved w/a figural panel or roundel on each side, flanked by lion heads hung w/floral swags, 18½" h., pr. 11,500.00

Jardinieres, zinc, female figure attired in a softly draped gown holding an urn upward above her head, raised on a waisted pedestal, signed "Carrier," late 19th c., overall 4' 6½" h., pr...10,925.00

Carved Marble Jardiniere on Figural Base

Jardiniere & pedestal base, marble, octagonal jardiniere carved w/leaf tips & masks, raised on a conforming pedestal & supported by a reclining lion on a low rectangular base, 5' 6" h. (ILLUS.)....................3,738.00

Model of a Retriever dog, cast iron, the standing animal w/its head raised, modeled fur detail on body & long, extended tail, painted reddish brown, probably J.W. Fiske & Co., New York, late 19th c., 52" l., 33½" h..9,200.00

Models of lions, bronze, the recumbent animal w/well-defined mane & head held erect, on a low footed rectangular base, 42" l., pr............3,738.00

Model of a Sphinx & a Putto

Models of Sphinx, terra cotta, the regal Sphinx depicted w/the figure of a frolicksome putto astride, 44" h., pr. (ILLUS. of one) 19,550.00

Planters, lead, rectangular, each w/four panels cast w/acorns & leaves, 47½" l., pr. 2,875.00

Carved Marble Planter

Planters, marble, globular, carved in the form of leaf tips, 13" h., pr. (ILLUS. of one) 4,888.00

Urn, cast iron, a leaf-tip & beaded lip above an oak leaf cast neck flanked by Janus handles ending in boar heads, the base further decorated w/berried oak leaves & a Greek key band, ending in a circular socle & a stepped plinth base, late 19th c., 35" h...3,450.00

Urns, cast iron, each cast w/foliage, ornate scroll handles, raised on paneled pedestal, stamped "J.W.

Fiske no. 21 & 23 Patd. June 1 1875, Barclay St. N.Y.," late 19th c., 4' h., pr. 9,200.00

Urns, terra cotta, each ovoid body centered by a crowned heraldic cartouche, the neck w/flaring rim & base decorated w/geometric designs, ornate double scroll handles, signed "GARIO ACRESTI ATALIA FIRENCE IMPRUNEIA 1898," ca. 1898, 39" h., pr. (damages) 4,600.00

Cast Iron Urn on Stand

Urns on stands, painted cast iron, ribbed body continuing to a leaf tip lip, raised on a circular socle ending in a stepped square base, late 19th c., 42" h., pr. (ILLUS. of one)..6,038.00

Well head, marble & wrought iron, octagonal form, the frieze carved w/a continuous rope, the body w/alternating panels carved w/heraldic shields, surmounted by a scrolled & spiral cast superstructure, 19th c., 9' 4" h. 12,650.00

GLASS

AGATA

Agata was patented by Joseph Locke of the New England Glass Co. in 1887. The application of mineral stain left a mottled effect on the surface of the article. It was applied chiefly to the Wild Rose (Peach Blow) line but sometimes was applied as a border on pale opaque green. In production for a short time, it is scarce. Items listed below are of the Wild Rose line unless otherwise noted.

Celery vase, bulbous base tapering slightly w/a gently flaring rim, green opaque ground decorated w/lacy gold trim on the rim & shoulder, 6⅞" h... $985.00

Toothpick holder, green opaque, squatty ovoid body tapering to a widely flaring rim, decorated around the rim w/a band of blue mottled stain w/a gold border band, 2¼" h. 770.00

Toothpick holder, squatty ovoid base tapering to a flaring rim, green opaque ground decorated w/lacy gold trim on the rim & shoulder 1,150.00

Tumbler, cylindrical, oily mottling w/blue spotting, 2½" d., 3⅞" h. 695.00

Tumbler, cylindrical, deep raspberry shading to creamy pink, decorated w/oily mottling & blue spotting, 2½" d., 3⅞" h. 695.00

Vase, 4½" h., cylindrical body w/squared scalloped rim, fine coloring 880.00

AKRO AGATE

This glass was made by the Akro Agate Company in Clarksburg, West Virginia between 1932 and 1951. The company was famous for their marble production but also produced many novelty items in various colors of marbleized glass and offered a popular line of glass children's dishes in plain colors and marbleized glass. Most articles bear the company mark of a crow flying through a capital letter A.

GENERAL LINE

Mexicali Powder Jar

Cup & saucer, demitasse, marbleized orange & white.............................. $15.00

Flowerpot, miniature, ribbed rim, green opaque, 2¾" h. 9.00
Flowerpot, miniature, ribbed rim, orange opaque, 2¾" h. 14.00
Flowerpot, scalloped rim, black amethyst, 3" h. 35.00
Jardiniere, ribbed & fluted rim, pumpkin opaque, No. 306CF, 5" h. 30.00
Lamp, marbleized orange & white, 9" h. 65.00
Planter, rectangular, blue w/decoration, No. 653, 8" l. 20.00
Powder jar, Colonial Lady cover, pink opaque, 6¼" h. 75.00
Powder jar, Colonial Lady cover, powder blue opaque base, white cover, 6¼" h. 65.00
Powder jar, Mexicali w/sombrero cover, marbleized orange & white (ILLUS.) 42.50
Powder jar, Mexicali w/sombrero cover, milk white opaque 40.00
Powder jar, Scottie Dog cover, white opaque 75.00
Smoking set: four ashtrays & cov. box; marbleized green & white, 5 pcs. 35.00
Vase, 6¼" h., scalloped rim, embossed graduated dart decoration, pumpkin opaque, No. 316 ....40.00
Vase, 6¼" h., tab handles, marbleized orange & white 30.00

CHILDREN'S DISHES

Bowl, cereal, Interior Panel patt., marbleized green & white 23.50
Bowl, cereal, Interior Panel patt., marbleized oxblood & lemon 35.00
Bowl, cereal, Stacked Disc & Panel patt., transparent cobalt blue 50.00
Creamer, Chiquita patt., transparent cobalt blue 24.50
Creamer, small, Raised Daisy patt., yellow opaque 45.00
Cup, small, Interior Panel patt., marbleized blue & white....................31.00
Cup & saucer, Chiquita patt., transparent cobalt blue 14.50
Cup & saucer, Stippled Band patt., blue opaque 39.00
Plate, dinner, 3¼" d., Interior Panel patt., marbleized blue & white 16.00
Plate, dinner, 3¼" d., Raised Daisy patt., blue opaque 14.50
Plate, dinner, 4¼" d., Concentric Rings patt., transparent cobalt blue 12.00
Sugar bowl, cov., Interior Panel patt., marbleized green & white 42.00
Sugar bowl, cov., Raised Daisy patt., yellow opaque 85.00
Teapot, cov., Octagonal-O patt., marbleized blue & white 23.00
Teapot, cov., Raised Daisy patt., medium blue opaque 52.50
Tumbler, Raised Daisy patt., yellow opaque 26.00
Tumbler, Stacked Disc & Panel patt., transparent cobalt blue, 2" h. 20.00

ALEXANDRITE

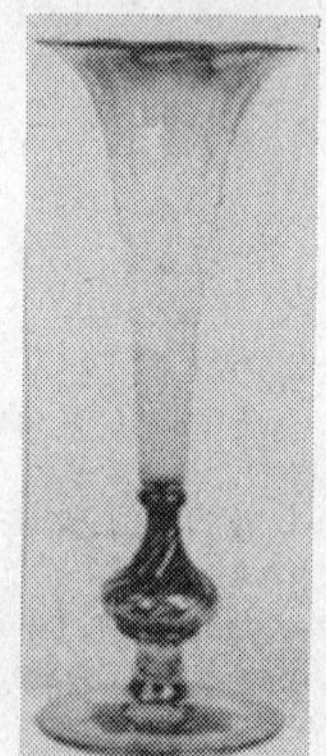

Alexandrite Trumpet-form Vase

This glass, shading from a yellowish color to rose to blue, was produced by Thomas Webb & Sons and Stevens & Williams of England. A somewhat similar ware was made by Moser of Carlsbad.

Bowl, 8½" d., free-form w/outswept rim, molded ribbed sides, attributed to Moser $125.00
Goblet, large bell-form bowl w/tiny optic honeycomb design, plain stem & round foot, Thomas Webb & Son., 4½" h. 747.50
Punch cup, barrel-shaped w/applied citron handle, 2¼" d., 2¾" h. 550.00
Vase, 4¼" h., Honeycomb patt. 765.00
Vase, 8¼" h., trumpet-shaped, round foot, swirl-molded compressed base (ILLUS.) 2,800.00
Wine, Optic patt., 4½" h. 950.00

AMBERINA

Amberina was developed in the late 1880s by the New England Glass Company and a pressed version was made by Hobbs, Brockunier & Company (under license from the former). A similar ware, called Rose Amber, was made by the Mt. Washington Glass Works. Amberina-Rose Amber shades from amber to deep red or fuchsia and cut and plated (lined with creamy white) examples were also made. The Libbey Glass Company briefly revived blown Amberina, using modern shapes, in 1917.

Amberina Cruet

Bar bottle w/original amber facet-cut stopper, Swirled Rib patt., 8" h. $350.00
Bonbon, Shape 3029, signed, Libbey Glass Co. 350.00
Bowl, ice cream, individual, 5" d., pressed Daisy & Button patt. 90.00
Bowl, 10" oval, pressed Daisy & Button patt. 350.00
Butter dish, cov., Diagonal Block patt. 235.00
Butter pat, pressed Daisy & Button patt. 110.00
Carafe, Reverse Amberina, Inverted Thumbprint patt., 7½" h. 275.00
Celery vase, square top w/ruffled rim, Diamond Quilted patt. 445.00
Cheese dish, cov., twelve-paneled cover w/cut finial, Optic patt., 9½" d., 7" h. 345.00
Compote, open, 10" h., ruffled rim, ball connector, flat disc base, Shape 3016, signed, Libbey Glass Co. 2,310.00
Creamer, globular base, slender neck w/flaring rim & pinched lip, applied angular amber handle, Swirl patt., 3⅜" d., 5" h. 135.00
Cruet w/original amber stopper, bulbous melon-ribbed body, applied amber handle, 6 ¾" h. (ILLUS.)........200.00
Ice cream set: master bowl & six plates; pressed Daisy & Button patt., 7 pcs. 925.00
Model of a pear w/stem 175.00
Pitcher, 4¾" h., flaring base below long angled sides to the flaring squared rim, applied reeded amber handle, Inverted Thumbprint patt., New England Glass Co....................345.00
Pitcher, milk, 5" h., bulbous, melon-ribbed body w/applied amber handle, Herringbone patt. 195.00
Pitcher, tankard, 6¾" h., Diamond Quilted patt., New England Glass Co. 770.00
Pitcher, 8" h., pleated rim, applied reeded clear handle 225.00
Punch cup w/applied amber handle, Inverted Thumbprint patt., Mt. Washington Glass Co. 135.00
Punch cup, Reverse Amberina, Inverted Thumbprint patt....................50.00
Rose bowl, round melon-ribbed body w/applied amber threading, 3½" h. 70.00
Spooner, Inverted Thumbprint patt., 4¾" h. 95.00
Syrup pitcher w/original silver plate top, ball-shaped, Inverted Thumbprint patt., New England Glass Co...450.00

Amberina Toothpick Holder

Toothpick holder, square rim, Diamond Quilted patt. (ILLUS.)........235.00
Tumbler, juice, Diamond Quilted patt., 2⅝" h. 125.00
Tumbler, Plated Amberina, embossed ribs, New England Glass Co., ca. 1880, 3¾" h. 1,320.00
Vase, 7" h., lily-form w/tricorner rim, New England Glass Co....................345.00
Vase, bud, 8" h., 2¼" d., bottle-shaped tapering to flaring rim, disc foot, applied clear spiral trim 195.00
Vase, 12" h., cylindrical w/three applied triangular ribbed feet, Swirled Rib patt., polished pontil......250.00

ANIMALS

Americans evidently like to collect glass animals and, for the past fifty years, American glass manufacturers have turned out a wide variety of animals to please the buying public. Some were produced for long periods and some were later reproduced by other companies, while others were made for only a short period of time and are rare. We have not included late productions in our listings and have attempted to date the productions where possible. Evelyn Zemel's book, American Glass Animals A to Z *will be helpful to the novice collector.*

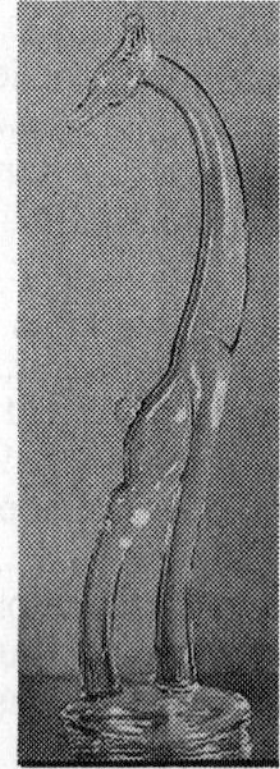

Giraffe by Heisey

Airdale Dog, clear frosted, unmarked, 6½" l., 5¾" h. $250.00

Angelfish book end, clear, A.H. Heisey & Co., 2¼ x 3½" wave base, 7" h. 115.00

Bear, Mama, clear, New Martinsville Glass Mfg. Co., 6" l., 4½" h. ....165.00 to 180.00

Chinese Pheasant, blue, Paden City Glass Mfg. Co., ca. 1940, 13¾" l., 5¾" h. ....125.00 to 150.00

Deer sitting, clear, Fostoria Glass Co., 1940-43, 1 x 2" base, 2¼" h. 45.00

Deer standing, clear, Fostoria Glass Co., 1 x 2" base, 4½" h. 42.00

Elephant book end, clear, New Martinsville Mfg. Co., 3¼ x 5¼" base, 6¼" l., 5¼" h. 80.00

Elephant figure w/trunk up, clear, A.H. Heisey & Co., 1944-53, large, 6½" l., 4¼" h. 425.00

Giraffe w/head turned, clear, A.H. Heisey & Co., 1942-52, 11" h.(ILLUS.) ....175.00 to 200.00

Goose, wings up, clear, A.H. Heisey & Co., 1942-53, 7½" l., 6½" h. .... 90.00 to 125.00

Hen, clear, A.H. Heisey & Co.,1948-49, 2¾ x 2½" base, 4½" h. 425.00

Horses, Clydesdale, clear, A.H. Heisey & Co., 1942-48, 8" l., 8" h., pr. ....400.00 to 450.00

Horse, Pony ashtray, clear, K.R. Haley, 5½" d. tray, pony 2½" h. at ears 23.00

Horse, Plug (Sparky), clear, A.H. Heisey & Co., 1941-46, 3½" l., 4¼" h. 95.00

Horse, Pony, standing, clear, A.H. Heisey & Co., 1940-52, 1½ x 2¼" base, 3" l., 5" h. ....75.00 to 100.00

Horse rearing book ends, clear, A.H. Heisey & Co., 3¼ x 6½ " base, 7¾" h., pr. 235.00

Horse rearing book ends, black, L.E. Smith, 1940s, 3 x 5¼" base, 5¾" l., 8" h., pr. 120.00

Horse Head (double heads) ashtray, clear, A.H. Heisey & Co. 45.00

Horse Head book ends, clear, A.H. Heisey & Co., 1937-55, 2¾ x 4¾" base, 7¼" h., pr. ....250.00 to 300.00

Pelican, clear, New Martinsville Glass Mfg. Co., 8¼" h. 85.00

Pouter Pigeon book ends, clear, Cambridge Glass Co., 4 x 5" base, 6" h., pr. 160.00

Pouter Pigeon book ends, clear, Paden City Glass Mfg. Co., 3 x 3¾" base, 6½" h., pr. 140.00

Rabbit, Bunnies, clear, ears up, ears back or ears lying down, New Martinsville Glass Mfg. Co., 1", each ....55.00 to 65.00

Seal w/ball candleholders, clear, New Martinsville Glass Mfg. Co., 7¼" h., pr. ....100.00 to 125.00

Starfish book end, clear, New Martinsville Glass Mfg. Co., 2¾ x 6¼" base, 7¾" h. 50.00

Swan dish, green opalescent, Imperial Swan, Imperial Glass Co., 1930s, 4½" h. 28.00

Swan dish, clear w/cobalt blue neck & head, New Martinsville Glass Co., 11" l. 85.00

Swan figure, wings up, clear, A.H. Heisey & Co., 1947-53, 7" h. ....475.00 to 525.00

Swan figure, Pall Mall patt., clear, Duncan & Miller Glass Co.,10½" h. ...60.00

Swordfish, blue opalescent frosted, Duncan & Miller Glass Co., 3¼" l., 5" h. 395.00

Tiger book end, head up, clear, New Martinsville Glass Mfg.Co., 3¼" x 5¾" base, 6½" h. 165.00

Tiger paperweight, black opaque, Imperial Glass Co. (Heisey mold), 1982-83, 8" l., 2⅔" h. 75.00

APPLIQUED

Simply stated, this is an art glass form with applied decoration. Sometimes master glass craftsmen applied stems or branches to an art glass object and then added molded glass flowers or fruit specimens to these branches or stems. At other times a button of molten glass was daubed on the object and a tool pressed over it to form a prunt in the form of a raspberry, rosette or other shape. Always the work of a skilled glassmaker, applied decoration can be found on both cased (two-layer) and single layer glass. The English firm of Stevens and Williams (which see) is renowned for the appliqued glass they produced.

Ewer with Applique Trim

Basket, rose bowl-shaped w/six-crimp top, creamy opaque w/amber applied twisted handle, applied amber branch & leaves, pink & white spatter applied flowers w/amber centers, 4½" d., 7" h.......................$195.00

Bowl, 4⅞" d., 5" h., bulbous sapphire blue body w/applied crystal scroll feet, six applied clear berry prunts around top w/three crystal fan-like applied designs, applied clear berry prunt on base, probably Webb.........195.00

Cornucopia-vase, shaded pink opalescent Diamond Quilted patt. body on clear scalloped foot, applied w/lavender spatter flowers & clear opalescent branch w/leaves & flowers, 3½"d., 8½" h.........................88.00

Decanter w/original blue faceted stopper, footed ovoid body tapering to tall slender neck w/applied blue handle, golden amber w/applied blue trim & applied blue salamander, 3¾" d., 12½" h. 175.00

Ewer, ovoid body w/flaring crimped rim, applied amber handle, creamy white opaque body applied w/a fine cranberry edging & an applied blue flower w/amber branch & green leaves, 2¾" d., 5¾" h. (ILLUS.).........88.00

Rose bowl, bulbous w/eight-crimp top, cased rose body applied w/large white flower & clear leaf & branch, white shading to opalescent lining, 3⅞" d., 2⅞" h. 85.00

Urn, cov., bulbous base w/domed lid, cranberry w/applied large clear flowers & leaves on sides, applied clear handle, feet & leaf top edge, applied clear finial on lid & clear flower prunt, 5½" d., 8¾" h..............495.00

Vase, 4⅝" h., 3⅛" d., bulbous thorny body, four-lobe top w/applied clear edging, pink ground w/applied flower & leaves decoration, applied clear wishbone feet..................................125.00

Vase, 6" h., 4½" d., footed trumpet-shape w/pinched together rim, lime green opalescent w/clear shell trim applied on sides..............................65.00

Vase, 12½" h., 5½" d., ovoid amethyst body w/a flaring six-petal-shaped rim w/applied sapphire blue edging, applied w/large green branches, leaves & small amber flowers, applied amber petal-shaped feet..295.00

ART GLASS BASKETS

Ruffled Art Glass Basket

Popular in the late Victorian era, these ornate hand-crafted glass baskets were often given as gifts. Sometimes made with unusually tall handles and applied feet, these fragile ornaments usually command a good price when they survive intact.

Cased, creamy white exterior, yellowish green interior, melon-sectioned w/scissor cut rim, applied clear handle, 6½" d., 6½" h. $150.00

Cased, pink & white candy stripe swirl exterior, white interior, bulbous w/ruffled rim, applied clear twisted thorn handle, 5½" d., 8" h. 175.00

Cased, shaded pink satin exterior, white interior, bulbous base w/eight-crimp rim, applied frosted handle, 3½" d., 5⅜" h. 125.00

Cased, white exterior, heavenly blue shaded satin interior, ruffled rim

w/applied clear frosted edging, applied clear frosted braided handle, 5¼" d., 6" h. 145.00
Cased, white exterior, pink interior, deeply ruffled rim, applied clear braided handle, 5½" d., 5½" h. 85.00
Cased, yellow exterior, clear interior, footed, rectangular w/applied clear twist handle, 4¾" w., 6⅜" h. 85.00
Creamy opaque, cylindrical body tapering to a ruffled fan-shaped rim, applied amber handle & edge trim, exterior decorated overall w/small blue, yellow & maroon flowers & green leaves, 4½ x 6", 6" h. 175.00
Green opalescent, eight-crimp rim, applied clear twist handle & pink & white spatter flower w/clear leaf & branch, 4" d., 6" h. 135.00
Lemon yellow opaque, ruffled rim, ribbed panels alternating w/embossed quilting, applied clear handle, 4⅛" d., 5" h. 85.00
Lime green shaded to white opalescent, exterior embossed w/florals & rope design, scalloped rim, applied clear braided handle, 5½" d., 7¾" h. 115.00
Pink opalescent Diamond Quilted patt., lightly ruffled rim, applied vaseline leaves & applied vaseline twist handle, 5" d., 6½" h. 145.00
Spangled, baby blue exterior, white interior w/silver mica flecks, tightly ruffled rim, applied clear feet & clear twisted thorn handle, 8¼" h. 275.00
Spangled, green w/mica flecks, molded Swirl & Swirl Rosette patt., rounded sides w/ruffled rim, applied clear twist handle, 5" d., 6½" h. 110.00
Spangled, maroon, green, yellow & white w/green mica flecks exterior, white interior, rounded sides w/ruffled rim & applied clear thorn handle, 4¼" d., 5½" h. 105.00
Spatter, pink, white & yellow exterior, yellow interior, melon-ribbed body w/flaring ruffled rim, applied angular thorn handle, 5½" d., 7½" h 175.00

BACCARAT

Baccarat glass has been made by Cristalleries de Baccarat, France, since 1765. The firm has produced various glasswares of excellent quality and paperweights. Baccarat's Rose Tiente is often referred to as Baccarat's Amberina.

Box, cov., Rose Tiente Swirl patt., 8" d., 2" h. $325.00
Cologne bottle w/original matching stopper, cylindrical body w/deep shoulder, a short cylindrical neck w/a flat flaring rim, Swirl patt., sapphire blue, original label, 2" d., 5" h. 75.00

Baccarat Cologne Bottle

Cologne bottle w/original bulbous stopper, cylindrical shouldered body tapering to a cylindrical neck w/a ringed neck, Rose Tiente Swirl patt., 3" d., 7¼" h. (ILLUS.) 75.00
Dresser set: covered powder jar & perfume bottle w/atomizer; clear w/intaglio cutting, signed Baccarat w/Marcel Franck fittings, 2 pcs. 295.00
Flower holder, bridge-shaped, five divisions for flowers, Swirl patt., sapphire blue, marked, 2 x 12", center 5" h. 195.00
Hurricane lamps, Rose Tiente Swirl patt. base, clear shade etched w/an inscription within a wreath, bobeche w/4½" l. prisms & screw on candleholders, base 8" h., overall 21½" h., pr. 1,125.00
Tumbler, cylindrical, Rose Tiente, molded sunburst design, 2⅞" d., 4" h. 55.00
Vase, 3½" h., goblet-shaped, decorated w/cut & enameled busts of Cleopatra, Mark Antony & Julius Caesar, satin finish 495.00
Vase, 4¼" h., paneled, green clover in base reflecting into the panels 50.00

BLOWN THREE MOLD

This type of glass was entirely or partially blown in a mold from about 1820 in the United States. The object was formed and the decoration impressed upon it by blowing the glass into a metal mold, usually of three but sometimes more sections, hinged together. Mold-blown glass actually dates back to ancient times. Recent research reveals that certain geometric patterns were reproduced in the 1920s and collectors are urged to read all recent information available. Reference numbers are from George L. and Helen McKearin's book, American Glass.

Blown Three Mold Bottle

Bottle, geometric, spherical body tapering to a slender cylindrical neck w/applied collared rim, pale green, 7¾" h., minor interior stain, minor open blisters inside neck, similar to GII-7 (ILLUS.) $3,740.00

Bottle, geometric, barrel-shaped body w/ribbed medial band, slender tall neck w/applied sloping lip, grass green, 8¼" h., GII-7 (slight roughness on bottom) 2,750.00

Bowl, 9" d., 5½" h., geometric, deep rounded sides w/folded rim, on applied round foot, clear, GII-18 (minor wear, small broken blister on bottom interior)........................3,630.00

Celery vase, geometric, cylindrical bowl w/deeply rolled rim, on applied knopped stem & round disc foot, clear, probably Pittsburgh, 7½" h. (GII-27) 1,320.00

Cologne bottle w/original Tam O'Shanter stopper, swirled ribs, sapphire blue, 5¾" h. (GI-3, type 2) 522.50

Cordial, geometric, small tapering conical bowl on an applied round foot, plain rim, clear, 2⅝" h. (GI-6) 302.50

Cruet stand bottle w/pressed wheel stopper, geometric, bulbous body above a cylindrical base, clear, pint (GII-18) 324.50

Decanter w/original pressed wheel stopper, miniature, geometric, clear, 3⅞" h., ¼ pint (GIII-21) 418.00

Decanter w/original bulbous patterned stopper, swirled ribs w/a body band molded "R U M," clear, quart (GIII-2, type 2) 302.50

Dish, geometric, round w/shallow sides & folded rim, clear, 5¾" d., 1" h. (GII) 93.50

Flip glass, geometric, slightly tapering cylindrical form, diamond point band, rayed base, 4¾" d., 5¾" h. (GIII-22) 198.00

Pitcher, miniature, 2⅛" h., geometric, applied handle, clear (GIII-12) 550.00

Salt dip, geometric, round bowl w/incurved sides raised on a short applied pedestal foot, cobalt blue, probably Boston & Sandwich, 3⅛" d., 1⅞" h. (GIII-25) 522.50

Tumbler, barrel-shaped, geometric, probably Boston & Sandwich, very pale blue, 3" d., 3⅛" h. (GII-18) 280.50

Wine glass, geometric, tapering conical bowl on applied ringed stem & round foot, 3⅞," h. (GII-19)..........440.00

BOHEMIAN

Ornate Cut & Enameled Pokal

Numerous types of glass were made in the once-independent country of Bohemia and fine colored, cut and engraved glass was turned out. Flashed and other inexpensive wares also were made and many of these, including amber- and ruby-shaded glass, were exported to the United States last century and in the present one. One favorite pattern in the late 19th and early 20th centuries was Deer & Castle. Another was Deer and Pine Tree.

Center bowl, yellow flashed cut to clear w/a floral design, 8" d.............$77.00

Compote, cov., 13" h., ruby-flashed cut to clear, the tapered bowl on a slender standard w/a circular foot, shaped cover & knopped finial, engraved w/running stags, castles & scrolls 137.50

Compotes, open, 8" d., oval bowls, ruby-flashed & etched to clear w/a stag & ferns, on a hexagonal foot, pr. 330.00

Decanter, ruby-flashed cut to clear Deer & Castle patt., 15" h. 215.00

Goblet, ruby-flashed, the deep rounded bowl facet-cut ruby to clear & raised on a paneled stem & round notched foot, the bowl w/a central ruby oval reserve etched w/a building titled "The President's House, Washington," ca. 1850, 6" h. 825.00

Pokals, cov., bulbous form on a tapered pedestal & circular foot, tall pointed finial on cover, cobalt blue cut to clear & enameled w/floral designs, one finial repaired, pr. (ILLUS. of one) 715.00

Tumbler, round tapering bowl facet-cut above the hexagonal ringed foot, the sides cut w/thirteen oval panels each featuring a different German building including "Schlofs," "Wilhelmshof," & "Marlafibein," each scene highlighted w/amber & cranberry stain, mid-19th c., 4¾" h. 302.50

Tumble-up set (water carafe w/tumbler lid), red cut to clear floral pattern, overall 8" h., the set 85.00

BRIDE'S BASKETS & BOWLS

These berry or fruit bowls were popular late Victorian wedding gifts, hence the name.

Amethyst shaded to lavender bowl w/pie crust rim, wide border of orange & white enameled flowers,11" d. $240.00

Cased bowl, blue shaded interior, embossed leaf pattern around bowl trimmed in gold, white exterior, pointed & crimped rim, resilvered frame w/ornate handle, 10" d...........295.00

Cased bowl, chartreuse interior, shaded pink exterior decorated w/gold leaves & branches & dainty white enameled flowers, ruffled rim w/applied clear edging & gold trim, ornately engraved silver plate frame w/tall decorative handle & ball feet, 12" d., 8¼" h. 595.00

Cased bowl, heavenly blue shaded satin interior enameled w/white flowers & heavy gold foliage decoration, white exterior, closely ruffled rim, 9¾" d., 3¼" h. 325.00

Cased bowl, pink shaded interior decorated w/dainty pink & white daisies, blue forget-me-nots & green leaves, white interior, ruffled rim applied w/clear ribbon candy edging, 10¼" d., 3" h. 225.00

Cased bowl, white interior, Peach Blow exterior, squared shape w/closely crimped sides & widely crimped corners, clear rim, polished pontil, no frame, 11" d., 3" h.............125.00

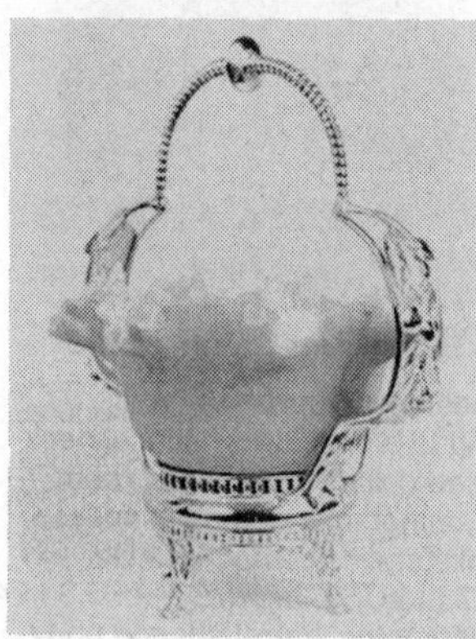

Satin Glass Bride's Basket

Cased bowl, white interior, yellow satin exterior w/blue ruffled rim, in ornate footed Pairpoint silver plate frame, bowl 9" d., overall 12" h. (ILLUS.) 450.00

Cranberry opalescent bowl, double crimped rim, vertical opalescent stripes radiating from center, no frame, 10⅝" d., 3¾" h. 150.00

Cranberry opalescent bowl, Spanish Lace patt. w/ruffled rim, original silver plate frame, 10¾" d. 295.00

Heavenly blue overshot bowl, deeply ruffled & crimped rim, ornate brass stand w/hanging brass rings, 7¾" d., overall 12" h. 188.00

Peach Blow bowl, eight-crimp top, polished pontil, silver plate frame w/grape & vine cluster at top, bowl 11½" d., 3¾" h., overall 14" h. (frame needs replating)....................225.00

White bowl, high tightly pleated back flaring down to a wide pleated front w/scrolls, decorated w/delicate pink roses & two little birds, in original silver plate frame decorated w/flowers & beading, 10½" d., overall 13" h. 350.00

BURMESE

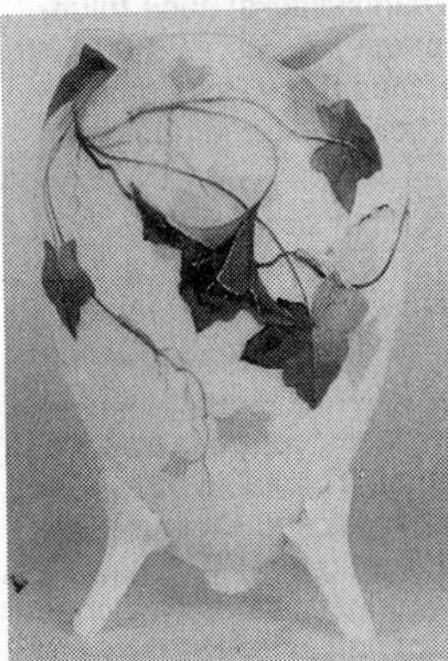

Burmese Vase by Webb

Burmese is a single-layer glass that shades from pink to pale yellow. It was patented by Frederick S. Shirley and made by the Mt. Washington Glass Co. A license to produce the glass in England was granted to Thomas Webb & Sons, which called its articles Queen's Burmese. Gundersen Burmese was made briefly about the middle of this century, and the Pairpoint Crystal Company is making limited quantities at the present time.

Bell, high domed bell w/flaring base, tall applied clear handle w/beehive-form finial, glossy finish, 11½" h. ...$450.00

Bowl, 6½" widest d., 2½" h., cylindrical base w/a flaring & folded over elongated oval rim, applied yellow rigaree trim on rim, Mt. Washington Glass Co. 750.00

Bowl-vase, small rounded bowl w/a widely flaring tri-lobed rim, raised on three small applied feet, 4" w., 2½" h. 80.00

Celery vase, footed, fluted rim, Mt. Washington Glass Co., 10" h. 425.00

Cologne bottle w/original stopper, Mt. Washington Glass Co., 4" d., 5" h....975.00

Creamer & sugar bowl, pitcher-shaped creamer w/applied yellow handle, globular open sugar bowl, creamer 3¾" h., sugar bowl 3½" d., 2" h., pr. 665.00

Cup & saucer, cylindrical cup w/applied yellow angled handle, wide & deep saucer, glossy finish 325.00

Dish, ruffled rim, satin finish, 4¾" d., 1½" h. 120.00

Finger bowl, nine-crimp top, satin finish, Mt. Washington Glass Co., 4⅜" d., 2¼" h. 225.00

Pitcher, 5½" h., slightly tapering cylindrical body in the Hobnail patt., applied yellow handle, Mt. Washington Glass Co. 605.00

Plate, 9" d., satin finish, Mt. Washington Glass Co. 225.00

Rose bowl, bulbous base tapering to a hexagonal rim, decorated w/lavender five-petal flowers & green & brown leaves, satin finish, unsigned Webb, 3" d., 3¼" h. 295.00

Rose bowl, spherical, six-crimp top, decorated w/bronze & gold-tinted chrysanthemums & leaves all outlined in gold, unsigned Webb, 3⅜" d., 3⅜" h. 650.00

Salt shaker w/original top, tomato-shaped, Mt. Washington Glass Co. 150.00

Toothpick holder, Diamond Quilted patt., satin finish 285.00

Tumbler, decorated w/yellow roses, Mt. Washington Glass Co., 3¾" h....565.00

Vase, 2½" h., 2" d., bulbous body w/collared hexagonal top, decorated w/flowers, leaves & branches 295.00

Vase, 4" h., 2¾" d., bulbous body tapering to a flaring neck w/crimped rim, decorated w/blue & white flowers & brown leaves, satin finish, unsigned Webb 295.00

Vase, 7" h., tapering egg-shaped body w/three-lobed rim, raised on three ribbed & pointed legs, enameled around the sides w/large ivy leaves & vines, signed by Thomas Webb & Sons (ILLUS.) 950.00

Vase, 10" h., cushion foot, expanding cylinder w/short narrow flaring cylindrical neck, decorated w/florals filled w/intricate lines in red, green, blue & gold, heavy gold outlining, Mt. Washington Glass Co. 1,250.00

Vase, 12½" h., bulbous base w/long stick neck, clear applied handles at the base of the neck, decorated overall w/dainty blossoms, shadow foliage & fragile gold branches 1,950.00

Vase, 14½" h., trumpet-form w/jack-in-the-pulpit tightly crimped rim, glossy finish, Mt. Washington Glass Co. 785.00

CAMBRIDGE

The Cambridge Glass Company was founded in Ohio in 1901. Numerous pieces are now sought, especially those designed by Arthur J. Bennett, including Crown Tuscan. Other productions included crystal animals, "Black Amethyst," "blanc opaque," and other types of colored glass. The firm was finally closed in 1954. It should not be confused with the New England Glass Co., Cambridge, Massachusetts.

Statuesque Line Compote

Ashtray, shell-shaped, pressed Caprice patt., Moonlight (pale blue) $9.00

Basket, etched Rose Point patt., Crystal, 7" h. 750.00

Bonbon, handled, Inverted Strawberry patt., clear, 5½" 40.00

Bowl, salad, 13½" d., pressed Caprice patt., Cobalt Blue 110.00

Bowl w/underplate: 9½" d. bowl w/ruffled rim, 10½" d. underplate; Strawberry (No. 2780) line, clear, 2 pcs. 98.00

Butter dish, cov., Gadroon (No. 3500) line, Crystal 40.00

Cake plate, handled, etched Rose Point patt., Crystal, 12" d. 85.00

Candleholders, two-light, pressed Caprice patt., w/prisms, Crystal, 6" h., pr. 140.00

Candlesticks, Pristine line, No. 499, Calla Lily design, Crystal, 6" h., pr. 54.00

Candlesticks, etched Diane patt., Crystal, 2½" h., pr. 35.00

Candy box, cov., footed, Sea Shell line, Charleton decoration, milk white, 6" h. 85.00

Claret, etched Rose Point patt., Crystal 55.00

Cocktail, Statuesque line, Dianthus (light pink) bowl, clear Nude Lady stem, 3 oz. 150.00

Cocktail shaker w/original glass top, etched Blossom Time patt., Crystal 85.00

Compote, open, 6½" d., 5" h., Tally-Ho line, Amber 30.00

Compote, open, 7" d., 9½" h., Statuesque line, Carmen bowl, clear Nude Lady stem (ILLUS.) 150.00

Console set: 9" d., ram's head-handled bowl & pair 9½" h. Doric Column candlesticks; Jade (blue-green opaque), 3 pcs. ......300.00 to 350.00

Cordial, etched Rose Point patt., Carmen bowl w/clear embossed base 150.00

Creamer & open sugar bowl, Decagon line, Crystal, 2 pcs. 34.00

Crown Tuscan cake plate w/open handles, Gadroon (No. 3500) line, 13" d. 98.00

Cruet w/original stopper, pressed Caprice patt., Crystal, 5 oz. 85.00

Cup & saucer, etched Cleo patt., Emerald (light green) 18.00

Decanter w/original stopper, etched Rose Point patt., No. 1321, Crystal 275.00

Figure flower holder, "Bashful Charlotte," Emerald, 13" h. 275.00

Figure flower holder, "Draped Lady," yellow, 8½" h. ....250.00 to 275.00

Figure flower holder, "Mandolin Lady," Forest Green (dark green), 9" h. 350.00

Figure flower holder, "Two-Kid," La Rosa (light to medium pink), 8¾" h. 210.00

Flower holder, Sea Gull, Crystal, 9½" h. 50.00

Goblet, pressed Caprice patt., Crystal, 7½" h. 14.00

Goblet, Statuesque line, Amber bowl, clear Nude Lady stem 155.00

Honey dish, cov., Gadroon (No. 3500) line, Crystal, Farberware cover w/embossed peony design, 5½" sq. 16.50

Ice bucket w/tongs, etched Apple Blossom patt., Topaz (vaseline) 140.00

Lemon plate, handled, pressed Caprice patt., Crystal, 6½" d. 10.00

Mayonnaise dish & underplate, etched Cleo patt., Crystal, 2 pcs. 45.00

Mug, beer, Everglade line, milk white 45.00

Oyster cocktail, etched Rose Point patt., Crystal 38.00

Pitcher w/ice lip, etched Rose Point patt., Crystal, 80 oz. 180.00

Plate, 7½" d., Decagon line, Moonlight 10.00

Plate, 8" d., etched Elaine patt., Crystal 12.50

Plate, sandwich, 11½" d., tab handles, etched Rose Point patt., Amber 16.00

Relish, pressed Caprice patt., Crystal, 12" l. 40.00

Salt & pepper shakers w/original tops, etched Chantilly patt., Crystal, pr. 25.00

Sherbet, pressed Caprice patt., Crystal 18.00

Child's Colonial Pattern Spooner

Spooner, child's, Colonial patt., Emerald (ILLUS.) 30.00
Tumbler, Apple Blossom etching, Emerald, 12 oz. 45.00
Urn, cov., Mt. Vernon line, Carmen 105.00
Vase, bud, 5" h., etched Rose Point patt., Crystal w/gold trim 70.00
Water set: 32 oz. pitcher & six 5 oz. tumblers; pressed Caprice patt., Moonlight, 7 pcs. 575.00

CARNIVAL GLASS

Earlier called Taffeta glass, the Carnival glass now being collected was introduced early in this century. Its producers gave it an iridescence that attempted to imitate that of some Tiffany glass. Collectors will find available books by leading authorities Donald E. Moore, Sherman Hand, Marion T. Hartung and Rose M. Presznick.

ACANTHUS (Imperial)

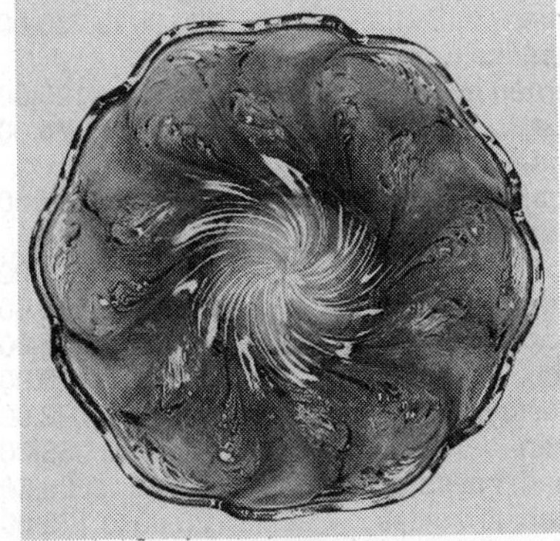

Acanthus Bowl

Bowl, 7" d., green $20.00
Bowl, 8" to 9" d., green 88.00
Bowl, 8" to 9" d., marigold (ILLUS.) 62.00
Bowl, 8" to 9" d., purple 95.00
Bowl, 8" to 9" d., smoky 85.00
Plate, 9" to 10" d., marigold 193.00
Plate, 9" to 10" d., smoky 250.00

ACORN BURRS (Northwood)

Berry set: master bowl & 5 sauce dishes; purple, 6 pcs. ....350.00 to 400.00
Berry set: master bowl & 6 sauce dishes; green, 7 pcs. 350.00
Butter dish, cov., green ....300.00 to 375.00
Butter dish, cov., marigold 178.00
Butter dish, cov., purple ....175.00 to 200.00
Creamer, green 90.00
Creamer, marigold 100.00
Creamer, purple 100.00
Creamer & sugar bowl, purple, pr. 250.00
Pitcher, water, marigold 325.00
Pitcher, water, purple ....350.00 to 400.00
Punch bowl & base, purple, 2 pcs. 795.00
Punch cup, aqua opalescent 1,800.00
Punch cup, blue 85.00
Punch cup, green 40.00
Punch cup, purple 30.00
Punch cup, white 55.00
Punch set: bowl, case & 5 cups; green, 7 pcs. ....1,200.00 to 1,600.00
Punch set: bowl, base & 6 cups; purple, 8 pcs. 1,500.00
Punch set: bowl, base & 6 cups; white, 8 pcs 4,000.00
Sauce dish, green 37.50
Sauce dish, marigold 30.00
Sauce dish, purple 45.00
Spooner, green 150.00
Spooner, marigold 88.00
Spooner, purple 100.00 to125.00
Table set: cov. sugar bowl, creamer, spooner & cov. butter dish; marigold, 4 pcs. 900.00
Table set, purple, 4 pcs 1,000.00
Tumbler, green 78.00
Tumbler, marigold 50.00
Tumbler, purple 58.00

ADVERTISING & SOUVENIR ITEMS

Basket, "Feldman Bros. Furniture, Salisbury, Md.," open edge, marigold ....50.00 to 75.00
Basket, "John H. Brand Furniture Co., Wilmington, Del.," marigold 60.00
Bowl, "Isaac Benesch," 6¼" d., purple (Millersburg) ....300.00 to 325.00
Bowl, "Bernheimer Brothers," blue 1,000.00
Bowl, "Dreibus Parfait Sweets," ruffled, smoky lavender 400.00
Bowl, "Horlacher," Peacock Tail patt., green 100.00

Bowl, souvenir, BPOE Elks, "Detroit, 1910," green, one-eyed Elk 1,000.00
Bowl, souvenir, BPOE Elks, "Detroit, 1910," marigold 845.00
Bowl, souvenir, BPOE Elks, "Detroit, 1910," purple, one-eyed Elk............385.00
Bowl, souvenir, Brooklyn Bridge, unlettered, marigold ....475.00 to 550.00
Bowl, souvenir, "Millersburg Courthouse," purple 550.00
Bowl, souvenir, Millersburg Courthouse, unlettered, purple 965.00
Card tray, "Fern Brand Chocolates," turned-up sides, 6¼" d., purple........175.00
Card tray, "Isaac Benesch," Holly Whirl patt., marigold.............50.00 to 70.00
Dish, "Compliments of Pacific Coast Mail Order House, Los Angeles, California" 700.00
Hat, "General Furniture Co." 1910, Peacock Tail patt., green 75.00
Hat, "Miller's Furniture - Harrisburg," basketweave, marigold........................75.00
Paperweight, souvenir, BPOE Elks, green...625.00
Paperweight, souvenir, BPOE Elks, purple (Millersburg) ....600.00 to 700.00
Plate, "Ballard, California," purple (Northwood) 900.00
Plate, "Brazier Candies," w/handgrip, 6" d., purple.......................500.00 to 600.00
Plate, "Fern Brand Chocolates," 6" d., purple...700.00
Plate, "Gervitz Bros., Furniture & Clothing," w/handgrip, 6" d., purple 1,350.00
Plate, "Greengard Furniture Co.," purple 625.00
Plate, "F.A. Hudson Furniture Co.," 7" d., purple (Northwood) 225.00
Plate, "Spector's Department Store," Heart & Vine patt., 9" d., marigold 450.00
Plate, "Utah Liquor Co.," w/handgrip, 6" d., purple...950.00
Plate, "We Use Brocker's," 7" d., purple 495.00

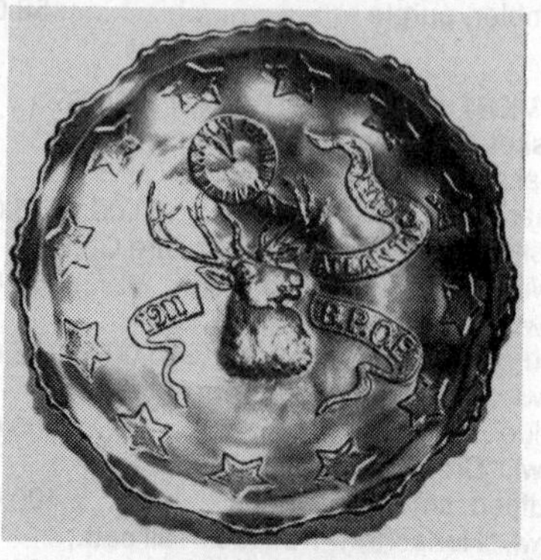

BPOE Elks Plate

Plate, souvenir, BPOE Elks, "Atlantic City, 1911," blue (ILLUS.) ....800.00 to 900.00
Plate, souvenir, BPOE Elks, "Parkersburg, 1914," 7Z\x" d., blue 1,050.00
Vase, "Howard Furniture," Four Pillars patt., green..80.00

AUSTRALIAN

Berry set: master bowl & 6 sauce dishes; Magpie, marigold, 7 pcs. 325.00
Bowl, 5½" d., Swan, marigold..............45.00
Bowl, 9" to 10" d., Emu, aqua............550.00
Bowl, 9" to 10" d., Emu, marigold 145.00
Bowl, 9" to 10" d., Kangaroo, marigold 100.00
Bowl, 9" to 10" d., Kangaroo, purple.....................................150.00 to 170.00
Bowl, 9" to 10" d., Magpie, marigold 115.00
Bowl, 9" to 10" d., Magpie, purple.......110.00
Bowl, 9" to 10" d., Swan, purple 175.00
Bowl, 9" to 10" d., Thunderbird, marigold 200.00
Bowl, 9" to 10" d., Thunderbird, purple 165.00
Bowl, 11" d., ice cream shape, Kookaburra variant, purple 300.00
Bowl, pin-up, purple.............................65.00
Cake plate, Butterfly & Bells, marigold 78.00
Compote, Butterflies & Waratah, aqua 135.00
Compote, Butterflies & Waratah, marigold ....175.00 to 200.00
Sauce dish, Kingfisher, marigold..........60.00
Sauce dish, Kookaburra, marigold 65.00
Sauce dish, Kookaburra, purple 45.00
Sauce dish, Swan, marigold..................65.00
Sauce dish, Thunderbird, marigold.......65.00
Sauce dish, Thunderbird, purple 85.00

BASKET (Fenton's Open Edge)

Amber................................200.00 to 250.00
Amberina, w/two rows, two sides turned up...125.00
Aqua 74.00
Aqua, w/two rows, jack-in-the-pulpit shape ....100.00 to 125.00
Aqua, w/two rows, two sides turned up 110.00
Aqua opalescent.................................145.00
Black amethyst 365.00
Blue 50.00
Celeste blue..92.00
Green...53.00
Green, hat shape 85.00
Green, low sides................125.00 to 175.00
Ice blue 195.00
Ice blue, w/two rows, open edge, six ruffled.............................225.00 to 295.00

Ice blue, w/three rows....................600.00
Ice green....................240.00
Ice green, w/three rows....................450.00
Marigold, 5" h., w/applied crystal handle....................75.00
Marigold....................40.00
Purple....................110.00
Red....................340.00
Red, hat shape....................400.00 to 450.00
Red, jack-in-the-pulpit shape....................425.00 to 450.00
Red, w/two rows, small....................325.00
Reverse Amberina....................650.00
Vaseline....................75.00 to 100.00
Vaseline, plain interior....................275.00
Vaseline, w/two rows, large....................75.00
White, w/two rows....................150.00
White, 6"....................200.00 to 250.00

BIG FISH BOWL (Millersburg)

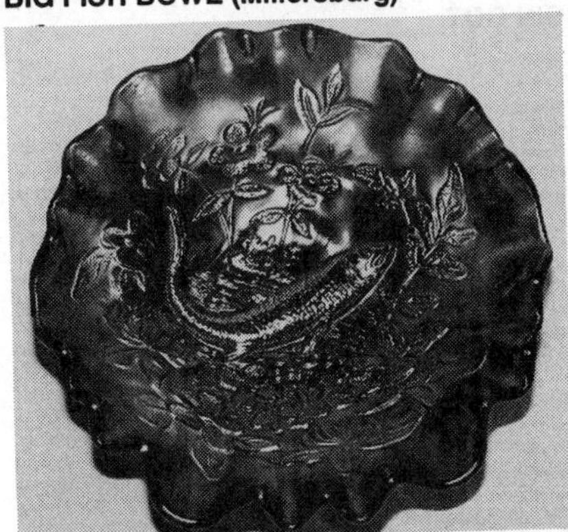

Big Fish Bowl

Green....................595.00
Green, square....................900.00 to 1,000.00
Marigold....................507.00
Marigold, ice cream shape....................550.00
Marigold, square....................850.00
Purple, ice cream shape....................660.00
Purple, ruffled (ILLUS.)....................704.00
Purple, square....................700.00

BLACKBERRY SPRAY

Bonbon, marigold....................30.00
Bowl, 7" d., marigold....................20.00
Compote, 5½" d., purple....................95.00
Hat shape, amber....................100.00 to 150.00
Hat shape, Amberina....................280.00 to 300.00
Hat shape, aqua....................75.00
Hat shape, jack-in-the-pulpit shape, crimped rim, aqua....................85.00
Hat shape, aqua opalescent....................475.00
Hat shape, jack-in-the-pulpit, crimped rim, clambroth....................27.00
Hat shape, jack-in-the-pulpit, crimped rim, vaseline....................65.00
Hat shape, green....................75.00
Hat shape, ice green opalescent....................350.00
Hat shape, red....................388.00
Hat shape, red slag....................475.00
Hat shape, Reverse Amberina....................450.00
Hat shape, vaseline....................70.00
Hat shape, vaseline w/marigold overlay....................54.00

BUTTERFLY & BERRY (Fenton)

Butterfly & Berry Pitcher

Berry set: master bowl & 5 sauce dishes; marigold, 6 pcs....................240.00
Bowl, 7" d., three-footed, marigold....................65.00
Bowl, 8" to 9" d., footed, blue....................55.00
Bowl, 8" to 9" d., footed, marigold....................72.00
Bowl, master berry or fruit, four-footed, marigold....................82.00
Bowl, master berry or fruit, four-footed, purple....................120.00
Bowl, master berry or fruit, four-footed, white....................250.00 to 275.00
Butter dish, cov., blue....................250.00
Butter dish, cov., green....................280.00
Butter dish, cov., marigold....................126.00
Centerpiece bowl, purple....................500.00
Creamer, blue....................85.00
Creamer, marigold....................70.00
Creamer, purple....................145.00
Pitcher, water, blue....................425.00
Pitcher, water, marigold (ILLUS.)....................225.00 to 275.00
Sauce dish, blue....................42.00
Sauce dish, green....................45.00
Spooner, blue....................120.00
Spooner, marigold....................62.00
Spooner, purple....................140.00
Sugar bowl, cov., blue....................120.00
Sugar bowl, cov., marigold....................82.00
Tumbler, blue....................60.50
Tumbler, green....................85.00
Tumbler, marigold....................39.50
Tumbler, purple....................325.00
Vase, 6" h., marigold....................35.00
Vase, 7" h., blue....................65.00
Vase, 8" h., marigold....................35.00
Vase, 9" h., blue....................80.00

Vase, 9" h., marigold 50.00
Vase, 9" h., purple 50.00
Vase, 10" h., blue 50.00

CARNIVAL HOLLY - See Holly Pattern

CHERRY OR CHERRY CIRCLES (Fenton)

Red Cherry Bonbon

Bonbon, two-handled, aqua....................280.00
Bonbon, two-handled, blue....................50.00
Bonbon, two-handled, marigold....................38.00
Bonbon, two-handled, red (ILLUS.) 7,250.00
Bowl, 5" d., fluted, blue....................30.00
Bowl, 5" d., marigold....................32.00
Bowl, 5" d., purple....................40.00
Bowl, 7" d., three-footed, marigold 42.50
Bowl, 7" d., three-footed, peach opalescent w/plain interior 90.00
Bowl, 10" d., vaseline w/ marigold overlay 75.00
Bowl, 10" d., ruffled, white 100.00
Card tray, aqua....................125.00
Plate, 6" d., blue 100.00
Plate, 6" d., Orange Tree exterior, marigold 80.00
Plate, 6" d., purple 275.00

CHERRY OR HANGING CHERRIES (Millersburg)

Banana compote (whimsey), blue 625.00
Banana compote (whimsey), green....................1,500.00
Bowl, 4" d., green 75.00
Bowl, 5" d., blue....................825.00 to 875.00
Bowl, 5" d., ruffled, marigold....................50.00
Bowl, 7" d., ice cream shape, marigold 112.00
Bowl, 8" to 9" d., ruffled, green 264.00
Bowl, 8" to 9" d., ice cream shape, green....................175.00 to 200.00
Bowl, 8" to 9" d., dome-footed, marigold 70.00
Bowl, 8" to 9" d., purple 60.00
Bowl, 9" d., Hobnail exterior, marigold 795.00
Bowl, 10" d., ice cream shape, green....................194.00
Bowl, 10" d., purple....................310.00
Bowl, 10½" d., ruffled, white 125.00
Bowl, ruffled, Hobnail exterior, marigold, large 468.00
Butter dish, cov., green....................227.00
Butter dish, cov., marigold....................190.00
Compote, green....................1,400.00
Creamer, green 77.00
Pitcher, water, marigold....................200.00
Pitcher, water, purple....................600.00
Plate, 7" d., purple 225.00
Spooner, green....................68.00
Spooner, marigold 75.00
Sugar bowl, cov., marigold 85.00
Tumbler, green 290.00
Tumbler, margold 200.00

CHERRY CIRCLES - See Cherry (Fenton) Pattern

COIN DOT

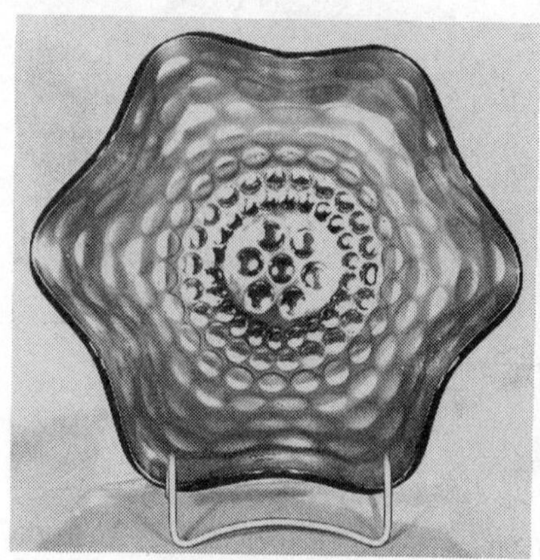

Coin Dot Bowl

Bowl, 6" d., green 25.00
Bowl, 6" d., ice cream shape-red....................1,500.00
Bowl, 6½" d., lavender....................30.00
Bowl, 6½" d., stippled, purple 32.00
Bowl, 7" d., blue....................30.00
Bowl, 7" d., green 30.00
Bowl, 7" d., marigold....................38.00
Bowl, 7" d., red 1,500.00
Bowl, 8" to 9" d., blue....................32.00
Bowl, 8" to 9" d., blue opalescent 300.00
Bowl, 8" to 9" d., green 42.50
Bowl, 8" to 9" d., stippled, green....................25.00
Bowl, 8" to 9" d., peach opalescent 173.00
Bowl, 8" to 9" d., purple (ILLUS.) 43.00
Bowl, 8" to 9" d., ruffled, vaseline 55.00
Bowl, 9½" d., ruffled, purple....................68.00
Bowl, 9½" d., stippled, purple 35.00
Compote, celeste blue opalescent 100.00
Compote, ice blue 450.00
Pitcher, water, marigold....................150.00
Plate, 9" d., aqua 80.00
Plate, 9" d., purple 90.00
Rose bowl, green....................80.00

Rose bowl, marigold 50.00
Tumbler, margold 50.00

DAISY & PLUME

Daisy & Plume Rose Bowl

Bowl, 8" to 9" d., three footed, green ..150.00
Bowl, 8" to 9" d., three footed, marigold 90.00
Candy dish, footed, blue 185.00
Candy dish, footed, marigold 50.00
Candy dish, footed, peach opalescent (Dugan) 100.00
Candy dish, footed, purple 75.00
Candy dish, footed, white 125.00
Compote, green 50.00
Compote, marigold 38.00
Compote, purple 55.00
Rose bowl, three-footed, blue 250.00
Rose bowl, three-footed, green (ILLUS.) 92.00
Rose bowl, three-footed, ice blue 900.00
Rose bowl, three-footed, ice green 900.00

DANDELION (Northwood)

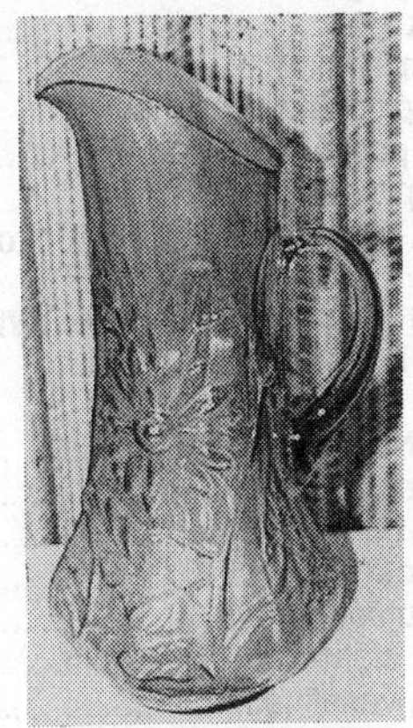

Dandelion Pitcher

Mug, aqua opalescent ....475.00 to 500.00
Mug, blue ....440.00 to 480.00
Mug, green ....500.00 to 600.00
Mug, ice blue opalescent 895.00
Mug, marigold ....375.00 to 400.00
Mug, Knights Templar, marigold 500.00
Mug, Knights Templar, purple 295.00
Pitcher, water, tankard, blue 260.00
Pitcher, water, tankard, green ....1,000.00 to 1,200.00
Pitcher, water, tankard, marigold (ILLUS.) ....400.00 to 450.00
Pitcher, water, tankard, purple ....650.00 to 750.00
Tumbler, blue 60.00
Tumbler, green ....75.00 to 100.00
Tumbler, ice blue 200.00
Tumbler, ice green 900.00
Tumbler, white 195.00
Water set: pitcher & 1 tumbler; white, 2 pcs. 2,500.00
Water set: pitcher & 2 tumblers; pastel marigold, 3 pcs. 875.00
Water set: pitcher & 6 tumblers; purple, 7 pcs. ....925.00 to 975.00

DIAMOND RING (Imperial)

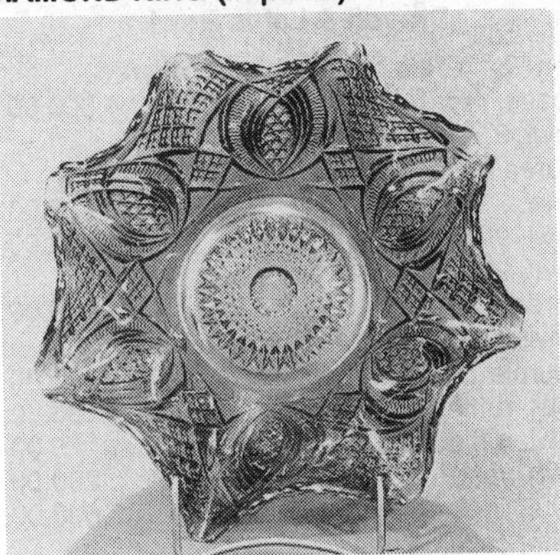

Diamond Ring Bowl

Bowl, 8" to 9" d., marigold 60.00
Bowl, 8" to 9" d., purple 75.00
Bowl, 8" to 9" d., smoky (ILLUS.) 40.00
Rose bowl, marigold 300.00
Sauce dish, marigold 22.50
Sauce dish, smoky 28.00

DRAGON & LOTUS (Fenton)

Bowl, 7" to 9" d., three-footed, blue 68.00
Bowl, 7" to 9" d., three-footed, green 75.00
Bowl, 7" to 9" d., three-footed, lavender 125.00
Bowl, 7" to 9" d., three-footed, lime green opalescent 300.00
Bowl, 7" to 9" d., three-footed, marigold 45.00
Bowl, 8" to 9" d., collared base, amber ....200.00 to 225.00
Bowl, 8" to 9" d., collared base, blue ..117.00
Bowl, 8" to 9" d., collared base, green 108.00
Bowl, 8" to 9" d., collared base, marigold 60.00

Bowl, 9" d., ice cream shape, collared base, amber....................150.00 to 200.00
Bowl, 9" d., ice cream shape, collared base, aqua opalescent................3,400.00
Bowl, 9" d., ice cream shape, collared base, blue....................................103.00

Dragon & Lotus Bowl

Bowl, 9" d., ice cream shape, collared base, red (ILLUS.) 4,500.00
Bowl, 9" d., ice cream shape, collared base, Reverse Amberina ....675.00 to 725.00
Bowl, 9" d., marigold..82.00
Bowl, 9" d., three-in-one edge, green...135.00
Bowl, ice cream shape, spade-footed, purple...100.00
Bowl, ruffled, blue................................86.00
Bowl, ruffled, purple..............................75.00
Bowl, vaseline......................................200.00
Plate, 9" d., marigold 2,600.00
Plate, collared base, blue.............................1,500.00 to 2,000.00

FARMYARD (Dugan)

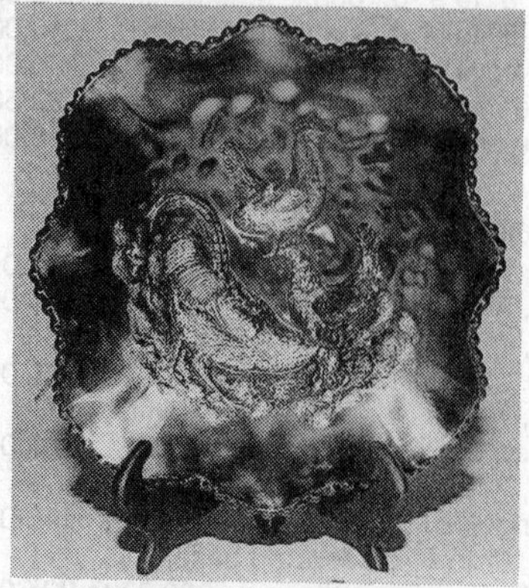

Farmyard Square Bowl

Bowl, purple....................................2,600.00
Bowl, fluted, purple..........................3,900.00
Bowl, ribbon candy rim, purple 3,500.00
Bowl, square, purple (ILLUS.) 2,900.00

Plate, 10" d., purple 6,000.00

FASHION (Imperial)

Fashion Pitcher

Bowl, 9" d., marigold.............................25.00
Bowl, 9" d., ruffled, smoky 40.00
Creamer, marigold................................25.00
Creamer, smoky 130.00
Creamer & sugar bowl, marigold, pr.....60.00
Creamer & sugar bowl, purple, pr.......325.00
Pitcher, water, marigold, (ILLUS.) ....100.00 to 125.00
Pitcher, water, purple........................950.00
Punch bowl & base, marigold, 12" d., 2 pcs. 104.00
Punch cup, marigold...........................15.00
Punch cup, red 325.00
Punch cups, marigold, set of 6 ....105.00
Punch set: bowl, base & 8 cups; marigold, 10 pcs. 325.00
Rose bowl, green................................425.00
Rose bowl, marigold, 7" d....................90.00
Tumbler, marigold.................................20.00
Tumbler, purple 175.00
Tumbler, smoky 90.00
Water set: pitcher & 3 tumblers; smoky, 4 pcs...................................700.00
Water set: pitcher & 6 tumblers; marigold, 7 pcs. ....300.00 to 350.00

FENTON'S FLOWERS ROSE BOWL - See Orange Tree Pattern

FINE RIB (Northwood & Fenton)

Bowl, master berry, 9" d., marigold.......35.00
Bowl, 10½" d., green 50.00
Bowl, purple..35.00
Compote, ruffled, green........................45.00
Plate, 9" d., eight-sided, marigold.........85.00
Sauce dish, vaseline..............................25.00
Vase, 6½ h., 5" d., blue 25.00
Vase, 6½ h., 5" d., green........................30.00
Vase, 6½ h., 5" d., marigold 25.00
Vase, 8½" h., blue 38.00
Vase, 8½" h., red 195.00
Vase, 9" h., green...................................65.00
Vase, 9½" h., vaseline (Fenton) 50.00

Vase, 10" h., amber (Fenton) 40.00
Vase, 10" h., aqua (Northwood) 70.00

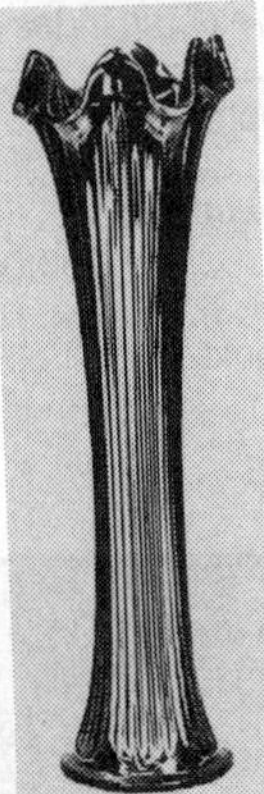

Fine Rib Vase

Vase, 10" h., blue (ILLUS.)..................40.00
Vase, 14" h., marigold 36.00
Vase, 15" h., blue 60.00
Vase, 16" h., marigold 45.00
Vase, 17" h., marigold 85.00

FLUTE (Imperial)

Flute Punch Set

Berry set: master bowl & 6 sauce dishes; marigold, 7 pcs. 135.00
Bowl, 8" to 9" d., marigold 28.00
Bowl, 8" to 9" d., purple 65.00
Butter dish, cov., marigold 60.00
Compote, green.......................................25.00
Creamer, breakfast size, marigold........50.00
Creamer, breakfast size, purple 60.00
Pitcher, water, marigold.......................275.00
Pitcher, water, purple...........................293.00
Punch set: bowl, base & 6 cups; purple, 8 pcs. (ILLUS.).....750.00 to 850.00
Rose bowl, marigold 24.00
Sauce dish, green....................................34.00
Sauce dish, marigold 15.00
Sauce dish, purple...................................50.00
Sugar bowl, open, breakfast size, amber..65.00
Sugar bowl, open, breakfast size, green..60.00

Toothpick holder, marigold 65.00
Toothpick holder, purple 80.00
Tumbler, aqua 175.00
Tumbler, cobalt blue 400.00
Tumbler, marigold.....................................40.00
Tumbler, purple 82.00
Tumbler, red 275.00
Tumbler, smoky 425.00
Vase, 9" h., aqua 70.00
Vase, 9" h., purple 82.00
Vase, 12" h., funeral, green 32.00
Vase, 17" h., green 65.00
Water set: pitcher & 6 tumblers; marigold, 7 pcs. 650.00

FROLICKING BEARS (U.S. Glass)

Pitcher, green ....5,000.00 to 7,000.00
Tumbler, green 9,500.00

FRUITS & FLOWERS (Northwood)

Fruits & Flowers Bonbon

Berry set: master bowl & 4 sauce dishes; purple, 5 pcs. 395.00
Bonbon, stemmed, two-handled, amber 375.00
Bonbon, stemmed, two-handled, aqua opalescent ....475.00 to 500.00
Bonbon, stemmed, two-handled, blue..163.00
Bonbon, stemmed, two-handled, ice green...450.00
Bonbon, stemmed, two-handled, lavender 650.00
Bonbon, stemmed, two-handled, marigold (ILLUS.).................................90.00
Bonbon, stemmed, two-handled, olive green...135.00
Bonbon, stemmed, two-handled, white ....375.00 to 400.00
Bowl, 6" d., ruffled, green 48.00
Bowl, 6" d., ruffled, marigold.....................60.00
Bowl, 6" d., ruffled, purple.........................48.00
Bowl, 7" d., blue...85.00
Bowl, 7" d., electric blue .....300.00 to 350.00
Bowl, 7" d., ruffled, ice green..................350.00
Bowl, 7" d., ruffled, marigold.....................15.00
Bowl, 9½" d., ruffled, Basketweave exterior, purple.......................................61.00

Bowl, 9½" d., ruffled, Basketweave exterior, purple 61.00
Bowl, master berry, 10" d., green 82.00
Bowl, master berry, 10" d., marigold....45.00
Bowl, 10" d., ruffled, purple....150.00
Bowl, piecrust rim, purple 225.00
Card tray, green....125.00
Plate, 7" d., green 170.00
Plate, 7" d., marigold 125.00
Plate, 7½" d., handgrip, purple ....150.00 to 175.00
Sauce dish, marigold 31.00
Sauce dish, purple....45.00

GOOD LUCK (Northwood)

Good Luck Ruffled Bowl

Bowl, 8" d., ruffled, blue....285.00
Bowl, 8" d., ruffled, stippled, blue 374.00
Bowl, 8" d., ruffled, blue w/electric iridescence....285.00
Bowl, 8" d., ruffled, stippled, blue w/electric iridescence....375.00 to 400.00
Bowl, 8" d., ruffled, green 263.00
Bowl, 8" d., ruffled, Basketweave exterior, green....250.00 to 300.00
Bowl, 8" d., ruffled, purple...200.00 to 225.00
Bowl, 8" d., ruffled, Basketweave exterior, purple 225.00
Bowl, 8" to 9" d., piecrust rim, aqua opalescent 1,800.00
Bowl, 8" to 9" d., piecrust rim, blue....403.00
Bowl, 8" to 9" d., piecrust rim, green....375.00 to 425.00
Bowl, 8" to 9" d., piecrust rim, marigold 170.00
Bowl, 8" to 9" d., ruffled, aqua opalescent....1,300.00
Bowl, 8" to 9" d., ruffled, green 800.00
Bowl, 8" to 9" d., ruffled, ice blue....4,200.00
Bowl, 8" to 9" d., ruffled, lavender....200.00 to 250.00
Bowl, 8" to 9" d., ruffled, marigold (ILLUS.) 125.00
Bowl, piecrust rim, stippled, ribbed exterior, blue w/electric iridescence 775.00
Bowl, ruffled, sapphire blue 1,300.00
Plate, 9" d., blue 425.00
Plate, 9" d., blue w/electric iridescence....1,250.00 to 1,275.00
Plate, 9" d., green....700.00
Plate, 9" d., marigold 500.00

GRAPE & CABLE

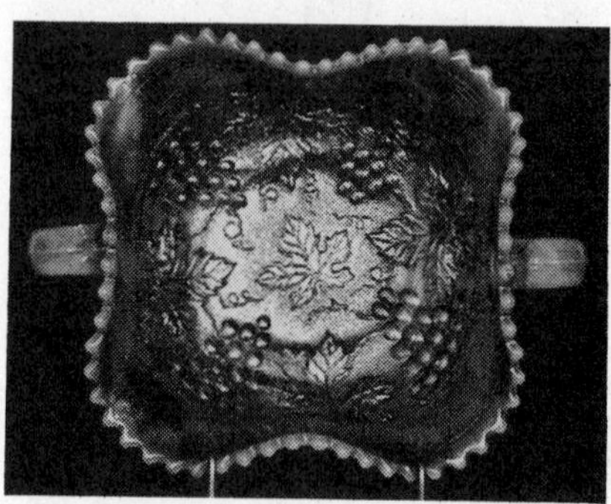

Grape & Cable Bonbon

Banana boat, banded rim, stippled, blue ....1,000.00 to 1,200.00
Banana boat, green....525.00
Banana boat, ice blue....550.00 to 600.00
Banana boat, ice green 750.00
Berry set: master bowl & 6 sauce dishes; marigold, 7 pcs. 275.00
Berry set: master bowl & 6 sauce dishes; purple, 7 pcs....375.00 to 400.00
Bonbon, two-handled, stippled, aqua opalescent (ILLUS.) 3,900.00
Bonbon, two-handled, blue....95.00
Bonbon, two-handled, stippled, marigold 45.00
Bonbon, two-handled, purple....68.00
Bonbon, two-handled, white ....650.00 to 750.00
Bowl, 7" d., ice cream shape, milk white w/marigold overlay (Fenton) ....150.00 to 250.00
Bowl, 7" d., ice cream shape, red (Fenton) 750.00
Bowl, 7" d., blue (Fenton) 40.00
Bowl, 7" d., ice blue 750.00
Bowl, 7" d., red (Fenton)....500.00
Bowl, 8" to 9" d., piecrust rim, blue w/electric iridescence....350.00
Bowl, 8" to 9" d., piecrust rim, stippled, blue....340.00
Bowl, 8" to 9" d., piecrust rim, green....147.00
Bowl, 8" to 9" d., piecrust rim, Basketweave exterior, purple 160.00
Bowl, 8" to 9" d., ball-footed, blue (Fenton) 85.00

Bowl, 8" to 9" d., ball-footed, green (Fenton) 76.00
Bowl, 8" to 9" d., ball-footed, pastel marigold (Fenton) 50.00
Bowl, orange, 10½" d., footed, Persian Medallion interior, blue (Fenton) ....225.00 to 250.00
Bowl, orange, 10½" d., footed, Persian Medallion interior, green (Fenton) ....225.00 to 250.00
Bowl, orange, 10½" d., footed, Persian Medallion interior, marigold (Fenton) 140.00
Bowl, orange, 10½" d., footed, Persian Medallion interior, purple (Fenton) 267.00
Bowl, orange, 10½" d., footed, green..............................300.00 to 350.00
Bowl, orange, 10½" d., footed, ice blue 1,250.00
Bowl, orange, 10½" d., footed, ice green............................950.00 to 1,150.00
Bowl, orange, 10½" d., footed, marigold 202.00
Bowl, orange, 10½" d., lavender.........395.00
Bowl, 10½" d., ruffled, Basketweave exterior, green................................100.00
Breakfast set: individual size creamer & sugar bowl; green, pr...................123.00
Breakfast set: individual size creamer & sugar bowl; purple, pr....................................200.00 to 250.00
Bride's basket, purple 2,975.00
Butter dish, cov., amber.....................155.00
Butter dish, cov., green......................180.00
Butter dish, cov., ice green 250.00
Candle lamp, purple ....500.00 to 600.00
Candle lamp shade, green 750.00
Candlestick, green 135.00
Card tray, horehound..............................80.00
Card tray, marigold 50.00
Card tray, purple......................................80.00
Centerpiece bowl, green.......................775.00
Centerpiece bowl, ice blue 825.00
Centerpiece bowl, ice green 910.00
Cologne bottle w/stopper, ice blue 950.00
Cologne bottle w/stopper, marigold 165.00
Compote, cov., large, green 425.00
Compote, cov., large, marigold........1,450.00
Compote, open, large, marigold ....300.00 to 350.00
Compote, open, small, purple............225.00
Compote, open, large, purple ....425.00 to 525.00
Cracker jar, cov., ice green.................800.00
Cracker jar, cov., marigold.................300.00
Creamer, marigold 90.00
Creamer, purple.....................................88.00
Creamer, individual size, green 65.00
Creamer, individual size, marigold 68.00
Cup & saucer, marigold 250.00
Cup & saucer, purple...........................450.00
Cuspidor, purple 3,000.00
Decanter w/stopper, whiskey, marigold ....600.00 to 625.00
Dresser set, purple, 7 pcs...............2,500.00
Dresser tray, blue 250.00
Dresser tray, purple 195.00
Fernery, ice blue.............................1,300.00
Fernery, purple ....650.00 to 700.00
Hatpin holder, ice blue....................2,500.00
Hatpin holder, ice green 1,700.00
Hatpin holder, lavender ......400.00 to 450.00

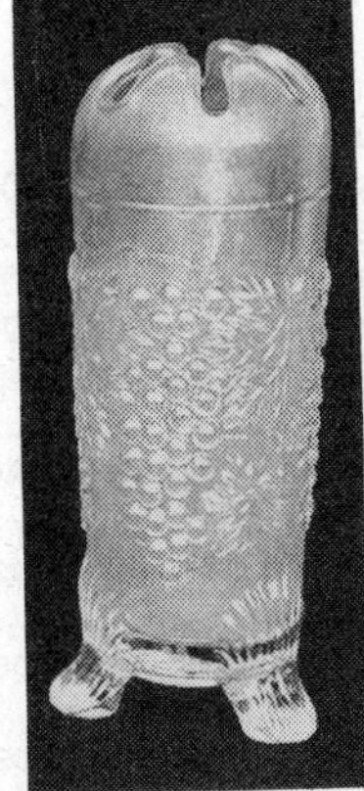

Grape & Cable Hatpin Holder

Hatpin holder, white (ILLUS.) 1,800.00
Hat shape, green ....225.00 to 250.00
Humidor, cov., stippled, blue 1,500.00
Humidor, cov., marigold......275.00 to 300.00
Humidor, cov., stippled, marigold 160.00
Humidor, cov., purple ....700.00 to 900.00
Ice cream set: master bowl & 1 individual dish; marigold, 2 pcs........425.00
Ice cream set: master bowl & 6 individual dishes; white, 7 pcs. 1,500.00
Perfume bottle w/stopper, marigold....417.00
Perfume bottle w/stopper, purple ....650.00 to 675.00
Pin tray, green 225.00
Pin tray, ice blue 900.00
Pin tray, marigold................140.00 to 150.00
Pin tray, purple ....250.00 to 275.00
Pitcher, water, 8¼" h., green 400.00
Pitcher, water, 8¼" h., marigold..........205.00
Plate, 5" to 6" d., purple (Northwood) ....130.00 to 140.00
Plate, 7½" d., turned-up handgrip, green...95.00
Plate, 8" d., green (Northwood) 140.00
Plate, 8" d., footed, marigold 92.00
Plate, 8" d., footed, purple 84.00
Plate, 9" d., marigold 250.00
Plate, 9" d., spatula-footed, green 165.00
Plate, 9" d., spatula-footed, ice green ....850.00 to 875.00
Plate, 9" d., marigold 109.00
Plate, 9" d., stippled, marigold 150.00
Plate, 9" d., stippled, marigold, variant 750.00

Plate, 9" d., stippled, purple 525.00
Plate, chop, 12" d., white 5,000.00
Plate, olive green 900.00
Plate, pastel marigold 300.00
Powder jar, cov., blue 600.00
Powder jar, cov., green 160.00
Punch bowl & base, purple, 11" d., 2 pcs. 450.00
Punch bowl & base, purple, 14" d., 2 pcs. ....500.00 to 525.00
Punch bowl & base, marigold, 17" d., 2 pcs. 1,100.00
Punch cup, aqua opalescent 895.00
Punch cup, blue 50.00
Punch cup, stippled, blue ....50.00 to 75.00
Punch cup, green 38.00
Punch cup, purple 25.00
Punch cup, white ....60.00 to 75.00
Punch set: 11" bowl & 6 cups; blue, 7 pcs. 1,550.00
Punch set: 11" bowl & 6 cups; white, 7 pcs. 1,750.00
Punch set: 14" bowl, base & 5 cups; purple, 7 pcs. 895.00
Punch set: 14" bowl, base & 6 cups; marigold, 8 pcs. 585.00
Punch set: 14" bowl, base & 6 cups; white, 8 pcs. 3,500.00
Punch set: 14" bowl, base & 8 cups; blue, 10 pcs. 2,300.00
Punch set, master: 17" bowl, base & 10 cups; white, 12 pcs. 6,000.00
Punch set, master: 17" bowl, base & 12 cups; marigold, 14 pcs. 2,500.00
Spooner, green 125.00
Spooner, marigold 42.00
Spooner, purple 100.00
Sugar bowl, cov., green 85.00
Sugar bowl, cov., marigold 85.00
Sugar bowl, cov., purple 104.00
Sugar bowl, individual size, green 60.00
Sugar bowl, individual size, marigold ...35.00
Sugar bowl, individual size, purple 68.00
Sweetmeat jar, cov., marigold 1,800.00
Sweetmeat jar, cov., purple ....225.00 to 275.00
Table set, green, 4 pcs. 525.00
Tumbler, green ....45.00 to 65.00
Tumbler, tankard, green .....200.00 to 225.00
Tumbler, tankard, marigold 48.00
Tumbler, tankard, stippled, marigold 65.00
Tumbler, tankard, purple ....45.00 to 55.00
Tumbler, tankard, stippled, purple 89.00
Water set: pitcher & 2 tumblers; blue, 3 pcs. 450.00
Water set: pitcher & 6 tumblers; marigold, 7 pcs. ....500.00 to 550.00
Water set: tankard pitcher & 6 tumblers; marigold, 7 pcs. ....700.00 to 800.00
Whimsey compote (sweetmeat base), purple 135.00
Whimsey punch cup, green 100.00
Whimsey punch cup, marigold 125.00
Whimsey teacup, purple .....100.00 to 125.00
Whiskey shot glass, marigold 165.00
Whiskey shot glass, purple 173.00

HANGING CHERRIES - See Cherry (Millersburg) Pattern

HEAVY GRAPE (Imperial)

Heavy Grape Punch Bowl

Bowl, 4" d., lavender 25.00
Bowl, 5" d., purple 150.00
Bowl, 6" d., green 32.50
Bowl, 6" d., marigold 45.00
Bowl, 6" d., purple 38.00
Bowl, 7" d., fluted, green 30.00
Bowl, 7" d., marigold 20.00
Bowl, 7" d., purple 42.50
Bowl, 8" to 9" d., green 58.00
Bowl, 10" d., purple 335.00
Bowl, square, purple 550.00
Nappy, handled, green 38.00
Nappy, handled, marigold 28.00
Nut bowl, six-footed, purple 75.00
Plate, 7" to 8" d., amber ......150.00 to 200.00
Plate, 7" to 8" d., blue-green 195.00
Plate, 7" to 8" d., smoky 125.00
Plate, chop, 11" d., amber 462.00
Plate, chop, 11" d., blue 400.00
Plate, chop, 11" d., smoky 2,500.00
Punch bowl & base, green, 2 pcs. (ILLUS.) ....250.00 to 300.00
Punch cup, amber 50.00
Punch cup, green 45.00
Punch cup, marigold 20.00
Punch cup, purple 38.00
Punch set: bowl, base & 4 cups; purple, 6 pcs. 800.00

HOLLY, HOLLY BERRIES & CARNIVAL HOLLY (Fenton)

Bonbon, two-handled, green 55.00
Bonbon, two-handled, marigold 110.00
Bonbon, two-handled, purple 65.00
Bowl, 5" d., marigold 25.00

Bowl, 5" d., scalloped, red 450.00
Bowl, 8" to 9" d., amber 125.00
Bowl, 8" to 9" d., lavender...175.00 to 200.00
Bowl, 8" to 9" d., light blue w/marigold overlay 200.00
Bowl, 8" to 9" d., marigold.......40.00 to 50.00
Bowl, 8" to 9" d., red, (Fenton) ....1,000.00 to 1,125.00
Bowl, 8" to 9" d., vaseline 85.00
Bowl, 8" to 9" d., white ....100.00 to 125.00
Bowl, 8" to 9" d., ice cream shape, blue 66.00

Holly Bowl

Bowl, 8" to 9" d., ice cream shape, green (ILLUS.) 103.00
Bowl, 8" to 9" d., ice cream shape, ice green 3,200.00
Bowl, 8" to 9" d., ice cream shape, marigold 80.00
Bowl, 8" to 9" d., ice cream shape, vaseline..130.00
Bowl, 8" to 9" d., ice cream shape, white 135.00
Bowl, 8" to 9" d., ribbon candy rim, amethyst ....100.00 to 125.00
Bowl, 8" to 9" d., ribbon candy rim, purple...............................100.00 to 125.00
Bowl, 8" to 9" d., ruffled, blue opalescent 1,400.00
Bowl, 8" to 9" d., ruffled, emerald green..300.00
Bowl, 8" to 9" d., ruffled, green..............................100.00 to 125.00
Bowl, 8" to 9" d., ruffled, red................................900.00 to 1,000.00
Bowl, 8" to 9" d., ruffled, vaseline 225.00
Compote, small, aqua w/marigold overlay ....100.00 to 125.00
Compote, small, blue..............................40.00
Compote, small, green ....50.00 to 75.00
Compote, small, purple.......100.00 to 125.00
Compote, small, red ....450.00 to 550.00
Compote, small, vaseline 70.00
Compote, ice green opalescent..........625.00
Compote, red......................................1,000.00
Dish, hat-shaped, amber, 5¾" 75.00
Dish, hat-shaped, Amberina 450.00
Dish, hat-shaped, blue, 5¾" 50.00
Dish, hat-shaped, green, 5¾" 36.00
Dish, hat-shaped, green w/marigold overlay 29.00
Dish, hat-shaped, marigold, 5¾" 30.00
Dish, hat-shaped, milk white w/marigold overlay.........................118.00
Dish, hat-shaped, moonstone............200.00
Dish, hat-shaped, purple, 5¾" 35.00
Goblet, blue 35.00
Goblet, green..70.00
Goblet, marigold 27.00
Goblet, red (Fenton) 429.00
Plate, 9" to 10" d., amethyst 1,050.00
Plate, 9" to 10" d., blue ....350.00 to 450.00
Plate, 9" to 10" d., celeste blue (Fenton) 9,500.00
Plate, 9" to 10" d., pastel marigold......200.00
Plate, 9" to 10" d., purple....400.00 to 600.00
Sauceboat, handled, purple..............110.00
Sherbet, blue 40.00
Sherbet, green......................................25.00
Sherbet, lime green 75.00

HOMESTEAD - See NU-ART HOMESTEAD PLATE

HORSE HEADS OR HORSE MEDALLION (Fenton)

Horse Heads Bowl

Bowl, 5" d., footed, marigold.................57.00
Bowl, 6" d., blue....................................60.00
Bowl, 6" d., collared base, marigold 85.00
Bowl, 7" to 8" d., amber 395.00
Bowl, 7" to 8" d., blue..........................115.00
Bowl, 7" to 8" d., green (ILLUS.)..........135.00
Bowl, ice cream shape, amber 280.00
Bowl, ice cream shape, blue...............235.00
Bowl, 7" d., ice cream shape, marigold 85.00
Bowl, 7" d., ice cream shape, purple ..425.00
Bowl, ruffled, collared base, Amberina 450.00

Bowl, jack-in-the-pulpit shaped, amber....................................495.00
Bowl, jack-in-the-pulpit shaped, blue...............................150.00 to 175.00
Bowl, jack-in-the-pulpit shaped, green...............................250.00 to 300.00
Bowl, jack-in-the-pulpit shaped, vaseline...............................400.00 to 425.00
Bowl, 7" to 8" d., blue.....................................750.00
Bowl, 7" to 8" d., marigold...200.00 to 225.00
Nut bowl, three-footed, amethyst.........225.00
Nut bowl, three-footed, blue 150.00
Nut bowl, three-footed, vaseline ....250.00 to 300.00
Rose bowl, blue 225.00
Rose bowl, marigold 136.00

IMPERIAL GRAPE (Imperial)

Basket, marigold.....................................80.00
Basket, smoky 118.00
Berry set: master bowl & 2 sauce dishes; purple, 3 pcs......................225.00
Berry set: master bowl & 4 sauce dishes; green, 5 pcs.........125.00 to 150.00
Bowl, 6" d., marigold.............................35.00
Bowl, 6" d., ruffled, purple.....................70.00
Bowl, 7" d., 2½" h., green 42.00
Bowl, 8" to 9" d., marigold.....................43.00
Bowl, 8" to 9" d., purple 120.00
Bowl, 10" d., green 40.00
Bowl, 10" d., marigold............................45.00
Bowl, 10" d., purple..............................117.00
Compote, clambroth 35.00
Compote, green......................................45.00
Compote, lavender swirled w/amber ..140.00
Cup & saucer, amber.............................65.00
Cup & saucer, green..............................85.00
Cup & saucer, marigold 80.00
Decanter w/stopper, green...............................125.00 to 150.00
Decanter w/stopper, marigold...............94.00
Goblet, green..35.00
Goblet, marigold 35.00
Goblet, purple 55.00
Goblet, smoky.........................75.00 to 100.00
Pitcher, water, amber 650.00
Pitcher, water, marigold........75.00 to 100.00
Pitcher, water, smoky ....300.00 to 400.00
Plate, 6" d., amber ....125.00 to 150.00
Plate, 6" d., green 60.00
Plate, 6" d., marigold 48.00
Plate, 8" d., green 50.00
Plate, 8" d., marigold 50.00
Plate, 8" d., purple ....75.00 to 100.00
Plate, 9" d., ruffled, clambroth 75.00
Plate, 9" d., flat, green 75.00
Plate, 9" d., ruffled, marigold ....50.00 to 100.00
Plate, 9" d., ruffled, purple 100.00
Plate, 9" d., ruffled, smoky 95.00
Rose bowl, amber.................................675.00
Rose bowl, green...................................65.00
Sauce dish, green..................................25.00
Sauce dish, ruffled, marigold.................20.00
Tray, center handle, amber 30.00
Tray, center handle, clambroth.............45.00
Tumbler, amber 98.00
Tumbler, aqua 130.00
Tumbler, green 28.00
Tumbler, lilac 59.00
Water bottle, purple ....150.00 to 175.00
Water bottle, smoky............................450.00
Water set: pitcher & 6 tumblers; marigold, 7 pcs. 225.00
Water set: pitcher & 6 tumblers; purple, 7 pcs. 700.00
Wine, marigold......................................28.00
Wine, purple 35.00
Wine, smoky 75.00
Wine set: decanter w/stopper & 6 wines; marigold, 7 pcs. 260.00
Wine set: decanter w/stopper & 6 wines; purple, 7 pcs. ....475.00 to 500.00

LUSTRE ROSE (Imperial)

Lustre Rose Bowl

Bowl, 7" d., three-footed, clambroth 75.00
Bowl, 7" d., three-footed, green............35.00
Bowl, 7" d., three-footed, marigold 42.00
Bowl, 8" to 9" d., three-footed, marigold (ILLUS.)................................40.00
Bowl, 8" to 9" d., three-footed, purple 117.00
Bowl, 8" to 9" d., three-footed, smoky 35.00
Bowl, 10½" d., three-footed, marigold 35.00
Bowl, 10½" d., three-footed, smoky......74.00
Bowl, 11" d., ruffled, collared base, green...85.00
Bowl, fruit, red..................................2,400.00
Bowl, whimsey, centerpiece, amber...250.00
Bowl, whimsey, centerpiece, purple ..550.00
Butter dish, cov., marigold 65.00
Butter dish, cov., purple.......................110.00
Creamer, marigold.................................37.00
Creamer, purple.....................................125.00
Fernery, amber 80.00
Fernery, blue 75.00
Fernery, green, 7½" d., 4" h..................60.00
Fernery, red 1,000.00

Pitcher, water, clambroth......................65.00
Pitcher, water, green 90.00
Pitcher, water, marigold........................85.00
Plate, 9" d., green 75.00
Plate, 9" d., marigold 60.00
Rose bowl, marigold..............................45.00
Rose bowl, purple...................................30.00
Sauce dish, clambroth 30.00
Sauce dish, marigold 12.00
Spooner, purple 125.00
Sugar bowl, cov., green..........................50.00
Tumbler, amber 17.00
Tumbler, marigold...................................25.00
Tumbler, purple 50.00
Tumbler, white 39.00
Water set: pitcher & 4 tumblers; purple, 5 pcs. 700.00
Water set: pitcher & 6 tumblers; marigold, 7 pcs. 250.00
Whimsey, flattened fernery, green......110.00

MILLERSBURG TROUT & FLY - See Trout & Fly Pattern

MORNING GLORY (Millersburg)

Morning Glory Pitcher

Pitcher, tankard, purple (ILLUS.) ....6,350.00 to 7,500.00
Tumbler, green 1,000.00
Tumbler, marigold...........................1,400.00
Tumbler, purple 1,300.00
Vase, 4¼" h., marigold 30.00
Vase, 6" h., green 79.00
Vase, 6" h., purple 73.00
Vase, 7" h., smoky..................................95.00
Vase, 8" h., purple 75.00
Vase, purple 125.00
Vase, funeral, 10 x 12" , marigold.......280.00
Vase, funeral, 9½ x 13" , purple 300.00

NU-ART CHRYSANTHEMUM PLATE (Imperial)

Amber 600.00
Marigold..495.00
Purple 1,200.00
White 700.00

NU-ART HOMESTEAD PLATE (Imperial)

Amber ....1,200.00 to 1,500.00
Blue 5,250.00
Emerald green 3,000.00
Green.................................750.00 to 850.00
Helios..395.00
Lavender..900.00
Marigold..400.00
Purple ....875.00 to 975.00
White 758.00

ORANGE TREE (Fenton)

Orange Tree Mug

Bowl, 8" to 9" d., blue.........................105.00
Bowl, 8" to 9" d., clambroth..................83.00
Bowl, 8" to 9" d., purple ....75.00 to 100.00
Bowl, 8" to 9" d., red 2,100.00
Bowl, 8" to 9" d., white 156.00
Bowl, 10" d., three-footed, blue 233.00
Bowl, 10" d., three-footed, green 235.00
Bowl, 10" d., Rose Tree interior, blue 1,100.00
Bowl, ice cream shape, marigold..........45.00
Bowl, ice cream shape, red 1,400.00
Bowl, ice cream shape, white 125.00
Bowl, moonstone 2,000.00
Bowl, peach opalescent..................1,900.00
Breakfast set: individual size creamer & cov. sugar bowl; blue, pr. 130.00
Breakfast set: individual size creamer & cov. sugar bowl; white, pr. 150.00
Butter dish, cov., blue 400.00
Butter dish, cov., blue w/electric iridescence...350.00
Butter dish, cov., marigold 250.00
Centerpiece bowl, footed, marigold, 12" d., 4" h. 80.00
Compote, 5" d., blue 62.50
Compote, 5" d., marigold 35.00
Creamer, footed, blue.............................80.00
Creamer, footed, purple..........................50.00
Creamer, individual size, blue 45.00
Creamer, individual size, purple 75.00
Creamer, individual size, white.............85.00
Creamer & sugar bowl, footed, blue, pr. 100.00
Goblet, blue 75.00
Goblet, green..190.00
Goblet, marigold 48.00

Hatpin holder, blue ....300.00 to 325.00
Loving cup, green 350.00
Loving cup, marigold ....175.00 to 200.00
Loving cup, purple 400.00
Mug, amber 114.00
Mug, Amberina 395.00
Mug, aqua...163.00
Mug, blue (ILLUS.) 57.00
Mug, lavender.....................................135.00
Mug, marigold w/vaseline base 150.00
Mug, purple..80.00
Mug, red ....350.00 to 400.00
Mug, sapphire blue.............300.00 to 350.00
Plate, 9" d., flat, clambroth..................215.00
Plate, 9" d., flat, green 2,000.00
Plate, 9" d., flat, marigold....225.00 to 250.00
Plate, 9" d., flat, Beaded Berry exterior, blue 550.00
Plate, 9" d., trunk center, flat, Beaded Berry exterior, marigold 185.00
Powder jar, cov., blue.........................105.00
Powder jar, cov., green.......................412.00
Powder jar, cov., marigold......65.00 to 70.00
Punch bowl & base, marigold, 2 pcs. 153.00
Punch bowl & base, white, 2 pcs. ....700.00 to 800.00
Punch cup, blue.....................................25.00
Punch cup, green 90.00
Punch set: bowl, base & 6 cups; blue, 8 pcs. ....500.00 to 525.00
Rose bowl, blue.....................................85.00
Rose bowl, red.................900.00 to 1,200.00
Rose bowl, white 275.00
Sauce dish, footed, blue.........................30.00
Sauce dish, footed, marigold..................21.00
Shaving mug, marigold..........................32.00
Shaving mug, marigold, large..............125.00
Sugar bowl, cov., marigold 110.00
Sugar bowl, cov., white........................100.00
Sugar bowl, open, individual size, marigold 40.00
Sugar bowl, open, individual size, purple 52.00
Tumbler, marigold..................................45.00
Tumbler, pastel marigold.......................49.00
Tumbler, purple 42.00
Tumbler, white.....................................100.00
Water set: pitcher & 6 tumblers; blue, 7 pcs. 700.00
Wine, clambroth.....................................65.00
Wine, marigold.......................................25.00

PANTHER (Fenton)

Berry set: master bowl & 4 sauce dishes; marigold, 5 pcs. 325.00
Bowl, 5" d., footed, aqua.....................425.00
Bowl, 5" d., footed, blue......................100.00
Bowl, 5" d., footed, clambroth...............35.00
Bowl, 5" d., footed, green 90.00
Bowl, 5" d., footed, marigold..................52.00
Bowl, 5" d., footed, red............................1,000.00 to 1,300.00
Bowl, 9" d., claw-footed, blue 390.00
Bowl, 9" d., claw-footed, green..............................625.00 to 675.00
Bowl, 9" d., claw-footed, marigold ....200.00 to 250.00
Bowl, 9" d., claw-footed, white............750.00
Bowl, berry, Butterfly & Berry exterior, marigold 35.00
Bowl, low, marigold..............................300.00

Panther Centerpiece Bowl

Centerpiece bowl, marigold (ILLUS.) ....575.00 to 600.00

PEACOCK AT FOUNTAIN (Northwood)

Peacock at Fountain Water Set

Berry set: master bowl & 2 sauce dishes; ice blue, 3 pcs. 640.00
Berry set: master bowl & 6 sauce dishes; blue, 7 pcs. 600.00
Bowl, master berry, blue......................325.00
Bowl, master berry, green 600.00
Bowl, orange, three-footed, aqua opalescent 1,100.00
Bowl, orange, three-footed, lavender..525.00
Butter dish, cov., marigold...................210.00
Butter dish, cov., purple......................275.00
Compote, ice green 1,400.00
Compote, marigold 400.00
Compote, purple 800.00
Compote, white.....................550.00 to 650.00
Creamer, marigold.................................65.00
Creamer, purple....................75.00 to 100.00

Pitcher, water, blue....................................450.00
Pitcher, water, marigold....................................250.00
Pitcher, water, white........950.00 to 1,000.00
Punch bowl & base, ice green, 2 pcs. 9,500.00
Punch bowl & base, marigold, 2 pcs. 900.00
Punch bowl & base, purple, 2 pcs. 1,500.00
Punch cup, aqua opalescent...........1,400.00
Punch cup, marigold....................................45.00
Punch cup, purple....................................38.00
Punch cup, white 75.00
Punch set: bowl, base & 5 cups; ice green, 7 pcs. 10,750.00
Punch set: bowl, base & 6 cups; purple, 7 pcs. 1,750.00
Punch set: bowl, base & 6 cups; ice blue, 8 pcs...............................7,000.00
Sauce dish, marigold....................................21.00
Sauce dish, purple....................................31.00
Sauce dish, white 50.00
Spooner, blue 150.00
Spooner, white....................................175.00
Sugar bowl, cov., ice blue....................265.00
Sugar bowl, cov., marigold 85.00
Table set, ice blue, 4 pcs................2,600.00
Table set, marigold, 4 pcs. 475.00
Table set, purple, 4 pcs. .....450.00 to 500.00
Tumbler, ice blue...............400.00 to 425.00
Tumbler, lavender....................................125.00
Tumbler, marigold....................................45.00
Tumbler, purple 55.00
Water set: pitcher & 5 tumblers; marigold, 6 pcs. 500.00
Water set: pitcher & 6 tumblers; blue, 7 pcs. 775.00
Water set: pitcher & 6 tumblers; purple, 7 pcs. (ILLUS.) 900.00

PEACOCKS ON FENCE (Northwood Peacocks)

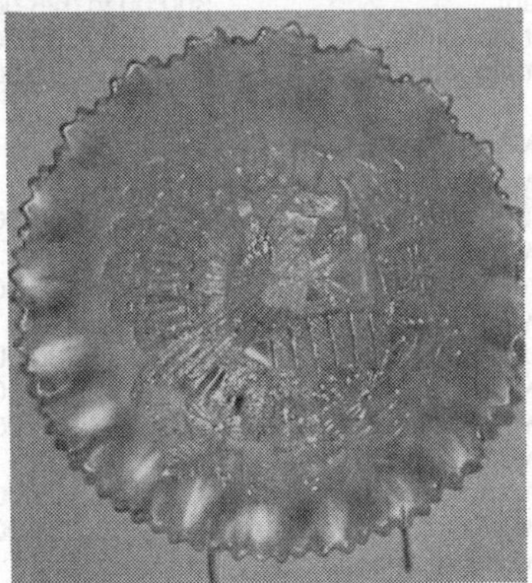

Peacocks on Fence Bowl

Bowl, 8" to 9" d., piecrust rim, aqua opalescent 3,000.00
Bowl, 8" to 9" d., piecrust rim, green..........................1,800.00 to 1,875.00
Bowl, 8" to 9" d., piecrust rim, blue w/electric iridescence.......................995.00
Bowl, 8" to 9" d., piecrust rim, lavender...550.00
Bowl, 8" to 9" d., piecrust rim, marigold (ILLUS.)............................288.00
Bowl, 8" to 9" d., piecrust rim, stippled, marigold............400.00 to 425.00
Bowl, 8" to 9" d., piecrust rim, pastel marigold ....325.00 to 350.00
Bowl, 8" to 9" d., ruffled rim, blue........525.00
Bowl, 8" to 9" d., ruffled rim, green.......................1,100.00 to 1,200.00
Bowl, 8" to 9" d., ruffled rim, ice blue 1,750.00
Bowl, 8" to 9" d., ruffled rim, ice green..1,400.00
Bowl, 8" to 9" d., ruffled rim, white......650.00
Bowl, 9" d., stippled, green.............1,100.00
Bowl, ruffled, lime green opalescent 4,000.00
Bowl, ruffled, ribbed back, white.........875.00
Plate, 9" d., ice blue......1,650.00 to 1,750.00
Plate, 9" d., ice green 450.00
Plate, 9" d., lavender ....1,100.00 to 1,200.00
Plate, 9" d., marigold 456.00

PINE CONE (Fenton)

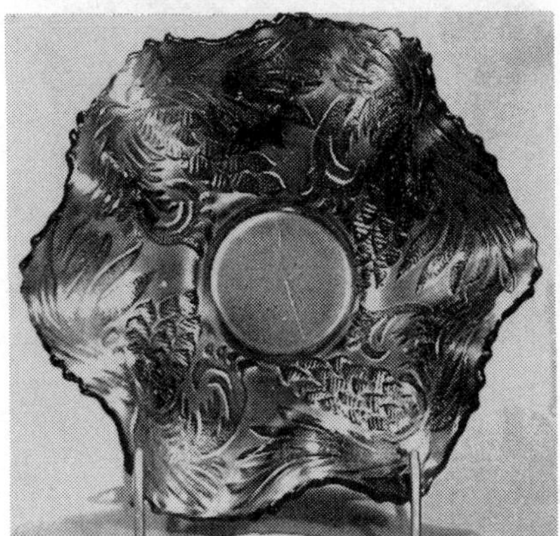

Pine Cone Bowl

Bowl, 5" d., blue (ILLUS.) 40.00
Bowl, 5" d., marigold............................40.00
Bowl, 5" d., purple...............................35.00
Bowl, 6" d., ruffled, blue 45.00
Bowl, 6" d., marigold 25.00
Bowl, 7" d., ruffled, blue 50.00
Bowl, 7" d., marigold............................28.00
Bowl, 7" d., ruffled, purple....................65.00
Plate, 6½" d., blue 122.00
Plate, 6½" d., green...........................200.00
Plate, 6½" d., marigold 50.00
Plate, 6½" d., purple...........................110.00
Plate, 7½" d., amber...........................425.00
Plate, 7½" d., blue 125.00

Plate, 7½" d., marigold 100.00
Plate, 7½" d., purple 65.00
Plate, 7¾" d., blue 225.00

ROSE SHOW

Bowl, 9" d., aqua................650.00 to 750.00
Bowl, 9" d., blue opalescent ....1,500.00 to 1,950.00
Bowl, 9" d., blue w/electric iridescence 1,250.00
Bowl, 9" d., green ....3,000.00 to 4,000.00
Bowl, 9" d., purple...........................1,275.00
Bowl, 9" d., sapphire blue 3,200.00
Bowl, 9" d., smoky 1,100.00
Bowl, 9" d., white ....350.00 to 400.00
Plate, 9" d., aqua opalescent...........8,000.00
Plate, 9" d., green 3,600.00
Plate, 9" d., ice blue......1,800.00 to 2,000.00
Plate, 9" d., marigold ....600.00 to 650.00
Plate, 9" d., moonstone 7,000.00
Plate, 9" d., pastel marigold ....1,000.00 to 1,500.00
Plate, 9" d., purple 1,500.00
Plate, 9" d., vaseline 3,400.00
Plate, 9" d., white...............................500.00

STAG & HOLLY (Fenton)

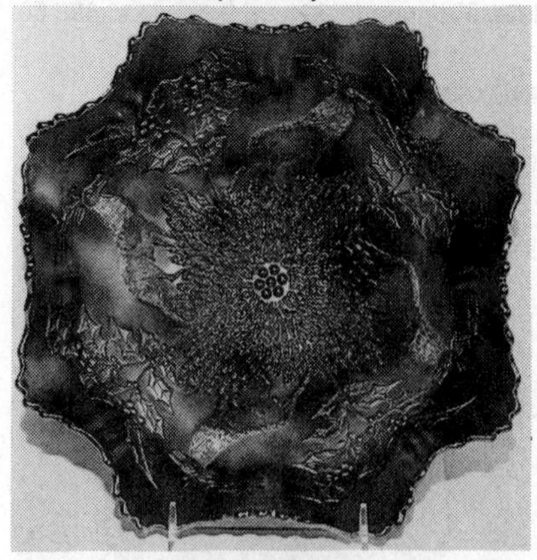

Stag & Holly Bowl

Bowl, 7" d., spatula-footed, blue ....125.00 to 175.00
Bowl, 7" d., spatula-footed, marigold 55.00
Bowl, 8" d., footed, ice cream shape, green...255.00
Bowl, 8" to 9" d., spatula-footed, blue ....225.00 to 250.00
Bowl, 8" to 9" d., spatula-footed, green..228.00
Bowl, 8" to 9" d., spatula-footed, purple 167.00
Bowl, 10" to 11" d., three-footed, amber.............................450.00 to 500.00
Bowl, 10" to 11" d., three-footed, aqua 800.00
Bowl, 10" to 11" d., three-footed, purple (ILLUS.) 435.00
Bowl, 10" to 11" d., three-footed, vaseline..........................175.00 to 275.00
Bowl, 11" d., flat, amber.....................750.00
Bowl, 11" d., flat, blue w/electric iridescence 450.00
Bowl, 11" d., ruffled, green w/marigold overlay 250.00
Bowl, 12" d., ice cream shape, blue ...325.00
Bowl, 12" d., ice cream shape, green...170.00
Plate, chop, 12" d., three-footed, marigold ....750.00 to 850.00
Rose bowl, blue, large 995.00
Rose bowl, marigold, large 275.00

STRAWBERRY (Millersburg)

Bowl, 6" d., ruffled, purple...................135.00
Bowl, 7" d., green 95.00
Bowl, 7" d., purple..............................115.00
Bowl, 8" to 9" d., marigold..................260.00
Bowl, 8" to 9" d., purple ......225.00 to 250.00
Bowl, 8" to 9" d., vaseline 1,250.00
Bowl, 9" w., tricornered, marigold 200.00
Bowl, 9½" w., square, green...............600.00
Bowl, 9½" w., square, ribbon candy rim, purple..400.00
Bowl, 9½" d., Basketweave exterior, marigold 55.00
Bowl, 9½" d., Basketweave exterior, purple...............................75.00 to 100.00
Bowl, 10" w., tricornered, ribbon candy rim, purple 450.00
Compote, marigold 275.00
Compote, purple 225.00

SWAN PASTEL NOVELTIES (Dugan)

Salt dip, amber 125.00
Salt dip, celeste blue 38.00
Salt dip, ice blue 40.00
Salt dip, ice green.................................35.00
Salt dip, marigold................100.00 to 125.00
Salt dip, peach opalescent ....300.00 to 325.00
Salt dip, pink 35.00
Salt dip, purple...................................272.00

TEN MUMS (Fenton)

Bowl, 8" to 9" d., ribbon candy rim, blue 140.00
Bowl, 8" to 9" d., ribbon candy rim, green..125.00
Bowl, 8" to 9" d., ribbon candy rim, purple 180.00
Bowl, 10" d., ruffled, blue....................130.00
Bowl, 10" d., footed, green 80.00
Bowl, 10" d., ribbon candy rim, green..175.00
Bowl, 10" d., footed, marigold.............225.00
Bowl, 10" d., ribbon candy rim, marigold 300.00
Bowl, 10" d., ruffled, marigold............105.00
Bowl, 10" d., ribbon candy rim, purple 110.00

Bowl, 10" d., ruffled, purple................155.00

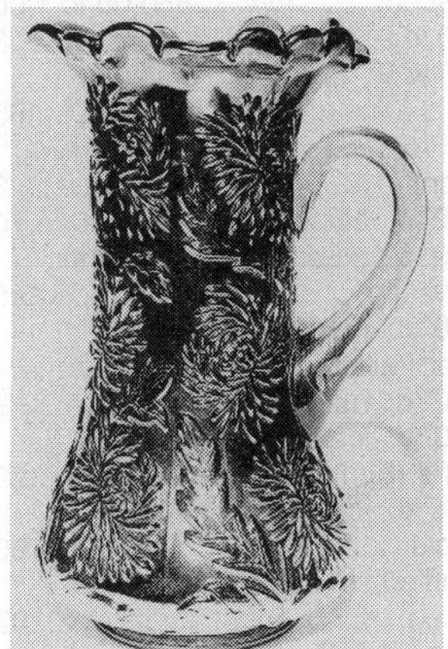

Ten Mums Pitcher

Pitcher, water, blue (ILLUS.) 1,650.00
Pitcher, water, marigold......................475.00
Tumbler. amber 65.00
Tumbler. blue.......................................75.00
Tumbler. marigold.................................50.00
Tumbler. white 153.00
Water set: pitcher & 1 tumbler; marigold, 2 pcs. 575.00

THREE FRUITS (Northwood)

Bowl, 5" d., marigold...........................30.00
Bowl, 5" d., purple...............................30.00
Bowl, 6" d., green 40.00
Bowl, 6" d., marigold...........................30.00
Bowl, 8" d., ruffled, green 75.00
Bowl, 8½" d., ruffled, blue....................95.00
Bowl, 8½" d., collared base, Basketweave & Grapevine exterior, green ...65.00
Bowl, 8½" d., dome-footed, green..............................150.00 to 175.00
Bowl, 8½" d., piecrust rim, marigold 60.00
Bowl, 8½" d., purple...........................100.00
Bowl, 9" d., ruffled, stippled, aqua opalescent 875.00
Bowl, 9" d., ruffled, blue.....................210.00
Bowl, 9" d., green 66.00
Bowl, 9" d., ruffled, green 100.00
Bowl, 9" d., stippled, purple 200.00
Bowl, 9" d., stippled, white.................762.50
Bowl, 9" d., dome-footed, Basketweave & Grapevine exterior, green ...70.00
Bowl, 9" d., dome-footed, Basketweave & Grapevine exterior, ice green...675.00
Bowl, 9" d., piecrust rim, stippled, ribbed exterior, green......................795.00
Bowl, 9" d., spatula-footed, aqua opalescent ....500.00 to 550.00
Bowl, 9" d., spatula-footed, emerald green..425.00
Bowl, 9" d., spatula-footed, ruffled, green...60.00
Bowl, 9" d., spatula-footed, purple......152.00
Bowl, 9" d., spatula-footed, white 360.00
Bowl, 10" d., ruffled, ice green...........375.00
Bowl, ruffled, stippled, footed, ice blue ....800.00 to 1,000.00
Bowl, ruffled, footed, Meander exterior, ice blue 450.00
Plate, 9" d., stippled, aqua opalescent ....1,850.00 to 2,000.00
Plate, 9" d., stippled, blue w/electric iridescence.......................800.00 to 900.00
Plate, 9" d., green 168.00
Plate, 9" d., marigold 113.00
Plate, 9" d., stippled, marigold 230.00
Plate, 9" d., purple 173.00
Plate, 9" d., stippled, purple...300.00 to 325.00Plate, 9½" w., 12 sided, green (Fenton) 150.00
Plate, 9½" w., 12-sided, marigold (Fenton) 150.00

TREE TRUNK VASE (Northwood)

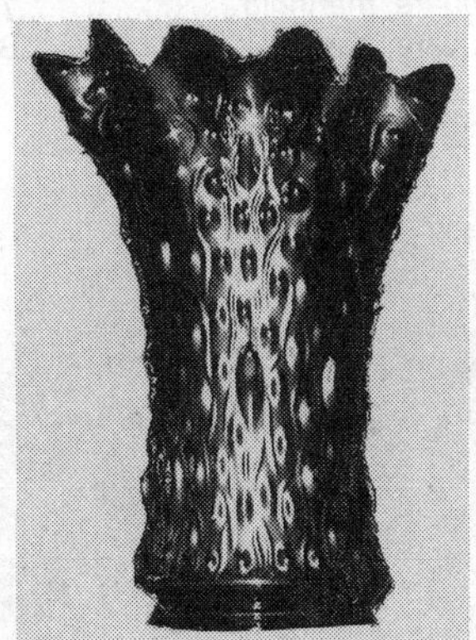

Tree Trunk Vase

6" h., purple, squatty..........150.00 to 175.00
6¼" h., squatty, marigold........55.00 to 60.00
6¾" h., marigold..................................75.00
7" h., green 45.00
7" h., ice blue 400.00
8" to 11" h., green ....35.00 to 45.00
9" h., aqua 95.00
9" h., white 100.00
9" to 12" h., aqua opalescent..............475.00
9" to 10" h., marigold 35.00
9" to 10" h., purple (ILLUS.) 52.50
10½" h., blue w/electric iridescence ...115.00
11" h., ice blue 350.00
12" h., ice green..................................440.00
12" h., marigold.................130.00 to 150.00
12" h., purple 185.00
13½" h., blue.......................375.00 to 400.00
14" h., purple 125.00
15" h., purple, w/elephant foot........1,300.00
17" h., white, funeral 1,000.00
18" h., green 550.00
18" h., purple 975.00

19" h., purple, funeral 1,800.00
20" h., cobalt blue, funeral..............1,300.00

TROUT & FLY (Millersburg)

Bowl, ice cream shape, green 850.00
Bowl, ice cream shape, lavender....1,350.00
Bowl, ice cream shape, marigold ....475.00 to 525.00
Bowl, ice cream shape, purple...............................595.00 to 650.00
Bowl, ribbon candy rim, green...........712.00
Bowl, ribbon candy rim, lavender 1,400.00
Bowl, ribbon candy rim, marigold 350.00
Bowl, ribbon candy rim, purple 575.00
Bowl, ruffled, green............450.00 to 500.00
Bowl, ruffled, lavender.....................1,800.00
Bowl, ruffled, marigold.......400.00 to 475.00
Bowl, ruffled, marigold, satin finish.....385.00
Bowl, ruffled, pastel marigold, satin finish 500.00
Bowl, ruffled, purple...........550.00 to 600.00
Bowl, ruffled, purple, satin finish.........675.00
Bowl, square, green......1,400.00 to 1,500.00
Bowl, square, marigold.......................700.00
Bowl, square, purple..........................825.00

VINTAGE or VINTAGE GRAPE

Vintage Plate

Bonbon, two-handled, blue (Fenton) 50.00
Bonbon, two-handled, green (Fenton)..50.00
Bowl, 6" d., green (Fenton)...................45.00
Bowl, 6" d., purple (Fenton)..................32.50
Bowl, 6½" d., ice cream shape, green 35.00
Bowl, 7" d., purple (Millersburg) ....50.00 to 75.00
Bowl, 7" d., ruffled, vaseline 110.00
Bowl, 7½" d., ice cream shape, blue 36.00
Bowl, 7½" d., ice cream shape, green 32.00
Bowl, 8" d., ribbon candy rim, Wide Panel exterior, blue 55.00
Bowl, 8" to 9" d., aqua opalescent.........................1,000.00 to 1,200.00
Bowl, 8" to 9" d., ruffled, aqua opalescent ....850.00 to 1,000.00
Bowl, 8" to 9" d., marigold (Fenton)......35.00
Bowl, 8" to 9" d., fluted, Persian blue 630.00
Bowl, 8" to 9" d., footed, purple (Fenton) 38.00
Bowl, 10" d., blue...............75.00 to 100.00
Bowl, 10" d., green, Hobnail exterior (Millersburg)....................................950.00
Bowl, 10" d., marigold, Hobnail exterior (Millersburg)........................575.00
Bowl, 10" d., ruffled, green 85.00
Bowl, 10" d., ice cream shape, vaseline (Fenton) 225.00
Bowl, 11" d., ice cream shape, marigold 600.00
Bowl, ruffled, domed base, celeste blue 825.00
Compote, 7" d., fluted, aqua opalescent 925.00
Compote, 7" d., blue (Fenton) 75.00
Compote, 7" d., fluted, green (Fenton) 46.00
Compote, 7" d., marigold (Fenton) 40.00
Compote, 7" d., purple (Fenton) 45.00
Cuspidor, marigold 2,300.00
Epergne, blue (Fenton).......................110.00
Epergne, green, large.........................235.00
Epergne, purple (Fenton) 130.00
Fernery, footed, blue (Fenton)..............85.00
Fernery, footed, green (Fenton) 75.00
Fernery, footed, red (Fenton) ....1,400.00 to 1,600.00
Ice cream set: master ice cream bowl & four 6" d. bowls; cobalt blue, 5 pcs. 450.00
Nut dish, footed, blue, 6" d. (Fenton)....70.00
Nut dish, footed, green, 6" d. (Fenton) 110.00
Plate, 6" d., blue 140.00
Plate, 6" d., purple 65.00
Plate, 6½" d., stippled, marigold...........50.00
Plate, 7" d., blue (Fenton) (ILLUS.) ....65.00 to 75.00
Plate, 7" d., green (Fenton) ....175.00 to 185.00
Plate, 8" d., green 165.00
Powder jar, cov., marigold (Fenton) 80.00
Powder jar, cov., marigold 75.00
Powder jar, cov., purple (Fenton) 100.00
Sandwich tray, handled, clambroth 28.00
Sandwich tray, handled, marigold 30.00
Sauce dish, blue 30.00
Sauce dish, blue, Hobnail exterior (Millersburg) 450.00
Tumbler, marigold (Fenton) 25.00
Wine, marigold (Fenton) 25.00
Wine, purple (Fenton)...........................32.00

VINTAGE GRAPE - See Vintage Pattern

WILD STRAWBERRY (Northwood)

Bowl, 6" d., green 55.00

Bowl, 6" d., purple....................................48.00
Bowl, 6" d., ruffled, purple...................100.00
Bowl, 7" d., marigold..............................85.00
Bowl, 10" d., green ....175.00 to 225.00
Bowl, 10" d., ice green.....................1,750.00
Bowl, 10" d., marigold............................85.00
Bowl, 10" d., purple.............................185.00
Plate, 6" to 7" d., w/handgrip, green...............................200.00 to 225.00
Plate, 6" to 7" d., w/handgrip, marigold...........................125.00 to 150.00
Plate, 6" to 7" d., w/handgrip, purple..125.00
Plate, 8" d., w/handgrip, green 100.00
Plate, 8" d., w/handgrip, purple...........150.00

WINDMILL or WINDMILL MEDALLION (Imperial)

Windmill Tumbler

Bowl, 7" d., marigold..............................40.00
Bowl, 7" d., purple..................................56.00
Bowl, 8" to 9" d., green 35.00
Bowl, 8" to 9" d., ruffled, marigold.........75.00
Bowl, 8" to 9" d., ruffled, purple 145.00
Bowl, 8" to 9" d., ruffled, vaseline 65.00
Bowl, 8" to 9" d., ruffled, smoky.............52.00
Bowl, 9" d., footed, marigold....................30.00
Bowl, 9" d., footed, purple.....................115.00
Dresser tray, oval, marigold.....................48.00
Pickle dish, aqua teal............................275.00
Pickle dish, green 50.00
Pickle dish, lavender................................70.00
Pickle dish, marigold................................28.00
Pickle dish, purple 50.00
Pitcher, milk, clambroth 45.00
Pitcher, milk, ice green 110.00
Pitcher, milk, marigold 60.00
Pitcher, milk, purple...........500.00 to 700.00
Pitcher, milk, smoky...............................225.00
Pitcher, water, marigold...........................78.00
Pitcher, water, purple..........450.00 to 500.00
Plate, 8" d., marigold 18.00
Sauce dish, clambroth 35.00
Sauce dish, green.....................................32.00
Sauce dish, marigold 20.00
Sauce dish, purple....................................35.00
Tumbler, green 39.00
Tumbler, marigold (ILLUS.) 35.00
Tumbler, purple 100.00
Water set: pitcher & 1 tumbler; marigold, 2 pcs. 130.00
Water set: pitcher & 2 tumblers; purple, 3 pcs. 1,200.00

WINDMILL MEDALLION - See Windmill Pattern

ZIPPERED LOOP LAMP (Imperial)

Zippered Loop Lamp

Hand, marigold, 4½" h. 1,200.00
Hand, marigold, medium 675.00
Sewing, marigold, small.........................325.00
Sewing, marigold, medium ....600.00 to 675.00
Sewing, smoky, medium ....950.00 to 1,000.00
Sewing, marigold, large (ILLUS.) ....550.00 to 575.00

(End of Carnival Glass Section)

CHOCOLATE

Smooth-Edged Dolphin Dish

This glass is often called Caramel Slag. It was made by the Indiana Tumbler and

Goblet Company of Greentown, Indiana, and other glasshouses, beginning at the turn of this century. Various patterns were produced, highly popular among them being Cactus and Leaf Bracket.

Animal covered dish, Dolphin, beaded top rim, Greentown $220.00
Animal covered dish, Dolphin, smooth rim, Greentown, 9" l., 4" h.. (ILLUS.) 375.00
Berry set: master bowl & five sauce dishes; Leaf Bracket patt., Greentown, 6 pcs......................................250.00
Butter dish, cov., small, Dewey patt., Greentown, 4" d. 105.00
Butter dish, cov., large, Dewey patt., Greentown, 5" d. 165.00
Compote, 8¼" d., Cactus patt., Greentown 240.00
Creamer, child's, Austrian patt., Greentown 190.00
Creamer, cov., Cactus patt., Greentown 85.00
Creamer, tankard-shaped, Shuttle patt., Greentown 95.00
Creamer & open sugar bowl, Dewey patt., pr..125.00
Mug, Herringbone patt., Greentown 85.00

Chocolate Serenade Mug

Mug, Serenade (or Troubador) patt., McKee, 3½" d., 5" h. (ILLUS.) 95.00
Salt & pepper shakers w/original tops, Leaf Bracket patt., Greentown, pr....................................150.00 to 200.00
Sauce dish, Leaf Bracket patt., Greentown 55.00
Spooner, Cactus patt., Greentown.......95.00
Sugar bowl, cov., Cactus patt., Greentown 145.00
Sugar bowl, cov., Dewey patt., Greentown ....100.00 to 125.00
Tumbler, iced tea or lemonade, Cactus patt., Greentown, 5" h. ....50.00 to 75.00
Tumbler, Fleur-de-lis patt., Greentown 110.00

CONSOLIDATED

The Consolidated Lamp and Glass Company of Coraopolis, Pennsylvania was founded in 1894 and for a number of years was noted for its lighting wares but also produced popular lines of pressed and blown tablewares. Highly collectible glass patterns of this early era include the Cone, Cosmos (which see), Florette and Guttate lines.

Lamps and shades continued to be good sellers but in 1926 a new "art" line of molded decorative wares was introduced. This "Martelé" line was developed as a direct imitation of the fine glasswares being produced by René Lalique of France and many Consolidated patterns resembled their French counterparts. Other popular lines produced during the 1920s and 1930s were "Dancing Nymph," the delightfully Art Deco "Ruba Rombic," introduced in 1928, and the "Catalonian" line, imitating 17th century Spanish glass, which debuted in 1927.

Although the factory closed in 1933, it was reopened under new management in 1936 and prospered through the 1940s. It finally closed in 1967. Collectors should note that many later Consolidated patterns closely resemble wares of other competing firms, especially the Phoenix Glass Company. Careful study is needed to determine the maker of pieces from the 1920-40 era.

A recent book which will be of help to collectors is Phoenix & Consolidated Art Glass, 1926-1980, *by Jack D. Wilson (Antique Publications, 1989).*

Bulging Loops

Pitcher, water, cased pink $360.00
Sugar shaker w/original top, blue opaque 450.00
Tumbler, cased yellow.........................45.00

Cone

Butter dish, cov., pink satin.................135.00
Pickle castor, cased pink, ornate silver plate frame, elaborate side & top trim, w/tongs 450.00
Sugar shaker w/original top, cased blue satin ....125.00 to 150.00
Syrup pitcher w/original top, squatty, cased blue 210.00
Syrup pitcher w/original top, squatty, cased pink.......................250.00 to 275.00
Water set: pitcher & four tumblers; blue opaque, 5 pcs. 285.00

Florette

Butter dish, cov., cased pink satin ....250.00 to 275.00

Florette Cracker Jar

Cracker (or biscuit) jar w/original silver plate rim, lid & bail handle, cased pink (ILLUS.) 295.00
Pitcher, water, pink satin 275.00
Spooner, cased pink, metal rim & handles 50.00
Sugar bowl, cov., cased pink satin 115.00
Toothpick holder, cased blue 65.00

Guttate

Guttate Syrup Pitcher

Celery vase, cased pink .....150.00 to 175.00
Pitcher, water, 9½" h., applied clear handle, cased pink satin 395.00
Salt shaker w/brass top, cased blue 52.00
Salt & pepper shakers, cased pink, pr. 75.00
Syrup pitcher w/original top, cased pink (ILLUS.) .....350.00 to 400.00
Water set: pitcher & four tumblers; cased pink satin, 5 pcs. 595.00

Later Lines

Ashtray, oblong, Santa Maria line, amber 45.00
Banana boat, oblong, Love Birds patt., Martelé line, three-color decoration on custard ground 500.00

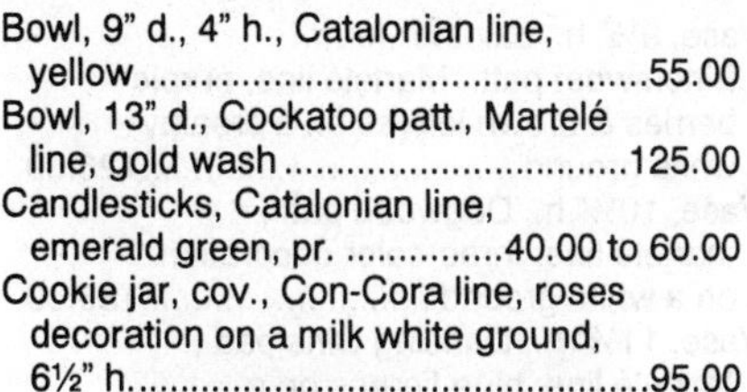

Bowl, 9" d., 4" h., Catalonian line, yellow 55.00
Bowl, 13" d., Cockatoo patt., Martelé line, gold wash 125.00
Candlesticks, Catalonian line, emerald green, pr. .....40.00 to 60.00
Cookie jar, cov., Con-Cora line, roses decoration on a milk white ground, 6½" h. 95.00

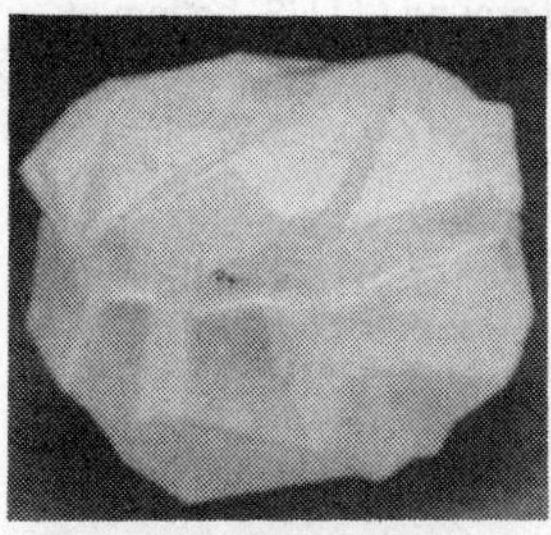

Ruba Rombic Dresser Jar

Dresser jar, cov., oblong, Ruba Rombic line, frosted amber, some staining, 5½" w., 4" h. (ILLUS.) 546.00
Lamp, table model, brass base & shade cap, Bittersweet patt., Martelé line, straw opal 165.00
Plate, 10" d., Dancing Nymph line, green frosted 150.00
Puff box, cov., Hummingbird patt., Martelé line, green wash, 4" d. 250.00
Vase, 6" h., ovoid, Dragonfly & Cattails patt., Martelé line, brown & coral decoration on a milk white ground .....95.00 to 110.00
Vase, 6½" h., flattened fan shape, shape No. 2201, Florentine line, green 185.00
Vases, 6¾" h., Ruba Rombic line, tall conical body on a flaring foot, green, pr. 770.00

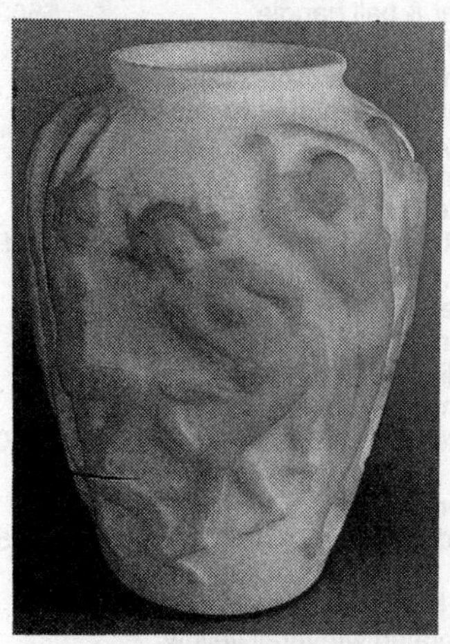

Dancing Girls Vase

Vase, 9½" h., baluster-form, Bittersweet patt., Martelé line, purple berries & brown leaves on a creamy white ground 125.00

Vase, 10½" h., Dogwood patt., Martelé line, three-color decoration on a white ground 135.00

Vase, 11½" h., Dancing Girls patt., Martelé line, blue figures on a custard ground (ILLUS. bottom of previous page) ....495.00 to 525.00

CORALENE

Creamer with Coralene Fruit

Coralene is a method of decorating glass, usually satin glass, with the use of a beaded-type decoration customarily applied to the glass with the use of enamels, which were melted. Coralene decoration has been faked with the use of glue.

Cracker jar, cov., Amberina body decorated w/coralene beaded fruit, branches & leaves, silver-plate rim, cover & bail handle $500.00

Creamer, ovoid body tapering to a slightly flaring cylindrical neck, applied pale amber handle, orange body decorated w/colored "fruit" coralene beading, enameled "Patent" mark, 2½" d., 3½" h. (ILLUS.) 265.00

Lamp, oil-type, square, white shaded to yellow dimpled satin glass base w/pink "seaweed" coralene beading, applied frosted leaf feet, clear chimney & frosted shade, marked "Patent" 600.00

Vase, 4" h., blue mother-of-pearl satin exterior w/yellow "wheat" coralene beading, white lining 475.00

Vase, 6" h., 4" d., ruffled & crimped rim, blue shaded to white satin body decorated w/overall yellow "seaweed" coralene beading 525.00

Vase, 8" h., ribbed body, soft yellow satin finish w/"drape" design yellow coralene beading, Mt. Washington Glass Co. 290.00

CRANBERRY

Cranberry Glass Cracker Jar

Gold was added to glass batches to give this glass its color on reheating. It has been made by numerous glasshouses for years and is currently being reproduced. Both blown and molded articles were produced. A less expensive type of cranberry was made with the substitution of copper for gold.

Basket, Optic Rib patt., applied clear "snake" handle, applied clear rigaree around the rim, twelve applied clear feet & applied clear berry prunt, 7½" h...$265.00

Bowl, 4" d., 5¼" h., rose bowl-shaped, applied clear reeded fans, six applied clear berry prunts around the rim, three applied clear scroll reeded feet & clear berry prunt 275.00

Box w/hinged lid, enameled white, yellow & blue flowers decorate the lid, gold scrolls around the sides, 4½" d., 3¼" h. 175.00

Cologne bottle w/atomizer, spherical body decorated w/white enameled designs, 3" d., 4¾" h. 95.00

Cracker jar, cov., square body, decorated overall w/gold florals & leaves, silver plate cover, rim & ornate bail handle, 4" w., 7¼" h. (ILLUS.)..........275.00

Creamer, Inverted Thumbprint patt., bulbous body tapering to a squared mouth, applied clear handle, 4"d., 4¾" h..135.00

Cruet w/original clear bubble stopper, cushion-footed ovoid body tapering to a cylindrical neck w/petal-shaped rim, decorated w/lavender thistle blossoms, green leaves & gold trim, applied clear handle, 3⅜" d., 8¼" h. 195.00

Decanter w/clear ball stopper, footed tapering cylinder w/slender ringed neck, enameled dainty blue & pale pink flowers & creamy yellow leaves decoration, applied clear pedestal foot, 3" d., 8½" h. 175.00

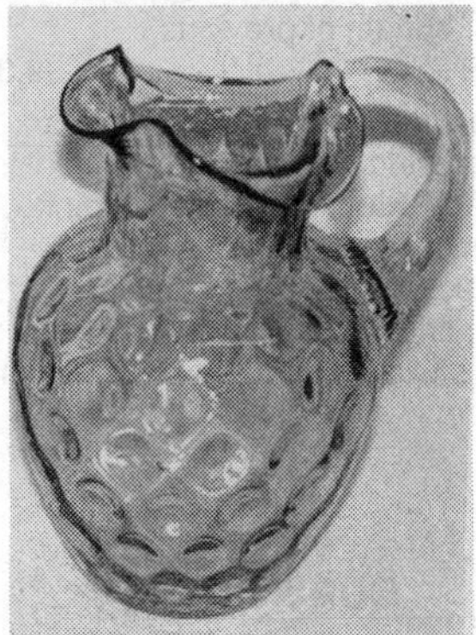

Inverted Thumbprint Pitcher

Pitcher, 6¼" h., 3⅞" d., Inverted Thumbprint patt., ovoid body tapering to a short cylindrical neck w/flaring rolled & fluted rim, applied clear reeded handle (ILLUS.) 118.00

Pitcher, 6½" h., 3⅝" d., Optic Rib patt., bulbous ovoid body w/squared neck & applied clear handle 100.00

Salt dip, master size, footed squatty bulbous body w/applied crystal rigaree around sides, applied crystal scalloped feet, 3¾" d., 2½" h 85.00

Sugar shaker w/original top, Venetian Diamond patt. 195.00

Toothpick holder, Inverted Thumbprint patt., bulging base tapering to a cylindrical neck 145.00

Vase, 4¼" h., 4¼" d., wide ovoid body tapering to a short flaring neck trimmed w/applied clear rigaree 60.00

Vase, 9⅝" h., 4⅛" d., footed funnel-shaped body tapering to cupped rim, mold-blown optic design w/applied clear spiraling rigaree around body ...75.00

Vase, 14" h., 3⅝" d., pedestal foot supporting an elongated ovoid body w/flaring trumpet-shaped neck, front decorated w/white enameled scrolling & white dotting 165.00

CROWN MILANO

This glass, produced by Mt. Washington Glass Company late last century, is opal glass decorated by painting and enameling. It appears identical to a ware termed Albertine, also made by Mt. Washington.

Crown Milano Syrup Pitcher

Box, cov., w/tiny applied feet, melon-ribbed, decorated overall w/enameled pansies & gold accents, 3½" d., 2½" h. $275.00

Cracker jar, cov., squatty melon-ribbed body decorated w/dainty multicolored flowers & ornate gold scrolling, original ornate silver plate cover, rim & bail handle, 5¼" d., 5¾" h. to top of handle 860.00

Creamer & cov. sugar bowl, creamy satin ground decorated w/h.p. lavender violets framed by pink blush edging & gold trim, paper label, creamer 3½" h., sugar bowl 4¼" h., pr. 920.00

Jardiniere, bulbous body decorated w/ten pansies w/ten medallions in violet, yellow & tan, heavy gold trim around the neck, signed on the bottom, 9¼" d., 7" h. 795.00

Syrup pitcher w/original silver plate top, melon-ribbed body, decorated w/enameled gold flowers & leaves & hundreds of blue, white, black, coral & turquoise enamel dottings on a soft butter cream ground (ILLUS.) 1,245.00

Vase, cov., 10½" h., decorated w/heavily enameled ivy leaves & vines in green & brown outlined in gold, lighter swirl designs on the cover, the background of the body & around the base 2,295.00

CRUETS

Amber, blown, bulbous body, applied blue handle, blue stopper, ca. 1880s $140.00

Amber, pressed, I.O.U. patt., original faceted stopper 110.00

Blue opalescent, blown, Christmas Bead & Panel patt., applied blue handle, original stopper 225.00

Clear, blown, Swirl patt., applied clear closed round handle, original ball stopper, 4½" h.....................................22.50

Clear, pressed, Peacock Feather patt., original stopper, 10" h. 125.00

Cobalt blue, blown, ovoid body tapering to a cylindrical neck & pinched spout, upper body decorated w/pink flowers & green leaves on a enameled gold ground, the lower body decorated w/white lacy dotting, applied cobalt blue handle, cobalt blue teardrop-shaped stopper, 2⅝" d., 6¼" h. 85.00

Cobalt blue, blown, ovoid body tapering to a cylindrical neck w/pinched lip, enameled w/bands of sanded gold leaves & white dot decoration, applied cobalt blue handle, original cobalt blue ball stopper, 3½" d., 8" h. 165.00

Cobalt blue, pattern-molded, bulbous body tapering to a slender neck w/high arched spout, applied strap handle, hollow ball stopper, Midwest, early 19th c., 7½" h. plus stopper (minor residue, slight check at handle).....................................1,210.00

Cranberry, blown, Moire satin finish, applied clear frosted handle, clear bubble stopper 295.00

Cranberry, blown, baluster-form body, cylindrical neck w/tricorner rim, enameled w/blue & white flowers & yellow leaves, applied clear handle, original clear bubble stopper, 3⅛" d., 8¼" h...195.00

Emerald green, pressed, Prize patt., w/original stopper.............................225.00

Green, pressed, Georgia Gem patt., gold trim, original stopper 350.00

Mold-Blown Cruet

Light blue, mold-blown, square body, cylindrical neck w/flared spout, enameled w/rust, blue, white & yellow flowers & leaves, applied amber handle, original amber facet-cut stopper, 3½" d., 7½" h...............165.00

Sapphire blue, mold-blown, 16-rib globular body tapering to a narrow neck w/high arched spout, applied hollow handle, original stopper, Midwestern, 7" h. plus stopper (ILLUS. bottom of previous column) 2,310.00

Sapphire blue, mold-blown, bulbous body tapering to a cylindrical neck w/pinched spout, decorated w/pink blossoms, orange flowers & pink branches, applied sapphire blue handle, original sapphire blue bubble stopper, 4" d., 8¼" h............165.00

CUP PLATES

Produced in numerous patterns beginning some 160 years ago, these little plates were designed to hold a cup while the tea or coffee was allowed to cool in a saucer. Cup plates were also made of ceramics. Where numbers are listed below, they refer to numbers assigned these plates in the book, American Glass Cup Plates, *by Ruth Webb Lee and James H. Rose. Plates are of clear glass unless otherwise noted. A number of cup plates have been reproduced. Also see CUP PLATES under Ceramics.*

L & R 87, plain round, 4⁷⁄₁₆" d. $16.00

L & R 95, octagonal, shields & tree-like devices in border, opal opaque 143.00

L & R 109, Thistle patt., octagonal w/incurved edges (some mold roughness on rim).............................55.00

L & R 174, round w/petaled rim, eight-petaled design in center, opal opaque 385.00

L & R 243, round w/small rim scallops, quatrefoil in center surrounded by small blossomheads, scrolls in border, opalescent (underfill on one scallop, mold roughness) 148.50

L & R 388, diamond point border, eight-petal center flower (minor rim nip) 30.00

L & R 465F, Heart patt., round, violet blue (several scallops missing or tipped) 302.50

L & R 563, Henry Clay, no name variant, opalescent (three tipped scallops, mold roughness) 467.50
L & R 572, round w/small rim scallops, Queen Victoria bust design (mold roughness) 132.00
L & R 610B, Ship Cadmus patt............30.00
L & R 655, Eagle patt., round, Pittsburgh (fin & mold roughness) ...126.50
L & R 691, round w/beaded rim, Lyre patt. (several beads tipped, overall mold roughness) 33.00

CUSTARD GLASS

This ware takes its name from its color and is a variant of milk white glass. It was produced largely between 1890 and 1915 by the Northwood Glass Co., Heisey Glass Company, Fenton Art Glass Co., Jefferson Glass Co., and a few others. There are 21 major patterns and a number of minor ones. The prime patterns are considered Argonaut Shell, Chrysanthemum Sprig, Inverted Fan and Feather, Louis XV and Winged Scroll. Most custard glass patterns are enhanced with gold and some have additional enameled decoration or stained highlights. Unless otherwise noted, items in this listing are fully decorated.

ARGONAUT SHELL (Northwood)

Argonaut Shell Cruet

Berry set, master bowl & 6 sauce dishes, 7 pcs. $575.00
Bowl, master berry or fruit, 10½" l., 5" h....................185.00 to 225.00
Butter dish, cov...............................282.00
Compote, jelly, 5" d., 5" h. 136.00
Creamer..145.00
Cruet w/original stopper (ILLUS.) 850.00
Pitcher, water....................................433.00
Salt & pepper shakers w/original tops, pr....................................325.00 to 350.00
Sauce dish..60.00
Spooner............................125.00 to 150.00
Sugar bowl, cov. 205.00
Toothpick holder................300.00 to 325.00
Tumbler 110.00

CHRYSANTHEMUM SPRIG (Northwood's Pagoda)

Chrysanthemum Sprig Tumbler

Berry set, master bowl & 10 sauce dishes, 11 pcs...............................975.00
Bowl, master berry or fruit, 10½" oval, decorated 165.00
Bowl, master berry or fruit, 10½" oval, undecorated.....................150.00 to 175.00
Butter dish, cov..................250.00 to 275.00
Celery vase...715.00
Compote, jelly, decorated..................115.00
Compote, jelly, undecorated................65.00
Condiment tray ....575.00 to 600.00
Creamer............................100.00 to 125.00
Cruet w/original stopper.....................334.00
Pitcher, water, decorated....400.00 to 475.00
Pitcher, water, undecorated..............................200.00 to 250.00
Salt & pepper shakers w/original tops, pr...210.00
Sauce dish...62.00
Sauce dish, blue trim 140.00
Spooner 110.00
Sugar bowl, cov., decorated 210.00
Sugar bowl, cov., undecorated...........145.00
Table set, cov., sugar bowl, creamer, cov. butter dish & spooner, 4 pcs. ...725.00
Toothpick holder w/gold trim & paint, signed 245.00
Toothpick holder, undecorated...........175.00
Tumbler (ILLUS.) 60.00
Water set, pitcher & 6 tumblers, 7 pcs. 800.00

GRAPE & CABLE - See Northwood Grape Pattern

GRAPE & THUMBPRINT - See Northwood Grape Pattern

INTAGLIO (Northwood)

Intaglio Butter Dish

Berry set, 9" d. footed compote & 6 sauce dishes, 7 pcs. 438.00
Bowl, fruit, 7½" d. footed compote 146.00
Bowl, fruit, 9" d. footed compote ....300.00 to 350.00
Butter dish, cov. (ILLUS.) 250.00
Compote, jelly.....................................100.00
Creamer...100.00
Creamer & cov. sugar bowl, pr. 275.00
Cruet w/original stopper 315.00
Pitcher, water.....................350.00 to 375.00
Salt shaker w/original top 85.00
Sauce dish...43.00
Spooner...130.00
Sugar bowl, cov. ....125.00 to 150.00
Table set, green stain, 4 pcs. 540.00
Tumbler 83.00

INVERTED FAN & FEATHER (Northwood)

Inverted Fan & Feather Berry Bowl

Berry set, master bowl & 6 sauce dishes, 7 pcs. ....575.00 to 600.00
Bowl, master berry or fruit, 10" d., 5½" h., four-footed, (ILLUS.) ....200.00 to 250.00
Butter dish, cov. 282.00
Compote, jelly....................350.00 to 425.00
Creamer..125.00
Pitcher, water.......................................650.00
Punch cup...265.00
Salt & pepper shakers w/original tops, pr. 495.00
Sauce dish...59.00
Spooner 140.00
Sugar bowl, cov. 215.00
Table set, 4 pcs. 800.00
Toothpick holder ....600.00 to 650.00
Tumbler ....75.00 to 100.00

IVORINA VERDE - See Winged Scroll Pattern

LOUIS XV (Northwood)

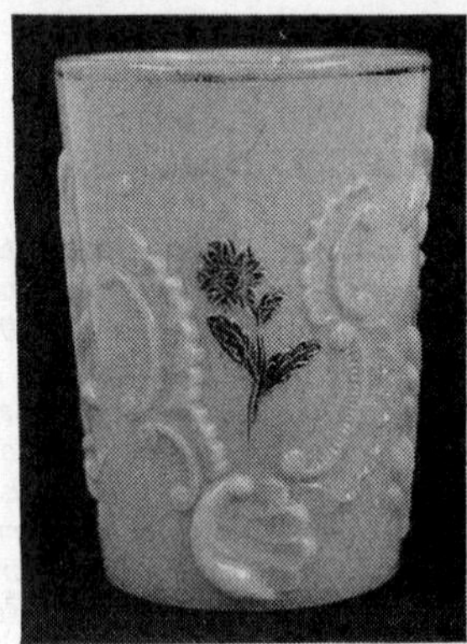

Louis XV Tumbler

Berry set, master bowl & 4 sauce dishes, 5 pcs. 425.00
Bowl, berry or fruit, 7¾ x 10" oval 142.00
Butter dish, cov. ....175.00 to 200.00
Creamer & cov. sugar bowl, pr. 250.00
Cruet w/original stopper 450.00
Pitcher, water..237.00
Salt shaker w/original top 80.00
Sauce dish, footed, 5" oval 40.00
Spooner ....60.00 to 75.00
Table set, 4 pcs. ....500.00 to 550.00
Tumbler (ILLUS.) 70.00
Water set, pitcher & 6 tumblers, 7 pcs. 800.00

NORTHWOOD GRAPE, GRAPE & CABLE or GRAPE & THUMBPRINT

Northwood Grape Cologne Bottle

Banana boat 325.00
Bowl, 7½" d., ruffled rim......................42.50
Bowl, master berry or fruit, 11" d., ruffled, footed..................................445.00
Butter dish, cov...................................250.00
Cologne bottle w/original stopper (ILLUS.) 550.00
Cracker jar, cov., two-handled ....575.00 to 600.00
Creamer ....125.00 to 150.00
Creamer & open sugar bowl, breakfast size, pr. ....100.00 to 125.00
Dresser tray ....275.00 to 325.00
Humidor, cov. 650.00
Pin dish..165.00
Plate, 7" d. 55.00
Plate, 8" w., six-sided 65.00
Plate, 8" d. 55.00
Punch cup...75.00
Sauce dish, flat 30.00
Sauce dish, footed.................................40.00
Spooner 135.00
Sugar bowl, cov. 150.00
Sugar bowl, open, breakfast size 62.00
Tumbler 50.00
Water set, pitcher & 6 tumblers, 7 pcs. 1,250.00

WINGED SCROLL or IVORINA VERDE (Heisey)

Berry set, master bowl & 5 sauce dishes, 6 pcs.....................................445.00
Bowl, fruit, 8½" d..................................165.00
Butter dish, cov.....................................176.00
Celery vase...350.00
Cigarette jar.......................145.00 to 175.00
Creamer, decorated...............................94.00
Cruet w/original stopper, decorated ....175.00 to 200.00
Cruet w/original stopper, undecorated 100.00
Match holder......................190.00 to 225.00
Pin tray, small 195.00
Pitcher, water, 9" h., bulbous..............230.00
Pitcher, water, tankard, decorated..................................300.00 to 375.00
Pitcher, water, tankard, undecorated..230.00
Powder jar, cov......................................99.00
Salt & pepper shakers w/original tops, pr..150.00
Sauce dish, 4½" d...................................36.00
Spooner 89.00
Sugar bowl, cov., decorated 135.00
Sugar bowl, cov., undecorated 95.00
Syrup pitcher w/original top 365.00
Toothpick holder 137.00
Tumbler 77.50
Water set, bulbous pitcher & 4 tumblers, 5 pcs. 550.00

(End of Custard Glass)

CUT GLASS

Cut glass most eagerly sought by collectors is American glass produced during the so-called "Brilliant Period" from 1880 to about 1915. Pieces listed below are by type of article in alphabetical order.

BASKETS

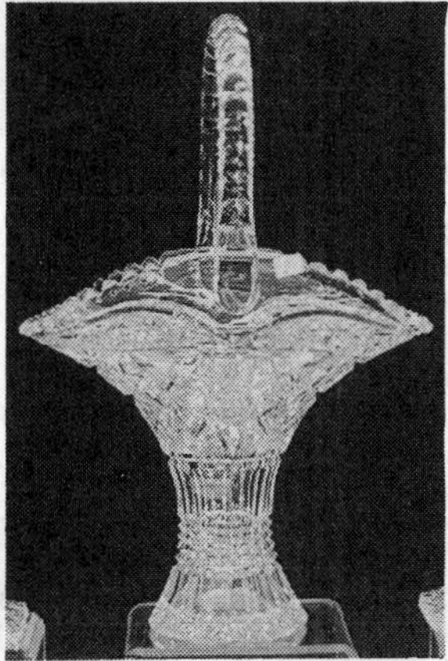

Brilliant Period Basket

Hawkes signed, Pattern No. 1298, hobstars & flashed stars, cut handle, 6½ x 8½"..$475.00
Hobnail & crosshatching, circular base tapering in & flaring out to a wide rim, thumbprint edge & applied handle, 19" h...............................2,530.00
Hobstars, pinwheel & crosshatching, twisted handle, 7" d., basket 1¾" h., overall 5¼" h. 310.00
Hobstars, cane & diamond point, 6" h..300.00
Hobstars, strawberry diamond & fan, St. Louis diamond handle, 4½ x 9" oval, overall 8" h. 825.00
Panel-cut waisted lower portion w/step-cutting at waist, the flaring upper section cut w/hobstars, cross-cut vesicas & other cutting, serrated rim, cut handle, 11" w., overall 16" h. (ILLUS.) 975.00

BOWLS

Banana, fan-shaped curving sides cut w/large hobstar each side, further cut w/St. Louis diamond at each end flanked by fans & triple notching, paneled stem, 16-point hobstar base, 3½" w., 6" l., 5" h...................325.00
Banana, two-part, bowl cut w/four 32-point hobstars separated by a flaring design of strawberry diamond, fan, notched prism & beading beneath a

Unusual Two-part Banana Bowl

scalloped & serrated rim, fitting into a base w/alternating fields of hobnail & strawberry diamond above a notched prism standard, 14-point serrated foot, bowl 8¾ x 12", 3¼" h., overall 9" h. (ILLUS.) 3,000.00

Berry, Libbey signed, hobstars & deeply cut stars, 8¼" d., 3½" h. 250.00

Cetus Pattern Bowl

Cetus patt., panels of cane alternating w/panels of hobstars, large hobstar in base, 10½" d. (ILLUS.).............2,600.00

Clark signed, central pinwheel w/rows of hobstars & hobnail beneath a cross-hatched border, 8¼" d............275.00

Fruit, hobstar & strawberry diamond vesicas alternating w/cane vesicas, on standard & domed base cut w/strawberry diamond & four-sided figures w/fans below, 8¾ x 10½", 8½" h..700.00

Fruit, pinwheel & fan cutting divided by vesicas centering a hobstar at the base, scalloped & serrated rim, 8" d...165.00

Fry signed, Chicago patt., crossed bars, low, 7¾" d. 500.00

Hawkes signed, Panel & Kohinoor patt., deep cut panels & diamonds of Harvard patt., 8" d., 3½" h................575.00

Hunt's Royal patt., Russian motif w/hobstar button, five-sided strawberry diamond lozenge & large hobstars, 7¾" d................................300.00

Ice, Libbey, middle section cut in a triangle of cross-cut diamond flanked w/strawberry diamond, a section of fans & another triangle of large hobnail, St. Louis diamond handles, 24-point hobstar footed base 400.00

Libbey signed, Delphos patt., vesicas of hobnail w/clear borders, surrounded by further hobnail, 10" d., 4¼" h. 600.00

Orange, large hobstar on each side & at each end in a circle of clear surrounded by cane, wavy ridged edge, low stem, star-cut foot, 6½ x 9", 6½" h.............................2,300.00

Rosette patt. variant, hobstars set in the center of notched prism, terminating in small fans, cane & vesica, 8" d. 175.00

Salad, Hawkes' Chrysanthemum patt., 9½" sq....................................900.00

Salad, Russian patt., 9¾" d. 250.00

Strawberry diamond & fan, low, 9½" d...125.00

BUTTER DISHES & TUBS

Cut Glass Covered Butter Dish

Covered dish, chain of hobstars w/notched prism, dome lid & matching underplate (ILLUS.)..........700.00

Tub, Hawkes signed, intaglio-cut florals & foliage, 3" d. base, 5" d. top, 4" h. 50.00

Tub, hobstars & crosshatching, hobstar base, raised handles, 5" d., overall at top of handles 3" h. 300.00

Tub, hobstar & nailhead cutting, 3½" d. base, 6½ d. top, 3" h...............40.00

Tub, cov., strawberry diamond & fan, w/matching underplate, the set........250.00

BUTTER PATS

Emerald green cut to clear, fans, triangles of cane w/center star, 3" d., set of 6....................................450.00

Hobstar Cluster patt., set of 6.............300.00

Persian (Russian patt. w/hobstar button) patt...70.00

CARAFES

Dorflinger's Marlboro patt., chain of hobstars w/fan & strawberry diamond, hobstar base, waisted form...220.00

Hawkes signed, Brunswick patt., chain of hobstars, zipper-type beading & flute, rayed base, 6" d., 7½" h. 325.00

Hobstars & pinwheel, step-cut neck, 6½" d., 8" h. 100.00

Peerless patt., fan, hobnail, hobstar & strawberry diamond, 9" h. 40.00

Strawberry diamond, fan & other cutting, star-cut base, notched prism neck, 6" d., 8" h.................................95.00

CHAMPAGNES, CORDIALS & WINES

Grecian Pattern Wine Glass

Champagne, Hawkes signed, Middlesex patt., hollow stem............120.00

Champagne, Hoare signed, Hindoo patt., hobstar & notched prism............60.0'

Cordials, Hoare's Richelieu patt., swirl motif, knopped stem w/teardrop, set of 4...1,100.00

Cordials, hobnail cutting, hob in teardrop stem, flashed star base, 3¾" h., set of 6................................180.00

Wine, cranberry cut to clear, Grecian patt., vesicas, fan & Russian, 4¾" h. (ILLUS.) 825.00

Wine, cranberry cut to clear, Russian patt. w/cut buttons, teardrop stem, rayed base, 4½" h............................350.00

Wine, hobstars separated by cross-cut diamond & strawberry diamond, faceted ball under bowl, double teardrop hollow stem, rayed base, bowl 2" h., overall 4¼" h. 30.00

CREAMERS & SUGAR BOWLS

Cut Glass Creamer & Sugar Bowl

Clark signed, hobstars & cross-hatching, strawberry diamond handle, pr...130.00

Clark signed, 24-point hobstar each side & nailhead diamond, cut handles, pr. 190.00

Cross-cut diamond & fan, wafer bases, sugar bowl w/cover, pr. 300.00

Hoare's Hindoo patt., chain of hobstars, beading & fan, pr..............320.00

Hobstars, fan & prism, pedestal base, notched handles, 4¼" h., pr. 425.00

Hobstars w/beaded vesicas beneath flashed fans, faceted knobbed stem, notched handles, notched foot w/16-point hobstar, 6" h., pr. (ILLUS.) 2,100.00

Hunt's Royal patt., Russian motif w/hobstar button, five-sided strawberry diamond lozenge & large hobstars, pr. 220.00

Strauss' Ulysses patt., round cov. sugar 5" d., 5½" h., milk-type creamer 4½" d., 5" h., pr. 850.00

DECANTERS

Russian Pattern Decanter

Chain of hobstars alternating w/fan, triple-notched handle, 20-point hobstar base, original lapidary-cut stopper...1,050.00

Harvard patt., bowling pin-form, matching stopper w/hobstar on top, overall 15" h. 1,300.00

Meriden's Plymouth patt., flashed hobstar w/strawberry diamond points 200.00

Russian patt., bulbous body, three ringed faceted neck, star-cut base, conforming teardrop stopper, 11½" h. (ILLUS.) 935.00

ICE TUBS

Meriden's Alhambra Pattern Ice Tub

Comet-type design w/a large shooting star in the base, the sides cut w/flashed fans, crosshatching, miters & further shooting stars, scalloped rim w/two rectangular handles, 5½" h. 187.00

Elite Cut Glass Company's Expanding Star patt., fan, hobstar & strawberry diamond, two handled, across handles 9" d. 300.00

Hoare's Carolyn patt., hobstars, cane, fan & beading, 5½" h. 725.00

Meriden's Alhambra patt., Wilcox signed sterling silver rim & handle (ILLUS.) 2,250.00

Straus' Corinthian patt., cane, hobstar, fan & strawberry diamond, 6" d., 5½" h. 160.00

JARS

Candy, hobstars, strawberry diamond & fan cutting on swelled cylindrical base, matching cover w/faceted finial, 8¾" h. 660.00

Caviar, cov., hobstars, cane, hobnail & strawberry diamond, rayed base, matching cut lid w/faceted finial, w/inner glass liner, 4¾" d., 7½" h. 1,300.00

Cracker, hobstar, cane, strawberry diamond, notched prism & fan, matching lid w/faceted finial, 6" d., overall 9" h. (ILLUS. top next column) 2,100.00

Deeply Cut Cracker Jar

Tobacco, Alhambra (Greek Key) patt., hobstars, cane & wide band of Greek key design, matching stopper, 24-point hobstar base, 6" d., 9½" h. 2,600.00

NAPPIES

Empire Cut Glass Company's Orinoco patt., 6" d. 30.00

Fry's Carnation patt., fan, hobstar & strawberry diamond, handled 60.00

Hawkes' Jupiter patt., 6" d. 170.00

Libbey's Princess patt., cross-cut diamond, fan & strawberry diamond, 6" d. 25.00

Strawberry diamond & fan, hobstar base, strawberry shape, handled, 5 x 6½" 80.00

PITCHERS

Libbey's Marcella Pattern Pitcher

Cider, Hawkes' Gladys patt., chain of hobstars, fan & strawberry diamond, 7½" h. 400.00

Milk, chain of hobstars, cane & cross-cut diamond, star-cut base, triple-notched handle, 8" d., 7½" h. 475.00

Tankard, Unger Brothers' Hobart patt., 11" h. 275.00

Water, Alhambra (Greek Key) patt., hobstars, cane & wide Greek key border, pedestal base, dentil edge at rim & base, 12¼" h. 5,750.00

Water, hobstar, cane & strawberry diamond fans, 32-point hobstar base, cut handle, fluted spout, 6" d., 9" h. 475.00

Water, Libbey's Imperial patt., cane, fan, hobstar & star, hobstar bottom, cut handle, 10½" h. 4,750.00

Water, Libbey's Marcella patt., cluster of hobstars around a hexagon center, cane. strawberry diamond & fans, 11" h. (ILLUS.) 6,000.00

Water, Pitkin & Brooks' Beverly patt., hobnail, hobstar, star & strawberry diamond, 6" d., 9" h. 700.00

PUNCH BOWLS & SETS

Elite Cut Glass Company's Expanding Star patt., fan, hobstar, star & strawberry diamond, 14" d. 300.00

Hobstars, cane, fan, deep miter cutting & other cutting, scalloped & serrated rim, on conforming base, 12" d., 12½" h., 2 pcs. 440.00

Punch set: 14" d. bowl, eight cups & 15" l. ladle; Hawkes' Holland patt., 10 pcs. 700.00

TRAYS

Hawkes Ice Cream Tray

American Cut Glass Company's Lansing patt., hobstars, flashed cross-cut hobstar vesicas & strawberry diamond, 14" d. 400.00

Bread, Clark signed, cane, hobstars & fan, further engraved w/leaf designs, rectangular w/rounded corners, 12½" l. 302.50

Celery, Empire Cut Glass Company's Plaza patt., 13" l. 75.00

Cranberry cut to clear, Russian patt., cranberry buttons & edges, remainder clear, 5¼ x 10½", 1½" h. 350.00

Eleanor patt., hobstars, cane, clear tusks & strawberry diamond, 12" d. 225.00

Hawkes' Grecian patt., vesicas, fan & Russian patt., butterfly-shaped, 9" w. 1,000.00

Hoare, scalloped sides centered by a large star surrounded by miters & stars, 15" d. 1,760.00

Ice cream, Hawkes' Gladys patt., chain of hobstars, fan & strawberry diamond, 16" l. (ILLUS.) 935.00

Ice cream, Hoare signed, Marquis patt., feather, hobnail, star & strawberry diamond, oval w/closed end handles, 10½ x 18" 1,175.00

Libbey signed, Snowflake patt., 12" d. 2,250.00

Taylor Bros. signed, chains of hobstars, strawberry diamond bow ties, 32-point hobstar base w/strawberry diamond points & fans between points, strawberry diamond rim, 9 x 14½" oval, 2¾" h. 1,700.00

VASES

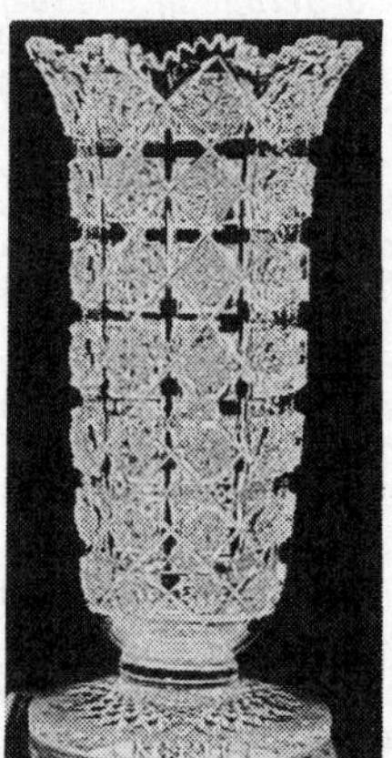

Sinclaire's Bird-in-a-Cage Pattern

Egginton's Victoria patt., beading, bull's-eye, hobstar & split oval, cylindrical form, 12" h. 209.00

Fry Glass Company's Vardin patt., trumpet-form, 9" h. 132.00

Hawkes signed, Brunswick patt., chain of hobstars, beading, fan & flute, 12" h., pr. 495.00

Hoare signed, stars, crosshatching & miters, waisted form, 6¼" h. 88.00

Libbey signed, cobalt blue cut to clear frosted, stylized geometric & bud design, baluster form, 9" h. 687.50

Sinclaire's Bird-in-a-Cage patt., urn-form w/scalloped & serrated rim, twenty-four point hobstar foot, 6" top d., 12" h. (ILLUS.) 5,000.00

WATER SETS

Pitcher & six tumblers, Libbey signed, stars, fan, strawberry diamond & miters, pitcher 9" h., 7 pcs. 1,320.00

Pitcher & six tumblers, Plymouth patt., flashed hobstar w/strawberry diamond points, 7 pcs. 130.00

Pitcher & six tumblers, Madeline patt., flashed hobstar, large leaves of cane & intaglio-cut cattails, hobstar base, pitcher 8½" h., 7 pcs. 250.00

CZECHOSLOVAKIAN

At the close of World War I, Czechoslovakia was declared an independent republic and immediately developed a large export industry. Czechoslovakian glass factories produced a wide variety of colored and hand-painted glasswares from about 1918 until 1939, when the country was occupied by Germany at the outset of World War II. Between the wars, fine quality blown glasswares were produced along with a deluge of cheaper, vividly colored spatterwares for the American market. Subsequent production was primarily limited to cut crystal or Bohemian-type etched wares for the American market. Although it was marked, much Czechoslovakian glass is mistaken for the work of Tiffany, Loetz, or other glass artisans it imitates. It is often misrepresented and overpriced.

With the recent break-up of Czechoslovakia into two republics, such wares should gain added collector appeal.

Basket, orange w/applied black trim & handle, 7½" h. $135.00

Basket, applied jet black handle & rim, red w/clear overlay, debossed floral decoration, signed 65.00

Basket w/applied pink spiral handle, red, yellow & white spatter body 180.00

Candlestick, free-blown w/a cylindrical socket w/a wide slightly dished drip pan upon a tapering columnar standard & wide thin disc foot, yellow w/applied black thin ribs ending in teardrops, components assembled in the Powlnoy manner, 9½" h. 316.00

Compote, 10" d., orange & black, oval mark 125.00

Figure of a black musician w/a guitar, 6½" h. 350.00

Figure of a doctor w/stethoscope, wearing jacket, tan pants, multicolored base, 8¾" h. 295.00

Rose bowl, Amberina w/controlled bubble design, original label, 5½" h. ..35.00

Vase, 4½" h., yellowish orange w/brown mottled exterior, signed 20.00

Vase, 6" h., tapering hexagonal form in bright green shading to pale green, engraved w/a floral design....165.00

Vase, 12" h., overlay, white cut to emerald green w/h.p. florals & gold trim, scalloped rim 250.00

DAUM NANCY

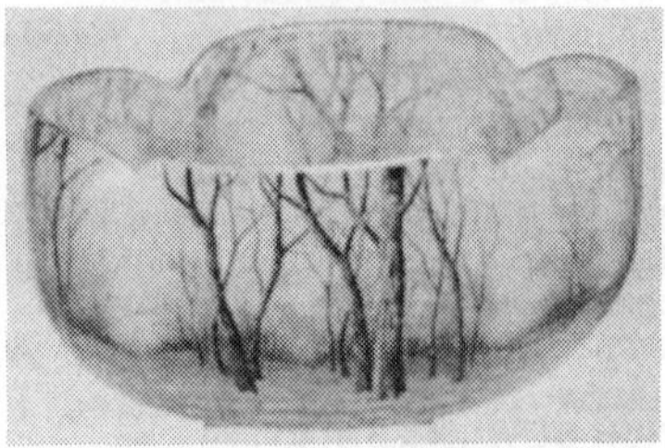

Daum Nancy Enameled Bowl

This fine glass, much of it cameo, was made by Auguste and Antonin Daum, who founded a factory in 1875 in Nancy, France. Most of their cameo and enameled glass was made from the 1890s into the early 20th century.

Bottle w/stopper, the cylindrical shouldered body w/a short neck & inset stopper w/flat, fan-shaped handle, mottled powder blue ground finely etched to depict swans on a lake w/grasses & trees in the foreground, enameled in white, green & black, the stopper trimmed w/gilding, enameled "DAUM NANCY" 3" h. $2,760.00

Bowl, 8" d., 3¾" h., low hemispherical vessel w/four lobes at the rim in grey mottled w/lemon yellow & tangerine, cut w/a winter landscape & enameled *en grisaille* w/charcoal black & frosty white, signed in enamel "Daum - Nancy" w/cross of Lorraine, ca. 1915 (ILLUS.) 2,875.00

Bowl, 11½" d., the acid-etched opalescent sides overlaid & enameled w/sprays of wildflowers & leafage in shades of rose, crimson & charcoal heightened w/gilding, signed in gilt enamel "DAUM - NANCY" w/cross of Lorraine, ca. 1910 ....2,013.00

Cameo bowl, 4" h., hemispherical w/three loop supports, the clear body splashed w/creamy white shading to deepest violet, overlaid & enameled in shades of violet, grass green & cherry red w/violet blossoms, buds & leafage, the lower section w/foliate strapwork heightened w/gilding, the loop supports in grey striated w/violet, signed in gilt "DAUM - NANCY" w/cross of Lorraine, ca. 1910 .... 4,313.00

Cameo lamp, table-type, the shouldered open conical shade & baluster-form base in grey mottled w/pale blue & violet, overlaid w/mottled shades of green, brown & yellow & cut w/lotus blossoms & leafage, the shade w/two applied & finely wheel-carved dragonflies, the base w/one, w/simple three-arm wrought-iron mount, shade & base signed in intaglio "DAUM NANCY" w/cross of Lorraine, ca. 1910, 9½" d., 19½" h. 50,600.00

Daum Nancy Art Deco Style Cameo Vase

Cameo vase, 6¾" h., flaring cylindrical body w/incurvate rim, raised on a cushion-form base, grey mottled w/white, overlaid in brilliant red & cut w/an Art Deco-style design of stylized clusters of ripe cherries pendent from leafy branches, inscribed "Daum Nancy" w/cross of Lorraine, ca. 1925 (ILLUS.) 1,495.00

Ewer, a pedestal foot supporting a tall, slender tapering cylindrical body w/a high, pointed spout, a long, arched applied handle, mottled pink ground shading to mottled green & brown w/a rough texture below, applied w/clear, brightly colored carved cabochon insects, their legs shallowly carved on the body, engraved "DAUM NANCY," 8¾" h. 6,325.00

Vase, 5⅝" h., the bulbous cylindrical neck above a bulbous base, applied scrolling side handles, in grey opalescent internally streaked w/orange & tangerine, cut w/a spray of blossoms & a dragonfly, the dragonfly enameled in pink, lavender, blue & amber & heightened in gilt, signed in gilt "Daum - Nancy" w/cross of Lorraine, ca. 1900 .... 28,750.00

Vase, 15" h., flaring cylindrical body w/an opened mouth, pale blue ground w/turquoise inclusions cased w/clear, raised on a circular foot, etched "Daum Nancy France" 1,725.00

DE VEZ & DEGUE

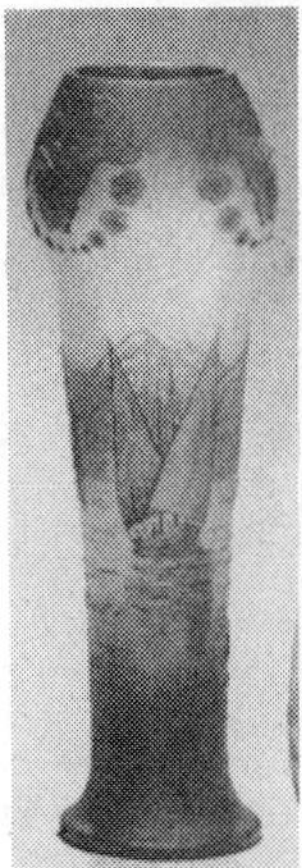

De Vez Cameo Vase

Cameo glass with the name DeVez was made in Pantin, France, by Saint-Hilaire, Touvier De Varreaux and Company. Some pieces made by this firm were signed "Degue" after one of the firm's glassmakers. The official company name was "Cristallerie de Pantin."

Cameo lamp, table model, 10½" d. domical shade raised on a baluster-form base w/round foot, mottled white & yellow overlaid in deep red & etched to depict morning glories, w/wrought-iron mount, shade & base w/cameo signature "Degue," overall 17¼" h. $2,300.00

Cameo vase, 6¾" h., ovoid body w/everted rim, grey cased over white, overlaid in orange & emerald green & cut w/a tranquil Dutch river landscape, signed in cameo, ca. 1920 .... 660.00

Cameo vase, 10" h., cylindrical body w/bulging neck, lemon yellow splashed w/cherry red, overlaid in cherry red & navy blue & cut w/a mountainous landscape w/boating in the near distance, the neck further cut w/butterflies within flowerhead surrounds, signed in cameo "deVez," ca. 1920 (ILLUS.) 880.00

Cameo vase, 18½" h., baluster-form, mottled blue ground overlaid in orange & brown, etched to depict trees, etched "Degue" 1,265.00

Vase, 15" h., ovoid body applied at the flat mouth w/three amethyst handles looping down the sides & joining a notched band, the body in clear internally decorated w/mottled shades of green, brown, yellow & blue, inscribed "Degue - Made in France," ca. 1928.........................1,495.00

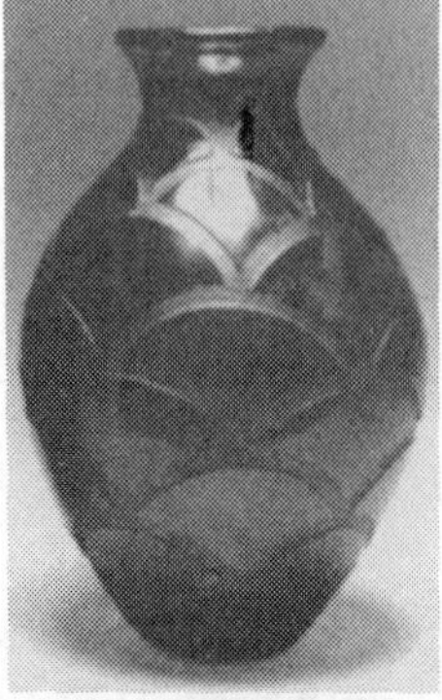

Degue Acid-Etched Vase

Vase, 17" h., large baluster-form body w/flaring rim, deep amethyst acid-etched w/row of deep intersecting arches, signed "Degue - Made in France," ca. 1925 (ILLUS.) 1,380.00

DEPRESSION GLASS

The phrase "Depression Glass" is used by collectors to denote a specific kind of transparent glass produced primarily as tablewares, in crystal, amber, blue, green, pink, milky-white, etc., during the late 1920s and 1930s when this country was in the midst of a financial depression. Made to sell inexpensively, it was turned out by such producers as Jeannette, Hocking, Westmoreland, Indiana and other glass companies. We compile prices on all the major Depression Glass patterns. Collectors should consult Depression Glass references for information on those patterns and pieces which have been reproduced.

ADAM (Process-etched)

Ashtray, clear, 4½" sq...........................$8.50
Ashtray, green, 4½" sq. 16.50
Ashtray, pink, 4½" sq...........................24.50
Bowl, dessert, 4¾" sq., green..............15.50
Bowl, dessert, 4¾" sq., pink 13.00
Bowl, cereal, 5¾" sq., green................37.00
Bowl, nappy, 7¾" sq., pink 18.50
Bowl, cov., 9" sq., green 75.00
Bowl, cov., 9" sq., pink..........................53.00
Bowl, 9" sq., pink 18.00
Bowl, 10" oval vegetable, green 22.50
Butter dish, cov., pink 76.00
Cake plate, footed, green or pink, 10" sq. 22.00
Candlesticks, green, 4" h., pr...............84.00
Candlesticks, pink, 4" h., pr 75.00
Candy jar, cov., green 96.50
Candy jar, cov., pink 82.00
Coaster, green, 3¼" sq. 17.00
Coaster, pink, 3¼" sq. 21.00
Creamer, green 17.50
Creamer, pink 16.00
Pitcher, 8" h., 32 oz., cone-shaped, green...37.00
Pitcher, 8" h., 32 oz., cone-shaped, pink 30.00
Plate, sherbet, 6" sq., green 7.00
Plate, sherbet, 6" sq., pink......................6.00
Plate, salad, 7¾" sq., green or pink......10.50
Plate, salad, round, pink 60.00
Plate, salad, round, yellow.................110.00
Plate, dinner, 9" sq., green 19.00
Plate, dinner, 9" sq., pink.......................26.00
Plate, grill, 9" sq., green or pink............17.00
Platter, 11¾" l., green 18.00
Platter, 11¾" l., pink..............................23.00
Relish dish, two-part, green or pink, 8" sq. 16.50

Adam Salt & Pepper Shakers

Salt & pepper shakers, footed, green, 4" h., pr. 75.00
Salt & pepper shakers, footed, pink, 4" h., pr. (ILLUS.) 60.00
Saucer, pink, 6" sq.................................6.50
Sherbet, pink, 3" h. 25.00
Sugar bowl, cov., green...................... 41.00
Sugar bowl, cov., pink 34.00
Tumbler, cone-shaped, green, 4½" h., 7 oz. 22.50

Tumbler, iced tea, pink, 5½" h., 9 oz. 55.00
Vase, 7½" h., green 53.00
Vase, 7½" h., pink 185.00
Water set: pitcher & 6 tumblers; pink, 7 pcs. 162.50

AMERICAN SWEETHEART (Process-etched)

Bowl, berry, 3¾" d., pink 38.00
Bowl, cream soup, 4½" d., Monax 106.00
Bowl, cream soup, 4½" d., pink 70.00
Bowl, cereal, 6" d., Cremax 8.00
Bowl, berry, 9" d., Monax 55.00
Bowl, berry, 9" d., pink 35.00
Bowl, soup w/flange rim, 9½" d., Monax 70.00
Bowl, soup w/flange rim, 9½" d., pink 58.00
Bowl, 11" oval vegetable, Monax 67.00
Bowl, 11" oval vegetable, pink 55.00
Console bowl, Monax, 18" d. 425.00
Creamer, footed, blue 95.00
Creamer, footed, Monax 8.50
Cup & saucer, ruby red 118.00
Lamp shade, Monax 545.00
Pitcher, 7½" h., 60 oz., jug-type, pink 530.00
Pitcher, 8" h., 80 oz., pink 440.00
Plate, bread & butter, 6" d., Monax or pink 4.50
Plate, salad, 8" d., blue 84.00
Plate, dinner, 9¾" d., Monax 22.00
Plate, dinner, 9¾" d., pink 30.00
Plate, chop, 11" d., Monax 13.50
Plate, salver, 12" d., Monax 16.00

American Sweetheart Plate

Plate, salver, 12" d., pink (ILLUS.) 15.00
Plate, salver, 12" d., ruby red 170.00
Plate, 15½" d., w/center handle, Monax 205.00
Platter, 13" oval, Monax 55.00
Platter, 13" oval, pink 40.00
Salt & pepper shakers, footed, Monax, pr. 270.00
Salt & pepper shakers, footed, pink, pr. 330.00
Sherbet, footed, pink, 4¼" h. 13.50
Sherbet, metal holder, clear 6.00
Sugar bowl, cov., Monax (only) 265.00
Sugar bowl, open, ruby red 100.00
Tidbit server, two-tier, Monax 70.00
Tidbit server, two-tier, pink 56.00
Tidbit server, two-tier, ruby red 220.00
Tumbler, pink, 3½" h., 5 oz. 67.00

BUBBLE, Bullseye or Provincial (Press-mold)

Bowl, berry, 4" d., clear or milk white 3.00
Bowl, berry, 4" d., green 9.50
Bowl, fruit, 4½" d., blue 9.50
Bowl, fruit, 4½" d., clear or milk white 3.50
Bowl, cereal, 5¼" d., green 12.00
Bowl, soup, 7¾" d., blue 13.00
Bowl, soup, 7¾" d., clear 7.00
Bowl, soup, 7¾" d., pink 10.00
Bowl, 8⅜" d., blue 13.50
Bowl, 8⅜" d., ruby red 24.00
Candlesticks, clear, pr. 12.00
Creamer, blue 29.00
Creamer, clear 6.00
Creamer, green 11.50
Creamer, milk white 4.00
Cup & saucer, clear 3.50
Cup & saucer, milk white 3.00
Lamps, clear (electric), pr. 56.00
Pitcher w/ice lip, 64 oz., clear 65.00
Pitcher w/ice lip, 64 oz., ruby red 48.00
Plate, bread & butter, 6¾" d., blue 3.50
Plate, bread & butter, 6¾" d., clear 2.00
Plate, dinner, 9⅜" d., green 15.00
Plate, dinner, 9⅜" d., ruby red 12.50
Plate, grill, 9⅜" d., blue 16.50
Plate, grill, 9⅜" d., clear 7.50
Platter, 12" oval, blue 13.00
Platter, 12" oval, clear 11.50
Saucer, blue, green or ruby red 3.50
Sugar bowl, open, blue 17.50
Sugar bowl, open, milk white 4.50
Tidbit server, two-tier, blue 44.00

Bubble Iced Tea Tumbler

Tumbler, juice, green, 6 oz. 10.50
Tumbler, juice, ruby red, 6 oz. 7.00
Tumbler, water, clear, 9 oz. 8.00

Tumbler, water, ruby red, 9 oz.................9.50
Tumbler, iced tea, clear, 4½" h.,12 oz. .10.50
Tumbler, iced tea, ruby red, 4½" h., 12 oz. (ILLUS.)....................................9.00
Tumbler, lemonade, clear, 5⅞" h., 16 oz. 13.00
Water set: pitcher & 8 tumblers; ruby red, 9 pcs. 130.00

CAMEO or Ballerina or Dancing Girl (Process-etched)

Bowl, sauce, 4¼" d., clear 6.50
Bowl, cream soup, 4¾" d., green..........98.00
Bowl, cereal, 5½" d., clear 6.50
Bowl, large berry, 8¼" d., green 35.00
Bowl, soup w/flange rim, 9" d., green ...47.00
Bowl, 10" oval vegetable, green 22.50
Bowl, 10" oval vegetable, yellow 37.00
Butter dish, cov., green.......................175.00

Cameo Footed Cake Plate

Cake plate, three-footed, green,10" d. (ILLUS.) 19.00
Candlesticks, green, 4" h., pr..............100.00
Candy jar, cov., green, 4" h. 58.00
Compote, mayonnaise, 5" d., 4" h., cone-shaped, green..........................28.00
Console bowl, three-footed, green, 11" d...63.00
Cookie jar, cov., green..........................44.00
Creamer, green, 3¼" h. 20.00
Creamer, yellow, 3¼" h. 16.00
Creamer, green, 4¼" h. 21.00
Decanter w/stopper, green, 10" h. 135.00
Decanter w/stopper, green frosted, 10" h..35.00
Domino tray, clear, 7" d. 85.00
Domino tray, green, 7" d. 145.00
Goblet, wine, green, 4" h. 59.00
Goblet, water, green, 6" h. 51.00
Goblet, water, pink, 6" h. 167.00
Pitcher, syrup or milk, 5¾" h., 20 oz., green..200.00
Pitcher, juice, 6" h., 36 oz., green.........48.00
Pitcher, water, 8½" h., 56 oz., jug-type, green...50.00
Plate, sherbet (or ringless saucer), 6" d., clear...2.00
Plate, sherbet (or ringless saucer), 6" d., green or yellow 3.50
Plate, dinner, 9½" d., yellow 7.50
Plate, sandwich, 10" d., green 14.00
Plate, sandwich, 10" d., pink.................57.00
Plate, dinner, 10½" d., trimmed, green...12.50
Plate, grill, 10½" d., yellow......................6.50
Plate, grill, 10½" d., closed handles, green...78.00
Plate, grill, 10½" d., closed handles, yellow 6.50
Platter, 10½" oval, green 18.00
Platter, 12", closed handles,yellow.......36.00
Relish, footed, three-part, green, 7½"...25.00
Salt & pepper shakers, green, pr. 64.00
Salt & pepper shakers, pink, pr. 950.00
Sherbet, pink, 3⅛" h. 83.00
Sherbet, yellow, 3⅛" h. 35.00
Sherbet, thin, high stem, green, 4⅞" h...26.00
Sugar bowl, open, yellow, 3¼" h. 13.00
Sugar bowl, open, green, 4¼" h. 20.00
Sugar bowl, open, pink, 4¼" h..............67.50
Tumbler, juice, footed, green, 3 oz. 61.00
Tumbler, juice, green, 3¾" h.,5 oz........25.00
Tumbler, water, green, 4" h., 9 oz. 25.00
Tumbler, water, pink, 4" h., 9 oz. 95.00
Tumbler, footed, green, 5" h., 9 oz. 25.00
Tumbler, yellow, 4¾" h., 10 oz. 83.00
Tumbler, green, 5" h., 11 oz. 27.50
Tumbler, yellow, 5" h., 11 oz. 58.00
Tumbler, footed, green, 5¾" h., 11 oz. 56.00
Vase, 8" h., green 27.50
Water bottle, dark green "White House Vinegar" base, 8½" h. 18.50

CHERRY BLOSSOM (Process-etched)

Cherry Blossom Pattern

Bowl, berry, 4¾" d., Delphite or pink 13.50
Bowl, berry, 4¾" d., green 15.50
Bowl, cereal, 5¾"d., green 30.00
Bowl, cereal, 5¾" d., pink 31.00
Bowl, soup, 7¾" d., green 54.00
Bowl, soup, 7¾" d., pink 57.00

Bowl, berry, 8½" d., pink 41.00
Bowl, 9" d., two-handled, Delphite........30.00
Bowl, 9" oval vegetable, Delphite 38.00
Butter dish, cov., green 79.00
Butter dish, cov., pink 67.00
Cake plate, three-footed, green, 10¼" d. 22.50
Cake plate, three-footed, pink, 10¼" d. 25.00
Coaster, green 11.50
Mug, green, 7 oz. 195.00
Mug, pink, 7 oz. 180.00
Pitcher, 6¾" h., 36 oz., overall patt., Delphite 77.00
Pitcher, 6¾" h., 36 oz., overall patt., green 56.00
Pitcher, 8" h., 36 oz., footed, cone-shaped, patt. top, pink 48.50
Pitcher, 8" h., 42 oz., patt. top, green (ILLUS.) 51.00
Pitcher, 8" h., 42 oz., patt. top,pink 51.00
Plate, sherbet, 6" d., Delphite 8.50
Plate, sherbet, 6" d., green 6.00
Plate, dinner, 9" d., green or pink 20.00
Plate, grill, 9" d., green 21.00
Plate, grill, 9" d., pink...........................22.00
Platter, 11" oval, green or pink 31.00
Platter, 13" oval, divided, pink 58.00
Salt & pepper shakers, green, pr. 1,085.00
Sandwich tray, handled, Delphite or green, 10½" d. 21.00
Sandwich tray, handled, pink,10½"d. ..19.50
Saucer, Delphite or green 4.00
Sugar bowl, cov., clear 15.00
Sugar bowl, cov., Delphite 35.00
Sugar bowl, cov., green 32.00
Sugar bowl, cov., pink 27.50
Tumbler, patt. top, green, 3½" h.,4 oz. (ILLUS. right) 21.50
Tumbler, patt. top, pink, 3½" h., 4 oz. 16.50
Tumbler, juice, footed, overall patt., Delphite, 3¾" h., 4 oz. 18.00
Tumbler, juice, footed, overall patt., green or pink, 3¾" h., 4 oz. 16.00
Tumbler, footed, overall patt., Delphite, 4½" h., 8 oz. 20.00
Tumbler, footed, overall patt., green, 4½" h., 8 oz. 28.50
Tumbler, footed, overall patt., pink, 4½" h., 8 oz..26.00
Tumbler, patt. top, green, 4¼" h., 9 oz. (ILLUS. left) 20.00
Tumbler, patt. top, pink, 4¼" h., 9 oz....17.50
Tumbler, footed, overall patt., Delphite, 4½" h., 9 oz...19.00
Tumbler, patt. top, pink, 5" h., 12 oz.....55.00
Water set: pitcher & 6 tumblers; green, 7 pcs. 165.00

JUNIOR SET:
Creamer, Delphite 36.00
Creamer, pink 38.00
Cup, pink 30.00
Cup & saucer, Delphite.........................37.00
Plate, 6" d., Delphite 10.50
Plate, 6" d., pink.......................................7.50
Saucer, pink...4.00
Sugar bowl, Delphite or pink................35.00
14 pc. set, Delphite.............................260.00
14 pc. set, pink 270.00

CUBE or Cubist, Jeannette Glass Co., 1929-33 (Press-mold)

Bowl, dessert, 4½" d., clear 3.50
Bowl, dessert, 4½" d., green...................6.50
Bowl, dessert, 4½" d., pink 5.00
Bowl, 4½" d., deep, clear.........................3.50
BBowl, salad, 6½" d., green 11.50
Bowl, salad, 6½" d., pink 9.50
Bowl, salad, 6½" d., ultramarine 55.00
Butter dish, cov., green..........................50.00
Butter dish, cov., pink 51.50
Candy jar, cov., green, 6½" h. 25.50
Creamer, clear, 2⅝" h.............................1.00

Cube Creamer

Creamer, pink, 2⅝" h. (ILLUS.) 3.50
Creamer, green, 3½" h. 8.00
Creamer, pink, 3½" h...............................5.50
Cup & saucer, green..............................17.00
Cup & saucer, pink 9.50
Pitcher, 8¾" h., 45 oz., green 211.00
Pitcher, 8¾" h., 45 oz., pink................139.00
Plate, sherbet, 6" d., clear 1.00
Powder jar, cov., three-footed, pink......21.50
Salt & pepper shakers, green or pink, pr...31.00
Sherbet, footed, green.............................7.00
Sherbet, footed, pink 5.50
Sugar bowl, cov., green, 3" h................18.50
Sugar bowl, cov., pink, 3" h. 16.00

Cube Sugar Bowl

Sugar bowl, open, pink, 2⅜" h. (ILLUS. previous page) 3.00
Tray for 3½" h. creamer & open sugar bowl, clear, 7½" 4.00
Tumbler, green, 4" h., 9 oz. 59.50
Tumbler, pink, 4" h., 9 oz. 45.00

DIAMOND QUILTED or Flat Diamond, Imperial Glass Co., late 1920s - early 1930s (Press-mold)

Bowl, cream soup, 4¾" d., black 17.50
Bowl, cream soup, 4¾" d., blue 15.00
Bowl, 5½" d., single handle, pink 7.00
Bowl, 7" d., crimped rim, black 21.50
Bowl, 7" d., crimped rim, blue 15.50
Candlesticks, flat or domed base, black, pr. 35.00
Candlesticks, flat or domed base, green, pr. 23.50
Compote, open, 6" h., 7¼" d., green 40.00
Console bowl, rolled edge, pink 33.00
Creamer, black 16.50
Creamer, blue 13.50
Cup & saucer, amber 7.50
Cup & saucer, green 10.00
Cup & saucer, pink 12.00
Ice bucket, black 72.50
Mayonnaise dish, three-footed w/plate, green, 2 pcs. 27.00
Pitcher, 64 oz., green 42.00
Plate, sherbet, 6" d., blue 4.50
Plate, luncheon, 8" d., blue 13.50
Plate, luncheon, 8" d., green or pink 5.50
Plate, sandwich, 14" d., pink 18.00
Sherbet, black or blue 10.50
Sugar bowl, open, green 7.50
Sugar bowl, open, pink 8.50
Tumbler, whiskey, green, 1½ oz. 6.50
Tumbler, iced tea, green, 12 oz. 9.00

DIANA, Federal Glass Co., 1937-41 (Press-mold)

Diana Demitasse Cup & Saucer

Bowl, cereal, 5" d., amber 11.00
Bowl, cereal, 5" d., clear 3.50
Bowl, cream soup, 5½" d., clear or pink 4.00
Bowl, salad, 9" d., amber 11.00
Bowl, salad, 9" d., clear 5.00
Bowl, salad, 9" d., pink 19.00
Bowl, 12" d., scalloped rim, clear 7.50
Candy jar, cov., round, clear 13.00
Coaster, amber, 3½" d. 13.00
Coaster, clear, 3½" d. 4.50
Coaster, pink, 3½" d. 6.50
Creamer, oval, amber 8.00
Creamer, oval, clear 3.00
Cup & saucer, demitasse, clear (ILLUS.) 10.00
Cup & saucer, demitasse, pink 40.00
Cup & saucer, amber 8.00
Cup & saucer, clear 4.50
Cup & saucer, pink 15.00
Plate, bread & butter, 6" d., amber or clear 1.50
Plate, dinner, 9½" d., pink 13.00
Plate, sandwich, 11¾" d., amber 10.50
Plate, sandwich, 11¾" d., clear 5.00
Platter, 12" oval, clear 4.50
Salt & pepper shakers, amber, pr. 89.00
Salt & pepper shakers, clear, pr. 22.00
Sugar bowl, open, oval, amber or pink 7.50
Sugar bowl, open, oval, clear 2.00
Tumbler, amber, 4⅛" h., 9 oz. 22.00
Tumbler, clear, 4⅛" h., 9 oz. 25.00
Junior set: 6 cups, saucers & plates w/round rack; clear, set 76.50
Child's cup, clear 4.50
Child's cup & saucer, clear 11.00

DOGWOOD or Apple Blossom or Wild Rose, MacBeth-Evans, 1929-32 (Process-etched)

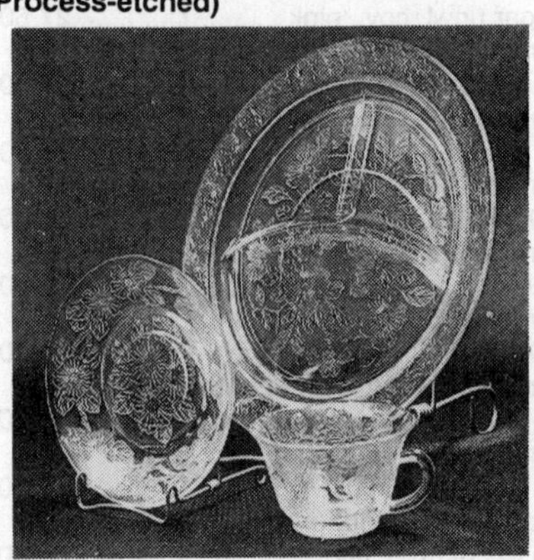

Dogwood Pattern

Bowl, cereal, 5½" d., green or pink 23.50
Bowl, berry, 8½" d., Cremax 31.00
Bowl, fruit, 10½" d., green 133.00
Bowl, fruit, 10½" d., pink 370.00
Cake plate, heavy solid foot, green, 13" d. 77.50
Creamer, thin, green, 2½" h. 37.00
Creamer, thin, footed, pink, 2¼" h. 17.50
Cup & saucer, Monax 39.00

Cup & saucer, pink (ILLUS.)................19.00
Pitcher, 8" h., 80 oz., American Sweetheart style, pink....................565.00
Pitcher, 8" h., 80 oz., decorated, green...415.00
Plate, luncheon, 8" d., clear...................4.00
Plate, luncheon, 8" d., green 6.50
Plate, grill, 10½" d., overall patt. or border design only, green..................15.00
Plate, grill, 10½" d., border design, pink...16.00
Plate, grill, 10½" d., overall patt., pink (ILLUS.) 17.50
Platter, 12" oval, pink........................400.00
Sherbet, low foot, green 40.00
Sherbet, low foot, pink.........................27.00
Sugar bowl, open, thin, green, 2½" h..40.00
Sugar bowl, open, thin, pink, 2½" h......15.00
Tumbler, decorated, pink, 4" h., 10 oz. 32.50
Tumbler, decorated, green, 4¾" h., 11 oz. 147.50
Tumbler, molded band, pink 15.00
Water set: decorated pitcher & 6 decorated tumblers; pink, 7 pcs.......298.00

DORIC, Jeannette Glass Co., 1935-38 (Press-mold)

Doric Salt & Pepper Shakers

Bowl, berry, 4½" d., green or pink 7.00
Bowl, cereal, 5½" d., green.................55.00
Bowl, cereal, 5½" d., pink 44.00
Bowl, large berry, 8¼" d., green 17.50
Bowl, 9" oval vegetable, green 27.00
Bowl, 9" oval vegetable, pink...............24.50
Butter dish, cov., green........................75.00
Butter dish, cov., pink 58.00
Cake plate, three-footed, green, 10" d...25.50
Candy dish, three-section, pink, 6" 9.00
Candy jar, cov., green, 8" h. 37.50
Candy jar, cov., pink, 8" h....................29.00
Creamer, pink, 4" h..............................11.50
Pitcher, 6" h., 36 oz., green or pink 32.00
Pitcher, 7½" h., 48 oz., footed, pink....425.00

Plate, sherbet, 6" d., green or pink 3.50
Plate, salad, 7" d., green 14.00
Plate, dinner, 9" d., pink........................13.00
Plate, grill, 9" d., green 15.00
Platter, 12" oval, pink...........................20.00
Relish tray, green, 4 x 4" 11.50
Relish tray, pink, 4 x 4"..........................12.50
Relish or serving tray, pink, 8 x 8" 19.00
Relish, square inserts in metal holder, pink 48.00
Salt & pepper shakers, green, pr. (ILLUS.) 35.50
Salt & pepper shakers, pink, pr. 32.00
Sandwich tray, handled, green or pink, 10" d. 13.00
Sherbet, footed, pink 11.00
Sugar bowl, cov., green........................28.50

Doric Sugar Bowl

Sugar bowl, cov., pink (ILLUS.) 23.00
Tumbler, green, 4½" h., 9 oz. 85.50
Tumbler, pink, 4½" h., 9 oz...................59.50
Tumbler, footed, green, 5" h., 12 oz. 94.00
Tumbler, footed, pink, 5" h., 12 oz........69.00

DORIC & PANSY, Jeannette Glass Co., 1937-38 (Press-mold)

Doric & Pansy Cup & Saucer

Bowl, berry, 4½" d., clear or pink............8.00
Bowl, berry, 4½" d., ultramarine 17.00
Bowl, large berry, 8" d., clear...............25.00
Butter dish, cov., ultramarine.............470.00
Creamer, pink 32.00

Creamer, ultramarine....160.00
Cup & saucer, clear....14.00
Cup & saucer, ultramarine (ILLUS.)....24.50
Plate, sherbet, 6" d., clear....8.00
Plate, dinner, 9" d., ultramarine....27.50
Salt & pepper shakers, ultramarine, pr....385.00
Sugar bowl, open, pink....32.00
Sugar bowl, open, ultramarine....138.00
Tray, handled, ultramarine, 10"....24.00
Tumbler, ultramarine, 4½" h., 9 oz....74.00

PRETTY POLLY PARTY DISHES
Creamer, pink....28.50
Creamer, ultramarine....33.50
Cup, ultramarine....29.50
Cup & saucer, pink....33.50
Cup & saucer, ultramarine....46.00
Plate, pink....6.50
Plate, ultramarine....12.00
Saucer, pink....5.50
Saucer, ultramarine....6.50
Sugar bowl, pink....27.50
Sugar bowl, ultramarine....37.00
14 piece set, pink....200.00
14 piece set, ultramarine....280.00

ENGLISH HOBNAIL, Westmoreland Glass Co., 1920s - '40s (Handmade - not true Depression)

English Hobnail Salt Dip

Ashtray, clear, various shapes....12.00
Basket, handled, clear, 5" h....25.00
Bowl, nappy, 4½" d., clear....7.00
Bowl, nappy, 4½" sq., green....8.00
Bowl, cream soup, 4¾" d., clear....6.50
Bowl, cream soup, 4¾" d., green....20.00
Bowl, 6" d., amber or clear....9.00
Bowl, grapefruit, 6½" d., clear....14.50
Bowl, fruit, 8" d., two-handled, footed, cobalt blue....120.00
Bowl, nappy, 11" d., blue....38.00
Bowl, 12" d., flared, green....40.00
Candlesticks, amber, 3½" h., pr....19.00
Candlesticks, blue, 3½" h., pr....33.50
Candlesticks, green, 8½" h., pr....67.50
Candlesticks, pink, 8½" h., pr....40.00
Candlesticks, turquoise, 8½" h., pr....61.00
Candy dish, cov., cone-shaped, amber, ½ lb....40.00
Candy dish, cov., urn-shaped, green, 15" h....300.00
Celery tray, clear, 12" l....17.00
Cigarette box, cov., clear....35.50
Cologne bottle, clear or green....28.00
Cologne bottle, turquoise....36.00
Cup & saucer, demitasse, clear....25.50
Cup & saucer, clear....8.00
Cup & saucer, turquoise....23.00
Dish, cov., three-footed, amber....60.00
Dish, cov., three-footed, clear....33.00
Goblet, cordial, clear, 1 oz....16.50
Goblet, wine, clear, 2 oz....17.00
Goblet, cocktail, amber or pink, 3 oz....15.00
Goblet, clear, 6¼ oz....16.00
Goblet, green, 6¼ oz....21.50
Goblet, pink, 6¼ oz....18.00
Ice tub, clear....65.00
Lamp, electric, clear, 6¼" h....30.50
Lamp, electric, amber, 9¼" h....71.00
Marmalade jar, cov., green....35.00
Marmalade jar, cov., pink....31.50
Oil bottle, clear, 2 oz....17.50
Parfait, footed, round, clear....19.00
Pitcher, 23 oz., clear....75.00
Pitcher, ½ gal., straight sides, clear....169.00
Plate, sherbet, 5½" or 6½" d., green....3.50
Plate, sherbet, 5½" or 6½" d., pink....2.50
Plate, luncheon, 8" round or square, amber....10.00
Plate, luncheon, 8" round or square, ice blue....25.00
Plate, luncheon, 8" round or square, pink....8.00
Plate, luncheon, 8" round or square, turquoise....15.00
Plate, dinner, 10" d., clear....7.50
Puff box, cov., clear....27.50
Salt & pepper shakers, amber, pr....72.50
Salt & pepper shakers, clear, pr....47.00
Salt & pepper shakers, green, pr....74.50
Salt dip, footed, clear, 2"....10.00
Salt dip, footed, cobalt blue, 2"....31.00
Salt dip, footed, green, 2"....14.50
Salt dip, footed, pink, 2" (ILLUS.)....15.00
Salt dip, footed, turquoise, 2"....16.50
Sherbet, footed, ice blue....23.00
Sugar bowl, open, footed or flat, clear....12.00
Sugar bowl, open, footed or flat, pink....19.50
Tumbler, whiskey, clear, 1½ oz....8.00
Tumbler, clear, 3¾" h., 9 oz....13.50
Tumbler, footed, clear, 9 oz....12.00
Tumbler, iced tea, clear, 4" h., 10 oz....8.50
Tumbler, iced tea, ice blue, 4" h., 10 oz....48.00
Vase, 7¼" h., amber....85.00
Vase, 7¼" h., clear....42.50
Vase, 7¼" h., pink....101.00

FLORAL or Poinsettia, Jeannette Glass Co., 1931-35 (Process etched)

Bowl, berry, 4" d., green or pink 16.00
Bowl, salad, 7½" d., green....................20.00
Bowl, cov. vegetable, 8" d., pink...........41.50
Bowl, 9" oval vegetable, green or pink 16.50
Butter dish, cov., green..........................84.50
Butter dish, cov., pink 86.50
Candlesticks, green, 4" h., pr.................73.50
Candlesticks, pink, 4" h., pr. 71.50
Candy jar, cov., green or pink...............36.00
Canister, cov., Jadite 28.00
Creamer, pink 14.50
Flower frog for vase, green.............1,200.00
Lamp, green 275.00
Lamp, pink 225.00
Pitcher, 5½" h., 24 oz., green 630.00
Pitcher, 8" h., 32 oz., cone-shaped, green 33.50
Pitcher, 8" h., 32 oz., cone-shaped, pink 32.00
Pitcher, lemonade, 10¼" h., 48 oz., green..230.00
Pitcher, lemonade, 10¼" h., 48 oz., pink 285.00
Plate, sherbet, 6" d., green or pink 6.00
Plate, salad, 8" d., green or pink...........10.00
Plate, dinner, 9" d., green 16.50
Platter, 11" oval, scalloped edge, pink..60.00
Refrigerator dish, cov., green, 5" sq. 54.00
Refrigerator dish, cov., Jadite, 5" sq.....21.50
Relish, two-part, oval, green.................15.00
Relish, two-part, oval, pink 16.00
Salt & pepper shakers, footed, pink, 4" h., pr 44.00
Salt & pepper shakers, flat, pink, 6" h., pr 51.50
Sugar bowl, cov., green........................26.50
Sugar bowl, cov., pink 20.00
Sugar bowl, open, green 10.00
Tray, closed handles, pink, 6" sq..........17.50
Tumbler, juice, footed, green or pink, 4" h., 5 oz...18.50
Tumbler, water, footed, green, 4¾" h., 7 oz. 18.50
Tumbler, lemonade, footed, green or pink, 5¼" h., 9 oz. 45.00
Vase, 6⅞" h., octagonal, clear............300.00
Vase, 6⅞" h., octagonal, green 505.00

(OLD) FLORENTINE or Poppy No. 1 Hazel Atlas Glass Co., 1932-35 (Process-etched)

Ashtray, clear, 5½" 18.00
Ashtray, green, 5½" 20.00
Bowl, berry, 5" d., cobalt blue or yellow 12.00
Bowl, berry, 5" d., green 11.00
Bowl, cereal, 6" d., clear or pink 20.00
Bowl, 8½" d., pink 31.00
Bowl, 8½" d., yellow..............................27.50
Bowl, cov. vegetable, 9½" oval, clear...45.00
Bowl, cov. vegetable, 9½" oval, green..40.00
Bowl, 9½" oval vegetable, yellow 27.50
Butter dish, cov., clear or green..........106.00
Butter dish, cov., pink 156.00
Butter dish, cov., yellow.......................146.00
Coaster-ashtray, yellow, 3¾" d.............26.00
Creamer, plain rim, clear 8.00
Creamer, ruffled rim, clear 30.00
Creamer, ruffled rim, cobalt blue 60.00
Creamer, ruffled rim, green 23.00
Creamer, ruffled rim, pink 26.00
Cup & saucer, pink or yellow 13.50
Nut dish, handled, ruffled rim, clear or pink 15.00
Nut dish, handled, ruffled rim, cobalt blue 44.50
Pitcher, 6½" h., 36 oz., footed, green ...39.00
Pitcher, 6½" h., 36 oz., footed, pink or yellow 43.00
Pitcher, 7½" h., 48 oz., clear.................59.00
Pitcher, 7½" h., 48 oz., green 75.00
Pitcher, 7½" h., 48 oz., pink...............100.00
Plate, sherbet, 6" d., clear 3.00
Plate, sherbet, 6" d., green 6.00
Plate, salad, 8½" d., pink.......................11.00
Plate, salad, 8½" d., yellow....................10.00
Plate, dinner, 10" d., clear 11.00
Plate, grill, 10" d., pink..........................15.50
Plate, grill, 10" d., yellow.......................13.00
Platter, 11½" oval, green 15.50
Platter, 11½" oval, pink.........................19.50
Salt & pepper shakers, footed, green, pr...34.50
Salt & pepper shakers, footed, pink, pr...46.00
Salt & pepper shakers, footed, yellow, pr...52.00
Sherbet, footed, clear or green, 3 oz......8.50
Sherbet, footed, pink, 3 oz......................9.00
Sugar bowl, cov., green or pink 25.50
Sugar bowl, cov., yellow 28.00
Sugar bowl, open, clear...........................8.00
Sugar bowl, open, ruffled rim, cobalt blue 45.00
Sugar bowl, open, ruffled rim, green 30.00
Sugar bowl, open, ruffled rim, pink 28.00
Tumbler, footed, green, 3¼" h., 4 oz. 8.00
Tumbler, juice, footed, clear, 3¾" h., 5 oz. 11.50
Tumbler, ribbed, clear, 4" h., 9 oz.........12.00
Tumbler, ribbed, pink, 4" h., 9 oz..........15.00
Tumbler, water, footed, yellow, 4¾" h., 10 oz. 19.00
Tumbler, iced tea, footed, green, 5¼" h., 12 oz. 16.00

FLORENTINE or Poppy No. 2, Hazel Atlas Glass Co., 1932-35 (Process-etched)

Bowl, berry, 4½" d., clear........................9.00

Bowl, berry, 4½" d., green....................11.00
Bowl, cream soup, plain rim, 4¾" d., green..11.50
Bowl, cream soup, plain rim, 4¾" d., pink 15.00
Bowl, 5½" d., green 45.00
Bowl, 5½" d., yellow...............................41.00
Bowl, cereal, 6" d., yellow......................35.00
Bowl, 8" d., clear....................................22.00
Bowl, cov. vegetable, 9" oval, green.......35.00
Bowl, cov. vegetable, 9" oval, yellow.....60.00
Bowl, 9" oval vegetable, green 22.50
Butter dish, cov., yellow.......................137.00
Candlesticks, green, 2¾" h., pr..............47.00
Candlesticks, yellow, 2¾" h., pr. 56.50
Candy dish, cov., clear 67.50
Candy dish, cov., green..........................95.00
Coaster, green, 3¼" d..............................13.00
Coaster, pink, 3¼" d. 17.50
Coaster, yellow, 3¼" d.............................20.00
Coaster-ashtray, clear, 3¾" d. 16.00
Coaster-ashtray, green, 3¾" d.................18.00
Compote, 3½", ruffled, cobalt blue 50.00
Compote, 3½", ruffled, pink 13.00
Condiment set: creamer, cov. sugar bowl, salt & pepper shakers & 8½" d. tray; yellow, 5 pcs. 161.00
Creamer, clear 6.50
Creamer, green 8.00
Cup & saucer, pink 11.50
Cup & saucer, yellow................................12.50
Custard cup, green 70.00
Custard cup, yellow 79.00
Gravy boat, yellow 50.00
Gravy boat w/platter, yellow, 11½" oval 81.00
Pitcher, 6¼" h., 24 oz., cone-shaped, yellow 142.00
Pitcher, 7½" h., 48 oz., straight sides, clear 52.50
Pitcher, 7½" h., 48 oz., straight sides, green..48.00
Pitcher, 8¼" h., 76 oz., clear.....................80.00
Pitcher, 8¼" h., 76 oz., pink 219.00
Pitcher, 8¼" h., 76 oz., yellow 400.00
Plate, sherbet, 6" d., clear 3.00
Plate, salad, 8½" d., green or yellow 8.00
Plate, dinner, 10" d., clear 10.50
Plate, dinner, 10" d., green 13.50
Plate, grill, 10¼" d., green 13.50
Plate, grill, 10¼" d., yellow.......................12.50
Platter, 11" oval, clear..............................10.50
Platter, 11" oval, green 14.50
Relish dish, three-part or plain, green, 10" 19.50
Relish dish, three-part or plain, pink, 10" 22.00
Salt & pepper shakers, yellow, pr. 44.00
Saucer, clear 3.00
Saucer, green...4.00
Sherbet, clear, green or yellow...............9.50
Sugar bowl, cov., clear 22.00
Sugar bowl, cov., green..........................19.00
Sugar bowl, cov., yellow.........................29.00
Tumbler, footed, yellow, 3¼" h., 5 oz. ..13.00
Tumbler, juice, clear, 3½" h., 5 oz. 9.00
Tumbler, juice, green, 3½" h., 5 oz.......12.00
Tumbler, juice, pink, 3½" h., 5 oz. 10.50
Tumbler, footed, yellow, 4" h., 5 oz. 15.00
Tumbler, blown, clear, 3½" h., 6 oz. 16.00
Tumbler, blown, green, 3½" h., 6 oz. 12.50
Tumbler, water, clear, 4" h., 9 oz...........10.00
Tumbler, footed, green, 4½" h., 9 oz. ...21.00
Tumbler, footed, yellow, 4½" h., 9 oz. ..30.00
Tumbler, blown, clear, 5" h., 12 oz. 19.50
Tumbler, iced tea, green, 5" h., 12 oz...26.00
Tumbler, iced tea, yellow, 5" h., 12 oz. 41.00
Vase (or parfait), 6" h., clear..................26.00
Vase (or parfait), 6" h., green 36.50
Vase (or parfait), 6" h., yellow...............54.50

MADRID, Federal Glass Co., 1932-39 (Process-etched)

Madrid Sugar Bowl

Ashtray, amber, 6" sq. 221.00
Ashtray, green, 6" sq. 195.00
Bowl, cream soup, 4¾" d., amber.........13.50
Bowl, sauce, 5" d., amber or pink 5.50
Bowl, soup, 7" d., blue 20.00
Bowl, soup, 7" d., clear 6.00
Bowl, soup, 7" d., green..........................15.50
Bowl, salad, 8" d., amber........................13.50
Bowl, salad, 9½" d., deep, amber 27.50
Bowl, 10" oval vegetable, amber 16.00
Bowl, 10" oval vegetable, blue...............33.50
Butter dish, cov., clear 49.00
Butter dish, cov., green...........................78.00
Cake plate, amber, 11¼" d. 15.00
Cake plate, pink, 11¼" d.........................12.00
Candlesticks, amber, 2¼" h., pr.............16.00
Console set: bowl & pair of candlesticks; amber, 3 pcs. 37.00
Console set: bowl & pair of candlesticks; iridescent, 3 pcs. 32.00
Console set: bowl & pair of candlesticks; pink, 3 pcs...36.00

Bowl, berry, 4½", green 20.00
Bowl, cereal, 5", pink 22.00
Bowl, salad, 9" octagon, green or pink 36.00
Bowl, salad, 9" octagon, yellow 93.00
Bowl, 10" oval vegetable, pink....................25.50
Bowl, 10" oval vegetable, yellow 49.00
Butter dish, cov., green or pink....................81.00
Butter dish, cov., yellow....................560.00
Cake stand, green, 10"....................19.50
Cake stand, pink, 10"....................23.50
Candy jar, cov., green 53.00
Cookie jar, cov., pink 48.00
Creamer, oval, green....................15.50
Creamer, oval, yellow 12.50
Cup & saucer, yellow....................10.50
Pitcher, 6" h., 37 oz., jug-type, green or pink....................48.00
Pitcher, 8" h., 60 oz., jug-type, green or pink....................49.50
Plate, sherbet, 5½", yellow 3.50
Plate, salad, 8", amber 8.00
Plate, salad, 8", green 12.50
Plate, dinner, 9", yellow 12.00
Plate, grill, 9", green 11.00
Plate, grill, 9", pink....................12.50
Plate, grill, 10½", closed handles, yellow....................5.50
Plate, sandwich, 11¼", handled, green....................15.00
Relish, pink, 7½"....................300.00
Relish, divided, green, 7½"....................24.50
Relish, divided, pink, 7½" 17.00
Salt & pepper shakers, green, 4½" h., pr....................46.00
Salt & pepper (or spice) shakers, green, 5½" h., pr. 39.00
Saucer, green....................9.00
Sherbet, footed, green or pink....................17.50
Sherbet, footed, yellow....................28.50
Sugar bowl, cov., green....................27.50
Sugar bowl, cov., pink 44.00
Tumbler, juice, green, 3" h., 5 oz....................27.50
Tumbler, juice, pink, 3" h., 5 oz. 23.00
Tumbler, water, yellow, 4" h., 9 oz....................20.50
Tumbler, footed, green, 5¼" h., 10 oz. 28.00
Tumbler, footed, pink, 5¼" h., 10 oz.....24.00
Tumbler, footed, yellow, 6½" h., 12½ oz. 22.50
Tumbler, iced tea, green, 5¼" h., 13 oz. 35.00
Vase, 8" h., green or pink 29.50
Vase, 8" h., pink frosted....................20.00

ROYAL LACE, Hazel Atlas Glass Co., 1934-41 (Process-etched)

Bowl, cream soup, 4¾" d., blue....................34.50
Bowl, cream soup, 4¾" d., clear....................11.50

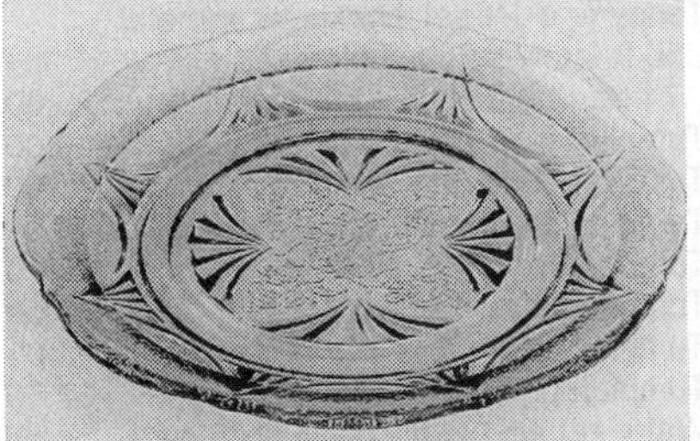

Royal Lace Plate

Bowl, berry, 5" d., green 28.00
Bowl, berry, 5" d., pink....................22.50
Bowl, berry, 10" d., green 24.00
Bowl, 10" d., three-footed, rolled edge, pink 47.50
Bowl, 10" d., three-footed, ruffled edge, clear 35.00
Bowl, 10" d., three-footed, straight edge, blue 70.00
Bowl, 11" oval vegetable, blue....................43.50
Bowl, 11" oval vegetable, clear....................14.00
Butter dish, cov., clear 65.00
Butter dish, cov., green....................250.00
Candlesticks, ruffled edge, blue, pr. ...132.00
Candlesticks, ruffled edge, clear, pr. 28.00
Candlesticks, ruffled edge, green, pr....42.50
Candlesticks, straight edge, clear, pr. ..32.00
Cookie jar, cov., blue 348.00
Cookie jar, cov., clear 38.00
Creamer, footed, green 24.00
Creamer, footed, pink....................17.00
Cup & saucer, green....................26.50
Cup & saucer, pink 18.50
Nut bowl, green 185.00
Pitcher, 48 oz., straight sides, blue.....146.00
Pitcher, 48 oz., straight sides, clear......37.50
Pitcher, 8" h., 68 oz., w/ice lip, pink......53.50
Pitcher, 8" h., 86 oz., without ice lip, pink 70.00
Pitcher, 8½" h., 96 oz., w/ice lip, blue 257.00
Plate, sherbet, 6" d., green or pink 8.00
Plate, luncheon, 8½" d., blue (ILLUS.) .31.00
Plate, luncheon, 8½" d., green or pink..15.50
Plate, dinner, 9⅞" d., blue 36.00
Plate, grill, 9⅞" d., pink....................17.50
Platter, 13" oval, blue....................46.50
Platter, 13" oval, clear....................14.00
Platter, 13" oval, green 30.00
Platter, 13" oval, pink....................32.50
Salt & pepper shakers, blue, pr. 225.00
Salt & pepper shakers, clear, pr. 39.50
Sherbet, footed, blue 34.50
Sherbet, footed, clear or pink 12.50
Sherbet, footed, green....................23.00
Sherbet in metal holder, amethyst....................34.00
Sherbet in metal holder, blue....................23.50
Sugar bowl, cov., clear 23.50
Sugar bowl, cov., green....................57.00
Sugar bowl, cov., pink 38.00

Toddy or cider set: cookie jar w/metal lid & 6 roly-poly tumblers; blue, 7 pcs. 125.00
Tumbler, blue, 3½" h., 5 oz. 40.00
Tumbler, clear, 4⅛" h., 9 oz. 11.50
Tumbler, green, 4⅛" h., 9 oz. 28.00
Tumbler, pink, 4⅛" h., 9 oz. 18.00
Tumbler, blue, 4⅞" h., 10 oz. 88.00
Tumbler, green, 5⅜" h., 12 oz. 42.00
Tumbler, pink, 5⅜" h., 12 oz. 37.50
Water set: 68 oz. pitcher & six 9 oz. tumblers; blue, 7 pcs. 360.00

ROYAL RUBY, Anchor Hocking Glass Co., 1939-60s (Press-mold)
(All items in ruby red.)

Ashtray, 4¼" sq. 4.50
Bowl, berry, 4¼" d. 6.00
Bowl, 4¾" sq. 6.50
Bowl, 7⅜" sq. 14.00
Bowl, soup, 7½" d. 12.00
Bowl, 8" oval vegetable 35.00
Bowl, salad, 11½" d. 30.50
Creamer, flat 7.00
Creamer, footed 8.00
Goblet, ball stem 10.00
Juice set, 22 oz. tilted pitcher & six 5 oz. tumblers, 7 pcs. 67.50
Pitcher, 22 oz., tilted or upright 30.50
Plate, luncheon, 7¾" d. 6.50
Plate, 8⅜" sq. 7.50
Playing card or cigarette box, divided, clear base 69.00
Popcorn set, 10" d. serving bowl and six 5¼" d. bowls, 7 pcs. 125.00
Punch bowl 37.50
Punch set, punch bowl, base & 8 cups, 10 pcs. 110.00
Sugar bowl, flat 7.00
Sugar bowl, footed 8.00
Sugar bowl w/slotted lid, footed 15.50
Tumbler, cocktail, 3½ oz. 10.50
Tumbler, iced tea, 13 oz. 11.00
Vase, 4" h., ball-shaped 5.00
Wine, footed, 2½ oz. 11.00

SANDWICH, Anchor Hocking Glass Co., 1939-64 (Press-mold)

Bowl, 4$\frac{5}{16}$" d., clear 4.50
Bowl, 4$\frac{5}{16}$" d., green 3.00
Bowl, berry, 4⅞" d., amber 3.00
Bowl, 5¼" d., scalloped, clear 7.00
Bowl, 5¼" d., ruby 17.00
Bowl, cereal, 6½" d., amber 13.50
Bowl, 6½" d., smooth or scalloped, green 41.00
Bowl, salad, 7" d., clear 7.00
Bowl, salad, 7" d., green 52.00
Bowl, 8" d., scalloped, clear 9.50
Bowl, 8½" oval vegetable, clear 6.50
Bowl, salad, 9" d., amber 23.50
Cookie jar, cov., clear 34.00
Cookie jar, green (no cover made) 17.00
Creamer, clear 4.50
Creamer, green 23.00
Cup & saucer, green 28.00
Custard cup, clear 4.00
Custard cup, ruffled, clear 12.50
Custard cup, green 3.00
Pitcher, juice, 6" h., green 154.00
Pitcher w/ice lip, 2 qt., clear 71.00
Pitcher w/ice lip, 2 qt., green 235.00
Plate, dessert, 7" d., amber 8.00
Plate, dinner, 9" d., clear 15.50
Plate, dinner, 9" d., green 74.00
Plate, snack, 9" d., clear 5.00
Punch bowl & base, clear 38.00
Punch bowl & base, opaque white 22.50
Punch set: punch bowl & 6 cups; clear, 7 pcs. 30.50
Punch set: punch bowl, base & 10 cups; opaque white, 12 pcs. 45.00
Sugar bowl, cov., clear 16.00
Sugar bowl, cov., green 24.00
Tumbler, juice, clear, 3 oz. 5.50
Tumbler, juice, green, 3 oz. 3.50
Tumbler, clear, 5 oz. 6.50
Tumbler, water, green, 9 oz. 4.00
Tumbler, footed, amber, 9 oz. 22.00
Tumbler, footed, clear, 9 oz. 27.00

SHARON or Cabbage Rose, Federal Glass Co., 1935-39 (Chip-mold)

Bowl, berry, 5" d., amber 7.00
Bowl, berry, 5" d., green or pink 11.00
Bowl, cream soup, 5" d., amber 24.50
Bowl, cereal, 6" d., green 24.00
Bowl, cereal, 6" d., pink 22.50
Bowl, soup, 7½" d., amber 42.00
Bowl, berry, 8½" d., pink 28.50
Bowl, 9½" oval vegetable, amber 17.00
Bowl, 9½" oval vegetable, green or pink 27.50
Bowl, fruit, 10½" d., pink 36.00
Butter dish, cov., amber 42.00
Butter dish, cov., green 74.50
Cake plate, footed, green, 11½" d. 48.50
Cake plate, footed, pink, 11½" d. 36.50
Candy jar, cov., amber 42.00
Cheese dish, cov., pink 805.00
Creamer, amber 12.00
Cup & saucer, green 26.00
Jam dish, amber, 7½" d., 1½" h. 31.00
Jam dish, green, 7½" d., 1½" h. 34.50
Pitcher w/ice lip, 9" h., 80 oz., amber 115.00
Pitcher w/ice lip, 9" h., 80 oz., green 322.00

Plate, bread & butter, 6" d., green or pink 6.50
Plate, salad, 7½" d., amber 15.00
Plate, dinner, 9¼" d., green or pink 17.00
Platter, 12¼" oval, amber 14.50
Platter, 12¼" oval, green 20.50
Salt & pepper shakers, green, pr. 61.00
Salt & pepper shakers, pink, pr. 48.50
Sherbet, footed, green 30.50
Sherbet, footed, pink 14.50
Sugar bowl, cov., amber 30.50
Sugar bowl, cov., green 43.00
Tumbler, amber, 4" h., 9 oz. 23.50
Tumbler, green, 4" h., 9 oz. 60.50
Tumbler, pink, 4" h., 9 oz. 36.00
Tumbler, footed, amber, 6½" h., 15 oz. 90.00
Tumbler, footed, clear, 6½" h., 15 oz. 16.50

TEA ROOM, Indiana Glass Co., 1926-31 (Press-mold)

Tea Room Creamer & Sugar

Banana split dish, flat, green, 7½" 98.00
Banana split dish, footed, clear, 7½" 46.00
Bowl, salad, 8¾" d., pink 52.00
Bowl, 9½" oval vegetable, green 69.00
Creamer, green, 3¼" h. 14.50
Creamer, green, 4" h. 14.50
Creamer & open sugar bowl on center-handled tray, green 55.00
Creamer & open sugar bowl on center-handled tray, pink (ILLUS.) 86.00
Cup & saucer, green 44.00
Cup & saucer, pink 63.50
Goblet, green, 9 oz. 77.50
Goblet, pink, 9 oz. 74.00
Ice bucket, green 70.00
Ice bucket, pink 85.00
Lamp, electric, clear, 9" 95.00
Parfait, green 63.50
Pitcher, 64 oz., green 160.00
Pitcher, 64 oz., pink 150.00
Plate, sherbet, 6½" d., pink 17.00
Plate, luncheon, 8¼" d., green 32.00
Plate, sandwich, w/center handle, pink 170.00
Relish, divided, green 22.50
Relish, divided, pink 13.00
Salt & pepper shakers, green, pr. 64.00
Salt & pepper shakers, pink, pr. 53.00
Sherbet, low, flared edge, clear 18.00
Sherbet, low, flared edge, green 27.50
Sherbet, tall footed, clear 27.50
Sugar bowl, cov., green, 3" h. 100.00
Sugar bowl, open, green, 4" h. 16.00
Sugar bowl, open, pink, 4" h. 14.00
Sugar bowl, open, rectangular, green 17.50
Sugar bowl, open, rectangular, pink 11.50
Sundae, footed, ruffled, clear 56.00
Sundae, footed, ruffled, green 135.00
Tray, rectangular, for creamer & sugar bowl, green 48.00
Tray w/center handle, for creamer & sugar bowl, pink 74.00
Tumbler, footed, clear, 6 oz. 28.00
Tumbler, footed, green, 6 oz. 42.00
Tumbler, footed, green or pink, 5¼" h., 8 oz. 30.00
Tumbler, footed, green, 11 oz. 62.50
Vase, 6½" h., ruffled rim, green 109.00
Vase, 9½" h., ruffled rim, amber 150.00
Vase, 11" h., straight, green 153.00
Vase, 11" h., straight, pink 105.00

WATERFORD or Waffle, Hocking Glass Co., 1938-44 (Press-mold)

Waterford Pattern

Ashtray, clear, 4" 5.00
Bowl, berry, 4¾" d., clear 5.50
Bowl, cereal, 5¼" d., pink 26.50
Bowl, berry, 8¼" d., clear 10.00
Butter dish, cov., pink 195.00
Cake plate, handled, clear, 10¼" d. 8.00
Cake plate, handled, pink, 10¼" d. 12.00
Creamer, oval, pink 12.00
Cup & saucer, clear (ILLUS. right) 9.00
Cup & saucer, pink 20.50
Goblet, amber, 5¼" h. 125.00
Goblet, clear, 5¼" h. 15.50
Pitcher, juice, 42 oz., tilt-type, clear 22.50
Pitcher w/ice lip, 80 oz., clear 29.50
Plate, salad, 7½" d., clear 4.50
Plate, salad, 7½" d., pink 10.00

Plate, dinner, 9⅝" d., clear 9.50
Plate, dinner, 9⅝" d., pink......................18.00
Plate, sandwich, 13¾" d., clear 8.50
Salt & pepper shakers, clear, short or tall, pr. 7.50
Sherbet, footed, clear 3.50
Sugar bowl, cov., oval, pink.................27.50
Sugar bowl, open, footed, clear (Miss America style) 2.00
Tumbler, footed, clear, 5" h., 10 oz. (ILLUS. left)..10.50
Tumbler, footed, pink, 5" h., 10 oz........17.50

WINDSOR DIAMOND or Windsor, Jeannette Glass Co., 1936-46 (Press-mold)

Ashtray, Delphite, 5¾" d.........................39.50
Ashtray, green, 5¾" d..............................44.50
Bowl, berry, 4¾" d., pink..........................8.00
Bowl, 5" d., pointed edge, clear 5.00
Bowl, 5" d., pointed edge, pink 18.00
Bowl, cream soup, 5" d., green or pink 23.00
Bowl, cereal, 5⅛" or 5⅜" d., clear...........7.00
Bowl, 7" d., three-footed, pink...............24.00
Bowl, 8" d., pointed edge, clear 11.00
Bowl, 8" d., pointed edge, pink 34.00
Bowl, berry, 8½" d., green 15.00
Bowl, berry, 8½" d., pink.......................17.00
Bowl, 9½" oval vegetable, clear...............8.50
Bowl, 9½" oval vegetable, green 23.00
Bowl, 10½" d., pointed edge, pink 107.50
Bowl, 7 x 11¾" boat shape, clear 17.50
Bowl, fruit, 12½" d., pink........................96.50
Butter dish, cov., clear 24.50
Cake plate, footed, green or pink, 10¾" d..19.00
Candlesticks, clear, 3" h., pr. 15.00
Candlesticks, pink, 3" h., pr. 81.00
Candy jar, cov., clear 11.00
Coaster, clear, 3¼" d. 7.00
Creamer, flat, green...............................12.50
Creamer, flat, pink 10.50
Creamer, footed, clear.............................5.50
Pitcher, 4½" h., 16 oz., Amberina red..600.00
Pitcher, 4½" h., 16 oz., clear..................19.50
Pitcher, 4½" h., 16 oz., pink.................113.00
Pitcher, 6¾" h., 52 oz., clear..................11.50
Plate, sherbet, 6" d., green 6.00
Plate, sherbet, 6" d., pink.........................4.50
Plate, salad, 7" d., green 17.50
Plate, dinner, 9" d., green or pink 19.00
Plate, sandwich, 10¼", handled, clear....7.00
Plate, chop, 13⅝" d., green or pink 40.00
Platter, 11½" oval, clear...........................7.00
Platter, 11½" oval, green 19.50
Relish, divided, pink, 11½" 187.50
Salt & pepper shakers, green, pr...........44.50
Salt & pepper shakers, pink, pr. 36.00
Sherbet, footed, green 13.00
Sherbet, footed, pink 9.50
Sugar bowl, cov., flat, clear 6.00
Sugar bowl, cov., flat, green..................23.00
Sugar bowl, cov., flat, pink.....................24.50
Sugar bowl, cov., footed, clear 6.00
Sugar bowl, cov., no lip, pink...............110.00
Tray, pink, 4" sq., without handles.........37.00
Tray, green or pink, 4⅛ x 9", w/handles 12.50
Tray, clear, 8½ x 9¾", without handles 12.00
Tray, pink, 8½ x 9¾", without handles 75.00
Tumbler, clear, 4" h., 9 oz.......................6.50
Tumbler, green, 4" h., 9 oz. 29.00
Tumbler, clear, 5" h., 12 oz......................9.00
Tumbler, green, 5" h., 12 oz. 42.50
Water set: pitcher & 6 each, 5 oz. tumblers, 9 oz. tumblers & 12 oz. tumblers; pink, in original box, 19 pcs.......................400.00

(End of Depression Glass Section)

DUNCAN & MILLER

Teardrop Champagne

Duncan & Miller Glass Company, a successor firm to George A. Duncan & Sons Company, produced a wide range of pressed wares and novelty pieces during the late 19th century and into the early 20th century. During the Depression era and after, they continued making a wide variety of more modern patterns, including mold-blown types and also introduced a number of etched and engraved patterns. Many colors, including opalescent hues, were produced during this era and especially popular today are the graceful swan dishes they produced in the Pall Mall and Sylvan patterns. The numbers after the pattern name indicate the original factory pattern number. The Duncan factory was closed in 1955. Also see ANIMALS and PATTERN GLASS in Glass section.

Ashtray, Caribbean patt. (No. 112), ruby $20.00
Ashtray, model of a duck, ruby 110.00

Bowl, 4¾" d., Puritan patt., pink.............9.00
Bowl, 6" d., handled, Teardrop patt. (No. 301), clear 4.00
Bowl, 7" d., Murano patt. (No. 127), pink opalescent..................................28.00
Bowl, 6½ x 11½", model of a Viking boat, clear ....150.00 to 175.00
Candlesticks, two-light, etched First Love patt., clear, pr. 110.00
Champagne, saucer-type, Teardrop patt., clear (ILLUS.).............................7.50
Cigarette box, cov., Caribbean patt., blue 73.00
Compote, 5" d., 3" h., Teardrop patt., clear 35.00
Cordial, Mardi Gras patt. (No. 42), clear 40.00
Cornucopia-vase, Three Feathers patt. (No. 117), clear, 8" h.................45.00
Creamer & open sugar bowl, Georgian patt. (No. 103), pink, pr. 30.00
Cruet w/original stopper, Early American Sandwich patt., clear, 3 oz. 35.00
Deviled egg plate, Early American Sandwich patt., green, 12" d.............35.00
Goblet, Canterbury patt., clear 12.00
Marmalade jar, cov., Teardrop patt., clear 37.00
Model of a swan, Pall Mall patt. (No. 30), ruby, 7" l.............................24.00
Model of a swan, Sylvan patt. (No. 122), blue opalescent, 12" l......350.00
Pitcher, 9½" h., w/ice lip, Canterbury patt., clear 90.00
Plate, salad, 8" d., Early American Sandwich patt., clear 10.00
Plate, 8½" d., Spiral Flutes patt., green..4.00
Punch set: punch bowl, 18" d. underplate & twelve cups; Caribbean patt., clear, cups clear w/applied ruby red handles, 14 pcs. 250.00
Relish dish, three-part, etched First Love patt., clear, 10½" l. 45.00
Salt & pepper shakers w/original tops, Mardi Gras patt., clear, pr. 37.50
Sugar bowl, cov., Bag Ware (No. 800), vaseline, ca. 1880s 80.00
Tumbler, old fashioned, Canterbury patt., clear, 8 oz. 7.50
Tumbler, juice, footed, cut Eternally Yours patt., clear, 5 oz......................20.00
Tumbler, juice, footed, Teardrop patt., clear, 4" h...9.00
Vase (cigarette holder), 3½" h., Grecian Urn line (No. 538), clear 12.50
Vase, 8" h., ruffled rim, Hobnail patt., blue opalescent.................................62.50
Wine, Mardi Gras patt., pr. 25.00

DURAND

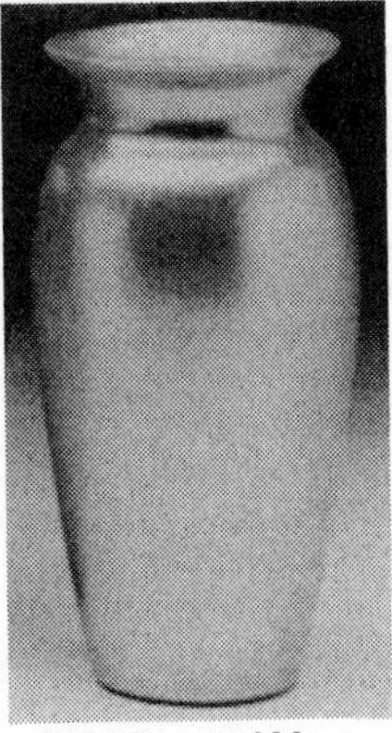

Gold Durand Vase

Fine decorative glass similar to that made by Tiffany and other outstanding glasshouses of its day was made by the Vineland Flint Glass Works Co. in Vineland, New Jersey, first headed by Victor Durand, Sr., and subsequently by his son Victor Durand, Jr., in the 1920s.

Center bowl, blue iridescence, signed, 14" w. $850.00
Jar, cov., wide tapering ovoid body w/a domed cover centered on the shouldered top, overall green & opal white swirled & 'crackled' surface, berry finial on the cover, overall iridescent finish, unsigned, 10" h. 990.00
Vase, 4½" h., gold iridescence, signed 395.00
Vase, 6³⁄₁₆" h., ovoid, amber iridescence decorated w/heart-shaped leaves & random trailing in pale green, inscribed "Durand - 1968-6," ca. 1920............................575.00
Vase, 8" h., simple baluster-form body w/flaring rim, overall smooth orangish gold iridescence, inscribed on base "V. Durand 1812-8" (ILLUS.) 575.00
Vase, 8¼" h., pyriform, King Tut patt., brilliant amber iridescence decorated w/lime green iridescent loopings & trailings, inscribed "Durand - 1706-8," ca. 1925 ....690.00
Vase, 12" h., "Moorish" type crackle glass, cushion foot tapering to a trumpet-form body w/ten molded ribs & overall crackled finish, ambergris w/gold iridescence, silver mark "V. Durand" on base 1,035.00

FENTON

Fenton Art Glass Company began producing glass at Williamstown, West

Virginia, in January 1907. Organized by Frank L. and John W. Fenton, the company began operations in a newly built glass factory with an experienced master glass craftsman, Jacob Rosenthal, as their factory manager. Fenton has produced a wide variety of collectible glassware through the years, including Carnival. Still in production today, their current productions may be found at finer gift shops across the country.

Basket w/wicker handle, Big Cookies patt., No. 1681, Mandarin Red, 10½" d., 5" h. $125.00

Basket, Hobnail patt., blue opalescent, 5½" h. 39.00

Basket, Coin Dot patt., French Opalescent, No. 1925, 6" h. 85.00

Bowl, 8½" d., rolled rim, Celeste Blue Stretch glass 40.00

Bowl, 9½" d., ruffled, No. 682, Emerald Crest.................................55.00

Bowl, 10" d., Diamond Optic patt., Mulberry...75.00

Butter dish, cov., Hobnail patt., No. 3977, milk white 16.00

Candleholders, cornucopia-shaped, Rose Crest, 6" h., pr. 75.00

Candlestick, Florentine Green Stretch glass, 8½" h. 38.00

Center bowl, oval, pedestal base, dolphin handles under wide flanged rim, No. 1608, Jade Green 45.00

Compote, open, 6" d., No. 206, Emerald Crest.................................25.00

Cookie jar, cov., Big Cookies (No. 1681) patt., Jade Green 125.00

Creamer, Coin Dot patt., No. 1942, cranberry opalescent, ca. 1944 ....55.00

Cruet, w/original stopper, Hobnail patt., No. 3863, milk white 19.00

Dresser bottle w/clear teardrop stopper, No. 711, bulbous body w/lady's leg neck, Beaded Melon patt., Peach Crest, 5½" h. 35.00

Epergne, three-lily, No. 4808, Diamond Lace patt., milk white..........50.00

Goblet, water, Lincoln Inn patt., Jade Green 25.00

Lamp, hurricane-type, No. 170, Diamond Optic patt., French Opalescent.......................................125.00

Model of an egg, pedestal base, Violets in the Snow decoration, ca. 1980 ....30.00

Novelty, top hat, Peach Crest, 4½" h...45.00

Pitcher, tankard, No. 8964, Hanging Heart patt., turquoise, 70 oz. ....150.00 to 175.00

Pitcher, ball-shaped w/ruffled rim, applied clear handle, Hobnail patt., cranberry opalescent, ca. 1948, 80 oz. 220.00

Plate, 8½" d., Silver Crest.......................30.00

Punch set: 10" d. bowl, underplate & eight punch cups; Hobnail patt., blue opalescent, 10 pcs. 500.00

Tidbit tray, three-tier, Ivory Crest, 6", 8½" & 13" d. 45.00

Vase, 4½" h., crimped rim, Hobnail patt., blue opalescent.........................20.00

Vase, 6" h., No. 7551, fan-shaped w/figural dolphin handles, Jade Green, ca. 1980 ....35.00

Vase, 12" h., swung-type, Hobnail patt., cranberry opalescent 145.00

Wine, Lincoln Inn patt., Jade Green 20.00

FINDLAY ONYX & FLORADINE

These wares were introduced by Dalzell, Gilmore & Leighton Co. of Findlay, Ohio, in January 1889. Onyx ware is a white-lined glass and was produced primarily in onyx (creamy yellowish-white) but also bronze and ruby, which are sometimes described as cinnamon, rose or raspberry. The raised flowers and leaves are silver colored or, less often, bronze. The Floradine line was made in ruby and autumn leaf (gold) with opalescent flowers and leaves and is not lined.

Findlay Onyx Celery Vase

Celery vase, creamy white w/silver flowers & leaves, 6½" h. (ILLUS.) ..$495.00

Creamer & cov. sugar bowl, creamy white w/silver flowers & leaves, pr. 1,050.00

Spooner, creamy white w/silver flowers & leaves, 4½" h. 425.00

Sugar shaker w/original top, creamy white w/silver flowers & leaves, 5½" h. ....450.00 to 475.00

Sugar shaker w/original top, unlined ruby w/white opalescent flowers & leaves 495.00

Tumbler, barrel-shaped, creamy white w/silver flowers & leaves, 2⅞" d., 3¾" h. 325.00

Tumbler, cylindrical, creamy white w/silver flowers & leaves, 3⅝" h. ....350.00 to 375.00

FOSTORIA

Fostoria Glass Company, founded in 1887, produced numerous types of fine glassware over the years. Their factory in Moundsville, West Virginia closed in 1986. Also see ANIMALS under Glass.

Ashtray, American patt., clear, 2⅞" d. ..$6.00

Ashtray, Coin patt., olive green 55.00

Bonbon, three-toed, American patt., clear 17.50

Bouillon cup, Fairfax patt., pink 10.00

Bouillon cup, footed, Versailles etching, blue 40.00

Bowl, 4" w., tri-cornered, Sylvan patt., clear w/gold trim 5.00

Bowl, 6¼" d., handled, Raleigh patt., Laurel cutting, clear 12.50

Bowl, 6½" d., three-footed, Chintz etching, clear 20.00

Bowl, 9¼" oval, Pioneer patt., green 22.00

Bowl, 10" d., Romance etching, clear...32.50

Bowl, 10½" d., three-footed, American patt., clear 22.00

Bowl, 11" d., flared rim, Colony patt., clear 32.00

Bowl, fruit, 12" d., footed, American patt., clear 185.00

Bowl, 12" d., three-footed, Oak Leaf etching, pink.......................................55.00

Bowl, 12" d., flared rim, Shirley etching, clear 48.00

Bowl, 12½" oval, 2⅞" h., Flame patt., Navarre etching, clear.........................50.00

Bowl, 13" l., oblong, Heirloom cutting, blue 45.00

Bowl, cream soup, w/underplate, Fairfax patt., blue 22.50

Butter dish, cov., American patt., clear, 1 lb. 175.00

Cake plate, two-handled, Baroque patt., Meadow Rose etching, clear, 10" d. 40.00

Cake plate, two-handled, Chintz etching, clear, 10" d. 40.00

Cake stand (or salver), American patt., clear, 10" sq., 7¼" h. 75.00

Candelabra w/prisms, Queen Anne patt., Everglades cutting, clear, pr. 200.00

Candlesticks, Baroque patt., Navarre etching, clear, pr. 50.00

Candlesticks, Shirley etching, clear, 5½" h., pr. 500.00

Candy box, cov., three-part, Meadow Rose etching, clear 80.00

Candy dish, cov., three-part, Chintz etching, clear 65.00

Candy jar, cov., urn-shaped, Coin patt., emerald green, 12½" h. 200.00

Celery dish, Baroque patt., yellow, 11¼" l. 25.00

Celery dish, handled, Sunray patt., clear, 10" l. 12.00

Celery dish, Wistar patt., clear, 9½" oval 22.00

Champagne, Chintz etching, clear 20.00

Champagne, Holly cutting, clear...........10.00

Cocktail, American patt., clear, 3½ oz. 14.00

Cocktail, Baroque patt., yellow, 3" h. 20.00

Cocktail, Colony patt., clear, 3½" oz.....12.50

Cocktail, Fairfax patt., pink 22.00

Cocktail, Holly cutting, clear, 5¼" h. 16.00

Compote, cov., jelly, 4½" d., 6¼" h., American patt., clear 25.00

Compote, 4", Sunray patt., clear..........18.00

Compote, 6½", Colony patt., clear........30.00

Compote, 8½", Coin patt., frosted ruby 75.00

Condiment bottle w/original stopper, American patt., clear 95.00

Console bowl, footed, Versailles etching, blue 40.00

Console set: bowl & pair of 3½" h. candlesticks; June etching, blue, 3 pcs. 145.00

Cordial, Chintz etching, clear, 1 oz.......55.00

Creamer, individual size, Baroque patt., blue 24.00

Creamer, footed, Fairfax patt., pink 10.00

Creamer & open sugar bowl, flared rim, footed, American patt., clear, pr. 16.00

Creamer & open sugar bowl, individual size, Baroque patt., blue, pr. 50.00

Cruet w/original stopper, Fairfax patt., pink 95.00

Cruet w/original stopper, Raleigh patt., clear 25.00

Cup & saucer, demitasse, Vernon etching, green 28.00

Cup & saucer, Baroque patt., clear 9.00

Cup & saucer, Fairfax patt., pink 11.00

Goblet, Acanthus etching, amber 30.00

Goblet, American patt., clear, 5½" h., 9 oz. 14.00

Goblet, Arcady etching, clear, 9 oz.......25.00

Goblet, Buttercup etching, clear, 10 oz. 22.00
Goblet, June etching, topaz 33.00

Lido Goblet

Goblet, Lido etching, clear, 12" h., 12 oz. (ILLUS.) 11.00
Goblet, Navarre etching, clear 28.00
Goblet, Queen Anne patt., clear, 10 oz. 18.00
Ice bucket w/metal tongs, Apple Blossom cutting, yellow 200.00
Ice bucket, Baroque patt., topaz 60.00
Marmalade jar, cov., handled, American patt., clear, 5½" 80.00
Mayonnaise bowl & underplate, Baroque patt., topaz, 2 pcs. 45.00
Mayonnaise bowl, underplate & ladle, Chintz etching, clear, 3 pcs. 47.50
Mayonnaise bowl, underplate & ladle, Romance etching, clear, 3 pcs. 55.00
Nut cup, footed, Fairfax patt., blue 20.00
Oyster cocktail, Beverly etching, amber 4.00
Oyster cocktails, Willowmere etching, clear, set of 4 ....24.00
Parfait, Fairfax patt., topaz, 7 oz. 10.00
Pitcher, 5" h., American patt., clear 20.00
Pitcher w/ice lip, 6½" h., footed, American patt., clear, 3 pt. 50.00
Pitcher w/ice lip, Colony patt., clear, 2 qt. 125.00
Plate, bread & butter, 6" d., Versailles etching, green 7.00
Plate, salad, 7" d., American patt., clear 10.00
Plate, 7" d., Mayflower etching, clear ...10.00
Plate, salad, 7½" d., Chintz etching, clear 14.00
Plate, salad, 7½" d., June etching, topaz 8.00
Plate, 8" d., Laurel cutting, clear 9.00
Plate, salad, 8½" d., American patt., clear 11.00
Plate, luncheon, 8½" d., Holly cutting, clear 12.00
Plate, luncheon, 8½" d., Meadow Rose etching, clear 15.00
Plate, dinner, 9" d., Colony patt., clear 17.50
Plate, dinner, 9½" d., Navarre etching, clear 40.00
Plate, dinner, 10" d., Seville patt., amber 20.00
Platter, 12" oval, Pioneer patt., green...22.00
Punch bowl & base, American patt., clear, 14" d. bowl, 2 pcs. 235.00
Punch set: punch bowl, base & ten cups; Coin patt., clear, 12 pcs. 525.00
Relish dish, two-part, Baroque patt., blue, 6½" l. 20.00
Relish dish, two-part, Holly cutting, clear, 8½" l. 25.00
Relish dish, boat-shaped, American patt., clear, 8½" l. 19.00
Relish dish, three-part, Fairfax patt., amber, 11½" l. 12.00
Relish dish, five-part, Navarre etching, clear, 13¼" l. 85.00
Salt & pepper shakers w/original tops, Baroque patt., topaz, pr. 90.00
Salt & pepper shakers w/original tops, Fairfax patt., pink, pr. 50.00
Sandwich server w/center handle, Chintz etching, clear, 12" d. 40.00
Sandwich server w/center handle, Colony patt., clear 29.00

American Iced Tea Tumbler

Sauceboat, Beverly etching, green.......55.00
Sauceboat & underplate, American patt., clear, 2 pcs. 45.00
Sauceboat & underplate, Fairfax patt., topaz, 2 pcs. 32.00
Sauceboat w/attached underplate, Pioneer patt., green 32.00
Sherbet, Coin patt., ruby........................50.00
Sherbet, Jamestown patt., green, 7 oz.. ....9.00
Sherbet, low, Laurel cutting, clear 10.00
Sherbet, Lido etching, clear, 6 oz. 7.00

Shrimp bowl, American patt., clear, 12¼" d. 325.00
Syrup pitcher w/original glass top & underplate, American patt., clear, 10 oz., 3 pcs. ....100.00 to 150.00
Toothpick holder, American patt., clear 35.00
Tumbler, whiskey, American patt., clear, 2 oz. 17.50
Tumbler, iced tea, footed, American patt., clear, 5½" h., 12 oz. (ILLUS previous page). 15.00
Tumbler, footed, Arcady etching, clear, 12 oz. 25.00
Tumbler, cocktail, Baroque patt., yellow, 3" h., 3½ oz. 10.00
Tumbler, footed, Colony patt., clear, 5¾" h., 12 oz. 9.00
Tumbler, water, Cynthia cutting, clear ..21.50
Tumbler, footed, Fairfax patt., blue, 6" h., 12 oz. 20.00
Tumbler, iced tea, Holly cutting, clear, 12 oz. 16.00
Tumbler, iced tea, Jamestown patt., clear 16.00
Tumbler, footed, Romance etching, clear, 6" h. 25.00
Tumbler, Versailles etching, green, 5¼" h., 9 oz. 25.00
Tumbler, iced tea, Wheat cutting, clear 15.00
Urn, cov., Coin patt., frosted emerald green, 12" h. 200.00
Vase, 8" h., Vesper etching, green 70.00
Vase, 10" h., flared rim, American patt., clear 48.00
Water set: pitcher & six tumblers; Rosby patt., clear, 7 pcs. 180.00
Water set: pitcher & six stemmed goblets; Vesper etching, green, 7 pcs. 375.00
Wine, Acanthus etching, amber 28.50
Wine, Holly cutting, clear 30.00
Wine, Lido etching, clear, 3 oz. 20.00
Wine, Navarre etching, clear 35.00

FRANCES WARE

Frances Ware Creamer

Frances Ware is the name of a decorative treatment for glass developed by Hobbs, Brockunier & Co., Wheeling, West Virginia, in the 1880s. It consists of decorating pieces with an amber-stained band around the rim and leaving the lower body in clear or frosted clear. This decoration was applied applied to Hobb's Hobnail pattern, their pattern No. 300 (Hobb's Block) or their swirled rib pattern, No. 326.

Butter dish, cov., frosted swirl w/amber rim $65.00
Creamer, frosted hobnail w/amber rim (ILLUS.) 60.00
Cruet w/original stopper, frosted hobnail w/amber rim 695.00
Finger bowl, frosted hobnail w/amber rim 25.00
Sauce dish, frosted hobnail w/amber rim 25.00
Spooner, frosted hobnail w/amber rim ..70.00
Syrup pitcher w/original top, frosted hobnail w/amber rim 350.00
Table set: cov. butter dish, cov. sugar bowl, creamer & spooner; frosted swirl w/amber rim, 4 pcs. 275.00
Toothpick holder, frosted hobnail w/amber rim 62.00
Tumbler, frosted hobnail w/amber rim ..45.00

FRY

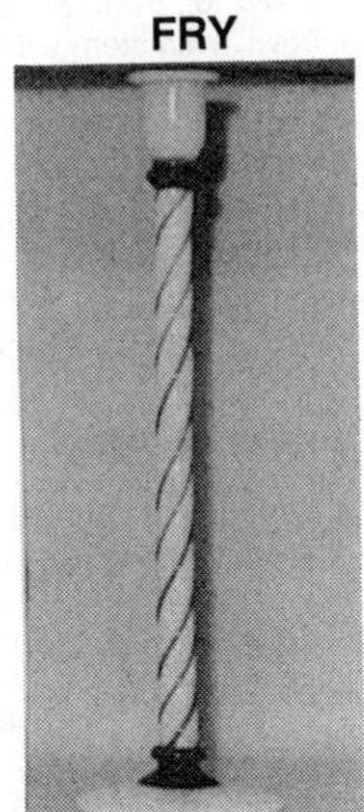

Fry Foval Candlestick

Numerous types of glass were made by the H.C. Fry Company, Rochester, Pennsylvania. One of its art lines was called Foval and was blown in 1926-27. Cheaper was its milky-opalescent ovenware (Pearl Oven Ware) made for utilitarian purposes but also now being collected. The company also made fine cut glass.

Collectors of Fry Glass will be interested in the recent publication of a good reference book, The Collector's Encyclopedia of Fry Glassware, *by The H.C. Fry Glass Society (Collector Books, 1990).*

Bell, Foval bell w/Delft blue handle & rim trim, 6½" h. $325.00

Bowl, 9¼" d., 5½" h., Foval, deep rounded & gently flaring white opal sides w/a jade green applied rim band & raised on a round applied jade green foot, No. 2504, w/a Fry company catalog No. 12, 2 pcs. 275.00

Bowl, 12" d., footed, Foval, w/applied Delft blue foot..................................285.00

Cake pan, Pearl Oven Ware, 9" d. 18.00

Candlesticks, Foval, bell-form socket above a blue connector to the twisted shaft wrapped w/a thin thread of blue, blue base connector to the round Foval foot, 16" h., pr. (ILLUS. of one) 495.00

Candlesticks, footed, clear & black striped decoration w/clear ball connector, pr. 500.00

Casserole dish, cov., Pearl Oven Ware, 8" d. 28.00

Coffeepot, cov., Foval w/applied jade green handle & finial on cover, 6½" h. 225.00

Compote, open, 6½" d., 9" h., Foval, Quilted patt. bowl, swirl stem w/open ring at the mid-point.........................350.00

Compote, open, 9" d., 5" h., Foval bowl w/Delft blue stem.....................235.00

Cup & saucer, Foval, applied green handle 59.00

Luncheon set: plate & goblet; Diamond Optic patt., clear w/black trim, 2 pcs. 150.00

Mug, iridescent green w/applied cobalt blue handle.............................35.00

Perfume bottle w/original turquoise stopper, Foval bulbous base............295.00

Pitcher, 9½" h., 5½" d., Diamond Optic patt., clear w/applied green handle 125.00

Platter, 9 x 12" oval, Foval, engraved w/flowers & ferns 65.00

Reamer, opaque green, embossed "F4/133/2/4" 30.00

Rose bowl, Foval w/three applied Delft blue feet.................................250.00

Vase, cov., 5" h., 7½" d., footed, Foval, sterling silver cover 299.00

Vase, 7½" h., Diamond Optic patt. (No. 2565), clear w/azure blue trim...150.00

Vase, 23" h., bulbous base tapering to a long pulled neck, clear w/applied black lines decoration 85.00

Wine, royal blue bowl w/clear twisted stem 20.00

GALLÉ

Gallé Enameled Bottle

Gallé glass was made in Nancy, France, by Emile Gallé, a founder of the Nancy School and a leader in the Art Nouveau movement in France. Much of his glass, both enameled and cameo, is decorated with naturalistic motifs. The finest pieces were made in the last two decades of the 19th century and the opening years of the present one. Pieces marked with a star preceding the name were made between 1904, the year of Gallé's death, and 1914.

Bottle w/original stopper, the wide flattened rectangular body w/a cylindrical neck at the top center fitted w/a flattened mushroom stopper, the body finely etched w/a cartouche reserve of a warrior on horseback against a gilt ground, the reverse w/a reserve of seated figures against a gilt ground, the ground elaborately etched w/Islamic-inspired foliate designs & further enameled inblack, white & red, 4½" h. $12,650.00

Bottle w/original stopper, flattened bulbous form w/bifurcated rim, the swirled celadon green body enameled en grisaille to depict an isolated lake scene w/architectural remains, framed by a curving branch in sienna & umber interspersed w/finely enameled shells in high relief, fitted w/a large tapered stopper decorated w/seaweed & a shell, all heightened w/gilding, enameled "CRISTALLERIE D'EMILE MODELE ET DECOR DEPOSES NANCY" & w/the maker's monogram, 9¼" h. (ILLUS. previous page) 23,000.00

Bowl, 4¾" h., clear deep rounded sides of shielf-form outline, composed of scalloped panels decorated w/hunting vignettes in gilt, carved w/scrolling vines & stylized floral designs, the border w/a shield diaper pattern trimmed w/burgundy & black enamel,enameled "Emile Gallé a Nancy" 2,875.00

Cameo bowl, 10" d., the bulbous opalescent body internally decorated w/olive green splashes, overlaid in rose & cut w/magnolia blossoms & leafage, the ground w/martelé, signed in cameo "Cristallerie - de Gallé - Nancy," ca. 1900 ....3,300.00

Cameo box, cov., wide & slightly tapering cylindrical sides, fitted w/a low, domed cover, frosted clear overlaid w/amethyst, the cover cut w/a dragonfly, the sides of the base cut w/a continuous leaf & berry design, cameo signature on base & cover, 2½" h. 1,045.00

Cameo compote, open, 8" h., conical w/incurvate rim, raised on a slender standard & circular foot, grey mottled w/pale tangerine, overlaid in lime green & dark amber & cut w/a pattern of vining hops & foliage, signed in cameo"Gallé," ca. 1900 ....2,645.00

Cameo lamp, table-top, the semi-spherical shade & bulbous ovoid base each w/a yellow & white frosted ground overlaid w/purplish blue& cut to represent flowering chrysanthemums, cameo signature on shade & base, shade 8¾" d., overall 12⅝" h. 20,700.00

Cameo vase, 4⅞" h., the double conical vessel w/short rolled lip w/grey sides shading to rich lemon yellow, internally decorated w/sea green & turquoise trailings suggesting algae, overlaid in amber, ochre & rich deep pumpkin & finely wheel-carved w/a Portuguese man-o-war, a starfish, sea grasses & other underwater vegetation, the sides partially martelé, signed in intaglio "Gallé," ca. 1900............10,350.00

Cameo vase, 6" h., spherical body tapering to a short, flared neck, clear frosted ground overlaid in lime green & umber, cut to depict a serene wooded lake scene, cameo signature 1,725.00

GOOFUS

This is a name collectors have given a pressed glass whose colors were sprayed on and then fired. Most pieces have intaglio or convex back designs. Several American glass companies, including Northwood Glass Co., produced this style ware early in the 20th century.

Bowl, 10¾" d., shallow, relief-molded red roses on gold $39.00

Bread tray, relief-molded Last Supper scene 50.00

Plate, 5¾" d., relief-molded rose & lattice decoration in red & gold 17.50

Plate, 7" d., relief-molded red on gold thistle design, advertising, molded into design "Henry Baack" 125.00

Vase, 7½" h., relief-molded red grapes on gold 20.00

Wall pocket, relief-molded bird & grapes decoration, 7¾" 55.00

GREENTOWN

Greentown glass was made in Greentown Indiana, by the Indiana Tumbler & Goblet Co. from 1894 until 1903. In addition to its famed Chocolate and Holly Amber glass, which see, it produced other types of clear and colored glass. Miscellaneous pieces are listed here. Also see PATTERN GLASS.

Animal covered dish, rabbit, teal blue $185.00

Butter dish, cov., Holly patt., clear ....150.00 to 200.00

Cake stand, Austrian patt., clear 110.00

Compote, open, Austrian patt., clear, 8 x 8" 65.00

Cordial, Austrian patt., clear 75.00

Cordial, Shuttle patt., clear 25.00

Creamer, child size, Austrian patt., canary, 2⅛" d., 3¼" h. 90.00

Cruet w/original stopper, Cord Drapery patt., clear 115.00

Mug, Indoor Drinking Scene, clear 45.00

Mug, Outdoor Drinking Scene, Nile green...85.00

Mug, Serenade (Troubador), amber, 4¾" h. 95.00

Nappy, cov., handled, Austrian patt., clear 20.00

Novelty, model of a dustpan, amber.....75.00

Novelty, model of a dustpan, blue (little roughness) 55.00

Pitcher, water, Fleur-de-lis patt.............35.00

Pitcher, water, Squirrel patt., clear 225.00
Sauce dish, footed, Herringbone Buttress patt., emerald green 85.00
Spooner, child's, Austrian patt., clear ...55.00
Toothpick holder, Holly patt., clear 85.00
Tumbler, Brazen Shield patt., cobalt blue 55.00
Vase, 6" h., Herringbone Buttress patt., emerald green....175.00
Vegetable bowl, Cord Drapery patt., clear, 7½" l. 25.00
Wine, No. 11 patt., clear 12.00

HEISEY

Numerous types of fine glass were made by A.H. Heisey & Co., Newark, Ohio, from 1895. The company's trade-mark -- an H enclosed within a diamond -- has become known to most glass collectors. The company's name and molds were acquired by Imperial Glass Co., Bellaire, Ohio, in 1958, and some pieces have been reissued. The glass listed below consists of miscellaneous pieces and types. Also see ANIMALS and PATTERN GLASS under Glass.

Ashtray, Empress patt., Sahara (yellow) $100.00
Banana split dish, footed, Greek Key patt., clear....33.00
Basket, Empress patt., Flamingo (pink), 7" h....475.00
Bowl, 11" d., footed, Empress patt., Zircon (blue-green) 795.00
Butter dish, cov., Lariat patt.,clear....125.00
Cake salver, Plantation patt., clear, 13"....135.00
Cake stand, Waverly patt., Orchid etching, clear, 12" 175.00
Candelabra, Old Williamsburg patt., Sahara, 20½" h., pr. 1,200.00
Candlesticks, Oak Leaf patt., pink frosted, pr....150.00
Candlesticks, Old Williamsburg patt., Sahara, 12" h., pr. 340.00
Candlesticks, two-light, Waverly patt., Orchid etching, clear, pr....100.00
Candy dish, cov., w/seahorse handles, Waverly patt., Rose etching, clear 187.00
Celery tray, oval, coarse Rib patt., clear, 9" l. 25.00
Champagne, Rose etching, clear 37.50
Champagne, Spanish patt., cobalt blue bowl w/clear stem, 5½ oz....85.00
Champagne, saucer-type, Spanish patt., Killarney cutting, clear....25.00
Champagne, saucer-type, Victorian patt., clear 12.50
Chip & dip set, Greek Key patt., clear, 2 pcs. 195.00
Cigarette box, cov., w/small horsehead finial, Puritan patt., No. 1489, clear 65.00
Cocktail shaker, cov., Orchid etching, clear, sterling silver top & base....160.00
Compote, jelly, 6¾" h., Rose etching, clear 40.00
Console set: bowl & pair of candle vases w/prisms & inserts; Ipswich patt., clear, bowl 11½" d., 5" h., 3 pcs. 375.00
Cordial, Carcassone patt., Old Colony etching, Sahara 145.00
Cordial, Lariat patt., w/Moonglo cutting, clear 110.00
Creamer & sugar bowl, Crystolite patt., clear, pr. 30.00
Creamer & sugar bowl, Petal patt., Moongleam (green), pr. 65.00
Cruet w/original stopper, Lariat patt., clear 125.00
Cruet w/original stopper, Pleat & Panel patt., Flamingo....75.00
Crushed fruit jar, cov., Greek Key patt., clear 335.00
Cup & saucer, Orchid etching,clear....49.50
Decanter w/original stopper, Coronation patt., clear 65.00
Domino sugar tray, Narrow Flute patt., Moongleam 60.00
Goblet, Carcassonne patt., Sahara, 9 oz. 35.00
Goblet, King Arthur patt., Moongleam 42.00
Ice bucket, Minuet etching, clear....150.00
Lamps, hurricane-type, Plantation patt., clear, 15" h., pr....675.00
Lemon dish, cov., w/dolphin finial, Queen Anne patt., clear, Farberware holder 70.00
Luncheon set: four cups & plates & dolphin-footed creamer & sugar bowl; Empress patt., Sahara, 10 pcs. 195.00
Marmalade jar, cov., Crystolite patt., clear, 6" h. 38.00
Mugs, Pineapple & Fan patt., emerald green, set of 3....80.00
Mustard jar, cov., Crystolite patt., clear 20.00
Mustard jar, cov., Twist patt., Flamingo 60.00
Nut cup, Empress patt., Flamingo 28.00
Nut dish, individual, footed, Colonial patt., clear 10.00
Oyster cocktail, Victorian patt. (No. 1425) clear, 5 oz. 11.00
Parfait, Old Glory patt., clear 27.50

Pitcher, Prince of Wales Plumes patt., clear w/gold trim, ca. 1890s 250.00

Heisey Puritan Pitcher

Pitcher, water, Puritan patt., clear, 3 qt. (ILLUS.) 115.00

Plate, 6" d., handled, Crystolite patt., clear 10.00

Plate, 6" d., Empress patt., Hawthorne (pale purple)......................................27.00

Plate, torte, 12" d., rolled rim, Lariat patt., clear 28.00

Plate, 13" d., Ridgeleigh patt., clear 32.00

Platter, 14" oval, Empress patt., Sahara 90.00

Pretzel jar, cov., etched Fisherman patt. 695.00

Punch cup, Victorian patt., clear...........12.00

Punch bowl & base, Greek Key patt., clear, 2 pcs. ....350.00 to 450.00

Relish dish, Crystolite patt., clear, 6" oval 20.00

Relish dish, three-part, Lariat patt., 10" l. 35.00

Salt shaker w/original top, Winged Scroll patt., green w/gold trim, early 20th c. 72.50

Salt & pepper shakers w/original tops, Empress patt., Sahara, pr. 135.00

Spooner w/underplate, Rhombic patt. (No. 365), clear, 2 pcs. 40.00

Syrup pitcher w/original top, Beaded Swag patt., milk white, early 20th c. 160.00

Toothpick holder, Beaded Swag patt., milk white w/floral decoration, early 20th c. 85.00

Tumbler, iced tea, footed, Rose etching, clear, 12 oz..........................40.00

Vase, 4" h., spherical, Empress patt. Sahara 145.00

Vase, 7" h., fan-shaped, Pineapple & Fan patt., emerald green w/gold trim, early 20th c. 30.00

Wine, Minuet etching, clear, 2½ oz. 35.00

Wine, Spanish patt., cobalt blue 200.00

HISTORICAL & COMMEMORATIVE

Admiral Dewey Covered Dish

Reference numbers are to Bessie M. Lindsey's book, American Historical Glass. *Also see MILK WHITE GLASS.*

Battleship Maine dish, cov., milk white, 7¼" l., No. 466 ....$95.00

Bryan (William J.) cup, cov., bust portrait of Bryan, "The People's Money" above, clear, overall 5" h., No. 336 ....67.00

Bunker Hill platter, "Prescott 1776 Stark-Warren 1876 Putnam," clear, 9 x 13½", No. 44 ....80.00 to 90.00

Civil War liquor glass, shield, flag w/thirty-five stars, inscribed "A Bumper to the Flag," 3½" h., No. 480 ....115.00

Columbia bread tray, shield-shaped, Columbia super-imposed against 13 vertical bars, amber, 11½ x 9½", No. 54 ....165.00

Columbus mugs, bust portraits of Columbus & George Washington, inscribed on base, "World's Columbian Exposition, 1893," clear, 2½" d., No. 2 ....80.00

Dewey (Admiral) dish, cov., ribbed base, amber, No. 387 ....230.00

Dewey (Admiral) dish, cov., tile base, milk white, 6¾" l., 4½" h., No. 390 (ILLUS.) 65.00

Emblem butter dish, cov., bullet finial, clear, No. 64 ....215.00

Emblem Tall Eagle jar, cov., model of an eagle w/eagle head cover, American shield at front base under a banner w/"E Pluribus Unum," milk white, 6¾" h., No. 55.......................195.00

Garfield cup plate, flaring rim, clear, 3" d., No. 297 ....100.00 to 125.00

Grant Peace plate, bust portrait of Grant center, maple leaf border, vaseline, 10½" d., No. 289 ....90.00

Harrison-Morton tray, bust portraits w/stippled ivy leaf border, clear, 8½ x 9½", No. 324 ....250.00 to 275.00

Indian match holder, milk white, 2¾" h., No. 12 ....65.00

Indian Chief plate, bust portrait of Indian center, milk white, 7½" d. 60.00

Kitchen stove dish, cov., amber, 4½ x 6¾", 4½" h., No. 149 ....300.00

Knights of Labor platter, amber, 11¾" l., No. 512 ....180.00 to 200.00

Liberty Bell plate, closed handles, scalloped rim w/thirteen original states & "100 Years Ago," clear, 8" d., No. 37 ....85.00

Louisiana Purchase Exposition plate, inscribed "World's Fair St. Louis, 1904," forget-me-not & openwork border, clear, 7¼" d., No. 105 ....17.50

Martyr's Mug

Martyr's mug, Lincoln & Garfield bust portraits & inscription, clear, 2⅝" h., No. 272 (ILLUS.) 100.00

McKinley Memorial platter, "It's God's Way" etc., clear, 8 x 10½", No. 356 ...60.00

Moses in the Bulrushes dish, cov., lid w/full figure of an infant, base w/design resembling rushes, milk white, 4" w., 5½" l., No. 214 ....90.00

Old Abe (eagle) compote, cov., clear, No. 478 ....130.00

Old Glory plate, Betsy Ross making first flag pictured in center, clear, 5½" d., No. 52 ....38.00

Old Statehouse tray, shows Independence Hall above "Old Statehouse, Philadelphia, Erected 1735," amber, No. 32 ....55.00

Railroad train platter, Union Pacific Engine No. 350, amber, 9 x 12", No. 134 ....225.00

Rock of Ages bread tray, clear, No. 236 ....85.00

Rock of Ages bread tray, clear w/translucent deep blue center, No. 236 ....165.00

Rock of Ages bread tray, clear w/milk white center, No. 236 ....155.00

Roosevelt (Theodore) platter, frosted portrait center, Teddy bears, etc. border, clear, 7¾ x 10¼", No. 357 ...175.00

Ruth statuette, Ruth shown as gleaner resting on one knee w/wisps of grain in each hand, "Gillender & Sons, Centennial Exhibition" inscribed on base, satin finish, clear, 4½" h., No. 216 ....75.00 to 100.00

Three Presidents platter, bust portraits of Garfield, Washington & Lincoln, inscribed "In Remembrance," clear, 10 x 12½", No. 249 ....70.00

Washington Centennial patt. platter w/bear paw handles, frosted center, "First in War," etc., clear, 8½ x 12", No. 27 ....130.00

Washington Bi-Centennial bottle, oval portrait medallion of Washington front & American eagle w/olive branches & thunderbolts in oval medallion reverse, "1732-1932," clear, qt., No. 262 ....22.50

Washington Monument paperweight, milk white, 2¾" sq. base, 5½" h., No. 255 ....175.00

Whisk broom dish, Daisy & Button patt. below handle, amber, 5" w., 7½" l. 65.00

HOLLY AMBER

Holly Amber Toothpick Holder

Holly Amber, originally marketed under the name "Golden Agate," was produced for only a few months in 1903 by the Indiana Tumbler and Goblet Company of Greentown, Indiana. When this factory burned in June 1903 all production of this ware ceased, making it very rare today. The same "Holly" pressed pattern was also produced in clear glass by the Greentown factory. Collectors should note that the St.

Clair Glass Company has reproduced some Holly Amber pieces.

Butter dish, cov. $1,500.00
Spooner, base 2⅝" d., top 3½" d., 4" h. 625.00
Toothpick holder (ILLUS.)...600.00 to 650.00
Tumbler ....350.00 to 375.00
Vase, 6" h., footed 485.00

IMPERIAL

Imperial Glass Company, Bellaire, Ohio, was organized in 1901 and was in continuous production, except for very brief periods, until its closing in June 1984. It had been a major producer of Carnival Glass (which see) earlier in this century and also produced other types of glass, including an Art Glass line called "Free Hand Ware" during the 1920s and its "Jewels" about 1916. The company acquired a number of molds of other earlier factories, including the Cambridge and A.H. Heisey companies, and reissued numerous items through the years. Also see ANIMALS under glass.

CANDLEWICK PATTERN

Ashtray, heart-shaped, No. 400/172, clear, 4½" $10.00
Basket, No. 400/173, clear, 5" h. 250.00
Bonbon dish, heart-shaped, No. 51H, clear w/gold trim, 6" w. 15.00
Candleholders, three-light, No. 400/115, clear, pr. 55.00
Candy box, cov., No. 400/59, clear, 5½" d. 45.00
Compote, 8", No. 400/48F, clear 75.00
Cordial, No. 3400, clear 35.00
Cruet w/original stopper, applied handle, No. 400/279, clear, 6 oz. 40.00
Cup & saucer, clear 11.50
Plate, bread & butter, 6" d., No. 400/1D, clear 6.50
Plate, salad, 7" d., 400/3D, clear 7.00
Punch bowl & underplate, 13" d. bowl No. 400/20B & 17" d. underplate No. 400/20V, clear, 2 pcs. 95.00
Relish dish, five-part, No. 400/209, clear, 13½" d. 65.00
Strawberry set: 7" d. plate & sugar dip bowl; No. 400/83, clear, 2 pcs. 55.00
Teacup & saucer, mallard cutting, No. 400/35, clear 15.00
Tumbler, juice, No. 400/19, clear, 5 oz. 12.00
Water set: 80 oz. pitcher No. 400/24 & six 12 oz. tumblers No. 400/19; clear, 7 pcs. 250.00

CAPE COD PATTERN

Bowl, cream soup, 5½", tab-handled, No. 160/198, clear 38.00
Bowl, 10" d., footed, No. 160/137B, clear 50.00
Candleholder, Aladdin style, No. 160/90, clear, 4" h. 125.00
Candleholders, two-light, No. 160/100, clear, pr. 100.00
Egg cup, No. 160/225, clear 15.00
Epergne, plain center, No. 160/196, clear, 2 pcs. 175.00
Plate, dinner, 10" d., No. 160/10D, clear 33.00
Salt & pepper shakers w/original tops, cobalt blue, pr. 90.00
Tom & Jerry punch bowl, footed, No. 160/200, clear 275.00

FREE HAND WARE

Graceful Free Hand Vase

Vase, 7" h., iridescent orange w/dark threading 165.00
Vase, 7⅜" h., 3½" d., cushion footed baluster-form w/flared rim, overall white decoration on butterfly blue iridescent ground, ca. 1924 ....350.00
Vase, 9¾" h., iridescent orange over opaque white 50.00
Vase, 10" h., baluster-form w/flaring foot & rim, opaque white heart & vine decoration on a translucent cobalt blue ground 495.00
Vase, 10" h., iridescent yellow orange exterior, blue interior 125.00
Vase, 11½" h., footed slender body w/rounded shoulders & expanded tooled trefoil rim, dark iridescent body decorated w/orange hearts & vines (ILLUS.) 660.00

MISCELLANEOUS PATTERNS & LINES

Animal covered dish, lion on lacy base, caramel slag 135.00

Animal covered dish, rooster on lacy base, jade green 135.00
Animal covered dish, rooster on lacy base, purple slag 175.00
Bowl, 9" d., Rose patt., red slag 65.00
Compote, cov., Frosted Panels patt., Rubigold 60.00
Vase, 8½" h., model of a dancing lady, red slag 98.00
Water set: pitcher & four tumblers; Frosted Panels patt., Rubigold, 5 pcs. 175.00

IOWA CITY GLASS

This ware, made by the Iowa City Glass Manufacturing Co., Iowa City, Iowa, from 1880 to about 1883, was produced in many shapes and patterns. The Frosted Stork pattern and pieces decorated with mottos and various animals are probably best known among collectors.

Goblet, Deer & Doe patt., clear $200.00
Goblet, Clear Stork patt. 150.00
Pickle castor, cov., Frosted Stork patt. 95.00
Plate, "Elaine," swan border 95.00
Platter, oval, "Be Industrious," clear beehive center, deer border 50.00
Platter, oval, "Be Industrious," clear beehive center, 1-0-1 border, 8 x 11½" 125.00
Platter, oval, Frosted Stork patt., 1-0-1 border, 8 x 11½" 58.00

JACK-IN-THE-PULPIT VASES

Maroon Opalescent Vase

Glass vases in varying sizes and resembling in appearance the flower of this name have been popular with collectors since the 19th century. They were produced in various solid colors and in shaded wares.

Cased, white exterior, shaded green interior, bulbous body w/applied clear petal-shaped feet, 5½" d., 6¼" h. $110.00
Cased, white exterior, shaded pink interior, swirling ruffled rim, 6½" d., 6½" h. 110.00
Chartreuse green opalescent, trumpet-form w/crimped rim, 4½" d., 7¼" h. 65.00
Maroon opalescent shaded to vaseline, trumpet-form w/ruffled rim 4¼" d., 7¼" h. (ILLUS.) 75.00
Orange shaded to vaseline, embossed ribbed bulbous base, applied vaseline leaf shaped feet, 3" d., 5½" h. 125.00
Spatter, tapering cylindrical body, green, white & pink spatter interior, green exterior w/diamond quilted design, 4¼" d., 6¾" h. 95.00
White opalescent w/applied ruffled green edging, 4½" h. 45.00

KELVA

Kelva was made early in this century by the C.F. Monroe Co., Meriden, Connecticut, and was a type of decorated opal glass very like the same company's Wave Crest and Nakara wares. This type of glass was produced until about the time of the first World War. Also see NAKARA and WAVE CREST.

Box w/hinged lid, Hexagonal mold, lid decorated w/a yellow rose on a mottled green ground, 3¾" d., 2½" h. $590.00
Box w/hinged lid, Octagonal mold, lip enameled w/pink & white flowers on a mottled green ground, 4" w., 3¾" h. 325.00
Box w/hinged lid, lid decorated w/white flowers & green leaves on a mottled rose ground, 4½" d., 2½" h. 425.00
Box w/hinged lid, lid decorated w/pink flowers on a mottled bluish grey ground, mirror inside the lid, 4½" d. 515.00
Humidor w/hinged cover, mottled blue ground, "Cigars" in gold across the front, 5" d. 795.00

Jewelry dish, dainty pink flowers on a mottled green ground, ornate ormolu handles & rim, signed, overall 4½" w 185.00

LACY

Large Lacy Dish

Lacy Glass is a general term developed by collectors many years ago to cover the earliest type of pressed glass produced in this country. "Lacy" refers to the fact that most of these early patterns consisted of scrolls and geometric designs against a finely stippled background which gives the glass the look of fine lace. Formerly this glass was often referred to as "Sandwich" for the Boston & Sandwich Glass Company of Sandwich, Massachusetts which produced a great deal of this ware. Today, however, collectors realize that many other factories on the East Coast and in the Pittsburgh, Pennsylvania and Wheeling, West Virginia areas also made lacy glass from the 1820s into the 1840s. All pieces listed are clear unless otherwise noted. Numbers after salt dips refer to listings in Pressed Glass Salt Dishes of the Lacy Period, 1825-1850, by Logan W. and Dorothy B. Neal. Also see SANDWICH GLASS.

Bowl, 5⅛" d., 1" h., round w/shallow sides and small rim scallops, starburst in center, hairpin border design, clear (several scallops tipped, mold roughness) $33.00

Bowl, cov., 7⅛" d., 5½" h., round flaring sides w/a galleried rim supporting a domed cover w/flora-form finial, a band of Roman arches & thistles around the sides, clear, Boston & Sandwich, ca. 1840 (one scallop slightly disfigured w/chip, two shallow spalls on top of rim)....................................715.00

Butter dish, cov., Roman Rosette patt., probably Pittsburgh, clear, 6½" d., 4" h. (one rim chip, overall scallop tipping) 495.00

Candlestick, a lacy Peacock Eye socket attached by multiple wafers to a plain square stepped base, 5¹¹⁄₁₆" h. (some corners w/shallow chips, others w/usual roughness) 1,100.00

Compote, open 6" d., 3¾" h., round w/deeply scalloped rim, Pine Tree & Shield patt., on applied short pedestal & plain round foot, clear (base appears to be lightly polished) 357.50

Dish, miniature, oval, scroll design, scalloped rim, clear, 2⅞" l. (minor chips) 60.50

Dish, round w/shallow sides, Princess Feather & Snail Shell design, attributed to New England, roughness, clear, 9¼" d., (ILLUS.) 385.00

Lamp, whale oil table-type, free-blown spherical font w/top opening tapering to a knopped stem applied w/a wide wafer to a pressed lacy Hairpin patt. foot, clear, Midwestern, ca. 1830, 7¼" h. 1,870.00

Pitcher & bowl set, miniature, each piece w/tiny flowers against a stippled ground, ca. 1840, clear, bowl 3¼" d., pitcher 2½" h., 2 pcs. (chips) 181.50

Plate, 5¼" d., round w/gently scalloped rim, Rose & Thistle patt., clear (light tipping on several scallops)...77.00

Salt dip, flaring casket-form on a flaring base, shell design on sides, reddish amethyst, probably Boston & Sandwich (SL 1) 715.00

Salt dip, cov., sleigh-shaped w/scrolled sides & feet, domed cover w/knob finial, clear, probably Boston & Sandwich, CD 2a (refracting small bubble on rim, some severe mold roughness on base & cover)............................412.50

Sugar bowl, cov., Gothic Arch patt., petal foot, peacock blue, ca. 1840, 5¾" h. (tiny spall on base rim, multiple flakes on circular disk under lid finial) 1,045.00

Tray, oblong, an overall design of delicate scrolls w/shell-form fans at the ends & a curved diamond in the center all on a finely stippled ground, attributed to Boston & Sandwich, clear, 7⅞ x 11⅝" (one scallop missing, another chipped) 1,100.00

Tureen, cover & undertray, miniature, oval, raised scroll designs on a stippled ground, clear, ca. 1840, 3" l., 3 pcs. (chips) 126.50

LALIQUE

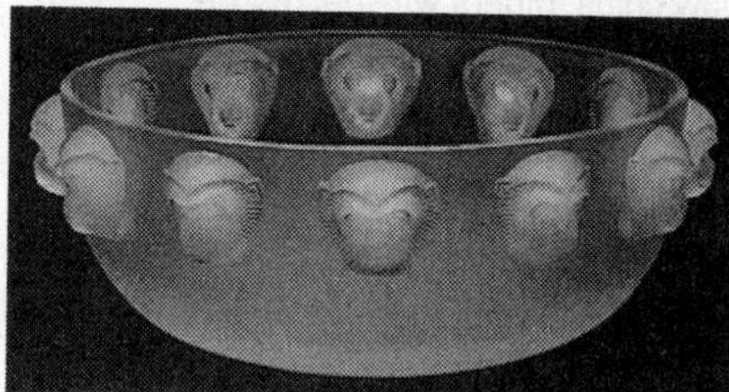

Lalique "Madagascar" Bowl

Fine glass, which includes numerous extraordinary molded articles, has been made by the glasshouse established by René Lalique early in this century in France. The firm was carried on by his son, Marc, until his death in 1977 and is now headed by Marc's daughter, Marie-Claude. All Lalique glass is marked, usually on, or near, the bottom with either an engraved or molded signature. Unless otherwise noted, we list only those pieces marked "R. Lalique" produced before the death of René Lalique in 1945.

Ashtray, "Feuilles," oval w/circular recessed cavetto in brilliant cobalt blue molded in low-relief w/leaves, inscribed "R. Lalique," introduced in 1928, 6⅞" l. $1,870.00

Bar pin, "Barrette Aubepines," a narrow rectangle of frosted clear molded in low-relief w/flowering stems, backed w/pale teal foil, brass backing w/a pin, stamped "LALIQUE" & w/artist's monogram, 2¾" l. 1,725.00

Bowl, 12½" d., "Muguet," flared sides molded w/lily-of-the-valley blossoms radiating from the center, stamped mark "R. LALIQUE FRANCE," opalescent w/blue patina 1,265.00

Bowl, 13" d., 4¾" h., deep rounded sides molded around the rim w/twelve monkey faces, opalescent, molded mark on rim "R. Lalique France" (ILLUS.) 6,875.00

Box, cov., "Veronique," the cover molded in low-relief w/two ribbon-tied bouquets, black, molded "R. LALIQUE," inscribed "France," introduced in 1919, 3⅛" d. 1,760.00

Clock, "Deux Colombes," the arched case molded in relief w/a pair of birds & flowers, opalescent, 9½" h. 3,960.00

Clock, "Naiades," the square frosted opalescent body molded in low-relief w/six swimming mermaids centered by a circular clock face, molded "R. LALIQUE," introduced1926, 4⅜" w., 4½" h. 3,450.00

Cordial set: a conical decanter w/a tall, slender neck & four-petal stopper & two slender cylindrical cordial tumblers; "Six Figurines," each piece in clear molded in relief w/narrow panels enclosing diaphanously-draped maidens w/brown patina in the recessed areas, decanter molded "R. LALIQUE," cordials engraved "R. Lalique - France," decanter 14" h., the set 3,850.00

Decanter w/original pointed spire stopper, "Sirenes et Grenouilles," bulbous body tapering to a slender tapering neck w/a flared rim, molded w/elongated panels of sinuous nudes amid surf w/frogs alternating w/wider ribbed panels, figural panels w/dark staining, engraving "R. Lalique France," 15½" h. 6,600.00

Vase, 4⅞" h., "Rennes," flaring ovoid body in frosted clear molded w/a frieze of stylized antelope, w/a frosted background of leafy foliage, acid-stamped "LALIQUE FRANCE" 403.00

Vase, 5⅛" h., "Moissac," the clear opalescent tapering conical body molded in high-relief w/vertical band of ribbed leaves, inscribed "R. LALIQUE FRANCE" 1,725.00

LIBBEY

In 1878, William L. Libbey obtained a lease on the New England Glass Company of Cambridge, Massachusetts, changing the name to the New England Glass Works, W.L. Libbey and Son, Proprietors. After his death in 1883, his son, Edward D. Libbey, continued to operate the company at Cambridge until 1888 when the factory was closed. Edward Libbey moved to Toledo, Ohio, and set up the company subsequently known as Libbey Glass Co. During the 1880s, the firm's master technician, Joseph Locke, developed the now much desired colored art glass lines of Agata, Amberina, Peach Blow and Pomona. Renowned for its Cut Glass of the Brilliant Period (see CUT GLASS*), the company continues in operation today as Libbey Glassware, a division of Owens-Illinois, Inc.*

Bowl, 2½" w., 5½" l., Amberina, rectangular, embossed vertical ribbing $285.00

Bowl, 6" d., 4" h., Amberina, paneled optic design w/ruffled rim, signed 595.00

Bowl, 6" d., Peking patt., pink, scalloped edge, Libbey-Nash series 100.00

Cocktail, Silhouette patt., clear bowl, frosted figural bear stem 75.00

Compote, open, 7½" d., 3¼" h., Amberina, a flattened & widely flaring rim on a rounded bowl raised on a short knop stem w/a round foot, marked "Amberina" & "Libbey" in a circle, ca. 1917...............................440.00

Libbey Silhouette Compote

Compote, open, 11" d., 7½" h., Silhouette patt., wide crystal bowl on an opalescent figural elephant stem, signed (ILLUS.)...............................385.00

Goblet, Silhouette patt., clear bowl, opalescent figural monkey stem, Libbey-Nash series 145.00

Maize salt shaker w/original top, condiment size, creamy opaque 95.00

Maize sugar shaker w/original top, creamy opaque w/blue husks 170.00

Maize tumbler, creamy opaque w/green husks trimmed in gold 135.00

Sherbet, Silhouette patt., clear bowl, black figural squirrel stem, signed, 4" h...145.00

Vases, 8" h., clear pedestal base, white opal ground w/pink pulled feather design, signed in pontil, pr...595.00

LOETZ

Unusual Loetz Bowl

Iridescent glass, some of it somewhat resembling that of Tiffany and other contemporary glasshouses, was produced by the Bohemian firm of J. Loetz Witwe of Klostermule and is referred to as Loetz. Some cameo pieces were also made. Not all pieces are marked.

Basket, applied clear handle, iridescent green, signed, 9½" d., 17½" h...$385.00

Bowl, 5½" h., the orange body w/rumpled rim set within an applied leaf-shaped iridescent blue base (ILLUS.) 1,150.00

Bowl, 10" d., 5½" h., yellow iridescent top portion w/flat flaring rim above a low-footed black base w/heavy blue mottled overlay forming a wavy border at midsection, design attributed to Dagobert Peche........3,500.00

Centerpiece, model of a large conch shell raised on a ruffled foot, gold decorated w/an iridescent oil spot design, 5½" h. 1,265.00

Ewer, the tall slender, curved neck pulled into a long peaked spout opposite a pulled strap handle, the wide squatty body w/a compressed shoulder, deep cobalt blue textured as elephant skin on the lower body & decorated w/silver iridescent spots, engraved "Loetz Austria," 10½" h...4,830.00

Garniture set: cov. box & pair of vases; footed vases w/black lower half & pink top, the compressed globular box w/black bottom section & pink top w/black ball finial, decorated w/black & white enameled designs, designed by Dagobert Peche, ca. 1916, box 5" h., vases 8⅛" h., 3 pcs. 1,725.00

Vase, 4" h., rounded shoulder, low wide neck, amber w/vertically arranged threading, applied rim & applied gold iridescent full-form fruits, leaves & stems......................467.50

Vase, 6" h., ovoid body tapering toward the everted & ruffled rim, the shoulder & neck deeply pinched, the gold iridescent ground decorated w/small circles interspersed w/large ruby red spots containing concentric rings, decoration attributed to Koloman Moser, ca. 1902............7,700.00

Vase, 8⅞" h., ovoid body tapering to a bulbous neck w/flaring rim, the lower body decorated w/raised upward-pulled "fork" devices in a row, the upper body & neck w/lime green iridescence, the lower raised designs in blue iridescence...........2,090.00

Vase, 13½" h., jack-in-the-pulpit type, free-blown floriform decorated w/striated gold amber pulled feather decoration w/gold & blue iridescent surface..1,430.00

MARY GREGORY

Small Mary Gregory Vase

Glass enameled in white with silhouette-type figures, primarily children, is now termed "Mary Gregory" and was attributed to the Boston and Sandwich Glass Company. However, recent research has proven conclusively that this ware was not decorated by Mary Gregory nor was it made at the Sandwich factory. Miss Gregory was employed by the Boston and Sandwich Glass Company as a decorator, however, records show her assignment was the painting of naturalistic landscape scenes on larger items such as lamps and shades but never the charming children for which her name has become synonymous. Further, in the inspection of fragments from the factory site, no paintings of children were found.

It is now known that all wares now called "Mary Gregory" originated in Bohemia beginning in the late 19th century and were extensively exported to England and the U.S. well into this century.

For further information see The Glass Industry in Sandwich, Volume 4, *by Raymond E. Barlow and Joan E. Kaiser, and the new book,* Mary Gregory Glassware, 1880-1990, *by R. & D. Truitt.*

Apothecary jar, cov., cranberry, white enameled girl gathering flowers w/a basket of flowers at her feet, ornate cover w/pointed finial, 16" h. $395.00

Box w/hinged lid, blue opaque, white enameled young girl wearing a hat & carrying a book on lid, 3⅛" d., 1⅝" h...195.00

Box w/hinged lid, cobalt blue, white enameled young girl in a fancy dress & bonnet & holding an umbrella while watching birds in the sky, background of florals & foliage on lid, sides decorated w/florals, brass frame w/ball feet, 5¼" d., 5½" h...550.00

Creamer, cranberry, white enameled young boy w/flowers 125.00

Decanter w/stopper, clear, white enameled young boy w/a telescope, 13½" h...60.00

Mug, electric blue, white enameled girl, 4" h...85.00

Toothpick holder, citron, white enameled girl standing in foliage watching a bird...............................250.00

Vase, 3" h., spherical footed body w/a flaring cylindrical neck, mold-blown optic ribbing, cranberry, white enameled young boy (ILLUS.) 225.00

Vase, 9⅝" h., 4¼" d., footed ovoid body tapering to a short cylindrical neck w/flared rim, opaque turquoise blue, white enameled young girl 225.00

Vase, 16¼" h., 5" d., footed baluster-form w/deep shoulder, a short cylindrical neck & a ringed wide cylindrical rim, amethyst, white enameled young girl tying her bonnet while a young boy kneels w/large mirror in front of her, ornate ormolu footed base 995.00

Water set: cov. tankard pitcher & six tumblers; clear, white enameled figures of children at play, hinged pewter lid on pitcher, 7 pcs. 680.00

McKEE

The McKee name has been associated with glass production since 1834, first producing window glass and later bottles. In the 1850s a new factory was established in Pittsburgh, Pennsylvania, for production of flint and pressed glass. The plant was relocated in Jeannette, Pennsylvania in 1888 and operated there as an independent company almost continuously until 1951 when it sold out to Thatcher Glass Manufacturing Company. Many types of collectible glass were produced by McKee through the years including Depression, Pattern, Milk White and a variety of utility kitchenwares.

Kitchenwares

McKee Water Dispenser

Bowl, 6" d., Chalaine Blue $45.00
Bowl, 9" d., Skokie Green....................15.00
Canister w/original glass cover, round, Chalaine Blue, 10 oz.........................50.00
Canister w/original glass cover, round, "Sugar," Chalaine Blue 55.00
Measuring cup, Skokie Green, 2 cup ...18.00
Refrigerator dish, cov., rectangular, French Ivory w/blue polka dots, 4 x 5"...33.00
Salt & pepper shakers w/original metal lids, Chalaine Blue, pr. 100.00
Salt & pepper shakers w/original tops, French Ivory w/blue polka dots, pr.....32.00
Salt & pepper shakers w/original tops, Roman Arch patt., black, 4½" h., pr...45.00
Water dispenser w/glass top, Skokie Green, 4½ x 5 x 11" (ILLUS.)...........225.00

Pres-Cut Lines

Bowl, 7" d., Rock Crystal patt., clear 15.00
Candlestick, Rock Crystal patt., amber, 8" h. 40.00
Champagne, Aztec patt., clear 17.00
Cheese & cracker server, Rock Crystal patt., ruby.............................175.00
Compote, 7" d., 3½" h., Rock Crystal patt., clear 38.00
Cordial, Rock Crystal patt., ruby, 1 oz. 60.00
Cracker jar, cov., Aztec patt., milk white 60.00
Creamer & open sugar bowl, Sunbeam patt., blue w/gold trim, pr...45.00
Goblet, footed, low, Rock Crystal patt., amber, 8 oz...............................50.00
Mayonnaise bowl & underplate, Rock Crystal patt., pink, 2 pcs. 25.00
Parfait, Rock Crystal patt., clear 25.00
Relish, five-part, Rock Crystal patt., clear, 12¼" d.....................................25.00
Sugar bowl, cov., footed, Rock Crystal patt., clear 36.00
Tumbler, Aztec patt., clear....................10.00
Tumbler, juice, Rock Crystal patt., clear 12.00
Vase, 11" h., footed, cylindrical, Rock Crystal patt., clear 55.00

Miscellaneous Patterns & Pieces

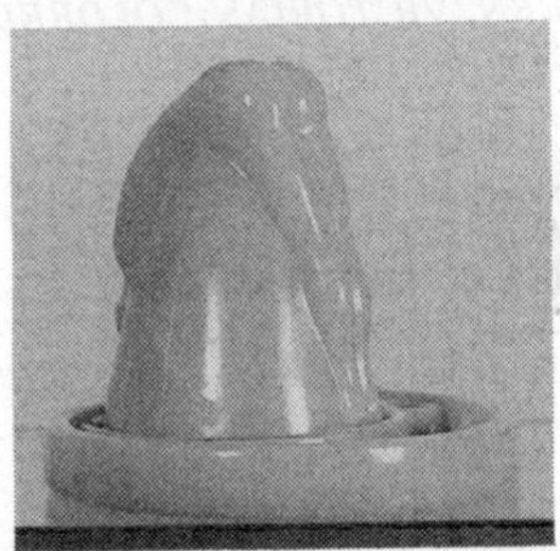

"Bottoms Up" Whiskey Tumbler

Animal covered dish, rabbit on split-ribbed base, milk white 325.00
Butter dish, cov., Wild Rose w/Bow-knot patt., green (worn old gold) 100.00
Candlesticks, Laurel patt., French Ivory, pr...25.00
Egg cup, French Ivory 6.50
Mug, Outdoor Drinking Scene patt., green opaque.......................................75.00
Mug, Serenade (Troubador) patt., blue opaque 55.00
Tom & Jerry set: bowl & twelve mugs; vaseline, all pieces signed, 13 pcs. 150.00
Tumbler, whiskey, w/coaster base, "Bottoms Up," French Ivory, 2 pcs. (ILLUS.) 50.00
Vase, 8" h., footed, triangular w/relief-molded nude on each side, opaque black 175.00

MILK WHITE

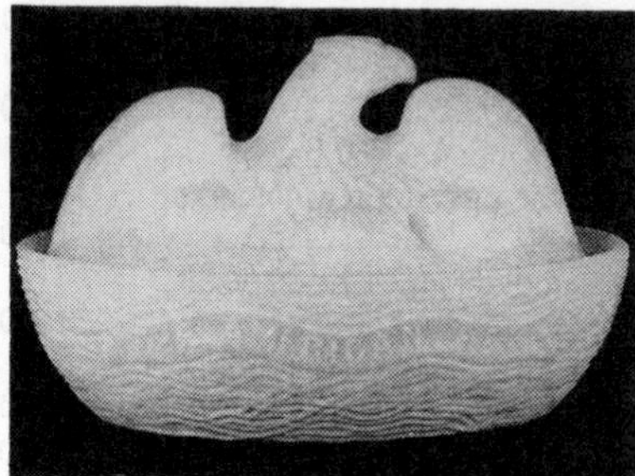

"American Hen" Covered Dish

This is opaque white glass that resembles the color of and was used as a substitute for white porcelain. Opacity was obtained by adding oxide of tin to a batch of clear glass. It has been made in numerous forms and shapes in this country and abroad from about the first quarter of the last century. It is still being produced, and there are many reproductions of earlier pieces. Also see HISTORICAL, PATTERN, VICTORIAN COLORED and WESTMORELAND GLASS.

Animal covered dish, "American Hen," eagle w/eggs inscribed "Porto Rico," "Cuba," & "Philippines," 6" l., 4" h. (ILLUS.) $66.00

Animal covered dish, Boar's Head w/glass eyes ....675.00 to 775.00

Animal covered dish, "The British Lion" on base, 6¼" l. 110.00

Animal covered dish, Chick & Eggs on lacy-edge pedestal base, Atterbury, 1880s ....75.00 to 100.00

Animal covered dish, Duck w/wavy base, glass eyes, Challinor, Taylor & Co., 5¼" h. 125.00

Animal covered dish, Hen on Basketweave base, Kemple Glass Co., mid-20th c. 55.00

Animal covered dish, Lion on scroll base, 5¾" l. 75.00

Bottle, model of an Octopus, tentacles winding around a large American coin, 4½" h. (no metal cap) 650.00

Bottle, model of a Sitting Bear, 10¾" h. 85.00

Bowl, 10" d., 4" h., Daisy patt., unpainted 70.00

Bowl, 10" l., 5¾" h., oblong, Shell patt., two ribbed & two petal feet 25.00

Box, cov., heart-shaped, embossed floral design highlighted w/touches of blue & gold 35.00

Butter dish, cov., Roman Cross patt. 50.00

Butter dish, cov., Versailles patt. w/pink decoration 45.00

Compote, open, 7½" h., Jenny Lind figural bust pedestal, ribbed bowl 85.00

Dresser tray, Chrysanthemum patt., 7½ x 10" 35.00

Egg cup, cov., model of a Hen on Nest, 2½" w., 2½" h. 175.00

Goblet, Blackberry patt. 38.00

Match holder, model of a bulldog head w/striker on back of the head, 2¼" h. 85.00

Model of a cat, sitting, 8" h. 200.00

Model of a tramp's shoe, 2⅛" h. 42.00

Mug, Bleeding Heart patt., 3¼" h. 60.00

Plate, 5½" d., Woof Woof ....50.00 to 75.00

Plate, 6" d., Dog and Cats, open leaf border 100.00

Plate, 7" d., Ancient Castle (Garfield Monument) 50.00

Plate, 7" d., Challinor's Forget-Me-Not patt. 40.00

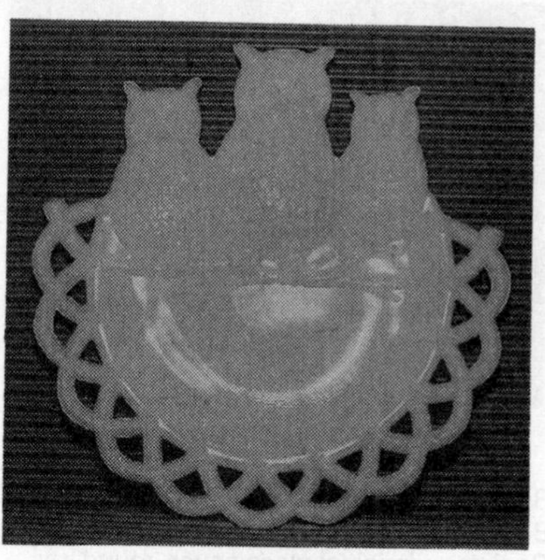

Three Owls Plate

Plate, 7" d., Three Owls (ILLUS.) 40.00

Plate, 7¼" d., Easter Bunny & Egg 60.00

Plate, 7¼" d., Lacy-Edge Indian, good paint 55.00

Plate, 8" d., Hearts & Anchor border 30.00

Plate, 8" d., Serenade 42.00

Plate, 8¼" d., Wicket border 35.00

Plate, 9" d., Angel Head, openwork border 30.00

Plate, 10½" d., Open Lattice Edge border, game bird in center 75.00

Platter, 9¾ x 13¼", Retreiver, lily pad border 110.00

Salt dip, figural turtle 45.00

Salt dip, model of a basket w/handle 35.00

Sugar shaker w/original top, h.p. Apple Blossom patt. 135.00

Sugar shaker w/original top, Little Shrimp patt. 75.00

Syrup pitcher w/original hinged tin

cover, pressed Blackberry patt., applied strap handle, ca. 1860, 7¼" h. 137.50
Syrup pitcher w/original metal top, Challinor's Tree of Life patt. 80.00
Table set: creamer, cov. sugar bowl, cov. butter dish, spooner; Versailles patt. w/h.p. rose decoration, 4 pcs. ..125.00
Whimsey, Easter Egg with Emerging Chick, 3¼" l. 40.00
Butter dish, cov., Roman Cross patt. 50.00
Butter dish, cov., Versailles patt. w/pink decoration 45.00

MOSER

Moser Decanters

Ludwig Moser opened his first glass shop in 1857 in Karlsbad, Bohemia (now Karlovy Vary, in the former Czechoslovakia). Here he engraved and decorated fine glasswares especially to appeal to rich visitors to the local health spa. Later other shops were opened in other cities and throughout the 19th and early 20th century lovely colorful glasswares, many beautifully enameled, were produced by Moser's shops and reached a wide market in Europe and America. Ludwig died in 1916 and the firm continued under his sons who were forced to merge with the Meyer's Nephews glass factory after World War I. The glassworks were sold out of the Moser family in 1933.

Box, cov., green, decorated w/a large yellow daisy on the cover, paper label "Glasfabrik, Karlsbad," 6" d., 4" h. $140.00
Center bowl, green, decorated w/intaglio-cut flowers, 9" d., 5" h. 425.00
Compote, open, 6¾" h., 7" d., dark amethyst, the exterior of the deep rounded bowl engraved w/a band of Amazon warriors highlighted in gold, the slender facet-cut pedestal flaring to a facet-cut round foot 357.50
Cordial set: decanter w/original stopper & four cordial glasses; smoky topaz decanter molded w/a frieze of nude women around the lower half, the glasses similarly decorated, decanter 10¼" h., 5 pcs. (stopper shortened) 247.50
Cup & saucer, amber decorated w/heavy gold scrolls & multicolored flowers 295.00
Decanters w/stoppers, footed cylindrical ovoid body tapering to a tall neck molded w/thin swirled ribbing below the arched spout, hollow bulbous stopper & applied strap handle, moss green enameled overall w/ornate & delicate flower blossoms & leaves in orange, green, blue & gilt, 8½" h., pr. (ILLUS.) 1,265.00
Pitcher, 6¾" h., Inverted Thumbprint patt., Amberina decorated w/four bunches of grapes highlighted w/applied yellow, red, blue & green glass beads, colorful three-dimensional bird below spout & overall decorative enamel & gold leaves, vines & tendrils, signed "Moser" 3,025.00
Sherbet & underplate, each in green heavily gilded & decorated w/small flowers, underplate 4½" d., sherbet 3¼" h., 2 pcs. 475.00
Syllabub set: 9" h. cov. bowl, six 3¼" h. footed mugs & 12¾" d. tray; handles & finial w/ribbed design, green ground decorated w/tiny flowers & flying insects, 8 pcs. 975.00
Toothpick holder, "Malachite," decorated w/enameled cherubs 225.00
Vase, 5" h., "Malachite," the deep green ovoid body tapering to a flat mouth & to a paneled foot, the sides deeply molded w/six nude women dancing below fruit-laden grapevines, polished highlights 522.50
Vase, 7" h., tapering ovoid body w/a short neck below a flattened rim cut w/five squared petals, aquamarine applied down the sides w/four S-form snakes decorated w/colorful enamel spots & interspersed w/enameled color blossoms 412.50
Vase, 8½" h., footed urn-form, dark amber w/the widely flaring rim cut

w/plain panels above a wide central panel engraved w/a continuous scene of Amazon warriors w/weapons on horseback, the bulbous base & flared pedestal foot further cut w/plain panels, the base signed in script "Made in Czechoslovakia Moser Carlsbad" 467.50

Moser Vase with Elephants

Vase, 11½" h., amethyst ovoid bottle-form w/a flattened, flaring rim, the bottom half cut w/graduated rings & w/further rings near the rim, the main body cameo-cut w/a continuous scene of elephants under palm trees, all enameled in white, gold & green, engraved signature (ILLUS.)...........................935.00

Vase, 13½" h., baluster-form, raspberry acid-cut to frosted clear in the form of raindrops, enameled w/two cranes striding through a swamp among lotus, iris & lily pads, trimmed w/gilt..................................660.00

Water set: 9½" h. tankard pitcher & six 4" h. matching tumblers; rim decorated w/white enameled chain w/heavy gold bands, body highlighted w/overall gold leaves speckled w/blue "jewels" & delicate branches w/coralene flowers on a clear ground, 7 pcs. 950.00

MT. WASHINGTON

A wide diversity of glass was made by the Mt. Washington Glass Company of New Bedford, Massachusetts, between 1869 and 1900. It was succeeded in 1900 by the Pairpoint Corporation. Miscellaneous types are listed below.

Rare Mt. Washington Punch Bowl

Bowl, 4½ x 4½", pillow-shaped, satin Diamond Quilted patt., creamy white ground decorated w/pink enameled florals & a yellow rim.....................$275.00

Bowl, 8½" d., 3½" h., "Napoli," clear ground, interior decorated w/h.p. flowers & exterior decorated w/gold outlining of the flowers, signed 500.00

Bride's basket, pink shaded to white satin Hobnail patt., w/applied blue rim, on a tall footed Barbour silver plate frame w/large parrots on the handles, bowl 9" d., 4¾" h., overall 13½" d.,...875.00

Flower holder, footed mushroom shape, pale blue shading to white, decorated w/small white & yellow flowers & green leaves, 5" d., 3½" h...200.00

Mustard pot, cov., bulbous ribbed body, decorated w/florals, silver plate rim & cover 300.00

Punch bowl on stand, decorated in the Royal Flemish manner, deep rounded bowl w/a flaring & notched rim, domed base, the bowl decorated w/three reserves of Palmer Cox Brownies in comic scenes involving a keg of ale, gilt scrolling trim, some gold loss, chip on base insert edge, 16" d., 13½" h. (ILLUS.) 18,400.00

Rose bowl, bulbous base w/rim flaring to twelve protruding "fingers," white satin ground decorated w/lavender pansies & yellow rim, 4" d., 3" h.......285.00

Salt shaker w/original top, egg-shaped, decorated w/enameled Shasta daisies & leaves, shaded pink ground 85.00

Salt & pepper shakers w/original two-piece metal tops, five-lobed apple-shaped body, matching decoration of pink & blue florals, pr. 150.00

Sugar shaker w/original metal top, egg-shaped, satiny white ground decorated w/purple violets 450.00

Vase, 6" h., 5¾" d., footed squatty bulbous body tapering to a short cylindrical neck flaring to a four-fold rim, twenty-four swirling molded ribs in body, decorated w/blue & white forget-me-nots, signed 965.00

Vase, 11½" h., decorated w/enameled spider mums & leaves & heavy gold branches, signed 895.00

MULLER FRERES

Muller Freres Cameo Vase

The Muller Brothers made acid-etched cameo and other fine glass at Luneville, France, starting in 1910 and until the outbreak of World War II in Europe.

Box, cov., oval, mottled orange & purple body etched & enameled w/red currants in naturalistic tones, enameled signature "Muller Fres Luneville," 7" l. $1,610.00

Cameo vase, 6¼" h., Art Deco style, squat ovoid body w/thick rolled rim, pale amber opalescent internally decorated w/gold & silver foil inclusions, overlaid in clear & deeply cut in an Art Deco type design of stylized butterflies, inscribed "MULLER FRES LUNEVILLE," ca. 1925 (ILLUS.) 2,013.00

Cameo vase, 8" h., ovoid body, mottled yellow overlaid in deep red & cut to depict a wooded river scene, cameo signature..............1,012.00

Cameo vase, 10¼" h., ovoid body tapering to a short, flaring neck, luminous orange overlaid in dark burgundy & black & acid-etched w/a riverside scene w/grasses & leafy trees, signed on the side "Muller Fres Luneville" 1,210.00

Cameo vase, 11¾" h., bottle-form, footed tapering cylindrical body below a tall slender stick neck w/flared mouth, grey infused w/lemon yellow, overlaid in deep teal blue & cut w/a wild windswept landscape w/rugged trees, signed in cameo, ca. 1925 ....575.00

Cameo vase, 14½" h., flaring cylindrical body raised on a cushion-form base, grey internally mottled w/lemon yellow & lavender, overlaid in blue, rose & purple & cut w/jack-in-the-pulpit blossoms & anemones, signed in cameo "MULLER FRES - LUNEVILLE," ca. 1925 ....1,840.00

Vase, 8½" h., baluster-form, opalescent yellow etched & enameled w/berries, cameo signature "MULLER Fres LUNEVILLE" 978.00

NAKARA

Like Kelva (which see), Nakara was made early in this century by the C.F. Monroe Company. For details see WAVE CREST.

Box w/hinged cover, decorated w/h.p. cupids on a blue ground, 3" d. $395.00

Box w/hinged cover, h.p. pink daisies decoration on a blue ground, 4" d., 2¾" h..310.00

Box w/hinged cover, Octagonal mold, lemon yellow shaded to deep peach ground decorated w/h.p. orchid-like blossoms in shades of orchid w/green foliage & white beading trim, 6" w. 485.00

Box w/hinged cover, Octagonal mold, shaded pale peach to brown ground decorated w/h.p. yellow flowers w/pink centers, 6¼" d., 4½" h. 960.00

Box w/hinged cover, Rococo mold, decorated overall w/dainty beaded flowers, 8" d. 1,150.00

Box w/hinged cover, Crown mold, cover decorated w/five h.p. roses on an olive green ground, sides w/similar decoration, 8" d.,5" h......1,350.00

Cigar humidor, cov., blue mottled ground decorated w/h.p. pink flowers, "Cigars" in gold on side 795.00

Humidor, cov., base decorated w/h.p. enameled florals & "Tobacco" in gold, 7" w., 7" h. 595.00

Humidor, cov., decorated w/an owl sitting in a tree, metal lid 1,220.00

Salt shaker w/original metal top, concave bulb shape, decorated w/a transfer scene of Niagara Falls applied over a tan painted background, 2⅝" h. 145.00

Vase, 8" h., squatty bulbous base tapering to a tall cylindrical neck, h.p. florals & white beading decoration on a blue shaded to yellow ground, w/decorative footed ormolu base 360.00

NEW MARTINSVILLE

The New Martinsville Glass Mfg. Co. opened in New Martinsville, West Virginia in 1901 and during its first period of production came out with a number of colored opaque pressed glass patterns and also developed an art glass line they named "Muranese" but which collectors today refer to as "New Martinsville Peach Blow." The factory burned in 1907 but reopened later that year and began focusing on production of various clear pressed glass patterns many of which were then decorated with gold or ruby staining or enameled decoration. After going through receivership in 1937 the factory again changed the focus of its production to more contemporary glass lines and figural animals. The firm was purchased in 1944 by The Viking Glass Company (now Dalzell-Viking) and some of the long-popular New Martinsville patterns are now produced by this still-active firm.

Ashtray, embossed w/"New Martinsville Centennial - 1838-1938" & a log cabin along the Ohio River, green ...$50.00
Book ends, model of an elephant, clear, pr. 185.00
Book ends, model of a prancing horse, clear, pr. 175.00
Bowl, 7 x 12" rectangle, Janice patt. (No. 4500 Line), ruby 40.00
Cordial, Moondrops patt. (No. 37 Line), cobalt blue 30.00
Dresser set: two cologne bottles w/original stoppers & cov. powder jar; Queen Ann patt. (No. 18 Line), clear, 3 pcs. 80.00
Liqueur set: decanter w/stopper & three liqueur tumblers; Moondrops patt., green, 4 pcs. 45.00
Pitcher, water, Moondrops patt., clear 50.00
Plate, torte, 18" d., Radiance patt. (No. 4200 Line), Prelude etching, clear 95.00
Relish dish, divided, Radiance patt., blue 24.00
Relish dish, five-part, Prelude etching, clear, 13" l. 85.00
Tumbler, Moondrops patt., ruby 12.00
Tumbler, water, footed, Prelude etching, clear 18.00

NORTHWOOD

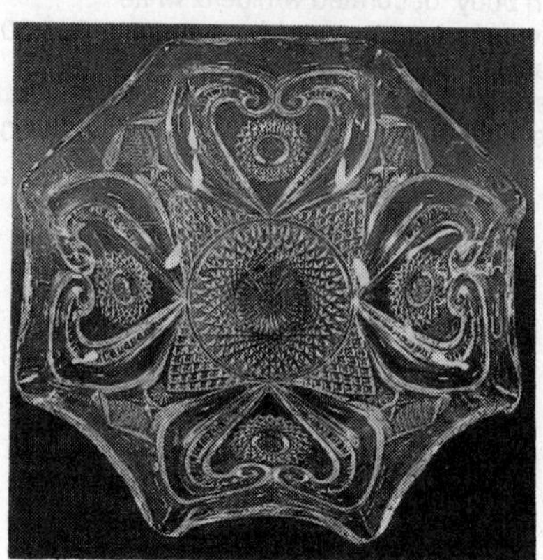

Northwood Valentine Bowl

Harry Northwood (1860-1919) was born in England, the son of noted glass artist John Northwood. Brought up in the glass business, Harry immigrated to the United States in 1881 and shortly thereafter became manager of the La Belle Glass Company, Bridgeport, Ohio. Here he was responsible for many innovations in colored and blown glass. After leaving La Belle in 1887 he opened The Northwood Glass Company in Martins Ferry, Ohio in 1888. The company moved to Ellwood City, Pennsylvania in 1892 and Northwood moved again to take over a glass plant in Indiana, Pennsylvania in 1896. One of his major lines made at the Indiana, Pennsylvania plant was Custard glass (which he called "ivory"). It was made in several patterns and some pieces were marked on the base with "Northwood" in script.

Harry and his family moved back to England in 1899 but returned to the U.S. in 1902 at which time he opened another glass factory in Wheeling, West Virginia. Here he was able to put his full talents to work and under his guidance the firm manufactured many notable glass lines including opalescent wares, colored and clear pressed tablewares, various novelties and, probably best known of all, Carnival glass. Around 1906 Harry introduced his famous "N" in circle trade-mark which can be found on the base of many, but not all, pieces made at his factory. The factory closed in 1925.

In this listing we are including only the clear and colored tablewares produced at Northwood factories. Specialized lines such as Custard glass, Chrysanthemum Sprig, Blue, Carnival and Opalescent wares are listed under their own headings in our Glass category. Also see under Pattern Glass ROYAL IVY and ROYAL OAK.

Berry set: master bowl & five sauce dishes; Parian Swirl patt., ruby w/enameled decoration, 6 pcs. $145.00
Berry set: master bowl & nine sauce dishes; Leaf Medallion (Regent) patt., purple w/gold trim, 10 pcs. 625.00
Bowl, 9" w., crimped rim, Valentine (No. 14) patt., clear (ILLUS.) 49.00
Bowl, 11" d., rolled edge, Jade Blue 50.00
Butter dish, cov., Gold Rose patt., green w/gold 100.00
Butter dish, cov., Panelled Holly patt., blue opalescent w/gold trim 375.00
Celery vase, Leaf Umbrella patt., ruby & white spatter 225.00
Compote, jelly, Leaf Medallion (Regent) patt., purple w/gold trim 80.00
Creamer, Cherry & Cable (Cherry Thumbprints) patt., clear 45.00
Cruet w/original stopper, Parian Swirl mold, Daisy & Fern patt., blue opalescent 80.00
Pickle castor, Leaf Mold patt. insert, vaseline w/cranberry spatter, satin finish, ornate silver plate frame, cover & tongs (resilvered) 375.00
Pitcher, water, Grape & Gothic Arches patt., green w/gold trim 100.00
Pitcher, water, Memphis patt., clear w/gold 90.00
Pitcher, water, Panelled Holly patt., white opalescent w/red & green.......225.00
Salt shaker w/original top, Leaf Mold patt., cranberry & white spatter 125.00
Salt shaker w/original top, Leaf Umbrella patt., Rose du Barry (cased mauve) 125.00
Spooner, Cherry & Cable (Cherry Thumbprints) patt., clear w/ruby & gold trim 75.00
Spooner, Leaf Mold patt., vaseline w/cranberry spatter, satin finish 90.00
Sugar bowl, cov., Apple Blossom patt., milk white 125.00
Sugar bowl, cov., Leaf Medallion (Regent) patt., purple w/gold trim 210.00
Sugar shaker w/original top, Leaf Umbrella patt., cased blue 220.00
Sugar shaker w/original top, Parian Swirl patt., ruby 285.00
Syrup pitcher w/original top, Ribbed Pillar patt., pink & white spatter 190.00
Table set: cov. butter dish, creamer & sugar bowl; Mikado patt., 3 pcs. 275.00
Toothpick holder, Leaf Umbrella patt., Rose du Barry (cased mauve) 225.00
Tumbler, Leaf Medallion (Regent) patt., purple w/gold trim 89.00
Tumbler, Netted Oak patt., milk white ..60.00
Water set: pitcher & six tumblers; Memphis patt., clear w/gold trim, 7 pcs. ....175.00 to 200.00

OPALESCENT

Presently, this is one of the most popular areas of glass collecting. The opalescent effect was attained by adding bone ash chemicals to areas of an item while still hot and refiring the object at tremendous heat. Both pressed and mold-blown patterns are available to collectors and we distinguish the types in our listing below. Opalescent Glass from A to Z *by the late William Heacock is the definitive reference book for collectors. Also see PATTERN GLASS.*

MOLD-BLOWN OPALESCENT PATTERNS

CHRYSANTHEMUM SWIRL

Chrysanthemum Swirl Cruet

Celery vase, blue...............................195.00
Celery vase, white 115.00
Cruet w/original stopper, cranberry (ILLUS.) 395.00
Pitcher, water, blue...........................495.00
Sugar shaker w/original top, cranberry..495.00
Tumbler, blue..92.50

COIN SPOT

Celery vase, ribbed mold, cranberry...210.00
Cruet w/original stopper, tapered mold, cranberry 235.00
Cruet w/original stopper, white 65.00

Mug, cranberry 95.00
Pitcher, 8" h., crimped rim, cranberry..150.00
Sugar shaker w/original top, blue 138.00
Sugar shaker w/original top, nine-panel mold, green 110.00
Syrup pitcher w/original metal top, bulbous-based mold, cranberry 395.00
Syrup pitcher w/original top, nine-panel mold, green 260.00
Toothpick holder, hat-shaped, white, 2½ x 5½" 50.00
Vase, 4¼" h., 5¼" w., square-top mold, canary 125.00
Water set: pitcher & two tumblers; square-top mold, cranberry, 3 pcs. ..635.00

HOBNAIL, HOBBS

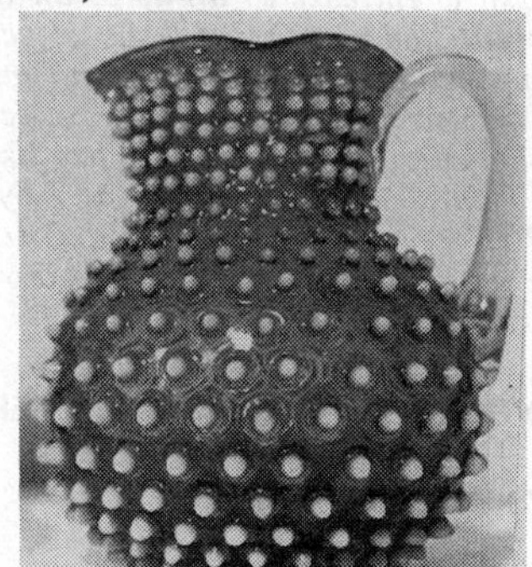

Hobnail Pitcher

Barber bottle w/original stopper, blue 175.00
Bowl, berry, 9" sq., 3" h., ruffled rim, cranberry..295.00
Cruet w/original stopper, cranberry 340.00
Pitcher, 5" h., w/square mouth, applied clear handle, cranberry (ILLUS.) 195.00
Spooner, vaseline.................................40.00
Syrup pitcher w/original top, cranberry..225.00
Tumbler, white 20.00
Vase, 5" h., triangular form, blue 65.00
Water set: pitcher & five tumblers; cranberry, 6 pcs. 340.00

REVERSE SWIRL

Bowl, master berry, blue........................65.00
Butter dish, cov., blue 225.00
Lamp, finger-type w/applied clear handle, cranberry............................425.00
Pitcher, water, canary 250.00
Salt & pepper shakers w/original tops, blue, 3⅜" h., pr...............125.00 to 150.00
Sugar shaker w/original top, canary ....250.00 to 300.00

Reverse Swirl Syrup Pitcher

Syrup pitcher w/original top, blue (ILLUS.)....................250.00 to 275.00
Toothpick holder, blue 100.00

SPANISH LACE

Spanish Lace Sugar Shaker

Bride's bowl, cranberry, 10" d., 4" h....250.00
Butter dish, cov., white 150.00
Celery vase, canary................75.00 to 95.00
Pitcher, water, cranberry ....900.00 to 950.00
Pitcher, tankard, white ....225.00 to 275.00
Rose bowl, white 65.00
Salt & pepper shakers w/original tops, blue, pr. 275.00
Sugar shaker w/original top, blue (ILLUS.) ....200.00 to 250.00
Sugar shaker w/original metal top, canary ....225.00 to 250.00
Sugar shaker w/original top, white........90.00
Tumbler, blue...82.00

PRESSED OPALESCENT PATTERNS

ARGONAUT SHELL

Banana bowl, canary, 7" l. 72.00
Compote, 7½" d., 4" h., blue 52.00
Cruet w/original stopper, white ....150.00 to 200.00

Spooner, blue 95.00
Sugar bowl, cov., blue 195.00
Tray, blue..90.00
Tray, canary..90.00

BEATTY RIBBED
Celery, blue 84.00
Creamer, individual, blue.......................50.00
Sauce dish, rectangular, blue 27.50
Sugar shaker w/original top, blue ....225.00 to 250.00
Sugar shaker w/original top, cranberry..435.00

DIAMOND SPEARHEAD
Berry set: master bowl & six sauce dishes; canary, 7 pcs. 275.00

Diamond Spearhead Butter Dish

Butter dish, cov., green (ILLUS.) 230.00
Celery vase, canary...........100.00 to 110.00
Compote, jelly, blue 125.00
Spooner, canary 100.00
Spooner, green.....................80.00 to 100.00
Sugar bowl, cov., canary 150.00
Toothpick holder, green.........................60.00
Tumbler, sapphire blue..........................65.00

DRAPERY
Bowl, 9" d., white 60.00
Butter dish, cov., blue w/gold trim.......175.00
Pitcher, water, blue w/gold trim ....200.00 to 250.00
Sauce dish, blue 36.00
Spooner, blue 72.00
Water set: pitcher & six tumblers; blue, 7 pcs. 775.00

FLUTED SCROLLS
Berry set: master bowl & six sauce dishes; blue, 7 pcs. 250.00
Bonbon, canary 50.00
Bonbon, green...45.00
Creamer, canary w/enameled flowers 75.00
Creamer, white 32.00
Cruet w/original stopper, blue............160.00
Puff box, cov., blue 45.00
Puff box, cov., canary 50.00
Spooner, blue 60.00

Sugar bowl, cov., blue ....100.00 to 125.00
Table set, canary w/floral decoration, 4 pcs. 600.00

JEWELLED HEART
Berry set: master bowl & four sauce dishes; white, 5 pcs. 150.00
Bowl, small, ruffled rim, white 23.00
Creamer, blue..65.00
Cruet w/original stopper, green 395.00
Tumbler, green 69.00

REGAL
Butter dish, cov., blue ....325.00 to 350.00
Celery vase, blue...................................165.00
Creamer, green 75.00
Pitcher, water, green 225.00
Spooner, green..55.00
Sugar bowl, cov., blue ....250.00 to 275.00

SCROLL WITH ACANTHUS

Scroll with Acanthus Jelly Compote

Bowl, master berry, blue.........................80.00
Compote, jelly, green (ILLUS.) 42.00
Creamer, blue..85.00
Cruet w/original stopper, white 95.00
Spooner, blue 85.00

SWAG WITH BRACKETS
Berry set: master bowl & two sauce dishes; blue, 3 pcs. 175.00
Butter dish, cov., canary .....225.00 to 250.00
Cruet w/original stopper, blue.............550.00
Tumbler, white 35.00
Water set: pitcher & six tumblers; blue, 7 pcs. 800.00

WATER LILY & CATTAILS
Bonbon, two-handled, blue....................35.00
Bowl, 8" d., green 50.00
Butter dish, cov., white 160.00
Spooner, blue 42.50
Tumbler, green 22.50

WREATH & SHELL
Berry set: master bowl & six sauce dishes: canary, 7 pcs. ......250.00 to 275.00
Butter dish, cov., blue ....250.00 to 295.00

Wreath & Shell Cuspidor

Cuspidor, lady's, blue (ILLUS.) 60.00
Salt dip, footed, green 75.00
Spooner, canary w/enamel decoration 135.00
Table set, white, 4 pcs. 395.00
Water set: pitcher & five tumblers; canary, 6 pcs. 795.00

(End of Opalescent Glass Section)

ORREFORS

Orrefors Enameled Bowl

This Swedish glasshouse, founded in 1898 for production of tablewares, has made decorative wares as well since 1915. By 1925, Orrefors had achieved an international reputation for its Graal glass, an engraved art glass developed by master glass blower Knut Berqvist and artist-designers Simon Gate and Edward Hald. Ariel glass, recognized by a design of controlled air traps, and the heavy Ravenna glass, usually tinted, were both developed in the 1930s. While all Orrefors glass is collectible, pieces signed by early designers and artists are now bringing high prices.

Bowl, 7¾" l., "Ravenna," the narrow curved clear vessel internally decorated w/red & blue overlapping designs, designed by Sven Palmquist, inscribed "ORREFORS - RAVENNA 533 - Sven Palmquist," ca. 1953 ....$2,300.00
Bowl, 9¼", 7" h., exposition-type, clear w/the tall upright sides enameled w/a scene titled "Sailor's Dream" featuring cavorting sailors & naked blonde women & a dance band w/tuba, accordion, bass & violin players, by Gunnar Cyren, signed "Orrefors Expo 682-68 Gunnar Cyren" (ILLUS.) 1,540.00
Decanter w/original stopper, the clear rectangular bottle engraved w/a cancan dancer balancing martini glasses on one foot & both hands, silvered-metal stopper, designed by Simon Gate, inscribed "S.G. 293.28," ca. 1922, 7⅝" h. 288.00
Vase, 6" h., "Graal," bulbous faceted clear body internally decorated w/tropical fish among aquatic plants in shades of green, designed by Edward Hald, signed "ORREFORS - SWEDEN - GRAAL - NU 454 - B - Edward Hald," ca. 1947 ....518.00
Vase, 11¼" h., "Kykaren," tapering cylindrical body decorated w/an engraved naked male diver viewed through horizontal ridges forming "waves" w/bubbles, applied black foot, designed by Vicke Lindstrand, inscribed "Orrefors Lindstrand 1343 A3R" 935.00

OVERSHOT

Popular since the mid-19th century, Overshot glass was produced by having a gather of molten glass rolled in finely crushed glass to produce a rough exterior finish. The piece was then blown to the desired size and shape. The finished piece has a frosted or iced finish and is sometimes referred to as "ice glass." Early producers referred to this glass as "Craquelle" and, although Overshot is sometimes lumped together with the glass collectors now call "crackle," that type was produced using a totally different technique.

Basket, opaque lemon yellow w/applied opaque lemon yellow handle, squatty bulbous body w/upright ruffled rim, molded swirling ribs, overshot exterior finial, overall gilt trim, 3½" d., 3¼" h. $110.00
Claret set: 9½" h. decanter w/ovoid glass body fitted w/a pewter pedestal foot, long handle & tall embossed neck w/ornate spout & hinged, domed cover & four glass-

Overshot Claret Set

bowled clarets fitted on turned pewter stems & domed feet; each piece in Rubina Crystal w/overshot finish, 5 pcs. (ILLUS.) 475.00
Compote, open, 9" d., 7" h., pedestal base, clear w/irregular h.p. gold design, attributed to the Boston & Sandwich Glass Company..............200.00
Finger bowl, paneled body w/flared rim, pink, 4⅝" h. 65.00
Goblet, clear w/applied cranberry snake stem 190.00
Pitcher, 5⅝" h., 3½" d., waisted cylindrical body w/flared rim, orange shaded to vaseline, vaseline applied handle 125.00
Punch bowl, cover & underplate, clear, large applied green snake handle on cover, the set 950.00
Vase, 13¼", baluster-form body w/flaring neck w/flat rim, brilliant fiery canary yellow w/applied turquoise blue neck & rim ring, attributed to the Reading Artistic Glass Works, Reading, Pennsylvania, associated w/Joseph Bornique, late 19th c.....2,415.00

PADEN CITY

The Paden City Glass Manufacturing Company began operations in Paden City, West Virginia in 1916, primarily as a supplier of blanks to other companies. All wares were hand-made, that is, either hand-pressed or mold-blown. The early products were not particularly noteworthy but by the early 1930s the quality had improved considerably and the firm continued to turn out high quality glassware in a variety of beautiful colors until financial difficulties necessitated its closing in 1951. Over the years the firm produced in addition to tablewares, items for hotel and restaurant use, light shades, shaving mugs, perfume bottles and lamps.

Bowl, 9" d., pedestal foot, etched Peacock & Rose patt., pink.............$75.00
Bowl, cream soup, footed Crow's Foot (No. 412) line, red 20.00
Cheese & cracker set, Simplicity (No. 700) line, pink w/heavy silver trim, 13" d., 2 pcs. 45.00
Cheese stand, Crow's Foot (No. 412) line, clear, 5" d., 3" h. 8.00
Console bowl, footed, Triumph (No. 701) line, pink w/floral cutting & gold trim, 12" d..45.00
Creamer, Party (No. 191) line, green 3.50
Cup & saucer, Crow's Foot (No. 412) line, amber 6.50
Cup & saucer, Crow's Foot (No. 412) line, red 10.00
Cup & saucer, Penny (No. 991) line, red..9.50
Goblet, Aristocrat line, red, 5¾" h.........12.00
Plate, 6" sq., Crow's Foot (No. 412) line, amber 1.25
Plate, 8½" sq., Crow's Foot (No. 412) line, amber 3.50
Platter, 6½ x 8¾" oval, Aristocrat line, red...18.00
Platter, 11¼" l., Crow's Foot (No. 412) line, amber..15.00
Platter, 9¼ x 12½" oval, Aristocrat line, red. 30.00
Rose bowl, footed, Gothic Garden etching, yellow 30.00
Salt & pepper shakers w/original tops, Party (No. 191) line, amber, pr. 18.00
Sandwich server w/center handle, Mrs. "B" line, amber 16.00
Sherbet, ball stem, Aristocrat line, ruby, 5 oz. 14.00
Tray w/handles, Crow's Foot (No. 412) line, amber, 10½" sq. 16.00
Vase, 5" h., elliptical-shaped, etched Lela Bird patt., ebony........................95.00
Vase, 8¼" h., Crow's Foot (No. 412) line, red 62.50

PAIRPOINT

Originally organized in New Bedford, Massachusetts, in 1880, as the Pairpoint Manufacturing Company, on land adjacent to the famed Mount Washington Glass Company, this company first manufactured silver and plated wares. In

1894, the two famous factories merged as the Pairpoint Corporation and enjoyed great success for more than forty years. The company was sold in 1939 to a group of local businessmen and eventually bought out by one of the group who turned the management over to Robert M. Gundersen. Subsequently, it operated as the Gundersen Glass Works until 1952 when, after Gundersen's death, the name was changed to Gundersen-Pairpoint. The factory closed in 1956. Subsequently, Robert Bryden took charge of this glassworks, at first producing glass for Pairpoint abroad and eventually, in 1970, beginning glass production in Sagamore, Massachusetts. Today the Pairpoint Crystal Glass Company is owned by Robert and June Bancroft. They continue to manufacture fine quality blown and pressed glass.

Pairpoint Covered Compote

Castor set: two square cruets w/original square cut stoppers, one square mustard jar w/original silver plate w/circular handle & a silver plate top holder w/ornate handle marked "Hartford"; clear w/cut & etched overall floral designs, the set $150.00

Compote, cov., 8¾" d., 13" h., clear deep rounded bowl on a knop stem & round foot, domed cover w/knop finial encasing a white rose & green leaves, the sides engraved w/a rosebush on trellis design, leafy floral bands on cover & foot (ILLUS.) 550.00

Cracker jar, cov., milk white w/h.p. blue Delft scenic decoration, silver plate rim, cover & handle, 5¾" h. 525.00

Pitcher, 12" h., green body & foot w/clear applied handle & "controlled bubble" knop stem 155.00

Tumbler, barrel-shaped, clear w/h.p. black enameled galleon under full sail & rim trim 235.00

Vase, 4½" h., footed spherical body, clear w/enameled floral decoration, "controlled bubble" ball connector on base, numbered in pontil 75.00

Vase, 12" h., trumpet-shaped green body, clear "controlled bubble" ball connector & green foot 95.00

Vase, 13" h., 6½" d., cobalt blue trumpet-shaped body & pedestal foot w/clear "controlled bubble" ball connector 235.00

Vases, 12" h., ruby body & foot, clear "controlled bubble" knop connector, pr. 300.00

PATE DE VERRE

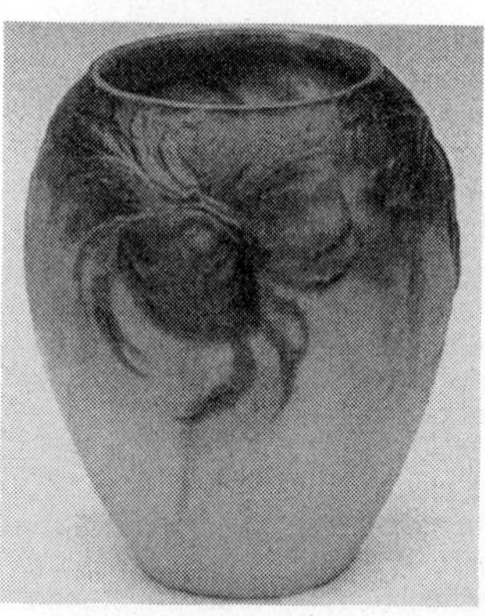

Pate de Verre Crab Vase

Pate de Verre, or "paste of glass," was molded by very few artisans. In the pate de verre technique, powdered glass is mixed with a liquid to make a paste which is then placed in a mold and baked at a high temperature. These articles have a finely-pitted or matte finish and are easily distinguished from blown glass. Duplicate pieces are possible with this technique.

Bowl, 3¾" d., circular, molded w/an abstract lotus pattern in various shades of green, molded signature "A WALTER NANCY" $633.00

Dish, shallow sides w/two scrolled handles, the mottled amber body molded w/stylized flowers & leaves, signed in the mold "G. ARGY-ROUSSEAU," 8¼" l. 5,175.00

Paperweight, figural, cast a stylized mouse lying spread-eagled on a circular base, in grey mottled w/rose, purple, ochre & green, molded factory mark "DECORCHEMONT," inscribed "D352," ca. 1950, 4" d., 2¼" h. 1,840.00

Vase, 5½" h., simple ovoid body w/closed rim, press-molded & carved, amethyst & frosted clear decorated w/three black & green molded crabs w/pincher claws & red eyes surrounded by naturalistic seaweed, impressed at center "G. Argy-Rousseau" & w/"France" on the base (ILLUS.) 5,500.00

Vase, 11¾" h., "Libation," ovoid, two portraits of an Egyptian woman carrying a water jug, w/broad frieze of repeating geometric devices between, executed in warm shades of orange, yellow & brown, impressed in mold "G. Argy-Rousseau" 38,500.00

Vide poche (figural dish), irregular contour, cast in low-, medium- and high-relief w/oak leaves & acorns, a beetle cast in full-relief at the center, in shades of lemon yellow, lime green, ochre, avocado & rust, signed in intaglio "DAUM - NANCY" w/cross of Lorraine, ca. 1920, 8¼" l. 3,450.00

PATTERN GLASS

Though it has never been ascertained whether glass was first pressed in the United States or abroad, the development of the glass pressing machine revolutionized the glass industry in the United States and this country receives the credit for improving the method to make this process feasible. The first wares pressed were probably small flat plates of the type now referred to as "lacy," the intricacy of the design concealing flaws.

In 1827, both the New England Glass Co., Cambridge, Massachusetts and Bakewell & Co., Pittsburgh, took out patents for pressing glass furniture knobs and soon other pieces followed. This early pressed glass contained red lead which made it clear and resonant when tapped (flint). Made primarily in clear, it is rarer in blue, amethyst, olive green and yellow.

By the 1840s, early simple patterns such as Ashburton, Argus and Excelsior appeared. Ribbed Bellflower seems to have been one of the earliest patterns to have had complete sets. By the 1860s, a wide range of patterns was available.

In 1864, William Leighton of Hobbs, Brockunier & Co., Wheeling, West Virginia, developed a formula for "soda lime" glass which did not require the expensive red lead for clarity. Although "soda lime" glass did not have the brilliance of the earlier flint glass, the formula came into widespread use because glass could be produced cheaply.

An asterisk (*) indicates a piece which has been reproduced.

ACTRESS

Bowl, cov. $110.00

Bowl, 6" d., flat 45.00

Bowl, 6" d., footed 50.00

Bowl, 7" d., footed 60.00

Bread tray, Miss Neilsen, 12½" l. 87.50

Butter dish, cov., Fanny Davenport & Miss Neilson .... 100.00 to 125.00

Cake stand, Maude Granger & Annie Pixley, 10" d., 7" h. 125.00

Cake stand, frosted stem .... 145.00 to 165.00

Celery vase, Pinafore scene 175.00

Cheese dish, cov., "Lone Fisherman" on cover, "The Two Dromios" on underplate .... 225.00 to 235.00

Compote, cov., 6" d., 10" h. 100.00

Compote, open, 10" d., 9" h. 100.00

Creamer, clear 70.00

Creamer, frosted 125.00

Goblet, Lotta Crabtree & Kate Claxton .... 75.00 to 85.00

Marmalade jar, cov., Maude Granger & Annie Pixley 110.00

*Pickle dish, Kate Claxton, "Love's Request is Pickles," 5¼ x 9¼" 45.00

Platter, 7 x 11½", Pinafore scene 100.00

*Relish, Miss Neilson, 5 x 8" 40.00

Relish, Maude Granger, 5 x 9" .... 75.00 to 95.00

Sauce dish, Maggie Mitchell & Fanny Davenport, 4½" d., 2½" h. 24.00

Spooner, Mary Anderson & Maude Granger 74.00

Sugar bowl, cov., Lotta Crabtree & Kate Claxton 97.00

ALASKA (Lion's Leg)

Alaska Butter Dish

Banana boat, blue opalescent .... 200.00 to 250.00

Banana boat, emerald

Berry set: master bowl & 4 sauce dishes; emerald green, 5 pcs. ....250.00 to 275.00
Bowl, 8" sq., blue opalescent ....150.00 to 200.00
Bowl, 8" sq., emerald green w/gold & enameling, w/silver plate stand....145.00
Bowl, 8" sq., vaseline opalescent....140.00
Bowl, 8" sq., vaseline opalescent w/enameled florals....225.00
Butter dish, cov., blue opalescent (ILLUS.) ....350.00 to 375.00
Butter dish, cov., emerald green w/enameled florals....200.00 to 250.00
Celery tray, blue opalescent w/enameled florals....250.00
Celery tray, emerald green.... 75.00
Celery tray, emerald green w/gold....85.00
Creamer, emerald green 48.00
Creamer, vaseline opalescent....68.00
Cruet w/original stopper, blue opalescent 260.00
Cruet w/original stopper, emerald green....275.00
Cruet w/original stopper, vaseline opalescent w/enameled florals ....200.00 to 250.00
Pitcher, water, blue opalescent 350.00
Pitcher, water, vaseline opalescent....350.00
Pitcher, water, vaseline opalescent w/enameled florals....425.00 to 500.00
Salt shaker w/original top, blue opalescent 85.00
Salt shaker w/original top, emerald green....70.00
Sauce dish, clear opalescent w/enameled florals....35.00
Sauce dish, emerald green.... 20.00
Sauce dish, emerald green w/enameled florals & leaves....38.00
Sauce dish, vaseline opalescent....38.00
Spooner, emerald green....34.00
Spooner, emerald green w/enameled florals 70.00
Spooner, vaseline opalescent 60.00
Sugar bowl, cov., emerald green w/enameled florals....73.00
Sugar bowl, cov., vaseline opalescent....210.00
Sugar bowl, cov., vaseline opalescent w/enameled florals....245.00
Table set, blue opalescent, 4 pcs. ....650.00 to 700.00
Tumbler, vaseline opalescent....77.00
Tumbler, vaseline opalescent w/enameled florals....80.00
Water set: pitcher & 6 tumblers; vaseline opalescent, 7 pcs. ....800.00 to 850.00

AMBERETTE - See Klondike Pattern

ARGUS (McKee & Brother, Pittsburgh)

Celery vase, flint....70.00
Champagne, flint 75.00
Champagne, flint, cut panels w/gilt florals 95.00
Creamer, applied handle, flint....105.00
Egg cup, flint....25.00 to 35.00
Egg cup, handled, flint....80.00
Goblet, flint 72.50
Goblet, Five-Row....55.00
Goblet, master size, flint....45.00
Mug, applied handle, flint....60.00
Salt dip, cov., master size, flint....90.00
Salt dip, open, master size, flint....35.00

Argus Spillholder

Spillholder, flint (ILLUS.)....45.00 to 55.00
Tumbler, footed, flint, 4" h....40.00
Wine, flint, 4" h....45.00
Wine (Hotel Argus), non-flint 18.00

ART (Job's Tears)

Banana stand 100.00
Bowl, 7" d., flared rim, footed....26.50
Bowl, 8" sq., shallow....34.00
Bowl, 8½" d....40.00
Bowl, 9¾" d....38.00
Bowl, rectangular....20.00
Butter dish, cov....45.00
Cake stand, 9" to 10½" d. 63.00
Celery vase....46.00
Compote, cov., 6" d., 10" h. 54.00
Compote, cov., 7" d. 65.00
Compote, open, 9" d., 7¼" h....48.00
Compote, open, 10" d., 9" h....50.00
Cracker jar, cov., 7" d., 8" h., to top of finial 5.00
Creamer....42.00
Goblet....54.00
Pitcher, water, 9½" h. 150.00
Relish, 4¼" x 7¾" 18.50
Sauce dish, flat or footed....14.00
Spooner....27.00
Sugar bowl, cov., engraved....48.00
Sugar bowl, cov., plain 41.00
Tumbler 30.00

ASHBURTON

Ale glass, flint, 6½" h. 85.00
Bitters bottle w/original pewter lid....65.00

Celery vase, scalloped rim, canary yellow, flint ....700.00 to 850.00
Celery vase, scalloped rim, clear, flint 135.00
Champagne, barrel-shaped, flint 85.00
Creamer, applied handle, flint ....275.00 to 325.00
Decanter, bar lip w/patent pewter-stopper, canary yellow, flint 1,600.00
Decanter, bar lip w/patent pewter stopper, clear, flint 155.00
Goblet, disconnected ovals 35.00
Honey dish, 3½" d. 9.00
Mug, applied handle, 3" h. 60.00
Pitcher, water, applied hollow handle, flint ....400.00 to 450.00
Pomade jar, cov., white opaque, flint..195.00
Sugar bowl, cov., flint 175.00
Tumbler, bar, flint...............................58.00
Tumbler, water, flint............................59.00
Wine, clear, flint 46.00
Wine, clear, knob stem 85.00
Wine w/cut design, clear w/gold trim ..125.00
Wine, peacock green, flint 650.00
Wine, non-flint.......................................30.00

ATLAS (Crystal Ball or Cannon Ball)

Butter dish, cov....................................50.00
Cake stand, 8" to 10" d. 28.00
Celery vase 39.50
Champagne, 5½" h. 37.00
Cordial 42.00
Creamer, flat or pedestal base 22.00
Goblet, engraved 30.00
Goblet, plain 30.00
Pitcher, milk, tankard, applied handle...45.00
Pitcher, water, tankard, applied handle 50.00
Salt dip, individual size 15.00
Salt dip, master size 20.00
Sauce dish, flat or footed 12.50
Spooner 30.00
Toothpick holder 25.00
Tray, water..65.00
Tumbler 28.00
Wine 25.00

BABY THUMBPRINT - See Dakota Pattern

BALDER - See Pennsylvania Pattern

BAMBOO - See Broken Column Pattern

BANDED PORTLAND

Berry set: master bowl & 8 sauce dishes; pink-stained w/gold trim, 9 pcs. 295.00
Bowl, berry, 9" d. 30.00
Butter dish, cov., pink-stained 150.00
Candlesticks, pr. 75.00
Celery tray, pink-stained, 10" oval........75.00
Celery tray, clear, 5 x 12" 25.00
Celery vase, clear.................................32.00
Cologne bottle w/original stopper, clear 51.00
Compote, cov., 8" d., high stand.........110.00
Creamer, individual size, clear 29.00
Cruet w/original stopper........................60.00
Dresser jar, cov., clear, 3½" d. 36.00
Goblet, clear 35.00
Goblet, pink-stained..............................68.00
Pitcher, water, 9½" h. 95.00
Pitcher, child's, pink-stained 32.50
Pomade jar, cov.....................................27.50
Punch cup...12.50
Relish, pink-stained, 4 x 6½" 28.00
Relish, 4 x 8½" oval 14.00
Salt & pepper shakers w/original tops, clear, pr. 55.00
Salt & pepper shakers w/original tops, pink-stained, pr. 85.00 to100.00

Banded Portland Sauce Dish

Sauce dish, 4½" d. (ILLUS.) 15.00
Spooner, pink-stained...........................75.00
Sugar bowl, cov., pink-stained............112.00
Sugar shaker w/original top..................50.00
Syrup jug w/original top, pink-stained 365.00
Toothpick holder, clear 41.00
Toothpick holder, pink-stained..............58.00
Toothpick holder, purple-stained 28.00
Tumbler 35.00
Vase, 6" h., flared, clear 32.00
Vase, 6" h., flared, pink-stained............35.00
Vase, 9" h. 42.00
Wine, clear..28.00
Wine, gold-stained................................35.00
Wine, pink-stained 75.00

BEADED GRAPE (California)

Bowl, 6½" sq., green............................28.00
Bowl, 7½" sq., green............................30.00
Bread tray, green, 7 x 10" 60.00
Butter dish, cov., square, clear 55.00
Butter dish, cov., square, green..................................70.00 to 80.00
Cake stand, green, 9" sq., 6" h.....................................75.00 to 85.00
Celery tray, green 40.00
Celery vase...32.00
Compote, cov., 4⅞" sq., 6" h., green 55.00
*Compote, cov., 8½" sq., high stand ..125.00

Beaded Grape Open Compote

Compote, open, 8½" sq., high stand, clear (ILLUS.)....72.50
Creamer, clear....35.00
Creamer, green....42.50
Cruet w/original stopper, green....115.00
*Goblet....35.00
Pitcher, water, round, green....78.00
*Plate, 8" sq., clear....27.50
*Plate, 8" sq., green....37.50
Relish, green w/gold, 4 x 7"....35.00
Salt shaker w/original top, clear....32.50
Salt & pepper shakers w/original tops, green, pr....75.00
*Sauce dish, green....15.00
Sauce dish, handled....15.00
Spooner....40.00
Sugar bowl, cov....54.00
Toothpick holder, clear....23.00
Toothpick holder, green....60.00
*Tumbler....27.50
*Wine, clear....35.00
*Wine, green....60.00

BEADED LOOP (Oregon, U.S. Glass Co.)

Berry set, master bowl & 6 sauce dishes, 7 pcs....65.00
Butter dish, cov....46.50
Cake stand, 9" to 10½" d....45.00
Celery vase, 7" h....29.00
Compote, cov., 7" d....95.00
Compote, open, jelly, clear....38.00
Compote, open, 7" d., clear....25.00
Creamer....35.00
*Goblet....39.00
Goblet, w/gold trim....32.50
Mug, footed....38.00
Pickle dish, boat-shaped, 7¼" l....12.00
Pitcher, milk, 8½" h....35.00
Pitcher, water, tankard....50.00
Relish....18.00
Salt shaker w/original top....25.00
Sauce dish, flat or footed....10.00
Spooner, clear....26.00
Spooner, ruby-stained....65.00
*Sugar bowl, cov....39.00
Toothpick holder....30.00
Wine....57.50

BEARDED HEAD - See Viking Pattern

BELLFLOWER

Bellflower Goblet

Bowl, 7½" d., 2" h....110.00
Bowl, 8" d., 4½" h., scalloped rim....95.00
Celery vase, fine rib, single vine....130.00
Compote, open, 4½" d., low stand, scalloped rim....85.00 to100.00
Compote, open, 6" d., low stand....59.00
Compote, open, 8" d., 5" h., scalloped rim, single vine....100.00
Compote, open, 8" d., 8" h., dome-footed, single vine....125.00
Cordial, fine rib, single vine, knob stem....150.00
Cordial, fine rib, single vine, plain stem....60.00
Creamer, fine rib, double vine, applied handle....160.00
Decanter w/bar lip, patent stopper, double vine, qt....385.00
Egg cup, fine rib, single vine....50.00
Goblet, barrel-shaped, fine rib, single vine, knob stem....54.00
*Goblet, barrel-shaped, fine rib, single vine, plain stem (ILLUS.)....48.00
Goblet, coarse rib....45.00
Honey dish, rayed center, 3¼" d....22.50
Honey dish, ringed center, 3½" d....22.50
Lamp, kerosene-type, 8½" h....175.00
*Pitcher, milk, double vine....350.00
Pitcher, water, 8¾" h., coarse rib, double vine....395.00
Plate, 6" d., fine rib, single vine....115.00
Salt dip, cov., master size, footed, beaded rim, fine rib, single vine....72.50
Sauce dish, single vine....20.00
Spooner, low foot, double vine....60.00
Spooner, scalloped rim, single vine....40.00
Sugar bowl, cov., double vine....55.00
Syrup pitcher w/original top, applied handle, fine rib, single vine, fiery opalescent....1,100.00
Tumbler, bar, fine rib, single vine....90.00
Tumbler, coarse rib, double vine....105.00
Wine, barrel-shaped, knob stem, fine rib, single vine, rayed base....100.00 to 125.00

Wine, barrel-shaped, fine rib, double vine, w/cut bellflowers 325.00

BIRD & STRAWBERRY (Bluebird)

Berry set: master bowl & 5 sauce dishes; w/color, 6 pcs. 525.00
Berry set: master bowl & 6 sauce dishes; footed, 7 pcs. ....150.00 to 200.00
Bowl, 5½" d., clear 24.00
Bowl, 7½" d., footed, w/color 70.00
Bowl, 9" d., flat, w/color 75.00
Bowl, 10" d., flat, w/color & gold trim ..115.00
Butter dish, cov., clear 87.50
Butter dish, cov., w/color ....175.00 to 225.00
Cake stand, 9" to 9½" d. 60.00
*Compote, cov., 6½" d., 9½" h. 145.00
Compote, cov., jelly 130.00
Creamer, clear 47.50
Creamer, w/color 125.00
Dish, heart-shaped 47.50
Pitcher, water 287.50
Plate, 12" d. 75.00
Punch cup 22.00
Sauce dish, flat or footed, clear 26.00
Sauce dish, w/color 34.00
Spooner, clear 49.00
Spooner, w/color ....100.00 to 125.00
Sugar bowl, cov. 65.00
Sugar bowl, open 32.00
Table set, 4 pcs. ....225.00 to 250.00
Tumbler, clear 52.50
Tumbler, w/color 95.00
Wine 55.00

BLUEBIRD - See Bird & Strawberry Pattern

BROKEN COLUMN (Irish Column, Notched Rib or Bamboo)

Bowl, 7" d. 40.00
Butter dish, cov. 85.00
Cake stand, 9" to 10" d. 90.00
Celery vase 55.00
Compote, cov., 5" d., high stand 80.00
Compote, open, jelly, w/red notches ..195.00
Cracker jar, cov. 100.00
*Creamer, clear 38.00
Creamer, w/red notches 245.00
Cruet w/original stopper 85.00
*Goblet 55.00
Marmalade jar w/original cover 100.00
Pickle castor, cov., clear, original ornate frame 250.00
Pickle castor, w/red notches, w/frame & tongs ....400.00 to 425.00
*Pitcher, water, clear 90.00
Pitcher, water, w/red notches 225.00
Plate, 5" d. 32.00
*Plate, 8" d. 40.00
Punch cup, blue 95.00
Punch cup, clear 25.00
Relish, w/red notches, 9" l., 5" w. 78.00
Salt shaker w/original top 55.00
*Sauce dish, clear 15.00
Sauce dish, w/red notches 32.00
*Spooner, w/red notches 125.00
*Sugar bowl, cov., clear 72.00
Sugar bowl, cov., w/red notches 150.00
Syrup pitcher w/metal top 130.00
Tumbler, clear 45.00
Tumbler, w/red notches 75.00
Vase, 6½" h. 30.00
Water set: pitcher & 5 tumblers; w/red notches, 6 pcs. 650.00
*Wine 85.00

BULL'S EYE

Ale glass 45.00
Celery vase, flint 75.00
Cordial, flint 85.00
Cruet w/original stopper 195.00
Decanter w/bar lip, flint, qt. 110.00
Egg cup, clear, flint, 3¾" h. .....45.00 to 55.00
Egg cup, jade green 385.00
Goblet, flint 72.00
Salt dip, individual size, rectangular 35.00
Tumbler, flat, flint 70.00
Wine, knob stem, flint 58.00

BUTTON ARCHES

Berry set: 8" d. master bowl & 6 sauce dishes; ruby-stained, 7 pcs. 158.00
Bowl, 8" d., ruby-stained, souvenir 45.00
Compote, open, jelly, 4½" h., ruby-stained 40.00
*Creamer, ruby-stained 37.50
*Creamer, individual size, ruby-stained 28.00
Cruet w/original stopper, ruby-stained 175.00
Goblet, clambroth 26.00
Goblet, clear 24.00
Mug, clear 18.00
Mug, ruby-stained 30.00
Pitcher, tankard, 8¾" h. 117.00
Punch cup, ruby-stained, souvenir 28.50
Salt dip 18.50
Salt shaker w/original top, ruby-stained 25.00
Sauce dish, clear 15.00
Sauce dish, ruby-stained 30.00
*Spooner, ruby-stained 42.50
Sugar bowl, cov., clear 45.00
*Sugar bowl, cov., ruby-stained 85.00
Syrup pitcher w/original top, clear 40.00
*Toothpick holder, ruby-stained 28.00
Toothpick holder, ruby-stained, souvenir 32.50
Tumbler, clambroth, souvenir 23.00
Tumbler, ruby-stained 42.50
Tumbler, ruby-stained, souvenir 39.50
Wine, clear 26.00
Wine, ruby-stained 37.50

CABLE

Butter dish, cov. 90.00

Celery vase....82.00
Champagne....250.00
Compote, open, 7" d., 5" h....52.50
Compote, open, 8" d., 4¾" h....70.00
Decanter w/stopper, qt. ......300.00 to 325.00
Egg cup, clambroth, flint....385.00
Egg cup, clear....55.00
Goblet....95.00
Honey dish, 3½" d., 1" h. 15.00
Lamp, whale oil, 11" h. 122.50
Plate, 6" d. 90.00
Salt dip, individual size....30.00
Salt dip, master size....36.00
Sauce dish....26.00
Spooner, chartreuse green....1,200.00
Spooner, clambroth w/gilt trim....850.00
Spooner, clear....35.00 to 45.00
Spooner, starch blue w/original gilt decoration of grape leaves....1,500.00
Tumbler, footed....335.00
Tumbler, whiskey....230.00

CABLE WITH RING

Creamer, applied handle, flint....165.00
Lamp, kerosene-type, w/ring handle, flint....195.00
Sauce dish, flint....14.00

CALIFORNIA - See Beaded Grape Pattern

CANNON BALL - See Atlas Pattern

CAPE COD

Bread platter....48.00
Compote, cov., 8" d., 12" h. 155.00
Compote, open, 8" d., 5½" h....45.00
Cruet w/original stopper....43.00
Goblet....47.00
Marmalade jar, cov. 65.00
Pitcher, water....95.00
Plate, 6" d. 35.00
Plate, 10" d., open handles....48.00
Sauce dish, flat or footed....16.00

CATHEDRAL

Cathedral Compote

Bowl, 6" d., crimped rim, blue....25.00
Bowl, 6" d., clear....16.00
Bowl, 7" d., clear....20.00
Bowl, berry, 8" d., amber....48.00
Butter dish, cov. 44.00
Cake stand, amber....55.00
Compote, cov., 8" d., high stand, blue....185.00
Compote, open, 9" d., 5½" h., amber ...65.00
Compote, open, 9" d., 5½" h., blue....65.00
Compote. open, 10½" d., 8" h., shaped rim, clear (ILLUS.)....55.00
Creamer....35.00
Cruet w/original stopper, amber....100.00
Goblet, amber....37.00
Goblet, clear....38.00
Goblet, ruby-stained....65.00
Relish, fish-shaped, amber....40.00
Sauce dish, flat or footed, ruby-stained....22.00
Sauce dish, flat or footed, vaseline....20.00
Spooner, clear....28.00
Spooner, vaseline....48.00
Sugar bowl, cov. 50.00
Tumbler....24.00
Wine, clear....26.00
Wine, vaseline....65.00

CHANDELIER (Crown Jewel)

Butter dish, cov. 100.00
Cake stand, 10" d. 75.00
Celery vase....40.00
Compote, open, 9¼" d., 7¾" h....57.00
Creamer....55.00
Goblet....50.00
Goblet, engraved....60.00
Inkwell....55.00
Pitcher, water, tankard, ½ pt.... 65.00
Pitcher, water, tankard, ½ gal....125.00
Salt dip, footed....36.00
Sauce dish, flat....16.00
Spooner....45.00
Tumbler....40.00
Waste bowl....25.00

CLASSIC

Bowl, open, 8" hexagon, open log feet....100.00 to 125.00
Butter dish, cov., open log feet....225.00
Celery vase, collared base....150.00
Celery vase, open log feet....165.00
Compote, cov., 6½" d., collared base....200.00
Compote, cov., 7½" d., 8" h., open log feet....220.00
Compote, open, 7¾" d., open log feet....150.00
Creamer, collared base....125.00
Creamer, open log feet....150.00 to 175.00
Goblet....275.00 to 300.00
Pitcher, water, collared base....225.00 to 275.00

Pitcher, water, 9½" h., open log feet...425.00
Plate, 10" d., "Blaine" or "Hendricks," signed Jacobus, each 215.00
Plate, 10" d., "Cleveland" 200.00
Plate, 10" d., "Warrior" ....150.00 to 175.00
Sauce dish, open log feet 40.00
Spooner, collared base 95.00
Spooner, open log feet 135.00
Sugar bowl, cov., open log feet 185.00

COLORADO (Lacy Medallion)

Banana bowl, two turned-up sides, blue 35.00
Banana stand, green 45.00
Berry set: 8" d. master bowl & five 4" d. sauce dishes; green w/gold, 6 pcs. 160.00
Bowl, 7" d., footed 25.00
Bowl, 7½" d., footed, turned-up sides, blue w/gold 50.00
Bowl, 9" d., green w/gold 45.00
Bowl, 9" d., footed, crimped edge, green...40.00
Bowl, 10" d., footed, flared & scalloped rim 45.00
Butter dish, cov., blue w/gold 260.00
Butter dish, cov., clear 85.00
Celery vase, green w/gold 70.00
Cheese dish, cov., blue w/gold 70.00
Compote, open, 6" d., 4" h., crimped rim 22.00
Creamer, blue, souvenir 60.00
Creamer, clear.......................................34.00
Cup & saucer, green..............................45.00
Mug, green, souvenir, miniature 22.50
Mug, green 30.00
Nappy, tricornered, green w/gold 29.00
Rose bowl, blue 60.00
Salt shaker w/original top, ruby-stained, souvenir...............................75.00
Sauce dish, blue w/gold.........................30.00
Sauce dish, clambroth 20.00
Sauce dish, clear 13.00
Spooner, blue w/gold.............50.00 to 60.00
Spooner, clear 40.00
Spooner, green w/gold 60.00
Sugar bowl, cov., clear, large 53.00
Sugar bowl, cov., green, large..............80.00
Sugar bowl, open, individual size, clear 20.00
Table set, green w/gold, 4 pcs. ....325.00 to 350.00
*Toothpick holder, blue w/gold 60.00
*Toothpick holder, clear w/gold 25.00
*Toothpick holder, green w/gold...........35.00
*Toothpick holder, green w/gold souvenir 30.00
*Toothpick holder, ruby-stained, souvenir 55.00
Tumbler, green w/gold...........................32.00
Tumbler, green w/gold, souvenir 30.00
Vase, 2½" h., green 45.00
Vase, 10½" h., blue 78.00
Water set: pitcher & 6 tumblers; green w/gold, 7 pcs. 450.00
Wine, clear...26.00
Wine, green w/gold................................40.00

COLUMBIAN COIN

Bowl, 8½" d., 3" h., frosted coins 75.00
Celery vase, frosted coins 110.00
Compote, cov., 8" d., frosted coins 157.00
Compote, open, 8" d., clear coins.........68.00
Creamer, gilded coins..........................125.00
Cruet w/original stopper, frosted coins 195.00
*Goblet, gilded coins.............................80.00
Lamp, kerosene-type, milk white, 8" h..400.00
Lamp, kerosene-type, frosted coins, 12" h. 180.00
Mug, frosted coins 120.00
Pitcher, milk, gilded coins 195.00
Relish, frosted coins, 5 x 8" 68.00
Sauce dish, flat or footed, frosted coins 42.00
Spooner, gilded coins............................77.50
Syrup pitcher w/original top, frosted coins 335.00
*Tumbler, clear coins 30.00
*Tumbler, gilded coins 55.00
Wine, frosted coins 145.00

COMPACT - See Snail Pattern

CORD & TASSEL

Cord & Tassel Creamer

Cake stand, 9½" d. 65.00
Compote, cov., 8" d. 75.00
Creamer (ILLUS.) 36.00
Goblet 38.00
Lamp, kerosene-type, applied handle ..85.00
Pitcher, water...98.00
Salt shaker w/original top, blue.............45.00
Spooner 23.00
Syrup pitcher w/original top, applied handle 110.00
Tumbler, water.......................................50.00
Wine 38.00

CROESUS

Berry set: master bowl & 6 sauce dishes; clear, 7 pcs. 300.00
Berry set: master bowl & 6 sauce dishes; green w/gold, 7 pcs. 395.00
Bowl, 7" d., 4" h., footed, purple w/gold 225.00
Bowl, 8" d., purple....175.00
Bowl, berry or fruit, 9" d., green....108.00
Bowl, berry or fruit, 9" d., purple....165.00
*Butter dish, cov., clear....98.00
*Butter dish, cov., green.....150.00 to 165.00
*Butter dish, cov., purple....200.00 to 225.00
Celery vase, gree w/gold....170.00
Celery vase, purple....300.00
Compote, open, jelly, green....225.00 to 275.00
Condiment tray, purple....90.00
*Creamer, green....80.00 to 100.00
*Creamer, purple....145.00
Creamer, individual size, purple, 3" h....130.00
Pitcher, milk, green....85.00
Pitcher, water, green....285.00
Pitcher, water, purple....400.00 to 500.00
Relish, boat-shaped, green....60.00
Salt shaker w/original top, green w/gold....100.00
Sauce dish, clear....23.00
Sauce dish, green w/gold....37.00
Sauce dish, purple w/gold....42.00
*Spooner, green....73.00
*Spooner, green w/gold....90.00 to 100.00
*Spooner, purple....80.00
*Spooner, purple w/gold....97.50
*Sugar bowl, cov., clear....78.00
*Sugar bowl, cov., green....110.00
Sugar bowl, cov., green w/gold....185.00
*Sugar bowl, cov., purple....150.00 to 175.00
*Sugar bowl, cov., purple w/gold....180.00
Table set, purple, 4 pcs....630.00
*Toothpick holder, green....65.00
*Toothpick holder, green w/gold....95.00
*Toothpick holder, purple....100.00 to 125.00
Toothpick holder, purple w/gold....130.00
*Tumbler, green....42.00
*Tumbler, green w/gold....54.00
*Tumbler, purple w/gold....70.00
Water set: pitcher & 5 tumblers; green, 6 pcs....450.00 to 500.00
Water set: pitcher & 6 tumblers; purple, 7 pcs....850.00 to 900.00

CROWN JEWEL - See Chandelier Pattern

CRYSTAL BALL - See Atlas Pattern

CUPID & VENUS (Guardian Angel)

Bowl, open, 8" d., footed....28.00
Bowl, 9" oval....50.00
Bread plate, amber, 10½" d....155.00
Bread plate, clear, 10½" d....45.00
Bread plate, vaseline, 10½" d....145.00
Butter dish, cov....110.00
Cake plate, 11" d....45.00
Celery vase....55.00
Champagne....110.00
Compote, cov., 7" d., high stand....110.00
Compote, cov., 7" d., low stand....65.00
Compote, open, 8½" d., low stand, scalloped rim....40.00
Cordial....85.00
Creamer....55.00
Goblet....67.00
Honey dish, 3½" d....15.00
Mug, 3½" h....40.00
Pitcher, milk....65.00
Pitcher, water....90.00
Relish, oval, 4½ x 7"....30.00

Cupid & Venus Sauce Dish

Sauce dish, footed, 3½" to 4½" d. (ILLUS.)....14.00
Spooner....35.00
Sugar bowl, cov....70.00
Wine....85.00

CURRIER & IVES

"Balky Mule" Water Tray

Bowl, master berry or fruit, 10" oval, flat w/collared base....35.00
Compote, cov., 7½" d., high stand....90.00
Compote, cov., 11½" d., amber....145.00
Compote, open, 7½" d., high stand, scalloped rim....50.00
Cup & saucer, blue....85.00
Cup & saucer, clear....42.50

Goblet, amber....95.00
Goblet, clear....30.00
Lamp, kerosene-type, 9½" h....80.00
Pitcher, milk....65.00
Pitcher, water, amber....145.00
Pitcher, water, clear....75.00
Salt shaker w/original top, blue....75.00
Salt & pepper shakers w/original tops, pr....65.00
Sauce dish, flat or footed....15.00
Spooner....35.00
Sugar bowl, cov....35.00 to 45.00
Syrup jug w/original top, amber....210.00
Syrup jug w/original top, blue....162.00
Syrup jug w/original top, clear....70.00
Tray, water, Balky Mule on Railroad Tracks, clear, 9½" d. (ILLUS.)....49.00
Tray, water, Balky Mule on Railroad Tracks, blue, 12" d....150.00
Tray, water, Balky Mule on Railroad Tracks, clear, 12" d....65.00
Tumbler, footed....38.00
Waste bowl....42.00
Wine, clear....25.00
Wine, ruby-stained....85.00

DAHLIA

Dahlia Water Pitcher

Bread platter, 8 x 12"....45.00
Butter dish, cov., clear....52.00
Cake stand, amber, 9½" d....75.00
Cake stand, blue, 9½" d....52.50
Creamer....28.00
Goblet....38.00
Mug, amber....45.00
Mug, blue....60.00
Pitcher, milk, applied handle....55.00
Pitcher, water, blue (ILLUS.)....125.00
Pitcher, water, clear....50.00
Plate, 7" d....18.00
Plate, 9" d., w/handles, apple green....42.50
Plate, 9" d., w/handles, clear....25.00
Relish, clear, 5 x 9½"....13.00
Relish, green, 5 x 9½"....25.00
Sauce dish, flat, amber....22.00
Spooner....35.00
Sugar bowl, cov., vaseline....60.00

Wine, amber....55.00
Wine, clear....32.00

DAISY & BUTTON

Daisy & Button Canoe

Banana boat, 14" l....45.00
Basket, silver plate handle, 6" h....125.00
Berry set: triangular master bowl & 4 sauce dishes; vaseline, 5 pcs....150.00
Bowl, 7 x 9½", sapphire blue....30.00
Bowl, 9" sq., amber....40.00
*Bowl, 10" oval, blue....65.00
Bowl, 10 x 11" oval, 7 ¾" h., flared, vaseline....95.00
Bowl, 11" d., amber....38.00
*Bread tray, amber....25.00
*Butter chip, fan-shaped....9.50
*Butter chip, round....6.00
Butter chip, square, amber....15.00
Butter chip, square, Amberina....75.00
Butter dish, cov., scalloped base....65.00
Butter dish, cov., square, clear....45.00
*Butter dish, cov., model of Victorian stove, green....215.00
Cake stand, blue....50.00
Cake stand, clear, 9" sq., 6" h....45.00
Canoe, vaseline, 4" l....18.00
Canoe, amber, 8" l. (ILLUS.)....35.00
Canoe, blue, 8" l....46.00
Canoe, blue, 11" l....60.00
Canoe, amber, 12" l....42.50
Canoe, green, 13" l....48.00
Castor set, 5-bottle, vaseline, in original frame....495.00
Celery tray, flat, boat-shaped, 4½ x 14"....90.00
Celery vase, square....65.00
Celery vase, triangular, amber....65.00
Compote, cov., 8½" d., low stand, amber....60.00
Creamer, child's, amber....25.00
*Creamer, blue....40.00
*Creamer, clear....29.00
*Cruet w/original stopper, amber....100.00
*Cruet w/original stopper, blue....95.00
*Cruet w/original stopper, clear....45.00
Cuspidor, blue....38.00
*Goblet, amber....32.00
*Goblet, blue....25.00
*Goblet, clear....22.50
*Hat shape, amber, 2½" h....29.00
*Hat shape, blue, 2½" h....35.00
*Hat shape, vaseline, 2½" h....38.00

*Hat shape, from tumbler mold, 4½" widest d. 55.00
*Hat shape, blue, from tumbler mold, 4¾" widest d. 45.00
Hat shape, clear, 8 x 8", 6" h. 85.00
Ice cream set: 2 x 7 x 9½" ice cream tray & two square sauce plates; amber, 3 pcs. 85.00
Match holder, wall-hanging scuff, clear 65.00
*Pickle castor, sapphire blue insert, w/silver plate frame & tongs 238.00
*Pickle castor, vaseline insert, w/silver plate frame & tongs 185.00
Pitcher, 5⅛" h., applied handle, amber 55.00
Pitcher, water, tankard, 9" h., amber ..125.00
Pitcher, water, bulbous, applied handle, ruby-stained buttons 325.00
Plate, 9" d., vaseline 40.00
*Plate, 10" d., scalloped rim, amber 28.00
*Plate, 10" d., scalloped rim, blue 35.00
Powder jar, cov., blue 38.00
Relish, "Sitz bathtub" 145.00
*Rose bowl, vaseline 38.00
*Salt dip, canoe-shaped, vaseline, 2 x 4" 12.00
*Salt shaker w/original top, corset-shaped, blue 25.00
*Salt & pepper shakers w/original tops, vaseline, pr. 50.00
Salt & pepper shakers, blue & amber, pr., w/clear glass stand 55.00
*Sauce dish, amber, 4" to 5" sq. 15.00
Sauce dish, Amberina, 4" to 5" sq. 115.00
*Sauce dish, blue, 4" to 5" sq. 16.00
*Sauce dish, vaseline, 4" to 5" sq. 20.00
Sauce dish, tricornered, vaseline 16.00
*Slipper, "1886 patent," amber 46.00
*Slipper, "1886 patent," blue 47.00
Slipper, ruby-stained buttons 80.00
•Spooner, amber 40.00
Spooner, Amberina, 5" h. 150.00
Spooner, amethyst 30.00
*Spooner, clear 30.00
Syrup pitcher, w/original pewter top, blue 175.00
Toothpick holder, fan-shaped, amber 35.00
Toothpick holder, square, blue 24.00
*Toothpick holder, three-footed, amber 30.00
Toothpick holder, three-footed, Amberina 170.00
*Toothpick holder, three-footed, electric blue 55.00
Toothpick holder, urn-shaped, clear 22.50
Toothpick holder, urn-shaped, vaseline 30.00
Tray, ice cream, handled, blue, 9¼ x 16½" 30.00
Tray, water, amber, 11" d. 95.00
Tumbler, water, blue 30.00
Tumbler, water, blue, pattern halfway up 30.00
Tumbler, water, clear 20.00
Waste bowl, vaseline 30.00
Whimsey, "canoe," wall hanging-type, ruby-stained buttons, 11" l. 110.00
Whimsey, "cradle," amber 45.00
*Whimsey, "dustpan," light blue 42.50
*Whimsey, "sleigh," amber, 4½ x 7¾" 225.00
Whimsey, "wheel barrow," vaseline 125.00
*Whimsey, "whisk broom" dish, amber 28.00
*Whimsey, "whisk broom" dish, blue 75.00
*Wine 20.00

DAISY & BUTTON WITH THUMBPRINT PANELS

Bowl, 7" w., heart-shaped, amber panels 42.50
Bowl, 8" sq., amber 28.00
Bowl, 9" sq., amber 28.00
Cake stand, vaseline, 10½" d., 7¼" h. 75.00
Celery vase, amber panels 125.00
Celery vase, clear 26.00
Creamer, applied handle, amber panels 68.00
*Goblet, amber panels 45.00
*Goblet, blue panels 55.00
Pitcher, water, vaseline 165.00
Salt shaker w/original top, amber panels 75.00
Spooner, amber panels 75.00
Tray, water, vaseline 95.00
Tumbler, amber panels 38.50
Tumbler, clear 25.00
Tumbler, vaseline 30.00

DAKOTA (Baby Thumbprint)

Dakota Engraved Celery Vase

Butter dish, cov., engraved 72.00
Butter dish, cov., plain 55.00
Cake stand, 8" d., engraved 50.00
Cake stand, 10¼" d., plain 58.00
Cake stand w/high domed cover 295.00
Celery vase, flat base, engraved (ILLUS.) 42.00

Celery vase, flat base, plain 35.00
Cologne bottle w/original stopper, 7" h...135.00
Compote, cov., jelly, 5" d., 5" h. 45.00
Compote, cov., 6" d., high stand, engraved ....75.00 to 100.00
Compote, open, jelly, 5" d., 5½" h., engraved 35.00
Compote, open, jelly, 5" d., 5" h., plain 36.00
Compote, open, 6" d. 30.00
Compote, open, 7" d., engraved 40.00
Creamer, table, plain 45.00
Creamer, hotel.....................................110.00
Cruet w/original stopper, engraved.....145.00
Goblet, clear, engraved 35.00
Goblet, clear, plain................................24.00
Goblet, ruby-stained, engraved 95.00
Goblet, ruby-stained, plain....................65.00
Pitcher, milk, jug-type, engraved, pt. ..235.00
Pitcher, milk, tankard, engraved, pt. ...145.00
Pitcher, milk, tankard, plain, pt. 90.00
*Pitcher, tankard, water, engraved, ½ gal. 254.00
Plate, 10" d. 63.00
Salt shaker w/original top 50.00
Sauce dish, flat or footed, clear, engraved 18.00
Shaker bottle w/original top, 5" h. 68.00
Shaker bottle w/original top, hotel size, 6½" h. 65.00
Spooner, engraved 35.00
Spooner, plain 40.00
Sugar bowl, cov., engraved 62.50
Sugar bowl, cov., plain 48.00
Tray, water, piecrust rim, engraved, 13" d...125.00
Tumbler, clear, plain 30.00
Tumbler, ruby-stained............................45.00
Waste bowl, engraved 75.00
Waste bowl, plain 58.00
Wine, clear, engraved............................40.00
Wine, clear, plain 30.00
Wine, ruby-stained.................................50.00

DEER & PINE TREE

Bowl, 5½ x 7¼"......................................45.00
Bread tray, blue, 8 x 13" 110.00
Bread tray, canary yellow, 8 x 13" 100.00

Deer & Pine Tree Bread Tray

Bread tray, clear, 8 x 13" (ILLUS.) 45.00

Butter dish, cov. 105.00
Cake stand 110.00
Celery vase...80.00
Compote, cov., 8" sq., high stand.......200.00
Creamer..62.50
*Goblet..50.00
Marmalade jar, cov. 110.00
Mug, child's, apple green.......................45.00
Mug, large, clear....................................37.50
Pickle dish 18.00
Pitcher, water.....................125.00 to 150.00
Sauce dish, flat or footed......................18.00
Spooner 45.00
Sugar bowl, cov. 62.50
Tray, water, handled, 9 x 15"..............135.00
Vegetable dish, 5¾ x 9" 50.00

DELAWARE (Four Petal Flower)

Delaware Banana Boat

Banana boat, green w/gold, 11¾" l.......90.00
Banana boat, rose w/gold, 11¾" l. (ILLUS.) 120.00
Berry set: boat-shaped master bowl & 5 boat-shaped sauce dishes; rose w/gold, 6 pcs. ....250.00 to 300.00
Bowl, 8" d., clear w/gold 55.00
Bowl, 8" d., green w/gold 50.00
Bride's basket, boat-shaped open bowl, green w/gold, in silver plate frame, 11½" oval 160.00
Bride's basket, rose w/gold, miniature 85.00
Butter dish, cov., clear 125.00
*Butter dish, cov., green w/gold..........125.00
Butter dish, cov., rose w/gold 165.00
Celery vase, rose band w/gold 45.00
Celery vase, green w/gold.....................82.50
*Creamer, clear w/gold 45.00
Creamer, green w/gold..........................58.00
Creamer, rose w/gold 55.00
Creamer, individual size, clear w/gold ..25.00
Cruet w/original stopper, green w/gold 185.00
Cruet w/original stopper, rose w/gold 325.00
Marmalade dish w/silver plate holder, green w/gold 45.00
Marmalade dish w/silver plate holder, rose w/gold 85.00
Pitcher, tankard, green w/gold............150.00
Pitcher, tankard, rose w/gold ....200.00 to 225.00
Pitcher, water, clear w/gold ....50.00 to 75.00
Pomade jar w/jeweled cover, rose w/gold 335.00

Powder jar, cov., green w/gold 225.00
Punch cup, clear 16.00
Punch cup, rose w/gold 45.00
Salt shaker w/original top 85.00
Sauce dish, boat-shaped, clear 18.00
Sauce dish, boat-shaped, green w/gold 35.00
Sauce dish, round, rose w/gold 24.00
Shade, gas, rose w/gold 295.00
Spooner, green w/gold 50.00
Sugar bowl, cov., clear 62.50
*Sugar bowl, cov., green w/gold 90.00
Sugar bowl, cov., rose w/gold...............90.00
Sugar bowl, individual size, rose w/gold 95.00
Table set, green w/gold, 4 pcs............400.00
Toothpick holder, green w/gold 101.00
Toothpick holder, rose w/gold.............125.00
Tumbler, green w/gold...........................40.00
Tumbler, rose w/gold 50.00
Vase, 6" h., green w/gold.......................65.00
Vase, 8" h., clear 105.00
Vase, 9½" h., green w/gold..................110.00
Vase, 9½" h., rose w/gold....................115.00
Water set: water pitcher & 4 tumblers; green w/gold, 5 pcs.........................550.00

DEWEY (Flower Flange)

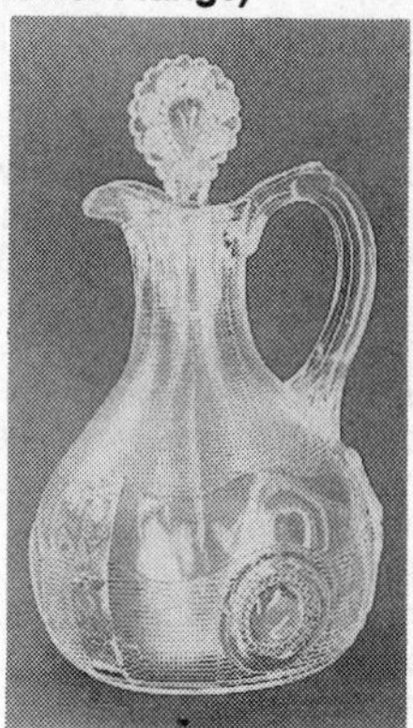

Dewey Cruet

Bowl, 8" d..35.00
*Butter dish, cov., amber 85.00
*Butter dish, cov., clear.........................55.00
*Butter dish, cov., green 80.00
Butter dish, cov., green, miniature........75.00
Creamer, cov., individual size...............45.00
Creamer, amber 60.00
Creamer & cov. sugar bowl, individual size, canary yellow, pr. 150.00
Cruet w/original stopper, amber 125.00
Cruet w/original stopper, canary yellow (ILLUS.) 170.00
Cruet w/original stopper, green...............................150.00 to 200.00
Mug, amber 60.00
Parfait, clear 40.00
Pitcher, water, amber 110.00
Pitcher, water, canary yellow..............145.00

Plate, footed, green 65.00
Salt shaker w/original top, amber 62.50
Sauce dish, canary yellow 35.00
Sauce dish, green...................................30.00
Sugar bowl, cov., clear 35.00
Sugar bowl, cov., green 75.00
Tray, serpentine shape, amber, small ..45.00
Tumbler, canary yellow..........................55.00
Tumbler, clear...45.00
Water set: pitcher & 6 tumblers; clear, 7 pcs. ....300.00 to 350.00

DIAMOND POINT

Diamond Point Creamer

Bar bottle, flint.....................................125.00
Butter dish, cov., flint 82.50
Celery vase, pedestal base w/knob stem, flint 90.00
Compote, open, 7" d., low stand, flint...67.50
Compote, open, 7" d., high stand, milk white 175.00
Compote, open, 10¼" d., high stand, milk white 350.00
Cordial, flint..195.00
Creamer, applied handle, flint (ILLUS.) 165.00
Cup plate, flint..60.00
Decanter w/original stopper, pt...........100.00
Decanter w/original stopper, qt...........165.00
Egg cup, canary yellow, flint ....300.00 to 350.00
Egg cup, clambroth, flint.....................135.00
Goblet, clear, flint...................................58.00
Goblet, amber, non-flint 25.00
Goblet, blue, non-flint 32.00
Goblet, clear, non-flint 35.00
Honey dish, clear, flint 18.00
Honey dish, milk white, flint 60.00
Honey dish, coarse points, non-flint 12.00
Pitcher, milk, applied handle, milk white, flint 550.00
Pitcher, water, bulbous, flint 350.00
Pitcher, water, non-flint..........................75.00
Plate, 8" d., milk white, flint.................125.00
Salt dip, cov., master size, flint 195.00
Sauce dish, flint, 4¼" d. 20.00
Sauce dish, non-flint, 3½" to 5½" d.......10.00

Spillholder, clear, flint 42.50
Sugar bowl, cov., flint 95.00
Sugar bowl, cov., non-flint 45.00
Toothpick holder, non-flint 35.00
Tumbler, flint..45.00
Tumbler, bar, flint....................................95.00
Wine, flint 100.00
Wine, non-flint...30.00

DIAMOND THUMBPRINT

Bowl, 7" d., footed, scalloped rim 95.00
Bowl, 8" d., footed, scalloped rim 100.00
*Butter dish, cov. ....150.00 to 200.00
Celery vase.........................175.00 to 200.00
Compote, open, 7" d., low stand, extended scalloped rim 125.00
Compote, open, 8" d., high stand 125.00
Compote, open, 11½" d., high stand ..300.00
Cordial, 4" h. 295.00
*Creamer, applied handle 200.00
Decanter w/bar lip, qt., 10½" h. 195.00
Decanter w/original stopper, qt...........225.00
*Goblet 450.00
Honey dish..25.00
Pitcher, water......................400.00 to 600.00
Sauce dish, flat 20.00
*Spooner...86.00
*Sugar bowl, cov. 150.00
Tray, serpentine shape, amber, small 45.00
*Tumbler ....50.00 to 90.00
Tumbler, bar, 3¾" h. 150.00
Tumbler, whiskey 150.00
Wine 235.00

DORIC - See Feather Pattern

EGYPTIAN

Egyptian Spooner

Bread platter, Cleopatra center, 9 x 12" 57.00
*Bread platter, Salt Lake Temple center 248.00
Butter dish, cov. 73.00
Celery vase...........................75.00 to 100.00
Compote, cov., 6" d., 6" h., sphinx base ....100.00 to 125.00
Compote, cov., 7" d., high stand, sphinx base 195.00
Compote, cov., 8" d., high stand, sphinx base 225.00
Creamer...45.00
Goblet 45.00
Pickle dish 20.00
Pitcher, water......................200.00 to 225.00
Plate, 10" d. 65.00
Plate, 12" d., handled 85.00
Relish, 5½ x 8½".......................................32.50
Sauce dish, flat 18.50
Sauce dish, footed 16.50
Spooner (ILLUS.) 45.00
Table set, 4 pcs. 295.00

EMERALD GREEN HERRINGBONE - See Paneled Herringbone Pattern

ENGLISH HOBNAIL CROSS - See Klondike Pattern

ESTHER

Esther Sauce Dish

Berry set: master bowl & 5 sauce dishes; green, 6 pcs. 215.00
Bowl, 8" d., clear.......................................35.00
Butter dish, cov., clear 75.00
Butter dish, cov., green............................145.00
Cake stand, 10½" d., 6" h. 50.00
Celery vase, amber-stained.....................125.00
Celery vase, clear 35.00
Compote, open, jelly, 5" d., green 60.00
Creamer, green 90.00
Cruet w/original stopper, clear, miniature 30.00
Cruet w/ball-shaped stopper, green.............................250.00 to 300.00
Goblet, amber-stained w/enamel decoration ....125.00 to 150.00
Goblet, clear 60.00
Pitcher, water, amber-stained ....200.00 to 250.00
Plate, 10¼" d. 30.00
Relish, clear, 4½ x 8½" 22.50
Relish, green, 4½ x 8½" 36.00
Salt & pepper shakers w/original tops, green, pr. 130.00
Sauce dish, clear, engraved (ILLUS.)...15.00
Sauce dish, green......................................25.00
Spooner, green 68.00
Sugar bowl, cov., green..........................125.00

Toothpick holder, amber-stained ....100.00 to 150.00
Toothpick holder, green....115.00
Tray, ice cream, clear....67.50
Tray, ice cream, green....145.00
Tumbler, clear....32.00
Tumbler, green w/gold....65.00
Water set: pitcher & 6 tumblers; green, 7 pcs. 545.00
Wine, amber-stained 75.00
Wine, ruby-stained, souvenir 75.00

EXCELSIOR

Excelsior Goblet

Bar bottle, flint, qt....70.00
Cake stand, flint, 9¼" h....150.00
Celery vase, flint....78.00
Champagne 85.00
Cologne bottle w/faceted stopper 95.00
Creamer, applied handle 275.00
Egg cup 47.50
Egg cup, double, fiery opalescent, flint 295.00
Goblet, flint (ILLUS.) 68.00
Platter, 9¼" l. 22.00
Spillholder, flint 76.00
Sugar bowl, cov. ....100.00 to 125.00
Tumbler, bar, flint, 3½" h. 60.00
Wine, flint....50.00

FEATHER (Doric, Indiana Swirl or Finecut & Feather)

Berry set, master bowl & 6 sauce dishes, 7 pcs....120.00
Bowl, 7 x 9" oval 24.00
Butter dish, cov., clear 60.00
Butter dish, cov., green....195.00
Cake stand, 8½" d....32.50
Cake stand, clear, 9½" h. 47.00
Celery vase....40.00
Compote, open, jelly, 5" d., 4¾" h., amber-stained....110.00
Compote, open, jelly, 5" d., 4¾" h., clear 23.00
Creamer, clear 38.00
Creamer, green 75.00
Cruet w/original stopper, clear....37.00
Cruet w/original stopper, green 250.00
Doughnut stand, 8" w., 4½" h. 36.00
Goblet, amber-stained....140.00

Feather Goblet

Goblet, clear (ILLUS.)....60.00
Pickle dish 15.00
Pitcher, milk 47.50
Pitcher, water, clear....60.00
Pitcher, water, green ....175.00 to 200.00
Relish, 8¼" oval, clear 18.00
Salt & pepper shakers w/original tops, green, pr. 225.00
Sauce dish, flat or footed, clear 14.50
Sauce dish, flat or footed, green....45.00
Spooner....30.00
Sugar bowl, cov., clear 46.00
Sugar bowl, cov., green....150.00
Syrup pitcher w/original top, clear 135.00
Syrup pitcher w/original top, green....315.00
Toothpick holder....85.00
Tumbler, clear....45.00
Tumbler, green 85.00
*Wine 37.50

FLORIDA - See Paneled Herringbone Pattern

FLOWER FLANGE - See Dewey Pattern

FOUR PETAL FLOWER - See Delaware Pattern

FROSTED LION (Rampant Lion)

Bowl, cov., 3⅞ x 6⅞" oblong, collared base 80.00
Bowl, cov., 4⅝ x 7 7/16" oblong, collared base 110.00
*Bread plate, rope edge, closed handles,10½" d. 78.00
*Butter dish, cov., frosted lion's head finial 90.00
Butter dish, cov., rampant lion finial....140.00
*Celery vase 70.00
Cheese dish, cov., rampant lion finial 425.00
Compote, cov., 5" d., 8½" h. 175.00

*Compote, cov., 6¾" oval, 7" h., collared base, rampant lion finial ....150.00 to 175.00
Compote, cov., 7" d., 11" h., lion head finial 150.00

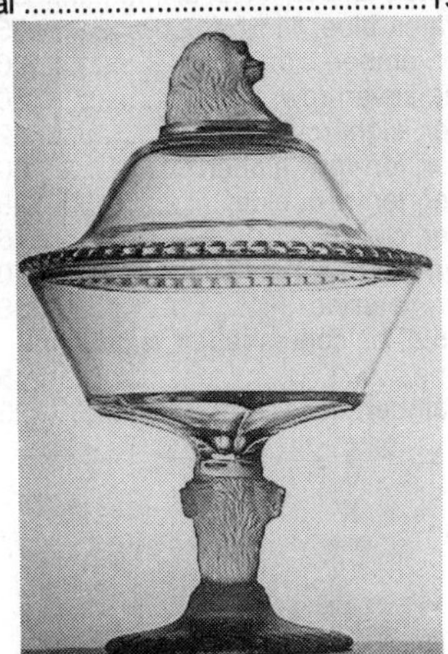

Frosted Lion Compote

Compote, cov., 8¼" d., high stand, frosted lion head finial (ILLUS.) 145.00
Compote, cov., 5½ x 8¾" oval, 8¼" h., rampant lion finial................185.00
Compote, open, 5" d., low stand...........62.00
Creamer................75.00
*Egg Cup 90.00
*Goblet................93.00
Marmalade jar, cov., rampant lion finial 145.00
*Pitcher, water ....525.00 to 550.00
Platter, 9 x 10½" oval, lion handles 95.00
Salt dip, cov., master size, collared base, rectangular 295.00
*Sauce dish, 4" to 5" d. 25.00
*Spooner................54.00
*Sugar bowl, cov., frosted lion's head finial 50.00
Sugar bowl, cov., rampant lion finial.....80.00
Table set, cov. sugar bowl, creamer & spooner, 3 pcs. 225.00

GALLOWAY (Mirror or misnamed Virginia)

Bowl, 9½" d., flat................30.00
Butter dish, cov................55.00
Cake stand, 9¼" d., 6" h. 52.00
Compote, open, 4¼" d., 6" h................33.00
Compote, open, 8½" d., 7" h................60.00
Creamer, clear................22.00
Creamer, rose-stained................75.00
Creamer, individual size, clear 19.00
Goblet................90.00
Mug, 4½" d. 37.50
Olive dish, 4 x 6"................19.00
Pitcher, milk................70.00
Pitcher, water................45.00
Punch cup................10.00
Relish, 8¼" l................14.50
Salt shaker w/original top 20.00
Salt & pepper shakers w/original tops, gold trim, 3" h., pr................47.50
Sauce dish, flat or footed................11.00
Spooner, clear 22.50
Spooner, rose-stained 80.00
Sugar bowl, cov., rose-stained 85.00
Sugar shaker w/original top 35.00
Syrup pitcher w/metal spring top 75.00
Table set, 4 pcs. ....225.00 to 275.00
*Toothpick holder, clear................22.50
*Toothpick holder, green 50.00
Tumbler 25.00
Vase, 9½" h. 32.00
Waste bowl 38.00
Water set: pitcher & 4 tumblers; rose-stained, 5 pcs................495.00
Wine 41.00

GOOD LUCK - See Horseshoe Pattern

GRAPE & FESTOON

Butter dish, cov., stippled leaf...............40.00
Compote, cov., 8" d., low stand, acorn finial, stippled leaf 55.00
Compote, cov., large, high stand, w/bird's nest finial 85.00
Creamer, stippled leaf 42.00
Egg cup, stippled leaf 20.00
Goblet, stippled leaf................23.00
Goblet, veined leaf................25.00
Mug................20.00
Pitcher, water, stippled leaf 90.00
Relish, stippled leaf 10.00
Salt dip, footed, stippled leaf 22.00
Sauce dish, flat, stippled leaf, 4" d..........9.00
Spooner, stippled leaf................25.00
Spooner, veined leaf................25.00
Wine, stippled leaf 50.00

GUARDIAN ANGEL - See Cupid & Venus Pattern

HEART WITH THUMBPRINT

Heart with Thumbprint Creamer

Banana boat, 6½ x 7½"................115.00
Berry set, master bowl & 5 sauce dishes,6 pcs. 125.00

Bowl, 7" sq., 3½" h....37.50
Bowl, 8" d., 2" h., flared rim....25.00
Butter dish, cov....125.00
Cake stand, 9" d., 5" h....150.00 to 175.00
Card tray, clear....19.00
Card tray, green....55.00
Celery vase....53.00
Compote, open, jelly, two handles, green....25.00
Cordial, 3" h....200.00 to 250.00
Creamer....39.00
Creamer, individual size, clear (ILLUS.)....30.00
Cruet w/original stopper....65.00
Goblet, clear....55.00
Goblet, green w/gold....125.00
Ice bucket....75.00
Lamp, kerosene-type, green, 9" h....250.00 to 275.00
Nappy, heart-shaped....42.50
Olive dish....19.50
Plate, 6" d....25.00
Punch cup, clear....22.50
Rose bowl, 3¾" d....55.00
Sauce dish....15.00
Spooner....55.00
Sugar bowl, cov., large....95.00
Sugar bowl, open, individual size, green w/gold....45.00
Syrup jug w/original pewter top....108.00
Syrup jug w/original pewter top, miniature, 4" h....100.00 to 125.00
Tray, 4¼ x 8¼"....30.00
Tumbler, water, clear w/gold....45.00
Vase, 10" h., trumpet-shaped....65.00
Waste bowl....85.00
Wine, clear....48.00
Wine, green w/gold....135.00

HOBNAIL

*Butter dish, cov., clear....85.00
Celery vase, footed, square, clear....20.00
*Cologne bottle, amber, 6½" h....37.50
*Cologne bottle, clear, 6½" h....22.00
*Creamer, fluted top, applied handle, amber, 2 x 3"....25.00
Creamer, three-footed, blue....25.00
*Creamer, individual size, amber....31.00
*Cruet w/original stopper, 4½" h....45.00
Egg cup, single....28.50
Egg cup, double....15.00
*Goblet....15.00
Mug, amber....30.00
Pitcher, 8" h., square top, amber....235.00
Pitcher, 8" h., square top, sapphire blue....265.00
Pitcher, water, blue....125.00
*Punch cup....22.50
*Rose bowl, 6" d., 5½" h....85.00
Salt shaker w/original top, blue....35.00
Spooner, ruffled rim, amber....35.00
*Spooner, clear....30.00
Spooner, frosted....35.00
*Sugar bowl, cov....20.00
*Toothpick holder, amber....39.00
*Toothpick holder, blue....25.00
Toothpick holder, vaseline....30.00
Tray, water, amber, 11½" d....55.00
Tray, water, blue, 11½" d....55.00
Tumbler, amber....30.00
Tumbler, seven-row, amber....20.00
*Tumbler, eight-row, amber....22.50
*Tumbler, ten-row, amber....60.00
*Tumbler, ten-row, blue....28.00
*Tumbler, clear....15.00
Tumbler, ten-row, ruby-stained....110.00
Tumbler, vaseline....38.00
*Vase, 5½" h., cone-shaped, ruffled rim, vaseline....45.00
*Wine, amber....25.00

Hobnail Wine

*Wine, clear (ILLUS.)....25.00
Wine, green....22.50

HONEYCOMB

*Butter dish, cov., non-flint, clear....45.00
Butter dish, cov., non-flint, clear w/gold....75.00
Cake stand, 9" d., 5¾" h., cable border....35.00
Celery vase, flint....60.00
Celery vase, New York Honeycomb, flint....45.00
Champagne, flint....40.00
*Champagne, non-flint....30.00
Claret, flint....50.00
Claret, New York Honeycomb, flint....45.00
Compote, open, 7" d., 7" h., flint....55.00
Compote, open, 8" d., 6¼" h., flint....110.00
*Creamer, non-flint....45.00
Decanter w/bar lip, flint, 10½" h....110.00
Decanter w/original stopper, flint, 13" h....110.00
Egg cup, flint....30.00
Egg cup, New York Honeycomb, flint....30.00
Goblet, flint....36.00
Goblet, flint, engraved....65.00
*Goblet, non-flint....14.00
Mug, flint....28.00
Mug, child's....35.00

Mustard pot, w/original pewter lid, etched, flint 75.00
Pitcher, milk, flint 90.00
Pitcher, water, 8½" h., molded handle, polished pontil, flint ....150.00 to 175.00
*Salt & pepper shakers w/original tops, non-flint, pr. 75.00
Sauce dish, flint 12.50
Spillholder, flint 40.00
Spooner, non-flint 23.00
Tumbler, bar 24.00
Tumbler, Vernon Honeycomb, flint 65.00
Wine, flint 35.00
*Wine, non-flint 10.00

HORN OF PLENTY (McKee's Comet)

Horn of Plenty Spillholder

Bar bottle w/original stopper, qt. 150.00
Bowl, 7½" d. 70.00
Bowl, 8" oval 110.00
Butter dish, cov. 125.00
Butter pat 16.00
Celery vase 200.00
Champagne 195.00
Compote, cov., 6¼" d., 7½" h. 250.00
Compote, open, 7" d., 7½" h., waffle base 110.00
Compote, open, 8" d., 6" h. 130.00
Compote, open, 9" d., 8½" h. 195.00
Compote, open, 10½" d., 9¾" h. 350.00
Creamer, applied handle, 7" h. 158.00
Creamer & cov. sugar bowl, pr. 325.00
Decanter, bar lip, pt. 110.00
Decanter w/original stopper, pt. 150.00
Decanter w/original stopper, qt. 175.00
Dish, 6¾ x 10", 2¼" h. 140.00
Egg cup, 3¾" h. 48.00
*Goblet 73.50
*Hat whimsey 350.00
Honey dish 18.00
*Lamp, w/whale oil burner, all-glass, 11" h. ....200.00 to 250.00
Plate, 6" d., clear 95.00
Relish, 5 x 7" oval 95.00
Salt dip, master size, oval 85.00
Sauce dish, 3½ to 5" d. 17.00
Spillholder, 4½" h. (ILLUS.) 80.00
Sugar bowl, cov. 120.00
*Tumbler, water, 3⅝" h. 85.00
Tumbler, whiskey, 3" h. 130.00
Tumbler, whiskey, handled 220.00
Wine 175.00

HORSESHOE (Good Luck or Prayer Rug)

Horseshoe Goblet

Bowl, cov., 5 x 8" oval, flat, triple horseshoe finial 295.00
Bowl, open, 7" d., footed 47.50
Bowl, open, 5 x 8" oval, footed 30.00
Bowl, open, 6 x 9" oval 27.50
*Bread tray, single horseshoe handles 50.00
Bread tray, double horseshoe handles 87.00
Butter dish, cov. 115.00
Cake stand, 7" d. 35.00
Cake stand, 10¾" d. 127.00
Celery vase 87.00
Cheese dish, cov., w/woman churning butter in base 275.00
Compote, cov., 7" d., high stand 75.00
Compote, cov., 8" d., low stand 210.00
Compote, cov., 8" d., high stand 175.00
Creamer 35.00
Doughnut stand 95.00
Goblet, knob stem 40.00
Goblet, plain stem (ILLUS.) 27.50
Marmalade jar, cov. 225.00
Pitcher, milk 90.00
Pitcher, water 128.00
Plate, 10" d. 86.00
Relish, 5 x 8" 5.00
Salt dip, individual size 17.50
Salt dip, master size, horseshoe shape 100.00
Sauce dish, flat or footed 14.00
Spooner 35.00
Wine 295.00

ILLINOIS

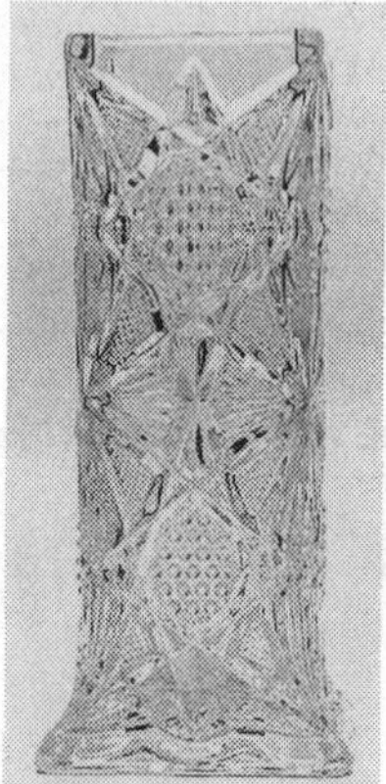

Illinois Straw Jar

Basket, applied handle, 7 x 7" 95.00
Bowl, 6" sq. 26.00
*Butter dish, cov., 7" sq. 75.00
Celery tray 35.00
*Celery vase 37.50
Cheese dish, cov., square 60.00
Creamer, small 25.00
Creamer, large.....................................40.00
Cruet w/original stopper.....................110.00
Doughnut stand, 7½" sq., 4¼" h. 65.00
Pitcher, water, tankard.........................75.00
Pitcher, water, tankard, w/glass lid 125.00
Pitcher, water, squatty, silver plate rim, clear 95.00
Pitcher, water, squatty, silver plate rim, green.......................................175.00
Plate, 7" sq. 25.00
Relish, 3 x 8½".....................................17.50
Sauce dish...14.00
Soda fountain (straw-holder) jar, cov., 12½" h. 250.00
Soda fountain (straw-holder) jar, no lid, 12½" h. (ILLUS.)..................110.00
Sugar shaker w/original pewter top 65.00
Toothpick holder 30.00
Vase, 6" h. 25.00
Vase, 9" h., 4" d. 41.00

INDIANA SWIRL - See Feather Pattern

IRISH COLUMN - See Broken Column Pattern

JACOB'S LADDER (Maltese)

Bowl, 7½ x 10¾" oval 25.00
Bowl, 9" d., flat.....................................40.00
Butter dish, cov., Maltese Cross finial ..55.00
Cake stand, 8" to 12" d. 52.00
Celery vase 38.00
Compote, cov., 8¼" d., high stand......128.00
Compote, open, 7" d., high stand 35.00
Compote, open, 8" d., high stand 42.00
Compote, open, 10" d., 5" h..................42.00
Compote, open, 10" d., high stand 55.00
*Creamer 35.00
Cruet w/original stopper, footed...........85.00
Dish, 8" oval 18.00
Goblet...65.00
Honey dish, open....................................9.00
Marmalade jar, cov. ....100.00 to 135.00
Pickle dish, Maltese Cross handle........18.00
Pitcher, water, applied handle 185.00
Plate, 6" d., amber 105.00
Plate, 6" d., clear 35.00
Plate, 6" d., purple 110.00
Relish, Maltese Cross handles, 5½ x 9½" oval 20.00
Salt dip, master size, footed 25.00
Sauce dish, flat or footed, blue 20.00
Sauce dish, flat or footed, canary 72.00
Sauce dish, flat or footed, clear 8.00
Spooner 25.00
Sugar bowl, cov. 65.00
Syrup jug w/metal top ....100.00 to 125.00
Wine 32.00

JEWEL & DEWDROP - See Kansas Pattern

JOB'S TEARS - See Art Pattern

KAMONI - See Pennsylvania Pattern

KANSAS (Jewel & Dewdrop)

Banana bowl 55.00
Bowl, 7½" d. 22.00
Bowl, 8½" d. 35.00
Bread tray, "Our Daily Bread", 10½" oval 42.50
Butter dish, cov. 65.00
Cake stand, 8" to 10" d. 48.00
Cake tray, "Cake Plate," 10½" oval 78.00
Celery vase 45.00
Compote, cov., 7" d., high stand.........125.00
Compote, open, jelly, 5" d......................42.00
Compote, open, 8" d., high stand 57.50
Creamer...47.00
Goblet 62.50
Mug, small, 3½" h. 30.00
Pitcher, milk 72.00
Pitcher, water...60.00
Relish, 8½" oval 28.00
Sauce dish, 4" d. 13.50
Spooner 75.00
Toothpick holder 55.00
Tumbler, water, footed...........................55.00
Wine 55.00

KING'S CROWN (Also see Ruby Thumbprint)

Banana stand 130.00
Bowl, berry or fruit, 8¼" d., flared rim ...27.00
Bowl, 9¼" oval, scalloped rim, round base 67.50
Butter dish, cov. 65.00
*Cake stand, 9" d. 85.00
Castor set, salt & pepper shakers, oil

bottle w/stopper & cov. mustard jar in original frame, 4 pcs. 325.00
Celery vase, engraved....................60.00
Celery vase, plain 48.00
*Compote, cov., 5" d., 5½" h., engraved 30.00
Compote, cov., 7" d., 7" h. 95.00
Compote, open, jelly 45.00
Compote, open, 7½" d., high stand 42.00
Compote, open, 8½" d., high stand 85.00
*Cordial 50.00
Creamer, clear 40.00
*Creamer, individual size, clear 16.50
Creamer, individual size, clear w/gold..29.50
*Cup and saucer 55.00
*Goblet, clear 30.00
Goblet, clear w/engraved moose, doe & dog 95.00
Lamp, kerosene-type, low hand-type w/finger hold 120.00
*Lamp, kerosene-type, stem base, 10" h. 180.00
Mustard jar, cov. 62.00
Pitcher, 5" h., souvenir....................40.00
Pitcher, tankard, 8½" h. 110.00
Pitcher, tankard, 13" h., engraved 122.50
*Plate, 8" sq. 70.00
Punch bowl, footed ....225.00 to 250.00
Punch cup 22.50
Relish, 7" oval 10.00
Salt dip, individual size 37.50
Salt & pepper shakers w/original tops, pr. 65.00
Sauce dish, boat-shaped....................22.00
*Sauce dish, round 17.00
Spooner 38.00
Toothpick holder, clear 28.00
Tray, square 29.00
*Tumbler, clear 22.00
Water set, bulbous pitcher & 6 goblets, 7 pcs. ....250.00 to 300.00
*Wine, clear 25.00
Wine, cobalt blue ....100.00 to 150.00

KLONDIKE (Amberette or English Hobnail Cross)

Klondike Butter Dish

Bowl, 6" sq., frosted w/amber cross ...200.00
Bowl, 7¼" sq., scalloped top, clear w/amber cross 185.00
Bowl, master berry or fruit, 8" sq., clear w/amber cross 85.00
Bread plate, clear w/amber cross, 8½ x 11" oval 120.00
Butter dish, cov., clear 150.00
Butter dish, cov., frosted w/amber cross (ILLUS.) ....450.00 to 475.00
Butter pat, clear w/amber cross............35.00
Celery vase, clear w/amber cross 138.00
Condiment set: tray, cruet, salt & pepper shakers; frosted w/amber cross, 4 pcs. 1,350.00
Creamer, clear w/amber cross 90.00
Creamer & open sugar bowl, frosted w/amber cross, pr. 200.00
Cruet w/original stopper, frosted w/amber cross ....700.00 to 750.00
Dish, oval, flat, shallow, clear w/amber cross 130.00
Goblet, clear 95.00
Lamp, kerosene-type, clear w/amber cross, 10" h. 155.00
Pitcher, water, clear....................50.00
Pitcher, water, clear w/amber cross ....250.00 to 275.00
Relish, boat-shaped, clear w/amber cross, 4 x 9" 115.00
Relish, boat-shaped, frosted w/amber cross, 4 x 9" 146.00
Salt shaker w/original top, clear w/ambercross 68.00
Salt & pepper shakers w/original tops, frosted w/amber cross, pr. ....200.00 to 250.00
Sauce dish, flat or footed, clear w/amber cross 22.50
Spooner, clear w/amber cross.............85.00
Spooner, frosted w/amber cross ....275.00 to 300.00
Sugar bowl, open, clear w/amber cross 75.00
Table set, frosted w/amber cross, 4 pcs. 950.00
Toothpick holder, clear 125.00
Toothpick holder, clear w/amber cross 375.00
Tumbler, clear w/amber cross 90.00
Tumbler, frosted w/amber cross.........145.00
Vase, 7" h., trumpet-shaped, clear 35.00
Vase, 8" h., trumpet-shaped, clear 50.00

LACY MEDALLION - See Colorado Pattern

LIBERTY BELL

Bowl, berry or fruit, 8" d., footed 95.00
*Bread platter, "Signer's", twig handles 100.00
Bread platter, w/thirteen original states, twig handles, 8¼ x 13" 85.00
Butter dish, cov. 100.00
Butter dish, cov., miniature 150.00
Compote, open, 8" d. 75.00

Creamer, applied handle....................110.00
*Goblet....................................45.00
Mug, miniature, 2" h.........................125.00
Mug, snake handle 300.00
Pickle dish, closed handles, 1776-1876 w/thirteen original states, 5½ x 9¼"oval.........................50.00
Plate, 6" d., closed handles, scalloped rim, w/thirteen original states 75.00
Plate, 6" d., no states, dated...............62.50
Plate, 8" d., closed handles, scalloped rim, w/thirteen original states 60.00

Liberty Bell Plate

Plate, 10" d., closed handles, scalloped rim, w/thirteen original states (ILLUS.) 95.00
Relish, shell handles, 7 x 11¼"............70.00
Salt dip...55.00
Salt shaker w/original pewter top........110.00
Sauce dish...25.00
Spooner...62.00
Sugar bowl, cov. 105.00
Table set, 4 pcs. ....400.00 to 450.00

LION, FROSTED - See Frosted Lion Pattern

LION'S LEG - See Alaska Pattern

LOG CABIN

Log Cabin Compote

Butter dish, cov......................................295.00
Compote, cov. (ILLUS.) 350.00
Compote, cov., "Lutteds Cough Drops" 325.00
*Creamer, 4¼" h. 132.00
Sauce dish, flat oblong 85.00
Spooner, clear 125.00
Spooner, sapphire blue 395.00
Sugar bowl, cov., 8" h., clear................250.00

LOOP (Seneca Loop)

Butter dish, cov., flint 195.00
Celery vase, flint.....................................75.00
Celery vase, non-flint..............................27.50
Compote, cov., 7" d., 9" h., flint 75.00
Compote, open, 8" d., 8" h., flint............85.00
Compote, open, 8" d., 8¼" h., milk white w/fiery opalescence................600.00
Compote, open, 9¼" d., 6½" h., flint.....65.00
Compote, open, 12¼" d., 9½" h., flint 400.00
Cordial, 2¾ h., non-flint 35.00
Creamer, clear, flint 60.00
Decanter, w/original stopper, flint, pt. 130.00
Egg cup, flint...22.00
Goblet, flint 25.00
Goblet, non-flint 12.00
Pitcher, water, applied handle, flint.....195.00
Salt dip, master size, flint........................25.00
Spooner, flint 32.00
Sugar bowl, cov., flint 100.00
Tumbler, footed, non-flint.........................35.00
Vase, 9⅝" h., flint.....................................75.00

LOOP & PILLAR - See Michigan Pattern

LOOP WITH STIPPLED PANELS - See Texas Pattern

MALTESE - See Jacob's Ladder Pattern

MASSACHUSETTS

Massachusetts Butter Dish

Banana boat, 6½ x 8½" 55.00
Bar bottle w/original pewter top, 11" h..80.00
Bowl, 6" sq. 18.00

Bowl, 8" l., pointed sides....................37.50
Bowl, master berry, 9" sq....................32.00
*Butter dish, cov., clear (ILLUS.) 55.00
Butter dish, cov., green........................65.00
Champagne 45.00
Creamer...32.00
Cruet w/original stopper........................42.00
Decanter w/stopper 88.00
Goblet..45.00
Mug, 3½" h., clear................................20.00
Mug, 3½" h., clear w/gold trim 24.00
Plate, 6" sq., w/advertising 90.00
Plate, 8" sq. 35.00
Punch cup..14.00
Relish, 8½" l...12.50
Rum jug, 5" h. 100.00
Sauce dish...15.00
Spooner 20.00
Sugar bowl, cov. 35.00
Toothpick holder 50.00
Tumbler, juice 19.00
Tumbler, water......................................25.00
Vase, 6½" h., trumpet-shaped, clear 22.00
Vase, 7" h., clear w/gold 24.00
Vase, 10" h., trumpet-shaped, green....60.00
Whiskey shot glass, clear 16.00
Wine, blue..110.00
Wine, clear...35.00

MICHIGAN (Paneled Jewel or Loop & Pillar)

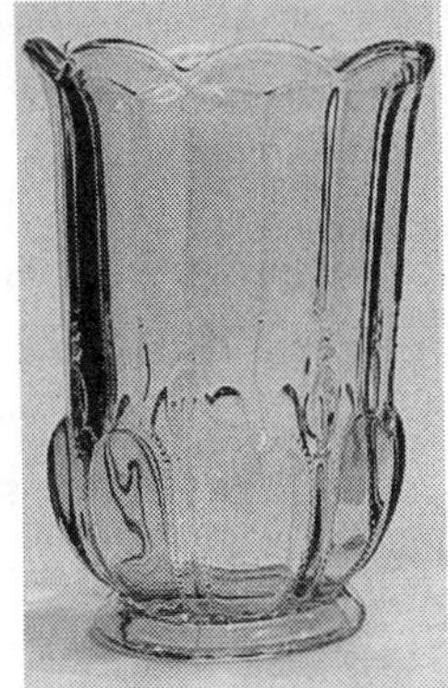

Michigan Celery Vase

Bowl, 8" d., clear 36.00
Bowl, 10" d...35.00
Butter dish, cov., blue-stained 175.00
Butter dish, cov., clear 60.00
Celery vase (ILLUS.) 45.00
Compote, open, jelly, 4½" d., blue-stained 125.00
Compote, open, 8½" d., high stand 65.00
Creamer, 4" h. 30.00
Creamer, individual size 45.00
Creamer, individual size, yellow-stained, enameled florals 55.00
Goblet, clear 35.00
Goblet, clear w/blue stain 40.00
Mug, yellow-stained, enameled florals 28.00
Pitcher, water, 8" h. 48.00
Pitcher, water, tankard, 12" h., clear.....75.00
Plate, tea, 6" d., yellow-stained w/pink florals 25.00
Punch cup, clear 6.00
Punch cup, enameled decoration 25.00
Relish, pink-stained 24.00
Salt shaker w/original top 27.50
Salt & pepper shakers w/original tops, individual size, pr. 75.00
Sauce dish, clear 13.00
Spooner, clear 40.00
Spooner, pink-stained............................71.00
Sugar bowl, cov., blue-stained 150.00
Sugar bowl, cov., child's, 4¾" h............40.00
Sugar bowl, individual size 22.00
Syrup jug w/pewter top 165.00
Table set, pink-stained, 4 pcs. ....350.00 to 375.00
*Toothpick holder, clear........................37.50
Toothpick holder, clear, enameled florals 45.00
Toothpick holder, pink-stained, gold trim ....275.00 to 300.00
Tumbler, pink-stained, gold trim 55.00
Tumbler, yellow-stained, enameled florals 35.00
Vase, 6" h., clear 35.00
Vase, 12" h. 24.00
Waste bowl 68.00
Water set: pitcher & 3 tumblers; yellow-stained, enameled florals, 4 pcs. 225.00
Wine, blue-stained................................40.00
Wine, clear..35.00
Wine, yellow-stained.............................50.00

MIRROR - See Galloway Pattern

MOON & STAR

Moon & Star Butter Dish

Bowl, cov., 6" d. 30.00
*Bowl, cov., 7" d...................................38.00

*Bowl, master berry, 8¼" d., 4" h..........35.00
Bowl, fruit, 9" d., footed........................35.00
Bread tray, scalloped rim, 6½ x 10¾"...65.00
*Butter dish, cov. (ILLUS.) 46.00
*Cake stand, 9" d.................................65.00
Cake stand, 10" d. 95.00
Celery vase..38.00
*Compote, cov., 6" d., high stand 55.00
Compote, cov., 7" d., 11" h. 70.00
Compote, cov., 13½" h. 125.00
Compote, open, 9" d., 6½" h.................35.00
*Creamer 52.00
*Cruet w/original stopper, applied handle 125.00
*Egg cup 35.00
*Goblet..45.00
Pickle dish, 8" l. 17.00
*Pitcher, water, 9¼" h., applied rope handle 150.00
Relish, oblong 20.00
Salt dip, individual size, footed 32.00
*Salt shaker w/original top 30.00
*Sauce dish, flat or footed, each...........20.00
*Spooner..45.00
*Sugar bowl, cov....................................60.00
*Syrup pitcher w/original top...............125.00
*Toothpick holder...................................21.00
*Tumbler, flat 85.00
*Wine...45.00

NOTCHED RIB - See Broken Column Pattern

OLD MAN OF THE MOUNTAIN - See Viking Pattern

OREGON No. 1 - See Beaded Loop Pattern

PANELED FORGET-ME-NOT

Paneled Forget-Me-Not Compote

Bread platter, 7 x 11" oval 35.00
Butter dish, cov. 40.00
Cake stand 45.00
Celery vase..40.00
Compote, cov., 7" d., 10" h. 67.50
Compote, cov., 8" d., high stand (ILLUS.) 78.00
Compote, open, 7" d., high stand 50.00
Compote, open, 8½" d., high stand 40.00
Creamer...32.00
Cruet w/original stopper........................55.00
Goblet, amethyst 750.00
Goblet, clear 35.00
Mustard jar, cov. 40.00
Pitcher, milk 60.00
Pitcher, water, amethyst 175.00
Pitcher, water, clear...............................65.00
Relish, handled, 4½ x 7¾".....................21.00
Relish, scoop-shaped, 9" l. 19.50
Sauce dish, flat or footed........................11.00
Spooner 30.00
Sugar bowl, cov. 35.00
Wine 125.00

PANELED HERRINGBONE (Emerald Green Herringbone or Florida)

Bowl, 6" d., ruby & amber-stained 55.00
Bowl, master berry, 9" sq., green 30.00
Butter dish, cov., clear 50.00
Butter dish, cov., green..........................73.00
Compote, open, jelly, 5½" sq., green....35.00
Cruet w/original stopper, green..............................100.00 to 125.00
*Goblet, clear 35.00
*Goblet, green 75.00
Pitcher, milk, green.................................75.00
Pitcher, water, clear................................42.00
Pitcher, water, green 85.00
*Plate, 9", green......................................35.00
Relish, 4½ x 8" oval, green.....................15.00
Sauce dish, green...................................12.50
Spooner, green.......................................25.00
Syrup pitcher w/original top, green..............................150.00 to 200.00
Tumbler, green 21.00
Wine, clear...22.50
Wine, green 48.00

PANELED JEWEL - See Michigan Pattern

PANELED THISTLE

Paneled Thistle Creamer

*Bowl, 8" d. 18.50
*Bowl, 8" d., w/bee....................................35.00
Bowl, 9" d., deep, w/bee....................................29.00
*Butter dish, cov., w/bee....................................50.00
Cake stand 38.00
Cake stand, w/bee....................................60.00
Candy dish, cov., footed, 5" sq., 6¼" h. 30.00
Celery vase....................................45.00
Compote, open, 5" d., low stand....................................19.00
*Compote, open, 6" d., high stand....................................45.00
Cordial 18.00
*Creamer (ILLUS.)....................................45.00
*Creamer, w/bee....................................60.00
Cruet w/stopper 45.00
*Goblet....................................34.00
*Honey dish, cov., square....................................60.00
Honey dish, open....................................10.00
Pitcher, milk 31.00
*Plate, 7" sq. 28.00
*Plate, 7" sq., w/bee 23.00
Plate, 9½" d. 26.00
*Relish, w/bee, 4 x 9½"....................................24.00
Rose bowl, 5" d., 2¾" h. 40.00
Salt dip, individual size 17.50
*Salt dip, master size....................................12.50
*Salt & pepper shakers w/original tops, pr. 65.00
*Sauce dish, flat or footed 14.00
*Spooner, handled....................................45.00
*Sugar bowl, cov....................................45.00
*Tumbler....................................30.00
Vase, 9¼" h., fan-shaped 25.00
Vase, 13½" h., pulled top rim....................................35.00
*Wine....................................24.00
*Wine, w/bee 30.00

PENNSYLVANIA (Balder or Kamoni)

Bowl, berry or fruit, 8½" d., clear w/gold trim 30.00
Butter dish, cov., clear....................................58.00
Butter dish, cov., green....................................85.00
Cake stand 45.00
Carafe....................................45.00
Celery tray, 4½ x 11" 28.00
Celery vase....................................22.50
Creamer, 3" h., clear w/gold trim, small 25.00
Creamer, 3" h., green w/gold trim, small 75.00
Cruet w/original stopper....................................44.00
Decanter w/original stopper, 10¾" h.....75.00
Goblet, clear 27.00
Goblet, clear w/gold....................................30.00
Pitcher, water....................................50.00
Punch cup, clear....................................10.00
Punch cup, clear w/gold 20.00
Salt & pepper shakers w/original tops, pr. 65.00
Sauce dish, round or square 12.50
*Spooner....................................21.00
Sugar bowl, cov., child's, green w/gold trim....................................145.00
Syrup pitcher w/original top 55.00
Table set, child's, 4 pcs. 250.00
Table set, 4 pcs. 225.00
Toothpick holder, clear 38.00
Tumbler, water, clear w/gold trim 25.00
Tumbler, water, ruby-stained....................................49.00
Tumbler, whiskey, clear....................................16.50
Tumbler, whiskey, green w/gold trim....25.00
Vase, 5¾" h., green 60.00
Wine, clear....................................16.00
Wine, green 25.00

POLAR BEAR

Polar Bear Waste Bowl

*Goblet, clear....................................125.00
Goblet, clear & frosted....................................175.00
Pitcher, water, clear....................................525.00
Tray, water, clear, 16" l....................................165.00
Tray, water, frosted, 16" l....................................250.00
Waste bowl (ILLUS.)....................................90.00

PORTLAND

Bowl, 8" d....................................25.00
Bowl, 10" d., flared....................................25.00
Butter dish, cov. 48.00
Cake stand, 10½" 55.00
*Candlestick....................................110.00
*Celery tray....................................25.00
Celery vase....................................42.50
Compote, cov., 6½" d., high stand......125.00
Compote, cov., 7" d., high stand.........100.00
Compote, cov., 8" d., high stand..........40.00
Compote, open, 7" d., high stand 45.00
Cordial 25.00
Creamer....................................40.00
*Creamer, individual size....................................18.00
Cruet w/original stopper....................................45.00
Goblet 39.00
Pitcher, water....................................52.50
Pitcher, water, miniature....................................26.00
Punch bowl, 15" d., 8½" h...150.00 to 175.00
Punch cup....................................18.00
Salt shaker w/original top 16.00
Sauce dish, 4½" d....................................10.00
Spooner....................................25.00
Sugar bowl, cov. 55.00
Sugar shaker w/original top 50.00
Table set, clear w/gold trim, 4 pcs. 350.00
Toothpick holder 27.00
Tumbler 25.00

Vase, 6" h., scalloped rim 28.00
Wine 29.00

PORTLAND MAIDEN BLUSH - See Banded Portland Pattern

PORTLAND WITH DIAMOND POINT BAND - See Banded Portland Pattern

PRAYER RUG - See Horseshoe Pattern

PYGMY - See Torpedo Pattern

RED BLOCK

Bowl, berry or fruit, 8" d. 85.00
Butter dish, cov. 95.00
Celery vase, 6½" h. 135.00
Creamer, large 80.00
Creamer, small, applied handle 35.00
Cruet w/original stopper 150.00
Decanter, whiskey, w/original stopper, 12" h. 175.00
Dish, rectangular, 5 x 7½" 55.00
*Goblet 40.00
Mug, plain, 3" h. 26.00
Mug, souvenir, 3" h. 42.00
Pitcher, 8" h., bulbous 225.00
Pitcher, tankard, 8" h. ....175.00 to 200.00
Salt shaker w/original top 49.00
Sauce dish, 4½" 35.00
Spooner 35.00
Sugar bowl, cov. 70.00
Tumbler, souvenir 32.00
Tumbler 35.00
*Wine 35.00

RIBBON (Early Ribbon)

Bread tray 35.00
Butter dish, cov. 72.50
Celery vase 38.00
Compote, cov., 8" d. 96.00
Compote, open, 8" d., low stand 40.00
Compote, open, 8" d., 8" h., frosted dolphin stem on dome base 295.00
*Compote, open, 5½ x 8" rectangular bowl, 7" h., frosted dolphin stem on dome base 295.00

Ribbon Waste Bowl

Compote, open, 8½" d., 4½" h. 50.00
Compote, open, 10½" d., frosted dolphin stem on dome base 395.00
Creamer 34.00
Dresser bottle w/stopper 125.00
*Goblet 35.00
Pitcher, water 120.00
Plate, 7" d. 34.00
Platter, 9 x 13" 60.00
Sauce dish, flat or footed 12.50
Spooner 30.00
Sugar bowl, cov., 4¼" d., 7¾" h. 72.00
Table set, 4 pcs. ....200.00 to 225.00
Waste bowl (ILLUS.) 42.50

ROSE IN SNOW

Bitters bottle w/original stopper 100.00
Bowl, 7" d., footed, canary 38.00
Butter dish, cov., round 55.00
Butter dish, cov., square 50.00
Cake plate, handled, amber, 10" d. 45.00
Cake plate, handled, blue, 10" d. 35.00
Cake plate, handled, clear, 10" d. 22.50
Cake stand, 9" d. ....100.00 to 150.00
Cologne bottle w/original stopper 95.00
Compote, cov., 6" d., 8" h. 85.00
Compote, cov., 7" d., 8" h. 95.00
Compote, open, 6" d., low stand 50.00
Compote, open, 8" sq., low stand 110.00
Compote, open, 8" d., high stand 70.00
Creamer, round 35.00
Creamer, square 39.00
Dish, 8½ x 11" oval, 1½" h. 130.00
*Goblet, amber 45.00
*Goblet, blue 85.00
*Goblet, clear 70.00
*Goblet, vaseline 32.00
Mug, blue, large 110.00
Mug, clear, 3½" h. 40.00
*Mug, applied handle, "In Fond Remembrance," yellow 35.00
Pitcher, water, applied handle 132.00
Plate, 5" d. 32.00
Plate, 6" d. 30.00
*Plate, 9" d., amber 40.00
*Plate, 9" d., clear 30.00
*Relish, 5½ x 8" oval, blue 65.00
*Relish, 5½ x 8" oval, clear 23.00
Relish, 6¼ x 9¼" 19.00
Sauce dish, flat or footed 10.00
Spooner, round 25.00
Spooner, square 28.00
Sugar bowl, cov., round 37.50
*Sugar bowl, cov., square 51.00
Tumbler 38.00

ROYAL IVY (Northwood)

Berry set: master bowl & 3 sauce dishes; craquelle, (cranberry & vaseline spatter), 4 pcs. 175.00
Bowl, fruit, 9" d., craquelle (cranberry & vaseline spatter) 235.00

Bowl, fruit, 9" d., frosted craquelle......150.00
Butter dish, cov., rubina crystal ....150.00 to 175.00
Creamer, clear & frosted 45.00
Creamer, rubina crystal 165.00
Cruet w/original stopper, craquelle (cranberry & vaseline spatter)..........495.00
Cruet w/original stopper, rubina crystal 295.00
Pickle castor, cased spatter (cranberry & vaseline w/white lining) insert, complete w/silver plate frame & tongs...........................300.00 to 350.00
Pitcher, water, cased spatter (cranberry & vaseline w/white lining)................325.00
Pitcher, water, clear & frosted 90.00
Pitcher, water, craquelle (cranberry & vaseline spatter) 350.00
Pitcher, water, rubina crystal 250.00
Rose bowl, frosted rubina crystal 95.00
Rose bowl, craquelle (cranberry & vaseline spatter) 180.00
Salt shaker w/original top, cased spatter (cranberry & vaseline w/white lining) 125.00
Salt shaker w/original top, rubina crystal 48.00
Spooner, clear & frosted.......................50.00
Spooner, frosted rubina crystal.............80.00
Sugar bowl, cov., frosted rubina crystal 200.00
Sugar shaker w/original top, cased spatter (cranberry & vaseline w/white lining) 300.00

Royal Ivy Sugar Shaker

Sugar shaker w/original top, frosted rubina crystal (ILLUS.) ....200.00 to 250.00
Syrup pitcher w/original top, cased spatter (cranberry & vaseline w/white lining) 490.00
Toothpick holder, craquelle (cranberry & vaseline spatter) 235.00
Toothpick holder, rubina crystal...........85.00
Tumbler, clear & frosted 52.50
Tumbler, craquelle (cranberry & vaseline spatter)...76.00
Tumbler, rubina crystal 66.00
Tumbler, frosted rubina crystal 70.00
Water set: pitcher & 5 tumblers; rubina crystal, 6 pcs. 595.00
Water set: pitcher & 6 tumblers; cased spatter (cranberry & vaseline w/white lining), 7 pcs. 955.00

RUBY THUMBPRINT

*Bowl, 8½" d. 90.00
Bowl, master berry or fruit, 10" l., boat-shaped 125.00
Butter dish, cov., engraved................225.00
Celery vase...100.00
Champagne, souvenir 45.00
*Claret..65.00
Compote, open, jelly, 5¼" h..................49.00
Compote, open, 7" d., engraved.........150.00
Compote, open, 7" d., plain 145.00
Compote, open, 8½" d., 7½" h., scalloped rim...................200.00 to 225.00
Cordial, engraved 40.00
Creamer, engraved..............................85.00
*Creamer, plain....................................60.00
Creamer, individual size 30.00
Cup, engraved 35.00
*Cup, plain 30.00
Cup & saucer, engraved.......................65.00
*Cup & saucer, plain............................60.00
*Goblet, plain 40.00
Goblet, souvenir 42.00
Pitcher, milk, 7½" h., bulbous 100.00
Pitcher, milk, tankard, 8⅜" h..............125.00
*Pitcher, water, tankard, 11" h. 132.00
*Plate, 8¼" d. 22.00
Sauce dish, boat-shaped......................28.00
*Sauce dish, round 20.00
*Sherbet...20.00
Spooner 65.00
Toothpick holder, engraved 47.50
Toothpick holder, plain 38.00
Tumbler, engraved 55.00
*Tumbler, plain 36.00
Water set, bulbous pitcher & 6 tumblers, w/engraved family names & dated 1897, 7 pcs. 595.00
*Wine 40.00

SAWTOOTH

Butter dish, cov., clear, flint 78.00
*Butter dish, cov., clear, non-flint..........50.00
Butter dish, cov., sapphire blue, non-flint 230.00
Cake stand, non-flint, 7½" d., 6" h. 30.00
*Cake stand, non-flint, 9½" d., 4½" h....75.00
Celery vase, knob stem, flint 45.00
Champagne, knob stem, flint................85.00
Champagne, non-flint 35.00
Compote, open, 7½" d., 5½" h..............38.00
Compote, open, 8" d., low stand, canary, flint 200.00

Compote, open, 9½" d., 10" h., flint....100.00
Creamer, applied handle, clear, flint....75.00
Creamer, applied handle, cobalt blue, flint....230.00
Creamer, miniature, non-flint....29.00
Decanter w/original stopper, flint, 14" h....145.00
Egg cup, cov., canary, flint....192.50

Sawtooth Covered Egg Cup

Egg cup, cov., clear, flint (ILLUS.)....100.00
Goblet, knob stem, flint....35.00
Goblet, knob stem, non-flint....25.00
Pitcher, water, applied handle, flint....215.00
Pomade jar, cov....60.00
Salt dip, cov., master size, footed, flint....100.00
Salt dip, master size, non-flint....22.00
Spillholder, flint....48.00
Spillholder, jagged sawtooth rim, sapphire blue, flint, 5½" h....700.00
Spooner, clear, non-flint....50.00
Spooner, cobalt blue, non-flint....85.00
Spooner, milk white, flint....75.00
Tumbler, bar, flint, 4½" h....58.00
Tumbler, bar, non-flint....32.50
Wine, flint....45.00
Wine, non-flint....18.00

SENECA LOOP - See Loop Pattern

SNAIL (Compact)

Banana stand, 10" d., 7" h..125.00 to 150.00
Bowl, 7" d., low....35.00
Butter dish, cov....95.00
Cake stand, 10" d....100.00
Celery vase....45.00
Cheese dish, cov....125.00
Compote, cov., 7" d., 8" h., engraved....185.00
Cracker jar, cov., 8" d., 9" h....295.00
Creamer, clear....58.00
Creamer, ruby-stained....70.00
Cruet w/original stopper....125.00
Goblet....100.00
Pitcher, water, tankard....110.00
Pitcher, wine, tankard....295.00
Plate, 7" d....46.00
Punch cup....32.50
Relish, 7" oval....22.50
Relish, 9" oval....31.50
Rose bowl, miniature, 3" h....36.00
Rose bowl, large....85.00
Salt dip, individual size....25.00
Salt dip, master size, 3" d....40.00
Salt shaker w/original top, clear....40.00
Salt shaker w/original top, ruby-stained....65.00
Sauce dish....18.00
Spooner, clear....42.00
Spooner, ruby-stained....75.00
Sugar bowl, cov., individual size....75.00

Snail Sugar Bowl

Sugar bowl, cov., plain (ILLUS.)....68.00
Sugar bowl, cov., ruby-stained....95.00
Sugar shaker w/original top....115.00
Syrup jug w/original brass top....110.00
Tumbler....45.00
Vase, 12½" h., scalloped rim....75.00

SPIKED ARGUS - See Argus Pattern

SPIREA BAND

Berry set: master bowl & 6 footed sauce dishes; blue, 7 pcs....150.00
Bowl, 8" oval, flat, amber....20.00
Butter dish, cov....45.00
Cake stand, amber, 8½" d....45.00
Cake stand, blue, 10½" d....80.00
Celery vase....25.00
Compote, cov., 7" d., low stand, amber....55.00
Creamer, amber....32.00
Creamer, blue....35.00
Creamer, clear....32.00
Goblet, amber....34.00
Goblet, blue....33.00

Spirea Band Goblet

Goblet, clear (ILLUS.)..........................20.00
Pitcher, water......................................45.00
Platter, 8½ x 10½", amber 24.00
Platter, 8½ x 10½", blue 35.00
Relish, blue, 4½ x 7"............................32.50
Salt shaker w/original top, blue............54.00
Spooner, amber....................................24.00
Spooner, vaseline.................................30.00
Sugar bowl, cov., blue 50.00
Sugar bowl, cov., clear 28.00
Wine, amber 23.00
Wine, blue...28.00
Wine, clear...15.50

TEXAS (Loop with Stippled Panels)

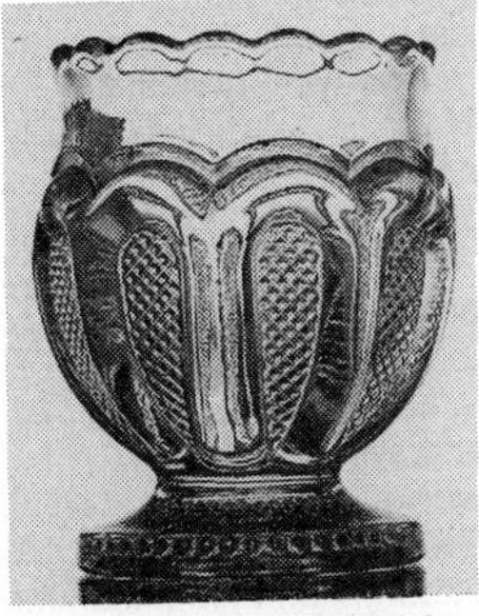

Texas Toothpick Holder

Cake stand, 9½" to 10¾" d. 62.50
Celery vase...75.00
Compote, open, jelly 100.00
Compote, cov., 6" d., 11" h. 165.00
Creamer...26.00
*Creamer, individual size......................18.00
Goblet, clear 38.00
Goblet, ruby-stained 110.00
Relish, handled, 8½" l..........................20.00
Salt dip, master size, footed, 3" d., 2¾" h. 22.00
Sauce dish, flat or footed 25.00
Spooner, ruby-stained 95.00
Toothpick holder, clear (ILLUS.)...........35.00
Toothpick holder, clear w/gold.............55.00
Vase, 7½" h., trumpet-shaped, pink-stained 95.00
Vase, bud, 8" h. 30.00
Vase, 9" h. 35.00
Vase, 10" h. 30.00
*Wine 115.00
Wine, ruby-stained..............................125.00

THISTLE, PANELED - See Paneled Thistle Pattern

THOUSAND EYE

Thousand Eye Butter Dish

Bowl, 8" d., 4½" h., footed, amber 35.00
Bowl, 11" rectangle, shallow, amber.....32.00
Bread tray, amber 32.00
Bread tray, apple green 52.00
Butter dish, cov., blue 145.00
Butter dish, cov., clear (ILLUS.)............50.00
Cake stand, blue, 8½" to 10" d. 88.00
Cake stand, blue, 12½" d. 60.00
Celery vase, three-knob stem, amber ..48.00
Celery vase, plain stem, amber 45.00
Compote, cov., 12" h. 115.00
*Compote, open, 6" d., low stand, amber 22.00
*Compote, open, 6" d., low stand, blue 38.00
Compote, open, 8" d., 3¾" h., apple green 40.00
Compote, open, 8" d., high stand, three-knob stem, vaseline.................58.00
Compote, open, 8" sq., low stand, apple green 65.00
Compote, open, 9½" d., low stand, amber 27.00
Creamer, amber 42.00
*Creamer, clear 35.00
Creamer, clear opalescent 95.00
Creamer & cov. sugar bowl, amber, pr. 100.00
Cruet w/original three-knob stopper, amber 135.00

Cruet w/original three-knob stopper, clear 32.00
Cruet w/original three-knob stopper, vaseline ....100.00 to 125.00
Egg cup, blue 65.00
Egg cup, clear 25.00
*Goblet, amber 30.00
*Goblet, apple green 40.00
*Goblet, blue 32.00
*Goblet, clear 28.00
*Goblet, vaseline Ï32.00
Lamp, kerosene-type, pedestal base, amber, 14" h. to collar 225.00
Lamp, kerosene-type, pedestal base, blue font, amber base, 12" h. 195.00
*Mug, amber, 3½" h. 28.00
*Mug, blue, 3½" h. 28.00
*Mug, clear, 3½" h. 20.00
*Mug, vaseline, 3½" h. 32.00
Mug, miniature, amber 30.00
Pickle dish, apple green 25.00
Pitcher, water, three-knob stem, blue 95.00
*Pitcher, water, clear 75.00
Pitcher, water, vaseline 60.00
Plate, 6" d., amber 22.50
*Plate, 6" d., clear 14.50
Plate, 8" d., amber 26.00
Plate, 8" d., apple green 25.00
*Plate, 8" d., clear 28.00
Plate, 8" d., vaseline 32.00
Plate, 10" sq., w/folded corners, blue 28.00
Plate, 10" sq., w/folded corners, clear 28.00
Platter, 8 x 11" 30.00
Salt & pepper shakers w/original tops, blue, pr. 75.00
*Salt & pepper shakers w/original tops, clear, pr. 65.00
Sauce dish, flat or footed, amber 12.50
Sauce dish, flat or footed, blue 16.00
*Sauce dish, flat or footed, clear 10.00
Spooner, three-knob stem, amber 52.00
Sugar bowl, cov., three-knob stem, amber 55.00
Sugar bowl, cov. 37.50
*Sugar bowl, open, three-knob stem 25.00
Syrup pitcher w/original top, amber 100.00
*Toothpick holder, amber 38.00
*Toothpick holder, blue 40.00
*Toothpick holder, clear 24.00
*Toothpick holder, vaseline 38.00
Tray, water, amber, 12½" d. 65.00
Tray, water, blue, 12½" d. 120.00
Tray, apple green, 14" oval 60.00
*Tumbler, apple green 39.00
*Tumbler, blue 30.00
*Tumbler, clear 18.00
*Wine, amber 20.00
*Wine, apple green 42.50
*Wine, blue 42.50
*Wine, clear 20.00
*Wine, vaseline 38.00

THREE FACE

Three Face Creamer

Butter dish, cov., engraved ....200.00 to 225.00
Butter dish, cov., plain 185.00
*Cake stand, 8" to 10½" d. 150.00
Celery vase ....100.00 to 125.00
*Champagne 165.00
Claret 152.00
Claret, engraved 265.00
Compote, cov., 4½" d., 6½" h. 100.00
*Compote, cov., 6" d. 125.00
Compote, cov., 7" d. 285.00
Compote, cov., 8" d., 13" h. 315.00
Compote, open, 6" d., high stand 80.00
Compote, open, 9½" d., high stand 160.00
*Cracker jar, cov. 1,250.00
Creamer (ILLUS.) 90.00
*Creamer w/mask spout 150.00
Goblet, engraved 150.00
*Goblet, plain 82.00
*Lamp, kerosene-type, pedestal base, 8" h. 165.00
Marmalade jar, cov. 225.00
Pitcher, water 450.00
*Salt dip 44.00
*Salt shaker w/original top 65.00
*Sauce dish 30.00
*Spooner 60.00
Spooner, engraved 100.00
*Sugar bowl, cov. 155.00
*Sugar shaker, w/original top 155.00
*Wine 85.00

THUMBPRINT, EARLY (Bakewell, Pears & Co.'s "Argus")

*Butter dish, cov. 115.00
*Cake stand, 8" to 9½" d. 275.00
*Celery vase, plain base 110.00
Celery vase, scalloped rim, pattern in base 155.00
*Compote, open, 6" d., low stand, scalloped rim 35.00
Compote, open, 7½" d., low stand 55.00
*Compote, open, 8" d., high stand 100.00
*Creamer 90.00

Early Thumbprint Goblet

Goblet, plain stem (ILLUS.) 38.00
Inkwell..350.00
Pickle dish 40.00
Pitcher, milk 90.00
*Pitcher, water, 8¼" h. ....300.00 to 400.00
*Sauce dish, clear 8.00
Sauce dish, milk white 75.00
Spillholder 48.00
*Sugar bowl, cov. 60.00
Sweetmeat bowl, 6½" d., 7" h. 190.00
*Wine, baluster stem 60.00

TORPEDO (Pygmy)

Bowl, 7" d., flat, clear 15.00
Bowl, 8" d. 32.50
Butter dish, cov. 75.00
Celery vase 40.00
Compote, cov., jelly 43.00
Compote, cov., 6" d. 78.00
Compote, cov., 7" d., 7¼" h. 65.00
Compote, cov., 8" d., 14" h. 135.00
Compote, open, jelly, 5" d., 5" h. 47.50
Compote, open, 8 x 10½", 8" h., ruffled rim 145.00
Creamer, collared base 55.00
Creamer, footed 37.50
Cruet w/original faceted stopper 75.00
Cup & saucer 65.00
Goblet, clear 50.00
Goblet, ruby-stained 80.00
Lamp, kerosene, hand-type w/finger grip, w/burner & chimney 125.00
Lamp, kerosene-type, 10" h. 185.00
Pickle castor, silver plate cover & tongs 250.00
Pitcher, milk, 8½" h. 95.00
Pitcher, water, tankard, 12" h. 75.00
Salt dip, individual size, 1½" d. 26.00
Salt dip, master size 45.00
Salt & pepper shakers w/original tops, pr. 95.00

Sauce dish 17.50
Spooner 40.00
Sugar bowl, cov. 95.00
Syrup jug w/original top, clear ....100.00 to 125.00
Tumbler, clear, engraved 55.00
Tumbler, ruby-stained 48.00
Wine, clear 90.00
Wine, ruby-stained 95.00

TREE OF LIFE - PORTLAND

Butter dish, cov. 110.00
Butter pat, green 20.00
Celery vase 100.00
Celery vase, in silver plate holder 135.00
Compote, open, 7½" d., scalloped rim 45.00
Compote, open, 7¾" d., 11" h., Infant Samuel stand, signed "Davis" 125.00
Compote, open, 10" d., 6" h., signed "Davis" ....100.00 to 125.00
Creamer, signed "Davis" 55.00
Creamer, blue, in silver plate holder ....175.00 to 200.00
Epergne, single lily, red snake around stem, 18" h. 450.00
*Goblet 50.00
Goblet, signed "Davis" 90.00
Ice cream set, tray & 6 leaf-shaped desserts, 7 pcs. 150.00
Mug, applied handle, 3½" h. 45.00
Pitcher, water, applied handle, clear 78.00
Plate, 7¼" d. 50.00
Powder jar, cov., red coiled snake finial on cover 350.00
Salt dip, individual size, footed, amber 65.00
Salt dip, footed, "Salt" embossed in bowl, clear 135.00
Sauce dish, leaf-shaped, blue 18.00
Spooner, in handled silver plate holder w/two Griffin heads 110.00
Sugar bowl, cov., clear, in silver plate holder 88.00
Sugar bowl, cov., clear 63.00
Syrup pitcher w/original metal top, blue opaque 100.00
Table set: cov. sugar bowl, creamer & spooner; in ornate silver plate holders, the set 180.00
Toothpick holder, apple green 125.00
Tray, ice cream, 14" rectangle 48.00
Waste bowl, amber 50.00
Waste bowl, clear 30.00
Waste bowl, green 45.00

TREE OF LIFE WITH HAND (Tree of Life-Wheeling)

Butter dish, cov. 125.00
Cake stand, frosted base, 11½" d. 85.00
Celery vase 47.00
Compote, open, 5½" d., 5½" h., clear

hand & ball stem 48.00
Compote, open, 5½" d., 5½" h., frosted hand & ball stem 65.00
Compote, open, 8" d., clear hand & ball stem 55.00
Compote, open, 9" d., frosted hand & ball stem 80.00
Compote, open, 10" d., 10" h., frosted hand & ball stem 95.00

Tree of Life with Hand Creamer

Creamer, w/hand & ball handle (ILLUS.) 75.00
Mug, applied handle, 3" h. 125.00
Pitcher, water, 9" h. 68.00
Sauce dish, flat or footed 19.00
Spooner 42.00

U.S. COIN

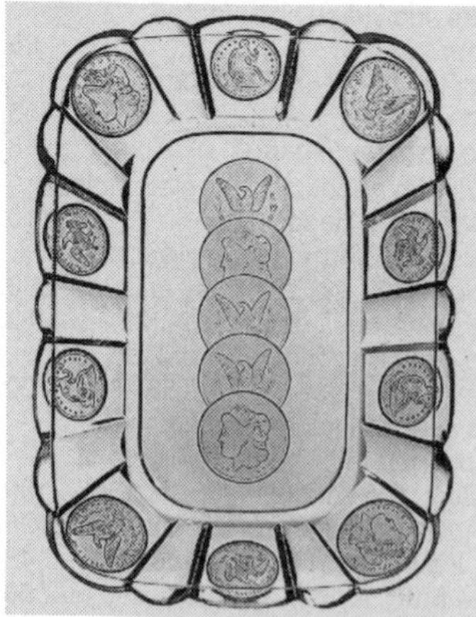

U.S. Coin Bread Tray

*Bowl, berry, 6" d., frosted coins, plate rim 400.00
Bowl, berry, 7" d., frosted quarters, plain rim ....300.00 to 350.00
Bowl, berry, 6" d., frosted coins, scalloped rim 800.00
Bowl, berry, 7" d., frosted quarters, scalloped rim 800.00
Bowl, berry, 9" d., frosted dollars, scalloped rim 1,200.00
Bread tray, frosted quarters & half dollars 230.00
*Bread tray, frosted dollars & half dollars (ILLUS.) ....350.00 to 395.00
Butter dish, cov., clear dollars & half dollars 490.00
Butter dish, cov., frosted dollars & half dollars ....400.00 to 500.00
Cake plate, frosted dollars & quarters, 7" d. ....400.00 to 450.00
Celery tray, frosted quarters 300.00
Celery vase, clear quarters 245.00
Celery vase, frosted quarters ....350.00 to 375.00
Champagne, flared rim, frosted half dimes 800.00
Claret, flared rim, frosted half dimes...600.00
*Compote, cov., 6" d., high stand, frosted dimes & quarters..350.00 to 400.00
Compote, cov., 7" d., high stand, clear dimes & quarters 300.00
Compote, cov., 9" d., high stand, frosted dollars 600.00
Compote, cov., 9" d., high stand, frosted dollars & quarters 1,500.00
Compote, open, 7½" d., high stand, straight rim, frosted quarters 495.00
Compote, open, 8¼" d., high stand, straightrim, frosted quarters 522.50
Compote, open, 9¾" d., high stand, straight rim, frosted quarters & half dollars ....350.00 to 400.00
Compote, open, 10½" d., straight rim, frosted quarters & half dollars 500.00
Compote, open, 7" d., low stand, straight top w/scalloped rim, frosted twenty cent pieces 450.00
Compote, open, 7" d., low stand, flared & scalloped rim, frosted twenty cent pieces 600.00
*Creamer, frosted quarters 450.00
Cruet w/original stopper, frosted quarters, 5½" h. ....625.00 to 650.00
Epergne, clear quarters & dollars 632.00
Epergne, frosted quarters & dollars....800.00
Finger bowl, straight rim, frosted coins 500.00
Finger bowl, flared rim, frosted coins 500.00
Goblet, straight top, frosted dimes, 6½" h. ....250.00 to 300.00
Goblet, straight top, frosted half dollar, 7" h. 400.00
Lamp, kerosene-type, square font, frosted dollars & quarters, 9½" h. ....400.00 to 450.00
Lamp, kerosene-type, square font, frosted half dollars & dollars, 10¼" h. 500.00

Lamp, kerosene-type, square font, frosted half dollars & dollars, 10¼" h. 500.00
Lamp, kerosene-type, round font, frosted quarters, 8½" h. 350.00
Lamp, kerosene-type, round font, frosted quarters, 9" h. 400.00
Lamp, kerosene-type, round font, frosted half dollars, 11½" h. 450.00
Lamp, kerosene-type, round font, frosted dollars, 11½" h. ....750.00 to 800.00
Lamp, kerosene-type, handled, clear quarters, 5" h. .....450.00 to 500.00
Lamp, kerosene-type, handled, frosted quarters, 5" h. 350.00
Mug, frosted dollars 350.00
Pickle dish, frosted half dollars, 3¾ x 7½" .....200.00 to 225.00
Pitcher, milk, frosted half dollars .....600.00 to 650.00
Pitcher, water, frosted dollars .....600.00 to 700.00
Preserve dish, clear half dollars in rim, dollars in base, 5 x 8" .....300.00 to 350.00
Sauce dish, flat, plain rim, frosted quarters, 3¾" d. .....125.00 to 150.00
Sauce dish, flat, plain rim, clear quarters, 4¼" d. 110.00
Sauce dish, flat, plain rim, frosted quarters, 4¼" d. 150.00
Sauce dish, footed, plain top, frosted quarters .....150.00 to 195.00
Sauce dish, footed, scalloped rim, frosted quarters 350.00
Spooner, clear quarters .....225.00 to 250.00
*Spooner, frosted quarters .....275.00 to 300.00
*Sugar bowl, cov., frosted quarters & half dollars .....350.00 to 400.00
Syrup jug w/original dated pewter top, frosted coins .....500.00 to 550.00
Toothpick holder, clear dollars .....150.00 to 175.00
*Toothpick holder, frosted dollars .....150.00 to 175.00
Tumbler, dollar in base, clear sides w/frosted 1882 coin 250.00
Tumbler, dollar in base, paneled sides w/clear 1878 coin .....150.00 to 200.00
Waste bowl -- See FINGER BOWL
Water tray, frosted coins 500.00
Wine, frosted half dimes 600.00

VIKING (Bearded Head or Old Man of the Mountain)

Apothecary jar w/original stopper 75.00
Bowl, cov., 8" oval 100.00
Bowl, 8" sq. 45.00
Butter dish, cov., clear 75.00
Butter dish, cov., frosted 85.00
Celery vase 55.00
Compote, cov., 7" d., low stand 82.00
Compote, cov., 9" d., low stand 110.00
Creamer 60.00
Egg cup 65.00
Marmalade jar, cov., footed 75.00
Mug, applied handle 62.50
Pickle jar w/cover 95.00
Pitcher, water, 8¾" h., clear 115.00
Pitcher, water, 8¾" h., clear & frosted 310.00
Relish 25.00
Salt dip, master size 35.00
Sauce dish, footed 18.00
Spooner 30.00

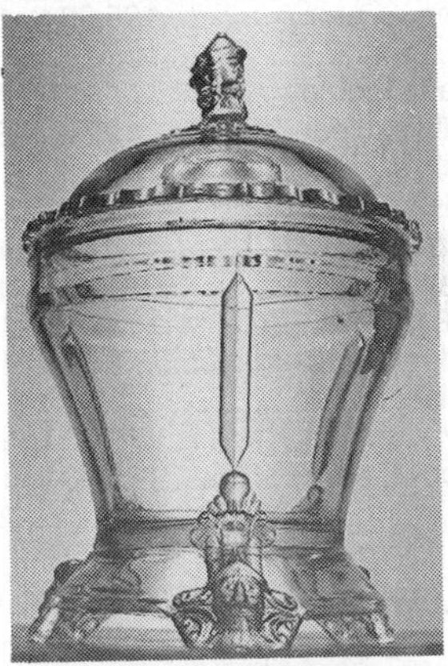

Viking Sugar Bowl

Sugar bowl, cov. (ILLUS.) 65.00

VIRGINIA - See Banded Portland Pattern

WESTWARD HO

Westward Ho Compote

Bowl, 8" 125.00
Bowl, 9" oval 95.00
Bread platter 115.00
*Butter dish, cov. .....125.00 to 150.00
*Celery vase 135.00
*Compote, cov., 4" d., low stand 100.00
Compote, cov., 5" d., high stand 95.00

*Compote, cov., 6" d., low stand.........120.00
Compote, cov., 6" d., high stand.........325.00
*Compote, cov., 4 x 6¾" oval, low stand...150.00
Compote, cov., 5 x 7¾" oval, high stand..............................200.00 to 225.00
Compote, cov., 8" d., low stand (ILLUS.) 325.00
Compote, cov., 6½ x 10" oval, low stand..............................225.00 to 250.00
Compote, open, 7" d., low stand.........175.00
Compote, open, 9" oval, high stand....100.00
*Creamer...........................125.00 to 150.00
*Goblet...75.00
Marmalade jar, cov. 295.00
Mug, child's, clear, 2½" h....................250.00
Mug, child's, milk white, 2½" h............175.00
Pickle dish, oval...................................65.00
Pitcher, milk, 8" h. 495.00
Pitcher, water.......................................405.00
Platter, 9 x 13" 170.00
Relish, deer handles 100.00
Sauce dish, footed..................35.00 to 40.00
Spooner...............................75.00 to 100.00
*Sugar bowl, cov................125.00 to 150.00
*Wine 225.00

WILDFLOWER

Wildflower Sauce Dish

Basket, cake, oblong w/metal handle 145.00
Bowl, 5¾ sq., vaseline..........................32.50
Bowl, 6½" sq., blue 35.00
Bowl, 7" sq...17.50
Bowl, 8" sq., 5" h., footed, amber 22.50
Butter dish, cov., flat, blue 50.00
Cake stand, apple green, 9½" to 11"....66.00
Cake stand, clear, 9½" to 11" 46.00
Cake stand, blue, w/bail handle..........225.00
Celery vase, amber 50.00
Celery vase, clear.................................35.00
*Champagne, amber 50.00
*Champagne, blue..................................50.00
*Champagne, clear.................................30.00
Compote, cov., 6" d., amber 40.00
Compote, cov., 8" d., clear ...75.00 to 100.00
Compote, open, 10½" d., 7½" h., blue 125.00
*Creamer, amber 35.00
*Creamer, blue 45.00
*Creamer, clear 35.00
*Creamer, vaseline.................................42.00
*Goblet, amber 36.00
*Goblet, apple green..............................40.00
*Goblet, blue..37.00
*Goblet, clear...30.00
*Goblet, vaseline 30.00
Pitcher, water, amber 65.00
Pitcher, water, apple green....................95.00
Plate, 10" sq., blue.................................45.00
Plate, 10" sq., clear................................21.00
Plate, 10" sq., vaseline 28.00
Platter, 8 x 11", apple green 47.50
Platter, 8 x 11", blue 45.00
*Salt dip, turtle-shaped, amber..............45.00
*Salt shaker w/original top, amber........35.00
Salt shaker w/original top, apple green..30.00
Salt shaker w/original top, blue.............55.00
Salt shaker w/original top, vaseline 55.00
Salt & pepper shakers w/original tops, vaseline, pr. 110.00
*Sauce dish, flat or footed, amber 13.50
*Sauce dish, flat or footed, apple green..22.50
*Sauce dish, flat or footed, blue............17.00
*Sauce dish, flat or footed, clear (ILLUS.) 12.00
*Sauce dish, flat or footed, vaseline 14.50
Spooner, amber.....................................30.00
Spooner, blue 35.00
Spooner, clear 22.00
Spooner, vaseline..................................34.00
*Sugar bowl, cov., vaseline 45.00
Sugar bowl, open, amber 25.00
Sugar bowl, open, blue..........................30.00
Syrup pitcher w/original top, amber..............................140.00 to 160.00
Syrup pitcher w/original top, blue 350.00
Tray, water, amber, 11 x 13" 45.00
Tray, water, blue, 11 x 13"....75.00 to 100.00
Tray, water, vaseline, 11 x 13" 50.00
Tumbler, amber 38.00
Tumbler, apple green 40.00
Tumbler, blue...45.00
Vase, 10½" h. 58.00
Waste bowl, amber................................48.00
Waste bowl, clear 28.00
Water set: pitcher, tray & 5 tumblers; apple green, 7 pcs. 318.00
*Wine, clear 50.00

WISCONSIN (Beaded Dewdrop)

Banana stand, turned-up sides, 7½" w., 4" h. 72.00
Bonbon, handled, 4" 24.00
Bowl, 6½" d..35.00
Bowl, 8" d...42.00
Butter dish, cov. 90.00
Cake stand, 8¼" d., 4¾" h. 42.50
Cake stand, 9¾" d. 45.00
Celery tray, flat, 5 x 10" 42.50
Celery vase...47.00

Compote, cov., 10½" d. 64.00
Compote, open, 6½" d., 3½" h.............30.00
Compote, open, 7" d., 4" h., tricornered, medium 25.00
Creamer, individual size 35.00
Cruet w/original stopper........................40.00
Cup & saucer.......................................55.00
Dish, cov., oval 26.50
Doughnut stand, 6" d. 40.00
Marmalade jar, cov. 125.00
Mug, 3½" h. 34.00
Nappy, handled, 4" d. 20.00
Pitcher, milk..75.00
Pitcher, water, 8" h. 65.00
Plate, 5" sq. 24.00
Plate, 6½" sq. 26.00
Punch cup...16.50
Relish, 4 x 8½".......................................20.00
Salt shaker w/original top 55.00
Sauce dish..14.00
Spooner 38.00
Sugar bowl, cov., 5" h. 95.00
Sugar shaker w/original top 63.00
Syrup pitcher w/original top, 6½" h. 75.00
*Toothpick holder...................................41.00
Tumbler 45.00
Vase, 6" h. 58.00

Wisconsin Wine

Wine (ILLUS.) 95.00

ZIPPER

Butter dish, cov......................................39.00
Butter dish, cov., ruby-stained...........100.00
Cheese dish, cov. 45.00
Creamer...35.00
Cruet w/original stopper........................36.00
Goblet 25.00
Pitcher, milk...55.00
Relish, 6 x 9½".......................................45.00
Sauce dish, flat or footed...........6.00 to 8.00
Sugar bowl, cov. 35.00
Sugar bowl, cov., ruby-stained 65.00
Toothpick holder, green w/gold 45.00
Wine, clear...30.00
Wine, ruby-stained.................................37.50

(End of Pattern Glass Section)

PEACH BLOW

Several types of glass lumped together by collectors as Peach Blow were produced by half a dozen glasshouses. Hobbs, Brockunier & Co., Wheeling, West Virginia made Peach Blow as a plated ware that shaded from red at the top to yellow at the bottom and is referred to as Wheeling Peach Blow. Mt. Washington Glass Works produced an homogeneous Peach Blow shading from a rose color at the top to pale blue in the lower portion. The New England Glass Works' Peach Blow, called Wild Rose, shaded from rose at the top to white. Gunderson-Pairpoint Co. also reproduced some of the Mt. Washington Peach Blow in the early 1950s and some glass of a somewhat similar type was made by Steuben Glass Works, the Boston & Sandwich Factory and by Thomas Webb & Sons and Stevens & Williams of England. Sandwich Peach Blow is one-layered glass and the English is two-layered.

Another single layered shaded art glass was produced early in this century by the New Martinsville Glass Mfg. Co. Originally called "Muranese," collectors today refer to it as "New Martinsville Peach Blow."

GUNDERSON - PAIRPOINT

Butter dish, cov. $250.00
Compote, 4½" d., 3" h., paper label....150.00
Cup & saucer, glossy finish 250.00
Toothpick holder 350.00

NEW ENGLAND

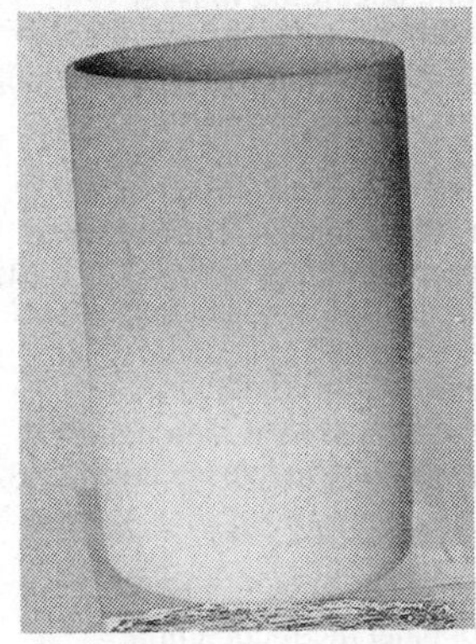

Tumbler with Satin Finish

Bowl, 5¼" d., 2½" h., scalloped rim 300.00
Celery vase, bulging cylindrical form w/pie crust crimped rim, 3½" d........545.00
Rose bowl, bulbous, seven-crimp top, satin finish, 2¾" d., 2⅝" h. 300.00

Tumbler, cylindrical, satin finish, 3¾" h. (ILLUS.) 475.00
Vase, 7" h., squatty bulbous base tapering to a tall slender 'stick' neck 239.00

WEBB

Bowl, 4" d., 2½" h., squatty bulbous shape, decorated w/heavy gold prunus & pine needles & a gold butterfly in flight, creamy white lining, satin finish 300.00
Pitcher, tankard, 9" h., signed....................385.00
Rose bowl, miniature, decorated w/gold flowers & butterfly, 2¼" d......385.00

Small Webb Decorated Vases

Vase, 3¼" h., 2¾" d., baluster-form, decorated w/gold prunus & branches, creamy white lining (ILLUS. right) 345.00
Vase, 3¾" h., 3¼" d., ovoid form tapering to a short neck w/slightly flaring rim, decorated w/silver flowers & heavy gold leaves, glossy finish (ILLUS. left) 325.00
Vase, 5" h., 3½" d., ovoid body tapering to a short flared neck, enameled w/two-colored birds, white flowers & gold foliage, creamy white lining, propeller mark 495.00
Vase, 7½" h., 4" d., squatty bulbous body tapering to a cylindrical neck, decorated w/heavy gold prunus blossoms, branches & pine needles, creamy white lining, glossy finish.....325.00

WHEELING

Cruet w/original facet-cut amber stopper, ovoid body tapering to a small cylindrical neck w/a high arched spout, amber applied reeded handle, 6¾" h. (ILLUS. top next column) 1,085.00
Flask, tooled lip, glossy finish, 4½" widest w., 7" h....................750.00

Wheeling Peach Blow Cruet

Pitcher, 4½" h., wide ovoid body tapering to a wide cylindrical neck w/flaring four-cornered rim, applied clear handle 785.00
Salt shaker w/original silver plate top, spherical body, glossy finish, 2½" h....................485.00
Tumblers, cylindrical, Drape patt., two w/satin & one w/glossy finish, 3¾" h., group of 3 ....460.00
Vase, 6½" h., 6½" d., bulbous, glossy finish 850.00
Vase, 8" h., "Morgan vase," tall ovoid body tapering to a slender ringed neck w/flaring lip, glossy finish (no stand) 770.00

PEKING

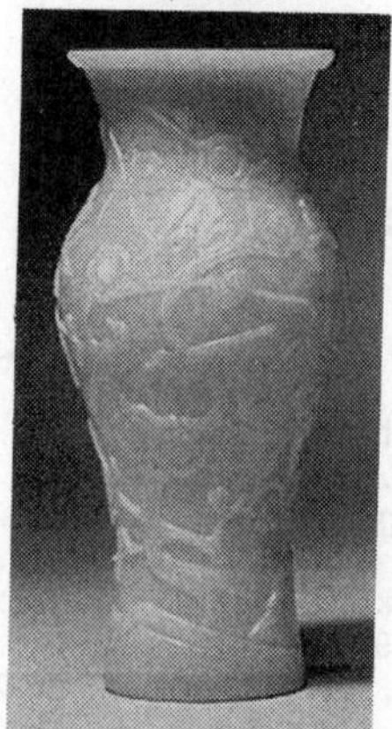

Fine Peking Glass Vase

This is Chinese glass, some of which has overlay in one to five colors, which has attracted collector interest. Peking Imperial glass is the most valuable.

Bowl, 7¾" d., the ruby red lobed body carved in relief w/seven panels of jardinieres filled w/flowers, each inscribed w/auspicious characters, Jiaqing period (ground rim chips) $2,875.00

Condiment set, chrysanthemum-form, consisting of an octagonal central bowl surrounded by eight radiating petal-shaped dishes, together w/a fitted fabric & cardboard circular box, 19th c., overall 18¼" d., the set 2,875.00

Jar, cov., ruby red, carved on each side w/scene of a horse & tree, early 19th c., 4¾" h. 2,310.00

Vase, 7" h., baluster-form w/flaring cylindrical neck, carved w/confronting archaistic *chilong* divided by mock tasseled rings between descending leaf-tips & rising lappets, egg yolk yellow, late 18th c. 12,650.00

Vase, 9" h., ovoid body tapering to a tall narrow cylindrical neck, opaque camellia leaf green swirled w/other greens, underside w/four-character Qianlong mark within double square, late 18th - early 19th c. 1,725.00

Vase, 12¾" h., bottle-form, finely carved through thick red to a snowflake white w/elegant ladies in palanquins followed by attendants & equestrian figures riding through a continuous landscape w/pavilions among rocky mountains & boldly carved leafy trees & pine trees issuing from massive rockwork encircling the base, all below a *ruyi* collar around the shoulders, surmounted by a tall cylindrical neck vigorously carved w/pavilions & military figures in a rocky landscape w/large pine boughs extending up the neck, the lip rimmed in red, the underside w/a large well-carved four-character Qianlong mark within a double square, Qianlong period (minute chips) 54,625.00

Vases, 8⅜" h., the yellow baluster-form body w/flaring rim carved in high relief w/songbirds perched among prunus & peony blossoms growing from rockwork formations, 19th c., pr. (ILLUS. of one) 920.00

PHOENIX

This ware was made by the Phoenix Glass Co. of Beaver County, Pennsylvania, which produced various types of glass from the 1880s. One special type that attracts collectors now is a molded ware with a vague resemblance to cameo in its "sculptured" decoration. Similar pieces with relief-molded designs were produced by the Consolidated Lamp & Glass Co. (which see) and care must be taken to differentiate between the two companies' wares. Some Consolidated molds were moved to the Phoenix plant in the mid-1930s but later returned and used again at Consolidated. These pieces we will list under "Consolidated."

Wild Geese Vase

Candy dish, cov., Phlox patt., tan on milk white ground $125.00

Compote, cov., Lacy Dewdrop patt., blue decoration on a milk white ground...125.00

Platter, 14" d., Jonquil patt., pearlized white on white satin ground 190.00

Vase, 6" h., 5" d., bulbous base w/short flaring neck, Aster patt., green on milk white ground.............125.00

Vase, 7" h., bulbous base w/trumpet-form sides, Bluebell patt., pearlized finish 63.00

Vase, 8¾" h., footed, tapering cylindrical body w/flaring rim, Primrose patt., green background w/frosted design.............................125.00

Vase, 9¼" h., pillow-shaped, Wild Geese patt., white birds on a blue ground (ILLUS.) 185.00

Vase, 11½" h., baluster-form, Dancing Girls patt., brown shadow figures on brown ground...................................495.00

PIGEON BLOOD

This name refers to the color of this glass, a deep blood-red. It was popular in the late 19th century and was featured in a number of mold-blown patterns.

Bowl, 4½" d., 2⅝" h., Inverted Thumbprint patt. $175.00

Bowl, 9" d., Torquay patt. w/resilvered silver plate rim................................110.00
Cracker jar w/original puffy lid, Torquay patt....................................650.00
Cruet w/original stopper, Torquay patt. ....800.00 to 850.00
Cruet w/original stopper, Venecia patt. 650.00
Pitcher, water, Torquay patt. ....375.00 to 395.00
Pitcher, water, Venecia patt...............350.00
Salt & pepper shakers w/original tops, Overlapping Petals patt., pr. 155.00
Syrup pitcher w/original metal cover, squatty form, Torquay patt. 425.00
Toothpick holder, Bulging Loops patt. 120.00

PILLAR-MOLDED

Rare Pillar-Molded Pitcher

This heavily ribbed glassware was produced by blowing glass into full-sized ribbed molds and then finishing it by hand. The technique evolved from earlier "pattern moulding" used on glass since ancient times but in pillar-molded glass the ribs are very heavy and prominent. Most examples found in this country were produced in the Pittsburgh, Pennsylvania area from around 1850 to 1870, but similar English-made wares made before and after this period are also available. Most American were made from clear flint glass and colored examples or pieces with colored strands in the ribs are rare and highly prized. Some collectors refer to this as "steamboat" glass believing that it was made to be used on American riverboats but most likely it was used anywhere that a sturdy, relatively inexpensive glassware was needed, such as taverns and hotels.

Decanter w/bar lip, eight-rib, clear, tapering conical form w/applied neck rings, 9¾" h. $82.50
Decanter w/matching ribbed pear-shaped stoppers, eight-rib, clear, bell-shaped body w/notched ribs tapering to ringed cylindrical neck, cut panels between the ribs on the shoulder, pr. 14" h...........................412.50
Pitcher, 7¼" h., eight-rib, deep amethyst, slightly tapering cylindrical body w/neck ring & wide slightly flaring rim, applied strap handle, tiny broken blister inside, wear, scratches (ILLUS.) 8,800.00
Pitcher, 10½" h., eight-rib, clear, bulbous base tapering in at mid-section & out at top, applied foot & handle 605.00
Sugar bowl, cov., eight-rib, clear, deep rounded bowl w/galleried rim, tall slender pyramidal cover w/button finial, on slender waisted applied stem & round foot, 10⅝" h. (small flake on top of finial at pontil) 1,870.00
Syrup jug w/original metal neck & cover, eight-rib, clear, ovoid footed base tapering to a cylindrical neck fitted w/hinged metal rim & spouted cover, applied strap handle, 11¼" h. 247.50
Vase, 8" h., eight-rib, clear, tall flaring tulip-form bowl w/swirled ribs at the top, applied knopped stem & disc foot (shallow chip on one rib)..........440.00

POMONA

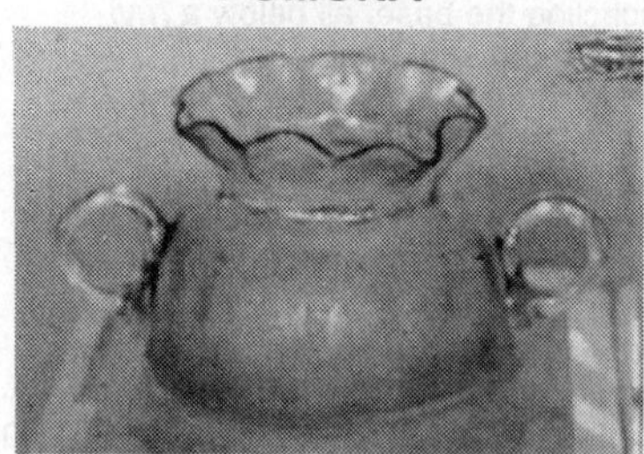

Pomona Open Sugar Bowl

First produced by the New England Glass Company under a patent received by Joseph Locke in 1885, Pomona has a frosted ground on clear glass decorated with mineral stains, most frequently amber-yellow, sometimes pale blue. Some pieces bore smooth etched floral decorations highlighted with staining. Two types of Pomona were made. The first Locke patent covered a technique whereby the piece was first covered with an acid-resistant coating which was then needle-carved with thousands of minute criss-

crossing lines. The piece was then dipped into acid which cut into the etched lines, giving the finished piece a notable "brilliance." A cheaper method, covered by a second Locke patent on June 15, 1886, was accomplished by rolling the glass piece in particles of acid-resistant material which were picked up by it. The glass was then etched by acid which attacked areas not protected by the resistant particles. A favorite design on Pomona was the cornflower.

Berry set: 8" d. master bowl & eight 4" d. sauce dishes; Inverted Thumbprint patt. w/turned in scalloped amber rims, 2nd patent, 9 pcs. $225.00

Bowl, 4" d., crimped & folded rim, 2nd patent 50.00

Bowl, 10" d., 4¼" h., upright crimped sides, pansy & blue butterfly design, 2nd patent 316.00

Celery vase w/ruffled rim & applied clear base, blue cornflower decoration, 1st patent, 6¼" h. 375.00

Creamer & open sugar bowl, squatty bulbous body w/Inverted Thumbprint patt., flaring ruffled amber rim & applied amber handles, 1st patent, pr. (ILLUS. of sugar bowl) 585.00

Cruet w/original bubble stopper, spherical body on applied crimped foot, applied handle, blue cornflower decoration, 2nd patent 650.00

Finger bowl, crimped rim, 1st patent ..140.00

Pitcher, tankard, 12¼" h., blue butterflies & gold grasses, 1st patent........747.50

Punch cup, blueberry decoration w/honey amber stain on rim, leaves & handle, 1st patent, 2⅝" d., 2¾" h...175.00

Toothpick holder, applied rigaree band around the neck, 2nd patent ...110.00

Tumbler, cylindrical, blue cornflower decoration, 2nd patent, 2½" d., 3½" h...145.00

Vase, 3" h., 6" w., fan-shaped w/ruffled rim, blue cornflower decoration, 1st patent 237.50

QUEZAL

These wares resemble those of Tiffany and other glasshouses which produced lustred glass pieces in the late 19th and early 20th centuries. They were made by the Quezal Art Glass and Decorating Co. of Brooklyn, New York, early in this century and until its closing in the mid-1920s.

Center bowl, deep flaring wide-ribbed bowl on a ribbed funnel base, blue shading to purple w/overall golden iridescence, signed, ca. 1900, 13⅛" d...$805.00

Taster, squared sides w/pinched dimples, gold iridescent interior & exterior, signed "Quezal" on base, 2¾" h...137.50

Vase, 7½" h., floriform, the opalescent sides decorated w/green striated feathering, the foot further decorated w/amber iridescent feathering, the interior in amber iridescence, inscribed "Quezal," ca. 1925.........1,035.00

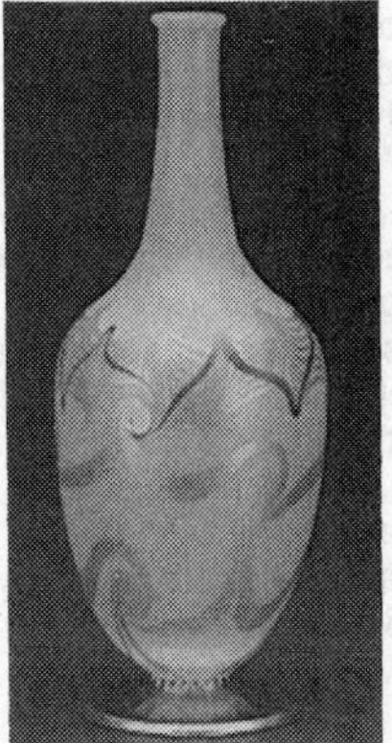

Decorated Quezal Vase

Vase, 9" h., footed ovoid body tapering to a slender 'stick' neck, Egyptian Revival style w/a creamy white body decorated w/a green zig-zag shoulder design above gold iridescent double hooked & pulled-feather design, by Martin Bach, foot inscribed "Quezal N.Y." (ILLUS.) ..2,300.00

Vase, 9¾" h., a cushion foot supporting a slender trumpet-form body w/a widely flaring & ruffled rim, opaque white ground decorated on the exterior w/green & gold pulled-feather designs & a band of gold iridescent hearts around the neck, etched "Quezal 6" 1,265.00

Vase, 13⅛" h., jack-in-the-pulpit form, the widely flaring ruffled rim above a slender stem & bulbous base in opalescent decorated w/finely pulled feathering in mint green & amber iridescence, the interior in amber iridescence, inscribed "Quezal," ca. 1920 ....4,600.00

PELOTON

Made in Bohemia, Germany and England in the late 19th century, this glassware is characterized by threads or filaments of glass rolled into the glass body of the objects in random patterns. Some of these wares were decorated.

Pitcher, 6½" h., bulbous ovoid body w/a cylindrical neck w/pinched spout, clear applied handle, the body w/clear threads interspersed w/pink, yellow, blue & white "coconut" threading....................$137.50
Plate, 6" d., ruffled rim, clear ground w/white, pink, blue & yellow "coconut" threading....................95.00
Rose bowl, footed bulbous body w/rim drawn up to four points, white opaque body w/deep pink, blue, yellow & white "coconut" threading, 3½" d., 3¾" h. 295.00
Vase, 3¼" h., 3⅞" d., bulbous body w/embossed ribbing & the top half pinched together to form two openings, shaded lavender to pink ground w/blue, pink, yellow & white "coconut" threading....................265.00
Vase, 3½" h., 3" d., spherical body w/ringed neck & flat ruffled rim, pinkish lavender ground w/white, pink, blue & yellow "coconut" threading....................195.00
Vase, 6⅛" h., 3¾" d., ovoid body w/embossed ribbing tapering to a flaring neck w/crimped rim, shaded lavender to pink ground w/blue, yellow, pink & white "coconut" threading....................275.00
Vase, 6¾" h., 5⅛" d., ovoid body w/embossed ribbing tapering to a flaring, crimped rim, cased clear ground w/royal blue "coconut" threading, white interior 225.00
Vase, 6¾" h., 5⅛" d., footed ovoid body tapering to a flat mouth, clear ground w/royal blue "coconut" threading....................145.00
Vase, 6¾" h., 5⅜" d., footed ovoid body w/a wide shoulder & short, wide neck w/flat rim flanked by small square handles, clear ground w/green "coconut" threading....................195.00

ROSE BOWLS

Amber, Hobnail patt., scalloped rim, three applied feet, 3" d., 5" h....................$75.00
Blue opalescent, Reverse Swirl patt., 3½" d., 4½" h. 40.00
Cased, pink exterior decorated overall w/heavy gold flowers & branches, white lining, base marked w/enameled red web & "E" (White House Glass Works, Stourbridge, England) on base, footed ovoid form, four-crimp top, 3" d., 3" h....................265.00
Cased satin, blue mother-of-pearl Ribbon patt., white interior, nine-crimp top, 3¾" d., 4" h....................275.00
Cased satin, shaded apricot mother-of-pearl Herringbone patt., white interior, eight-crimp top, 3¾" d., 4" h....................195.00
Cased satin, shaded pink exterior decorated w/creamy white morning glory & green leaves, white interior, applied frosted petal feet, egg-shaped, four-crimp top, 4½" d., 5½" h....................135.00
Golden amber air-trap zipper pattern, twelve-crimp top, registry number on base, miniature, 2½" d., 2¼" h. 118.00
Sapphire blue w/air-trap bubbles, egg-shaped, crimped top, engraved registry number, 2½" d., 2" h. 95.00

RUBINA CRYSTAL

Rubina Cologne Bottles

This glass, sometimes spelled "Rubena," is a flashed ware, shading from ruby to clear. Some pieces are decorated, others are plain.

Cologne bottle w/clear facet-cut stopper, cut-paneled cylindrical body, 2¾" d., 6¼" h. (ILLUS. right) $88.00
Cologne bottle w/original facet-cut stopper, cylindrical shouldered body w/a short neck & flared rim, overall lacy stippling, gold band trim on shoulder & rim, St. Louis, France, 3" d., 7½" h. (ILLUS. left) 110.00
Condiment set: rectangular salt dip, mustard pot & pepper shaker w/original silver tops & ball-footed silver plate holder w/angular handle; overall cut design, 3⅝" d., 5¼" h., the set....................195.00
Spooner, Venecia patt....................110.00
Sugar shaker w/original top, Hobb's Optic patt. 195.00

Tumbler, Hobnail patt., 4" h....................65.00
Vase, 10" h., 2⅛" d., slender trumpet-form, decorated w/engraved fern-type foliage....................68.00
Water set: pitcher & two tumblers; Hobnail patt., 3 pcs....................250.00

RUBINA VERDE

This decorative glass, popular in the late 19th and early 20th centuries, shades from ruby or deep cranberry to green or greenish-yellow.

Celery vase, decorated w/applied rigaree & h.p. cherry blossoms & butterflies, 6" d., 12" h....................$265.00
Cruet w/original facet-cut greenish yellow stopper, applied greenish yellow handle, Inverted Thumbprint patt., 7" h....................485.00
Pickle castor, corset-shaped Inverted Thumbprint patt. insert, w/ornate footed silver plate frame w/matching tongs, marked Tufts....................395.00
Pitcher, water, Hobnail patt....................450.00
Vase, 8¼" h., 1⅞" d., tall slender waisted cylindrical form, decorated w/applied clear rigaree spiralling trim around body, applied clear petal feet....................95.00

RUBY-STAINED

Majestic Ruby-Stained Butter

This name derives from the color of the glass - a deep red. The red staining was thinly painted on clear pressed glass patterns and refired at a low temperature. Many pieces were further engraved as souvenir items and were very popular from the 1890s into the 1920s. This technique should not be confused with "flashed" glass where a clear glass piece is actually dipped in molten glass of a contrasting color. Also see PATTERN GLASS.

Berry set: master bowl & four sauce dishes; Bar & Flute patt., 5 pcs....................$160.00
Bowl, berry, individual, Bar & Flute patt....................20.00
Butter dish, cov., Heavy Gothic patt. ..155.00
Butter dish, cov., Majestic patt., 7½" d., 6" h. (ILLUS.)....................110.00
Butter dish, cov., Tacoma patt....................80.00
Butter dish, cov., Triple Triangle patt....90.00
Compote, 8¼ x 8½", open, Scroll with Cane Band patt....................220.00
Creamer, Almond Thumbprint patt., 4½" h....................20.00
Creamer, Arched Ovals patt....................45.00
Cruet w/original stopper, Button Panel patt....................369.00
Cruet w/original stopper, Zippered Swirl & Diamond patt....................85.00
Goblet, Beaded Dart Band patt....................25.00
Goblet, Swag Block patt....................50.00
Pitcher, water, Carnation patt., w/gold trim....................265.00
Pitcher, water, Ladder with Diamond patt....................250.00
Sauce dish, Millard patt....................25.00
Sugar bowl, cov., Heavy Gothic patt....................125.00
Sugar bowl, cov., Triple Triangle patt....................35.00
Syrup pitcher w/original top, Beauty patt....................395.00
Table set: cov. butter dish, creamer, cov. sugar bowl & spooner; Diamond Band with Panel patt., 4 pcs....................190.00
Toothpick holder, Box-In-Box patt., w/enameled floral decoration....................145.00
Tumbler, Diamond & Sunburst Variant patt....................29.00
Water set: pitcher & six tumblers; Diamond Band with Panel patt., 7 pcs....................145.00
Wine, Block Band patt....................24.00

SANDWICH

Numerous types of glass were produced at The Boston & Sandwich Glass Works in Sandwich, Massachusetts, on Cape Cod, from 1826 to 1888. Those listed here represent a sampling. Also see PATTERN GLASS and LACY in the "Glass" section.

All pieces are pressed glass unless otherwise noted.

Bowl, 6" d., lacy, Rayed Peacock Eye patt., clear....................$135.00
Candlestick, Dolphin patt., the petal-

form dark blue socket on a short knob stem applied w/a wafer to the milky clambroth figural dolphin pedestal on a double-step square foot, ca. 1850, 9¾" h. 715.00

Sandwich Columnar Candlestick

Candlesticks, dark blue petal socket atop a milky clambroth columnar standard w/stepped, square base, ca. 1850, minor base chips, heat check in one socket, 9¼" h., pr. (ILLUS. of one) 1,320.00

Candlesticks, Acanthus Leaf patt., opaque blue hexagonal leaf-molded socket applied w/a wafer to the baluster-form acanthus leaf-molded milky clambroth pedestal & domed, leaf-molded hexagonal foot, 10⅞" h., pr. (very minor flakes under foot) 1,870.00

Cologne bottle w/original steeple-shaped stopper w/air trap, ring-necked bottle, dark green 250.00

Compote, open, 9½" d., 6¾" h., Petal & Loop patt., moonstone..............1,650.00

Salt shaker, "Christmas" salt w/dated metal top w/agitator, amber, lid signed "Dana K. Alden, Boston" 65.00

Salt shakers, "Christmas" salt w/dated metal top w/agitator, in original box labeled "Dana K. Alden's World Renowned Table Salt Bottles," two amethyst, one each cobalt blue, pale aqua blue, vaseline & amber, set of 6 (one top & agitator badly corroded) 715.00

Spill holder, Sandwich Star patt., clear 75.00

String holder, domical, overlay, cut thumbprint design w/cobalt blue cut to clear 275.00

Sugar bowl, cov., lacy, octagonal Acanthus Leaf patt., deep emerald green, 5½" h. (usual mold roughness) 17,600.00

Sugar bowl, cov., lacy, Gothic Arch patt., opaque blue w/lightly 'sanded' surface, 5¼" h. (small chips).........1,375.00

Vase, 9¼" h., ovoid opaque moonstone Sawtooth patt. body raised on a blown jade green pedestal foot & w/a tall blown jade green slender trumpet neck w/flattened ruffled rim, ca. 1860....1,980.00

SATIN

Satin glass was a popular decorative glass developed in the late 19th century. Most pieces were composed of two layers of glass with the exterior layer usually in a shaded pastel color. The name derives from the soft matte finish, caused by exposure to acid fumes, which gave the surface a "satiny" feel. Mother-of-pearl satin glass was a specialized variety wherein air trapped between the layers of glass provided subtle surface patterns such as Herringbone and Diamond Quilted. A majority of satin glass was produced in England and America but collectors should be aware that reproductions have been produced for many years. Also see ROSE BOWLS and WEBB under Glass.

Basket, flaring cylindrical base, rim pinched at middle forming a double lobed top, applied clear frosted handle, bridal white mother-of-pearl Herringbone patt., rich pink interior, 3 x 4¾", 5 ¾" h. $325.00

Basket, bulbous base flaring to a fan-shaped crimped rim, applied frosted clear twisted thorn handle, applied clear edge trim, shaded heavenly blue mother-of-pearl Herringbone patt., white interior, 8¼" d., 9¼" h. ...550.00

Bowl, 5½" d., 4¾" h., deep rounded sides w/deeply lobed rim, rich blue shaded to light blue mother-of-pearl Diamond Quilted patt., applied w/three frosted thorny log tubes at the sides continuing down to form the feet 395.00

Bowl, 9¼" d., 3⅜" h., footed, rounded sides w/turned-down ruffled rim, chartreuse mother-of-pearl Diamond Quilted patt., white exterior, applied frosted rim edging & three applied frosted thorn feet...........................425.00

Cracker jar, cov., ovoid body, shaded pink to white & decorated w/pink & white carnation-like flowers & green leaves, resilvered cover, rim & bail handle, 5" d., 7½" h.........................225.00

Creamer, squatty bulbous base tapering to a wide cylindrical neck w/pinched lip, applied frosted blue

handle, heavenly blue mother-of-pearl Raindrop patt., 3¼" d., 4½" h. 225.00
Cruet w/original stopper, ovoid body tapering to a slender neck w/rolled rim, applied clear frosted handle, shaded apricot mother-of-pearl Diamond Quilted patt., white lining 1,450.00
Ewer, footed ovoid shouldered base, flaring cylindrical neck w/tricorner rim, applied clear frosted handle, shaded pink decorated w/dainty blue flowers, creamy white water lilies & green leaves, white interior, 3⅝" d., 8⅜" h. 118.00
Rose bowl, bulbous, eight-crimp top, heavenly blue mother-of-pearl Ribbon patt., white interior, 4" d., 2¾" h. 235.00
Rose bowl, bulbous, eight-crimp top, applied clear frosted petal feet, shaded heavenly blue enameled w/blue & creamy white flowers & tan buds, 4½" d., 4¾" h. 135.00
Salt shaker w/original top, shaded pink mother-of-pearl Diamond Quilted patt., white interior, 5½" h. 175.00
Sugar shaker w/original metal top, ovoid base w/short bulbous neck, heavenly blue mother-of-pearl Herringbone patt., white lining, 6¼" h. 650.00
Vase, 4¾" h., 6" d., squatty bulbous body tapering to a flaring three-petal rim, heavenly blue mother-of-pearl Ribbon patt., white interior 495.00
Vase, 7" h., 4" d., ovoid body tapering to a cylindrical neck w/flaring & crimped rim, shaded heavenly blue mother-of-pearl Diamond Quilted patt., white lining 198.00
Vase, 9½" h., 4½" d., squatty bulbous base tapering to a tall cylindrical stick neck, shaded rose to green, white interior, marked Webb 495.00

SILVER DEPOSIT - SILVER OVERLAY

Silver Deposit and Silver Overlay have been made commercially since the last quarter of the 19th century. Silver is deposited on the glass by various means, most commonly by utilizing an electric current. The glass was very popular during the first three decades of this century, and some pieces are still being produced. During the late 1970s, silver commanded exceptionally high prices and this was reflected in a surge of interest in silver overlay glass, especially in pieces marked "Sterling" or "925" on the heavy silver overlay.

Tall Silver Overlay Vase

Bowl, 12¼" d., 3⅛" h., three-footed, clear w/silver overlay flowers & scrolls $65.00
Flask, flat w/rounded shoulders, clear w/scrolling hallmarked silver overlay, hinged silver cover, 5" h. 275.00
Plate, 10" d., black w/silver overlay, marked "D. Rockwell Silver Co." 245.00
Vase, 5½" h., iridescent amethyst body applied w/angular Secessionist-style silver overlay bands, bands marked "Sterling," Austria, early 20th c. 440.00
Vase, 8" h., expanding cylinder w/short flared mouth, rose red w/white lining, overlaid w/scrolling floral overlay, stamped "Sterling 680" (small bruise at side) 357.50
Vase, 12" h., slender trumpet-shaped body on a thin round foot, green overlaid overall w/a silver spiderweb-style design 374.00
Vase, 14" h., bulbous top w/wide flat mouth, the sides tapering to a slender body w/a cushion foot, dark green overlaid w/willowy carnations & interlaced leaves, marked on the base by the Alvin Mfg. Co., Providence, Rhode Island, ca. 1905 (ILLUS.) 2,760.00

SLAG

Originally named "Mosaic" glass by makers in the late 19th and early 20th century, collectors today also refer to this variegated glass as 'marble' or 'agate.' It is produced by mixing together milk white glass with another color, most often dark purple, to produce a swirled effect. Blue, green and caramel colors are also found and the rarest type is 'pink slag,' made only in the Inverted Fan & Feather pattern in the early 20th century. Reproductions of slag have been produced, most notably by the Imperial Glass Corp., so care is needed when purchasing some pieces.

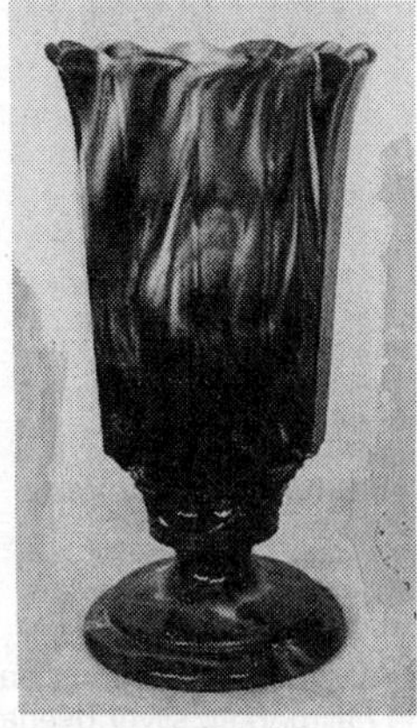

Fluted Celery Vase

Animal covered dish, Hen on nest w/lacy edge, rust, 8" l. $250.00
Bread tray, Tam O'Shanter patt., purple 275.00
Celery vase, Fluted patt., purple (ILLUS.) 95.00
Cruet w/original stopper, Inverted Fan & Feather patt., gold trim, pink......1,100.00
Mug, Bird in Nest patt., purple 85.00
Sauce dish, Inverted Fan & Feather patt., pink 225.00
Sugar bowl, cov., Challinor's Flying Swan patt., butterscotch 185.00
Toothpick holder, Scroll with Acanthus patt., purple 125.00
Water set: 8" h. pitcher & six tumblers; Water Crane patt., blue, 7 pcs. 275.00

SPANGLED

Spangled glass incorporated particles of mica or metallic flakes and variegated colored glass particles imbedded in the transparent glass. Usually made of two layers, it might have either an opaque or transparent casing. The Vasa Murrhina Glass Company of Sandwich, Massachusetts, first patented the process for producing Spangled glass in 1884 and this factory is known to have produced great quantities of this ware. It was, however, also produced by numerous other American and English glasshouses. This type, along with Spatter, which see below, is often erroneously called "End of Day."

A related decorative glass, Aventurine, features a fine speckled pattern resembling gold dust on a solid color ground. Also see "Art Glass Baskets" under Glass.

Spangled Glass Bowl

Basket, spherical w/eight-crimp top, applied clear thorn handle, rose exterior w/mica flecks, white lining, 4⅛" d. 7¼" h. $195.00
Bowl, 8" d., 2¾" h., flattened ruffled rim, shaded gold w/mica flecks interior, white underside (ILLUS.) 95.00
Candlestick, hollow baluster-form standard w/flared foot & down-turned flared lip, black amethyst w/ mica flecks, 18" h. 220.00
Ewer, ovoid body tapering to a cylindrical neck w/a three-petal rim, cased orange ground w/mica flecks, white lining, 4" d., 8½" h..................125.00
Pitcher, 8" h., melon-ribbed body tapering to a cylindrical neck w/ruffled rim, clear applied handle, deep cranberry shaded to pink exterior w/blue, pink, yellow & black spatter & mica flecks, white interior 295.00
Tumbler, tapering cylindrical form, green w/mica flecks, 2⅝" d., 3⅞" h. ...45.00
Vase, 5" h., 4¼" d., jack-in-the-pulpit shape, green, brown & white spatter w/silver mica flecks 79.00

SPATTER

This variegated-color ware is similar to Spangled glass but does not contain

applied on a clear, opaque white or colored body. Much of it was made in Europe and England. It is sometimes called "End of Day."

Also see "Art Glass Baskets" under Glass.

Spatter Glass Pitcher

Basket, rectangular-shaped footed bowl w/slightly ruffled edge, applied clear twisted thorn handle, maroon, white, green, blue & yellow spatter exterior w/embossed Basketweave patt., white lining, 4¼ x 5", 5½" h...$100.00

Candlesticks, baluster-shaped w/cushion foot & w/molded swirled ribbing, maroon, green, blue, yellow, white & pink spatter, 3⅞" d., 8¾" h. .135.00

Creamer & open sugar bowl: tankard-shaped creamer w/clear applied handle & petal-shaped feet, squatty bulbous, open sugar bowl w/clear applied petal feet; deep maroon, blue, white, green & creamy spatter, 2⅝" d., 4½" h. creamer, 5" d., 3" h. sugar bowl, pr. 88.00

Decanter w/original heart-shaped clear stopper, ovoid body tapering to a slender cylindrical neck w/petal-shaped spout, applied clear handle, blue & white spatter, 3½" d., 8¾" h...135.00

Ewer, pedestal cushion foot supporting an ovoid body tapering to a flaring neck w/tricornered rim, applied clear handle, yellow & white spatter exterior decorated w/enameled yellow flowers & leaves & a butterfly outlined in pale pink, yellow lining, 3¾" d., 11" h. 118.00

Jar, cov., slightly domed cover w/applied clear knob finial, cylindrical sides w/applied clear shell trim beneath rim, maroon, yellow, blue & aqua spatter, white lining, 3⅝" d., 5¾" h. 68.00

Pitcher, 6¾" h., 6" d., bulbous spherical body tapering to a short cylindrical neck w/pinched lip, clear applied reeded handle, orange & yellow spatter, yellow lining (ILLUS.) 175.00

Vase, 7¼" h., 5" d., cushion foot supporting an ovoid body tapering to a slightly flaring cylindrical neck, clear applied angular shoulder handles, clear cased yellow & white spatter enameled w/purple & white flowers, green leaves & a grey & white bird decoration........................195.00

STEUBEN

Most of the Steuben glass listed below was made at the Steuben Glass Works, now a division of Corning Glass, between 1903 and about 1933. The factory was organized by T.G. Hawkes, noted glass designer, Frederick Carder, and others. Mr. Carder devised many types of glass and revived many old techniques.

ACID CUT BACK

Steuben Acid Cut-Back Vase

Vase, 9" h., bulbous ovoid body on a small footring, the wide shoulder tapering to a short cylindrical flaring neck, greenish yellow ground overlaid in turquoise blue iridescence & cut w/a band of stylized leaping gazelles against stylized scrolling foliage, geometric rim & base bands, unsigned $4,400.00

Vase, 9¾" h., footed wide cylindrical body w/a wide shoulder to a short, flared neck, white overlaid in Jade green & acid-etched to depict stylized carnations (ILLUS.) 920.00

Vase, 10" h., tall flat hexagonal body, olive green opalescent ground overlaid w/turquoise blue iridescence, cut w/a geometric stylized scene of a hunter w/drawn bow & a leaping gazelle in a jungle landscape, unsigned, ca. 1925...........4,675.00

AURENE

Aurene Candlestick & Punch Bowl

Bowl, 12" d., shallow incurved sides, on three applied prunt feet, overall blue iridescence, shape No. 2586, engraved mark "Aurene 2586".........770.00

Candlesticks, ovoid candle socket w/flattened flaring rim raised on a stem w/a rope twist upper section, on a circular slightly domed foot, overall gold iridescence, signed "Aurene 686," 10" h. (ILLUS. of one, left)...880.00

Aurene Cordial Set

Cordial set: cylindrical decanter w/pointed stopper, four conical glasses & a round tray w/deep upright sides; gold iridescent finish, each piece signed "Aurene 2025," tray 6¼" d., decanter 8¾" h., the set (ILLUS.)...................................2,860.00

Punch bowl, deep rounded sides w/a flat rim, raised on a small, thick round foot, overall gold iridescence, shape No. 2852, signed "Aurene 2852," chips on foot edge, 12" d., 5½" h. (ILLUS. right) 605.00

Vase, 4⅜" h., footed ovoid body tapering to a wide, flat rim, rich turquoise blue iridescent ground decorated around the shoulder w/a band of striated scrolling lappets in pinkish amber iridescence, signed "Aurene 650".................................7,370.00

Vase, 11½" h., bulbous spherical top w/flaring rim raised on a tall very slender stem above a domed disc foot, gold iridescent ground w/green heart & vine & white blossom inclusions around the top, inscribed "Aurene 578"................................2,750.00

BRISTOL YELLOW

Champagnes, shape No. 7336, 4" d., 8" h., pr. 170.00

Nut dish, pedestal base, decorated w/black Jade threading, 3 x 5".........195.00

Pitcher, tankard, 9" h., quilted pattern body w/black Jade threading on the upper rim, shape No. 6829..............325.00

Vase, 8½" h., wide slightly flaring cylindrical body w/airtrap bubbles & applied random threading in brilliant yellow around the upper half, marked 220.00

CALCITE

Console set: 10" d. bowl & pair of 6" h. candlesticks; bowl w/everted rim w/blue Aurene interior & Calcite exterior, candlesticks w/slightly domed foot & wide rim in blue Aurene w/Calcite upper stem, candleholders shape No. 3581, the set...1,870.00

Finger bowl & underplate, Calcite exterior, iridescent gold Aurene interior, 2 pcs. 335.00

Vase, triple-bud, 12 3⁄16" h., a tall widely flaring central trumpet flanked by a pair of shorter slightly curved trumpets w/elongated jack-in-the-pulpit rims, all attached to a domed disc base, overall iridescence, ca. 1920...1,375.00

CINTRA

Candlestick, lavender w/small bubbles throughout, 10½" h. 1,425.00

Lamp, table model, green baluster-form body overlaid in Alabaster & acid-etched w/stalks of bearded wheat & grasses, fleur-de-lis mark at lower edge, mounted w/matching wheat design gilt-metal base & fittings & gazelle finial, 14½" h. (ILLUS. top next column) 1,210.00

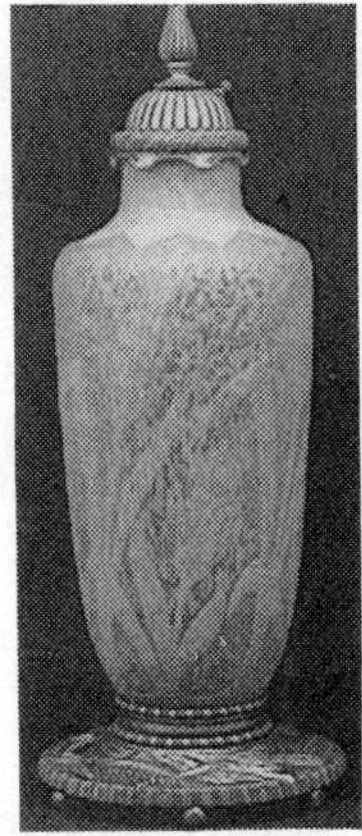

Cintra Table Lamp

Perfume bottle w/pointed stopper, ovoid facet-cut body w/the black & white Cintra interior veiled by controlled air bubbles, cased in heavy crystal, ca. 1925, 9" h. (minor chips) 4,600.00
Wine, opal 385.00

CLUTHRA

Cluthra Handled Vase

Plate, 6½" d., pink, signed 85.00
Vase, 7" d., 4½" h., bowl-form w/a wide squatty body widest at the middle & angling sharply toward the flat rim & base, bubbly green top shaded to white at the base 467.50
Vase, 10¾" h., classic footed baluster-form body w/a wide flaring neck w/rolled rim, applied opal loop handles at the shoulder, double-cased crystal w/bubbled swirling light amethyst between layers, base stamped "Steuben" in script, shape No. 2959 (ILLUS.) 1,870.00

GROTESQUE

Grotesque Bowl

Bowl, 8" l., 4¾" h., four-lobed, ruffled sides, amethyst shading to clear, shape No. 7276 ....425.00
Bowl, 11½" l., 6¼" h., four-lobed oblong ruffled sides in blue Jade, fleur-de-lis mark, minor interior surface wear (ILLUS.) 3,850.00
Vase, 11" h., paneled tulip-form raised on a pedestal foot, green shading to clear, shape No. 7090 ....475.00

IVRENE

Bowl, 10" d., 4¼" h., small foot supporting a deep & widely flaring body in iridescent white w/an unusual thin blue Aurene rim band 770.00
Vase, 5" h., 4½" d., mushroom-shaped body tapering to cylindrical neck w/flaring rim, polished pontil 110.00
Vase, 10" h., footed spherical base below a tall, widely flaring neck w/twelve molded ribs & a ruffled rim, shape No. 7565, marked 550.00

JADE

Plum Jade Bowl-Vase

Bowl-vase, the wide squatty bulbous cased plum Jade body acid-etched in the Canton motif w/a scrolled etched ground, Alabaster lining, 8" d., 4⅛" h. (ILLUS.) 2,970.00
Cup & saucer, green Jade, unsigned 175.00

form body w/a widely flaring ruffled neck, applied serpentine loop handles down the shoulders, shape No. 8002, 15" h. 350.00

Vase, 5½" h., 9" l., green Jade, rectangular block form w/Alabaster lion head medallions at each end, shape No. 6381 ....357.50

POMONA GREEN

Compotes, open, 7" h., shallow bowl w/flaring rim, raised on a hollow baluster shaped stem & pedestal base, shape No. 7032, pr. 300.00

Vase, 6½" h., paneled trumpet-form body raised on a ringed, platformed base, green & topaz, shape No. 7188, signed................................95.00

SELENIUM RED

Candlesticks, short cylindrical socket w/flattened, flared rim raised on an ovoid standard, cupped pedestal base, shape No. 6626, 7" h., pr. 725.00

Vase, 12" h., tall slender lightly paneled ovoid body tapering to a flaring rim in deep red, raised on a low domed red foot, signed "STEUBEN - F. Carder," ca. 1920s 1,725.00

Wine w/twisted stem, signed 75.00

VERRE DE SOIE

Verre de Soie Console Bowl

Console set: 9¾" d. bowl & pair of candlesticks; the footed bowl in a diamond quilted design w/flat & widely flaring sides w/applied Pomona green threading around the top half, the matching candlesticks w/wide slanted rims w/applied Pomona green threading above deep flaring cylindrical sockets on short slender stems flaring to a wide round foot, strong iridescent finish, minute breaks in threading, candlesticks 4½" h., 3 pcs. (ILLUS. of bowl) 440.00

Vase, 10" h., baluster-form w/flared mouth, engraved overall floral decoration 357.50

MISCELLANEOUS WARES

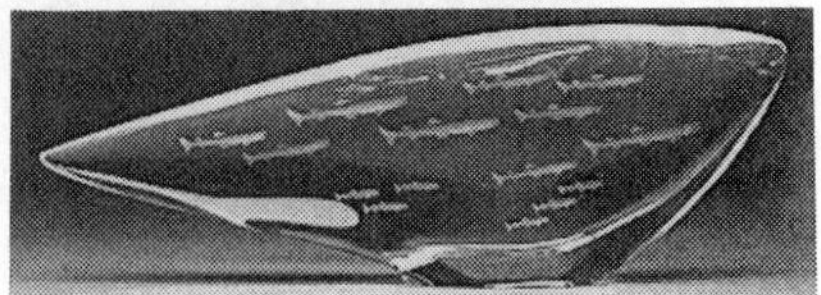

"Salmon Run" Sculpture

Centerpiece, six tall clear triangular vases of various heights tapering down & conjoining on a circular foot, ca. 1925, unsigned, 15¼" h. 1,035.00

Sculpture, "Salmon Run," tapering oblong crystal form engraved w/a school of salmon, masterwork designed by James Houston, engraved by George Thompson, number 14 of a series of 20, w/original red leather & velvet box, 18" l. (ILLUS.) 13,200.00

Sculpture, "Tree of Life," clear crystal in a stylized branched tree-form engraved & frosted w/real & surreal portraits, designed by Jacob Landau, executed by Donald Pollard, shape No. x3295, 14¼" h...16,500.00

STEVENS & WILLIAMS

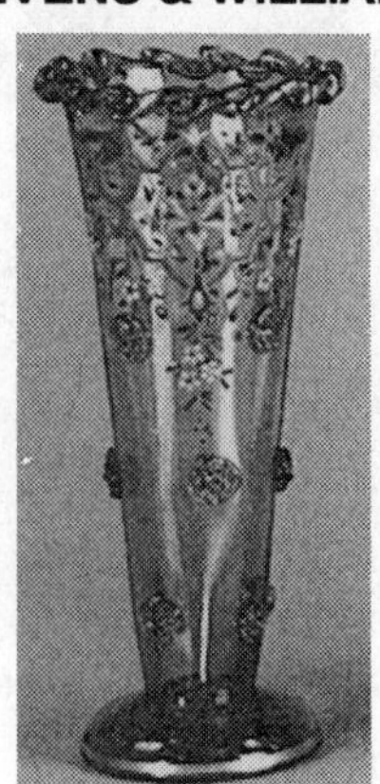

Stevens & Williams Enameled Vase

This long-established English glasshouse has turned out a wide variety of artistic glasswares through the years. Fine satin glass pieces and items with applied decoration (sometimes referred to as "Matsu-No-Ke") are especially sought after today. The following represents a cross-section of its wares.

Basket, narrow ribbed body of clear cased pink w/mica flecks, the scalloped rim w/applied amber ribbon edge, applied twisted amber handle, 5" d., 7½" h $275.00

Bowl, 4¾" d., 3⅛" h., squatty bulbous body w/flaring & lobed rim, creamy white exterior decorated w/applied amber rim edging & large applied amber ruffled leaves on each side, pink lining, applied berry prunt on base 145.00

Bowl, 7⅜" d., 3¾" h., satin glass, three-lobed clover leaf-form top w/tightly crimped rim, shaded gold to aqua mother-of-pearl satin Swirl patt., robin's egg blue lining 895.00

Cameo mustard pot, cov., ovoid body in white overlaid w/deep pink & cameo cut w/detailed flowers, leaves & vines, silver plate rim & cover, 1⅞" d., 3¼" h. 225.00

Cameo vase, 5" h., 3" d., squatty bulbous body tapering to a tall slender stick neck w/flaring ruffled rim, white overlaid w/pink & intaglio-cut w/leaves, grasses & dots, unsigned 295.00

Creamer, bulbous body w/scissor-cut top & applied amber handle, creamy white exterior decorated w/applied blue flowers & green leaves, pink lining, 2¾" d., 2⅞" h. 275.00

Cruet w/original light blue bubble stopper, light blue bulbous body tapering to a cylindrical neck w/pinched spout, decorated w/overall white crackle design, applied angled blue handle, 4" d., 8" h. 145.00

Rose bowl, ovoid body w/box-pleated top, blue & light blue vertical stripes, 4½" d., 4½" h. 145.00

Rose bowl, satin glass, ovoid body w/box-pleated top, shaded pink mother-of-pearl satin Basketweave patt., creamy white lining, 4½" d., 6" h. 425.00

Sweetmeat jar, cov., barrel-shaped, cranberry ground w/overall white crackle design, silver plate cover w/finial, rim & bail handle, 3⅜" d., 3⅛" h. 145.00

Vase, 4" h., 3¾" d., bulbous body w/widely fluted rim, milk white exterior decorated w/applied red cherries w/clear stems & leaves, pink lining 150.00

Vase, 6⅜" h., 3½" d., satin glass, pedestal footed squatty bulbous body tapering to a cylindrical neck w/flaring, scalloped rim, heavenly blue satin mother-of-pearl Swirl patt., white lining 195.00

Vase, 7½" h., 4½" d., ovoid creamy white body w/ruffled rim applied w/amber edging, the exterior applied w/three large ruffled leaves in green, amber & cranberry wrapping around the sides, deep rose lining 225.00

Vase, 9¾" h., 4½" d., footed baluster-form body w/unevenly flared & ruffled rim, four applied pink & white flowers w/amber & green branches, applied amber loop branch feet & handles, deep rose shaded to paler rose exterior, white lining 795.00

Vase, 12" h., 4" d., bulbous base tapering to a wide cylindrical neck w/scalloped rim, deep coral decorated w/applied white opalescent rim edging & four large ruffled leaves wrapping around the body, creamy white lining 395.00

Vases, 10" h., footed tall trumpet-form body in smoky amber applied w/amber rigaree around the rim & w/flattened amber prunts around the sides, enameled w/stylized florals in blue, red & green w/gilt trim, slight gilt wear, pr. (ILLUS. of one) 247.50

TIFFANY

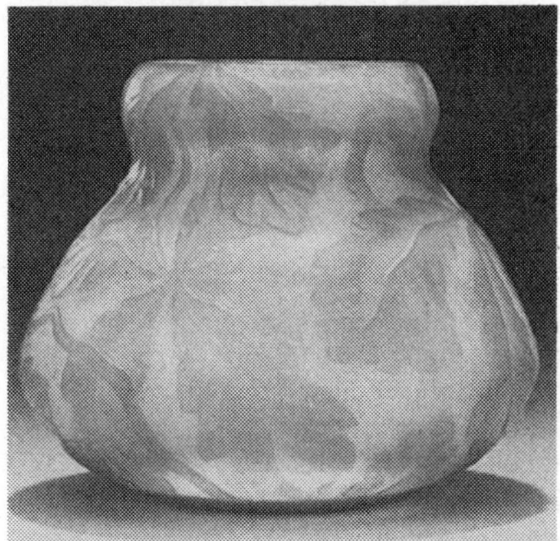

Tiffany Cameo Vase

This glassware, covering a wide diversity of types, was produced in glasshouses operated by Louis Comfort Tiffany, America's outstanding glass designer of the Art Nouveau period, from the last quarter of the 19th century until the early 1930s. Tiffany revived early techniques and devised many new ones.

Bonbon, stretched bluish green opalescence on ribbed bowl

w/internal herringbone decoration, foot inscribed "L.C.T. Favrile 1700," 5" d., 3" h. $550.00

Bowl, 2¾" h., low bulbous body in deep amber decorated w/applied raised trailing devices in silvery-blue iridescence against a deep purple & dark blue iridescent ground, inscribed "L.C.T.Q9917," ca. 1902 ....2,070.00

Bowl, 8" d., 3¾" h., footed, the deep body w/widely flaring sides & a flattened rim, overall gold iridescence, marked "L.C. Tiffany - Favrile 1848," w/a paper label 770.00

Cameo vase, 7" h., squatty bulbous gourd form in lemon yellow overlaid in butterscotch & deeply wheel-carved to depict overall woodbine leaves & vines, engraved "L.C. Tiffany Favrile 9815 A" (ILLUS.) ...6,050.00

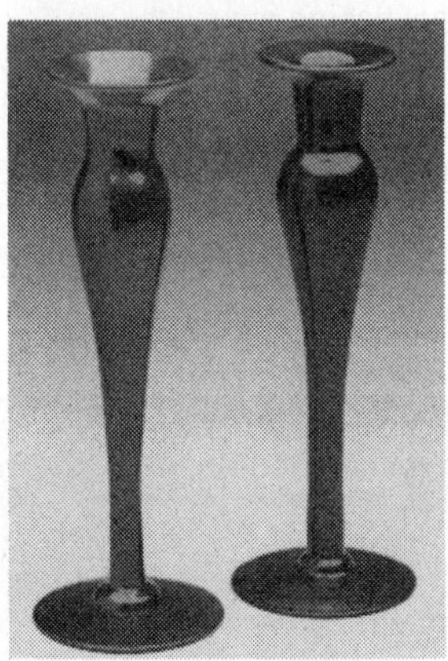

Tiffany Candlesticks

Candlesticks, flaring socket above a bulbous tapering shaft on a disc foot, lustrous crimson red, inscribed "L.C.T. Favrile," one w/partial paper label, 8¾" h., pr. (ILLUS.) 2,200.00

Center bowl, low foot, geometric floral devices within a diamond quilted pattern on the flared pastel aqua opalescent bowl, rim w/narrow stretched border, 11¼" d., 3½" h. 990.00

Compote, open, 6¾" d., 4¾" h., a small shallow bowl w/a wide flat rim raised on a slender pedestal w/round foot, dark cobalt blue decorated w/overall stretched purplish blue iridescence, signed on base "L.C. Tiffany Favrile 1838"...880.00

Creamer & sugar bowl, tankard creamer w/applied handle, squatty bulbous open sugar bowl; gold iridescent, signed "L.C.T.," creamer 1⅞" d., 2⅞" h., sugar bowl 3¼" d., 1⅝" h., pr. 750.00

Goblet, the wide waisted bowl w/flaring rim tapering at the base to a small ring wafer above a tapering slender stem on a slightly domed round foot, overall gold iridescence, signed "L.C.T. F1774," 8" h.............275.00

Sherbets, "Prince" patt., widely flaring bell-shaped bowl on a short stem & round foot, overall gold iridescent finish, signed "L.C.Tiffany Favrile," 3½" h., set of 6................................935.00

Tumblers, barrel-shaped, gold iridescent finish, two marked "LCT," 3¼" h., set of 9................................825.00

Vase, miniature, 2⅝" h., gently paneled ovoid body w/a short cylindrical neck, pale amber decorated w/loopings & trailings around the upper section, overall gold iridescence, w/original Tiffany Glass and Decorating Company paper label, early 20th c. 690.00

Vase, 8½" h., ovoid body tapering slightly to a wide, flat mouth, internally-decorated, the ambergris body lightly molded w/21 ribs & decorated w/green, opal & brownish amethyst double hooked feathers, chains & zig-zag internal designs, overall iridescent finish, signed "L.C.T. A1634" 1,430.00

Vase, 11¼" h., waisted floriform body w/everted rim, opalescent decorated w/pulled fine-lined green feathering, raised on a slender shaped stem above a domical foot further decorated w/green feathering, inscribed "L.C. Tiffany-Favrile V352," ca. 1904 ....2,588.00

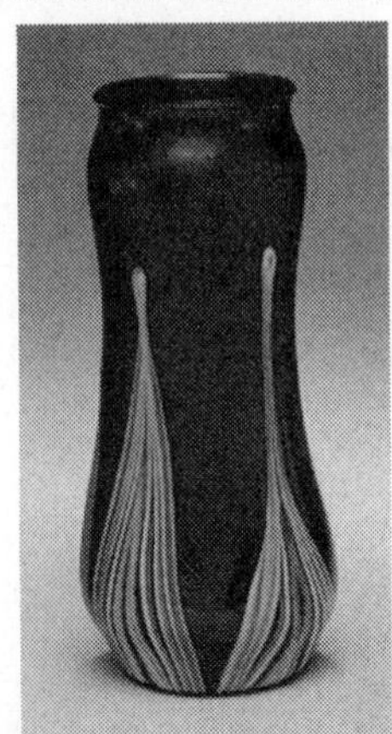

Tiffany "Pulled-Feather" Vase

Vase, 14" h., waisted cylindrical body

in deep cobalt blue decorated w/a green & white striped pulled-feather design, engraved "L.C. Tiffany - Favrile 0769 1" (ILLUS.) 2,860.00
Wines, shallow waisted bowl raised on a faceted stem & circular foot, brilliant amber iridescence decorated about the waist w/opalescent scrolling lappets, inscribed "L.C.T.," 1892-1928, 5" h., set of 12 ....4,400.00

TIFFIN

A wide variety of fine glasswares were produced by the Tiffin Glass Company of Tiffin, Ohio. Beginning as a part of the large U.S. Glass Company early in this century, the Tiffin factory continued making a wide range of wares until its final closing in 1984. One popular line is now called "Black Satin" and included various vases with raised floral designs. Many other acid-etched and hand-cut patterns were also produced over the years and are very collectible today. The three "Tiffin Glassmasters" books by Fred Bickenheuser, are the standard references for Tiffin collectors.

Basket, flower, No. 6553, clear...........$85.00
Candy dish, cov., coralene florals decoration on Black Satin ground......88.00
Carafe, etched Roses patt., clear.........72.00
Champagne, etched Flanders patt., pink 36.00
Console set: 13" d. bowl w/deep everted rim & pair of candleholders; Fontaine etching, bowl No. 8153, candleholders No. 9758, twilite, 3 pcs. 385.00
Creamer & sugar bowl, etched Fuchsia patt., clear, pr. 50.00
Goblet, etched Cherokee Rose patt., clear, 8" h. 18.00
Goblet, etched Classic patt., clear........28.00
Goblet, Franciscan patt., citron............10.00
Parfait, etched Byzantine patt., clear....22.00
Plate, 8" d., etched Flanders patt., yellow...11.50
Sherbet, etched Classic patt., clear......22.00
Sherbet, etched Fuchsia patt., clear.....25.00
Tumbler, iced tea, footed, Fuchsia patt., clear 30.00
Tumbler, juice, footed, etched Persian Pheasant patt., clear, 5 oz. 15.00
Vase, 5" h., etched Poppy patt., black amethyst 85.00
Vase, 6" h., four-footed, cut Twilight patt., clear 85.00
Wine, etched June Night patt., clear.....35.00

VENETIAN

Venetian glass has been made for six centuries on the island of Murano, where it continues to be produced. The skilled glass artisans developed numerous techniques, subsequently imitated elsewhere.

Bowl, 17½" d., free-form scalloped rim, pale blue shaded to electric blue ground & decorated w/gold swirls $245.00
Centerpiece, blown as a large reclining blossom & stem, moonlight blue opalescent leaves & clear corkscrew vines, 18" l. 65.00
Cordial set: baluster-form decanter & six goblets; smoke-colored, the decanter w/mermaid-form finial & interior white mermaid, the goblets w/mermaid-form stems, decanter 8½" h., the set 385.00
Figure of a sea nymph riding on a wave, clear w/gold accents, 10" h....330.00
Figures of a man & woman, dressed in gold & white embossed swirl 18th century style court clothing, 11" h., pr..450.00
Goblet, bowl w/embossed swirl design, clear w/gold flecks, on a dolphin-form stem 375.00
Model of a bird, white & blue, on clear pedestal, 8" h. 40.00
Model of an elephant, turquoise, 10" l. 40.00
Model of a pheasant, clear w/blue accents, 15½" l. 135.00
Models of roosters, orange & clear spangled, 7" h., pr. 140.00
Salt dips, model of a swan, amethyst ground w/gold flecks, 3¼", set pf 6..150.00
Stemware set: fourteen goblets, eleven wines, fourteen aperitifs & ten cordials; each w/ruby bowls etched w/grapevines & raised on a knopped stem & circular foot monogrammed "OMD," the set 825.00
Vase, 7¾" h., tapering squared form, red cased clear decorated w/colorful millefiore canes, filligrana sections & ribbons in the Zanfirico technique....550 00

VENINI

Founded by former lawyer Paolo Venini in 1925, this Venetian glasshouse soon developed a reputation for its fine quality decorative glass and tablewares. Several noted designers have worked for the firm over the years and their unique pieces in the modern spirit, made using traditional techniques, are increasingly popular with collectors today. The factory continues in operation.

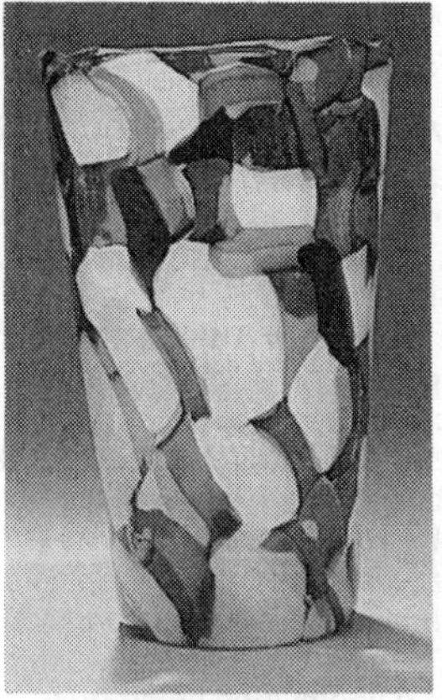

Venini Vase

Bottle w/original stopper, "Inciso," the short ovoid vessel w/mushroom-shaped stopper in clear cased in red, designed by Paolo Venini, unsigned, ca. 1956, 5¼" h. $575.00

Bowl, 5½" d., 3¼" h., "Pulegoso," heavy pale blue squared body w/minute bubbles & gold foil inclusions, stamped "Venini Murano Made in Italy" 467.50

Centerpiece, irregular form in olive green encased within corrugated clear & molded w/deep ridges resembling a large cabbage leaf, probably designed by Tony Zuccheri, inscribed "venini - italia," ca. 1966, 18" d. 920.00

Decanter w/stopper, "vetro battuto," ovoid body w/cylindrical neck, topaz w/a hammered finish, acid-stamped "venini murano ITALIA" & "BOTTLE MADE IN ITALY," 7¼" h. 748.00

Figure of a gentleman, combining the "mask" & "patchwork" series, composed of black mask face, hat, trousers & shoes w/opaque white lattimo hair, beard, collar, stockings & gloves w/four fingers on the right hand & five fingers on the left, his coat of transparent red, blue & green pezzato squares, designed by Fulvio Bianconi, stamped on base "Venini Murano Italia," 14" h. 3,575.00

Light fixture, hanging-type, the shade in cased white decorated w/green, amethyst & red stripes, suspended from a simple rod standard, ca. 1955, 6" d. 115.00

Model of a chicken, "filigrano" glass, the clear curved tubular body w/white threading, a crimped tail & applied white comb & crimped white base, by Tommaso Buzzi, acid-stamped "venini - italia," ca. 1932, 7¼" h. 1,725.00

Vase, 6¼" h., "Fazzoletto," slumped handkerchief form, turquoise bluish-green exterior, white interior, acid-stamped mark "Venini Murano Italia" 247.50

Vase, 10" h., 'vetro pezzato arlecchinó, slightly flaring cylindrical form w/undulating rim, clear, white, milky pale blue, blue, pale green, green & red in an overall patchwork design, acid-etched mark "venini murano ITALIA," designed by Fulvio Bianconi (ILLUS.)..........................4,950.00

VERLYS

This glass is a relative newcomer for collectors and is not old enough to be antique, having been made since the 1930s in France and the United States, but fine pieces are collected. Blown and molded pieces have been produced.

Ashtray, Birds & Bees patt., clear.......$45.00

Bowl, 6" d., Pine Cone patt., clear 50.00

Bowl, 14" d., Water Lilies patt., clear..100.00

Bowl, 19" d., decorated w/relief-molded goldfish, clear......................250.00

Box, cov., topaz w/chrysanthemum decoration, 5¼" d. 375.00

Charger, Birds & Dragonflies patt., 12" d., signed 89.00

Console bowl, Water LIly patt., clear, signed, 15" d. 100.00

Vase, 5" h., footed ovoid body tapering to a short cylindrical neck, molded overall w/flying butterflies, fiery opalescent, inscribed "Verlys" on base 172.50

Vase, 9½" h., Alpine Thistle patt., topaz 525.00

VICTORIAN COLORED GLASS

There are, of course, many types of colored glassware of the Victorian era and we cover a great variety of these in our various glass categories. However, there are some pieces of pressed, mold-blown and free-blown Victorian colored glass which don't fit well into other specific listings, so we have chosen to include a selection of them here.

Inverted Thumbprint Pitcher

Animal covered dish, Cow on oval paneled base, black opaque..........$500.00

Animal covered dish, Lion on picket base, opaque blue w/white head, 5½" l. 85.00

Box w/hinged cover, free-blown, cobalt blue, lacy-style, decoration w/enameled dainty white leaves & gold flowers around sides w/gold dots, scallops w/dainty white leaves in reserves, 2" d., 1¼" h. 145.00

Box w/hinged lid, free-blown, cobalt blue, decorated w/white enameled daisies & leaves on cover, 2" d., 1¼" h. 135.00

Cracker jar, cov., free-blown, barrel-shaped, lime green enameled w/overall decoration of dainty blue forget-me-nots, green leaves & lavender foliage, resilvered cover, rim & bail handle, 4¾" d., 6½" h. 225.00

Cracker jar, cov., free-blown, barrel-shaped, lime green decorated overall w/sprays of dainty pink & blue flowers & green leaves, resilvered rim, handle & cover, 5" d., 6¾" h. 225.00

Creamer, mold-blown, bulbous body w/squared mouth, Inverted Thumbprint patt., amber body & applied amber handle, ca. 1880s, 5" h. 30.00

Decanter w/original spear-shaped amethyst cut to clear bubble stopper, bulbous amethyst cut to clear body w/eight-cut panels, short cylindrical neck, pattern cut under scalloped foot, 3⅞" d., 11" h. 145.00

Pitcher, 8" h., 5½" d., mold-blown Inverted Thumbprint patt., footed ovoid body tapering to a short cylindrical neck, applied angular handle, aqua blue decorated w/large white & yellow blossoms & green leaves & branch (ILLUS.)................165.00

Salt dip, master-size, chartreuse green w/green threaded decoration, clear applied snail feet, 1¾" d., 1¼" h. 65.00

Salt shaker w/original top, Challinor's Forget-Me-Not patt., Nile green 40.00

Syrup pitcher w/original top, Inverted Thumbprint patt., blue, Hobbs, Brockunier & Co. 140.00

Toothpick holder, Jefferson Optic patt., blue 65.00

Tumble-up (water carafe w/tumbler lid), free-blown, footed spherical body w/cylindrical neck fitted w/a tumbler, sapphire blue enameled w/large white flowers & leaves, 4⅞" d., 7¾" h., 2 pcs. 195.00

Vase, 6⅞" h., 6½" d., ovoid melon-ribbed body w/widely flaring rolled & crimped rim w/applied clear edging, clear applied feet w/gold trim, sapphire blue, decorated overall w/dainty pink & white flowers & tan leaves 325.00

Vases, 4¼" h., 2¾" d., squatty bulbous bases tapering to a trumpet-form neck w/slightly flaring & scalloped rim, cobalt blue decorated w/white daisies w/yellow centers, pink buds & green leaves, pr. 125.00

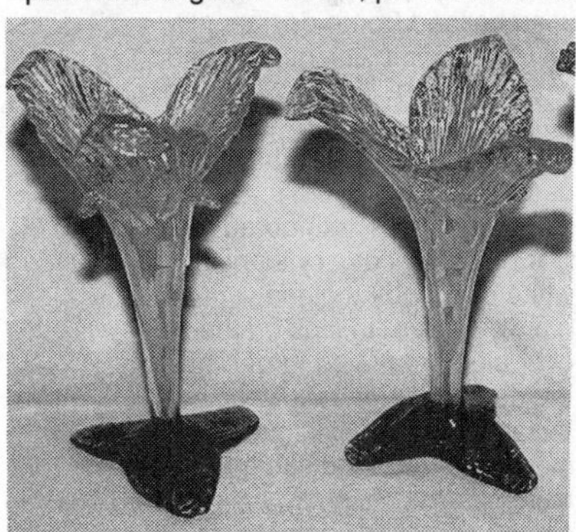

Flower-Form Vases

Vases, 8⅛" h., 5⅜" w., flower-form w/large flaring triple-petal rim w/pink opalescent tips spattered w/pink specks then shading to yellow & clear, green three-leaf applied foot, pr. (ILLUS.) 185.00

WAVE CREST

Now much sought after, Wave Crest was produced by the C.F. Monroe Co.,

Meriden, Connecticut, in the late 19th and early 20th centuries from opaque white glass blown into molds. It was then hand-decorated in enamels and metal trim was often added. Boudoir accessories such as jewel boxes, hair receivers, etc., were predominant.

Box w/hinged lid, Egg Crate mold, lid decorated w/central floral decoration of pink & maroon flowers & green leaves on a shaded light green ground, 3" d., 2½" h. $225.00

Box w/hinged lid, Egg Crate mold, pink ground decorated w/clusters of blue flowers, raised gold borders surround floral groupings, wide gilt-metal mounting, 4½ x 4¾" 550.00

Box w/hinged lid, Helmschmied Swirl Mold, lid decorated w/dainty pink & gold flowers & green leaves, shaded blue to white ground, 5½" d., 3½" h. 350.00

Box w/hinged lid, Embossed Rococo mold, h.p. blue flowers on a pink ground, raised on an ornate gilt-metal footed base, 5" w., 6" l. 875.00

Box w/hinged lid, Hexagonal mold w/embossed scrolling, top & sides decorated w/shaded pink florals & green foliage on a soft green ground, 8½" w., 6" h. 1,250.00

Card holder, upright rectangular form w/embossed frame design, gilt-metal rim, cloth lining, decorated w/delicate pink flowers & a blue border 310.00

Cigar holder, plain cylindrical body decorated w/h.p. florals, gilt-metal handled rim & scroll-footed base 250.00

Cigar humidor, cov., cylindrical, the white opal body molded w/florals & h.p. w/"Cigars" in pink on the side over blue enameled forget-me-nots, the domed cover decorated w/an Indian on horseback, gilt-metal hinged mounts, red flag mark on base 660.00

Cologne bottles w/original scroll-molded creamy white stoppers, cylindrical body w/deep scroll-molded shoulder, a short cylindrical neck w/a flaring rim, enameled w/dainty blue flowers, green leaves & foliage & heavy gold scrolling on a creamy white ground, pr. 925.00

Cracker jar, cov., barrel-shaped, panels of yellow flowers w/pink centers & green leaves decorate a soft pink ground, silver plate rim, cover & bail handle, 5½" d., 7¼" h. 350.00

Cracker jar, cov., Egg Crate mold, decorated w/h.p. lavender, green & tan florals on a white shaded to pale blue ground, 5" d., 9"h. 650.00

Creamer & cov. sugar bowl, decorated w/h.p. cupids & whimsical scrolling, creamer w/gilt-metal lipped rim & handle, sugar bowl, w/gilt-metal rim, cover & bail handle, pr. ..100.00

Ferner, Egg Crate mold, decorated w/light pink spider mums, no liner, 7" sq...345.00

Glove box w/hinged lid, pink w/blue floral decoration, 4 x 8½" 875.00

Humidor w/original brass cover & finial, cream & brown bulbous cylindrical body decorated w/three bulldog heads & "Three Guardsmen," 5⅛"d., 6½" h. 525.00

Photo receiver, Egg Crate mold, the body decorated w/clusters of pink & blue flowers & light green foliage on a creamy white ground, ornate gilt-metal rim 395.00

Salt & pepper shakers w/original tops, hexagonal, Embossed Rococo mold, decorated w/h.p. florals, pr.....145.00

Sugar shaker w/original top, Helmschmied Swirl mold, alternating panels of blue scrolls & yellow flowers 480.00

Syrup pitcher w/original top, Helmschmied Swirl mold, white & beige swirls highlighted w/lavender & gold florals 295.00

Vase, 9" h., 1¼" rim d., squatty bulbous body tapering to a tall cylindrical neck, decorated w/shaded pink to burgundy mums, deep green enameled swags & a deep green enameled rim w/white dotting, footed gilt-metal base..........595.00

Vase, 13½" h., footed, burnt orange ground decorated w/large purple orchids on the front & back, signed 1,095.00

WEBB

This glass is made by Thomas Webb & Sons of Stourbridge, one of England's most prolific glasshouses. Numerous types of glass, including cameo, have been produced by this firm through the years. The company also produced various types of novelty and "art" glass during the late Victorian period. Also see in "Glass" BURMESE, ROSE BOWLS, and SATIN & MOTHER-OF-PEARL.

Webb Scenic Cameo Vase

Bowl, 4" d., 2½" h., deep rounded sides below the flat rim, ruby cut to green in a floral wreath & swag design, star-cut base $220.00

Cameo bottle w/ornate sterling silver cap & rim, cylindrical, red overlaid in white & cameo-cut w/butterflies, flowers & leaves, 5" h. 600.00

Cameo lamp, miniature, a tapering conical shade above an ovoid base, each in brilliant sapphire blue w/white cameo-cut blossoms, leaves & a butterfly in flight on the base & a morning glory vine on the shade, mounted w/a gilt-metal Silber Burner, four-sided medallion Webb mark on base, w/chimney, 8¾" h. plus chimney.................................3,300.00

Cameo vase, 5" h., gourd-form body, cranberry shading to amber cased over creamy opalescent white, overlaid in white & cut w/cyclamen blossoms, buds & foliage w/a butterfly & dragonfly in flight, unsigned, ca. 1890 ....1,840.00

Cameo vase, 8⅝" h., "The Pet Parrot," cylindrical w/rounded base & low disc foot, low collared mouth, the medium blue sides overlaid in white & finely cut on the obverse w/a young maiden clothed in classical drapery seated on a stone coping, gazing at a parrot perched on her right hand, an urn & flowering leafage at her feet, between leaftip & flower borders & acanthus leafage, the foot further carved w/flowerheads, impressed "WEBB" & titled, ca. 1890 (ILLUS.)...........31,050.00

Cracker jar, cov., glossy cased peach blow w/engraved diamonds & other geometric devices, sterling silver rim, cover w/ball finial & bail handle marked "Tiffany & Co. Makers," including finial 7¼" h. 935.00

Vase, 4¼" h., 2⅝" d., ovoid form w/short cylindrical neck, rich blue decorated w/gold flowers, branches & leaves, a gold dragonfly reverse, creamy white interior........................225.00

Vase, 8¼" h., 4¾" d., baluster-form, creamy opaque decorated w/gold prunus blossoms & branches cascading down from the rim & a large gold bee in flight......................245.00

Vases, 7¼" h., 5" d., spherical body tapering to a short, cylindrical neck w/slightly flaring rim & applied angular bronzy handles, shaded orange decorated w/heavy gold maidenhair fern, small daisies & a gold butterfly on the back, white lining, pr. 495.00

WESTMORELAND

Westmoreland Cat on Lacy Base Dish

The Westmoreland Specialty Company was founded in East Liverpool, Ohio in 1889 and relocated in 1890 to Grapeville, Pennsylvania where it remained until its closing in 1985.

During its early years Westmoreland specialized in glass food containers and novelties but by the turn of the century they had a large line of milk white items and clear tableware patterns. In 1925 the company name was shortened to The Westmoreland Glass Company and it was during that decade that more colored glasswares entered their line-up. When Victorian-style milk glass again became popular in the 1940s and 1950s, Westmoreland produced extensive amounts in several patterns which closely resemble late 19th century wares. These and their figural animal dishes in milk white and colors are widely collected today but buyers should not confuse them for the antique originals. Watch for Westmoreland's "WG" mark on some pieces. A majority of our listings are products from the 1940s through the 1970s. Earlier pieces will be indicated.

Animal covered dish, Cat on a lacy base, glass eyes, opaque blue, copied from the Atterbury original (ILLUS.) $55.00
Animal covered dish, Chick and Eggs, milk white, copied from the Atterbury original 95.00
Animal covered dish, Hen on nest, chocolate brown w/iridizing, gold yellow & green trim, copied from antique original 125.00
Animal covered dish, Lamb on picket base, Green Marble, copied from antique original, 5½" l. 65.00
Animal covered dish, Rooster on ribbed base, milk white w/blue head, copied from antique original, 5½" l.....95.00
Ashtray, Beaded Grape (No. 1884) patt., milk white, 6½" 9.00
Banana stand, Doric (No. 3) patt., milk white 30.00
Basket, oval w/open handle, Paneled Grape (No. 1881) patt., milk white 28.00
Butter dish, cov., Old Quilt (No. 500) patt., milk white, ¼ lb. 34.00
Candlesticks, model of a dolphin w/hexagon base, milk white, 9" h., pr. 125.00
Console set: 9½ x 12" oval, footed bowl w/flared rim & two 4" h. candlesticks; Paneled Grape patt., milk white, 3 pcs. 85.00
Creamer, Old Quilt patt., milk white......14.00
Creamer & open sugar bowl, Della Robbia patt., milk white, pr. 24.00
Cruet w/original stopper, Della Robbia patt., milk white 18.00
Cup & saucer, English Hobnail patt., milk white 15.00
Goblet, water, Della Robbia patt., colored trim, 6" h., 8 oz. 37.50
Gravy boat & underplate, Paneled Grape patt., milk white, 2 pcs. 52.50
Honey dish, cov., Beaded Grape patt., milk white 14.00
Honey dish, cov., Old Quilt patt., milk white 20.00
Pitcher, water, 12" h., Paneled Grape patt., milk white, 1 qt. 50.00
Punch set: 5 qt. punch bowl, 18" d. underplate, twelve cups & ladle; Paneled Grape patt., milk white, 15 pcs. 550.00
Syrup pitcher w/original top, Old Quilt patt., milk white 30.00
Table set: cov. butter dish, cov. sugar bowl, creamer & spooner; Ring & Petal (No. 1875) patt., cobalt blue, 4 pcs. 600.00
Vase, 12" h., Paneled Grape patt., milk white 50.00
Water set: 9" h. pitcher & six 6" h. tumblers; Paneled Grape patt., clear, 7 pcs. 200.00
Wine set: decanter w/original stopper & eight 2 oz. wines; Paneled Grape patt., milk white, 9 pcs. 185.00

(End of Glass Section)

GLOBE MAPS

Table Model Globe by Malby

Celestial globe, table model, turning within a brass meridian ring, mounted in a wooden frame w/baluster- and ring-turned legs joined by turned X-form stretchers, Merriam Moore & Co., Troy, New York, second quarter 19th c., 12" h. (imperfections) $1,210.00
Celestial globe, table model, mounted within a brass meridian ring, in a wooden frame on baluster- and ring-turned legs joined by turned X-stretchers, Gilman Joslin, Boston, Massachusetts, second quarter 19th c., 14½" h. (imperfections) 2,420.00
Celestial & terrestrial globes, table models, each in a carved mahogany stand w/brass meridian & four reeded curved supports above a ribbed melon-form pedestal above a tripod base composed of curved sabre legs w/acanthus-carved knees & ending in paw feet, J. Wilson & Sons, Albany, New York, ca. 1830, 24" h., pr. 34,500.00
Celestial & terrestrial globes, table models, mahogany, each within a brass meridian ring, the rim w/the months & zodiac signs, on a spiral gadrooned stand & cabriole legs w/pointed pad feet, joined w/a compass stretcher, one compass lacking glass, some restorations,

Malby's, England, the celestial dated 1860, mid-19th c., 17" d., 25" h., pr. (ILLUS. of one) 7,150.00

Celestial & terrestrial globes, floor models, mahogany, each mounted within a brass meridian ring, on an urn-form stand & splayed legs centered by a compass stretcher, w/turned feet, Regency period, England, first quarter 19th c., the terrestrial dated 1816, 16" d., 36" h., pr. 15,400.00

Terrestrial globe, table model, turned mahogany & engraved brass, the sphere pivoting within a circular support on ring-turned legs joined by turned stretchers, the globe inscribed "...Terrestrial globe containing all the late discoveries and geographical improvements...," England, dated 1833, 17" d., 15" h......1,610.00

GOLLIWOGS

The Golliwogs, charming black characters introduced in a book by Bertha Upton in 1889, were as popular in England as were Raggedy Ann and Andy in the United States. They were widely used as advertising premiums and also can be found in a series of books, as banks, dolls and perfume bottles.

Birthday card, Golliwog w/bears & Scottie dog..$20.00

Book, "Golliwog's Circus," 1903, 28 full pages illustrated 245.00

Doll, black cloth body, dressed in English blue coat & red & white striped pants, ca. 1920, 16" h. 250.00

Figure, yarn, black & red, original string tag w/"Good Luck Golly Wog" poem, 1922, 2½", h...........................55.00

Perfume bottle, figural, spherical frosted glass bottle body w/a wide disc collar, smiling black head stopper w/fuzzy hair, original paper label, produced by deVigny, Paris, France, 1920s, 6" h..........................330.00

Tea set, child's: cov. teapot, cov. sugar bowl, creamer, five cups & saucers & five plates; china, decorated w/dancing Golliwogs, colorful, Royal Rudolstadt, Germany, 18 pcs. 295.00

GRANITEWARE

This is a name given to metal (customarily iron) kitchenwares covered with an enamel coating. Featured at the 1876 Philadelphia Centennial Exposition, it became quite popular for it was lightweight, attractive, and easy to clean. Although it was made in huge quantities and is still produced, it has caught the attention of a younger generation of collectors and prices have steadily risen over the past five years. There continues to be a consistent demand for the wide variety of these utilitarian articles turned out earlier in this century and rare forms now command high prices.

Graniteware Kettle

Bacon platter, brown & white swirl ...$295.00

Bacon press, green & white swirl 35.00

Baking pan, Chrysolite swirl 125.00

Baking pan, Iris swirl...........................195.00

Bedpan, grey mottled 17.50

Berry bucket, cov., blue & white swirl, tin lid, bail handle....................150.00

Berry bucket, cov., miniature, grey mottled 110.00

Berry bucket, cov., blue & white mottled 125.00

Bowl, blue & white swirl, 15½" d., 4¼" h...60.00

Bucket, grey mottled, miniature, 3½ x 3½" 65.00

Cake pan, blue & red mottled 25.00

Candleholder, red, leaf-shaped 55.00

Canning funnel, grey mottled................35.00

Chamber pot, cov., child's, blue & white speckled 15.00

Chamber pot, cov., cobalt blue & white swirl 135.00

Chamber pot, open, grey mottled 30.00

Chocolate dipper, grey mottled, tubular handle 155.00

Coffee biggin, cov., red checked design, 4-piece 185.00

Coffee boiler, cov., black & white speckled, bail handle & fixed base handle, marked "USN," 3 gal. 55.00

Coffee boiler, cov., blue & white mottled 65.00

Coffee boiler, cov., emerald green & cream swirl, large....................................335.00
Coffee boiler, cov., grey mottled...........45.00
Coffee boiler, cov., Iris swirl................285.00
Coffee boiler w/tin lid, blue & white swirl, w/bail handle...........................145.00
Coffee percolator, cov., deep medium green exterior, white interior, pear-shaped w/gooseneck spout, graniteware basket, 10½" h. 45.00
Coffeepot, cov., tin lid w/wooden knob, blue speckled, 1 cup 200.00
Coffeepot, cov., gooseneck spout, brown & white swirl 250.00
Coffeepot, cov., cobalt blue, 8½" base, 9" h...40.00
Coffeepot, cov., cobalt blue& white swirl, w/black wooden handle 245.00
Coffeepot, cov., white w/enameled flowers decoration, pewter trim, 11" h...175.00
Coffee urn, cov., blue & white mottled 250.00
Colander, blue & white swirl inside & out 125.00
Colander, blue & grey swirl...................75.00
Colander, brown & white swirl 45.00
Colander, grey mottled, w/rim base, 12" d..55.00
Colander, Iris swirl 75.00
Colander, violet shaded to deep violet 36.00
Cream can, cov., grey & white swirl, w/tin lid & wire bail handle, ½ gal.....115.00
Creamer, small, blue & white spatter..110.00
Cuspidor, blue & white swirl, with paper label 130.00
Custard cup, cobalt blue & white swirl...65.00
Dipper, blue & white swirl 63.00
Dipper, brown & white swirl 35.00
Dipper, grey mottled 15.00
Dishpan, blue & white swirl, round, two-handled, large 100.00
Double boiler, cov., cobalt blue & white swirl, "Belle" shaped bottom ...295.00
Double boiler, cov., grey mottled..........55.00
Dustpan, cream & green........................98.00
Dustpan, grey speckled.........................98.00
Egg skillet, grey mottled, w/indentations 175.00
Foot tub, blue & white swirl, oval, large...60.00
Fruit jar filler, grey mottled, marked "Acme" 39.00
Funnel, blue & white swirl...................125.00
Funnel, grey mottled, marked "Agate, Seconds"...45.00
Funnel, grey mottled, seamed, riveted, w/hanging ear 40.00
Hot plate, twin, electric, green & white mottled overall, chrome legs, dual controls 20.00
Jelly roll pan, blue & white relish 60.00
Kettle, cov., blue & white swirl, w/bail handle (ILLUS.).................................140.00
Kettle, cov., robin's-egg blue w/white speckling, dark blue handles & trim, cat's eye knob lid 85.00
Liquid measure, grey mottled, 1 qt. 45.00
Loaf pan, grey mottled, large w/low sides 25.00
Lunch bucket, cov., w/insert tray & thermos, grey mottled 125.00
Lunch pail w/tin lid, grey spatter 65.00
Milk pan, cobalt blue & white swirl........45.00
Molasses pitcher, cov., grey mottled ..165.00
Mold, melon-shaped w/tin bottom & band, grey mottled 145.00

Graniteware Muffin Pan

Muffin pan, 8 cup, cobalt blue & white swirl (ILLUS.) ....225.00 to 275.00
Muffin pan, 12 cup, grey mottled, Agate Ware...45.00
Mug, blue & white swirl.........................30.00
Mug, grey mottled w/red trim 12.00
Mug, red w/black trim 10.00
Mush mug, iris & white swirl 165.00
Pan, handled, blue & white swirl, 8" h...50.00
Pie pan, blue & white swirl....................22.00
Pie pan, Chrystolite 45.00
Pitcher, water, grey mottled, Agate Ware 28.00
Pitcher, water, white, large 27.50
Preserving kettle, cov., blue & white swirl 67.00
Pudding pan, blue & white swirl, large 100.00
Pudding pan, red & white swirl 130.00
Rice canister, cov., solid blue 80.00
Roaster, cov., blue & white swirl, large 95.00
Roaster, cov., cobalt blue, Savory Jr., Republic Metalware Company 60.00
Salt box, cov., hanging-type, top tab embossed "Salt," grey mottled, marked "L & G Manufacturing," 11" l. 400.00
Saucepan, cov., grey mottled, Agate Ware 25.00
Saucepan, cov., robin's egg blue & white swirl, 3 qt. 75.00
Scoop, grey mottled, 6" l......................115.00
Slop jar, cov., cobalt & blue swirl, 3 gal. 315.00

Soap dish, hanging-type, cobalt blue & white swirl 120.00
Soap dish, hanging-type, w/insert, light blue & white swirl 55.00
Spoon, blue & white speckled, 6" l. 22.50
Table, child's, rectangular, white, decorated w/colorful alphabet, circus scene, nursery rhymes, numbers, etc., on turned wooden legs.............175.00
Tea kettle w/tin lid, gooseneck spout, blue & white swirl, w/bail handle 70.00
Teapot, cov., gooseneck spout, blue & white swirl 125.00
Tea strainer, blue & white swirl.............50.00
Tea strainer, grey spatter 25.00
Upcooker, cov., black & white 60.00
Utensil holder w/four utensils & drip pan, red & white, 5 pcs. 265.00
Wash basin, salesman's sample, blue & white swirl 125.00
Water dispenser, cov., w/copper spigot, grey mottled, Agate Ware, 30" h...120.00

HATPINS & HATPIN HOLDERS

HATPIN HOLDERS

China, white, decorated w/h.p. blue & purple berries $115.00
Nippon china, gold & floral bands at top & bottom 145.00
Nippon china, purple & blue berries w/gold accents 180.00
R.S. Prussia china, green to deep green calla lilies 165.00
Ruby glass enameled w/pink & blue daisies & gold sprays & dotting........110.00

HATPINS

Advertising "Economy Stoves & Ranges," 10" l. 52.00
Brass, Art Deco knob design, head 1½" l., shank 8½" l. 95.00
China, white decorated w/flowers.........60.00
Copper, figural Indian Chief head 65.00
Gold (18k yellow), slightly dished disc, woven design w/a spray of articulated flowers w/gem-set tips, Italy 275.00
Moonstones, gold (14k yellow) & gems, the semi-ovoid moonstones set in a gold wire twist & beadwork mount, accented w/alternating diamonds & rubies, Austrian hallmarks, Victorian, pr. 1,650.00
Rhinestone, pink faceted head in a Tiffany-style setting...........................45.00
Silver plate, Art Nouveau style shield-shaped head w/a profile of a lovely lady wearing a hat & w/long flowing hair, head 1¾ x 2¼", 8" l. 115.00
Sterling silver, horse head in horseshoe 35.00

HEINTZ ART METAL WARES

Beginning in 1915 the Heintz Art Metal Shop of Buffalo, New York began producing an interesting line of jewelry and decorative items, especially vases and desk accessories, in brass, bronze, copper and silver. Their distinctive brass and bronze wares overlaid with sterling silver Art Nouveau and Art Deco designs are much sought after today. Collectors eagerly search for pieces bearing their stamped mark consisting of a diamond surrounding the initials "HAMS." Around 1935 the firm became Heintz Brothers, Manufacturers.

Heintz Desk Set

Compote, open, a wide & deep rounded bowl w/a molded rim decorated w/a sterling silver inlay Greek key band, long angled handles from the rim to the base of the bowl, raised on a short pedestal w/a wide flaring domed foot w/stepped edge, marked, 11½" d., 5½" h. (dullness to interior patina) ...$82.50
Desk set: blotter pad w/four corners, inkwell, hand-held blotter, perpetual calendar, letter opener, pen tray, spherical-base desk lamp; each piece w/silver inlaid poppy blossom & leafy sprig, the lamp w/a conical pierced poppy pattern shade missing its silk lining, marked, the set (ILLUS.) 1,650.00
Humidor-trophy, cov., the wide slightly rounded cylindrical container set on a very wide stepped & domed foot w/curved angular handles running from the rim to the foot, the stepped & domed cover w/button finial, decorated near the rim w/a silver overlay band of two thin lines joining stylized quatrefoil devices,

presented by the Los Angeles Optimist Club Golf tournament, fine dark patina, No. 2628, 8¼" d., 10" h. 165.00

Lamp, table model, mushroom-shaped shade pivoting within a harp support raised on a slender standard w/flaring foot, bronze w/verdigris patina overlaid w/sterling silver weed decoration on shade & base, felt bottom, 7½" d., 10" h. 495.00

Lamp, table model, silver, bronze & mica, the shade decorated w/a broad band of reticulated jonquils backed by mica panels, the base decorated w/jonquils overlaid in silver, fine dark brown patina to bronze, no signature visible, 8¾" d., 14¾" h. (uneven edge to shade, replaced mica) 660.00

Vase, bud, squatty bulbous base tapering to a tall slender neck, overall silver-plate finish overlaid w/a design of stylized slender weeds up the front, marked, No. 3663, 3½" d., 6" h. 247.50

Vase, ovoid w/short collared neck, sterling silver overlay depicting clusters of Japanese cherry blossoms & branches on a cleaned medium brown patinated ground, die-stamped "HAMS - 3700 - STERLING ON BRONZE," 4¾" d., 8" h. 275.00

Vase, tall slightly tapering cylindrical form, silver overlay decoration of a group of three long-stemmed blossoms joined by scroll devices, early dark verdigris patina, inscribed "uoz-Pxx," pre-1913, 3" d., 8½" h. (small dent in base) 247.50

Vase, tall cylindrical form w/closed rim, silver overlay full-length cattails, No. 3608A, impressed mark, 10" h. 357.50

Tall Heintz Art Metal Vase

Vase, expanding cylinder w/rolled rim, sterling silver overlaid decoration of poppies on a green patinated bronze ground, die-stamped "HAMS - SILVER-ON-BRONZE- pat.," 5½" d., 11" h. (rim slightly irregular) 550.00

Vase, tall ovoid body w/a short cylindrical neck, silver inlaid design of tall swamp grass up the side, fine dark patina, marked, minor irregularity at the rim, 5½" d., 12½" h. (ILLUS. previous column) 385.00

HOLIDAY COLLECTIBLES

For collectors Christmas offers the widest selection of desirable collectibles, however, other national and religious holidays also were noted with the production of various items which are now gaining in popularity. Halloween-related pieces such as candy containers, lanterns, decorations and costumes are the most sought after category after Christmas and other holidays such as Thanksgiving, Easter and the 4th of July have relatively few collectibles available for collectors. Also see CHRISTMAS TREE LIGHTS and CHRISTMAS TREE ORNAMENTS, EGG REPLICAS, and VALENTINES.

EASTER

Candy container, chalkware, rabbit w/egg basket, blue & brown paint, glass eyes, marked, 7¾" h. $49.50

Model of an egg, papier-maché, red background decorated w/bunnies & children playing 40.00

HALLOWEEN

Candy container, bisque, figure of pumpkin man, Germany, 1930s 65.00

Candy container, composition, figure of a witch, Germany, 4" h. 210.00

Candy container, papier-maché, figure of a devil, Germany, 1950s, 7" h. 32.00

Candy container, papier-maché, figure of pumpkin man, Germany, 1950s, 5½" h. 28.00

Candy container, papier-maché, figure of a witch, Germany, 1950s, 6" h. 22.00

Candy container, papier-maché, figure of a witch, West Germany, 7½"" h. 32.00

Candy container, papier-maché, model of a black cat, Keystone, West Germany, 6" h. 375.00

Candy container, papier-maché, model of a black cat w/horn, Germany, 1950s, 7" h. 35.00
Candy container, papier-maché, model of a cat, early, 8" h. 110.00
Candy container, papier-maché, model of a cat, Germany, 1950s, 5" h. 22.00
Candy container, papier-maché, model of a cat w/black wire neck, Germany, 1950s, 5½" h. 28.00
Candy container, papier-maché, model of a pumpkin, Germany, 1950s, 4" h. 22.00
Candy container, papier-maché, model of a pumpkin, Germany, 1950s, 6" h. 32.00
Die-cut decoration, cardboard, witch w/orange honeycomb tissue pull-up arms 42.00
Jack-o-lantern, metal, 6" h. 35.00
Noisemaker, tin, lithographed, Germany, 1930s 75.00
Party hat, orange cardboard decorated w/a black die-cut witch 7.50

HORN

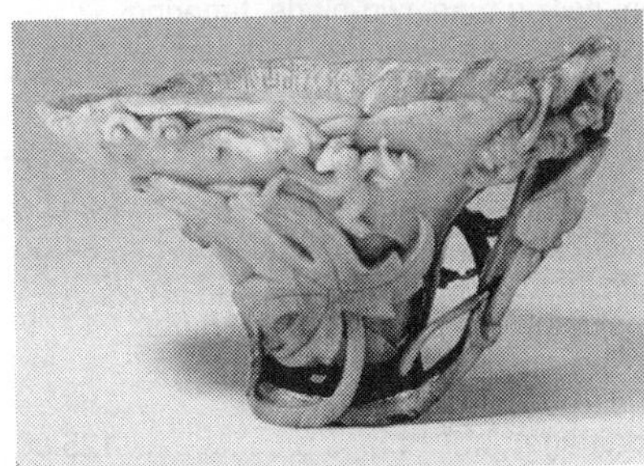

Chinese Libation Cup

The hard keratinous substance that forms the horns and hoofs of animals can be worked to produce a wide range of items, both utilitarian and decorative. Powder horns are probably the most readily recognized items available, but spoons, tumblers, jewelry and haircombs also abound. The horn furniture, popular in this country during the 1880s, incorporates whole animal horns of the Texas Longhorn and other steers to form the framework. Excluding furniture, most horn items, even those with scratch-carved decoration, are moderately priced. Also see POWDER HORNS & FLASKS.

Box, cov., oval w/waisted sides, tooled geometric designs, decorative iron finial, 3½" w., 2⅞" h. $220.00
Cup, engraved w/Masonic symbols & initials "WA," 3½" h. 192.50
Figure of Shoulao, carved standing turned to one side, wearing long flowing robes billowing out to the sides, w/one hand grasping a reticulated peach, the other holding a gnarled staff, the smiling face framed by bushy eyebrows, moustache & long beard, China, 18th - 19th c., 6¼" h. 2,185.00
Libation cup, rhinoceros horn carved as a mallow bloom on a vine extending around the sides bearing large serrated leaves w/a pair of *chilong* amid entwined budding magnolia branches trailing up one side & onto the interior, the interior rim encircled w/an archaistic inscription, the underside signed *yuan yuan* within a double gourd, China, early 18th c., minor chips, 7" w., 4¼" h. (ILLUS.) 12,650.00
Tablespoon, carved cow horn, w/dark patina, 9¾" l. 30.00

HORSE & BUGGY COLLECTIBLES

Bridle & bit, leather w/snaffle bit w/silver rondeles, Yuma, Arizona $55.00
Catalog, "Murray Line," 1909, buggies, buckboards, delivery wagons, harness, saddlery, etc., 8 x 10", 192 pp. 95.00
Figure of a cowboy, carved & painted white oak, standing full-bodied figure of a smiling cowboy w/painted tin teeth, smoking a cigarette, wearing a black-painted tin hat brim, red & white gingham shirt w/black buttons, collar & cuffs, black & blue painted pants & black cowboy boots, composed of six sections held together by steel rods, Connecticut or Massachusetts, ca. 1920, 5'9" h. 11,500.00
Fly cover, for horse, leather mesh 45.00
Hitching post, cast iron, the finial in the form of a tiny standing black stable boy wearing a peaked cap, mounted atop a slender tapering fluted columnar base, late 19th c., 5'4" h. 1,495.00
Hitching posts, cast iron, stylized model of a horses' head w/a crimped mane mounted atop an oval ribbed column base, 19th c., 15¼" h., pr. (ILLUS. top next page) 1,840.00

Horse Head Hitching Posts

Riding crop, stag horn handle & wrapped shank, 28½" l. 126.50
Riding crop, stag horn handle w/silver inlay, leather-covered shank, 24" l. 104.50
Saddle, high-backed, "Clark Saddle Co.," Portland, Oregon..................250.00
Saddle, high-backed, "J.C. Welcome," Burns, Oregon, "A" fork, new strings, new sheepskin 300.00
Sign, "Acme Cowboy Boots," painted metal & neon, a 3-D molded plastic cowboy boot in red, cream, white & yellow to the left of a shaped rectangular sign w/yellow neon spelling out "Acme..Boots," the word "Cowboy" printed in yellow at the center, new cord & plug, 20¼" l., 12½" h. (minor scratches & soiling) 825.00
Spurs, large rowl, wide band, marked "Crockett," pr. 135.00
Spurs, silver-inlaid steel, Crockett/Renalde, pr. 450.00
Spurs, silver-inlaid steel, made in Mexico, pr. 650.00
Spurs, silver-plated steel, Mexican transitional style, pr. 225.00

HOUSEHOLD APPLIANCES

Labor saving devices for the housewife as well as appliances to improve the quality of life of the American family began to proliferate in the 19th century. The introduction of electricity helped expand the field even more and today early appliances, especially electric models, are increasingly collectible. Many serious collectors search for early fans and toasters in particular, but old coffee makers, steam irons and vacuum cleaners also have dedicated enthusiasts. All pieces listed are electric unless otherwise noted. Also see LAUNDRY ROOM ITEMS.

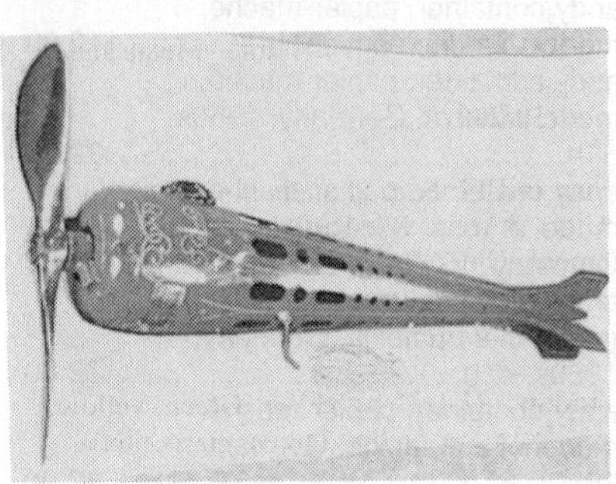

Unusual Ceiling Fan

Buffet server, "Chase No. 27011 Lurelle Guild" $145.00
Coffeepot & cover w/glass finial, percolator-type, "Universal Percolator Co., Landers Frary & Clark" 300.00
Curling iron, "Hotpoint," by Edison Appliance 45.00
Fan, "General Electric," brass blades, patented August 1895..................250.00
Fan, "Westinghouse," 11" cage 65.00
Fan, ceiling-type, two-blade, tapering metal body w/wood tip, dark red w/yellow highlights, silver blades, minor paint chipping, 36" l. (ILLUS.) 467.50
Ice cube breaker, "Lightning"..................80.00
Juicer, "Sunkist," 1940s (unused) 34.00
Knife sharpener, "Constellation," molded black plastic w/white metal insert & white feet, designed by George Nelson, 3 x 5" (some damage)..................125.00
Mixer, "Chicago," w/Jadite bowl..................45.00
Mixer, "Dormeyer," w/original bowls & beaters, ca. 1940s 45.00
Mixer, "Hamilton Beach," ten-speed electric deluxe model w/milk white glass bowls 25.00
Sewing machine, "Household," treadle-type, walnut cabinet..................165.00
Sewing machine, "Singer, Model 20," in original box..................145.00
Television, "Motorola Model 9T1," Bakelite cabinet 175.00
Toaster, "Crocker-Wheeler Elec. Mfg. Co. Toast-O-Later, Model J" (some scratches) 149.00
Toaster, "General Electric," porcelain, third model 185.00
Toaster, "Kenmore," rounded corners ..35.00
Toaster, "Seneca," flip-down sides 21.00
Toaster, "Universal Model E984T," w/flip-down sides 40.00

ICART PRINTS

Morning Cup

The works of Louis Icart, the successful French artist whose working years spanned the Art Nouveau and Art Deco movements, first became popular in the United States shortly after World War I. His limited edition etchings were much in vogue during those years when the fashion trends were established in Paris. These prints were later relegated to the closet shelves and basements but they have now re-entered the art market and are avidly sought by collectors. Listed by their American titles, those appearing below have been sold within the past eighteen months. All prints are framed unless otherwise noted.

Apache Dancer, 1929, 13¼ x 20¼" ....$800.00 to 1,000.00
Autumn, 1928, 6½ x 9" ....800.00 to 1,000.00
Autumn Leaves, 1926, 17 x 21" (margin trimmed, laid-down) 1,265.00
Baby Doll, 1924, unframed, 13½ x 18¼" (time-darkened) 1,150.00
Basket of Apples, 1924, unframed, 12 x 16½" (time-darkened, mat burn, foxing) 1,035.00
Behind the Fan, 1922, 14¾ x 19" (laid-down, slight margin soiling) ..1,035.00
Belle Rose, 1933, 16¼ x 20⅞" ....1,400.00 to 1,500.00
Birds of July, 1926, unframed, 11⅞ x 16½" (laid-down, margin time-darkening, foxing) 1,150.00
Conchita, 1929, 14 x 21" (glued down, time-darkened, mat burn) 1,150.00
Fair Model, 1937, unframed, 11⅛ x 19" (glued to mat)..............2,530.00
Fallen Nest, 1924, 14⅞ x 18¾" 1,150.00
Faust, 1928, 13 x 20½" (laid-down, margin trimmed)..............................920.00
Forbidden Fruit, 1926, 13 x 17½"..................1,000.00 to 1,500.00
Fruit, 1926, unframed, 14 x 19¾" (glued to mat, time-darkened, mat burn) 1,150.00
Gay Senorita, 1939, 17½ x 21½".....1,495.00
Gay Trio, 1936, 10⅞ x 18⅜"...........4,600.00
Hydrangeas, 1929, 16⅛ x 20½" oval (glued to mat, slight time-darkening) 1,150.00
Lady of the Camelias, 1927, 16¾ x 21" oval (margins trimmed).......................................2,200.00
Laziness, 1925, 15 x 19" (glued to mat, time-darkened).......................1,495.00
Letter (The), 1923, 12⅝ x 17½" (foxing, slight time-darkening)..........920.00
Look, 1928, unframed, 13⅞ x 18½"..................................1,380.00
Madame Bovary, 1929, 16 x 20" oval (laid-down, loss to one corner, residue on margins) 990.00
Mardi Gras, 1936, framed, 18½ x 18½" (glued to mat, mat burn) 6,613.00
Martini, 1932, 12½ x 16⅝" (trimmed slightly)..4,313.00
Morning Cup, 1940, unframed, 17¼ x 19", slight mat burn, (ILLUS.) 2,300.00
Pals, 1923, unframed, 16¼ x 20½" (some mat burn, foxing, small hole in border) 2,760.00
Parasol (The), First Cherries, 1928, unframed, 14 x 17½" oval (slight time-darkening & soiling) 1,100.00
Perfect Harmony, 1932, 13⅛ x 17⅜" (margin trimmed, laid-down) 2,875.00
Pink Slip (The), 1939, 11⅛ x 18⅞" ..1,840.00
Red Gate (The), 1925, unframed, 12¼ x 17" (slight soiling) 1,725.00
Scheherazade, 1927, unframed, 13⅜ x 20⅜" 1,840.00
Silk Robe (The), The Silk Dress, 1926, 15 x 18½" 1,955.00
Sleeping Beauty, 1927, framed, 15½ x 19½" oval (time-darkened, laid-down, mat stain).....................1,495.00
Speed, 1927, 14¾ x 24½" (glued to mat, mat burn, time-darkened)..........................2,500.00 to 3,000.00
Speed II, 1933, 16⅛ x 26" (laid-down, minor time-darkening & foxing) 2,875.00
Spilled Milk, 1925, unframed, 16¼ x 21¾"..................................1,265.00
Symphony in White, 1932, framed, 15 x 18⅞" (time-darkening, glued to mat, mat burn) 2,070.00
Venus, 1928, 13⅜ x 18⅞" oval........1,610.00
Winter, 1928, 6¾ x 9" 920.00

Youth, 1930, framed, 15⅜ x 24" (time-darkened, soiled margins, laid-down) 2,588.00

ICONS

Virgin of Kazan Icon

Icon is the Latin word meaning likeness or image and is applied to small pictures meant to be hung on the iconostasis, a screen dividing the sanctuary from the main body of Eastern Orthodox churches. Examples may be found all over Europe. The Greek, Russian and other Orthodox churches developed their own styles, but the Russian contribution to this form of art is considered outstanding.

Apparition of the Virgin to St. Sergei, Russia, 17th c., 8⅝ x 11¼" $1,980.00

Calendar icon for the month of April, depicting the saint or saints honored on each day, Russia, early 19th c., 13½ x 17¾"....................................1,265.00

Calendar icon for the month of September, painted in miniature w/all the saints & feasts for each day of the month, Central Russia, ca. 1600, 14½ x 17⅞".......................13,200.00

Christ Pantokrator, silvered riza, Russia, late 19th c., 4 x 5" 275.00

Christ, the Virgin Mary & various saints, depicted in three registers, w/brass riza, Russia, late 19th c., 10½ x 12"..357.50

Dormition of the Holy Virgin, Russia, 18th c., 10½ x 12¼" 1,035.00

Hodigitria Mother of God, w/silver & enamel oklad, Moscow, Russia, ca. 1895, 6⅞ x 8¾"............................2,300.00

Mother of God, the silver oklad w/a border of fruiting vine, Moscow, Russia, ca. 1910, 7½ x 8¾"..........1,495.00

St. George Slaying the Dragon, Russia, 19th c., 11¾ x 14" 1,265.00

St. Nicolas, hagiographical-type, painted in the center w/St. Nicholas, surrounded by scenes from his life, partly-gilded oklad, silver & niello frame, Moscow, Russia, 1888, 12 x 14"..1,320.00

Saints Samon, Guri, Aviv, the Upper border painted w/the Holy Visage, Russia, 17th c., 10½ x 12½" 4,600.00

Triptych icon, the central panel painted w/the New Testament Trinity, one wing painted w/the Presentation of the Virgin in the Temple, the Descent into Hell, the Hodigitria Virgin & the Decollation of St. John the Baptist, the other wing painted w/selected saints, each panel within a brass frame, Russia, 18th c., 5⅝ x 15" open 3,680.00

Virgin of Hodigitria, silver & enamel, Russia, ca. 1900, 8 x 10½" 385.00

Virgin of Kazan, silver-gilt & enamel, hallmarked riza, Russia, late 19th c., 9 x 11" (ILLUS.) 550.00

Virgin Iverskaya, Russia, 18th - 19th c., 10½ x 12½" 550.00

Virgin of Tenderness, silver-gilt oklad, w/silver filigree robes, Russia, ca. 1900, 5⅝ x 7" 1,265.00

Vladimir Mother of God, w/brass oklad, Russia, late 18th c., 16½ x 19¾"..................................2,185.00

INDIAN ARTIFACTS & JEWELRY

Covered Iroquois Basket

Basket, Cherokee, woven cane, rectangular w/slightly rounded ends, geometric design in red, black & natural, 6¾ x 14", 7½" h. plus bentwood handle $115.50

Basket, Eastern Woodland, Iroquois, woven splint, oblong w/squared base, decorated w/stylized vegetable-dyed potato stamp flowers & leafage w/details in red & green w/stationary ash handles & rim, 12½" l., 4¾" h. 575.00

Basket, cov., Eastern Woodland, Iroquois, woven splint, circular wrapped rim above rounded sides w/a square bottom, overlapping cover w/pointed top, decorated w/stylized vegetable-dyed potato-stamp flowers & details in red & green, w/oversized bentwood ash carrying handle, attributed to J.H.S., 11" d., 8" h. (ILLUS.) 2,558.00

Basket, cov., Eastern Woodland, Iroquois, woven splint, the slightly domed lid w/ash rim fitted on a circular basket w/square base, decorated w/hearts & flowers in vegetable-dyed potato stamp w/detail in green & red, initialed "J.H.S.," late 19th c., 12¼" d., 9½" h. 2,875.00

Basket, Pima, woven willow, round w/wide, shallow sides, five woven male figures in dark martynia around the sides, 10⅞" d. (very soiled, two hanging holes in center, small paint stain, few missing stitches) 825.00

Navaho Germantown Chief Blanket

Blanket, Navaho, Germantown Chief-type, finely woven wool in dark forest green, red & natural w/a band of serrate diamonds down the center against a striped ground & half-diamonds in bands down the sides, corner tassels, very minor staining, 56 x 70" (ILLUS.) 10,450.00

Book, "By Canoe & Dog Train Among the Cree & Salteaux Indians," by Rev. Young, ca. 1890 ....30.00

Bowl, Apache, basketry, round w/wide, shallow sides, woven martynia & willow in geometric narrow bands, ca. 1890, 11¾" d. (two small hanging holes in center)..577.50

Bowl, Pima, basketry, martynia & willow in an early fret design, 18" d. (stitch wear, soiling, five small hanging holes, rim chip)..................770.00

Jar, Acoma, pottery, water-type w/a squatty bulbous body tapering to a wide, flat mouth, decorated w/a wide band of red ochre & umber birds & stylized florals on a white polished slip ground, concave base w/unusual four-lobe design, ca. 1900, 7¾" d., 6½" h. (minor wear, chip near rim) 687.50

Jar, Acoma, pottery, water-type w/a bulbous ovoid body tapering to a wide flat mouth, decorated in polychrome w/various geometric banded designs in umber & dark & light ochre on a white slip ground, late 19th c., 11" d., 10⅛" h. (hairline, rim chips, glaze chips) 8,580.00

San Ildefonso Redware Jar

Jar, San Ildefonso, redware, bulbous ovoid form tapering to a flat mouth, decorated on the upper two-thirds w/bands of stylized blossoms & scrolls in red ochre & black on a cream ground, glued rim chip & minor wear, 10" d., 9½" h. (ILLUS.) 1,402.50

Jar, Santo Domingo, pottery, wide bulbous body w/two long angled spouts w/flared ends joined by an arched handle at the top, black paneled design on buff slip w/red ochre underbody, by Monica Silva, ca. 1925, 10¼" d., 14" h. (minor wear, glaze damage from old sticker) 990.00

Jar, Zuni, pottery, globular w/large mouth, overall polychrome design in umber w/red ochre on a white slip ground, well defined band break, bottle bottom, late 19th c., 12½" d., 9⅛" h. (wear to glaze & painting, one area at bottom very worn)......2,350.00

Jars, Hopi, pottery, cylindrical, umber & ochre thunderbird design on a creamy orange slip ground, marked w/ear of corn symbol for Corn-woman, scratches, some wear &

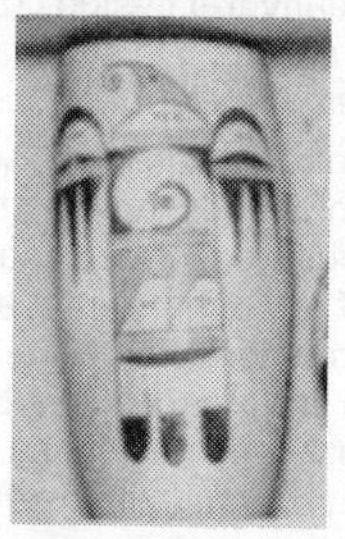

Hopi Pottery Jar

small broken firing bubble, 10" h., pr. (ILLUS. of one) 530.00

Knife sheath, Sioux, beaded leather, clear violet & red w/blue & white beads, wrapped leather tassel end, 12½" l. 60.00

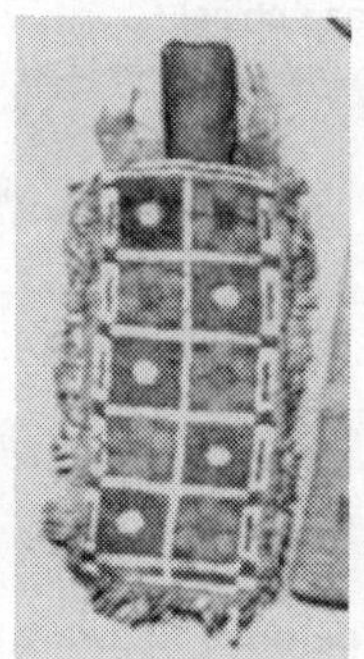

Great Lakes Knife Sheath

Knife sheath, woman's, Great Lakes, rectangular beaded leather, stylized blossomheads arranged in beaded squares of alternating red, gold, blue & white, fringe border on three sides, contains old knife, 4" w., 10½" l. plus straps, 2 pcs. (ILLUS.) 440.00

Moccasins, Ponca, beaded leather, spot-beaded in pink, green, white, yellow & white heart red, made in 1910 by the daughter of Chief White Eagle, marked on soles "Robert M. Glesaner, 1910," 6⅜" l., pr. 412.50

Moccasins, man's, Sioux, beaded leather, the front & sides beaded overall w/checked triangular designs in green, yellow, blue & rose on an opal white ground, collected at Fort Yates, North Dakota, ca. 1910, 9¾" l., pr. (minor bead loss).............550.00

Model of a canoe, woodlands, birch bark, traditionally made & pitched, from the Red Lake Chippewa Indian Reservation, ca. 1930s, 63" l. (bark split at one end) 1,045.00

Olla, Papago, basketry-type, yucca & martynia, a terrace design w/stylized "I's" interspersed w/stacked arrowheads, 9½" d., 11¾" h. (minor wear, few mission rim stitches).................770.00

Peace medal, silver, oval, spread-winged American eagle obverse, Indian & George Washington exchanging peace pipe reverse & "George Washington, President 1793," probably by Wilkerson, Mansfield, Ohio, w/chain, 3 x 4⅜"....220.00

Early Indian Photographs

Photographs, one showing an Indian encampment w/Scarcee Indian Saskio & family in front of their tepee, the other shows Scarcee Indians Mutsmamakan & his squaw in front of their tepee w/horses to the side, matted & framed, ca. 1900, 25" w., 12" h., pr. (ILLUS.) 176.00

Pillow, Iroquois, beaded & needlepoint, decorated w/a large bird flanked by "1888" & "E.L." on a red ground w/lace trim, 8" l. 82.50

Pipe bag, Sioux, beaded rawhide, geometric beading in two shades of blue & red on a white ground w/red, green & orange quillwork, 26" l. plus long fringe (wear, some damage).......................................1,100.00

Pipe bowl, Tlingit, carved wood in the figure of a seal, raven, eagle & whale, polychrome trim, brass bowl, hole in end for reed stem, good wear, made for tribal use, 3¼" l., 2" h...1,540.00

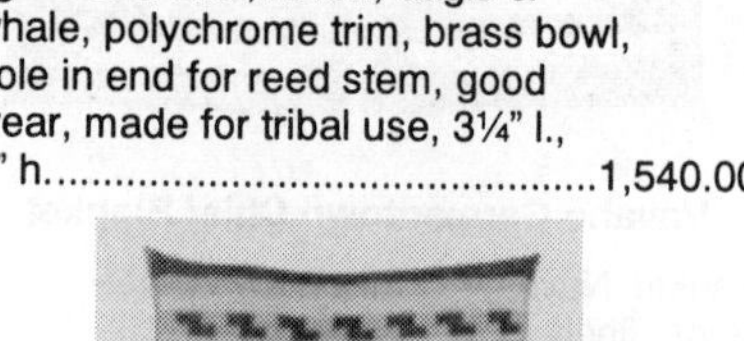

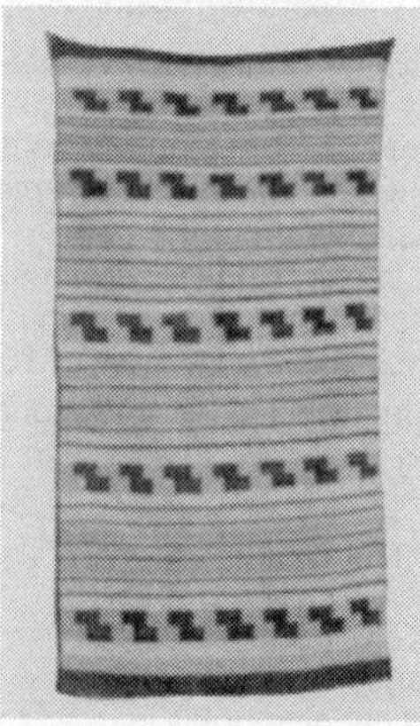

Navaho Child's Blanket Rug

Rug, Navaho, child's traditional-style,

bands of staggered small blocks alternating w/wide bands of narrow stripes, faded red & yellow, rust, black & natural, ca. 1890-1910, 32½ x 62" (ILLUS.) 450.00

Rug, Navaho, Storm patt., carded grey, black, natural & Ganado red, small soiled area in one corner, 36 x 46"..350.00

Rug, Navaho, Western Reservation, Storm patt., mixture of hand-carded black, grey, red & natural w/some commercial grey yarn, 36 x 59" 400.00

Early Storm Pattern Rug

Rug, Navaho, probably Crystal area, early Storm patt., dark brown, natural, carded tan & red, a few loose stitches along edge, 42 x 66" (ILLUS.) 600.00

Rug, Navaho, Two Grey Hills geometric design in gold, tan, grey & black on a natural ground, hand-carded wool, ca. 1950, unused, 47 x 60"..650.00

Rug, Navaho, cotton type w/hand-carded red, dark brown, arbrush grey & natural wool, featuring a large rectangle in the center framing a cross & w/a small diamond at each corner, within a rectangular zigzag border, fine sheen & no wear, ca. 1900, 47 x 65" 1,320.00

Rug, Navaho, Northwest Reservation, two large serrate diamonds around crosses w/further crosses flanking the diamonds, diamond band border, in dark brown, red, arbrush tan & natural hand-carded & spun wool, fine sheen, stains, color bleeding & wear at ends, 49 x 73" 687.50

Rug, Navaho, interlocking triangle design in red, dark brown, carded tan & natural, bright analine orange yarn in selvage & ends, ca. 1895, 50 x 74" (minor breaks in orange yarn, minor soiling & stains).............750.00

Rug, Navaho, early West Reservation, tan, brown & natural wool w/orangish red band of central diamonds & zigzag border bands, lovely sheen, 62 x 74" (some staining) 935.00

Large Navaho Ganado Rug

Rug, Navaho, Ganado, a large long banded cross in the center flanked by smaller crosses & a Greek key band border, red, dark brown, carded tan & natural, some bleeding, a few selvage & warp breaks w/small holes, ca. 1910, 65 x 84" (ILLUS.) 500.00

Rug, Navaho, Tes Nos Pas, finely carded & woven wool, wide border of angular H-devices, central Storm patt. in black, grey, tan, red, dark green, orange & natural, 60 x 98" (minor staining) 4,895.00

Rug, Navaho, Storm patt. in carded greys & tans, dark brown, black, Ganado red & natural white, woven by Norma Bitsue, 1960s, 108 x 156"..................................30,000.00

Runner, Navaho, hand-carded & spun wool, West Reservation type w/Tes Nos Pas border, serrated diamonds & triangles in red, white, black & brown on a pale gold ground, 24 x 144" 1,925.00

Saddle blanket, Navaho, Germantown-type, woven wool, stepped & interwoven bands form large diamonds centered by swastika, in black, purple & white on a red ground, two pairs of hands woven, one on each side of where the cinch would go, ca. 1885, 25 x 31" plus fringe (warp break, very minor moth damage, stiff spot) 2,475.00

Tab bag, Crow, beaded flap in light

& dark blue, red, greasy yellow & white, end tabs have vermillion stain, ca. 1890, tab 10" l. 1,300.00

Tray, Apache, coiled basketry, geometric & quadruped design in martynia willow, ca. 1900, 18¼ x 20⅝", 4½" h. (removable paint drip on six stitches) 3,500.00

IVORY

Ivory Allegorical Figure

Charger, oval, the center w/an oval scene depicting the crowning of the Queen, the outer rim decorated w/various court scenes, further adorned w/ivory petals, mid-19th c., 25" l. (losses & age cracks) $7,475.00

Corset busk, carved whale ivory, the slender shaft w/heart-shaped top carved w/a heart enclosing the initials "F.S.," an anchor, a pot of flowers & a spray of leaves, decorated w/red, green & sepia inks, 19th c., 13¼" l. 825.00

Figure, allegorical, a kneeling nude looking down w/one arm raised, on a circular base & raised on a green marble base, late 19th c., 12" h. (ILLUS.) 4,600.00

Figures of Lohan, each standing monk w/naturalistic features, well-carved wearing long flowing robes falling in contoured folds & each carrying a unique attribute, accompanied by an animal or a boy, the heads w/eyes & further details picked out in black, the ivory all w/natural dark-stained veining, China, 19th c., set of 18 (splits, minor chips & losses)..................43,125.00

Tankard, the cylindrical body carved w/a continuous battle scene, the hinged lid w/a kneeling soldier, the handle in the form of a trumpeter, mid-19th c., 13¼" h. (age cracks) 10,350.00

Tusk, upright form carved overall w/figures of various gods climbing among delicate foliage, India, 19th c., 9¼" h.................................165.00

Vase, baluster-form base below a tall trumpet-form neck, the body carved on one side w/a pair of confronted *chilongs* w/a *lingzhi* in its jaws, the body & bifurcated tail undulating around the sides, the neck carved w/a larger *chilong* in high-relief, its tail encircling the neck, the flared base w/ribbed bands, China, 19th c., 5¼" h...1,380.00

JADE

18th Century Jade Wine Pot

Bowl, moghul-style, the thin stone carved around the sides w/eight foliate leaf-form panels enclosing upright blooming stems, divided by flowerheads & between bands of foliate scroll, w/two thin reticulated flora-form handles, raised on a flowerhead forming the footring, the stone faintly suffused w/white overall, China, across handles 7" w. $3,450.00

Brushwasher, oval, carved on the exterior on one side w/a boy grasping a peach & peering over the sides into the interior at a smaller recumbent boy, the yellow stone suffused w/russet brown & white, China, 17th c., 5" l.........................6,900.00

Dish, chrysanthemum-form, thinly carved on the interior & exterior w/rows of overlapping petals, the interior & underside w/a central flowerhead encircled by three rows of overlapping petals, greenish grey speckled w/grey, China, 18th c., 6½" d. 1,495.00

Figure of a mythical beast, carved in Six Dynasties style, in a recumbent position, the head turned sharply back w/bulging eyes & finely incised mane & tail, dark green, China, 18th c., 3" l. 2,070.00

Koro, cov., raised on masked paw feet, the body carved w/flowers interrupted by thick foliate handles w/loose rings, the matching cover w/three small loose rings & floral knop, bright green, China, 5¼" h. 19,550.00

Model of an elephant, recumbent animal w/a boy riding on his back w/a string of cash, yellow w/deep reddish brown patches, China, late Ming Dynasty, 5" l. 9,775.00

Model of a ram, recumbent animal w/legs tucked under body, the head held forward w/long curving horns trailing on the back, polished white w/a pale green tint, China, 18th c., 3¼" l. 2,588.00

Vase, quadrangular-form, carved & incised on each side w/a *taotie* mask above archaistic pendant blades encircling the body, above bats soaring amid concentric wave & *ruyi* lappets further repeated around the incurving neck, set w/ two elephant-head-form handles, the white stone broadly suffused w/apple green & a splash of spinach green, China, 6¼" h. 2,875.00

Vase, *fang-gu* form, squared body in an archaic bronze form flaring at the top & base, carved on the rounded center section of each side w/a *taotie* mask between leaftip blades infilled w/dense geometric designs, the fitted angled cover w/rectangular knob, greenish yellow w/splashes of taupe, China, Qianlong Dynasty, 6½" h. 27,600.00

Wine pot, cov., oval, carved on one side w/dragons rising up from water & descending from swirling clouds, the reverse w/a phoenix, the spout emerging from a carved dragon head, opposite a dragon-form handle, raised on four masked splayed feet, pale grey, China, 18th c., 6½" h. (ILLUS.) 4,600.00

JEWELRY

Also see INDIAN ARTIFACTS & JEWELRY.

ANTIQUE (1800-1920)

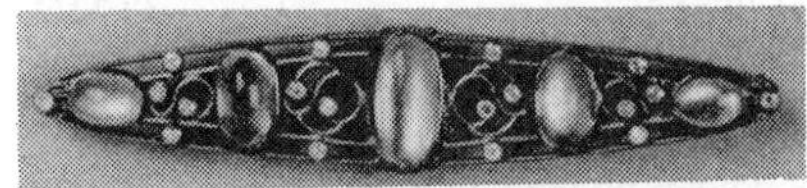

Arts & Crafts Bar Pin

Bar pin, gold (14k), moonstone & diamond, Arts & Crafts style, pierced narrow oblong gold bar bezel-set w/five oval cabochon moonstones accented w/18 bezel-set diamonds, early 20th c. 3¾" l. (ILLUS.) $1,870.00

Bracelet, bangle-type, diamond & pearl, centered by a button pearl flanked by two mine-cut diamonds further enhanced w/a graduated diamond top, in a platinum top 14k gold mount, Austrian hallmarks, Edwardian 2,530.00

Bracelet, bangle-type, gold (14k yellow) & diamond, the center designed w/a lily blossom set w/diamonds, flanked by smaller diamonds, in a three-row hinged mount, early 20th c. 1,320.00

Bracelet, bangle-type, gold (14k pink) & onyx, rectangular onyx plaques mounted in mill grained gold, Victorian 935.00

Bracelet, bangle-type, gold (14k) & pearls, Art Nouveau style, centered by three freshwater pearls within a foliate motif accented by engraved scrolled sides, hallmarked 715.00

Victorian Snake Bracelet

Bracelet, bangle-type, gold (18k), sapphire & pearl, the hinged bangle set in the upper half w/a coiled snake accented w/wire-twist & beadwork, the head set w/an oval sapphire & red stone eyes, the body inset w/small pearls & sapphires, hallmarked, Victorian, minor dents (ILLUS.) 1,760.00

Bracelet, gold (14k), textured gold hands holding two interlocking ovals accented w/blue enamel gloves on a flexible bracelet, European hallmark, Victorian 1,980.00

Bracelet, gold (14k), centered w/a lion's head holding a diamond in its mouth, enhanced by red stone eyes, joined by tapering oval plaques, Victorian (solder) 165.00

Bracelet, gold (18k yellow), composed of filigree oval links, French hallmarks 715.00

Brooch, gold (14k), diamonds & enamel, center set w/diamonds in a star shape, highlighted w/blue enamel & flanked on either side w/star-set diamonds, Victorian......1,650.00

Edwardian Gold Bracelet

Bracelet, gold (15k yellow) & seed pearls, heavy curb link suspending three pavé-set seed pearl hearts, Edwardian (ILLUS. of part) 550.00

Bracelet, opal & pearl, Arts & Crafts style, oval opal doublet plaques alternating w/blister pearls within an 18k gold foliate mount, 14k gold plunger, signed "Oakes" 4,070.00

Bracelet, silver, diamond & gold, charm-type, an 18k white gold chain composed of long twist links suspending eleven charms, most figural in silver set w/tiny diamonds, forms include a pheasant, quail, swan, dog, crown & painted portrait, also accented w/pearls on some charms, Edwardian.......................3,575.00

Bracelets, bangle-type, gold (18k), fine wire-twist edging & small beadwork sprigs on each side, in a fitted velvet box marked "J.E. Caldwell & Co.," Victorian, pr. (minor dents)...1,980.00

Bracelets, bangle-type, gold-filled, plain bands decorated w/black enamel floral tracery, Victorian, pr. ..247.50

Brooch, agate, large oval stone set within a silver frame, Victorian 110.00

Victorian Amethyst Brooch

Brooch, amethyst & gold, cross-shaped gold mount set w/large oval & pear-shaped foil-backed amethysts, Victorian (ILLUS.) 770.00

Brooch, Berlin ironwork, oblong lacy pierced quatrefoil w/Gothic roundels centering a putti & suspending three pear-shaped pierced foliate drops, in a fitted box, Victorian 1,870.00

Brooch, black opal, diamond & platinum, the flattened heart-shaped opal surmounted by a diamond-set bow within a platinum mount, Edwardian (opal crazed) 1,045.00

Brooch, diamond & enamel, Art Nouveau style, a figure-8 18k gold frame mounted across the center w/a diagonal band of five old European-cut diamonds surrounded by tiny enameled flowers along the edges, early 20th c. 660.00

Brooch, diamond & 18k gold, oval form w/a small lobe extended at each quadrant, set overall w/old mine-cut diamonds, scrolled openwork gold mount, antique......3,630.00

Brooch, garnets & silver-gilt, rose-cut garnets surrounding a cabochon suspending swags of garnets in a silver-gilt mounting, late Victorian......................................1,210.00

Brooch, gold (14k yellow) & diamond, modeled in the form of a lady's hand holding an old mine-cut diamond, w/black enamel tracery cuff, Victorian...1,430.00

Brooch, gold (14k), seed pearl & sapphire, Art Nouveau style, in the form of a large, long-winged butterfly, the delicate openwork design set in the body & along the wing edges w/seed pearls, the veins in the wings accented w/bezel-set sapphires, American-marked, 5¼" l. 2,860.00

Brooch, micro-mosaic & 18k gold, a quatrefoil design against a turquoise mosaic ground, within a circular gold twist wire frame, Castellani, Victorian.......................................2,310.00

Brooch, *plique-a-jour* enamel, moonstone, diamond & yellow gold, Art Nouveau style, a barbell form w/trefoil ends, silver & amber *plique-a-jour* set w/small diamonds & a central cabochon moonstone, by Georges Fouquet, stamped "G. FOUQUET 10777," France, early 20th c., 3¼" l. 9,775.00

Brooch, silver, Art Nouveau style, the relief-molded bust profile of an exotic woman within a double snake

Art Nouveau Silver Brooch

frame, signed "William Link," ca. 1902 (ILLUS.) 412.50

Brooch, silver-gilt, *plique-a-jour* enamel, diamond & ruby, Art Nouveau style, modeled in the form of a dragonfly, the veined wings in *plique-a-jour* enamel shading from rose to pale green, the body set w/old mine-cut diamonds, the eyes w/ruby cabochons, ca. 1900, 2¼" l. 1,495.00

Cameo brooch, carved shell, depicting the full figure of a classical woman in flowing drapery, within an 18k gold mount w/wire twist & beadwork, Victorian 1,870.00

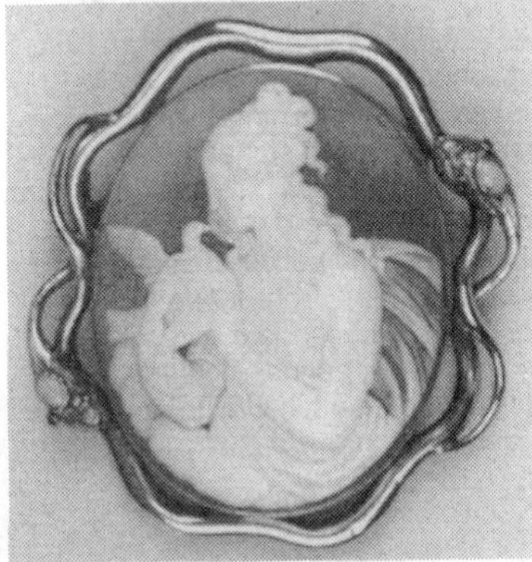

Victorian Cameo Brooch

Cameo brooch, carved shell, depicting the figure of a lady holding a dove, within a 15k yellow gold double snake frame, each snake head set w/turquoise & red eyes, some shell crazing, Victorian (ILLUS.) 660.00

Cameo brooch, gold (15k) & lava, depicting an angel holding two cherubs within a gold beaded frame...330.00

Cameo necklace, choker-type, carved lava, composed of 20 oval lava profiles of classical women within gilt frames spaced by chain link & stitched to a ribbon, Victorian 770.00

Cameo pendant, agate, oval, cut w/a bust portrait of Mary Queen of Scots wearing a tall lacy collar, the frame accented w/seed pearls & suspended from a florette & ribbon band trimmed in seed pearls, Gibbs Version by Augustus Saint-Gaudens, 1872, commissioned by Montgomery Gibbs for his wife 6,600.00

Cameo pendant, tourmaline & 14k yellow gold, pink tourmaline carved to depict the bust of a pharoah, mounted within a gold rope frame...1,760.00

Cameo pin-pendant, hardstone, depicting the profile of a lady within a 14k rose gold mount, highlighted w/scrolls & beadwork, 10k gold pin stem, Victorian 935.00

Cameo ring, onyx & 14k rose gold, a carving of a bird, w/wings in the form of a ram's head & classical male, in a gold mount, Victorian 770.00

Chain, gold (14k), fancy link-type w/reeded oval links highlighted by chased & openwork plaques, Victorian, 23" l. 1,100.00

Chain & slide, gold (14k), double curb link chain w/beaded detail, slide highlighted w/black enamel tracery & small pearls, Victorian, 66" l. (minor solder)...............................2,200.00

Chatelaine, parcel-gilt sterling silver & mixed metal, the belt hook in tab form w/rounded top applied & engraved w/Japanesque designs, suspending a cloisonné enamel bead, three perfume bottles of different sizes & designs & an *aide memoire* notepad w/ivory leaves & a silver pencil; one bottle hand-hammered & applied w/copper butterflies & dragonflies, another w/flip top & engraved Japanese figures, all hanging from links of chain, maker's mark of Tiffany & Co., New York, ca. 1875, overall 9" l. (one bottle cap missing).........1,610.00

Choker, seed pearl, the delicate band composed of alternating rosette motifs joined by three individually decorated rows of seed pearl chains, now mounted on a velvet band, Victorian, 13" l. 747.00

Cloak fasteners, silver, modeled as Medusa heads, Victorian 110.00

Cross, gold (18k yellow), diamond & pearl, the pierced gold cross highlighted by small leaves, rose-cut diamonds & centered by a button pearl, suspended from an oval link chain, ca. 1910, 22" l. 880.00

Cross, onyx, pearls & gold, the onyx cross centered by pearls & yellow gold, Victorian 275.00

Cross, *pietra dura*, wide flat form inlaid w/white roses & blue flowers on a vine, w/an 18k gold wire & beaded top & pendant loop, Victorian (minor nicks) 440.00

Cuff buttons, micro-mosaic & 15k yellow gold, designed as spaniel dogs, one w/light coloring against a light ground, the other dark against a dark ground, in gold mounts, Victorian, pr....................357.50

Cuff buttons, moss agate & 14k gold, each w/a plaque of moss agate set in gold prong mounts, Victorian, pr. (minor dent) 110.00

Cuff links, gold (18k), Art Nouveau style, each designed w/the head of a lion within a shaped circular frame, a bezel-set diamond held in the open mouth, pr....................550.00

Coral & Pearl Earrings

Earrings, coral & freshwater pearl, dangle-type, a pearl & coral cluster above a gold bow highlighted w/pearls & coral above large coral bead drops w/a tiny pearl dangle below, some solder, antique, pr. (ILLUS.) 412.50

Earrings, gold (14k yellow), textured spheres enhanced w/a black enamel tracery floral motif, Victorian 275.00

Earrings, gold (15k), Etruscan Revival style, ram's head suspending amphora w/wire detail (minor dent to back of one urn)....................1,890.00

Earrings, woven human hair, three acorns in a dangle style, ca. 1850, pr....................165.00

Lavalier, gold (18k) & lapis lazuli, centrally set w/a lapis button within an oval openwork wire-twist frame accented w/beadwork, suspending lapis teardrop-shaped terminals, on a fine foxtail link chain, minor solder, Victorian....................770.00

Locket, gold (14k yellow) & enamel, designed as an oval picture locket shielded by an enamel-decorated butterfly w/retractable wings folding to reveal a hidden picture, Victorian....................747.00

Locket, gold (14k), sardonyx & bloodstone, gold profile of a classical male w/a diamond wreath mounted on sardonyx, reverse w/bloodstone tablet, Victorian....................275.00

Horseshoe-shaped Locket

Locket, gold (15k), designed as a horseshoe w/textured hoof, compartment containing a five-leaf clover & engraved, signed "Pierret," Victorian (ILLUS.) 1,320.00

Locket, gold (15k yellow), coral & enamel, the oval polished body decorated on the front w/two interwoven horseshoe motifs, one defined by half pearls, the other by light pink coral, each w/blue enamel borders, Victorian....................488.00

Tiffany Black Opal Necklace

Locket & chain, gold (14k), a circular locket w/a monogram, suspended from a gold link chain, highlighted w/bezel-set sapphires flanked to two seed pearls, Victorian, 70" l., 2 pcs. 1,045.00

Necklace, black opal & gold, composed of a large triangular black opal within a wirework gold setting & suspending a large teardrop-form black opal, from Tiffany & Company, New York (ILLUS.) 7,700.00

Necklace, diamond, composed of clusters of arched leafy swags set w/diamonds each centered by a spread-winged swallow set w/diamonds, in silver-topped yellow gold, suspended from a later fancy link silver chain, antique, 15½" l....4,675.00

Necklace, freshwater pearl, designed as a festoon platinum necklace w/white & pink pearls, highlighted w/bezel-set diamonds, Edwardian 1,650.00

Necklace, gold (14k), composed of round beads w/wire twist decoration, Victorian, 14½" l. 1,210.00

Necklace, gold (18k), Etruscan Revival style, woven necklace w/a fringe of bead & wire twist ends, accented w/tiny frogs suspending gold urns, maker's mark "JB" for John Brogden, in fitted box 7,150.00

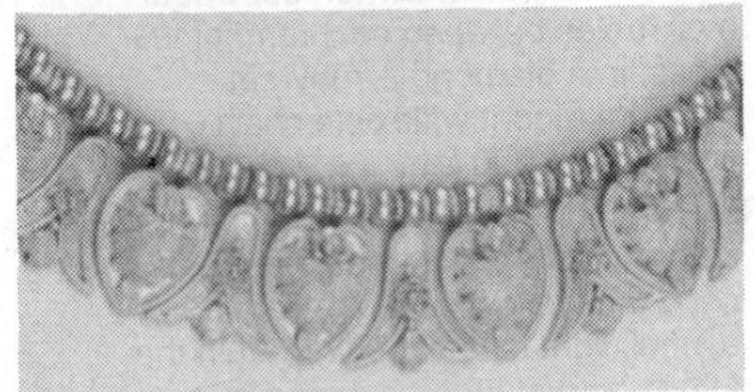

Fine Etruscan Revival Necklace

Necklace, gold (18k), Etruscan Revival style, composed of lotus & palmette drops of twisted wire & granulations suspended along a bead chain, ca. 1860, 14⅝" l. (ILLUS. of part) 20,900.00

Necklace, topaz, diamond & pearl, designed as a delicate platinum festoon chain centrally set w/a rectangular-cut topaz within a delicate diamond-set floral mount, suspending a pear-shaped topaz highlighted w/pearls & w/tiny pearls along the chains, Edwardian 1,540.00

Pendant, aquamarine, fresh water pearl & enamel, Art Nouveau style, centrally set heart-shaped aquamarine accented w/a diamond within an enameled ribbon, suspending two fresh water pearls & a teardrop-shaped aquamarine, attached to an 18k gold rope chain, 14" l. 825.00

Pendant, black opal, set w/a pear-shaped black opal highlighted at the top by a collet-set foliate frame & cable link chain, 16½" l. 1,320.00

Pendant, diamond, sunburst form, the wavy sun rays set w/diamonds centered by a 7.5 mm grey button pearl, in a platinum & 18k gold mount w/diamond pendant loop, Victorian 3,630.00

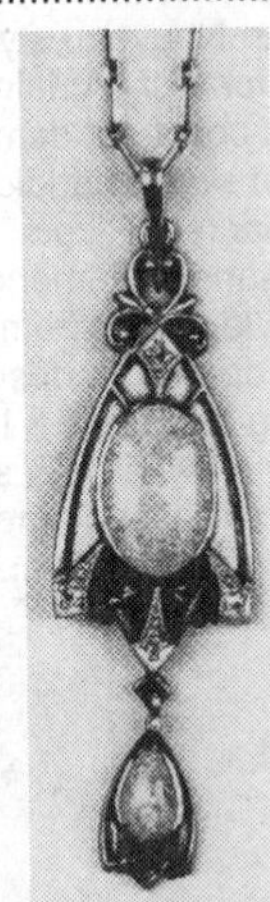

Arts & Crafts Pendant

Pendant, enamel & opal, Arts & Crafts style, an oval opal within a frame of green & blue *guilloché* enamel highlighted by rose-cut diamonds w/a smaller drop below, on a 'paper clip' gold chain, early 20th c., 20" l. (ILLUS.) 2,860.00

Pendant, gold (14k yellow), depicting a lady w/flowing hair in a repeating floral motif, w/an amethyst top 330.00

Pendant, gold, pearl, amethyst & *plique-a-jour* enamel, shaped triangular form w/a central pyriform panel set w/an amethyst cabochon & flanked by wing-form panels in *plique-a-jour* enamel shading from rose to green, pearl drop, ca. 1900, 2⅛" l. 690.00

Pendant, sterling silver, Art Nouveau style, stylized foliate design in a textured finish highlighted by seed pearls & cabochon garnets 715.00

Pendant, sterling silver & abalone shell, circular section of abalone shell within a foliate design mount, suspended from a 'paper clip' chain, marked "Kalo," 15" l. 715.00

Pin, diamond, model of a winged caduceus, the stem entwined w/snakes & wings set w/diamonds, pearl terminals at the top & bottom, ruby-set in silver-topped yellow gold, Victorian (two diamonds missing) 2,860.00

Pin, diamond & 18k gold, a simple open circle gold mount set w/old European-cut diamonds, Victorian....................................1,760.00

Pin, enamel, opal & silver, Arts & Crafts style, abstract design in blue & green enamel & set w/three opals in a silver mounting, marked "T.F." for Theodore Fahrner......................632.50

Pin, gold (14k), Art Nouveau style, modeled in the form of a griffin, highlighted by a collet-set demantoid & a diamond-set sword handle w/pearl finial, marked "Rikers" 1,210.00

Pin, gold (14k) pearls & diamonds, Arts & Crafts style, round frame surrounding an openwork design of delicate scrolling blossoms & leaves on vines, accented w/large & small pearls & small collet-set diamonds, attributed to Edward Oakes 3,080.00

Victorian Bowknot Pin

Pin, gold (14k yellow), platinum, ruby, diamond & sapphire, a bowknot w/a textured finish accented by platinum dots, a ruby, diamond & sapphire, patent dated "November 4, 1879" (ILLUS.) 1,320.00

Pin, gold (15k yellow) & turquoise, the bombé buffed star-shaped pin chased & embedded w/turquoise beads, the reverse w/window displaying woven hair, Victorian 258.00

Ring, agate, the square plaque set within a 14k gold beaded frame, Victorian...302.50

Ring, aquamarine & diamond, a center oval aquamarine surrounded by diamonds, set within a pierced platinum top gold mounting, signed "Kohn," Edwardian......................2,530.00

Ring, citrine & 14k yellow gold, the citrine seal depicting a rampant lion, within a gold chased floral mount, Victorian...412.50

Ring, diamond solitaire, round European-cut stone weighing approximately .95 ct, in a 14k yellow gold mount, antique 1,980.00

Ring, diamond & topaz, centrally set w/a rectangular cushion-cut topaz surrounded by mine-cut diamonds, within a 14k yellow gold foil-back openwork wire mount, w/silver top, Georgian 880.00

Ring, garnet & 18k gold, Arts & Crafts style, three cabochon garnets bezel-set in a three-lobed hand-made gold wire frame early 20th c. 330.00

Ring, gold (14k), Art Nouveau style, designed as a sea monster w/the head at the top & the scaly body forming the undulating shank, patent-dated 1897, Newark, New Jersey 1,100.00

Ring, gold & enamel, memorial-type, beaded borders, chased on a black enamel ground w/the inscription "HENRY COBB OB:5 FEB 1772 AE: 61," marked inside "TS" in rectangle twice, Thomas Shields, Philadelphia, ca. 1772 ....1,150.00

Ring, opal, diamond & 18k yellow gold, Art Nouveau style, centrally set w/an oval opal within a green *guilloché* enamel & diamond highlighted mount, signed Marcus & Co. 3,850.00

Ring, ruby & diamond, set w/five old oval European-cut diamonds arranged in a cross w/four tiny diamonds at each corner, set w/four oval rubies between each arm of the cross, in a diamond & ruby-set platinum mount w/flexible chain shank, ca. 1900 ....1,870.00

Ring, sapphire & 14k yellow gold, Arts & Crafts style, centered by a collet-set 9 mm yellow sapphire flanked by a small light blue sapphire within the foliate gold mount, attributed to Edward Oakes 2,750.00

Watch chain, gold (14k), fancy links w/matching fob & swivel clasp, Victorian, 15" l. 440.00

Watch chain, gold (14k), composed of fancy links 605.00

Watch chain, gold (15k), designed as alternating round & oval-shaped links w/wire twist & bead detail, Victorian, 14" l. (minor dents)...........660.00

Watch chain, woven human hair, w/gold fittings, attached watch fob containing old Victorian photo...........70.00

Watch chain & slide, gold (14k), a loop-in-loop chain w/a shield-shaped slide accented by black enamel & seed pearls, Victorian, 46" l. (ILLUS. top next column) 1,430.00

Watch chain & slide, gold (14k), open link chain fitted w/two slides set w/opals, ¾" l. slides, 26" l. chain......200.00

Victorian Watch Chain & Slide

Watch chain & slide, gold (15k), fancy links w/bead terminals, removable slide enhanced w/an applied textured leaf decoration, 60" l. 1,320.00

SETS

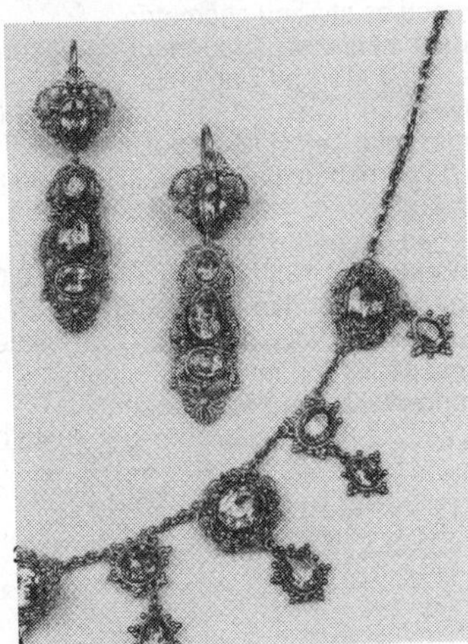

Georgian Necklace & Earrings Set

Brooch & earrings: bog oak, the brooch carved as a large quatrefoil w/two large round medallions above fine chains suspending a rosette-carved crossbar further suspending three small balls & long teardrops, the matching earrings w/crossbars & drops, Victorian, the set 440.00

Brooch & earrings: onyx & seed pearl, oval brooch accented w/a seed pearl center medallion, conforming earrings, each in 14k mountings, the set 385.00

Brooch & earrings: pietra dura, oval brooch decorated w/flowers within a 14k gold mount, w/matching earrings, in fitted box, Victorian, the set 1,100.00

Cameo brooch & earrings: yellow gold & lava, the circular brooch depicting a full figure putti holding a bunny, w/matching earpendants, in yellow gold mountings, the set....................550.00

Necklace & earrings: lapis & 18k gold, Etruscan Revival style, lapis beads w/wire twist & beadwork finials suspended from a gold foxtail chain, completed by a clasp, the earrings of conforming design, marked "Roma," necklace 15½", the set....2,750.00

Necklace & earrings: pink tourmaline & 14k gold, a gold canetille necklace set w/large round tourmalines & tourmaline drops, & a pair of dangle-type tourmaline earrings, in a fitted box, Georgian, the set (ILLUS.) 3,520.00

Pendant & earrings: enamel, pearl & 18k gold, the pendant w/a blue enamel center accented by pearls within a white enamel frame, highlighted by wire-twist & beadwork, w/matching earrings, Victorian, the set (minor dent to pendant drop) 1,650.00

Pin & earrings: moss agate & yellow gold, the oval pin & teardrop-shaped earrings each framed in a conforming twisted wire border, Victorian, the set 862.00

Pin & earrings: onyx cameo, the round onyx cameo pin depicting the profile of a lady within a pearl & gold frame, w/matching earrings, Victorian, the set 1,100.00

Pin, bangle bracelet, pendant earrings & two buttons: gold (15k) & garnet, each set w/a single carbuncle highlighted w/a wire twist & bead decoration, further embellished w/a tassel, the set 3,850.00

MODERN - 1920s - 1960s

The bright sparkling jewelry so popular from the 1920s through the 1960s has again come into its own. The baubles of rhinestones (faceted glass with a foil backing), colored glass stones and faux *pearls were affordable to a large segment of the population with prices ranging from very low — less than a dollar for a rhinestone dress clip — to well over $100 for a well-designed article utilizing sterling silver mountings set with fine Austrian crystal. Some pieces were in excellent taste, resembling fine jewelry, while others were flamboyantly fake with a multitude of rhinestones interspersed with brilliantly colored glass stones. Also see BAKELITE.*

Bracelet, Bakelite, bangle-type, black w/butterscotch polka dots 300.00

Bracelet, Bakelite, bangle-type, feather carved design, yellow, 1" w. 135.00

Bracelet, Bakelite, hinged, cream set w/multicolored rhinestones 40.00

Bracelet, diamond & platinum, Art Deco style, diamond-set double-row spaced by four collet-set diamonds accented w/foliate & X-links (some solder) 4,400.00

Bracelet, green & black onyx & 18k yellow gold, Retro style, the flexible band composed of gold oval cut-out links interspersed w/alternating green & black onyx sugar loaf shapes 575.00

Bracelet, cuff-style, lacquered metal, the wide band enameled in geometric devices & zigzags in Chinese red, black & gunmetal grey, incised "JEAN DUNAND," ca. 1925, 3⅜" w. 7,425.00

Bracelet, multicolored cabochon stones & pewter-tone metal, marked "Schiaparelli" 125.00

Bracelet, pearls & aquamarine crystal beads, three-strand, marked "Demario" 85.00

Bracelet, sterling silver, four swirled naturalistically engraved segments linked by alternating single & double dome links, impressed mark in oval "Spratling Silver" & a circle w/"Spratling - Made in Mexico," by William Spratling, 20th c., 8" l. 825.00

Brooch, 1¾" d. blue cabochon stone surrounded by two rows of clear rhinestones, marked "Pauline Rader," overall 2 x 2¼" oval 120.00

Brooch, diamond & emerald, Art Deco style, rectangular w/flower & bow design in diamonds at one side, the remaining sides set w/diamonds, accented in the four corners w/emeralds 1,650.00

Brooch, gold (14k bicolor), model of a butterfly w/stylized polished gold wings, the body set w/citrines & a tourmaline, diamond eyes & ruby antennae, Lester & Co., ca. 1940 ....825.00

Brooch, large baroque pearl surrounded by rhinestones, marked "Weiss" 60.00

Brooch, model of a hummingbird w/mother-of-pearl wings & red & turquoise enameled body, marked "Boucher" 85.00

Brooch, sterling silver & glass, modeled as an abstracted eye w/a brilliant gazing yellow center, designed by Sam Kramer, stamped "STERLING" & artist's monogram, ca. 1950, 3" l. 2,185.00

Clip, gold (18k yellow), modeled in the form of a stylized hand w/two bangles accented w/a white & yellow fringed glove, ca. 1940s 880.00

Cuff links, platinum, diamond & sapphire, square w/clipped corners, set w/single-cut diamonds & synthetic sapphires, in an engraved platinum mounting w/white gold findings, pr. 660.00

Cuff links, silver-gilt, octagonal, cast w/heads of ancient maidens, one Egyptian inspired, the other Nordic, one impressed "LALIQUE," ca. 1920s, ½" d., pr. 2,875.00

Earclips, opal & diamond, Art Deco style, each designed as a flower, centered by a black opal highlighted by rose-cut diamonds, in platinum mounts w/white gold backs, pr. (nick to one opal) 2,090.00

Earrings, Bakelite, hoop-type, brown w/yellow polka dots, pr. 95.00

Earrings, diamond & white gold, Art Deco style, chandelier-type, designed as stylized geometric pendant motifs, set throughout w/assorted full- and single-cut diamonds, pr. 2,415.00

Earrings, gold (14k yellow), designed as a fluted ribbon, ca. 1950s, pr. 330.00

Earrings, gold (14k yellow), flat discs w/reeded edges, w/screw-backs, hallmarked, ca. 1950s, pr 110.00

Earrings, lavender rhinestones, drop-type, marked "Weiss," pr. 35.00

Earrings, pearls & rhinestones, model of a snowflake, marked "Kramer," pr. 40.00

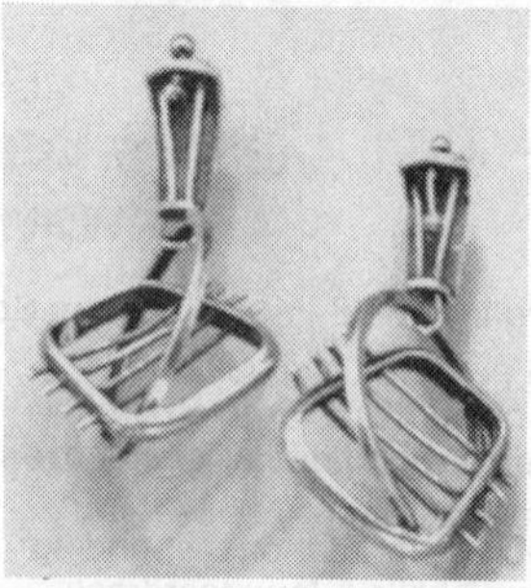

Sterling Silver Earrings by Wiener

Earrings, sterling silver, formed of circles & rectangles resembling mobiles, impressed "ED WIENER" & "STERLING," pr. (ILLUS.) 575.00

Jabot (two-section pin), diamond, ruby & platinum, Art Deco style, the curved upper portion set w/calibre-cut rubies, red spinels, round diamonds & straight baguettes over a heart-shaped section set w/round diamonds & inset w/rubies 2,750.00

Necklace, black glass beads w/silvery blue highlights, sterling silver clasp, five-strand, marked "Carnegie" 95.00

Necklace, champagne-colored pearls, ten-strand, marked "Miriam Haskell" 225.00

Necklace, choker-type, tiny gold-tone beads, marked "Monet" 17.50

Necklace, seed pearls & clear rhinestones, marked "Vendome," 14½" l. 75.00

Pendant, gold (14k yellow) & gems, depicting a lion w/a radiating frame set w/diamonds, citrines & rubies suspending pink tourmalines, baroque pearls, green beryls & onyx, ca. 1950s 550.00

Pendant, sterling silver, concentric faceted circles centered by a round amethyst cabochon, signed "Georg Jensen no. 143," made by Bendt Gabrielson, ca. 1950 ....825.00

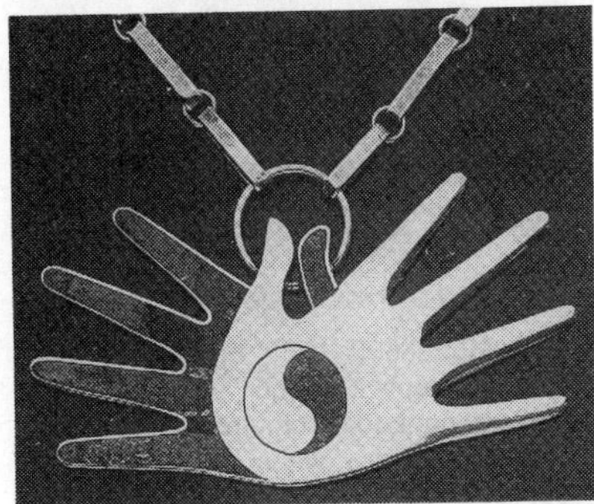

Sterling Silver & Turquoise Pendant

Pendant, sterling silver & turquoise, modeled in the form of two hands, the fingers extended at either side, one hand in silver, the other inlaid w/turquoise, suspended on a heavy silver link chain, pendant stamped "WILLIAM SPRATLING TAXCO MEXICO - 925," necklace 17" l. (ILLUS.) 1,380.00

Pin, antiqued sterling silver, solid spherical shape w/embossed flowers overall, marked "Joseff Hollywood," 2½" d. 225.00

Pin, Bakelite, deeply carved lovebirds, red 250.00

Pin, Bakelite, model of an anchor, red 85.00

Pin, Bakelite & rhinestones, model of a horse, red 95.00

Pin, blue rhinestones, model of a butterfly w/trembling wings, marked "Weiss," 2" 125.00

Pin, diamond & onyx, Art Deco style, designed as a circle w/a bow at the top, set w/diamonds, the inner curve of the circle further set w/French-cut onyx, platinum mounting 2,860.00

Pin, gold (14k pink) & ruby, free-form bow design w/ruby center, ca. 1940s 220.00

Pin, lavender rhinestones, model of a leaf, marked "Boucher" 65.00

Pin, Lucite, model of a hat, red 35.00

Pin, multicolored rhinestones, model of a Christmas tree, marked "Hollycraft," 1¾ x 2½" 48.00

Pin, purple rhinestones, model of a butterfly, marked "Eisenberg Ice" 175.00

Pin, rhinestones, model of a bow, marked "Jomaz" 35.00

Pin, silver-tone metal w/rhinestones, model of a flame, marked "Vendome" 12.00

Pins, sterling silver, large green stone body w/clear accent stones, model of a frog, marked "Coro," pr. 165.00

Pin, sterling silver, model of a bee, marked "Trifari" 175.00

Pin, sterling silver & marcasite, model of a peacock, marked "Alice Caviness" 50.00

Pin, sterling silver w/gold wash set w/three emerald green stones, model of a bouquet, marked "Corocraft Sterling," 3½" l. 65.00

Pin, vermeil (gold-plated sterling silver) & rhinestones, model of a flower, marked "Corocraft" 55.00

Ring, diamond, onyx & platinum, Art Deco style, solitaire-type w/central European-cut diamond surrounded by calibre-cut onyx, platinum mounting 1,760.00

Ring, jade, Art Deco style, set w/a central jadeite cabochon approximately 13.5 x 19.5 mm, flanked by three diamond baguettes, in a platinum mount 7,700.00

Ring, star sapphire, diamond & platinum, the oval cabochon pale blue sapphire retained by a fancy mounting w/graduating shoulders, set throughout w/round & marquise-cut diamonds 1,725.00

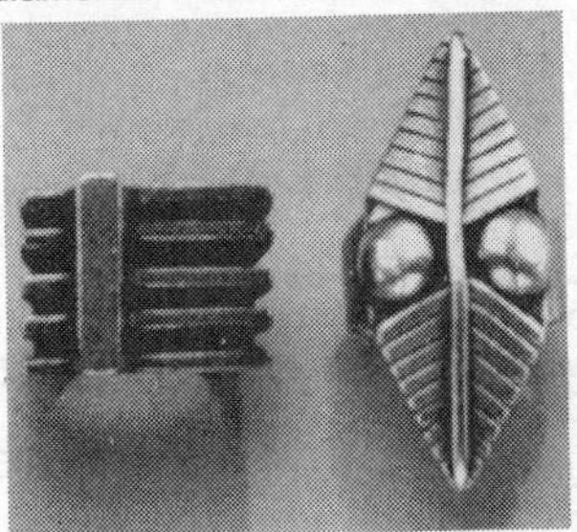

Sterling Silver Rings by De Patta

Ring, sterling silver, the face in the form of two opposing leaves centering two spheres, impressed maker's mark, Margaret De Patta, ca. 1938 (ILLUS. right)....................575.00

Ring, sterling silver, channeled top conjoined by a right-angle bar, impressed "STERLING" & "DE PATTA," Margaret De Patta, ca. 1948 (ILLUS. left)............................920.00

Scarf pin, Bakelite, carved in the form of a feather, rose pink........................38.00

SETS

Bracelet & earrings: sterling silver, hinged bracelet decorated w/dancing Orientals, matching earrings; marked "Siam Sterling," 3 pcs. 50.00

Bracelet & necklace: pearls, red crystal beads & rhinestones; marked "Trifari," 2 pcs.................................165.00

Bracelet & necklace: pearls & red, white & blue stones; marked "Eisenberg," 2 pcs...........................110.00

Bracelet, brooch & earrings: multi-colored rhinestones, brooch & earrings in the form of a crown; marked "Weiss," 4 pcs. 195.00

Necklace & earrings: bluish green mottled glass accented w/aurora borealis stones; marked "Hobé," 3 pcs. 225.00

Necklace & earrings: emerald green & clear rhinestones w/six strands on a gold mesh chain, matching drop-type earrings; marked "Hobé," 3 pcs. 135.00

Necklace, bracelet & earrings: six-strand gold-tone metal necklace & bracelet w/black cabochon clasps surrounded by red aurora borealis stones, matching earrings; marked "Hobé," 4 pcs. 150.00

Pin & earrings: large bluish grey rhinestones in the form of a question mark, matching earrings; marked "Ledo," 3 pcs.....................................75.00

Pin & earrings: pink enamel, model of a flower; marked "Original by Robert," 3 pcs. 85.00

JUKE BOXES

Rock-Ola Model CM 39, countertop model, 1939, original condition, w/new buttons...........................$2,950.00

Rock-Ola Model 1422, 1946.........................4,000.00 to 5,000.00

Rock-Ola Model 1484, 1960, wall mount-type.......................................900.00

Seeburg "Mayfair," 1939, 78 rpm, w/remote teardrop speaker..........4,000.00

Seeburg Model A, 33⅓ rpm (reconditioned).............................2,450.00

Seeburg Model 100-B, 1950-51 (restored) 3,900.00

Seeburg Model 201, 200 selection model, 1958 ....1,045.00

Seeburg Model W, "Hideaway," 1953...350.00

Wurlitzer Model 412, 1936, original condition 2,800.00

Wurlitzer Model 500, 1939 (restored).......................................5,600.00

Wurlitzer Model 600

Wurlitzer Model 600, 1938, the glazed front revealing twenty-four selections flanked by columns of illuminated plastics, within veneered case, restored (ILLUS.)................5,500.00

Wurlitzer Model 700, 1940, restored...5,000.00

Wurlitzer Model 750E, 1941 ....9,500.00

Wurlitzer Model 780, 1941...........................6,000.00 to 7,000.00

Wurlitzer Model 800, glass front, 24 selections, 1940...........................8,900.00

Wurlitzer Model 1050, early style cabinet, w/all optional equipment, 1973 (restored) 8,600.00

Wurlitzer Model 1100, 1948-49 (restored) ....6,500.00 to 7,500.00

Wurlitzer Victory Model, 1943-45.................10,500.00 to 11,500.00

KEWPIE COLLECTIBLES

Rose O'Neill's Kewpies were so popular in their heyday that numerous objects depicting them were produced and are now collectible. The following represents a sampling.

Rare Kewpie Figures

Bank, bisque, pink w/six playful white Kewpies, "Koin Keeper," 5 x 5½" (small chip) $175.00

Camera, "Kewpie Kamera," sold by Sears & Roebuck, 1915, mint in original box 300.00

Cake topper, bisque, Kewpie Huggers, 2¼" h. 200.00

Doll, celluloid, big side glancing eyes, movable arms w/starfish-type hands, 10" h. 195.00

Figure, bisque, Kewpie Doodle Dog, white animal w/black markings & blue wings, 4" h...........................2,000.00

Figure, bisque, Kewpie Governor, 2½" h...300.00

Figure, bisque, Kewpie "Hottentot," black finish, jointed at shoulders, original paper sticker reading "Gluck-kind," Germany, very large (ILLUS. left) 6,000.00

Figure, Kewpie "Little Traveler," w/Doodle Dog, 2¼" h., Japan...........400.00

Figure, bisque, Kewpie "Little Traveler," w/umbrella & bag, two stickers, signed on feet, Germany, 3½" h...350.00

Figure, bisque, Kewpie Soldier, labeled, 4" h. 600.00

Figure, bisque, reclining on stomach, labeled, 3" h. 450.00

Figure, bisque, seated w/elbows on knees, signed "Rose O'Neill," 4½" h...150.00

Figure, bisque, standing Kewpie w/jointed shoulders, 9" h. (ILLUS. right) 550.00

Figure, rubber, sitting position, signed "Rose O'Neill," made by Cameo 20.00

Figures, bisque, Bride & Groom figures w/original clothing, used on a wedding cake in 1920s, pr. 650.00

Figure group, bisque, two Kewpies reading book, signed, 3½" h. 850.00

Pillow cover, linen, depicts Kewpie, marked "Rose O'Neill" 145.00

Pitcher, Jasper Ware, blue ground w/white relief Kewpies, 3½" h. 275.00

Plate, china, decorated w/six Kewpies, marked "Royal Rudolstadt, Germany" 65.00

Tea set, child's: cov. teapot, cov. sugar bowl, creamer & six cups & saucers; porcelain, colorful groups of Kewpies on each piece, pink lustre trim, Germany, 15 pcs.........1,750.00

KITCHENWARES

Reading Hardware Apple Parer

Also see FIREPLACE & HEARTH ITEMS, METALS - IRON, and WOODENWARES categories.

Apple parer, cast iron, "Goodell Co.," pat. May 24, 1898 ....$80.00

Apple parer, cast iron, four-gear, "Reading Hardware Co., Reading, Pennsylvania," 1878 first patent date (ILLUS.) 70.00

Apple parer, cast iron, "E.C. Simmons Keen Kutter," 1890s 110.00

Apple parer, cast iron, "Sinclair, Scott Co., Made in U.S.A.," three-gear, w/heart motif on one wheel................65.00

Batter pitcher, jade green glass, Fire King...10.00

Beater jar, "Ladd Mixer No. 1," clear glass paneled & footed bowl base w/fitted metal top w/handle, early 20th c., 1 qt. 225.00

Butter churn, "Dazey No. 4," glass jar w/metal lid & mechanism & wooden paddles ....80.00 to 100.00

(Kitchenwares continued on page 708)

Patents for Kitchen Collectibles: Finding the Geniuses Behind It All

by Linda Campbell Franklin

Thomas Alva Edison defined genius as "1% inspiration and 99% perspiration." It's also the secret of successful invention, but just when we collectors begin a litany of thanks for the ingenious gadgets we love we notice that Edison also wrote "There is no substitute for hard work." Tracing inventions from the U.S. Patent Office's first century is profitable fun, although the search needs inspiration and perspiration in the same ratio as genius.

An early Patron Saint of Kitchen Substitutes for Hard Work (i.e. labor-saving devices) was Moses Coates, a mechanic from Chester County, Pennsylvania, who on February 4, 1803, got the first apple parer patent. No exact Coates models are known, but early hand-made wooden parers of that type bring $175.00 and up. Collectors also celebrate, among others, Horatio Keyes, David H. Whittemore, J.D. Seagrave, and E.L. Pratt of Worcester, Massachusetts, whose October 4, 1853 parer was probably the first practical parer with a mechanically-guided blade. Mass-production (and interchangeability) of cast-iron gears by 1850 set off a "furious battle to perfect the paring machine," says John Lambert, founder of Apple Parer Enthusiasts (see Research & Resources).

Many parer patents were granted in 1857, but with no corresponding leap in pie pan or pie trimmer patents. You do wonder if the All American Apple Pie didn't come of age in 1857, although a new recipe was needed in 1867, when nutmeg graters had *their* great year! In 1857, baseball was already the All American sport and the country was in turmoil over slavery, the 'Mormon War' took place and there was a financial panic. Lambert suspects that 1855-56s crop of really "great designs" (including the turntable parer) spurred others to "top that" if they could. In 1867, Reconstruction Acts were instituted in the aftermath of the Civil War, Charles Dickens visited the U.S., and Russia sold us Alaska.

By 1890, when there were over 100 parer patents, the market had a "shake-out." A few earlier designs including the Reading '78, Little Star, and White Mountain were left and continued to be featured for many decades in hardware stores and mail-order catalogs. A newish variation of the "White Mountain," Model #300, is still manufactured today by the White Mountain Freezer Company.

U.S. patent records reveal that a booming canning industry may have precipitated the decline of apple parer patents. Peeled apple segments were ready in a jiffy with a can opener (hundreds of *those* were patented, beginning with one in 1858). The canning industry itself, which began circa 1840, was the biggest labor-saving "device" between the wheel and 1930, when Clarence Birdseye began to freeze food in little boxes! Instead of having a parer clamped to the kitchen counter all fall (not to mention mechanical pineapple eye snips, tomato corers, corn shellers, raisin seeders, wheat berry grinders, peach parers, meat tenderizers, cabbage cutters, pea shellers, and the like) you could bypass picking, sorting, washing, and parboiling with boxes or tins of food ready to cook or serve straight out of the can!

Established in 1790 "to promote the progress of useful arts" the U.S. Patent Office granted 8,500 to 10,000 unnumbered patents through 1835; we have only sketchy information on many of them. From 1836 to 1890, it granted 443,986 numbered patents, 20,438 design patents, 11,136 reissues, and 18,774 trademarks. We laugh to read that in 1833 Patent Office Commissioner John D. Craig wanted to resign because he believed that everything "seems to have been done."

Within two years he was succeeded by the more optimistic Henry Ellsworth, under whom, starting in 1836, the burgeoning flood of worthwhile and worthless patents were numbered as granted, on Tuesday of every week.

For at least 60 years many shall-we-say undeserving inventions were patented. Even if well-intentioned, many neither claimed something truly new, nor even described something that would work, let alone save labor. Those silly if imaginative inventions, which patent collectors love to find and photocopy, didn't satisfy what Judge Learned Hand called a requisite for a valid subject for patent: "a new display of ingenuity." In an 1838 *Franklin Institute Journal,* the editor chastised one patentee thusly: "We cannot well conceive of a less promising affair than the foregoing, but things are not stopped in the Patent Office merely because they are trifling." It was relatively cheap and easy to get a patent, and there was a slim chance to make a fortune.

The *New York Times* reported on December 14, 1890 that:

> "2,400 women have secured patents but very few have made much money with them with the exception of the lady who was so fortunate as to hit upon the fluting iron ... The women who have secured patents have been mostly thrifty housewives, and their inventions have been generally in the nature of kitchen utensils and domestic articles."

That article was based on a Patent Office publication: an 1809-1888 chronological listing of "Women Inventors," giving names, patent numbers, inventions, and dates. Among women's patents we find cookstoves, ice-cream freezers, butter-workers, washing-machines, a combination of sofa and bathing tub, vegetable-graters, culinary boilers, and – beginning in the 1840s – a lot of "improvements on" mincing-knives, sieves, pie-tubes, bathroom racks, pastry-rollers, dish-washers, strawberry-hullers, flour-sifters, cake-stirrers, etc. The 1870s brought a spate of housekeeping helpers including a canning funnel, an egg-poaching pan, a fruit-fork, and an ever-useful "pantaloon tree," for drying those voluminous unmentionables. Sarah Sewell, Mark Centre, Ohio, patented a combined washing-machine and teeter or seesaw (#330,626), November 17, 1885. A lot of today's day-care centers could use one of those. Predominant in most years were inventions relating to sewing, clothing, corsetry and, as an indication of the hard work involved, laundering and ironing. Many women besides famous Mrs. Potts (the probable "fortunate" lady cited by the *New York Times*) got patents on sad irons and fluting irons.

Hundreds of women's patents, including domestic science ones, were little machines. Sarah Cooper, Morrisonville, Pennsylvania, patented (#196,743) an "improvement in apple quartering and coring machines" on November 6, 1877; Emma Orendorff, Delavan, Illinois, patented (#199,704) an "Improvement in apple-corers" on January 8, 1878. Another collecting specialty, eggbeaters, is represented by Sarah A. Ulmer, Portland, Maine, whose tin churn-like eggbeater (#224,117) was patented February 3, 1880. Ulmer's beater was manufactured and is in at least one collection. Scores of them may be out there. Others patentees included Katherine Livingood, Womelsdorf, Pennsylvania, eggbeater (#282,738) on August 7, 1883; Hannah Zephyrene Gibson, Oberlin, Ohio, eggbeater (#293,648), February 19, 1884; Eugenia Kilborn, Cedar Rapids, Iowa, eggbeater (#303,022), August 5, 1884; and Edith A. Marsh, New Albany, Indiana, eggbeater (#345,709), July 20, 1886. All are possible finds, especially in or near the patentees' hometowns.

An article in *House Furnishing Review* of January 1903 noted inventions recently viewed at the Woman's Department of the Mechanics' Fair in Boston. Described as "the most original and unique invention" was Philadelphian Lydia C. Sharples' bread-making machine. It was already being manufactured by The Scientific Bread Machine Co., Philadelphia. It took her three years, but Sharples made her own working patent model, of cardboard, tin and wood, and I bet her dyspeptic husband, for whom she wished to make digestible bread, was a happy man!

Probably the most inexpensive, tantalizing pursuit for collectors of cooking or housekeeping tools is patent research. It's so absorbing that more time can be spent researching the genius behind the tool than in finding it (or earning the money to buy it). One devoted patent collector is Don Thornton, whose remarkable eggbeaters compelled him to search out their inventors' thought processes as revealed in application specifications. Thornton says that "The *Official Gazette* is the history of America in the form of millions of illustrated short stories!" He recommends hanging out at a patent depository library, preferably one with patents on microfilm and also hardbound copies of indices and *Official Gazettes*, which have pictures and short descriptions of every patent, including design patents and trademarks. The good ones don't stop at 1900, either; Don has made great finds in 1940s and '50s *Gazettes*.

Pictures and claims help determine what if any parts are missing from a piece, or how something is supposed to work. And monetary value is affected by patent knowledge in other ways. About ten years ago I bought a humorously waggly sheet brass and iron wire eggbeater which screw-clamped to a shelf edge. I paid more than I'd ever paid before, but the dealer said it would have been more *if it had been a patented piece*. A few years later the patent drawing for it was found. Now the somewhat rough sawn edges of heavy sheet brass seemed a sign that it might be a production prototype, not a one-off piece. The value went up 300% and I sold it. Us patent junkies get hooked by suspenseful searches for patents for things we have, or think we have. At an auction I bought a cast-iron gadget billed as a "pea sheller." The only mark was "Dec. 4, 1855"; it had felt-covered wringer-like rollers, and a trough. Pop them ol' peapods, thought I. A year later, by chance, I was browsing the *Gazette's* precursor (see Research), the patent report for 1855, and there was a picture of my gadget! It's a knife scourer. The felt pads held scouring powder or pumice, and the trough caught the pasty mess of pumice and water. I don't know if the value went up or down, depends on which class of gadget is most sought-after. An embossed "patent" date on a gear may actually be the date an impatient inventor sent an application to Washington; or it may have been made up so that a gadget already in production would seem patent-protected. Always check a perpetual calendar to confirm that a date found on an object fell on Tuesday. As a break from the "hard work" we love serendipitous finds of funny-looking inventions found by browsing *Gazettes*. Lucky Don Thornton lives near a patent library where he searches a year's index, sees how interesting the drawing looks in the *Gazette*, puts a microfilm reel on a machine, spins the crank to his target patent, and makes a photocopy right then. Instant gratification!

You can also be a P.I. [Patent Investigator] by (A) using your own three-volume *Subject-Matter Index of Patents*, (B) consulting the *Official Gazette* of the Patent and Trademark Office (P.T.O.), at regional patent depository libraries, and (c) ordering photocopies of specific patents (typically you'll get a full-page drawing, plus one to four pages of inventor's claims). Order photocopies from the P.T.O. ($2.00 each, PS Center, CPK-1, Washington, DC 20231), or Rapid Patent Service, which provides libraries with sets of microfilmed patents (see Research). For years I got patent copies from the P.T.O. by sending an object's name and date, and sometimes the inventor. Now this germane information is called "narrative comment" by P.T.O., which will only fill an order by patent number. Your local library can advise you on the closest of over 50 depository libraries around the U.S. that have bound (or microfilmed) issues of the weekly *Official Gazette* from 1873 on, or others that have at least some years on microfilm.

Tracking down the thoughts and hopes of inventors no matter how deluded they were, is a hobby in itself. It's a form of virtual reality for the browser – what might have been, what could be out there. If you are feeling jaded about finding a rare apple parer, or an idiosyncratic eggbeater, or a brilliantly efficient can opener to add to your collection, consider taking an *Official Gazette* sabbatical!

Research & Resources

U.S. Patents: *Subject-Matter Index of Patents for Inventions Issued by the United States Patent Office from 1790 to 1873, inclusive.* Ayer Co. Pubns, POB 958, Salem, New Hampshire 03079, ISBN 0405077378, $158.00

Early Unnumbered U.S. Patents 1790-1836. Research Publications, 1980. Order from Rapid Patent Service, 1921 Jefferson Davis Hwy. Ste#1821-D, Arlington, Virginia 22202. 1-800 336-5010. For inventors, RPS does patent searches, patent drawings, etc. For collectors, if your depository library doesn't have the years you need, RPS does individual photocopies made off microfilm. They have other books & microfilm on patents, including design patents, pertinent if only the design of something (for example a fancy muffin pan or ice-cream mold) was patentable. Before writing or calling, try to make your query concise. They're friendly, but also very busy.

Journal of the Franklin Institute, Franklin Institute, Philadelphia, 1820s to 1850s. A large selection entitled "Mechanics' Register" disseminated details of American patents, often with pithy remarks. Editor Thomas P. Jones became Commissioner of Patents in 1828/29.

Report of the Commissioner of Patents for the Year _____ Arts and Manufacturers. Published as a report to the House of Representatives, about 40,000 copies were printed each year, most for the use of the Congressmen. I believe these bound, 2- and 3-volume reports started in the 1840s. One volume each year has illustrations; another has claim precis.

Official Gazette of the U.S. Patent & Trademark Office, Washington, D.C. Began 1873; continues today. Contains brief patent claims & pictures, plus indices of inventor, object and assignor. Individual volumes occasionally show up for sale at antiquarian booksellers.

British patents dating back to 1617 A.D. are represented by specifications and abstracts by the Science Reference & Information Service of the Patent Office Library. I've bought through antiquarian booksellers 115pp-150pp illustrated tri-annual "Abridgments" for Class 28, Cooking and Kitchen Appliances, Bread-making, and Confectionery patents. In 1900, the British Patent Office was preparing illustrated abridgements for some 146 classes, covering the period 1617 to 1854. I've never seen them. Reference materials at the Library are open to the public, but our kind of historical research cannot be undertaken by SRIS staff. For services available from the B.P.O., write Head of Marketing & Publicity, The Patent Office, State House, 66-71 High Holborn, London WC1R 4TP, England. By the way, it's frustrating to work with British patents because in their system, it's the *application* that gets the number! Copies of some British and other foreign patents can be ordered through RPS.

Books relating to invention:

Mechanical dictionaries: Various late 1800s early 1900s books with 1000s of mechanical drawings of gears, parts and motives to use in making or inventing a gadget or machine.

Patent process books: More or less detailed, about developing ideas, applying for patent, and defending a claim. One is Munn & Co.'s *The U.S. Patent Law: Instructions How to Obtain Letters Patent,* 1867.

Norman, Donald A. *The Psychology of Everyday Things,* Basic Books, 1988. Delves into the thinking behind gadgets.

Collectors' resources emphasizing patents: SASE to each for order info.

Fisher, Charles, *Hazelcorn's Price Guide to Old Electric Toasters, 1906-1940.* H.J.H. Publications, POB 1066, Teaneck, NJ 07666.

Franklin, Linda C. *300 Years of Kitchen Collectibles;* also *300 Years of Housekeeping Collectibles.* $25.50 each ppd USPS. From author: 2716 Northfield Rd., Charlottesville, Virginia 22901. I *don't* do patent searches.

Smith, Wayne. *Ice Cream Dippers. An Illustrated History,* 1986+. Well researched & illustrated. From author, Box 418, Walkersville, MD 21793.

Thornton, Don. *Beat This: The Eggbeater Chronicles,* 1994. Brand new book. From Off Beat Books, 1345 Poplar Ave., Sunnyvale, California 94087-3770.

International Society of Apple Parer Enthusiasts. For info: John Lambert, 117 E. High St., Mt. Vernon, Ohio 43050.

Periodical articles:

Amram, Fred. "Collecting Inventions by Women," *The Antique Trader Weekly,* March 30, 1988.

Ferguson, Eugene S. "Elegant Inventions: The Artistic Component of Technology." *Technology & Culture,* July 1978.

Levy, Marion. "There's Fascination in Apple Parers," *The Antique Trader Weekly,* October 24, 1979.

McAndrews, Glenn. Column "Patent Penning," in *AntiqueWeek,* 1990-1991.

ABOUT THE AUTHOR

Linda Campbell Franklin is a long-time kitchen gadget collector and researcher and her book, 300 Years of Kitchen Collectibles, *is a standard reference for collectors of kitchen appliances and utensils.*

Due to her busy schedule Ms. Franklin is not able to do specific patent research for others nor can she provide pricing information on pieces readers may own. Anyone writing her should include a stamped, self-addressed envelope for a reply.

ILLUSTRATIONS & PRICES

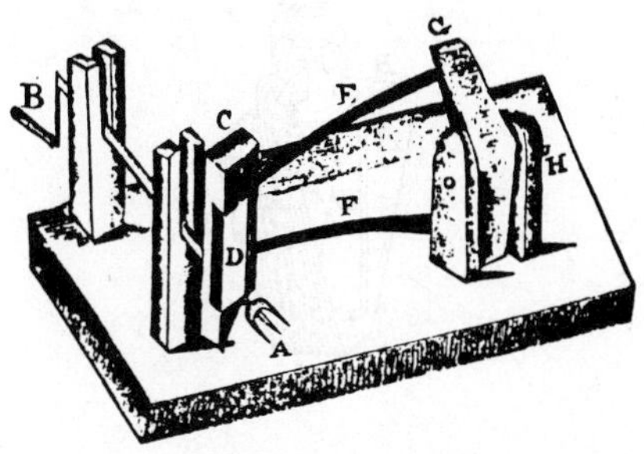

Fig. 1. Moses Coates unnumbered apple parer patent, Feb. 4, 1803 from 1804 book

The Domestic Encyclopedia, by Anthony Willich.

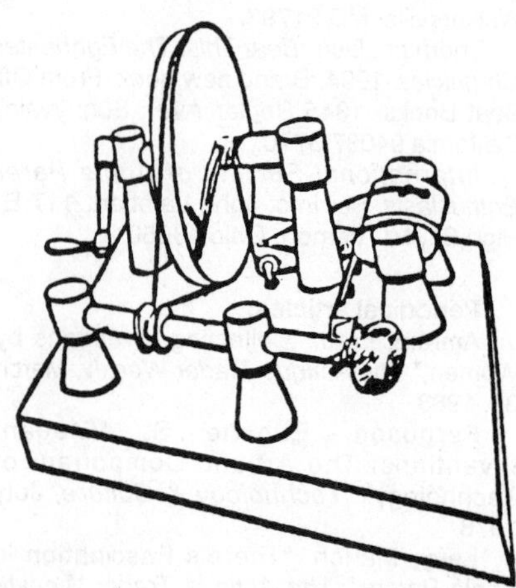

Fig. 2. G.H. Hubbard, Shelburne Falls, MA, bench-type apple parer & slicer, patent #16,517, Jan. 27, 1857. Red-painted turned wood, leather thong. John Lambert found one recently, so it was manufactured! ....**$300.00 to $400.00**

Fig. 5. Charles P. Shaw, Biddeford, Maine, pie trimmer & crimper, #30,592, pat'd Nov. 6, 1860. Wheel (a) is corrugated rather than serrated, to crimp. Probably wood and iron if it exists. **$100.00**

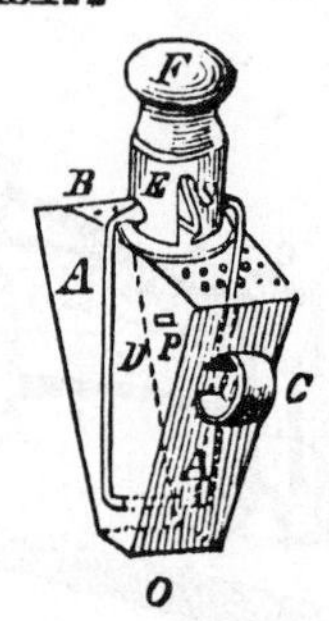

Fig. 3. Nathan Ames, Saugus, MA, nutmeg grater patent #18422, granted October 13, 1857.

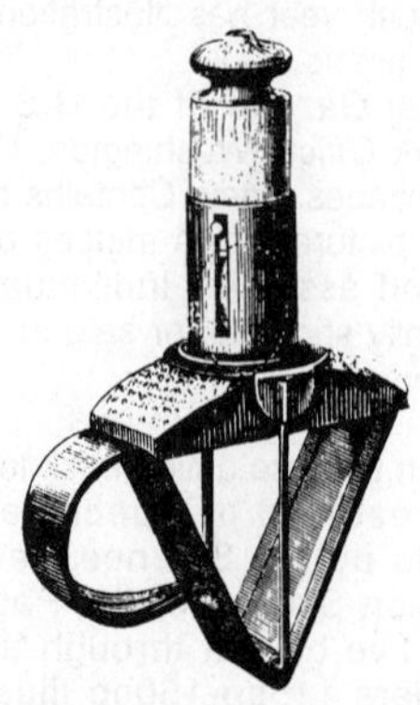

Fig. 4. Nutmeg grater, tin & wood, about 5" l., the Ames' patent. From an 1871 American Agriculturist. Slightly later ones have rounded oblong grip handles. . . . .**$125.00 to $150.00**

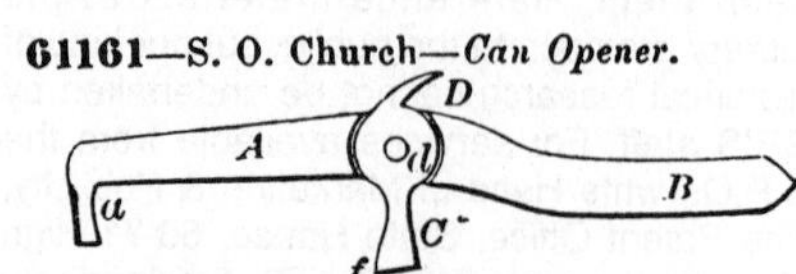

Fig. 6. S.O. Church, West Meriden, CT, assignor to himself and S.S. Wilcox. Can opener, #61,161, Jan. 15, 1867. This levered opener almost undoubtedly the origin of "church key" nickname for prying openers.

Fig. 7. A prize patent drawing - the silly side of patent collecting. Andrew Jackson, Jr., "Eye Protector for Chickens," pat'd June 16, 1903. Jackson claimed this as protection "from other fowls that might attempt to peck them. It will not interfere with the sight of the fowl."

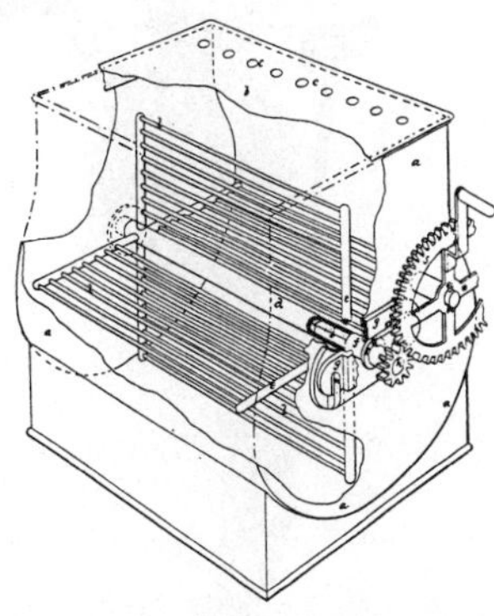

Fig. 8. Sarah A. Ulmer, Portland, Maine, mixer & eggbeater, #224,117, pat'd Feb. 3, 1880. Shapely tin container, earliest known tin container rotary mixer. Known in one collection, 7" h. . . . . **$275.00 - $300.00.**

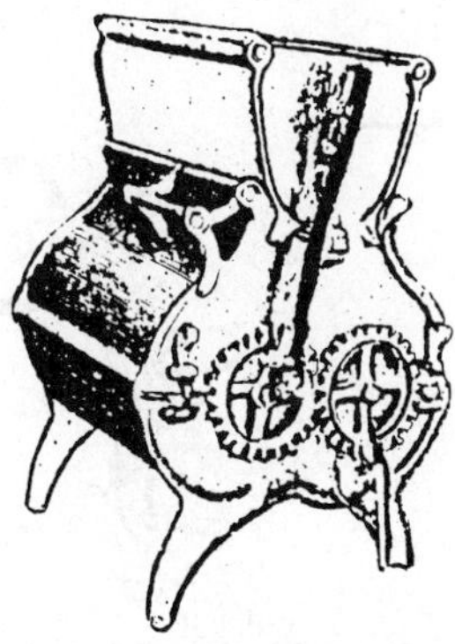

Fig. 9. Lydia C. Sharples, Philadelphia, bread-making machine, heavy tin, cast iron crank & gears. Pat'd 1902; manufactured by Scientific Bread Machine Co. (ILLUS. right) . . . . **$100.00 - $150.00.**

Fig. 12. Miller's screw-clamp, wig-wag egg-beater, cutout sheet brass, iron, wire, 9½" l.............................. **$325.00 - $400.00**

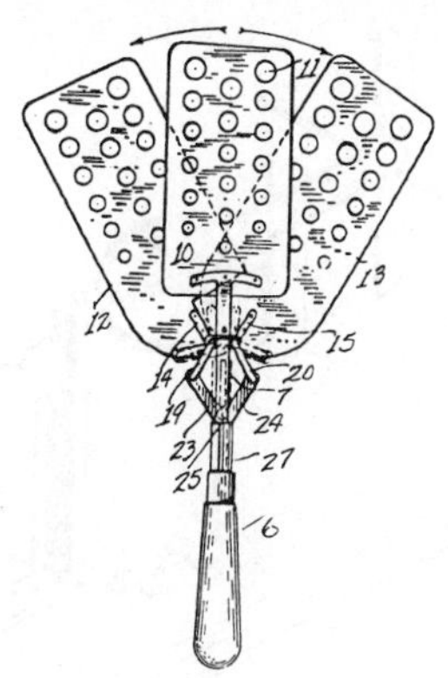

Fig. 10. Minnie Greene & Lois Udey, El Segundo, CA, "kitchen utensil" - expanding cake turner, tiller handle. Pat'd Dec. 8, 1936. Tin & wood, 12½" l., marked "Coradon" or "Gadget Mfg. Co." . . . . **$15.00 to $20.00**

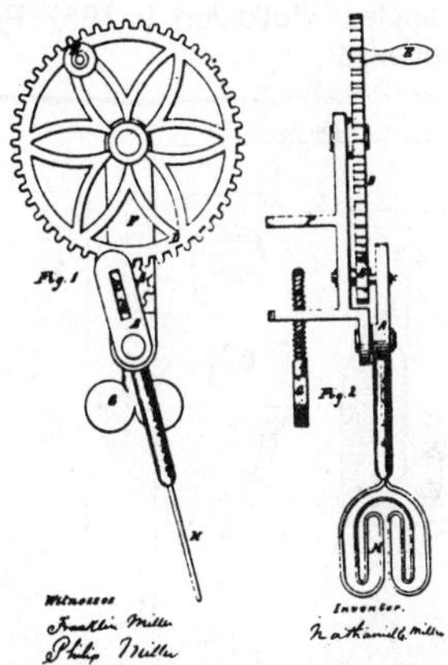

Fig. 11. Nathaniel C. Miller, Stroudsburg, PA. Eggbeater #138,094, pat'd Apr. 22, 1873.

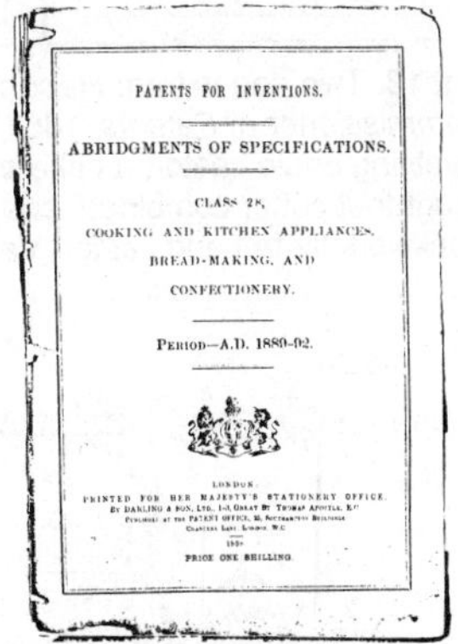

PATENTS FOR INVENTIONS.

ABRIDGMENTS OF SPECIFICATIONS.

CLASS 28,

COOKING AND KITCHEN APPLIANCES, BREAD-MAKING, AND CONFECTIONERY.

PERIOD—A.D. 1889-92.

LONDON:

PRINTED FOR HER MAJESTY'S STATIONERY OFFICE.

PRICE ONE SHILLING.

Fig. 14. Cover of British patent *Abridgments of Specifications* for Class 28 cooking patents, 1889-92 . . . . **$30.00**

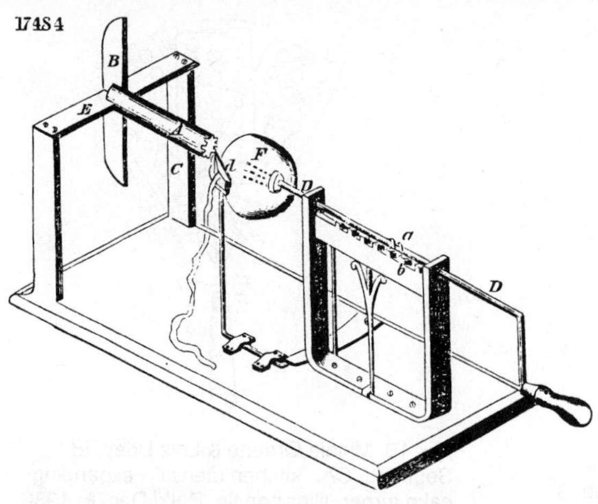

Fig. 15. C.F. Bosworth, Petersham, MA, #17,484, "Machine for paring, coring, and slicing apples." Pat'd Jun. 9, 1857. Probably does not exist.

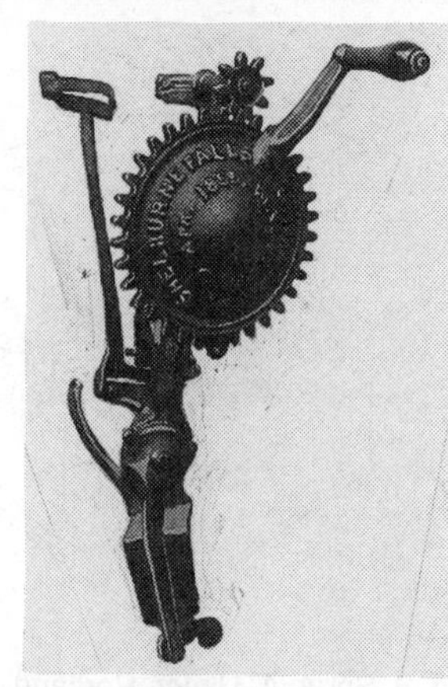

Fig. 21. Hubbard's "all-metal Maxam," Shelburne Falls. Says "Apr. 1855" on it, but pat'd Jan. 27, 1857. 11½" h. Very brittle iron, found usually with broken pieces, complete **$400.00**

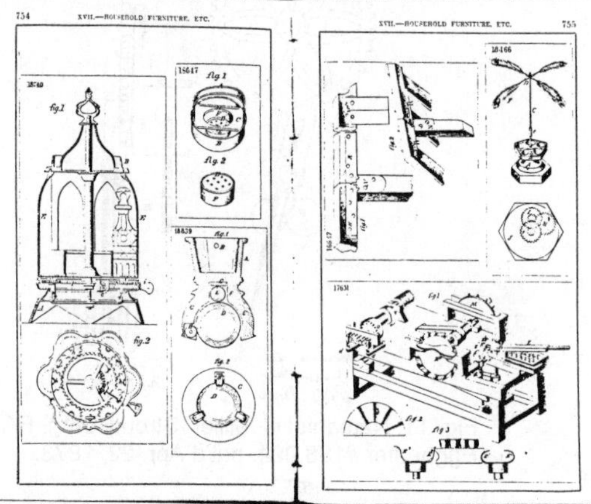
754 XVII.—HOUSEHOLD FURNITURE, ETC.

XVII.—HOUSEHOLD FURNITURE, ETC. 755

Fig. 13. Two pages from *Report of the Commissioner of Patents*, 1857, showing a revolving bottle castor, a cake-cutter & doughtnut cutter combined, and at far right a clockwork fly-fan and castor. Value of book **$300.00**

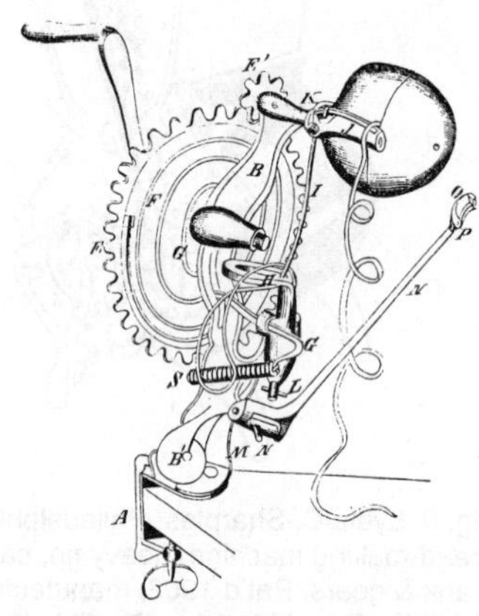

Fig. 20. G.H. Hubbard, Shelburne Falls, MA, #16,517, apple paring & slicing machine, known as the "all metal Maxam." Says "S.N. Maxam" on it, but pat'd Jan. 27, 1857 by Hubbard's widow. Maxam himself did hold a parer patent, from 1855. Note spiral on large concave cast iron gear.

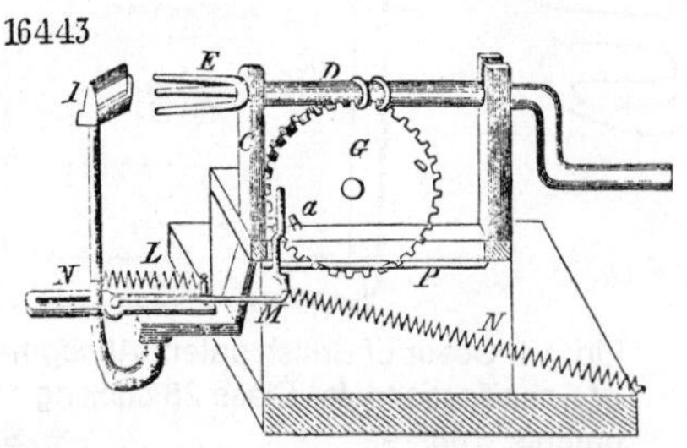

Fig. 16. J.O.M. Ingersoll, Ithaca, NY, #16,443, apple parer. Pat'd Jan. 20, 1857. Probably never made.(ILLUS. left)

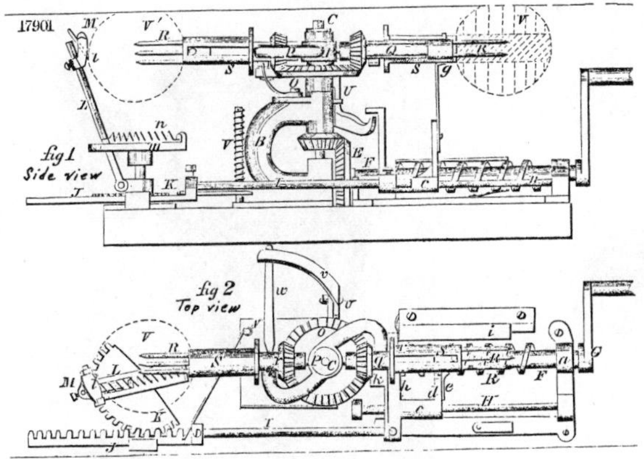

Fig. 17. P.W. Thickins, Brasher Iron Works, NY, #17,901, apple parer & slicer. Pat'd July 28, 1857. One collector believes he just missed getting part of one; the Iron Works address strengthens claim. Many parts, and easily broken.

Fig. 27. Browne's parer, close to the patent, but possibly modified. Cast iron, marked "Nonpareil" (without comparison), and "pat. pend. 1854," though probably patented in 1856. Earliest clamp-on and very rare. 8¼" h. . . . .**$500.00+**

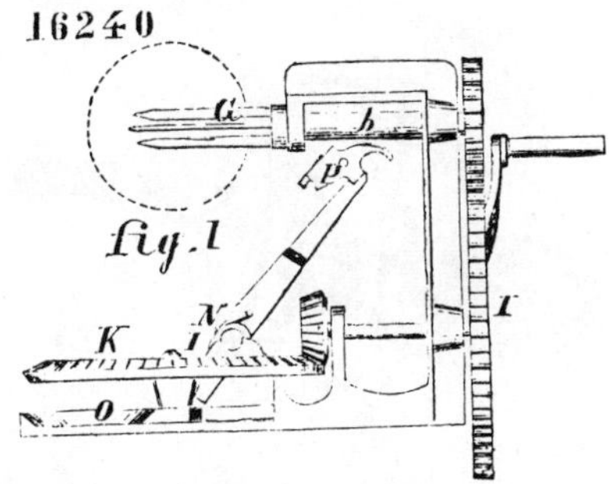

Fig. 18. Horatio Keyes, Leominster, MA, #16,240, apple parer. Pat'd Dec. 16, 1856. Two are known, one has partial paper label; cast iron very brittle **$400.00**

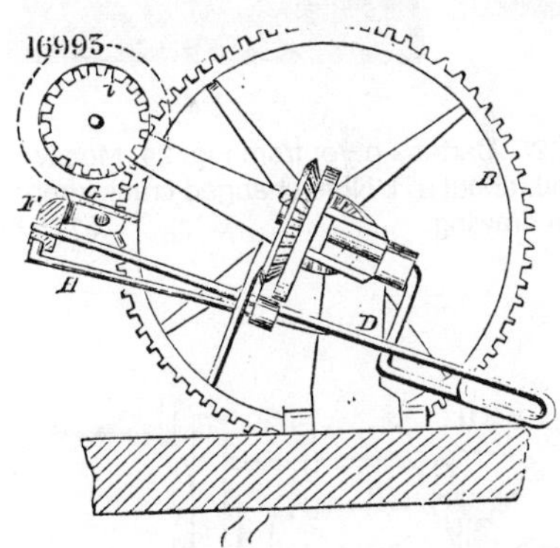

Fig. 22. J.J. Parker, Marietta, OH, #16,993, apple parer. Pat'd Apr. 7, 1857.

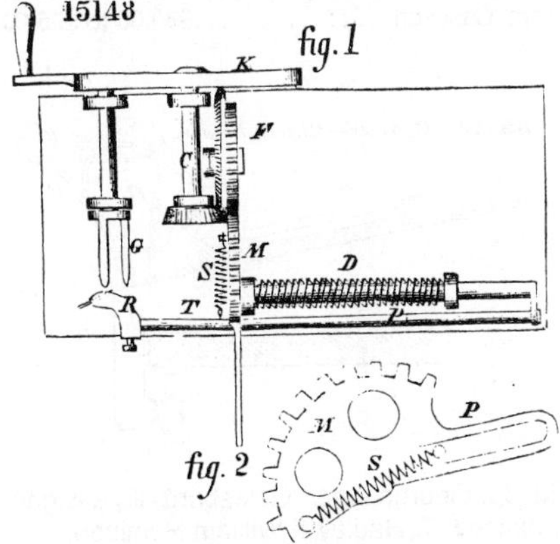

Fig. 19. J.D. Seagrave, Worcester, MA, #15,148, machine for paring apples. Pat'd Jun. 17, 1856. Known as the "Big Wheel Seagrave." **$150.00**

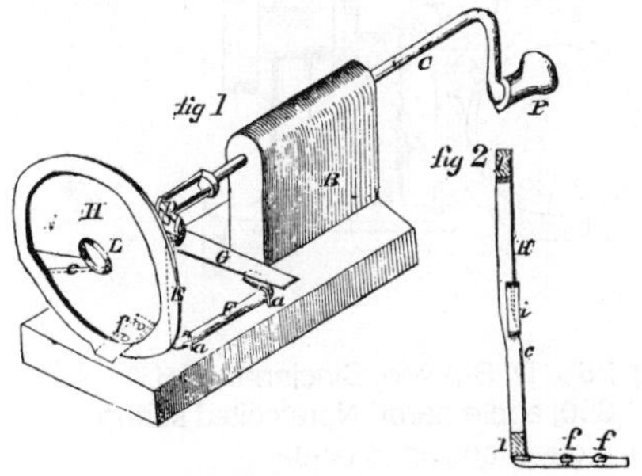

Fig. 24. C.P. Carter, Ware, MA, #15,603, apple parer. Pat'd Aug. 26, 1856.

Fig. 23. Parker's parer, shown in Fig. 22. Cast iron; note horseshoe motif of big 5½" diam. gear. . . . . **$400.00 to $500.00**

Fig. 28. Apple parer called by collectors the "ultimate Union," marked "Pat. Nov. 11, 1866 Pat. Apr. 6, '80," but really a David H. Whittemore, pat'd Nov. 20, 1866. Cast iron. . . . . **$300.00+**

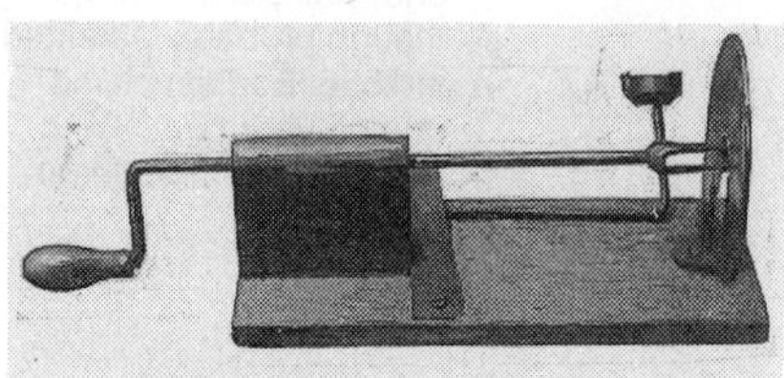

Fig. 25. Carter's parer from Fig. 24. Mostly wood, about 9" l. Note changed crank knob from drawing. **$125.00**

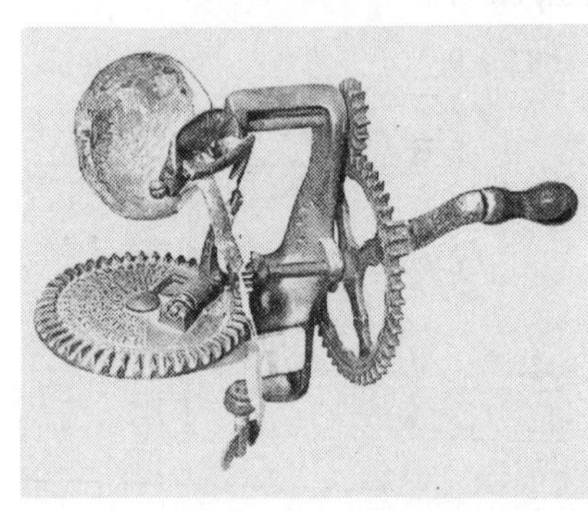

Fig. 29. First continuous turntable parer, pat'd by Horatio Keyes, Leominster, MA, Jun. 17, 1856 & Dec. 16, 1856. Mfd. by Lockey & Howland. "The parer for the million" - a million sold in the first 10 years. Cast iron. . . . . **$60.00 to $75.00**

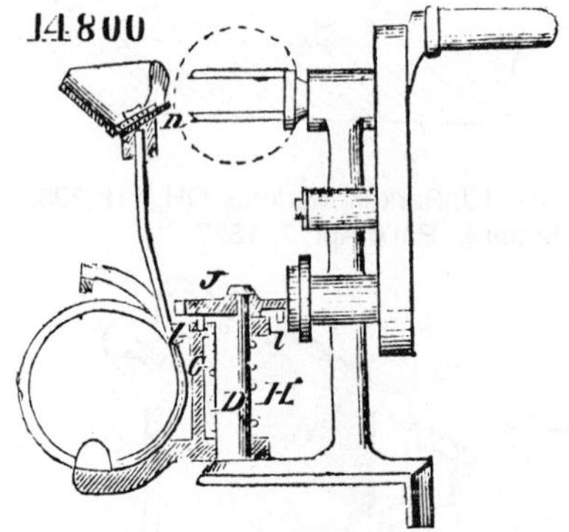

Fig. 26. J.D. Browne, Cincinnati, OH, #14,800, apple parer. Note coiled spring which gave tension to blade.

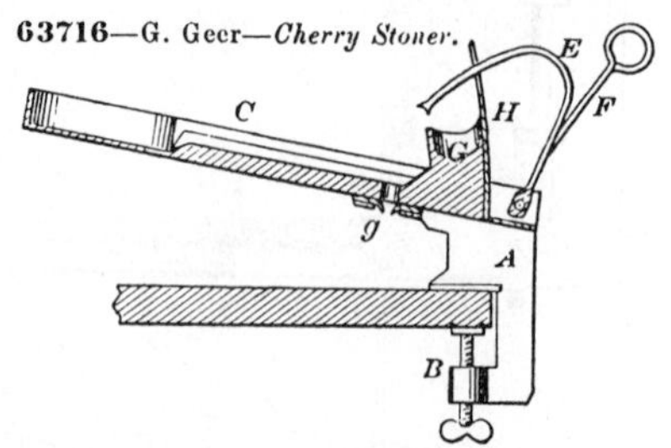

Fig. 30. George Geer, Galesburg, IL, assignor to himself, T. Hadley & William Hamilton, #63,716, cherry stoner, pat'd Apr. 9, 1867.

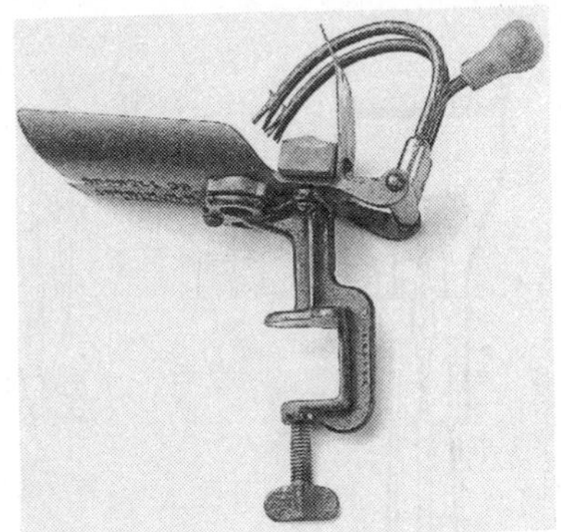

Fig. 31. "The Family Cherry Stoner," manufactured by Goodell Co., ca. 1895 version, but unmistakably the Geer patent with its curved forked plungers and tilted hopper pan. Cast iron, 8" h. . . . . **$35.00 to $50.00**

Fig. 34. Cherry pitter, manufactured by New Standard Co., Mt. Joy, PA, nickeled cast iron, 10" h. **$75.00**

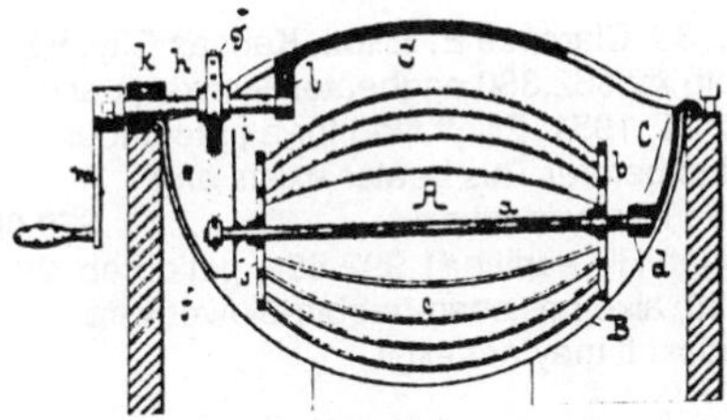

Fig. 32. Jacob L. Newcomer, Baltimore, MD, #318,786, eggbeater with a pan and iron frame. Pat'd May 26, 1885.

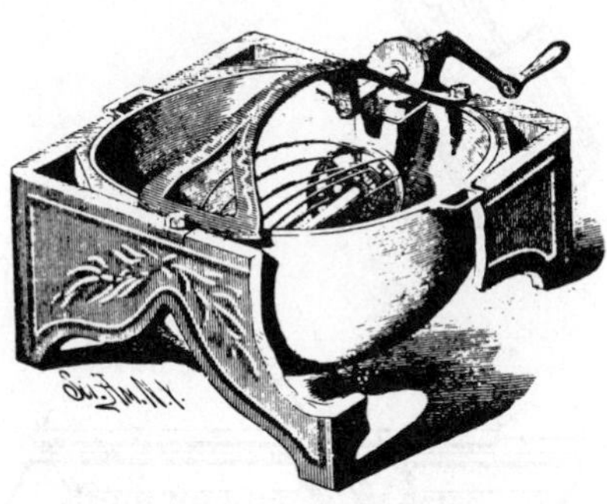

Fig. 33. "Newcomer's Improved Egg Beater," in cutaway view showing the inset (and removable) pan. Shows painted & decorated wooden box, and pinstriped iron brace. This picture from *Scientific American*, another great 19th century source for patent information. . . . . **$200.00 to $300.00**

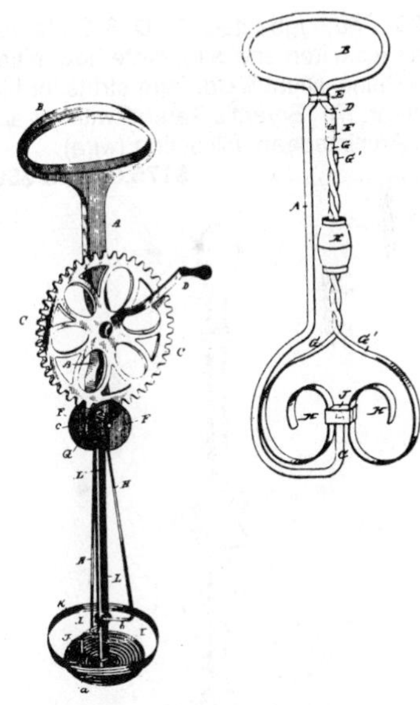

Fig. 35. Patent drawings for eggbeaters in the next picture. (Left) George H. Thomas, Chicopee Falls, MA, #331,662, pat'd Dec. 1, 1885. Note how gear was changed during manufacture. (Right) Charles A. Bryant, Wakefield, MA, #319,191, pat'd June 2, 1885.

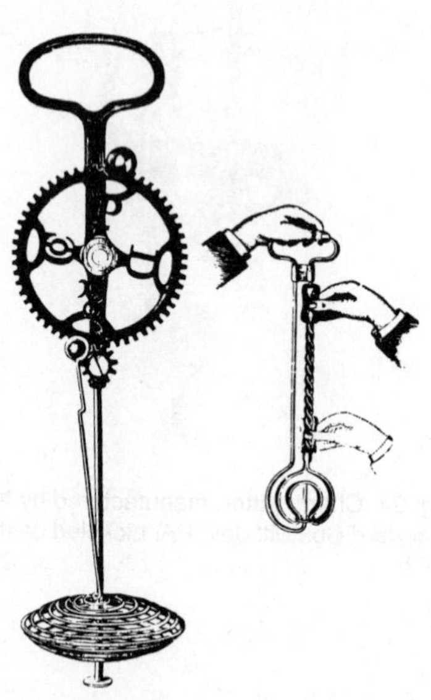

Fig. 36. Two eggbeaters: "P.D. & Co.'s" rotary turbine (cast iron and wire) Note how initials of the Paine, Diehl & Co. form struts for big cast gear. (R) "Bryant's Patent" with up-and-down Archimedean drill action (wire). ....**$175.00 and $30.00**

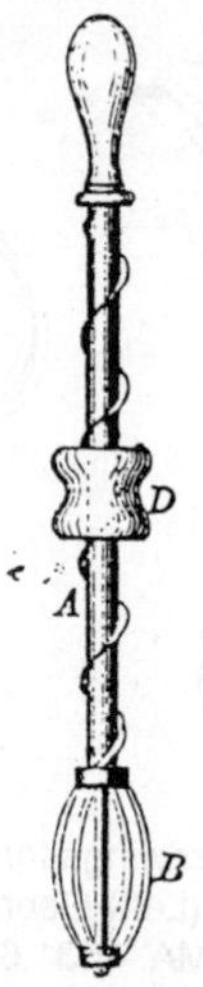

Fig. 37. Frederick Ashley, New York, NY, #28,047, eggbeater, pat'd May 1, 1860. This works on Archimedean principle, but the wooden (?) or iron (?) shaft has a wire wrapped around it. Early version of this type.

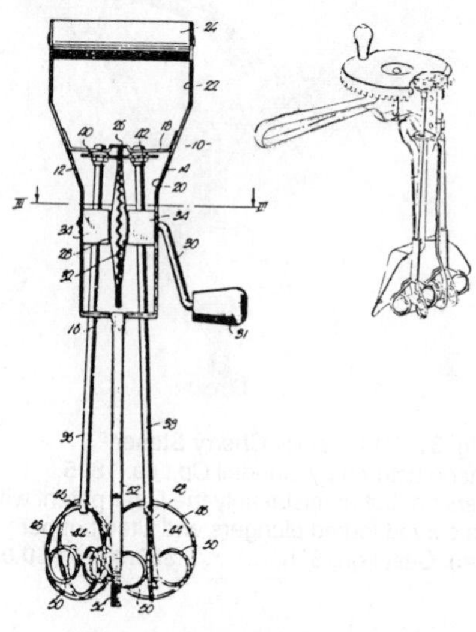

Fig. 38. Clarence E. Elliott, Kansas City, KS. (Left) #2,562,380 eggbeater & mixer, pat'd Jul. 31, 1951. Elliott filed for a patent four years before! This beater exists and looks nearly identical. ....**$30.00** (Right) His earlier #1,992,654, pat'd Feb. 26, 1935, also has soap-bubble-blower wire blades! It may not exist.

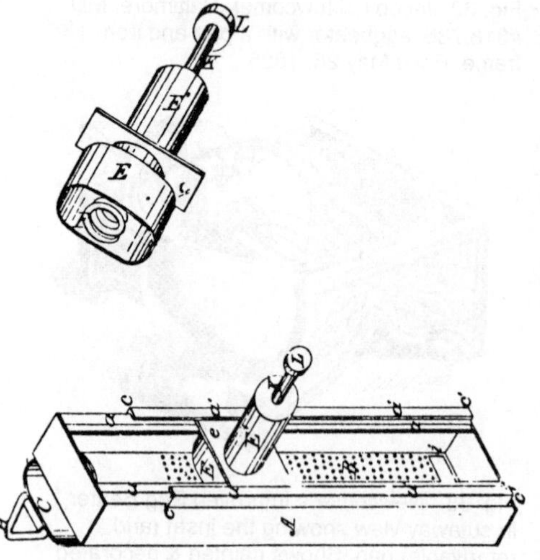

Fig. 40. Richard H. Chinn, Washington, DC, #66,675 nutmeg grater, pat'd Jul. 16, 1867. This one exists, but with no marks. All tin, sliding, spring-loaded hopper, 6¼" l. .**$200.00**

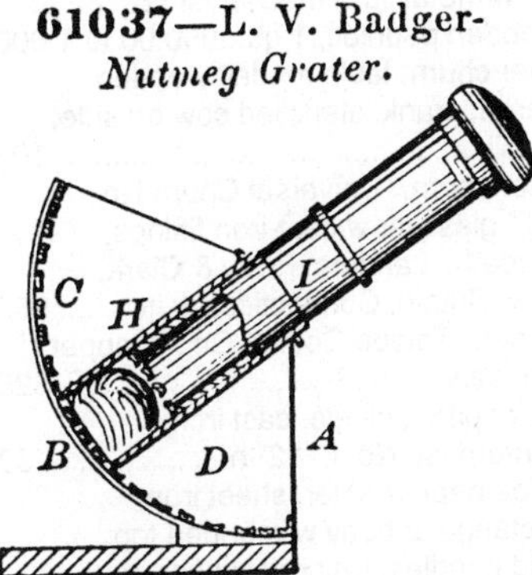

Fig. 41. L.V. Badger, Chicago, IL, #61,037 nutmeg grater, pat'd Jan. 8, 1867. Resembles one in Fig. 3, but grating surface is on inside of curve.

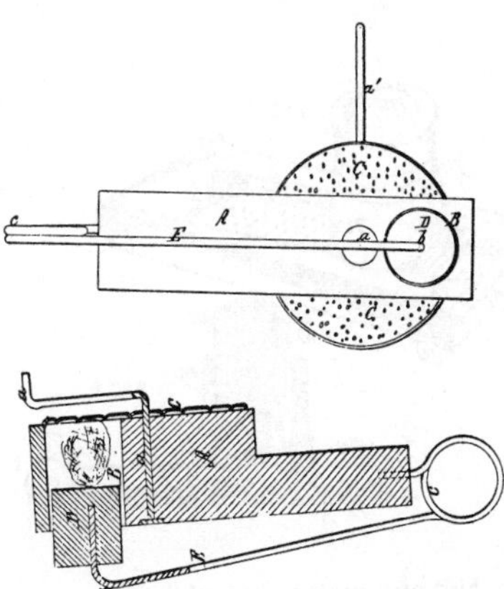

Fig. 42. R.W. Whitney & Joseph P. Davis, South Berwick, ME, #67,010 nutmeg grater, pat'd Jul. 23, 1867.

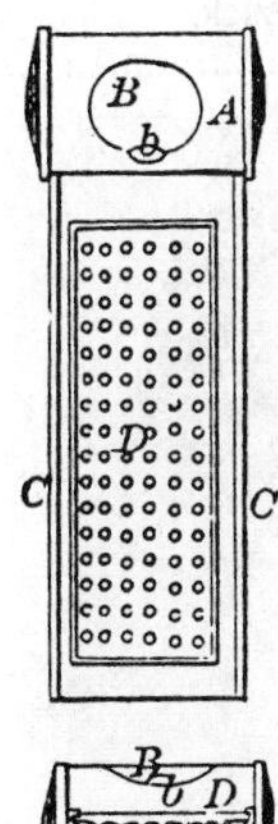

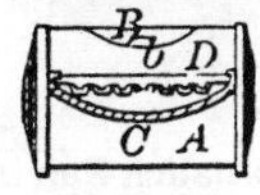

Fig. 39. William Bradley, Lynn, MA, #61,511 nutmeg grater, pat'd Jan. 29, 1867. The grating plate could be "slipped out for renewal."

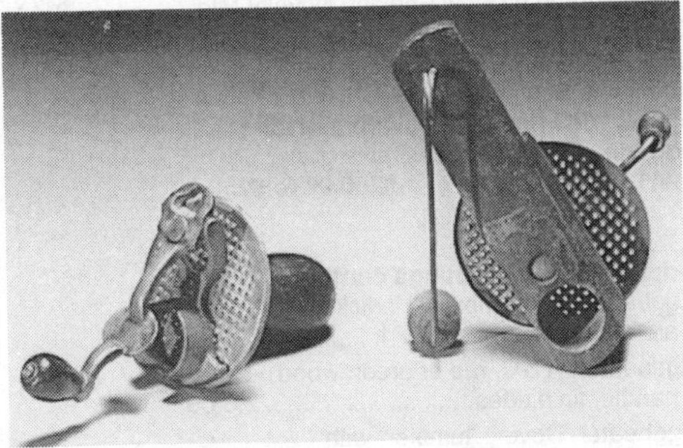

Fig. 43. (Right) Whitney & Davis grater. Tin, wood and wire, 5⅛" l. **$125.00**
(Left) "GEM" nutmeg grater, wood, iron, tin, mfd. by Caldwell Mfg. Co., Rochester, NY. Advertised in 1907 but probably modernized modification of much earlier rotary patent.

Additional Price Listings:

Apple parer, corer, slicer, "Little Star," cast iron clamp-on ....$35.00 to $50.00

Apple parer, homemade wooden, mid-19th c., with steel blade 150.00

Apple parer, White Mountain, turntable-type, cast iron 45.00

Bread machine, Universal, tin "bucket," cranked blades 100.00

Cherry pitter, three legs, Scott Mfg. Co., cast iron, 12" l.............85.00 to 125.00

Cherry pitter, four legs, end "spout," cast iron & often mounted to board, 10½" l. ....100.00 to 125.00

Cherry pitter, "New Standard," tinned or nickeled cast iron, cranked, 10" h..................................35.00 to 50.00

Cream whip, "Fries," tin churn-like vessel, 10½" h. ....100.00 to 125.00

Eggbeater, "Aluminum Beauty," cast & sheet aluminum, 10¾" l. 30.00

Eggbeater, "Taplin's Light Running" center drive, nickeled iron, wood, 12¼" l. 60.00

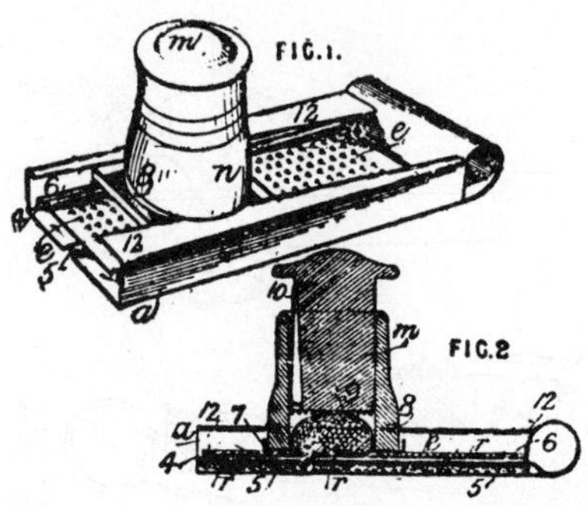

Fig. 44. Nutmeg grater: One of the big mysteries still needing research! Go to it. Looks like T.L. Holt's patent of March 18, 1889, and some are so marked, on top of the wooden nutmeg container. Advertised as the "Monitor" (reference to Civil War warship), manufactured by New England Novelty Mfg. Co., Boston. Later advertised as "The Unique," by Steel Edge Stamping & Retinning, Boston. Also looks like A.J. Boult's Apr. 1, 1889 *British* patent, from which this drawing comes. Very desirable grater, 4½" l. . . . . **$200.00 to $250.00**

Additional Price Listings continued:

Eggbeater, drink mixer, "Horlick's," archimedean action, 9½" l. 28.00

Eggbeater, A & J, red or green wood handle, tin blades................................6.00

Eggbeater, Dover, "tumbler" with small blade "ball" at end of long blades, tin & cast iron, 10¾" l. 55.00

Ice cream scoop, "Gilchrist" #31, squeeze action, nickeled brass, 10½" l. ....75.00 to 100.00

Ice cream disher of "key scraper" type, conical, tin & iron. Most are.......45.00

Meat grinder, "Enterprise #12," tinned cast iron, with accessory blades 40.00

Meat & food chopper, "American" or "Starrett", pat'd 1865, #1 or 2, 10" diameter revolving container with cast-iron "derrick"-like works ....150.00 to 200.00

Raisin seeder, cast iron, ornate frame & stand with three legs, 6½" h. 200.00

Sausage stuffer, "Stow's" lever action, cast iron on board 150.00

(End of Special Focus)

(Kitchenwares continued from page 695)

Butter churn, "Dazey No. 10," glass jar w/metal lid & mechanism & wooden paddles, 1 qt....950.00 to 1,000.00

Butter churn, table model, wooden barrel, crank, stenciled cow on side, small 195.00

Butter churn, "Universal Churn No. 15," glass jar w/cast-iron fittings, made by Landers, Frary & Clark, New Britain, Connecticut, 1 qt. 950.00

Canner, "Toledo Cooker Co.," Copper Conservo, 1907 ....325.00

Cherry pitter, single, cast iron, "Enterprise No. I," 12" h. 32.50

Coffee bean roaster, sheet iron, rectangular body w/rounded top, end handles, cylindrical hopper, hand crank, 13" h. 38.50

Cornstick pan, cast iron, seven-ear, "Griswold No. 262," 4¼ x 8½"............75.00

Cornstick pan, cast iron, seven-ear, corn or wheat stick,"Griswold No. 272," corn or wheat stick, 5¾ x 13¼"..68.00

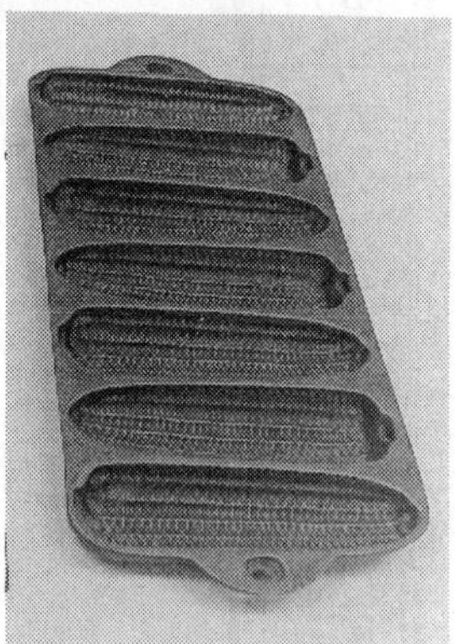

Griswold Cornstick Pan

Cornstick pan, cast iron, seven-ear, "Griswold Crispy Corn Sticks, No. 273," 5¾ x 13¼" (ILLUS.) ....75.00 to 95.00

Cornstick pan, cast iron, seven-ear, "Griswold No. 283," 7⅝ x 14"...........250.00

Cornstick pan, cast iron, seven-ear, "Krusty Korn Kob - Tea Size - Wagner Ware, Sidney Ohio - No. 1317," 4¼ x 8½"........................100.00

Cornstick pan, cast iron, seven-ear, "Krusty Korn Kob, -Jr., Wagner Ware, Sidney, Ohio, Pat'd. July 6, 1920," 4¼ x 8½"................75.00 to 100.00

Cream whipper, tin, table top model, on legs w/top & handle, 6" h. plus legs 90.00

Cup & saucer, turquoise blue glass, "Fire-King" logo, Anchor Hocking Glass Co. 6.00

Dipper, round brass bowl w/a long, slender, flattened wrought-iron handle, bowl 2½" d., handle 8" l.........71.50

Dipper, round brass bowl w/long slender flattened & slightly flaring wrought-iron handle, bowl 2½" d., handle 9" l. 99.00

Dipper, brass & wrought iron, small brass inlay in handle, 14¾" l. 71.50

Dipper, brass bowl w/long well-shaped wrought-iron handle, 2¾" bowl, overall 17¼" l. 93.50

Dish covers (flyscreens), wire screen, w/turned wood finials, nested set of 5, 6½" to 9½" d., the set..................185.00

Dough scraper, wrought iron, 4¼" w. 33.00

Dutch oven, cov., cast iron, "Griswold No. 11" 450.00

Dutch oven, cov., cast iron, "Griswold No. 12" 98.00

Egg beater, cast iron, "Cyclone," Browne Mfg. Co., Kingston, New York, perforated flanges, patent dated 1901, 11¾" l. 125.00

Egg pan, cast iron, "Griswold No. 562" 75.00

Flour sifter, table top model, pine, "Blood's - Pat. 9/17/1861," 9 x 9 x 13" 375.00

Food chopper, kidney-shaped metal blade mounted w/a cylindrical bone & composition-inlaid black & white handle, 19th c., 7" h. 357.50

Food chopper, graniteware, "Chopette," green..............................27.00

Food chopper, "Keen Kutter No. 12" 45.00

Food chopper, "Universal No. 3" 11.00

Food cover, clear blown glass, w/folded rim & applied handle, 8¼" d., 7" h. 165.00

Food grinder, cast iron, "Keen Kutter No. 11" 15.00

Fork, wrought iron, two-tine, simple handle w/hanging hook, marked "J. Metzger," 18¼" l...............................126.50

French waffle iron, cast iron, restaurant-type, "Griswold No. 7," ca. 1890s 750.00

Fruit press, cast iron & sheet metal, "Enterprise Mfg. Co. No. 1," patented September 30, 1879 ....65.00

Grater, punched tin & wood, the half-round tin cylinder w/fine punched holes mounted on a pine backboard w/a round disc handle terminal punched w/a hanging hole, old finish, 13½" l. 137.50

Griddle, cast iron, "Griswold No. 6" 39.50

Griddle, cast iron, "Griswold No. 9," w/handle 50.00

Jagging wheel, carved bone, serrated wheel fitted into a ring-turned shaft w/a rounded handle tip, 19th c., 6½" l. (minor imperfections) 302.50

Jar, cov., clear blown glass, slender w/straight sides, tin lid, 3½" d., 6¾" h. 192.50

Juice reamer, caramel glass, marked "Sunkist" on the side 265.00

Kraut (or cabbage) cutter, pine, heart cut-out crest & chip-carved bottom edge, old red paint, 21¼" l. 330.00

Lemon squeezer, cast iron, "Arcade No. 2," w/ironstone insert..................85.00

Meat fork, wrought iron, three-tine, long & slender flattened handle w/small loop at end, handle stamped "G.D. Miller," 25" l. 77.00

Mixing bowl, splash-proof, turquoise blue glass, "Fire-King," Anchor Hocking Glass Corp., 8½" d...............15.00

Mug, jadite green, "Fire King" 6.00

Nutmeg grater, "Dazey No. 867" 85.00

Patty mold, cast iron, "Griswold No. 72" 50.00

Pitcher, utilitarian crockery, Grape Cluster in Shield patt., green & cream, 8" h.....................................125.00

Popover pan, cast iron, "Griswold No. 10 948" 28.00

Poppy seed grinder, brass hopper, wooden handle, marked "Czechoslovakia" 100.00

Potato ricer, porcelain...........................75.00

Early Rack & Utensils

Rack & utensils, wrought iron, the rack w/twisted & arched upper frame centering the large initials "M - B" above a flat bar w/four hooks suspending a ladle, skimmer, spatula & two-tine fork, possibly Pennsylvania, late 18th - early 19th c., overall 16" w., 27½" h., the set (ILLUS.)............................1,840.00

Refrigerator dish, cov., square, amber glass, Federal, 4 x 4" 8.00

Salt & pepper shakers, milk white glass w/red dots, Hocking Glass Co., pr. 25.00

Skillet, cast iron, "Griswold No. 3," small emblem....................................18.00
Skillet, cast iron, "Griswold No. 4" 45.00
Skillet, cast iron, "Griswold No. 12," large emblem 105.00
Skillet, cast iron, "Wagner No. 3"..........19.00
Spatula, wrought iron, well-shaped blade, 16" l. (minor edge damage on blade) 66.00

Early American Wafer Iron

Wafer iron, cast iron, scissor form w/projecting wrought-iron handle, each circular mold half cast on the interior w/the seal of the United States w/a spread-winged American eagle & shield, the eagle clutching arrows & an olive branch, sixteen stars above a banner inscribed "E Pluribus Unum," 1796-1803, overall 29" l. (ILLUS.) 1,725.00
Waffle iron, "Cruso No. 8," embossed w/rooster, H.S.B. Co. 115.00
Waffle iron, cast iron, "Stover No. 8," w/stand 45.00
Waffle iron, cast iron, "Wagner Ware No. 8," square, w/stand, patent dated "Feb. 22, 1910" 110.00

KNIFE RESTS

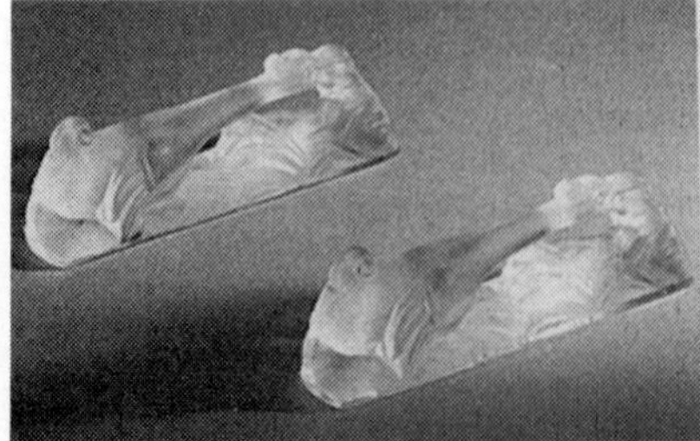

Frosted Glass Knife Rests

Cut glass, cranberry, pointed ends, 3¼" l., pr. (small chips) $121.00
Glass, "Libellule," triangular prism molded w/a tail & the impression of a dragonfly in flight, frosted finish, each inscribed "Lalique," introduced 1919, 3⅞" h., set of 5.......................920.00
Glass, molded as a stylized swan w/outstretched neck, frosted grey, each molded "COLETTE," ca. 1925, chip to one, 4" l., set of 6 (ILLUS. of two) 920.00
Silver plate, bird in hoop 50.00
Silver plate, figural, each in the form of a different stylized elongated animal or bird, impressed "Gallia," w/original box, 20th c., each 3¾" l., set of 12 ....4,830.00
Sterling silver, models of racing horses, Art Deco style, 3½" l., pr. 75.00

KNIVES

Knives of all types are collectible today but especially popular are better quality pocket types from the late 19th and early 20th century. Even more modern knives by such makers as Case and Remington are sought after. Overall condition of the knife's blade(s) and handle are very important in pricing with mint, unsharpened knives bringing premium prices. Also see ADVERTISING ITEMS.

Advertising, "Tuf Nut" pocketknife, two-blade, engraved "Demand Tuf Nut Work Clothes" $25.00
Case two-blade pocketknife, No. 6207, "Mini Trapper," 3½" l. closed 150.00
Colt, three-blade pocketknife, No. 703, ca. 1970 ....49.00
Hayward Empire two-blade pocket-knife, gold-filled handle engraved w/"BPOE Elks" 45.00
Keen Kutter four-blade pocketknife, No. K357, pearl handle, 3½" closed (weak back spring)..........................95.00
L & K four-blade pocketknife, gentleman's-type, gold handle w/engraved serpent, Germany, 3" l. (some wear) 65.00
Marbles Arms folding hunting knife, stag handle, large 650.00
Remington two-blade jackknife, No. R675...75.00
Remington one-blade jackknife, No. R2075...135.00
Remington two-blade penknife, No. R6854, pearl handle....................60.00
Remington scout knife, No. R-S3333, bone handle, acorn shield.................75.00

Richards, Sheffield pipe smoker's knife, two silver blades & tamping block on end 16.50

Winchester two-blade pocketknife, No. 2115, pearl celluloid handle, 2⅞" l. closed 110.00

LACQUER

Chinese Cinnabar Lacquer Box

Most desirable of the lacquer articles available for collectors are those of Japanese and Chinses origin, and the finest of these were produced during the Ming and Ching dynasties, although the Chinese knew the art of fashioning articles of lacquer centuries before. Cinnabar is carved red lacquer.

Armchairs, the arched scroll-pierced back w/a serpentine crestrail above the oval seat, raised on square tapering legs w/incurved scrolled toes ending in ball feet, the whole painted w/lotus blossoms w/trailing foliate scrolls in tones of iron-red, black, green & yellow on a brown ground, Chinese Export, 19th c., pr...$1,925.00

Box, cov., cinnabar, the cover w/a circular medallion containing a jardiniere filled w/coral & the babao beneath a chun character centered w/a medallion of Shoulao & flanked by a pair of dragons amid clouds, the cover & box w/four reserved figures in landscape settings, on a diaper ground w/bands of ruyi scrolls at the rims, all carved through the red, yellow & green layers, chips, cracks, repairs, China, 18th c.,12¼" d. (ILLUS.) 1,725.00

Document box, rectangular, comprising two stacked trays & a cover, the whole supported on four squat cabriole legs, the top & sides w/a black rectangular panel set on a placed aogai ground, each panel featuring subtle overlapping circles in gold & centered w/a red lacquer mon, 19th c.,11 x 13" (chips, cracks & losses)...........................1,380.00

LAUNDRY ROOM ITEMS

The "good old days" weren't really all that good when Monday "wash day" and Tuesday "ironing day" came around. There was a lot of hard work involved in scrubbing clothes on the washboard and smoothing out the wrinkles with the hefty flatiron or "sadiron" (sad=heavy). Today collectors can look back with some nostalgia on those adjuncts of the laundry room, curious relics of the not too distant past.

IRONS

Charcoal iron, cast-iron base, wooden handle supported by ornate wrought-iron holder, bird finial, worn black paint, 8" h. (pins holding handle damaged)............................$60.50

Electric iron, "Hotpoint," three-settings, weighs 15 lbs., last patent 1924...60.00

Electric iron, "Pyrex," clear glass w/cobalt blue bottom........................800.00

Electric iron, "Sunbeam," patent dated "Dec. 22, 1924," small, in handled case 40.00

Fluting iron, cast iron, "Star," by American Machine Co., crank handle & clamp, black paint w/red & gold stripes, w/two slugs (some paint wear) 140.00

Goffering iron, iron & brass, a bullet-shaped brass cylinder at the top on a ring-turned iron standard w/a tripod base w/arched legs, good detailings, 19th c., 12¾" h................110.00

Sadiron, "Downs & Co. No. 2" 50.00

Sadiron, "Sensible No. 4," 4" l. 22.00

Sleeve iron, "Sensible No. 1," w/detachable handle..........................35.00

SPRINKLING BOTTLES

Ceramic, figural Chinese man, wearing blue & white clothes, perforated metal cap, 8½" h. (ILLUS. top next page) 27.00

Ceramic, figural Chinese man, marked "Sprinkle Plenty," yellow & green glaze....................................28.00

Ceramic, model of an elephant.............30.00

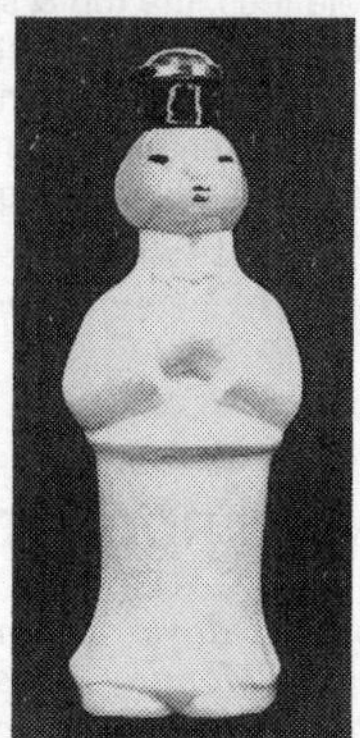

Chinese Man Sprinkling Bottle

Ceramic, model of a poodle..................85.00
Ceramic, model of a Siamese cat.........60.00

WASHBOARDS

Corrugated metal, "Scanti Andi," for lingerie, depicts lady in underwear, ca. 1920s, 8½ x 18½"......................25.00
Glass insert, wooden frame, "Cupples Co."..22.00
Glass insert, wooden frame, marked "National No. 701," 24" h. 45.00
Glass insert, wooden frame, "Top Notch - The Glass King," large 35.00

MISCELLANEOUS ITEMS

Clothes & towel drying rack, wall-type, metal holder slides rods up & out, advertising backplate, "American Wringer Co.," horseshoe pictured......65.00
Wash boiler, cov., copper, oval w/end handles 225.00
Wringer, wooden, "Horseshoe Brand," patent dated 1888..............................45.00
Wringer, wooden, hand-made, consisting of rollers & cogs mounted on a pine board, dated "1873" 90.00

LIGHTING DEVICES

Also see ART DECO, CANDLESTICKS & CANDLEHOLDERS, FIRE FIGHTING COLLECTIBLES, HEINTZ ART METAL WARES, METALS, RAILROADIANA, ROYCROFT ITEMS, MOVIE MEMORABILIA, and WORLD'S FAIR COLLECTIBLES. Also see various listings in the "Glass" and "Ceramics" categories.

LAMPS

FAIRY LAMPS

These are candle burning night lights of the Victorian era. Best known are the Clarke Fairy Lamps made in England, but they were also made by other firms. They were produced in two sizes, each with a base and a shade. The Fairy Pyramid Lamps listed below usually have a clear glass base and are approximately 2⅞" d. and 3¼" h. The Fairy Lamps are usually at least 4" d. and 5" h. when assembled and these may or may not have an additional saucer or bottom holder to match the shade in addition to the clear base.

Fairy Pyramid Lamps

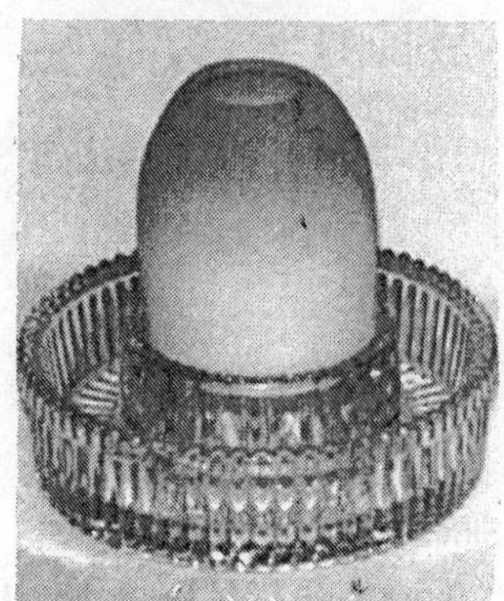

Burmese Shade on Clarke Base

Apple green embossed swirl frosted glass shade on marked "Clarke" clear glass base, 3" d., 3¾" h. $110.00
Burmese satin glass shade, on marked "Clarke" clear glass base, Webb, 2¾" d., 4" h. 175.00
Burmese satin glass shade on marked "Clarke" clear flower bowl base, 5" d., 4½" h. (ILLUS.) 245.00

Decorated Burmese Fairy Lamp

Burmese satin glass shade decorated w/colored prunus blossoms & leaves, w/a matching crimped Burmese base & a marked "Clarke" clear glass insert, 3¾" d., 5¼" h. (ILLUS.) 1,250.00

Cranberry Overshot swirl glass shade, marked "Clarke" clear glass base, 3" d., 3¾" h. 110.00

Cranberry swirl glass shade w/mica flecks & irregular green threading, marked "Clarke" clear glass base, 2⅞" d., 3½" h. 165.00

Frosted apple green embossed swirl glass shade, marked "Clarke" clear glass base, w/unlighted original "Burglar's Horror" candle, 3" d., 3¾" h...150.00

Rose Diamond Quilted patt. mother-of-pearl satin glass shade, marked "Clarke" clear glass base, 3" d., 3½" h...145.00

Spatter glass shade w/applied clear rigaree, matching base, 4" h. 100.00

Verre Moire (Nailsea) glass shade, green w/white loopings, on marked "Clarke" clear glass base, 3½" h..250.00

Verre Moire (Nailsea) glass shade, frosted cranberry w/opaque white loopings, marked "Clarke" clear glass base, 2¾" d., 3¾" h. 245.00

Yellow opaque w/white spatter glass shade on marked "Clarke" clear glass base, 3" d., 3¾" h. 125.00

Fairy Lamps

Blue Diamond Quilted mother-of-pearl satin glass shade, marked "Clarke" milk white glass base, 3¾" d., 5⅞" h...375.00

Burmese satin glass shade decorated w/colored prunus blossoms on a matching base w/turned-down ruffled edge & matching insert, 6" h...1,400.00

Burmese Fairy Lamp & Epergne

Burmese fairy lamp & epergne, three Burmese satin glass shades decorated w/prunus blossoms in a gilt-metal footed stand fitted w/four Burmese glass flower holders w/ruffled rims, w/clear glass lamp bases, 7" w., 8" h. (ILLUS.) 3,100.00

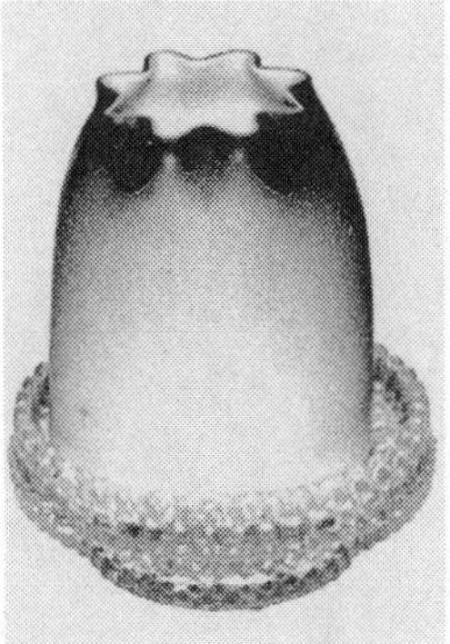

Green Satin Fairy Lamp

Green satin glass shade w/crimped top, on a marked "Clarke" clear glass base, shade attributed to Thomas Webb, 3¾" d., 4¾" h. (ILLUS.) 245.00

Pink Swirl patt. mother-of-pearl satin glass shade, matching ruffled base, 5½" d., 5" h. 530.00

Verre Moire (Nailsea) glass shade, frosted blue w/opaque white loopings, matching ruffled base w/a marked "Clarke" clear insert cup, 5½" d., 5½" h. 650.00

Verre Moire (Nailsea) glass shade, frosted blue w/white loopings, matching wide ruffled base w/a marked "Clarke" clear glass candle cup, base 8" d. 350.00

Figural Fairy Lamps

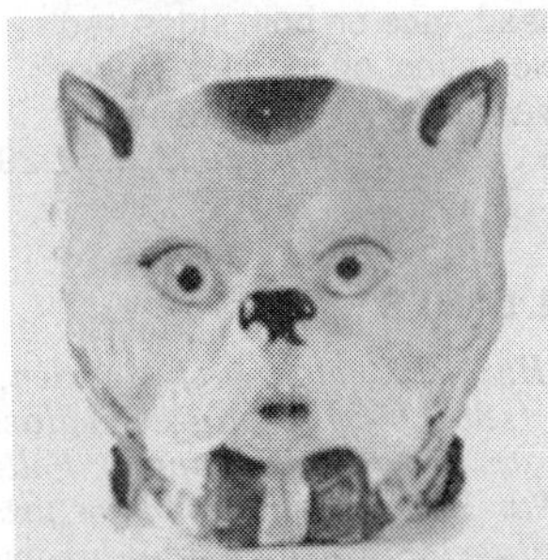

Three-Face Figural Fairy Lamp

Bisque, figural cat head shade w/green eyes, 3¼" h. 125.00

Bisque, figural dog, cat & owl faces, three relief-molded faces w/colored trim & glass eyes, minor roughness on rim, 4" h. (ILLUS.) 350.00

Bisque, figural lion's head shade w/glass eyes, brown painted decoration, 2½" d., 3½" h. 245.00

Bisque, figural owl head w/painted trim & glass eyes, 4" h. 275.00

Rabbit Fairy Lamp

Bisque, figural rabbit in seated position, colored trim & red glass eyes, 4¾" h. (ILLUS.) 550.00

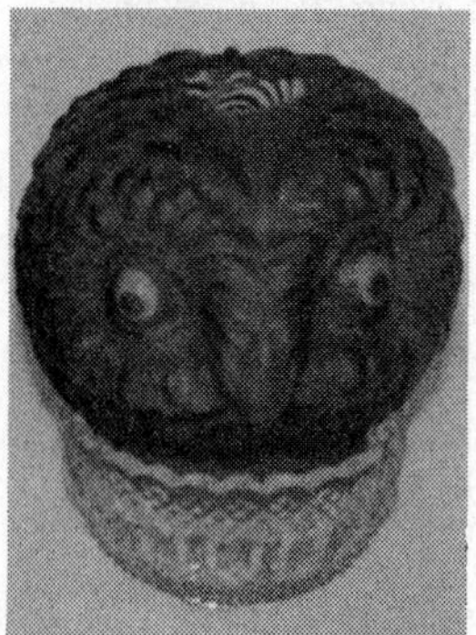

Glass Owl Head Fairy Lamp

Glass, frosted apple green figural owl's head, face on both sides, red enameled eyes, on marked "Clarke" clear glass base, 3⅜" d., 4½" h. (ILLUS.) 295.00

HANDEL LAMPS

The Handel Company of Meriden, Connecticut (1885-1936) began as a glass and lamp shade decorating company. Following World War I they became a major producer of decorative lamps which have become very collectible today.

Boudoir lamp, 7" w. squared, arched & domed glass shade w/scalloped rim, reverse-painted w/a continuous hilly landscape, shade signed "Handel 6154," on a slender bronzed-metal standard w/a squatty base w/four scroll feet on a square plinth, flat chip on interior shade rim, 15" h. (ILLUS.) 1,760.00

Handel Boudoir Lamp

Boudoir lamp, 10" d. domical shade in chipped & sand-finished grey glass painted on the interior w/a pair of exotic parrots perched in leafy branches, painted in shades of red, blue, yellow, green & black, against a mottled bright yellow-ochre ground, raised on a simple molded patinated metal standard, w/finial, shade signed in enamel "HANDEL 7013," base w/woven label "HANDEL - Lamps," ca. 1915, 13¾" h. 3,738.00

Mantel lamps, a cylindrical "Teroma" glass shade h.p. w/a continuous mountainous landscape, one signed "Bedigie," both shades marked "Handel 6990," fitted w/a bronzed-metal domed cap w/finial & raised on a slender pedestal base w/domed foot, cap wires loose, overall 15½" h., pr. 2,310.00

Night light, the pointed egg-form shade in grey textured glass reverse-painted w/lemon yellow & enameled on the exterior w/two birds perched in rose bushes alternating w/trellised roses, in shades of green, mauve, blue & charcoal grey, fitted into a low pierced Chinese-style base painted ivory, shade signed "Handel 7098," 7½" h. 403.00

Piano lamp, domed, half-round cylindrical glass shade reverse-painted w/a zig-zag band design in yellow & brown against a green ground, raised on a pivoting copper base, shade signed "Handel 6001

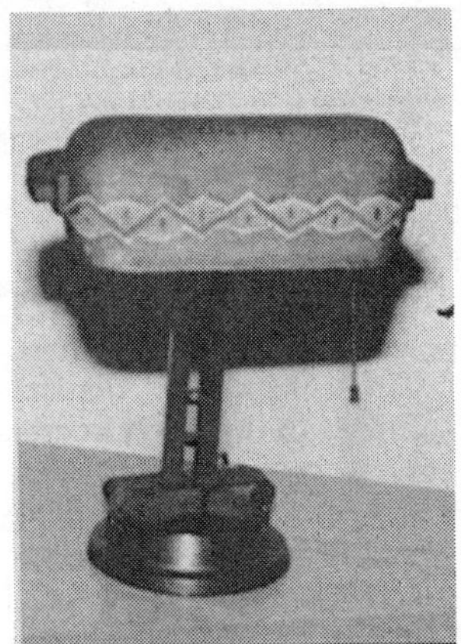

Handel Piano Lamp

GS," cloth label on base, shade 8" l. (ILLUS.) 1,870.00

Table lamp, 8" d. conical slag glass shade overlaid w/copper-plated hammered metal & cut w/a series of stylized tulips & leaves, the base w/a double-bar standard on an arched brace set upon a domed metal foot w/cut-out slag glass windows, original dark patina, shade signed, overall 13¾" h. 1,210.00

Table lamp, 16" d. domical reverse-painted glass shade decorated w/finely detailed pink, maroon & white ball-shaped hydrangea blossoms against a green leafy ground, signed at the edge "Handel 6739," mounted on a slender cylindrical bronzed metal Handel base w/round foot, overall 22" h...9,625.00

Table lamp, 17¾" domical reverse-painted glass shade w/chipped ice & sanded glass painted w/sprays of roses & leafage in rich jewel-like shades of pink, red, yellow, green & blue reserved against a rainbow-hued ground further painted w/two butterflies in flight, on a patinated metal standard composed of three scrolling legs raised on a tiered circular foot, shade signed in enamel "HANDEL 6688 R," impressed "HANDEL Lamps PAT'D No - 979664," base w/cloth label, overall 23½" h. 16,500.00

Table lamp, 18" d. domical reverse-painted glass shade, chipped ice & sanded finish, grey painted on the reverse w/a woodland landscape in shades of green, brown, blue, violet & black, raised on a heavy baluster-form patinated metal base cast w/wide leaves, w/cap & finial, shade signed "HANDEL 6754," base impressed "HANDEL," retains woven label, ca. 1920, overall 25" h...7,150.00

Handel Exterior-Decorated Lamp

Table lamp, 18¼" d. domed conical glass shade w/chipped & sand-finished exterior decorated w/a band of spatulate leafage reserved against a ground decorated w/spongework in shades of lime, olive & emerald green, the interior painted mustard, raised on a patinated metal base cast w/leafy trees, shade signed "HANDEL #5565 - U.S. Patents - No. 979664," ca. 1920, 22¾" h. (ILLUS.) 3,850.00

Handel 'Tulip' Lamp

Table lamp, a domical reverse-painted glass shade decorated w/large tulips against a leafy ground, shade signed "Handel 7040," raised on a bronzed-metal slender baluster-form base w/original paper label, 24" h. (ILLUS.).....................9,350.00

MINIATURE LAMPS

Our listings are arranged numerically according to the numbers assigned to the various miniature lamps pictured in Frank R. & Ruth E. Smith's book, Miniature Lamps, *now referred to as Smith's Book I, and Ruth Smith's sequel,* Miniature Lamps II. *All references are to Smith's Book I unless otherwise noted.*

Clear glass Bull's Eye patt. stem lamp, Nutmeg burner, advertised in Butler Brothers "Our Drummer" 1912 catalogue, 5" h. base (no chimney), No. 112 ....65.00

Beaded Swirl Lamp

Embossed beaded swirl, smoky green glass shade & base, Hornet burner, 4" d., 8½" h., No. 370 (ILLUS.) 395.00

Light green glass Fish-scale patt. stem lamp, Nutmeg burner, clear glass chimney, 5" h., No. 116 ....150.00

Milk white glass "Apple Blossom" lamp, embossed flowers & beading, light green band around top of base & shade & pink & green flower decoration, Nutmeg burner, 7¼" h., No. 194 ....235.00

Milk white glass w/embossed beaded panels & boats, windmill & lighthouse on base & vertical rows of beading on globe-chimney shade, Hornet burner, 7¾" h., No. 215 ....300.00 to 325.00

Red satin glass embossed base & petal-molded globe-chimney shade, Nutmeg burner, clear glass chimney, 9" h., No. 284....................275.00

Frosted clear glass base & ball-shaped shade w/embossed scrolls, flowers & faint spiderweb, Nutmeg burner, clear glass chimney, 8¼" h., No. 292 ....400.00 to 450.00

Milk white glass base & globe-chimney shade embossed w/Beaded Swirl patt., Hornet burner, 8¾" h., No. 369 ....200.00 to 250.00

Yellow & brown porcelain figure of man beside barrel base, English burner, clear glass chimney, 3½" h. base, No. 487 ....245.00

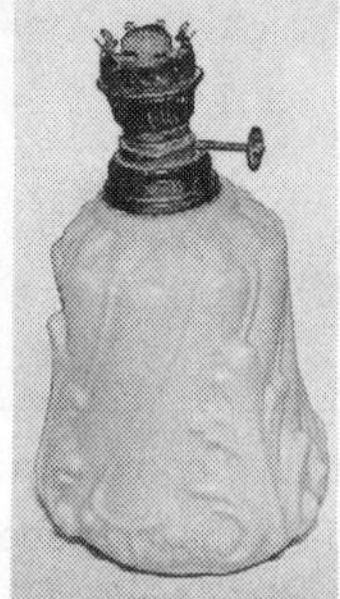

Pink Embossed Lamp Base

Shaded pink satin glass embossed w/swirled panels & large acanthus leaves up the sides around the base, white lining, original burner, base only, 3¾" d., 5¾" h., Book II, No. 517 (ILLUS.) 118.00

Not in Smith

Milk White Lamp w/Beaded Shade

Milk white bulbous stepped base w/a ring of ribbing around the top, h.p. blue blossoms & green leaves, yellowish green beaded shade w/long bead fringe, 3⅛" d., 7½" h. (ILLUS.) 275.00

Shaded pink satin glass w/bulbous squared base molded in bold relief w/large bull's-eyes framed by indented rings & scroll bands, white

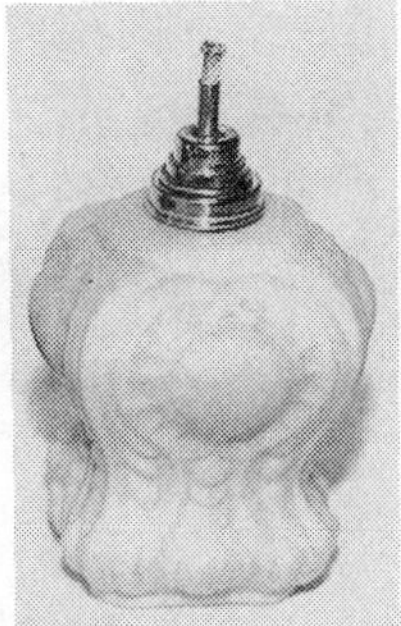

Embossed Pink Satin Glass Base

lining, partial burner, base only, 3⅜" d., 5¼" h. (ILLUS.) 115.00

PAIRPOINT LAMPS

Well known as a producer of fine Victorian art glass and silver plate wares, between 1907 and 1929 the Pairpoint Corporation of New Bedford, Massachusetts also produced a wide range of decorative lamps.

Pairpoint Boudoir Lamp

Boudoir lamp, 6½" w. square pyramidal glass 'Vassar' shade reverse-painted w/colorful floral medallions on a frosted ground, raised on a silvered-metal standard cast as a figural draped cherub standing on a round foot on a stepped onyx & metal base, base signed & numbered "E3018," worn silver on base, 14½" h. (ILLUS.) 880.00

Boudoir lamp, 9¼" d. "Puffy" glass shade painted on the interior w/roses & butterflies in shades of yellow, rose, green, blue & black reserved against a patterned pale violet ground, raised on a slender baluster-form patinated-metal standard w/a footed disc base, shade printed "The Pairpoint Corpn.," the base impressed "PAIRPOINT MFG. CO." w/monogram & numbered "3047," w/finial, chips to upper shade rim, overall 16¼" h. 1,495.00

Table lamp, 12" d. "Puffy" domical 'Lotus' reverse-painted glass shade, pink & white blossoms against a green leafy ground, rim marked in gold "Pat. Applied For," raised on a slender baluster-form gilt-metal standard molded w/leaves & framed by four undulating wires continuing up to form a support for the shade ring, the four-lobed base molded w/wide leaves, base signed & numbered "3082," 19½" h. 8,800.00

Pairpoint "Puffy" Rose Lamp

Table lamp, 13" d. "Puffy" domical 'Rose' reverse-painted glass shade, yellow blossoms on a leafy green ground, marked "Pat. Applied For," raised on a silvered-metal slender standard flanked by serpentine arms supporting the shade ring, the foot base w/wide scrolled leaves, base marked & numbered "3083," silver worn on base, 21" h. (ILLUS.).......7,150.00

Table lamp, 14" d. "Puffy" tapering cylindrical 'Stratford' shade in grey frosted glass painted on the reverse w/a band of multicolored rose blossoms & leafage w/two hummingbirds in flight, the ground painted white w/strips of leaves & stylized foliage, raised on a four-arm support above a shaped patinated metal four-sided standard cast w/swirling leafage, shade unsigned, base w/impressed factory marks, ca. 1915, 22" h. 5,750.00

Pairpoint Table Lamp

Table lamp, 16" d. tapering open drum-form glass shade reverse-painted w/stylized Persian influenced repeating floral & leafy scroll design, mounted on a gilt-metal ribbed vasiform standard above a knop stem & ribbed pedestal foot, base marked, 22" h. (ILLUS.) 1,430.00

Table lamp, 17¼" 'Exeter' patt. frosted grey glass shade reverse-painted w/a rural scene depicting a horse-drawn wagon harvesting the fall's bounty, corn stalks in a field & a cluster of farm buildings, all in sunset colors of orange, brown, lavender, green & rust, raised on an urn-form base cast w/gadrooning & leaves, w/finial, shade w/printed label "The Pairpoint Corp'n," ca. 1915, 22¾" h...............................2,588.00

Table lamp, 17½" d. domical reverse-painted 'Bombay' shade decorated w/a continuous lakeside wooded landscape, raised on a gilt-metal standard w/a central shaft framed by three slender inswept legs all resting on a round green marble plinth, base signed "Pairpoint" & numbered "D3095," 25½" h. 3,100.00

Table lamp, 17½" d. conical reverse-painted 'Carlisle' glass shade decorated w/two peacocks on a wall in a flower-filled formal landscape, marked "The Pairpoint Corp.," raised on a bronze squatty urn font atop three slender legs centered by a baluster-turned post all above a tripart foot, base marked "D3070," worn finish on base, 22" h. (ILLUS.) 3,300.00

Pairpoint Lamp with Peacocks

TIFFANY LAMPS

Lamps were just one product of the well known Tiffany Studios of New York, founded by Louis Comfort Tiffany. Lamp production began in the 1890s and continued into the early 1930s.

Tiffany Candle Lamp

Candle lamp, a pair of Favrile glass cylindrical shafts supporting bronzed metal sockets & raised on bronze arms issuing from a bronze & Favrile glass bulbous base, fitted w/filigree metal shades, base stamped "Tiffany Studios - New York," 12" h. (ILLUS.)...................2,420.00

Chandelier, "Daffodil," the 29" d. conical leaded glass shade w/beaded edges, the mottled blue 'fractured' glass ground decorated w/a profusion of amber & yellow daffodils w/green stems, tag stamped "TIFFANY STUDIOS NEW YORK," 41" h. 19,550.00

Desk lamp, a 7" d. domical damascene style glass shade w/green wavy swirled iridescent decoration cased in pearl opal suspended within a swing adjustable bronze harp frame above a ribbed cushion foot, shade signed "L.C.T. Favrile," base impressed & numbered "418," 13½" h. 3,080.00

Desk lamp, "American Indian," 12¼" d. conical glass shade w/curved lower border composed of rows of rectangular tiles in striated amber & green, green & white, orange, red & white & deepest dark brown opalescent glass, raised on an American Indian bronze base, w/finial, shade impressed "TIFFANY STUDIOS NEW YORK 1586," base impressed "TIFFANY STUDIOS - NEW YORK - 536," 1899-1928, 17⅜" h. 19,550.00

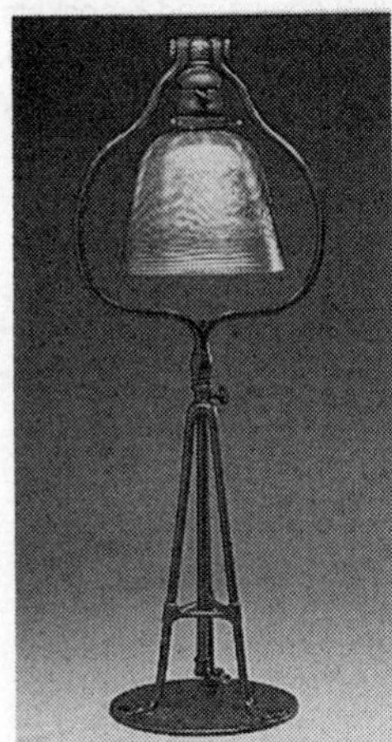

Tiffany Favrile & Bronze Desk Lamp

Desk lamp, the elongated domed green glass shade decorated w/rainbow iridescent gold waves, supported by bronze telescoping harp-arms w/tripod standard on flattened circular foot, shade inscribed "L.C.T.," base inscribed w/initial "P" & stamped "TIFFANY STUDIOS NEW YORK 438," 25½" h. (ILLUS.) 4,025.00

Floor bridge lamp, a 10" d. domical glass shade w/a gold iridescent exterior w/pulled dimple decoration & a white lining suspended in a gilt-bronze swing adjustable harp standard w/a tripod base ending in spade-shaped feet, shade signed "LCT Favrile," base impressed "Tiffany Studios New York 423," overall 4'7" h. 4,675.00

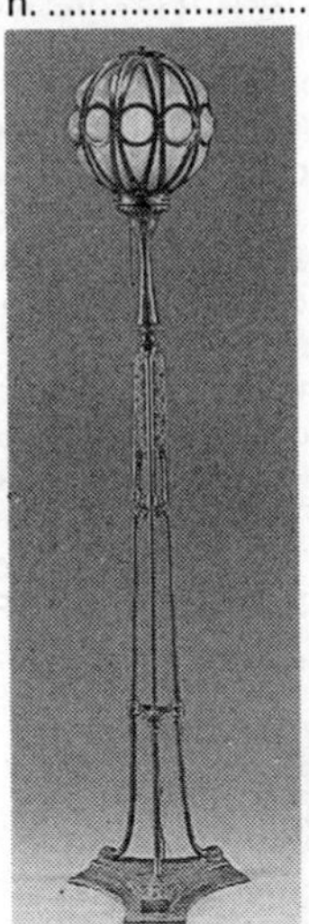

Unusual Tiffany Floor Lamp

Floor lamp, Favrile glass & bronze, the 12" d. spherical shade in bronze pierced w/a geometric pattern & blown w/deep green opalescent glass, fitting into a pierced mount above a tripod standard wrought w/coiling & scrolling devices, the legs ending in stylized paw feet further mounted on a shaped triangular base, w/finial, shade impressed "D878S," base impressed "TIFFANY STUDIOS - NEW YORK - 376," 1899-1928, 5'9½" (ILLUS.) 11,500.00

Floor lamp, "Helmet Rose," the 24" d. flaring domical leaded glass shade w/heavily mottled yellow flowers w/mottled green leaves against a striated caramel ground shading to blue below & stamped "TIFFANY STUDIOS NEW YORK," the slender bronze base w/scroll tendrils & stamped "TIFFANY STUDIOS NEW YORK 379," overall 5'6" h. 63,000.00

Floor lamp, "Laburnum," 21¼" d. gently lobed domical leaded glass shade w/irregular lower rim composed of clusters of laburnum blossoms in various shades of mottled ochre, amber & golden yellow, w/leafage in various shades of green, against a deep cobalt blue mottled ground, raised on a junior bronze floor base wrought w/applied stringing above a circular base cast w/radiating leafage, further raised on four petal-form feet, w/pigtail finial, shade unsigned, base impressed "TIFFANY STUDIOS — NEW YORK - 979," 1899-1928, 5'7½" h. 140,000.00

Floor lamp, "Oriental Poppy," 26" d. domed leaded glass shade decorated w/a profusion of deep ruby & crimson blossoms w/striated blue centers among mottled green leaves all against a mottled blue & yellow ground, the bronze base w/a band of vertical ribbing on the standard terminating in scrolls on the broad circular foot, on five ball feet, w/green-brown patina, shade stamped "TIFFANY STUDIOS NEW YORK 1902," the base stamped "TIFFANY STUDIOS NEW YORK 375," 6'7" h. 442,500.00

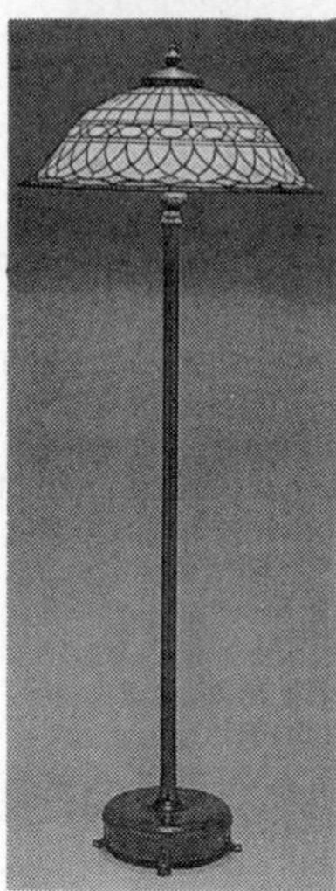

Tiffany "Roman" Floor Lamp

Floor lamp, "Roman," 25" d. broad domical leaded glass shade w/flaring rim, composed of radiating rectangular tiles in striated pale green & white opalescent glass, above a medial band of lozenge & quatrefoil shaped tiles in textured pale green glass, the lower border of interlacing design also in pale green & white striated opalescent glass, raised on a cylindrical bronze standard above a cushion-form base raised on four petal-form feet, w/finial, shade impressed "TIFFANY STUDIOS NEW YORK 1564," base impressed "TIFFANY STUDIOS - NEW YORK - 584," 1899-1928, 5'4" h. (ILLUS.) 10,350.00

Leaded Glass & Bronze Lantern

Lantern, the six leaded glass sides decorated w/bright mauve, violet & pink iris sprays among green leaves against a mottled & streaked variegated blue sky, the mount finely cast as vertical iris leaves above a pierced bronze root-form bottom panel centering a matching circular hinged door, greenish brown patina, w/two original chains, rod & sockets, 13¼" d., 23¼" h. (ILLUS.) 176,000.00

Tiffany "Lily" Lamp

Lily table lamp, twelve-light, the bronze base w/greenish patina composed of a cluster of lily pads, buds & leaves issuing twelve slender, arched central stems each fitted w/a ribbed gold iridescent blossom-form shade, shades marked "LCT," base impressed "Tiffany Studios - New York 382," 21" h. (ILLUS.) 20,900.00

Stick lamp, the bulbous cased glass shade decorated w/iridescent damascene trailing fitting into a vented socket above a bulbous cup set w/amber iridescent cabochons, raised on a slender shaped bronze standard continuing to a circular base cast as an inverted flowerhead, shade inscribed "L.C.T.," base impressed "TIFFANY STUDIOS - NEW YORK - 1285, 1899-1928, 22½" h. 4,600.00

Student lamp, the 6¼" d. domical metal shade pierced w/pine needles encasing deep green glass, adjustable bronze rod standard, rich brown-green patina, shade unsigned, base impressed "TIFFANY STUDIOS - NEW YORK - 304," 1899-1920, 19¾" h. 2,875.00

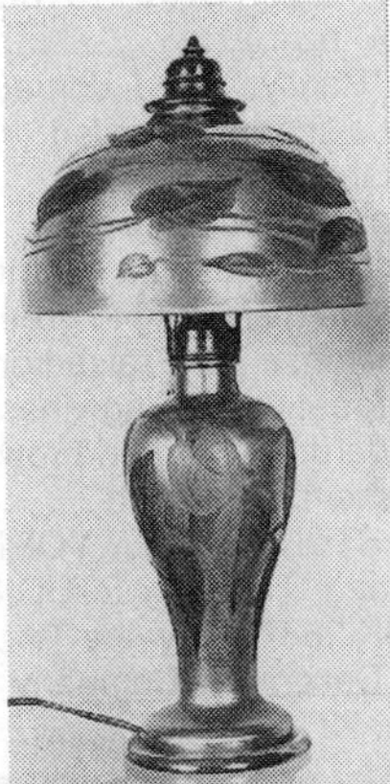

Favrile Glass Table Lamp

Table lamp, Favrile glass, the domical gold iridescent Favrile glass shade intaglio-cut w/a band of heart-shaped green leaves, raised above a matching baluster-form base, shade signed "279N L.C. Tiffany - Favrile," base signed "L.C. Tiffany - Favrile," 15" h. (ILLUS.) 4,070.00

Table lamp, three-light, each inverted bell-form amber iridescent glass shade fitting into a vented socket above a curved arm about a central urn, raised on a waisted fluted standard, further raised on a stepped molded bronze base cast w/radiating gadrooning & leafage, greenish brown patina, shades inscribed "L.C.T. Favrile," base impressed "TIFFANY STUDIOS - NEW YORK - 310," 1899-1928, overall 22" h. 3,850.00

Table lamp, "Crocus," 16" d. domical leaded glass shade composed of four bouquets of mottled white glass crocus blossoms tinged w/pale yellow & pink, against a striated green & white opalescent glass

Tiffany "Crocus" Lamp

ground, the lower border in olive green rippled glass, raised on a paneled bronze standard library base, w/finial, the shade impressed "TIFFANY STUDIOS - NEW YORK," base impressed "TIFFANY 1899-1928, 21½" h. (ILLUS.) 17,250.00

Table lamp, "Daffodil," the 13⅞" d. domical leaded glass shade composed of daffodil blossoms & leafage, the blossoms in beautifully mottled shades of golden amber, yellow & orange opalescent glass, the leafage in various shades of green striated opalescent glass, against a ground of purple, blue & green striated glass, raised on a simple paneled bronze stick base, w/finial, shade impressed "TIFFANY STUDIOS NEW YORK 1426," base impressed "TIFFANY STUDIOS - NEW YORK - 533," 1899-1928, 21½" h...13,800.00

Tiffany "Dragonfly" Lamp

Table lamp, "Dragonfly," the 14" d. domical leaded glass shade composed of six dragonflies w/outspread wings in purple & blue striated opalescent, the wings overlaid w/bronze filigree, against a tessellated ground of green & white striated opalescent set w/emerald green cabochons, raised on a shaped standard above an inverted mushroom cap base, w/finial, shade impressed "TIFFANY STUDIOS NY 585," base impressed "TIFFANY STUDIOS - NEW YORK - 337," 1899-1928, 18¼" h. (ILLUS.) 12,650.00

Table lamp, "Empire Jewel," the 22¼" w. octagonal shade composed of sloping panels, each set w/oval stylized foliate medallions composed of opalescent 'jewels' reserved against a charcoal grey ground within 'jeweled' opalescent & striated pink, lime green & yellow glass tile borders, on a paneled silvered bronze standard & circular dished base, shade impressed "TIFFANY STUDIOS - NEW YORK 1953," base impressed "TIFFANY STUDIOS - NEW YORK - 532," 1899-1920, overall 25¾" h. 25,300.00

Tiffany "Laburnum" Lamp

Table lamp, "Laburnum," the deep gently paneled 21" d. domical shade w/irregular lower rim composed of pendant clusters of laburnum blossoms in shades of mottled golden yellow & pale amber opalescent glass, w/leafage in various shades of green striated glass, against a deep purple & cobalt blue striated glass sky shading to delicate turquoise at the lower rim, raised on an adjustable bronze cylindrical standard cast w/coiling tendrils continuing to a cushion-form base cast w/radiating leafage, raised on four petal-form feet, shade unsigned, base impressed "TIFFANY STUDIOS - NEW YORK - 6852," 1899-1928, overall 31½" h. (ILLUS.).............77,000.00

Table lamp, "Linenfold," 12½" w. hexagonal shade composed of rectangular amber 'linenfold' panels above ruffled 'linenfold' border tiles, the four-sided gilt-bronze standard & square base cast w/geometric stringing, shade impressed "TIFFANY STUDIOS NEW YORK 1948," base impressed "TIFFANY STUDIOS - NEW YORK," 1910-20, overall 19¼" h. 6,600.00

Table lamp, "Pansy," 16" d. domed leaded glass shade w/mottled apricot & sapphire blue pansy blossoms amid mottled green foliage & stems, against a geometric ground of cream shading to green below, the bronze base raised on four curved feet w/scrolling vines along standard, all w/green-brown patina, shade tag stamped "TIFFANY STUDIOS NEW YORK," base stamped "TIFFANY STUDIOS NEW YORK 26877" & w/the Tiffany Glass and Decorating Company monogram, 22" h. 28,750.00

Tiffany "Peony" Lamp

Table lamp, "Peony," the 22" d. domical shade w/incurvate lower rim, composed of peony blossoms in various stages of development from newly emerging buds to mature full-blown blossoms, in shades of red, mauve, rose, lavender, orange & pink striated opalescent glass, the leaves in various shades of green opalescent w/multicolored striations, against a ground of green & blue glass shading to green & white, raised on a bronze tree trunk standard, w/finial, shade impressed "TIFFANY STUDIOS NEW YORK 1505-3," base impressed "TIFFANY STUDIOS - NEW YORK - 553," 1899-1918, 33½" h. (ILLUS.) 107,000.00

Table lamp, "Pomegranate," 16" d. domical leaded glass shade composed of mottled green segments banded by a yellow border design of stylized pomegranates, signed "Tiffany Studios - New York," raised on a slender bronze standard w/dished & footed base impressed "Tiffany Studios - New York," 21" h. 7,150.00

Table lamp, "Pond Lily," 20½" d. conical shade w/straight lower rim, composed of full-blown water lily blossoms & buds in various shades of striated pink, mauve, pale violet & white striated opalescent glass, some of the blossoms tinged w/pale yellow, the leafage in various shades of mottled green, blue & white mottled & striated opalescent glass, against a ground of deep cobalt blue striated rippled glass, raised on a bronze standard composed of twisted stems swirling to the circular base, w/finial, shade impressed "TIFFANY STUDIOS NEW YORK 1490-22," base impressed "TIFFANY STUDIOS - NEW YORK - S220 - 443," 26¾" h......................................145,500.00

Table lamp, "Pony Apple Blossom," 10¼" d., shouldered domical leaded glass shade w/irregular lower rim, the yellow-centered pink & white flower clusters among green leaves on a mottled green & white ground, all above an open network of branches at the top, stamped "TIFFANY STUDIOS NEW YORK 884-10," the tree-form bronze base cast in low-relief w/interlacing gnarled roots, w/a brownish green patina, stamped "TIFFANY STUDIOS NEW YORK 29721," w/company monogram, overall 17" h..36,800.00

Table lamp, "Swirling Leaf," 18" d. domical shade w/straight lower border composed of radiating graduated rectangular tiles in green & white striated opalescent glass, w/medial band of swirling lemon leaves in violet, purple, green & white striated opalescent glass, raised on a simple paneled gilt-bronze stick base on a circular molded base cast w/integral lug feet, w/replaced finial, shade impressed "TIFFANY STUDIOS - NEW YORK," base impressed "TIFFANY STUDIOS - NEW YORK - 531," 1899-1928, 27" h. (ILLUS.) 6,900.00

Tiffany "Swirling Leaf" Lamp

Table lamp, "Woodbine," the 20" d. domical leaded glass shade w/mottled blue woodbine flowers against a striated & mottled green ground, stamped "TIFFANY STUDIOS NEW YORK," the bronze stick base w/dished foot & rich brown patina, stamped "TIFFANY STUDIOS NEW YORK," w/finial, 31" h..20,700.00

MISCELLANEOUS LAMPS

Early Argand Lamp

Aladdin, Model A-102, peach Venetian table lamp, w/burner, 1932-33..90.00

Aladdin, Model No. B, Colonial table lamp, green moonstone font, w/bracket, complete w/burner..........150.00

Aladdin, Model B, Colonial table lamp, white moonstone font, w/wall bracket, complete w/burner 150.00

Aladdin, Model B-98, Queen table lamp, rose moonstone, complete w/burner..325.00

Aladdin, Model B-130, Orientale table lamp, ivory, w/ No. 701 glass shade...215.00

Aladdin, Model C-164, Brazil table lamp, glass font, shelf lamp w/burner, 1974-75..............................80.00

Argand lamp, patinated bronze, urn-form font cast w/doves above a cylindrical support w/stylized pilasters, the font hung w/prisms, burner supports a baluster-form frosted & etched shade, B. Gardiner, New York City, mid-19th c., electrified, 18" h., pr. (ILLUS. of one) 1,840.00

Art Deco Table Lamp

Art Deco table lamp, wrought iron, the base w/a central openwork section cast w/stylized vines & leaves, on a narrow rectangular stepped foot, supporting a long pleated cloth shade, by Edgar Brandt, impressed "E. BRANDT," ca. 1925, 19" w., 20½" h. (ILLUS.) 5,175.00

Art Nouveau figural lamp, patinated bronze, cast as the figure of an Art Nouveau maiden standing w/her hair braided & pulled into a topknot, wearing a long draped gown & holding her arms out to the sides w/a blossom-form socket in each hand, after Julian Caussé, inscribed "J. Caussé," early 20th c., casting flaw in head, greenish gold patina, 18" h. (ILLUS. top next column).......805.00

Figural Art Nouveau Lamp

Austrian table lamp, silver-plated metal & iridescent glass, cast as a large blossom w/leaf-form base, the stem entwined w/a small garden snake, the blossom-form shade in opalescent glass decorated w/pink oil-spotting & cobalt blue trailing, Wurttembergische Metallwarenfabrik (WMF), Austria, base w/impressed factory marks, glass unsigned, ca. 1900, 13⅜" h.................................2,300.00

Victorian Banquet Lamp

Banquet lamp, kerosene-type, blown glass & cast metal, the bulbous onion-form green blown glass font lightly frosted & h.p. w/large stylized gold flowers & buds & raised on a scroll-cast pedestal base, w/scroll feet, w/burner & matching green glass tulip-form shade w/ruffled top, w/chimney, 7¼" d., 17" h. (ILLUS.) ..425.00

Betty lamp (early grease lamp) w/hanger, brass, w/decorative detail, 5" h. plus hanger (pick missing).......115.50

Betty lamp (early grease lamp) w/hanger, sheet iron, shallow oblong form w/end spout, an upright angled handle at the back fitted w/twisted long pick, worn black paint, 3¾" h. plus hanger 220.00

Betty lamp (early grease lamp) w/hanger, wrought iron, heart finial on font cover, old gold paint, 4" h. plus hanger 192.50

Betty lamp (early grease lamp) w/hanger, polished brass lid w/heart finial, found in Warren, Ohio, 4" h. plus hanger (wick pick missing) 159.50

Betty lamp (early grease lamp) w/hanger, wrought iron, tooled w/initials "J.S." & "1827, NO 29," 5" h. plus hanger (light rust) 770.00

Chromed-metal & bronze desk lamp, Art Deco style, the domical chromed-metal shade pendent from a curved support above a conforming bronze base, designed by Donald Deskey, manufactured by Deskey-Vollmer, New York, ca. 1927-29, unsigned, 12" h. 1,380.00

Edgar Brandt table lamp, glass & bronze, the conical shade in grey glass mottled w/orange, lavender & purple, fitting into a standard cast as a flaring cobra mounted on a circular basket-woven base, shade impressed "DAUM - NANCY" w/cross of Lorraine, base impressed "BRANDT," ca. 1925, 21¼" h......20,700.00

Gilt-bronze piano lamp, the hammered domical shade set w/a band of amber glass bosses & applied w/cast bronze bats w/outspread wings, pendent from a curved arm rising from a shaped base also mounted w/a bat, further mounted on black marble, Germany, ca. 1900, 17" l., 13½" h. 3,163.00

Kerosene table lamp, cut-overlay glass, squatty inverted pear-shaped font in blue cut to clear w/overall dots, on a columnar brass pedestal w/stamped brass intertwined bands, on a square black marble foot, New England, mid-19th c., 9½" h. 546.00

Kerosene table lamp, nickeled-metal base w/plain bulbous font on a pedestal foot embossed w/a band of lunettes above the pierced bottom edge, w/an umbrella-form milk glass shade w/paneled lower edge fitted on a shade ring, by Bradley & Hubbard, early 20th c., 21" h. (minor shade chipping at top edge) 165.00

Kerosene table lamp, clear pressed flint glass, Bigler patt., on a paneled pedestal w/round foot, pewter collar, 7½" h. (pinpoint flakes) 71.50

Kerosene table lamp, pressed glass, clear Thumbprint & Fleur-de-Lis patt. font, opaque white glass conical base, clear shade w/engraved decoration, brass collar, connecter & burner, overall 21½" h. 220.00

Kerosene table lamp, "Ripley Marriage Lamp," pressed translucent starch blue fonts attached to a moonstone central match holder attached w/a brass collar to an opaque white pressed base, marked "D.C. Ripley & Co. - Pat. Pending," ca. 1870, 12⅛" h. (small unseen chip under base, trace of mold roughness, plaster at connector deteriorated) 990.00

Kerosene table lamp, pressed glass, clear Zig Zag & Diamond patt. font, opaque white spherical shaft decorated w/h.p. floral design, pedestal base 125.00

Lacemaker's lamp, aqua blown glass, spherical font w/top opening applied to a multiple-knop stem on a flattened wide dished foot, applied angled side handle on stem, 19th c., 5¾" h. 907.50

Lard lamp, tin, brass label plate "N. & H. Gufford, 117 Court St. Boston," 6½" h. 275.00

Lard lamp, tin, Kinnear patent-type, 7¼" h. 220.00

Slag Glass Table Lamp

Leaded glass table lamp, 16" w. octagonal shade w/a pierced-metal floral design gridwork overlaid on & centering rows of green, yellow & red slag glass inserts, slender green patinated metal standard on octagonal weighted base, attributed to Bradley & Hubbard, frame bent slightly, 18" h. (ILLUS.) 747.50

Leaded glass table lamp, 20½" d. domical shade w/an uneven bottom edge & composed of red ripple glass blossoms w/yellow centers, smooth green leaves on brown stems against a yellowish green slag ground, mounted on a slender lobed telescoping bronzed metal quatraform base, attributed to Handel, several glass segments cracked, 25" h. 1,840.00

Leleu (Jules) floor lamp, ivory inlaid mahogany, the octagonal standard w/paneled octagonal base inlaid w/ivory beading, w/finial & pleated shade, Jules Leleu, France, ca. 1935, 23" d., 6' h. 6,325.00

Loetz table lamp, iridescent glass & gilt-bronze, the bell-form shade in amber iridescent glass decorated w/raised swirling trailing pendent from a curved standard cast w/a dragonfly w/outspread wings, supported by a triangular leaf-form base, unsigned, Austria, ca. 1900, 19¼" h. 3,163.00

Millefiore boudoir lamp, the bulbous mushroom-shaped blown glass shade raised on metal fittings above a matching slender baluster-form base, shade & base composed of multi-colored floral canes, gilt-metal fittings, overall 14" h. 880.00

Peg lamp, clear cut glass, squatty bulbous form cut around the sides w/starburst panels alternating w/plain panels, brass fittings & collar, ca. 1850, 4" d. 93.50

Sparking lamp, miniature, blown glass, spherical font w/top opening for burner, on applied ringed stem & round foot, 3¼" h. (chip on edge of foot) 440.00

Whale oil table lamp, blown & pressed glass, the blown tapering conical font attached by multiple thin wafers to an ornate scroll-molded triangular paw footed pressed lacy base, clear, 10⅛" h. (missing collar) 660.00

Whale oil lamps, brass, bell-form ring-turned font on a baluster-shaped standard on turned round foot, fitted w/single burner, American-made, mid-19th c., 6" h., pr. 748.00

Wilkinson table lamp, 21" d. domical leaded glass shade composed of eight rippled pink tulips spaced by white & lavender panels above yellow ovals w/green leaves below, mounted on a slender bronzed metal foliate-cast base marked "Wilkinson Brooklyn, N.Y.," some glass cracks, 27½" h. 2,875.00

OTHER LIGHTING DEVICES

CHANDELIERS

Art Nouveau Chandelier

Art Deco, frosted & clear glass & chrome, set w/clear glass rods enclosed by chromed supports, the lower section w/frosted glass panels, ca. 1930, 24¼" d., 33" h. 3,450.00

Art Nouveau style, patinated & gilt-metal, double oval structure held by four converging arms, molded w/an interlacing clematis vine, some buds fitted w/sockets, green, gold & black painted patina, early 20th c., 35" h. (ILLUS.) 978.00

Baroque-Style Chandelier

Baroque-Style, brass, eight-light, the turned standard w/a spherical pendant supporting eight scrolled candlearms, each w/stylized fans, w/an upper tier w/eight similarly scrolled arms w/reflectors, 19th. c., damages to arms, 23" d., 26" h. (ILLUS.) 2,588.00

Charles X, ormolu, five-light, center font-form supporting five acanthus cast branches w/reeded drip pans & fitted w/scrolled decoration, suspended from later chains, France, early 19th c., 11" d., 25½" h. 2,875.00

Degue signed, molded & frosted glass w/a central dome & four side panels, each molded w/foliate devices, conjoined by foliate spandrels, each panel molded "Degue," ca. 1925, 18" d., 36" h. 2,530.00

Handel signed, painted glass & gilt-metal, the spherical etched iridescent shade painted w/large cobalt blue parrots perched in green & rust branches against a cream background, the parrots w/reverse painting, supported by a gilt-metal mount, the shade signed "HANDEL 6996," 10" d. shade, overall 33" h. 2,530.00

Louis XV-Style, gilt-bronze & glass, six-light, of cage-form w/a central standard supporting scrolled candle branches w/alternating spires, overall hung w/pendants, 43" h.....2,588.00

Louis XVI Chandelier

Louis XVI style, gilt-stenciled painted tole, the circular corona pierced w/arches & mounted w/rams' heads, centering a single lamp w/cylindrical shade, suspended from large link chains joined at an upper crown w/large leaves, France, early 19th c., 16½" d., (ILLUS.) 1,150.00

Regence-Style, gilt-bronze, 16-light, the baluster-shaped standard supporting two tiers of foliate candle branches, ending in masks, overall cast w/ram's heads, busts, scrolls & foliage, late 19th c., 38" h. (electrified) 8,625.00

Tiffany signed, leaded glass & bronze, "Nasturtium," the octagonal paneled shade w/irregular border decorated w/nasturtium vines & blossoms against a trellis, in brilliant tones of apricot, cherry, pale violet, orangish red & mint green, supported by an adjustable chain, pole & cap framework, w/rich chocolate patina, shade stamped "TIFFANY STUDIOS NEW YORK," shade 24" d., overall including hardware 57" h. 17,250.00

Tinware & turned wood, eight-light, the ring-turned standard w/eight wire projecting candlearms ending in cylindrical candle cups w/crimped drip plates, 22¼" h. (lower section of column replaced) 575.00

Wrought-iron, four-light, a hook-ended bar supporting a sawtooth rachet ending in four upturned bar arms ending in candlesockets, 31" h. 748.00

LANTERNS

Early Kerosene Barn Lantern

Barn lantern, kerosene-type, tin & glass, clear beveled glass tapering sides above a square metal font base w/old worn brown japanning, square pierced vent cap w/arched strap across top & a wire bail handle, the burner marked "Holmes, Booth & Haydens, Waterbury, Ct.," 19th c., 8¾" h. (ILLUS.) 214.50

Candle lantern, tin & glass, a large clear blown spherical globe on a low cylindrical tin font base & supporting a cylindrical tin vent band w/a pointed cover w/large ring handle, 10¼" h. plus ring handle (minor rust) 275.00

Candle lantern, tin & glass, semi-circular tin frame w/glass front, hinged door in back, traces of old black paint on exterior, old white on interior, replaced ring handle at the top, 11" h. plus ring handle 264.00

Hand lantern, kerosene-type, brass font, red cast glass globe, marked "Works Progress Administration of Ohio" 150.00

Hand lantern, tin w/pressed paneled globe, bottom w/removable font marked "N.E. Glass Co. Patented Oct. 24th, 1854," circular ring handle, traces of old black paint, 12" h. plus handle 412.50

Hanging lantern, Arts & Crafts style, glass & copper, hammered copper w/overhanging top, grid pattern over "hammered" glass panels, unmarked Gustav Stickley, Model No. 830, 6" sq., 11" h. (cleaned patina) 550.00

Early Skater's Lanterns

Skater's lantern, brass, a clear pear-shaped globe on a burner & domed brass font, w/a domed pierced cap w/wire bail handle, small holes in bottom, 7" h. (ILLUS. left) 77.00

Skater's lantern, tin & glass, clear pear-shaped glass globe, domed tin font & domed pierced vent cap, wire bail handle, 6¼" h. 55.00

Skater's lantern, tin & glass, clear pear-shaped glass globe, domed tin font & domed pierced vent cap, marked "Jewel," some rust, w/wire bail handle, 7" h. (ILLUS. right) 49.50

SHADES

Cameo Glass Shade

Cameo glass, widely flaring bell-form, pink cut to creamy white in a delicate design of floral wreaths & ribbons, each w/impressed signature "Thos. Webb & Son Cameo," England, 19th., 6" d., 4¼" h., pr. (ILLUS. of one) 1,500.00

Handel, 10" d. conical leaded glass shade, w/straight lower border & irregular rim, composed of tapering rectangular sections of mottled & striated green, amber & yellow opalescent glass above a lower border composed of simple flowerheads in pink & yellow striated opalescent glass w/yellow glass centers & leafage in various shades of green striated opalescent glass, unsigned, ca. 1915 ....1,380.00

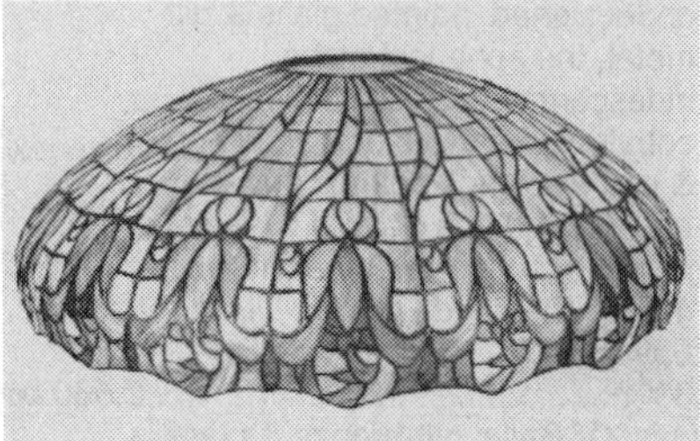

Leaded Shade with Florals

Leaded glass, hanging-type, 24" d. domical shade w/tuck-under scalloped rim below yellowish amber & pastel green stylized blossoms band, attributed to Duffner and Kimberly, no electrical fittings (ILLUS.) 1,725.00

Lime Green Glass Shade

Lime green glass, bell-form w/crimped & ruffled rim, molded w/an overall dewdrop effect, 8¾" d., 7" h., pr. (ILLUS. of one) 295.00

Lustre Art, trumpet-form, iridescent butterscotch snakeskin design, signed, set of 5 ....1,250.00

Lustre Art, waisted cylindrical form, iridescent hooked-feather design in blue, unsigned, set of 9..............2,700.00

Nuart, Pearl Lustre, scalloped interior panels, Imperial, 4⅞" d., 4½" h. 45.00

Pairpoint, domical open-topped

boudoir lamp-sized "Puffy" glass 'Concord' shade, reverse-painted & molded w/asters & wild roses, marked in gold "Patented," 6½" d., ...1,210.00

Quezal, baluster-shaped, green-gold iridescent "Autumnal" leaves w/random threading on silvery white ground, gold iridescent lining, 6" h., set of 9 ....1,800.00

Quezal, bell-form, gold iridescent pulled-feather design on white, white interior 215.00

Quezal, bulbous w/ruffled rim, iridescent gold hooked-feather design 250.00

Quezal, tulip-shaped, white pulled-feather design on gold iridescent ground, 6" h., set of 7 ....1,400.00

Quezal, widely flaring w/scalloped rim, green pulled-feather design, gold iridescent interior 175.00

Steuben, bell-form, brown Aurene leaf & vine decoration on Calcite, gold Aurene interior, 4½" h. 175.00

Steuben, bell-form, gold Aurene, signed, 5¾" h., set of 2 ....200.00

Steuben, bell-form, gold & green iridescent King Tut patt. on Calcite, gold Aurene lining 325.00

Steuben, tulip-shaped w/lightly scalloped rim, green iridescent pulled-feather design w/gold border on Calcite, white iridescent interior, signed, set of 6 ....1,200.00

Tiffany, domical, the opalescent sides decorated w/brilliant amber iridescent damascene sworls, inscribed "L.C. Tiffany Favrile," 1899-1920, 7" d. 2,645.00

Tiffany, "Hollyhock," conical leaded glass shade composed of flower clusters in pink, magenta & white among green leaves, all set against blue striated w/magenta sky shading to mottled green below, stamped "TIFFANY STUDIOS NEW YORK 625-7," 28" d., 45" h. 33,350.00

Verre Moire Glass Shade

Verre moire (Nailsea), bell-form w/crimped & ruffled rim, blue shaded to clear, opaque white loopings, satin finish, 2" d. base, 5½" d., 4¼" h., pr. (ILLUS. of one) 265.00

MAGAZINES

All magazines are in excellent, complete condition unless otherwise noted.

American Boy, 1921, February, stories by Leo Edwards, Heyliger, Kelland & Mills, also toy ads $12.00

American Boy, 1925, April, Harrison Cady cover 23.00

American Druggist, 1933, December 8.00

American Sportsman, 1908, June 25, harness, trotting horses, races, etc., 12 pp. 12.00

Atlantic Monthly, 1973, August, Marilyn Monroe cover & story "Marilyn Jewish Princess" 13.50

Ballyhoo, 1931, Vol. 1, No 1, humorous-type 35.00

Black Cat, 1906, November 25.00

Boy's Life, 1960, November 3.50

California Real Estate, 1932, June, city & county facts, roster of Western Realtors 18.00

Child Life, 1929, June, complete w/doll pages 6.50

Collier's, 1901, February 9, article by Nicholas Tesla, "Talking With The Planets" 12.50

Collier's, 1902, July 5, Leyendecker cover, King Edward VII coronation preparations, Queen, family, etc. 12.50

Collier's, 1956, March 2, Prince Rainier & Grace Kelly cover & inside article 14.00

Cosmopolitan, 1952, October, Queen Elizabeth II on cover 20.00

Craftsman, October 1903 through March 1904, bound 75.00

Delineator, 1936, April 4.00

Ebony, 1946, Joe Louis on cover 30.00

Electrical Record, 1913, November 20.00

Esquire, 1938, December 45.00

Everybody's, 1913, August 14.00

Farm Mechanics, 1923, June 8.00

Fortune, 1931, March 15.00

Graphic Arts, 1911, January, Vol. 1, many nice color illustrations, Jessie Willcox Smith full page color "Mother & Child" 13.50

Harper's Weekly, 1872, November 30, Boston fire on cover 10.00

Harper's Weekly, 1893, March 4, President Harrison on cover, also picture of President Cleveland, his cabinet & his home 8.00

Hot Rod, 1955, June, Indy 500 preview 10.00
House & Garden, 1939, July 50.00
Inland Printer, 1906, color full page Ault Wiborg illustration "Cow Puncher Girl" 15.00
Ladies' Home Journal, 1914, September, fashion issue 17.00
Ladies' World, 1917, w/Charlie Chaplin paper doll, uncut 45.00
Life, 1936, December 28, illustrated article on "Gone With the Wind," Metropolitan opera's ballet on cover ..45.00
Life, 1942, March 30, Shirley Temple on cover 20.00
Life, 1944, June 19, General Eisenhower on cover 25.00
Life, 1944, December 11, Judy Garland on cover 15.00
Life, 1945, November 12, Ingrid Bergman on cover 10.00
Life, 1953, September 14, Casey Stengel on cover 25.00
Life, 1955, July 18, Audrey Hepburn on cover 25.00
Life, 1955, August 5, Ben Hogan on cover 55.00
Life, 1960, August 15, Marilyn Monroe & Yves Montand on cover 28.00
Life, 1960, December 26, special 25 year issue 12.00
Life, 1961, January 31, Clark Gable on cover 32.00
Life, 1962, April 13, complete w/baseball cards, Elizabeth Taylor & Richard Burton on cover 125.00
Life, 1962, September 28, Don Drysdale on cover 14.00
Life, 1964, May 29, Jackie Kennedy on cover 10.00
Life, 1964, August 7, Marilyn Monroe on cover 40.00
Life, 1965, May 7, John Wayne on cover 10.00
Life, 1971, October 29, David Cassidy on cover 15.00
Literary Digest, July-December 1905, bound volume 65.00
Literary Digest, 1935, April 20, Babe Ruth cover & story 25.00
Literary Digest, 1935, April 27, Mussolini on cover 20.00
Look, 1937, November 23, color Joan Crawford cover, color Robert Taylor back cover 12.00
Look, 1950, August 29, William Boyd as Hopalong Cassidy on cover 18.00
Look, 1950, December 5, Esther Williams on cover 20.00
Look, 1956, October 16, James Dean on cover 15.00
Look, 1956, December 25, Lucille Ball & family on cover 15.00
Look, 1960, July 5, Marilyn Monroe & Yves Montand on cover 15.00
Look, 1960, August 2, John & Pilar Wayne on cover & story 10.00
Modern Mechanics, 1932, May 10.00
National Geographic, 1917, October, "Our Flag" Number 25.00
National Geographic, 1936, January through June, six months bound 8.50
National Lampoon, 1973, September...12.00
Newsweek, 1940, May 20, Churchill & Chamberlain on cover, Churchill takes over as Prime Minister 25.00
Newsweek, 1956, June 25, Mickey Mantle double photo on cover 69.00
Newsweek, 1963, December 2, John F. Kennedy Memorial issue 20.00
Pictorial Review, 1920, lovely lady cover, colorful full page advertisements including Cream of Wheat w/black mammy & Coca-Cola, also Dolly Dingle dolls 50.00
Playboy, 1955, April 65.00
Popular Mechanics, 1924, January 10.00
Popular Science, 1923, November 10.00
Popular Science, 1929, June 10.00
Power Magazine, 1897, January through December, bound 265.00
Printing Art, 1912, October, Ault Wiborg ad & other unique color ads 13.50
Puck, 1889, February 6, article on trusts, politics, etc., nice color illustrations 12.00
Puck, 1892-1893, August through February, seven months bound 255.00
Radio News, July 1926 through June 1927, full year bound 40.00
Saturday Evening Post, 1906, January 27, scene of long-haired woman kneeling, entitled "The False Gods," by J. C. Leyendecker 8.50
Saturday Evening Post, 1908, November 21, Thanksgiving issue, J.C. Leyendecker cover illustration of grandmother making pie 42.00
Screen Book, 1939, December, Deanna Durbin on cover 20.00
Screen Guide, 1943, Ingrid Bergman on cover 32.00
Screen Play, 1936, September, Joan Bennett on cover 20.00
Sir, 1942, w/"I Wouldn't Strip for Hitler," Vol. 1, No. 1 ....40.00
Sports Illustrated, 1961, October 2, Roger Maris on cover 30.00
Sunset, 1909, January 10.00
Sunset, 1915, October, Pan-Pacific edition 15.00
Theatre Arts, 1939, October, Helen Hayes (Ladies & Gentleman) on cover, Marx Bros., etc., inside 12.00

Time, 1938, July 11, Walter Winchell on cover & in feature article 25.00

Time, 1941, March 17, Henry Ford cover 24.00

Time, 1941, August 4, Charles DeGaulle in uniform on cover 30.00

Time, 1942, September 21, Nazi Field Marshal Fedor Von Bock on cover 34.00

Time, 1944, May 1, Lt. General Omar Bradley on cover..............................15.00

Time, 1945, November 12, Blanchard & Davis on cover................................20.00

Time, 1947, April 14, Brooklyn Dodgers, Leo Durocher, on cover......24.00

Time, 1950, April 10, Ted Williams on cover 45.00

Time, 1951, June 25, Sugar Ray Robinson on cover............................25.00

TV Guide, 1966, January 22, David Janssen on cover..............................15.00

TV Life, 1954, No. 6, Rosemary Clooney on cover, feature stories on Lucy & Desi, Dorothy Dandridge, Jack Webb & Sid Caesar..................23.00

Vicks, 1880, January through December, bound, 392+ pages, twelve full page floral color plates......38.00

Woman's Home Companion, 1911, February, Harrison Fisher lovely lady on cover, Dottie Darling & Kewpies color page, color Cream of Wheat ad, Jack & Betty cut-outs page missing.....................................40.00

MARBLES

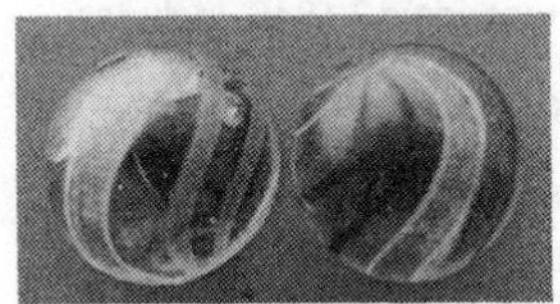

Lutz-type Marbles

Bennington-type, blue mottled, 2" d...$115.50

Bennington-type, blue & brown mixed, set of 10 ....15.00

Bennington-type, blue, brown & blue-green, lot of 50.........................135.00

Glass, Akro Agate, for Chinese Checker game, mint in box 29.00

Glass, blue oxblood, ⅝" d....................15.00

Glass, Indian Swirl, red, ¾" d. 65.00

Glass, latticino-type, lacy yellow core w/red & blue mixed outer swirled stripes, 2⅛" d. 192.50

Glass, Lutz-type, solid core, lime green w/solid white core & two goldstone bands, 13/16" d..................176.00

Glass, Lutz-type, thin bands of bluish green, white & goldstone, 13/16" d......231.00

Glass, Lutz-type, wide clear w/bands of goldstone, one marble trimmed in white & bands of dark blue, the other trimmed in white & bands of robin's-egg blue, ⅞" d., lot of 2 (ILLUS.) 250.00

Glass, Lutz-type, banded, clear w/two bands of goldstone trimmed in white & four bands of yellow, 1 7/16" d. 632.50

Glass, "onionskin," speckled red, pink, turquoise, blue, white, yellow, 2" d. (chip on pontil) 350.00

Glass, "onionskin," mottled lobes of red, yellow & green, 2¾" d. (small ding)..475.00

Glass, opalescent, vaseline, ½" d.........10.00

Glass, open core-type, swirled red, white, blue, green & yellowcore w/white outer bands, 1 15/16" d. 110.00

Glass, slag-type, blue & milky white, ⅝" d...5.00

Glass, slag-type, purple & milky white, ¾" d..8.00

Glass, sulphide, w/bear, 1¾" d. 135.00

Glass, sulphide, w/bird, 2½" d. (ground spot on base)......................203.50

Glass, sulphide, w/Christ on the cross 1,000.00

Glass, sulphide, w/crane holding fish 550.00

Glass, sulphide, w/figure "8"..............875.00

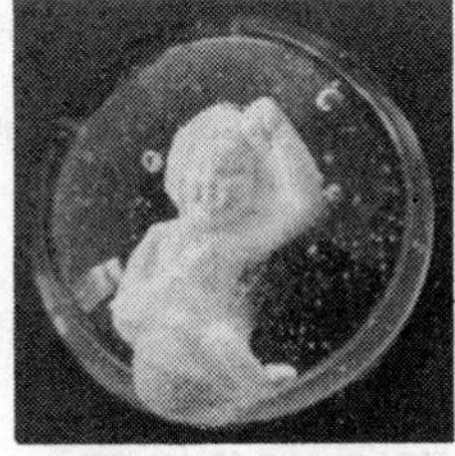

Sulphide Marble with Seated Girl

Glass, sulphide, w/seated girl washing hair, polished, 1½" d. (ILLUS.).........300.00

Glass, sulphide, w/man wearing hat sitting on stump, polished, 1¼" d. 250.00

Glass, sulphide, w/owl 175.00

Glass, sulphide, w/pink cow 1,300.00

Glass, sulphide, w/rabbit, 2" d. 115.00

Glass, sulphide, w/rabbit, amber tinted, 2" d. 325.00

Glass, sulphide, w/rearing horse, 1¾" d...95.00

Glass, sulphide, w/squirrel, 1⅝" d. (minor wear)......................................132.00

Glass, white clambroth w/green & red lines, ⅝" d. (two small chips) 90.00

Glass, white clambroth w/red lines, 11/16" 185.00

MATCH SAFES & CONTAINERS

Advertising container, stoneware, cylindrical tapering sides, impressed label w/shield & eagle "American Brew Co. Rochester, N.Y." highlighted in blue & w/blue base stripe, 2¾" h. $126.50

Advertising safe, pocket-type, leather, "Rice & Hutchins Shoes" 35.00

Advertising safe, "Schlitz" in banner around a globe, Milwaukee around the edge, leather covered base w/cigar cutter on bottom 85.00

Advertising safe, wall-type, lithographed tin, "Ceresota Prize Bread Flour," die-cut young child cutting a large loaf of bread on a large barrel forming the holder, browns & pale green w/black lettering, 2½" w., 5½" h. (touch up on back, scratches at nail holes & edges, very minor rust) 253.00

Advertising safe, lithographed tin, "Wise Wives Work Wonders With Solarine," 3½ x 4 x 5" 150.00

Advertising safe, wall-type, barrel-shaped, "B.F. Hollenbach & Sons Groceries" 55.00

Advertising safe, wall-type, "Osborne Harvesting Machines" 145.00

Brass container, hanging-type, model of an open umbrella, 3 x 5" 55.00

Brass safe, figural cat peeking out of a boot, striker on base, 1¼ x 1¾" 185.00

Brass safe, figural mouse, 1 x 2" plus leather tail & ears 175.00

Brass safe, horseshoe-shaped, embossed horse on front, 2 x 2¼" ...195.00

Brass safe, model of a slipper, hinged cover, cigar cutter on back of heel, ⅞ x 3" 195.00

Brass safe, model of a stein, embossed figures of a lady & man standing by a tree on front & back, 1 x 1⅝" 175.00

Cast iron container, man's head 55.00

Cast iron container, table model, model of an alligator, "C&C Co., Fla," 8" l. 235.00

Cast iron container, table model, in the form of a crying child w/drum, old dark patina, 5⅝" l 55.00

Cast iron container, wall-type, double urn, 1867 ....65.00

Cast iron container, wall-type, grotesque face of Bacchus 150.00

Cast iron container, wall-type, w/game pouch, horn & bird, 1870 ....80.00

Nickel plate safe, figural bust of King Alfred, striker on base, 1¾ x 2" 375.00

Nickel plate safe, figural pig, striker on base, 1½ x 2½" 135.00

Silver plate safe, stylized Art Nouveau relief-molded florals, 1½ x 3" 75.00

Sterling silver safe, pocket-type, scene of golfer swinging, ¼ x 1¾ x 2 ½" 110.00

Yellowware container, table model, designed in the form of a dung beetle on a leaf, removable lid, 6" l. (chips) 71.50

MEDICAL COLLECTIBLES

Book, "Consumptive's Guide," by Dr. Potter, New York, 1852, 176 pp.......$80.00

Book, "The Elements of Surgery," by Samuel Mihles, M.D., 1764, London, second edition, illustrated w/copper plates, leather cover, 368 pp. (end papers missing) 185.00

Book, "Historie de la Medecine," by Daniel Le Clerc, Paris, 1702 ....375.00

Book, "Health Knowledge," by Medical Book Distributors, Vol. I, 1927 w/ anatomical pull-outs 35.00

Book, "People's Medical Lighthouse & Advisor," by H.K. Root, M.D., 1857, Saratoga Springs, 472 pp. 20.00

Book, "The People's Common Sense Medical Advisor," by R.V. Pierce, M.D., 1886 ....20.00

Book, "Practical Bacteriology Blood-work Parasitology," by Stitt, 1916 ......35.00

Book, "Thomson's Conspectus of Pharmacopoeias of London, Edinburgh, Cublin Physicians US Pharmacopoeia," 1846, includes prescriptions, etc., 313 pp. 45.00

Chart, "Chart of Sinovsoidalogy," 1915, Ultima Physical Appliance Co., 17 x 22" 45.00

Cigarettes, quack medicine for bronchial asthma, paroxysms, hay fever, colds, Blosser, 24 in original box 75.00

Dentist's chair, w/bracket table & cuspidor, "Wilkerson," ca. 1877 ....3,750.00

Dentist's drill, foot pedal-driven, black enamel w/gold leaf trim, White Mfg., 1895 ....475.00

Doctor's medical bag, cowhide 85.00

Lens kit, "Doctor's Eye," w/leather case 150.00

Machine, "Myofasciatrom Model RV3," quack medical device in walnut box 75.00

Machine, "Williams Perfection Electro-Magnetic Machine," quack medical device, oak case, original & in working condition 195.00

Medicine container, tin, "Gall Salve," Bickmore 15.00

PIll making machine, "Whitall, Tatum & Co.," cast-iron w/brass molding, gold stenciling, microscope-shaped 165.00

Phrenological head, composition, a stylized human head w/the bald scalp divided into segments, 19th c., 11" h..825.00

Splints, spring-type, one for arm & the other for the leg, marked "Pat. 1885 - Perfection Process Fracture Spring Splints, James Wallace MD, inventor & sole proprietor," pr. 13.00

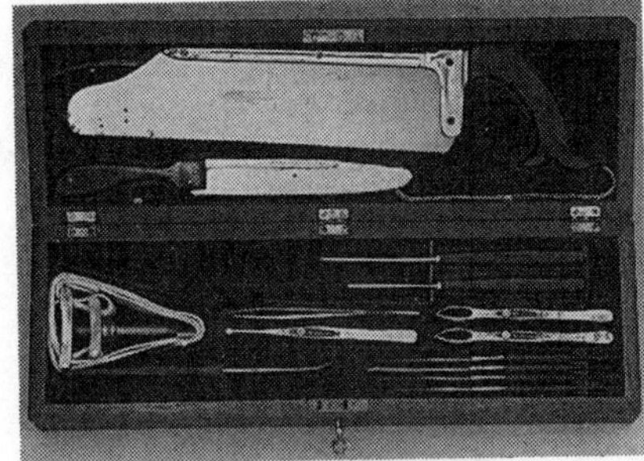

19th Century Surgeon's Kit

Surgeon's kit, composed of two saws, forceps, two Liston knives, three scalpels, tourniquet, sutures & five other instruments, most w/ebony handles, complete in a velvet-lined fitted brass-bound mahogany case w/key, by W.F. Ford, ca. 1860, case 15½" l. (ILLUS.) 2,875.00

Surgical instruments, in a folding leather case marked "Codman and Shurtleff Surgical and Dental Instruments, 13 Tremont Street, Boston," further fitted in a mahogany case labeled "G. Tiemann & Co., Manufacturers, 67 Chatham Street, New York," together w/a leather-bound book, 'The Physician Hand Book" dated 1879, the group 6,050.00

METALS

ALUMINUM

Buffet server, cov., w/handled undertray, Tulip patt., flower & ribbon handles, "Rodney Kent No. 440," 2 pcs. $18.00

Coaster, hammered, depicts golfer, Wendell August..................................15.00

Dish, cov., hammered, w/Bakelite handles, Cellini, Chicago, 5 x 8 x 12" 135.00

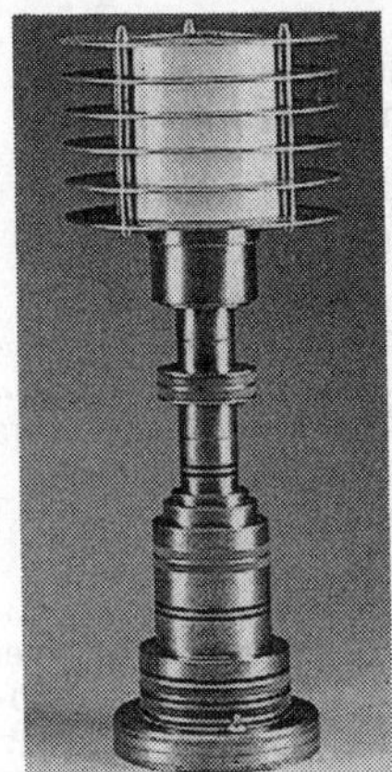

Unique Aluminum Lamp

Lamps, table model, modernistic design w/a cylindrical, multi-stepped base tapering up to a multi-disc shade enclosing a frosted glass cylinder, the base decorated w/rust & black bands, probably manufactured by Pattyn Products Company, ca. 1935, 20" h., pr. (ILLUS. of one) 8,800.00

Lazy Susan breakfast server: toast rack, two cov. glass jelly pots w/spoons, & cov. butter dish; Ribbon & Tulip design, unused w/original tag, Rodney Kent Co., the set............28.00

Tray, hammered, birds on branch decoration, basketweave handle, Farberware, 13½" l. 15.00

Tray, hammered, Marlin fish scene, w/double fish hook handles, Wendell August, 17 x 23" 120.00

Vase, hammered, w/glass liner, exquisite pine decoration, Arthur Armour, 11½" h...............................200.00

Wall panel, rectangular, decorated w/multicolored enameled copper Navajo-style figures embedded in a sanded ground, probably designed for the S.S. United States, ca. 1952, 7' l., 42" h. 1,150.00

BRASS

Card tray, relief scene of the landing of Columbus center, 3¾ x 5¼"...........92.00

Centerpiece bowl, the wide-mouthed oval body w/broad flattened lip, raised on a simple oviform foot, by Professor Waldemar Raemisch, signed "RAEMISCH - GERMANY," ca. 1930, 12⅞" l. 1,495.00

Charger, round w/wide flanged rim w/molded edge, engraved in the center w/a large coat of arms surmounted by a crown, France, mid-18th c., 21½" d.......................3,220.00

Kettle, spun, iron bail handle, deep slightly flaring cylindrical sides, marked "American Brass Kettle," 12½" d. 49.50

Kettle shelf, cast, grill-work top, 6 x 10", 5" h. 104.50

Kettle stand, cut-out design of squirrels on top, paw feet, 6 x 10¾" 115.50

Memo clip, oblong w/embossed floral design, marked "Merry Phipson Parker's Letter Clip," 6" h. 49.50

Paperweight, bust of a pharoah, w/enameled base..............................95.00

Toasting fork, adjustable, w/weighted conical base, stamped "Patent No--" (dents in base) 165.00

18th Century Brass Wall Sconces

Wall sconces, single-light, surmounted by a shell, the oval reflector plate below w/petal-form surround, the dished drip plate below centering a molded candlecup, English or Continental, second half 18th c., 10" w., 18¾" h., pr. (ILLUS.) 3,105.00

BRONZE

Figural Bronze Chalice

Ashtray, floor model, a reticulated quatraform dish raised on a ribbed columnar shaft above a matching openwork platform base raised on four paw feet, 30" h. 137.50

Censer, lobed body w/three legs supporting a cylindrical neck cast in light-relief w/angular scrolls, beneath two upright loop handles on the everted rim, the domed wood cover carved in the form of a furled lotus leaf & surmounted by a turquoise pierced knob, raised on a similar carved wood base, 18th c., overall 11¼ " h. 2,300.00

Chalice, figural, cast as the head of Bacchus, brown patina, 3½" h. (ILLUS.) 403.00

Cigarette box w/hinged lid, the rectangular lid cast w/a young goat herd carrying clusters of grapes, w/two leaping goats in the distance, cedar-lined, designed by Rockwell Kent, impressed "RK," ca. 1930, 6½" l. 230.00

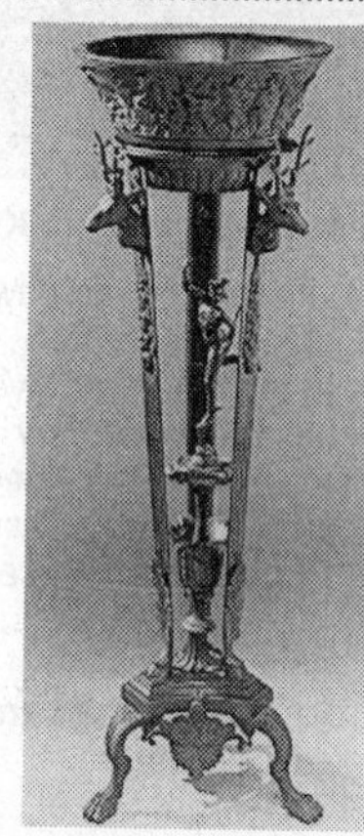

Ornate Bronze Jardiniere & Stand

Jardiniere & stand, the bowl w/a continuous allegorical band, supported by a tripod stand headed by deer heads & ending in hoof feet, enclosing a figure of Mercury, raised on scrolled legs & paw feet, patinated finish, overall 42" h., 2 pcs. (ILLUS.) 2,300.00

Lamp, figural table model, cast as the figure of dancer Loie Fuller in swirling gossamer & voluminous gown, the portion swirling overhead enclosing two small light fixtures, gilt finish, inscribed "Raoul Larche" & impressed "Siot-Decauville - fondeur - Paris," France, ca. 1900, 18" h. 13,200.00

Medal, awarded to René Lalique, oval, cast w/leafage & artistic trophies, the reverse inscribed

"Concours - 1893 - Artistes et Industriels - Orfevrerie - Vase a Boire -2me Prix - Mr. R. Lalique," in original fitted red leather presentation box stamped "UNION CENTRALE - DES - ARTS DECORATIFS - 1893," 2⅞" l., 2 pcs. 2,588.00

Model of a cat w/rifle, marked "Austria," 2" h. 245.00

Mold, two-piece, for casting pewter spoons, 9" l. 330.00

Tray-lamp, the irregular shallow circular tray cast in medium- & full-relief along the rim w/thistle pods & thorny leafage, one pod rising from the surface & hinged to enclose a small light fixture, gilt finish, inscribed "A.Marionnet," ca. 1900, 13¼" l. 3,025.00

Urn, campana-form, a wide slightly flaring cylindrical body w/a wide flattened rim w/gadrooned rim, the body sides cast in high-relief w/a continuous Bacchanalian scene of putti, loop twig handles at base of bottom, raised on a short paneled pedestal continuing to a deep domed base w/a grapevine border, late 19th c., 16½" d., 14" h. 990.00

Vase, tapering cylindrical body w/compressed bulbous base, cast w/trailing ivy vines & a grasshopper in full-relief, black patina, inscribed "HUGO ELMQUIST," ca. 1900, 12" h. 2,875.00

Vase, tapering cylindrical form w/wide flaring rim, decorated w/alternating ribs, vertical panels & curvilinear devices, impressed "Tiffany & Co. 28215B," 15" h. 990.00

CHROME

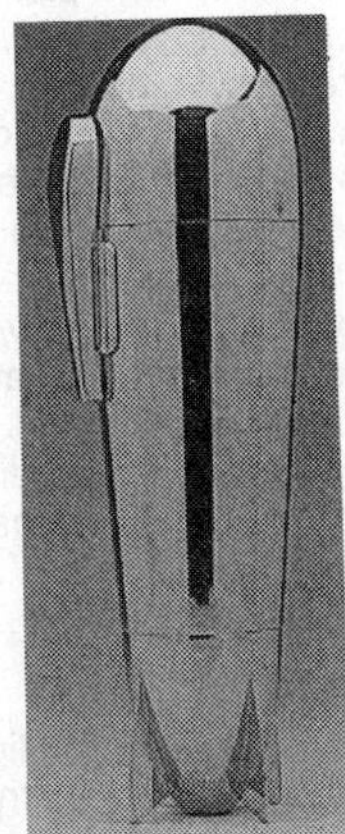

Chrome "Zeppelin" Cocktail Shaker

Buffet server, electric, by Lurelle Guild, "Chase," catalog No. 27011 ..295.00

Champagnes, an inverted cone sitting atop a slender stem & joined by five discs, on a round foot, w/plastic label, each 9½" h., set of 12 ....518.00

Cocktail set: cylindrical cocktail shaker w/horizontal striations around the base & on the cover & topped w/a dark blue plastic stopper, six footed cordials of cobalt blue glass mounted on stepped chrome feet & a round chrome tray; all pieces w/the Chase company mark, ca. 1930, tray 11¾" d., shaker 12" h., the set 276.00

Cocktail shaker, the streamlined Zeppeliln-shaped body disassembling into 19 pieces, comprising four glasses, funnel, corkscrew & cover, jigger, cover to form a second jigger, covers & gondola housing four spoons, several pieces stamped "GERMANY," ca. 1929, w/fitted suede case, 12" h. (ILLUS.) 3,220.00

Coffee set: cov. coffeepot, open sugar bowl & creamer; Art Deco style, each labeled "Sunbeam," made by The Chicago Flexible Shaft Co., Design Pat. D-92668, ca. 1930s, the set 75.00

Corn set: a circular cobalt blue glass tray w/chrome rim, chrome oil server & salt & pepper shakers; designed by Russel Wright, manufactured by Chase, all stamped w/company logo, tray 6" d., shakers 5⅛" h., the set 115.00

Microphone, grey enameled domed base below a cylindrical chrome stem supporting a circular microphone, 1930s, 12" h. 460.00

Smoking set: a rectangular cigarette case & lighter; each etched w/geometric designs, in original box, impressed Ronson mark & serial numbers, ca. 1930, box 4$\frac{5}{16}$ x 7½", the set 161.00

Wine bucket, flaring cylindrical body w/two applied circular handles, one side cast w/a square medallion w/a young Bacchus & two leaping goats in the distance, designed by Rockwell Kent, impressed "RK" & the Chase company mark, ca. 1930, 9¼" h. 575.00

COPPER

Ashtray w/matchbox holder, shallow rimmed bowl, matchbox holder & two cigarette rests on rim, wood-grained surface, monogramed, w/glass liner, marked "Hand wrought by Fred Brosi - Ye Olde Copper Shoppe San Francisco," 3¾" x 6½"......................................165.00

Enameled Copper Box

Box, cov., Arts & Crafts style, round tapering sides & low-domed cover centered by a round enameled floral medallion in red & green outlined in black on a blue ground, Boston school, unsigned, ca. 1910, original brown patina, 4¾" d., 2¾" h. (ILLUS.) 385.00

Candlesticks, Arts & Crafts style, hand-hammered, a shallow dished base centered by a cylindrical standard below a shallow flaring socket, an applied riveted handle near the top, hammered finish, Gustav Stickley Model 74, early 20th c., 10" h., pr..........................1,380.00

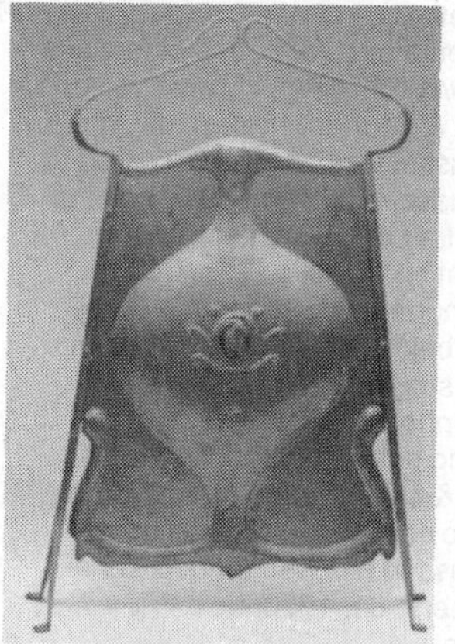

Art Nouveau Copper Fire Screen

Fire screen, Art Nouveau style, shaped rectangular screen framed in wrought iron & continuing on to form legs, central ceramic insert w/blue glaze, unsigned, England, ca. 1900, 18¼" w., 28½" h. (ILLUS.) 330.00

Humidor, Arts & Crafts style, hand-hammered, rectangular flat cover w/domed central section w/upright angled handle, the conforming base on short scrolled & riveted tab feet, original dark patina, unmarked, early 20th c., 6¼ x 10½" 165.00

Kettle, iron bail handle, dovetailed construction, rim stamped "J.P. Schaum, Lancaster, Pa.," polished, 22" d., 14" h. (battered) 165.00

Mug, cylindrical dovetailed body w/wrought copper strap handle, early, 6" h. 137.50

Pitcher, cov., tankard-type, Arts & Crafts style, hand-hammered, the tall tapering cylindrical body w/a heavy hammered band around the base and around the top third, angled handle, low-domed cover also covering the rim spout, original dark red patina, marked w/artist's cipher, England, early 20th c., 6" d., 12" h. 137.50

Planter, Arts & Crafts style, hand-hammered, wide shallow form w/upright & slightly incurved sides w/an applied decoration of continuous ivy vines, brown & green patina, impressed metal tag mark of L. LaGatta, early 20th c., 9¼" d., 3" h...550.00

Plaque, designed in the form of an oversized charger w/deeply depressed center & a broad rim embossed w/large stylized pods, original reddish brown patina, impressed clamp mark of Gustav Stickley, Model No. 345, 20" d. (minor wear to patina) 5,775.00

Sauce pan, cov., cylindrical body w/dished flat cover, double cast-iron long handle, marked "D.H. & M. Co., N.Y.," 5" d. plus handle 110.00

Teakettle, cov., dovetailed construction, bulbous body w/rounded shoulder to a short rim fitted w/a low domed cover, swan's-neck spout & hinged strap handle, handle stamped "W. Powell," 6" h. plus handle 742.50

Tray, Arts & Crafts-style, hand-hammered, oval w/low flared sides & a flared rim, mounted w/angled loop end handles, Dirk Van Erp mark, early 20th c., 17" l. 605.00

Tray, hand-hammered, circular w/four lobes at corners, the lobes & flat rim applied w/cut-outs accented by raised rivets, impressed w/windmill mark & "Dirk Van Erp" in box, early 20th c., 12½" d. 1,870.00

IRON

Bill clip, cast, round dome form, figural bas relief duck & "A. Silz, Poultry & Game," 2½ x 4" oval 95.00

Book press, cast, a rectangular metal platform w/rounded ends supporting a large arched framework composed of a pair of stylized dolphins w/gold paint centered by a long screw for the rectangular pressing plate & w/a large round handle at its top, old black paint, 19th c., 10¾ x 20" 440.00

Bundt pan, cast, "Griswold No. 965" 950.00

Cigar cutter, cast, counter-type, embossed "King Alfred 10¢ Cigar," 3" clock at top 1,550.00

Fork, hand-wrought, three-tine 'claw,' well shaped flattened ribbed handle w/eye hanger, stamped "M. Moles," overall 17¾" l.....................................99.00

Griddle, cast, flat thick disc w/a long flat, tapering handle ending in a flat knob, handle 12½" l., griddle 13" d. (pitted)..115.50

Ice tongs, hand-wrought, ca. 1800, 16" l...23.00

Lawn sprinkler, cast, model of a frog, Grey Iron Casting, Mt. Joy, Pennsylvania 140.00

Mailbox, cast, wall-mount, "Griswold" 135.00

19th Century Cast Iron Dog

Model of a dog, cast, the figure of a dog in a playful stance in the full round w/molded fur & curled tail, late 19th c., probably America, 37" l., 24" h. (ILLUS.) 5,750.00

Muffin pan, cast, six cups, "Griswold's Erie No. 18"......................................125.00

Muffin pan, cast, thirteen cups in the shape of stars, hearts, circles & scalloped circles, marked "Reids Pan Dec. 1870," 9 x 16¾" 159.50

Paperweight, cast, bust of Henry Clay on a rectangular base w/rounded edges, 3 x 4¾"...............................121.00

Pencil sharpener, cast, "Planetary," by A.B. Dick, dated 1895 ....350.00

Pin tray, cast, figural parrot, painted, 2½" l...35.00

Shooting gallery target, cast, model of a battleship, rusted red paint, 10" l. ...93.50

Shooting gallery target, cast, model of a full-bodied simple stylized bird, old gold repaint, 3¼" h.........................104.50

Shooting gallery target, cast, model of an Indian in a canoe, 9" l. (damage, very rusted).......................................77.00

Skillet, cast, "Griswold No. 8," large pattern..24.00

Skillet, cast, "Griswold No. 9," w/slant letters 36.00

Skillet, cast, "Wagner Ware No. 8" 16.00

Teakettle, cov., cast, gooseneck spout, marked "Baster," dated 1863 ....115.00

Toasting rack, hand-wrought, hearth-type, a long rotating bar w/squared bars w/twisted details above a tripod base, 16" l. 115.50

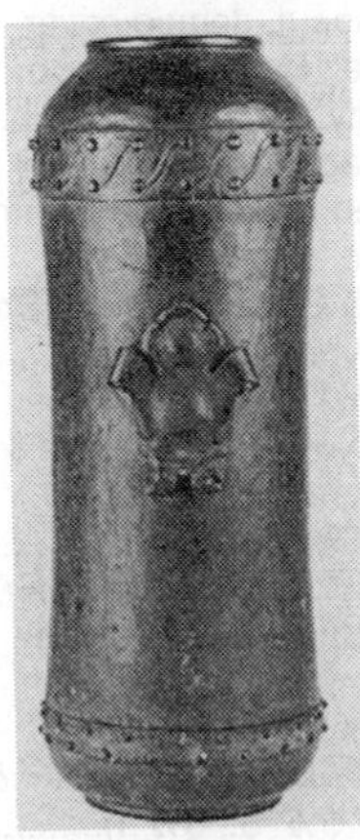

Cast Iron Umbrella Stand

Umbrella stand, cast, decorated w/a riveted band at top & base w/an applied medallion at midsection, hammered finish, unsigned, 24½" h. (ILLUS.) 440.00

Waffle iron w/stand, cast, hearts & diamonds design, No. 7 in circle in center & on handle, 6¾" d., 5" l. handle 158.00

PEWTER

Basin, touch mark of Semper Eadem, Boston, 1725-72, polished, 8" d., 1⅞" h. (minor wear) 440.00

Bowl, oval, open handles, flowers & leaves design, Kayserzinn, No. 4322, 13" l. 145.00

Bread tray, raised floral design, impressed "KAYSERZINN" & numbered "322," 7½ x 13" 350.00

Candlestick, stepped circular base, turned shaft, short cylindrical candle socket w/flaring rim, Roswell Gleason, Dorchester, Massachusetts, 1821-71, 7" h. 330.00

Candlesticks, a waisted cylindrical socket above a tall tapering cylindrical shaft above a ringed, domed foot, Henry Hopper, New York, New York, ca. 1840, marked, 10" h., pr. 880.00

Chalice, tall slightly waisted cylindrical cup on a short stem w/domed round foot, unmarked American, mid-19th c., 5¾" h. 192.50

Charger, Robert Palethorp, Jr., Philadelphia, 1817-22, 13" d., (wear & scratches) 357.50

Coffeepot, cov., tall 'lighthouse' style, Roswell Gleason, Dorchester, Massachusetts, 1821-71, 10⅝" h. (minor dents)..................................687.50

Coffeepot, cov., bulbous base, gooseneck spout, domed cover w/turned finial, Boardman & Co., New York City, 1825-27, 11½" h......330.00

Communion flagon, tall cylindrical body w/ringed middle & flaring ring-stepped base, domed cover w/thumb lift & C-scroll handle, Smith & Feltman, Albany, New York, 1849-52, 10½" h. 550.00

Compote, Art Nouveau style, iris & butterfly decoration, unmarked Kayserzinn, 9¾"................................85.00

Cracker jar, cov., hammered finish, spherical w/embossed lily pads around the rim, impressed "H - MADE IN ENGLAND - TUDRIC PEWTER - MADE BY LIBERTY & CO - 01562," 5½" d., 5½" h.............385.00

Flagon, cov., tapering cylindrical body w/band at middle & above base, ringed foot, C-scroll handle w/thumbpiece, shaped spout, stepped domed cover, Roswell Gleason, Dorchester, Massachusetts, 1821-71, 10" h.......................495.00

Inkstand, central cylindrical well w/pen holes around the top rim & a central porcelain insert, on a wide, flat, flanged base, marked "S (crown) O," possibly England, early to mid-19th c. 70.00

Lamp, table-type, a whale oil burner in the acorn-shaped font on a short cylindrical stem above the shallow wide dished foot w/a small strap handle at one side, unmarked American, 19th c., 5½" h. (foot slightly battered) 247.00

Measure, haystack-type, marked "Gill," England, 3¾" h.......................192.50

Measures, tankard-form, bulbous sides, strap handle, set of eight in graduated sizes from one-quarter gill to one gallon, from 2" to 10¼" h., the set 2,200.00

Pewter Mug by Samuel Hamlin

Mug, tapering cylindrical body flaring slightly at the molded base, lower body w/narrow raised band, scrolling strap handle, touch mark of Samuel Hamlin, Providence, Rhode Island, first quarter 19th c., 6" h. (ILLUS.) 2,300.00

Covered Pewter Water Pitcher

Pitcher, cov., water, baluster-form body w/scroll handle, domed hinged cover w/turned finial, touch mark of Roswell Gleason, Dorchester, Massachusetts, 1821-71, 8½" h. (ILLUS.) 302.50

Pitcher, cov., water, bulbous w/low flaring foot, scroll handle & flaring spout, hinged stepped cover w/turned finial, Sellew & Co., Cincinnati, Ohio, 1832-60, 9¼" h. 742.50

Plate, "Love" touch, Pennsylvania, ca. 1750-93, 7⅞" d. (minor wear & corrosion).......................................297.00

Plate, flanged rim, marked "Townsend & Compton, London," England, late 18th - early 19th c., 8⅛" d. (wear, scratches) 110.00

Plate, John Skinner, Boston, 1760-90, smooth brim, 9¼" d...........................357.50

Plate, Roswell Gleason, Dorchester, Massachusetts, 1821-71, 10⅞" d...247.50

Plate, Samuel Pierce, Greenfield, Massachusetts, 1792-1830, 11¼" d. 495.00

Porringer, pierced scrolling 'crown' tab

handle marked on the back "SG," possibly by Samuel Green, Jr. of Boston, early 19th c., 5¼" d., ...275.00

Porringer, 'Old English' style pierced tab handle, Boardman & Sherman, Hartford, Connecticut, 1810-50, 4" d..605.00

Teapot, cov., wide rounded cup-form body raised on a short pedestal foot, the rounded shoulder tapering to a short wide neck w/flared rim, domed cover w/disc finial, swan's-neck spout & C-scroll painted handle, Smith & Co., Boston, Massachusetts, 1847-49, 8" h.........................302.50

Teapot, cov., tapering shouldered cylindrical body on flaring foot, black painted scroll handle, swan's-neck spout, domed cover w/ornate finial, George Richardson, Boston, 1818-28, 9¼" h. 605.00

Teapot, cov., wide slightly tapering cylindrical body w/flared base & rim, domed cover w/disc finial, swan's-neck spout & S-scroll handle, Freeman Porter, Westbrook, Maine, ca. 1835-60.......................................440.00

Tea set: cov. teapot, cov. sugar bowl, cov. creamer & tray; the semi-circular teapot & wedge-shaped sugar bowl & creamer, each w/a hinged lid & spherical Bakelite knob, fitting into the circular tray raised on four stepped feet, all four pieces fitted w/solid angular black Bakelite handles attached w/brass rivets, designed by Gene Theobald, each stamped "Pewter - by - Wilcox" & numbered, ca. 1928, tray over handles 8½", 4 pcs. 4,025.00

Time lamp, a bulbous glass bulb at the top surrounding a bar w/time notations above a shallow covered burning fluid font angled to the side of the tall slender shaft raised on a flaring round base, unmarked, Europe, 19th c., 15½" h. (minor imperfections) 330.00

Tumbler, flaring sides, Thomas Danforth Boardman, Hartford, Connecticut, 1804-60 & later, 2¾" h. 77.00

SHEFFIELD PLATE

Coffee & tea service: cov. coffeepot, cov. teapot, open sugar bowl & creamer; each w/a flaring oval form w/scrolled handles, bright-cut neoclassical decoration, Walker & Hall, Sheffield, England, together w/a handled silver plate tray, the set..357.50

Coffee urn, cov., plain vasiform body over a spreading base on ball feet, lion head & ring handles, monogrammed, England, 19½" h. (minor dents, rosing) 495.00

Sheffield Plate Tureen & Wine Coolers

Soup tureen, cov., *bombé* oval form raised on four large scroll feet decorated w/shells & leaves, reeded rod end handles rising from lion masks, gadroon shell & foliate borders, matching ring finial on domed cover, body & cover engraved w/a crest & coronet within Garter motto, marked by T. & J. Creswick, ca. 1825, overall 16" l. (ILLUS. bottom) 4,025.00

Wine coolers, fluted campana-form, large loop handle at lower sides, engraved w/arms above a band of water leaves, grapevine border, detachable rims & liners, J. Watson & Son, England, ca. 1830, 10" h., pr. (ILLUS. top) 3,450.00

SILVER, AMERICAN (Sterling & Coin)

Early American Silver Caster

Beakers, paneled baluster-form body w/flared rim & a hammered surface, marked on bases "SPECIAL HAND-WORK," Tiffany & Co., New York, New York, ca. 1909, 4" h., set of 6 ...2,645.00

Bowl, child's, deep round sides & scalloped rim, the sides divided into four panels each w/a relief scene depicting a scene from the nursery rhyme "Sing a Song of Sixpence" framed by interlaced flowering tendrils, Tiffany & Co., New York, New York, ca. 1905, 5⅛" d. ...1,495.00

Bowl, *Martelé*, the fluted base below a leaf-flanked lobed body & wide rolled ruffled & lobed rim w/chased daisies & other flowers surrounded by tendrils, Gorham Mfg. Co., Providence, Rhode Island, ca. 1902, 10¾" d. ...2,415.00

Butter dish, cov., circular, raised on three hoof feet headed by foliage, the rim engraved w/a crest & motto below an applied beaded band, w/pierced interior grille, the domed cover repoussé & chased w/panels of ivy on a matted ground above a similar bead band & surmounted by a bud finial, Tiffany & Co., 1859-70, 6⅝" d. ...1,320.00

Cann, baluster-form on molded rim foot, w/foliate scroll handle, Paul Revere, Boston, 1765-95, 5⅛" h. ...13,200.00

Caster, cov., footed baluster-form w/corded girdle, the cover pierced & engraved w/panels of latticework & w/a slender baluster-form finial, the foot engraved w/contemporary initials "MTE" conjoined, marked by Jacob Gerritse Lansing, Albany, New York, ca. 1770, 5" h. (ILLUS.) ...4,888.00

Cheese scoop, w/shovel bowl, knopped stem & reeded rectangular handle w/foliate decoration, engraved initials "MC," maker's mark of A.E. Warner, Baltimore, Maryland, Baltimore assay office mark & dominical letter "D," 1823, 9⅜" l. ...1,320.00

Coffeepot, cov., bulbous baluster-form body raised on a short pedestal w/domed foot, based on German 18th c. rococo designs w/shell fluting, asymmetrical shellwork cover & conforming scroll handle & spout, J.E. Caldwell, Philadelphia, ca. 1850-60, 13½" h. ...1,265.00

Creamer, pyriform, on three scroll feet, w/wavy rim & scroll handle, engraved under base "S" over "S*E," the front later engraved "MES to LES," Samuel Casey, Exeter & South Kingston, Rhode Island, 1750-70, 3⅞" h. ...1,100.00

Silver Goblet with Scene

Goblet, octagonal cylindrical bowl raised on an octagonal pedestal foot, the sides of the bowl chased w/a lakeside landscape w/swans & sailboat, houses & a fountain behind, all framed by leafy scrolls & two rococo cartouches, one inscribed, Hyde & Goodrich, New Orleans, ca. 1849, 7½" h. (ILLUS.) ...4,888.00

Pitcher, faceted vase shape, the shoulder bright-cut w/stylized foliage & reeded scallops, w/angular handle, the rim applied w/a die-rolled band of leaves on a reeded ground, the side engraved w/a coat-of-arms, crest & motto, maker's mark of Baldwin Gardiner, New York, ca. 1830, 7¾" h. ...7,150.00

Pitcher, vase-shaped, w/flaring rim & angular handle, the side applied w/conjoined initials "OE," spot-hammered surface, maker's mark of Lebolt & Co., Chicago, ca. 1915, 9⅛" h. ...1,430.00

Plates, shaped circular form, the lobed depressions headed by applied stylized flowerheads, the applied oval & reed rim w/foliate scrolls & shells at intervals joined by scrolls, engraved under bases "MCT 1902," each marked, Tiffany & Co., New York, 1891-1902, 9⅞" d., set of 18 ...17,600.00

Porringer, circular w/pierced three hole handle, maker's mark of Thauvet Besley, New York, ca. 1740, 7⅞" l. ...2,860.00

Punch bowl, deep hemispherical bowl w/rolled gadrooned rim & raised on a short pedestal w/a wide domed base raised on short shell & scroll-work feet, the bowl chased w/rococo ornament including morning glory & engraved w/a foliate monogram, William Gale & Son, New York, 1852, 13¼" d. 2,990.00

Sauceboat, oval, hammered surface, four ball feet, w/long-handled spoon, marked "LEBOLT HAND-MADE STERLING," early 20th c., 3¼ x 6¾", 2 pcs. 440.00

Soup ladle, circular shell bowl, the downturned rounded stem engraved w/feather-edge border, maker's mark of Lewis Fueter, New York, ca. 1770, 15" l. 2,420.00

Sugar nippers, scissor-form, the join engraved w/flowerheads, w/shell tips, the loop handles engraved "M" & "S," John Ball, Concord, Massachusetts, 1750-60, 4¾" l. 2,420.00

Victorian Silver Tea Set

Tea & coffee service: cov. teapot, cov. coffeepot, cov. sugar bowl & creamer; Classical Revival style w/ovoid footed bodies & domed covers, each piece w/die-rolled zigzag borders, chased strapwork borders & bud finials, monogrammed on one side & engraved on the other w/the date "Jan. 14th 1870," Ball, Black & Co., New York, coffeepot 11½" h., 4 pcs. (ILLUS.) 2,185.00

Tea tray, oval w/molded rim & raised border etched w/interlaced running foliage enclosing flowerheads, loop end handles, the center engraved w/a monogram within an oval of spreading petals, Tiffany & Co., New York, New York, ca. 1915, overall 28¾" l. 4,888.00

Vegetable tureen, cov., Chrysanthemum patt., a squatty oval body w/loop end handles & a rolled, flattened rim cast w/blossoms & leaves, raised on tall curved leaf & blossom legs, the stepped, domed & ribbed cover w/a twisted leaf finial, Tiffany & Co., New York, 1902-07, marked, overall 11½" l. 5,750.00

Wine syphon, of typical hooped form, complete w/vacuum pump w/ivory handle, the valve w/a serrated disc tap, Baldwin Gardiner, Philadelphia or New York, ca. 1820-30, 15" l. (repaired) 1,150.00

SILVER, ENGLISH & OTHERS

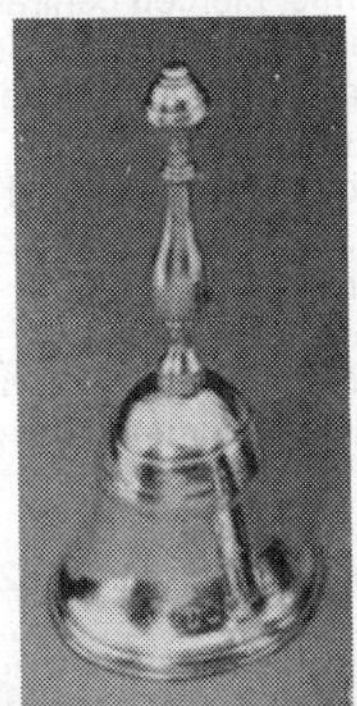

English Table Bell

Bell, table-type, molded borders & baluster-form handle, Peter & Ann Bateman, London, 1791, 4¼" h. (ILLUS.) 1,265.00

Argyle, cylindrical body w/slender S-form spout & raffia-covered C-scroll side handle, the cavity sides filled through a capped spout, low domed cover w/bud finial, Andrew Fogelberg, London, 1773, 4½" h. 2,300.00

Basket, oval, pierced & chased w/exotic birds & flowers, on four openwork supports, Edwin Charles Purdie, London, 1897, 11¾" l. 2,300.00

Beaker, of Aztec inspiration, cylindrical w/slightly incurved body, applied w/four semi-circular loops joined by a reeded band, marked on the base & stamped "Jean Puiforcat, Made in Mexico," ca. 1945, 5½" h. 1,265.00

Bidet, pear-shaped dish, the interior engraved w/a foliate monogram, the flat everted rim chased w/rococo ornament on a matte ground, maker's mark "GL," Paris, France, ca. 1875, 18" l. 3,450.00

Bowl, lobed & fluted w/applied brackets for spoons, engraved w/the initials "GA," Venice or Padua, Italy, ca. 1770, 5" oval 690.00

Bowl, embossed in high-relief w/iris

blossoms & leaves, incurvate rim formed by blossoms, gilt interior, Japan, ca. 1900, repairs, 13" d. ...3,163.00

Brandy bowl, the shallow oval body lobed into eight panels, each engraved w/a vacant cartouche, flat interlaced ribbon rim handles, spreading rim foot, handles w/later inscriptions underneath, Sigusmund Zshammer, Amsterdam, Holland, 1684, overall 9⅛" l. 3,738.00

Brazier, typical form pierced w/formal foliage & ovals & engraved w/contemporary arms, pierced central dish, on three panel feet w/wood terminals & a straight turned wood handle, Louis XV period, Jean-Baptiste Leroux, Lille, France, 1767, 6¾" d. 2,875.00

Cake basket, round, the sides embossed & pierced w/fruit & flowers, matching openwork swing handle, on a scroll-trimmed base, the center engraved w/contemporary arms, George IV period, Robert Gainsford, Sheffield, 1824, 13" d. 2,013.00

Silver Casket from India

Casket, rectangular w/an overhanging hinged stepped cover, the cover & sides embossed w/a dignitary smoking his hookah surrounded by numerous attendants, borders of foliage & flowerheads, raised on four elephant head feet, India, late 19th c., 15" l. (ILLUS.)...................2,875.00

Casters, cov., plain pear shape w/molded borders, engraved w/identical crests, the covers pierced w/formal flowers & foliage, ball finials, George I period, Samuel Welder, London, 1715, 4½" h., set of 3 ....1,438.00

Center bowl, boat-form, lightly hammered surface, fluted sides & molded scroll feet w/block terminals, maker's mark "AD," Copenhagen, Denmark, 1922, 13" l. 1,265.00

German Neo-Gothic Centerpiece

Centerpiece, Neo-Gothic style, a low hexagonal bowl surmounted by figures of a lion & a dragon, the knob above the hexagonal base set w/hardstones, metal liner, F. Gleichen, Germany, 1897, 15¾" h. (ILLUS.) 8,050.00

Coffee percolator, campana-form raised on curved rosewood blocks above a disk-form base, reeded borders, slip-lock rosewood lid, w/concealed electrical element, the base stamped "Jean E. Puiforcat," Paris, France, ca. 1930, 8¼" h. 8,050.00

Coffeepot, cov., paneled pear-shape, scrolled wooden handle, Birmingham, England, 1919-20, 7½" h. 247.50

Coffeepot, cov., tall pear-shaped body on a domed round foot & tapering to a stepped domed cover w/a baluster-form finial, shell-fluted swan's-neck spout capped by a leaf, ornate scroll wooden handle, the body flat-chased & engraved at the neck w/strapwork enclosing diaper & three masks, George II period, Dublin, Ireland, 1738, 9¾" h. 3,450.00

Coffee urn, cov., horizontal barrel-shaped body applied w/ribbed hoops, the foot resting on a square pedestal supported by four reeded ball feet, each side applied w/a lion mask w/ring handles, the spigot finial missing, the body engraved w/the Royal Arms, the cover w/a reeded ball finial, engraved w/the Royal Badge, w/removable heating-rod holder & cover, George III period, William Fountain, London, 1801, 8¾" l. (ILLUS. top next column) 3,450.00

English Royal Coffee Urn

Compote, open, flared bowl on leaf & berry stem centered by a bud, on stepped circular base, designed by Johan Rohde, Georg Jensen Silversmithy, Copenhagen, Denmark, stamped w/London import marks for 1927, numbered 242, 7⅛" d. 1,430.00

Cup, cov., two-handled, vase-form, engraved w/contemporary arms in a beaded frame decorated w/ribbon-tied laurel swags above crossed oak sprays, loop handles rising from leaves, reel-shaped cover w/urn finial, beaded borders, George III period, Hester Bateman, London, 1784, 14¾" h. 3,738.00

Dish, serving, round w/shaped gadroon rim, engraved w/a later initial "H" & marquess' coronet, George II period, John Jacobs, London, 1754, 13" d. 1,725.00

Dish cross, of typical form, w/pear-shaped crested lamp, sliding supports & beaded borders, George III period, William Plummer, London, England, 1777, extended 11⅜" l...2,310.00

Entree dishes, cov., rectangular, the borders decorated w/shells, flowers & fruit, the domed cover w/matching border & also chased w/a band of leaves & berries, engraved w/contemporary arms & crests, matching detachable ring finials, Benjamin Smith II, London, England, 1818, 12¾" l., pr. 6,600.00

Ewer, helmet-shaped on a stepped, domed foot, vertically lobed & fluted, the body applied w/two molded girdles, faceted harp-shaped handle, Martin Muller II, Augsburg, Germany, 1732-33, 8" h. (repairs to foot) 2,300.00

Ewer, ovoid body raised on a short flaring pedestal, the cylindrical neck flaring to a tall, arched spout, C-scroll long handle, the body lightly chased near the base w/alternating formal foliage & sprays of bulrushes, borders of leaftips, the handle rising from an anthemion partly chased w/matted leaves & topped by an oval patera, Jean-Charles Cahier, Paris, France, 1819-38, 12½" h. (ILLUS.) 4,600.00

French Silver Ewer

Jardiniere, Art Nouveau style, shaped oval form on four openwork leaf feet extending from the openwork sides composed of elaborately entwined foliage & flowerheads enclosing a vacant cartouche on one side & engraved "SLM" on the other, surmounted at one end by a classical maiden holding a stringed instrument & at the other end by a girl holding pipes, w/copper liner, marked under base "GEBR. FRIEDLANDER," Berlin, Germany, ca. 1900, 22" l. 9,200.00

Ladle, front-tipt handle & naval engraving, London, England, 1889-90, 13" l. 275.00

Meat platter, oval w/shaped molded rim, Carl Gottfried Haase, Breslau, Germany, ca. 1770, 18" l. 1,610.00

Early English Silver Mug

Mug, footed baluster-form body chased w/swags of flowers & bands of rococo ornament including reeds & shellwork, the foot chased to match, leaf-capped double-scroll handle applied w/strapwork pendent from a mask, engraved w/a crest, gilt interior, George II period, Aymé Videau, London, 1740, 5⅜" h. (ILLUS.) 5,290.00

Pitcher, water, barrel-form, the sides designed as banded staves, Boucheron, Paris, France, 19th c., 10¼" h. 2,970.00

Pitcher, modernistic bulbous pigeon-breasted body tapering to a short neck w/flared spout & w/a long swept handle from the top rim to almost the base, designed by Henning Koppel in 1952, marked by Georg Jensen, Denmark, 11¼" h. 10,925.00

Porringer, Art Nouveau style, deep rounded bowl raised on a flaring trumpet base, two widely outswept wirework loop handles w/forked ends joining the rim to the foot, designed by C. R. Ashbee, mark of the Guild of Handicraft, London, England, 1903, length over handles 9½" 2,530.00

Mexican Silver Punch Set

Punch set: bowl, twenty-four cups, ladle & tray; the deep rounded & footed bowl w/rosewood solid tab handles, the cups w/angular wood handles, wooden handle on ladle, Mexico, post-1950, tray 26¼" d., the set (ILLUS.) 4,888.00

Salt dips, *bombé* rectangular form w/curved everted tops w/gadroon rims, on a stepped rectangular base, gilt interior, engraved crest, George III period, Richard Sibley, London, 1818, 3¾" l., set of 6 ....1,265.00

Salt & pepper shakers, figural, modeled as a whimsical owl perched on a ribbed sphere atop a domed foot cast w/scallops, hardstone eyes, Georg Jensen, Denmark, 20th c., 2½" h., pr. 440.00

Samovar, cov., bulbous ovoid body tapering to a wide flat beaded rim below the domed cover w/a stylized fruit basket finial, the sides fitted w/carved stylized acanthus ebony handles & a similar tap handle over the scroll & berry tap, raised on a wide cyindrical pedestal divided into panels engraved w/leafy scrolls, on a black wood base, w/an electric socket, marked by Georg Jensen, Denmark, ca. 1925-32, 12" h. 18,400.00

French Sauce Boats

Sauce boats, double-lipped boat-shaped in the Louis XV style, molded foliate borders & detachable undertrays, by Puiforcat, Paris, France, retailed by Cartier, early 20th c., 9¾" l., pr. (ILLUS.) 1,955.00

Soup ladle, oval waved fluted bowl, the handle terminal cast in the form of an elaborate rococo cartouche decorated w/trailing flowers, a tree & shells, George II period, Elizabeth Oldfield, London, 1754, 14" l. 1,725.00

Soup tureens, cov., round squatty pear-form body on a flaring pedestal base, stepped domed cover w/floral finial, base & cover chased & embossed overall in low-relief w/meandering flowering plants, Spanish Colonial or Central American, second half 19th c., 13½" l., pr. 6,325.00

Sugar box, cov., rectangular w/hinged flat-domed cover, applied thin leaf-tip borders, w/lock, maker's mark "SS," probably Frankfort-am-Main, Germany, ca. 1800, 7⅜" l. 2,588.00

Russian Silver Tankard

Tankard, cov., tapered cylindrical form w/relief 'staves' beneath rim & at base, w/hinged cover & bifurcated thumbpiece, engraved decoration on sides & cover, Moscow, Russia, 1888, 5¼" h. (ILLUS.) 1,150.00

Tea & coffee set: cov. teapot, cov. coffeepot, cov. sugar bowl & cov. creamer; Art Deco style, each of oval box form, raised on a reeded base in the form of two conjoined circles, reeded shoulders, the covers w/a raised cruciform design extending to downswept C-scroll handles partly bound w/thread, traces of gilding on the raised panels & handles, signature of Jean E. Puiforcat, France, ca. 1930, coffeepot 5⅜" h., 4 pcs. 24,150.00

Tea & coffee set: cov. coffeepot, cov. teapot, cov. sugar bowl & creamer; rococo-style w/pear-shaped tapering bodies w/ornate scroll handles, spouts & feet, each piece applied w/cartouches enclosing engraved arms & a coronet, Maison LaVallee, F. Nicoud Sucr., Paris, France, ca. 1880, coffeepot 9¾" h., 4 pcs. 2,875.00

Tea & coffee set: cov. coffeepot, cov. teapot, cov. sugar, creamer & waste bowl; shallow footed waste bowl, the other pieces w/squatty bulbous pear-shaped smooth bodies on small curved feet, the handles formed by elongated arches curving back to form a foot, Taxco, Mexico, 20th c., 5 pcs. 825.00

Tea & coffee service: cov. teapot, cov. coffeepot, cov. sugar bowl, creamer, waste bowl, sugar nips, kettle on lamp stand & rectangular tray w/openwork blossoms at the corners; Blossom patt., each piece except sugar nips engraved w/names & date "1924," Georg Jensen Silversmithy, Copenhagen, Denmark, ca. 1920-24, tray 21¾" l., coffeepot 7¾" h., 8 pcs. 18,700.00

Tea kettle, cover & lampstand, squatty bulbous melon-lobed body cased w/bunches of flowers & w/rustic oak branch overhead handle & spout, the cover cast in the form of a leafy canopy w/an oak spray finial, the base w/an openwork apron of rococo ornament raised on scrolled legs, Paul Storr, London, stamped "STORR & MORTIMER," the chained keys by Hunt & Roskell, 1840, overall 15¼" h. (ILLUS. top next column) 4,600.00

Victorian Tea Kettle & Stand

Teapot, cov., oval cylindrical body w/flat cover & ivory finial, the sides w/fine vertical reeding, straight angled reeded spout, wooden C-scroll handle, Wm. Plummer, London, England, 1809, 5" h. 825.00

Mexican Silver Teapot

Teapot, cov., tapered quadrangular form, one side embossed w/the coronation of Montezuma, the other side w/a presentation to Montezuma of the new palace staff, figural finial, Mexico, early 20th c., 7¾" h. (ILLUS.) 1,035.00

Tea set: cov. tea kettle & stand w/burner, cov. teapot, open sugar bowl & creamer; classical oblong fluted bodies chased w/a ribbon & floral band, Barnard, London, 1888-95, 5 pcs. 880.00

Teaspoons, 'fancy-back' type, the back of the acorn-shaped bowl decorated w/a hen & chicks in a barnyard scene, the rounded terminals of the handle decorated w/rococo ornaments, George II period, London, ca. 1750, set of 12..1,610.00

Tea tray, two-handled, rectangular w/gadroon border, the corners decorated w/shells, w/raised handles, Henrik Tallberg, St. Petersburg, Russia, 1826, 17½" l...2,760.00

Tea tray, rectangular, the gadroon rim decorated at intervals w/shells & foliage, matching end loop handles, the center engraved w/contemporary arms below a foliate mantle, raised on four winged paw feet, George IV period, John Mewburn, London, 1822, 31½" l..11,500.00

English Colonial Tea Urn

Tea urn, cov., spherical body w/a partly fluted cover w/a ball finial, ring handles at the sides & raised on a ribbed slender pedestal upon a stepped square base w/ball feet, engraved w/bright-cut borders & crests, maker's mark "RG" & pseudo-hallmarks imitative of London, 1803, probably English Colonial, possibly India, early 19th c., overall 18½" h. (ILLUS.)...2,300.00

Toast rack, an arched base on four flattened ball feet, a row of seven slender rods issuing from each side & joined by crossbars w/knob terminals, designed by Christopher Dresser, made by Hukin & Heath, England, dated 1881, 5¼" l...........1,430.00

Tray, square w/rounded corners & a crimped rim band, stamped on the base "ENTW. PROF. OTTO PRUTSCHER, MUSTER GES. GESCHUTZT," Vienna, Austria, ca. 1910-20, 10½" w..........................1,150.00

Tray, shaped circular form w/a shell & scroll decorated rim band, the interior decorated w/chased flowers & scrolls & an engraved coat-of-arms, on three scroll feet, George II period, J. Morison, London, England, 1759-60, 13½" d..................2,750.00

Tray, round w/a shaped molded rim applied w/alternating male & female bacchic masks, the center engraved w/slightly later arms on a drapery mantle, on four scroll & shell legs, George II period, Frederick Kandler, London, 1736, 18¾" d...................5,463.00

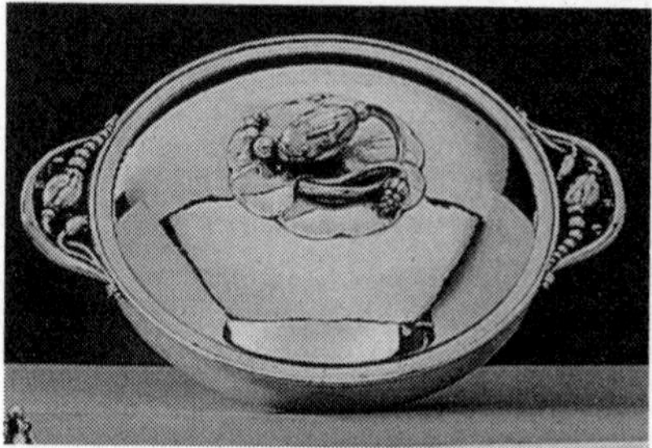

Georg Jensen Vegetable Dish

Vegetable dish, cov., round w/D-form rim handles pierced w/stylized blossoms, the low domed cover centered by an applied blossom & bud finial, marked by Georg Jensen, Denmark, 1925-32, overall 12¼" l. (ILLUS.) 6,670.00

Wine coasters, silver-gilt, round bottom w/shell & scrollwork rim on the slightly *bombé* low sides pierced & chased w/scrolling foliage & panels of diaper on a matte ground, the base plates chased w/spiraled lobes & engraved w/crest & baron's coronet, William IV period, Paul Storr, London, 1832, 5¾" d., pr.....6,325.00

Wine taster, shallow saucer-shaped bowl on a domed base, engraved w/arms w/lion supports, Regence period, Gabriel Tillet, Bordeaux, France, 1722-23, 4¼" d. 4,600.00

SILVER PLATE (Hollowware)

Bonbon basket, bail handle, grape clusters & leaves on handle & perimeter of wire basket, 2 x 7½", 7½" h...275.00

Cake basket, embossed pedestal base, swing handle, interior engraved w/four different birds, leaves, Meriden Britannia Co., No. 1822, 10" d., 14" h. including swing handle..................................175.00

Center bowl, shallow, supported by a standing allegorical figure resting on a spreading circular foot, Gorham Mfg. Co., Providence, Rhode Island, ca. 1880, 13" h. 715.00

Coffee urn, cov., bulbous urn-form body on tall decorated feet, a crown-shaped rim w/rows of tiny flowers, ornate curved handles & a serving spout w/ivory handle, the body chased overall w/florals, w/burner in base, Hartford Silver Plate Co., ca. 1880s, 17" h. 350.00

Coffee & tea service: cov. coffeepot, cov. teapot, sugar bowl, creamer & waste bowl; Remembrance patt., Reed & Barton, 5 pcs. 500.00

Mirror plateau, inset mirrored top surrounded by a frame of star-cut medallions w/beaded outer border & petal-shaped prongs on inner border, raised on five feet, 12" d. 125.00

Mirror plateau, elaborate scrolling & foliate decoration framing circular inset mirror, 20½" d. 440.00

Nut bowl, model of a nut w/a large seated squirrel on a branch forming the handle, Reed & Barton, late 19th c. (resilvered) 395.00

Spoonholder, round step-up base, figural stem of a Victorian lady in a fancy draped dress holding a large umbrella w/slots for twelve spoons, loop handle, 10" d. umbrella, 8" h. 285.00

Sugar bowl - spoonholder, the bowl decorated w/heavy repoussé designs, the rim w/prongs to hold twelve spoons, Meriden Silver Plate Co., ca. 1880 (resilvered) 175.00

Vase holder w/vase, modeled as a bushy-tailed squirrel seated on a mound base beside an opalescent pale green bud vase, Meriden (resilvered) 275.00

Ornate Victorian Water Set

Vases, hexagonal slightly tapering form, decorated w/a band of incised Gothic-style design around the rim, marked "GORHAM CO., SPECIAL, 1637," 6" w., 10" h., pr. 770.00

Water set: a cylindrical covered pitcher w/finely ribbed upper & lower bands & a wide center band engraved w/cranes, tilting within an arched frame w/ornately scroll-molded feet set upon the rim of a flaring ribbed circular dish base w/inset drip tray & raised on paw feet, the rim of the base w/supports for two matching goblets & the front w/a full-figure flying horse projection, American-made, late 19th c., 21½" w., 25" h. (ILLUS. left column) 2,320.00

SILVER PLATE (Flatware)

ALHAMBRA (Rogers)

Cold meat fork 35.00
Demitasse spoon 10.00
Sugar tongs, large 60.00

ASSYRIAN HEAD (1847 Rogers Bros.)

Cheese scoop 75.00
Salt spoon, master 15.00
Soup ladle 125.00
Teaspoon 12.00

DAFFODIL (1847 Rogers Bros.)

Cream soup spoon 15.00
Fruit spoon 12.50
Ice cream fork 20.00
Salad fork 8.00
Seafood fork 10.00

DUNDEE (1847 Rogers Bros.)

Berry spoon, large 30.00
Butter knife, twisted handle 15.00
Dinner knife 12.00
Luncheon fork 12.00
Luncheon knife 12.00
Salt spoon, master 12.00
Sugar spoon 15.00
Tablespoon 18.00
Teaspoon 8.00
Youth fork 15.00

FIRST LOVE (1847 Rogers Bros.)

Cold meat fork 25.00
Cream soup spoon 15.00
Dessert fork 18.00

FLORAL (1835 R. Wallace)

Berry spoon 85.00
Chocolate spoons, set of 4 ....100.00
Dinner knife 25.00
Pickle fork, long-handled 45.00

Soup ladle, large.....100.00
Tablespoon.....18.00

KING CEDRIC (Oneida Community)
Butter knife, individual, flat-handled.....13.00
Butter knife, master, flat-handled.....15.00
Cocktail fork.....14.00
Cold meat fork.....34.00
Cream soup spoon.....18.00
Iced tea spoon.....17.00
Sugar spoon.....16.00

LA VIGNE (1881 Rogers)
Bouillon spoon.....53.00
Citrus spoon, gold-washed bowl.....30.00
Demitasse spoon.....12.00
Dinner knife, hollow-handled.....80.00
Pastry fork.....48.00

OLD COLONY (1847 Rogers Bros.)
Berry fork.....29.00
Bread knife, large.....68.00
Ice cream spoon.....30.00
Nut pick.....25.00
Soup ladle.....95.00
Sugar tongs.....75.00
Tomato server.....75.00

STERLING SILVER (Flatware)

ARABESQUE (Whiting Mfg. Co.)
Berry spoon.....150.00
Cheese scoop, bright-cut, gold-washed bowl.....350.00
Cream ladle.....85.00
Demitasse spoon.....25.00
Dessert spoon.....25.00
Dinner fork.....45.00
Ice cream set: ice cream slice & 12 ice cream spoons; bright-cut, 13 pcs......750.00
Pastry fork.....85.00
Serving spoon w/gold-washed bowl.....95.00
Soup ladle.....400.00
Tablespoon.....55.00
Teaspoon.....15.00

Cactus (Georg Jensen)
Bouillon spoon.....65.00
Dinner fork.....110.00
Fruit knife.....75.00
Gravy ladle.....200.00
Lemon fork, 2-tine.....65.00
Server, flat.....95.00

Empire (Whiting Mfg. Co.)
Berry spoon.....110.00
Dinner knife.....60.00
Pickle fork.....35.00
Sugar shell.....35.00
Tablespoon.....48.00

ENGLISH KING (Tiffany & Co.)
Asparagus fork.....750.00
Berry spoon, conch.....495.00
Cold meat fork.....115.00
Fish serving fork.....350.00
Game knife.....1,050.00
Gravy ladle.....275.00
Ice cream fork.....85.00
Iced tea spoon.....75.00
Ice tongs.....675.00
Luncheon fork.....65.00
Olive spoon.....150.00
Youth fork & knife, pr......95.00

HERALDIC (Whiting Mfg. Co.)
Bonbon server, scalloped edge.....55.00
Dessert spoon.....28.00
Luncheon fork.....22.00
Mustard ladle.....80.00
Olive fork.....75.00
Pastry fork, 3-tine.....45.00
Pie server.....245.00
Sardine tongs.....295.00

KINGS (Dominick & Haff)
Bouillon ladle.....225.00
Demitasse spoon.....16.00
Dinner fork.....50.00
Dinner knife.....48.00
Egg spoon.....30.00
Gumbo spoon.....39.00
Luncheon knife.....38.00
Oyster ladle.....225.00
Teaspoon.....19.00
Tablespoon.....70.00

LILY OF THE VALLEY (Gorham Mfg. Co.)
Butter fork.....19.00
Butter spreader, hollow handle.....12.00
Cream soup spoon.....19.00
Iced tea spoon.....21.00
Luncheon fork.....21.00
Luncheon knife.....17.00
Olive fork.....16.00
Salad fork.....24.00
Salad serving fork.....65.00
Teaspoon.....12.50
Tomato server, pierced.....65.00

MAZARIN (Dominick & Haff)
Asparagus fork.....275.00
Bouillon spoon.....19.00
Claret ladle.....150.00
Dessert spoon.....25.00
Dinner fork.....25.00
Soup spoon, oval.....25.00
Sugar sifter.....95.00
Sugar tongs.....95.00
Teaspoon.....15.00

PLYMOUTH - New Plymouth (Gorham Mfg Co.)
Bouillon spoon.....8.00
Butter serving knife.....30.00
Cocktail fork.....8.00

Demitasse spoon 15.00
Dinner fork 22.00
Dinner knife 22.50
Ice spoon, pierced 300.00
Mustard ladle 45.00
Olive spoon, pierced 24.00
Salad serving fork 125.00
Soup ladle 200.00

RENAISSANCE (Dominick & Haff)

Berry spoon, 7⅜" l. 235.00
Citrus spoons, set of 6 ....255.00
Claret ladle 185.00
Cocktail fork 40.00
Ice cream fork 45.00
Jelly cake knife 400.00
Lettuce fork 145.00
Sauce ladle 450.00
Strawberry fork 38.00
Sugar tongs 68.00

ROCOCO (Dominick & Haff)

Grapefruit spoon 30.00
Ice cream spoon 35.00
Luncheon fork 20.00
Luncheon knife 25.00
Parfait spoon 25.00
Pie server, silver blade 150.00
Seafood fork 22.00
Serving spoon 35.00

VERSAILLES (Gorham Mfg. Co.)

Versailles Pattern

Asparagus fork 585.00
Berry spoon, shell-shaped bowl, gold-washed 395.00
Bonbon spoon, gold-washed bowl 225.00
Butter spreader 32.00
Coffee spoon 19.00
Cold meat fork 150.00
Cream soup spoon 65.00
Dinner fork 56.00
Dinner knife 58.00
Dinner service: 12 each dinner knives, lunch knives, salad forks, bouillon spoons, dessert spoons, dinner forks, lunch forks, butter spreaders, demitasse spoons, 24 teaspoons, 6 tablespoons, pair of salad servers & 1 each butter knife, jelly spoon, serving fork, sauce ladle & berry spoon: in fitted wooden chest, 145 pcs. 10,350.00
Orange knife 60.00
Punch ladle, 12¾" l. 195.00
Salt spoon, master 47.00
Soup ladle 425.00

WAVERLY (R. Wallace & Sons)

Berry spoon 60.00
Honey spoon 75.00
Horseradish spoon 45.00
Ice cream knife 165.00
Jelly server 70.00
Sherbet spoon 25.00
Sugar sifter 250.00

TIN & TOLE

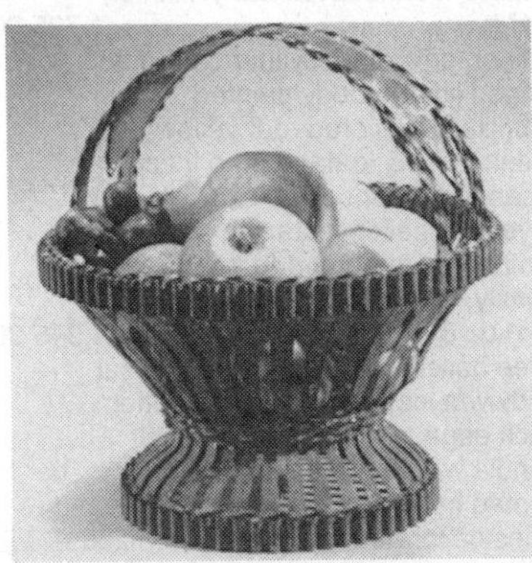

Reticulated Cut Tin Basket

Apple tray, tole, square w/outward flaring scalloped sides painted w/white borders decorated w/brightly colored red berries & green foliage, the sides & bottom in gold highlighted w/yellow leaves & pinstriping, all on a black japanned ground, probably Connecticut, early 19th c., 11½" w., 3¼" h. 6,325.00

Basket w/overhead handle, cut-tin, the openwork footed basket w/ornate wide handle & crimped rims retaining traces of original red & blue paint, filled w/an assortment of painted stone fruit representing apples, grapes, peaches & plums, America, 19th c., 10" h. (ILLUS.) 2,300.00

Bouquet of flowers, tin, Anniversary-type, eight blossoms w/well-defined petals & foliage, 16" l. 550.00

Bread tray, tole, rectangular w/deep canted sides & rounded tab end handles, original dark brown japanned ground w/brown crystalized center framed by a yellow band, the sides decorated w/stylized florals in yellow, green, black, olive & red, 12¾" l. (wear) 302.50

Candle mold, tin, ten-tube, rectangular top & base, tubes slant to center, strap handle at top side, 10¾" h. 170.50

Candle sconces, tin, miniature, the scalloped sunburst backplates continuing to projecting candlearms supporting circular drip pans, probably Pennsylvania, ca. 1840, 4⅜" d., 7½" h., pr. 4,025.00

Canister, cov., tole, the circular box w/fitted hinged lid & wire loop handle decorated w/a broad white band w/red blossoms & green leaves heightened w/scallops of bright yellow on a black japanned ground, Connecticut, early 19th c., 4¾" h...1,725.00

Canister, cov., tole, cylindrical w/fitted hinged lid, the body painted w/brilliantly colored red; yellow & green fruits & leafage on a black japanned ground w/borders of white & yellow scallops, stars & feathering, attributed to the Filley Family, Connecticut, early 19th c., 8¾" d., 8⅜" h.................................4,945.00

Coffee boiler, cov., tole, wide conical body w/a loop handle at the bottom back edge, a rim spout, wire bail handle w/wooden grip & a low-domed cover w/loop handle, the sides decorated w/sprays of stylized red roses on a black ground, probably Pennsylvania, late 19th c., overall 18" h.......................................748.00

Coffeepot, cov., tole, slightly tapering cylinder, strap handle, angled spout, slightly domed cover w/knob finial, original dark brown japanning w/band of floral & foliate decoration in yellow, red, green, white & black, 11" h. (some wear, lid has slight battering & replaced wooden finial) 495.00

Creamer, cov., tole, tapering cylindrical body w/pointed rim spout & strap handle, low domed cover, worn original black ground w/stylized floral decoration in red, yellow & green, 4⅛" h. (minor battering).....220.00

Document box, cov., tole, rectangular w/low-domed cover centered by a loop ring handle, decorated w/original dark brown ground w/a white rim band & yellow commas & floral decoration in green, red & black, 8" l. (some wear) 302.50

Figures of peasants, tole, a man & woman in Tyrolean peasant costume, each standing w/a tapering cylindrical receptacle on their back, on green rectangular base, Europe, 19th c., 15¾" h., pr. (some restoration to paint)............6,038.00

Jardinieres, tole, figural, one modeled as a standing male Blackamoor, the other as a female Blackamoor, each in period costume & carrying on their back a tall stave-form cylindrical container, raised on a *faux marbre* rectangular base, decorated in shades of red, green, brown, black & trimmed w/gilt, Italy, 14" h., pr. (losses) 4,888.00

Match container, tole, wall-type, the arched & crimped backplate, pierced for hanging, w/an angular pocket decorated w/red, yellow & green leafage & flowers on a black japanned ground, probably Pennsylvania, early 19th c., 4¼" w., 8" h. 690.00

Model of a top hat, tin, anniversary gift, the brim gently curved, 8" h. (light rust) 297.00

Models of lady's slippers, tin, the pair of low-heeled slippers w/high, pointed backs & curled pointed tongues, the fronts applied w/molded flowers, 10th anniversary gift, 19th c., 10" h., pr...920.00

Mug, tole, tapering cylindrical form w/strap handle, decorated w/a green & yellow long-tailed bird perched in a fruit & flower spray, all on a black japanned ground, Pennsylvania, early 19th c., 5¾" h. 8,338.00

Pattern, barn painter's, tin, in the shape of an irregular five-pointed star, Lancaster County, Pennsylvania, 39½" d., ...165.00

Pitcher, tin, base flaring outward to midsection & then tapering to collared neck, C-scroll handle, punched & tooled sunburst designs, 11" h...137.50

Tin American Eagle Wall Plaque

Plaque, wall-type, tin, the cut & repoussé flat spreadwing figure of an American eagle w/individual realistically layered feathers, America, early 20th c., 44" w., 29" h. (ILLUS.) 1,093.00

Syrup jug w/hinged lid, tole, tapering cylindrical form w/strap handle, decorated w/brightly colored red, yellow & green tulips & leafage within white scallops on a black japanned ground, probably New England, early 19th c., 4" h. 1,495.00

Tea caddy, cov., tole, wide cylindrical body below a slightly domed top centered by a short, small neck w/cap, worn original dark brown japanning w/stylized florals in red, green & yellow, 5¾" h. 165.00

Tea canister, cov., tole, tall octagonal body tapering at the shoulder to a wide mouth w/a domed cover, an overall gilt ground w/each panel decorated w/a tall Chinese figure & trimmed w/green scrolls, England, first half 19th c., 26" h. 1,955.00

Top hat, tin, Anniversary-type, tall crown & slightly curved brim, 6¼" h. 275.00

Tray, tole, rectangular w/cut corners, flaring rim, the center painted w/seven red fruits w/yellow stems all on a black ground, yellow inner border band, probably Pennsylvania, 19th c., 17½" l. 460.00

Tray, tole, oval w/pierced end handles, black ground decorated in the center w/a wide gilt-scroll oval frame surrounding a h.p. colored scene of a seated classical maid & a lion, wide gilt-scroll border band, England, early 19th c., 30" l. (some restoration to paint) 5,463.00

MINIATURES (Paintings)

Portrait of Stephen Decatur

Bust portrait of Alexander I, three-quarters dexter, in uniform, wearing three orders & blue sash, peach sky background, signed "Isabey" (Jean Baptiste Isabey) right edge, in an oval gilt-rimmed frame, ca. 1810, 1⅞" h. $2,415.00

Bust portrait of Stephen Decatur, water-color on ivory, the young naval officer depicted wearing a high-collared uniform w/epaulettes & gold braid fastenings across the front of his jacket, in an oval frame w/beaded decoration, attributed to William Sheys (active ca. 1810-20), 2½" l. (ILLUS.) 4,950.00

Bust portrait of a young gentleman, water-color on ivory, posed three-quarters sinister, wearing a high collar, dark cravat, striped vest & dark coat, signed "Ladd," note on backboard inscribed "W.L. Ladd Pinxt. Del. Boston," oval within a gilt-metal oval liner & raised conforming wooden frame, all within a square outer frame, 19th c., 1¾ x 2⅛" 302.50

Bust portrait of a gentleman, three-quarters dexter, w/dark grey jacket, white waistcoat w/stars & white jabot against a reddish grey ground, signed & dated by James Peale, 1796, in an oval gold pendant frame, 2¾" h. 1,725.00

Bust portrait of a young lady, water-color on ivory, her blonde hair arranged in an ornate coiffure, the reverse w/an arrangement of hair & seed pearls on opalescent glass, unsigned, French School, early 19th c., within a narrow oval metal frame, 1⅞ x 2⅝" 440.00

Bust portrait of a lady, three-quarters sinister, wearing low-cut white dress w/red brooch & shawl, curly brown hair, against a grey-beige ground, attributed to John Wesley Jarvis, ca. 1805, in an oval gold pendant frame w/glazed reverse, 2½" h. 690.00

Bust portrait of a young man, water-color on paper, identified on backboard as Sereno Clark together w/notes on the artist & sitter, attributed to Alpheus Chapin, 1787-1870, rectangular frame w/eglomise mat w/oval opening, overall 3¼ x 4¼" 550.00

Bust portrait of Napoleon, water-color on ivory, shown three-quarters sinister, signed "Duval," black lacquered frame, 4⅝" w., 5½" h. 279.00

Bust portrait of an old woman, water-color on paper, primitive depiction of the woman wearing a white lace bonnet & black dress against a blue & green ground, old gilt frame, 5⅝" w., 6⅜" h. 495.00

Bust portrait of a young woman, on ivory, her hair parted in the center & gently pulled back, in an oval wide molded frame, 19th c., 4⅛ x 4¾" 247.50

Half-length portrait of a gentleman, almost full-face of a stocky man w/light brown long hair, wearing a blue jacket, white waistcoat & cravat, against a beige-grey ground, signed w/initials "IP" & dated "1795," attributed to James Peale, in gold oval pendant frame w/blue & white enamel trim, glazed compartment on reverse w/woven hair, 2½" h.........3,220.00

Half-length portrait of a mother & child, the seated mother in a red velvet dress, the blonde daughter in white dress w/blue bow & standing w/her arms around her mother's waist, greyish green background, Continental School, probably France, ca. 1815, in a circular gilt-metal rim frame, 3½" d..................1,955.00

Half-length portrait of a nobleman, in a suit of armor w/red ermine-trimmed cape, shoulder-length powdered hair, lace collar fixed w/intaglio brooch, Continental School, ca. 1725, in gold & foil-backed ruby bordered silver locket frame, 2⅜" h. 805.00

MINIATURES (Replicas)

American Federal Chest of Drawers

Andirons, brass, ball & steeple finial above a cylindrical plinth, on spurred arched cabriole legs w/pad feet, 19th c., 6¼" h., pr........................$2,070.00

Blanket chest, painted & decorated pine, rectangular top w/cotter-pin hinge opening to a deep well, the top painted w/a red & green tulip, the front w/a small red house flanked by trees on rolling hills, the sides w/tulips, raised on bracket feet, Johannes Weber, Lancaster County, Pennsylvania, ca. 1800, 6⅝" l., 4⅝" h..................................1,610.00

Blanket chest, painted wood, rectangular top w/molded edge opening to a deep well, plain nailed side, painted green, 19th c., 9¾" l., 4¾" h. (imperfections) 990.00

Boots, leather, hightop-style, handmade, 8½" h., pr. (some wear) 275.00

Box, cov., curly figured hardwood, sliding puzzle-type domed lid, 3½" l. 302.50

Bucket, pine & walnut, stave construction w/alternating pine & walnut staves & two metal bands, wire bail handle w/wooden handhold, old varnish finish, 4½" d., 3⅜" h..49.50

Carousel, painted metal, comprising pairs of polychrome-painted elephants, horses, dogs & deer, each mounted w/metal poles on a yellow-painted circular platform, a canvas tent above & hung w/three lights, motorized, a brass plaque inscribed "R.M. Spahr Maker York PA 1921," 22" d., 17" h. (motor not working) 2,875.00

Chest of drawers, American Empire style, cherry & mahogany veneer, rectangular top over a long ogee-front drawer flanked by stripe-inlaid stiles above two long drawers w/wooden knobs flanked by S-scroll pilasters down the sides, mid-19th c., 12¾ x 13¼", 14½" h...........467.50

Chest of drawers, Federal style, mahogany, hinged rectangular top lifting over a fitted well above a conforming case w/four long drawers w/ivory pulls & keyhole escutcheons, on ring-turned feet, New York, 1815-25, 8¼ x 13", 13" h. (ILLUS.) 1,430.00

Chest of drawers, French Empire style, gilt-metal mounted walnut, orange & beige marble rectangular top above a flush frieze drawer overhanging a pair of long drawers w/round brass pulls & keyhole escutcheons flanked by columns, raised on bun feet, French Provincial, early 19th c., 13 x 25½", 20" h..1,725.00

Fire bucket, painted leather, cylindrical, painted on the front w/an elaborate portrait medallion "Franklin

Hose" & centering a portrait of Benjamin Franklin, all on a bright red ground highlighted w/gilding, signed by A. Cook, Boston, ca. 1860, single ring handle, 2⅞" h. 24,150.00

Footstool, painted & decorated pine, rectangular top w/demilune sides on bootjack supports, the top painted w/red flowers & green foliage & highlighted in gilt & black on a yellow ground within a red & black reserve, the sides & supports w/green foliage w/black highlights, inscribed on the underside in pencil "Center County," Landis Valley, Pennsylvania, early 19th c., 4¼ x 8", 4½" h. 2,300.00

Salt box, butternut, wire nail construction, scratch-carved compass star designs, old patina, 3¼" w., 3½" h. 357.50

Side chair, slat-black, painted wood, two arched slats painted w/flowers centered by leaves & flanked by turned stiles painted w/geometric designs above a rush seat, on turned legs w/flattened ball feet joined by round box stretchers, original yellow paint, 19th c., 16⅜" h. (seat damaged) 437.00

Trunk, rectangular w/flat top, worn original leather covering w/brass stud trim, original lock & key, 6" l. 192.50

Miniature Shaving Stand

Shaving stand, curly maple veneer, a rectangular mirror w/beveled wood frame swiveling between scrolled uprights on a rectangular case w/a single dovetailed drawer w/a small opalescent glass pull, on small ball feet, mid-19th c., veneer missing on one end, 7¾" l. (ILLUS.) 302.50

MOLDS - CANDY, FOOD & MISC.

Also see BUTTER MOLDS & STAMPS.

Cake, lamb, cast iron, "Griswold No. 866" ....$100.00 to 150.00

Cake, sheep, cast iron, 12½" h. 38.50

Candle, tin, eight-tube w/rectangular top & base plates & small loop handle at side of top, 11" h. 104.50

Candle, floor model, 24 tin tubes mounted in a rectangular pine framework w/bootjack ends, old worn patina, 7 x 19½", 16¼" h. 1,100.00

Candy, bird, carved wood, two-part, rectangular w/six openings, 11¾" l. 38.50

Candy, eagles w/shields, cast lead, three birds in a row, two-part, 8¼" l. 186.50

Chocolate, American eagle w/shield & banner marked "Liberty," tin, two-part, marked "JAB 10," 4½" h. 49.50

Minstrels Chocolate Mold

Chocolate, black minstrel boys, each playing a different musical instrument, tin, three separate joined by flat straps, marked "11/27 Germany," very minor rust, 10" l., 6" h. (ILLUS.) 82.50

Chocolate, cat in seated position, tin, two-part, 3⅜" l. 71.50

Chocolate, dog in seated position, tin, two-part, w/clips, 4⅝" l. 49.50

Chocolate, duck wearing Tyrolean hat, tin, two-part, marked "REI 23011," 5¾" h. 33.00

Egg-Shaped Mold with Rabbits

Chocolate, egg-shaped & embossed

w/Easter rabbits on parade, tin, two-part, marked "JAB 13," 7½" l., 6¾" h. (ILLUS.) 38.50

Chocolate, egg-shaped & embossed overall w/stars, tin, two-part, 4" h. 60.50

Chocolate, elephant w/trunk down, tin, two-part, w/clips, 4¼" l. 82.50

Chocolate, elf w/basket of eggs on his back riding a large running rabbit on a grassy base, tin, two-part, marked "REI 6526," 4½" l. 66.00

Chocolate, girl standing & hugging large rabbit, tin, two-part, marked "21889S," 7" h. 88.00

Chocolate, Jack O' Lantern w/wide grin, tin, folding two-part type 66.00

Chocolate, Kewpie w/arms at side, tin, two-part, marked "JAB 10," 5" h. 110.00

Chocolate, Kewpie standing w/one hand on stomach, one at mouth, tin, two-part, marked "REI 17499," 11" h. 170.50

Chocolate, lion, standing w/head forward, tin, two-part, w/clips, 6½" l. 66.00

Chocolate, owl, tin, two-part, w/clips, 4⅜" l. 49.50

Chocolate, pig in upright position, tin, two-part, w/clips, marked "Made in Germany," 3⅛" l. 71.50

Chocolate, rabbit sitting upright w/a pack on its back, tin, two-part, 11¼" h. 44.00

Chocolate, rabbit walking, tin, marked "Made in U.S.A.," 10½" h. 115.50

Chocolate, rabbit sitting w/basket in front, tin, two-part, w/clips, marked "Made in Germany," 7½" h. 104.50

Rooster Chocolate Mold

Chocolate, rooster standing, tin, two-part, marked "EPP 4689," 4½" h. (ILLUS.) 38.50

Chocolate, rooster, tin, two-part, w/clips, 6" h. 60.50

Chocolate, rooster, tin, 10½" h. 104.50

Chocolate, Santa Claus w/basket, tin, two-part, w/clips, 6½" h. 115.50

Chocolate, Santa Claus w/pointed hood & arms at front, solid nickel silver, two-part, marked "7," 5" h. (very minor tarnish) 77.00

Chocolate, wild boar, tin, two-part, w/clips, 4⅝" l. 71.50

Chocolate, witch w/pointed hat riding broomstick, tin, two-part, 6" h. 93.50

Chocolate, zeppelin "Hindenburg," tin, two-part, marked "REI 25647," 11½" l. 121.00

Food, artichoke-like fruit, copper, half-round form, 8½" l. 220.00

Food, fish, copper, oval, design stamped in the top, tin-washed, 4¼ x 5¼" 99.00

Food, fish leaping, copper, detailed scales & fins, 10" l. 220.00

Food, geometric, copper, round domed form w/eight-lobed ring at top centered by an indentation w/a star, 10" d. 165.00

Food, lion, tin, oval w/fluted sides & well-formed lion in top, 5¼" l. 44.00

Food, rabbit, tin, oval w/scalloped edges, design stamped in top, 2¾ x 3½", set of 4 ....66.00

Food, shell-shaped, half-round flaring & finely ribbed form, 9" l. 274.50

Food, Turk's turban, redware w/yellow slip wavy line & polka dot decoration, 9½" d. (some wear, small glaze flakes) 1,567.50

Food, Turk's turban, redware, white slip rim w/brown wavy line design, 12" d. (rim chip) 71.50

Ice cream, rabbit running, pewter, hinged two-part, 4½" l. 115.50

MOTHER-OF-PEARL HANDLED FLATWARE

Berry spoon, silver plate bowl w/embossed fruits & flower, 8" l. $10.00

Butter knife, sterling silver blade, w/"W" monogram 14.00

Carving set, sterling silver ferrules, 2 pcs. 32.50

Cheese knife, sterling silver blade 16.00

Dinner forks & knives, silver-gilt tines & blades, 6 each, the set 66.00

Fruit knives, Sheffield blade, set of 5 ....75.00

Fruit knives, sterling silver fittings, Landers Frary & Clark, Aetna Works, set of 6 in original box 180.00

Knives, carved mother-of-pearl handles, blunt silver plate blades, marked "Meriden Cutlery Co.," 8" l., set of 12 ....275.00

Luncheon knives, sterling silver blades, w/"W" monogram, set of 6 ....78.00

Meat fork, large, w/sterling silver ferrule, fancy....................................65.00
Nut picks, set of 4..................................35.00
Pickle fork, sterling silver tines, $6\frac{3}{8}$ l.....18.00

MOVIE MEMORABILIA

BOOKS

"Doris Day" coloring book, 12 x 15"....$25.00
"Dracula," press book, starring Bela Lugosi, Universal Pictures, 1931 ..5,500.00

"Dracula's Daughter" Press Book

"Dracula's Daughter," press book, starring Otto Kruger, Gloria Holden & Marguerite Churchill, Universal Pictures, 1936 (ILLUS.) 1,100.00
"Duke: The Real Story of John Wayne," inscription & autograph inside front cover, paperback...........250.00
"Gone With the Wind," by Margaret Mitchell, movie edition, illustrated w/scenes from the movie, soft cover, second printing, New York, 1940.......45.00
"Heroes of the Silent Screen," 1972, biographies & pictures of 30 stars, hardcover, 244 pp., 7 x 10"...............25.00
"Jeanette MacDonald" coloring & cut-out book, Merrill No. 3461.................45.00
"Stars of Photoplay," w/149 sepia art portraits & biographies, stars include Valentino, Beery, Bennets, Pickford, M. Davies, Pitts, Buck Jones, etc., from Photoplay magazine, 1924........35.00

COSTUMES

Bette Davis, "The Virgin Queen," 20th Century Fox, 1955, a pair of size seven suede shoes w/ornate gun metal beading on the front, worn by Davis in the scene where she, as Queen Elizabeth I, crosses a puddle, marked "B. Davis" on the bottom, w/a movie still showing Davis wearing the shoes, the group..1,035.00

"The Wizard of Oz" Dress

Judy Garland, "The Wizard of Oz," MGM, 1939, blue & white gingham pinafore w/a white cotton blouse finished at the sleeves & neck w/blue scalloped trim, together w/a delicate white cotton petticoat & Garland's two blue socks w/red stains, label w/star's name, includes a still of Garland wearing this costume, the group (ILLUS.).......48,400.00
Jean Harlow, "Libelled Lady," MGM, 1936, black silk lace evening gown lined w/pale pink silk crepe, designed by Dolly Tree, w/studio label, w/two movie stills showing Harlow wearing the dress, 3 pcs. (lace torn in back & at shoulder strap)...3,300.00
Katharine Hepburn, "Song of Love," MGM, 1947, black satin repp Victorian-style dress w/bustle & train fastens in front w/hidden hook & eye border, bronze satin sleeves covered w/black crocheted lace....1,265.00
Charlton Heston, "Ben-Hur," MGM, 1959, tunic & belt, brown ultra suede tunic worn by Heston in the movie, trimmed on the bottom & sleeves in chain mail, the tunic bordered w/bronze-tone buttons, marked inside the collar "Property of MGM - 53," w/a brown leather belt w/brass-tone buttons & plates, 2 pcs. 5,060.00
Vivien Leigh, "Gone With The Wind," MGM, 1939, black straw hat w/wide rim scalloped at the back, w/a wide light pink silk ribbon across the front ending in long ties, label w/star's name, along w/a movie still showing Leigh wearing the hat, the group (ILLUS. top next page)..................6,600.00
Vivien Leigh, "That Hamilton Woman," United Artists, 1941, black velvet gown w/the V-neck bodice trimmed

"Gone With The Wind" Hat

w/black lace & two full-length panels of crystal beading in a design of wheat clusters tied w/bows, w/designer label of Rene Hubert, w/a movie still of Leigh wearing the gown, 2 pcs. 3,850.00

"Niagara" Black Silk Negligee

Marilyn Monroe, "Niagara," 20th Century Fox, 1952, black silk negligee w/an appliqued pink rose at the bodice, star's name label, w/photograph of star wearing it, 2 pcs. (ILLUS.) 7,700.00

Munchkin costume, "The Wizard of Oz," Metro-Goldwyn-Mayer, 1939, vest, gold felt & cotton w/covered buttons, 22" l. 660.00

Leonard Nimoy, "Star Trek III: The Search for Spock," Paramount Pictures, 1984, pair of ears worn by Nimoy in his role of Mr. Spock, w/note of authenticity from Nimoy & autographed photo, 3 pcs. 1,100.00

Jane Russell, "The French Line," RKO, 1953, black leotard, decorated w/rhinestones & three large cut-out ovals in the torso, designed by Russell & Howard Greer, w/a Japanese ad for the movie, 2 pcs. 2,750.00

James Stewart, "How The West Was Won," MGM, 1963, pair of buckskin pants worn by Mr. Stewart, tan fringed style w/a side zipper, front & rear maroon flaps, marked inside waistband "J. Stewart" 2,530.00

Elizabeth Taylor, "Little Women," MGM, 1949, coat worn by Ms. Taylor in the movie, wool blend in mustard yellow trimmed on the collar, yoke & sleeves in green & mustard plaid w/matching buttons, fully lined in mustard crepe 1,035.00

Dick Van Dyke, "Mary Poppins," Disney, 1964, brightly striped pink, orange & gold jacket worn in the animated park scene, full red lining & a Western Costume Co. tag which reads "No. 2764-1 Dick Van Dyke Chest 39½, sleeve 17½," w/a photo of Van Dyke wearing the jacket, the group 4,370.00

LOBBY CARDS

"Animal Crackers" Lobby Card

"Animal Crackers," starring the Marx Brothers, caricature bust portraits of the four brothers at the left side, the right side w/a color photograph of Groucho & two women, Paramount, 1930 (ILLUS.) 1,210.00

"Beau Hunks," starring Stan Laurel & Oliver Hardy, sepia-tone scenes from the movie, MGM, 1939, set of 2 .....660.00

"The Broadway Melody," scene depicting cast of musicians & singers gathered in a semi-circle around a man, MGM, 1929 .....660.00

"Cabin in the Sky," starring Ethel Waters, Eddie "Rochester" Anderson & Lena Horne, each card w/a photographic scene from the movie & caricature by Al Hirschfeld, MGM,

1943, set of 8 ....1,100.00

"Double Indemnity," starring Fred MacMurray, Barbara Stanwyck & Edward G. Robinson, various scenes from the movie featuring the stars & other cast members, Paramount, 1944, set of 8 ....880.00

"The Gold Rush," starring Charlie Chaplin, large color scene of cabin interior w/two men fighting & Chaplin cowering on other side of room, black & white photo of Chaplin seated to left of interior scene, United Artists, 1925 ....1,430.00

"The Hunchback of Notre Dame," starring Lon Chaney, scene of the hunchback & Esmerelda on a cobblestone street w/a robed man in the background, Universal, 1923 ....1,650.00

"Jezebel," starring Bette Davis & Henry Fonda, scene of the stars & another woman on a veranda, Warner Brothers, 1938 ....550.00

"Metropolis" Lobby Card

"Metropolis," black & white photo scene of two men & a female robot, Paramount, 1926, linen-backed (ILLUS.) 4,670.00

"The Phantom of the Opera," starring Lon Chaney, scene of woman & army officer to left side & silhouette of the phantom at right, Universal Pictures, 1925, title card 3,850.00

"The Scarlet Empress," starring Marlene Dietrich, scene of Dietrich wearing a fur-trimmed off-the-shoulder gown & gazing provocatively over one shoulder, single jumbo card, Paramount, 1934, 14 x 17" 1,840.00

"The Scarlet Letter," starring Lillian Gish, MGM, 1926, 11 X 14", set of 8...2,860.00

"The Seven Year Itch," starring Marilyn Monroe & Tom Ewell, each w/a color photo scene from the movie, 20th Century Fox, 1955, set of 8 ....990.00

"The Son of the Sheik," starring Rudolph Valentino, scenes of Valentino & various cast members, United Artists, 1926, set of 6 ....1,650.00

"Tarzan" Lobby Cards

"Tarzan, The Ape Man," starring Johnny Weismuller, Neil Hamilton, C. Aubrey Smith & Maureen O'Sullivan, various color scenes from the movie, MGM, 1932, set of 4 (ILLUS. of part) 3,575.00

POSTERS

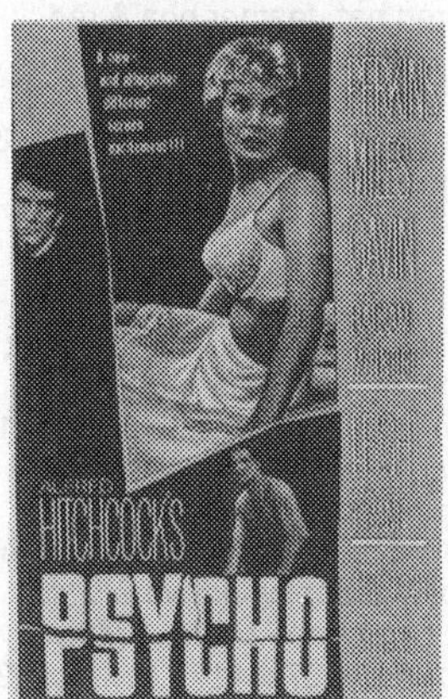

"Psycho" Poster

"Any Wife," starring Pearl White, color scene of the star plummeting from a large bridge into a river, one-sheet, William Fox, 1922, linen-backed, 27 x 41" 7,150.00

"A Sainted Devil," starring Rudolph Valentino, picture of Valentino dressed as an Argentinian gaucho, standing w/hand on one hip & smoking a cigarette, one-sheet, Paramount, 1924, linen-backed, 27 x 41" 8,250.00

"The Bank," starring Charlie Chaplin, large bust portrait of Chaplin w/eyes closed & mouth open as if sneezing, one-sheet, Essanay, 1915, paper-backed, 27 x 41" 16,675.00

"The Birth of a Nation," scene of a hooded & robed Klansman wearing a helmet w/a tall slender point & holding a flaming cross aloft, astride a rearing horse w/red & white Klan trappings, one-sheet, Epoch, 1916, linen-backed, 27 x 41" 49,500.00

"David Copperfield," starring W.C. Fields, Lionel Barrymore, Madge Evans & Maureen O'Sullivan, color portraits of the main characters to either side centering a book lettered w/the title & names of the cast members, one-sheet, MGM, 1935, linen-backed, 27 x 41" 1,870.00

"Der Blaue Engel" (The Blue Angel), starring Emil Jannings, Marlene Dietrich, color bust portraits of the stars, UFA, Germany, 1929, linen-backed, 38 x 85" 27,500.00

"Don Juan," starring John Barrymore, large full-length color portrait of the star, one-sheet, Warner Brothers, 1926, linen-backed, 27x 41" 7,150.00

"Every Day's a Holiday," starring Mae West & Edmund Lowe, half-length portrait of Mae West wearing a feathered hat, feather boa & red gown, standing w/one hand on her hip, one-sheet, Paramount, 1937, linen-backed, 27 x 41' 2,090.00

"The Ghost Breakers," starring Bob Hope & Paulette Goddard, painted scene of the stars & a black man w/a green & blue caricature of a ghost hovering above, three-sheet, Paramount, 1940, linen-backed, 41 x 81" 1,320.00

"Go West," starring Groucho, Chico & Harpo Marx, caricature of the brothers & a beautiful woman on the back of a galloping brown & white horse, one-sheet, MGM, 1940, linen-backed, 27 x 41" 2,200.00

"The Kid," starring Charles Chaplin, scene of Chaplin in his trade-mark 'little tramp' outfit holding the hand of a young boy dressed in overalls & a large cap, both looking back over their shoulders, one-sheet, First National Attraction, 1921, linen-backed, 27 x 41" 27,500.00

"The Last of the Mohicans," starring Randolph Scott, Binnie Barnes & Henry Wilcoxon, scene of Indian warrior & British officer fighting on cliff at upper left, bust portraits of Scott & Barnes lower right, one-sheet, Reliance, 1936, linen-backed, 27 x 41" 550.00

"Life Begins for Andy Hardy," starring Mickey Rooney, Judy Garland & Lewis Stone, color bust drawing of an astonished Mickey being kissed on the cheek by Judy, one-sheet, MGM, 1949, linen-backed, 27 x 41" 660.00

"Little Annie Rooney," starring Mary Pickford, scene of Pickford as Annie looking angrily over a board fence lettered w/her name & the movie title in "chalk," three-sheet, United Artists, 1925, linen-backed, 41 x 81" 5,060.00

"The Littlest Rebel," starring Shirley Temple & John Boles, color bust portrait of Shirley smiling & giving a salute above a small scene of horsemen, a cannon & explosion, one-sheet, 20th Century Fox, 1935, linen-backed, 27 x 41" 3,850.00

"Lloyds of London," starring Freddie Bartholomew & Madeleine Carroll w/Tyrone Power, scene of ships engaged in battle w/bust portraits of lovers center, & young Freddie to the left, six-sheet, 20th Century Fox, 1936, linen-backed, 81 x 81" 7,590.00

"The Maltese Falcon," starring Humphrey Bogart & Mary Astor, bust photo of Bogart holding a gun at upper right, full-length photo of Astor at lower left wearing a deep red gown, three-sheet, Warner Brothers, 1941, 41 x 81" 6,600.00

"The Merry Widow," starring Mae Murray & John Gilbert, scene of two men in uniform fighting as lovely young blonde tries to stop them, three-sheet, Metro Goldwyn, 1925, linen-backed, 41 x 81" 3,910.00

"Mississippi," starring Bing Crosby, W.C. Fields & Joan Bennett, bust portrait of Crosby singing to Bennett w/Fields, wearing a captain's cap, looking on, against a background of a paddlewheel boat & the river, one-sheet, Paramount, 1935, paper-backed, 27 x 41" 2,750.00

"Nanook of the North," three individual color bust portraits of various cast members & drawing of dog sled in distance w/large sled dog in foreground, one-sheet, Pathe', 1921, linen-backed, 27 x 41" 6,050.00

"Ninotchka," starring Greta Garbo with Melvin Douglas & Ina Claire, central portrait of Garbo in a glamorous pose beneath photos of Garbo & Douglas, three-sheet, MGM, 1939, linen-backed, 41 x 81" 1,610.00

"The Painted Lady," starring George O'Brien & Dorothy MacKaill, one-sheet, Fox, 1924, linen-backed, 27 x 41" 5,720.00

"The Perils of Pauline," 6th episode in 2 parts, 'The Abduction,' color drawing of the bound & gagged Pauline being carried by a masked man, one man unconscious on the ground & another man in the background, one-sheet, Eclectic Film Co., 1914, linen-backed, 27 x 41" 6,050.00

"The Petrified Forest," starring Leslie Howard & Bette Davis w/Humphrey Bogart, bust portraits of the stars center above a depiction of Bogart in lower left corner, three-sheet, Warner Brothers, 1936, 41 x 81" 13,200.00

"The Postman Always Rings Twice," starring Lana Turner & John Garfield, full-length color scene of the stars standing, he w/his hand on her arm, one-sheet, MGM, 1946, linen-backed, 27 x 41" 3,575.00

"The Private Life of Henry VIII," starring Charles Laughton, bust portrait of Laughton top center above title & scene of Laughton holding a beautiful young woman, three-sheet, United Artists, 1933, paper-backed, 41 x 81"..............14,950.00

"Psycho," starring Anthony Perkins, one-sheet, Universal, 1960, 27 x 41" (ILLUS.) 495.00

"Pygmalion," starring Leslie Howard w/Wendy Hiller, caricature of George Bernard Shaw wearing a sandwich board advertising the movie, artwork by Al Hirschfeld, one-sheet, MGM, 1938, linen-backed, 27 x 41" 2,200.00

"Rain," starring Joan Crawford w/Walter Huston, large color bust portrait of the star, one-sheet, Atlantic Picture, reissue, ca. 1937, linen-backed, 27 x 41" 9,350.00

"Romance & Riches," starring Cary Grant w/Mary Brian, large color bust portraits of stars below grey & white action scene at top corner, one-sheet, Grand National, 1937, linen-backed, 27 x 41" 660.00

"Senor Daredevil," starring Ken Maynard & Dorothy Devore, color bust portrait of Maynard in cowboy hat & scarf holding a revolver forming the background, small picture of man on rearing horse lower right, one-sheet, First National Picture, 1926, linen-backed, 27 x 41" 1,210.00

"The Seven Year Itch," starring Marilyn Monroe & Tom Ewell, large color bust painting of Marilyn waving & holding a pair of men's shoes, a small figure of Tom Ewell to lower right, one-sheet, 20th Century Fox, 1955, linen-backed, 27 x 41" 1,870.00

"She Done Him Wrong," starring Mae West with Cary Grant, Paramount, 1933, three-sheet, linen-backed, 41 x 81" 4,620.00

"Sleepy-Time Donald," Walt Disney production featuring Donald Duck, scene of Donald sleepwalking on the edge of the roof of a tall building, one-sheet, Walt Disney Productions, 1947, linen-backed, 27 x 41" 3,300.00

"Some Like It Hot" Poster

"Some Like It Hot," starring Marilyn Monroe, Tony Curtis & Jack Lemmon, central scene of Marilyn winking & w/an arm around Tony Curtis & Jack Lemmon dressed in women's clothing, one-sheet, United Artists, 1959, linen-backed, 27 x 41" (ILLUS.) 880.00

"The Son of the Sheik," starring Rudolph Valentino, one-sheet, United Artists, 1926, linen-backed, 27 x 41" (ILLUS. top next page).................................13,200.00

"The Son of the Sheik" Poster

"Sunset Boulevard," starring Gloria Swanson, William Holden & Erich von Stroheim, depiction of Swanson w/an anguished expression against a bright red background above a bust photograph of Holden in the arms of another woman, half-sheet, Paramount, 1950, linen-backed, 22 x 28" 990.00

"The Virginian," starring Gary Cooper & Walter Huston, half-length color portrait of the stars in Western attire against a barren desert background w/mountains in the distance, one-sheet, Paramount, 1929, linen-backed, 27 x 41" 9,350.00

"The Walking Dead," starring Boris Karloff, six-sheet, Warner Brothers, 1936, linen-backed, 81 x 81" 28,600.00

"White Christmas" Poster

"White Christmas," starring Bing Crosby, Danny Kaye, Rosemary Clooney & Vera-Ellen, one-sheet, Paramount, 1954, 27 x 41" (ILLUS.) 385.00

"Wings," starring Charles Rogers, Clara Bow & Richard Arlen, scene of airplanes flying in formation above two planes in combat w/one going down in flames, one-sheet, Paramount, 1927, linen-backed, 27 x 41" 4,950.00

MISCELLANEOUS

Academy Award (Oscar), 1939, presented to Vivien Leigh for her 'Best Actress' performance in "Gone With The Wind" (MGM), gold-colored bronze, 12" h...............510,000.00

Ashtray, bronze, slightly rounded flattened square form featuring an etched profile of Alfred Hitchcock in the center, designed by Wah Ming Chang for Bronze Originals of California, from the estate of Alfred Hitchcock, 8" w. 1,840.00

Biscuit tin, depicts Madeleine Carroll, star of "The Thirty-Nine Steps," oval, England, ca. 1930s 65.00

Errol Flynn Cigarette Case

Cigarette case, sterling silver, formerly owned by Errol Flynn, rectangular w/cut corners, line-incised top w/central small reserve engraved "EF," inscribed on the inside "Good Luck Errol - J. (John) Barrymore," w/letter of authenticity, 4½" l., 2 pcs. (ILLUS.) 7,150.00

Doll, Marilyn Monroe, depicting her character in "How To Marry A Millionaire," TriStar, mint in box 45.00

Lobby or drive-in insert, "A Bedtime Story," starring Maurice Chevalier & Helen Twelvetrees, profile caricature of Chevalier w/his straw hat tilted to cover one eye, his lower lip in an exaggerated pout, portrait & colorful lettering against a black background, Paramount, 1933 .....1,320.00

Lobby or drive-in insert, "College," starring Buster Keaton, caricature bust portrait of the star at top, further

"College" Insert Card

small caricatures at lower right & left, United Artists, 1927, 14 x 36" (ILLUS.) 3,575.00

Lobby or drive-in insert, "Dr. Jekyll and Mr. Hyde," starring Fredric March & Miriam Hopkins, half-length color depiction of the star forming background, small full-length scene of a man & woman w/their arms around each other at lower right, Paramount, 1931, 14 x 36" 7,700.00

Lobby or drive-in insert, "Metropolis," drawing of a huge grey futuristic building against a starry sky crossed w/orange light beams, a single airplane flying in front of the building, Paramount, 1926, 14 x 36" ..33,000.00

Lunch box & thermos, "The Black Hole," the box w/a scene of a space vehicle entering the black hole, the thermos depicts the characters from the film, 1979, mint condition, 2 pcs. 150.00

Magazine, "Modern Screen," 1952, October, Elizabeth Taylor cover, M. Lanza, Lucy & Desi, Lana Turner, etc., inside......................................10.00

Magazine, "Photoplay," 1932, November, Joan Crawford cover, features on Clara Bow, Spanky McFarland, Novarro, Chaplin, etc. 10.00

Magazine, "Photoplay," 1946, August, June Allyson cover............................15.00

Magazine, "Photoplay," 1948, April, Betty Grable cover 10.00

Magazine, "Screen Stories," 1951, August, Alice In Wonderland cover....25.00

Magazine, "Silver Screen," 1936, Barbara Stanwyck cover, Shirley Temple contest inside 35.00

Movie advertising slide, "Goodrich Water Bottles," glass, hand-colored, depicts baby & dog, 3¼ x 4" 30.00

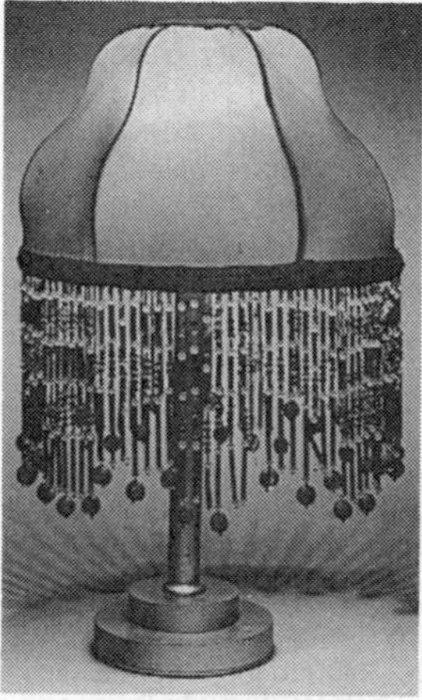

Original "Casablanca" Lamp

Movie prop, table lamp from "Casablanca," used in Rick's Cafe, fitted w/a low, long beaded fringe, marked on the bottom "Casablanca 007," along w/10 movie stills & a pop-up book entitled "The Great Movies Live," lamp 17" h., the group (ILLUS.) 12,100.00

Movie prop, the tiller from the boat 'The African Queen,' used in the 1951 movie of the same name, made of ash & mounted w/a brass band inscribed "To Katie With enduring affection from the "African Queen" - May-September 1951," presented to Katharine Hepburn by director John Huston, framed w/a personal note from Ms. Hepburn, tiller 12¾" l. 18,400.0

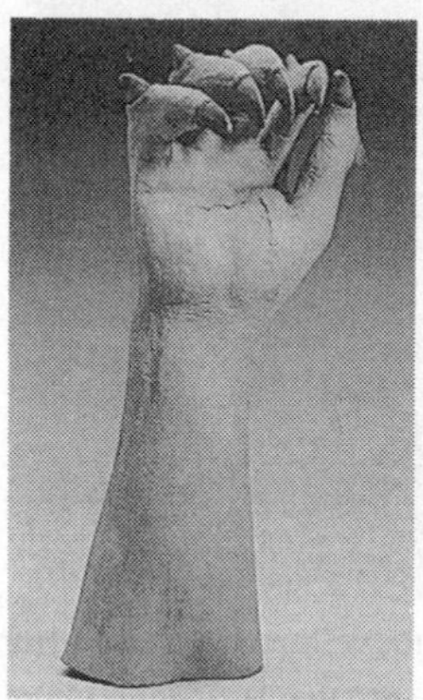

Prop from "The Thing"

Movie prop from "The Thing," RKO, 1951, a molded rubber arm of the monster, painted green & yellow (ILLUS.) 1,045.00

Movie title slide, "Behind the Front," starring Wallace Beery, glass, hand-colored, ca. 1920s, 3¼ x 4" 20.00

Movie title slide, "Only the Brave," starring Gary Cooper, glass, hand-colored, ca. 1930s, 3¼ x 4" 35.00

Movie title slide, "Street of Chance," starring William Powell, glass, hand-colored, ca. 1930s, 3¼ x 4" 25.00

Photograph, from "The Incredible Shrinking Man," Universal, 1957, depicts Grant Williams w/nail prying cheese from mouse trap, framed.......15.00

Photograph, autographed black & white photo of Marilyn Monroe wearing a dress made from a potato sack advertising "U.S. No. 1 Idaho Potatoes," signed in green ink "To Gregory Best Wishes Marilyn Monroe," 8 x 10" 5,060.00

Program, "The Gaucho," starring Douglas Fairbanks, silent film, from Grauman's Chinese Theatre, 1927....15.00

Program, "La Dolce Vita," Anita Ekberg on cover, directed by Federico Fellini, late 1950s...............35.00

Program, "The Ten Commandments, " 1923...35.00

Record album, movie soundtrack from "Jack The Ripper," 1960 ....25.00

Record album, movie soundtrack from "The Wild One," Marlon Brando on cover 30.00

Tray, serving-type, lithographed tin, "The Greatest Show On Earth," movie cast shown, 1952 ....75.00

Window Card from "Ben-Hur"

Window card, "Ben-Hur," profile bust portraits of a man & woman above scene of chariot race, MGM, 1926, linen-backed, 14 x 22" (ILLUS.) 1,430.00

Window card, "The Broadway Melody," depicting showgirls in various costumes, each holding a letter to spell out the name of the movie, MGM, 1929, 14 x 22" 2,750.00

Window card, "Tarzan Escapes," starring Johnny Weissmuller & Maureen O'Sullivan, dramatic color drawings depicting Tarzan in a log pen w/large elephant in background & two scenes of Tarzan & Jane, MGM, 1936, 22 x 28" 770.00

Writing tablet, Lana Turner on cover, unused 5.00

MUCHA (Alphonse) ARTWORK

A leader in the Art Nouveau movement, Alphonse Maria Mucha was born in Moravia (which was part of Czechoslovakia) in 1860. Displaying considerable artistic talent as a child, he began formal studies locally, later continuing his work in Munich and then Paris, where it became necessary for him to undertake commercial artwork. In 1894, the renowned actress Sarah Bernhardt commissioned Mucha to create a poster for her play "Gismonda" and this opportunity proved to be the turning point in his career. While continuing his association with Bernhardt, he began creating numerous advertising posters, packaging designs, book and magazine illustrations and "panneaux decoratifs" (decorative pictures).

Salon des Cent Poster

Calendars, "Tete Byzantines," lithographed in color, each w/a profile bust portrait of an exotic young woman w/an ornate headdress framed by a round reserve above two boxes w/the months of the year, one woman blonde, the other brunette, 1900, framed, 18 x 25⅞", pr. $12,650.00

Cloth panel, rectangular, velveteen printed in color w/the central image of a redheaded maiden surrounded by flowering vines in shades of green, brown & tan, imprinted signature, probably printed by Hines, Stroud & Co., London, England, ca. 1900, 27 x 33½".......3,738.00

Plaques, composition, round, cast in low- & medium-relief w/bust profile portraits of exotic Art Nouveau maidens, in shades of dark brown, chocolate brown & silver, inscribed "Mucha," ca. 1898, 8" d., pr. 2,300.00

Poster, "Bernhardt - American Tour," lithograph in color depicting actress Sarah Bernhardt standing & holding a palm frond, signed in the plate, 1895, framed, 29 x 77½" 13,800.00

Poster, "La Samaritaine," lithograph in color depicting Sarah Bernhardt in the role of Photine standing beside a tall vase, signed in the plate, 1897, framed, 22½ x 68½" 13,800.00

Poster, "Monaco Monte-Carlo," depicting a beautiful young woman seated w/her legs drawn up to one side, stylized circular floral arrangements behind her & another similar semi-circular arrangement at the front, printed in colors by F. Champenois, Paris, 1897, 30 x 43⅝" (5" tear at lower right corner, tear at center left margin, minor losses to edges)...5,750.00

Poster, "Salon des Cent," lithograph printed in color by F. Champenois, Paris, depicting a half-length nude portrait of a young woman holding a quill pen & paint brush, loose sheet, 16¼ x 24" (ILLUS.) 7,475.00

Poster, "Sarah Bernhardt" in a semi-circle above a bust portrait of the actress depicted w/a crown of lilies in her long hair, the background composed of stars in varying sizes, printed in colors by F. Champenois, Paris, France, 1897, loose sheet, 20⅞ x 30³⁄₁₆" (slightly time darkened)...2,530.00

Poster, "Vin de Incas," lithograph printed in colors by F. Champenois, Paris, 1899, framed, 5³⁄₁₆ x 14⅝" (some abrasions in upper right, upper corners taped to sheet).......1,150.00

Print, "Automne," lithograph in color of a young Art Nouveau maiden standing amid autumn leaves & fruiting vines & holding a dish, by F. Champenois, Paris, late 19th c., loose sheet, on canvas, framed, 20 x 39" (time-darkened, mat burn) 4,600.00

Prints, "Heures du Jour" (The Times of the Day), four color lithographs printed in colors by F. Champenois, Paris, France, 1899, framed, 33¼ x 44½", set of 4.....................6,900.00

Prints, "Les Etoiles," "Clair de Lune," "Etoile du Matin," & "Etoile Polaire," each w/a different allegorical figure of a young woman, each w/a floral or leaf border band, in various conditions, generally good condition, lithographed in color by F. Champenois, Paris, 1902, each 11½ x 29½", set of 4 ....34,500.00

MUSICAL INSTRUMENTS

Loud Brothers Piano Forte

Accordion, "Guerrin & Co.," San Francisco, California, mint in case $550.00

Banjo, "Concertone," four-stringed, w/case...180.00

Banjo, "Gretsch Broadkaster," mother-of-pearl fretboard.................350.00

Flute, "Calura," tin, painted black & gold, in original box...........................55.00

Harmonica, "Bohm System - The Bluebird," sailing vessel trademark, Bohm System, Germany....................45.00

Harmonica, "Hohner - Auto-Valve-Harp," M. Hohner, Germany, 4½" l., w/box & instructions..........................65.00

Harmonica, "Hohner - Echo Harp," M. Hohner, Germany, 6¾" l., w/box........95.00

Harmonica, "Hohner - Melodica," alto, w/keys 30.00

Harmonica, "Hohner - Tremolo Concert Harp," Model No. 683, four keys, 192 reeds, in original case 145.00

Harmonica, "Magnus," black plastic, w/instructions & original box 25.00

Organ, pump-type, "Estey," Eastlake cabinet, 11 stops, 122 reeds, 1891, restored 1,400.00

Organ, pump-type, "Mason & Hamlin," ca. 1886 ....1,500.00

Piano, grand, "Chickering," cherry, square case, Serial No. 18920,1858 ....15,000.00

Piano, grand, "Wm. Knabe," rosewood, square case, 1850s, good condition 8,000.00

Piano, grand, "Lindeman & Sons," rosewood, square case, 82 keys, 1861, restored 7,000.00

Piano, grand, "Steinway," Empire style w/turned, fluted & carved legs, lyre pedal frame & scrolled edge music rack, ebony refinishing, Serial No. 102914, ca. 1901, 56" w., 7'10" l. 7,425.00

Piano, upright, "Geo. H. Davis," ornately carved ebony case, marked "patented 10/28/1873, #23153," Germany, restored 9,950.00

Piano, upright, "Errard," the rectangular case by L.W. Collman fitted w/gilt-bronze leaftips, flowerheads & a pair of candelabra, carved w/foliage, columns & a lyre & incised decorations, the whole w/panels fitted to simulate grillwork, Victorian, 5'1" w., 45" h. 5,175.00

Piano forte, "Loud Brothers," rosewood, the rectangular top w/ebonized line inlay & outset rounded corners enclosing the keyboard over a conforming case w/ebonized line inlay stenciled gilt line & anthemion decoration as well as applied ormolu banding over two short scroll & anthemion-carved drawers over four robust tapering cylindrical acanthus-carved & lobed legs, on brass castors, Philadelphia, Pennsylvania, ca.1830, 28 x 67½", 36" h. (ILLUS.) 4,370.00

Pitch pipe, "Hotliners Trutone," Model No. P10, w/original box....................20.00

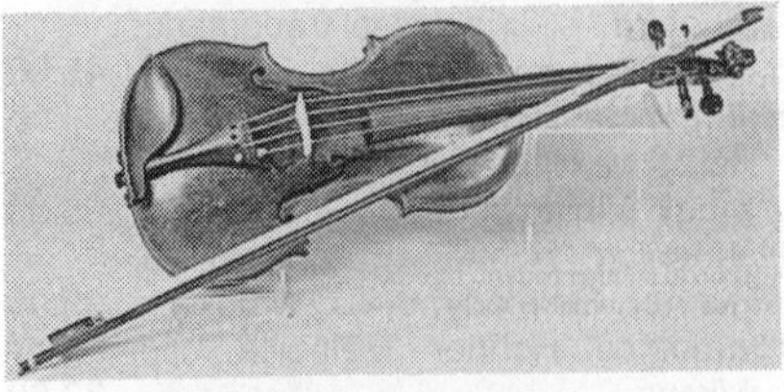

Violin by Johann Lippold

Violin, "Johann Georg Lippold," inscription inside instrument reads "Muficalifeher Infrrumentenmacher In Neukirchen, 1792" (ILLUS.) 1,760.00

MUSICAL INSTRUMENTS, MECHANICAL

Band organ, "Mortier," console cabinet, 101 keys & includes organ pipes, xylophone, snare drum, triangle & exposed accordion, fully chromatic, w/40 books of new, popular music, made in Belgium, 1937 ....$100,000.00

Band organ, "Mortier," console cabinet w/three moving figures, 539 pipes & six percussion instruments, 14' w. 118,000.00

Band organ, "Wellershaus," 56 keys, 191 pipes, two drums & cymbal, ca. 1875, 8' w. 18,000.00

Band organ, "Wurlitzer Model 125," w/external horns, cymbal, bass & snare drum 20,000.00

Barrel organ, "Gavioli," 25 key Uniflute, inlaid cart, portable hand-cranked model, plays ten tunes, Paris, France 8,500.00

Calliope, "National," 53-note (unrestored) 10,000.00

Coin-operated piano, "Seeburg Style A," w/mandolin & orchestrion bells 8,250.00

Cornet, 'Cornetino,' chromed metal, playing eighteen notes, complete w/instruction leaflet & 12 paper rolls, early 20th c., 15" l. 690.00

Orchestrion, "Coinola X," ca. 1920 ....16,000.00

Orchestrion, "Hupfield Atlantic," weight driven (original exterior finish, interior restored) 12,000.00

Photoplayer, "Wurlitzer Style O," double-tracker piano w/mandolin, pipes, two side chests, full traps horse trot, fire gong, etc., unrestored w/extra parts 8,500.00

Reproducing piano, grand, "Fischer Ampico," Queen Anne art case, 5' 6" 22,500.00

Reproducing piano, grand, "Knabe Ampico," Italian Renaissance art case fully carved w/statues, further carved w/eight busts of composers on the rim & matching bench, 6' 4" (restored) 150,000.00

Reproducing piano, grand, "Steck Duo-Art," art case w/double legs & matching bench, w/150 rolls, 1928 ....12,000.00

Reproducing piano, grand, "Stroud Duo-Art," 1933, original finish, w/bench & rolls, 5' 4" (mechanism rebuilt) 5,500.00

Reproducing piano, grand, "Weber Duo-Art," No. 74562, w/bench & rolls, 4' 8" (restored stack) 4,800.00

Reproducing piano, grand, "Welte Mignon," mahogany case, w/25 rolls, 6' 6" 15,000.00

MUSIC BOXES

Swiss Music Box on Stand

Automaton-type, singing bird box, silver & enamel, rectangular, enameled translucent blue over a *guilloché* ground, the cover further enameled w/birds perched on branches w/a cherub directing the song, raised on four scroll supports, the actuating slide set w/five cabochon sapphires, w/London import marks for 1937, 4" l. $2,300.00

Automaton-type, singing bird box, silver-gilt & enamel, enameled translucent green over foliage, the front w/drawer, the top opening to reveal a brightly-plumed singing bird, Continental, 5¾" l. 2,875.00

Imperial Symphonion (American) disc music box, mahogany case, double comb, plays 15¾ d. discs, w/12 discs, the group 3,900.00

Regina (American subsidiary of Polyphon Musikwerke, Rahway, New Jersey) disc music box, floor model, mahogany case w/turned spindles in top gallery, plays 20¾" d. discs 12,500.00

Samuel Troll Fils, Geneva (Swiss) cylinder music box on stand, burl walnut & tulipwood-inlaid cabinet set upon a table stand w/shaped rectangular top w/a shaped apron w/drawer & writing slide, on simple cabriole legs on casters, double-combs w/dampers, bellows & ten bells, interchangeable 19½" l. cylinders playing six tunes each, late 19th c., overall 34 x 59", 43" h. (ILLUS.) 14,850.00

Woog (Swiss) cylinder music box, rosewood veneered lid w/fruitwood floral inlay & boxwood stringing, playing six airs as listed on original tune sheet, lever wound, Serial No. 48266, ca. 1890, 11 cm cylinder, 16¾" w. (two teeth repaired on comb) 518.00

NAPKIN RINGS

Children on Teeter-Totter Napkin Ring

Napkin rings were popular dining table adjuncts in the late 19th and early 20th century. The most valuable today are the figural silver plate examples produced in abundance between 1880 and 1900. All rings listed here are silver plate unless otherwise noted.

Apple & leafy branch on ring $58.00

Bird on triangular ring supported by a horse base, Pairpoint.......................110.00

Bird w/wings spread supporting ring, four ball feet 120.00

Boy standing w/dog next to ring, Meriden..195.00

Boys (2) in caps w/earmuffs roll an ornately decorated ring, on rectangular base, Middletown Silver Plate..235.00

Cherub sitting on top of large ring 220.00

Cherubs (2) holding six-sided ring......100.00

Children on teeter-totter w/ring between, on shaped base, Simpson, Hall, Miller & Co. (ILLUS.)...............600.00

"Comin' Thru' the Rye," barrel-form on pedestal legs, No. 1468 ....65.00

Dog begging & sitting on an American shield decorated w/stars & stripes, Wilcox, 2½" h. 185.00

Horse pulling ornate wheeled cart w/heavily decorated ring, Meriden...325.00

Horseshoe base holding triangular ring etched w/florals & a hummingbird, all pulled by a figural flying bird, Pairpoint...235.00

Hummingbird perched on ornament next to ring, highly detailed, Derby ..295.00

International Exposition of 1935, souvenir-type, brass, set of 4............20.00
Kittens standing on hind legs holding ring...175.00
Leaf w/strawberry next to floral-engraved ring, large..............................75.00
Nude cherub boy pushing square ring on rectangular base, Tufts 275.00
Rectangular base w/pleated rim w/floral etched ring set on the base at an angle & held up by two busts of classical women facing in opposite directions, Southington Silver Co. 325.00
Triangle on four ball & claw feet, wishbones front & back, engraved leaves & "Best Wishes," openwork floral border, Meriden........................73.00

Wolf with Napkin Ring

Wolf, standing w/head raised beside an engraved ring, on an oblong scrolled base w/four ball feet, Barbour Silver, 3" h. (ILLUS.) 275.00

NAUTICAL ITEMS

Early Ship Painting

The romantic lure of the sea, and of ships in general, has opened up a new area of collector interest. Nautical gear, especially items made of brass or with brass trim, is sought out for its decorative appeal. Virtually all items that can be associated with older ships, along with items used or made by sailors, are now considered collectible for technological advances have rendered them obsolete. Listed below are but a few of the numerous nautical items sold in recent months.

Barometer, ship's, mahogany, w/reeded melon finial over indicator, spiral-reeded body enclosing a thermometer, adjustable brass bracket, J. Blair, 45 Prince St., Bristol, England, early Victorian, mid-19th c., 37" h.......................$5,520.00
Book, "500 Sailling Records of American Built Ships," by Carl C. Cutler, published by The Maine Historical Association, 1952..............45.00
Deck watch, two-day, small nickel lever movement, 17 jewels, adjusted to three positions, bi-metallic compensation balance, cam-wheel regulator, silvered matte dial w/up & down scale for 50 hours & constant seconds below, applied baton numerals, gimbaled & mounted on a square removable mahogany base within an outer mahogany traveling box, both signed "Longines," ca. 1940, outer box 22 cm w. 2,475.00
Half-model of the U.S. Battleship Massachusetts, carved & painted wood, mounted against a seascape w/name lower center, 36" w., 30" h. (some losses) 605.00
Marine chronometer, two-day, gilt spring detent, polished steel helical hairspring, diamond end-stone, bi-metallic compensation balance, silvered matte dial, Roman numerals, subsidiary seconds & up & down scale for 55 hours, mounted in gimbals, w/two-tier mahogany box w/brass details, lid inset w/maker's plaque, Peter L. DeMory Gray, New York, ca. 1890, outer box 18 cm w. 1,650.00
Octant, brass fittings & ivory plates within an ebony case, case w/label of "John Bliss & Co. 110 Wall Street" & pencil inscription "John A. Ryder South Orrington, Maine," octant labeled by "Walker, Liverpool," England, 19th c. 412.50
Painting, oil on canvas, a three-masted sailing ship flying the American ensign of 1795, other sail-vessels in the background, late 18th - early 19th c., unsigned, framed, scattered old retouching, 23 x 30¾" (ILLUS.) 11,550.00

Print, "New-York Clipper Ship Challenge...," lithographed in color by Endicott & Co., additional hand-coloring, full inscription beneath the scene, dated 1852, framed, sheet size 23½ x 32½" 3,300.00

Print, "View of the Stone Fleet Which Sailed from New Bedford, Nov. 16th, 1861," lithographed in black & blue w/additional hand-coloring, after Benjamin Russell, printed by Louis Prang & Co., 1862, framed, 17 x 26¼" (staining, toning, foxing, minor creases & tears).....................605.00

Sea chest, painted pine, rectangular, original old blue paint, Massachusetts, ca. 1820, 16 x 36", 14½" h...1,045.00

Inlaid Ebony Sextant

Sextant, bone-inlaid & brass-mounted ebony, marked by Spencer & Co., London, England, ca. 1860, in a mahogany case, 13½" l. (ILLUS.) 575.00

Ship model, carved & painted wood, the "H.M.S. Bounty," fitted w/complete rigging & flags, on a wooden base, England, in glass showcase, 9 x 23½", 20½" h..........................1,150.00

Model of the Steamer "America"

Ship model, carved & painted wood, model of the steamer "America," polychrome paint, w/wooden cradle, early 20th c., 27" l., 19½" h. (ILLUS.) 770.00

Ship model, carved & painted wood, the steam yacht "Vamoose," Rhode Island, 1891, enclosed in a glass-sided case, 12 x 51", 14" h. 1,650.00

Ship's compass, brass, gimballed in wooden case, printed card signed "Wm. Helffricht, Philadelphia," 19th c., 7" d.....................................220.00

Spyglass, metal, marked "Blackford Emery, London, Day or Night," 19th c., 24½" l. (imperfections) 220.00

Telescope, three-draw, brass, marked "The Lord Bury Telescope, J.H. Steward, 457 Strand, London," 19th c. 220.00

NETSUKE

These decorative toggles were used by the Japanese to secure an inro, tobacco pouch or other small personal articles by means of a cord slipped through a kimono sash (obi). They are carved of ivory and other materials. There are many reproductions.

Figure of "Inch Boy" sitting on a man's clog, ivory, 1¼" h. $330.00

Figure of Sennin, wood, rich patina, 4¼" l...302.50

Model of a cat w/a rabbit & a bird at its feet, ivory, signed "Masanao"...1,100.00

Model of a lotus pod w/a demon underneath, ivory, signed, 1¼" h. 247.50

Model of a Shishi, ferocious beast w/a ball, wood, 2¼" h. 192.50

Model of two quail on a tassel of millet, ivory, signed "Shigetsugu," late 18th - early 19th c. 852.50

NUTTING (Wallace) COLLECTIBLES

In 1898, Wallace Nutting published his first hand-tinted pictures and these were popular for more than 20 years. An "assembly line" subsequently colored and placed a signature and (sometimes) a title on the mat of these copyrighted photographs. Interior scenes featuring Early American furniture are considered the most collectible of these photographs.

Nutting's photographically illustrated travel books and early editions of his antiques reference books are also highly collectible.

BOOKS

"Connecticut Beautiful," first edition....$32.50

"England Beautiful," first edition 65.00
"Massachusetts Beautiful," 1935. ....40.00
"New Hampshire Beautiful," second edition 30.00
"Photographic Art Secrets," first edition 315.00
"Virginia Beautiful," first edition 42.50

PRINTS

The Bridesmaid's Procession

All Sunshine, 13 x 16", exterior scene, England..100.00
Arched Lane (The), 13 x 16", exterior scene 70.00
Bower For The Wedding, 5½ x 9", exterior scene 195.00
Bridesmaid's Procession (The), 10 x 18", exterior scene (ILLUS.).....100.00
By a Cottage Door, 13 x 17", exterior scene, France 245.00
Call at the Manor (A), 12 x 16", interior scene 265.00
Capture of a Red Coat (The), 13 x 16", exterior scene of a man in a red jacket near a girl w/a red dress..650.00
Chambord on the Casson, 13 x 16", exterior scene, France 150.00
Chopping Bowl (The), 11 x 13", interior scene 205.00
Colonial Belle (A), 11 x 17", interior scene 50.00
Coming Out of Rosa (The), 8 x 10", exterior scene 125.00
Connecticut Blossoms, 12 x 16", exterior scene 55.00
Corner Cupboard (The), 10 x 14", interior scene 75.00
Cosmos and Larkspur, 13 x 16", floral arrangement in stoneware vase 900.00
Cress Brook Road, 18 x 22", exterior scene 175.00
Delicate Stitch (A), 15 x 19", interior scene 90.00
Dell Road (The), 13 x 16", exterior scene 185.00
Dream and Reality, 10 x 12", exterior scene 55.00
Fair Vale (The), 10 x 12", exterior scene, Ireland 135.00
Final Glance (The), 10 x 16", interior scene 115.00
Fine Point (A), 13 x 15", interior scene 105.00
Good Night, 14 x 17", interior scene...154.00
Goose Chase Quilt (The), 11 x 17", interior scene 132.00
Great Wayside Oak (The) 7½ x 9½", exterior scene 180.00
Heart of the Orchard (The), 10 x 12", exterior scene 150.00
Hollyhock Cottage, 8 x 10", foreign exterior scene, England.....................71.50
Honeymoon Windings, 13 x 16", exterior scene 60.50
Ivy and Rose Cloister, 14 x 17", exterior California Mission scene 200.00
Jane, 11 x 17", exterior scene w/girl descending porch stairs....................90.00
Joyous Anniversary (A), 10 x 12", exterior scene, Ireland 95.00
Joy Path, 9 x 11", exterior scene, England..115.00
Langdon Door (The), 13 x 16", exterior scene, black & white close-up view of large doorway, pencil-signed 115.00
Last Furrow (The), 13 x 16", exterior scene w/man plowing w/two white horses 340.00
Little River with Mt. Washington (A), 10 x 16", exterior scene 70.00
Maid and a Mirror (A), 11 x 17", interior scene 135.00
Maine Coast Sky (A), 10 x 12", seascape 195.00
Mary's Little Lamb, 14 x 17", exterior scene in England 160.00
Morning Errand (A), 12 x 16", exterior scene in California 575.00
Natural Bridge (The), 13 x 16", exterior scene 260.00
Old Senate Chamber, 13 x 16", interior scene, Maryland 275.00
Old Time Romance (An), 12 x 15", interior scene 190.00
Pause at the Bridge (A), 10 x 12", exterior scene 165.00
Pomperaug Water, 13 x 22", exterior scene 105.00
Print, miniature, 4 x 5", exterior scene w/a country road & clusters of birch...40.00
Sailing Among Windmills, 10 x 16", exterior scene, Holland 155.00
St. Mary's in May, 13 x 16", exterior scene, England 80.00
Sewing a Rag Rug, 7½ x 9½", interior scene 200.00
Shimmering Gold, 10 x 16", exterior 50.00
Sip of Tea (A), 7½ x 9½", interior scene 170.00
Southern Colonial Room (A), 11 x 14", interior scene 85.00
Spring Flowers, 13 x 16", exterior scene, England 285.00
Summer Opulence, 8 x 10", floral arrangement in golden vase 425.00

Thatched Dormers, 8 x 10", exterior scene, France 55.00
Vista of Amalfi (A), 8 x 10", exterior scene, Italy 120.00
Warm Spring Day (A), 14 x 17", exterior scene w/sheep 125.00
Way Through the Orchard (The), 13 x 16", exterior scene 60.50
Where Trout Lie, 9 x 12", exterior scene 75.00
Winding Way (A), 13 x 16", exterior scene 190.00
Wisteria Gate, 10 x 16", exterior scene in California 235.00
Work Basket (The), 10 x 12", interior scene 95.00
Yosemite Waters, 11 x 13", exterior scene 215.00

MISCELLANEOUS ITEMS

Christmas card, a scene of birch trees above "Christmas Greetings," 4 x 6" 95.00
Mirror, wall-type, half-round ring-turned columnar sides, "Early Mother Instinct" print at top of little girl & cradle by fireplace, 10 x 18" 415.00
Photographic glass negative, original for "Flowering Time," Nutting #158, 8 x 10" 125.00
Silhouette, 7 x 8", little lamb follows Mary to school 95.00

OCCUPIED JAPAN

American troops occupied the country of Japan from September 2, 1945, until April 28, 1952, following World Ward II.. All wares made for export during this period were required to be marked "Made in Occupied Japan," Now these items, mostly small ceramic and metal trifles of varying quality, are sought out be a growing number of collectors.

Ashtray, china, w/figural Boston Bull dog & fire hydrant at edge $25.00
Cheese dish, cov., ceramic, figural cottage 70.00
Creamer & cov. sugar bowl, ceramic, figural cottage, pr. 50.00
Cuckoo clock, wooden, figural owl, eyes move when running, Terpuka Clock Co. Ltd., 10" h. 265.00
Figure, 18th c. gentleman musician playing lute dressed in green tricornered hat, pink jacket, striped pants & flowing cape, w/gold trim, bisque, 10" h. 60.00
Figure of a boy leaning on a fence, china, 9½" h. 38.00
Figure of a boy playing an accordion, china, 3¾" h. 10.00
Figure group, lady seated at piano, man playing violin, h.p. bisque, Andrea, base 5 x 10", 8" h. 300.00
Jam pot, cov., ceramic, basketweave bottom w/a cluster of fruit on the cover 20.00
Jam pot, cov., ceramic, basketweave bottom w/a cluster of fruit on the cover 20.00
Model of a Terrier dog, porcelain, 6½" h. 35.00
Mug, bust of grinning man w/prominent white teeth & wearing a black bow tie & green cap, 5½" h. 45.00
Mug, bust of old gentleman w/grey beard & mustache & wearing a green cap, 5½" h. 45.00
Teacup & saucer, overall floral decoration & gold trim 15.00
Teapot, cov., ceramic, figural cottage...59.00
Toy, windup celluloid, minstrel monkey playing a mandolin 145,00
Toy, windup celluloid, walking camel....95.00
Vase, tulip-shaped, decorated w/three Colonial ladies around base, nearing green, yellow, pink dresses, h.p. roses, china, 6¾" h. 50.00

OFFICE EQUIPMENT

Early Check Writing Machine

By the late 19th century business offices around the country were becoming increasingly mechanized as inventions such as the typewriter, adding machine, mimeograph and dictaphone became more widely available. Miracles of efficiency when introduced, in today's computerized offices these machines would be cumbersome and archaic. Although difficult to display and store, many of these relics are becoming increasingly collectible today.

Adding machine, "Comptometer," ca. 1920s $95.00
Adding machine, Fell & Farrant," fine original condition 65.00
Check writing press machine, metal case, punches numbers in checks, working, early 20th c., 4½ x 5½", 5½" h. (ILLUS.) 33.00
Dictating machine, "Edison E" 245.00
Labeling machine, "Monarch Marking System," w/print box 95.00
Mimeograph, "Edison No. 4," in wood case 75.00
Pencil sharpener, "Climax No. 2" 45.00
Pencil sharpener, "Corspring Crosby," automatic crank-type 125.00
Pencil sharpener, mechanical, "Planetary Pencil Pointer," ca. 1896 ....185.00
Ticker tape machine, wooden, tall slightly tapering octagonal case w/flaring octagonal base, original glass top & paper roll w/extra roll, "Dow-Jones" tag on side & a long clipboard hung at the side, 17" w., 38" h. (overall soiling) 550.00
Typewriter, "Blickensderfer No. 5," w/wood case, manual & accessories ....100.00 to 125.00
Typewriter, "Corona No. 3," folding model w/case ....100.00 to 125.00
Typewriter, "Gunka No. 5" 250.00
Typewriter, "Hammond No. 12" 50.00
Typewriter, "Oliver No. 5" ....50.00 to 75.00
Typewriter, "Oliver No. 9," w/manual & original accessories 60.00
Typewriter, "Royal No. 5" 75.00
Typewriter, "L.C .Smith & Bros. No. 8" 35.00

L.C. Smith Typewriter

Typewriter, "L.C .Smith & Corona Typewriter, Inc.," black metal w/gold lettering, early 20th c., soiled, scratches, 9¼ x 11½" (ILLUS.) 27.50

OLYMPIC GAMES MEMORABILIA

First begun in Ancient Greece as a Pan-Hellenic festival of athletic games, as well as choral poetry and dance contests, the Games were held every four years until the 4th century A.D. Not until 1896 were the Olympics revived under the leadership of Baron deCoubertin of France. The first modern Games were held in Athens, Greece and have continued throughout this century with lapses during the two World Wars. It was in 1924 that the first Winter Olympics were initiated so the numbering for the Summer and Winter Olympics does not coincide. Posters, pins and other items from past Olympiads are today highly collectible.

Book, "Olympic Committee Report," 1936, Berlin summer games, includes photographs of the opening ceremonies & Hitler, Hindenburg & Jesse Owens, etc., includes statistics, hardcover, 490 pp. $75.00
Book, "Olympic Committee Report," 1948 ....45.00
Book, "Olympic Committee Report," 1952 ....40.00
Book, "Olympic Committee Report," 1956 ....40.00
Flag, 1972 Munich summer games, 10 x 25' 250.00
Hand puppet, 1980 Moscow summer games, Misha Bear, packaged, ca. 1979 ....30.00
Pin w/ribbon, 1932 Lake Placid winter games, "Official" 5.00
Plate, ceramic, 1968 Mexico City summer games, torch w/Mexico, gold leaf, Staffordshire, England, 7" d. 60.00
Plate, ceramic, 1972 Munich summer games, underglaze-blue decoration, Winterling 30.00
Postcard, original photograph of the U.S. Olympic track team, 1912 ....15.00

OPERA GLASSES, LORGNETTES & EYEGLASSES

Eyeglasses, silver, marked "P & B", octagonal shape, green glass w/fold-in side lens, (one side lens chipped), w/metal case, 19th $95.00
Lorgnette, diamond & platinum, Art Deco style, rectangular w/pointed end & short handle, set w/diamonds in a pierced platinum mount..........2,860.00

Lorgnette, 10k yellow gold, pierced openwork design case & handle.....440.00

Lorgnette, 14k gold, Art Nouveau style, centered by a collet-set diamond in a textured gold foliate mount, 6½" l.................................1,870.00

Lorgnette, 14k gold, Art Nouveau style, scrolled design w/collet-set rubies & sapphire (missing stones & oxidation to gold) 1,540.00

Lorgnette, 14kt yellow gold, polished finish w/scroll-work handles & top....440.00

Lorgnette, gold & enamel, enameled translucent canary yellow over a guilloche ground & applied w/gold arrows, the lenses opening by means of a diamond-set collar, Faberge', marked w/initials of Workmaster Henrik Wigstrom & 56 standard (14k), St. Petersburg, ca. 1900, 5 ⅝" l................................13,800.00

Lorgnette, platinum, gold & gems, the short beaded platinum & white gold handle mounted w/a diamond bail & bridge retaining spring-loaded double lens, highlighted by a sapphire ring & terminals 920.00

Ornate Art Deco Lorgnette

Lorgnette, platinum, diamond & onyx, Art Deco style, the frame centered w/an old European-cut diamond within a geometric black onyx & diamond mount enhanced by calibre-cut onyx in a platinum mount, can be used as a clip, clasp needs repair (ILLUS.) 5,775.00

Lorgnette, platinum, seed pearl & onyx, Art Deco style, the lorgnette w/an onyx & diamond handle suspended from a seed pearl chain spaced w/onyx beads & navette shaped links, 41" l........................1,760.00

Opera Glasses, mother-of-pearl, marked "La Tour" 155.00

Quizzing glass (monocle), gold (14k), designed as a snake head handle holding a small ring, the coiled body around the glass, Georgian 825.00

PAPER COLLECTIBLES

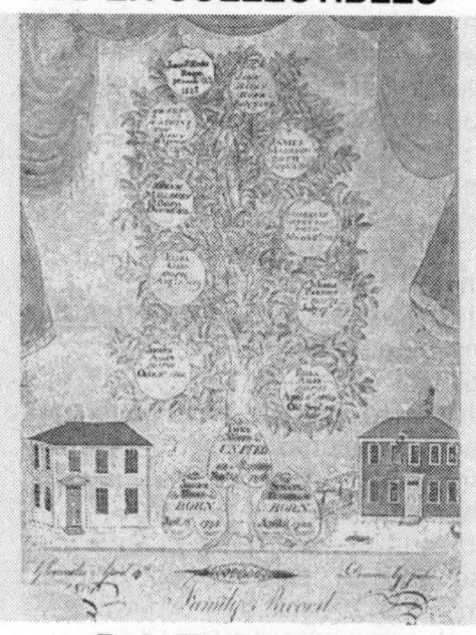

Early Family Record

Also see CHARACTER COLLECTIBLES, FIRE FIGHTING COLLECTIBLES, FRATERNAL ORDER ITEMS, MAGAZINES, MUCHA ARTWORK, PAPER DOLLS, POLITICAL ITEMS, RADIOS, ROYCROFT ITEMS, SIGNS & SIGNBOARDS, STEAMSHIP COLLECTIBLES and WORLD'S FAIR COLLECTIBLES.

Broadside, "Cleveland, Medina & Seville Stage Line, Via Berea on and after Nov. 20th, 1866...," printed in black on a white ground, in beveled frame w/worn red graining, 12½" w., 16½" h. (some damage & tape stains) $319.00

Broadside, theatrical, "The Soldier's Daughter," starring Mrs. H.A. Perry, creative typography, 1865, 8½ x 19¼"...45.00

Calendar, 1904, Paul de Longpre roses, 4 pp. 135.00

Calligraphic drawing, pen & ink on paper, a folk art-style drawing of a very tall giraffe nibbling the top of a very tall tree on the left side, a large spread-winged eagle to the top right above a banner & inscription dated "June 19th, 1883," in narrow frame, 15½ x 24" (paper darkened w/minor foxing..............................1,320.00

Calligraphic drawing, pen & ink on heavy paper, rectangular, a pair of large leaping stags at the top flank the small bust of a man above a crest flanked by eagles above a shield all above a wide landscape scene across the bottom centered by an open book, inscribed "Book keeping, Commercial Arithmetic, Business and Ornamental Penmanship, etc. - taught by H.J.

Schiffert, Allentown, Pa.," in wide ebonized frame w/gilt liner, early 20th c., 29¼ x 37" 1,650.00

Confederate $500 bond, 1863, Jackson vignette, pink, No. 9,158 of 34,361 issued, unframed, 13½ x 13¾" 65.00

Confederate $1,000 bond, 1863, Old Custom House, Richmond vignette, No. 2,285 of 2,404 issued, unframed, 12¼ x 13½" 55.00

Family benefit notice, Confederate Army, member of the 63rd Virginia Regiment, unframed, 2½ x 6" 30.00

Family record, water-color on paper, swagged draperies at the top above a large leafy tree w/roundels printed w/the names & dates of family members, inverted hearts at the base w/the names & marriage date of the parents flanked by two two-story houses, record of the Hicks Family of Gloucester, Massachusetts, signed "Joshua Pool," dated "1800," 10 x 14" (ILLUS.) 2,860.00

Label, "Heinz," original barrel label in full color, 1930s (slight aging) 10.00

Newspaper, "Daily Graphics," New York, July 14, 1874, cover story on the Philadelphia Baseball Athletic Club 75.00

Newspaper, "The Emancipator & Weekly Chronicle," Boston, February 5, 1845, abolitionist paper, copy owned by James Gillespie Birney, contains speech of his Ohio honor, advertisement of his biography & debate of Oregon question 40.00

Playbill, "Arsenic & Old Lace," w/Boris Karloff on cover, 1941 ....20.00

Playbill, "Damn Yankees," w/Gwen Verdon on cover, New York City, 1955 ....25.00

Playbill, "Palace Two-A-Day," w/Judy Garland on cover, New York City, 1951 ....27.00

Playbill, "Peter Pan," w/Mary Martin on cover, 1954 ....30.00

Playing cards, souvenir-type, Yellowstone Park, 53 views, Haynes Photo Studio, early 75.00

Print, "The War for the Union 1862 - A Bayonet Charge," by Winslow Homer, printed in "Harper's Weekly," 2 pp. 50.00

Program, "Miss America Pageant, Official Program, Atlantic City, 1955" 21.00

Slave document, estate appraisal of Henry Reed, seven slaves by name & rental, 1863, 8 x 10" 145.00

Slave document, estate appraisal, 20 entries including negro boy Moses, 1862, 2 pp., 7½ x 10" 87.00

Souvenir book, "City of Charm," Havana, Cuba, ca. 1930, 68 pgs. 20.00

Spencerian penmanship exercise, pen & ink on paper, a pair of birds at the top flanking the inscription "Plain and Ornamental - Penmanship," above rows of alphabets & other examples of penmanship, signed "H.J. Schiffert 1904," matted & framed, 22½ x 26½" (minor stains) ..126.50

View book, "Atlantic City, Playground of the World," 1928, many photos, 22 pgs. 28.00

PAPER DOLLS

(Also see CHARACTER COLLECTIBLES category.)

Advertising, "Dennison's," black child, articulated limbs, tissue paper clothing, ca. 1920, 9" h. $65.00

Advertising, "Enameline," die-cut figure of a stocky girl golfer, ca. 1890s 116.50

Advertising, "Lion Coffee," Little Red Riding Hood, 3 pcs. 125.00

"Air Hostess & Pilot," 1950s, Merrill......23.00

"Barbie Design-a-Fashion," uncut, 1971 ....20.00

"Dollies," uncut book, Saalfield, 1918...55.00

"Fairy Princess," 1958, Merrill, uncut....30.00

"It's A Date," 1956, Whitman 35.00

Jack & Jill's New Frocks & Frills, uncut, Regensteiner, 1925....................35.00

Mary Martin, uncut book, Saalfield No. 1539, 1944 ....75.00

"Old Lady in the Shoe," uncut book, Whitman, 1940....................68.00

Partridge Family, uncut in original box, Whitman No. 5137, 1971 ....18.00

Shirley Temple, uncut book, Saalfield No. 4420, 1959 ....40.00

"Sunshine Family," uncut, 1978............20.00

PAPERWEIGHTS

Advertising, "The A.P. Smith Mfg. Co.," embossed metal rectangle showing the building of A.P. Smith Mfg. Co., East Orange, N.J., an upright figural fire hydrant in the top center, 3¾ x 6½," 3½" h. (hydrant loose, minor wear) $93.50

Advertising, cast iron, "Crane Paper Co.," figural elephant, ca. 1855-1905, 1 x 2 x 4" 85.00

Baccarat "'Bouquet de Marriage' Mushroom" weight, the tuft composed entirely of white stardust canes w/salmon whorl cane centers about a central grouping of similarly colored star canes encompassing a cobalt blue, red & white arrowhead cane flower w/a star silhouette stamen, framed w/a white gauze cable at the periphery within cobalt blue spiral threads & mercury bands, star-cut base, 2¹¹⁄₁₆" d........2,645.00

Baccarat "Concentric Millefiori Mushroom" weight, the tuft composed of three rows of millefiori canes comprising: coral cogwheel canes lined w/green trefoils & star silhouettes; white stardusts w/red centers & cobalt blue, red & white arrowhead canes w/red star silhouette centers about a central composite cane grouping of green shamrocks & red whorl canes within a basket of elongated white staves lined in yellow w/pink centers encompassed by a white gauze cable within cobalt blue spiral threads & mercury bands, star-cut base, 3³⁄₁₆" d. (minor wear) 1,955.00

Baccarat Faceted Sulphide Weight

Baccarat "Faceted Sulphide" weight, the clear glass set w/a sulphide depicting a hunter & his dog in a woodland scene, set on a ruby-flashed ground circular foot, cut w/a decagonal window & geometric facets, (small chips & surface wear), 3⅜" d. (ILLUS.) 2,070.00

Baccarat "Garlanded Butterfly" weight, the insect formed w/two shaded orange, red, purple, yellow & white millefiori cane wings overlapping two smaller marbled & brightly colored wings w/a a purple gauze cable body, two blue eyes, a black head & antennae encompassed by a garland of white, pink & green cogwheel composite canes alternating w/ green, red & white star silhouette canes, star-cut base, 3³⁄₁₆" d. (minor scratches to surface) 3,450.00

Baccarat "Primrose" weight, the clear glass set w/six rounded red petals w/white stripes about a white stardust stamen w/a cobalt blue whorl cane center, growing from a curved green stem w/six leaves & seven further leaves about the flower, 2⁷⁄₁₆" d. 978.00

Bacchus "Close Millefiori" weight, the clear glass set w/assorted millefiori canes in shades of claret, green, purple, yellow, turquoise, blue & white including silhouettes of women, leaves & stars, England, 19th c., 3⁷⁄₁₆" d. (surface wear)......2,300.00

Clichy "Concentric Millefiori Colorground" weight, the clear glass set w/six pink & white stardust canes divided by green pastrymold canes at the periphery above a row of coral pastrymold canes, an inner row of white edelweiss canes & a central pink & green rose cane, set on an opaque cobalt blue ground, 2½" d. 1,725.00

Clichy magnum "Chequer" weight, the clear glass set w/three concentric rows of assorted brightly colored millefiori canes including a large pink & green rose cane at the periphery & a smaller similarly colored rose cane near the center encompassing a claret, green & white composite pastrymold cane, divided by short lengths of white latticino tubing, 4⅜" d...................9,488.00

Clichy "Pansy" weight, the clear glass set w/a flower composed of two upper purple shaded petals above three lower yellow petals edged in purple & similarly colored markings about a green stamen center, growing from a curved green stem w/seven shaded green leaves & a purple bud pendant from an elongated green stem, 2¾" d. 1,380.00

Millville-type weight, multicolored segmented mushroom on a pedestal foot, 3½" d., 3¾" h. 115.00

New England "Faceted Upright Bouquet" weight, the clear glass set w/four millefiori canes in shades of yellow, red, and cobalt blue, three flowers in shades of red, white & cobalt blue, each w/similarly colored millefiori cane stamens among six green leaf tips, set on a white latticino ground, cut w/a window & two rows of six side printies divided by vertical ribs, 2 11/16" d. 2,185.00

New England "Poinsettia" weight, blue blossom w/green & white latticino ground, 19th c., 3" d. 431.00

St. Louis Double Clematis Weight

St. Louis "Double Clematis" weight, the clear glass set w/two rows of five overlapping ribbed & pointed petals in shades of lilac & turquoise about a yellow stamen center, growing from a curved green stem w/two serrated leaves & a further leaf about the flower, set on a white latticino ground, 2 15/16" d. (ILLUS.) 1,495.00

St. Louis "Faceted Upright Bouquet" weight, the clear glass set w/a central white flower formed w/a cobalt blue, green & white composite pastrymold cane stamen encompassed by four smaller flowers in shades of amber, coral, cobalt blue & white, joined by a cluster of several green leaves framed in a cobalt blue & white spiral torsade & mercury bands, cut w/six side printies & a star-cut base, 2¾" h. 1,955.00

St. Louis "Plum" weight, the clear glass set w/two bright cobalt blue plums w/yellow stems pendent from an ochre forked branch w/three serrated green leaves, 2¾" d. 575.00

St. Louis "Strawberry" weight, the clear glass set w/a strawberry in different stages of growth as a central flower composed of five white ribbed petals about a shaded blue & green pastrymold cane stamen & two red berries below, growing from a curved green stem w/three green leaves, set on a white latticino ground, 2 11/16" d. 863.00

Sandwich "Weedflower-type Pansy" weight, the clear glass set w/a flower composed of two cobalt blue upper petals & two lower pink & white striped petals & one w/pink, blue & white stripes about a red, white & blue composite cane stamen w/gold flecks, growing from a curved green stem w/two leaves & a further leaf about the flower, 2⅝" d. 690.00

Stankard (Paul) "Cattleya Orchid Colorground" weight, the clear glass set w/a flower composed of five shaded pink petals about a white stamen, growing from a long curved variegated green stem w/two leaves, set on an opaque green ground w/a white ground below, signed w/a single "S" cane & engraved "26676 66/75," 3" d. 920.00

Stankard (Paul) magnum "Environment" weight, the clear glass set w/four flowers, each stamen center w/red pistils, three pale yellow buds, two variegated green buds & three red berries, growing from creeping vines in shades of green, w/a black & yellow bee w/two translucent brown wings approaching the berries, set on a sandy ground, signed w/a single "S" cane & engraved "A155 1983," 4⅛" d. 4,600.00

PAPIER-MACHE´

Large Papier-Maché Vase

Various objects including decorative adjuncts were made of papier-maché, which is a substance made of pulped paper mixed with glue and other materials or layers of paper glued and pressed and then molded.

Candy container, figural Belsnickle, white coat w/mica flecks, red fiber trim & worn green feather tree, 8" h. (cracks along seam, base damage).....................................$275.00

Candy container, model of a rabbit standing w/paws raised, glass eyes in removable head, Germany 225.00

Candy container, model of a rooster, egg-shaped body w/spring legs & neck, 9" h. 95.00

Model of an owl, perched on a conical base & facing the viewer, worn original paint, 13¾" h. (edge damage, small holes)..........................33.00

Model of a pig w/spring legs, squeals when legs are moved, ca. 1900.......175.00

Sewing box on stand, a large spherical box decorated on the top w/a panel depicting a cathedral, opening at the center to reveal various sewing compartments & an opened well, raised on a tripod base w/bold S-scroll legs, decorated overall w/gilt florals & bands & mother-of-pearl inlay,Europe, mid-19th c., 38" h.................................2,200.00

Tea caddy, cov., rectangular, the cover lacquered w/a scene of an angel embracing a young girl in an interior, the inside w/two lidded compartments, Lukutin, Russia, ca. 1900, 9⅜" l. 2,070.00

Tray, oval w/everted rim, centered by a plain surface painted w/a masted ship in a large harbor, Regency period, England, early 19thc., 16½" l. 990.00

Tray, rounded rectangular dished top decorated overall w/gold flower sprays & scrolls on a black lacquer ground, on a later faux bamboo stand, the legs joined by an X-form stretcher, Victorian,mid-19th c., 26½ x 34½", 19" h.........................2,640.00

Vases, 39" h., baluster form w/flared rim, decorated overall w/birds building nests, floral sprays, parrots on branches & fish swimming in a lotus-filled pond in green, orange, pink & gilt against a black ground, India, pr. (ILLUS. of one) 715.00

Writing desk, Victorian style, the upper section w/a slanted writing flap & welled compartment surmounted by two cupboard doors enclosing four drawers below an arched mirrored superstructure, the whole lifting to reveal a game board above a single fitted frieze drawer, raised on four spiral-turned front legs joined by a heavy framework to the two columnar back legs, black ground decorated overall w/very ornate inlaid mother-of-pearl & scrolling gilt designs, Europe, mid-19th c., 24½" w., 4' 6½" h. 6,600.00

PARRISH (Maxfield) ARTWORK

*During the 1920s and 1930s , Maxfield Parrish (1870-1966) was considered the most popular artist-illustrator in the United States. His illustrations graced the covers of the most noted magazines of the day-*Scribner's, Century, Life, Harper's, Ladies' Home Journal *and others. High quality art prints, copies of his original paintings usually in a range of sizes, graced the walls of homes and offices across the country. Today all Maxfield Parrish artwork, including magazine covers, advertisements and calendar art, is considered collectible but it is the fine art prints that command the most attention.*

"The Knave of Hearts" Cover

Advertisement, magazine, Youth's Companion, 1919, February 20, "Peter, Peter, Pumpkin Eater," for Ferry's Seeds, full-page, matted......$95.00

Advertisement, magazine, "Jell-O," small 'King & Queen' 75.00

Advertisement, magazine, Saturday Evening Post, 1924, September 20, for Edison-Mazda lamps, full-page, matted 65.00

Book, "The Arabian Nights," illustrated by Maxfield Parrish, 1909 .....100 to 125.00

Book, "The Golden Age," by Kenneth Grahame, illustrated by Maxfield Parrish. 1899 ....125.00 to 150.00

Book, "Italian Villas and Their Gardens," by Edith Wharton, illustrations by Maxfield Parrish, 1904...............................200.00 to 250.00

Book, "King Albert's Book," illustrated by Maxfield Parrish, 1914 ....100.00

Book, "The Knave of Hearts," by Louise Saunders, illustrated by Maxfield Parrish, 1925, Charles Scribner's Sons, black cloth board covers, first edition (ILLUS. of cover) 1,050.00

Book, "Knickerbocker's History of New York," by Washington Irving, illustrated by Maxfield Parrish, 1915 edition ....150.00 to 175.00

Book, "Maxfield Parrish - The Early Years," by Skeeters, published by Nash, fine dust jacket ......250.00 to 275.00

Book, "Poems of Childhood," by Eugene Field, illustrated by Maxfield Parrish, first edition, 1904 ....150.00 to 175.00

Book, "Wonder-Book and Tanglewood Tales (A)," by N. Hawthorne, illustrated by Parrish, 1910 ....150.00

Booklet, "Jell-O," illustrated by Maxfield Parrish, 1924, framed, 8½ x 10½" 65.00

Calendar, 1927, for Edison-Mazda, entitled "Reveries," small, complete 395.00

Calendar, 1929, for Edison-Mazda, entitled "Golden Hours," small, complete 300.00

Calendar, 1929, for Edison-Mazda, entitled "Golden Hours," large, complete 650.00

Calendar, 1931, for Edison-Mazda, entitled "Waterfall," small (no pad) ...495.00

Calendar, 1933, for Edison-Mazda, entitled "Sunrise", 8 x 18"................225.00

Calendar, 1937, for Brown & Bigelow Publishing Co., entitled "Twilight," large, framed, complete, 16 x 20"....295.00

Calendar, 1942, for Brown & Bigelow Publishing Co., entitled, "Thy Templed Hills," w/original frame & backing, 12 x 16" 225.00

Calendar, 1952, for Brown & Bigelow Publishing Co., entitled "Lights of Welcome," large...............................110.00

Calendar print, 1926, for Edison-Mazda, entitled "Enchantment," small 250.00

Calendar print, 1931, for Edison-Mazda, entitled "Waterfall," small, cropped..125.00

Calendar print, 1931, for Edison-Mazda, entitled "Waterfall," large...............................700.00 to 750.00

Calendar print, 1941, for Thomas D. Murphy Co., entitled "White Birches," 9 x 11"...................................95.00

Calendar print, 1941, for Brown & Bigelow Publishing Co., entitled "Winter Twilight,"small.......................65.00

Calendar print, 1943, for Brown & Bigelow Publishing Co., entitled "A Perfect Day," medium 65.00

Calendar print, 1946, for Edison-Mazda, entitled "Valley of Enchantment," large 300.00

Calendar print, 1948, for Brown & Bigelow Publishing Co., entitled "Mill Pond," large 250.00

Magazine, American Heritage, 1970, December, includes a Maxfield Parrish article & portfolio of color paintings 6.50

Print, "Cassim in the Cave of Forty Thieves," Dodge Publishing Co., from "Arabian Nights," 1906, 9 x 11"..90.00

Print, "Circés Palace," Dodge Publishing Co., from "A Wonder-Book and Tanglewood Tales," 1908, framed, 9 x 11"......................................150.00

Print, "Cleopatra," House of Art - Reinthal Newman, 1917, medium, framed, 15 x 16"..............................695.00

Print, "Daybreak," House of Art - Reinthal Newman, 1923, small, framed, 6 x 10"...............................100.00

Print, "Daybreak," House of Art - Reinthal Newman, 1923, medium, framed, 10 x 18" ....200.00 to 225.00

Print, "Daybreak," original blue frame & braided blue silk hanging cord, 12 x 24"..255.00

Print, "The Dinkey-Bird," from "Poems of Childhood," 1905, 11 x 16"...........................225.00 to 275.00

Print, "Dreaming," House of Art - Reinthal Newman, 1928, medium, framed, 10 x 18"..............................450.00

Print, "Garden of Allah," House of Art - Reinthal Newman, 1918, small, framed, 4½ x 8½"...........................100.00

Print, "Garden of Allah," House of Art - Reinthal Newman, 1918, large, framed, 15 x 30"..............250.00 to 295.00

Print, "Garden of Allah," House of Art - Reinthal Newman, 1918, small, w/mirror, 4½ x 8½" 300.00

Print, "The Lute Players," House of Art - Reinthal Newman, 1924, small, framed, 6 x 10"...............................125.00

Print, "The Lute Players," House of Art - Reinthal Newman, extra large, framed, 18 x 30"..............................550.00

Print, "Old King Cole," Dodge Publishing Co., for Collier's, 1896, framed 6½ x 25"..............................850.00

Print, "Prince Codadad," Dodge Publishing Co., book illustration, 1906, 9 x 11"...................125.00 to 150.00

Print, "Prosperina & Sea Nymphs," for Dodge Publishing Co., 1910, 9 x 11" 250.00

Print, "Queen Gulnare," Dodge Publishing Co., 1907, framed 9 x 11" 150.00

Print, "Reveries," House of Art - Reinthal Newman, 1928, small, framed, 6 x 10" 225.00

Print, "Wild Geese," House of Art - Reinthal Newman, 1924, framed, 12 x 15" .... 225.00 to 250.00

Puzzle, jigsaw-type, "The Page," 1926, w/box 145.00

Tie rack, "Old King Cole," by Pyraglass Products 115.00

PERFUME, SCENT & COLOGNE BOTTLES

Gold Scent Flask

Decorative accessories from milady's boudoir have always been highly collectible and in recent years there has been an especially strong surge of interest in perfume bottles. Our listings also include related containers such as pocket bottles and vials, tabletop containers & atomizers. Most readily available are examples from the 19th through the mid-20th century, but earlier examples do surface occasionally. The myriad varieties have now been documented in several recent reference books which should further popularize this collecting specialty.

BOTTLES & FLASKS

Agate w/gold & enamel mounting, carved in the form of Pantaloon, leaning against a tree trunk which is the perfume container, the figure of Pantaloon w/diamond eyes & diamond jacket buttons, the gold base-mount chased w/scrolls, the stopper in the form of a bird, the neck inscribed "Pour La Plus Belle" on a white enamel ground, probably England, 19th c., 3" h. $5,175.00

Clambroth glass, teardrop-shaped, hinged lid & chain w/finger ring, h.p. decoration of raised enameling & gold highlights, attributed to Boston & Sandwich Glass Works, Sandwich, Massachusetts, 4½" l. 120.00

Clear cut glass, horn-shaped, spiral cutting, hinged brass top & fittings, 4½" l. 110.00

Clear glass, "Ambre Antique," by Coty, mint in box 55.00

Clear glass, "Matchabelli," crown-shaped bottle w/cross stopper, ½ oz. 55.00

Clear glass, "Tzigane" by Corday, flacon-type, designed by Rene Lalique, 3¾" h. 350.00

Clear glass, "Shocking de Schiaparelli," cube-form stopper, w/original box 90.00

Cobalt blue glass, decorated w/elaborate gold trim & raised enameled flowers, engraved hinged brass top & chain w/finger ring 185.00

English cameo glass, bulbous body, light blue overlaid in blue & cut overall w/delicate flowers, sterling silver screw lid, 2½" h. 450.00

Fiery opalescent mold-blown glass, flattened ovoid form w/sunburst design, 19th c., 2⅞" l. 621.50

Gold, swirl-fluted, w/hinged cover, late 19th c., 2½" h. (ILLUS.) 1,495.00

Gold-Mounted Rock Crystal Bottle

Rock crystal, gold & enamel, gold cagework chased w/scrolls, foliage, birds & squirrels, also enameled in multicolors, w/a bird-form stopper, probably England, ca. 1820, 3⅞" h. (ILLUS.) 3,450.00

Sapphire blue frosted glass, spherical, decorated w/enameled pink & white flowers w/yellow centers & yellow leaves, w/silver dome-shaped screw-on top, 3" d., 3¾" h. 195.00

VINTAGE PHONOGRAPHS

THE EVOLUTION OF THE REVOLUTION

No. 1,174—Vol. XLVI.]
NEW YORK, MARCH 30, 1878.
[Price 10 Cents.

By Louise D. Paradis

"Mary Had A Little Lamb" were the first words recorded on a tin cylinder and played back on a phonograph. Thomas Edison was the genius who set the wheels in motion eventually bringing recorded music into our homes, dance parlors and even The White House. He began making the first "talking machine" on December 1, 1877 and it was only five days later, on December 6, that Edison's landmark recording of a simple nursery rhyme was played by that first phonograph. This successful demonstration was conducted in the research office of Edison's Menlo Park, New Jersey laboratory.

The first Edison phonographs consisted of cylinders covered with tin foil, a diaphragm and a horn which amplified the sound. Edison described his invention (as illustrated right) to *Frank Leslie's Illustrated Newspaper* as follows: "This mouthpiece is simply an artificial diaphragm. Turn it over and you see this thin disk, (3) of metal at the bottom. Whenever you speak in the mouthpiece the vibrations of your voice jar the disk, which, as you see, has in its centre a fine steel point. Now for the other part of the machine. Here is a brass cylinder, grooved something like the spiral part of screw, only much finer. I wrap a sheet of tin-foil around the cylinder, and shove the mouthpiece up to it so that the tiny steel point touches the tin-foil above one of the grooves. I then turn the cylinder with a crank, and talk into the mouthpiece. The vibrations arouse the disk, and the steel point pricks the tin-foil, leaving perforations resembling the old Morse telegraphic alphabet. They are really stereoscopic views of the voice, recording all that is said, with time and intonations. It is a matrix of the words and voice, and can be used until worn out. Now let us reset the cylinder, so that the steel point may run over the holes or alphabet made when we talk in the

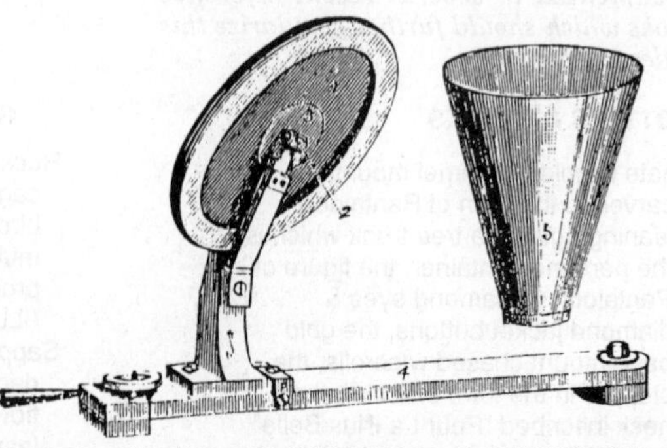

NEW JERSEY.—EDISON'S PHONOGRAPH FOR RECORDING AND REPRODUCING SOUND.

mouthpiece. The thin metal disk rises, and, as the steel point trips from perforation to perforation, opening the valves of the diaphragm, the words, intonation and accent are reproduced exactly as spoken through the funnel" (5).

The early phonographs were hand-cranked, not electric, and were considered by many to be nothing more than noisy contraptions. In addition, the quality of the early tin foil cylinder recordings could vary widely as each one was an original recording. The cylinders were made by combining tin foil and lead; the softer lead metal was necessary in order to record the human voice. However, probably the most serious problem facing the new invention was that the cylinders could not be removed from the "talking machine," and they would wear out after only two or three playbacks, virtually rendering the new machine inoperable.

Another hurdle to be overcome was that the only way multiple recordings could be made was to set up several cylinder recorders and then record a singer, musician or orchestra. Variations in quality were inevitable, as the same performance was being recorded by the various machines over and over again. The end result being (especially after three or four repeat performances) tired voices, strings out of tune, etc.... Many skeptics thought the phonograph would never last. Soon, however, the public eagerly awaited the opportunity to purchase this new and novel gadget so that they could listen and, in a sense, travel to places where they otherwise could probably never reach.

Charles Cros was another early pioneer in the recording field. Born in Fabrezan, France on October 1, 1842, he became a poet, physicist, artist and musician. He was intrigued with the arts, literature and scientific research which led him to author a variety of artistic and scientific documents.

His fascination with early inventions and writing led to his first published essay which described the process of color photography. Probably the most revolutionary document of his career was a letter written to the Academie des Sciences, Paris, France in April, 1877. It began, "A Process For The Recording and Reproduction of Phenomena Perceived by the Ear..." His research document on the sound recording process evolved out of his study of photography. Even though his sound recording process was well described, Mr. Cros was unable to find a machinist able to devise the necessary equipment, so he eventually abandoned the idea.

Cros later described his sound recording process to his friend Abbé Lenoir, who published an article describing the Cros process of recording and reproduction research by using the term "phonograph." This term later became synonymous with the developing technology.

After Edison's initial success, many inventors became intrigued by the new phonograph. Competition naturally followed and with it came a wealth of new developments in the fledgling industry. As new entrepreneurs entered the market, each gave a distinguishing name to his phonograph. By 1888 the phonograph was commonly referred to as the "talking machine."

Another famous and familiar inventor, Alexander Graham Bell, became interested in the development of the "talking machine." He had received the Prix Volta award and a considerable financial prize from the Academie des Sciences in Paris for his work in developing the telephone. By May, 1886 he submitted a patent for the "graphophone." Bell's partners in this new venture were his cousin, Chichester Bell and physicist Charles Sumner Tainter, who had developed a hard wax composition. This new material was developed for the cylinder disc recordings since it was easy to impress and rendered a more pleasing sound than the noisy tin foil-covered cylinder.

When Mr. Bell first patented his "graphophone," Mr. Edison filed a lawsuit. Edison also believed that Bell had simply reversed the order of his words. However, Edison realized that he needed the newly developed wax cylinders, and Bell needed the sapphire needle that had been developed by Edison. So a cross-licensing agreement was reached from the common vision of these ingenious inventors.

Mr. Jesse H. Lippincott was a major investor with Mr. Edison and Mr. Bell, and they formed the North American Phonograph Company. This company divided the United States into 33 territorial companies and was instrumental in distributing phonographs and cylinders from New York to California. The Columbia Phonograph Company was one of these original companies. The main goal of this newly formed organization was to advertise and promote sales of the cylinder records that were being used by both versions of the new talking machine.

In 1888 Emile Berliner demonstrated the first disc record on his "gramophone." That disc record was made of zinc. He accomplished the recording by coating the zinc disc with wax, the recording stylus etched the recorded material on the wax, then the disc was exposed to acid and the record was ready. This new recording method produced a recording that was somewhat more audible and of a more consistent quality. It was also less expensive and numerous copies could be made from the master disc. However, the sound produced by Mr. Berliner's "gramophone" was still quite similar to the other hand-operated phonographs of the time. He realized that in order to attract a broader public to his new phonograph he needed to develop a motor that would operate the machine more quietly and play the record at a more even and consistent speed.

In 1896 Mr. Berliner successfully contracted with machinist Eldridge Johnson to make a silent and long running motor for the gramophone. Eventually, Mr. Johnson acquired the assets of the Berliner Gramophone Company, and formed the "Victor Talking Machine Company." He also adopted the famous trade-mark design of Nipper, the terrier dog attentively listening to "His Master's Voice."

The year 1897 also marked Columbia Phonograph Company's introduction of the "Eagle Graphophone" with an exceptionally ingenious marketing strategy just in time for the upcoming Christmas season. As the first truly affordable "talking machine," the "Eagle" was named in order to reflect its $10.00 retail price and symbolize the $10.00 Eagle coin in use at the time. The "Eagle" was a world-wide success and helped to firmly establish the phonograph industry.

Initially both the phonograph and the recording business offices operated by the Columbia Phonograph Company were located in Washington, D.C. The introduction of the affordable "Eagle" graphophone created international demand for the now affordable equipment, so Columbia decided to merge the parent companies, Bell's American Graphophone Company and Columbia Phonograph Company, to form the Columbia Disk Graphophone Company.

During the early days of the industry both Edison and Columbia created many machines to capture the attention of buyers. Both developed a treadle attachment that could be fitted on the household sewing machine and the music played by pumping the foot pedal. Coin-operated "talking machines," the predecessor of the juke box, were also very popular. Edison even marketed a water-powered phonograph that was attached to a hand-operated water-pump. As these unusual devices are highly sought after by collectors, you may want to examine your grandmother's sewing machine a little closer.

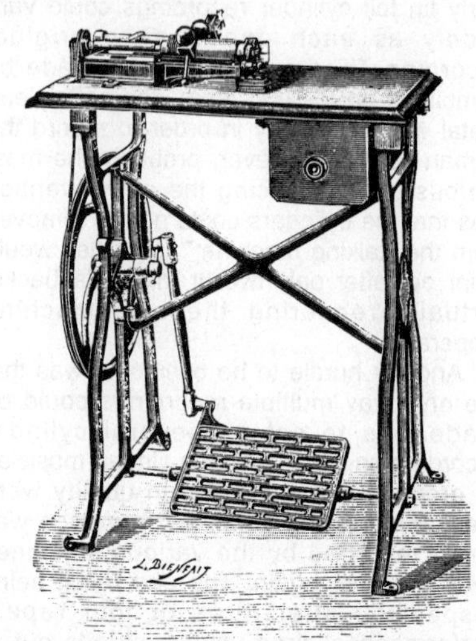

Edison also marketed a talking doll in 1889 fitted with a hand-cranked voice mechanism. The Simon & Halbig Doll Company of Germany provided Edison with lovely bisque heads for the doll, and the torso is made of metal. The doll was only made for a short period of time and today is popular with both doll and phonograph collectors.

Columbia supplied the market with a wide variety of cylinder phonograph models until 1912. Continual improvements were made on the motor, tone arm and the horns. In the early years of production, in order to meet the consumer's demands for improved models, Columbia often pieced together Graphophones using some parts from previous models and some newly "improved" parts. Some collectors say it is difficult to find two identical Columbia Disk Graphophones. For instance, you may find two machines with the same motor and tone arm, but one may have the hand-crank on the side while the other is located in the back. But as the industry developed, the parts became much more standardized and records show that up to 2,000 Columbia disk machines were being produced each day.

Victor, Edison and Columbia all began to produce the new internal horn "talking machine," which became very popular and eventually brought to a close the production of the external horned-phonographs. New names such as Amberola and Victrola were given to the new sleek "talking machines." Women were instrumental in the growing popularity of the internal horn machine, as they now viewed the phonograph, in the lovely mahogany or quarter-sawn oak cabinets, as an attractive piece of parlor furniture.

Another early industry entrepreneur was Henri Lioret. He was born in 1848 in Moret-sur-Losing, France, the son of a watchmaker. Upon Henri's completion of college he carried on the family business in Paris. He became fascinated with the Edison phonograph at the 1889 Paris Exposition Universelle. Around that same time he was asked by Emile Jumeau (the famous dollmaker) to give his beautiful dolls the ability to speak to their playmates. Thus, in 1893, the first French "talking machine" was lovingly placed in what became popularly known as the "Bebe Phonographe."

The talking bebe was far superior to previous talking dolls as its phonographic device used a replaceable celluloid cylinder hidden in the doll's chest. Henri Lioret patented his celluloid cylinder in France on November 28, 1893. They came with a variety of speeches and songs. A "Bebe Phonographe" recently sold at McMasters Doll Auctions, in Cambridge, Ohio and commanded $950.00.

Lioret then marketed his Lioretgraph No. 2 cylinder-type phonograph in 1895, in order to meet the demands of the French public. His clockmaking expertise along with the celluloid cylinders, offered the French consumer a well-developed, pleasant sounding phonograph. The Lioretgraph was also reasonably priced and became very popular in Europe.

Another fascinating story connected with the development of the phonograph business in France centers on Charles Pathé. In the summer of 1894, Pathé was strolling through a carnival in Vincennes, France and became fascinated by the crowds of people who were willing to pay to listen the the Edison "talking machine." Desiring a business of his own, he sought funds and within a few weeks Pathé had purchased his own Edison phonograph and a variety of cylinder discs. With his new purchases Pathé began entertaining enthralled crowds at festivals throughout Paris and the surrounding villages.

Pathé's venture was a success and he eventually expanded his business by importing the Edison phonographs from E.O. Kumberg in London, England. He also began his own recording studio and cylinder production business in order to supply the demand for cylinders featuring French recording artists.

The Pathé Freres company was formed in 1896 when his brother Emile joined the company. The company continued to import American phonographs, but by the end of the 19th century they began to produce their own version of the phonograph, which was very similar in design to the American phonograph, as illustrated here.

Pathé Cylinder Phonograph

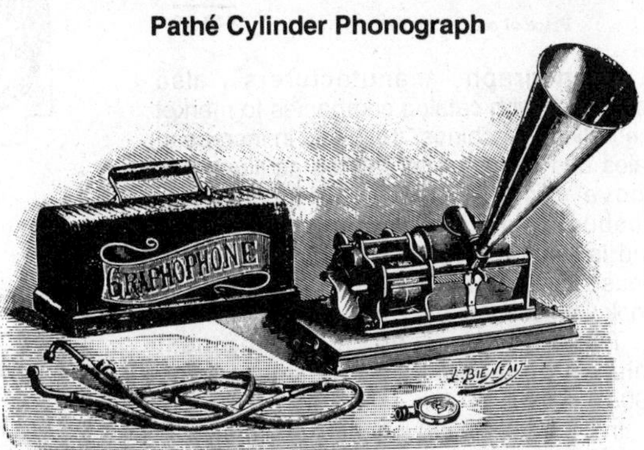

Eagle Graphophone

The Pathé cylinder-disc phonographs eventually distinguished themselves from their American counterparts by being adorned with a wide variety of flaring morning glory-form horns.

The Pathé Brothers continued to adopt the developments being made in the phonograph industry and marketed their own disc machines in 1906, called the "Pathé phone." By 1929 the company became part of the Societe Pathé Marconi, which was a union of the Gramophone, Columbia and Pathé companies.

By the beginning of the 20th century, many new companies, both in the United States and Europe, had entered the "talking machine" market. In order to remain competitive and to attract buyers to purchase a newly developed machine, new disc records, or a new horn, advertising in magazines and newspapers became vitality important to the many manufacturers wishing to promote their products.

GRAPHOPHONE
The GRAPHOPHONE

OUR HOME ENTERTAINMENT OR EXHIBITION OUTFIT.

No. 6400. Our **Home Entertainment** or **Exhibition Outfit** consists of the following pieces:

One graphophone talking machine and oak carrying case, one recording diaphragm, one automatic extra loud reproducing diaphragm, one speaking tube, one bottle of oil and one screw driver, complete.... **$25.00**

12 Musical and Talking Records, your own selection.... **6.00**

1 Hearing Tube for three persons.... **3.00**

1 Small Horn for concert work.... **1.00**

Price of outfit complete.... **$35.00**

Phonograph manufacturers also contracted with catalog companies to market the "talking machines," resulting in increased sales and profits. The catalog ad illustrated above appeared in the 1897 Sears, Roebuck and Company Consumer Guide and is reprinted by permission of Chelsea House Publishers, a division of Main Line Book Co.

The advertisement (shown top next column) appeared in a magazine dated 1908.

In 1877 the latest scientific wonder was the "speaking" phonograph. Soon afterwards music by the finest orchestras, songs of the most famous vocalists, and speeches by the great people of the time could be recorded and enjoyed in the comfort of the home or by a gathering at a local theatre. In a remarkable vision of the future, the *Scientific American* on December 22, 1877 wrote, "It is already possible by

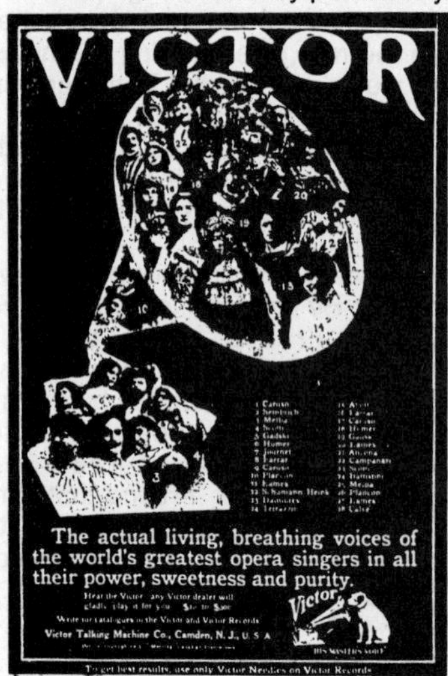
VICTOR
The actual living, breathing voices of the world's greatest opera singers in all their power, sweetness and purity.
Victor Talking Machine Co., Camden, N.J., U.S.A.
Victor

Magazine Advertisement

ingenious optical contrivances to throw stereoscopic photographs of people on screens in full view of an audience. Add the talking phonograph to conterfeit their voices, and it would be diffucult to carry the illusion of real presence much further."

A Phonograph Exhibition

A special thank you to:

Allen Koenigsberg
The Antique Phonograph Collector Club
Magazine: The Antique Phonograph Monthly
502 E. 17th Street
Brooklyn, NY 11226

If you are interested in receiving a back issue of their publication or wish to make an inquiry about an unusual phonograph, send a stamped, self-addressed envelope along with your request. Many books and reference materials are also available from this source.

Also, a special thank you to Merritt's Antiques, Inc. for permission to use their photographs of Edison phonographs.

Recommended references:

The Illustrated History of Phonographs, by Daniel Marty, published by Dorset Press, New York. 1981.

Look for the Dog, An Illjustrated Guide to Victor Talking Machines by Robert W. Baumbach, published by Stationery X-Press, P.O. Box 207, Woodland Hills, Ca 91364, 1981.

The Compleat Talking Machine by Eric Reiss, published by The Vestal Press, Ltd., Vestal, New York 13850, 1986.

About the Author

Louise Paradis is an Editorial Assistant for the Antique Trader Book Division and is a contributing author to *The Antique Trader Weekly*. She is a graduate of the University of Wisconsin-Platteville and enjoys researching and writing on popular trends in antiques and collectibles.

PRICE LISTING:

(The prices are based on those received from auction houses and antiques shops in Pennsylvania, Ohio and Illinois. The values of early phonographs can vary widely based on their condition and whether or not they contain original parts.)

COLUMBIA

Columbia Gramophone Eagle, bell-shaped horn, wooden cabinet, ca. 1897 ....$350.00 to 495.00

Columbia Gramophone No. 60, bell-shaped horn, wooden cabinet, ca. 1888 (ILLUS. top next column) ....400.00 to 600.00.

Columbia AH with front mount, brass bell-shaped horn, oak cabinet, ca. 1902-05.......................................1,000.00

Columbia AK, nickel-plated bell-shaped horn, wooden cabinet, ca. 1904-08..................800.00 to 1,000.00

Columbia AR, brass bell-shaped horn, mahogany cabinet, 1903 ....1,700.00

Columbia Gramophone No. 60

Columbia BI Sterling, nickel-plated morning glory horn, oak cabinet, 1906-10.......................1,000.00 to 1,200.00

Columbia BII Improved Sterling, nickel-plated morning glory horn, oak cabinet, with pillar-shaped corner decoration, ca. 1909-11......................1,500.00 to 1,600.00

Columbia BII Sterling, wooden horn, oak cabinet, wiith pillar-shaped corner decoration, 1909-11...........2,500.00

Columbia BD, nickel-plated morning glory horn, mahogany cabinet, ca. 1906-10...............1,300.00 to 1,500.00

Columbia BS, coin-operated, table top model, wooden cabinet with a curved glass front, ca. 1898 (ILLUS.) 3,000.00

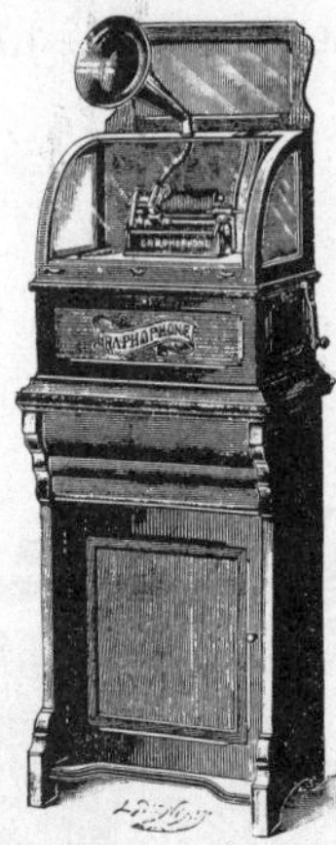

Columbia BS, coin-operated, floor model, wooden cabinet with curved glass front, ca. 1898 (ILLUS.)............3,000.00

EDISON

Edison Class M, brass witch hat horn, oak cabinet, ca. 1893..............................10,000.00

Edison Concert Model A, brass, long auditorium horn, oak cabinet, ca. 1899-1900.......................2,000.00

Edison Home Model A, brass morning glory horn, oak suitcase-type cabinet, ca. 1896-1901....................750.00

Edison Fireside Model A, metal miniature morning glory horn, oak cabinet, ca. 1909-12..............750.00 to 800.00

Edison Gem, first model, with built in reproducer which cannot be removed from the carrier, small Edison black japanned tin horn, metal case, 1890-1900 ....1,100.00

Edison Standard Model B, small metal bell-shaped horn, oak cabinet, ca. 1906-08..........................600.00 to 650.00

Edison Triumph Model A, brass & metal large morning glory-shaped or big bell-shaped horn, oak cabinet, ca. 1901-05...........................850.00 to 900.00

Edison Triumph Model E, brass & metal cygnet (question mark shape) horn, oak cabinet, ca. 1910-11......................1,100.00 to 1,200.00

Edison Gem, third model, silver decal reading "Gem" on top of horn, all metal case, ca. 1905-08...850.00 to 950.00

Edison Home Model C, painted green metal morning glory horn, oak cabinet, ca. 1896-1901 (ILLUS.)..650.00

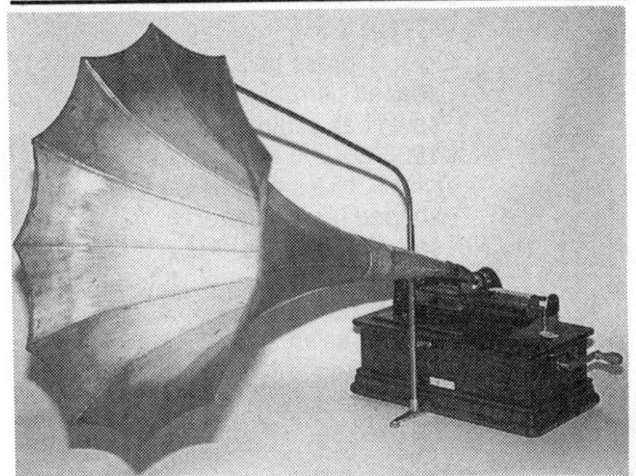

Edison Home Model H, painted red morning glory horn, oak cabinet (ILLUS.).........650.00

Edison Standard Model C, large (30") brass horn, oak cabinet (ILLUS.).................550.00

Edison Standard Model H, reproduction bell-shaped horn, oak cabinet (ILLUS.)....................475.00

Edison Home Model H, painted red morning glory horn w/floral decoration (ILLUS. top next page)..650.00

Edson Standard Model H, black-painted metal, morning glory horn, oak cabinet, ca. 1906-08 (ILLUS. center next page)...........750.00

Edison Home Model C, Reproduction bell-shaped horn, oak cabinet (ILLUS.)......................550.00

Edison Amberola

Edison Amberola Model 30, internal horn, oak cabinet (ILLUS.)......................................425.00

Edison Amberola Model 50, internal horn, mahogany cabinet (ILLUS.)....450.00

VICTOR

Victor I, brass bell-shaped horn, quarter-sawn oak cabinet, ca. 1903-20......................1,050.00

Victor II, brass bell-shaped horn, quarter-sawn cabinet, ca. 1902-20......................1,175.00

Victor II, oak horn, quarter-sawn oak cabinet, ca. 1902-20...2,500.00

Victor III, oak horn, oak cabinet, ca. 1902-20......................3,200.00

Victor III, brass bell-shaped horn, oak cabinet, ca. 1902-20 (ILLUS. below)......1,500.00 to 1,800.00

Victor IV, mahogany horn, mahogany cabinet, ca. 1902-20...4,000.00

Victor E (Monarch Junior), front mount, brass bell-shaped horn, wooden cabinet, ca. 1902-05......................1,100.00

Victor Monarch, back or front mount, brass bell-shaped horn, quarter-sawn oak cabinet, ca. 1901-05......................1,100.00

Victor P, front mount, brass bell-shaped horn, oak cabinet, ca. 1902-06......................1,050.00

Victor Z, steel bell-shaped horn, wooden cabinet, ca. 1903-08...1,400.00

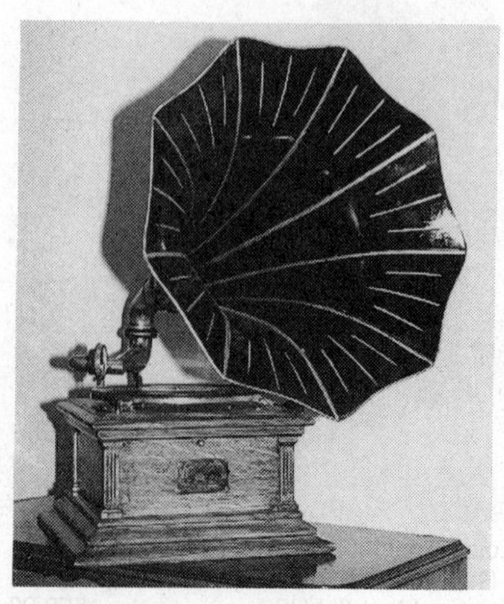

Victor III Model

Victrola Internal Horn Machines

Victrola IX, quarter-sawn oak cabinet, ca. 1905 ....250.00 to 325.00

Victrola No. 835, Art Deco cabinet, veneered walnut cabinet, ca, 1928-29...525.00

Victrola XVI, internal horn, mahogany floor model cabinet, gold-painted, ca. 1907-21 (ILLUS.) ....700.00 to 900.00

Victrola IX, internal horn, mahogany table model cabinet, ca. 1911-25 (ILLUS.) ....375.00 to 425.00

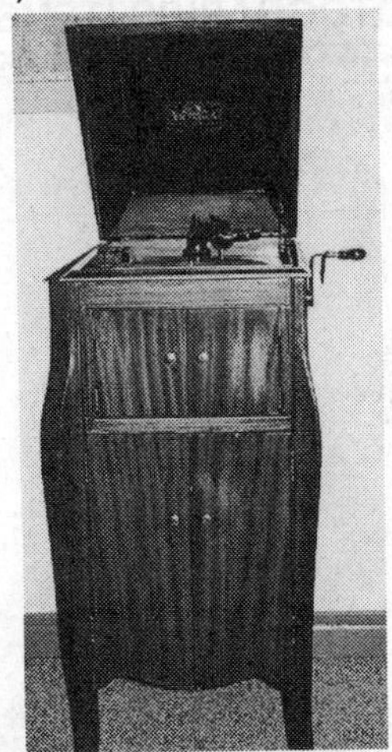

Victrola X, internal horn, mahogany floor model cabinet, ca. 1910-21 .....495.00

MISCELLANEOUS:

The Standard Talking machine Company, metal morning glory horn, dovetailed oak cabinet, ca. 1903 (ILLUS. top next page).................1,000.00

Sonora, internal horn, Queen Anne-style mahogany floor model cabinet, labeled with "Highest Award for Tone at Panama-Pacific Exposition," 1915 (ILLUS. top next page)........................700.00 to 800.00

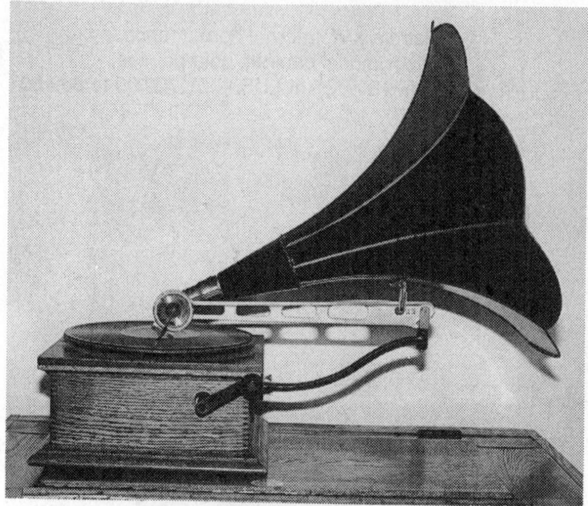

Standard Talking Machine

Sonora Floor Model Machine

(End of Special Focus)

PHOTOGRAPHIC ITEMS

Rare Ambrotype of Indian Chief

Ambrotype, depicting Chief Maungwudas of the Ojibway tribe of Pennsylvania, 1/6th plate (ILLUS.) $3,190.00

Ambrotype, depicting a Civil War Union soldier....................................50.00

Cabinet photograph, William F. Cody (Buffalo Bill) by Anderson, New York City....................................180.00

Cabinet photograph, young girl w/waist length hair & basket 15.00

Cabinet photograph, General George Washington Curtis Lee, of the Confederate Army...........................150.00

Cabinet photograph, General Fitzhugh Lee, of the Confederate Army 150.00

Cabinet photographs, funeral floral arrangements, ca. 1885, pr................25.00

Camera, Conley, safety folding-plate model, red bellows, patent dated 1907..65.00

Camera, Eastman Kodak 1A Jr. manual, 1916 ....5.00

Camera, Eastman Kodak Autographic Junior 1A, w/leather case 45.00

Camera, Eastman Kodak Beau Brownie, the rectangular body w/geometric design on the face in royal & robin's-egg blue, designed by Walter Dorwin Teague, in a green faux leather case, 1930s, case 5¼" h. 345.00

Camera, Eastman Kodak Brownie No. 1A, folding-type................................20.00

Camera, Eastman Kodak Brownie No. 2, folding-type, maroon bellows, ca. 1904..50.00

Camera, Eastman Kodak No. 3, cartridge-type, ca. 1900..................175.00

Camera, Eastman Kodak Hawkeye Model B #2A, folding cartridge-type...50.00

Camera, Eastman Kodak Rainbow Hawkeye No. 2, folding model C, 1933..55.00

Camera, Eastman Kodak Six-16, chrome Art Deco designs on brown enamel 85.00

Camera, Eastman Kodak Special No. 2 ....35.00

Camera, Eastman Kodak Target Hawkeye Six-16 ....18.00
Camera, Eastman Kodak Vest Pocket, Model B, 1931 ....35.00
Camera, Imperial, 5 x 7 view, Wollensak, F-8 to F-250, No. 13, wood & brass 485.00
Camera, Minolta No. 1611, in box 25.00
Camera, Polaroid Model 110A 175.00
Camera, Polaroid Model No. 360, w/electronic strobe & carrying case 150.00
Camera, Voightlander AVUS folding plate camera w/two holders, holder pack & case 120.00
Camera, Zeiss Contaflex, w/case & strap, ca. 1953, Germany, in mint condition 65.00
Camera, Zeiss Ikon, Carl Zeiss Jena 4.5, first coupled range finder, pre-World War II, 2½ x 4¼" 50.00
Carte de visite, General Banks 25.00
Carte de visite, John Wilkes Booth & the Devil 125.00
Carte de visite, Major Decker, (P.T. Barnum's midget) 32.00
Carte de visite, Admiral Dot (P.T. Barnum's midget) 32.00
Carte de visite, Lieutenant General U.S. Grant 60.00
Carte de visite, Horace Greeley 50.00
Carte de visite, Stonewall Jackson, of the Confederate Army 150.00
Carte de visite, Andrew Johnson, by Brady 100.00
Carte de visite, Abraham Lincoln, Salisbury Bros. & Co., Providence, Rhode Island 50.00
Carte de visite, President Abraham Lincoln w/family 25.00
Carte de visite, General Meade 25.00
Carte de visite, Thomas Nast, by Sarony 125.00
Carte de visite, Graziella Ridgeway, soprano 22.00
Carte de visite, General Sherman 25.00
Carte de visite, Tom Thumb (P.T. Barnum's midget) 32.00
Carte de visite, Giddeon Wells 65.00
Cartes de visite, Tom Thumb's wedding & reception, set of 2 ....30.00
Catalog, Kodak & Kodak Supplies, 1916, 64 pp. 15.00
Daguerreotype, baby in long white dress, case 2⅜ x 2 13/16" 32.00
Daguerreotype, baby w/high boots (case has minor damage) 90.00
Daguerreotype, carpenter w/elaborate saw 450.00
Daguerreotype, mother & daughter, hand-tinted, 1850 ....45.00
Daguerreotype, cased, beautiful young lady 50.00
Daguerreotype, young man holding hat 70.00
Daguerreotype, lovely woman playing a concertina 225.00
Daguerreotype, young child holding a cat, sixth plate, in a pressed leather case, 2½ x 2¾" 357.50
Movie camera, Paillard, 8mm, w/instructions, sun filter & box, ca. 1940s 48.00
Mug shots, Chicago Police Department, 1903-26, set of 15 ....150.00
Photograph, interior scene of saloon w/bartender, fixtures & bar, ca. 1900, 6 x 8" 115.00
Photograph, police patrol wagon w/police chief & fire chief posing in front of wagon company storefront ..125.00
Photographic paper, Agfa Ansco, one full box, ca. 1930s 12.00
Tintype, blacksmith 100.00
Tintype, Civil War drummer boy seated w/drum, cased 210.00
Tintype, Civil War soldier, thermoplastic case 175.00
Tintype, seated child, Stoddard Studios, w/cardboard, glassine sleeve, Victorian 18.00
Tintype, two young cowboys, one w/gunbelt 75.00
Tintype, man w/mustache, hand-colored full plate 40.00

PIE BIRDS

A pie bird is a small, hollow device with a stem that allows steam to escape from a double-crust pie, Usually in the form of a bird with an open beak, they can be found in china, pottery or metal. Various figural examples are listed below.

China, bear, standing & yowling, grey fur $89.50
China, black chef dressed in yellow 95.00
China, black mammy dressed in pink ...65.00
China, black mammy w/large mouth, England 50.00
China, chef holding a pie, England 50.00
China, duck, colorful decoration 25.00
China, owl dressed in shirt & tie, England 50.00

PINCUSHION DOLLS

These china half figures were never intended for use as dolls, but rather to serve as ornamental tops to their functional pincushion bases which were discreetly covered with silk and lace skirts. They were produced in a wide variety of forms and quality, all of which are now deemed collectible, and were especially popular during the first quarter of this century.

Our listings are arranged numerically, when possible, according to the code numbers assigned in The Collector's Encyclopedia of Half-Dolls *by Frieda Marion and Norma Werner.*

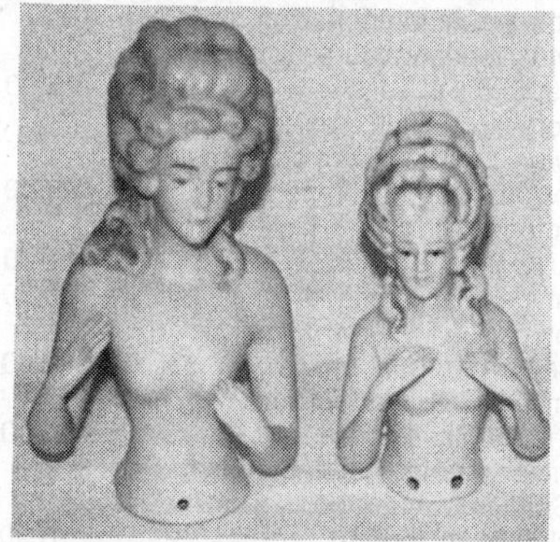

Bisque & China Half Figures

Bisque half figure of a lady, fancy grey hair in horizontal curls flowing over her shoulders, both hands free, impressed "5275," 5⅛" h. (ILLUS. left) $145.00

China half figure holding rose, Dressel & Kister (MW108-501) 225.00

China half figure of a lady, wearing an elegant large white hat w/red ribbon & lavender & yellow plumes, a narrow black band encircling her throat, holding a small green fan, modeled camisole, incised Goebel crown mark & "1202/3" w/"Bavaria" (MW 217-501) 300.00

China half figure of a lady, molded curly hair w/ribbon & flowers decoration, arms away from body w/one hand extended, incised "15278" & "GERMANY," 3½" h. (MW 307-403) 250.00

China half figure of a lady, ornate coiffure w/top knot & rows of curls at the sides cascading to her shoulders, wearing an off-the-shoulder top w/short flounced sleeves, one hand to her breast the other to her throat, incised "GERMANY 15501," 3½" h. (MW 311-403) 125.00

China half figure of "Carmen," Germany, attached to clothes brush (MW 364-401) 125.00

China half figure of a lady, swept back chestnut hair held by a gold comb, nude w/arms away from body, one hand near the waist & the other slightly raised, the fingers beautifully detailed, "Made in Germany" in blue script, 5¾" h. (MW 407-501) 500.00

China half figure of a lady, head slightly tilted & wearing a plumed hat, low-cut bodice w/full sleeves, one hand holding a wide-spread fan & the other raised to her breast, "4345 - Germany" (MW 511-411) 55.00

China half figure of a lady, head tilted & wearing a domed cap w/flowers molded at sides, one arm behind back, other at front holding a neck ribbon at bodice, "5160 - Germany," 3¼" h. (MW 512-310) 52.50

China half figure of a lady, long bunches of curls at each side of slightly tilted head, one hand at shoulder, other holding fan at shoulder, row of bows down front of bodice, "7942 - Germany," 3½" h. (MW 512-412) 65.00

China half figure of a young woman wearing a bonnet, her arms akimbo, wearing a short sleeved top w/lacing at the front, incised "5715 Germany," 3" h. (MW 514-305) 95.00

China half figure of a lady wearing a wide-brimmed hat, arms away from body & one hand raised to her breast, thought to represent the English actress, Mrs. Siddons, as painted by Gainsborough, incised "3379," 4½" h. 325.00

China half figure of a Spanish dancer, one hand at her waist, the other raised w/hand to cheek, wearing a comb in her hair, "4347 - Germany," 3½" h. (MW 564-401) 45.00

China figure of 1920s bathing beauty, seated, h.p. bathing suit & cap, 2" h. (MW 731-271) 150.00

China half figure of a lady, ornate coiffure w/rows of rolled curls, both hands free & raised to her breast, 4" h. (ILLUS. right) 95.00

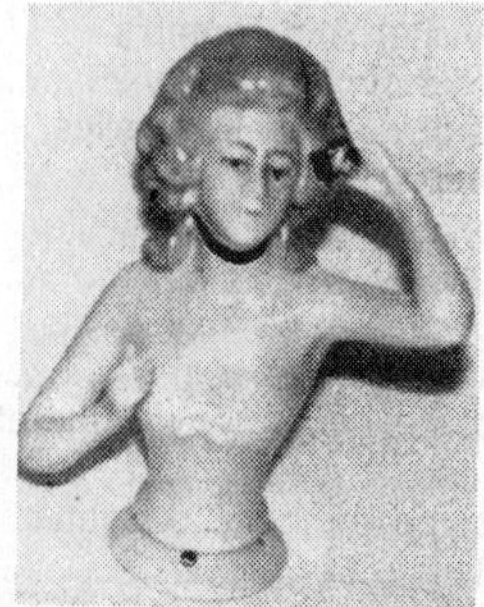

Graceful China Half Figure

China half figure of a lady, ornately styled curly grey hair, one arm raised to place a flower in the hair, the other hand free, wearing white bodice, incised "1501," 4" h. (ILLUS.) 85.00

China half figure of a "flapper," her arms crossed, incised "3030 Germany" 30.00

China half figure of young girl w/blonde curls, arm out, incised "5287" 30.00

PIN-UP ART

1941 Calendar with Lady of Mystery

Calendar, 1934, large color illustration at the top of a standing nude woman w/her back to the viewer & holding a long sheer green drape across her back, in an interior w/checkered floor & pillars in the background, titled "Where Unimagined Beauty Dwells," small calendar sheets at the bottom, 19 x 30" (tears at fold mark) $176.00

Calendar, 1939, Earl Moran, 15 x 33" 175.00

Calendar, 1940, a young blonde woman sitting w/her legs crossed & wearing a low-backed green dress, sitting sideways & looking up at a large parrot on a roost, titled, "Pretty Polly," red, yellow, green & blue bird, artist-signed, calendar sheets below, 16 x 33½" (fold marks, very minor soiling) 176.00

Calendar, 1941, "Lady of Mystery," exotic lady standing wearing a feathered outfit, after a painting by Edward M. Eagleston, produced by V.P. Wright, signed, fold mark, very minor soiling, 16 x 33½" (ILLUS.) 93.50

Calendar, 1943, "Modern Eve," Earl Moran nude, 16 x 34" 150.00

Calendar, 1946, Alberto Vargas, w/envelope 60.00

Calendar, 1947, Alberto Vargas, for "Esquire" 48.00

Calendar, 1951, "Erbit," nude model by Gillette Elvgren 80.00

Calendar,1953, "Esquire," w/envelope 65.00

Calendar, 1954, Earl Moran, 12 pgs 65.00

Calendar, 1955, George Petty, for "Esquire" 80.00

Calendar, 1956, George Petty, for "Esquire" 80.00

Calendar, 1957, "Playboy Playmate Calendar," Jayne Mansfield pictorial, w/original wrapper 55.00

Calendar, 1958, "Playboy Playmate Calendar," 20.00

Calendar, 1959, Zoe Mozert, girl in red wearing white stole, 16 x 33" 35.00

Calendar, 1964, "Playboy Playmate Calendar" 30.00

Calendar, 1967, "Playboy Playmate Calendar" 12.00

Calendar, 1972, "Playboy Playmate Calendar," w/jacket 25.00

Calendar top, 1950s, Jayne Mansfield, large 45.00

Candy box, stunning color image of sensual 1930s beauty by Billy Devorss, 11 x 16" 150.00

Date book, Alberto Vargas prints, for "Esquire," 1945 ....45.00

Magazine, "American Weekly," 1921, June, "The Suppliant," cover by Vargas 65.00

Magazine, "Flirt," 1952, April, cover by Peter Driben 8.00

Magazine, "Laff," 1948, girl in bikini, cover by Helen Mann 11.00

Magazine, "Playboy," 1954, August 125.00

Magazine, "Playboy," 1954, November 125.00

Magazine, "Playboy," 1955, August 75.00

Magazine, "Playboy," 1956, December 60.00

Magazine, "Playboy," 1957, January 35.00

Magazine, "Playboy," 1969, "Fifteenth Holiday Anniversary Issue" 24.00

Painting, original oil by Saul Levine, color vignettes of a lovely blonde against a dark background, used for the back cover of the paperback "Someone is Bleeding" (ILLUS.top next column) 2,894.00

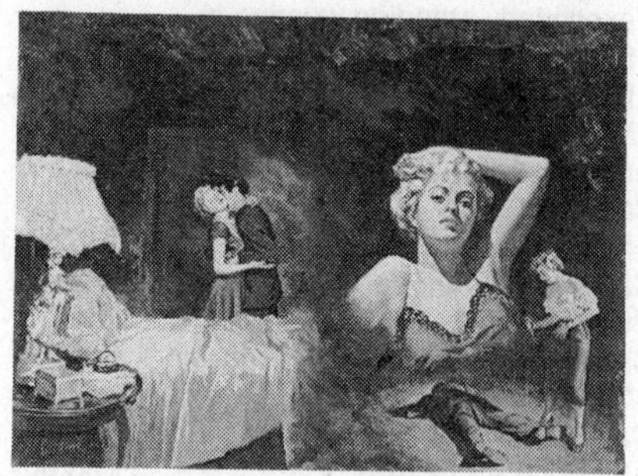

Saul Levine Oil Painting

Playing cards, illustrated by Elvgren, 1950s, boxed, mint & sealed 95.00

Playing cards, Alberto Vargas illustrations, all different, full deck, w/original illustrated box 65.00

Playing cards, double deck, classic artwork by Alberto Vargas, in "Esquire" alligator case 95.00

Print, "Adorable," by Rolf Armstrong, original mat, framed 75.00

Program, "Moulin Rouge," 1960, cover illustration by Vargas................45.00

Sheet music, "Dear Heart," illustrated by Rolf Armstrong 20.00

PIPES

Carved Meerschaum Pipe

Meerschaum, bowl carved w/a bacchanalian scene of putti & a reclining nude lady, amber stem, w/a fitted case, 8⅝" l. (ILLUS.) $660.00

Meerschaum, bowl carved as a bearded, gruff looking man wearing a hat w/a sash hanging at the back ...50.00

Meerschaum, bowl carved as a black man's head w/hat, amber stem, 4¼" l. 300.00

Meerschaum, bowl carved w/deer, a standing buck, doe & fawn beside the bellflower-form bowl, amber & meerschaum stem, amber mouth piece, damages, w/fitted case, 11⅝" l. (ILLUS.) 467.50

Meerschaum Pipe with Deer

Meerschaum, bowl carved as the head of a gentleman in a plumed beret, stained highlights, amber stem, w/fitted case, 6⅛" l. 330.00

POLITICAL, CAMPAIGN & PRESIDENTIAL ITEMS

Also see BOOKS, PRESIDENTIAL & HISTORICAL FIGURES

CAMPAIGN

William Henry Harrison Apron

Apron, 1840 campaign, Harrison (William Henry), silk, painted decoration depicting the log cabin associated w/the "Tippecanoe and Tyler Too" campaign, lacks ties, very good condition, 21" w., 21½" h. (ILLUS.) $1,870.00

Bandana, silk, 1892 campaign, Harrison (Benjamin) & Reid (Whitelaw), 18 x 18" 125.00

Bar soap, 1980 campaign, Carter (James) 18.00

Bubble gum cigars, 1968 campaign, Nixon (Richard), "Win With Dick" on cigar, photo of Nixon on box, box of 24 ....25.00

Clicker, 1968 campaign, Nixon (Richard), "Veterans for Nixon" 25.00

Coin, 1860 campaign, Lincoln

(Abraham) & Hamlin (Hannibal), ferrotype of Lincoln on one side & Hamlin on reverse 375.00

Coin, 1924 campaign, LaFollette (Robert) & Wheeler (B.K.), "Progressive Party" & embossed portraits, bronze, 7/8" d. 125.00

Coin, 1932 campaign, Roosevelt (Franklin D.) & Garner (John N.), "Good Luck," embossed portraits of Roosevelt & Garner & a swastika, 1 1/4" d. 40.00

Jacket, paper, 1968 campaign, Nixon (Richard), white background w/blue stars & large red block lettered "Nixon" printed overall, Mars Disposables Mfg. Co. 175.00

License plate attachment, 1936 campaign, Landon (Alfred) & Knox (Frank), model of a sunflower 35.00

Match book, 1928 campaign, Smith (Al), "Elect Al Smith," "Vote For Repeal" on reverse side, red, white & blue 45.00

Medal, 1916 campaign, "Charles Evans Hughes for President" 38.00

Newspaper, 1948 campaign, "Harry S Truman For President," eight page tabloid, portrait cover 45.00

Newspaper, 1960 campaign, Kennedy (John), poster-like front page w/"Kennedy for President, Leadership for the 60s" & JFK portrait 60.00

Pennant, 1952 campaign, GOP Republican National Convention, w/elephant's head & building shown, Chicago, Illinois 25.00

Pin, 1896 campaign, McKinley (William) & Hobart (Garret), mechanical brass bug w/photo of McKinley & Hobart on the collapsible wings, works 275.00

Pin, 1928 campaign, Smith (Alfred E.), model of a derby, metal 22.50

Pin, 1964 campaign, Goldwater (Barry), elephant head wearing eye glasses 10.00

Pinback button, 1968 campaign, Nixon (Richard) & Agnew (Spiro) jugate, 3 1/2" d. 22.00

Pinback button, 1984 campaign, Mondale (Walter) & Ferraro (Geraldine) jugate, 1 3/4" d. 10.00

Ribbon, 1860 campaign, Lincoln (Abraham), central portrait from a photographic image, mounted on a light blue silk ribbon, 1 7/8 x 2 1/4" (fiber loss) 330.00

Ring, 1928 campaign, Hoover (Herbert), metal enameled diagonally w/the name "Hoover" & the date "1928" 30.00

Snuff box, 1848 campaign, General Zachary Taylor, gilt & lacquered, round, the cover w/a portrait of Zachary Taylor inscribed "Old 'Rough and Ready'—the Hero of the War with Mexico," 3 1/2" d. (minor imperfections) 1,150.00

Songbook, 1912 campaign, Teddy Roosevelt Bull Moose Party, 62 pp. 35.00

Stickpin, 1896 campaign, Bryan (William J.), celluloid 68.00

Stickpin, 1904 campaign, Roosevelt (Theodore), "Our Choice," brass 65.00

Textile, 1840 campaign, Harrison (William Henry), cotton w/brown roller-printed design w/central scene of "William Henry Harrison" on a horse w/sword drawn encircled by vignettes depicting scenes from his career, framed, 28 1/4" w., 26 1/2" h. (stains, tear in bottom border design & old sewn repairs) 660.00

Textile block, 1852 campaign, white cotton roller-printed overall w/small round bust portraits of candidate Franklin Pierce surrounded by eagles, foliage & flowers in red, orange, blue, grey & black, in an early beveled bird's-eye maple frame w/a wide black eglomisé mat w/oval opening, 9 x 10 1/2" 412.50

Watch fob, 1904 campaign, Roosevelt (Theodore) & Parker (Alton), w/original leather strap, metal 30.00

Watch fob, 1908 campaign, Taft (William H.) & Sherman (James), brass, bust in horseshoe, metal 75.00

NON-CAMPAIGN

Plaster Bust of George Washington

Bust of George Washington, oval, molded & sculptured plaster, inscribed under the shoulder "C.C. Wright F.," Charles Cushing Wright (1796-1854), in an ornate beaded oval frame, 5 1/2 x 6 1/2" (ILLUS.) 2,875.00

Cuff links, brass, model of Lyndon B. Johnson's cowboy hat, engraved "L.B.J.," pr. 13.00

Inaugural button, 1789, George Washington, copper, depicting an eagle surmounted by a star, 34 mm. (lacks shank, worn & patinated surface) 440.00

Inaugural button, 1789, George Washington, brass, "GW" w/linked states border, 34 mm. d. 935.00

Inaugural invitation, 1965, Lyndon B. Johnson, framed 10.00

Inaugural program, Roosevelt (Franklin) & Garner (John N.) inauguration, 1937 ....50.00

Inaugural program, Roosevelt (Franklin) & Wallace (Henry A.) inauguration, dated January 20, 1941 ....40.00

Inaugural program, Truman (Harry) & Barkley (Alben) inauguration, 1949 ...45.00

Menu, 1924 Democratic National Convention, large....................24.00

Pass, to the Senate floor, signed by Senator Harry Truman, 1939 ....175.00

Plaque, cast iron, bust of William McKinley, old polychrome paint w/some touch-up, 11¼" h. 82.50

Playing cards, John F. Kennedy, "Kennedy Kards," complete deck.......22.50

Spoon, features Harry Truman at top of handle & "Berlin Airlift" in bowl.......45.00

Spoons, silver plate, representing each of the Presidents from George Washington through Dwight Eisenhower, engraved bowl w/President's picture on handle, set 325.00

Textile, cotton, portrait of "Washington" standing beside a horse within a star-filled oval frame beneath a shield decorated w/stars & stripes, all against a vertically striped ground, in olive brown, red & blue on a white ground, 17½" w., 25" h. (wear, fading & color bleeding, edges have holes from being attached to a stretcher) 550.00

Textile, cotton, blue & white roller-printed depicting the first six Presidents & a spread-winged American eagle w/"E Pluribus Unum" & "Les Presidents des Etats-Unis," France, framed, 27¾" w., 26¼" h. (minor stains) 467.50

Textile, commemorative, black copper engraving on silk w/portrait labeled "G. Washington, born Feb. 11th, 1732 Died Oct. 14th, 1799," upper portion appliqued in black silk w/a top hat, framed, 17¼" w., 24¼" h. (top corners cut, wear, stains & small tears) 550.00

Textile, commemorative, printed silk, bust of "Washington" in medallion flanked by crossed flags, bugles, oak leaves & acorns, surmounted by a spread-winged American eagle & "First in War, First in Peace..." all within a border of battling ships, in black, olive green, mustard yellow & red, framed, 29½" w., 24¾" h. (minor stains) 4,510.00

Textile, commemorative, printed cotton, scene titled "The Death of General Washington," surrounded by various sized paneled inscriptions, early 19th c., in old gilt shadowbox frame, 27 x 31" (age stains, tear) 275.00

Ticket, 1896 Republican National Convention, St. Louis, Missouri, ornate engravings 35.00

Ticket, 1936 Democratic National Convention, FDR portrait engraving ..20.00

Ticket, 1940 Republican Convention, Lincoln portrait engraving 20.00

Walking stick, carved & painted wood, the square ball top surmounting several registers of double portrait busts of Presidents Washington through Cleveland, w/metal tip, America, late 19th - early 20th c., 39" h....................6,050.00

POSTCARDS

Also see ADVERTISING ITEMS.

Advertising, "Daniel Webster Cigars," colorful, ca. 1910 ....$20.00

Advertising, "Ford Motor Company," two interior & three exterior photographs, ca. 1920, set of 5 ....30.00

Advertising, "Goodyear Tires," combination of Will Rogers photo & cartoon, 1929....................22.00

Advertising, "Humphrey's Witch Hazel Ointment," illustration of ointment tube, colorful, ca. 1915 ....10.00

Battleships, pictures the U.S.S. Olympia, Massachusetts, Brooklyn & Wisconsin, 1905, set of 4 ....40.00

Boxers, early real photograph 15.00

Cat w/green glass eyes, mechanical-type 22.50

Flood & Ice Gorge of Cincinnati, 1918, set of 4 ....20.00

"House of David" band, real photo........38.00

Independence Day, depicts cherubic children, firecrackers, flags, etc., highlighted w/gilt trim, Raphael Tuck artwork, set of 5 ....50.00

Memphis State Fair, pumpkin-shaped, opens out to 12", depicts women watching steeple chase, 1909 ....15.00

New York City skyscrapers, souvenir folder-type, 1930s 24.00

Railroad wreck, Boonville, New York, 1908, set of 6 ....85.00

Valentine greeting, Curtis Publishing, 1906, mint unused condition, set of 8..45.00

POSTERS

(Also see DISNEY COLLECTIBLES, MOVIE MEMORABILIA and MUCHA (Alphonse) ARTWORK.

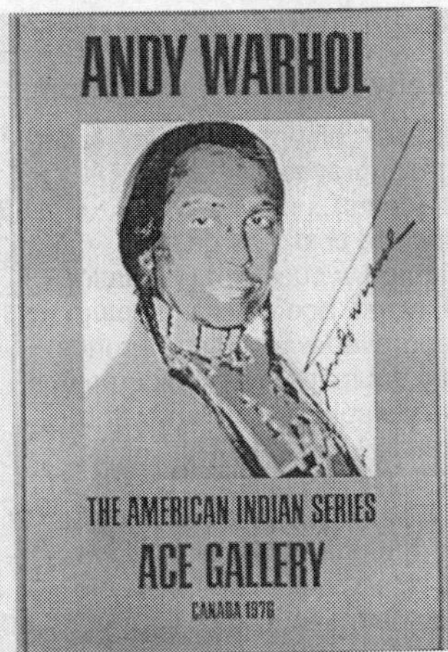

Andy Warhol Poster

Art gallery, "Andy Warhol - The American Indian Series - Ace Gallery - Canada 1976," signed by Warhol in black pen, glazed & framed, 34 x 50" (ILLUS.) $1,035.00

Jimi Hendrix Concert Poster

Concert poster, "Jimi Hendrix Experience - Vanilla Fudge - Soft Machine - Eire Apparent...," held in Seattle, Washington at the Seattle Center Coliseum, September 6, 1968, photo of Hendrix head in the center, framed 18 x 24" (ILLUS.) ..1,725.00

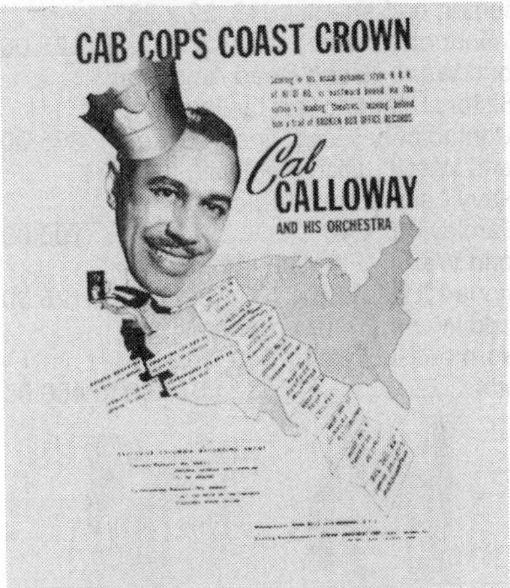

Cab Calloway Concert Tour Poster

Concert tour, "Cab Cops Coast Crown...Cab Calloway and His Orchestra," w/a picture of Calloway's head & a listing of concert dates from October through December on his eastbound tour, late 1940s - early 1950s, 22 x 30" (ILLUS.) 575.00

Chat Noir Poster

Magazine, "Prochainement - la tres illustre Compagnie du Chat Noir...," lithograph printed in colors by Charles Verneau, Paris, France, ca. 1900, design by Theophile-Alexandre Steinlen, laid down on linen, small black mark on top left, $14\frac{1}{4}$ x $24\frac{1}{2}$" (ILLUS.) 2,185.00

Medicine show, "Clifton Comedy Co.," black-face patent medicine show, Donaldson Litho, ca. 1920, 20 x 30"..125.00

Movie, "Walt Disney's Victory Through Air Power," battle scenes around the border, text & large plane in the center, half-sheet, 1943, 22 x 28" (minor edge wear) 125.00

World War I, "Don't Read American History, Make It," art by James Montgomery Flagg, linen-backed 385.00

World War II, "Dish it out with the Navy," signed by McClelland Barclay, 28 x 40" 100.00

World War II, "Fly With the Marines," signed "HHL," 28 x 40" 125.00

World War II, "Four Freedoms," by Norman Rockwell, 1943, set of 4 ....375.00 to 400.00

"Don't Get Hurt" Poster

World War II, "I need you on the job *full time*...Don't Get Hurt," soldier looking down the barrel of a machine gun, red & black lettering, marked "U.S. Government Printing Office: 1943-0-539038," fold marks, very minor soiling, 28½ x 40½" (ILLUS.) 33.00

"Keep him flying!" Poster

World War II, "Keep him flying! - Buy War Bonds," pilot climbing into the cockpit of a fighter plane, green plane, green & yellow lettering, signed "Schreiber '42," corners missing, fold marks, minor soiling, 28½ x 40" (ILLUS.) 55.00

World War II, "The US Marines Want You," 28 x 40" 75.00

POWDER HORNS & FLASKS

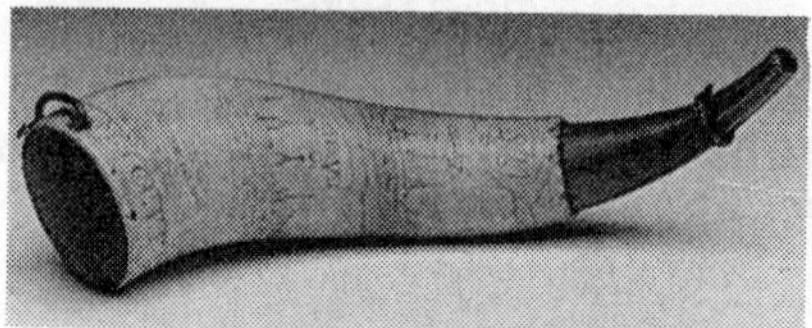

Early Engraved Powder Horn

Copper flask, embossed hunter & dog design, engraved "J.W. Selly," 8¼" l. (dents) $82.50

Horn, incised compass design highlighted w/buckshot, old patina, 7½" l. (wear, age cracks, no plug) ...115.50

Horn, engraved w/woodland scenes, military equipage, ship & figures of a soldier pursuing an Indian, w/the inscription "JONATHAN CARPENTER'S HORN - CAMP AT BARNERD - SEPT. YE 1ST 1780," 9½" l. (the plug is a later addition, minor loss to butt end, small hole in body near spout) 4,600.00

Horn, engraved w/a large heart sprouting feathers surrounded by small hearts, scallops & a fish, probably Pennsylvania, late 18th c., 10" l. 1,035.00

Horn, relief-carved design of an animal w/a horse's head & a lion's body, inscription w/partial pitch inlay reading "Un requerdo," 10½" l. (cracks, wear) 55.00

Horn, French & Indian War era horn engraved w/images of New York, Albany, Rhode Island, Long Island, Amboy "Beses House" & three forts & inscribed "John Williams Com'y in Col: E & F Ret" & "Croun Point August 27 1759," 13½" l. (ILLUS.) 8,250.00

Revolutionary War Powder Horn

Horn, engraved w/a register of fighting soldiers beside a naval scene, the inscription "Levi Gaschet, his horn, Nov. ye 30th, 1775: maid (sic) in Dorchester in Gage's. War," surrounded by swags below a register of trees, the spout faceted, minor loss to end, second line of inscription may be later, 15" l. (ILLUS.) 9,200.00

PURSES & BAGS

Early Gold Mesh Bag

Beaded, black rose tambour, cathedral dome frame, elaborate clasp, France $195.00

Beaded, center design of peacock & roses, tricolored fringe, lg. 265.00

Beaded, cut steel, diamond design, bead fringe top & bottom, 6 x 9" 65.00

Beaded, cut steel in a diamond design, fringed top & bottom, gathered w/chain top 98.00

Beaded, silver & clear beads in swag design, fancy fringes, 6 x 8½" 75.00

Black velvet, long rectangular body embroidered overall w/metallic thread in a scrolling vine design w/large serrated leaves set w/colored cabochon stones to resemble pearls, strap handle from end to end.................................71.50

Enameled mesh, Art Deco design in black & white, Whiting & Davis, large...200.00

Enameled, black & gold diamond designs, Mandalian Mfg. Co., 3½ x 7" 125.00

Enameled mesh, decorated w/birds of paradise, Mandalian Mfg. Co., mint in box, 8½" l. 125.00

Enameled mesh, spectacular double peacocks decoration, Mandalian 235.00

Enameled mesh, pink & blue on cream geometric floral design, Whiting Davis, 3¾ x 7" (fringe cut) 95.00

Gold mesh, 9k, round, w/coin-like disc in center engraved "1900"...............325.00

Gold (14k red & yellow) & diamond, in the form of an eight-panel cylinder, engine-turned neo-classical design decoration, the hinged top set on each side w/a diamond, w/chain handle & ring...................................977.00

Gold mesh, 14k yellow gold Art Nouveau style change purse w/a pointed bottom & three ball drops, the arched & ornately chased frame engraved "X-mas 97," hallmarked (ILLUS.) 357.00

Gold mesh, 14k yellow gold, pearl fringes, chain handle & sapphire thumbpieces, ca. 1920s 1,200.00

Gold mesh, 14k yellow gold, w/an etched closure & a cabochon sapphire clasp, highlighted by a slide handle & beaded tassel, hallmarked 467.50

Gold, 14k yellow gold & diamond, the rectangular gold frame highlighted w/diamonds, suspending a zigzag pattern mesh bag & change purse, w/a cabochon sapphire & yellow gold oval link handle 2,860.00

Lucite, lunch box-style, gunmetal grey, Wilardy, New York, 1950s 50.00

Petit point, outdoor scene in center cartouche w/people, trees, house, dog, etc., surrounded by scrolls & multi-colored flowers, tan background, enameled & beaded clasp & frame, original silk lining, France...165.00

Silver mesh, ball chain fringing at center & bottom, sapphire blue stone thumbpieces, Germany, 6 x 7"..65.00

Silver mesh, dolphins decoration on top, chain w/ring in center, ball fringe base, marked "U," 4 x 6" 275.00

Sterling silver, clutch-type, designed as a stylized duck, the highly polished body hinged, further enhanced by a woven black silk cord strap threaded through the gracefully arched neck, signed "Tiffany & Co. Peretti," 5¾" l. 632.00

Sterling silver mesh, cathedral-style, w/tassel, 7" l. 88.00

Velvet, green velvet bag, silver frame containing blister pearls, demantoid garnets & three-facet rose-cut simulated diamonds 247.50

Velvet, wide #800 grade silver frame w/pierced openwork design of adults & childrens, medallions chain 175.00

Collectible Table Top Radios

1930 to 1960

by HARRY POSTER

As with most collectibles, table top radios have undergone significant changes over the years, and radio collectors find some very collectible, while others are shunned. After the initial series of very large wooden cabinets in the 1920s and early 1930s, most of the radio manufacturers decided to produce "portable" table top sets in addition to their console model radios. There was a definite need for smaller sets, and once most of the homes in the United States were wired with electricity, small radios became a reality. During this period, some of the table radios being produced were referred to as "miniature" in the trade literature, although many were still oversized.

For those regions where electricity was slow in coming, "farm sets" were sold. Some console size farm sets do turn up, but generally the farm sets were wooden table top radios, about the size of AC/DC models, but with a large area inside the cabinet where oversized batteries could be stored. Even the largest farm sets are quite light because of the lack of a transformer and other electrical components used to convert alternating electricity into direct current. With very few exceptions, farm sets are worth one half, or less, of the value of a similar AC/DC model.

RCA, General Electric, FADA, Westinghouse and dozens of other lesser known manufacturers were producing thousands of different table top radios in the 1930s; generally in wood or wood-like cabinets. At some point pressed wood was used to fabricate intricate designs in what had become mostly breadbox-shaped wooden table sets. In the mid-1930s, Emerson produced the Mickey Mouse radio; it was a great use of pressed wood which allowed Mickey Mouse and several other Disney characters to be featured on the front and sides of the set. But, for every notable table top, there were dozens of less interesting sets, such as the Emerson Model 414, produced the same year as the Mickey Mouse set, but which was simply a rectangular table top radio with a few flourishes on the edges.

Other sets from the period included those covered by "leatherette" and cloth (these are mostly shunned by the collectors), and some sets were even produced with a cardboard or paperboard case (only the more interesting examples are popular). Sparton and several other companies began producing small sets with mirror covering the cabinet on some of these table tops, and nearly all of the mirrored radios are very popular, and valuable, today.

This is not to ignore the interesting wooden and veneer cabinets which were being produced throughout the 1930s. Although most collectors tend to ignore, or pay only a minimal price for, the square or rectangular shaped table sets, some of these wooden sets did feature unusual styling. Emerson produced a series of interesting table top radios with veneer across a very rounded top; Admiral, Crosley and Zenith often accented the cabinet design using unusual dial features. Some collectors look for those sets which used "electric eye" tubes above or within the dial, while some single out wooden table tops with unusually styled speaker protrusions.

By the late 1930s, many plastic-like compounds were produced and perfected, which allowed the portable sets to be made and sold in an unbelievable number of designs, colors, and even color combinations. FADA sold Bakelite radios, first with simple brown, black or white cases, then with chrome trim, and later in a variety of colorful cabinets; RCA sold small sets in a variety of colors plus brown and white; Emerson perfected the miniature radio in one or more bright colors, including patriotic red, white and blue! All told, at least 17 companies were offering brightly colored plastic radios (in trade-name materials including Plaskon, Bakelite, and Catalin), and dozens of companies were selling table sets in pressed wood, paper, cloth-covering, and leatherette cabinets.

Many of the colorful "plastic" radio cases

from the 1930s and 1940s now actively sought by collectors were composed of exotic materials which could be formed into colored cabinets which were cheaper and easier to make than the wooden table top radios they were designed to replace. And, the designers of the period were able to mold contemporary shapes into the cases without regard to the limitations of wood and veneers. "Deco" styled asymmetrical cases, and those with intricate cut-outs and appliqués, were now possible.

Two- and three-tone sets were easily crafted, as were those which featured inserted grills, knobs and trim in a similar or contrasting color scheme. Wood, and even pressed wood, did not stand up to the intricate detailing given to many of these small cabinets. The new plastics did not peel, warp or get ragged edges, although the passage of time has proven difficult for most, if not all, of the non-wooden cases.

Collectors actively search for the brightest Plaskon and Catalin radios, but many look for the unusually designed or intricate cases made in less colorful Bakelite and similar substances. Catalin radios are about the only collecting area where square lines and lack of detail do not lower the prices paid or, at least, the prices asked. In general, Catalin prices are dependent on the color and condition, with reds, blues and greens worth more than yellows, and the maker, with Bendix, DeWald and a few others at the bottom and FADA, Air King and Motorola at the top.

By the Second World War, actual plastics (as we know them today) were designed, and then used in table top radio cabinets. Most manufacturers had eliminated Bakelite and other early materials by the 1950s, and when truly subminiature table top radios were introduced, these new plastics were used.

Most radio collectors avoid late 1940s and more modern plastic sets, with only a few exceptions. Some of the mid- and late-1950s table top radios were "coat pocket" sized transistor sets with a wire handle which doubled as a support to allow table top operation. These transistor "table tops" about 4 inches by 8 inches, and have AM band only, with Conelrad "Civil Defense" marks at two places on the dial, in case of nuclear attack! The larger tube-type table tops from the 1950s and 1960s, whether of wood, Bakelite, plastic, or some combination, are usually shunned by the collectors. Except for a few with outlandish style, most tube sets produced after 1950 sell for well below $50 at the radio meets.

The rep-wood, or pressed wood, cabinets were made popular by RCA, Emerson, and a few other companies. In general, they are worth a little less than wooden table tops from the period. But, unusually styled, or theme sets, are often worth much more. RCA sold a series of sets at the 1939 New York World's Fair, which featured the '39 Fair plus the Golden Gate Exposition model. These two sets are worth around $1,000 in mint condition, but similar, plain table tops from the series, in pressed wood, are worth well under $100.

Emerson pressed and sold a rep-wood Mickey Mouse radio, and a few other sets which featured Disney characters, now worth around $1,000, but they too sold pressed cabinet model radios which are worth $50 or less. In general, the collectors will pay a significant price if a theme is shown; they will shun cabinets that were pressed just to offer a cheaper-than-wood cabinet. And, most of the radios which were cloth or leatherette covered, are valued at under $100, with most under $25.

When a wooden table top is encountered, a few things will indicate if it is a valuable set, or one which might be ignored. Sets trimmed in chrome, such as those by Majestic, are usually worth $100 or more. And the black and chrome series from RCA are worth $1,000 or more. Those with strange lines or accents (not just pretty features!) might be valued at $50 to $100 or so, and those with simple square or rectangular design, are nearly always worth under $50. Some wooden sets are worth more, but most reflect these guidelines.

A few tests will usually show if the "plastic" radio at hand is valuable, very valuable, or just a common table top. First, if your table top is brown, black, or white, it probably will sell for under $50, but large or unusual features sometimes put the value at over $50. And, if you luck across an Air King "skyscraper" shaped set, even the more common white or brown models might sell for a few thousand dollars. Most 1950 or later plastic radios, regardless of shape, size or color, will sell for under $50.

If you have a colored (other than white, black or brown) plastic set from the 1930s or 1940s, check the bottom. If it's much brighter in color than the top and sides, you may have a Catalin set, with a value of $500 to $5,000 or more. Catalin is usually very thick, and when sold, the radio was highly polished, so no ripples could be detected. Often the trim and knobs were in a contrasting color, although many one-color Catalins were sold.

Sparton produced the most common of

the mirrored cabinet radios; the circular Blue Bird, and the rectangular "3-Knob" and "4-Knob" models, are most often found. If the cabinets and mirrors are very clean and complete, prices around $2,000 or so are usually reported. (The floor model Sparton "Nocturne," a round four-foot high mirrored set, is one of only a few floor model radios which is worth significantly more than the equivalent table top sets: a mint Nocturne is worth well over $10,000!). Mir-ray, Troy, and a few other manufacturers produced rectangular wooden sets with mirror covering the cabinets, but these makers' sets are less common, and often less valuable.

Most table top and portable tube-type sets have little value. The vast majority sell for under $50, if they sell at all. Paper, cloth, and leatherette styles fall into this category. If the back opens, and batteries go into the set, even if there is a cord (for battery or AC/DC operation), suspect the worst. And, in general, nearly any radio with a phonograph or record player built-in will be shunned by most radio collectors!

If your portable radio uses transistors, rather than tubes, there is a chance you have a popular set. Most of the coat-pocket/table top transistor radios from about 1955 to 1960 will be worth between $25 and $200, with the leather or cloth covered sets at the low end, and the plastic sets at the high end. Sometimes the hardest part of evaluating the transistor set is determining the date of manufacture. Usually looking for the "CD" marks on the dial is an indication that the set was made before the late 1960s. And, most transistor sets with AM band only are more popular than multiband radios. Early sets were made in Japan or the USA, and most Hong Kong, Taiwan, and sets from other countries have no collector value yet.

ABOUT THE AUTHOR

Harry Poster has been collecting and dealing in both radios and vintage TVs since 1982. He travels to radio meets and antiques shows from Chicago and West Virginia, to New York state and New Hampshire. Plus, he buys and sells both radios and TVs mail-order, across the USA, and around the world. Chilton Books has recently published his second illustrated price guide, Poster's Radio and Television Price Guide, 1920-1990. *To ascertain the approximate value of your crystal, tube or transistor radio, or older television, and where to sell it, please send a photo and a SASE to: Harry Poster, P.O. Box 1883, So. Hackensack, NJ 07606.*

PRICE LISTING

Air King:

Model 52, skyscraper-shaped Plaskon radio, brown or black.....$2,500.00

Model 911, wooden table top with push-buttons, simple styling 25.00

Model 9562, large leatherette 1957 transistor table top 100.00

Model A-520, battery portable with handle on top 35.00

Airline:

"Lone Ranger," Bakelite set with character, 1951 (ILLUS.) 400.00

Arvin:

Model 140-P, cloth covered portable, handle on top, metal trim 15.00

Model 441-T, "Hopalong Cassidy" metal trimmed table top, red or black 200.00

Model 746P, plastic portable from 1953, metal grill and metal handle.....25.00

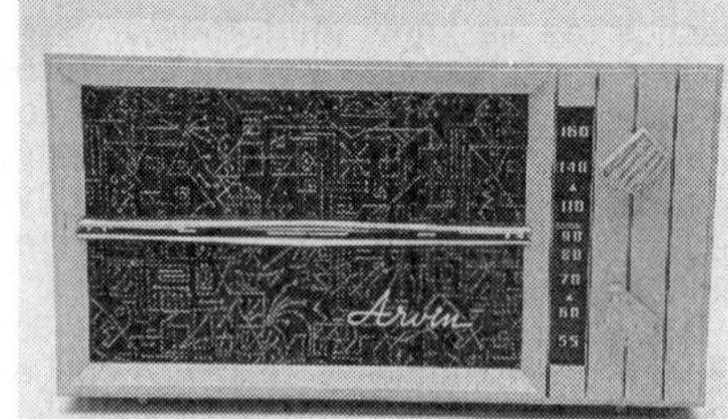

Model 2564, wide plastic set with irregular knobs, 1957 (ILLUS.)...........45.00

Belmont:

Model 6D-111, 1940 brown Bakelite set with pushbuttons (ILLUS. bottom previous page) 85.00

Benrus:

Brass-tone radio from 1955, large clock face on dial (ILLUS.) 75.00

Crosley:

Model 9-113, simple brown table top with long dial, 1949 ....15.00

Model 11-119, painted Bakelite set with unusual dial (ILLUS.) 100.00

Model 56-TD, unusual Bakelite from 1947, "rocket-ship" styling.................85.00

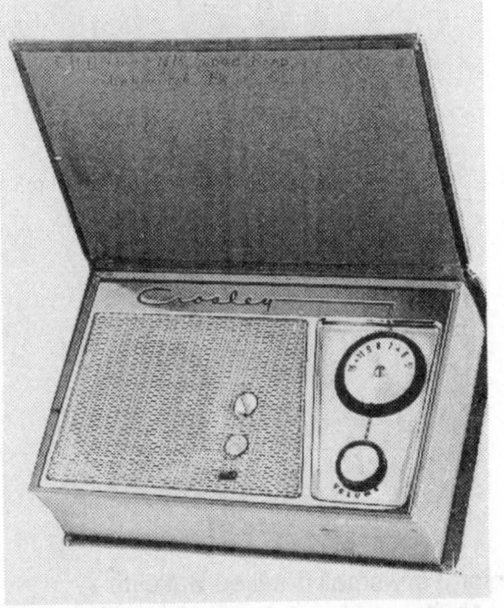

Model F5, Musical Chef, with mechanical tuner in simple plastic set 30.00

Model JM-8, "Book-shaped" transistor and tube radio, unusual style (ILLUS. bottom left)..........................100.00

DeWald:

Model 500-A, brown or white painted Bakelite, rounded sides 35.00

Model 501-A, Lyre-shaped Catalin table top in yellow or brown 400.00

Model K-701A, oversized plastic transistor radio, DeWald's first (ILLUS.) 200.00

Emerson:

Model 375, "5+1" grill bar Catalin set, red body.......................................2,500.00

Model 400, "Aristocrat" with yellow, green, or brown body, ea. (ILLUS.) .400.00

Model 536, cloth covered portable from 1947..15.00

Model 646, maroon plastic portable from 1950..25.00

Model 888, large transistor radio with wire support-handle 85.00

Model 911, very rectangular plastic transistorized table top........................45.00

Model BT-245, tall table top Catalin tombstone-shape in blue (ILLUS.) 5,000.00

"Mickey Mouse" pressed-wood table top from 1934, all original (ILLUS.) 1,500.00

FADA:

5F50, small yellow Catalin set, inserted red grill, mint (ILLUS.) 2,000.00

Model 110, wooden Art Deco table top with light and dark wood 65.00

Model 845, plastic bodied "cloud" shaped radio, various colors...........150.00

Model 1000, "Bullet," yellow Catalin body, with maroon Catalin trim (ILLUS.) 700.00

Model P-80, plastic portable with small Catalin knob, front opens 45.00

Kadette:

Clockette, green Crystlin plastic, 1937, clock-like front (ILLUS.) 1,300.00

Junior, very small detailed Bakelite case, brown, two-tube model (ILLUS.) 150.00

Motorola:

Model 77XM, rounded 1948 Bakelite radio, brown and white (ILLUS.) 25.00

Philco:

Transitone 53-560, rectangular black Bakelite from 1953 (ILLUS.) 20.00

Model F675-124, simple leatherette covered tube radio (ILLUS.)...............15.00

RCA:

Model 1BT29, 1959 all transistor coat pocket/table top (ILLUS.) 60.00

Standard:

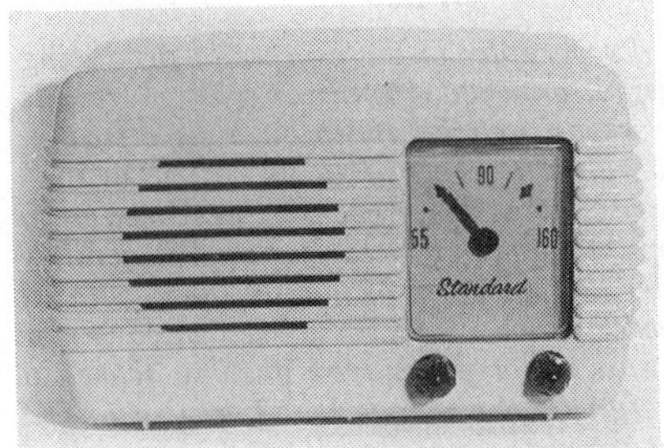

Bakelite table top in colored Bakelite, blue body (ILLUS.) 250.00

Stewart Warner:

Model 07-511, Deco Bakelite set with large pointer (ILLUS.) 85.00

Zenith:

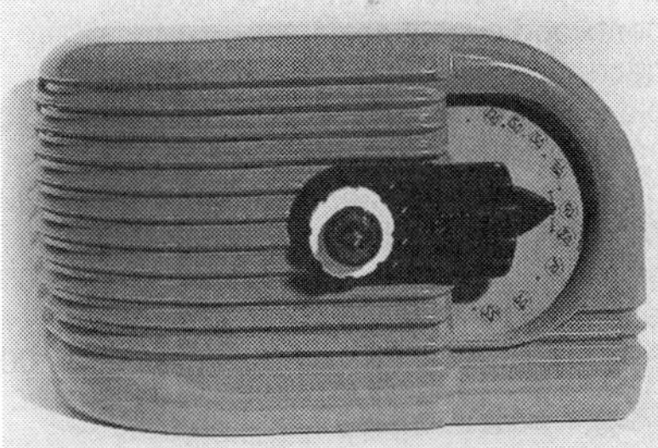

Model 6D311, curved Bakelite set with large attached antenna (ILLUS.)......100.00

Model T521, 1955 plastic rectangular clock radio, black and red (ILLUS.)....30.00

PYROGRAPHY

Pyrography is the process of producing designs on wood, leather or other materials by using heated tools or a fine flame. Commonly referred to as "burnt-wood" wares, creating these articles became a popular home craft earlier in this century after the invention of the platinum-pointed needle which could be safely heated. Prior to this a hot poker was used to scorch a design in the wood. But because of the accuracy the needle allowed, burning a design into wood became a hobby with many and companies issued kits with all the tools necessary to create the design on a pre-stamped softwood box or article. A wide variety of designs were available including flowers, animals and scrolls. Women were popular subjects and the rights to Charles Dana Gibson's famous "Gibson Girl" were obtained by Thayer and Chandler Co. of Chicago who also sold items pre-stamped with the Sunbonnet Babies. Modest prices are still associated with burnt-wood wares unless the overall workmanship or design is exceptional.

Box, cov., scene of a Dutch girl w/buckets, goat carts & geese, 2 x 5 x 7" $26.00

Box w/hinged cover, decorated w/flowers on sides & bird on top, brass fittings, 3 x 8 x 15" 195.00

Box w/spring-latched cover w/handle, bentwood oval, sides & top decorated w/a band of scrollwork, old patina, 10¼" l. 192.50

Pencil box, engraved "B.D.F.," w/a bear, deer & fox 30.00

Plaque, scene of a bulldog, 18 x 22" oval 45.00

Plaque, scene of boy & cat, Flemish Art, 12" d. 20.00

RAILROADIANA

B & O Centenary Demitasse

Badge, "DL&W" (Delaware, Lackawanna & Western), 'Lieutenant' $130.00

Badge, "Erie," 'Lieutenant' 110.00

Book, "Narrow Gauge in the Rockies," by Beebe & Clegg, 1958, autographed, numbered vol., w/original box.................................150.00

Book, "Northern Pacific - Main Street of the Northwest," 1968, pictorial history, 208 pp. 25.00

Book, "North Shore, America's Fastest Interurban," 1964, first edition, several photographs, hard cover 20.00

Book, "Rules for the Government of the Maintenance of Way," 21 pp. of fold-out schematics, screw binding, hard cover, 68 pp. 25.00

Booklet, "Burlington Zephyr," w/layout diagram & photos, ca. 1933..............34.00

Booklet, "UPRR" (Union Pacific Railroad), 1947 "Colorado," 32 pgs..........18.00

Booklet, "Union Pacific Railroad," entitled "Progress," information & photos on the "Streamline Train," 1934 ....30.00

Bookmark, "Texas & Pacific Railway," aluminum, heart-shaped, early 90.00

Bowl, cereal, "Union Pacific Railroad," china, Portland Rose patt. 350.00

Bread tray, "P&LE" (Pittsburgh & Lake Erie Railroad), ornate silver plate, early 1900s, 6½ x 15½" 95.00

Butter pat, "Atchison, Topeka & Santa Fe," china, California Poppy patt. (no back stamp) 25.00

Butter pat, "Pennsylvania Railroad," china, Purple Laurel patt. backstamped 70.00

Butter pat, "RI" (Rock Island Lines), 1924, silver plate, 3" d. 50.00

Butter pat, "Union Pacific Railroad," china, Winged Streamliner patt..........25.00

Cabinet, ticket master's, 21 drawers on each side w/roll-top covers, painted black wooden top, 30 x 40 x 62" 995.00

Calendar, 1909, "Toledo Chicago Railroad," chromatic pictures of ladies in feather costumes, 4 pp. 150.00

Calendar, 1935, "Great Northern Railroad" 75.00

Calendar, 1937, "Chesapeake & Ohio Railroad," 4 pp. 85.00

Calendar, 1970, "Illinois Central Railroad," wall-type, fold-out-type, depicts passenger train interior scene, original mailing envelope, 10 x 15" 7.00

Clock, pendulum-type, "Bureau of Standards Certified Railroad Times," 34" l. pendulum, 18" w., 64" h. case 2,000.00

Conductor's whistle, "Pennsylvania Railroad," brass 27.00

Creamer, "PRR" (Pennsylvania Railroad), silver-soldered, seamless, "5115, PRR" on bottom, International Silver Co. 100.00

Creamer w/hinged lid, "NYC&HR" (New York Central & Hudson River Railroad), silver plate, ca. 1900 ....95.00

Creamer w/hinged lid, "UPRR" (Union Pacific Railroad), silver plate, ca. 1910 ....95.00

Creamer & cov. sugar bowl, "Chicago & Eastern Illinois Railroad," Art Deco-style, silver soldered, Reed & Barton, 4½" h., pr. 195.00

Crumb tray, "Chicago, Burlington & Quincy RR," Burlington Route, silver plate 55.00

Cup, "Southern Pacific Co.,," china, Prairie-Mountain Wildflowers patt. 55.00

Cup & saucer, demitasse, "Baltimore & Ohio Railroad," china, Centenary patt., Scammells, blue & white, 1927 (ILLUS.) 85.00

Cup & saucer, "C.M.S.T.P.& P.R.R." (Chicago, Milwaukee, St. Paul & Pacific Railroad), china, marked "Theo Haviland" 150.00

Cup & saucer, "Chicago, Milwaukee, St. Paul & Pacific RR," china, Olympian patt., gold lettering inside cup, Lenox China............100.00 to 150.00

Cuspidor, "Central Pacific Railroad," brass w/emblem................................30.00

Diary, "Cotton Belt Route - St. Louis Southern Western Railroad Lines," 1948, never used 12.50

Dish, "Chesapeake & Ohio Railroad," china, Washington patt., Buffalo China, 9" l. 600.00

Egg cup, "Southern Pacific Railroad," china, Prairie-Mountain Wildflowers patt. 225.00

Fire grenade, "Chicago-Northwestern Railroad," embossed metal cylinder 225.00

Lantern, "Chicago, Milwaukee & St. Paul Railroad," brass top, bell bottom, red cast globe 275.00

Lantern, "Colorado & Southern Railroad," bell bottom, 80% tin, clear etched globe ....325.00 to 350.00

Lantern, "D&H" (Delaware & Hudson Railroad), clear globe.......................250.00

Lantern, "Great Northern Railroad," clear cast globe..............................200.00

Lantern, "Great Northern Railroad," 100% tin, clear tall globe.................145.00

Lantern, "New York Central Railroad," red globe, bell bottom, embossed, "Dietz, No. 6"....................................100.00

Lantern, "NYNH&H" (New York, New Haven & Hartford Railroad), Dietz Vesta model, clear globe 55.00

Lantern, "NYC" (New York Central Railroad), Dietz Vesta model, clear globe 55.00

Lantern, "NYNH&H RR," (New York, New Haven & Hartford), two-color globe, Adams, Westlake, ca. 1887 ..150.00

Lantern, "Northern Pacific Railroad," red cast globe 200.00

Lantern, "Richmond, Fredericksburg & Potomac," Handlan model, clear globe 48.00

Lantern, "Wheeling & Lake Erie," Dietz Vesta model, red globe, brass frame...60.00

Lantern, conductor's, brass, clear globe etched "A. Carter," base stamped "Blake"s Patent 1852," 14½" h. (imperfections) 990.00

Lantern, presentation-type, nickel plated, clear glass globe engraved "J.D. Carr," base marked "St. Louis R.W. Supplies," 19th c., 16" h. 385.00

Magazine, "The Railway Age," 1886, May, several ads, railroad cars, bridges, wheels, tools, spikes & other railroad related equipment........15.00

Menu, "Pennsylvania Railroad," 1935, 8 pgs. 20.00

Model of a train car, combination passenger - baggage car, wood w/metal fittings, painted red & inscribed "Independence - Lawrence - No. 4," late 19th c., w/original packing crate, 54" l. (imperfections) 990.00

Napkins, "Chicago, Burlington & Quincy," white cotton w/'California Zephyr' interwoven in center, 14" sq. 10.00

Oil can, "D&RG" (Denver & Rio Grand Railroad), large 82.00

Padlock, "Santa Fe Railroad," w/dust cover, Keen Kutter 475.00

Padlock, "Southern Pacific Railroad," Keen Kutter 650.00

Padlock & key, "Michigan Central Railroad," brass 200.00

Paperweight, "Rock Island Railroad," clear glass, round, ca. 1880...............85.00

Pass, "Atchison, Topeka & Santa Fe," 1963 ....10.00

Plate, "Erie Railroad," china, Centennial patt., blue & white, 1951 ....25.00

Plate, "Chesapeake & Ohio Railroad Lines," china, George Washington patt. 395.00

Plate, "Union Pacific Railroad," china, Circus series, clown, 8¾" d. 290.00

Plate, "Union Pacific Railroad," china, Circus series, monkey w/pipe 300.00

Plate, dinner, "Union Pacific Railroad," Desert Flower patt. 75.00
Plate, "New York Central Railroad," china, DeWitt Clinton patt., 7½" d. 30.00
Plate, "New York Central Railroad," china, Mercury patt., 9" d. 45.00
Plate, "Pennsylvania Railroad," china, Mountain Laurel patt., 7¼" d. 25.00
Plate, "Pennsylvania Railroad," china, Mountain Laurel patt., 9¼" d. 45.00
Plate, "Southern Pacific Railroad," china, Prairie-Mountain Wildflowers patt., 7" d. 35.00
Plate, "Southern Pacific Railroad," china, Prairie-Mountain Wildflowers patt., 9½" d. 65.00
Plate, "Union Pacific Railroad", china, Zion patt., 9½" d. 400.00
Platter, "C&O" (Chesapeake & Ohio), china, George Washington patt., Buffalo/Syracuse, 10½" l. 69.00
Platter, "CB&Q" (Chicago, Burlington & Quincy), china, Violets & Daisies patt., 8½ x 12½" oval 375.00

Indian Tree Platter

Platter, "New York, New Haven & Hartford RR," china, Indian Tree patt., 12" l. (ILLUS.) 75.00
Platter, "Southern Pacific Railroad," china, Sunset patt., 6½ x 9" 110.00
Playing cards, "Chesapeake & Ohio Railroad," Peake, Chessie's Old Man, sealed pack.................................35.00
Playing cards, "Union Pacific," double deck 17.50
Sauce dish, "Union Pacific Railroad," china, Desert Flower patt. 35.00
Service plate, "Missouri Pacific Lines," china, State Capitals patt., diesel engine w/state capitals border, "Route of the Eagles," by Syracuse China, 10½" d. ....225.00 to 250.00
Station cash book, "Illinois Central Railroad," 1946, hard cover, 13 x 17"..10.00
Strong box, tin, "N.Y. N.H. & H. RR" (New York, New Haven & Hartford Railroad), 15 x 18 x 24" 75.00
Sugar bowl, cov., tab-handled, "The Pullman Co.," silver plate 95.00
Sugar bowl, cov., "PRR" (Pennsylvania Railroad), silver-soldered, "SX0891, 14 oz., Keystone" on bottom, International Silver Co. 100.00
Switch key, "Burlington Northern Railroad" 28.00
Switch key, "Penn Central Railroad," brass 20.00
Switch lock, "Kansas City Southern Railroad" 87.50
Switch lock, "Rock Island Railroad," case hardened brass w/key 65.00
Syrup pitcher w/attached undertray, "Seaboard Air Line Railway," silver plate, ca. 1925, 8" h. 95.00
Tablecloth, "Chicago, Burlington & Quincy," white cotton w/'California Zephyr' interwoven in center, 42 x 44" 15.00
Timetable, "Lackawanna Railroad," 1937 ....15.00
Timetable, "New York & Harlem Railroad," compliments of Woodlawn Cemetery, ca. 1900.........14.00
Timetable, "Southern Pacific Railroad," 1957 ....15.00
Timetable & connections booklet, "Colorado Midland Railroad," 1904, colorful litho of Indian & mountain scene, also w/Wells Fargo information 390.00
Timetable & map, employee's, "UP" (Union Pacific), 1939 ....15.00

REVERSE PAINTINGS ON GLASS

Compote of Fruit Painting

Bust portrait of Benjamin Franklin in silhouette, background paper has grey ink wash laurel wreath & facsimile signature "Benj. Franklin," old gilt frame, 10¾" w., 12¾" h. $192.50
Compote filled w/fruit, a blue & white paneled & footed compote filled

w/large pieces of fruit in yellow, red, green, white, purple & tan, against a black background w/white scrolls, in a carved period wood frame painted red w/gold highlights, 15½ x 21" (ILLUS.) 7,188.00

Landscapes, each w/a Chinese gentleman w/young courtesans playing musical instruments or w/fans at a pavilion terrace w/a river in the background, in later floral-etched giltwood frames w/an old framer's paper of James Bolton, Bristol, England, dated "8/7/88," China, late 18th c., 17 x 43¾", pr. 14,950.00

Portraits of Chinese ladies, each seated at a round table which holds a vase w/a large blossom, leafy willow branches across the top, against a mirrored ground, in flat reeded frame w/wire loop hanger at the top, China, 18th c., 11½ x 16", facing pr. (losses) 605.00

River scene, depicting the side wheeler steamship "Ohio" in brilliant colors, poplar frame, 12½" w., 10½" h. 275.00

Silhouettes, two facing pairs featuring busts of men, each w/title of "Daniel Webster," "Franklin Pierce," "Lloyd N. Rogers" or "Millard Fillmore," each within a rectangular gilt band surrounded by a narrow églomisé black matting within a beveled rosewood veneer frame, ca. 1850, 11½ x 13" 412.50

Victorian House Painting

Victorian house in a landscape w/flowers, colorful, some painting applied to the top surface as well as the reverse, in original carved giltwood frame, probably New York State, late 19th c., 28 x 36" (ILLUS.) 3,450.00

Water scene, depicting the paddle steamer "Citizen" underway w/large trails of smoke issuing from the two smokestacks, probably America, 19th c., 6¾ x 8½" 385.00

ROYALTY COMMEMORATIVES

QUEEN VICTORIA (1837-1901)

Golden Jubilee Fairy Lamp

Cup & saucer, china, depicts Victoria & Albert w/children in color, "The Royal Family," under picture, Staffordshire $275.00

Fairy lamp, 1887 Golden Jubilee commemorative, crown-shaped cranberry overshot glass shade, on a marked "Clarke" clear glass candle cup, 3" d., 4¼" h. (ILLUS.)....195.00

1897 Diamond Jubilee Inkwell

Inkwell, white metal & brass, 1897 Diamond Jubilee commemorative, detailed bust of Queen Victoria in white metal, crown cover hinges back to reveal inkwell, square brass base, back w/"Victoria Regina 60 years 1897," w/registry mark & maker's marks, 6" d., 7¼" h. (ILLUS.) 350.00

Match safe, nickel plate, 1887 Golden Jubilee commemorative, rectangular, the front embossed w/a bust of Queen Victoria & banners w/"Jubilee 1837-1887," back-stamped "Perry & Co.," 2½" sq. 110.00

Match safe, thermoplastic, 1897 Diamond Jubilee commemorative, book-shaped, embossed bust of Queen Victoria on front....................110.00

Medallion, brass, 1887 Golden Jubilee commemorative, star-shaped, 2" w. 40.00

1897 Diamond Jubilee Pitcher

Pitcher, stoneware, 1897 Diamond Jubilee commemorative, barrel-shaped body, brown & tan design, two bust portraits of the Queen from 1837 & 1897 & "She brought her people lasting good" enclosed within a banner, marked "Doulton," 4⅛" d., 7¾" h. (ILLUS.) 275.00

Plate, china, 1887 Golden Jubilee commemorative, rectangular w/cut corners, overall round vignettes including a portrait of Victoria & Prince of Wales, allegorical figures & a world globe, gilt border, 9½" h. (age cracking, worn gilt)....................33.00

EDWARD VII (1901-10)

Edward VII Match Safe

Match safe, silver plate, rectangular w/an embossed bust portrait of Edward, 1½ x 2" (ILLUS.) 100.00

Mug, clear glass w/etching of King Edward VII and Queen Alexandra 85.00

Pinback button, celluloid, 1902 coronation commemorative, color portrait depiction of the King & Queen 34.00

Plate, china, 1902 coronation commemorative, Edward & Alexandra depicted, fluted rim, Foley, 7" d. 55.00

Tumbler, water, porcelain, 1902 coronation commemorative, Regent China 65.00

GEORGE V (1910-36)

Compact, Silver Jubilee commemorative, 1910-1935, portraits of King George & Queen Mary 55.00

Sugar bowl, open, porcelain, 1911 coronation commemorative, Shelley China 45.00

Tumbler, china, 1911 coronation commemorative, Stoke-on-Trent mark..52.50

EDWARD VIII (1936, Abdicated)

Bowl, china, 1937 coronation commemorative, Edward's likeness w/crown in center surrounded by crests of ten Empire nations, Wedgwood, 10" d............................350.00

Cup & saucer, china, 1937 coronation commemorative, Royal Chelsea patt. 40.00

Mug, china, "To Commemorate the Investiture of HRH Edward Prince of Wales by George V," w/portrait, Grafton, 1911 ....75.00

Plate, china, 1937 coronation commemorative, Homer Laughlin......49.00

GEORGE VI (1936-52)

Book, 1937 coronation commemorative, published by Illustrated London News 35.00

Creamer, china, 1937 coronation commemorative, Aynsley, 4" h. 25.00

Egg cup, china, 1937 coronation commemorative, portraits of King George & Queen Elizabeth...............15.00

Handkerchief, 1937 coronation commemorative, King George & Queen Elizabeth 25.00

Mug, porcelain, 1937 coronation commemorative, by Midwinter 75.00

Newspaper, "Illustrated London News," 1937 Coronation Week issue 55.00

Plate, china, commemorating King George VI & Queen Elizabeth's visit to the United States, depicts British coat-of-arms, 1939............................35.00

Plate, clear pressed glass, 1937 coronation commemorative 125.00

Rattle, celluloid, 1937 coronation commemorative, red, white & blue, w/portraits, musical, 8½" l. 85.00

Stamps, 1937 coronation commemorative, England, 60 stamps, complete set........................85.00

ELIZABETH II (1952-)

Album, 1953 coronation commemorative, 95 pp. 50.00

Book, 1953 coronation commemorative, published by Illustrated London News 35.00

Coloring book, 1953 coronation commemorative 15.00

Cracker tin, commemorating the 1959 opening of the St. Lawrence Seaway, Prince Philip & Queen Elizabeth..28.00

Cup & saucer, china, 1953 coronation commemorative, Johnson Brothers ...35.00

Mug, china, commemorating 1959 royal visit to Canada, Shelley China 75.00

Pin tray, china, 1953 coronation commemorative, Staffordshire 25.00

Pin tray, china, 1977 Silver Jubilee commemorative 19.00

Plate, china, 1953 coronation commemorative, Tuscan Bone China, 4" d. 30.00

Spoon, gold-plated, commemorating 1959 royal visit to Canada 50.00

Toffee tin, 1953 coronation commemorative, colorful portraits of Queen Elizabeth II & Prince Philip.....55.00

ROYCROFT ITEMS

Elbert Hubbard, eccentric entrepreneur of the late 19th century, founded Roycroft Shops and established a craft community in East Aurora, New York in 1895. Individuals were trained in the trades of bookbinding, leather tooling and printing. Craft-style furniture in the manner of Gustav Stickley and known as "Aurora Colonial" furniture was produced. A copper workshop, begun in 1908, turned out numerous items. All of these, along with those pieces of Buffalo Pottery china which were produced exclusively for use at the Roycroft Inn and carry the Roycroft symbol, constitute a special category associated with the Arts and Crafts movement.

Ashtray on stand, hand-hammered copper, slightly domed round foot w/embossed flower supports four tall slender strap legs topped by a dished holder w/an overhead handle w/matchbox bracket & set w/an ashtray, original condition, orb mark, 7½"d., 29¼"h. (ashtray possibly re-patinated).................................$1,100.00

Book, "The Philistine," by Elbert Hubbard, leather covers w/ad pockets, 1907 ....37.00

Rare Roycroft Bookcase

Bookcase, oak, a rectangular top w/broken-crown deep molding above a frieze band carved w/"Roycroft," above a tall glazed door w/beveled glass flanked by reeded sides above a base drawer w/incised orb & cross marks flanked by shaped foot brackets, original medium finish, Model No. 84, 15½ x 31½", 5'h. (ILLUS.)...........11,000.00

Book ends, hand-hammered copper, decorated w/one large embossed poppy blossom, original dark patina, orb mark, 5½" w., 5½" h., pr. 440.00

Book stand, oak, a rectangular overhanging top above lower shelves w/exposed tenons & keys, metal company tag, 13¾ x 26", 26⅛" h...460.00

Bowl, hand-hammered copper, round w/shallow incurved sides & raised on three small pointed feet, red patina, impressed mark, 10¼"d., 4⅛" h. (traces of brass wash) 440.00

Bowl, hand-hammered copper, deep rounded bulbous sides w/inverted rim, on three small knob feet, original dark patina, orb mark, 10"d., 4¼" h. (some pitting to finish) 330.00

hammered copper, a slender cylindrical shaft on a round poppy blossom-form foot, the bell-shaped socket w/rolled rim, original patina, orb mark, 3¾" d., 8" h., pr. 412.50

Candlesticks, hand-hammered copper, Princess-type, two slender square columns support a dished bobeche & cylindrical candle cup, on a slightly domed rectangular foot, fine original dark patina, orb mark, 8" h., pr. 522.50

Candlesticks, hand-hammered copper, slender cylindrical shaft on a round base, the cylindrical socket w/rolled rim, original patina, orb mark, 4" d., 10" h., pr. 550.00

Candlesticks, hand-hammered copper, tall thin stems twisted above the flat disc base, cylindrical candlecup w/wide rim, dark copper wash, die-stamped orb & cross mark, 5" d., 12½" h., pr. (some wear to patina) 550.00

Chamberstick, hand-hammered copper, the round dished base centered by a candle socket w/wide flat rim, a long flat handle w/curled end extends from rim of socket, original patina, marked, 5¾" d. (minor wear) 110.00

Roycroft Chest of Drawers

Chest of drawers, chestnut, a low backrail between short stiles above the rectangular top slightly overhanging the case w/three long drawers, oval covered pulls, paneled sides, original medium finish, carved "Roycroft" on the backrail, 20½ x 44", 37" h. (ILLUS.) 1,760.00

Compote, open, hand-hammered copper, footed deep rounded bowl w/flattened flared rim, the sides stamped w/wide arched panels, original patina, orb mark, small dent at rim, 9" d., 3½" h. 330.00

Conference table, Mission-style, extension-type, oak, round top slightly overhanging a deep apron above six heavy octagonal legs ending in large ball feet, made for the Roycroft Inn, minor restoration to finish & color, unmarked, 84" d., 30" h. 4,400.00

Console set: 11" d., 3" h. closed-rim bowl & pair of candlesticks; acid-etched silvered copper, the candlesticks w/slender square shafts on domed square base, a cylindrical socket w/a wide squared & flared rim, all w/orb mark, 3 pcs. ..275.00

Desk set: calendar, pen tray, letter rack, letter opener, ink blotter & pad w/four corners; hand-hammered copper, each piece w/an overall hammered design, original patina, orb mark, blotter pad 10 x 21", the set 742.50

Dining chairs, Mission-style, oak, the narrow slats in the back between tall rectangular stiles, the top slat w/an impressed orb mark, tacked-on hard leather seat insert, square tapering legs w/rungs, original color & leather, added varnish, Model No. 27, 37" h., pr. 715.00

Humidor, cov., copper, smooth cylindrical body, domed cover w/inverted pear finial, original reddish patina, orb mark, 5¼" d., 8¼" h. 110.00

Roycroft Desk Lamp

Desk lamp, a mushroom-shaped hammered brass shade raised on a hammered brass slender shaft w/flaring base, original patina, orb & cross mark, 5" d., 14" h. (ILLUS.) 935.00

Lamp, table model, the round shade w/a low pyramidal hammered wood-grained copper top above the flat copper rim pierced w/long rec-

copper rim pierced w/long rectangular panels lined w/mica, raised on a slender square paneled copper pedestal on a paneled flat rectangular foot, original patina, orb mark, 8" d., 15" h. 1,210.00

Roycroft Table Lamp

Lamp, table model, a hammered copper domical shade w/riveted strapwork framing mica sections, raised on a slender hammered copper shaft on a disc foot, impressed mark, Model No. 902, cleaned, 10" d., 15" h. (ILLUS.) 1,430.00

Lamp, table model, hand-hammered copper & leaded glass, the 18¼"d. conical shade of bright apple green leaded glass w/a checkered band of lavender around the rim, raised on an ovoid copper base w/a riveted narrow band & oval ring handles, on a flaring round foot, green plastic light switch pulls, marked, 22½" h...6,050.00

Mirror, wall-type, oak, plain flat rectangular sides w/hanging hooks & chains at the top, original dark finish & hardware, unmarked, 23 x 29"..660.00

Rocking chair without arms, oak, the tall back w/a flat crestrail above five vertical slats, tacked-on leather seat, original medium finish, orb & cross mark, 19 x 21", 40" h. (ILLUS. top next column) 550.00

Tray, hand-hammered copper, circular body w/flanged incised rim, riveted handles, original dark patina, die-stamped orb & cross mark, 16" d. (some wear)...........................330.00

Tray, hand-hammered copper, heavy gauge, round w/a wide flat rim

Roycroft Rocking Chair

w/'stitched' edge & riveted loop handles, restored dark patina, stamped orb mark, 18½" d...............605.00

Vase, hand-hammered copper, cylindrical, heavy sides decorated w/a band of embossed stylized roses near the rim, die-stamped orb & cross mark, 3" d., 6" h. (repatinated)..605.00

Vase, hand-hammered copper & silver, cylindrical, heavy copper body overlaid in nickel silver w/a stylized band, die-stamped w/orb & cross mark, 3" d., 6½" h. (loss of patina)..825.00

Vase, inlaid copper, cylindrical body w/four full-length angular buttresses, the surface hammered in a wood grain pattern, inlaid w/four small silver squares near rim, die-stamped orb & cross mark, 4¼" d., 8" h. (minor wear to patina)...................2,420.00

Vase, bud-type, nickel silver & glass, Viennese Secessionist style, three narrow metal stems joined at the top by a rim & attached to a slightly domed metal foot, inset w/a long clear glass tube, probably designed by Dard Hunter, Secessionist-style orb mark, 2¾" d., 8½" h. 1,760.00

Vase, hand-hammered copper, tall cylindrical body flared at the base & w/a gently scalloped rim, an incised band w/a cluster of stylized bell-shaped blossoms near the top, original dark patina, orb mark, 3½" d., 9½" h. (minor wear).............605.00

Vase, hand-hammered copper, American Beauty-type, squatty footed base w/riveted shoulder sloping to a cylindrical neck w/widely flaring rim, original dark finish, custom-made w/factory-drilled hole in side for lamp cord, stamped orb mark, 8¼" d., 10½" h. 880.00

Vase, copper, Etruscan-style, footed wide squatty low base tapering to a tall slender cylindrical neck w/flared rim, original dark patina, minor pitting, stamped orb mark, 9" d., 15½" h. 715.00

Vase, copper, Etruscan-style, flattened base & tall flaring neck, covered in a fine & unusual verdigris patina, die-stamped orb & cross mark, 9" d., 15¾" h. 2,310.00

Writing desk, lady's, Mission-style, oak, a thick rectangular top overhanging a wide hinged slant-front w/long hammered copper hinges opening to a fitted interior above a single long drawer w/copper bail handles, on square tapering legs ending in MacMurdo feet, excellent original dark finish, minor wear, orb mark, Model No. 91, 19 x 37½", 44" h. 3,410.00

RUGS - HOOKED & OTHER

HOOKED

Boy in Pony Cart Hooked Rug

Amorous scene of a young blonde-haired maiden galloping away w/her lover on a horse w/the figure of Cupid leading them to a church, the jilted swain in the background carrying a rifle over "Let Love Be Your Guide," worked in brown, light blue, green & maroon stitches, New England, ca. 1925-45, mounted on a stretcher, 30 x 51" $19,550.00

Basket of pansy-like flowers in the center in rich solid colors on an intense blue ground, within an oval border of similar flowers & an outer black border, made by Susie Lopp-Glick, Leola, Lancaster Co., Pennsylvania, ca. 1943, 24 x 39" 220.00

Basset hound puppies, a comical row of five tan puppies w/details in green, yellow & black, ca. 1940-50, 22 x 35" 2,070.00

Bear, standing animal in navy blue-black on a grey ground w/a pink border, 22 x 32½" 577.50

Blacksmith shop scene, a square blacksmith shop w/a large white horse being shoed in the center background, a wagon, boy & a dog in the foreground, worked in various dark colors, 32 x 34" 291.50

Boy in pony cart center scene, crocheted yarn edge, rich colors, early 20th c., 17 x 33" (ILLUS.)........330.00

Cat & flowers, central figure of a white cat, enclosed by a leafy floral border & corner medallions, worked in pink, blue & green on a variegated grey ground, 19th c., 39 x 46" 3,850.00

Children, boys & girls at various activities such as marbles, roller skating, jump rope & a tea party, lettered at bottom edge "APPROPRIATE GAMES" and in the upper corners "FOR BOYS" and "FOR GIRLS," worked in various tones of beige, pink, blue, grey & red fabric, ca. 1930, 33¼ x 49¼" (some minor stain) 4,400.00

Cottage scene w/windmill, pond & road flanked by flowers, worked in multicolored yarns, wide black cloth binding, 25½ x 36½" (some wear & small holes)....................................175.00

Floral bouquet center surrounded by meandering vines w/blossoms & leaves, the whole within a scalloped rose blossom border, worked in bright tones of red, blue, green, beige & brown shirred fabric, New England, early 19th c., 4'1" x 5'2" 7,425.00

Floral gridded blocks (48), room-size, scarlet, peach & sepia floral bouquets on a cream ground, w/pale green sashing w/cream scrolls & peach roses at all crosspoints, w/pale green border, late 19th - early 20th c., 9' 10" x 13' 9½" 2,750.00

Florals, runner-type, composed of alternating rows of colored quatrefoils alternating w/sytlized blossom heads all within a dark band border, worked in browns & blues w/other colors, 30 x 80" 605.00

Florals, an oval floral bouquet in a central medallion framed by long leafy scrolls flanking smaller floral clusters, worked in browns, mauve, pink, blue, lavender & off-white on a beige ground, 38 x 72" 440.00

Flowers in Pot Hooked Rug

Flowers in a pot, large rose-like blossoms on leafy stems, similar blossoms in lower corners, various colors, 19th c., minor loss, 32 x 40" (ILLUS.) 880.00

Foxes, two white-tailed foxes, one seated & the other standing & looking at the viewer, in an open landscape w/leafy trees & fir trees, worked in tones of beige, green, black, lavender & white, early 20th c., 32¼ x 55" (some minor stains) 1,150.00

Geometric design, worked in red, yellow, green, beige, black & pink fabric in an optical Baby Blocks pattern, late 19th - early 20th c., 53½ x 85¼" (some minor wear)....2,875.00

Geometric design, worked in tones of beige, grey, salmon pink, red & black fabric in a Log Cabin pattern of concentric squares, late 19th c., 53½ x 89½" (some minor wear)....1,955.00

Geometric design, room-size, concentric diamonds composed of herringbone bands worked in green, beige, black, blue & pink fabric, all within a striped border, late 19th - early 20th c., 11 x 15'....................5,175.00

Horse & dogs, worked in beige, red, slate blue & black fabric, at the center the figure of a stylized horse, having an abstract symbol in the center, w/four red legs & tail, flanked by two small dogs, a heart, stars, a pair of shoes & clover leaf devices, the whole within beige corners, late 19th c., mounted on a stretcher, 37 x 44" (some fabric loss & wear) 13,225.00

Horses, large prancing horses flanking a three-story house w/trees, w/diamond border, initialed "M.M." above the horses, worked in red, green, yellow, blue & brown fabric, New England, third quarter 19th c., 3'4" x 5'¾" 3,575.00

Landscape scene, worked in brown, green, blue, grey, white, red & pink, the view centered by a gambrel-roofed house amid trees & a flagpole, a river scene on the left & a road & church on the right, the whole within a black border, probably New England, early 20th c., 33 x 64½" 2,300.00

Man on horseback smoking a pipe, worked in red, beige, brown, black & blue fabric, a parrot in the upper left & a cat in the upper right & a large red & blue dog below, probably Pennsylvania, late 19th - early 20th c., mounted on a stretcher, 40⅜ x 41¾" 1,840.00

Paisley Design Hooked Rug

Paisley design, square form composed of bold swirls worked in purple, green, violet, red & gold depicting stylized leaves & four peacock plumes, the corners w/stylized foliate designs, surrounded by a slate blue border, late 19th - early 20th c., several repairs, 94½" sq. (ILLUS.) 4,180.00

Parrot, 'Waldoboro' style, so-called for the town of Waldoboro, Maine where the style was originally developed, worked in bright green, red, maroon, beige & lavender fabric depicting the central figure of a red parrot w/glass eye perched on a leafy branch, the corners w/blossoms & leafage, executed in a tufted technique, w/a braided brown wool border, mounted on a stretcher, Maine, late 19th c., 28 x 44" 2,300.00

Parrot, worked in beige, pale blue, green, red & black fabric, at center the figure of a small stylized & exuberantly depicted red & orange parrot standing on one foot, surrounded by stylized blossoms & foliage, probably New England, early 20th c., 24½ x 73¼" (some wear & fading)..................................460.00

Pennsylvania-German motifs including potted tulips, stars, hex signs & distelfinks worked in orange, slate & navy blue on red & black fabric, Pennsylvania, late 19th c., 35 x 61" 920.00

Stag in stylized angular landscape, the large animal w/a button eye in the foreground w/a cottage & pointed mountains in the background, worked in various colors, 23 x 38" 275.00

The Three Bears, Momma, Pappa & Baby Bear dressed & marching in a row carrying bowls of porridge, worked in brown, green, red, pink & beige, wide dark border bands, late 19th - early 20th c., 28½ x 44" 1,725.00

Trout, the large fish surrounded by wavy water worked in shades of purple, blue, cream, green, brown, beige & red within a dark rectangular border, late 19th c., 18½ x 32" (minor fading, some wear) 467.50

OTHER

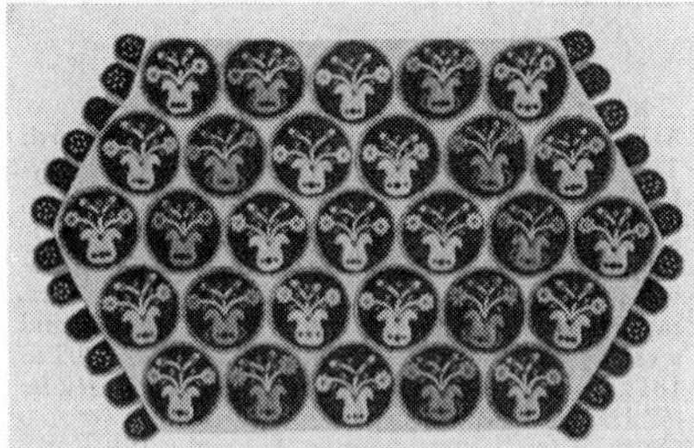

Unusual Penny Rug

Penny rug, the center composed of small wool discs in olive green, green & maroon, the corners in red filled w/floral embroidery, 28 x 46" (wear, holes, repairs) 187.00

Penny rug, unusual design composed of brightly colored red, yellow, green & pink wool & flannel patches arranged in a pattern of circles each containing a vase of flowers, all stitched on a hexagonal pink cotton ground bordered w/embroidered scallops, late 19th c., some minor wear, 29 x 48" (ILLUS.) 2,588.00

Penny table rug, composed of wool appllique discs in shades of red, yellow, orange, green, blue, tan & brown, late 19th - early 20th c., 25¾" w., 61" l. (ILLUS. top next column) 825.00

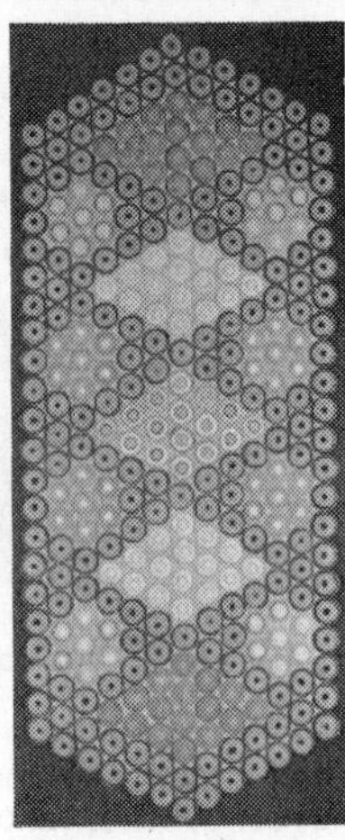

Penny Table Rug

Shirred rug, a four-petal blossom surrounded by a mosiac roundel in the center flanked by scattered diamonds & heart-shaped blossoms on leafy stems in each corner within chain-link & sawtooth border bands, worked in red, green, beige & blue, 19th c., 27 x 42" (some fabric loss) 920.00

Shirred wool, long rectangular form w/the center panel decorated w/a variety of stylized flowers, the narrow border band w/a running blossom & vine design, worked in shades of blue, red, green, brown & cream wool, 19th c., 29 x 62" 2,750.00

Wool carpet, room-size, Art Deco design of overlapping fanned shell-like motifs in shades of green, ca. 1930s, 9'1" x 11'9" (wear) 1,100.00

Wool felt rug, wide pointed ends & sawtooth sides, composed of small embroidered & appliqued diamonds in colorful designs of four-petal flowerheads or pinwheel & ball devices against a black felt ground, 23 x 34¼" 385.00

Wool & wool felt table rug, composed of red, brown, yellow, green, beige & blue fabrics w/the figures of two small horses flanking a spray of roses, surrounded by a field of concentric layered circles appliqued on a beige ground bordered by scalloped red & brown wool & wool felt borders, mounted on a stretcher, New England, third quarter 19th c., 23 x 33" (some fabric loss & wear) 1,725.00

Woven carpet, room-size, Aubusson, pale celadon field w/polychrome floral sprigs overall within a narrow bead border, open saffron outer border, France, Charles X period, ca. 1825, 5'11" x 7'8" (minor repairs & rewoven areas) 5,750.00

Woven pile rug, room-size, Rose &

Ribbon patt., the rose ground filled w/floral sprigs enclosed by ribbon & vine borders, within an outer interlaced & ribbon-entwined border, 11'10" x 17' 2,420.00

Woven rag rug, room-size, cotton material woven in bands of lavender, magenta & cranberry, 20th c., 10 x 12' 1,610.00

Woven Rag Rug

Woven rag rug, room-size, woven in irregular stripes in tones of maroon, green, navy blue, yellow & brown, possibly Amish, Pennsylvania, late 19th - early 20th c., 6' 4" x 14' 2" (ILLUS. of part) 3,738.00

Yarn-sewn rug, a large snowflake device in the center framed by a large, wide flower wreath above the inscription along the bottom edge "Augustine W. Phillips," worked w/bronze, brown, green, yellow, blue & pink fabric, probably Pennsylvania, ca. 1830, 4' 6" x 5' 2" (some fraying & fabric loss) 13,800.00

SALESMAN'S SAMPLES

The traveling salesman or "drummer" has all but disappeared from the American scene. In the latter part of the 19th century and up to the late 1930s, they traveled the country calling on potential customers to show them small replicas of their products. Today these small versions of kitchenwares, farm equipment, and even bathtubs, are of interest to collectors and are available in a wide price range.

Axe head, "Keen Kutter" $350.00

Clothes boiler, copper, oblong............175.00

Egg carrier, "Star Egg Carrier," wooden, dated April 15, 05, 1½ x 3½ x 4½" 18.00

Furnace, "Sunbeam," in original carrying case 775.00

Hat, w/original tin box, "Dobbs," excellent condition 30.00

Miner's lunch pail, nickel-plated brass, by Lisk...390.00

Pitch fork, "Diamond Edge," w/decal ..450.00

Refrigerator, "General Electric Home-Freezer Refrigerator," white plastic, w/card reading "Your General Electric Home-Freezer Refrigerator will be along soon," in cardboard box (card w/soiling & aged corners) 38.50

Sample Signboard

Signboard, wood w/reverse-painted on glass advertisements in red on a black background & gold lettering, in original carrying case, overall flaking & discoloring of lettering, 12" w., 24" h. (ILLUS.) 88.00

Buck Junior Cast Metal Stove

Stove, kitchen range-type, "Buck's Stove & Range Co.," cast metal, 20" l., 18½" h. (ILLUS.) 500.00

Stove, kitchen range-type, "Karr," blue porcelain & nickel-plated cast iron, highly detailed down to the tiny pot holder..4,950.00

Early Smith Corona Typewriter

Typewriter, "L.C. Smith & Corona Typewriters, Inc. - Syracuse, New York," flip-top mechanism, w/original carrying case, soiling, minor wear (ILLUS.) 44.00

Early Washing Machine

Washing machine, "A. & D. Shultz, Reading, Pa.," hand-crank model, wood slat-sided tub w/metal bands mounted in a framework w/metal crank mechanism, late 19th c. (ILLUS.) 160.00

Washing machine wringer, "Star," cast iron, embossed markings "Pat. Oct. 19, 1875, Nov. 2, 1875, July 3, 1877," 14" l., 11" h. (very minor rust)..55.00

SCALES

Balance scale, countertop, brass, the projecting arms supporting two circular dished trays, balancing on a columnar standard, fitted w/a lift, on a black-painted weights box w/drawer, signed "Jones & McDonald," New York, first half 19th c., overall 21" h. $1,265.00

American-Made Balance Scale

Balance scale, countertop, brass, w/two projecting arms supporting two circular dished trays, the columnar standard fitted w/a crank, on a circular base, marked "Henry Troemner, MAKER, Philadelphia," first half 19th c., 30¾" h. (ILLUS.) 2,875.00

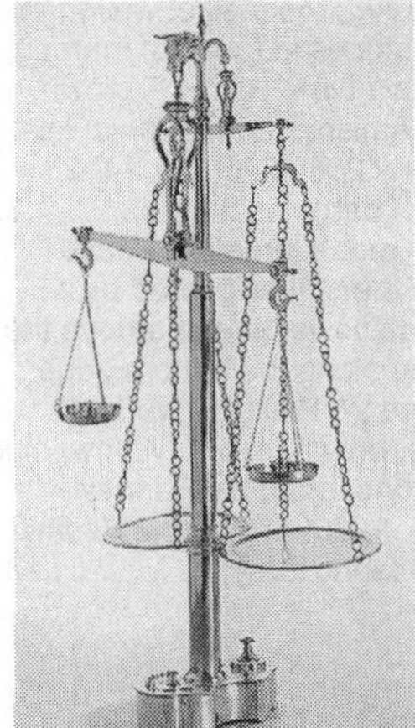

English Balance Scale

Balance scale, countertop, brass, columnar stem w/a figural ox head finial above pairs of small & large arms each supporting circular trays, the shaped base fitted to hold fifteen graduated weights, variously impressed w/letters, England, late 19th c., overall 5'7" h. (ILLUS.) ...12,650.00

Balance scale, countertop, oak & marble w/weights & brass pans, 9 x 21", 8" h.......................................60.00

Candy scale, countertop, brass, visible mechanism, ornate trim, "Brandford," 3 lb. 300.00

Candy scale, countertop, brass, "Computing Scale Co., Canada," 5 lb. 200.00

Candy scale, countertop, cast iron w/bronze trim, "IBM Canada," 2 lb. ..200.00

Coin-operated sidewalk scale, lollipop-type, porcelain, "Watling".....800.00

Egg scale, "Jiffy-Way," mint in box.......30.00

Gold scale, brass, original red paint w/black label w/eagle & "Miners Improved Gold Scale. Manufactured expressly for California, Germany," in oval tole case, 7¼" l. (some wear)...192.50

Gold scale, mahogany frame, glass case, drawer w/ivory pulls, Henry Troemner, 10 x 20", 20" h. 650.00

Jeweler's scale, oak w/marble top & glass lid, Henry Troemner, 7 x 14", 7½" h. 200.00

Jeweler's scale, w/six weights, Eastman Studio scale, made by Kodak (avoirdupois weight) 95.00

Milk scale, brass, "Forschners," mint in box 90.00

Platform Scale with American Shield

Platform scale, countertop, brass & glass, an upright brass fan-shaped frame around the scale chart above a large blue & white painted American shield, on an oblong platform base w/a scroll-cast apron & legs, restored, 2 lb., 9" l., 10¼" h. (ILLUS.) 357.50

Toledo Platform Scale

Platform scale, countertop, green porcelain w/brass trim, upright fan-shaped face in white w/black numbers beside the four-prong support for the brass pan, marked "Toledo," restored, 3 lb., 14" l., 14½" h. (ILLUS.) 121.00

SCIENTIFIC INSTRUMENTS

French Wheel-type Barometer

Barometer, stick-type, mahogany, the rounded case top above the glass bulb & thermometer, a narrow body w/round wood column enclosing the glass tube, bulbous base pendant, Abraham Optician, Exeter, England, mid-19th c., 37" h. $747.50

Barometer, stick-type, mahogany, the swan's-neck crest above a rectangular bowed glass panel w/engraved 'silvered' register, the long bowed body above an urn-form covered pendant, signed "Cary, London," England, early 19th c., 40" h. 2,530.00

Barometer, stick-type, rosewood veneer, a cove-molded flat pediment above a rectangular glass plate over the dial, long slender case centering a thermometer, round bottom drop, ivory dials, marked "W. Cray Optician, London Bridge," England, 19th c., 37½" h. (glass over thermometer & several pieces of molding missing) 495.00

Barometer, stick-type, walnut, rounded top enclosing the barometer register & a thermometer over a long slender drop framing the tube, ending in a circuar section enclosing the reservoir, E.C. Spooner, Boston, Massachusetts, mid-19th c., 42" h. 220.00

Barometer, wheel-type, Neoclassical style, giltwood, the circular barometer dial at the base & surmounted by a rectangular thermometer all flanked by trailing laurel leaves w/shell-carved cresting, ending in an acorn terminal, Europe, third quarter 18th c., 16" w., 40¼" h. (dial distressed) 1,380.00

Barometer, wheel-type, mahogany, the swan's-neck pediment over a case w/etched steel "Damp/Dry" indicator & thermometer, the base w/barometer dial & maker's signature plate for T. B. Corti, Glasgow, Scotland, George III period, late 18th c., 39" h. 1,870.00

Barometer, wheel-type, painted & parcel-gilt, an oval painted barometer within an oval molded case surmounted by a pair of lovebirds within a laurel wreath perched on a torch & quiver of arrows terminating in ribbon-tied laurel swags, losses to carving, Louis XVI period, France, last quarter 18th c., 20" w., 33" h. (ILLUS.) 1,725.00

Clinometer, brass, in mahogany case, signed "Watkin Clinometer - J. Iticks Maker, London 1896," case stamped "E.R. Watts & Son London," case 9½" l. 230.00

Compass, dip-type, brass, signed "W. & L.E. Gurley - Troy, N.Y.," mid-19th c., 4¾" d. 287.50

Compass, prismatic-type, brass, green printed card, signed "Ellio Bros., Strand London," 3" d. 230.00

Compass, surveyor's, cased brass, dial signed & case labeled "W. & L.E. Gurley, Troy, N.Y.," 19th c., case 7½" l. 770.00

Compass, surveyor's, brass, cased, Europe, 19th c., case 8" l. 172.50

Compass, surveyor's, in mahogany case, dial signed "Richard Patten, New York," case w/partial paper label, 19th c., case 14½" l. 690.00

Compass, surveyor's, in mahogany case, dial signed "William J. Young, Philadelphia," case labeled, complete w/Jacob's staff & survey chain, second quarter 19th c., case 15½" l. 862.50

Compass, surveyor's, cased brass, dial signed "Hagger & Brother, Baltimore," w/Jacob's staff, mid-19th c. 1,045.00

Compass, surveyor's, mounted in a mahogany case, marked by B. Pike and Sons, New York, early 19th c. 546.00

Microscope, brass, "Bausch & Lomb," Serial No. 11, double pillar Y base, ca. 1880 ....525.00

Protractor, brass, vernier-arm-type, signed "Messer, Lond," 6" d. 144.00

Sighting level, surveyor's, cased brass, marked "Chas. Schott maker, Nashville," mid-19th c., 14½" l. 412.50

Sighting level, surveyor's, cased brass, signed "Stackpole & Brother, New York," w/tripod base, mid-19th c. 467.50

Sundial, wooden, painted markings & decoration, metal gnomon, 19th c., 7⅛" sq. 440.00

Telescope, w/two interchangeable lenses, on tripod, Bardou & Son, Paris, France, in mahogany case, 35¾" l., tripod 63½" h....................1,430.00

Thermometer, silver & ivory, the domed oval base w/four paw feet applied w/a collar of foliage & shells & fitted w/an elephant tusk mounted w/an engraved silver register & glass thermometer, both curved to follow the tusk, marked on base & numbered "10755-1568," Tiffany & Co., New York, ca. 1885, 10" h.....1,150.00

Universal equinoctial dial, engraved & silvered brass, the hinged silvered chapter ring w/signature of maker, W & S Jones, Holborn, London, & w/folding gnomon w/latitude scale above a compass within a glazed case, on adjustable leveling feet, together w/a velvet-lined leather case w/printed label "Gedney King, Mathematical Instrument Maker No. 29 State Street, Boston," late 18th - early 19th c., 5" l., 2 pcs...............1,495.00

SCOUTING ITEMS

Scout rules and regulations, handbooks and accouterments have changed with the times. Early items associated with the Scouting movements are now being collected. A sampling follows.

BOY SCOUT

Award pin, adult, sterling silver, "Silver Beaver," mint in box......................$125.00

Book, "Boy Scouts Motorcycles," by Ralph Victor, 1911, illustrated by Mendel, Platt and Rich......................20.00

Book, "Boy Scouts of the Air in the Lone Star Patrol," by Gordon Stuart, 1916, Reilly and Britton......................18.00

Book, "Projects for Scouts," by the Rural Scouting Service, 1947 ....10.00

Book, "Stories of Boy Scouts Courageous," by Franklin Matthews, 1944, D. Appleton and Company.......15.00
Calendar, 1958, illustrated by Norman Rockwell, 16 x 33" 55.00
Coin, commemorative, 1950 Jamboree 25.00
Craft kit, 'Beadcraft Outfit," Official Boy Scout, complete with instructions..28.00
Cutlery set, folding-type, knife, fork & spoon, wire handles, George Schrade Knife Co., 1942-46, in leather case, the set 30.00
First aid kit, tin, dated 1928, w/unopened contents........................40.00
Handbook 1929-30 ....23.00
Handbook, 1937 ....35.00
Handbook, 1948 ....15.00
Handbook for Scoutmasters, 1947.......18.00
Handkerchief, souvenir, 1960 Colorado Jamboree 30.00
Hat, Scout master's, w/box dated 1942 (box rough) 50.00
Match holder, metal tube w/ screw cap 20.00
Merit badge sash, w/26 Merit badges, ca. 1930s 32.00
Neckerchief, Cub Scout, 1950s 12.00
Neckerchief, souvenir, 1937 National Jamboree 40.00
Neckerchief, souvenir, 1953 National Jamboree 20.00
Neckerchief, souvenir, 1957 National Jamboree 20.00
Neckerchief slide, brass, embossed w/George Washington & Boy Scouts, ca. 1930 ....24.00
Sheet music, "The Boy Scout Dream," 1915 ....20.00
Uniform, 1950 yellow Valley Forge patch, Eagle Order patch & Leader's patch, ca. 1940s 125.00
Wrist watch, marked "Boy Scouts of America, National Council, New York," 1930s 175.00
Wrist watch, Cub Scout model, 1950s 75.00

BROWNIE SCOUT

Equipment catalog, 1954.....................10.00
Handbook, 1954 ....8.00
Uniform, 1940s 14.00

CAMPFIRE GIRLS

Sheet music, "Camp Fire Girls March," 1916...16.00
Uniform, w/moccasins, satchel & picture of owner wearing it in 1918 ..200.00

GIRL SCOUTS

Book, "Blue Book of Policies & Procedures," paperback, 1931 ....25.00
Canteen, tin w/cloth cover 15.00
Cup, folding-type, 1950s.........................5.00
Diary, 1954 ....5.00
Handbook, "Leader's Nature Guide," 1942 ....5.00
Handbook, "Weather Handbook," 1942 ....5.00
Handbook, 1958 ....7.50
Hat, beret-style, 1950s 8.00
Pin, depicts Girl Scout w/blonde hair wearing a hat & scarf, plastic, ca. 1950 ....50.00
Sheet music, "Girl Scouts Together," 1949 ....5.00
Uniform, khaki-colored cloth, 1920s 50.00
Uniform, leader's dress, w/emblems & badges, 1930s 50.00

SCRAPBOOKS & ALBUMS

Album, photograph, miniature-type, red leather cover, w/21 tintypes.....$150.00
Album, photograph, brown-embossed cover decorated w/celluloid leaves, berries & bird's nest w/eggs, gilded edges, includes 28 tintypes, 42 pp., 2 x 5 x 6" 85.00
Album, photograph, celluloid cover decoration w/roses, contains many Victorian photos, velvet stand..........195.00
Album, photograph, leather-bound, beveled glass insert in cover w/reverse-painted scene of Romeo & Juliet, brass latch, photos included, overall 6 x 7½" (spine damage, overall wear) 40.00
Album, photograph, leather & gilt covers w/twin clasps, containing a collection of Civil War cartes de visite, including several Civil War officers, 1860s 395.00
Album, photograph, papier-maché & lacquer, the cover decorated w/a scene of a peasant girl carrying pails of water through a dark forest, Russia, ca. 1885, 12" l. 690.00
Album, photograph, cover w/scene of a young girl & mother playing piano, stenciled floral velvet base, holds cabinets, tintypes & cartes de visite...145.00
Album, photograph, printed velvet fabric cover w/mirror, brass corners, ornate mirrored stand, Victorian 165.00
Album, postcard, Halloween, Santas, early views, Winsch's, Tuck's, signed artists, etc., set of over 400 cards 300.00
Album, postcard, containing 49 views of Yellowstone National Park, dated 1920...75.00

Album, Victorian trade cards including blacks, 32 pp. 245.00

SCRIMSHAW

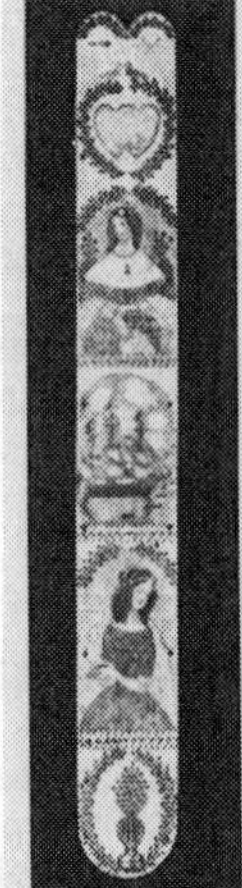

19th Century Corset Busk

Scrimshaw is a folk art by-product of the 19th century American whaling industry. Intricately carved and engraved pieces of whalebone, whale's teeth and walrus tusks were produced by whalers during their spare time at sea. In recent years numerous fine grade hard plastic reproductions have appeared on the market so the novice collector must use caution to distinguish these from the rare originals.

Corset busk, engraved whalebone, rounded ends, engraved w/a full-length portrait of a woman, "Zerviah," an American man-of-war passing a lighthouse & a fort, early 19th c., 13" l. $880.00

Corset busk, engraved whalebone & baleen, decorated w/a three-masted ship, fashionable ladies, floral wreaths, birds & Cupid's bow in red, green, blue, sepia & black inks, back w/baleen engraved w/similar designs, loss of heart-shaped inlay, 19th c., 14½" h. (ILLUS.) 3,450.00

Ditty box, cov., miniature, engraved whalebone & pine, finger-lappet construction, the fitted lid w/a painted pine top, the sides delicately engraved w/a two-masted sailing ship, a trumpeting angel & a large seven-bay clapboard house, fastened w/five delicate cut diamond-head fingers, probably New Bedford, Massachusetts, ca. 1840, 3 x 4", 1¾" h.......................6,900.00

Horn book, whalebone, red & black letters, heart-shaped handle, 4¼" h. 632.50

Porpoise jaws, carved w/ships under sail & a church, 19th c., 14¾" l. 302.50

Walrus tusk, decorated along its length w/a giraffe, elephant, leopard, native huts & a three-masted sailing ship, 19th c., 17" l. (some wear) ...1,760.00

Whale's tooth, carved w/a two-masted sailing ship & a fashionable lady, 19th c., 4½" h. (small age cracks)....715.00

Whale's tooth, the side engraved w/a scene of a three-masted ship w/American flag, 4½" l. 852.50

Whale's tooth, etched on one side w/a lone maiden under a berried branch standing next to a furled American flag & holding in one hand her handkerchief & in the other her pocket, both w/red pigment; the other side w/a ship sinking under the stars, a winged trumpeting angel & a sailing vessel, mid-19th c., 4¾" h...805.00

Whale's tooth, engraved w/a scene of a fashionable lady, 19th c., 5½" h. (losses at tip) 495.00

SEWING ADJUNCTS

Pincushion-Spool Stand Combination

Darning cotton holder w/pincushion on lid, Mauchline ware, round, decorated w/roses & forget-me-nots decal J. & P. Coats label.................$38.00

Darning egg, cased glass, red, white & blue, ca. 1890, 2¾ x 4"................175.00

Pincushion, advertising, "Success Manure Spreaders," tin w/cloth insert 95.00

Pincushion, dressmaker's, monogrammed linen cover, 22" d. 45.00

Pincushion, flattened silk-embroidered ball w/pink, green, yellow & white silk stitches on an overall stitched black silk ground, probably New England, early 19th c., 2½" d. 1,380.00
Pincushion, sterling silver, model of a lady's high-heeled slipper w/cloth insert, marked "Sterling," 3½" l. (cloth insert worn) 110.00
Pincushion, pink velvet, model of a strawberry w/green felt leaves, 2¾" d., 4¾" h. 85.00
Pincushion-spool stand, exotic woods w/ivory fittings, two tiers w/central domed pincushion, sailor-made, imperfections, late 19th c., 10" h. (ILLUS.) 715.00
Sewing box, carved & painted wood, rectangular lid w/carved pear handle, the front facade w/a beehive flanked by vines & grape clusters, old brown paint, on bun feet, probably New England, 19th c., 12 x 19½", 13" h. 1,150.00
Sewing box, poplar, cylindrical w/flat extending rim at base & top, cover w/turned handle, original yellow varnish & red & black stenciled decoration w/arrows & foliate designs, 9" d., 7" h. 605.00
Sewing chest, mahogany, w/hinged lid, divided fold-out compartments, Norway, extends to 40", 23" h., ...95.00
Sewing chest, painted pine, constructed in the form of a miniature tall chest of drawers, the rectangular molded top above two short & three graduated long drawers continuing to a scalloped apron on bracket feet w/black striping on a red ground to simulate rosewood, the top w/original pincushion, New England, mid-19th c., 4 x 11", 13½" h. 805.00
Spool cabinet, "J. & P. Coats," oak, two-drawer, 1920s 255.00
Stiletto, ivory 18.50
Tape measure, brass, model of a turtle, ca. 1890s 75.00
Tape measure, celluloid, figural Indian boy 115.00
Tape measure, celluloid, figural Mammy 165.00
Tape measure, celluloid, model of a bear standing on all four feet 57.00
Tape measure, celluloid, model of a Scottie dog & pup 62.00
Tape measure, nickel-plated brass, model of a turtle, w/script writing "Pull My Head But Not My Leg" 225.00
Tatting shuttle, sterling silver, relief floral decoration 125.00

SHAKER ITEMS

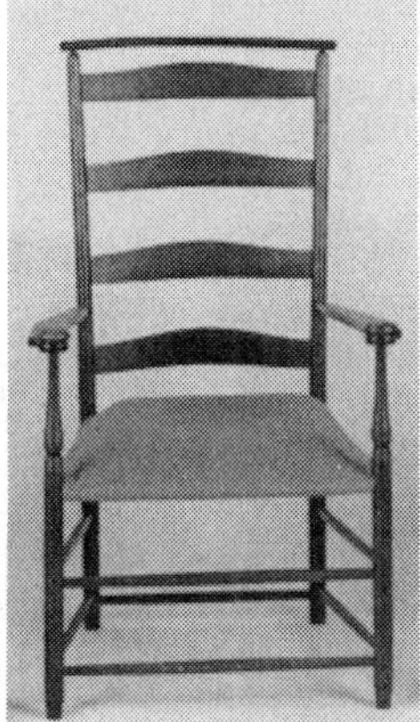

Shaker Armchair

The Shakers, a religious sect founded by Ann Lee, first settled in this country at Watervliet, New York, near Albany, in 1774 and by 1880 there were nine settlements in America. Workmanship in Shaker crafts is an extension of their religious beliefs and features plain and simple designs reflecting a chaste elegance that is now much in demand though relatively few early items are available.

Armchair, a round crest bar about four slightly arched slats in the back between simple turned stiles above the flat & shaped open arms w/mushroom handgrips above baluster-turned arm supports, replaced cloth seat, simple turned legs joined by double rungs in the front & sides & s single rung in back, model No. 6, Mt. Lebanon, New York, 1880-1920 (ILLUS.) $880.00
Basket, round, woven splint, wrapped rim, Sabbathday Lake, Maine, 16" d., 7¾" h. plus bentwood handle (minor damage) 198.00
Blanket chest, pine, rectangular top opening to a well w/large till w/dovetailed drawer, molded base, bracket feet, Mt. Lebanon, New York, 16½ x 37½", 18" h. (refinished, back feet have glued repairs, minor edge damage).............................1,320.00
Box, cov., painted round bentwood, single-lappet on cover & triple-lappets on base, old dark bluish green paint, 10½" d. (minor wear & age crack in lid band).......................495.00
Box, cov., painted oval bentwood, double lappet on base, original vivid putty graining in tones of tobacco-amber & yellow, the top banded in

mint green & black & ornamented w/hand-lettered serified writing in black, "Sugar," Maine Community, ca. 1835, 10 x 13¾", 4½" h. 4,025.00

Butter churn, stave construction w/wooden bands, worn old red paint, Mt. Lebanon, New York, 14½" h. plus dasher (handle damaged) 247.50

Candlestand, cherry, circular top above an expanding cylindrical standard on a tripod base w/spider legs, underside signed "Made by Thomas Hammond - Annie W (illegible) 1883," Thomas Hammond, Jr., 1791-1880, Harvard, Massachusetts, 17" d., 27" h. 6,050.00

Chest of drawers, pine, rectangular top w/molded edge above a case w/seven graduated long drawers, shaped apron, bracket feet, a New Hampshire community, early 19th c., 36" w., 6' 2" h. 4,400.00

Shaker Cupboard & Chest of Drawers

Cupboard w/chest of drawers, walnut, a rectangular top w/a cove-molded cornice above a single four-panel cupboard door above a mid-molding over a case of four long drawers w/wooden knobs, simple bracket feet, attributed to Daniel Baird, Union Village, Ohio, ca. 1832, 19 x 39½", 8'½" h. (ILLUS.) 11,000.00

Dipper, bentwood, cylindrical w/turned wood handle, painted ochre, 5½" d. plus handle (imperfections)..............220.00

Foot warmer, walnut, dovetailed case w/ball feet, tin-lined interior w/whale oil lamps, worn black velvet covering on top, wire bail handle, Mt. Lebanon, New York, 7 x 8" 275.00

Goblet, walnut, low foot w/short stem supporting the cylindrical bowl w/ring-turning at base, slightly flaring lip, together w/a letter stating it was purchased from Sister Clark & Eldress King, Canterbury, New Hampshire, in 1954, 4¼" h. 137.50

Grater, punched tin, half-round punched tin section attached to a wooden backboard, Mt. Lebanon, New York, 29" l. 49.50

Ladder, painted wood, nine rounded rungs flanked by slender side rails, labeled "L.A. Shepard, Canterbury, N.H.," 12" w., 9' 1" h....................1,650.00

Mule chest (box chest w/one or more drawers below a storage compartment), child's, pine, rectangular top w/slightly overhanging edge lifting above a deep compartment over a single long drawer w/turned wooden knob, bracket feet, original red stain, Canterbury, New Hampshire, 16¼ x 33¼", 24¾" h.....................8,250.00

Music sheet, double-sided, ink on paper, marked "Shaker tune No 1" & "Shaker tune No 2" on one side & "Jeffersons Liberty" on the reverse, attributed to Enfield, Connecticut Community, 19th c., framed, 7½" l., 3½" h...863.00

Pantry box, cov., bentwood, oval, two lappet construction in base & single-lappet on cover, base carved w/initials "E.R.," painted ochre, 5½" l. 3,575.00

Pen wiper, composed of a bisque doll w/grey felt dress & pink ribbon, Sister Mildred, Sabbathday Lake, Maine, 2⅜" h. 110.00

Pincushion, maple, large green velvet cushion mounted on a maple screw stand on a circular base, 10½" h. (incomplete) 770.00

Rocking chair, child's, maple, the cylindrical stiles w/turned acorn finials centering the three arched slats above a woven seat, on cylindrical front legs w/rounded tops, joined by cylindrical box stretchers, late 19th - early 20th c., 28½" h. (left rocker replaced) 345.00

Rocking chair without arms, ladder-back type, three curved & gently arched slats between plain turned stiles w/turned acorn finials, paper rush seat, turned legs joined by double stretchers on front & sides & single stretcher at back, refinished w/red stain, size No. 3, Mt. Lebanon, New York, 33" h. (new paper rush seat) 220.00

Rocking chair w/arms, maple, a slender rod crestrail above a tall ladder back w/four slightly arched slats above flat shaped arms on baluster-turned arm supports flanking the old tape seat, double rungs at the front & sides, original surface, Model No. 6, New Lebanon, New York, 43" h. (some surface abrading)..747.50

No. 7 Shaker Rocker

Shaker rocker w/arms, a slender shawl bar at the crest above four slightly arched slats between simple stiles, flat shaped arms w/mushroom handgrips above baluster-turned arm supports, replaced tape seat, simple turned legs joined by double rungs in the front & sides & a single rung in the back, original surface, model No. 7, Mount Lebanon, New York, 1880-1930, minor repairs, 34" h. (ILLUS.) 747.50

Shaker Sewing Steps

Sewing steps, painted wood, three-tier open steps w/solid sides & an open back w/brace, original chrome yellow paint, mid-19th c., 13¼ x 13¼", 17¼" h. (ILLUS.) 2,090.00

Sewing table, painted finish, the rectangular top w/shaped three-quarter gallery above a conforming case fitted w/a single short drawer, on square tapering legs, painted red, 18⅛ x 18½", 29¾" h. 2,530.00

Side chair, tilting-type, maple, the three arched slats flanked by rounded cylindrical & steam-bent stiles w/bulbous acorn finials, over a trapezoidal caned seat on tapering cylindrical legs, the rear fitted w/wooden ball-in-socket tilters, joined by seven cylindrical box stretchers, possibly Enfield, New Hampshire, ca. 1850, 42½" h. 1,380.00

Storage box, cov., oval, maple & poplar bentwood, triple lappet construction, New England, 19th c., 6½ x 9½", 4" h................................259.00

Birch Shaker Table

Table, birch, rectangular top w/breadboard ends widely overhanging an apron w/a single long drawer w/small wooden knob, on turned & tapering legs w/knob feet, old shellac finish, inscribed under top in pencil, probably Canterbury, New Hampshire, early 19th c., 17¼ x 27½", 24½" h. (ILLUS.) 9,350.00

Table, cherry & birch, rectangular top overhanging a deep apron w/single drawer w/turned wooden knob, on square tapering legs, old shellac finish, probably Canterbury, New Hampshire, early 19th c., 18 x 26", 26" h. (imperfections)...................1,650.00

Tea kettle, cov., tin, canted sides & sloping shoulder, straight spout, cover w/squared handle, wide swivel handle, Mt. Lebanon, New York, 7" h. plus handle (old soldered repairs)...165.00

Wood bin, poplar, rectangular narrow top above sides slanting out to frame the opening, turned pegs added to ends, layers of old worn paint, Union Village, 19 x 35", 38¼" h...385.00

SHEET MUSIC

Also see ADVERTISING ITEMS and CHARACTER COLLECTIBLES.

"The Perfect Song"

"Amelia Earhart's Last Flight," by McEnery, 1939....................................$23.50
"The Burning of Rome," by E.T. Paull...25.00
"The Continental," 1934, by Conrad & Magidson, from "The Gay Divorcee," Fred Astaire & Ginger Rogers on cover 30.00
"Dat Lovin' Rag," by Smally & Odar, 1908 ....20.00
"Der Fuehrer's Face," 1942, by Oliver Wallace, Donald Duck & Hitler on cover 22.00
"Girl of Mine," 1917, by Harold Freeman, cover by Rolf Armstrong 17.00
"I've Lost You, So Why Should I Care," 1916, by Richard Howard, photo of Theda Bara on cover 26.00
"The Little Ford Rambled Right Along," 1914, by Fay Foster & Byron Gay 5.00
"The Midnight Fire Alarm," 1900, by Harry J. Lincoln & E.T. Paull, cover by E.T. Paull.............................25.00
"Napoleon's Last Charge," 1910, by Edward Ellis, battle scene on cover by E.T. Paull 30.00
"Oh, Mr. Man Up in the Moon," from "Dimples," Shirley Temple on cover..35.00
"On the Good Ship Lollipop," 1934, by Sydney Clare & Richard Whiting, from "Bright Eyes," Shirley Temple on cover 16.00
"The Perfect Song," 1929, by Clarence Lucas & Joseph C. Brill, musical theme of the Pepsodent Hour, photo of Amos & Andy on cover, very minor soiling (ILLUS.)......27.50
"Princess Pocahontas March & Two-Step," 1903, w/cover photo 35.00
"Roosevelt the Peace Victor," 1905, w/Theodore Roosevelt on cover 55.00
"Short'nin Bread," 1928, by Jacques Wolfe, pictures mammy 20.00
"Silver Sleighbells," 1906, by E.T. Paull, cover by E.T. Paull...................32.00
"The Song of the Alumnae Albany Female Academy," 1850s 40.00
"The Storm King," March Galop, 1902, by E.T. Paull, cover by E.T. Paull 29.00
"Texas Roundup in The Spring," 1935, pictures cowboy & horse..........18.00
"We'll Stand by the Flag March," by E.T. Paull, colorful cover by E.T. Paull 95.00
"When I Grow Up," 1935, by Edward Heyman & Roy Henderson, from "Curly Top," Shirley Temple on cover 16.00

SIGNS & SIGNBOARDS

Cow Brand Baking Soda Ad

Apothecary, gilded zinc, in the form of a mortar & pestle, 19th c., 28" h. (imperfections) $522.50
Baking soda, "Cow Brand Baking Soda," printed cardboard, a colorful picture of a brown & yellow cedar waxwing bird on a branch, wood-grain-style border w/white lettering, Church & Dwight Co., ca. 1918, very minor soiling, 11 x 14½" h. (ILLUS.) 88.00
Beer, "Champagne Velvet Beer," tin on cardboard, rectangular, comic color scene of an older fisherman carrying a fry pan & box of beer & tiptoeing away from his campsite as skunks explore his creel, 14¼ x 19¼" (some paint chipping & pitting)..88.00
Beer, "Iron-City Tech Beer," printed cardboard, designed as a scoreboard in black & yellow

w/inning numbers & highlights in white, red & blue lettering across the center reading "Iron-City Tech Beer - Every Taste a Treat - Sensation of the Year," 18 x 25" (very minor bent corners)....................................77.00

Bootmaker's Trade Sign

Bootmaker, painted metal, made as a fully dimensional lady's boot w/an articulated top & vamp & a small boot near the top, painted black, flaking & pitting, probably American-made, 19th c., 9" w., 14" h. (ILLUS.) 460.00

Self-framed Grape-Nuts Sign

Breakfast cereal, "Grape-Nuts," self-framed tin, a color scene of a young girl wearing a cape & walking beside a large St. Bernard carrying her book bag, printed across the bottom "To school well fed on GRAPE-NUTS—"There's a Reason," wide molded gold self-frame, minor wear, early 20th c., 20¼" w., 30¼" h. (ILLUS.) ....1,200.00 to 1,300.00

Butcher shop, carved & painted pine & gesso, model of a large realistically-carved pig, painted a reddish pink w/an iron corkscrew tail, suspended on wrought-iron hooks, early 20th c., 30" l., 15" h..3,450.00

Camera film, "Kodak Verichrome Safety Film," porcelain, made to resemble a box of film in yellow w/black print & a red check bottom border, double-sided, 24¼" l., 12½" h. (edge wear, scratches & some flaking) 220.00

Candy, "Raspberry Charms," lithographed paper, black background w/red & green lettering, a tipped box of red raspberries & a package of the candy on the left side, text reads "Raspberry - a specialty 'tasty' one of the eleven luscious flavors of Charms," "Made by Charms Co., Newark, NJ," framed, 12¾ x 22¼" (very minor crease marks along edge) 220.00

Candy, "Whitman's Chocolates," porcelain, long rectangular form w/dark green ground printed w/white lettering reading "Agency - Whitman's Chocolates and Confections - Since 1842," white border band, 39½" l., 13½" h. (minor chipping, scratches, rust & edge wear) 132.00

Champagne, "Korbel Sec California Champagne," painted metal, a scene of a young woman w/her brown hair pulled back into a bun holding a large cluster of grapes at the left, a large bottle to the right, lettering reads "Korbel Sec California Champagne - Fermented in the bottle," framed, 13 x 19".........203.50

Chocolates, "Ox-Heart Chocolates & Cocoa," painted tin, rectangular, yellow, cream, blue & red embossed lettering on a dark blue ground w/red border, round Ox-Heart logo w/cherries to the side in red, green, blue & yellow, 4½ x 19½" (very minor paint scratches) 147.50

Nebo Cigarettes Cardboard Sign

Cigarettes, "Nebo, the Gloriously Good Cigarette," cardboard, blue & yellow lettering above woman in scanty costume & jewels, water staining, piece missing by "N" in "Nebo," frame has scratches & chips, 22" w., 30" h. (ILLUS.) 180.00

La Preferencia Cigar Sign

Cigars, "La Preferencia Cigar," lithographed paper, pretty woman dressed in red, white & yellow lettering, impressed lettering in frame at bottom, minor creases & watermarks, minor soiling, 25" w., 35" h. (ILLUS.) 1,600.00

Clothier, "Ethan Allen - Clothier," die-cut painted tin, cut-out figure of a smiling fat man standing on a rectangular box, printed across his front "Delighted with the Clothes Sold By" & on the box "Ethan Allen Clothier - Marshall," green & white w/black lettering & trim, 12" w., 35¾" h. (overall paint loss & scratches) 330.00

Porcelain Coal Sign

Coal, "C.F. & I. Coals - for More Heat!," porcelain, rectangular, red & black lettering & three red devils w/black buckets of coal in one corner, red border, minor chipping at mounting hole, 20" l., 9" h. (ILLUS.) 313.50

Cobbler, "John Newman," painted wood, the cobbler's name above a depiction of a man's boot & a lady's high button shoe over "Made and Repaired," late 19th c., 13½" w., 39¾" h. 990.00

Concrete company, "Rhode Island Concrete Co. - 3 Custom House Street," porcelain, rectangular w/a wide dark blue border w/white block lettering, the center w/a brown & white rectangular reserve w/a scene of two men pushing a roller on a sidewalk, 13 x 21" (overall scratches & chipping) 429.00

Dog food, "Melox Dog Foods," porcelain, a blue background w/a large white & black standing terrier above a red ball printed "Melox Dog Foods," printed across the bottom in white "The Foods that Nourish," 18" w., 26" h. (edge chipping, minor scratches) 825.00

Drug company, "Evergreen Drug Co.," reverse-painted glass, white ground printed w/"Prescriptions - Compounded Exactly as Your Doctor Orders" over a logo above "Evergreen Drug Co." across the bottom, lettering in blue & logo in red, gold, black & blue, golden border & lettering at bottom, wooden frame, 18" l., 12" h. (minor scratches & paint flaking) 44.00

Exterminating product, "Common Sense Exterminator - Kills Rats and Roaches," painted tin, black ground w/pink & cream lettering, a rectangular reserve in the lower right w/a black gentleman rat walking upright & wearing a top hat & dress coat while reading a newspaper, black rat in pink coat, 7½ x 8¼" (nail hole in center, minor denting & overall rust) 165.00

Farm implements, "John Deere Quality Farm Implements," painted tin, rectangular, black ground w/large red & golden yellow lettering, a central square featuring a leaping stag in yellow & black, 48" l., 18" h. (minor paint chips) 385.00

Sleepy Eye Flour Sign

Flour, "Sleepy Eye Flour & Cereals Free - If Not The Best - Ask the Man," lithographed die-cut tin, profile portrait of Chief Sleepy Eye, real tassel suspended from the tip of his headdress feather, imperfections, 13½" h. (ILLUS.) 1,650.00

Flour, "White Rose Flour," painted wood, rectangular, sky blue ground & painted white lettering reading "White Rose Flour Bakes Better Bread," white molded frame, 74" l., 26" h. (scratches, overall light paint loss) 412.50

Gasoline, "Texaco," porcelain keyhole style, round upper section w/large red star w/green "T" below "Texaco" in black, lower rectangular section in white w/black lettering "L.G. Johnson - Consignee," 11" w., 12½" h. (minor staining of red, soiling) 330.00

Hotel Schenley Sign

Hotel, "Hotel Schenley - Pittsburgh," porcelain, rectangular, white lettering on a black ground band across the top above a pale blue ground w/the hotel in shades of orange & black below black lettering "On Lincoln Highway at Schenley Park," also "Garage" in lower corner, edge wear, chipping, top corner bent, 27½ x 60" (ILLUS.) 1,320.00

Ice cream, "Banquet Ice Cream," reverse-painted glass, rounded-front, white ground w/gold & red lettering reading "We Serve Banquet Ice Cream - Inviting - Delicious," red & pink ice cream in a dish & a soda in the center, early 20th c., 23" w., 37" h. (scratch across one letter) ..1,320.00

Ice cream, "Borden's Ice Cream," painted metal w/flanged end, rectangular, double-sided, red & white background, a large yellow daisy framing Elsie the Cow's head at the left, "Borden's Ice Cream" in contrasting colors to the right, 24" l., 15" h. (minor fading & chipping & staining) 330.00

Sonny Ice Cream Cones Sign

Ice cream cones, "Sonny Sugar Cones - 5¢," lithographed cardboard, color bust portrait of a smiling boy & orange & blue ice cream cone on the right w/blue lettering on white in the center, framed, very minor wear, 9½ x 20½" (ILLUS.) 137.50

Insurance company, "City of New York Fire Insurance Company," painted embossed tin, rectangular, red & gold lettering on a black ground, a large oval reserve in the center w/a skyline of New York City, 25" l., 18" h. (minor scratches & denting) 302.50

Kitchen ranges, "Wrought Iron Range Company," lithographed paper, rectangular, a color design w/the brand at the top center above a large factory vignette, smaller factory & stove vignettes around the sides in pink, yellow, blue & green, early 20th c., in a wooden frame, 16½ x 22½" (soiling, crease marks)..330.00

Locksmith Trade Sign

Locksmith, "Yale," carved & painted wood, model of a large key inscribed "Yale - Yale & Towne Mfg. Co. - Stamford, Conn. U.S.A. - Yale," early 20th c., 16 x 42" (ILLUS.).....2,875.00

Medicine, "Pepto-Bismol," die-cut cardboard in a bottle shape, pink w/black cap & red & black lettering, reads "Pepto-Bismol - For Upset Stomach...Controls Common Diarrhea," 10⅞" w., 27¼" h. (soiled, edge wear) 49.50

Optician, wood, model of a large pair of wire-rimmed eyeglasses, yellow & gold around spectacles framing large blue eyes w/pink trim, 54" l., 15" h. (soiling, minor paint loss & cracking) 880.00

Paint, "Martin-Senour Paints and Varnishes," die-cut cardboard stand-up type, cut-out three-quarter length portrait of a painter standing wearing a cream-colored cap & jacket & brown pants & pouring red paint out of a bluish green can, cream-colored wording beside him reading "Top to Bottom - 100% Pure," box-form panel across the bottom printed in blue w/"Martin-Senour - Paints and Varnishes - Sold Here," 24½" w., 38½" h. (edge wear, one taped spot on bottom) 198.00

Paint, "Sapolin," hardboard canvas, rectangular w/three oval reserves w/portraits of Lincoln, Washington & Theodore Roosevelt against a dark ground, a small plaque below the portraits reads "This frame is gilded with Sapolin gold enamel - Mfg. by Gerstendorfer Bros. N.Y., U.S.A.," in a wide gilt plaster frame molded w/a scrolling leaf band & molded on the inner liner "SAPOLIN," early 20th c., 21" l., 13½" h. (soiling, very minor cracking on frame) 71.50

Patent medicines, "Dr. D. Jayne's Family Medicines," reverse-painted glass, silver & foil lettering on a black ground, gold inner border, wooden frame, 21¾" l., 11½" h. (minor scratches & paint loss) 121.00

Planters Peanuts Sign

Peanuts, "Planters Salted Peanuts," die-cut tin, counter-type, a figure of Mr. Peanut at each end flanking a rectangular block w/"Planters Salted Peanuts - Only Genuine When Sold in Our Trade Mark Bag" (ILLUS.)..1,650.00

Radio, "RCA Victor Radio," print, black & white design w/Pierrot & Pierrette balancing on opposite ends of a seesaw sign above a 1920s radio cabinet, a box w/type between them & another box of type in the lower right, framed, 8¾ x 10¾" (wrinkles in print, chips on frame) 33.00

Railroad crossing, porcelain, white cross w/black lettering mounted w/white reflectors, 41" h. (minor wear) 121.00

Razor, "Keen Kutter," cardboard, rectangular, a three-quarter length portrait of a man shaving on the left side, a razor in the upper right, advertising down the center w/"Always Ready to Shave - The Razor That Fits The Face - Keen Kutter...," black & red lettering, early 20th c., 20¾" l., 10¾" h. (crease in one corner, small dent mark) 33.00

Columbia Grafonola Sign

Record player, "Columbia Grafonola," painted tin, rectangular, a young man & woman on the left w/a floor model grafonola on the right, "Columbia Grafonola - "Don't get up - it stops itself - The Non-Set Automatic Stop is only one of many exclusive features on this Modern Phonograph - Chas. W. Norton - Farmington, Maine," yellow ground w/green, blue, black, red & brown, overall scratches, scuff marks, minor paint loss, early 20th c., 17½ x 23½" (ILLUS.) 220.00

Refrigerators, "North Star Refrigerators," porcelain, rectangular, crossed scrolls up the sides & a large star near the top, reads "Agency For North Star Refrigerators - The Indiana Manufacturing Company - Peru, Indiana," blue & white lettering on red, blue & yellow ground, 8" w., 16" h. (overall touch-up)..165.00

Shoes, "The Friendly Five - $5," porcelain, shield-form w/black ground & yellow trim & profile portraits of two colonial gentlemen shaking hands beside a large shoe over "Widths AAAA to EEEE," black & yellow lettering, very minor rust at edges, 18 x 24" (ILLUS. top next column) 346.50

Friendly Five Shoe Sign

Shoes, "Hamilton, Brown Shoe Co.," lithographed paper, a colorful scene in pastels of George & Martha Washington dancing, printed across the top "Hamilton, Brown Shoe Co. - Keep The Quality," the company emblem between the dancers' feet & printed in script across the bottom "American Lady Shoe - American Gentleman Shoe," late 19th - early 20th c., 29¾" w., 39¾" h. (creases, wear, minor staining) 231.00

Soft drink, "Barq's," painted tin, rectangular w/embossed white & red lettering reading "Drink Barq's - 'It's Good,'" bottle to the right, all on a dark blue ground w/cream & red border, 11⅝" x 29½" (minor rust, wrinkled, bent corner, scratches, soiling) 82.50

Soft drink, "Fruit bowl," painted metal flanged-type, a large bottle to the left on a yellow ground, "Drink Fruit Bowl" in red, green & cream, dark green border, 1950s, 18½" l., 14" h. (overall minor scratches) 143.00

Soft drink, "Green River," painted tin, rectangular, silhouetted scene of the sun setting over a long jungle river, embossed orange lettering reading "Green River - In Bottles," green & blue ground, red & black border, ca. 1920, 12 x 19½" 209.00

Hires Root Beer Sign

Soft drink, "Hires," painted metal, rectangular, cartoon-like figure of a man holding a bottle, printed "Drink Hires - It hits the Spot - Try a bottle and you'll buy a case," yellow ground w/blue border & red letters, rust around mounting holes, minor scratches, bottom left tip of corner gone, early 20th c., 9 x 16" (ILLUS.) 302.50

Soft drink, "Moxie," die-cut tin on wood, half-length portrait of the Moxie Man pointing at the viewer above a rectangular signe reading "Drink Moxie," white letters on red w/a yellow border, 12" w., 12½" h. (overall scratches & paint loss) 143.00

Soft drink, "Nehi," painted tin, rectangular, bottle in oval reserve at the right in cream, red & blue, "Drink Nehi," w/name in oversized letters at the left, red letters on yellow ground w/a green & red checked border, 45" l., 18" h. (warped, scratches) 82.50

Spark plugs, "AC Spark Plug," die-cut painted metal, flange-type, a round circle at the top framing a cartoon horse standing & taking a shower in a bath tub, square lower section w/rounded corners reads "Registered - A.C. Spark Plug Cleaning Station," cream & red at top, blue ground w/yellow, red & cream below, 10½" w., 15¼" h. (very minor scratches, bent corner) 220.00

Stove polish, "The Rising Sun Stove Polish," color lithographed paper, a large interior scene of a young woman standing & holding a handwritten letter thanking her husband for the stove polish, delivery boy in the background, a black maid seen through the kitchen door in the background, the letter dated "July 1879," woman wearing a pink dress, maid in blue & white, matted & framed, 23 x 29½" (minor soiling) 1,430.00

Tavern, "Doty Tavern," carved & oil painted on wood, decorated w/images on both sides in an oval w/"T. Doty" in gilt lettering below, the panel within a molded edge & flanked by baluster-turned stiles, suspended from wrought-iron spiral-turned hooks, overall 42½" w., 50" h., including suspension 70½" h. (weathered, including paint loss) 6,050.00

Telephone, "Public Telephone," flange-mounted porcelain, round w/a circle w/white letters framing a center picture of an early desk-top telephone, early 20th c., 16" d., 16" h (minor chipping) 385.00

Telephone Office Sign

Telephone office,"Telephone Office," porcelain, oval w/arrow across the center w/the Bell System logo for Southern Bell, blue & white, minor scratches, 21½ x 32½" (ILLUS.) 467.50

Tires, "Armstrong Tires," painted tin, rectangular, red ground w/yellow & black-outlined yellow lettering reading "Unconditionally Guaranteed -Armstrong Tires," 23 x 35" (overall paint chipping).........33.00

Mayo's Plug Tobacco Sign

Tobacco, "Mayo's Plug," porcelain, rooster standing on a tobacco crate, blue lettering, chipping around mounting holes, 6½" w., 13" h. (ILLUS.) 375.00

Washing machine, "The Maytag - The Way to Her Heart," die-cut metal, flange-type, the die-cut heart center w/a color picture of the Maytag washer, red ground w/yellow & black lettering & brown washer, ca. 1920s, 17" w., 18" h. (ILLUS. top next column) 8,800.00

Watchmaker, carved & painted wood, depicting a large open-faced pocketwatch w/Roman numerals & winding stem at top, old weathered surface, New England, late 19th c., 21" d., overall 29" h. 1,540.00

Maytag Washer Sign

Watchmaker's Sign

Watchmaker, trade sign, reverse-painted glass, model of a large reverse-painted double-dial pocket watch w/Arabic numerals & centering the name "W.D.Hebert," set into a gilt-painted iron frame marked "C.W.T. Co.," ca. 1915, 35" h. (ILLUS.) 374.00

Whiskey, "I.W. Harper Whiskey," vitrolite, a colorful scene of the interior of a log cabin w/hunting items, a hunting dog & a large bear skin hanging on the wall all printed on milk glass, titled "Here's Happy Days," copyrighted in 1909, framed, 24½ x 30½" 825.00

Wine, "La Salle Wines," self-framed tin on cardboard, an evening scene w/a young woman wearing a red dress seated on a moonlit terrace, light blue lettering reads "Preferred by thousands - LaSalle Wines," ca. 1930s, 11 x 14½" (scratches in upper right & around edges)................165.00

Work clothes, "Sweet-Orr Pants - Shirts

- Overalls," painted tin, rectangular, yellow ground w/black letters, a cream square in the center w/two teams of men in a tug of war, white panel w/black lettering across the bottom reads "P.A. Stief and Sons - 9-15 N. Oak St. - Mt. Carmel, Pa.," 72" l., 48" h. (minor denting, rust spottings & scratches) 148.50

SILHOUETTES

Silhouette of a Family

These cut-out paper portraits in profile were named after Etienne de Silhouette, Louis XV's unpopular minister of finance and an amateur profile cutter. As originally applied, the term was synonymous with cheapness, or anything reduced to its simplest state. These substitutes for the more expensive oil paintings or miniatures were popular from about 1770 until 1850 when daguerreotype images replaced the vogue. Silhouettes may be either hollow-cut, with the head cut away leaving the white paper frame for mounting against a dark background, or the profile itself may be cut from black paper and pasted to a light background.

Bust portrait of a gentleman facing right, wearing a high-collared jacket & high-collared shirt, heavy ink & gold wash trim, in a flat rectangular black lacquer frame w/oval gilded liner, 4½ x 5¼" $467.50

Bust portrait of a man, hollow-cut, facing right, his hair tied in a queue, black silk backing, old molded frame, 4¼ x 4⅞"...............................247.50

Bust portrait of a young man facing left, hollow-cut, wearing a high-collared jacket, back marked "Edward Bowman, April 28, 1848," in dark beveled wood frame, 4⅜ x 4⅝" 192.50

Bust portrait of a youth, hollow-cut, facing right, embossed label "Museum" (stamped backwards, Peale Museum), inscribed in ink "Papa, H.A.M.," framed, 5½" w., 7' h. 247.50

Bust portrait of Napoleon cut-out in black velvet & framed by a needlework wreath, mounted on satin, narrow giltwood frame labeled "Alice VanLeer Carnick," overall 8⅝ x 9¼" h. (some wear & stains) ...247.50

Bust portrait of a young woman facing left, hollow-cut, her hair pulled back & up into a large bun, in a beveled wood frame, 5 x 6¾" 137.50

Bust portraits of a lady & gentleman, hollow-cut, she facing right her hair pulled back into a large bun & w/ink & water-color trim showing an Empire style gown w/puffed sleeves & a narrow white collar, he facing left & w/ink & water-color trim showing a high-collared jacket & tall white collar, in similar embossed brass rectangular frames w/oval openings, early 19th c., 4½ x 5⅛", pr...715.00

Family group portrait, depicting Dr. Hugh Caldwell in an elaborate frock coat & his wife wearing a flounced & embroidered gown, posed w/their two small children, a dog & pot of flowers, free-cut black paper w/bronzing mounted on white paper w/wash, by William J. Hubard, ca. 1828, framed, 12 x 19" (ILLUS.) ...3,220.00

Full-length portrait of a man, standing & facing left, wearing a long jacket, white brushed details, ink wash landscape background, in an early bird's-eye maple veneer frame w/gilded liner, early 19th c., 13¾ x 15¾" 522.50

Full-length portrait of a young lady, facing right, her hair pulled back into a bun & w/side curls, wearing a flounced dress, brushed gilt & polychrome gouache detail, initialed "F.R.," in beveled bird's-eye maple frame w/gilt liner, early 19th c., 10¾ x 14¾" 880.00

SNUFF BOTTLES & BOXES

The habit of taking snuff (powdered tobacco meant for inhaling) began in 17th century France and reached its peak during the 18th century, spreading to England, elsewhere on the Continent, and even to China, probably introduced there by Spanish or Portuguese traders. In Europe, tightly hinged porcelain or metal boxes were considered desirable containers to house the aromatic snuff. Orientals favored bottles of porcelain or glass, or carved of agate, ivory or jade. By mid-19th century the popularity of snuff declined.

BOTTLES

Finely Carved Ivory Snuff Bottle

Clear glass five-color overlay, seal-type, of flattened teardrop shape, decorated in yellow, blue, red, green & brown w/a scene of birds & butterflies flying over flower vases & vessels, w/a cat on one side, all on a clear ground, Yangzhous School, China, 1800-50 ....$1,150.00

Enameled copper, flattened round body, decorated w/colorful Oriental figural scenes, 2½" h. 126.50

Ivory, carved in high-relief w/nine *fu* lion pups, each w/bushy mane & tail, chasing beribboned brocade balls around the sides, all on a scrolling wave ground, between *ruyi* & key-fret borders, the underside w/a black incised four-character mark, the matching cover w/a lotus blossom, Qianlong mark & period, China (ILLUS.) 13,800.00

Jade, rounded form, well-carved white stone w/two monster-mask & mock-ring handles, China..........................920.00

Overlay glass, carved through the opaque amberish yellow overlay to the translucent amber ground w/a clambering *chilong* on each side, the oval footrim also carved from the yellow overlay, China, 1750-1850..1,265.00

Overlay glass, spherical fruit form, the tomato red body carved through overall w/white trailing clouds, the green glass stem & spoon centered on a fruit collar, the base incised w/a four-character Qianlong seal mark, China, Qianlong Dynasty, 2" h....63,000.00

Rock crystal, carved on each side w/pierced rockwork & pine boughs, China, 1800-80 ....1,035.00

Soapstone, stylized relief carving, brown shaded to white, 3" h.............60.50

BOXES

Snuff Box with Dog Scene

Agate, shaped oval form, the body of mottled brown agate, the cover w/a gold border chased w/foliage & scrolls, molded thumbpiece, probably England, ca. 1750, 2¾" l. 3,738.00

Birch bark, flattened oval form w/the hinged cover engraved w/designs & German inscriptions, 4" l. (some wear) 93.50

Enamel, modeled in the form of a finch, w/red face & yellow beak, brown wings, the hinged base decorated w/flowers on a white ground, South Staffordshire, England, ca. 1770, 2¼" h................805.00

Enamel, modeled in the form of a head of an Ethiopian, the hinged cover decorated w/a courting couple in a garden setting, w/gilt-metal mount & thumbpiece in the form of a flowerhead, the base decorated w/a flowerspray, the interior of the cover decorated w/a flowerspray, the interior of the cover decorated w/a rural landscape, Continental, late 18th c., 2½" h. 2,300.00

Gold, shaped rectangle w/canted corners & molded rims, the hinged cover engraved w/a coat-of-arms & helm within an elaborate foliate scroll cartouche enclosed by a reeded border w/flowerheads at each corner, the base engraved w/a crest within an elaborate foliate scroll, scalework, rocaille & ribbon cartouche, the interior cover w/an engraved presentation inscription dated April 14, 1747, maker's mark

"FN," probably for Francis Nelme, George II period, London, England, ca. 1740, 2⅝" l. 13,200.00

Gold, vari-colored, engine-turned, the hinged cover chased w/a reserve of vari-colored flowers on a matted ground, the corners similarly decorated, Switzerland, ca. 1815, 3⅜" l. 2,300.00

Gold & enamel, oval, enameled overall in sky blue, the cover enameled w/a miniature of cupid w/a young lady bordered by pearls, cover edged w/pearls, Switzerland, late 18th c., 2¾" l. 5,463.00

Gold & enamel, oval, enameled translucent orangish yellow over an engine-turned ground, the cover mounted w/a miniature of a lady w/putti, Switzerland, ca. 1780, 2¾" l. 3,788.00

Gold & enamel, the cover enameled w/a lion attacking a deer & w/foliage on a cream ground, the border enameled w/birds & foliage on a translucent green ground, the lobed sides & base similarly enameled, the interior of the cover enameled w/a doe on a blue ground, surrounded by foliage, Persia, 19th c., 3¾" l. 10,350.00

Papier-maché, round, the top decorated in polychrome w/a scene of revelers in a gentleman's club, England, 4³⁄₁₆" d. (craquelure, minor loss) 660.00

Porcelain, all-white, the base molded as a wicker basket w/loop handles at the ends, the cover w/a rose surrounded by two daisies, an acorn & leaves, the rim & cover rim w/a contemporary reeded silver mount (wear), Mennecy, France, Paris discharge mark for 1750-56, date letter "K" for 1750 & unclear maker's mark, ca. 1750, 2½" l. 1,035.00

Purpurine & micro-mosaic, oval, the hinged cover set w/a micro-mosaic of a female hound w/her pups, the male hound standing beside her, in original leather case, Rome, Italy, ca. 1810, 3½" l. (ILLUS.)..............6,325.00

Silver, flattened oval form, the lid machine-tooled in the center w/a rayed sun design & w/a narrow leaf edge band, indistinct marks, 3" l. 203.50

Wood, carved in the form of a Pug dog w/protruding tongue & bulging eyes, the hinged mother-of-pearl cover w/gilt mounts & shell-form thumbpiece, ca. 1765, 2¾" h. 6,900.00

SODA FOUNTAIN COLLECTIBLES

The neighborhood ice cream parlor and drugstore soda fountain are pretty much a thing of the past as fast-food chains have sprung up across the country. Memories of the slower-paced lifestyle represented by the rapidly disappearing local soda fountain have spurred the interest of many collectors today. Anything relating to the soda fountains of old and the delicious concoctions they dispensed are much sought-after.

APPLIANCES

Malted milk mixer, porcelain, Champion Jr. Mixer, Model K2 -Serial No. M-2316 - Premier Industries Corporation, New York, U.S.A., 17" h. (very minor scratches) $49.50

Malted milk mixer, "Gilchrist No. 22".....95.00

Malted milk mixer, "Hamilton Beach," cream enamel w/polished chrome name plate band, each head w/three-speed setting & independent operation 265.00

Malted milk mixer, "Hamilton Beach No. 18," black porcelain finish..........125.00

Malted milk mixer, "Hamilton Beach No. 33," green porcelain finish.........135.00

ICE CREAM SCOOPS & SERVERS

"Benedict Indestructo No. 4," round, nickel-plated brass, wooden handle, patented July 1928, 10" l. 35.00

"V. Clad Co.," conical w/heart-shaped turn-key, steel w/flat steel handle, patented November 12, 1878, 8" l. 40.00

"Dover Springless Ice Cream Disher," round, nickel-plated brass, wooden handle, patented May 1929, 10" l. 85.00

"Dover Double Slicer," No. D-11, size 20...750.00

"Gem Spoon Company - Trojan," round, nickel-plated brass, wooden handle, patented November 1916, 10¼" l. 50.00

"Gilchrist No. 31," size 10, round nickel-plated brass, wooden handle, patented in 1915, 11" l. (finger wear, dent)..80.00

"Gilchrist No. 31," size 16, round, nickel-plated brass, wooden handle, patented in 1915, 11" l. 35.00

"Gilchrist No. 31," size 20, round, nickel-plated brass, wooden handle, patented in 1915, 11" l. 33.00

"Glad's No. 10," mechanical, 2¾" d., 7" l. 45.00

"Hamilton Beach 31," chromium-plated brass, wooden handle, patented in 1932, 10" l. 40.00

"Hamilton Beach Model 60" 55.00
"Hamilton Beach Model 160B" 27.00
"Keiner-Williams Stamping Co.," conical bowl, steel w/steel wire loop handle, "KW" on ornate wing nut, 1905 patent 40.00
Magic Ice Cream sandwich wafers scoop 295.00
"Mosteller No. 6," removable mechanism 395.00
"New Gem Mfg. Company," round, nickel-plated brass, wooden handle, ca. 1932-40, in original box, 10½" l. 150.00
"United Products Company," banana split scoop, nickel-plated brass, wooden handle, ca. 1930, 11½" l. ....700.00 to 750.00

CONTAINERS & DISPENSERS

Johnston's Hot Fudge Container

Container, counter-type, "Johnston's Instant Hot Fudge," electric, metal w/stoneware lining, hinged cover, silver background & silver lettering on a red & black oval, brown top & base, w/spoon, minor scratches (ILLUS.) 110.00

Hires Punch Bowl

Punch bowl - dispenser, "Hires Rootbeer," pottery, the deep round bowl on a pedestal base, color transfers of the Hires boy holding a foaming mug above the word "Sparkling," etc., "Drink Hires Rootbeer" around the sides, metal spigot on one side, professionally restored, Villeroy & Boch, Germany, early 20th c. (ILLUS.) 22,000.00

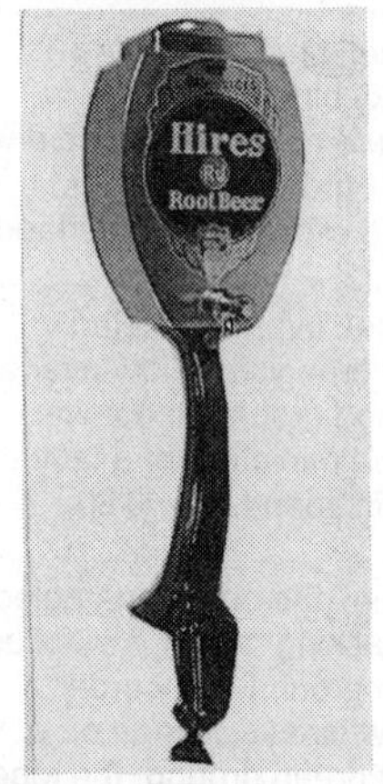

Hires Syrup Dispenser

Syrup dispenser, "Hires Root Beer," metal, the flattened oblong container w/spigot printed in cream & blue "Hires Root Beer," blue handle, metal pedestal w/clamp for attaching to the counter, lettering rubbed off seal, 22" h. (ILLUS.).......................220.00

SOUVENIR SPOONS

All spoons are sterling silver and teaspoon size unless otherwise noted.

Alaska, figural totem pole handle, dated "1916" $49.00
Arizona, Indian figural profile handle, canoe & tent on reverse, "Grand Canyon" in bowl 35.00
Arkansas, full-figure black boy w/watermelon handle, Arkansas Traveler in bowl 95.00
Art Nouveau, patented design of tulips & scrolls handle, "1904" & "Womens Christian Temperance Union" in bowl, 6" 1. ....35.00
Betsy Ross at spinning wheel on handle, "Daughters of the American Revolution" in bowl 85.00
California, bear figural top of handle, "Golden Gate, San Francisco" in bowl 55.00

California, "City of Angels, Los Angeles" on handle, "Mission of San Gabriel" in bowl....45.00

California, Laguna Beach, California & artist's palette on handle, plain bowl....15.00

California, Muir Woods & cut-out redwood tree on handle, plain bowl....15.00

California, Richardson Grove, California & cutout tree on handle, plain bowl....15.00

Camp Grant in bowl, World War I era, figural soldier handle....15.00

Canada, Indian full-figure handle, "Toronto" in bowl....35.00

Colorado, figural woman diver handle, "Glenwood Springs" in bowl....38.00

Florida, alligator figural handle, "Jacksonville, Fl." engraved in bowl....55.00

Florida, orange branch w/full-figure alligator on handle, oranges in gold-washed bowl, Jacksonville, Florida in bowl....55.00

Illinois, Chicago skyline handle, "Masonic Temple" in bowl....65.00

Illinois, Peoria Courthouse & Soldiers Monument in bowl, monogrammed handle....40.00

Iowa, model of a fish handle, "Okaboji" in bowl....50.00

Iowa, rose on handle, bowl engraved "Sioux City, IA"....27.50

Maryland, turtle & seashells figural handle, Baltimore Monument in bowl, Justis & Armiger, Baltimore, 1891....65.00

Missouri, full enameled bowl of "St. Louis Union Station"....125.00

Nebraska, Indian head figural handle, "Crawford, NE" engraved in bowl....85.00

Nebraska, water lily handle, "Wayne, Nebraska" in bowl....35.00

New York, Indian figural profile handle, bow & arrows on reverse, "Niagara Falls" in bowl....35.00

New York, New York City on handle, Brooklyn Bridge engraved in bowl....35.00

New York, Woolworth Building figural handle, "New York" engraved in bowl....20.00

Oregon, figural beaver handle, "Mt. Hood" in bowl....33.00

Oregon, Mt. Hood, Oregon engraved in bowl, beaded handle....30.00

Salem Witch second design, figural witch, crescent moon, rope & cat handle, Daniel Low, ca. 1891, demitasse....125.00

Thousand Islands & side-wheeler in the rapids on handle, engraving of coastline in bowl....35.00

Virginia, figural head of George Washington w/sword, his tomb, monument & the White House on the handle, Christ Church, Alexandria, Virginia in bowl....40.00

Washington state, Chief Seattle figural Indian handle, Mt. Rainier engraved in bowl....30.00

Washington state, figural Indian handle, "Mt. Rainier" in bowl, demitasse....25.00

Washington state, Indian totem pole figural handle, Olympic Range & Seattle engraved in bowl....30.00

SPICE CABINETS & BOXES

Grain-Painted Spice Cabinet

Cabinet, grain-painted, the rectangular case w/sloped hinged lid opening to a deep well, the upper case containing 15 small drawers, the lower portion containing seven small drawers, raised on bootjack feet, grain-painted overall to resemble a more exotic wood, probably Pennsylvania, early 19th c., 6½ x 19", 29" h. (ILLUS.)....$18,400.00

16th Century Spice Cabinet

Cabinet, oak & pine, rectangular top over case w/central door composed of light & dark squares, some w/turned knobs, black bands flanking & at top & bottom, base w/sawtooth design, refinished, some imperfections, possibly Massachusetts, ca. 1700, 7 x 14½", 14¼" h. (ILLUS.) 990.00

Cabinet, painted wood, rectangular top over twelve drawers, on turned legs, old mustard yellow paint, turned pulls, probably New England, mid-19th c., 5¼ x 12", 23¼" h. (minor imperfections) 935.00

Italian Renaissance Spice Cabinet

Cabinet, walnut, Italian Renaissance, rectangular molded top over case w/three long drawers within a beveled molded surround, on bracket feet, 17th c., 14½ x 23", 20½" h. (ILLUS.) 1,100.00

Queen Anne Spice Cabinet

Cabinet, walnut, Queen Anne, bonnet top style, the swan's neck crest w/rosette-carved terminals surmounted by three flame-form finials, the arched paneled door w/lock opening to an interior fitted w/thirteen drawers of various sizes, fluted pilasters flanking, the molded base on ogee bracket feet, Philadelphia area, Pennsylvania, ca. 1755, 10½ x 15", 29" h. (ILLUS.) 51,750.00

Tin box, cov., rectangular, original black paint w/red striping, contains six square canisters w/stenciled labels 104.50

Tin box, cov., round, worn original brown japanning w/gold stenciled "Spices" on side, contains six (of seven) small round spice boxes w/stenciled labels, 7¼" d. 115.50

STANHOPES

Stanhopes are optical novelties, sometimes referred to as "peephole" viewers, that take their name from the English scientist, Lord Charles Stanhope, who developed the tiny (under ⅛" d.) round lens with two convex faces enclosed in a metal tube to enlarge images concealed in bone, ivory or celluloid jewelry and miniatures. Most were designed as souvenir items of various locations such as Niagara Falls, but some held religious images or risque views.

Celtic Cross, carved bone, scene of holy apparition inside $35.00

Charm, barrel-shaped, white plastic, Niagara Falls scene inside 22.00

Charm, binoculars, Graf Zeppelin inside 45.00

Charm, church building, silver-colored metal, Lord's Prayer inside 45.00

Cross, carved simulated wood, St. Anne DeBeaupre Basilica inside 55.00

Cross on chain, silver colored metal w/five rhinestones, Lord's Prayer inside, mint in box 45.00

Needle case, model of an umbrella, carved ivory, photos of Versailles inside 150.00

Manicure set, celluloid, folding-type, w/three implements, pictures of Niagara Falls inside 45.00

Quill pen, carved ivory, St. Anne DeBeaupre Basilica inside 65.00

Ring, man's, aluminum, w/nude scene inside, Victorian 225.00

Ring, man's, w/scene of nude lady on bicycle inside 95.00

STATUARY

Bronzes, and other statuary, are increasingly popular with today's collectors. Particularly appealing are works by "Les Animaliers," the 19th century French school of sculptors who turned to animals for their subject matter. These, together with figures in the Art Deco and Art Nouveau taste, are available in a wide price range.

BRONZES

Figure of a Maiden by Cambos

Alliot, Lucien Charles, figure group of a girl & pheasant, greenish brown patina, inscribed "L'ALLIOT. BRONZE," France, early 20th c., 16 x 31" $1,610.00

Anfrice, C., figures of Semiramis & Cleopatra, standing women in exotic costumes each holding a mirror, on round socle bases w/Egyptian-style designs & titles, signed "Anfrice," silvered patina, 19th c., 15" h., pr. (worn finish) 1,840.00

Bouval, Maurice, bust of a maiden, titled "Poppy," a young woman w/her head raised & eyes closed, large poppy blossoms in her hair w/the stems & large leaf drooping down to her chest, rubbed bronze patina, signed "M. Bouval," France, ca. 1900, 13¾" h.................................8,625.00

Cambos, Jean-Jules, figure of a young maiden standing wearing a low-cut slip & dipping one foot into water, brown patina, signed "J. Cambos" w/a foundry mark, metal label on front of base, France, early 20th c., 30" h. (ILLUS.) 4,313.00

Caussé, Cadet Julian, bust of an Art Nouveau maiden, titled "Violette," the young woman w/long hair raised on a rockwork pedestal w/violet blossoms at her bosom, dark greenish brown patina, signed "J. Caussé," impressed "LU/19" foundry stamp, France, ca. 1900, 22½" h...2,760.00

Chiparus, Demetri, "Dourga," the standing figure of a woman w/outstretched arms, wearing an elaborate beaded costume, her head & hands carved in ivory, silver & gilt patinas, brown & white stepped onyx base, base inscribed "D. Chiparus," ca. 1925, 24⅝" h. (losses to hands) 17,250.00

Colinet, Claire-Jeanne-Roberte, figure of a dancer, the maiden depicted on tiptoe, her arms gracefully raised above her head, her breasts exposed above a swirling skirt, her upper body, head & legs carved from ivory, on a brown onyx socle, inscribed "Cl.J.R. Colinet," ca. 1925, 11⅝" h..7,188.00

De Lotto, figure of a young boy, standing nude on one foot & holding up one leg to examine the foot, brown patina, signed "De Lotto," raised on a marble pedestal, overall 6' h. 5,500.00

Demanet, Victor, figure of an archer, the nude male seated on a rock & bracing one leg against another rock while drawing his long bow, rich greenish brown patina, inscribed "Victor Demanet," stamped "BRONZE - FRANCE," early 20th c., 24" h...2,185.00

Winged Nymph by Drouot

Drouot, Edouard, figure of a winged nymph in a racing position flying w/arms outstretched, medium brown patina, on a stepped marble base, inscribed "E. Drouot," France, ca. 1900,15⅞" h. (ILLUS.) 2,300.00

Garreau, Georges, figure of a reclining nude woman w/a dove, blackish brown patina w/natural highlights, inscribed "g. garreau," on a black Belgian marble base, early 20th c., 16" h...............................1,725.00

Gerome, Jean Leon, maiden & a tiger, a large roaring tiger w/its front paws standing atop a collapsed maiden, gilt patina, France, 19th c., 19" h. (ILLUS. top next page).................8,800.00

Maiden & Tiger by Gerome

Gilbert, A., the dancing figure of a woman in a patterned Harlequin suit painted silver & brown, her face & hands carved in ivory, mounted on a checked pyramidal base in black marble & white onyx, signed "A. Gilbert," France, ca. 1925, 14½" h. 4,888.00

Gruber, A., bust of a maiden, the lovely young woman, her head turned to sinister, w/long flowing hair continuing to the shaped square plinth, a corsage of lilies nestled to her bosom, dark golden brown patina, inscribed "A. Gruber," ca. 1900, 7" h. 575.00

Jennewein, Carl Paul, figure of a nude young boy standing atop a leaping dolphin, brown patina, inscribed "C.P. JENNEWEIN," first half 20th c., 12" h. 5,750.00

Kéléty, Alexandre, model of a seagull, the soaring bird supported by one wing on a stepped Belgian marble rectangular base, rich greenish brown patina, inscribed "KELETY," France, early 20th c., 24¼" h. 575.00

Kuchler, Rudolf, "Nude with Snake," nude young woman standing w/hands clasped beneath her chin, a large snake coiled about her feet, light brown patina, inscribed "R. Kuchler fec.," 16" h. 920.00

Lanceray, Eugene, figure group depicting a peasant man on his sleigh drawn by three horses, signed, Russia, 1872, 12" l. 2,185.00

Landowski, Paul Maximilien, figure group of a tall, hooded woman w/long braids standing behind a small child, polished bronze patina, France, ca. 1925, 21⅛" h. (ILLUS. top next column) 1,495.00

Woman & Child by Landowski

Lavroff, George, model of polar bears, stylized animals in a fighting embrace, on a carved white marble oblong base, inscribed "G. Lavroff" & "1867," silvered finish, ca. 1925, 11½" h. 3,450.00

Mars-Vallett, Marius, figure of Sarah Bernhardt in the role of 'La Princesse Lointaine,' the standing woman wearing a close-fitting openwork headdress, a loose blouse w/full sleeves & open down the front, & a long robe, on a stepped mottled green marble base w/bronze corner mounts, the figure parcel-gilt on the head, arms & chest, inscribed "Mars Vallett" & stamped "G121," impressed w/the Siot-Decauville foundry seal, late 19th - early 20th c., 23¾" h. ...9,775.00

Ofner, Josef, bust of an Art Nouveau maiden, her head raised & her eyes closed, w/large poppy blossoms in her hair & stems trailing down her shoulders, chocolate brown patina, stained wood oval base, signed "J.OFNER," ca. 1900, 13½" h. 2,588.00

Dancer Figure by Paris

Paris, Roland, figure of a dancer, the standing woman dressed in an exotic caped costume w/shell-shaped headdress, painted in red, gold & patterned black, her arms & face carved in ivory, mounted on a hexagonal yellow veined stepped marble base, inscribed "ROLAND PARIS," ca. 1925, some losses to paint, 23⅛" h. (ILLUS.) 19,350.00

Pompon, Francois, model of an owl, the stylized figure w/large eyes & lightly indicated wings, on a shaped base, inscribed "POMPON" & stamped w/the Valsuani foundry seal, brown patina, 7⅛" h. 2,070.00

Pradier, Jean Jacques, "Rebecca at the Well," depicting a maiden nude but for a drape about her hips dipping water in a jug, brown patina, inscribed "J. Pradier - E. de Labroue ft." & dated "1859," 12¼" h...........4,600.00

Resch, Walter Sebastian, figure of a dancer, inscribed "W.S. Resch," rubbed greenish brown patina, Germany, ca. 1920, on wooden socle, 21¼" h. 1,495.00

Tereszczuk, P., figure group "Piggy-back," a young boy in a Commedia d'el Arte costume carries on his back a young girl in costume, carved ivory faces, inscribed "P. Tereszczuk" & a foundry mark, dark brown patina, green marble base, Poland, ca. 1925, 7½" h...............1,150.00

Vienna bronze, model of a dog on a chair 210.00

Vienna bronze, model of a dog w/an umbrella 175.00

Villanis, Emmanuel, bust of a young maiden, head turned w/downcast eyes, a headband in her long hair, on a square flaring base titled "CARMELA," olive & black patinas, signed "E. Villanis," stamped "SOCIETE DES BRONZES DE PARIS" & numbered "2106," ca. 1900, 24¼" h...............................3,680.00

Zach, Bruno, figure of a standing woman in a riding outfit & holding a riding crop in her crossed arms, rubbed golden bronze patina, on a stepped white onyx base, signed "Bruno Zach," foundry stamp "BROMA," Germany, ca. 1925, 26" h...11,500.00

MARBLE

Bazzanti, figure of a boy, standing in front of a tree stump wearing a jacket, shirt & kneebreeches, holding a bouquet in one hand, Florence, Italy, 19th c., signed, 44¾" h...4,950.00

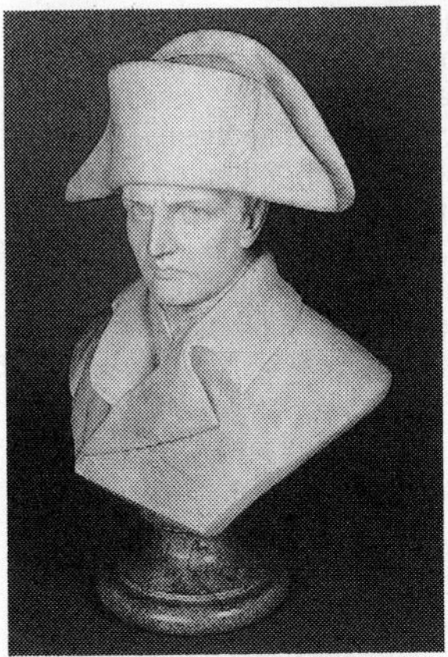

Bust of Napoleon

Besji, Professor G., bust of Napoleon I, signed on the back "Professor G. Besji, Galleria A. Falli," Italy, late 19th c., 20¼" h. (ILLUS.) 1,980.00

Bouraine, Marcel, "Awakening," figure of a seated nude, one leg tucked under her body, the other knee raised, one hand raised to her shoulder, signed "BOURAINE," France, early 20th c., 13¾" h.......3,450.00

Bust of Diana

Bust of the goddess Diana, her head turned to dexter, weathered patina, late 19th c., 25½" h. (ILLUS.).......2,875.00

Bust of a young girl, her head tilted downward w/her long curly hair falling around the sides, wearing a necklace but nude except for a wrap at the lower chest, the base edge roughly finished, mounted on a black marble base, late 19th c., 21" h...2,588.00

Figure of an Indian woman representing the continent of America, the half-nude figure w/her arms holding her curled legs &

wearing a feathered headdress in her long, curly hair & a w/feather dress around her waist, raised on a large columnar white marble base w/octagonal foot, attributed to Emmanuele Caroni, third quarter 19th c., overall 6'1½" h. 85,000.00

Figure of Mercury, nude & seated on a draped tree stump holding a pipes of Pan, Italy, 19th c., 32" h. 3,450.00

Figure of a Slave Girl

Figure of a "Slave Girl," standing half nude w/an animal skin skirt, her hands & one ankle shackled & chained to a rock, after the antique, 19th c., 4'10½" h. (ILLUS.)..........11,000.00

Figure of Venus de Milo, the armless half-nude woman draped around the waist, Italy, late 19th c., 37" h. (minor base chips) 825.00

Figure of a water carrier, a standing lady in classical dress holding a bowl in one hand & a small ewer in the other, set upon a fluted columnar base, late 19th c., 4'8" h. 3,300.00

Lapini, C., figures of children, a little girl wearing a slip & seated cross-legged in a rush-seat chair looking down at her handkerchief & a little boy wearing a long shirt & seated w/one leg tucked under in a rush-seat chair, holding a small book in one hand & reading, on notched square bases inscribed w/proverbs, signed "C. LAPINI FIRENZE 1892," Italy, late 19th c., 28" h., pr. 19,550.00

Model of a lamb, recumbent sleeping animal w/legs tucked around the body, on a rectangular base w/cut corners, late 19th c., 8" l., 3½" h. ..3,163.00

Moreau, Auguste, figure group of Venus & Cupid, Venus seated on a

Figure of Venus & Cupid

tall rock & nude except for a cap & a drapery across one leg, small winged cupid by one leg, inscribed "Aug. Moreau," together w/a marble pedestal, losses & restoration, France, 19th c., 35½" h. (ILLUS.) 12,650.00

Moreau, Math, figure of a young maiden wearing short diaphanous gown holding a bird at her breast, another at her feet, posed semi-seated against a vine-covered tree stump, on a circular mound base, base signed "Math Moreau," 31½" h...2,200.00

Nannini, R., bust of a woman, inscribed "R. Nannini Firenze 1892," Italy, w/associated green marble socle, 23½" h. 3,738.00

Villani, E., figure of a young boy, sitting nude on a stool & holding a wooden box mouse trap, signed "E. Villani" & "P. Barzanti Florence," Italy, late 19th c., 38" h. 5,750.00

OTHER MATERIALS

Busts of Apollo & Athena

Alabaster, bust of George Washington, late 19th c., 11" h. (some pitting) 770.00

Alabaster, busts of Apollo & Athena, after the antique, signed "P. Bazzanti, Florence," Italy, late 19th c., 18½" h., pr. (ILLUS.) 1,430.00

Alabaster Figure of a Woman

Alabaster, figure of a kneeling woman, half nude, wearing a turban & holding a snake in one hand, signed "A. Germany," Italy, ca. 1900, minor damage, 14¼" h. (ILLUS.) 715.00

Ivory, figure of a maiden clutching rose blossoms, one arm across her bosom, the other across her torso, mounted on a red & white marble socle, inscribed "Joe Descomps," France, ca. 1925, 8⅜" h..............4,313.00

Ivory, figure of a nude girl, w/one leg up & clasped in her hands, seated on the edge of a green onyx socle, inscribed "F. Preiss," Germany, ca. 1925, 4⅝" h.................................2,300.00

Lead Statue of a Boy

Lead, figure of a standing nude boy, nearly life-size, on a rock on an Italian silvered-metal base in the form of a reverse Corinthian column, 4'3" h. (ILLUS.) 4,600.00

Stone, figure of a woman bent under the weight of the sheaf of wheat she is carrying, signed "r. diligent," Raphael-Louis-Charles Diligent, France, early 20th c., 16" h. plus wooden base 2,070.00

Stone, stylized model of a reclining polar bear, his head on his front paws, on a low base w/irregular jagged edges, R. Abel Philippe, France, early 20th c., 23¾" h......16,100.00

Terra cotta, bust of Caesar Augustus, his mantle decorated w/an allegorical scene, raised on a circular ebonized socle, Europe, 19th c., 23" h...............................3,450.00

Terra cotta, bust of a young girl, the 18th c. child w/her hair pulled back & w/tight curls above her ears, wearing a low-cut gown, inscribed "Gaig...?," on a turned walnut socle, 20" h. 690.00

STEAMSHIP MEMORABILIA

The dawning of the age of world-wide airline travel brought about the decline of the luxury steamship liner for long-distance travel. Few large liners are still operating, but mementoes and souvenirs from their glamorous heyday are much sought-after today.

Book, "The Queen Mary - A Book of Comparisons," statistics, illustrated, published by Cunard White Star Line, 20 pp. (edge wear)..................$35.00

Butter pat, "Red Star Line," china, 1898...125.00

Coffee cup, "Vaccaro Line, Standard Fruit & Steamship Co.," china, T.A. Lotz Co., New Orleans, Louisiana 30.00

Customs receipt, "Cunard Lines," liner "Lusitania," dated September 7, 1910...20.00

Ice tub, "Eastern Steamship Lines," china 75.00

Menu, "Holland America Line," 1952....12.00

Menu, "Cunard Lines," liner "Queen Elizabeth," 1948..................................9.00

Paperweight, "American President Lines," brass, in original box 85.00

Passenger list, "Cunard Lines," liner "Queen Elizabeth," 1948......................9.00

Passenger list, liner "Queen Mary," 1948...9.00

Passenger list, "S.S. Regina," 1926 .....15.00

Playing cards, "Home Line Steam-ship" 15.00

Playing cards, "Swedish American Lines," w/slip case 18.00

Program, "S.S. Normandie," for charity fete-farewell party at sea, 1937 ....30.00

Rug, Art Deco style, the pale grey ground w/central pale yellow & mint green geometric design w/yellow strip side borders, designed for use on the liner "Normandie," ca. 1935, 2' 11" x 5' 690.00

Stock certificate, "Cunard Lines," 1909 ....30.00

Timetable, deck plans, etc., "American Lines," 1914 Atlantic crossing 24.00

Wallet, ship's purser, depicts the ship "F. Missler Bremen," ca. 1930 ....10.00

STEIFF TOYS & DOLLS

From a felt pincushion in the shape of an elephant, a world-famous toy company emerged. Margarete Steiff (1847-1909), a polio victim as a child and confined to a wheelchair, planned a career as a seamstress and opened a shop in the family home. However, her plans were dramatically changed when she made her first stuffed elephant in 1880. By 1886 she was producing stuffed felt monkeys, donkeys, horses and other animal forms. In 1893 an agent sold her toys at the Leipzig Fair. This venture was so successful that a catalog was printed and a salesman hired. Margarete's nephews and nieces became involved in the business, assisting in its management and the design of new items. Through the years, the Steiff Company has produced a varied line including felt or plush animals, Teddy Bears, gnomes, elves, felt dolls with celluloid heads, Kewpie dolls and even radiator caps with animals or dolls attached as decoration. Descendants of the original family members continue to be active in the management of the company still adhering to Margarete's motto "For our children, the best is just good enough."

Bear on wheels, w/original button, cast-iron wheels, 26" l. $2,050.00

Beaver, brown mohair, felt paws, tail & mouth, button in ear & stock tag, 9" h. 125.00

Camel (Dromedary), tan mohair body w/velvet face & legs, glass eyes, straw-stuffed, 1950s, 5½" ...85.00 to 95.00

Deer: "Bambi," velvet body, mohair chest & tail, sewn nose & mouth, 9" h. 65.00

Dog: "Peky," terrier, unjointed white plush mohair body w/black & brown spots, glass eyes, sewn nose & mouth, applied ears, w/chest tag, mint condition, 6" h. 40.00

Dog, Poodle, long & short black mohair, ca. 1940, 9" 65.00

Duck on wheels, quacks & waddles when pulled, original chest tag 195.00

Fish: "Flossie," multicolored mohair, glass eyes, felt lips & mouth, no identification, mint condition, 11" l......90.00

Giraffe, gold & orange velvet, w/button in ear & tag, 6" h. 95.00

Giraffe, gold & brown mohair, w/original buttons, 28" h. 385.00

Goat: "Snucki," white mohair body, black velvet legs, glass eyes, no identification, 8" h. 75.00

Hedgehog dolls: "Mecki" & "Micki," felt jointed body w/rubber head, cotton & felt clothes & leather shoes, 1950s, each 9" h., pr. 190.00

Koala bear, long & short tan mohair, jointed body, sewn nose & mouth, glass eyes, 1950s, 5" h. 120.00

Lamb, white mohair, glass eyes, sewn nose & mouth, w/tag in ear, 1950s, mint, 9" h. 325.00

Lion, standing, cream & brown mohair, glass eyes, working squeaker, button in ear, 10" h. 225.00

Lion, gold mohair, life-size display animal, 1960s 3,500.00

Lizard, multicolored felt, glass eyes, 1959, 10" l. 65.00

Monkey (chimpanzee): "Jocko," long curly brown mohair, fully jointed w/button in ear & tag "Made in U.S. Zone Germany," 18" h. 135.00

Monkey on a cart, stuffed animal w/grey mohair fur, beige felt trim, glass eyes & ear button, on a metal cart w/four wooden wheels marked "Steiff," 10" h. (very good condition) 395.00

Reindeer, tan mohair, felt antlers, glass eyes, sewn nose & mouth, 12½" h. 275.00

Rooster, multicolored felt, glass eyes, metal felt-covered legs, w/identification, mint condition, 6½" h. 245.00

TEDDY BEARS

Teddy bear, "Teddy Baby," gold mohair, jointed body, chest tag & U.S. Zone Germany tag, 3½" h........900.00

Teddy bear, beige mohair, glass eyes, fully jointed, long feet, chest tag, w/original yellow tag in ear, ca. 1957, mint condition, 6" h. 250.00

Teddy bear, silver plush, black shoebutton eyes, brown stitched nose & mouth, felt pads, swivel limbs, straw-stuffed, button in left ear, ca. 1910, 9½" h. (minor worn patches, a few moth holes to pads) 805.00

Teddy bear, light brown wool, wearing a red, tan & beige shirt, a blue jacket & short pants, ca. 1910, 13½" h.......518.00

Teddy bear, long gold plush fur, black shoebutton eyes, black stitched nose & mouth, felt pads, swivel limbs, growler, button in left ear, very good condition, ca. 1915, 23½" h. (small holes at edges of pads, several moth holes to pads) 4,025.00

STEINS

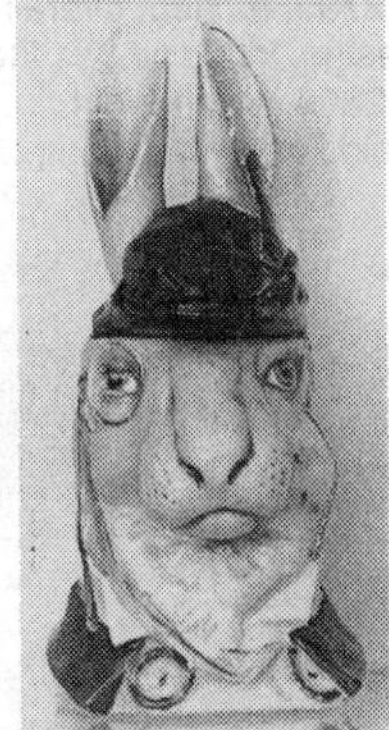

"Gentleman Rabbit" Stein

Advertising, "Budweiser," 1980 Holiday, Ceramarte $80.00

Advertising, "Budweiser," 1981 Holiday, Ceramarte 155.00

Character, "Gentleman Rabbit," porcelain, rabbit wearing hat w/feather, jacket & shirt w/wing collar, w/a monocle in his eye, C.G. Schierholz & Sohn, ca. 1900, 1/2 liter (ILLUS.) 2,640.00

"Nun" Character Stein

Character, "Nun," porcelain, in black & white habit, lithophane in base depicts monk w/lady, w/pewter mounts, 4" d., 7¼" h., ½ liter (ILLUS.) 345.00

Columbia Art Pottery, depicts monk reading a newspaper, pewter lid, 3 liter 100.00

Glass, green w/white enameling, white lattice design w/fancy coat of arms in center, "Anno 1667" below, green glass inset hinged lid w/green finial, green applied handle, pewter mounts, 4⅝" d., 14¼" h....................395.00

Glass, iridized champagne beige-flashed, matching applied handle, white enamelled scrolls & sprays around center, w/pewter figured hinged lid, 3⅞" d., 9¼" h., ½ liter 245.00

Mettlach, No. 171, grey & tan w/blue band w/relief-molded white figures representing the twelve months, inlaid lid, 3½" d., 5¾" h., ¼ liter ....150.00 to 175.00

Mettlach, No. 485, white relief-molded continuous scene of musicians & dancers on a tan background, inlaid lid, ½ liter 230.00

Mettlach, No. 675, relief-molded barrel w/hoops at top, base & middle, inlaid lid, ½ liter 150.00

Mettlach, No. 1005, relief-molded tavern scenes, inlaid lid, 1 liter.........376.00

Mettlach, No. 1028, molded tree trunk form w/an oval panel w/white relief-molded figures of a man carrying hat & walking w/a young woman, inlaid lid, ½ liter 185.00

Mettlach No. 1146, etched scene of students drinking in a tavern, signed "C.Warth," inlaid lid, ½ liter....................365.00

Mettlach Tavern Scene Stein

Mettlach, No. 1403, etched scene depicting a man bowling in a tavern, signed "C. Warth," inlaid lid, ca. 1898, ½ liter (ILLUS.) ....375.00 to 450.00

Mettlach, No. 1508, etched tavern scene, inlaid lid, ½ liter 550.00

Mettlach, No. 1642, tapestry scene of man drinking, pewter lid, 1 liter 395.00

Mettlach, No. 1725, etched scene w/lovers w/man holding a stein, inlaid lid, ¼ liter 375.00

Mettlach, No. 1940, relief-molded Yale University emblem, pewter lid, 3 liters 1,150.00

Mettlach, No. 2036, character, model of an owl, the bird's head forming the lid, a crest at its feet inscribed "BIBITE," stoneware lid, ½ liter 900.00

Mettlach Stein No. 2057

Mettlach No. 2057, etched scene of dancing peasants, inlaid pewter lid, top repaired, .3 liter (ILLUS.) 350.00

Mettlach No. 2094, etched scene of lady playing fiddle & people dancing, inlaid lid, ½ liter 500.00

Steins No. 2136 (left) & 2123 (right)

Mettlach No. 2123, etched, scene of drinking knight, signed "Schlitt," inlaid lid,½ liter (ILLUS. right)........1,485.00

Mettlach No. 2134, etched scene of gnome in nest holding two steins, inlaid lid, .3 liter 2,970.00

Mettlach No. 2136, etched & PUG, Anheuser Busch Brewery, inlaid lid, ½ liter (ILLUS. left)......................3,190.00

Mettlach No. 2248, relief scene depicting peasants dancing, inlaid lid, .3 liter 210.00

Mettlach No. 2278, relief-molded w/four panels of sports scenes on a colored ground, inlaid lid, ½ liter ....250.00 to 300.00

Mettlach No. 2359, relief four-panel decoration w/figures in each, inlaid lid, .3 liter 225.00

Mettlach No. 2430, etched, scene of Cavalier drinking, inlaid lid, 3 liter 495.00

Mettlach No. 2582, etched jester performing on table in front of tavern, signed "Quidenus," inlaid lid,1 liter ....450.00 to 500.00

Mettlach No. 2799, etched, overall Art Nouveau design, inlaid lid, 2.1 liter ..675.00

Mettlach No. 2808, etched, girl bowling, inlaid lid, ½ liter.................475.00

Steins No. 3156 (left) & 2917 (right)

Mettlach No. 2917, etched & relief, Munich Child & scenes of Munich, "Heim," inlaid lid w/figural lion & shield, ½ liter (ILLUS. right) 3,300.00

Mettlach No. 2921, etched, scene of hunter drinking in front of campfire, inlaid lid, 2.8 liter 900.00

Mettlach No. 2936, etched, Elk's Club stein,inlaid lid, ½ liter 495.00

Mettlach No. 2966, tapestry, a scene of a man seated on an upright barrel & holding a stein of beer in one hand & a long cane under his other arm, pewter lid, ½ liter 357.50

Mettlach No. 3000, etched, three panels w/women, pewter lid, ½ liter 300.00

Mettlach No. 3156, etched, Chicago stein w/three buildings pictured, inlaid lid w/gold dome & eagle, ½ liter (ILLUS. left) 2,860.00

Mettlach No. 3251, etched, hunter & young girl, inlaid lid, ½ liter 345.00

German Porcelain Stein

Porcelain, cylindrical w/two molded bands, the front decorated w/an oval reserve of a colorful city & landscape titled "Gruss aus Rothenberg" & framed by purple & pink flowers, lithophane castle scene in the base, domed pewter lid & thumbrest, Germany, ½ liter, 4" d., 8¾" h. (ILLUS.) 110.00

Pottery, buff & green embossed tavern scene, finial w/two full-figured elves seated on barrel drinking, impressed "Germany," 10" h. 105.00

Pottery & Stoneware Steins

Pottery, cylindrical, cream ground printed w/a rectangular color tavern scene flanked by scrolling gold leaves, domed pewter lid & ball thumbrest, Sarreguemines, France, 1 liter, 4" d., 9½" h. (ILLUS.) 195.00

Stoneware pottery, blue & grey, cylindrical w/molded bands, embossed tavern scene on the front, scrolls on the back, domed pewter cover & thumbrest, Germany, 1 liter, 4½" d., 10¼" h. (ILLUS. right) 145.00

Owl Stoneware Stein

Stoneware pottery, figural, modeled as a large owl w/molded feathers, the head forms the lid, pewter lid band & thumbrest, Merkelbach & Wick, Germany, ½ liter (ILLUS.) 175.00

Stoneware pottery, bulbous ovoid body tapering to a cylindrical neck w/a low domed metal lid w/knob finial, etched designs, Muskau, Germany, late 17th c., 1½ liter 3,300.00

Wood, burl, cylindrical w/scroll-carved feet, low domed cover, Norway, 1½ liter 1,100.00

Norwegian Rosemaled Stein

Wood, cylindrical w/knob feet, domed cover w/turned three-ring knob, heavy S-scroll handle, h.p. rosemaled band of stylized florals, Norway, 1½ liter (ILLUS.) 2,035.00

STEREOSCOPES & STEREO VIEWS

Hand stereoscope viewers with an adjustable slide may be found at $30.00 to $50.00 each in good condition. Elaborate table models are priced much higher. Prices of view cards depend on the subject material and range from less than $1.00 to $10.00, or more.

STEREOSCOPES & VIEWERS

Stereoscope, Keystone Eye Comfort, Model 40, crinkled brown metal finish, w/twelve view cards including eye exercises, the set $75.00

Stereo viewer, Keystone Monarch, aluminum frame 60.00

Stereo viewer, Underwood & Underwood, wooden frame, w/70 photographic cards, mint in box, the set 225.00

STEREO VIEWS

Airplane, Ford Tri-Motor mail & passenger plane in Chicago, Illinois 20.00

Airplane, U.S. Mail plane in Cleveland, Ohio, ca. 1920s...............20.00

Battleship "Maine" wreck, ca.1899 ....8.00

Black Family in cotton field, 1899.........19.00

Black male workers & uniformed black male leading goat cart w/white children, ca. 1890 ....18.00

Black people eating sugar cane 40.00

Black transposition-type, "April Foll No. 316," F.G. Weller, Littleton, NH...10.00

Chippewa squaw & papoose, Keystone 15.00

Civil War, picket guard w/prisoners near Lewinsville, Pennsylvania..........45.00

Indian child standing in large basket, Keystone...15.00

Katen Yance, Sioux warrior in battle stance, Keystone 20.00

London, England, "Old Curiosity Shop," set of 5 ....22.00

Palestine (100 cards), Jerusalem (25 cards) & Rome (50 cards), Underwood & Underwood, boxed set of 175 cards 175.00

Professor Lowe's balloon ascension, ca. 1860s 250.00

San Francisco earthquake scenes, complete set of 25 cards....................75.00

World War I scenes, Germans at the front, including the Kaiser, set of 14 ....37.00

STICKPINS

Advertising, "Burk Pork Packers," Philadelphia, Pennsylvania, model of a pig, ca. 1900 ....$28.50

Advertising, "Lipton Tea," model of a leaf 23.00

Advertising, "Moline Carriage," model of a carriage 25.00

Advertising, "Moline Plow Co.," figural chubby man w/corn...........................45.00

Advertising, "New Departure Coaster Brake," depicts Victorian girl on bike 60.00

Advertising, "Old Dutch Cleanser," depicts cleaning lady in blue enamel, early 85.00

Crystal & 18k gold, reverse-painted depicting jockey silks in blue & white polka dots w/yellow helmet, dated on back "April 6, 1899," in gold mounting, French hallmarks 825.00

Diamond, ruby & platinum, a collet-set old European-cut diamond in an etched mount, highlighted by a synthetic ruby, on a 14k white gold pin 660.00

Enamel & pearl, designed as a white enameled hand holding a baroque pearl, accented w/a rose-cut diamond bracelet & ring...............1,430.00

Gold, 14k, Arts & Crafts style, scarab set within the yellow gold mount, marked "Winn" 440.00

Gold (14k), in the form of an eagle's claw clutching a diamond, marked w/initials of Workmaster Alfred Thielemann & 56 standard, Fabergé, St. Petersburg, Russia, ca. 1900, 3" l...................................1,650.00

Gold (14k), modeled in the form of a gargoyle holding a cultured pearl in its mouth, within a plique-a-jour enamel top, marked by Whiteside & Blank 3,300.00

Gold (14), modeled in the form of an oak leaf w/a pearl & diamond-set acorn, marked w/initials of Workmaster Oskar Pihl in Cyrillic & 56 standard, Fabergé, St. Petersburg, Russia, ca. 1890, 3" l. 5,225.00

Gold (14k) & demantoid garnets, model of lizard set in garnets, in a chased gold mounting, Edwardian era...660.00

Gold (18k yellow) & pearl, Art Nouveau style, depicting a griffin holding a pearl in its mouth, hallmarked, France 220.00

Gold & enamel, Art Nouveau style, the lozenge-shaped top sculpted w/a female nude her arms to her sides, each hand holding a lily blossom & pad, further small pad leaves at the tip & base of the top, all against a celadon _guillouche_ enameled ground, inscribed "LALIQUE," early 20th c., 3⅝" l.....7,150.00

Ruby, diamond & 14k yellow gold, the twisted gold stem surmounted by a horseshoe defined by a band of seventeen small round diamonds & a conforming row of twenty-three rubies 690.00

Sapphire & 14k yellow gold, Art Nouveau style, central collet-set sapphire within an ornate gold frame w/a geometric design, marked "Whiteside & Blank" 357.50

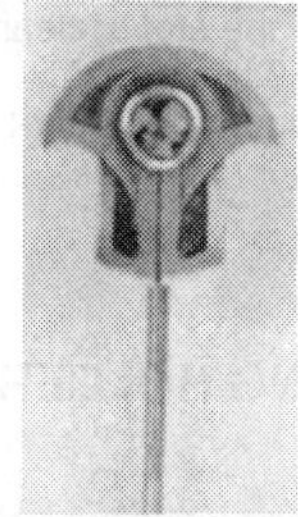

Arts & Crafts Stickpin

Sapphire, enamel & 14k gold, Arts & Crafts style, the arched head collet-set in the center w/a sapphire framed by blue enamel (ILLUS.) 220.00

Tourmaline, diamond & platinum, a pink tourmaline surrounded by rose-cut diamonds in a platinum top, 18k yellow gold stem, French hallmarks 302.50

STIRRUP CUPS

Russian Silver Stirrup Cup

The stirrup cup was a type of small tumbler, used in the late 18th and early 19th centuries, which held a single drink to be consumed by the hunter while on horseback. In the most familiar form, the bowl was made in the form of a fox's head or more rarely a hound's head. While these were made primarily of earthenware at a number of English potteries, examples are also found made of silver, glass and other materials.

Prattware, naturalistically modeled as the head of a fox w/slightly bared teeth, pricked ears (right w/a small chip), brown eyes & an ochre coat sponged around the eyes & muzzle in brown, the curly nape of his neck picked out in brown above the brown-edged rim (two small chips), & his chin uncolored, ca. 1810, 4¾" l. $1,265.00

Silver, modeled in the form of a horse's head, gilded interior, Samuel Arnd, St. Petersburg, Russia, ca. 1860, 3" h. (ILLUS.) 4,888.00

Staffordshire earthenware, models of fox heads, brown coat & white mask w/black & ochre eyes, rose muzzle, black-sponged nose & crimson nostrils & mouth, pricked ears (one w/tips chipped) w/rose interiors, wearing an ochre collar, 4 11/16" l., pr. 1,725.00

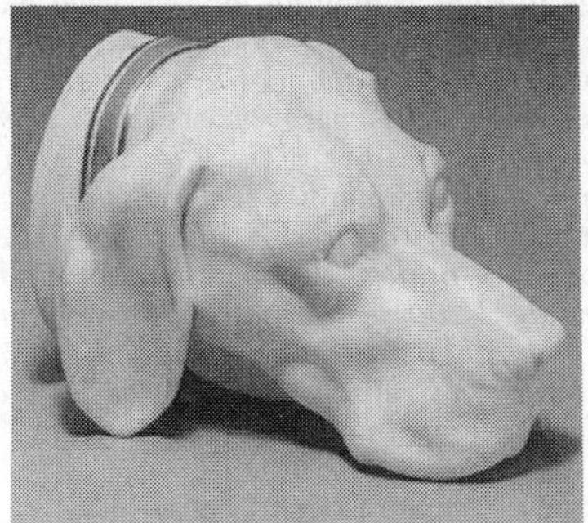

Parian Hound Head Stirrup Cup

Staffordshire parian, naturalistically modeled as the head of a hound wearing a gilt-edged orange collar, the back of the neck pierced w/a hole for suspension, ca. 1850-60, repaired chips on edge of rim & right ear, 7¾" l. (ILLUS.) 1,150.00

Staffordshire pearlware, modeled in the form of a fox head w/slightly bared teeth & pricked ears (minor chips), all but his eyes covered in a light brown glaze, ca. 1785, 5⅝" l. (the rim w/two small hair cracks & a restored chip) 690.00

Staffordshire pearlware, model of a hound's head, brown-spotted coat (two glaze chips), a salmon-shaded muzzle, black nose, iron-red mouth & black & grey eyes, the rim edged in brown (enamel chips), painter's numeral "3" in iron-red, ca. 1825, 5 1/16" l. 575.00

Staffordshire pearlware, modeled as the head of a small Pug dog w/an ochre coat & white chin, orange mouth, upraised protruding grey eyes & eyelashes, grey-edged ears, wearing a grey-edged collar decorated w/grey four-dot clusters & incised circlets, 1790-1800, 2⅞" l. (repaired) 1,150.00

Staffordshire stoneware, modeled in the form of a fox head, the unglazed coat well delineated & w/incised whiskers & pricked ears, the gilt-edged & dashed collar & the interior glazed, 4 7/16" l. (rim chip) 690.00

STOVES

The thought of a family gathered companionably around the parlor stove on a cold winter's evening, or of an apple pie baking in the wood-burning cookstove, brings to some a longing for the "good old days." On a more practical note, many people turned to wood-burning stoves during the 1970s energy crisis when they discovered wood was plentiful and by far cheaper than commercial fuels. Aside from the primary function, a handsome old parlor stove adds a distinctive touch with its ornate design and an old cookstove can turn a kitchen into a real family room. Whatever the reason, there has been a renewed interest in old stoves of all types.

Cookstove, "Home Comfort," grey granite w/light grey wheat sheaf panels, water reservoir, top warming ovens, two bars & all hardware $1,000.00

Cookstove, "Quick Meal," blue granite 1,950.00

Parlor stove, cast iron, "Corona," the rectangular top w/rolled edge centered by a large, full-length standing figure of George Washington as the statesman wearing blue-painted swagged robes & holding a rolled document, two narrow doors on the front, the lower door embossed "Corona," the top corners suspending white-painted iron tassels, raised on four tall, simple cabriole legs, Corona Stove Company, late 19th c., 5' 9" h. 14,950.00

Parlor stove, cast iron, "Estate Stove Co., Hamilton, Ohio," coal burning type w/vent oven, nickel-plated banding & ornate top w/urn finial, ca. 1860, 6' h. 5,500.00

Parlor stove, cast iron, "Round Oak," complete, 16" 550.00

Parlor stove, cast iron & sheet iron, an urn finial atop an arched sheet iron heat exchanger w/applied cast ornaments resting atop two small, short & one wide central chimney resting atop the rectangular cast stove w/a pair of doors & cast scrolls across the front, on a oblong rectangular base raised on short legs w/paw feet, brass finials at the front corners of the stove, cleaned & polished, mid-19th c., 40½" h.. ....495.00

Parlor stove, decorated w/Delft-type tiles on three sides, France..........1,000.00

STRING HOLDERS

Kitten with String String Holder

Before the widespread use of paper bags, grocers and merchants wrapped their goods in paper, securing it with string. A string holder, usually of cast iron was, therefore, a necessity in the store. Homemakers also found many uses for string and the ceramic or chalkware wall-type holder became a common kitchen item.

Cast iron, Dutch girl $39.00

Ceramic, model of a Scottie dog head 125.00

Chalkware, bust of a baby yawning, shelf sitter-type 55.00

Chalkware, bust of a sailor boy 65.00

Chalkware, kitten w/a ball of string, 4 x 6" (ILLUS.) 46.00

Chalkware, monkey on ball of twine, 4 x 8" 55.00

SUGAR SHAKERS

Called "muffineers" by the English who favored sifting a small amount of sugar on their muffins, sugar shakers are a popular collectible. All listed have their original tops unless otherwise noted.

China, decorated w/a colorful scene of two prancing Kewpies against a pale blue ground, Germany $89.00
Glass, Argus Swirl patt., milk white decorated w/tiny orange bubbles & yellow florals 85.00
Glass, Argus Swirl patt., shaded pink to white 'peach bloom' color 195.00
Glass, lime green, tapering cylindrical form w/a pressed button band pattern around the base, resilvered domed top w/pointed finial, 2½" d., 6" h. 50.00
Nippon porcelain, tapering hexagonal body w/rounded top & side handle near top, white ground decorated w/h.p. pink flowers outlined in gold, green leaves & gold edging, marked, 3¾" d., 5¼" h. 95.00
Silver plate, cylindrical w/side handle & domed top pierced w/a star design, chased around the bottom half w/blossoms & leaves, marked "Wilcox," late 19th c., 3" d., 5" h. 95.00

SUNBONNET BABIES COLLECTIBLES

Bertha L. Corbett, creator of these faceless children, proved a figure did not need a face to express character. Her pastel drawings appeared in "Sunbonnet Primer" by Eulalie Osgood Grover, published in 1900. Later Miss Corbett did a series showing the babies at work, one for each day of the week, and they became so popular advertisers began using them. Numerous objects including cards and prints with illustrations of, or in the shape of, the Sunbonnet Babies are now being collected. Also see ROYAL BAYREUTH under Ceramics.

Book, "Sunbonnet Babies ABC Book," 1929, by Eulalie Osgood Grover $65.00
Book, "The Overall Boys," by Eulalie Osgood Grover, 1905...........................45.00
Book, "The Overall Boys in Switzerland," by Eulalie Osgood Grover, 1915 ....45.00
Book, "The Sunbonnet Babies in Holland," by Eulalie Osgood Grover, 1915 ....45.00
Book, "The Sunbonnet Babies in Italy," by Eulalie Osgood Grover, 1922 ....45.00
Table runner, crocheted, Sunbonnet girl holding a parasol & walking her dog, white, 14 x 17" 34.00

TEDDY BEAR COLLECTIBLES

Early Mohair Teddy Bear

Theodore (Teddy) Roosevelt had become a national hero during the Spanish-American War by leading his "Rough Riders" to victory at San Juan Hill in 1898. He became the 26th President of the United States in 1901 when President McKinley was assassinated. The gregarious Roosevelt was fond of the outdoors and hunting. Legend has it that while on a hunting trip, soon after becoming President, he refused to shoot a bear cub because it was so small and helpless. The story was picked up by a political cartoonist who depicted President Roosevelt, attired in hunting garb, turning away and refusing to shoot a small bear cub. Shortly thereafter, toy plush bears began appearing in department stores labeled "Teddy's Bears" and they became an immediate success. Books on the adventures of "The Roosevelt Bears" were written and illustrated by Paul Piper under the pseudonym of Seymour Eaton and this version of the Teddy bear became a popular decoration on children's dishes. Also see STEIFF.

Hot water bottle, decorated w/Teddy bears, 1950s $25.00
Pinback button, celluloid, "Teddy Bear Bread" premium 42.50
Plate, child's, china, illustrated w/the Roosevelt Bears, hot air balloon scene & verse 75.00
Plate, china, illustrated w/the Roosevelt Bears, scene titled "Up San Juan Hill," mint condition 275.00

Target, cloth, features a Roosevelt-style bear, advertising giveaway from American Printing Co., 1906, 17 x 24" 95.00

Teddy bear, brown mohair, swivel head w/black glass bead eyes, black floss mouth & nose w/horizontal stitching, applied ears, jointed shoulders & hips, long feet, 4" (small spot of mohair missing from side of face) 425.00

Teddy bear, gold mohair w/hump back, shoe button eyes, straw stuffing, long snout, hand-stitched nose & mouth, Ideal, ca. 1915, 14" 345.00

Teddy bear, white mohair, fully jointed, glass eyes, ca. 1930, 16" 525.00

Teddy bear, yellow mohair, straw-stuffed body, pink felt feet, 19" 195.00

Teddy bear, yellow mohair, glass eyes, new pads, 20" 265.00

Teddy bear, mohair, straw-stuffed body w/back hump, fully jointed, glass eyes, 24" 1,300.00

Teddy bear, golden mohair, straw-stuffed body, jointed, button eyes, sewn nose & mouth, early 20th c., 24" (ILLUS.) 1,850.00

Teddy bear, long tan hair, brown paws, brown plastic eyes, black stitched nose & mouth w/a sweet expression, England, ca. 1940, 38" 173.00

TELEPHONES

Western Electric Candlestick Phone

Candlestick-type, "Western Electric - Made in U.S.A." at base, "Freehold 8-1064" on label above mouthpiece, black finish, scratches overall & wear to paint where handled, 11¼" h. (ILLUS.) $126.50

Desk-type, French-style, "Western Electric," mounted on a three-tier brass-plated cast-iron round stand, working 75.00

Wall-type, "Kellogg," oak case 185.00

Wall-type, "Monarch," oak case 220.00

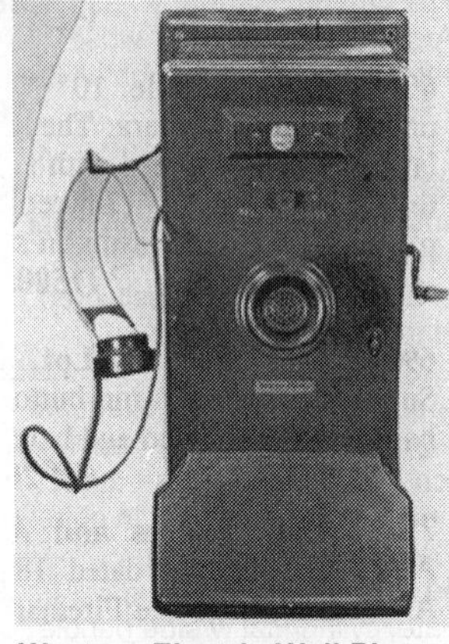

Western Electric Wall Phone

Wall-type, "Western Electric," wood & metal, olive green w/black receiver, crank on one side, w/headpiece receiver, scratched & soiled, 9" w., 20½" h. (ILLUS.) 126.50

Wall-type, "Western Electric," oak case, ca. 1919 ....350.00

TEXTILES

BEDSPREADS

Candlewick, two-piece w/cut corners, white on white floral design on homespun cotton, all hand-sewn, 72 x 84" (minor stains) $192.50

Chenille, large blue peacock w/pink, white, green & yellow tufting, 91 x 101" 245.00

Embroidered, red birds & flowers, full-size, ca. 1920 ....95.00

Hand-crocheted, Snowflake patt. w/Popcorn stitch, 2" l. hand-knotted fringe, overall 90 x 100" 185.00

Hand-crocheted, Star & Popcorn patt., scalloped edges, twin-size, pr. 295.00

Linen, homespun natural material w/a white on white woven design, 69 x 99" 214.50

COVERLETS

Jacquard, single weave, one-piece, a large central floral medallion flanked by spread-winged eagles at each corner, scrolling foliage borders, edge labels reading "M. by H.

Stager, Mount Joy, Lancaster Co., Pa. Warranted Fast Coller (sic)," faded olive green, orange, red & natural white, 77" sq. (overall & fringe wear) 357.50

Dated 1848 Coverlet

Jacquard, single weave, two-piece, floral star medallions w/vining rose borders & eagle corners w/Knox County, Ohio 1848," navy blue, deep salmon red, yellowish green & natural white, 69 x 77" (ILLUS. of part) 467.50

Jacquard, single weave, two-piece, four-flower medallions, diamonds, rose & vintage borders, corner labeled "Loudonville, Ohio 1868 wove by Peter Grimm," red, blue & natural white, 69 x 86" 1,100.00

Jacquard, single weave, two-piece, four rose & four leaf medallions w/bird, tree & basket of flowers border, corner blocks signed "Susan Frank, Fancy Coverlet wove by G. Heilbronn, Basil, Ohio," navy blue, royal blue, tomato red & natural white, 68 x 88" (minor wear, a little fringe loss, minor stains).................440.00

Floral Coverlet Dated 1840

Jacquard, single weave, two-piece, floral medallions w/rose border & corner blocks signed "Michael Franz, Miami County, Ohio 1840," navy blue & natural white, minor wear & light stains, 67 x 90" (ILLUS. of part) 605.00

Jacquard, single weave, two-piece, four rose medallions in the center, rose borders & corners labeled "Woved by A. Wolf, Ohio, AD 1848 for Martha Wood," tomato red, teal blue, navy blue & natural white, 72 x 86" (minor wear & stains).........357.50

Jacquard, single weave, two-piece, floral pattern w/vintage border, corners labeled "Jacob Daron 1845, Barbara Good," red, green, blue & natural, 82 x 84"..............................357.50

Jacquard, double woven, one-piece, a large star center w/realistic birds, deer & capitol buildings in borders, red, navy blue, olive green & natural white, 75 x 82" (minor stains)...........440.00

Jacquard, double woven, one-piece, star center w/eagles & flowers, olive green, navy blue, magenta red & natural white, 80 x 90" (wear, small holes & fringe incomplete) 192.50

Early Commemorative Coverlet

Jacquard, double woven, one-piece, floral medallions w/eagle, Masonic & Independence Hall borders, corners w/"Agriculture & Manufactures are the foundation of our independence, July 4, 1825, H. Sutherland, Gnrl. Lafayette," navy blue & natural white, wear & holes, no fringe, 76 x 94" (ILLUS. of part) 495.00

Jacquard, double woven, two-piece, overall vining floral design, corners labeled "Cadiz, Ohio," navy blue, tomato red & natural white, 76 x 82" (minor wear, stains) 440.00

Jacquard, double woven, two-piece, snowflakes & pine trees design, navy blue, tomato red & natural white, fringe at one end, 76 x 84" 770.00

Jacquard, double woven, two-piece, Hempfield Railroad patt. w/floral center & railroad borders in navy blue & natural white, 77 x 85" (some wear & small holes) 2,860.00

Large Blue & White Coverlet

Jacquard, double woven, two-piece, central medallion framed w/two wide leafy scroll rings surrounded by small birds & sprigs framed by large spread-wing American eagles w/banners within leafy scroll & pagoda border & narrow arrow device border band, maker's initials "CAW" & dated 1858 & 1860, some fabric loss & minor discoloration, blue & white, 92" sq. (ILLUS.).......1,035.00

Linsey-woolsey, consisting of two thicknesses of linsey-woolsey, the glazed top w/alternating coral & gold broad stripes heightened w/herringbone quilting within broad coral linsey-woolsey borders heightened w/overlapping shell quilting, the reverse a solid piece of gold linsey-woolsey, New England, late 18th c., 88 x 100" (some staining & repair)...........................1,265.00

Linsey-woolsey, composed of three panels of glazed worsted fabric in tones of pale lavender & aqua blue, the side panels elaborately quilted w/delicate floral vines & blossoms on a ground heightened w/fine scale diagonal line quilting, the central panel in a silvery aqua blue heightened w/diamond quilting, backed w/bronze & beige fabric, probably Pennsylvania, early 19th c., 96 x 100" (some fading & repairs) 805.00

Overshot, one-piece, optical pattern in pastel shades of pink & blue w/white, 76 x 98" (minor wear).........104.50

Overshot, two-piece, plaid pattern in navy blue, teal green & deep salmon red, 72 x 82" (some wear & small holes) 154.00

Overshot, Chain & Checkerboard patt., double-woven in two pieces w/a center seam, worked in red, white & blue wool & linen, probably New England, early 19th c., 76 x 96" (some small holes)........................1,035.00

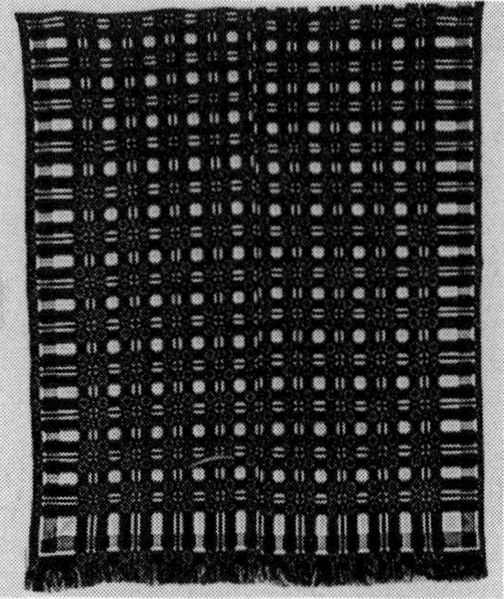

Early Overshot Coverlet

Overshot, Snowball patt., double-woven in two pieces w/center seam, worked in red, white & blue wool & linen, pine tree borders & original fringe, probably New England, early 19th c., 76 x 80" (ILLUS.).................575.00

LACE

Battenburg

Dresser scarf, 54" l. 65.00

Table centerpiece, scalloped edge, 14" d...48.00

Table centerpiece, drawn-work square in center, lace corners, 16" sq...74.00

Table centerpiece, very large 10" w. butterflies at corners, overall 30 x 80"...65.00

Tablecloth, drop-pointed edges, ca. 1933, 72" l.......................................375.00

Tea cozy, flower design, 16" w., 12" h..72.00

Other Laces

Alencon lace tablecloth, banquet-size, w/twelve matching napkins, France, ca. 1949, never used 495.00

Cluny lacy tablecloth, scalloped solid center w/5" w. Cluny lace border, 22" d...72.00

Filet lace table centerpiece, a design of men w/horns & women dancing in the center, 3" to 4" w. lace border, beige, 18" d...58.00

Filet lace table runner, a large design

of ladies w/flower baskets at each end, 6 x 23" filet lace oval center, overall 16 x 50" 135.00

Tatted lace centerpiece, composed of six fancy circles, beige, 12 x 17"........78.00

LINENS & NEEDLEWORK

Apron, hand-crocheted, pale pink w/blue stripes at bottom & down sides, 13 x 17" 23.00

Apron, hand-crocheted w/raised flower on pocket, light green & pink, 20" l. 36.00

Bed tick, homespun linen, red embroidered initials "M.M.," 61 x 67" 16.50

Blanket, woven wool, overall blue & white checkered design, one-piece w/hand-sewn hems, 19th c., 62 x 80" (small holes) 115.50

Embroidered Chair Cushion

Chair cushion, embroidered & appliqued, the top & sides embroidered w/flowers & leaves in shades of red, green, white, yellow & brown on a black ground, the underside panel covered in a printed chintz w/a basket of flowers in shades of peach & brown, Pennsylvania, ca. 1830, restuffed, 16 x 19" (ILLUS.) 2,588.00

Crib spread, hand-crocheted, squares w/flowers, rabbits, cats, squirrel, deer, pigs, etc., 40 x 66" 198.00

Mattress cover, single-size, homespun linen, overall small blue & white check design, machine-sewn, button closure, 19th c., 30 x 70" (small holes & repair)...........82.50

Mattress cover, homespun linen, overall small plaid design in natural white & red w/natural linen backing, machine-sewn, 19th c., 51 x 64".......220.00

Napkins, dinner-type, damask, five groups of six each from 24" sq. to 27 x 33", some w/"G" monogram, 30 pcs. 75.00

Pillow shams, turkey red embroidery on white, "I Slept & Dreamed" on one, "I Woke & Found" on the other, pr. 85.00

Pillow shams, turkey red embroidery on white, two birds w/heart-shaped wreath of flowers, 1½" ruffle, red edge, single thickness, 27½ x 30", pr. 125.00

Pillows, worked in *gros* & *petit point*, one depicting a gentleman & ladies at leisure by a bird bath, the other a classically dressed soldier w/ladies in waiting, within foliate borders & tasseled edges, England, 13 x 15", pr. 2,640.00

Show towel, homespun linen, pink cross-stitch embroidery w/stars, two chairs, flowers & "Leo Sartman 1834," 19" w., 51" l. 99.00

Show towel, homespun cotton, decorated w/three large cut-work panels featuring a large center starburst surrounded by flowers & birds, Pennsylvania, 15" w., 53" l.....330.00

Show towel, homespun linen w/pink cross-stitch embroidery of stars, flowers, initials & the date "1834," applied fringe, Pennsylvania German, 17½ x 57" 137.50

Show towel, homespun cotton w/wool embroidery, various stylized embroidery designs including flowers, birds, stars, hounds & hunters, hearts & the inscription "Elizabeth Musser 1846," worked in red, pink, olive green & ivory, Pennsylvania, 18" w., 57" l...............302.50

Show towel, natural dark linen homespun w/wool embroidery, finely detailed stitches forming rows of stylized designs including flowers, birds, initials & the inscription "Susanna Denlinger was born - the year 1825," a cut-work panel w/deer at the bottom, worked in rich colors of red, pink, two shades of blue, olive green & white, Pennsylvania, 17½" w., 68" l. (minor stains, top edge worn & frayed) 412.50

Table centerpiece, hand-crocheted w/a fancy initial "H" & rosettes across the bottom, beige, 10 x 12" 32.00

Table centerpiece, hand-crocheted, a design of cupid dancing in the center, 11" sq. 36.00

Table centerpiece, hand-crocheted w/the initial "E" in the center encircled w/flowers, white, 12 x 18" 36.00

Table centerpiece, hand-crocheted w/three butterflies, ecru, 9 x 15½" 30.00

Tablecloth, homespun cotton w/a blue & white checkered pattern, hand-sewn off-center seam & hand-hemmed edge, 19th c., 58 x 78"......214.50

Tablecloth, ecru linen, cut-work & satin stitch, 72 x 120"....................145.00

Tablecloth, hand-printed linen, decorated w/mustard yellow & olive green rectangles connected by grey bands on a greige ground, designed by Frank Lloyd Wright for Taliesin, produced by Schumacher, w/red logo "Design 101 - An Exclusive Schumacher Hand Print - The Taliesin Line of Frank Lloyd Wright," 48 x 60" 550.00

Tablecloth, light & dark blue cross-stitched pineapple border, 56 x 80" ...65.00

Tablecloth, white linen w/5" w. band of satin stitch embroidery around border, 68 x 108" 100.00

Tablecloth & napkins, "Moravian Art Linen, ecru & brown tones, pull-work, cross-stitch in deer design, Czechoslovakia, 50 x 70" tablecloth & eight napkins, 9 pcs....................125.00

Tablecloth & napkins, ecru linen w/two large Cluny lace medallions & edge trim, twelve matching napkins, tablecloth, 136" l., the set................225.00

Table piece, crocheted w/initial "J" in center, roses at sides, 15 x 18"..........36.00

Arts & Crafts Table Runner

Table runner, embroidered linen, Arts & Crafts style, three purple grape clusters & leaves on each end, scalloped edges, early 20th c., 30" l. (ILLUS.) 192.50

NEEDLEWORK PICTURES

Needlework embroidery on canvas, depicting a stylized landscape w/a woman & child in kneepants in the foreground & unusual birds, large flowers & fruit-filled tree, worked in shades of rose, blue, green & tan, frame inscribed "wrought by Mary Elliot," the backboard inscribed "...M.E. Noyes," possibly Boston, 18th c., framed, 13" sq. (some losses) 6,050.00

Early Silk Needlework Picture

Needlework embroidery on silk, floral swags & willow branches & wheat stalks above an oblong reserve w/the scene of two couples in a landscape w/a large willow tree at center & a village in the distance, ribbon-tied floral sprigs & willow branches at the bottom, probably Connecticut, early 19th c., in a giltwood frame, minor scattered discoloration, 16½ x 18½" (ILLUS.) 3,190.00

Needlework embroidery on silk, depicting a shepherdess w/two sheep standing next to a tree, a house in the background, the oval surrounded by a bow-tied swag & flowering vines, embroidered & painted in tones of green, red, pink, brown & blue silk & French knot threads, attributed to Miss Patten's School of Hartford, Connecticut, ca. 1800, 14½" w., 18" h. (minor discoloration to silk) 2,875.00

Needlework embroidery & water-color memorial picture, a scene w/a large willow tree overhanging a tall monument to the left w/a lady standing nearby, a church, leafy tree & smaller headstones to the right, inscribed "Sacred to the memory of Thomas Clark...1812," Albany, New York, framed, 13¾ x 19½" (some staining & fiber loss) 517.50

Needlework embroidery & water-color, scene of standing Lady Liberty holding a standard w/a flag inscribed "I am free" & holding a cornucopia within a large oval reserve framed by a meandering leafy flowering vine, done in tones of green, blue, pink, yellow & red silk, French knot & gilt metallic threads trimmed w/silver sequins, sewn oval reserve border w/silver sequins, made by Susan Shearer, Palmer, Massachusetts, dated 1805, framed, 12½ x 15½" 8,625.00

Needlework silk embroidery, a small central oval vignette of cottages amid trees, surrounded by a wide ground filled w/flower sprigs & birds, in a narrow tortoiseshell frame, Charles I period, England, early 17th c., 22½ x 23½" 3,680.00

Needlework wool petit point on canvas, a landscape scene w/a shepherdess, a bird in her hand & a dog by her side, w/the figure of a boy in the background flying a kite, worked in blue, green, red & beige, England, mid-18th c., framed, 25⅛ x 27" (losses) 3,738.00

QUILTS

Appliqued Album Quilt

Appliqued Album quilt, composed of sixteen squares, each w/a different stylized design including flowers, an eagle, wreaths, hearts, hands, etc., in shades of red, green & yellow calico against a white quilted ground, minor stains, 19th c., 76" sq. (ILLUS.) 1,210.00

Appliqued Album quilt, worked in 69 blocks of variously alternating appliqued chintz & calico squares including compass star, bird-in-heart, tulip, flower garlands & flower-in-urn, all surrounding a larger central chintz square appliqued in a blue floral wreath & centering a presentation inscription to Rev. & Mrs. Bartolette, April 8, 1845, the blocks inscribed in pen, cross-stitch or stamp w/the names of the donors, all quilted according to design of individual squares, together w/a history of the congregation of the Amwell Baptist Church, Flemington, New Jersey, dated 1845, 92½ x 103" 8,050.00

Appliqued w/*broderie perse* center block w/an exotic bird perched atop a tree of life on a white double diamond quilted ground framed by a blue chintz sashing surrounded by numerous *broderie perse* flora & bird details further enclosed by a chintz *guilloché* border surrounded by a continuous chintz diamond border framed by a wide blue chintz border, white binding, America, ca.1830, 108 x 110" 9,900.00

Appliqued Fleur-de-Lis Quilt

Appliqued Fleur-de-Lis patt., composed of sixteen moss green & red & white printed calico four-arm fleur-de-lis patches mounted on a white cotton ground intricately quilted w/feather wreaths & baskets of flowers, the borders w/appliqued large diagonal floral sprays, some fading, probably Massachusetts, ca. 1850, 88" sq. (ILLUS.) 1,840.00

Appliqued Flying Goose patt. variant, composed of variously printed red, coral, brown, green & turquoise calico & chintz patches, the central field delicately worked w/a latticework of red & yellow & calico alternating w/brown & green chintz patches, the whole surrounded by a broad undulating flowering vine border w/blossoms in *broderie perse* as well as calico appliques, the white cotton field w/small scale flower, outline & diagonal line quilting, many of the chintz patches retain their original glazing & the quilt retains its original cotton tape edging, signed on the back in cross-stitch "Sarah H Mead 1848," Greenwich, Connecticut, dated 1848, 101 x 104" (some minor staining & discoloration)..............15,525.00

Appliqued Oak Leaf patt., composed of brightly colored red, slate blue, green & beige printed calico patches mounted on a crisp white cotton field w/herringbone & wreath quilting, Cumberland County, Pennsylvania, ca. 1860, 80" sq. (some minor fading)..1,380.00

Appliqued Rose of Sharon Quilt

Appliqued Rose of Sharon patt., composed of ornate entwining leafy vines & flowers in green, red, pink, yellow & orange against a white quilted ground, a meandering floral border band, Ohio, mid-19th c., 82" sq. (ILLUS.) 1,760.00

Appliqued Sunflower variant patt., large scalloped blossoms flanked by four trumpet-form blossoms on leafy stems, in red, teal blue, goldenrod & pink calico on white quilted ground, machine-sewn applique, hand-quilting, made by Margaret Holloway, central Missouri, late 19th c., 72 x 84" (minor stains & repair) 1,100.00

Appliqued Tree of Life patt., composed of slate grey, green, blue, red, yellow & orange patches w/four fruit-laden trees flanking pots of tulips & birds all within a meandering grapevine border w/small yellow, red & coral birds against a white cotton ground w/outline & circle quilting, probably Pennsylvania, 20th c., 80 x 88"...2,300.00

Victorian Crazy Quilt

Crazy quilt, appliqued & embroidered, composed of brightly colored silk, velvet & damask odd-shaped patches arranged in a series of squares w/lavishly colored embroidery in the form of flowers, the whole within dark maroon velvet borders, Coester Family, Bridgeport, Connecticut, ca. 1855, 64" sq. (ILLUS.) 1,265.00

Crazy quilt, appliqued & embroidered, worked in multicolored silk & velvet fabrics framed by multicolored embroidery & decorated w/a variety of designs including fish, pocketwatch, Holy Bible, spectacles, flowers, thimble & scissors, the quilt w/the Lord's Prayer executed in appliqued silk & embroidery, red silk border, America, ca. 1890, 67 x 69"........11,000.00

Commemorative Crazy Quilt

Crazy quilt, appliqued, composed of variously printed red, blue, beige & brown calico patches arranged in a series of squares made up of odd-shaped patches, at the center a printed fabric depiction of "The America's Cup Race between the Puritan and the Cenesta, Sept.85," the reverse w/a patriotic printed fabric commemorating the World's Fair, Chicago, 1892, 72 x 80" (ILLUS.) 1,150.00

Crib-size, pieced Bow Tie patt., worked in several solid colors against a black ground, Mennonite, 26 x 32½" 522.50

Streak of Lightning Crib Quilt

Crib-size, pieced Streak of Lightning patt., unusual double-sided quilt, the front composed of beige, pink, blue, black & lavender patches, the reverse in black & pink fabric in a crisscross pattern, the field decorated w/cable quilting, Amish, Pennsylvania, ca. 1930, some fabric loss & fading, 30 x 36" (ILLUS.) 690.00

Crib-size, pieced Tumbling Blocks patt., composed of various woven & patterned men's suit fabrics in tweed & worsteds in tones of grey & brown along w/red, grey & black flannel patches, within an inner border of diamonds on points accentuated w/copper pinheads, the outer border w/broad lengths of tan & black wool & flannel, trimmed w/red & yellow floral brocade fabric, probably Indiana, late 19th - early 20th c., mounted on a stretcher, 50 x 52"..3,163.00

Pieced Bar patt., composed of dusty coral, forest green, purple & greyish blue wool & cotton patches, the field w/diamond, flowerhead, star & feather quilting, Amish, probably Lancaster County, Pennsylvania, late 19th c., 68 x 72" (some minor stain & fabric loss) 1,840.00

Pieced Barn Raising patt., composed of brightly colored blue, yellow, red, green & pink solid & printed calico patches, narrow inner red & yellow zigzag border, the whole within a broad red & black calico border, the reverse w/broad stripes of brown & black calico, wide scale diagonal & outline quilting, probably Pennsylvania, ca. 1880, 88" sq. 1,840.00

Pieced Carolina Lily patt., composed of two shades of green, pink & blue w/embroidered stems, heightened w/quilting, Mennonite, 74 x 80" 935.00

Pieced Church patt., composed of twelve blocks each w/a stylized church w/pointed front pediment w/round stylized clock face, variously printed & solid calico & cotton patches, some patches tied w/silk ribbon & trimmed w/embroidery, Moravian, probably Pennsylvania, late 19th c., 76 x 84" (some minor stains & fabric loss).............1,495.00

Pieced Diamond-in-the-Square patt., the central diamond embellished w/elaborate tulip-quilting framed by burgundy sashing w/blue corner blocks w/pinwheels, star & chevron stitching surrounded by tulip-quilted green spandrels enclosed by burgundy sawtooth-quilted sashing & blue floral-quilted corner blocks framed by a purple flower basket-quilted border w/blue wreath-stitched corner blocks, wool & cotton, the backing initialed "M.B.," Amish, Lancaster County, Penn sylvania, ca. 1920, 75 x 77" 3,850.00

Pieced Double Wedding Ring patt., composed of red, brown, slate blue, jade green & coral wool patches, mounted on a black ground heightened w/flowerhead & concentric ring quilting, Amish, western Pennsylvania or Ohio, ca. 1890, 80" sq. (some minor wear) 2,185.00

Pieced Fan patt., composed of red, beige, slate blue, purple & black wool & wool plaid fabric, sewn w/silk thread embroidered in turkey tracks stitch w/flowers, hearts & butterflies, dated "1876," Cape Cod, Massachusetts, some minor wear & fading, 64 x 80" (ILLUS. top next page)....2,875.00

Pieced Flower Basket patt., worked in burgundy & petal pink cotton & wool on a teal Princess Feather-quilted ground, surrounded by burgundy Princess Feather-stitched sashing, w/burgundy binding, Amish, Lancaster County, Pennsylvania, ca. 1910, 70 x 76" 9,900.00

Pieced Flying Geese patt., composed of brightly colored bands of calico &

Pieced Fan Pattern Quilt

glazed chintz alternating w/white cotton bands decorated w/feather & line quilting, New England, third quarter 19th c., 98 x 104" (some minor stains) 1,265.00

Pieced Lone Star patt., composed of red, navy & teal blue patches on a goldenrod ground, machine-sewn binding, by Mary Green Knietzing, Louisville, Kentucky, 1922, penciled pattern intact, 78 x 88" 605.00

Pieced Monkey Wrench patt., worked in blue prints alternating w/yellow calico, 67 x 83" (minor overall wear & light stains) 385.00

Pieced Nursery Rhyme Quilt

Pieced Nursery Rhyme design, one w/small pieced squares arranged to show stylized figures & four trees surrounded by letters reading "Jack and Jill - Went Up The Hill - To Fetch - A Pail of Water," all against a white quilted ground, the second w/a similar central scene surrounded by the inscription "Jack Fell Down - Broke His Crown - and Jill Came - Tumbling After," also against a white ground, early 20th c., each 70 x 90", pr. (ILLUS. of one)..2,200.00

Pieced Ohio Star patt., thirty blocks worked w/pieced blue stars on black flower-stitched blocks on a copper spade-quilted ground, black vine-stitched inner border, copper scrolling vine-stitched outer border, burgundy binding, initialed "BM" and dated "1916," Amish, Ohio, 1916, 67 x 77" 4,950.00

Pieced Star of Bethlehem Quilt

Pieced Star of Bethlehem patt., composed of olive green, yellow, gold, navy blue & rose-printed & solid calico patches, the field w/small scale & intricate flower & wreath quilting, the whole within broad borders of stars & pink & yellow chintz, probably Pennsylvania, mid-19th c., some minor stains & discoloration, 114 x 116" (ILLUS.) 7,130.00

Pieced Sunburst patt., composed of red, black & blue calico patches forming sunbursts w/bright yellow centers arranged in four rows of three each within bright yellow, red, white & blue calico squares, the whole decorated w/diamond & line quilting, Kentucky, third quarter 19th c., 70 x 88" 920.00

Pieced Tree of Life patt., composed of green calico patches arranged on a white ground decorated w/floral & line quilting, within a green calico border & binding, third quarter 19th c., 77 x 90" (ILLUS. top next page)...920.00

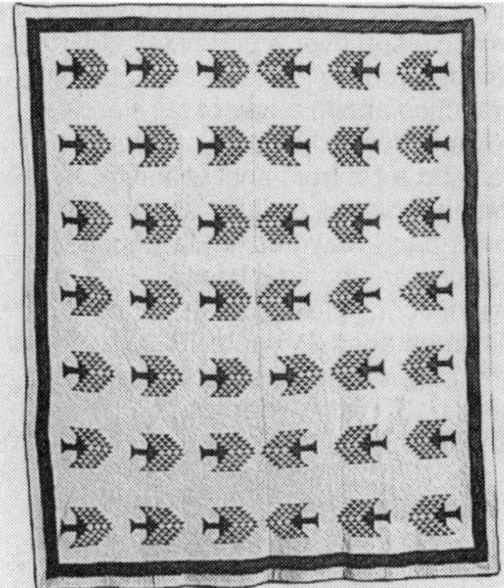

Pieced Tree of Life Quilt

Pieced Triple Irish Chain patt., composed of vividly colored olive green & red patches mounted on a white cotton ground elaborately quilted w/floral sprays, leafage & diamond stitching, the whole within double red & green sawtooth borders, Mary Elizabeth McCauley, Towson, Maryland, ca. 1870, 80" sq. (minor fading)................................1,495.00

Pieced Tumbling Blocks patt., composed of blue, maroon & grey solid patches within blue & black borders, decorated w/line & seed quilting, Amish, Ohio, 20th c., 60 x 80" 805.00

Pieced Weathervane patt., composed of pale green & blue print & red & white polka dot on green patches against a white ground w/bull's-eye quilting, a solid green border stripe, blue & white check backing, reputed to be by Mrs. Clarence Hooley, Lancaster County, Pennsylvania, 78 x 82".......................................1,210.00

Stuff-work, all-white cotton, at center a spread-winged American eagle perched on a mound, inscribed w/the date "March the 20th, 1850" within a circular laurel wreath surround, the inner borders w/swags & clusters of tulips, the outer border a double laurel vine, the design raised in stuff-work against a ground heightened w/diamond quilting, probably Pennsylvania, ca. 1850, 80 x 84" (some minor wear)..........2,750.00

Trapunto bride's quilt, all-white cotton field elaborately quilted w/a large basket of blossoms & vines surrounded by a meandering grape cluster & grapevine border, the field w/scallops, Lancaster County, Pennsylvania, early 19th c., 92 x 108" (minor discoloration) 1,725.00

Trapunto Crib Quilt

Trapunto crib quilt, all-white cotton ground w/elaborate & extensive trapunto decoration, the center w/a large cornucopia filled w/floral blossoms within a feather wreath roundel surrounded by wide undulating grape cluster & vine borders, original tatted cotton fringe, probably Pennsylvania, early 19th c., some small stains & discoloration, 36" sq. (ILLUS.) 1,380.00

Wool worsted, composed of five narrow indigo blue panels stitched together & quilted w/an overall pattern of luxuriant floral, grape cluster & star designs, the background heightened w/diagonal line quilting, initialed "D.W. (Dolly Whittaker) at the top, probably Hartland, Vermont, ca. 1800, 100 x 100" (some small fabric loss & repairs) 715.00

SAMPLERS

Early Unframed Sampler

Alphabet & numerals above "Elizabeth Stone was born in Danvers Janury (sic) 30th worked this in the 10th year of her age 1796," over a pair of trees & vining flowers, three sides w/a continuous zigzag border, worked in pink, green & cream silk on a linen ground, framed, 7½" w., 11½" h. 3,080.00

Alphabets & numerals above a pair of urns over leafy branches & the inscription "Wrought by Elizabeth Bigelow, Marlborough, Aged 11 Yeaf," all within a flowering vine border w/a small house in the lower left corner, worked in silk threads in shades of green, pink, bittersweet, yellow & black on linen, unframed, 9½ x 10" (ILLUS.) 1,045.00

Alphabets & numerals above a pious verse & inscription, a small two-story house flanked by pairs of trees at the bottom, all within a meandering floral vine border, worked in variety of green, brown, blue & red silk stitches on a linen ground, inscribed "Wrought by Lucy P. Blankinship - 1841," probably Massachusetts, framed,16¼" sq. (some fading & discoloration) 288.00

Sampler with Wide Floral Border

Alphabets w/inscription "Wrought by Caroline Darling, Marlborough - August 1819 aged 11 years," inscription framed by small grapevines, all within a box surrounded by a wide meandering floral vine border centering baskets of flowers at the top & bottom, worked in silk threads on linen, framed, 13½ x 17¼" (ILLUS.) 3,850.00

Family record, needlework on linen w/a band of delicate blossoms & leaves across the top & down the sides above a small oval reserve w/inscription over a pair of tall slender trees w/inwardly arching branches above a pair of tall slender columns topped by pots of flowers & flanking a central panel w/family member names & dates all above a lower band w/two boxed inscriptions flanking an unboxed central inscription, signed & dated "Lucy A. Kinsman aged 11 years 1823," probably Massachusetts, framed, 16½ x 18" (very minor scattered discoloration) 2,530.00

STEVENGRAPHS

Centennial Exhibition Bookmark

Bookmark, "Centennial - 1776-1876 - USA," above "The Father of His Country," & a bust portrait of George Washington above a verse & a scene at the Philadelphia Centennial Exhibition, framed (ILLUS.)..............135.00

Bookmark, "Marriage of Princess Louise & Marquise of Lorne," 1871....45.00

Bookmark, "Unchanging Love," framed...85.00

Print, "Columbus Leaving Spain," ca. 1893, framed...................................225.00

"The Good Old Days"

Print, "The Good Old Days," stage-coach scene, signed on front & original Thomas Stevens label on back, framed (ILLUS.)......................135.00

Print, "Lady Godiva Procession," framed 150.00

Print, "The Landing of Columbus," ca. 1893, framed.................................225.00

"The Present Time"

Print, "The Present Time - 60 Miles An Hour," early railroad scene, framed (ILLUS.) 285.00

Print, "Wellington & Blugher at Waterloo," framed 185.00

TAPESTRIES

Aubusson Tapestry

Aubusson, a large central oval medallion w/a pair of lovers in a garden, framed by floral swags in green, red, pink & brown, France, 19th c., 36½ x 80", pr...................9,900.00

Aubusson, each rectangular panel woven w/a central medallion surrounded by scrolls supporting a ribbon w/a pendent basket of flowers & fruit above a scallop shell surrounded by flowers, within trellis & scroll borders, woven w/metallic threads & wool in chestnut, pink, pale blue & salmon, France, 19th c., 9' 4" l., pr. (ILLUS. of one).............9,900.00

Aubusson fragment, a Biblical - mythological subject depicting three women in classical dress w/a ewer & jewels, France, late 17th c., 76 x 138" (repairs, minor splits) 5,775.00

Brussels, a Biblical scene depicting two women in a garden w/an angel approaching overhead, three men in the background & a city in the distance, fruit & floral wide border band, weaver's mark of Wilhelm de Pannemaker in lower right, town mark in lower left selvage, Belgium, 16th c., 77 x 108" (areas of reweave, splits) 12,100.00

Brussels garden-style, a large scene of a formal garden w/fountains, grotto & hens, trophy & flower border in vivid colors, early 18th c., 9' 7" x 10' 4" (minor areas of reweave & repair) 22,000.00

Flemish Biblical Tapestry

Flemish Biblical scene, the large central scene depicting a king wearing a turban & a soldier standing by a burning altar, mountains in the distance, floral urn & game park borders, Flanders, late 16th c., 5' 7" x 9' 8" (ILLUS.) 4,950.00

Flemish fragment, a mythological scene of three women in classical dress walking in a wooded landscape, Belgium, late 17th - early 18th c., 64½ x 83" (splits, minor repairs)..4,070.00

Flemish hunting scene, the large central panel decorated w/mounted hunters, dogs, deer & various animals in a woodland setting, a wide border of floral urns & trophies, late 16th - early 17th c. (border separate, repairs).......................15,400.00

Flemish "Verdure" Tapestry

Flemish "verdure" style, the large scene w/three figures in a forest landscape, one seated w/a bird & cage, one seated w/a cat & the third standing, Flanders, late 17th c., repairs, 6' x 8' (ILLUS.) 4,950.00

Flemish "verdure" style, depicting a stag hunt in the foreground flanked by elegant couples & farmers in the distance, beyond a castle w/moat & boats, on the edge of a forest w/mountain village in the distance, the borders w/allegorical figures & couples in oval medallions, Flanders, 17th c., 11' 4" x 14' 3" 31,900.00

(End of Textiles Section)

THEOREMS

Basket of Fruit Theorem

During the 19th century, a popular pastime for some ladies was theorem painting, or stencil painting. Paint was allowed to penetrate through hollow-cut patterns placed on paper or cotton velvet. Still-life compositions, such as bowls of fruit or vases of flowers, were the favorite themes, but landscapes and religious scenes found some favor among amateur artists who were limited in their ability and unable to do freehand painting. Today these colorful pictures, with their charming arrangements, are highly regarded by collectors.

Basket of fruit on velvet, yellow basket w/wrapped rim & foot & center handle filled w/large pieces of fruit & serrated leaves, shades of green, blue, yellow, red & brown, paper label attached to original cardboard backing, Cordelia Lane, early 19th c., framed, 6¾ x 8⅛" $2,530.00

Basket of fruit, water-color on paper, simple low basket w/curled handles filled w/a variety of fruits depicted on leafy branches, unsigned, framed, 10 x 14" 1,870.00

Basket of fruit, water-color & pen & ink on white velvet, a woven straw basket brimming w/peaches, pears, a melon, grapes & berries on a sawtooth edged mat, in what appears to be the original grain-painted Federal frame, American School, ca. 1830, 12¾ x 16½" (ILLUS.) 920.00

Basket of fruit & vegetables, water-color on velvet, colorful array of peaches, pears, plums & squash in a blue & yellow striped basket against a white ground, American School, ca. 1830, framed, 13 x 20" ..805.00

Bouquet of flowers on velvet, profusion of large blossoms in old faded shades of brown & dark green w/traces of blue & gold on a gold ground, in a contemporary gilt frame, 24½" w., 28¼" h. (minor damage & small hole) 440.00

Bowl w/fruit & vining grapes on velvet, Oriental Export-type bowl on its side surrounded by various varieties of fruit & grape clusters in soft old faded shades of blue, brown, green & gold, contemporary frame, 28½" w., 24¾" h. 660.00

Landscape w/deer *en grisaille* on paper, framed, 19th c., 8¼ x 10½" (very minor foxing) 345.00

Pear on cotton, naturalistically colored fruit w/leaves in yellow, red & shades of green, in decorated frame, 5¾" w., 8" h. 170.50

Primrose bush, water-color & ink on paper, a small tree w/large open blossoms, buds & pointed serrated leaves, signed "Painted by Sally Stearns 1857," framed, 6¾ x 8¼" (light staining, tears in lower edge) ..825.00

TOBACCO JARS

Bisque, decorated w/playing cards on four sides, a pipe on the lid, all against a black ground, Germany, 6½" w., 4½" h. $375.00
Majolica, figural bust of an alpine man 150.00
Majolica, figural bust of an Arab, 6" h. 155.00
Majolica, figural bust of a carpenter....125.00
Porcelain, figural bust of a young black girl, her turban forming the lid 425.00

TOOLS

Ice pick, "Winchester No. 9502" $45.00
Inclinometer, "Warren Knight," in box 135.00
Level, cast iron & brass, marked "The Davis Level & Tool Co. Springfield, Mass...patd...1883," 24" l. 165.00
Level, "Keen Kutter No. K624," cast iron 100.00
Line level, embossed cast iron, marked "Stanley - Pat. Feb. 18 '90," works (minor wear) 33.00
Mallet, maple burl beetle, 11" l. 20.00
Mallet, burl, 12" l. 27.50
Plane, "Stanley No. 1" 75.00
Plane, "Stanley No. 2" 175.00
Plane, "Stanley No. 2C" 300.00
Plane, gauge-type, "Stanley No. 4" 82.50
Plane, "Stanley No. 5¼" 75.00
Plane, "Stanley No. A18" 85.00
Plane, "Stanley No. 45" w/two boxes of blades 115.00
Plane, "Stanley No. 48" 70.00
Plane, "Stanley No. 55," new condition in original box 465.00
Plane, "Stanley No. 62" 270.00
Plane, "Stanley No. 100½" 110.00
Plane, "Stanley No. 140" 97.50
Plane, "Stanley No. 147" 85.00
Plane, "Stanley No. 289" 175.00
Plane, "Ward's Master Plow No. 45," w/blades, in original box 125.00
Plane, "Winchester No. W5C" 65.00
Plane, "Winchester No. W130" 115.00
Plane, "Winchester No. 3025" 75.00
Plane, "Winchester No. 3026C" 70.00
Rule, folding-type, "Stanley No. 66¾"...35.00
Rule, folding-type, "Stanley No. 87," ivory, four-fold, 2' l. 650.00
Rule, folding-type, "Stanley No. 90," ivory, four-fold, 1' l. 230.00
Rule, folding-type, "Stephens & Co. No. 83," ivory, four-fold, 2' l. 850.00
Spoke shave, chamfer-type, "Stanley No. 65" 95.00
Trammel points, "Stanley No. 2" 30.00

TOOTHPICK HOLDERS

Reference numbers listed after the holders refer to the late William Heacock's books, Encyclopedia of Victorian Colored Pattern Glass, Book 1 *or* 1000 Toothpick Holders.

Pansy Toothpick Holder

Amber cut glass, Art Deco style, tulip-shaped w/a scalloped rim & flattened, squared sides, cut w/diamond designs, 1½" w., 2¾" h. $55.00
Blue glass, pressed Hobnail patt., round (Book 1, No. 146) 35.00
Canary opalescent glass, pressed Ribbed Spiral patt. (Book 1, No. 252) 75.00
Clear glass, pressed Box-In-Box patt. (Book 1, No. 31) 30.00
Clear glass, pressed Brazillian patt. (Book 1, No. 33) 20.00
Clear glass, pressed Buckingham patt. (1000, No. 737) 25.00
Clear glass, pressed Czarina patt. (1000, No. 599) 25.00
Clear glass, pressed figural Cat on a Pillow 85.00
Clear glass, pressed figural monkeys on tree trunk 140.00
Clear glass, pressed Fashion patt. (1000, No. 654) 20.00
Clear glass, pressed Grated Diamond & Sunburst patt. (1000, No. 631) 20.00
Clear glass, pressed Intaglio Sunflower patt. (1000, No. 673) 25.00
Clear glass, pressed Paddlewheel & Star patt. 25.00
Clear glass, pressed Quartered Block patt. (1000, No. 618) 22.50
Clear glass, pressed Queen's Necklace patt. 50.00
Clear glass, pressed Spearpoint Band patt. (Book 1, No. 288) 30.00
Clear glass, pressed Sunbeam patt. (1000, No. 114) 25.00

Clear glass, pressed Whirligig patt. (1000, No. 633) 22.50
Clear glass, pressed Winsome patt. (1000, No. 616) 20.00
Cranberry-stained glass, pressed Wedding Bells patt. (Book 1, No. 320) 135.00
Cut glass, Art Deco style, clear w/black enamel trim & frosted panels, 2⅛" d., 2⅝" h. 75.00
Emerald green glass, pressed The Prize patt. (Book 1, No. 244) 125.00
Emerald green glass, pressed Trophy patt. (1000, No. 235) 18.00
Emerald green glass w/gold, pressed Winged Scroll patt. (1000, No. 163) 450.00
Green glass, pressed Tree of Life patt. (1000, No. 197) 50.00
Milk white glass, painted Stork patt. (1000, No. 404) 35.00
Milk white glass, pressed Coiling Serpent patt. (1000, No. 387) 45.00
Peach-stained glass, pressed Jefferson Optic patt., decorated w/gold scrolls & white enameled daisies (1000, No. 139) 85.00
Pink opaque glass, pressed Pansy patt., Book 1, No. 224 (ILLUS.)..........75.00
Pink opaque glass, pressed Sunset patt. (Book 1, No. 295) 80.00
Ruby-stained glass, Brittanic patt. (Book 1, No. 34) 110.00
Silver plate, figural dog reclining beside a holder w/an applied shield on the front, (1000, No. 826) 30.00
Silver plate, figural squirrel w/nut........140.00
White opalescent glass, pressed Bead Swag patt., decorated w/roses (1000, No. 309) 60.00

TOYS

Also see ADVERTISING ITEMS, CHARACTER COLLECTIBLES, COCA-COLA ITEMS, DISNEY COLLECTIBLES, MARBLES, STEIFF TOYS & DOLLS and TEDDY BEAR COLLECTIBLES.

Early Cast-Iron Packard

African Safari animal, Zebra, wooden, painted eyes, Schoenhut (Philadelphia), reduced size $375.00
Airplane, "Spirit of St. Louis," pressed steel, Metalcraft Corp. (St. Louis, Missouri), Model No. 800 ....300.00
Airport toy set, cast metal, a hanger building in orange, green, red & grey, two red, blue & orange gas pumps & two silver planes, Louis Marx (New York, New York), ca. 1930s, 1½" to 3" h., the set.............522.50
Air rifle, pump-type, "Quackenbush - No. 4," w/extra dart barrel & unopened box of 100 slugs dated "1883" 650.00
Automobile, Cadillac sedan, cast metal, Tootsietoy (Dowst Mfg. Co., Chicago, Illinois), ca. 1927................50.00
Automobile, Chevrolet Coupe, cast iron, painted grey & black w/nickeled wheels, Arcade Mfg. Co. (Freeport, Illinois), ca. 1927, 8¼" l. 1,850.00
Automobile, Ford Model T Touring sedan, cast iron, Arcade, ca. 1925 ....575.00
Automobile, Lincoln sedan, pressed steel, John C. Turner (Wapakoneta, Ohio), 27" l. 4,675.00
Automobile, Packard sedan, cast iron, unusual blue paint, engine hood opens, metal disc wheels, all-original, Hubley Mfg. Co., Lancaster, Pennsylvania (ILLUS.) 27,500.00
Bakery wagon, horse-drawn, cast iron, w/driver, Arcade Mfg Co., 12" l. 295.00
Battery-operated, "Airport Saucer," saucer spins around, rotating within enclosed airport w/two moving airplanes & flashing tower................145.00
Battery-operated, "Balloon Vendor," clown holds balloons w/one hand & rings bell w/other, mint in box 350.00
Battery-operated, "Buttons Puppy with a Brain," Louis Marx, 12" 175.00
Battery-operated, "Charleston Trio," Louis Marx 950.00
Battery-operated, "Charlie, The Drumming Band Clown," plays drums & cymbals w/hands & feet, mint in box 250.00
Battery-operated, "Charlie Weaver Bartender" ....80.00 to 100.00
Battery-operated, "Crap Shooting Monkey," monkey shakes dice in cup & rolls them out, Cragston, Japan (ILLUS. top next column) ....150.00 to 200.00
Battery-operated, "The Drinking Captain," standing figure by a lamp-post, smoke comes from tattoo in shirt, Japan, mint in box..................175.00
Battery-operated, "Good Time Charlie," sits on garbage can near lighted lamppost kicking his foot,

Battery-Operated "Crap Shooting Monkey"

drinking from flask, smoking cigar & blowing smoke from mouth, face turns red, wearing top hat & tails 145.00

Battery-operated, "Happy Santa," tin & cloth w/vinyl face, Santa's head moves & he plays the drums & cymbals, Alps-Shojo Ltd. (Tokyo, Japan), ca. 1950 ....225.00

Battery-operated, "Indian Joe" playing drums ....75.00 to 100.00

Battery-operated, "Jumbo, The Bubble Blowing Elephant," mint in box 100.00

Battery-operated, "Mambo, The Drumming Elephant" 160.00

Battery-operated, "Mr. McPooch," dog w/pipe & wearing a red plaid coat & hat, walks, barks, nods head & wags tail, mint in box...............................120.00

Battery-operated, "Mother Bear," plush bear in tin rocking chair rocks & moves in knitting motion, w/box ...125.00

Battery-operated, "Nutty Mad Indian," original box 130.00

Battery-operated, "One-Arm Bandit," three actions, Cragston, 1960s, includes a sign 3 x 3¼", overall 6¼" h...60.00

Battery-operated, "Picnic Bear," mint in box 170.00

Battery-operated, "Picnic Bunny," mint in box 170.00

Battery-operated, "Piggy Cook," mint in box ....150.00 to 175.00

Battery-operated, policeman on motorcycle, lithographed tinplate, w/turning front wheel & rubber tires, Nomura (Japan), 11½" l....................500.00

Battery-operated, "Santa Claus," on skates or skis, Alps-Shojo Ltd., mint in box 250.00

Battery-operated, "Santa Claus," rings bell & eyes light up, w/box 125.00

Battery-operated, "Smoking Grandpa," tin, old man in rocking chair smokes & rocks, Japan, w/box ....200.00 to 225.00

Battery-operated, "Smoking Papa Bear," green coat 145.00

Battery-operated, "Struttin Sam," tin, black man on drum-shaped stage, ca. 1950s, 10½" h., ...375.00

Battery-operated, "Telephone Bear"...195.00

BB gun, "Bull's Eye Pistol," w/brown bottle of lead BBs, target stamp, loading device & original lithographed box, patent dated "Feb. 26, 1924" 350.00

BB gun, Daisy Model 25, Daisy Manufacturing Co., excellent condition 150.00

BB gun, Daisy Model 36 ....85.00

BB gun, Daisy Model 40, Daisy Manufacturing Co. 250.00

BB gun, pistol-type, Daisy Model 118, "Targeteer," Daisy Manufacturing Co. 70.00

BB gun, "Spittin Image," Model 1894, near mint in box 150.00

BB gun, "Matchless Repeater," cast iron & brass, 1890s 950.00

Blocks, building-type, wood, "Sifo's Mailbag of Blocks from the Land of Hiawatha," No. 142, in original cloth bag 55.00

Blocks, building-type, lithographed paper-on-wood, a series of seven blocks & three domes which line up to form a model of the U.S. Capitol building, 19th c., 19½" l. (worn paper) 1,375.00

Blocks, nesting-type, lithographed paper-on-wood, each graduated square block decorated w/a colorful scene & letter of the alphabet, late 19th c., set of 10 (some wear & taped repair) 302.50

Early Toy Blocks

Blocks, puzzle-type, lithographed paper on wood, titled "Baby Bunting ABC and Picture Cubes," various color scenes of animals & the alphabet, in original wooden box, copyrighted in 1884, McLoughlin Bros., (New York, New York), set of 8 (ILLUS. top) 500.00

Blocks, puzzle-type, lithographed paper on wood, "The Fairyland R.R. Blocks," flattened rectangular blocks w/Punch & Judy scenes & the alphabet on one side & railroad cars & numbers on the other side, late 19th - early 20th c., set of 9 (ILLUS. middle row) 575.00

Blocks, puzzle-type, lithographed paper on wood, New York Central R.R. train set, #61 toy engine pulls two wooden-wheeled cars w/lift-off tops, alphabet & pictorial blocks stored inside the railroad cars, late 19th - early 20th c., the set (ILLUS. bottom row) 1,700.00

Blocks, puzzle-type, lithographed paper, titled "Three Kittens in a Tub," in original box, the set 300.00

Early Paddle Wheel Boat

Boat, paddle-wheel steamboat, cast iron, marked on the side of the wheel "City of New York," late 19th c. (ILLUS.) 1,045.00

Britains (soldiers), "Beefeaters, Outriders, Footmen of the Royal Household," Set No. 1475 ....225.00

Britains (soldiers), "Cowboys," Set No. 183, set of 7 ....150.00

Britains (soldiers), "George VI Coronation Coach," Set No. 1470....175.00

Britains (soldiers), "Indians," Set No. 150, set of 7 ....150.00

Britains (soldiers), "Military Police," Set No. 2201, set of 8 ....150.00

Britains (soldiers), "Mounted Arabs," Set No. 164, set of 5 ....225.00

Britains (soldiers), "Mounted Canadian Government Guard," Set No. 163, set of 5 ....225.00

Britains (soldiers), "Seaforth Highlanders," Set No. 5188 ....195.00

Britains (soldiers), "16th C Knights," mounted & foot soldiers, Set No. 1307, 9 pcs....................150.00

Bus, double-decker, lithographed tin, marked at top "Bico Bus to Joyville," w/windup mechanism, metal disc wheels, painted green & yellow, early 20th c., Distler (Germany), 9" l. (ILLUS. top next column) 3,025.00

"Bico Bus to Joyville"

Bus, "Greyhound," tin, KKK (Japan), mint in box, 7" l. 110.00

Bus, "Inter-City," die-cast metal, Buddy L (Moline Pressed Steel Co., E. Moline, Illinois), 1928, 24" l....................500.00 to 550.00

Bus, cast iron, sight-seeing type embossed "Seeing New York 1899," Kenton Hardware Co. (Kenton, Ohio), 10" l. 2,970.00

Cannon, "Boy Ranger Machine Gun," cast-iron w/wooden-spoked & rimmed wheels, shoots marbles, marked "Patd. June 1903," Kilgore Mfg. Co. (Westerville, Ohio), 19" l....495.00

Cap pistol, "Atomic Disintegrator," Hubley Mfg. Co. mint in box....................395.00

Cap pistol, "Big Bill," cast iron, Kilgore Mfg Co. 85.00

Cap pistol "Fanner 50," Mattel, Inc. (Hawthorne, California) 65.00

Cap pistol, "Flintlock Jr.," Hubley, w/box 42.00

Cap pistol, "National," cast iron 42.50

Cap pistol, "Navy Colt 34," Hubley Mfg Co. ....150.00 to 175.00

Cap pistol, "Nichols Stallion 38," near mint in box 150.00

Cap pistols & twin holster set, "Nichols Stallion - 250," the set 95.00

Cap pistols & twin holster set, "Kilgore Americans," Keystone Mfg. Co. (Boston, Massachusetts), the set 500.00

Chemistry set, No. 12024, A.C. Gilbert Co. (New Haven, Connecticut), the set 40.00

Circus animal, Alligator, wooden, glass eyes, Schoenhut, regular size 500.00

Circus animal, Bear (brown), wooden, painted eyes, Schoenhut, regular size 450.00

Circus animal, Bear (brown), wooden, glass eyes, Schoenhut....................650.00

Circus animal, Giraffe, wooden, glass eyes, Schoenhut, regular size, 11" h. (ILLUS. top next page) 495.00

Circus animal, Monkey, wooden, original clothes, Schoenhut....................275.00

Circus animal, Ostrich, wooden, glass eyes, Schoenhut ....725.00 to 750.00

Schoenhut Giraffe

Circus animal, Ostrich, wooden, painted eyes, Schoenhut 400.00

Circus animal, Tiger, wooden, painted eyes, Schoenhut, reduced size........275.00

Circus cage wagon, cast iron, "Overland Circus" polar bear wagon, pulled by a pair of white horses w/riders, w/driver, Kenton Hardware Co., unused in original box, polychrome paint, 14" l. ....600.00 to 650.00

Circus performer, "Ringmaster," wooden w/wooden head, Schoenhut, reduced size 325.00

Clockwork mechanism, battleship, tinplate body painted in two tones of grey w/black lining & portholes, dusty pink deck, two large & four smaller guns, two lifeboats, four funnels, two masts, two anchors on chains, adjustable rudder, three-blade screw, winding key, Bing (Germany), ca. 1920, 29" l. (completely restored & repainted).........2,185.00

Clockwork Black Musicians

Clockwork mechanism, black minstrel musician - banjo player, seated wearing cloth outfit, on a rectangular wooden base, Jerome Secor Mfg. (Bridgeport, Connecticut), late 19th c. (ILLUS. center) 25,300.00

Clockwork mechanism, black minstrel musician - bones player, seated & wearing colorful cloth outfit, on a rectangular wood base, Jerome Secor Mfg., late 19th c. (ILLUS. right)..12,650.00

Clockwork mechanism, black minstrel musician - tambourine player, seated wearing a colorful cloth outfit, on a rectangular wood base, Jerome Secor, late 19th c. (ILLUS. left)...............................38,500.00

Early Clockwork Boxers

Clockwork mechanism, boxers, two black men standing atop a rectangular wood platform, wearing worn cloth outfits, Ives Corp. (Bridgeport, Connecticut), late 19th c. (ILLUS.)..........................14,300.00

Clockwork mechanism, dancing clown, lithographed tin plate, two-dimensional figure printed in red, white & blue & shown holding a small pig, jointed at hips & knees, background shallow box containing mechanism printed in sepia tones w/scenes of other clowns & circus figures, American-made, early 20th c., 7" h. (key arbor crudely cut, winding key replaced, slight surface rust)..748.00

Clockwork mechanism, Ferris wheel, painted tin w/twelve enclosed gondolas & steam station house on wooden lithographed platform, Germany, ca. 1890 ....650.00

Clockwork mechanism, racing car, Alfa Romeo CIJ P2 w/the body finished in cream, numbered "2" in red, well-detailed w/leather bonnet straps, filler caps, front grill, brake lever, steerable front wheels, rubber tires w/diamond pattern, France, late 1920s, 21" l. (some retouching to paint)..2,530.00

Early Clockwork Woodchopper

Clockwork mechanism, woodchopper, man standing holding an axe above a log, dressed in ragged cloth outfit, raised on a rectangular wood platform, Ives Corp., late 19th c. (ILLUS.) 27,500.00

Construction bucket loader, hand-operated, pressed steel, painted dark green, used to load earth haulers, William Doepke Mfg. Co. (Rossmoyne, Ohio) 650.00

Cork gun & holster, metal, Tomboy, mint condition.....................................65.00

Covered wagon, cast iron, pulled by a black & a white horse, w/driver, fabric cover for wagon, Kenton Hardware Co., unused condition in original box, 15" l. 522.50

Covered wagon w/horses & driver, lithographed tin, Northwestern Products Co. (St. Louis, Missouri), w/four page booklet 135.00

Erector set, A.C. Gilbert (New Haven, Connecticut), Model No. 9½, all motorized, in blue steel case 225.00

Erector set, A.C. Gilbert Model No. 10051, w/instruction booklet, set 60.00

Farm animal, Bulldog, wooden, painted eyes, Schoenhut, regular size 550.00

Farm animal, pig, wooden, painted eyes, leather ears, woven tail, Schoenhut, ca. 1925, 3¾" h.............325.00

Farm animal, Reindeer (or Deer), wooden, glass eyes, Schoenhut, regular size 650.00

Fire ladder truck, metal, Kingsbury Mfg. Co. (Keene, New Hampshire), 36" l. 1,200.00

Fire pumper truck w/hydrant, pressed tin, complete w/ladders & hose, hydrant connects w/garden hose & sprays water, Tonka, 17" l. 325.00

Fire pumper wagon, horse-drawn type, cast iron, w/original driver & two horses, Hubley Mfg. Co., 13" l...350.00

G.I. Joe "Adventure Team" set, "Danger of the Depths," in original box 175.00

G.I. Joe, French Resistance Fighter, Action Soldiers of the World series, complete w/sweater, pants, boots, beret, shoulder holster w/revolver, radio set, bayonet, grenades, MAS machine gun & Croix de Guerre, no scar, Hasbro Mfg. Co. (Pawtucket, Rhode Island), near mint condition ..290.00

G.I. Joe, German Soldier, Action Soldiers of the World series, complete w/jacket & pants, boots, helmet, backpack, belt w/pouches, Luger in Holster, 9 mm Schmeisser machine gun, stick grenades & Iron Cross, no scar, Hasbro Mfg. Co., near mint..320.00

G.I. Joe, Green Beret, complete w/four-pocket jacket & side pocket pants, green beret w/insignia, boots, camouflage scarf, camouflage radio set, M-16 rifle, belt w/holster & .45 pistol & grenades, hard head figure, Hasbro Mfg. Co., near mint.............300.00

G. I. Joe, Imperial Japanese Soldier, Action Soldiers of the World series, complete w/jacket, pants, boots, helmet, backpack, belt w/pouches, pistol & holster, rifle & bayonet, w/medal, no scar, Hasbro Mfg. Co., near mint..500.00

G.I. Joe, Marine, brown eyes, painted blond hair & scar, wearing camouflage fatigues, marked on lower back "Made in England by Palitoy under license from Hasbro, 1964"..50.00

G.I. Joe, Navy Shore Patrol, complete w/blue jumper w/zipper to armpit, pants w/flap, boots, white Shore Patrol helmet, white duffle bag, armband, white belt w/holster & .45 pistol & nightstick, hard head figure, Hasbro Mfg. Co., near mint condition 200.00

G.I. Joe, Russian Infantry Man, Action Soldiers of the World series, complete w/jacket & pants, boots, fur hat, belt, binoculars w/case, ammo box, D.P. machine gun w/bi-pod & drum clip, anti-tank grenades & Lenin medal, no scar, Hasbro Mfg.Co., near mint 320.00

G.I. Joe, West Point Cadet, complete w/parade jacket & white pants, shoes, parade hat & plume, sash, sword belt, sword & scabbard & white M-1 Garand, hard head figure, Hasbro Mfg. Co., near mint condition 300.00

Grain Loader farm vehicle, green steelplate, black rubber Goodyear tires, yellow "Barber Greene" decal w/green lettering on each side of loader ramp, 16½" l., 12" h. (minor rust & scratches) 187.00

Grocery store set, wooden, includes counter w/paper cutter, 24 built-in drawers w/porcelain labels, two built-in floor to ceiling glass showcases, over 65 cans, bottles, boxes, etc., complete, 14½ x 15 x 38" 1,200.00

Hansom cab, cast iron, covered cab w/passenger, driver sitting on box at front driving single white horse, vehicle w/large spoked wheels at back & smaller ones at front, Kenton Hardware Co. (Kenton, Ohio), unused condition in original box, 15¾" l. 500.00

Horse-drawn cart, tin, foliate-embossed cart w/red & gold japanning, on two spoked cast-iron wheels, pulled by a prancing brown horse, 9½" l. (wear & axle resoldered) 110.00

Horse-drawn Tinplate Omnibus

Horse-drawn omnibus, tinplate, finished in red, grey & beige w/stenciled design & "Prospect Park" on sides, the high-wheeled, rear-entrance vehicle pulled by one white & one gold horse, both on wheels, Althof-Bergmann (New York, New York), ca. 1880, restoration, overall 16½" l. (ILLUS.) 13,800.00

Ice Wagon, cast iron, red & yellow ice wagon, pulled by a large trotting brown horse, w/driver & accessories including plastic "ice" & tongs, Dent Hardware Co. (Fullerton, Pennsylvania), ca. 1910, 15" l. (paint worn) 748.00

Ironing board, wooden w/folding legs, painted red, ca. 1910 ....30.00

Ironing board cover set, "Little Sweetheart," Wolverine Co. (Pittsburgh, Pennsylvania), in package 12.00

Jack-in-the-box, wooden box w/colorful lithographed paper covering, the comic figure in top hat w/papier mache head w/polychrome paint & a cloth-covered body, marked "Made in Germany," early 20th c., 6¾" h. (nose damage) 165.00

Jump toy, carved and painted pine, comprising two figures of men w/goatees & moustaches & wearing porkpie hats, suspended above a platform w/a dog, each of the figures suspended from a wire spring w/allows the figures to dance when the crank is turned, probably Pennsylvania, early 20th c., 12½" l., 15¼" h. 4,600.00

Painted Canvas Knock-Over Toy

Knock-over toy, painted canvas, the swell-bodied animal painted w/long lashes & whiskers, in chalk pink & grey, w/wooden base, America, early 20th c., 13½" h. (ILLUS.) 288.00

Log cart, cast iron, two black & white oxen pull a four-wheeled cart w/a large log, driver sits sideways to drive the team, Kenton Hardware Co., ca. 1910, 15½" l. 1,035.00

Matchbox combine, "Massey Harris," Lesney's Matchbox Toys (London, England) 385.00

Matchbox tractor, "Massey Harris 745D," Lesney's Matchbox Toys, near mint condition 650.00

Microscope set w/case, 1945, A.C. Gilbert Co. (New Haven, Connecticut) 125.00

Motorcycle, "Harley Davidson," lithographed tin, w/three moving pistons, TN, Japan 695.00

Motorcycle w/policeman, cast iron, the blue uniformed officer rides an elaborate red & silver Indian motorcycle w/black rubber tires,

Hubley Mfg. Co. (Lancaster, Pennsylvania), early 20th c., 9" l. (some paint wear) 368.00

Motorcycle w/sidecar, cast iron, nickel-spoked wheels, 4" 225.00

Music box, in the form of a giant screen TV, 1973, Fisher-Price, Inc. (East Aurora, New York) 45.00

Hand-Painted Noah's Ark

Noah's ark, wood, h.p. multicolored boat w/Noah & a wide assortment of hand-carved animals under the hinged rooftop, some small repairs to the figures, Germany, ca. 1895, 15" l. (ILLUS.) 978.00

Ocean Liner "St. Louis"

Ocean liner, "St. Louis," lithographed paper on wood, replica of the turn-of-the century American passenger liner w/large black hull, two decks, twin stacks, six lifeboats, wheel horse, masts & flags, on auxillary wheels, R. Bliss Mfg. Co. (Pawtucket, Rhode Island), ca. 1895, 34½" l. (ILLUS.) 2,990.00

Optical toy, "Zoeatrope," wood on cardboard, a brown cylindrical open-topped drum w/13 vertical slits, pivots on a wooden base allowing the lithographed paper strips, inserted inside, to appear to be moving, Milton Bradley & Co. (Springfield, Massachusetts), ca. 1870, 11¼" x 11¼" x 14¾" 575.00

Panorama toy, "Historiscope," consisting of five lithographed rolls enacting a panorama of the history of America, in a built-in cardboard stage, Milton Bradley, ca. 1800, boxed, 2¼ x 5¼ x 8¾" 437.00

"Western Panorama"

Panorama toy, "Western Panorama," consisting of a/linen scroll w/14 colorful western scenes mounted in a wooden frame w/turning wooden dowels, McLoughlin Brothers (New York, New York), ca. 1895, 1¾ x 10¾ x 12½" 403.00

Pedal car, "Auburn," steel construction, boat tail, finished in red & black w/red lining & leatherette interior, chromed details including steering wheel, windshield, lamps, mascot, bumpers, disc wheels w/black rubber rims, 1932, rebuilt & restored, 56½" l. 3,105.00

Pedal car, "Chrysler," finished in ivory & two-tone brown, w/chromed details including steering wheel, windshield, seven lights, bumpers, rear grill, w/spare wheel, painted vents on bonnet, black tires w/white sidewalls, Steelcraft, 1932, completely restored & rebuilt, 51" l. 8,050.00

Pedal car, "Cord," finished in black lined in red, w/red leatherette interior, chromed details include horizontal strips on hood & radiator, front & rear lights, steering wheel, disk wheels w/black rubber tires, maker unknown, 1935, restored, 57½" l. 6,900.00

Pedal car, "Duessenberg," finished in red & black lined red, w/supercharged appearance, two windshields, cast steering wheel, red leatherette interior, chromed bumper, headlights, horns, steering wheel, spare wheel, open disc wheels w/black rubber rims, American National Co. (Toledo, Ohio), 1932, completely restored & rebuilt, 62½" l. 4,600.00

Pedal car, "Kiddillac," finished in rose pink, black & silver, black rubber-rimmed whitewall tires, w/steering wheel, early 1950s, 44" l. 1,035.00

Pedal car, "LaSalle Skipper," finished in silver w/maroon wheel arches & lining, maroom leatherette interior, chromed accessories include windshield, bumpers, mascot, pierced silver painted disk wheels w/black rubber rims, spare wheel, 1938, extensively rebuilt & restored, 52" l. 2,415.00

Pedal car, "Lincoln Zephyr," finished in deep blue & black w/silvered details including mascot, headlights, chromed steering wheel, bumpers, black leatherette interior, blue disk wheels w/black rubber tires, Steelcraft, 1939, completely restored & rebuilt, 40½" l. 2,760.00

Pedal tractor, Oliver, Model No. 1800 ....300.00

Pedal vehicle, "Atomic Missile," red jet-form body w/cream trim & red lettering, cream seat & steering wheel, three-wheeled, unplayed-with, 24½ x 45", 24" h. 330.00

Pedal vehicle, jet plane, three-wheeled, finished in silver w/red & black detailing, red steering wheel & seat, black rubber-rimmed tires, fully restored, overall 45" l. 1,035.00

Pedal vehicle, tractor, finished in red w/gold-painted radiator grill, steering wheel, black rubber-rimmed metal tires, 35" l. (some surface rust) 690.00

Penny toy, automobile, open touring car in gold w/red & green lithographed decoration w/a tan uniformed chauffeur, Germany, ca. 1980, 3½" l. 288.00

Penny toy, automobile, open phaeton w/original driver, olive green & black, Germany, ca. 1912, 4½" l. 196.00

Penny toy, bus, double-decker model w/driver, finished in red & light grey, marked "General - NS 293," Germany, ca. 1915, 3½" l. 322.00

Penny toy, man standing in front of a pool table w/his cue stick pulled back, lithographed tin, Germany, 1916 ....165.00

PEZ candy dispenser, plastic, Frankenstein, 4½" h. 150.00

PEZ candy dispenser, plastic, Jiminy Cricket, 4½" h. 30.00

PEZ candy dispenser, plastic, Lion w/crown, 4½" h. 30.00

PEZ candy dispenser, plastic, Maharajah, 4½" h. 25.00

PEZ candy dispenser, plastic, Peter Pez, 4½" h. 65.00

PEZ candy dispenser, plastic, Psychedelic Eye, 4½" h. (one sticker) 275.00

Santa Claus PEZ Dispenser

PEZ candy dispenser, plastic, Santa Claus, full-bodied, ca. 1950s, 4½" h. (ILLUS.) 215.00

PEZ candy dispenser, plastic, Sheik, 4½" h. 35.00

PEZ candy dispenser, plastic, Thor, the Mighty Viking, ca. 1960s, 4½" h. 173.00

PEZ candy dispenser, plastic, Wolfman, 4½" h. 160.00

PEZ candy dispenser, plastic, one modeled w/the head of an airline pilot wearing a blue captain's hat w/black brim & earphones, the other modeled as a blonde stewardess wearing a light blue hat, ca. 1970s, 4½" h., pr. 207.00

Piano, player-type, "Pianolodeon," electric, J. Chien & Co. (New York, New York), w/six music rolls 300.00

Pipsqueak toy, painted & molded composition, cat & kitten, modeled as a curled up mother cat w/a small kitten on a bellows base, ca. 1880, 2 x 4½" (bellows inoperable) 230.00

Pipsqueak toy, painted composition, exotic bird w/gilded & painted colors of orange, magenta, purple, yellow & green iridescent plumage, mounted on spring legs on a squeaking bellows base, ca. 1884, 7¾" h. (some paint wear) 173.00

Play set, bus terminal, wood pressed board & plastic, includes traffic cop, bus, car & working luggage conveyor, loudspeaker record player calls out towns, Keystone Mfg. Co. (Boston, Massachusetts), early 1950s, mint in box 625.00

Play set, fire department, wood pressed board & plastic, includes three fire vehicles, working alarm, doors & other equipment, Keystone, early 1950s, mint in box 625.00

Play set, "Soldier of Fortune," consisting of 25 standing tin plate soldiers, a lithographed tin firing toy cannon & two boxes of ammunition, Louis Marx & Co. (New York, New York), 1930s, in original illustrated box 650.00

Play set, "US Armed Forces Training Center," Series 1000, fearing guided missiles, Marx, 90% complete, in original box 250.00

Pop gun, "Daisy," double-barrel, wood stock 65.00

Pop-Up Kritter, "Stoopy Storky," red w/blue beek & yellow legs & creamy white webbed feet, on a blue guitar-shaped base, Model 410, Fisher-Price, Inc., 1931-32 (mint condition) 200.00

Printing press, cast iron, w/box of Gothic letters, 1800s, 4 x 8" 255.00

Pull toy, airplane w/pilot, "Super Jet," Model 415, Fisher-Price, Inc., 1952 ....125.00

Pull toy, bear, "Teddy Xylophone," bear plays five nickled metal keys w/drumsticks, Model 752, Fisher-Price, Inc., 1946-47 ....175.00

Pull toy, bear, "Tiny Teddy," bear playing a xylophone, Model 636, Fisher-Price, Inc., 1958-61 ....55.00

Pull toy, burro, "Bucky Burro," colorful animal w/acetate ears & spring tail emits a hee-haw sound as he bucks while pulling a two-wheeled cart w/a spring-mounted driver, Model 166, Fisher-Price, Inc., 1955-57, 13½" l. 235.00

Pull toy, clown, "Squeaky the Clown," seated figure on wheels, w/rotating arms, bobbing head that squeaks, large red nose, wearing red costume w/star design & green ruff at neck, Model 777, Fisher-Price, Inc., 1958-59 ....105.00

Pull toy, dog, "Butch the Pup," felt ears & wagging acetate tail, Model 333, Fisher-Price, Inc., 1951-53 ....130.00

Pull toy, dog cart w/driver, cast iron, a black cart on two red wheels, blue-suited driver, pulled by a large yellowish white dog, Wilkins Toy Co. (Keene, New Hampshire), ca. 1915, 9½" l. (worn paint on dog) 863.00

Pull toy, dog cart w/girl driver, cast iron, a red cart on two yellow cast wheels & driven by a girl in a blue & white dress, pulled along by a large black dog, John Harris, ca. 1895, 7" l. 437.00

Pull toy, donkey, "Kicking Donkey," large rubber ears, rope tail, leg action w/sound & rubber on all wheels for traction, Model 175, Fisher-Price, Inc., 1937-38 ....175.00

Pull toy, duck, "Baby Duck Tandem Cart," duckling pulling two two-wheeled carts, Model 75, Fisher-Price, Inc., 1953-54 ....85.00

Pull toy, duck, "Walking Duck Cart," duck w/revolving plastic feet pulling colorful two-wheeled cart, Model 305, Fisher-Price, Inc., 1957-64 ....85.00

Pull toy, elephant, "Go'N Back Jumbo," circus elephant w/beaded pull string, Model 360, Fisher-Price, Inc., 1931-1934 ....510.00

Pull toy, elephant on wheels, tinplate, large grey elephant wearing a red & yellow rug, stands on a four-wheeled green platform, attributed to George Brown, ca. 1890, 9" l. 690.00

Pull toy, fire truck, "Winky-Blinky Fire Truck," wheeled truck w/smiling face at front, ladders & other equipment lithographed on sides, three firemen figures riding in truck, Model 200, Fisher-Price, Inc., 1954-59, 12" l. ....50.00 to 75.00

Pull toy, fish, "Sunny Fish," colorfully lithographed body on wheels, spring-mounted wooden tail that wiggles up & down w/the body, concealed bell, Model 420, Fisher-Price, Inc., 1955, 6¾" l. 80.00

Pull toy, "Gaston," cast iron, Gaston, w/oversized comic 'nodder' head, seated in a two-wheeled carriage drawn by a single tan & gold horse, Kenton Hardware, ca. 1910, 9¾" l. ..322.00

Pull toy, horse, "Buddy Bronc," a young buckaroo bounces up & down on his pony, Model 430, Fisher-Price, Inc., 1938 ....300.00

Pull toy, horse, "Pony Chime," two lithographed wooden ponies pulling a musical roller chime illustrating the nursery rhyme "Ride a Cockhorse to Banbury Cross," Model 137, Fisher-Price, Inc., 1962, 13½" l. 75.00

Pull toy, horse on dumbbell-shaped wooden platform w/small metal wheels, brown fur w/black mane & tail, 30" l., 27" h. (fur worn, some missing, split seams, some rust on wheels) 330.00

Pull toy, horse on wheeled platform, brown hair cloth w/straw stuffing, on a thin rectangular board platform w/arched front, the horse w/glass eyes, partial harness & horsehair tail, painted platform w/replaced small pewter wheels, 19th c., 27" l., 26½" h. (mane replaced, one wheel damaged) 385.00

Pull toy, horse on wheeled platform, the horse w/a strong black burlap body w/black leather ears, open mouth, horsehair mane, yellow saddle, on a rectangular wooden platform w/small wheels, ca. 1910, 38" l. 863.00

Pull toy, "Humpty Dumpty," Humpty w/smiling face on one side & a crying face on the other, movable eyes on both sides, roller-type arms, tummy & feet & a bell on each arm, Model 757, Fisher-Price, Inc., 1957 ....200.00

Pull toy, mouse, "Merry Mousewife," wears a maid's hat, sweeps w/her plastic broom & squeaks, Model 662, Fisher-Price, Inc., 1962-64 ....30.00

Pull toy, monkey on a horse, carved & painted pine, the stylized figure of a monkey holding a yellow top hat & wearing a red coat seated on the back of a dappled grey horse w/leather ears, mounted on wrought-iron wheels w/an elongated wooden handle, head turns from side to side & right arm holding the top hat moves up & down when toy is pulled, New York, ca. 1860, 31½" l., 16" h. 4,888.00

Pull toy, mule on wheels, "Go'N Back Mule," oilcloth ears & rope tale, Model 350, Fisher-Price, Inc., 1931-33 ....950.00

Pull toy, rabbit, "Running Bunny Cart," rabbit pulling a colorful two-wheeled cart, Model 311, Fisher-Price, Inc., 1958, 10½" l. 85.00

Pull toy, rabbit, "Running Bunny," Model 733, Fisher-Price, Inc., 1938-41, 7" l. 95.00

Pull toy, racing scull w/rowers, cast iron, the long narrow boat w/eight action rowers pulling at the oars in unison guided by a facing coxswain, in brown shell w/simulated green water, the whole on four large notch-cut four-spoke cast wheels, Ideal (Brooklyn, New York), ca. 1895, 14½" l. (one oar replaced) 3,450.00

Pull toy, rocking horse on wheeled platform, the dark brown rocking horse w/a stiff brown mane & tail, & a yellow & tan harness, mounted on a wood rocker attached to a rectangular red wheeled platform, Germany, ca. 1920, 31 x 38" 460.00

Pull toy, rooster on wheeled platform, papier-maché bird w/original bright polychrome paint on spring legs, mounted on a wooden base w/tin wheels, marked "Ultrahart" on bottom, 8¼" h. (minor wear) 687.50

Pull toy, seal, "Susie Seal," balancing a plastic ball on her nose, waddling yellow front flappers, emits an "arf-arf" sound, Model 460, Fisher-Price, Inc., 1961-63, 6¾" l. 30.00

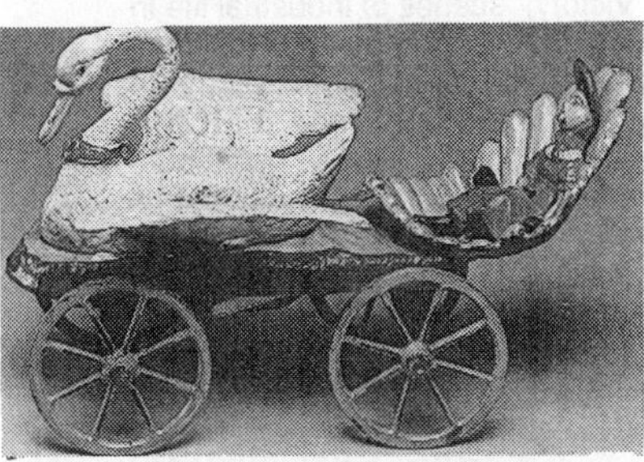

Swan Chariot Pull Toy

Pull toy, swan chariot, cast iron, girl in a light brown dress & hat in a pink-painted shell-form seat, on a platform painted taupe & brown w/white swan to front, articulated wings of swan flap as the toy moves along on yellow-painted spoked wheels, early repainting to swan, some paint loss & chips, bellows replaced, America, ca. 1885, 10½" l. (ILLUS.) 6,900.00

Pull toy, train engine, "Whistling Engine," air-pump action, model 617, Fisher-Price, Inc., 1957.............40.00

Puppet w/record, "Kilroy the Kop," wooden, Effanbee (new York, New York), mint in box & original instructions, 1945...........................135.00

Rare Fallows Horse Push Toy

Push toy, horses, tinplate & cast iron, large black horses w/red & gold trim ride between two 7" d. cast wheels, leather reins, long wooden push pole to the rear, restored, James Fallows & Sons (Philadelphia, Pennsylvania), ca. 1895, overall 30" l. (ILLUS.) 2,185.00

Puzzle, jigsaw-type, "First Ringing of the Liberty Bell," color lithograph, complete w/200 pieces, ca. 1880, near mint in original box, 9 x 12"........85.00

Puzzle, jigsaw-type, wooden, "Victory," scenes of industrial life in Europe, United States, & England, made in England, unopened.............26.00

Railway toy, printed wood, a 27" d. raised platform, a paper on wood lithographed trolly car & a paper on wood waiting platform depot w/ladder, original wooden box for car & depot, Shepard Hardware Co., ca. 1890, 11 x 27"........................2,300.00

Riverboat, cast iron, "City of New-York," painted in beige, yellow & green w/red piping, featuring red side wheels, a black stack & a wheelhouse, Harris Toy Co. (Toledo, Ohio), late 19th c., 15½" l. 1,035.00

Robot, "Attacking Martian," battery-operated, in original box 300.00

Robot, "Big Loo," battery-operated, plastic, 1960s..............................1,052.00

Robot, "Mars King," battery-operated, tin, arms move when walking, lighted space scenes on chest, loud siren, no box 275.00

Robot, "Moon Explorer," battery-operated, he walks, eyes light, arms swing, the clock hands revolve, & colored wheels revolve in two windows on either side of the clock, a piston-lever operates in a lower window, insertion of an antenna starts the action, mint in box 50.00

Robot, "Piston Head Robot," battery-operated, plastic & tin, walks & head contains moving lighted pistons, Japan, early 1970s, mint in box........65.00

Robot, "Planet Robot," windup, sparky, wrench hands, flashing dome atop head, grey, excellent working condition, K.O. (Japan), 1960s 495.00

Robot, "R-1," battery-operated, lithographed tin, robot face above tank-like body on treads, near mint condition 450.00

Robot, "Space Explorer," battery-operated, tin & plastic, spaceman walks & stops as door drops down to reveal a screen w/lighted, moving space scene.................................215.00

Robot, "X-9 Space Robot Car," battery-operated, mint in box........3,850.00

Robot, "X-70," battery-operated, walking model w/a "tulip-form" head opening to reveal a TV camera, marked "Kitahara #121," ca. 1960s, 12" h. (slight crack in battery compartment)..................................775.50

Sand pail, lithographed tin, decorated w/tropical birds, Ohio Art Company (Bryan, Ohio), large 45.00

Sand toy, cat chasing mouse, Victorian 295.00

School room set, painted wood, "District School," consisting of seven wooden standing figures, painted & w/hinged arms, plus five figures in chairs, desk, eight open wooden books & a teacher figure, Charles M. Crandall (Corington, Pennsylvania), ca. 1875, box 2½ x 6 x 10", the set..978.00

Service station, lithographed tinplate, "Roadside Rest Service Station," a coffee stand, twin gas pumps w/original glass light & accessories including motor oil cases, oil stand, water bucket & raised auto jack w/electric light underneath, Louis Marx, ca. 1935, 5 x 10 x 13½" 460.00

Sewing machine, "Kayanee," U.S. Zone Germany, mint in box 65.00

Sewing machine, "Lindstrom's Little Miss, Model 203," blue w/colorful stenciling, ca. 1930s, w/original box 135.00

Sewing machine, "Little Missy," black & gold picture of pretty child's face, ca. 1889, Lindstrom 210.00

Sewing machine, "Singer Model 20," cast iron, 1920s 60.00

Sewing machine, "Stitch Mistress," metal, w/original box & instructions..65.00

Sewing machine, "Stitchwell," cast iron, w/original wooden box 150.00

Sled, child's size, wood & steel, sturdy wood platform w/steel-edged runners, h.p. in dark red & detailed in yellow, ca. 1905, 39" l. 368.00

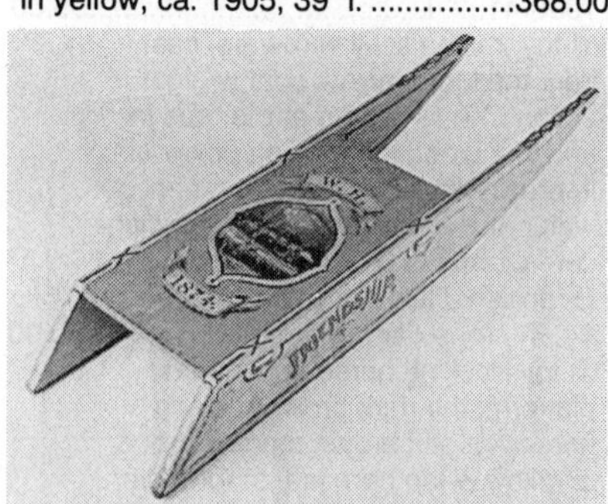

Painted & Decorated Wooden Sled

Sled, child's size, painted & decorated wood, platform w/central scene w/initials "W.H." above & "1874" below, runners stenciled "Friendship," highlighted w/gilt decoration, 42" l. (ILLUS.)............1,100.00

Sled, child's size, painted & decorated wood, red w/stenciled design, curved wooden runners 425.00

Steam shovel, cast iron, "Panama," a swiveling red cab sits on treads, encasing a nickeled spring-activated shovel, Hubley, early 20th c., 9" l. (paint wear) 1,265.00

Speedboat, steam fired, hull repainted white & grey lined w/red, w/short funnel, adjustable rudder, three-blade screw, Bing, Germany, ca. 1910, 19¼" l. 546.00

Stove, "Perfection," cast iron, brass-plated, w/warming shelf on top, 4½" d., 10" w., 8½" h.......................260.00

Stuffed animal, cat, seated black velvet animal w/stitched details & glass eyes, 7" h. (one eye cracked) 137.50

Taxicab, cast iron, painted orange w/black trim & printed on the doors "Yellow Cab Co.," & "Phone 30," screen grille, lights, rear tire, orange & white solid disc wheels, w/driver, Arcade Mfg. Co. (Freeport, Illinois) ca. 1925, 9" l. 3,220.00

Taxicab, cast iron, "Red Top" cab in red, white & black w/a nickled driver & white rubber tires, Arcade, ca. 1924, 7¾" l. 1,380.00

Taxicab, "Parmelee Yellow Cab," cast iron, yellow & black w/nickled grille & rear license plate, original embossed rubger wheels, Arcade, 1935, 8" l.......................................3,220.00

Tea kettle, cov., cast iron, "Griswold No. 0," colonial design, swirl handle, swinging cover, w/footed iron trivet 235.00

Tea kettle, cov., cast iron, "J.J. Siddons No. 70," w/brass handle & brass lid, w/iron trivet w/rattail handle, 1½ pt. 275.00

Tractor, "John Deere," die-cast metal, w/high lift, 1950s, 13" l. 150.00

Tractor, "Oliver," cast iron, w/driver, 2¾" 100.00

Tractor w/road scraper scoop, cast iron, finished in green w/red wheels, driver, silvered scoop operated by a hand chain, Hubley, early 20th c., 9¼" l. 483.00

Train car, "No. 4 Electric Rapid Transit" double engine motor car, finished in tan & orange w/gold lettering, eight wheels, nine cut-out windows to each side, electric motors, standard gauge, Lionel, 1908-13, 14" l. (some paint loss to sides & roof).................................7,475.00

Train engine, keywind, cast iron, a six-wheeled engine painted black & red w/a tall stack, bell, lamp, turning cow catcher & a keywind motor placed in the cab, Welker & Crosby (Brooklyn, New York), ca. 1880, 11½" l. 1,840.00

Train, engine & tender, Carette gauge I 4-4-0 style, live steam type, finished in NER green & black lined yellow & black, numbered "1870" to side of cab, control levers & water gauge glass to cab, front headlamps, w/matching six-wheeled tender lettered "NER" to sides, length over buffers 23" (paint loss to side of boiler) 4,600.00

Train engine & tender, brass & steel, coal fired live steam "Earlham Hall" locomotive numbered "7930" on brass plaque & w/curved brass nameplate over wheels, cab w/sliding roof panel, center lever opening firebox door, pressure gauge, water gauge glass, safety, finished in green & black, w/matching six-wheel "Great Northern" tender & length of brass display track on wood board base, engineered model 3½" gauge, engine & tender 47" l. 1,495.00

Marklin Train Engine & Tender

Train engine & tender, Marklin gauge I 'RI' 0-4-0 style, spirit fired live steam-type, finished in black lined red, gold & silver, cab w/water gauge glass & whistle, w/matching four-wheeled tender, engine lacks lamps & cow catcher, surface losses & some rust (ILLUS.) 633.00

Train engine & tender, Stevens Model Dockyard 4-4-0 style, brass & steel, coal fired live steam model finished in Great Northern Railway green lined black & white, w/brown undercarriage, cab w/water gauge glass, reverse, safety, whistle, opening fire-box door, cast wheels, brass boiler, numbered on oval plaque to side of cab "5443," w/matching six-wheeled tender lettered "GNR" to side w/maker's plaque, 8" gauge, England, early 20th c., overall 61" l. 6,038.00

Train set, paper-on-wood, a highly lithographed "Jack and Jill" engine & tender together w/a "Mother Goose" passenger car depicting many children in all the windows, Reed Toy Co. (Leominster, Massachusetts), ca. 1895, overall 38" l., the set (loose wheels) 2,070.00

Train set, cast iron, clockwork floor-type, a pair of "WHIST" passenger cars w/cut-out profiles of passengers at windows pulled by a small black & red locomotive, Hubley, ca. 1906, overall 24" l., the set 1,150.00

Train set, cast iron, consisting of an early engine No. 999, tender, passenger car, "Vanderbilt," & a combination buffet & baggage car, marked on sides "New York Central & Hudson," cars in dark brown w/maroon roofs, Pratt & Letchworth, ca. 1900, overall 60" l., the set (small chip on locomotive cab, cars playworn) 4,830.00

Train set, paper-on-wood, consisting of an engine, a baggage car & a marked "Pawtucket" passenger car, all highly lithographed & marked "New York Central," Bliss, ca. 1890, 28" l., the set (paper missing on cow catcher) 920.00

Train set, floor model, tinplate, a tank locomotive w/two cast driving wheels, in green & black detailed in gold & red, w/red-lined yellow passenger car w/one opening door on each side, a blue-lined yellow passenger car, & a brown baggage ca, Marklin, ca. 1902, locomotive 10¾" l., 4 pcs. (some restoration & repainting)....................................4,025.00

Train set, a 0-4-0 tank locomotive in black-lined red, white & silver, the cab w/two sets of hinged opening doors, control levers at rear, w/lengths of racked track & blue-painted girder supports for raised portions of track, Gauge I, Marklin, Germany, ca. 1900, locomotive 8" l., 26 pcs. 5,750.00

Truck, Bell Telephone Mack truck, cast iron, red truck w/open top & flat roof jutting over cab, embossed "BELL TELEPHONE" on sides, w/a detachable tow & cable pulley, trailer & pole, Hubley, ca. 1930, 13" l...2,185.00

Truck, coal dump truck, cast iron, red & green, the load can be dumped by pulling a lever at the driver's right, Hubley, ca. 1922, 9½" l................1,380.00

Truck, delivery, "Mack," cast iron, red open cab w/driver, orange cage-type rear carriage w/opening doors, lettered "Junior Supply Co., New York, Philadelphia," on yellow

Dent Cast Iron Delivery Truck

spoked wheels, Dent Hardware Co. (Fullerton, Pennsylvania), ca. 1925, 15½" l. (ILLUS.) 9,775.00

Truck, dump-type, "Mack," cast iron w/steel frame, grey body w/metal spoked wheels, stickers on each door, w/driver, Arcade, ca. 1925, 12" l., 5⅜" h. (overall paint chipping) 935.00

Truck, oil tanker, steelplate, a "L" high cab painted black, the tank in dark green, the chassis & wheels in red, spigot at rear, turning front wheels, two oil cans included, Buddy-L (Moline Pressed Steel Co., E. Moline, Illinois), ca. 1925, 25" l. 1,725.00

Truck, pressed steel, "Baggage Line," the high covered cab in black w/a vivid yellow open bed w/slatted sides, two chains for tailgate, turning front wheels, Buddy L, ca. 1928, 26" l. (some flaking paint on bed)...2,185.00

Truck, tank-type, "Mack," cast iron, green body w/"Gasoline" in raised letters painted white on tank & "Mack" in raised letters painted white on door, white rubber tires, Arcade, ca. 1925, 13¼" l., 4¾" h. (one rear tire missing rubber, minor chip on right square edge rail) 1,650.00

Truck, "Hercules Motor Express," tinplate, open cab & slatted back, painted black & orange w/red metal wheels, movable rear tailgate, sign on the side, Chein, ca. 1930, 20" l. ..748.00

Wagon, buckboard & driver, cast iron, four-wheeled yellow buckboard w/driver, pulled by two white goats on wheels, early 20th c., 13½" l. 368.00

Wagon, child's size, painted wood, upright sides of narrow slats, wooden wheels w/steel bands, steel fittings, old worn white repaint, found in North Carolina, 33" l. plus tongue...379.50

Wagon, milk-type, painted & stenciled tinplate, four-wheeled blue & gold milk wagon w/a driver's seat & a stenciled picture of a cow & "Pure Milk" on either side, pulled by a white horse, George Brown & Co. (Forestville, Connecticut), 13½" l. (paint worn) 322.00

Wagon, transfer-type, cast iron, green & red painted wagon w/open top, w/driver & drawn by two brown & one white trotting horse, Dent, early 20th c., 19½" l. 1,265.00

Washing machine, "Little Miss," ca. 1940, Marx 135.00

Windup carved wood & cloth "George Washington," the carved wood figured of Washington standing & wearing period style clothes & dancing atop a tinplate drum, the drum w/lithographed eagle, probably created for the American Centennial in 1876, 9½" h. 5,175.00

Windup celluloid black baby, crawls & turns head 265.00

Windup celluloid boy playing xylophone, Occupied Japan 225.00

Windup celluloid monkey playing banjo, Occupied Japan 175.00

Windup tin automobile, couple w/rumble seat, finished in lavendar & purple, operating front headlamp, turning wheels & a bumper, Kingsbury, ca. 1930, 12½" l. (slight paint scratches, motor skips) 253.00

Windup tin automobile, "1948 Buick," No. 100, Schuco Toy Co. (Nuremberg, Germany), excellent condition 175.00

Windup Tin German Automobile

Windup tin automobile, "Ta-Ra-Ra-Bumm" auto w/clown driver & two clowns in the back seat, as car moves forward the clowns' heads move back & forth, Ebo (Germany), ca. 1915, 7" l. (ILLUS.) 4,830.00

Windup tin "Baggage Porter," Unique Art Mfg. Co., Inc. (New York, New York), near mint 195.00

Windup tin bird in birdcage, the multicolored bird perched on a branch w/rocks & flowers at the bottom of the cage, a gold wire cage rests on a tinplate base w/large key, the bird's head moves from side to side, the tail shifts back & forth & the bird's beak opens & closes while a chirping nose is emitted, start & stop control on bottom of base, 21" h. 805.00

Windup tin "Charlie Chimp Hula Expert," chimp w/hula hoop around his waist, 1950s, Japan, mint in box 95.00

Windup tin "Clown on Roller Skates," near mint in original box 400.00

Windup tin "Crawling Baby," plastic & cloth, TN (Japan) ca. 1950, mint in box 75.00

Windup tin "Dare Devil," a black & white lithographed zebra kicks his hind legs at a cowboy driver of a two-wheeled cart, Lehmann (Germany) Model No. 752, early 20th c., 7" l. 253.00

Windup tin "Dora the Driver," Marx, near mint 235.00

Windup tin drummer, lithographed decoration w/a tall rounded hat & dress uniform, Louis Marx & Co., 9" h. (light wear on drum) 185.00

Windup tin "Fire Chief Siren Coupe," hard rubber tires, w/box, 14¾" l. 375.00

Windup tin "Flying Circus," elephant supports a flying plane & flying clown, Unique Art Mfg. Co. 600.00

Windup tin "George Washington Bridge," each side of the bridge lithographed w/Hudson River scenes, the bridge features suspension cables & the twin arches, a small bus travels to & fro across the space, Bueschel, ca. 1936, box encased in Plexiglas, 25" l. 1,610.00

Windup tin, "Ham and Sam," consisting of one dancing figure beside seated piano player, on wood-effect base, mechanism under piano, w/start/stop lever, LineMar (Japan), ca. 1950, good condition, 5½" h. 575.00

Windup tin "Jenny the Balky Mule," Ferdinand Strauss Corp. (New York, New York) 215.00

Windup tin "Monkey, the Sheriff," monkey wearing cowboy hat & carrying two guns, 1950s, Japan, mint in box 95.00

Windup tin "New Century Circle," a man in a three-wheeled vehicle, seated under an umbrella twirled by a black servant in a back seat, man removes his hat in greeting, Lehmann, Model No. 345, early 20th c., 5" l. 322.00

Windup tin paddle wheel boat, large green & white boat w/a pair of smoke stacks & covered passenger deck, on a wheeled stand, marked "St. Louis," Marklin (Germany), early 20th c., 31" l. 19,550.00

Windup tin "Roller Coaster," includes two cars, J. Chein & Co., ca. 1938, mint in box 390.00

Windup tin "Ski Jumper," skier flips over on bottom of slope, Wolverine Co. (Pittsburgh, Pennsylvania), mint in box 225.00

Windup tin tank, "Sparkling Tank," 1930s, Louis Marx & Co., w/box 130.00

Windup tin tractor, "Sparkling Climbing Tractor," Louis Marx & Co., w/box 185.00

Windup tin & felt bear, "Cubby the Reading Bear," Japan, mint in box ..100.00

Windup tin & wood battleship "New Jersey," finished in dark grey & green, painted portholes, triple screws, three stacks, searchlights, cannon, ventilator, gun turrets & flags, Orkin, ca. 1920, 35" l. 1,265.00

Windup wooden dog, "Puppy Back-Up," Fisher-Price, Inc., No. 365, 1932-36..145.00

TRADE CARDS

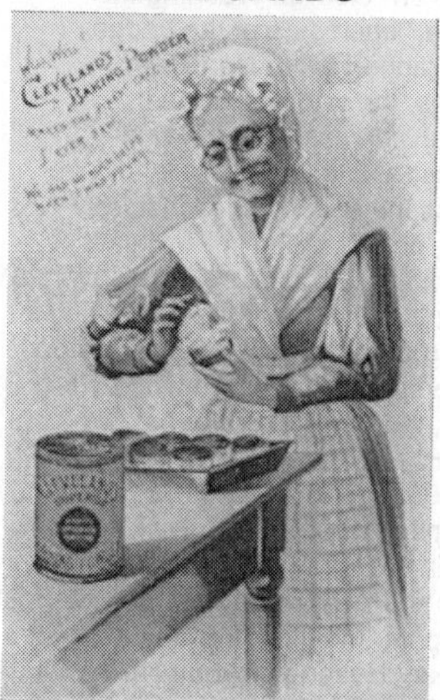

Baking Powder Trade Card

The Victorian trade card evolved from informal calling cards and hand-decorated notes. From the 1850s through the 1890s, the American home was saturated with these black-and-white and chromolithographed advertising cards given away with various products.

Baking powder, "Cleveland's Baking Powder," scene of elderly woman sampling warm muffins from a pan, can of the product in the foreground (ILLUS.) $27.50

Billiards, "Burrows Home Billiards," die-cut model of a colorful butterfly, advertising on the reverse 12.00

Cigarettes, "Hassan Cigarettes," "Indian Life in the '60s," 1910, set of 22...130.00

Cleaner, "Bon Ami," pictures baby chicks in baskets, 1904.....................10.00

Clipper ship, "Silas Fish - Sutton & Co's Dispatch Line for San Francisco...," large gold vignette of a fish w/'Silas Fish' overprinted in red & blue, other lettering & frame lines in purple, ca. 1850s (little glue residue on reverse) 5,060.00

Clockwork toys, "Crawling Baby" pictures early clockwork bisque toy & "For Sale By The National Toy Company - 299 Broadway, New York - A Natural Creeping Baby," 2½ x 4" 145.00

Cocoa, "Van Houten's Cocoa," mechanical-type, bust portrait of an unhappy man looking into a cup marked "Imitation," opens to show man happy w/Van Houten's..............24.00

Engine oil, "Eldorado Engine Oil," winter landscape featuring the "Ice Palace at St. Paul 1886," advertising across the top reading "Use Eldorado Engine Oil - It is the Best," advertising on the reverse, black & white 20.00

Furniture, "Lang & Nau Furniture, Brooklyn," detailed Victorian parlor interior w/numerous pieces of furniture, reverse w/advertising for the spring 1883 season, in bluish green..60.50

Ginger, "Sanford's Ginger," black comical, caricature of a black girl seated on a huge watermelon & holding a black baby in a cradle made from a watermelon rind, bright colors 19.00

Graniteware, "Gramote Iron Ware Is 'All the Gossip'," scene of three old ladies gathered around a table, one serving coffee to the other two using graniteware pieces............................48.50

Ink, "Stafford's Inks Last forever...," hold-to-light-type, charming bust portrait of a sleeping Victorian toddler, held to light the child opens her eyes 22.00

Insurance, "Continental Insurance Company," snowy winter landscape w/children rolling large balls of snow, some forming the word

"Continental," one ball dated "1882," advertising statement for 1882 on the reverse, in shades of sepia 35.00

Lamp oil, "Home Light Oil," colorful scene of Uncle Sam supplying various figures representing countries of the world from a large barrel, titled "Uncle Sam supplying the World with Home Light Oil" 39.50

Patent medicine, "Dr. Morse's Indian Root Pills," mechanical-type, shows a sick-looking Victorian lady w/baby, opens to show the lady & baby healthy & happy in a Victorian interior, scarce 66.00

"Everett Piano" Card

Piano, "Everett Piano - 'For Sale Only by Fisher and Ogden - Oneonta, N.Y.'....," hold-to-light-type, shows a scene of Victorian ladies, gentlemen & children looking into a large glass store window, held to light shows a man watching a lady playing a piano, ca. 1880s (ILLUS.) 44.00

Railway, "Mount Washington Railway," central oval reserve w/a landscape of Mount Washington in the distance, wording in outer frame, Boston departures on the reverse 27.50

Sewing machine, "White Sewing Machine Co.," mechanical-type, shows a cross, ugly family struggling w/an old sewing machine, opens to show them transformed into a happy, handsome family 50.50

Silver company, "Gorham Manufacturing Co.," a design of a tea kettle on stand marked "Tea Kettle - Celtic," drawing of Celtic crosses in a landscape in the upper border, Gorham trademark in the lower right, the kettle in silver & vignette scene in green, gold lettering, information on the Celtic period on the reverse 22.00

Sleds, "Flexible Flyers," fanciful scene of children sledding down a steep hill & taking off to become soaring birds, on a grey background, advertising on the reverse 39.50

Stoves, "Acorn Stoves," mechanical-type, shows unhappy Victorian couple w/bad food in a cold room, opens to show a warm, happy couple 26.50

Thread, "J. & P. Coats' Spool Cotton - Ye Skilful Fisherman...," mechanical-type, comic, scene of a rustic fisherman & a boy holding a spool of thread on a dock w/a small fish getting away, opens to show man catching a large fish w/Coats' thread...22.00

TRADE CATALOGS

Atlas Portland Cement, 1924, 42 pp., 11 x 14" $39.00

Belknap Hardware & Manufacturing, 1955, Louisville, 4,000 pp. 65.00

Birge Wall Paper, 1912, room illustrations, Mission, Arts & Crafts, etc. 140.00

Blees-Moore Instrument Co. 1901, surgical instruments, 645 pp., 6¾ x 9¾" 126.00

Bradley Swim Togs (men & women), 1930, die-cut cover, color illustrations 20.00

Cartier, Inc., New York, 1930, "The Book of Gifts," 16 pp. 35.00

Craftsman Furniture Made by Gustav Stickley, January 1909, 6 x 9" (tears to paper cover, contents good condition but for one tear) 192.50

Carson, Pirie, Scott & Co., 1925, jewelry, watches, silverware, etc., 346 pp. 50.00

De Laval Cream Separators, 1952, 21 pp. 15.00

Elkhart Carriage & Harness Mfg Co., 1904, 240 pp. (minimal cover damage) 98.00

Fischer Equipment Co., 1900, includes moto-vehicles (electrical), buggies, surreys, phaetons, etc., 24 pp., 6 x 9" 83.00

Ft. Dearborn Watch Co., 1928, watches, lamps, fixtures, etc., 612 pp., 9 x 12" 105.00

Goldsmith Athletic Goods, 1922, baseball, football, etc., well illustrated 38.00

Gong Bell Mfg., 1919, fine gongs & bell toys, Connecticut, 34 pp., 6 x 9" 50.00
Good Year, 1937, Spring & Summer, auto supplies, bicycles, radios, etc., 30 pp. 35.00
Gusmer (A.) & Co., 1924, brewery machinery, casks, etc., 6 x 9¼" 48.00
Holmes & Idle, 1889, ladies & children's collars & cuffs, 90 models pictured, 28 pp., 3 x 6" 32.00
Iver Johnson Sporting Goods Co., 1903, guns, rifles, bicycles, etc., 120 pp., 9¼ x 12" 73.00
Kingman Plow, 1910, farm implements & vehicles, hard cover, 221 pp., 6½ x 9¾" 88.00
Krones System of Industrial Drawing, 1893, Krone Bros., New York 55.00
Larkin & Co., 1916-17, No. 76 ....45.00
Larkin & Co., 1924-25, pictures furniture & premiums 40.00
Lowney's Chocolates, 1905, colorful Art Nouveau graphics, product illustrations 57.50
Luden's Easter Candies, 1934, detailed pictures of their Easter line on glossy paper, some in color, 65 pp. 31.00
Marshall Field & Co., Jewelry Department, 1903, hard cover 89.00
May & Malone Co., 1931, assortment of merchandise including section of fountain pens, hardcover, 704 pp. 75.00
McCormick, 1898, farm machinery, illustrated, color covers 95.00
Mills,(Thomas) & Brothers, Manufacturers of Confectioners' Machinery & Equipment, 1924, candy making machines, toys & chocolate molds, starch & fruit drop patterns, store display items, scales, etc., 219 pp. (some cover wear) 140.00
Montgomery Ward, 1917, Spring & Summer 65.00
Montgomery Ward, 1953-54, Fall & Winter 25.00
National Target & Supply Co., ca. 1930, guns, etc., 131 pp. 60.00
Netter Bros., 1898, pure rye whiskies, brandies, rums, etc., 32 pp., 5¼ x 8" 33.00
P & O Vehicles, 1915, buggies, wagons, surreys & accessories, 92 pp. 76.00
Pardee (Lucius,) 1875, groceries, wines, liquors, Havana cigars, etc., some illustrations, 64 pp., 5½ x 7¾" 63.00
Remington Firearms & Ammunition, 1923, No. 107, 192 pp. 42.50
Riker's Drug Store, 1905, medical & health supplies 38.00
Root (A.I.) Co., 1903, bee keeper's supplies 12.00
Ross (L.P.), 1905, spring, footwear for men, ladys & boys, 72 pp., 6 x 9½" ...40.00
Savage Arms Company, 1905, No. 15, color cover, 48 pp., w/original envelope 52.50
Schmelrer's, 1916, bicycles & supplies, 14 pictures of bicycles, 162 pp., 5½ x 7¾" 47.00
Schwahn-Seyberth Co., Eau Claire, Wisconsin, ca. 1915, harness & harness parts 85.00
Schwarz (F.A.O.), 1944, toy catalog 74.00
Sears, Roebuck and Co., 1910, camera catalog, Art Nouveau cover, 72 pp. 95.00
Sears, Roebuck and Co., Mid-Summer Book, 1945, 139 pp. 20.00
Shapleigh Hardware Co., 1957, Keen Kutter, leather-bound 525.00
Spiegel, 1947, Christmas, large toy section 45.00
Spirella Corsets, 1924, 128 pp. 35.00
Stanley Rule & Level Co., 1907, No. 34, 144 pp. 49.50
Stark Bros. Fruit Trees, ca. 1925, Louisiana, MO, 64 pp. 18.00
True Fruit, 1912, soda fountain requisites, brilliant color illustrations 65.00
Victor Red Seal Records, 1923, 105 pp. 15.00
Webster Sterling Silverware & Novelties, 1952, baby items, serving pieces, dresserwares, etc., 72 pp. 52.00
Western Ranchman Outfitters, Cheyenne, Wyoming, 1951-52, fall & winter, saddles, spurs, Western clothes, etc., 70 pp. 40.00
Westinghouse Co., 1885, threshing machines & engines, 30 pp., 5¾ x 9¼" 84.00
White Mfg. Co., 1900, hearse accessories, plumes, rails, emblems, door handles, etc., 37 pp. 38.00
Williams (Charles) Store, Christmas, 1929 ....100.00
Wyeth Hardware, 1927, 2,417 pp., hardcover 150.00

TRAMP ART

Tramp art flourished in the United States from about 1875 into the 1930s. These chip-carved woodenwares, mostly in the form of boxes or other useful items, were made mainly from old cigar boxes although fruit and vegetable crates were also used. The wood is predominantly edge-carved and subsequently layered to create a unique effect. Completed items were given an overall stained finish which was sometimes further enhanced with painted highlights. Though there seems to be no written record of the artists, many of whom were itinerants, there is a growing interest in collecting this ware.

Box, cov., rectangular w/a hinged cover, two pyramidal stacks of chip-carved blocks on the cover & the front & back sides & a single stack at each end, 9½" l. $93.50

Box w/drawers, the rectangular case w/one drawer above the other, overall chip-carved decoration, old alligatored varnish finish, 6" h. (minor edge damage) 200.00

Frame w/mirror, nearly square mirror surrounded by a layered chip-carved frame composed of stars & circles w/tulips in the corners centering a scalloped flowerhead at the crest, trimmed w/gilding & red velvet, ca. 1930, 33½ x 38" 4,600.00

Picture frame, criss-cross style w/laminated jigsaw work w/chip-carved & carved doubled spread-winged eagle crest, old brown finish, porcelain button trim, one eagle w/old repair, minor edge damage, 14 x 17½" 247.50

Wall pocket, shaped pointed crest w/diamond design, conforming pocket, overall chip-carving, 10½" w., 7½" h. 110.00

TRAYS, SERVING & CHANGE

Anheuser-Busch Tray

Both serving & change trays once used in taverns, cafes and the like and usually bearing advertising for a beverage maker are now being widely collected. All trays listed are heavy tin serving trays, unless otherwise noted.

American Line, colorful center scene of steamship under sail, printed at the top border w/"Compliments American Line" & along the bottom edge w/"Philadelphia - Queenstown - Liverpool," ca. 1910-20, 4¼" d., (change)..$115.00

Anheuser-Busch, St. Louis, Missouri, maiden holding Eagle & "A" logo symbol aloft surrounded by winged cherubs, ca. 1900, 13½ x 16½" oval (ILLUS.) 750.00

Cottolene Shortening, depicts blacks picking cotton (change)....................125.00

Dobler Brewing Co., Albany, New York, half-length color profile portrait of a lovely dark-haired lady wearing a low-cut gown 100.00

Fairy Soap Change Tray

Fairy Soap, little girl w/violets sitting on large bar of soap, change (ILLUS.) 95.00

Globe-Wernicke Furniture, depicts 1930s couple (change) 55.00

Green River Whiskey, black man & horse in front of building w/"She Was Bred in Old Kentucky," 12" d...............................500.00 to 600.00

Heath & Milligan Mfg. Co., Chicago, Illinois, "Best Prepared Paint," 1920s (change)..100.00

J. Hungerford Smith Co., "True Fruit Flavors Make Our Fountain Famous," Rochester, NY, 11 x 13½"...85.00

Iroquois Indian Head Beer & Ale, Buffalo, New York, Indian head profile in center 50.00

Mascot Cut Tobacco, depicts a cottage scene, artist-signed (change)..95.00

McAvoys Malt Marrow, scene of a boy w/his dog, 15" d. 475.00

Miller High Life Beer Tray

Miller "High Life" Beer, Milwaukee, Wisconsin, scene of young lady wearing a red striped dress & pointed hat & sitting on a crescent moon, 14" d. (ILLUS.) 82.50

Old Reliable Coffee, w/pretty lady, ca. 1907, approximately 5" d. (change)...148.00

Red Raven Splits, oval, scene of an elderly fat man wearing a top hat & sitting asleep w/a bottle & red raven on the table in front of him, titled "It's a Dream," change, 4⅜ x 6⅛" (some scratches) 95.00

Robert Burns Cigars, Savage Mfg. Co., depicts Robert Burns, ca. 1930 ....150.00

TRIVETS

George Washington Trivet

When numbers are noted following trivets listed below they refer to numbers in the long out-of-print books, Trivets, Book 1 *and* Trivets, Old and Re-Pro, Book 2, *both by Dick Hankenson. A recent comprehensive book will also be of great help to collectors.* A Collector's Guide to Trivets & Stands, *by Rob Roy Kelly and James Ellwood, was released by Golden Era Publications, Lima, Ohio, in 1990. All trivets are cast iron except where otherwise noted.*

Child, dog & hat within a lacy rectangular framework w/rounded corners, lacy handle, 11" l. $137.50

Cleveland (Grover), bust portrait within horseshoe, black paint...........115.50

"Colt" w/long-tailed "C" in center of angled bars, spade-shaped, Book 1, No. 130 ....95.00

Columns & arcs, rectangular w/ornate oval handle 10" (short hairline in center)...71.50

Eagle & "God Bless Our Home," spread-winged bird perched on an arrow above horseshoe lettered "God Bless Our Home" around the outer edges, "Welcome" around a smaller horseshoe centering an anchor within the curve, 10"..............93.50

Florals, shaped triangular form, star within a circle handle, 9" l. 71.50

Garfield (James), bust portrait within horseshoe lettered "Garfield," Book 2, No. 3 ....82.50

George Washington bust portrait in relief center, Book 1, No. 17 (ILLUS.) 71.50

Girl's face within a circle, within a square foliate surround, large ring handle, 8"...93.50

Heart & openwork, heart handle, 9½" l. 126.50

Lincoln Drape (or Broom & Wheat), rectangular w/scrolls flanking tassels (brooms), center wheat stalk, ring & heart handle, Griswold, Book 1, No. 27 ....25.00

Lyre-form, wrought iron & brass, tooled decoration, penny feet, wooden handle, 11" l., 7" h. 220.00

Ober Large Leaf, embossed in large script on reverse "OBER," Book 2, No. 20 ....115.50

Odd Fellows, brass, three circles & hand & heart in center, wreath frame, three-ring handle, Book 1, No. 13 ....75.00 to 100.00

Pinwheel-type, round w/narrow oval handle, 7½" l. 82.50

Scrolls centering three hearts within a circular frame, six small tab feet, worn blue fired enamel, 8" d. 93.50

Spade tulip, spade-shaped w/scrolling tulips in center, 10" l., Book 2, No. 45 ....93.50
Starflower within a circle, spade-shaped w/fans in corners, 9½" l. 60.50
Tulip, stylized openwork blossom, marked "S.B. Miller," 8" l. 49.50
"Uneedit Gas Iron" & Rosenbaum Mfg. Co., New York" embossed in recessed panels, Book 1, No. 147.....40.00

VALENTINES

Early Pennsylvania Valentine

Folk art-type, folded & pin-pricked paper fraktur-style, square w/lightly scalloped edge, decorated in the center w/a four-petal design surrounded by stylized pin-prick hearts & German inscriptions within an outer border of water-color floral swags in red, blue, yellow & mauve, dated "1839," Pennsylvania, unframed, 8¼" sq. (minor damage & stains) $990.00
Folk art-type, folded paper decorated on both sides in water-color, ink & graphite w/squares of hearts, floral bands & romantic inscribed verses, Pennsylvania, mid-19th c., 12½" sq. (ILLUS.) 1,650.00
Shellwork, in hinged double octagonal case, one side w/geometric design centering a heart, the other w/similar geometric design centering "FORGET ME NOT," late 19th c., 8½" w. (minor imperfections) 1,430.00
Shellwork, in hinged double octagonal case, decorated w/compass rose & heart patterns, 19th c., 13¾" w. (losses) 2,860.00

VENDING & GAMBLING DEVICES

Carnival Wheel of Fortune

Arcade, "Boop-A-Doop," Pace Mfg. Co., 1932 ....$575.00
Arcade, "Kenney's League Leader," 1-cent operation, one button releases the ball & another button releases the bat, J.H. Kenney & Co. 775.00
Arcade, "The Wizard," wooden cabinet, Mills Novelty Co., ca. 1904 ......475.00
Arcade, "World Series," Rock-Ola Mfg., 1933 ....625.00
Candy vendor, "Owl Gum," oak cabinet, single column, Mill's Novelty Co., ca. 1905 ....250.00
Fortune vendor, "Swami," also holds menus & napkins 65.00
Gambling, Bally's "Reliance" dice countertop slot machine, 5-cent play, ca. 1936 ....4,900.00
Gambling, Caille's "Cadet" countertop slot machine, 10-cent play, 1936-39 (restored) 1,900.00
Gambling, Caille's "Silent Sphinx" countertop slot machine, 5-cent play, ca. 1932 ....2,600.00
Gambling, carnival wheel of fortune, horse race-type, a large colorful wheel w/a scene of a different racing horse for each of the ten numbers, number reel at the top, on a tripod base, early 20th c., imperfections, wheel 33" d., 46" h. (ILLUS.)............990.00
Gambling, Eagle's "Eagle" countertop slot machine, 25-cent play, front case decorated w/a grey eagle & red, yellow & blue trim, jackpot symbol to side of window at top, "#270015" on side by handle, ca. 1910, 15" d., 16" w., 26" h. 1,595.00
Gambling, Groetchen's "Columbia" countertop slot machine, 25-cent play 1,100.00

Gambling, Jennings' "Four Star Chief" countertop slot machine, 5-cent play, 1936 ....2,800.00

Gambling, Jennings' "Rockaway" countertop pocket payout slot machine, 1-cent play, 1931-33....1,150.00 to 1,200.00

Gambling, Jennings' "Standard Chief" countertop slot machine, 25-cent play, 1946-56 (restored) 1,200.00

Gambling, Jennings' "Sun Chief" countertop slot machine, $1-play, 1949....2,200.00

Gambling, Jennings' "Today" countertop slot machine, 5-cent play, 1926....1,450.00

Gambling, Mills' "Black Cherry" countertop slot machine front on pre-World War II machine, 50-cent play, ca. 1936 ....1,500.00 to 1,600.00

Gambling, Mills' "Blue Front" countertop slot machine, 25-cent play (restored)....2,200.00

Gambling, Mills' "Cherry" ("Bursting Cherry") countertop slot machine, 10-cent play, 1937 ....2,100.00

Gambling, Mills' "Cherry" ("Bursting Cherry") countertop slot machine, 25-cent play, 1937 (restored)....1,275.00

Gambling, Mills' "Chicago" upright floor model slot machine, 50-cent play, ca. 1912 ....12,500.00

Gambling, Mills' "Diamond" countertop slot machine, 10-cent play....1,150.00

Gambling, Mills' "Four Jacks" countertop slot machine, 5-cent play 1,375.00

Gambling, Mills' "Twentieth Century" upright slot machine, single wheel, 25-cent play, ca. 1902 ....12,500.00

Gambling, Pace's "Chrome Comet" countertop slot machine, 25-cent play, 1939 ....2,100.00

Gambling, Pace's "Comet" countertop slot machine, 1-cent play 1,050.00

Gambling, Watling's "Blue Seal" countertop slot machine w/front vendor, 25-cent play (restored)....3,300.00

Gambling, Watling's "Blue Seal" countertop slot machine w/side vendor, 25-cent play (restored)....2,400.00

Gambling, Watling's "Rol-A-Top Bell" countertop slot machine, w/cornucopia of coins, etc., 10-cent play, 1935-46 (ILLUS. top next column) 3,800.00

Golf ball vendor, "Sportsman," Jennings, 1934-36 ....5,300.00

Gum vendor, "Columbus Model 34," clear glass cylindrical dome w/porcelain base & cover, Columbus Vending Co., 1936 ....550.00

Gum vendor, "Cop Directing Traffic (Stop & Go)," policeman holding a stop & go sign, short porcelain case, 1-cent operation, Pulver Mfg. Co. 665.00

Watling's "Rol-A-Top Bell"

Gum vendor, Penny King "4 In 1," Art Deco style machine w/a chromium finish, base rotates, ca. 1937, original condition....675.00

Gum vendor, Pulver "Foxy Grandpa," case w/Foxy Grandpa inside, ca. 1900 ....2,000.00

Match vendor, "1¢ Match," Columbus Vending Co., 16" h.....150.00

Peanut vendor, George E. Bayle Co. "Bayle's Salted Peanuts," oak cabinet w/glass window, ca. 1910 ....1,600.00

Peanut vendor, "Silver King Hot Nut," aluminum base w/curved chute embossed "Try Some," clear glass globe w/ruby hobnail glass top w/flashing light, Silver King Corp., 1947 ....95.00

Postage stamp dispenser, porcelain, tall upright case w/a porcelain front in white in brown w/a stepped design, brown & white lettering, reads "U.S. Postage Stamps" at the center below stamp windows & coin slots for 5¢ & 10¢, pull levers at the bottom, 6" sq., 14" h. (no key, chipping to porcelain on top)....110.00

Trade stimulator, "Imp," Groetchen, w/cigarette reels, 5-cent operation, in original factory box & original keys, 1940s....350.00

Trade stimulator, "Official Sweepstakes," racing horses revolve on a track, 1-cent play, w/gumball prize, Rock-Ola Mfg. Co., 1935 ....1,400.00

VICTORIAN WHIMSEYS

Hats, boots and slippers are just a few of the knickknacks turned out in the Victorian era, in both glass and ceramics. Dishes were made in the shape of stoves;

bowls were shaped as wide-brimmed hats; toothpick holders as coal scuttles. We list only a few of the wide assortment of Victorian whimseys that abounded in the late 19th century.

GLASS

Birdcage fountain, clear mold-blown, tapering ovoid body w/a flared rim & Tam O'Shanter stopper, small water trough pulled-out at base of body, ca. 1850, 5¼" h. $88.00

Boot, lady's high-top, amber pressed Daisy & Button patt., spur on back & strap across instep, smooth toe, ca. 1880s, 5¼" l., 5½" h. 35.00

Boot, lady's high-top, clear pressed Daisy & Button patt., spur on back & strap across instep, smooth toe, ca. 1880s, 5¼" l., 5½" h. 65.00

Boot w/turned-up toe, blown spatter glass w/swirled band design, applied clear leaf across front & clear rigaree around top, ca. 1890, 5" l., 3¾" h. 95.00

Button hook, free-blown w/long clear teardrop-form handle tapering to the colored glass hooked end, handle applied w/colored flowers, 6⅜" l. 44.00

Hat, blue mold-blown Swirl patt., one side upturned, 6½" w. 120.00

Hat, clear mold-blown, low crown w/wide rolled rim, made from a soda water bottle & embossed "Lake City Soda," ca. 1900, 4¼" d., 1¾" h. 137.50

Shoe, lady's high-heel style, clear pressed glass, three sunbursts on each side, row of hobnails around top, bow at front, Sowerby, England, ca. 1885, 7½" l., 3½" h. 150.00

Top hat, aqua, mold-blown in bottle mold, tall cylindrical crown & wide ruffled & deeply folded rim, embossed "Hunt & Miller - New Milford - Conn.," ca. 1900, 5⅜" d., 4" h. (some minor interior stain) 192.50

Top hat, blown medium green glass, cylindrical w/wide gently rolled rim, 5½" h. (broken blisters) 38.50

VINAIGRETTES

These were originally tiny boxes, usually silver, with an inner perforated lid enclosing a sponge soaked in aromatic vinegar to lessen offensive orders. Later versions made of glass in this country contained perfumes.

Cowrie shell, w/silver mounting, serrated rim, the gilt interior w/inner cover pierced & chased in a floral trellis pattern, George III period, Joseph Willmore, Birmingham, England, 1808, 1¼" h. $1,980.00

Enamel, circular design depicting mythological scenes in multi-colored enamel (some chipping to enamel) 275.00

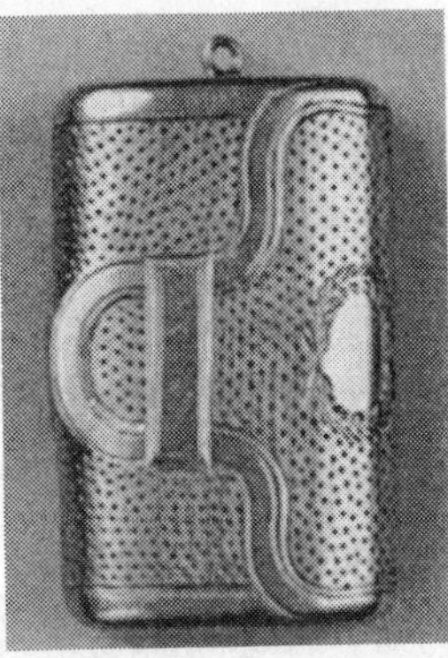

Silver-Gilt Purse-Form Vinaigrette

Silver-gilt, designed as a rectangular purse decorated w/an engraved floral design, English hallmarks, 1816, pendant bail soldered at top (ILLUS.) 330.00

Sterling silver, modeled in the form of a purse w/relief design, chain handle, gilt interior, Birmingham, England hallmarks for John Turner, 1792, ⅞" l. 236.50

Sterling silver, modeled in the form of a lady's handbag w/tooled design, chain handle, gilt interior, Birmingham, England hallmarks for Joseph Taylor, 1821, 1" l. 203.50

Sterling silver, modeled in the form of a tooled purse, chain handle w/ring, gilded interior, Birmingham, England, hallmarks for S. Pemberton, 1790, 1¼" l. 214.50

Sterling silver, rectangular, Birmingham, England, 1817-18, 1½" l. (monogam removed) 192.50

Tiger Claw Vinaigrette

Tiger claw, surmounted by the figure of a reclining gold tiger above a garnet atop a chased high carat gold mount, Victorian (ILLUS.) 3,850.00

WARTIME MEMORABILIA

Since the early 19th century, every war that America has fought has been commemorated with a variety of war-related memorabilia. Often in the form of propaganda items produced during the conflict or as memorial pieces made after the war ended, these materials are today quite collectible and increasingly important for the historic insights they provide. Most commonly available are items dating from World War I and II and since the fall of 1989 marked the fiftieth anniversary of the beginning of World War II, there should be added interest in this collecting field.

CIVIL WAR (1861-65)

Souvenir spoon, GAR (Grand Army of the Republic), model of a musket on the handle, 1894 Pittsburgh Encampment.................................$75.00

Sword, foot officer's, engraved blade, marked, "Horstman & Son, Philadelphia" 325.00

Walking stick, metal handle embossed w/"Army Quartermaster Corps," hollow wooden shaft, ca. 1860 ....265.00

Watch fob, bronze, imprinted "Union For Ever" 30.00

SPANISH-AMERICAN WAR (1898)

Book, "Official History of the Spanish American War," colored maps & many pictures, 1899, Leslie 35.00

Bust of Admiral Dewey, composition, titled "He Remembered the Maine - May 1 '98," 7⅞" h. (chipping & soiling overall).................................93.50

Print, picture of the U.S. Battleship Maine, paper on glass w/a chain frame, white ship on sea green water, signed "F.N. Atwood, '95," 8" sq. (minor soiling & watermarks) ...33.00

Print, picture of the U.S. Battleship Maine, 1898, lists dates, names, weight & size, date of sinking, framed & matted 85.00

WORLD WAR I (1914-18)

Advertisement, three-fold counter display-type, arched top above the three panels, each w/a different color scene w/"Buy Liberty Bonds...," red & blue lettering, light blue ground, soiled, stained, edge wear, fading, torn folds & top bent, 39" w., 27" h. (ILLUS.) 33.00

Liberty Bonds Counter Display

Airplane propeller, wood w/copper armor, original decals, 8' l.............1,200.00

Book, "History of 7th English 5th Division – 1917-1919".........................20.00

Book, "Leslie's Photographic Review of the Great War," 1920 edition, hard cover 12.50

Book, "The Wonder of War in the Air," by Rolt-Wheeler, illustrated, 1917......28.00

Box, wooden, marked "Red Cross," w/hat, razor kit & green wool bandages 125.00

Lugar, German Erfurt Military, 9mm, 4" l. barrel....................................1,400.00

Medallion, bronze, commemorative of "The Great War for Civilization," lists allied countries...................................30.00

WORLD WAR II (1939-45)

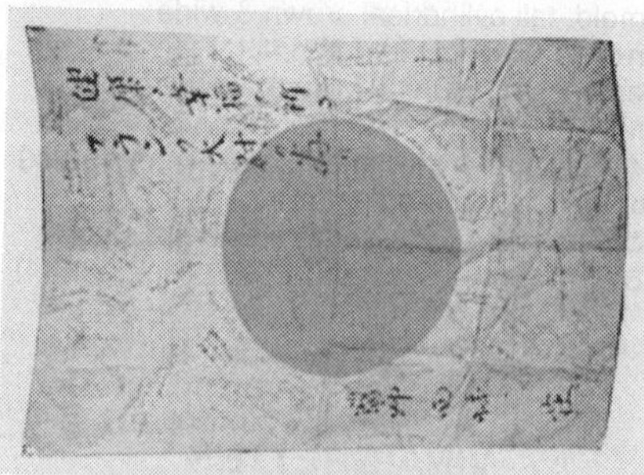

Captured Japanese Flag

Bar & medal, Merchant Marine Pacific War Zone, in box 25.00

Bayonette & scabbard w/frog, German, Mauser 35.00

Book, "The Empire State at War," 1949, Hartzell publishers, New York, 423 pgs...28.00

Chamber pot, miniature, china,

interior w/illustration of Hitler & reads "Chums, what would you do?," England, 2" h. 45.00

Fishing reel, miniature, made from George VI coins, Trench Art 45.00

Flag, Japanese, captured by U.S. servicemen who signed their names & addresses across the front, overall soiling, 26 x 36" (ILLUS.) 110.00

Gas mask, United States Navy, in bag, unused 28.00

Hat pin, gold & silver, Merchant Marine Captain 85.00

Helmet, American, grey, shore patrol-type 50.00

World War II Souvenir Pillow

Pillow, satin w/yellow & blue fringe, cream ground w/blue, yellow & red lettering, a red & yellow airplane, yellow, blue & red flowers, yellow & blue emblems & small red & blue stars, reads "United States Army Air Forces – Technical Training School – Greetings From – Gulfport Field – Mississippi," small tear in back, soiled, overall fading, 16 x 18" (ILLUS.) 11.00

Pillow cover, yellow satin, square, blue planes flying at top & blue pilot figures at the bottom w/a red plane to the right, the center w/a ribbon banner around "U.S. Air Force - Morrison Field - W. Palm Beach, Fla." in red, fringe border, 16 x 17" (minor paint loss & soiling)................11.00

Scarf, silky cloth, square, printed around the sides w/airplanes, propellers, hangers & a winged emblem w/flags, "U.S. Air Forces" across the bottom, yellow w/red & blue lettering, 23½" sq. (wrinkled)......22.00

Sword & scabbard, German, Infantry officer-type, lion's head hilt w/red eyes, made by Eickhorn 350.00

Transfer pictures (tattoos), four sheets w/pictures of Roosevelt, Chiang Kai-shek, Stalin, Marshall, MacArthur & Eisenhower, over 150 pictures, on original store card 85.00

Tumbler, ceramic, "R.A.F. British War Relief Society" 95.00

WATCHES

Lady Elgin Pendant Watch

Hunting case, lady's, American Waltham Watch Co., Waltham, Massachusetts, serial no. 4137721, porcelain enamel dial w/Roman numerals & subsidiary seconds dial, engraved tri-color gold case, late 19th c. $198.00

Hunting case, lady's, Elgin National Watch Co., Elgin, Illinois, serial no. 2753486, stem wind movement, porcelain enamel dial w/Roman numerals & subsidiary seconds dial, engraved 14k yellow gold case w/scalloped edge 247.50

Hunting case, lady's, Illinois Watch Co., Springfield, Illinois, serial no. 3550419, 21-jewel "A. Lincoln" movement, porcelain enameled dial w/Arabic hour & minute ring & subsidiary seconds dial, engraved 14k yellow gold case, early 20th c...302.50

Hunting case pendant, lady's, Lady Elgin, 14k gold, Art Nouveau floral overlay on green *guilloché* enamel accented w/two small diamonds, suspended from a dragon watch pin accented w/green enamel, some enamel loss (ILLUS.) 1,210.00

Hunting case, man's, American Waltham Watch Co., 19-jewel "Riverside" movement, porcelain enameled dial w/Roman numeral hour & Arabic numeral minute ring, subsidiary seconds dial, engraved 14k yellow gold case, early 20th c...247.50

Hunting case, man's, D.C. Jaccard, St. Louis, Missouri, serial no. 83551, stem set movement, porcelain enamel dial marked "Special, Mermod, Jaccard & Co., St. Louis," & w/Roman numerals & subsidiary seconds dial, engine-turned 14k yellow gold case 220.00

Open face, man's, European Watch & Clock Co., Inc., 19-jewel eight adjustment movement, Art Deco, platinum, the circular beveled rock crystal case centered by an engine-turned oyster enamel dial signed "Cartier - France," w/blued steel arrow hands & an outer chapter ring w/rose diamond Roman numerals, the triangular bail numbered 05220 - 3943 & w/French hallmarks 8,050.00

Open face, man's, Patek Philippe & Co., Geneva, Switzerland, serial no. 882010, 18-jewel movement, cream dial w/Arabic numerals & subsidiary dial for seconds, 18k yellow gold case w/monogram on back, signed on dial, case & movement 1,100.00

Open face, man's, Vacheron & Constantin, 21-jewel movement, 18 size, 18k yellow gold case, triple signed 1,980.00

Open face pendant, lady's, Meylan, Switzerland, serial no. 23599, 18-jewel movement, silver dial signed Hodgson, Kennard and Co., Boston, black Arabic numerals, case no. 192459, w/a *guilloché* enamel back cover & frame, highlighted by rose-cut diamonds, & a diamond-set platinum bail, suspended from a platinum link chain highlighted by enamel bars, & a 14k white & yellow gold chatelaine bar pin.................1,320.00

WATCH FOBS

Antique Fob with a Citrine

Advertising, "Bradstreet & Clemens Co., Grand Island, Nebraska," horseshoe-shaped w/two horses in center, ca. 1920s $45.00

Advertising, "Bulldog 'Won't Bite' Tobacco," enameled metal 95.00

Advertising, "Cooks Linen, St. Louis, Missouri," metal, scene of chefs in kitchen 60.00

Advertising, "East Tennessee Packing Company," brass, figural 50 lb. Selecto Ham, 1" l. 15.00

Advertising, "Freihofers Fine Bread," celluloid 20.00

Advertising, "Gold Acorn Plug Tobacco," w/chain.............................95.00

Advertising, "John Deere," mother-of-pearl, shield-shaped, no strap 85.00

Advertising, "Kellogg's Corn Flakes," brass, cereal box-shaped, ca. 1940...95.00

Advertising, "Leroy Plow Co., Miller Bean Harvester," celluloid & brass 125.00

Advertising, "Samuel Rosenthal & Bros.," oval w/embossed scene of a seated boy holding up pants, New York City, ca. 1890s..........................32.00

Advertising, "Twinkies Shoe Co.," brass w/inset compass 295.00

Advertising, "Walters & Dunbar Stockyard - Chicago" 35.00

Advertising, "Wyandotte Chemical," depicts an Indian...............................50.00

Citrine, the oval stone mounted in an ornate chased foliate mounting, possibly of pinchbeck, leafy scrolls continue to the suspension ring, antique (ILLUS.)...............................825.00

Fraternal, "Dairyman's Association," depicts three cow heads, 1913 ....35.00

Gold mesh & charm w/blood red intaglio-cut stone on one side & striped agate on other........................65.00

WEATHERVANES

Early Auto Weathervane

Angel Gabriel, painted & decorated sheet iron, the silhouette form figure w/outstretched body in flight, holding a trumpet, w/flaring dress, on rod mount w/rectangular base, 19th c., 59" l., 33" h.................................$1,725.00

Automobile, early touring car, copper silhouette-style w/sheet fenders & hollow tires, ca. 1910, missing one headlight, 31" l., 13" h. (ILLUS.)....1,430.00

Bull, molded sheet metal, full-bodied animal depicted standing in profile, America, 19th c., 27½" l., 19" h.....3,300.00

Butterfly, sheet-metal silhouette-type, standing w/wings up, a row of pierced circles around the outer edge of the wing w/larger pierced circles on the wing by the body, America, late 19th c., 23" l., 16½" h..1,540.00

Dove Weathervane

Dove, molded copper, the full-bodied bird w/repoussé feathers perched on an orb above an arrow directional, weathered overall verdigris, L.W. Cushing & Co., Waltham, Massachusetts, late 19th c., some imperfections, 23" l., 24½" h. (ILLUS.) 8,050.00

Eagle, molded & gilded copper, the full-bodied bird w/repoussé feather detail, raised wings in flight, perched on an orb in an arrow directional, mounted in a black metal base, third quarter 19th c., 31½" l., 24" h. 2,300.00

Fox hunt scene, painted sheet metal, a silhouetted vignette showing two hunters on horseback jumping a rail fence w/two dogs in the lead, double thickness of metal painted black, mounted on a large horizontal wrought-iron bar, ca. 1920, 54" l., 28" h..920.00

Goddess of Liberty, painted copper & zinc, attributed to Cushing and White, Waltham, Massachusetts, late 19th c., 19½" h. (later paint decoration over partial gilt) 23,100.00

Horse, molded copper & zinc, the gilded swell-bodied prancing animal w/left foreleg raised, the head & neck of cast zinc w/molded mane detail, w/a ridged & repoussé sheet-metal tail, mounted on a rod above wrought-iron directionals, attributed to J. Howard & Co., West Bridgewater, Massachusetts, third quarter 19th c., 23" l., 19" h. (restorations to gilding) 8,625.00

Horse & rider, molded & gilded copper, swell-bodied prancing animal w/ridged cut sheet copper mane & tail w/the upright figure of a top-hatted rider, covered in gilding & old polychrome, mounted on a rod in a black metal base, 26½" l., overall 26" h. (restoration to gilding) 8,913.00

Steam Locomotive Weathervane

Locomotive, steam-type, sheet metal, silhouette-type w/smoke billowing from stack, late 19th c., wear to paint decoration, 64" l. (ILLUS.) 2,310.00

Racing car & driver, molded & gilded zinc, early auto w/molded body w/cast zinc tires & the figure of a driver behind the wheel, mounted on a rod w/a cast-iron directional, early 20th c., 30½" l. (some bullet holes & corrosion) 690.00

Ram, molded & gilded copper, well-detailed full-bodied figure of a standing ram w/modeled repoussé fleece & applied curled sheet copper horns, exceptional overall original gilt & verdigris patina, attributed to the L.W. Cushing & Sons Company, Waltham, Massachusetts, third quarter 19th c., mounted on a rod, 36" l., 31" h.................................48,875.00

Rooster, molded zinc & sheet copper, swelled bodied stylized standing bird, the head, body & legs cast in zinc w/sheet copper tail & feet, the tail repoussé w/pin-pricked outlines, retains traces of gilding & several coats of old polychrome, mounted on a rod supported by a tapered yellow-painted wood standard w/ball, J. Howard & Co., West Bridgewater, Massachusetts, late 19th c., 12" w., overall 4'2" h.........2,990.00

Stag, gilded copper, full-bodied leaping animal above a log & leafy branches, attributed to Harris & Co., Boston, Massachusetts, late 19th c., 32" l. 17,050.00

WHISTLES

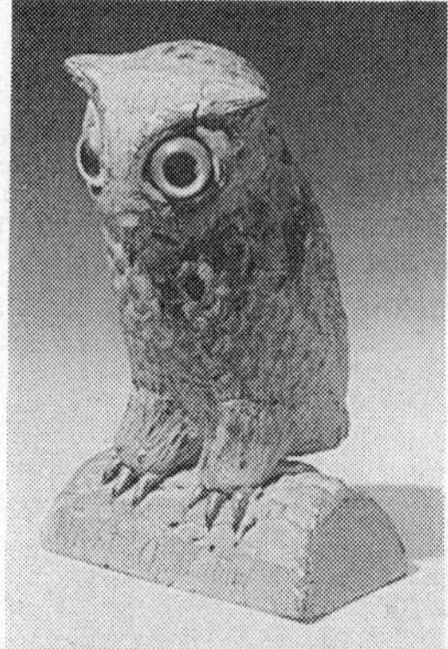

Unusual Stoneware Whistle

There are many types of whistles—devices used to produce whistling sounds by means of breath, air or steam forced through them. We distinguish between working steam whistles such as those used on boats, trains or in early factories as a warning, summons or command, and the small whistles used by individuals, some of which were meant to be a whimsey or toy.

Small Whistles

Pottery, miniature model of a bird, black glaze, 1¾" h. (small chips) $27.50

Pottery, model of a standing bird, blue & white glaze, 3" h. (tail ground flat) 55.00

Redware, model of a rabbit, marked "Germany" 90.00

Stoneware, the molded hollow model of an owl w/details picked-out in yellow & brown glaze & fitted w/yellow & black glass eyes, perched on a base, incised w/the inscription "Night Operator," & signed on the base "Anna, Ill. 1890," owl hoots when blown, some firing cracks, 5½" h. (ILLUS.)................3,300.00

Steam Whistles

Brass, boat, "Buckeye," 11" l. 295.00

Brass, boat, "Lunkenheimer," 10" l. 275.00

Brass, locomotive, "Lunkenheimer," 24" l. 550.00

WIENER WERKSTATTE

Wiener Werkstatte Figure Group

The Wiener Werkstatte (Vienna Workshops) were co-founded in 1903 in Vienna, Austria by Josef Hoffmann and Koloman Moser. An offshoot of the Vienna Secession movement, closely related to the Art Nouveau and Arts and Crafts movements elsewhere, this studio was established to design and produce unique and high-quality pieces covering all aspects of the fine arts. Hoffmann and Moser were the first artistic directors and oversaw the work of up to 100 workers, including thirty-seven masters who signed their work. Bookbinding, leatherwork, gold, silver and lacquer pieces as well as enamels and furniture all originated from these shops over a period of nearly thirty years. The finest pieces from the Wiener Werkstatte are now bringing tremendous prices.

Box, cov., glass & silvered metal, plain clear rectangular box w/a flat metal cover decorated w/four beaded panels each enclosing a beaded diamond, two lines of beading around the narrow edge, designed by Josef Hoffmann, probably executed by Alfred Mayer, ca. 1910-20, marked 3¾ x 5¼" ...$1,380.00

Box, cov., silver & enamel, rectangular sarcophagus-form, the hinged cover insect w/an enameled plaque painted in translucent & opaque shades of yellow, red, green & blue w/a an elegant girl reclining on a chaise below a giant flowering stylized plant, the enameled signed w/initial "L," ca. 1910, 5" h.............4,025.00

Brooch, gold (18k), finely cast w/flowers & leafage, attributed to Dagobert Peche, impressed "WW," flower mark & "18K," together w/the original leather presentation box stamped "WW," ca. 1915, 1⅝" l. ...5,175.00

Bust of a woman, the stylized head in shades of blue, green, white & orange, by Gudrun Baudisch, impressed "WW - MADE IN AUSTRIA - 346 - GB," 8" h. (minor chips) 2,760.00

Centerpiece, hammered brass, the ribbed melon-form cup applied w/two coiling looping handles, raised on a ribbed inverted trumpet-form base, designed by Josef Hoffmann, impressed "WIENER - WERK - STATTE," "JH" monogram & "MADE IN AUSTRIA," ca. 1924, length across handles 11½", 7⅜" h. 9,200.00

Figure group, ceramic, modeled as a stylized hillside surmounted by stylized figures of a young couple, one side w/a boy w/a pair of birds, the other w/a flutist, glazed in blue, yellow, green & cream, attributed to Lotte Calm, impressed "WW LC 18," 11" h. (ILLUS.) 575.00

Tazza, painted metal, round flat top w/a low pierced gallery raised on four flat reticulated legs joined by reticulated incurved stretchers, painted white, designed by Josef Hoffmann, ca. 1905, 9½", 4⅛" h. 977.00

Vase, clear glass, the footed bell-form body enameled in light blue, dark blue & red w/a border design of classical nude maidens alternating w/flowers above striped borders, designed by Wally Wieselthier, signed in enamel "V. WIESEL-THIER. WW," ca. 1920, 6" h. 1,725.00

Vase, brass, the tulip-form body raised on a floriform pedestal in ribbed hammered brass, impressed "JH" monogram, "MADE IN - AUSTRIA" & "WIENER - WERK - STATTE," ca. 1925, 11½" h. 6,325.00

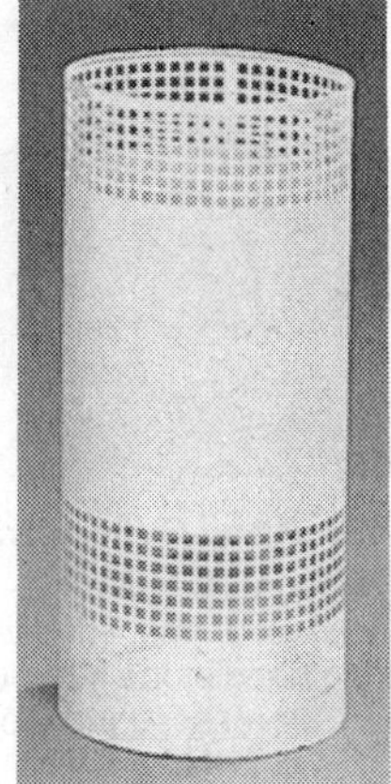

Wiener Werkstatte Waste Basket

Waste paper basket, metal, cylindrical w/small square pierced holes at the top & near the base, repainted white, worn, designed by Josef Hoffmann, ca. 1905-06, 9⅝" d., 20½" h. (ILLUS.) 2,300.00

WOODENWARES

The patina and mellow coloring, along with the lightness and smoothness that come only with age and wear, attract collectors to old woodenwares. The earliest forms were the simplest and the shapes of items whittled out in the late 19th century varied little in form from those turned out in the American colonies two centuries earlier. Burl is a growth, or wart, on some trees in which the grain of the wood is twisted and turned in a manner which strengthens the fibers and causes a beautiful pattern to be formed. Treenware is simply a term for utilitarian items made from "treen," another word for wood. While maple was the primary wood used for these items, they are also abundant in pine, ash, oak, walnut, and other woods. "Lignum Vitae" is a species of wood from the West Indies that can always be identified by the contrasting colors of dark heartwood and light sapwood and by its heavy weight, which causes it to sink in water.

Also see KITCHENWARES.

Large Burl Bowl

Apple box, decorated pine, outward flaring sides, grain-painted on both sides in yellow & brown w/stripes & dots w/entwined black & yellow lines, New England, early 19th c., 10⅛" w., 2½" h. (cracks to bottom)...$460.00

Apple butter scoop, carved pine, one-piece construction w/ U-shaped handle, 7 x 17½" 230.00

Bowl, cov., deep rounded bowl w/incised rings & a flaring rim, raised on a short ring-turned stem on a ring-turned round foot, the ring-turned domed cover w/pointed button finial, attributed to Pease of Ohio, worn varnish finish, 4½" h. 275.00

Bowl, cov., ash burl, deep & wide rounded sides on a small, thick footring, decorated w/incised bands, the domed cover w/a wide mushroom finial, good figure, scrubbed finish, 7¼" d., 5¾" h. 3,520.00

Bowl, burl, shallow rounded flaring sides, good figure, scrubbed finish, old notch in rim, 7" d., 2" h. 170.50

Bowl, ash burl w/good figure, slightly rounded sides, 6¼" d., 2⅛" h. 330.00

Bowl, flared rim, ring-turned detail near base, on low standard & circular ring-turned foot, old worn varnish, attributed to Pease of Ohio, 19th c., 7" d., 3⅝" h. 330.00

Bowl, burl, oblong boat shape, the upswept ends w/pierced handholds, good figure, old worn patina, 14¼ x 15½", 6½" h. 4,400.00

Bowl, ash burl w/good figure, hanging hole in rim, good old scrubbed patina, 15½" d., 6¾" h. (age cracks & holes in bottom & minor age cracks in rim) 1,210.00

Bowl, burl, deep rounded sides to a small flat bottom, 19th c., 15⅞" d. (ILLUS.) 550.00

Bucket, cov., stave construction w/three metal bands, iron hasp & iron bail handle, painted & stenciled "Boston Oyster Company," New England, early 20th c., 12¼" h. (some paint & wood loss) 302.50

Bucket, tapering cylindrical stave construction w/two iron bands, old dark green repaint over red, wire bail handle w/wooden handgrip, 5¾" h. 159.50

Butter churn, barrel-shaped, stave construction w/six iron bands, old worn red paint, inset wooden cover & stick dasher, 24" h. 165.00

Butter churn, dasher-type, tapering cylindrical shape, stave construction w/wire bands, old dark finish, 19th c., 24" h. plus dasher 275.00

Butter paddle, burl, wide oblong rounded bowl curving up to rounded side handle, excellent figure, color & patina, 19th c., 10" l. 522.50

Butter paddle, curly maple, bird-head hook handle, good old finish, 11" l. 99.00

Butter scoop, burl, wide round & curved blade tapering to a curved rounded handle w/hook end, good figure, soft finish, 11½" l. 583.00

Carrier, bentwood, round w/the exterior of the deep sides decorated w/original rosemaled polychrome floral decoration on a red ground, arched bentwood center handle w/inscribed date "1873," 15" d., 5¾" h. plus handle (some wear, bottom board covered w/contact paper) 660.00

Cheese (or butter) press, all-wood, floor model w/trestle construction, on shoe feet, old green repaint, 19th c, 28" l., 31½" h. 71.50

Compote, open, wide shallow bowl w/flared sides raised on a short thick pedestal w/flared foot, old worn red & greenish exterior paint, interior w/greyish scrubbed finish, 12" d., 5¾" h. 550.00

Cookie board, small rectangular board divided into eight blocks each w/a different carved design including an eagle, squirrel, rooster & sheaf of wheat, 3 x 7" 412.50

Cookie board, mahogany, the nearly square board carved in the center w/a round medallion framing a large spread-winged American eagle above a standing figure of George Washington flanked by figures of ladies representing Liberty & Justice further flanked by two large cornucopias, inscribed in a banner above the eagle "E Pluribus Unum," probably by J. Conger, New York, New York, old finish, 19th c, 11¾ x 12" 2,640.00

Corset busk, indented top w/notched corners & rounded bottom end, inscribed w/two joined hearts at the top above various floral, geometric & fish designs inlaid w/sealing wax, early 19th c., 13¾" l. 825.00

Cranberry scoop, wood, tin & galvanized hardware cloth, box-form w/long pointed teeth & a center bar handle, side branded "W.B. Sherman", 18" l. (post holding hardware cloth broken) 137.50

Fine Mahogany Cutlery Tray

Cutlery tray, rectangular w/a molded base & scalloped rims, fitted w/a center pivoting handle, the inte-rior w/two dividers, impressed mark on bottom "T.S. BOSTON," possibly Thomas and/or John Seymour, Boston, Massachusetts, ca. 1805, 10½ x 12½", handle 5¾" h. (ILLUS.) 5,750.00

Cutting board, a round one-piece poplar board tapering at one end w/a squared tab handle w/half-round cut-out hand hole, old finish, 19 x 23"....159.50

Dough box, cov., the rectangular lid w/old red paint lifting to a deep well w/canted sides, notched handles in lid & box, early 19th c., 13 x 27", 8" h....250.00

Dough box on stand, cov., poplar, the rectangular top lifting above a deep canted well raised on baluster- and knob-turned splayed legs, old red finish, 19¾ x 42", 27¾" h. (tape residue on top & paint cleaned off in spots)....836.00

Dough box on stand, cov., a rectangular walnut cover w/old dark brown paint above a deep poplar dovetailed box w/simple end handles & canted sides on heavy splayed legs joined by an H-stretcher, 22¾ x 47" (wear & edge damage on two-board top)....1,540.00

Drying rack, pine, mortised & pinned construction, one bar at center, another across the top, vertical bars at either side ending in shoe feet, worn old dark patina, 37½" w., 44¾" h....302.50

Drying rack, pine, three-bar, two tall slender chamfered square posts joined by three crossbars, on shaped shoe feet, old dark patina, 47" l., 5' 4" h....192.50

Goblet, turned, slightly tapering cylindrical bowl on a ring-turned stem w/flaring round foot, decorated w/wide red & green bands, attributed to Pease of Ohio, 3½" h....55.00

Hay rake, all-wood, five flaring, curved & pointed tines w/cross braces near their joins to the long handle, old soft finish, 19th c., 74" l....220.00

Jar, cov., miniature, flaring bell-form ring-turned footed bowl w/a low-domed cover w/pointed knob finial, worn varnish finish, attributed to Pease of Ohio, 2" h....192.50

Jar, cov., miniature, small turned spherical body on a low foot & flaring at the rim, w/a slightly domed cover w/pointed knob finial, wire bail handle w/wooden hand grip, worn varnish finish, attributed to Pease of Ohio, 2¾" h....605.00

Jar, cov., turned, bulbous body tapering to a flattened rim supporting a low domed cover w/disc finial, on a low foot, wire bail handle w/wooden handgrip, old

Turned Wooden Jar

worn patina, attributed to Pease of Ohio, 19th c., small hole in bottom at age cracks, 6¼" h. (ILLUS.)....302.50

Jar, cov., the ovoid form w/original turned lid & finial decorated overall in green & red feathered paint on an ochre yellow ground, inscribed in pencil on the bottom in 19th c. script "Crandall," Midwestern, probably Ohio, early 19th c., 6½" h. 1,840.00

Keg, cov., stave construction w/black-painted metal bands, black stenciled label "Kerosene Oil," brass spigot, wire bail handle w/wooden handgrip, 9½" h....220.00

Kraut cutter, walnut board w/molded edges & mounted w/an angled iron blade, the rounded & lobed flat end handle pierced w/a small heart, old finish, 7¼ x 22½"....170.50

Mortar, burl, wide turned ovoid body on a thick, flaring foot, turned rings, old dark finish, 7" h. (filled age cracks)....60.50

Pastry (or butter) roller, turned, narrow rolling cylinder w/carved vining design, elongated ovoid handles, soft patina, 14" l. (minor chips on edge of cylinder)....225.50

Pestle, kitchen-type, curly maple, turned, mushroom finial, good soft patina, 11¾" l....71.50

Pickle bucket, cov., stave construction, tapering cylindrical form w/three metal bands, worn original yellow paint & red bands, black stenciled label "Sweet Pickles...," wire bail handle & inset cover, 13" h. 192.50

Plate, hand-turned w/lightly molded rim, scrubbed finish, slightly out of round, 6" d....313.50

Plate, tiger stripe maple, 19th c., 10" d....522.50

Rolling pin, curly maple, one-piece w/turned & shaped handles, 21" l....148.50

Salt box, cov., hanging-type, mahogany, a wide crest w/a raised center tab w/hanging hole above scalloped sides over the rectangular slant lid on the storage compartment above a narrow drawer, old mellow refinishing, 8½" w., 13¾" h. 577.50

Shovel, grained maple, one-piece hand-hewn & carved construction, open "D" handle, early 1800s, 3' l. 150.00

Soap dish, round cylindrical form w/molded rim, old dark patina, 3" d., 1½" h. 33.00

Spoon, curly maple, long oval bowl tapering to a long, slender turned handle, good color, 17" l. (minor age cracks in bowl) 93.50

Early Storage Barrel

Storage barrel, cov., stave construction, tapering cylindrical form fastened w/four buttonhole lappets, original red paint, New England, early 19th c., age cracks & wear, 20½" h. (ILLUS.) 633.00

Storage bin, cov., cherry, upright cabinet-style w/a narrow rectangular top above a hinged slant-top opening to a deep well w/interior drawer, dovetailed base raised on tall bracket feet, old mellow refinishing, lid ends restored, feet repaired, 13½ x 25", 27¼" h. 2,420.00

Sugar bucket, cov., stave construction w/three lappet bands, flat cover, bentwood swing handle, old worn light green repaint, 12" h. 275.00

Violin case, painted & decorated, the tapering oblong case w/arched lid, painted red & decorated w/an American eagle & shield flanked by the inscription "BG" & "Musician," second half 19th c., 30½" l. (some minor paint loss) 467.50

WOOD SCULPTURES

American folk sculpture is an important part of the American art scene today. Skilled wood carvers turned out ship's figureheads, cigar store figures, plaques and carousel animals of stylized beauty and great appeal. The wooden shipbuilding industry, which had originally nourished this folk art, declined after the Civil War and the talented carvers then turned to producing figures for tobacconist's shops, carousel animals and show figures for circuses. These figures and other early ornamental carvings that have survived the elements and years are eagerly sought.

Bust of a man, carved & painted, the cartoon-like rendering of a bald-headed man w/protruding eyes & sticking out his tongue, painted in flesh tones w/pink shirt collar, early 20th c., 20" h. $1,725.00

Cigar store figure of a black native figure, carved standing figure wearing a tobacco leaf skirt, one arm down at side, the other raised & movable to offer a cigar, black pitch tar-covered, on round base, late 19th c., 4' 8" h. (one foot restored, overall soiling) 9,350.00

Cigar store figure of an Indian princess, carved & painted pine, shown standing & wearing a gilded diadem of red & green feathers, blue gown & red shawl over fringed leather stockings, on a composition base w/tin plates around the sides inscribed "Battle Ax Plug," Samuel Robb, New York, late 19th c., overall 5' 8" h. (some restoration to paint) 33,350.00

Dummy boards, one painted as a young girl holding a bouquet & dressed in an elaborate dress w/lace borders, the other as a young boy wearing a similar outfit & holding a rose upon which the Madonna & Child are seated, Europe, 19th c. in the 18th c. style, paint losses to boy, 34¼" & 35¼" h., pr. 1,650.00

Figure of a boxer, carved & painted pine, the realistically rendered & finely sculpted figure standing w/muscles tensed, fist raised in a boxing stance, clad in navy blue painted boxing shorts w/an orange sash & black tie shoes, flesh-toned body, possibly from a gymnasium or circus, American-made, late 19th c., 6' 5" h. 46,000.00

Figure of a cowboy, carved & painted white oak, standing full-bodied figure of a smiling cowboy w/painted tin teeth, smoking a cigarette, wearing a black-painted tin hat brim, red & white gingham shirt w/black buttons, collar & cuffs, black & blue painted pants & black cowboy boots, composed of six sections held tegether by steel rods, Connecticut or Massachusetts, ca. 1920, 5' 9" h...........11,500.00

Figure of George Washington, carved & painted, depicting Washington astride his charger, Jack, w/his hat raised, on a rectangular base, America, ca. 1845, 10½" l., 14" h...6,600.00

Figure of Uncle Sam, carved & painted pine, carved in the full round, the high-stepping figure w/black-painted hair, eyes, eyebrows & goatee, wearing a grey-painted top hat, blue waistcoat w/nail head buttons, red & white striped trousers & black shoes, his left arm raised across his chest & his left leg extending forward, now mounted on a white-painted rectangular metal base, American-made, late 19th - early 20th c., 19¼" h. ...3,450.00

Model of an eagle, carved & painted pine, the full-bodied, spread-winged bird w/cross-hatched body & comb & lappet-carved wings, perched on a green mound, Wilhelm Schimmel, Cumberland Valley, Pennsylvania, ca. 1880, 17" w., 9½" h..............17,250.00

Model of a penguin, carved & painted, base inscribed "Char. H. Hart... Gloucester Mass. Maker," ca. 1930, 7" h...550.00

Model of a raven, carved & painted pine, carved in the full round, shown standing w/incised eyes & feather detail, on cast metal legs, painted black, New England, ca. 1920-30, some age cracks & paint loss, 44" l., 27" h...7,475.00

Lady Ship's Figurehead

Ship's figurehead, carved & painted pine, small three-quarter length figure of a red-haired lady wearing a green dress w/white collar, probably New England, ca. 1860, some repaint & restorations, 23" h. (ILLUS.) 4,313.00

Ship's figurehead, three-quarter length young woman, carved in the round, her flowing tresses & face tilted upwards, wearing a draped dress & holding a book in one hand, retaining traces of blue, red & white polychrome, mounted on a carved socle now on a black wood pedestal base, ca. 1850, 5' h.....................13,800.00

Whirligig, carved & painted wood, figure of a soldier in a two-tone blue uniform w/tin belt, buttons, sword & medal, his tin hat has "Prince Albert" tobacco advertisements, the arms form paddle blades, applied facial features are well-made replacements, mounted on old wooden stool base, 15¾" h. plus base (paint very worn) 1,155.00

Washerwoman Whirligig

Whirligig, carved & painted wood & sheet metal, the full-bodied figure of a washerwoman wearing a black-painted tin bonnet & black apron & standing at a washboard in a grey-painted tub all made of sheet metal, the figure mounted in a green-painted wood platform fitted w/black, red & white propeller & tail, the figure scrubs when the propeller turns, now mounted on a black-painted metal rod & base, early 20th c. 28" l., 32½" h. (ILLUS.) 4,888.00

WORLD'S FAIR COLLECTIBLES

There has been great interest in collecting items produced for the great fairs and expositions held through the years. During the 1970s, there was particular interest in items produced for the 1876

Centennial Exhibition and now interest is focusing on those items associated with the 1893 Columbian Exposition. Listed below is a random sampling of prices asked for items produced for the various fairs.

1876 PHILADELPHIA CENTENNIAL

Printed Cotton Quilt

Book, "The Illustrated History of the Centennial Exhibition of 1876," worn leather binding, 6 x 9" $27.50

Booklet, pocket-type, "Centennial Souvenir 1876 Philadelphia," containing a fold-out group of photos of all of the pavilions w/a locator map, 3¾ x 4¾" 65.00

Books, "The Masterpieces of the Exposition 1876: Vol. I, "Fine Art;" Vol. II, "Industrial Art;" & Vol. III, "History, Mechanics, Science;" leather-bound, the set....................375.00

Bust of Abraham Lincoln, opaque white glass w/satinized finish, Gillinder & Sons, 6" h....................375.00

Bust of Shakespeare, frosted clear glass, Gillinder & Sons, 5" h. 125.00

Cup & saucer, George Washington commemorative, dated 1876, Copeland, large (some wear) 60.00

Figure of Buddha, amber glass, Gillinder & Sons 115.00

Harmonica, by Wilhelm Thie, in original box 200.00

Jigsaw puzzles, lithographed paper on wood, five assembled puzzles of the buildings of the Philadelphia Centennial framed to hang together, along w/a framed document, a framed etching of the Art Gallery & a dozen colored cards of the Centennial also framed together, puzzles by George Chinnock, 8 pcs. 1,265.00

Paperweight, clear glass, oval, illustrates Memorial Hall....................125.00

Paperweight, glass, model of a lion, Gillinder & Sons, 2½" d.,....................85.00

Plate, depicts Memorial Hall in center & "The Union Forever - Centennial 1776-1876" embossed around the border, Staffordshire, 6" d....................145.00

Pot lid, "Philadelphia Exhibition 1876," transfer-printed multi-colored scene of Memorial Hall, 4¼" d. (lid was broken in half & professionally reglued)....................99.00

Quilt, printed cotton, tied construction, each block w/three Fair scenes center w/"International Exhibition 1876" & "Philadelphia," portrait & scene vignettes in each corner, some fiber loss, patches & discoloration, 82 x 86" (ILLUS.)....................495.00

Slipper w/bow, glass, satin finish, Gillinder & Sons 110.00

Toothpick holder, frosted glass, model of a chick by an egg, w/"Just Out," Gillinder & Sons 67.00

Trade Card with Fair View

Trade card, "Philadelphia Shafting Works," front features panoramic bird's-eye view of the Exhibition grounds at Fairmount Park, reverse w/advertising (ILLUS.) 50.50

Trade card, "John Russell Cutlery Co.," folding-type, one side w/advertising surrounding a vignette of the 'J. Russell & Co. Green River Works,' other side w/five small vignettes of various Exhibition buildings, advertising on reverse 71.50

Vase, frosted clear glass, model of a hand holding sheaf of wheat, "Centennial 1876," Gillinder & Sons, 7" h....................55.00

1893 COLUMBIAN EXPOSITION

Book, "A Week at the Fair," 168 pp. 45.00

Book, "Columbian Exposition, Chicago, Vol. II," large 35.00

Book, "Columbian Exposition Official Guide Book" 27.00

Book, "Columbian World's Fair Atlas,"

illustrated w/Fair buildings, Chicago scenes, all state maps, territories, maps of the world, etc., 192 pp..........35.00

Book, "World's Fair Columbian Exposition 1893," Columbus & Columbia, 13 illustrations in oil colors, over 500 engravings, diagrams & maps, fold-out colored map of Chicago & the Fair, leather bound, 880 pp., excellent condition 215.00

Booklet, advertising "Aultman Machine Co.," color lithographs 145.00

Booklet, advertising "Fairbank's Cottolene," cover illustration of their exhibit at the Columbian Exposition, inside advertising on a detachable card, 4 pp..37.50

Booklet, advertising, "Singer - The Universal Sewing Machine," die-cut, round shape w/a classical figure holding a small sewing machine over a world globe on the cover, all-color w/Exposition & sewing scenes, 8 pp...33.00

Bookmark, "Star Spangled Banner," silk, in original paper folder, Phoenix Silk Manufacturing 135.00

Coin, bronze, depicts U.S. Government Building, marked on reverse "U.S. Treasury Department Exposition 1893," 1½" d. 12.50

Dresser scarf, views of the Fair, mint condition 95.00

Grapefruit spoons, silver plate, each w/a different Fair scene, set of 6........75.00

Lamp with Scene of Columbus

Lamp, kerosene, scene on font depicting the landing of Columbus over "1492 Landing of Columbus 1892," shade decorated w/bust portrait of Columbus, 17" h. (ILLUS.) 375.00

Model of a hatchet, glass, bust portrait of George Washington on the blade beneath "The Father of His Country," reverse of blade has "World's Fair 1893," on the handle "Libbey Glass Co. Toledo, Ohio," 8" l. 100.00

Needle case, barrel-shaped, transfer design of Women's Building 195.00

Plate, china, six-scallop rim, transfer scene of the Electrical Building center 50.00

Paperweight, clear glass w/illustration of "Transportation Building, Columbian Exposition" 45.00

Photographs, portfolio of the World's Fair, series of sixteen books published by Werner Co., Chicago, original & in excellent condition, the set 135.00

Pitcher, water, clear glass, etched Columbus portrait 325.00

Plate, china, transfer scene of the Machinery Hall, blue & white, Wedgwood, England, 8" d. 50.00

Postcards, each w/different depiction of U.S. Grant, set of 8 ....65.00

Purse, shell sides, depicts the landing of Columbus, marked "World's Columbian Exposition, Chicago 1893," 2 x 2½" (small chip on back) 21.00

Rose bowl w/crimped top, opalescent satin glass, transfer scene of Fair building, 4 x 4½" 60.00

Scarf, silk, embroidered ship in one corner, "World's Fair 1893 J.E. Knopf" in opposite corner, 18" sq.........8.00

Shovel w/"Beckwith's Round Oak, Dowagiac, MI" marked on scoop 80.00

Spoon, demitasse, sterling silver, Fisheries Building 30.00

Stereo view cards, various Fair views, 1894, set of 26 ....110.00

Sugar bowl, open, two-handled, Peach Blow glass, hand-applied souvenir inscription on side, New England Glass Co., 2½" h..............450.00

Table cover, crocheted, full figure Columbus w/name & "America" under figure, dated "1492-1892," 29" sq. (couple small separations).....65.00

Teaspoon, silver plate, depicts Columbus & name on handle w/eagle 9.00

Teaspoon, sterling silver, twisted handle, bust of Columbus, marked "World's Fair 1893" in bowl 30.00

Teaspoon, sterling silver, Lady Liberty on handle 70.00

Tea tile, porcelain, Fair building pictured 50.00

Textile, "Souvenir World's Columbian

Exposition, Chicago, 1893" above elongated oval containing a scenic overview of the Fair, the sides of vignettes of Fair scenes & people, red & black printed on white cotton, unframed, 25" w., 21½" h. (wear, stains, edges frayed & sewn tear) 55.00

Token, scene of the landing of Columbus on one side, Administration Building on the other..............20.00

Henderson Company Trade Card

Trade card, "C.M. Henderson & Co. Shoes," vignette scene of the Art Palace above a Victorian toddler on hands & knees drawing, advertising on the reverse (ILLUS.) 11.00

Trade card, "Nelson Morris & Co.," die-cut model of a ham, opens to show stages of the butchering process and mentions their exhibit at the World's Fair, sepia & brown.....72.50

Tumbler, clear glass, w/etched Electricity Building.............................45.00

Watch case opener, metal, "H. Muhr & Sons" on front, "World's Columbian Exposition 1893" on back..40.00

Watch fob, four-section w/eagle & landing of Columbus 60.00

Wrapping tissue, w/five Exposition buildings illustrated, 18 x 20" 28.00

1901 PAN-AMERICAN EXPOSITION

Book, "Souvenir of the Great Pan-American Exposition," all photographs..20.00

Bucket, miniature, wooden, expanding cylindrical body w/three sets of hoops, wire bail handle w/wooden handhold, lettered "Pan American 1901," probably by Pease of Ohio, 2¼" h. plus handle 60.50

Model of a buffalo, white clay w/a brown & green glaze, marked "Expo 1901," 6½" l. (chips)..........................71.50

Paperweight, glass, rectangular, photo of Temple of Music Building & portrait of President McKinley 25.00

Photogravure, engraving of Government & Fisheries Buildings, 12½ x 16½"......................................15.00

Lithographed Cotton Pillow Cover

Pillow cover, lithographed cotton, printed w/buffalo heads in corners & American continents in center, red, white & blue satin ribbon edge, 26" sq. (ILLUS.) 165.00

Playing cards, single deck 65.00

Spoon, demitasse, sterling silver, figural Indian bust handle, Agriculture Building in bowl & Electric Tower on reverse 25.00

Spoon, jelly, Electric Building in bowl (some wear on handle) 15.00

Teaspoon, silver plate, figural Indian Chief handle, dated 1901..................15.00

Teaspoon, sterling silver, full figure Indian w/buffalo on handle.................30.00

Teaspoon, sterling silver, "Pan American Expo, 1901," official spoon, "Electric Tower" in gilt bowl....55.00

Tumbler, clear glass, depicts the Horticultural Building.........................20.00

Tumbler, clear glass, buffalo decoration...18.00

1904 ST. LOUIS WORLD'S FAIR

Booklet, "Louisiana Purchase," Lewis...23.00

Cup, china, colorful depiction of the Palace of Varied Industries, marked Austria...45.00

Cup, metal, collapsible, "Palace of Mines & Metallurgy, St. Louis, 1904," patented Feb. 23, 1897 ....110.00

Cup, enameled steel, "Official Souvenir Cup. The World's Fair, St. Louis 1904," 2¾" h. (chips) 33.00

Matchsafe, leather, embossed decoration 25.00

Model of a shoe, white porcelain w/gold trim, pictures Electricity Building 65.00

Napkin ring, aluminum.........................10.00

Nut bowl, porcelain, master size, footed, Palace of Machinery pictured, unmarked Nippon 85.00
Paperweight, glass, seashells inside 18.50
Postcards, various Fair scenes, unused, set of 10 .... 45.00
Teaspoon, sterling silver, "Buffalo to Steam Engine" on handle, information on reverse of handle, "Festival Hall - Cascades" on bowl 50.00
Teaspoon, sterling silver, "Louisiana Purchase Expo, St. Louis, 1904," on handle, "Transportation Building" in bowl 65.00

1909 ALASKA-YUKON-PACIFIC EXPOSITION

Rose bowl, china, footed, "Palace of Agriculture," depicts Japanese girls, etc. 225.00
Scarf, silk, landmarks & logo in black, 15" sq. 65.00
Teaspoon, sterling silver, "Alaska Yukon Pacific Expo Machinery Hall" in bowl 75.00
Teaspoon, sterling silver, Manufacturing Building in bowl, full information on back of bowl 50.00
Teaspoon, sterling silver, w/logo, Seward & date on handle, U.S. Government Building in bowl, totem pole & Mt. Rainier on handle reverse 50.00
Watch fob, sterling silver, Art Nouveau style, colorful enamel decoration of a woman, 1½" 125.00

1933-34 CHICAGO "CENTURY OF PROGRESS"

World's Fair Hanging Lamp

Ashtray, molded rubber tire w/amber glass insert embossed "Century of Progress" & "Firestone," 5½" d. 33.00
Badge & ribbon, "American Legion Convention," bronze, Fort Dearborn & Indian pictured 22.00
Bank, lithographed tin, "Century of Progress," Canco, 1934 .... 55.00
Book, "Official Pictures of a Century of Progress Exposition," soft cover, 1933 .... Ï30.00
Booklet, advertising, "Firestone" 10.00
Booklet, official photos of Fair in color, Lyford cover 37.50
Calendar, perpetual-type w/gold-colored metal stand 28.00
Coin, copper, elongated cent 10.00
Harmonica, Art Deco style enamelled decoration, Germany, mint in box 60.00
Lamp, hanging-type, colorful city skyscrapers depicted in orange, green, blue, grey, white & yellow above "A Century of Progress Chicago 1934," marked "Pat. 87, 543 Other Patents Pending," 3½" d., 5½" h. (ILLUS.) 220.00
Letter opener, brass w/red lettering, "Chicago World's Fair - Science Carillon," curved, small 15.00
Mirror, pocket-type, celluloid w/wooden handle 20.00
Model of a key, bronze w/logo & Fair building 20.00
Mug, copper, w/Fair logo 16.00
Paperweight & pencil holder, model of a bulldog, painted cast iron, mint 125.00
Pencil, mechanical, Fair decoration, mint w/original box 55.00
Plate, china, depicts various Fair buildings, 8½" d. 30.00
Playing cards, Fair scenes on backs, complete w/two jokers, in original box 28.00
Pocketknife, steel w/blue enamel decoration, pictures comet & "Chicago" 85.00
Postcard, General Motors Building 8.00
Postcards, souvenir pack of Fair views, Donneley Deeptone 27.50
Scrapbook, contains tickets, photographs, maps, etc., 1933 .... 125.00
Sponge, figural Dutch Cleanser's Cleanser girl, in original box 70.00
Teaspoon, sterling silver, east view of Administration Building in bowl 20.00
Teaspoon, sterling silver, Fort Dearborn & Administration building in bowl 20.00
Teaspoon, sterling silver, Chicago Hall of Science in bowl 15.00
Thermometer, w/framed Sky Ride picture, 5 x 7" 24.00
Tie clip w/logo 15.00
Tray, metal, rectangular w/rounded corners & a flanged rim, the center w/a marbleized brown & gold design around a central rectangular gold &

brown scene of the Ford Company building above "A Century of Progress," 12 x 17½" (minor edge chipping) 71.50

1933 Visitor Ribbon

Visitor ribbon, embossed metal top framing white cardboard insert lettered "VISITOR," above a red ribbon lettered "CENTURY OF PROGRESS CHICAGO 1933" over a round bottom section w/Fair logo & further lettering in blue & white, minor soiling & fold marks, 2" w., 3½" h. (ILLUS.) 16.50

1939-40 NEW YORK WORLD'S FAIR

New York World's Fair Snow Dome

Autograph book, blue w/gold embossing, depicts Trylon & Perisphere 85.00

Book, "1939 Fair in Pictures," 48 pgs. 17.00

Book, "Seeing New York World's Fair," w/two pages of punch-out buildings, McLoughlin Bros. 75.00

Booklet, fold-out type, hotel listings & color map, features Trylon & Perisphere 24.00

Cake plate, ceramic, depicting color scene of Trylon & Perisphere, together w/serving knife, 2 pcs. 75.00

Compact, mother-of-pearl & rhinestones, Trylon & Perisphere in rhinestones against a mother-of-pearl ground....................................85.00

Envelope w/cachet, "Railroads on Parade," posted 5/30/39 ....4.00

Pennant, small, dated October 17, 1940, the closing day of the Fair..........8.00

Pillow covers, colorful depictions of the Trylon on one & Perisphere on the other, 11 x 17", pr. 60.00

Pinback button, "I Was There," ½" d.....10.00

Plate, Old New York, commemorating the inaugural of George Washington at Federal Hall, New York, Wedgwood, 10½" d. 45.00

Playing cards, double deck, depicts various sights including the Trylon & Perisphere, boxed set.......................64.00

Postcards, souvenir-type, mint in package, set of 10 ....15.00

Purse, embossed leather, depicts Trylon & Perisphere 22.00

Sheet music, picturing Father Knickerbocker 30.00

Snow dome (paperweight), glass dome enclosing a view of the Fair, colorful specks float when dome is shaken, on a black base w/Trylon & Perisphere logos & "New York World's Fair," 4" h. (ILLUS.) 49.50

Spinner, Communication Building pictured 14.00

Swizzle stick, glass, marked "Ruby Foo's Sundial Restaurant" 12.50

Tie rack, leather, embossed decoration 40.00

Tie tack, Scottie dog, Fair emblem w/chain connecting "40" to dog..........65.00

1939 GOLDEN GATE INTERNATIONAL EXPOSITION

Ashtray, china, w/logo, date in center, Panoramic view border in soft colors, Homer Laughlin.....................75.00

Booklet, official guide, color cartograph fold-out, first edition, 1940 ....30.00

Comb & metal case w/logo & panoramic buildings, original comb 50.00

Postcard book, Treasure Island & Golden Gate "Night & Day" lithographed views 30.00

Postcards, miniature packet, Fair views..15.00

1962 SEATTLE WORLD'S FAIR

Cigarette lighter, metal, figural Space Needle, 10½" h. 45.00

Doll, "Miss Seattle World's Fair," in domed case, 1962 ....75.00
Plate, ceramic, relief-molded Space Needle 18.00
Tumblers, frosted glass, set of 7 different 65.00

1964-65 NEW YORK WORLD'S FAIR

Ashtray, tin, depicts Unisphere 15.00
Bank, dime register bank-type 50.00
Book, children's, dinosaur pop up-type 35.00
Book, "New York State Vacation Lands," 1965, World's Fair edition 15.00
Calendar, 1964, desk-type, metal 22.00
Guide, "Official Guide 1964-1965 New York World's Fair" 10.00
Hat, man's, black felt, size 7, in large World's Fair box by Adam of 5th Avenue 100.00
Magazine, "National Geographic," April, 1965, World's Fair issue 10.00
Model of Vatican Pieta Building 20.00
Pin, model of "Unisphere," U.S. Steel exhibit, mint in package 10.00
Plaque, plastic, model of "Unisphere," U.S. Steel exhibit 15.00
Plate, Unisphere in center, 6" d. 18.00
Postcards, various Fair scenes, set of 44 ....44.00
Program, "General Motors Futurama," colorful cover 27.50
Thermometer, model of the Unisphere 17.50
Tray, red, depicts eight different attractions w/Unisphere in center, 12" d. 30.00
Tumbler, glass, depicts Science Hall, 6½" h. 16.00
Viewmaster reel set, Fair scenes 25.00

WRITING ACCESSORIES

Early writing accessories are popular collectible and offer a wide variety to select from. A collection may be formed around any one segment—pens, letter openers, lap desks or inkwells—or the collection may revolve around choice specimens of all types. Material, design and age usually determine the value. Pen collectors like the large fountain pens developed in the 1920s but also look for pens and mechanical pencils that are solid gold or gold-plated. Also see METALS.

INKWELLS & STANDS

Amber cut glass well, square shape w/ large dimples in sides, facet-cut hinged lid, 2¾" d., 4½ " h. $245.00
Blown-three-mold glass well, geometric, cylindrical body w/disc mouth, pontil scar, light olive green, probably Mt. Vernon Glassworks, Vernon, New York, ca. 1820-40, GII-15, 2¼" d., 1¾" h. 2,860.00
Blown-three-mold glass well, geometric, cylindrical body w/diamond point band, disc mouth, pontil scar, yellowish olive green, Coventry Glass Works, Coventry, Connecticut, ca. 1820-40, GII-2, 2½" d., 1⅞" h. 132.00
Brass stand, Modern style, the rectangular tray raised on riveted angular feet, w/pierced triangular end handles, centered by a cylindrical well w/hinged cover & pellet finial, designed by Jan Eisenloffel, ca. 1900, 10¾" l., 3½" h. 330.00
Bronze well, figural, a 4" h. chickadee perched on a hinged-top acorn holding the well, another chickadee on an evergreen bough alongside, Schute, Vienna, Austria, 19th c., ...550.00
Bronze well, figural, cast as a mean dog chained to a post, his head hinged to reveal an inkwell, stamped "TIFFANY & CO. - UNION SQUARE," ca. 1875, 5¼" l. 920.00

Figural Ceramic Inkstand

Ceramic inkstand, figural, modeled as three children seated on a raised mound at the edge of a small pond & giggling at the sight of three huddling frogs staring back at them, the ends of the oblong base fitted w/covered inkwells, glazed in mottled tan, brown & celadon green, designed by Max Blondat for Emile Decoeur, signed "MAX BLONDAT - E. DECOEUR - Céramiste," France, ca. 1900, 15" l., 10" h. (ILLUS.) 1,840.00
Lacy glass stand, pressed, irregular rectangular-form w/overall raised scrolling & four scrolled feet, possibly Boston & Sandwich Glass Works, Sandwich, Massachusetts,

clear, 6" w., 9½" l., 3" h. (minor chips & roughness, inkwell inserts are missing) 357.50

Mold-blown glass well, melon-form w/28 vertical ribs, sheared mouth, pontil scar, yellowish olive, probably Pitkin Glass Works, Manchester, Connecticut, 1783-1830, 2⅝" d., 2" h...1,980.00

Pewter & enamel well, Art Nouveau design, the wide, low-domed body decorated w/raised stylized whiplash designs trimmed w/bluish green enamel buttons, low-domed cover, glass insert, impressed mark "English Pewter - 0521," early 20th c., 5" d., 1½" h..........................275.00

Porcelain well, figural, modeled w/two young boys fighting over a bird's nest, raised on a grapevine decorated base, Europe, 19th c., 10½" l. 385.00

Pottery well, redware w/a grey salt glaze & traces of old gold paint, short cylindrical form w/a flat top pierced w/four small holes & a slightly raised larger center hole, 3½" d. (hairline, small chips).............71.50

Sapphire blue pressed glass stand, an oblong scalloped tray centered by three removable bottles, each w/a silver plate lid, the center bottle probably a sander, marked "Baccarat," w/original paper label, France, 3½ x 9¾", 3½" h. 395.00

Staffordshire pottery well, figural, a black, brown & white Spaniel dog reclining beside a well on a cobalt blue-painted oblong base, 19th c., 5" l. (light wear on black).................155.00

Sterling Silver & Agate Inkwell

Sterling silver & agate well, egg-shaped form raised on four legs w/paw feet, overall engraved designs set w/various faceted & buff top agates, a faceted citrine at the top, vermeil interior, Scottish hallmarks, ca. 1899 (ILLUS.) 1,430.00

Vaseline cut glass well, pyramidal shape, faceted hinged lid, 3½" w., 3¼" h..195.00

LETTER OPENERS

Fuller Brush Letter Opener

Advertising, "Fuller Brush," figural Fuller Brush man, white plastic (ILLUS.) 7.50

Advertising, "Hogan Steel," brass.........25.00

Brass, depicts a shield showing Carew Tower, Cincinnati, fancy handle.........22.00

Celluloid, full-figure cat on handle, cat opens mouth to hold pencil.............185.00

Silver plate, Art Nouveau style, handle blends into blade forming a Russian wolfhound, 11" l. 47.50

Silver & shaded enamel, the handle enameled in a stylized floral design in muted tones, tortoiseshell blade, marked "K. Fabergé" in Cyrillic w/Imperial warrant & 88 standard, Moscow, Russia, ca. 1910, 12¾" l...3,910.00

Sterling silver, in the form of an arrow w/a chased tip & etched feather, Shiebler (slight damage to feather, minor solder)..................................220.00

PENS & PENCILS

Advertising mechanical pencil, "What Cheer Clay Products Co., What Cheer, Iowa' 47.50

Eversharp "Doric" fountain pen, marbleized blue body, ca. 1930s.........275.00

Eversharp "Gold Seal Doric" fountain pen, Morocco (burgundy & pearl) body, ca. 1931 ....65.00

Eversharp "Skyline" fountain pen, blue w/gold-filled cap, ca. 1940s..................69.00

Grieshaber fountain pen, jumbo-sized, black & gold marbleized body, 14k gold tip, 1920s..................................250.00

Parker "Blue Diamond 51" fountain pen, blue body, 1946..................................75.00

Parker "Lady Duofold" fountain pen, orange body, 1920s....................................125.00
Parker "No. 16" fountain pen, gold-plated filigree & black Vulcanite body, ca. 1912....................................785.00
Parker "75" fountain pen, solid sterling silver body, 1965, mint in box.............115.00
Sheaffer "Lifetime Triumph" fountain pen, green marbleized body, 1940s....100.00
Sheaffer "Lifetime Triumph" mechanical pencil, gold-filled top, black barrel, ca. 1945 ....150.00
Sheaffer No. 2 fountain pen, jade marbleized body, ca. 1915................150.00
Sheaffer "Sovereign" fountain pen, No. 73S, black body, ca. 1950 ....35.00
Sheaffer "Stratowriter" ballpoint pen, gold-filled body, ca. 1947 ....400.00
Sheaffer "Valiant Snorkel" fountain pen, black body, 1952 ....55.00
Waterman "Hundred Year" fountain pen, navy blue body, 1939 ....475.00
Waterman "Ideal No. 512" fountain pen, silver-gilt filigree over black body 350.00
Waterman "Ideal No. 0552½V" lady's fountain pen, engraved gold-filled body, 1925....................................85.00
Waterman "No. 52V" fountain pen, red ripple body, 1920s....................................95.00
Waterman "No. 52½V" fountain pen & mechanical pencil, brown, brown ripple hard rubber w/gold-filled trim, 1925, the set....................................125.00

YARD LONG PRINTS

These out of proportion colorful prints were fashionable wall decorations in the waning years of the 19th century and early in the 20th century. They are all 36" wide and between 8" and 10" high. A wide variety of subjects, ranging from florals and fruits to chicks and puppies, is available to collectors. Prices for these yard-long prints have shown a dramatic increase within the past years. All included in this list are framed unless otherwise noted.

"A Yard of Youth," from Youth's Companion 100th Anniversary, F.L. Martini, unframed (some foxing on ends)....................................$150.00
Maud Humphrey children 140.00
Morning Glories, unframed..................45.00
Poppies & asters, signed "Clarkson," in original gold frame 110.00
"Roses & Hydrangeas," signed Paul DeLongpre 85.00

YARN WINDERS

Floor model reel, carved & turned maple, four shaped arms w/turned spindles above a shaped support, on a heart-shaped base, branded "E. Frost," New England, 19th c., 44½" h....................................$385.00
Floor model reel, mixed hard- & softwoods, six baluster-turned arms on a box-form upright on a rectangular board base raised on three widely canted turned legs, chip-carved details & branded label "N. Lindsay, Reading," old dark patina, 19th c., overall 30" h. (wear, damage to edge & gear box, renailing) 93.50
Table model yarn "swift," Shaker-style, maple w/cup finial, original iron clamp, 26" w. expanded, 24" h....................................195.00
Table model yarn "swift," pine, eight vertical slats swiveling on a center spindle w/heart-shaped wrought-iron screws, New England, mid-19th c., 32" h....................................198.00

ZEPPELIN COLLECTIBLES

Badge, pilot's, sterling silver, hallmarked $550.00
Badge, pilot's, silver, Germany...........180.00
Button, tunic-type, brass, depicts zeppelin, globe & swastika 35.00
Pin, sterling silver, model of a zeppelin, large ....75.00 to 80.00
Place mat, marked "First Day Dinner," "First Europe Pan American Flight," from the Graf Zeppelin, 1929..........150.00
Postcard, advertising, "Tidewater Oil Co. - carried on board the Graf Zeppelin," illustration of zeppelin, 1929....................................35.00
Postcard w/cancelled stamp, carried on the USS Akron, 1932 ....65.00
Stickpin, figural zeppelin marked "LZ129" 45.00
Toy, model of a large zeppelin, papier-maché w/wooden wheels & cone tail, debossed "Los Angeles" on both sides, ca. 1920, 14" l., 3" h. (minor soiling, small dent in bottom)....................................88.00
Toy, windup tin, model of the Graf Zeppelin, by Schilling, 1960s, 9½" l....................................95.00

INDEX

* Denotes "Special Focus" section